Wissenschaftliche Untersuchungen
zum Neuen Testament · 2. Reihe

Herausgegeben von
Martin Hengel und Otfried Hofius

115

B. J. Oropeza

Paul and Apostasy

Eschatology, Perseverance,
and Falling Away
in the Corinthian Congregation

Mohr Siebeck

B. J. OROPEZA, born 1961; 1990–1995 Research Associate, Christian Research Institute, Rancho Santa Margarita, CA; 1989–1999 Instructor of Theology, Victory Outreach International, La Punete, CA; 1998–1999 Visiting Assistant Professor of Religion, George Fox University, Newberg, OR; 1999–2000 Adjunct (Assistant) Professor of Religion, George Fox University, Newberg, OR.

Die Deutsche Bibliothek – CIP Einheitsaufnahme

Oropeza, B. J.:
Paul and apostasy : eschatology, perseverance and falling away in the Corinthian congregation / B. J. Oropeza. - Tübingen : Mohr Siebeck, 2000
(Wissenschaftliche Untersuchungen zum Neuen Testament : Reihe 2; 115)
ISBN 3-16-147307-8

© 2000 J.C.B. Mohr (Paul Siebeck) Tübingen.

The book was typeset by Martin Fischer in Reutlingen using Times typeface, printed by Gulde-Druck in Tübingen on non-aging paper from Papierfabrik Niefern and bound by Heinr. Koch in Tübingen.

Printed in Germany

ISSN 0340-9570

To My Mother

Preface

My interest in questions related to apostasy, perseverance, and eschatology arose from my previous research and studies which often focused on new religious movements that had (what would be considered by many as) extreme apocalyptic views. At the University of Durham in England I had the opportunity to concentrate more on aspects related to the New Testament. Some additional information was included during my professorship at George Fox University. The fruit of my endeavours are compiled in this present work. Many people have assisted me along the way. At Durham I wish to thank all the faculty and students who participated in the New Testament Seminar classes on Monday nights. I wish to thank especially Professor James D. G. Dunn and Dr. Loren Stuckenbruck, my doctoral supervisors, for critically assessing the many pages of my rough drafts, for providing helpful feedback, and for directing me to relevant sources. I wish to thank Dr. Alan Ford and Dr. Natalie Knödel for their assistance regarding questions related to computers. They know the many hours I spent staring in front of the Macintosh SE/30 screen in the Computer Room of the Theology Department. I also wish to thank the secretarial department, especially Margaret Parkinson, for assisting with information on the technicalities of this thesis. Other people who deserve to be mentioned for their feedback or some other means of assistance are as follows: Prof. C. K. Barrett, Dr. Stephen Barton, Dr. Mark Bonnington, Dr. Marco Conti, Dr. Alan Ford, Dr. Larry Hurtado, Dr. Natalie Knödel, Dr. Leena Lybeck, Dr. James McGrath, Prof. I. Howard Marshall, Doug Mohrmann, Astrid Pallash, Elizabeth Raine, Dr. Brian Rosner, Stephen Ross, Jerry Truex, Tet-Lim Yee, and Ian Yorkston.

I also wish to thank my wife Cathie and son Jared for their support and the long hours they spent waiting for me to come home many evenings. As well, I thank my mother, Magda Sanchez and her husband Henry, for their financial assistance. Finally, I would like to thank those many people who assisted us financially, or helped in some way or another in reference to Cathie's cancer. All the people from the King's Church in Durham, who are too numerous to mention, thank you. Those who sacrificed for us in very exceptional ways were Brian and Rhoda Clarke, Reverend Peter and Ruth Scott, Richard and Janet Bagnall, and Iris Prizeman. Other people connected with Victory Outreach who assisted or provided some means of support were Reverend Sonny and Julie Argunizoni, and their secretary Kathy Clark, Reverend Brian and Vivian Villalobos, Reverend Mike and Johann Pike, Reverend Mitchell and Nellie Peterson, Alex and Leah Newcomb, and Laura Richardson. Other people and organisations who helped or encouraged us in special ways include Zina and Jim Hopson, Danny and Maggie Gallardo, Fr. C. K. and Debbie Robertson, Jerry and Vangie Truex, Ian and Valerie Yorkston, Andrew and Vicki Carver, Daniel and Diane Koh, Atty Fujiwara and family, Tet-Lim and Josephine Yee, Desra Percaya, Dr. Gillian Baughton, Angie Stephenson, Dr. Michael Richardson, Steven Rwaminyinyo, "Rushty," Anthony Moss, Kate Silverton from BBC, Student Ministries International, and the Macmillan Cancer Relief Fund. In the States, special thanks to Reverend Eldon and Doreen Babcock and all the people from the church in Sherwood who helped us out.

At George Fox University I wish to thank the faculty for the use of facilities in the Religion and Library departments. Laurie Lieggi, Sandy Maurer, and Charles Church deserve special mention. A very special thanks to Jenae Donohue, my assistant at GFU. Special thanks also to Prof. Dr. Martin Hengel, Prof. Dr. Otfried Hofius, and Herrn Georg Siebeck for publishing this book in the scholarly series, *Wissenschaftliche Untersuchungen zum Neuen Testament*.

Newberg, Oregon, July 1999   B. J. Oropeza

Table of Contents

Chapter 1

Introduction: Perspectives on Apostasy and Perseverance

1. Apostasy and Perseverance in Church History

Whether Judas Iscariot betraying Christ, or Christians renouncing their faith due to severe persecution, heresy, temptation, or sceptical reasoning, apostasy has plagued the church throughout the ages. There remains a much needed enterprise to explain apostasy in comprehensible terms. The definition Richard Muller has offered is that apostasy (ἀποστασία and *apostasia*, respectively) is "a wilful falling away from, or rebellion against, Christian truth. Apostasy is the rejection of Christ by one who has been a Christian, the ultimate or final apostasy being the so-called unforgivable sin, the *peccatum in Spiritum Sanctum* (q. v.), the sin against the Holy Spirit; apostasy is also one of the characteristic evidences of antichrist."[1] Although this statement may be valid, there is warrant for attempting a more refined meaning by examining the matter more closely in light of recent biblical interpretative methods. The aspect of apostasy which will be significant for this study is the notion of "falling away" from the faith; the antipode of the perseverance of the saints: "die Beharrung, Bewährung und Kontinuität des Glaubens in der Geschichte."[2] A thorough overview of approaches on apostasy and perseverance throughout the entire history of the church is beyond the scope of this study. Nevertheless, since the interpretation of some recent New Testament scholars often seem coloured by their respective traditions arising from earlier theological conflicts – especially those from Calvinist and Arminian persuasions – a brief background for this discussion is in order. I will attempt a preliminary overview of some of the most significant tensions in its history.[3]

---

[1] Muller, DLGT, 41.

[2] Moltmann (1986), 5:226–27.

[3] Unfortunately, few sources specifically trace questions related to apostasy and the perseverance of the saints throughout its history. It was important to compile a list of works which were helpful in this pursuit. See appendix for sources.

1.1 Pre-Reformation Perspectives on Apostasy and Perseverance

If Christianity emerged from a Jewish matrix, then it seems important to mention the relationship between the two groups in reference to apostasy. The earliest Christians did not entirely abandon their Jewish roots when they accepted Jesus as Messiah. Perhaps it is correct to suggest that the Christians were in some sense understood as "heretics" to Jewish groups who thought themselves to be more traditionally Jewish.[4] It seems that at least Pauline Christianity posed a threat to other Jews, especially over the area of Gentile and Jewish relationships. Paul was portrayed by his opponents as teaching apostasy (ἀποστασία) from Moses (Acts 21:21).[5] J. T. Sanders suggests that even though the Jewish *birkat ha-minim* (blessing/curse on heretics) in the Eighteen Benedictions (c. 80 C. E.) may not have originally included a curse against the Nazarenes, Jewish Christians still may have been the primary focus of the curse. After the Jewish war, expulsion from the synagogues rather than sporadic persecution of the Christians became a factor in Jewish-Christian relationships, and John's Gospel seems to reflect this pattern[6] (e.g., John 9:22, 34). Three observations follow from this. First, it seems unlikely that Jewish Christians would not be included at least among the heretics of this curse. Second, if they were being banished from some of the synagogues, this would indicate some sense of defection from the beliefs of the Jews who expelled them. Third, while the boundaries between Christianity and early Judaism may be rather blurred before 70 CE, a more definite parting of the ways began to take place afterwards. By the time of Justin Martyr's *Dialogue with Trypho the Jew* (c. 155), the boundaries between the two groups are defined better.[7]

A survey of the warning passages in the New Testament warrants that at least three basic dangers threatened the early Christian communities: deception and heresies from within the body of believers, persecution from external powers, and temptations arising from vices associated with the practises of non-Christians.[8] Persecution, for example, is stressed in Hebrews and 1 Peter. Issues

---

[4] Cf. GROSSI (1992), 1.376.

[5] The subject of apostasy was not unimportant to Jewish tradition. See appendix for listings. Feldman maintains that Judaism and Christianity were the only ancient religions to teach "exclusionary 'conversion'" (1993:288). Kippenberg, however, adds that while exclusivity was foreign to Greco-Roman religions, the limits of toleration were reached when citizens defected from their ancestral religion. For examples of the phenomenon, see KIPPENBERG, 1987:1.354.

[6] J. T. SANDERS (1993), 58–61.

[7] Along with Sanders' work, other studies on early Jewish-Christian relationships include DUNN (1991); MEISSNER (1996); SEGAL (1990); MAIER (1982); BARCLAY (1995a), 89–120; NEALE (1993), 89–101; HARVEY (1985), 79–96; and RÄISÄNEN (1983), 543–53.

[8] Scholars normally recognise these topics within the respective writings. See for example the general introductions of R. BROWN (1997) and EPP & MACRAE, eds. (1989). Natu-

related to false teachers/teachings are found in the Johannine and the Deutero-Pauline writings, 2 Peter, and Jude. The *paraenetic* sections of the Pauline writings and James focus on vices and virtues. These and other early texts helped to shape the trajectory of Christian response to the phenomenon of defection in the post-apostolic era. The Christians were to persevere through various types of opposition, standing firm against temptation, false doctrine, hardships and persecution.

1.1.1 Challenges to the Faith: Sedition and Vices

Vices related to sedition not only threatened the unity of the Corinthian congregation in Paul's time but also a generation later when Clement of Rome (c. 96) writes to the congregation. The latter attempted to settle a faction related to the members' deposition of the established leaders in the congregation. In his letter the Corinthians are exhorted in the virtue of obedience and are to cast aside vain toil, strife, and jealousy, which lead to death. God appoints judgement and torment for the doubters and double-minded who turn aside to disobedience. Such people are prefigured in the example of God's judgement against Lot's wife, who was not in accord with her godly husband (*1 Clem.* 9–11). The Corinthian instigators are warned to repent and submit to the presbyters – it would be better for them to humble themselves than be exalted but cast out from the "hope of God" (57:1–2; cf. *2 Clem.* 6:7). Similar to Clement, Ignatius of Antioch (c. 107) writes that the Christians who follow a schismatic person will not inherit the kingdom of God, yet the Lord is able to forgive anyone who repents and returns to the unity of God and the bishop (Ign. *Phld.* 3:2; 8:1). He exhorts his readers to avoid heresy and hold fast to apostolic teachings.

In the epistle of Barnabas (c. 100), the author sets Christians before two ways, which are described in the metaphors of light and darkness in terms of the abstaining from or practising of vices (*Barn.* 18–21). If the Christians fail to learn more accurately about their salvation, the prince of evil may gain an entrance through deceit and hurl them away (ἐκσφενδονήσῃ) from their life (*Barn.* 2:10). The readers are to take heed in the last days and flee from the lawless works of the evil way, for God will judge all according to their deeds. Those who slumber over their sins will be cast out from the Lord's kingdom (*Barn.* 4). The Didache (c. 100) also maintains two ways: the way of life or death. The way of life is associated with loving God and one's neighbour. It involves abstaining from vices mentioned in the Ten Commandments or related to bodily lusts, sorcery, and idolatry (including meat sacrificed to idols). The way of death includes the practice of these vices (*Did.* 1–6).

---

rally, I am not claiming that these topics were the only important themes in the respective writings or that there is no overlap of ideas among the sources.

The vice of covetousness is a significant danger in Polycarp's epistle to the Philippians (2nd c.). Here it is written that a former presbyter named Valens and his wife apparently committed some act of covetousness. The writer hopes that the Lord would grant them repentance. The person who does not refrain from coveting will be defiled through idolatry and punished "as one of the Gentiles who know not the judgement of God" (Pol. *Phil.* 11). Presbyters are instructed to turn back members who have gone astray, and they are to refrain from both false Christians and the love of money (Pol. *Phil.* 6). A more generalised admonition against vices is found in an ancient homily where the author exhorts his Christian audience to repent from the evil deeds of the flesh. If they desire worldly things, they will fall away from the path of righteousness and suffer eternal punishment (2 Clem. 5–8).

If a warning against vices and call to repentance marks a facet of apostasy in the patristic writings of the late first and early second centuries, the Shepherd of Hermas epitomises this aspect. Those who have sinned grievously and committed apostasy are beckoned to return. Falling away and repentance are portrayed in complex ways, and this perhaps compliments the multifaceted nature of earliest Christian discourses on the issue. Contrary to the book of Hebrews, which seems to teach that baptised Christians are not given a second chance once they fall away (cf. Heb. 6:4–6; 10:26–31), the Shepherd of Hermas affirms that apostates may be forgiven while a gap of time remains before the final eschaton. A refusal to respond to this offer will result in final condemnation. Those who have denied the Lord in the past are given a second chance, but those who deny him in the coming tribulation will be rejected "from their life" (*Herm. Vis.* 2.2).

In the vision of the tower under construction (the church), numerous stones (believers) are gathered for the building. Among the rejected are those who are not genuine Christians; they received their faith in hypocrisy. Others do not remain in the truth, and others who go astray are finally burned in fire (*Vis.* 3.6–7). Some others are novices who turn away before they are baptised, and still others fall away due to hardships, being led astray by their riches. They may become useful stones, however, if they are separated from their riches. The penitents receive 12 commands; salvific life depends on their observance (*Herm. Man.* 12.3–6). Repentance would become unprofitable for the Christian who falls again after restoration (*Man.* 4.1:8; 3:6).

In the Parables, rods of various shapes and sizes represent different kinds of believers: the faithful, rich, double-minded, doubtful-minded, and hypocritical deceivers. These are allowed to repent – if they do not, they will lose eternal life (*Herm. Sim.* 8.6–11). Apostates and traitors who blaspheme the Lord by their sins are completely destroyed (*Sim.* 8.6:4). Another parable describes apostates as certain stones which are cast away from the house of God and delivered to women who represent 12 vices. They may enter the house again if they follow virgins who represent 12 virtues. Certain apostates became worse than they were before they believed and will suffer eternal death even though they had fully known God. Nevertheless, most people, whether apostates or fallen ministers, have an opportunity to repent and be restored (*Sim.* 9.13–15, 18 ff). Hermas and his audience are to persevere and practise repentance if they wish to partake of life (*Sim.* 10.2–4).

Penance is stressed in the Shepherd of Hermas and becomes a recognisable discipline developed in the patristic era.[9] Those who committed serious sins were to do public penance which included confession, exclusion, absolution, and restoration (*exomologesis*). Bishop Callistus I (d. c. 222) introduced penance reforms which were interpreted by Hippolytus as giving license to loose morals. Callistus allegedly permitted those who sinned "unto death" (1 John 5:16) to remain in the church, affirming that tares are permitted to grow along with the wheat and that Noah's ark housed both clean and unclean animals (Hipp. *Refut.* 9.7). More normative was the view that penance may be granted one time after baptism and that some sins (such as idolatry and adultery) were more heinous than others. Some sins were in fact too grievous to be forgiven (*peccata irremissibilia*).[10] Eternal condemnation or lifelong excommunication awaited the person whose sin was irremissible (cf. Tert. *De Paen.* 7; Clem. *Strom.* 2.13; Orig. *De Orat.* 28).[11] More lenient approaches seemed to be adopted on a wider scale after the persecutions of Decius and Diocletian claimed many defectors.[12]

1.1.2 Deception and Heresies

Prior to the establishment of ecumenical creeds, we may question the boundaries of what would be considered a true deviation from the Christian faith and whether the term "apostate" aptly categorises the people from multifarious heretical or heterodox systems.[13] No doubt, the apologists of the early church – who refuted groups such as the Gnostics, Marcionites, Montanists, Encratites, and

---

[9] On further issues related to penance, see WATKINS (1961); HEBBLEWAITE & DONOVAN (1979).

[10] For examples of sin categorisation, see BASIL, *Epistles* 188, 199, 217.

[11] Cf. QUASTEN (1992), 2:31–34, 69–71, 84–85, 299–302, 380–81; J. KELLY (1978), 216–19.

[12] In Spain, however, the Council of Elvira (c. 306) ordered lifelong excommunication with no hope of reconciliation even at death.

[13] Beugnet makes some interesting distinctions between heretics and apostates (1907:1.1602–03). The two terms may frequently overlap in meaning, especially when a person abandons one faith for another (e.g., Ammonius Sakkas and Julian the Apostate defected from some form of Christianity and became Neoplatonists). Perhaps a useful distinction for the early church is that apostates normally renounce/abandon their faith (whether or not they actually join another religious system), while heretics embrace a faith that deviates from the faith of those who oppose them. On distinction and overlap between heresy and schism in the patristic era, see references in GROSSI (1992:1.376).

Monarchians – believed themselves to be defending the apostolic faith. An intensive examination of this sort, however, is beyond our current study.[14] The aspect of heresy I wish to consider is this: early Christians frequently believed that apostasy came by way of deceivers at the instigation of the devil, and terrible consequences awaited such people.

The final section of the Didache echoes the Synoptic tradition (Matt. 24:4–13, 15, 21–26; Mark 13:5ff; Luke 21:8ff; cf. 2 Thes. 2:3ff; Rev. 13:13–14) when it warns against apostasy through the deception of false prophets in the last days. In those days it is said that sheep will be turned into wolves and a world deceiver will appear and do great signs and wonders. Though many will fall away and be destroyed (σκανδαλισθήσονται πολλοὶ καὶ ἀπολοῦνται), those who endure in their faith will be saved (*Did.* 16).

In the letter of Ignatius to the Ephesians, the readers are exhorted to avoid corrupting the faith. They should not be deceived by the teachings of the prince of this world. People who are led astray will suffer unquenchable fire and be robbed of the life set before them (Ign. *Eph.* 16–17). Similarly, apostates in the Apocalypse of Peter (2nd c.) will suffer eschatological judgement involving floods of fire and darkness (*Apoc. Pet.* 5).

The eschatological scheme of Irenaeus (c. 130–200) describes the beast of the Apocalypse as leading astray the inhabitants of the earth. This figure embodies in his own person all apostasy, evil, and false prophecy. He likewise possesses the number 666 – he is the summation of both 600 years of wickedness caused by the apostate angels before the Deluge and 6000 years of apostasy related to the age of the world (*Adv. Haer.* 5.28–29). Irenaeus claims that when Polycarp met Marcion the heretic, he promptly denounced him as the "first-born of Satan" (Iren. *Haer.* 3.3:4 cf. Pol. *Phil.* 7). Justin Martyr (c. 100–165) views the devil himself as apostatising from the will of God (*Dial. Tryph.* 125:4f).

Tertullian (c. 160–225) compares heresies with idolatry and concludes that both have been introduced by the devil (Tert. *De Praescr.* 40). Heresy could end up destroying even people who were thought to be faithful – the very disciples of Jesus turned away from him in John's Gospel (John 6:66). For Tertullian, no one is a Christian except the one who perseveres to the end (*De Praescr.* 3).[15]

In the view of Eusebius (c. 260–340), Simon Magus was the author of heresy (cf. Acts 8:9–24), and the devil is to be blamed for bringing the Samaritan magician to Rome and empowering him with deceitful arts which led many astray (Eus. *Hist. Eccl.* 2.13). The magician was supposedly aided by demons

---

[14] Here the reader may wish to consult more thorough analyses on heresy in works such as LÜDEMANN (1996); FREND (1985); H. BROWN (1984); PRESTIGE (1977); W. BAUER (1977); J. T. SANDERS (1993).

[15] On patristic use of defection in John 6:66, see DOIGNON (1992), 111–14; TANCA (1984), 139–146.

and venerated as a god, and Helen, his companion, was thought to be his first emanation (Just. *Apol.* I.26; *Adv. Haer.* 1.33; cf. Iren. *Haer.* 1.23:1–4).[16] Simon's successor, Menander of Samaria, was considered to be another instrument of the devil; he claimed to save humans from the aeons through magical arts. After baptism, his followers believed themselves to be immortal in the present life. It is stated that those who claim such people as their saviours have fallen away from the true hope (Eus. *Hist. Eccl.* 3.26). Basilides of Alexandria and Saturninus of Antioch followed Menander's ways. Adherents of the former declared that eating meat sacrificed to idols or renouncing the faith in times of persecution were matters of indifference. Carpocrates is labelled as the first of the Gnostics. His followers allegedly transmitted Simon's magic in an open manner. Eusebius asserts that the devil's intention was to entrap many believers and bring them to the abyss of destruction by following these deceivers (*Hist. Eccl.* 4.7).

The use of anathemas and excommunications became the normative means of handling heresy. Hippolytus (c. 170–236) affirmed that there was no place for the heretic in the church; expulsion from the earthly Eden was their lot. Cyprian (c. 258) viewed the heretics as those who lose their salvation because they put themselves outside the unity of the church.[17] Cyril of Alexandria (c. 444) anathematised Nestorianism, and creeds (such as the Athanasian) declared anathemas on those who did not hold to the tenets of the creed. The condemnation of heretics gave way to abuse as church and state distinctions were blurred after the time of Constantine.

1.1.3 Persecution and Perseverance: Martyrdom and Lapsis

The *Martyrdom of Polycarp* is sometimes considered to be the first of the "Acts of the Martyrs."[18] In this document Polycarp is killed for refusing to confess Caesar as Lord and offer incense; he refuses to revile Christ (*Mart. Pol.* 8 ff; similarly, Ign. *Rom.* 7). Other Christians did not always follow his example. Some fell into idolatry in the face of persecutions.[19]

---

[16] In the Acts 8 account of Simon, S. Brown argues that the magician himself was not a true apostate because he was never a Christian in any "full sense": unlike other Samaritan converts in the narrative, he did not receive the gift of the Spirit (1969: 110–12).

[17] GROSSI, 1:367; J. KELLY (1978), 201. Studies on excommunication include: HYLAND (1928); VODOLA (1986); DOSKOCIL (1958); GAUDEMET (1949), 64–77; BOUDINHON (1913), 6:678–91.

[18] Cf. QUASTEN, 1:77.

[19] Cf. e.g., FOAKES-JACKSON (1908), 1:623 who cites Pliny's report (*Ep.* 10.96). For the sake of brevity, no concentrated effort will be made to verify the historicity of information presented in this overview. It will have to suffice to assume that the authors intended to portray their information as true and "factual" from their point of view. One may call into question the actual amount of defectors in church history, but this does not nullify the affirmation that many *did* defect.

Stirred by his own experience under the Diocletian (c. 284–305) persecution, Eusebius wrote *Collection of Martyrs* and emphasised persecution and martyrdom in his *History of the Church*. He describes Christians who persevered and others who fell away. Polycarp and Germanicus were found to be faithful in the persecution at Smyrna (c. 160), but Quintus threw away his salvation at the sight of the wild beasts (Eus. *Hist. Eccl.* 4.15). During Marcus Aurelius' reign (c. 161–80), Eusebius affirms that the Christians confessed their faith despite their suffering from abuse, plundering, stoning, and imprisonment. It is recorded that in Gaul some became martyrs, but others who were untrained and unprepared (about 10 in number) proved to be "abortions" (ἐξέτρωσαν), discouraging the zeal of others. A woman named Biblias, who had earlier denied Christ, confessed him and was joined with the martyrs. Certain defectors did likewise, but others continued to blaspheme the Christian faith, having no understanding of the "wedding garment" (ie., Matt. 22:11ff) and no faith (*Hist. Eccl.* 5.1).

During the reign of Decius (c. 249–51), the Christians of Alexandria are said to have endured martyrdom, stoning, or having their belongings confiscated for not worshipping at an idol's temple or chanting incantations. But some readily made unholy sacrifices, pretending that they had never been Christians, while others renounced their faith or were tortured until they did (*Hist. Eccl.* 6.41). In his account of the Diocletian persecution, Eusebius commends the heroic martyrs but is determined to mention nothing about those who made shipwreck of their salvation, believing that such reports would not edify his readers (8.2:3).[20] He recollects Christians who suffered in horrible ways which included their being axed to death or slowly burned, having their eyes gouged out, their limbs severed, or their backs seared with melted lead. Some endured the pain of having reeds driven under their fingernails or unmentionable suffering in their private parts (8.12).[21]

Eusebius commends the forgiving attitude of the faithful toward Christians who fell during persecution. He was apparently writing against the unmerciful conduct of the Novatians, who argued that lapsed (*lapsi*) believers should not be admitted back into the church (*Hist. Eccl.* 5.2:8; 6.43; cf. Cyp. *Ep.* 50[47]; 52[48]). Cyprian, the bishop of Carthage (c. 258), classified the persecuted believers into 6 categories: 1) those who made sacrifices [to gods or emperor] (*sacrificati*); 2) those who burned incense but did not eat sacrifices (*turificati*); 3) those who bought the certificate of sacrifice (*libellatici*); 4) those who fled (*stantes*); 5) those who refused to sacrifice and lived (*confessores*); and 6) those who confessed Christ and died (*martyres*). Many of the lapsed believers desired

---

[20] Croix maintains that there was a large number of defectors during the persecutions of the early fourth century (1954:82).

[21] See also FREND (1965), ch. 15.

to return to the church after the Decian persecution was over, seeking reconciliation through the *confessores*. The amount of time spent in penance for lapsed Christians apparently depended on how severely they were afflicted, and it was often granted to those who were near death (cf. Cyp. *De Lap.*; *Ep.* 18[12]; Peter of Alexandria, *On Penance*).[22] Cyprian wrote that defectors who celebrate the eucharist without penance do violence to the body and blood of Christ and sin more against the Lord than when they had denied him (*De Lap.* 16). Ambrose (c. 339–97) criticised the Novatian's use of Hebrews 6:4–6 (ie., that it is impossible for apostates to have a second chance to repent) and argued that such passages were to be harmonized with the less strenuous writings of Paul.[23] Consequently repentance was made possible because what is impossible with humans is possible with God (*De Paen.* 2.2).

The Donatists stressed the importance of the priest's involvement with the sacraments and claimed that the church was a visible institute of the elect. They refused to accept the consecration of Caecilian, the bishop of Carthage (c. 311), because his consecrator had betrayed the faith in the Diocletian persecution – traitors needed to be rebaptised or remain outside of the church. Augustine (c. 358–430) contended for the validity of such appointments, arguing that the true administrator of the sacraments was Christ. Rebaptism or reordination was not necessary.[24] On the issue of sin and penance, Augustine affirmed three categories: repentance of sins before baptism, daily forgiveness for post-baptismal venial sins, and formal penance for mortal sins which the church was able to remit through the keys of Peter (cf. Matt. 16:18–19).[25] Defectors could be accepted back into the church through proper penance. No sin was beyond forgiveness except persistent impenitence until death, which Augustine seemed to equate with blaspheming the Spirit. He warns that the Donatists, who continue to shun the Catholic church, were in danger of the unpardonable sin (*Sermo* 71).[26]

Regarding ecclesiology, Augustine believed that not everyone who received "birth" in the church belong to it except those who persevere and do not lack charity (Aug. *De Bapt.* 1.10[13]). For Augustine, there is an invisible communion of believers which is not entirely equated with the visible church. More than this, even people who seem to be part of the invisible fellowship may not possess the gift of perseverance, and others who are presently heretics or unconverted may eventually inherit eternal life. Thus, the elect are not precisely the same as either the visible or invisible church – they are those who persevere to the end (Aug. *De Bapt.* 5.27–28[38–39]; *De Corrept. et Gra.* 38–42; *De Dono*

---

[22] Cf. SATO (1992), 628–29; BEUGNET, 1:1605; H. BROWN, 197.
[23] Ambrose believed that Paul was the writer of the Hebrews epistle.
[24] HÄGGLUND (1968), 125ff.
[25] J. KELLY, 437–38.
[26] Cf. TIPSON (1984), 306–307.

Persev. 21).[27] Augustine also affirmed that individuals could not be certain about their predestination and salvation until they departed from this life. The number of those who will persevere is kept hidden so that no Christian will become high-minded. The graces of justification and salvation could still be lost (*De Corrept. et Gra.* 40; *De Dono Persev.* 1, 33).

1.1.4 Apostasy and Perseverance in the Middle Ages

As the Medieval church involved itself in the affairs of the state, sin and apostasy were dealt with primarily in terms of penance, excommunication, or judicial punishment. Pope Innocent III (1160–1216) defended excommunication as a distinct penalty which was intended as a medicinal corrective for the offender. Civil laws such as found in the Theodosian Code (c. 439) and Justinian Code (c. 529) deprived apostates of wills, possessions, and sometimes the right to live.[28] Fear of abandonment to Judaism or paganism seemed common. Legal abuse in this regard eventually devolved into the Inquisition. In Spain (e.g., 1480–92), it was directed at apostates and Marranos (Jews who outwardly converted to Christianity but who practised Judaism in secret). Certain Christians among the Turks and Moors, on the other hand, defected in order to enjoy advantages reserved for Muslims.[29]

The problem of sin often seemed to overshadow any comfort related to salvation. Not only were seven deadly sins identified in this period (pride, gluttony, sloth, anger, lust, covetousness, envy), but Alexander of Hales and Peter Lombard's *Sentences* recognised six species of sins against the Spirit (despair, presumption, impenitence, obstinacy, assaulting the known truth, envy of another's grace). Thomas Aquinas (c. 1225–74) wrote regarding three ways the church had understood the blasphemy of the Spirit: 1) attributing Christ's works to the demonic; 2) final impenitence; and 3) a special sin committed through malice.[30] Penance was available for the person who had not committed the unpardonable sin. Private confession, however, eventually replaced public penance. The Fourth Lateran Council (1215) affirmed that every baptised church member was to make private confessions of sin at least once a year.

Questions about the church's relationship with apostate monarchs are also significant at this time. Emperor Frederick II (1215–50), for example, was excommunicated by the pope four times. The papacy viewed him as the Antichrist

---

[27] Cf. Hägglund, 128–29, 139; J. Kelly, 416. The issue of apostasy is perhaps better related to the Augustinian debate with the Donatists; perseverance, on the other hand, arises more out of the Pelagian controversy.

[28] Some of the codes seem directed against defectors to Judaism. See codes and penalties in Bouché (1935), 1:644–50; Guzzetti (1968), 1:75; Beugnet, 1:1607; Foakes-Jackson, 1:624–25.

[29] Cf. Foakes-Jackson 1:625. On Islam and apostasy, see Zwemer (1924).

[30] For more precise nuances, see Tipson, 307–09.

when he opposed the church. Thomas Aquinas argued that if a prince falls away, he forfeits the allegiance of his Christian subjects. Apostates are to be excommunicated from the church and are severed from God altogether (*Summa Theologica* IIa IIae, Q. 12 Art. 1–2).

The common heretic fared worse. After excommunication the individual was to be delivered to the "secular tribunal to be exterminated thereby from the world by death" (*Summa Theologica* IIa IIae, Q. 12 Art. 3 f). Heretics were granted penance upon return, but if they fell again and returned, they were admitted penance and then delivered to be executed. Altogether Aquinas distinguished three types of falling away: apostasy *a fide* (falling from the faith); apostasy *ab ordine* (abandonment of clerical state); and apostasy *a monachatus* (abandonment from a monastic lifestyle).[31]

On the issue of perseverance, Aquinas elaborated on Augustine and integrated Aristotle's *Nichomachean Ethics*. For Aquinas, perseverance is to be understood in three ways that are essentially mental, ethical, and theological in perspective.[32] First, perseverance signifies a mental habit in which one is able to stand steadfast and not be moved by sadness. Secondly, it is a habit whereby a person "has the purpose of persevering in good unto the end," and third, "perseverance is called the abiding in good to the end of life." The third view requires divine assistance. Those who are justified by grace and desire to be continually kept from wickedness must pray to God for such perseverance, for "to many grace is given to whom perseverance in grace is not given" (*Summa Theologica*, Ia IIae Q. 109, Art. 10; cf. Q. 114, Art. 9).

Another view, which was attributed to William of Occam (1285–1347) and discussed at the Council of Trent, suggested that God had chosen certain privileged individuals – such as the apostles and Mary, the mother of Jesus – and he willed them to be saved without the basis of any foresight of the good which they might do. But such individuals were few. In reference to the majority, God willed that all humanity be saved, and he provides them with the means necessary to this end, but they are free to reject them.[33]

John of Damascus (c. 675–749) is perhaps one of the best representatives of Eastern Christian thought in the Medieval period. He wrote a compendium (περὶ αἱρέσεων ἐν συντομίᾳ) on 103 heresies in his *Fount of Knowledge*. Included among the heretics are the Monothelites and Ishmaelites (Islam). Barbarism, Scythism, Hellenism, and Judaism are considered the archetypes of all heresies (*On Heresies* 1–4; 99; 101). In his *Exposition of the Orthodox Faith*, he writes that God does not compel virtue but Christians have it in their own power to abide in virtue and follow God or dwell in wickedness and follow the devil.

---

[31] For elaboration, see VON HOVE (1913), 1:624–26
[32] Cf. DAVIS (1991), 214.
[33] Cf. NUTTAL (1951), 3.

Two kinds of abandonment exist which are related to the providence of God. The first concerns matters of guidance and training, as when God permits misfortune to overtake Christians in order to bring about more restoration. God sometimes allows Christians who are puffed up in virtue and righteousness to fall away into sexual immorality so as to enlighten their understanding of self-weakness and humility. In such cases, the fallen individuals confess and are restored. The second form of abandonment is complete and hopeless. No restoration takes place; the person chooses to remain blind and incurable. Such a person, like Judas, is handed over to total destruction (*Orthodox Faith* 2.29–30).

Summary

Several observations in relation to apostasy and perseverance in Pre-Reformation history should be distilled at this point. First, as we have examined, threats to the Christian faith often came by way of three basic venues. Heresy seems to have persisted in one form or another throughout the eras. In earliest Christianity, the believers themselves were sometimes considered as deviants from early Judaism. In the patristic era, they often handled heresy through apologetic refutations. This approach eventually gave way to a more exacting judicial system and Inquisition, which at times directed their efforts against defectors or potential defectors to Judaism. The patristic sources also affirm that a number of vices were a source of temptation for members in the congregations. Apostasy in such cases would normally involve a turning away from Christianity back into practices such as idolatry. The Medieval church often seemed preoccupied with personal sin and forgiveness through penance. Christian defection as a result of persecution was another problem. Our sources claim that in the face of death, many believers remained faithful, but many others fell away through renouncing Christ or making sacrifices to other gods. The combination of church and state in the Middle Ages alleviated the problem of persecution for the Christians, but other religious groups were not as fortunate.

Second, those who committed apostasy were punished by means of expulsion. If they did not leave the church on their own, they would be excommunicated. Still, contrary to the Novatians and Donatists, the hope of restoration was possible in many cases, but a continual habit of backsliding and returning to the church was not acceptable. If the offenders refused to repent and return to the church, they were to suffer the loss of eternal life. In the Middle Ages, apostates would be handed over to the civil authorities for punishment or execution if they failed to repent.

Third, the notion of perseverance involved patient endurance through persecutions and temptations. Even in the Augustinian system, the Christian who had the gift of perseverance was expected to struggle to the end against sinning and falling away. The believers did not know whether or not they had the gift until the end of their earthly existence. Personal certainty of salvation was to be earnestly prayed for.

Finally, not all apostasies were the same. The phenomena of a "mixed church" and genuine apostates are both recognised. Public renunciation of Christ and the bribery of officials were two unequal ways of avoiding persecution. Defection under torture would be evaluated differently than other forms of abandonment. Some vices were thought to be more heinous than others. Some traitors remained traitors while others confessed Christ again, at the price of martyrdom. Questions regarding the restoration of lapsed Christians gave rise to mixed reactions. While the church fathers would affirm the reality of the phenomenon of apostasy, it would be misleading to assume that Hermas, Tertullian, Cyprian, Augustine, John of Damascus, Thomas Aquinas and the others all shared the same opinions. Perspectives on apostasy and perseverance were as divers as the circumstances in which they occurred. Therefore, unity of phenomenon and diversity of thought would not be a wrong way to describe the concept of apostasy which we find in the church's history. The post-Reformation challenge, as we will notice, did not resolve this diversity, it only amplified it.

1.2 The Post-Reformation Debate about Apostasy and Perseverance

1.2.1 Reformation and Counter-Reformation Perspectives

In the view of the Reformation advocates, the punitive God of the Medieval church was being replaced by a merciful saviour. For Martin Luther (1483–1546) the assurance of personal salvation could be known by every believer through the hearing of God's message. Luther had taken a strong stand against free-will, but both Luther and his successors held that it was possible for a Christian to fall away through unbelief. He recognised that the danger of apostasy accompanied the Christian journey and that there was no room for a false sense of self-confidence.[34] The believers are justified by faith alone (*sola fide*), and they are recognised as *simul justus et peccator*, and yet unbelief is able to completely undermine the state of the righteous. Luther writes regarding the believer, "Even if he would, he could not lose his salvation, however much he sinned, unless he refused to believe. For no sin can condemn him save unbelief alone."[35] Final perseverance remained uncertain – Christians are secure in Christ but they are insecure in themselves. This position reflected the early Lutheran

---

[34] Cf. PFÜRTNER (1964:97, 100–103) who also cites Luther's commentary on Hebrews (Heb. 3:16 re: 1 Cor. 10:1–4, 12), where the Reformer warns, "We must therefore fear lest through apostasy we should lose again the beginning of a new creature" (Weimar 57–3, 154f; cf. *Works* 29:157–8).

[35] LUTHER (1970a), 182; cf. (1970b), 281.

confessions such as the Augsburg Confession (1530), the Formula of Concord (1576), and the Saxon Articles (1592).[36]

In the Counter-Reformation, the Council of Trent (1545–63 [esp. Sixth Session, 1546–47]) comprehended final perseverance as a gift which is linked to secretive predestination. No person "so long as he is in this mortal life, ought so far to presume as regards the secret mystery of divine predestination, as to determine for certain that he is assuredly in the number of the predestinate" (ch. 12; cf. canons 15–16). The Roman Catholic church concluded that apostasy could take place because some who receive grace do not persevere in grace until the end. Final perseverance cannot be received by merit; rather, a just person receives this gift by seeking it in persistent prayer, and it becomes the ground for meriting the attainment of eternal salvation. Thus, the church viewed this perseverance in terms of "living and dying in the grace of Christ."[37] Vestiges of thoughts from Augustine and Aquinas are evident in this viewpoint.

The Eastern Orthodox church reflected the tendency of John of Damascus and earlier fathers such as John Chrysostom and Cyril of Jerusalem in rejecting aspects of grace that might infringe on human freedom. Rejecting Augustinianism, the church maintained a form of synergy in which divine grace and human will, though unequal, cooperate together. In this system justification is first a product and gift of the divine grace, and it secondarily comes through human faith. A fall from faith and good works involves a fall from grace.[38] The church nevertheless agreed with Augustine on the aspect that there may be "sheep" without the church and "wolves" within.[39] The mystery of the church is that its members are imperfect; they may sin by abusing and misusing their human freedom, yet these individuals become something *different* corporately – the sinless Body of Christ. For the eastern churches, chrismation (confirmation) is not only a sacrament in which one becomes a full member of God's people, it is also a means by which apostates to Islam might again be reconciled to Christianity. Protestants and some Roman Catholics have also been received by this church through chrismation.[40]

If the common belief in the Middle Ages was that the Christian church would persevere and prevail to the end, this perspective seemed to be especially challenged by groups in the Radical Reformation which believed that the church had become apostate. These groups were sometimes isolated from other forms of Christianity and were said to distinguish people as either Christians or agents of wickedness. Excommunication seemed to play an important role in these

---

[36] Augsburg Confession: Art. 12; Saxon Articles: Art. 4, 3; Formula of Concord: Art. 4 neg. 3.

[37] CONNELLY (1967), 11:154.

[38] Cf. KARMIRIS (1973), 75–81; WARE (1972), 226–27; CONSTANTELOS (1982), 65–66.

[39] WARE, 248–252.

[40] Cf. WARE, 285–86.

communities. The early Mennonites attempted to unify a confession of faith among different congregations – the main disagreement occurred over attitudes toward those who had left the community.[41] Generally, their doctrine asserted that God provides the remedy from sin for everyone through Christ and saves those who believe and persevere. Like the Arminians, they believed that election was conditional (Waterland Confession, Art. 7). During the Calvinism-Arminian controversy, however, some apparently sided with the Calvinists.[42] The Anabaptists which are condemned in the Augsburg Confession (1530) are described as contending that some may obtain sinless perfection in this life. They also denied that a person "once justified can lose the Spirit of God" (Part 1, Art. 12).

John Calvin (1509–64) held to the Reformation view of justification and knowledge of personal salvation, but he also opined that those who are elect believers would finally persevere and could have assurance of this. Final perseverance is grounded in predestination and election. In God's eternal decree, God predestined some to eternal life and others to eternal condemnation (*Institutes* 3.21:5; cf. 3.2.15–40, 14.6–9, 18–20, 24.6f). For Calvin, biblical passages on apostasy found in Hebrews (6:4–6; 10:26–29) were applied to the subject of sinning against the Holy Spirit. The unpardonable sin could be committed by certain people in the church and thus expose them as reprobate and having false faith. The Lord uses the fear of final apostasy in order to safeguard true believers against it. Only the ones who ignore the threat are in real danger of falling away.[43] It is possible for an elect believer to fall away from God's grace temporarily, but if the person is truly elect, he/she will eventually be restored.[44]

In the Reformed tradition Zacharias Ursinus (1534–83), one of the authors of the Heidelberg Catechism, stressed soteriology and the *ordo salutis* which included (among other things) "effectual calling, conversion, faith, justification, regeneration, good works, perseverance, resurrection to glory, and eternal life" (*Explicationes Catecheseos* col. 215).[45] Similar to Calvin, Ursinus held that the elect could fall but not permanently, and the reprobate could appear to be gifted in accordance with the faithful church members, but only temporarily.[46]

William Perkins (1558–1602) became one of the most influential Calvinists in England. In his system the reprobate could plummet through five stages of apostasy even if that person had experienced the five positive benefits listed in Hebrews 6:4–6 (*A Golden Chaine* 53). Eventually, the false Christians would:

---

[41] Cf. LATOURETTE (1975), 2:785.
[42] SCHAFF, 3:844.
[43] TIPSON, 310–11.
[44] Cf. DAVIS, 218.
[45] MULLER (1986), 109.
[46] MULLER, 110.

1) be deceived by sin; 2) harden their hearts; 3) become perverted and wicked; 4) refuse the Word they once accepted; and 5) fall away. The final stage is equated with sinning against the Spirit.[47] Perkins' influence in this area was later evident in Sebastian Benefeld's collection of sermons entitled *The Sinne against the Holy Ghost Discovered* (1615) and Thomas Bedford's *The Sinne unto Death* (1621). The former stressed that Christians should be on guard against apostasy, the latter claimed that those who fear apostasy could take comfort that they are far from it, but those who are without fear are in grave danger of committing it.[48]

The contention of Jacobus Arminius (1560–1609) with the theology of Francis Gomarus and Theodore Beza was centred against supralapsarianism, the doctrine that predestination includes God's decree to permit Adam to fall; election and reprobation are thus decreed before the fall. In his *Declaration of Sentiments,* Arminius posited that, in relation to predestination and foreknowledge, God decrees (in the antecedent will of God): 1) the salvific and mediating roles of Christ; 2) the reception of those who repent and believe in Christ to effect their salvation, and the abandonment to damnation of the impenitent; and 3) the administration in a sufficient and efficacious way the means necessary for faith and repentance according to divine wisdom and justice. God then decrees (in the consequent will of God) the saving and damning of persons based on God's foreknowledge of who would believe and persevere and who would not.[49]

Although Arminius denied having taught final apostasy in his *Declaration of Sentiments*, in the *Examination of the Treatise of Perkins on the Order and Mode of Predestination* he writes that a person who is being "built" into the church of Christ may resist the continuation of this process. Concerning the believers, "It may suffice to encourage them, if they know that no power or prudence can dislodge them from the rock, unless they of their own will forsake their position."[50] A believing member of Christ may become slothful, give place to sin, and gradually die altogether, ceasing to be a member.[51] The covenant of God (Jer. 23) "does not contain in itself an impossibility of defection from God, but a promise of the gift of fear, whereby they shall be hindered from going away from God so long as that shall flourish in their hearts."[52] If there is any consistency in Arminius' position, he did not seem to deny the possibility of falling away.

---

[47] Cf. TIPSON, 313–14.

[48] TIPSON, 314ff.

[49] ARMINIUS (1968), 1:653f. See MULLER (1991); BANGS (1971); and PRAAMSMA (1968), 22–38 for fuller treatments.

[50] ARMINIUS, 3:455 cf. 1:667.

[51] ARMINIUS, 3:458.

[52] ARMINIUS, 3:458; cf. BANGS, 216–19, 348–49.

1.2.2 From the Remonstrance and Synod of Dort to the Twentieth Century

The Dutch confessions of the *Remonstrance* (1610) and the *Canons of the Synod of Dort* (1619) perhaps mark the zenith of the debate between Calvinists and Arminians. The Arminian perspective of apostasy is often attributed to Arminius' successor, Simon Episcopius, who produced it as the fifth point of the *Remonstrance*. This article denied that those who receive grace cannot finally lose it. The Arminians claimed that believers are incorporated into Christ and receive the assisting grace of the Holy Spirit so that wickedness could not pluck them out of Christ's hand (John 10:28), but it had not been established that grace could not be lost if the believers abandoned the things of Christ. The Synod of Dort responded with their five points; the last of these held that since Christian believers are the elect, they will never finally fall away. At times they might lose a sense of their full assurance due to grievous struggles, but they will eventually escape all temptation. If a true saint loses a sense of God's favor, such a disposition would not be permanent (Canons of Dort 5.5, 9–11).

The Calvinist and Arminian debate in Holland influenced some in England to address perseverance more clearly. Prior to that time, the Thirty-Nine Articles (1562) were written and reflected a moderate form of Calvinism.[53] Article 17 addresses predestination and election in terms of an *ordo salutis* which flows from grace to calling, justification, adoption, and conformity into Christ's image. At length, by God's mercy, the chosen vessels attain "everlasting felicity." But none of the articles directly focused on the issues of perseverance, reprobation, and falling away. After the debate in Holland began, Samuel Hoard defended Arminianism while John Davenant supported Calvinism. Arminian influence grew as was evident in the House of York Conference (1626). Eventually, the English church split into Arminian and Calvinist-Puritan camps.[54]

Still not all Puritans were Calvinists. John Goodwin presented the Arminian position of falling away in *Redemption Redeemed* (1651). For Goodwin, the Calvinist position seemed to permit vile practices that were exempt from punishment. In 1654 John Owen responded with the Calvinist position in *The Doctrine of the Saints' Perseverance Explained and Confirmed*. The Arminian position was said to lead to moral collapse by its stress on faulty human will. Some people may have "tasted" of the heavenly gifts (Heb. 6:4–6), but they were not genuinely Christians if they fall away. The Arminian view was that "tasting" the gifts essentially meant fully experiencing them (cf. Heb. 2:9); hence, genuine believers could fall away. Responses and rebuttals went back and forth with works such as Goodwin's *Triumuiri* (1658) and the Calvinist response by Thomas Watson's *A Body of Practical Divinity* (1692).[55]

---

[53] Cf. Bickenell (1925), 20–21; Schaff, 1:622–23.

[54] Cf. Gavin (1978), 280–310; Tipson, 321ff.

[55] Goodwin (1651), (1658); Owen (1980); Thomas Watson (1965); cf. Wakefield (1960), 253–58.

In 1647 the Westminster Confession supported the Calvinist position that "They whom God hath accepted in his Beloved, effectually called and sanctified by his Spirit, can neither totally nor finally fall away from the state of grace; but shall certainly persevere therein to the end, and be eternally saved" (ch. 17). Confessions such as that of the Society of Friends (1675), espoused the possibility of apostasy by resisting the inward grace of God. Yet for the Quakers, "such an increase and stability in the truth may in this life be attained, from which there can not be a total apostasy" (prop. 9).

The Amyraldism movement sought a middle position between Calvinism and Arminianism by claiming that the atonement was universal but efficacious only to the elect. Richard Baxter also attempted to posit a middle ground. In his work entitled *Catholicke Theologie* (1675), he claimed that final perseverance is not based on certainty; certainty can result in lewdness in conduct while uncertainty encourages carefulness. Hence, no one could be certain of his/her final salvation if he/she does not continue in love and faith. Nevertheless, God does not abandon any who do not first abandon God.[56] Baxter claimed he was confident that "none of the Elect shall ever fall away; and persuaded, that all the Rooted, through-Christians, are Elect. But yet I dare not say, that *I am Certain of this*, that all are elect to salvation, and shall never fall away totally and finally, who sincerely Believe and are Justified."[57] Good works express faith and are a necessary means to final justification.[58] Though Baxter's views and *via media* position were often criticised, his influence continued into the next century.

Philip Doddridge (1702–51), influenced by Baxter, opposed rigid forms of Calvinism without embracing Arminianism. Doddridge suggested that passages related to warning the saints against apostasy are "the means by which God continues his saints in their holy course, it being still true, that continued holiness is absolutely necessary in order to [sic!] their salvation, with which the *certainty* of their salvation in that way is not by any means inconsistent" (Lecture 179).[59] Anglican and Episcopalian "neutrality" regarding Calvinism and Arminianism appeared in later works such as Richard Laurence's *An Attempt to Illustrate those Articles of the Church of England which the Calvinist Improperly Consider as Calvinistical* (1805) and bishop William White's *Comparative Views of the Controversy between the Calvinists and the Arminians* (1817).[60]

---

[56] BAXTER (1675), Ninth Days Conference, Second Crimination; Tenth Days Conference, Fifth Crimination; The First Part: Of God's Nature, Knowledge, and Decrees of God, 24.685–89; Pacifying Principles, 18.257–276.

[57] BAXTER, *The Right Method For a Settled Peace of Conscience, and Spiritual Comfort* (1653), pp. 651f. Cited from Nuttal, 22.

[58] Cf. SCHREINER (1998), 61, whose information is from BEOUGHER (1990).

[59] DODDRIDGE (1804), 5:243.

[60] Cf. PRICHARD (1982), 23–51.

The subject of apostasy and perseverance was relegated to a less significant aspect of the Calvin-Arminian debate in the eighteenth century as the subjects of antinomianism, early unitarianism, and Enlightenment perspectives came to the forefront. Still questions about perseverance were being discussed and debated in the American colonies and England. Jonathan Edwards opted for assurance through self-examination of religious affections and godly living. In his *Religious Affections* (1746), gracious affections are confirmed by the witness of the Holy Spirit in the believer's spirit (e.g., Rom. 8:16).[61] Edwards and other New England Calvinists seemed to be concerned about the spreading influence of Arminianism in the area. His contentions often centred on subjects related to free-will.[62] For Edwards, perseverance involved obedience and godly living: "They that will not live godly lives, find out for themselves that they are not elected; they that will live godly lives, have found out for themselves that they are elected" (Miscellaneous Remarks 7:1).[63] The saints are to be cautious and pray regardless of the promise that they will persevere. They must take care and obey God, for "if Christians cease to care to persevere, that very thing is a falling away" (Misc. Rem. 7:16 cf. 9, 29). Responding to the possibility that a righteous man might die in his sin and have his prior righteousness rejected (cf. Ezek. 18:21–24), Edwards claims that such a person only *seems* to have righteousness. True believers never finally fall away and perish (Misc. Rem. 7:24–26). Apostates, then, were never genuine believers.

George Whitefield and John Wesley (the former a Calvinist and the latter an Arminian), who had been colleagues since the time of the Oxford Holy Club in 1729, became divided over issues such predestination, election, and perseverance even though both were considered non-controversialists.[64] Wesley rejected the Calvinist notion of perseverance in his works entitled *Serious Thoughts upon the Perseverance of the Saints* and *Predestination Calmly Considered* but he affirmed the doctrine of assurance related to salvation on the ground that believers had an inner testimony of the human spirit (which combines revelation, experience, and logic) and the Holy Spirit (which gives a subjective kind of assurance).[65] Assurance, however, seemed to be marked by a kind of *scala perfectionis*:[66] 1) some Christians have faith which is mixed with fear and doubt; 2) some Christians have the full assurance of faith in which they possess a present assurance; and 3) very few Christians have the full assurance of hope in which they have assurance of their final perseverance. In affirming these degrees, Wesley's position was not much different than that of Occam and Catholicism.

---

[61] Cf. OROPEZA (1995), 153.
[62] Cf. RICH (1987), 641–55.
[63] EDWARDS (1974), 2:596–603.
[64] Cf. HARRISON (1937), 193.
[65] NOLL (1975), 161–77; W. ABRAHAM (1989), 233.
[66] Cf. STOEFFLER (1965), 136.

Normally, Wesley affirmed that "we speak of an assurance of our present pardon; not ... of our final perseverance."[67] It is possible for certain believers to lose all assurance because it is possible for them to lose their salvation.

Howell Harris attempted to mend the breach between Whitefield and Wesley, hoping that the Wesley brothers would receive "further Light" and not oppose the Calvinist understanding of election and perseverance. Later on he came to affirm that he and they preached "two Gospels, one sets *all on God*, the other *on Man*; the one *on God's Will*, the other on *Man's Will*."[68] John Gill responded to Wesley's work in 1752 with *The Doctrine of the Saint's Final Perseverance*. Two years later Wesley responded with *An Answer to all which the Rev. Dr. Gill has printed on the Final Perseverance of the Saints*.[69]

In the nineteenth century the Calvinist-Arminian controversy waned in the wake of the development of theological liberalism and biblical criticism which appeared to modify the sharper dogmatism of the two camps.[70] Friedrich Schleiermacher (1830) took wind out of the debate by holding to a form of universal restoration. His own version of perseverance might be described this way: a regenerate person could not do an act so as to lose the grace of regeneration.[71]

In the Baptist tradition, however, *The New Hampshire Confession* reflected Calvinism while Free Will Baptists espoused Arminianism. J. R. Graves introduced Southern Baptist Landmarkism with perseverance in terms of the "security of the believers."[72] The question of apostasy and perseverance also found audience through systematic theological works from authors such as Heinrich Heppe (1851), Charles Hodge (1871–73), Robert Dabney (1878), and W. T. G. Shedd (1894) who held to the Calvinist perspective, and Thomas Rahlston (1874), William Burt Pope (1875–76), John Miley (1892–94), and J. A. Beet (1906) who stood for Arminianism.[73] In terms of the debate, then, the nineteenth century might be considered the period of the systematisation of the doctrines. Since that time, this contention in systematic theologies has not developed much further. Still both Calvinists and Arminians wrote more extensive works on the subject: Patrick H. Mell's *Predestination and the Saints'*

---

[67] Letter to Dr. Lavington, Bishop of Exeter (Nov. 19, 1751); cf. *Journal of John Wesley* 2.83 (Wesley, 1931:3.305).

[68] Letter from H. Harris to John Cennick, 27 October, 1740; extract reprinted in SELL (1983), 61–62. On Whitefield's view, see WHITEFIELD (1960 reprint), esp. 573–87; SELL, 61ff.

[69] Cf. SELL (1983), 81–82.

[70] Cf. HARRISON, 223.

[71] SCHLEIERMACHER, *The Christian Faith* sec. 111 (1926:510–17).

[72] MOODY (1981), 362. Moody's own affirmation of the doctrine of apostasy marks a later point of departure from the normative Southern Baptist position.

[73] Although Charles Finney is often considered an advocate for Arminianism, it seems that he held to some form of the perseverance of the saints (FINNEY, 1957:544–619). PETERSON (1990:122) notes that the Bethany Fellowship omits FINNEY'S section on perseverance in their 1976 reprint of Finney's *Lectures*.

Perseverance, Stated and Defended (1851) and Albert Nash's *Perseverance and Apostasy: Being an Argument in Proof of the Arminian Doctrine* (1871) are two examples.[74]

In the first half of the twentieth century, those who addressed the issue did not seem to add any significant advancements. Representative systematic works in this area are exemplified by the theologies of Louis Berkhof for the Calvinists (1939) and H. Orton Wiley for the Arminians (1941–49).[75] Karl Barth, on the other hand, believing that Jesus was the only elect and reprobate human, affirmed a type of universalism.[76] New movements in the twentieth century, such as those found in the dispensational and Pentecostal schools, merely drew sides on the issue with the former moderately siding with Calvinism and the latter with Arminianism.[77] More recently, proponents from the dispensational school have been some of the leading figures behind the American evangelical debate over the doctrines of grace and assurance. But these "in-house" debates often presuppose final perseverance, and from there a contention about grace, repentance, and aspects related to present assurance of final perseverance ensues. Carson demonstrates that some of the main advocates of this controversy lack scholastic and exegetical sophistication.[78]

Although both the Calvinists and Arminians read Scripture in light of their views, such debates had little to say about one's method of interpreting biblical texts. Essentially, both sides addressed the issue of perseverance and apostasy by selecting texts to reinforce their respective dogmatic positions while either ignoring or briefly explaining away the opposing view. Both positions often revived old arguments from their predecessors, sometimes knowingly, sometimes unknowingly. Other traditions also focused primarily on theological aspects of apostasy and perseverance without breaking fresh ground in the biblical domain. With the rise of various methodological approaches to biblical writings in the twentieth century, however, new possibilities for understanding apostasy and perseverance have been opened up.

---

[74] For further listings, see the appendix and bibliography.

[75] Some other works in this century include BOETTNER (1932), MURRAY (1955), SELLERS (1987), and SCHREINER & WARE, eds. (1995) for the Calvinists; STEELE (1899), JESSUP (1938) (1942), SHANK (1961), and PINNOCK, ed. (1975), (1989) for the Arminians. Cf. HEGLE (1961) and PETERSON (1990:119–25) for more examples.

[76] BARTH (1957), 2.2; cf. BRUNNER (1950), 1:346–53.

[77] Representative systematic works of the latter include PEARLMAN (1937) and E. WILLIAMS (1953); the former, CHAFER (1947) and THIESSEN (1949). Representative works from other traditions which include apostasy and perseverance are listed in the appendix.

[78] CARSON (1992), 1–29. Peterson writes that a debate of similar magnitude arose in Westminster Chapel in England, which was generated by teachers such as R. T. KENDALL (1983) and has implications as to whether British Calvinism stems more from Beza than Calvin (1990:119f).

1.3 Recent Approaches to the Question of Perseverance and Apostasy

In the last several decades, relatively little scholarly work has been carried through in the area of apostasy and perseverance. Some works have focused on philosophical aspects of this area or have studied sociological and demographic dimensions.[79] Most of the recent approaches have used either the systematic theological or the traditio-historical method as their starting point. The last two approaches do not, of course, exhaust the ways of interpreting this subject, but they are currently the most prominent. Below are some of the most significant works of recent years which draw on these methods.[80]

1.3.1 The Classical-Theological Approach to Perseverance and Apostasy: G. C. Berkouwer

During the second half of the twentieth century, G. C. Berkouwer has made a theological contribution in the area of apostasy and perseverance with his work entitled *Faith and Perseverance* (1958). Berkouwer combines the early Protestant confessions with biblical Scripture to arrive at his perception of perseverance. He suggests that passages which seem contrary to the doctrine of perseverance are a means which God uses to lead the saints to trust God.[81] Obedience is therefore an important factor. Yet passages that seem to warn against the danger of apostasy do not exhaust the reality of God's grace.[82] Perseverance, which is realised in the believer through prayer, preaching, and sacraments, can only be maintained in faith through God's grace. Thus, perseverance is a gift which is sealed by faith. Christians persevere when they cease to trust themselves and rest in God's persevering grace.[83] Berkouwer concludes, "When the Reformed fathers spoke about the consolation of perseverance, they had God's grace in mind. Hence, the doctrine of perseverance, as long as it recognises its dependence on grace, can never be a mere abstraction which makes an eventless continuity of life."[84]

Berkouwer's argument that biblical admonitions are a means by which God brings about perseverance is nothing new.[85] This view is not without its weaknesses. If the elect were not admonished, would they then be able to fall away?

---

[79] See for instance WOLTERSTORFF (1990), 396–417; CRAIG (1991), 65–74; and HELM (1993), 103–09 for the former; BROMLEY, ed. (1988); HUNSBERGER (1983), 21–38; and HADAWAY (1992), 26–34 for the latter.

[80] For other recent exegetical works on the subject, see the appendix.

[81] BERKOUWER (1958), 97–121.

[82] Berkouwer writes, "If anything is certain it is this, that according to the Scriptures God's grace does not stop at the limits of human freedom of choice" (1958:90).

[83] BERKOUWER, 234–36 cf. 106, 213.

[84] BERKOUWER, 238.

[85] Cf. DODDRIDGE (1802–06) before Berkouwer's time and SCHREINER (1998) afterwards.

If not, exactly what special distinction or significance does the warning motif have in the New Testament? Are we to assume that, along with grace, the warnings are necessarily effectual for the elect but not the non-elect? Even if we suppose that this is conceivable, in view of other options, is it the most probable? Namely, if Berkouwer stripped away his Reformed presuppositions, would he have honestly arrived at the same conclusions? His perspective lacks evidence from the New Testament authors themselves. Did *they* believe that the very hearing or reading of their warnings worked or necessitated effectual perseverance among the elect? If we were to examine the warning passages in light of their respective contexts, would we not consider it a better option to affirm that at least some of the writers assumed their recipients were genuine believers who were in real danger of apostasy? It seems that Berkouwer's interpretation is put forth more *for the sake of the Reformed system* than for the sake of being entirely true to the full impact of the warning passages.

Berkouwer begins his study by citing Reformed confessions before moving to biblical scripture.[86] It comes as no surprise, then, that he subsumes perseverance under the rubric of grace and does not carefully examine passages which may be associated with apostasy. Doctrines central to the Reformed confessions become the presupposition to which all biblical passages conform. On the other hand, another theological method does no better if someone begins with passages that may be related to apostasy, but then reads into this a system that misinterprets passages on perseverance, election, and predestination. If systematic theologians mitigate either the doctrine of apostasy by means of election, or election by means of apostasy, their approach often becomes little more than a rehashing of old Calvinist or Arminian dogmas with perhaps the added benefit of adopting and systematising biblical passages that have been interpreted through traditio-historical exegesis.[87]

Missing from Berkouwer and other theological works is the analysis of passages in light of their own social-historical, cultural, and rhetorical milieus. One should attempt to understand what a biblical subject meant to the original recipients. A faulty starting base inevitably leads to a faulty trajectory. Berkouwer's assumptions convince only those who share his Reformed opinions. To those outside the system, his arguments sound like cases of special pleading. Another related problem is that the systematisation of passages has a tendency to make Paul, John, the Synoptic texts, and other New Testament writers or writings say essentially the same thing without presenting any real diversity on the issues of perseverance and apostasy.

---

[86] BERKOUWER, 19.

[87] Berkouwer's view partially prompted Shank's work (1961), a Wesleyan-Arminian response to perseverance and apostasy (1961:165–78). Sellers' work (1987), which defends the Calvinist view, in turn, responds back to Shank.

1.3.2 The Traditio-Historical Approach to Perseverance and Apostasy:
I. Howard Marshall and D. A. Carson

In his book entitled *Kept By The Power of God: A Study of Perseverance and Falling Away*, I. Howard Marshall rightly notes that New Testament scholars have not adequately explored the topic of sanctification in relation to perseverance and apostasy. Too often they have given this subject over to the dogmatician, whether Calvinist or Arminian. Regarding these perspectives, Marshall writes, "The only hope of a *rapprochement* between these two points of view would appear to lie in a thorough study of the New Testament evidence."[88] He commends Berkouwer for emphasising the assurance of final salvation, but he criticises him for not facing up to the real danger described in New Testament warning passages. He also criticises Rudolf Bultmann for going to the opposite pole in making faith seem purely dependent on human effort and providing no comfort or assurance in perseverance.[89] His work takes tradition-history into account as he begins his study by examining texts which may have influenced New Testament thought. These sources include the Hebrew scriptures, the Dead Sea Scrolls, and "Rabbinic" literature.[90]

Marshall believes that Jewish literature has much to say about national apostasy. God forsakes those who forsake him, and those who forsake him may never return (Jer. 14:10ff; 15:6; Ps. 78:59–60). Regarding transgressions committed by individuals, he writes that a person who commits "witting" sin would have been "cut off" from the community of believers. Such a person's sin must not contaminate the camp (cf. Exod. 12:15; Lev. 7:20f; Num. 15:30f; Josh. 7; Isa. 22:14). Regarding the Qumran community, he concludes that the group seemed to hold a form a predestination which did not preclude the potential for members to fall away. He finishes the chapter by affirming that for the Pharisees, the tension between divine foreknowledge and human freedom is not worked out; "it was enough to state the fact of a human freedom which might lead to righteousness or apostasy."[91]

Marshall then proceeds to the New Testament of which he covers a different corpus in each chapter. For the Synoptic Gospels, he affirms that theoretically, one could be a disciple of Christ without attaining the coming kingdom, but it is very difficult to ascertain if any of the disciples fell away in this sense. Judas may have been a nominal disciple and Peter's abandonment was only temporary. In any case, he states that there is no affirmation that perseverance is a special grace that is guaranteed to some disciples.[92] In other New Testament

---

[88] MARSHALL (1969), 6 cf. 207.
[89] MARSHALL, 200–207; cf. BULTMANN (1951), 1:320–22.
[90] MARSHALL, 9–28.
[91] MARSHALL, 29.
[92] MARSHALL, 70. S. BROWN, on the other hand, affirms Judas as an apostate in Luke's Gospel (1969:82–97).

writings Marshall suggests more firmly that the writers warn against apostasy as a potential threat among the Christian community; hence, there is a need for them to persevere.[93] Marshall concludes that the possibility of falling away should drive believers to a renewed faith. Nevertheless, they should not become overwhelmed by fear of apostatising because God gives sufficient strength to those who persevere.[94]

Marshall rightly looks into the Hebrew scriptures and early Jewish traditions in an attempt to find how they may have influenced the New Testament writers, some of whom appear to have been brought up in the Jewish faith.[95] This approach sets Marshall apart from Berkouwer because he focuses on the ideas and presuppositions that may have influenced the New Testament writers themselves instead of how their interpreters in church history have understood them. Marshall's approach provides a safeguard against reading into the New Testament too much of one's own theological presuppositions. Unfortunately, his preliminary survey of Jewish literature is very brief. Marshall's conclusion suggests that his concerns are partially pastoral. In his introduction, he notes the problem of church membership loss in the 1960s prompted his study of this theme. He is concerned with a phenomenon that often occurs in religious communities wherein a person who was once a faithful religious adherent at point A is no longer so at point B. Marshall thus relates the question of perseverance to the Calvin-Arminian problem of the doctrine of assurance. Along these lines D. A. Carson responds to Marshall and others in an article entitled, "Reflections on Christian Assurance."[96]

Carson asserts that arguing for a hypothetical warning or a loss of service or rewards as opposed to a loss of salvation in certain New Testament passages such as Hebrews 6:4–6 and 1 John 2:19 "are desperate expedients that responsible exegesis will happily avoid."[97] Such views cannot be sustained in many cases without torturing the texts. Carson affirms that falling away occurs, but the issue for him is whether those who fall away are genuine believers. He suggests that Marshall diminishes the force of passages which affirm ultimate perseverance by stressing passages that refer to apostasy and human responsibility to persevere. One example of the former is John 6:37–40 in which Carson affirms that Jesus will keep and preserve those whom the Father has given

---

[93] MARSHALL, 86–88, 106–114, 129, 145f, 165–67.

[94] MARSHALL, 205–06.

[95] On Paul's Jewish background, for instance, see JEREMIAS (1969), 88–94.

[96] For Carson, the basis of assurance is Christ and his work, and "failure to persevere serves to undermine assurance" (1992:28–29). He defines assurance as "a Christian believer's confidence that he or she is already in a right standing with God, and that this will issue in ultimate salvation" (1–2). For a list of studies on assurance, see the appendix.

[97] CARSON, 14. For further criticisms of these viewpoints, see also SCHREINER (1998), 32–62.

him.[98] He also cites 1 John 2:19, among other passages, in maintaining that "genuine faith, by definition, perseveres; where there is no perseverance, by definition the faith cannot be genuine."[99]

In Carson's earlier work entitled *Divine Sovereignty and Human Responsibility: Biblical Perspectives in Tension*, he begins by examining the impact of the Old Testament and early Jewish literature upon the New Testament texts and affirms that God's sovereignty and human responsibility are held in a balance of tension.[100] For Carson, the Hebrew scriptures indicate that apostasy does not dissolve election because a remnant of Israelites always remain after they rebel against God and are punished (cf. Mic. 2:12; 4:7; Isa. 1:9). The elect may be a smaller group than the "covenant people" as a whole, but only the former will enjoy the new covenant (Isa. 10:20ff; 11:11–16; 55:3; Jer. 31:33; 32:37f; 50:5).[101] Carson also notes the variety of opinions among early Jewish writings.[102] He then examines the subject of election in the Gospel of John and affirms that the elect could never finally fall away.[103]

Several observations and reflections are worth noting in relation to Carson and Marshall. First, Carson applies a traditio-historical method to the subject of apostasy. Like Marshall, he examines early relevant Hebrew and Jewish traditions to shed light on the interpretation of the New Testament writers. However, his criticism that Marshall diminishes the importance of the weight of perseverance passages seems problematic. Carson refers to only a few passages which appear to describe inauthentic Christians (e.g., Matt. 7:15–23; 1 John 2:19) and

---

[98] CARSON, 16. Here Marshall questions whether the will of God may be frustrated by human sin. W. Abraham, on the other hand, suggests that 6:36–40 is a chiasm which juxtaposes responsibility and security under the sovereignty of God (1989:248).

[99] CARSON, 17. Here Carson seems to agree with Gundry Volf (see below) whom he refers to in his article in a rather favourable manner although he does express some criticisms of her work (14–16).

[100] CARSON (1981), 197ff. Carson considers this tension as the mystery of compatibilism (1992:24–25). Somewhat similar is Borchert who stresses assurance without mitigating the warning passages. Both are held in tension as part of the mystery of the divine-human relationship (1987:esp. 211). Schreiner criticises Borchert's conclusion by suggesting that such a position seems to embrace a contradiction (1998:52). The questionable assumption here is whether the words of the New Testament authors should be understood with the same rigors of logic that theologians use today. Certainly, paradoxes, double-meanings, hyperbole, and other ancient forms of language found in the NT render untenable an endeavour to employ the stricter views of logic to the texts consistently (e.g., Tit. 1:12–13; Luke 14:26; 1 Cor. 10:4; John 6; cf. DAMER, 1987 for more possible examples).

[101] CARSON (1981), 31.

[102] CARSON (1981:60–78) notes that some Jewish literature states that the number of elect is determined by God (cf. 4 Ezra 4:36), while Qumran literature narrows the elect to the remnant (cf. 1 QM 12.1; 13:7–10; 14:8–10). Some apocalyptic literature might view the Messiah as God's elect one (1 En. 39:6; 40:4f; 45:3f; 46:3f; 61:8; Apoc. Abr. 31.1). The "Rabbis" generally believed the Jews were an elect people; thus, individual Jews are automatically elect unless they opt out of the religious community.

[103] CARSON, 195.

then adds to these verses certain hypothetical "if" passages (e.g., Col. 1:22–23; 2 Pet. 1:10–11; Heb. 3:6, 14) to support his view that "genuine faith is tied to perseverance; transitory faith is spurious."[104] Perhaps some who fell away were never genuine believers (e.g., 1 John 2:19 – provided the assumption that the Johannine writer is adequately representing his opponents!), but this does not mean that *all* the accounts or warnings of apostasy in the New Testament may be understood this way. Marshall seems correct in affirming that "the 'mixed Church' theory is accordingly not adequate to explain *the whole* of the New Testament."[105] Some cases may involve genuine believers while others do not.

Second, both Carson and Marshall rightly take to task a view of assurance which mitigates the warning passages and discourses that encourage obedience. Marshall asserts that "whether I am a Calvinist or not, I must heed the encouragements and warnings, in the former case to show that I am a real and not a seeming believer, and in the latter case for fear that I might fall away from the real faith that I have."[106] An observation related to this point is that humans may never be free from all the problems of anxiety which personal assurance is perhaps wrongly intended to resolve. The existentialists have helped others appreciate this point.[107] The Christian life seems to involve an aspect of working out personal salvation with "fear and trembling" (cf. Phil. 2:12). Assurance and anxiety may have their proper place, especially if they help prevent *desparatio* and *presumptio*.

A third reflection is this. On a socio-phenomenological level, statistics on the numerous accounts of apostasy in the world (past and present) appear to demonstrate the reality of the phenomenon.[108] Priests, ministers, bishops, missionaries, Sunday school teachers, theologians, and laypersons have all been known to abandon their faith, and this happens regardless of one's interpretation of the warning passages. If some apply Carson's interpretation to the phenomenon, perhaps they could explain certain cases as people who were never genuinely converted. Carson's view may have limited benefits in this regard. However, if some take this view a step further and reply that every case of apostasy never

---

[104] CARSON (1992), 17. Contrariwise, the "if" passages, when read in light of their respective situations, are often interpreted as affirming a potential threat of the falling away of genuine believers (e.g., 2 Pet. 2:1–22; and McKNIGHT [1992:21–59] on the Hebrews passages).

[105] MARSHALL, 200. (Emphasis mine.) A few examples which are mentioned by Marshall that would seem to support his view include Hebrews 6:4ff; 2 Peter 2:1; and Revelation 22:19.

[106] MARSHALL (1990b), 314; cf. also COOK (1993), 150–51.

[107] Cf. Hunt who also writes, "The believer can never simply sit back, as though the full experience of his faith were already realized" (1971: 239).

[108] Cf. the research and statistics of HADAWAY (1992), 26–34; HADAWAY and Roof (1988), 194–200; BROMLEY (1988), 9–25; Nelson and BROMLEY (1988), 47–61; HUNSBERGER (1983), 121–38; (1980), 158–70; cf. GREELEY (1971), 125–34; SATO, 619–21; BARBOUR (1994), and historical examples above.

involved a genuine convert, they are making a sweeping statement which seems insufficient and does not correspond to the various cases of the phenomenon. Many apostates do appear to have been genuine Christians, and the explanation that they all "lacked" the gift of perseverance is too shallow when no consistent and objective criteria has been established to determine who *has* the gift. Those who make such a claim have yet to provide a consistent way to determine who is genuine and who is not *before* the apostasy occurs.[109] Hence, sweeping explanations of this sort become insufficient when made to cohere with the phenomenon of apostasy found in the external world.

One final observation is that the traditio-historical approach which both Carson and Marshall use did not prevent them from arriving at different conclusions about apostasy. Both examine the Johannine text, for example, but they emphasise different motifs. Marshall stresses that John's use of "abiding" (μένω) in Christ is similar to – if not the same as – persevering in Christ (cf. John 14:10; 15:4ff; 1 John 2:28; 2 John 7–11). Those who do not continue abiding in Christ are cast out (John 15:6).[110] Carson stresses the new birth and sonship of believers and that they were given to Christ by God (cf. John 1:12f; 3:3–7; 6:35f; 17:2f).[111] True apostates could not be genuinely saved in the first place (1 John 2:19). Conversely, Marshall claims that John allows for the idea of a mixed church but John still warns against failing to persevere (1 John 2:24; 2 John 8).[112] In such a view the reality of inauthentic believers does not preclude that everyone who falls away was never saved to begin with. In any case, many issues related to apostasy and perseverance remain unresolved despite the sophisticated exegesis of Marshall and Carson.

1.3.3 Judith Gundry Volf's Contribution to the Study of Perseverance and Apostasy

Perhaps the most important study of recent times on the subject of apostasy and perseverance is represented by Judith Gundry Volf's work entitled *Paul and Perseverance: Staying In and Falling Away*.[113] Her approach might best be considered as topical-exegetical. She covers the major writings of Paul but leaves out the disputed texts of 1 and 2 Timothy, Titus, Ephesians, and Colossians.

---

[109] Cf. R. PERKINS (1988), 58. Likewise, some apostates, when they still professed Christianity, could have very well affirmed that they too had present assurance of final perseverance.

[110] MARSHALL (1969), 171–86.

[111] CARSON (1981), 181–195.

[112] MARSHALL, 184–87; cf. MARSHALL (1978), 152.

[113] GUNDRY VOLF (1990). Marshall, who does not hold to Judith Gundry Volf's position, has said that Gundry Volf's work "bids fair to be the most detailed and acute study of the topic thus far" (1990b:308).

Gundry Volf's evaluation arose from the reexamination of Paul's gospel by E. P. Sanders who has argued that for Paul, salvation is by grace, while judgement is by works. One does not observe the law in order to enter into a state of being "in" grace; rather, one must keep the law to stay in. Both Paul and most early Jewish writings emphasise that works function as a way of "staying in."[114] Sanders also maintains that Paul thought heinous, uncorrected sin could lead to one's exclusion from salvation.[115]

Beginning with Sanders' conclusion as her starting point, Gundry Volf attempts to answer the questions, "Does Paul assume that Christians will remain in salvation? If so, on what basis? What, if anything, can disrupt this continuity, and to what extent can it do so?"[116] At the beginning of her endeavour, she admits that her exegetical conclusions are theologically similar to the classic Reformed position. Nevertheless, she assures the reader, "my intent is to uncover what Paul, unaware of theological systems formed after his time, believed about continuity in [the] Christians' salvation."[117]

In the first of four sections, she examines the matter of Paul's perspective on the salvific continuity of the saints. There is an eschatological tension between the Christian's present and final salvation in which Gundry Volf explores the question of whether Paul believed the saints would "stay in" the faith during the imminent tribulation of the eschaton. She gathers a battery of texts beginning with the *ordo salutis* or "golden chain" in Romans 8:29–30.[118] Because the elect are "foreknown" (προγινώσκειν) and "predestined" (προορίζειν), she asserts that God's saving work involves the individual's final salvation, as expressed in the term "glorification."[119] The saved are considered (individual) objects, with God as the subject of salvation throughout the entire saving process. Whatever the obstacles, God will complete the work God started in the Christian because God is faithful in fulfilling his eternal purposes.[120]

Part two of her work explores Pauline texts which create a tension with her argument from part one because they have been interpreted by some scholars to underscore the possibility that ethical failure can disrupt a person's salvation. These texts include the "destruction" of weak congregation members by means of the liberty of stronger members in reference to eating and drinking (Rom. 14:1–23; 1 Cor. 8:7–13), the chastisement of Christians who practice grievous

---

[114] E. P. SANDERS (1977), 543; (1983), 10, 147.

[115] E. P. SANDERS (1983), 105 (cf. 112): "... those who deny their faith lose the salvation which faith brings."

[116] GUNDRY VOLF, 1.

[117] GUNDRY VOLF, 2–3.

[118] Other scriptural references Gundry Volf examines in this section are 2 Thessalonians 2:13–14, 1 Thessalonians 5:9, Romans 8:23, 2 Corinthians 1:22, 5:5, and Philippians 1:6.

[119] Gundry Volf interprets προγινώσκειν as "God's prior choice, not prior knowledge" and προορίζειν as "God's eternal determination of the elect to a goal" (9).

[120] GUNDRY VOLF, 13, 33, 80.

sins (1 Cor. 11:27–34; 5:1–5), the warning to beware or else one may fall into sin (1 Cor. 10:12), and the exclusion from the kingdom of heaven of those who practice sinful vices (1 Cor. 6:9–11; Gal. 5:19–21). She concludes that unethical behaviour in a Christian setting does not indicate a loss of one's salvation. Rather, such behaviour constitutes evidence for an inauthentic Christianity. Those who continually practice unethical behaviour are not truly converted in the first place. Alternatively, God may chastise a genuine Christian who falls into sin, but this is not the same as saying that he or she will be eternally condemned.[121]

In part three, Gundry Volf attempts to answer the question of whether a person's salvation can be undermined through unbelief. In Romans 9–11 she finds that Israel's current state of unbelief is only temporary. God's election of Israel to salvation will prove to be irrevocable on the day when "all Israel shall be saved" (Rom. 11:26). She admits, however, that Paul's warning that the Gentiles could be "cut off" because of their boasting allows for the possibility that those who do not put their trust in God's grace may fall away.[122] Nevertheless, Paul does not expect the worst to happen because final salvation rests in a faithful God whose acting grace preserves the elect.[123]

The final section addresses the continuity of Paul's own salvation experience.[124] In passages such as 1 Corinthians 9:23–27 Gundry Volf claims that Paul's introverted struggle is not with his own salvation; rather, it involves his desire not to fall into divine disapproval regarding his apostolic mission. In other passages Paul establishes his personal conviction that he will continue in the faith (Rom. 6:5; 8:11; 2 Cor. 4:14). That Paul's message to the saints might be in vain is for the sake of argument only, according to Gundry Volf – but she admits it is possible that some of these passages envision the possibility of falling away. Ultimately, however, such passages are not permitted to play a significant role in her thesis since "it is also possible to interpret these texts as not presupposing final loss of salvation, and compelling arguments for any view are lacking …"[125]

---

[121] GUNDRY VOLF, 155–57.

[122] GUNDRY VOLF, 197. In part three she also exegetes Galatians 5:1–4 (a passage referring to the falling away from grace of the one who seeks to be justified by circumcision), and 2 Corinthians 13:5 (a passage referring to self-examination lest one falls short of being Christian).

[123] Gundry Volf states, "God will do so [keep the elect] not apart from their faith in the gospel, but accompanied by their faith, though that faith is not necessarily a constant in the process of salvation, which derives its essential continuity instead from divine initiative" (229).

[124] Gundry Volf notes that Paul also struggles with the notion of whether he himself has run in vain in Philippians 3:11–12. Moreover, he considers whether his labour among other Christians has been in vain (Phil. 2:16; 1 Thes. 3:5; Gal. 2:2; 4:11; 1 Cor. 15:2; 2 Cor. 6:1).

[125] GUNDRY VOLF, 282.

Gundry Volf has contributed to the subject of apostasy and perseverance by examining the issue more carefully in light of one New Testament author.[126] She thus avoids the problematic method of many Calvinists and Arminians who have attempted to create a completely homogenous explanation to the subject at the expense of making all the New Testament writers say essentially the same thing. Nevertheless, a few criticisms are worth noting regarding Gundry Volf's approach. First, she approaches the subject of apostasy topically. She claims that "the grouping of texts with common *topoi* lets their parallelism, nuances and contrasts come to light more easily."[127] She adds, "This arrangement does not overlook the possibility that Paul's epistles reflect a general development in his theology. But other factors affecting interpretation – especially historical and literary contexts – seem in this case to unlock more doors to Paul's meaning than do chronological considerations."[128] Problematic in her approach is the seemingly arbitrary starting point: her exegetical foundation rests on a Reformed understanding of election and predestination, which she then presupposes when examining texts that might reflect apostasy. Paul's warning passages thus tend to be reinterpreted in light of God's predetermined election of individuals to final salvation.

We can observe this limitation in her conclusion to part four. After examining several passages in which Paul is concerned that his labour among some of his converts might be in vain, Gundry Volf writes that Galatians 4:11 and 2 Corinthians 6:1 might allow for a real danger of falling away, but it is also possible that they do not mean this at all. Since arguments are lacking for any view, she maintains that "the texts in question cannot play a decisive role in the discussion of perseverance. By the same token, passages where Paul's meaning is plain ought to take precedence over the ambiguous ones in the attempt to formulate a concluding statement on Paul's view of staying in salvation."[129]

One cannot help but ask what makes the perseverance passages "plain" and the ones which conflict with them "ambiguous"? This question becomes especially poignant when we notice that only one section of her work establishes the foundation upon which she bases her argument for perseverance while the other three sections are devoted to explaining the passages which potentially contradict her foundation. If an unconditional election that stresses individualism is rightly the starting point for perseverance in Pauline theology, why does Paul seem to write much more about the dangers of falling away?

It seems that even though she wishes to let Paul speak for himself, the thrust of her arguments have already been compiled in favour of the position she

---

[126] In recent memory, Schuyler Brown also pursued an important study of this sort in reference to the Lukan texts (1969).

[127] GUNDRY VOLF, 4.

[128] Ibid.

[129] GUNDRY VOLF, 282.

wishes to support. The *analogia fidei* of her work begins with a Calvinist view of election. The emphasis on the work of God and believers as mere objects of salvation seems to fit well with classic Reformed theology. On the other hand, she does allow for the *possibility* of falling away; nevertheless, her presuppositions seem to direct her away from the conclusion that certain texts may point to falling away as a *real occurrence* that could culminate in a loss of salvation.

A second weakness from her work stems from the first. By studying Paul and perseverance topically, Gundry Volf emphasises individual Pauline *passages*, not Pauline epistles in their entirety. A topical approach to individual Pauline passages can fail to take into consideration the situation unique to the audience for which Paul wrote each of his letters. Both Joest and Watson have recognised that Paul's messages of grace and justification may often be directed to different audiences and in a different frame of mind than his warning statements. Both despair (*anfechtung*) and false security (*securitas*) are problems that arise among various congregation members in differentiating circumstances, and Paul has to encounter both issues.[130] In Gundry Volf's work, the texts from Romans, Corinthians, and Galatians are often sprinkled throughout her study without adequate recognition that Paul was addressing particular situations in his letters. Missing in Gundry Volf's method is a proper focus on the historical-cultural milieu of each of these letters as a whole. This basic issue is too often left aside and not integrated into her thesis.

Gundry Volf's treatment of 1 Corinthians exemplifies the limitations of her method. She critically examines ten different passages from 1 Corinthians in all: 1:8,9; 5:1–5; 6:9–11; 8:7–13; 9:23; 9:27; 10:12; 10:13; 11:27–34; 15:2. The order they appear in her work, however, is quite different. The texts of 10:13 and 1:8,9 are examined in chapter 2 under the heading of "Tension in Continuity," 8:7–13 appears in chapter 3 ("Destruction of the Weak"); 11:27–34, 5:1–5, and 10:12 in chapter 4 ("Punishment of the Disobedient"); 6:9–11 in chapter 5 ("Exclusion of Evildoers from the Kingdom"); 9:27 and 9:23 in chapter 8 ("Paul's Hope"); and 15:2 in chapter 9 ("Believing in Vain"). This approach does injustice to the fact that these passages are interrelated. Paul originally provided these instructions to a young church as its adherents underwent factional and ethical problems. Likewise, Romans 8:29–30 functions as her foundation text on perseverance while Romans 9–11 is examined under a different heading related to apostasy some 150 pages later.[131]

---

[130] Joest (1968); N. Watson (1983), 212ff.

[131] The connection between Romans 8 and 9–11 may add an important dimension to the study of election and perseverance if these chapters are taken together. Gundry Volf's view of election and predestination in chapter 8 might need to be reinterpreted once we read it in light of chapters 9–11 where Paul speaks of the "cutting off" of some of the elect of Israel and warns that the same thing could happen to the Christian Gentiles (cf. this work ch. 5:2.2f).

Finally, Gundry Volf divorces 1 Corinthians 10:12 from 10:13 without giving enough recognition that 10:12 functions as the climax of an entire pericope on apostasy beginning in 10:1. In addition, the wilderness journey in 10:1–13 is closely related to the foot race metaphor in 9:24–27 which, in turn, is closely related to a longer literary context of meat sacrificed to idols spanning from 8:1 to 11:1. The ramifications of idolatry, fornication, factions, and related problems in Corinth are almost completely missing in Gundry Volf's evaluation of this verse. All the chapters in part two of her work (chapters 3–5 where she attempts to explain apparent apostasy passages) involve aspects of potential apostasy related to situations at the church in Corinth. Despite the significance of 1 Corinthians for Paul's understanding of perseverance and apostasy, Gundry Volf's topical-exegetical method does not observe properly the unifying structures and dynamics which may have conditioned both the Corinthian congregation and Paul's response to their contingent situation.

1.4 Evaluation of the Recent Debate

We find some significant shortcomings in Gundry Volf's work, as noted above. Her superb exegesis does not nullify the fact that her starting point remains arbitrary. In this respect, her approach is not so different than Berkouwer's systematic method and thus suffers from some of the same setbacks. The latter openly starts with the Reformed creeds and then looks at the entirety of the New Testament scriptures – in a superficial way – to arrive at a theology of perseverance. The former, though examining passages on perseverance in a more thorough manner, begins with Pauline texts which she interprets very much along the lines of the Reformed tradition. Other Pauline texts which are more problematic for her are then interpreted with this presupposition.

In keeping with the Calvinist idea of the perseverance of the saints, Carson affirms, like Gundry Volf, that if a person fell away from the faith, he/she was never a true disciple in the first place. Yet Carson asserts that there is ultimately an unresolved tension between election and the sovereignty of God on the one hand, and human responsibility and freedom on the other. On the other end of the spectrum, Marshall's view falls much in line with the Arminian tradition. Hence, in theological terms, it seems that even a serious exegesis of New Testament passages on perseverance and apostasy could result in one's position ending somewhere within the continuum marked by Calvinism and Arminianism. This occurrence is frequently the case, it seems, because a number of theologians and biblical exegetes from Calvinist or Arminian persuasions have often assumed that a unilateral conception is maintained by the various New Testament authors – as though these authors all believed and thought alike on apostasy and perseverance irrespective of different circumstances, time, education, and cultural and ethnic backgrounds. Studies such as Dunn's *Unity and Diversity in the New Testament* have demonstrated that the New Testament apostles and saints did not always think and believe alike (e.g., Gal. 2).[132]

If unity and diversity in relation to apostasy and perseverance marks the history of the church (as we have examined), it might also seem to describe earliest Christianity. Whereas the author of Hebrews offers no hope of restoration after apostasy (Heb. 6:4–6), the writer of James *does* (James 5:19–20). If the Johannine writer understands apostates as false believers, this does not mean that 2 Peter must do the same. Perhaps the Shepherd of Hermas holds for us an example of the proper paradigm when it depicts numerous levels of apostasy and endurance. Some believers are genuine and persevere, some are not genuine, and some are genuine but fall away. Some are restored while others are not.

Another observation is that if Gundry Volf's work correctly distils the major Pauline passages on perseverance and apostasy in his undisputed letters, then Paul gives more warnings than words of perseverance to the readers of his letters.[133] Hence, a further examination of Paul's view of apostasy seems in order. Perhaps more issues and resolutions could be addressed if new questions and approaches were explored. In reference to the Johannine disagreement between Marshall and Carson, for instance, we may want to ask a different set of questions: who were the opponents of John in his literature? What social dynamics might have coloured John's reaction toward those who fell away? What social and ethical issues are at stake? Social and rhetorical questions might shed new light when examining passages related to apostasy. We will now examine these approaches.

2. Rhetorical Approaches to New Testament Interpretation

The New Testament writers often exhort their readers to enact or refrain from certain beliefs or practices. It would therefore seem important to make an attempt at understanding such authors' communication to their readers in terms of speech and argumentation. Rhetorical questions may be important for our study because rhetoric involves persuasion. Yehoshua Gitay rightly comments that "Rhetoric, the art of persuasion, is concerned with an audience who may not share or may even oppose the speaker's/author's ideas, concepts, or ideolo-

---

[132] Even the homogenous atmosphere of the early Christians portrayed in Acts 2 is all but lost by the time we read Acts 21. A very conservative reader might object that diversity in scripture mitigates his/her notion of "divine inspiration." But what if the "divine" intended that unity and diversity be found in the scriptures?

[133] Of course more could have been said about the presumption of the law keepers in Romans 2:1–16, Paul's view of death in relation to believers in Romans 8:1–13, and so forth.

gies. Rhetorical analysis reveals the speaker's strategy of appealing to or mastering the audience's mind."[134]

2.1 George A. Kennedy: The Rhetorical Method

In *New Testament Interpretation through Rhetorical Criticism*, George A. Kennedy has provided certain theoretical concepts which underlie the use of classical rhetoric with the objective of supplying another tool for interpreting the New Testament. For Kennedy, "The ultimate goal of rhetorical analysis, briefly put, is the discovery of the author's intent and of how that is transmitted through a text to an audience."[135] Kennedy argues that "Paul could not expect to be persuasive unless there was some overlap between the content and form of what he said and the expectations of his audience."[136] Kennedy maintains that one must understand some classical rhetoric if one wishes to comprehend Paul's words when he addresses Greek-speaking audiences.[137]

Kennedy notes that according to Aristotle (*Rhetoric* 3.1.1358a), there are three types of rhetoric: 1) judicial (legal), which involves persuading an audience to make a judgement about the past; 2) deliberative (political), involving persuasion to take an action in the future; and 3) epideictic (ceremonial), involving the holding or reaffirming of a present position. He associates the first with speeches found in Acts and 2 Corinthians, the second with the Sermon on the Mount (Matt. 5–7), and the third with the Magnificat (Luke 1:46–55).[138]

The arrangement of judicial speeches normally contains several aspects to the composition including *proem, narratio, propositio, probatio, refutatio,* and *epilogue.*[139] Kennedy informs us that the arrangement of deliberative speeches often takes on a simplified form of the judicial speeches. This arrangement includes *proem, proposition, proof,* and *epilogue.* Kennedy gives an example of rhetorical arrangement by selecting 1 Corinthians chapter 1:

---

[134] GITAY (1993), 136.

[135] G. KENNEDY (1984), 12.

[136] G. KENNEDY, 10.

[137] It is evident that Paul addresses a primarily Gentile audience in at least some of his messages (cf. ch. 2 below).

[138] G. KENNEDY, 19–20. These categories would be considered a sub-category of the 5 parts of rhetoric as commonly taught in ancient Greek schools: invention (planning a discourse and arguments), arrangement (positioning of the various parts into a coherent whole), style (choosing the language and figures of speech in the composition), memory (delivery preparation), and delivery (instructions on speech and gestures). The three species of rhetoric come under the first category of the five parts (cf. KENNEDY, 13–14; D. WATSON, 1992:699). An excellent overview on rhetorical method is presented in D. WATSON (1988), ch. 1.

[139] G. KENNEDY, 23–25.

Proem or *Exordium*	Introduction and the obtaining of goodwill towards the speaker	1 Corinthians 1:4–9
Narratio	Exposition of facts or background information	1 Corinthians 1:11–12
Propositio or *Partitio*	Listing of proposition(s) into separate headings	1 Corinthians 1:10
Probatio	Supporting the proposition(s) with arguments	1 Corinthians 1:12–17
Refutatio and *Digressio*	Refuting the opposing view(s) – also includes motivation and attendant circumstance(s), if a *digression* is included	*Refutatio:* (1 Corinthians 1:12–17) *Digressio:* 1 Corinthians 1:18–29
Peroratio or *Epilogue*	Summary and emotional appeal to take action	1 Corinthians 1:30–31

According to Kennedy, the shortest rhetorical units in biblical literature should be at least 5 or 6 verses long. Their normal length takes up a good portion of a chapter or even several chapters. He adds, "One rhetorical unit may be enclosed within another, building up a structure which embraces the whole book. In rhetorical criticism it is important that the rhetorical unit chosen have some magnitude. It has to have within itself a discernible beginning and ending, connected by some action or argument."[140] Kennedy, however, does not specify whether he believes 1 Corinthians 1 is judicial or an exceptional deliberative case. We will observe that 1 Corinthians consists of some deliberative rhetorical units, and these units are comprised of warnings to the congregation. With this point in mind, I will now turn to a work which applies rhetorical criticism more specifically to the text of 1 Corinthians.

2.2 Margaret Mitchell: Rhetorical Method Employed in Paul's Letter to the Corinthians

A different application of rhetorical method is represented by Margaret Mitchell. She argues that 1 Corinthians is a unified letter which, as a whole, is the product of deliberative rhetoric. The primary function of the letter for Paul was to warn against factionalism, that is, to foster reconciliation among the various Chris-

---

[140] G. KENNEDY, 34.

tian groups at Corinth.[141] The prothesis (πρόθεσις) of the 1 Corinthians is found in 1:10 where Paul exhorts the congregation to be in unity, having the same mind and purpose, and that there should be no divisions among them. Mitchell suggests that Paul's deliberative rhetoric is characterised by 1) a focus on future time as the subject of deliberation; 2) the use of appeals or ends (the advantageous appeal – τὸ συμφέρον – being the most distinctive); 3) demonstration by example or παράδειγμά; and 4) subjects of deliberation; in the Corinthian case, factionalism and concord.[142] The thesis statement is then followed by the epistolary body, a statement of facts (1:11–17), and four proofs: the censure of factionalism (1:18–4:21); integrity against defilements (5:1–11:1); manifestation of factionalism in coming together (11:2–14:40); and the resurrection and final goal (15:1–57).

In the largest "proof" section (5:1–11:1), Paul offers advice on divisive issues which can result in defilement: fornication, solidarity issues (5:1–7:40), and meat sacrificed to idols (8:1–11:1). The last of these contains two separate treatments on idol meats (8:1–13; 10:23–11:1) and two examples as proofs (9:1–27; 10:1–13). Mitchell posits that 1 Corinthians 9:1–27 is generally a positive proof while 1 Corinthians 10:1–13 supports Paul's argument against discord in the congregation by appealing to negative examples for the church *not* to follow.[143] Since the latter text is clearly one of Paul's warning passages, we will focus on this text. The παράδειγμά in this passage compares the Corinthians with the Israelites in the wilderness. Despite their common identity as God's people, the Israelites still rebelled against God by committing vices such as coveting, idolatry, and fornication. Mitchell cites Philo and Josephus who both refer to the wilderness episode as a faction or στάσις.[144] Paul is thus saying that idolatry, fornication, testing the Lord, and murmuring can divide the Corinthian church.

This construal leads Mitchell to suggest that Paul may not be rebuking a Corinthian misconception that immunity is obtained through the sacraments (1 Cor. 10:3–4). She finds little support for this idea in the context. Although several contemporary or nearly contemporary sources seem to link ritual to "magical power" (e.g., Ignatius *Eph.* 20.2), Mitchell responds, "Nowhere is it said that the Corinthians (or Israelites!) engaged in the eating of idol meats or in sexual immorality because they believed that the magical powers of the Eucharist would protect them from harm."[145] The sacramental language in

---

[141] M. MITCHELL (1991), 1. Mitchell contends that both Paul and the Patristic fathers attempt to censure the heresies of schism in the Corinthian congregation (e.g. CLEMENT of Rome seems to agree with the Corinthian theme of factionalism – 1 CLEMENT 47).

[142] M. MITCHELL, 19, 23.

[143] M. MITCHELL (47–48) notes that Paul often cites the Hebrew Bible in 1 Corinthians (5:6–8; 6:16–17; 9:8–10, 13; 10:18; 11:2–16; 14:21; 15:32).

[144] M. MITCHELL, 139: Philo *Post Cain* 182–85 cf. *Vit Mos.* 1.24; *Ebr.* 99; Josephus *Antiq.* 3.295; 4.140.

[145] M. MITCHELL, 251–52.

1 Corinthians 10:1–13 is intended to convey that Israel was unified at the beginning; however, because of factions, harm came to virtually everybody.

The rhetorical device used by Paul in this section is the argument of "then and now" involving "a comparison of fortuitous, divinely assisted beginnings with later misfortunes. The application to the Corinthians will be made explicit in 10:14–17 (it is, however, already present in this passage in 10:6, 11)."[146] The Corinthian community is conceived so much in terms of a body that the very survival of the community is at stake due to the factions. Thus, for Mitchell, 1 Corinthians 10:12 reads: "even if you think you yourselves stand, you will indeed fall if others do."[147]

The way Mitchell has woven together the outline of 1 Corinthians through the theme of factionalism and concord is impressive. She maintains the unity of 1 Corinthians 8:1–11:1, for instance, by classifying 9:1–27 (sometimes considered a digressive apologetic for Paul's apostolic authority with little relation to the larger context) as an exemplary argument on the proper use of freedom for the common good.[148] Her approach assists the reader to look at 1 Corinthians in a rhetorical rather than theological way. This adds a new dimension to the study of this epistle.

There are some weaknesses, however, in Mitchell's handling of the passage under examination. The theme of unity and discord in her argument is at times emphasised at the expense of a reconstruction of specific reasons why unity at

---

[146] M. MITCHELL, 252. An alternative rhetorical explanation on 1 Corinthians 8–10 comes from Countryman who suggests that Paul uses a devise employed by Cicero and others in which the first and last arguments are the strongest. In the first argument, Paul grants the "strong" in Corinth their premise that foods, idols, and physical purity are irrelevant. Nevertheless, when the strong participate in such things, they can cause the "weak" to stumble (chs. 8–9). In the second argument (10:1–13), which is weaker, Paul warns that strong Christians should not be overconfident. According to Countryman, Paul adds nothing new here ethically to the situation. In the third argument (10:14–22), another weak argument, Paul affirms that although idols are nothing, there are such things as demons. In the final argument, Paul returns again to his stronger first argument (1988:102–03). Countryman suggests the Pauline tradition had virtually nothing to say regarding physical aspects of sexual purity. Impurity consists of property ethics, or "getting the better of someone else; in other words, impurity is competitive greed – mainly for influence in the community or for sexual property" (109). Countryman concludes that there are no NT rules against bestiality, masturbation, homosexuality, polygamy, and pornography (243). His view of 1 Corinthians 8–10 is not convincing. By reducing the importance of 1 Corinthians 10:1–13, he does not adequately appreciate the integratedness of the entire idol meat pericope and the rhetorical importance of Paul's argument concerning sin and judgement. (This may be why he also diminishes the significance of the vice lists in 6:9–11 and 10:5–10.) Impurity may involve competitive greed, but Paul does not seem to reduce it to this definition alone. The role of body in the Corinthian church in relation to the *cosmos* constitutes a significant factor in Paul's concept of purity as we will discuss below.

[147] M. MITCHELL, 254.

[148] M. MITCHELL, 185. For a summary of terms and *topoi* related to her theme of factionalism in Corinth, see 180–83.

Corinth was a problem. It may be the case that the view of salvific "immunity" through sacraments is not as weak as Mitchell claims: the Corinthians argued about which leader had baptised them (1 Cor. 1:11–17), and some were apparently being baptised for the dead (15:29). It seems they overemphasised the importance of baptism (cf. ch. 3.1.4 below). Perhaps as members of the body of Christ, with an inflated view of eschatology, some of the Corinthian members believed themselves exempt from sin and judgement.

Mitchell's interpretation of 1 Corinthians 10:12 is also questionable. She argues that the body imagery was so crucial that the sin of some led to the destruction of practically all. But in relation to divine judgement, this verse seems to address the "some" who could fall from the sins described in 10:7–10 more than the "all" who partook in spiritual benefits of 10:1–4. Paul's repetitive use of the third person singular in verse 12 seems hard to reconcile with her paraphrased version which uses the second person plural to strengthen her case. Mitchell's rhetorical viewpoint does add to the importance of factions at Corinth, but this does not mean that they must consistently remain Paul's primary concern throughout every passage of the letter.

2.3 Rhetorical Methods in Light of This Study

Mitchell's insights contribute a new dimension to studies on 1 Corinthians. Her work supports the idea that in certain passages, Paul is using a persuasive means of communicating his message to his readers. He seems to use deliberative rhetoric in warning passages because he wishes to convey some very crucial instructions to the Corinthian congregation.[149] Thus a rhetorical perspective of Paul's warnings may be helpful in interpreting the points that Paul wished to emphasise, and 1 Corinthians 10:1–13 seems to provide an excellent example of this. Nevertheless, Mitchell's exclusive focus on the Corinthian congregation itself does not seriously entertain the idea of a contrast between those "inside" and those "outside" the congregation. Such notions are important in the letter for understanding baptism as an entrance ritual, and why Paul – perhaps prompted by a transitional state of eschatological dualism – draws up boundaries for the Corinthians. We will now turn to such issues.

---

[149] Synofzik demonstates that Paul often derives the concept of judgement and recompense from traditional material as a tool for his arguments (1977). But see corrections given by N. WATSON (1983), 211–12.

3. Social and Cultural Anthropological Approaches
to New Testament Interpretation

The social sciences have provided an important venue for New Testament interpretation. Cultural anthropological studies contribute by furnishing models that
can assist in our interpreting the symbolic universe of various cultures. Two
such models which I have found to be influential for New Testament studies are
Mary Douglas' concept of purity and Victor Turner's analysis of ritual and
liminality. Dale Martin, A. J. M. Wedderburn, and Jerome Neyrey are among
the scholars who have utilised socio-anthropological conceptions in relation to
the New Testament, which may be important for this study.[150] Anthropological
models help break down complex human activity into simple abstract representations in order to comprehend human experience.[151]

3.1 Mary Douglas: Purity and Contamination

3.1.1 Purity and Boundaries

In her work *Purity and Danger*, Mary Douglas maintains that cultural rituals of
purity and impurity create a "unity in experience" in which symbolic patterns
are developed and disparate elements are given meaning.[152] In Douglas' view,
"Reflection on dirt involves reflection on the relation of order to disorder, being
to non-being, form to formlessness, life to death."[153] She suggests that dirt or
uncleanness is "matter out of place" which must be approached by means of
order. Dirt cannot be included if a culture wishes to maintain orderly patterns.
This perspective helps one gain insight into the area of pollution.[154] Douglas
writes: "In short, our pollution behaviour is the reaction which condemns any
object or ideal likely to confuse or contradict cherished classifications."[155]

She discerns clean and unclean categories described in Leviticus and Deuteronomy, and affirms that holiness essentially means separateness. However, if

---

[150] My use of the expression "socio-anthropology" seeks to combine the disciplines of
cultural anthropology and sociology (social-scientific method). I do this because the two
disciplines are not easy to distinguish when related to New Testament studies. This is perhaps even more true when assessing the Corinthian situation in which terms such as "group,"
"body," and "community" play significant roles.

[151] Cf. MALINA (1983), 24.

[152] DOUGLAS (1966), 2–3.

[153] DOUGLAS, 5.

[154] DOUGLAS, 40. Douglas notes that their are only two real differences between Western
and primitive cultural perspectives on defilement: 1) Western society avoids dirt through the
use of hygiene instead of religious ritual; and 2) Western society has knowledge of patho-
genic organisms (35–36).

[155] DOUGLAS, 35.

one is to avoid a conception that the Old Testament distinguishes between clean and unclean categories in an arbitrary manner, one must also understand holiness in terms of wholeness or completeness: "In short the idea of holiness was given an external, physical expression in the wholeness of the body seen as a perfect container."[156] Hence, understanding the idea of dirt may advance our comprehension of purification rules in relation to the body. For Douglas, it is not possible to interpret rituals involving saliva, breast milk, excrement, and the like unless we perceive the human body as symbolising the larger society. There is an analogous relationship between human and social bodies in reference to purity and danger.[157]

In *Natural Symbols* Douglas provides a "group/grid" anthropological axis which assists her in interpreting the control of social bodies and their boundaries.[158] She gives the example of a witch hunting community to demonstrate how the model works. The community interprets the cosmos in a dualistic manner of good versus evil, and it prescribes clearly marked external boundaries. But when the community announces it is being attacked by internal deviance, it tends to either split over the issue, or expel the alleged culprits. Douglas classifies this type of community as a "strong" group which has confused internal markers. It appears in the strong group/weak grid quadrant of her axis.[159] One of the most prominent advocates of Douglas' "group/grid" is Bruce Malina, who adapts her model to New Testament studies. This enterprise arose out of his dissatisfaction with the current models for interpreting the New Testament.[160] After explaining how one classifies various groups and societies in the quadrant, he applies the model to Paul's view of the Law and the New Testament view of fasting.[161]

---

[156] DOUGLAS, 51–52. Thus, perversion (תֶבֶל), the antithesis of holiness, is essentially a mixing or confusing of categories (Lev. 18:23f; 19:19). Douglas affirms that holiness as wholeness involves wholeness of body, undertakings, species and categories of creation, and straight dealing as opposed to double-dealing (53).

[157] Cf. DOUGLAS, 114–15.

[158] Douglas defines the grid as the "rules which relate one person to others on an ego-centred basis" and the group as "the experience of a bounded social unit" (1970:viii). The latter is also understood in terms of the claims it makes, the boundaries it prescribes, and the rights and privileges it conveys over its members (1978:7).

[159] DOUGLAS (1970), 105, 112–13.

[160] Malina expands upon Douglas' model by defining the "grid" as the vertical axis which charts various demarcations regarding "socially constrained adherence that persons in a given group usually give to the symbol system – the system of classifications, definitions, and evaluations – through which the society enables its members to bring order and intelligibility to their experiences." The "group" is the horizontal axis that plots the degree of "social pressure exerted upon an individual or some subgroup to conform to the demands of the larger society, to stay within the 'we' lines marking off group boundaries" (1986), 13.

[161] MALINA (1986), chs. 6, 9.

3.1.2 Evaluation

When using Douglas' work on cultural purity as a heuristic model for New Testament passages, one discovers some interesting observations. For example, 1 Corinthians 8–14 contains a similar motif to Douglas' idea of disorder, mixture, and confusion as definitions describing pollution and perversion. One of the dangers of Christians eating at an idol temple is the confusion of mixing the Lord's table with the table of demons (10:14–23). Impropriety in worship and disorder at the Lord's table instigated Paul to exhort the Corinthians to do all things decently and in order. That which is out of place must be done away (1 Cor. 11, 14).

Douglas also expounds on the aspect of bodily wholeness. This is an important dimension in relation to the Corinthian church. As we noted earlier in Mitchell, schism and division are set against unity and solidarity in the church at Corinth. Paul stresses the corporate aspect of the community of God, which he defines as the body of Christ (1 Cor. 6:12ff; 12). In 1 Corinthians 12:13 the Corinthian congregation has been baptised into a solidarity in Christ, and here Paul seems to echo Galatians 3:27–28 which stresses that all social status distinctions disappear.[162] With respect to Corinth, I will explore the possibility that certain misperceptions about status distinctions related to baptism and conversion led to some of the problems Paul attempted to correct at Corinth.

Additionally, Douglas explains that wholeness extends to the idea of social completeness. Half finished projects, though not necessarily unclean in themselves, are to be completed (Deut. 20:6–7).[163] This notion might have some significance when we examine the cultural-anthropological concept of liminality (3.2 below). My study will attempt to test the validity of the idea that, contrary to the Corinthian congregation's inflated eschatological notions, the Corinthians had not reached a final state of perfection. Douglas' insights on purity seem helpful for this study, and their appropriateness will be observed in the following chapters.

Nevertheless, not all of Douglas' anthropological studies seem equally helpful for various New Testament studies. The Douglas-Malina group/grid model may assist in discerning nuances regarding a smaller community's cultural and social boundaries, but when applied to at least one early Christian community, the model ends up with differing results. Urban von Wahlde adapts the group/grid model and applies it to the Johannine community. He believes the Johannine community developed through a process of three stages. The first stage that is reflected in the earliest version of John's Gospel depicts the Johannine community as Jewish Christians (strong group/low grid). The second version of the

---

[162] I am assuming with the majority of scholars that Galatians was written earlier than Corinthians.
[163] DOUGLAS (1966), 51–52.

Gospel demonstrates a conflict between the community and the religious authorities called "the Jews." Still, the community sees itself as primarily Jewish Christians, but it also sees itself as mostly independent of the parent Jewish community (strong group/low grid both start weakening). In the third version of the Gospel a split within the Johannine community occurs over the issues of Christology and ethics. At this third stage, the Johannine community moves toward harmony with the Petrine tradition and the "Great Church" (strong group/ high grid) while the dissidents became a weak group/low grid community.[164]

A similar study with different results comes from Jerome Neyrey's work *An Ideology of Revolt*, which is Christological in scope. Neyrey attempts to answer what it meant to the Johannine community that Christ was "equal to God" and "not of this world," both terms expressing a revolt against former cultural ideologies.[165] Taking the symbolic categories adopted from Mary Douglas, Neyrey applies the Douglas-Malina group/grid axis to the Johannine community. Unlike von Wahlde, however, he arrives at a different three-stage interpretation of the community. In the first stage, the Johannine community focused on missiology. It was at that time a strong group/low grid community emphasising purity and strong group boundaries. During what Neyrey calls the second or replacement stage, the community remained a strong group but with a rising grid. Finally at the "high Christology" stage, the community became a weak group/low grid community emphasising such motifs as spontaneity and love.[166]

Although the differences between von Wahlde and Neyrey are not entirely blatant, it appears that the adaptation of the Douglas-Malina group/grid could become rather arbitrary. This might be expected to some extent, given that various interpreters may have different agendas and may be asking different sorts of questions. More pointedly, however, J. T. Sanders argues that this model does not give an explanation for social changes, it can only help indicate that change has occurred.[167] Nevertheless, if the model helps to illuminate social change, it may still prove to be beneficial. Still, there may be also a tendency to fit the biblical data into the model to the extent that some of the writer's intentions are lost or undermined. In the process of using the group/grid model, certain characteristics of a congregation might be ignored or oversimplified.[168]

With moderate alterations, Jerome Neyrey adopts the symbolic categories of the Douglas-Malina group/grid to some of the motifs in Pauline literature. Neyrey argues that a symbolic universe is made up of a community's perception of six major categories which are 1) purity and patterns of order; 2) rites and ceremonies; 3) body and social perception; 4) sin and deviance; 5) cosmol-

---

[164] VON WAHLDE (1995), 379–89.
[165] NEYREY (1988), 6, 111, 175.
[166] NEYREY, 130–76.
[167] J. T. SANDERS (1993), 113 cf. 106.
[168] Cf. ROHRBAUGH (1987), 108.

ogy; and 6) evil and misfortune. He then applies these categories to the apostle Paul in an attempt to understand Paul's symbolic universe.[169] According to Neyrey's model, the Corinthian congregation best fits the weak group/low grid quadrant; there is a low regard for purity, blurred boundaries between society and self, individualistic propensities, personal ethics, uncontrolled bodies, and a welcoming of spirit possession.[170] Paul, on the other hand, seems to be somewhere in the strong group/low grid region: strong but not overbearing purity notions, concern for expelling pollutants, group membership values, controlled bodies, a view of sin which coordinates individual with society, and a sense of danger regarding the demon possessed.[171]

But these categories are not entirely correct. The Corinthians' apparently high regard for the Lord's Supper and baptism rituals (1 Cor. 1:11–17; 10:1–4; 11:16ff) seems to contradict the weak group/low grid quadrant's anti-ritualistic notion.[172] Again, there seems to be no indication from the letter that all forms of spirit possession would have been welcomed in the Corinthian congregation or that the congregation's discernment was so poor that they would not be able to discern the difference between demonic and Spirit possession. Despite the disorder in worship, Paul never seriously questions that it is the Spirit of God who influences them (1 Cor. 14).[173] In any case, the group/grid model does help provide a general description that Paul and the Corinthian congregation members have conflicting cosmologies along the lines of purity, outside boundaries, and perceptions of the body. Beyond this, the model's usefulness seems to diminish in this situation. Perhaps a better application might be to analyse potential changes in the congregation's attitudes by examining both of Paul's letters to the Corinthians, but an intensive examination of this sort is beyond the scope of this present work. For this study we will pursue ideas related to purity but will adopt other models than the group/grid axis in reference to social bodies and their boundaries (cf. 3.3 below).

---

[169] NEYREY (1990), 11–20.

[170] NEYREY (1986), 134; cf. (1990), ch. 5.

[171] Ibid.

[172] We will elaborate on these rituals in ch. 3.

[173] 1 Corinthians 12:3 might be interpreted as an indication that some Corinthians were cursing Jesus under spiritual inspiration. More likely, Paul seems to be indicating what may have actually occurred in a certain Hellenistic religious setting (cf. FEE, 1987:578–82). If such an event did occur in congregation, this still would not necessarily indicate that it was uttered by a congregation member or that the members accepted the curse as coming from the Spirit of God.

3.2 Victor Turner's Liminality Phase

3.2.1 Ritual and Pilgrimage Processes

Victor Turner describes liminality as a transitional state and process used to categorise cultural-religious phenomena. Liminality appears in rites of passage, pilgrimages, millennial groups, monasticism, and so forth. The liminal period is called by Turner the "'moment in and out of time.'"[174] He derived the concept from Arnold van Gennep's rites of passage "which accompany every change of place, state, social position and age ... All rites of passage or 'transition' are marked by three phases: separation, margin (or *limen*, signifying 'threshold'), and aggregation."[175] The liminal stage is characterised by ambiguity, says Turner, "Thus, liminality is frequently likened to death, to being in the womb, to invisibility, to darkness, to bisexuality, to the wilderness, and to an eclipse of the sun or moon."[176] The neophyte in the liminal stage is represented as possessing nothing and having no status. The neophyte's self-control is tested during the liminal stage which is often considered dangerous or pollutant because it is not readily accessible to classification.[177] An important relational aspect of liminality is *communitas*, a phenomenon one experiences through comradeship, lowliness, sacredness and homogeneity with other "liminars" who have broken down or reversed the hierarchical barriers of the structured society.[178] Accordingly, the liminal stage is unstructured or prestructured.

Turner's liminality is also found in the phenomenon of pilgrimage. Here the liminal stage is marked by a release from mundane obligations and structure. Pilgrimages may be short-term, long-term, or permanent. The transient is a pilgrim who renounces world and home. Pilgrimages may have a character of separation or initiation in which the liminal period is much longer than many rites of passage. Turner observes that certain Buddhists, Hindus, and Medieval palmers spent their entire life on pilgrimages.[179] He maintains that monasticism is an example of permanent liminality. For Turner, Benedictine monasticism shares a number of liminal features with the *Mukanda* (circumcision) of the Ndembu tribe, even though one is a form of permanent liminality while the other is not. Monks, hippies, nomads, millennial groups, and court jesters are

---

[174] TURNER (1969), 96; cf. TURNER (1979), 16.

[175] TURNER (1969), 94. VAN GENNEP (1960:vii, 11) defines the three phases as separation (*séparation*), transition (*marge*), and incorporation (*agrégation*).

[176] TURNER, 95.

[177] TURNER, 109. On a similar note, Douglas observes the importance and danger involved in transitional states. They are dangerous because, like unborn babies, they are difficult for the cult to define. Douglas affirms that in certain initiation-segregation stage rituals, boys can end up dead. To go out into the margins is to expose oneself to the powers that could either kill or elevate an individual (1966:96–97).

[178] V. & E. TURNER (1978), 250.

[179] TURNER (1974), 182, 285; (1979), 21f; V. & E. TURNER, 2, 250.

all examples of people who live in a state of long-term liminality.[180] Turner observes that this aspect of transition may also be extended to art and literary forms. The main characters in Bunyan's *Pilgrim's Progress*, Chaucer's *Canterbury Tales*, and "2001: A Space Odyssey" embark upon extended liminal quests.[181]

3.2.2 Evaluation

Turner's studies point us to a couple of important observations. First, such anthropological models as his are concerned with the observation of cultural patterns which exist among various cultures, past and present. Turner developed his studies by consolidating numerous cultural-religious systems including major religious bodies such as Islam, Judaism, Christianity, Buddhism, and so forth.[182] The model of liminality presents a mapping on how many cultures operate, though it does not prescribe how those cultures *must* operate.[183] Hence, liminality is a general pattern which helps classify the process of change. Second, the Christian life may also be seen as in a state of marginality. Turner writes, "'The Christian is a stranger to the world, a pilgrim, a traveller, with no place to rest his head.' Transition has here become a permanent condition."[184] Turner's observation of *communitas* shares characteristics in common with a number of enthusiast religious groups in history.[185] Turner also compares liminality with the characteristics of millenarian movements. In such groups sexual distinctions are minimised, property is shared, and an absolute leader is desired, among other things. But when the community's prophecies fail, the group becomes more institutionalised.[186]

A number of New Testament scholars have recognised the importance of Turner's concepts, including Wayne Meeks, Mark McVann, and A. J. M. Wedderburn.[187] Wedderburn's use of Turner stems from his argument against the idea that Christian baptism as a participation in Christ's death and resurrection originated in the initiation rites of the mystery religions.[188] Parallels between

---

[180] TURNER (1969), 107 ff.

[181] TURNER (1974), 182. Turner also writes that one should not limit the combination of potential liminal patterns, for liminality is an "experimental region of culture, where new elements and new combing rules may be introduced" (1979:21–23; cf. V. & E. TURNER, 2). The concept of liminality would thus seem to extend beyond strict ritualism.

[182] TURNER (1974), 166, 182; (1967), 102–03; cf. VAN GENNEP, 88–93.

[183] Cf. EVANS-PRITCHARD (1962), 13–28. On the justification of the use of cultural interpretation in reference to Turner's symbolism, see HANSEN (1975), 1–6, 98–101.

[184] TURNER (1969), 107.

[185] E.g., HEYD (1985), 279–89.

[186] TURNER (1969), 111–112, 129.

[187] MEEKS (1983a), 88–89, 156–57; WEDDERBURN (1987), 380–92; MCVANN (1991), 151–57; MCVANN (1993), 14–20. An entire issue of *Semeia* has also been dedicated to this subject (MCVANN, ed. 1995).

[188] WEDDERBURN, 3.

early Christian and mystery initiations may have emerged instead from similar presuppositions: both would fall under the rubric of "rites of passage" from a death event to a kind of transformation, and both "drew it from the general stock of ideas of their time, and indeed of most other times as well. This was an imagery that was current then in their environment as it has been and is in a multitude of other cultures."[189] Wedderburn maintains that Paul's reversing of societal values marking the new era (e. g., Gal. 3:28) resembles the liminal existence described by cultural anthropologists. He suggests that early Christian initiation, as described by Paul, appears to set the converts in a state of liminality in which they must live out the remainder of their earthly existence.[190]

Wedderburn's suggestions seem correct. The structures of Paul's thoughts may have been influenced by the resource of ideas on liminality observed in many cultures, including the traditions of the ancient Israelites – traditions with which Paul was no doubt familiar. The Hebrew scriptures seem to contain rites of passage similar to many other cultures, including rites related to birth, circumcision, and death.

Reference	Separation	Liminal period	Aggregation
Leviticus 12:2–8	Mother's pregnancy terminates in birth	Mother is declared unclean from 40 to 80 days	Mother is once again declared clean and can have sexual relations with her husband
Leviticus 12:3; Luke 2:21	Birth of a male infant	Seven days without identity	Circumcision on the eighth day
Genesis 44:32 ff 50:11; 1 Sam. 31:11–13; cf. 2 Sam. 12:15–24	Death of a loved one	Period of mourning	Commencement of regular activities again
Deuteronomy 21:10–14	Captivity of a foreign woman by an Israelite male during war	The woman's head is shaved, her nails cut, and she is granted time to mourn for her relatives	After the period of mourning, the Israelite could have sexual relations with the woman

---

[189] WEDDERBURN, 391 cf. 380–82.
[190] WEDDERBURN, 386–87, 392.

The Nazarite vow is another example of liminality (Num. 6). The vow was marked by the Nazarite's uncut hair and abstinence from wine. Samson and perhaps Elijah are two examples (Judges 13; 2 Kings 1:8; Luke 1:17). John the Baptist, who lived in the wilderness, seems to be an example of the marginal Nazarite existence (Luke 1:13ff, 80; 3:2–4; Mark 1:2–8). Also, his ministry may be seen as bringing others into an initiation process with a new status in view (Matt. 3:1ff; Luke 3:1ff). All three of these individuals are characterised as living on a special diet, residing in the wilderness, and having God's spirit (Judg. 15; 1 Kings 19; Luke 3:1–6).[191] The role of Jesus functioned in a similar way after his baptism. As a liminal prophet, he enters the wilderness to fast and be tempted of the devil before he makes his public appearances in the power of God's spirit (Matt. 4:1–11; Luke 4:1–14). He stressed a lifestyle comparable to a state of perpetual marginality (Mark 10:28–31; Luke 9:57ff). These appear to be prime examples of what Turner calls the marginal existence.

The lives of the Hebrew heroes may be viewed as other examples of long-term odysseys. They have experienced a separation from the old life and are on their way to the new one. Edmund Leach affirms that religious thinking consists of a mediation of opposites. The crossing of thresholds, then, may be important to religious studies because inspired sacred persons "almost always experience their inspiration in a 'betwixt and between' locality, described as 'in the wilderness', which is neither fully in This World nor in The Other."[192] He thus interprets many Old Testament accounts in light of Turner's studies on liminality states. Leach compares Abraham, Joseph, and Moses as three examples of liminars who left a "Land of Suffering" to enter a "Wilderness" phase, and then make it to a "Land of Plenty."[193] Other prominent examples include Jacob, who fled from Esau before his name was changed to Israel, and David, who fled from Saul before becoming king of Israel. Differently, Lot's wife is a negative reminder of perpetual liminality in the wilderness: she became a pillar of salt between Sodom and the hills of Zoar when she looked back at the destruction of her former residency.[194]

Ronald Hendel views the tripartite "rites of passage" as reflecting Israel's escape from Egypt, its encounter with God in the wilderness, and its final homeward destination in the promised land.[195] In a similar manner, Robert Cohn considers the wilderness in Torah traditions as a "buffer zone" between Israel and Egypt. He concludes that it was during the Israelites' wilderness trek that the conceptions of liminality and *communitas* affected the social and religious values of the people in a revolutionary way. The wilderness narrative may re-

---

[191] Compare also the Nazarites with the nomadic Rechabites (Jer. 35).
[192] LEACH (1983a), 15–16.
[193] LEACH (1983b), 44.
[194] Cf. AYCOCK (1983), 116–117.
[195] HENDEL (1989), 374–5.

flect the historic situation of a new religious movement which found its cultivation "betwixt and between" the "structure" of Egypt and Canaan. Cohn suggests that liminal categories may contribute to appreciating the actual social process of historic Israel.[196] The values Israel experienced in the wilderness continued to reassert themselves in the proceeding eras so that during the later Israelite exile, "the reactualization of liminality drew people to the wilderness story as a paradigm of their own experience ... The narrative thus became a repository for traditions expressing the ambiguities of liminality, the possibilities of communitas, and the limiting values of structure."[197] The Israelites learned behavioural lessons about patience, faith, and humility from these examples. Hence, transition periods became a means to test and build the character necessary for a new status. Thus, we have noted that the ancient Hebrew and Christian traditions contain examples similar to the ritual process, and they also describe various examples of perpetual or long-term marginality.

With such a rich tradition of liminal patterns, it seems unlikely that Paul would *not* have made a connection between transitional episodes and the Israelite or Christian community's existence. Paul himself is said to have taken a type of Nazarite vow (Acts 18:18). We might even assume that Paul experienced a similar period of marginality after he went to Arabia, or when he escaped Jerusalem and went to Tarsus, living in an obscure state for a number of years (Gal. 1:17–21 cf. Acts 9:30; 11:25). In 1 Corinthians 10:1–12 Paul may have in mind the liminal journey of both communities when he depicts Israel's "baptism" and their journey through the desert.[198] Behind his narrative might underlie an assumption in common with many cultures – a liminal or marginal process which Paul wishes to convey to the Corinthians who are encouraged to share certain traits with marginal groups, traits such as separation, healing, renewal, and a form of egalitarianism (1 Cor. 1:26ff; 11:17–34; 12–14 cf. 4:7ff). A similar concept of liminality which we have surveyed would appear to be in the mind of Paul at least with reference to structures associated with wilderness imagery derived from his Jewish heritage. Israel's episode in the wilderness would be an example for him of a life-time journey or liminal state beginning with Israel's separation from Egypt and ending with its inheritance of the promised land. A further study of this process seems warranted.

While Turner's studies do not always relate to New Testament passages, the combination of initiation and wilderness patterns in 1 Corinthians 10:1–13

---

[196] COHN (1981), 20–21 cf. 3, 22.

[197] COHN, 23.

[198] On the use of baptism with Turner's liminality, see McVANN (1991), 151–57. The wilderness is seen as a symbol for liminality not only by Turner but also van Gennep. The latter notes that deserts are often considered neutral zones. This is especially true in classical Greek texts, where neutral zones were used for market places or battlefields. Thus, the person who travels between two countries "wavers between two worlds" (VAN GENNEP, 18–19, 24).

prompt us to suggest that this pericope may be one in which some of Turner's insights do shed fresh light if not taken to extremes.[199] Notions of bodily purity and contamination, boundary markers, social identity, and rites of passage can be observed, with modifications, over a wide range of cultures and periods, including Greco-Roman and Jewish cultures. Such investigations might provide new ways of looking at the tapestry of discourse in the New Testament. As we have observed earlier in this chapter, apostasy arises from within a religious *community*. For Paul that community is often described as the "body of Christ" in 1 Corinthians. Social dimensions might therefore place our text in sharper relief, and it is precisely this benefit which we hope to capture by interacting with socio-anthropological models like Turner's.

On the other hand, there is a chance that the use of such a model might "clutter up" or detract from our arguments. But I believe this possibility can only be properly determined at the risk of using the models. Risk, creativity, and transformation do have their proper places in an interdisciplinary environment. It is my opinion that if comparative and heuristic approaches provide interesting ideas and encourage the interaction of different disciplines, then they do serve at least a minimal purpose. Some investigations, of course, produce more than this. If the application of liminality is not necessary to establish my arguments, this does *not* mean that it is not beneficial for this study. The next section will consider some other ways cultural anthropological models have been used in New Testament studies.

3.3 Socio-Anthropological Approaches to Apostasy

Although socio-anthropological models may be helpful when interpreting the New Testament, very little has been done on the question of apostasy even though this topic relates closely to cultural and sociological issues. Below are a few attempts by scholars who have applied socio-anthropological models to subjects related to apostasy.

3.3.1 Dale Martin: Boundaries of the Social Body

In his book entitled *The Corinthian Body,* Dale Martin argues that a theological difference in the Corinthian church stems from different perceptions about the body. Paul, along with the "weak" in the church – and lower status Graeco-Roman society in general – holds to clearer theological and ethical boundaries

---

[199] At the end of the third stage of the ritual process, for instance, the neophyte returns to the structural society. The transformed pilgrim often goes home. Obviously, Paul or the traditions he echoes would not want Israel to go back to Egypt!

than do the upper-class, well-educated "strong." Instead of upholding the hierarchical constitution of the body as a microcosm of society, Paul takes issue with the "strong" by emphasising instead a reversal of status in the apocalyptic world.[200]

In reference to sin and judgement in Corinth, Martin believes that two disease aetiologies are at the heart of the problem. The "strong" operate on an aetiology of balance – diseases normally arise due to physiological imbalances in the body. Paul, on the other hand, holds to the common Christian belief of invasion aetiology – diseases arise from external sources and must be extricated from the body.[201] Regarding the excommunication of the offender in 1 Corinthians 5:1–5, Paul's primary concern is to expunge the man before he pollutes the entire body of Christ.[202]

The apostate's consignment to Satan, though a secondary issue with Paul, reveals Paul's apocalyptic war between the flesh and spirit (Martin uses "sarx" and "pneuma"). Martin argues that "since no secure boundary separates the offender's body from the church's body, the offender's presence in the church represents an invasion of sarx into the church itself. The pneuma that needs to be saved is both the pneuma of the man and that of the church; the sarx that must be destroyed is both that of the man and that of the church."[203] Mere contact with the *cosmos*, however, does not threaten the body; in the same message, Paul does not advocate complete separation from non-believers (1 Cor. 5:9–12). A disguised pollutant, according to Martin, is the real threat for Paul because it could penetrate the boundary between *cosmos* and the body of Christ.[204]

Regarding eating meat sacrificed to idols in 1 Cor. 8–10, Martin notes that the "strong" have knowledge or *gnosis* on the matter while the "weak" do not. Unlike some of the contemporary philosophers of the time, Paul believes in *gnosis* as a kind of talisman of magical proportions which protects those who have it from demonic pollution. The weak, on the other hand, are not privileged with this protection; thus, their "conscience" (συνείδησις) could become defiled. Since Paul believes that *gnosis* cannot be learned, he does not encourage the "strong" to teach *gnosis* to the "weak"; instead, they are to refrain from their liberty for the sake of the weak.[205]

---

[200] D. MARTIN (1995), xv–xvii, cf. 59–67.

[201] D. MARTIN, 163–64.

[202] D. MARTIN, 168–69. Paul seems to be in keeping with the Jesus tradition that an excommunicant should be treated "as a Gentile and a tax-collector," or in other words, a nonbeliever (Matt. 18:15–17).

[203] D. MARTIN, 174.

[204] D. MARTIN, 170. However, the degree of influence that disease aetiology plays on Paul's perspective in 1 Corinthians 5 is difficult to determine. Paul's reason for expelling the fornicator seems to have more to do with the ideas of expulsion he is deriving from the Deuteronomic tradition (cf. Deut. 17:7). Nevertheless, Israel's perception of expulsion may itself presuppose a purity model emphasising external disease and extrication (see Douglas above).

[205] D. MARTIN, 181–83.

I would prefer a less exotic view. In chapter 8 the weak are encouraged to eat, but due to their pre-Christian idolatrous upbringing, they lacked the ability to hold consistently the viewpoint that an idol is not a god. Hence, they would believe they had sinned against God by eating an offering in honour of another deity.[206] From Paul's perspective, this self-condemnation could no doubt lead them into real idolatry.[207] If this interpretation is correct, Paul has a pragmatic reason for not instructing the weak with *gnosis* about this issue. Since his primary concern is to counter division (cf. 2.2), he may have thought that the weak – convinced that any form of eating idol meat was wrong – would not readily accept his correction. Perhaps he feared they would begin to question his apostolic authority as some other members were apparently doing. Rather than being the potential cause of more strife in the Corinthian body, Paul gives up some of his rights for the sake of the weak and urges the strong to do likewise.

Nevertheless, Martin's observations prompt some provocative issues. His insights lead us to understand that Paul considers expulsion necessary because the contamination that could result is a real threat to the body. His approach thus points us in a direction which stresses the importance that contamination plays in a community setting. What might add to Martin's view is the importance of how 1 Corinthians 10:1–13 fits with his discussion on the body and its boundaries.[208] Were some of the Israelites who rebelled in the wilderness expunged so that the others might not get contaminated? If so, what might Paul be warning the Corinthians by his use of wilderness examples?

3.3.2 Jerome Neyrey: Entrance and Exit Rituals

We have observed that Martin's approach shows the importance of the body in relation to the Corinthian situation. In *Paul, In Other Words*, Jerome Neyrey suggests that the primary distinction between Paul and his opponents' perception of the body hinges on the areas of purity, ritual, body, personal identity, and sin/deviance. In general the Corinthians have little regard for concerns about body pollution and boundaries, and they are strongly individualistic. Paul on the other hand, has a strong concern for purity and boundaries, and he holds to strong corporate orientations.[209]

Neyrey claims that there are both entrance and exit rituals which denote the marking of boundaries. Rituals may involve status transformation in the case of

---

[206] Cf. FEE (1987), 378ff; MURPHY-O'CONNOR (1978), 550, 552.

[207] This would seem to be similar to the notion that a former alcoholic could lose self-control and fall back into drinking spells by seeing a "stronger" person drink a glass of wine.

[208] D. MARTIN, 54–56. Martin does not address the fact that 1 Corinthians 10:1–13 carries all three of the major motifs that he mentions earlier in his book. They are "allness," "status," and "apocalypticism."

[209] NEYREY (1990), 128 cf. 108–09.

entrance rituals, or status reversal in the case of exit rituals; "Paul's most noted entrance ritual is baptism."[210] This he relates to Victor Turner's ritual method. Neyrey notes that from Paul's perspective, circumcision has now become a ritual of exit (cf. Phil. 3:5–7). The letter to the Galatians exemplifies this exit ritual. Neyrey argues that in keeping with Paul's binary categories of spirit/flesh, Sarah/Hagar, and other such categories, Paul warns that those baptised believers who find themselves returning to circumcision become apostate, crossing back over the boundary from faith/spirit to works/flesh.[211] Neyrey continues that for Paul, those who cut the foreskin are themselves "cut off" from Christ (Gal. 5:2–4, 12; 6:12–14 cf. 4:30).[212] What does not belong to the body must be expelled. The person who is expelled from Christ thus suffers a status degradation. Boundaries are set by excommunication, which is a "now" exit ritual, and divine judgement, which is a "future" separation ritual (cf. Matt. 13:24–30, 47–50).[213] On the other hand, the Judaizers who preach "another gospel" also set their own boundaries that Paul warns will "shut you out" of the kingdom (Gal. 4:17).[214] Neyrey writes: "Galatians, then reflects Paul's incessant boundary making, a perception of two mutually exclusive systems or ways of serving God. The boundary is legitimated in history (3:6–13; 4:21–31), exemplified in experience (1:15–17; 3:1–5) and illustrated by specific practices (2:16–17; 5:4)."[215]

Neyrey's assessment of the Galatian situation in reference to apostasy opens up some provocative questions if asked of the Corinthian congregation. Neyrey notes that Paul's most important entrance ritual is baptism and that excommunication is one of his exit rituals. Utilising this model, what insight could we uncover concerning Paul's use of baptism and judgement in reference to Israel in 1 Corinthians 10:1–13? Applying the categories of Paul's symbolic universe to the Corinthian situation, what insights can we uncover regarding purity, body, cosmology, and individualism in relation to apostasy? In this study I will attempt to explore such questions.

4. The Purpose and Scope of This Study

Issues related to apostasy and perseverance have been discussed and debated throughout the span of church history. The Calvinists and Arminians have normally systematised biblical doctrine to posit one claim or another without much

---

[210] NEYREY, 87; cf. 79–80.

[211] NEYREY, 72, 89, 190–92.

[212] Neyrey claims that Paul wishes the Judaizers would mutilate themselves (Gal. 5:12). There is a play on the word "cut" (ἀποκόπτω). The Judaizers would thus be "cut off" from the Jewish system by becoming permanently unclean (cf. Lev. 21:20f; 22:24; Deut. 23:1).

[213] NEYREY, 89–91.

[214] NEYREY, 191.

[215] NEYREY, 190–91.

progress. Differently, Judith Gundry Volf's work on this issue focuses on one particular New Testament author rather than many. In this regard she has done a great service by attempting to decipher Paul's own view of perseverance and falling away. Nevertheless, her method does not adequately incorporate some of the more recent interpretative methods. As we have noted earlier, this also seems to be the case with other prominent studies related to the subject. More specifically, rhetorical and socio-anthropological studies throw the issue of being "in" and "out" into a much sharper relief than other recent studies have allowed. Moreover, Gundry Volf's topical method does not adequately address the situation in the Corinthian congregation, which is where Paul addresses the subject of falling away perhaps more than in any of his other letters. (Her work examines more passages in 1 Corinthians than any of Paul's other letters.)[216] In this letter, Paul's discussion in 1 Corinthians 8–10 seems to be his most prolonged discourse related to the question of apostasy, and the wilderness message in 10:1–13 appears to be the longest concentrated pericope focusing on divine judgement as it relates to this issue. Gundry Volf's work does not integrate the elements of idolatry, apostasy, and perseverance in this passage. This raises strong suspicions that her work has overlooked aspects of Paul's communication that require more attention than a topical investigation may have permitted.

My purpose in this study is to present a thorough examination of 1 Corinthians 10:1–13. I will explore the possibility that this passage reflects a rhetorical argument attempting to deter potential judgements against some of the congregation members. Paul gives an extended warning that members should not conduct themselves in a manner which resembles the Israelites who, after crossing the Red Sea, were overthrown in the wilderness because of their rebellions. I will be investigating the passage in detail, considering the Corinthian situation and adding insights associated with recent interpretative methods. However, I do not plan to create a socio-anthropological perspective on apostasy at the expense of other biblical disciplines. In fact, an intertextual study will often be the focus due to the nature of the passage under consideration. It is necessary to carefully examine the traditions Paul may be referring to in this pericope. I wish to pursue, then, an eclectic approach which draws on traditio-historical exegesis, intertextuality, rhetorical, and socio-anthropological methods with the objective of discovering fresh insights into the passage.[217] Although I will have the question of apostasy and perseverance in mind, I do not wish to read this into everything Paul is writing. It will therefore be necessary to understand as much as possible about what Paul is actually saying rather than attempt to force meanings where they may not fit.

---

[216] N. Watson also confirms that warnings of coming judgement "are more prominent in 1 Corinthians than anywhere else" (1983:214f).

[217] In some ways my method is similar to that of Vernon Robbins' socio-rhetorical criticism (1996a,b).

Chapter 2

The Corinthian Situation and Meat Sacrificed to Idols

1. The Situation in Corinth

Before we examine 1 Corinthians 10:1–13, the structural and argumentative continuity or discontinuity between this passage and the larger context of 8:1–11:1 must be established.[1] In the larger pericope Paul gives instruction to the Corinthian congregation regarding their previous inquiries about the validity of eating meat sacrificed to idols (8:1, 4).[2] From this point it is apparent that the "strong" members of the congregation were justifying their eating of idol meat by affirming they had knowledge that idols were not real deities, and so they posed no threat to or influence on the food which is offered to them. Other Christians with a weaker "conscience" (συνείδησις), who had come out of an idolatrous background, would have found it offensive to eat such food (8:7).[3]

Some scholars have argued that the weak are only a hypothetical group and that Paul is the one who has the problems with idol meat.[4] But Paul appears to agree with the strong that one could eat idol meat as long as it does not offend others (10:23–33). Moreover, Paul's language best fits the assumption that both the strong and weak appear to be actual groups (cf. 8:7, 10).[5] Paul also may be implying that he himself ate idol foods on occasions (1 Cor. 9:4 cf. 10:30).[6] This would at least be hypothetically consistent with his pastoral principle to be-

---

[1] For an overview on various interpretations by recent scholars regarding idol meats in Corinth, see HORRELL (1996), 106ff; GARDNER (1994), 1–10; GOOCH (1993), 135–55.

[2] Κρέα in 8:13 indicates that meat is the precise food in this context.

[3] The force of ἕως ἄρτι in 8:7 suggests the position that the weak were former idolaters. This also implies that the idol meat situation in Corinth – unlike the situation in Acts 15 – is not a conflict between Jew and Gentile Christians, but a conflict among a primarily Gentile audience (cf. MURPHY-O'CONNOR, 551–54). It seems difficult to believe that former Jews would have been involved in any form idolatry. Also, Paul's distinction between the "weak" and "Jews" in 1 Cor. 9: 20, 22 should not be overlooked. The "weak" and the "strong" are somewhat oversimplified terms to designate the two groups in dispute (e.g., the "strong" are better classified in Corinth as those who have γνῶσις). For the sake of brevity and dialogue, I will use the terms nonetheless. Paul appears to have γνῶσις with the strong (8:1).

[4] E.g., GOOCH, 61–72; HURD (1965), 117–25. The primary reason for hypothetical groups often seems to be that 8:9–13 and 10:28–29 are hypothetical statements.

[5] In 8:10 the "third class condition" (ἐάν + subjunctive) is not an unreal condition like the "second class" (cf. ZERWICK, *Gram.*:103ff; BURTON, *Syntax*:100–12).

[6] Cf. BRUNT (1981), 26; FEE (1987), 402; BAILEY (1983) 166; HURD, 126–27, 130–31.

come all things to all people (including those without the law) that he might save some (1 Cor. 9:19, 21–22). If his primary objective was to bring the Gospel to the Gentiles (cf. Gal. 1:15–16; 2:2 ff), it seems difficult to accept that Paul would refuse a meal offered to him by those he was trying to reach (cf. 1 Cor. 10:27, 30–31). The serious tone of Paul's message, and his emphasis on how the situation disrupts relationships, seems best explained by the reality of the positions of the weak and strong. Gardner writes, "Paul had to face people who were eating this meat and the seriousness of that problem is amply illustrated by his use of words like μολύνω (8:7), πρόσκομμα (8:9), ἀπόλλυμι (8:11), and σκανδαλίζω (8:13)."[7]

2. Unity and Disunity in the Message on Meat Sacrificed to Idols

2.1 The Problem of Unity in 1 Corinthians 8:1–11:1

The apparent discontinuity of Paul's message in 1 Corinthians 8:1–11:1 has led some scholars to argue that the passage consists of more than one source. In an effort to explain the apparent disjunction of Paul's words 9:24–10:22 (or 10:1–22) is sometimes assigned to a separate epistle ("A"), and 8:1–9:23 and 10:23–11:1 are said to form another letter ("B"). The former, argues Schmithals, is concerned with the worship of idols and it treats only *cultic* meals. The latter focuses on meat sacrificed to idols with no indication that some in Corinth wished to take part in idol worship.[8] More recently Lamar Cope has suggested that Paul did not originally write 10:1–22 – it came from an early midrash.[9] Others have suggested or assumed that 10:1–13 or 10:1–22 was a midrash or homily carefully composed prior to its present form in the Corinthian setting.[10]

2.1.1 The Unity of Sections "A" and "B"

Nevertheless there are viable reasons to argue for the unity of Paul's thought in 1 Corinthians 8:1–11:1, as a number of scholars have pointed out.[11] The Deuteronomic tradition (which is commonly echoed by Paul in his arguments) ap-

---

[7] GARDNER, 21.

[8] SCHMITHALS (1971) 14, 92–95; cf. WEISS (1910), 211–13, 250 f; VON SODEN (1951), 254–55. For a summary of early reconstructions, see MERKLEIN (1984), 154–56; HURD, 41–47.

[9] Cope, (1990), 114–123.

[10] E.g., MEEKS (1982), 64–78; SANDELIN (1995), 257–73; ERIKSSON (1998), 167; ELLIS (1978), 209. Less affirmative are COLLIER (1994), 55–75; YEO (1995), 156–58; and HORRELL (1997), 95 f.

[11] E.g., HURD, 115–42; MERKLEIN, 153–83; W. WILLIS (1985), 267–96; PROBST (1991), 361–68; MALHERBE (1995), 231–55; BOUTTIER (1981), 205 ff; and SMIT (1996), 577–91. Hurd's argument from text tradition should not be overlooked. Hurd writes that scholars who

pears as an underlying source which pervades the entire discussion on idol meats, and it appears to be the source of Paul's adaptation of the *Shema* in 8:4– 6 (cf. Deut. 6:4f).[12] Not only does Paul adapt the *Shema* to contrast monotheism with idolatry, but his argument may also presuppose a unity amongst the Corinthian members based upon the solidarity and love of God as emphasised in the Deuteronomic tradition. Hence, discord between the strong and weak over the issue of idol meats would tend to violate this message of love which is at the centre of the early Christian messages (e.g., Matt. 22:37–41; cf. Lev. 19:18).[13] Mitchell has also demonstrated on rhetorical grounds that the content of 10:1– 22 is concerned with the major theme of the letter: unity and discord (cf. 10:10, 17).[14] This theme undergirds the entire discussion. Paul echoes the monotheism/idolatry motif in the Deuteronomic tradition again in 1 Corinthians 10:18– 22 where he discusses fellowship with demons and provoking the Lord to jealousy (cf. Deut. 32:17, 21; 6:14–15). Hence, this motif from the Deuteronomic tradition is used by Paul in both the hypothetical "A" and "B" letters. Paul also cites the Exodus tradition of the golden calf in 1 Corinthians 10:7 (Exod. 32:6) but focuses on the eating and drinking which takes place at the event. This implies a continuum between the discussion on idol meats in 8:1–13 and the warning against idolatry of 10:1–22.

---

argue for separate letters in 8:1–11:1 find "no hint either in the evidence of the manuscripts or in the patristic literature that 1 Corinthians ever circulated in any arrangement except the one which is traditional" (132). This observation certainly places the burden of proof on those who would apportion the text.

[12] Paul borrows from the Deuteronomic tradition in 1 Corinthians 10:1–13 (see chs. 3.5.4; 5.3.2 above; cf. OROPEZA 1998a:57–68). Paul's terms and motifs used in relation to the entire letter and found also in 10:1–13 (*pneumatikos,* vice list, eating/coveting, fleeing sin, "now" eschatology, etc.) renders unlikely the position that this section was not written by Paul or was written by him prior to the Corinthian context (cf. ch. 4:2.3 for problems with Meek's position on 10:1–13).

[13] Cf. WRIGHT (1991), 49. Against Wright, Horrell suggests that Paul's discussion of love is grounded in a Christological praxis and that 8:4–6 is a claim made by the strong (1997:86, 90, 105–06). However, language strikingly similar to "ἐξ οὗ τὰ πάντα ... δι' οὗ τὰ πάντα" in relation to God and/or Christ (8:6) is used in other Pauline contexts, suggesting that 8:6 is more likely to have originated from Paul (1 Cor. 11:12b; Rom. 11:36; Col. 1:16; cf. Eph. 1:22–23). It may be better to view 8:1–3 as the basis for a love praxis in Christ and Paul's echo of the *Shema* (8:6 cf. vv. 4–5) is his theological presupposition against idolatry. The former is emphasised in chapters 8–9 and 10:23ff, while the latter is stressed in 10:1–22. I find it unnecessary to choose between a theological and practical ground for the text. On the other end of the spectrum, Smit goes too far in claiming that 10:1–22 does not discuss a social issue but a theological/idolatrous one (1997:43, 46, 53; cf. WALTER, 1979:425–36). He does not seem to consider the interrelationship between the two. The paradigms for social unity are both the monotheistic unity (8:1–6) and solidarity of eucharistic fellowship (10:16f) which are diametrically opposed to fellowship with idols/demons (cf. 10:20–22).

[14] M. MITCHELL (1991), 237–58. Tomson notes the rhetorical unity of the chapters by Paul's stress on "all ... not all" (e.g., 8:1, 7; 9:19; 10:2, 23, 33 – TOMSON, 1990:192). For aspects of the communal unity in 1 Corinthians 6–14 see D. E. SMITH (1981:325–34).

In addition, one may note the similarities between the situation in Romans and that in Corinth over the issue of table fellowship. Romans 14:1–15:4 has in common with 1 Corinthians 8–10 the problem of strong Christians offending weaker ones by what they eat. In both letters, as well as both "A" and "B" in 1 Corinthians, Paul's argument includes citations from the scriptures of Israel's tradition which are then used to claim that what happened to Israel in former times was for Paul and the Christians' instruction (1 Cor. 9:9–10; 10:6–7; Rom. 15:3–4).[15]

2.1.2 The Relationship of Idol Meats with 1 Corinthians 9

Another problem with the unity of chapters 8–10 rests in the function of chapter 9. Paul seems to be diverted from his subject into a discussion about financial matters and his apostolic "authority" (ἐξουσία). The unity of Paul's thought in chapters 8 and 9, however, seems linked together by Paul when he uses himself as an example beginning in 8:13.[16] When this verse is read in light of chapter 9 we find that Paul claims he would never eat meat if it causes a weaker person to fall even though he has the apostolic right (ἐξουσία) to eat and drink, to marry, to refrain from physical labour, and more emphatically, to be supported through his preaching. He does not always exercise his ἐξουσία on these matters, however, because the preaching of Gospel (i.e. the message of salvation) must not be offensive at the expense of his rights. In order for Paul to partake of the eschatological blessings of the Gospel, he himself must run the course of Christian living with self-control or else he would be disqualified (9:23–27).[17] In chapter 9, then, Paul uses himself as an example to convince the strong that they should also exercise self-control by refraining from their right to eat at the expense of the conscience of the weak.

Paul uses the athletic metaphor of running a race in 9:24–27 to suggest that unless he makes an effort to control himself, he will not attain the victor's crown at the end of the race. The aspects of completion and rejection in relation to movement/distance is then altered and expanded by Paul in chapter 10. He

---

[15] Cf. W. WILLIS, 274–75; HURD, 133–34. Von Soden writes, "Man vergleiche noch im einzelnen den parallelen Aufbau beider Abschnitte [Rom. 14–15 and 1 Cor. 8, 10] und die Wiederkehr der gleichen Motive in denselben Gedankenzusammenhängen bei völliger Freiheit und gegenseitiger Unabhängigkeit des Ausdrucks hier und dort" (1951:257). Similarly (but failing to recognise the importance of Romans 15:4) is HINZ (1973), 409.

[16] It is significant that beginning in 8:13 Paul often writes in the first person until 10:1. He concludes the major sections of this subject using himself as an example (8:13; 9:19–23; 9:26–27; 10:33–11:1). Cf. D. WATSON (1989), 307–08.

[17] Other significant links between 9 and the larger context are as follows: 1) the voluntary non-use of ἐξουσία links 8:9 with 9:4–6, 12, 18; 2) the freedom and slavery motif is found in both in 9:1 (which is closely linked to 8:13) and 9:19–23 (cf. vv. 16–17); 3) 9:23 links the earlier argumentation with 9:24–10:22. For further discussion on the connections between 9:23 and 24, and 10:13 and 10:14 see FEE, 432, 464.

warns that the Corinthians must also set a sober course for their lives in terms of a journey, lest they, like the children of Israel in the wilderness, fail to reach their destination because of idolatry or other vices (10:1–13). Paul's charge to the Corinthians to flee from idolatry in 10:14 is his resolution to the problem in 10:7.[18] Verse 14 provides the bridge between 9:24–10:13 and the following argument in 10:15–22 where Paul addresses the sensibility of his imperative language to flee idolatry in 10:14.[19] This verse brings Paul back into a final discussion on idol meats and refraining from one's right to eat for the sake of others in 10:23–11:1.[20] Thus, the unity of Paul's thought in 8:1–11:1 may be maintained.

2.2 The Unity of 1 Corinthians 8:1–11:1 in Light of Rhetorical Discourse

Regarding the quality of coherence in 1 Corinthians 8:1–11:1 Margaret Mitchell has argued for the rhetorical unity of the passage with 8:1–13 as Paul's first treatment of the idol meat situation, 9:1–27 and 10:1–13 as two exemplary arguments, 10:14–22 as the second treatment of the situation, and 10:23–11:1 as a final appeal to advantage. Mitchell has also noted that the subject of unity and discord arises repeatedly throughout the text as it does throughout the entire epistle.[21] The pericope of 10:1–13 thus stands as one example of factionalism in Mitchell's epistolary body of the letter – 1:10–15:58 Epistolary Body:

a) 1:10 Thesis Statement
b) 1:11–17 Statement of Facts
c) 1:18–15:57 Proofs
   (1) 1:18–4:21 First Proof: Censure of Factionalism
   (2) 5:1–11:1 Second Proof: Integrity Against Defilement, Advice on Divisive Issues

---

[18] The Israelite wilderness example is the focus of 10:1–11, and 10:12–13 seem to contain the final conclusions drawn from the wilderness episode. There is also exegetical support for delimiting 10:1–13 as a distinct unit as we will discuss in upcoming chapters and §3 below.

[19] Cf. FEE, 464. The connection between 10:14 is so close to what precedes it that GARD-NER (149, 155) includes the verse in the pericopes before (10:1–14) and after it (10:14–22). Notice that Paul does not say to flee from an idol temple or idol meats but to flee from idolatry (10:14). Nevertheless, he believes the former two could devolve into the latter.

[20] The connections between chapters 8–9 and 10:23–11:1 are significant. Hurd lists fifteen similarities (129–30); Fisk mentions nine (1989:65–67). Perhaps the most significant similarity between the two passages is that of the central theme: the strong should not be a stumbling block to the weak in terms of what they eat. They should seek the benefit of many. In the latter passage, however, the subject matter is more general, and the strongs' right to eat meat is more pronounced (cf. 10:29b-30).

[21] M. MITCHELL, 1, 19, 23. In an similar manner Witherington suggests that in 1 Corinthians 8–10 Paul utilises an *egressio* pattern of A–B–A. In this framework 1 Corinthians 10:1–13 may be an *exemplum* under one of the rubrics of Quintilian's *paradeigma* that adduces some past action to persuade an audience of whatever point the user wishes to make (WITHERINGTON, 1995:191, 217).

Mitchell's outline provides a coherent way of looking at the letter as a whole in rhetorical categories which would have been accessible for Paul in the first century.[22] Moreover, unity and discord do run through the entire letter beginning with Paul's exhortation in 1:10 and ending with his appeal for the members to submit to the house of Stephanas (16:15–18). Mitchell's outline therefore seems quite plausible.[23]

In addition, a perspective of 1 Corinthians 10:29b–10:30 which emphasises deliberative rhetoric may ease the tension between this passage and Paul's argument in the context of 8:1–11:1. The former passage has been problematic with regard to coherence because it seems that in this passage Paul turns against the weak by justifying the liberty of the strong. It is not that Paul now approves of the liberty of the strong against the weak so that he contradicts what he wrote earlier; rather, he may be utilising a form of rhetoric which recollects what was affirmed earlier in his argument. Duane Watson suggests that Paul is using a diatribe in 10:29b-30 in a form known as deliberative rhetoric of recapitulation. This style of rhetoric aims at the weak points of the opponent. In this case Paul reiterates in 10:23–11:1 the weak points of the strong: 1) a lack of respect for others; 2) a defense of eating despite offending others (through the blessing over the food).[24] Consequently, it appears that Paul intends to add persuasiveness to his message by using deliberative argumentation.[25] In this light, the

---

[22] For examples of some elements of ancient deliberative rhetoric which are found in 1 Corinthians, see M. MITCHELL, 20–64.

[23] Differently, Linda Belleville has argued for the structural and thematic coherency of 1 Corinthians on examining the letter's structure in light of first century epistolary conventions and forms (1987:15–37). She observes that chapters 8 and 10 are introduced by two distinct disclosure formulae: "we know that ..." (8:1–9:27); "I do not want you ignorant ..." (10:1–22). Belleville suggests that these indicate two topics: 1) idol food, and 2) idol worship (28–29 cf. 37). The topics may be somewhat oversimplified (cf. § 2.3 below), but as long as the texts are not taken as mutually exclusive categories, it can be argued that the form of the texts implies a diversity of subject matter under a common theme which runs from 8:1 to 11:1.

[24] D. WATSON, 311.

[25] D. WATSON, 312, 318.

range of overlapping problems and solutions in 1 Corinthians 8:1–11:1 might be depicted in the outline below:

1. Problem 1: Eating idol meats may become a stumbling-block to weaker congregation members (1 Cor. 8:1–13)
   Solution 1: Refrain from exercising one's ἐξουσία as does Paul (1 Cor. 8:13–9:23)
   Solution 2: Exercise one's self-control as does Paul (1 Cor. 9:24–27)
2. Problem 2: Eating idol meats may lead to idolatry (1 Cor. 10:1–13)
   Solution 1: Exercise one's self-control (1 Cor. 9:24–27)
   Solution 2: Flee from idolatry (1 Cor. 10:14)
3. Problem 3: Eating idol meats may open the way to a communion with demons (1 Cor. 10:15–21)
   Solution: Do not let it to happen (1 Cor. 10:21–22 cf. v. 14)
4. Recapitulation of Problem 1 (1 Cor. 10:23–11:1)
   Recapitulation and expansion of Solutions 1 and 2 (1 Cor. 10:24–25, 27–29a, 31–11:1).

2.3 Coherency in Paul's Argument Regarding Meat Sacrificed to Idols

Although a majority of recent scholars argue for the literary unity of 1 Corinthians 8:1–11:1, they disagree over the nature of that unity. Bruce Fisk summarises the position held by the majority of scholars and a second position held by Gordon Fee. He correctly gets to the heart of the issue: the majority, in essence, argue that Paul primarily focuses on marketplace idol meats that were previously used in idol worship (1 Cor. 8:1–13; 10:23–11:1), and secondarily, pagan temple worship (1 Cor. 10:1–22). Fee, on the other hand, argues that 8:1–13 and 10:1–22 focus on pagan temple worship, and 10:23–11:1 emphasises marketplace idol meat. A summary of Fee's arguments may be seen on the following chart:[26]

Problems with the Majority View	Fee's Alternative
1 Corinthian 8:10 focuses on dining in an idol temple, not merely eating idol meats.	1 Corinthians 8 and 10 show that the strong were eating cultic meals in pagan temples (cf. 1 Cor. 8:10; 10:1–22).
1 Corinthians 8:4–6 closely parallels the idolatrous practises of 10:14–22.	In 1 Corinthians 8 Paul challenges the strong's knowledge on the ethical basis of love, and in 10:1–22 he condemns their idolatrous behaviour.

---

[26] FISK, 53. He lists in the first camp CONZELMANN (1975), 146–80; BARRETT (1968), 188 ff; BRUCE (1971), 78–102; MURPHY-O'CONNOR, 547–49; THRALL (1965), 60–77; and SONGER (1983), 364–66. On Fee's view see FEE (1980), 172–97, and (1987), 357–491.

1 Corinthians 8 discourages eating idol meats but 10:23–11:1 encourages it.	1 Corinthians 10:23–11:1 shows for the first time that Paul considers idol meats sold in the market place to be morally neutral.
1 Corinthians 8:1–10:22 is dispropor-tionate in intensity if the problem stems from Corinthian quarrels about the propriety of eating market idol meat.	
1 Corinthians 8:7, 10 show that Gentile Christians are under discussion, but it seems unlikely that they would be so sensitive toward mere market-place idol meats.	

While Fisk recognises Fee's contribution to the Corinthian situation and the problems Fee raises regarding the majority view, he criticises Fee's position on several points, including his interpretation of εἰδωλόθυτος.[27] But perhaps the most crucial problem with Fee's argument is that it is not able to explain ad-equately why Paul is lenient toward idol meats in chapter 8 if idolatry or a pagan cultus is primarily in view both here and in 10:1–22. A similar error is made by Paul Tomson, who places too much emphasis on the first letter's con-nection with fornication and Paul's boundaries in 2 Corinthians 6:11–7:1. He argues that Paul is against any kind of eating of idol meat, and this viewpoint leads him to paraphrase 10:29b and virtually ignore 10:30f where Paul seems to permit the eating of idol food.[28] The apparent contradiction between chap-ters 8 and 10 may be explained if some activities in a cultic setting are morally objectionable for Paul while others are not.[29]

---

[27] Against Fee's suggestion that εἰδωλόθυτος means "meat eaten in an idol's temple" (cf. 1 Cor. 10:19), for instance, Fisk suggests on semantic ground (distinguishing between mean-ing and referent) that εἰδωλόθυτος is best defined as "meat offered to idols" and that the usage of the word is determined by the respective context in which it appears. He also rightly argues that εἰδωλόθυτος (1 Cor. 8:1, 4, 7, 10; 10:19) and ἱερόθυτον (1 Cor. 10:28) are virtu-ally synonymous for Paul in the text. In the latter verse, it seems that Paul places ἱερόθυτον on the mouth of a Gentile because they probably used the word on a normal basis instead of the more Jewish (and apparently more pejorative) εἰδωλόθυτος. The former word may be understood as "sacrificed to a divinity" ("holy-offered") implying the Gentile belief that idols are in fact gods (56–59; see also BRUNT, 1981: 28–29 ftn.7). This does not necessarily mean that the informant in 10:28f is the unbeliever who invited the Christian to dine. It seems that the one who may be offended is still the weak Christian (cf. 8:10); Paul's use of ἱερόθυτον may reflect the weak's belief that idols were gods (cf. 8:7) or the non-offensive language commonly used by Christians in the presence of unbelievers. It is also possible that Paul's thought arbitrarily shifts from a generic informant to a weak Christian.

[28] TOMSON, ch. 5, esp. 196–99, 202–03, 208, 216–19.

[29] Cf. FISK, 59–61. In chapter 8 Paul suggests that idol meat *in itself* is not contaminated (1 Cor. 8:8 cf. vv. 1, 4). He also argues that idol meat can only contaminate based on a

We may be able to probe a little further than this. Paul seems to be implying that there is an entire range of idol meat predicaments a Christian may find him- or herself in. While it is true that both idol meats and fornication can be understood as cultic practices in 1 Corinthians (1 Cor. 10:7–8 cf. 6:12–20), Paul's exhortation regarding idol meat is not *because* it is a cultic practice (8:10; 10:27 ff). Apart from 1 Corinthians, εἰδωλόθυτος appears in early Judeo-Christian literature in Acts 15:29; 21:25; Rev. 2:14, 20; 4 Macc. 5:2; Did. 6:3. While some have argued that εἰδωλόθυτος has a cultic connotation in Acts and Revelation,[30] this is no indication that meat sacrificed to idols should *always* be located in a cultic milieu or shunned as such. The problems in 4 Maccabees and the Didache seem concerned with the eating of idol meats rather than where they are eaten.[31] To this list can be added the discussion on idol foods in the Sibylline Oracles (cf. 2.95) and Joseph and Aseneth (8:5; 10:12–13; 11:8; 21:13f). These references do not clearly place such food in a cultic situation; rather, idol food seems to defile because it has been contaminated by idols. In Joseph and Aseneth 10:12–13, for instance, Aseneth seems to be in her own private chamber when she throws her royal dinner consisting of idol food out of her north window.[32] In Paul's case, εἰδωλόθυτος is neither condemned nor necessarily forbidden.

Some have affirmed that what is at stake in the Corinthian situation is not the eating or location of the idol meats *per se*, but the *nature* of idol meats.[33] Perhaps even more precisely, the problem with idol meats is more a question of *who* than *what*. Social dissimilarities seem to be at the heart of the problem: in chapter 8 the problem rests in a disunity of fellowship between the strong and weak over idol meats; in chapter 10:1–22, the problem centres on Christians sharing in a unified fellowship with idolaters and demons. It is significant that Paul begins the pericope (8:1–3) by rebuking the strong's high-mindedness about the issue of idol meats and offers love (ἀγάπη) as the alternative to knowledge (γνῶσις). For Paul the immediate threat of idol meats was relational: through the strong's knowledge that idols were not gods (8:1, 4–6) they were defiling the conscience (συνείδησις) of the weak and destroying their faith as a result (8:7–12). The importance of this sociological observation should not be understated since Paul again returns to the same problem at the end of his idol meat discussion in 10:23–11:1.

---

person's belief (1 Cor. 8:7). Although Paul warns the strong of the danger of offending other Christians, he does not warn them of any danger of their participating in idolatry (1 Cor. 8:9). The strong actually seem to practise reclining in an idol's temple, yet Paul does not bother to identify this as idolatrous (cf. 8:10). Moreover, the only mention of sin in chapter 8 has to do with violating the weak (8:12).

[30] E.g., WITHERINGTON (1993).

[31] *Contra* WITHERINGTON, 240–42, 247.

[32] For further Jewish examples against pagan foods, see BONNINGTON (1994), 186–91, 216–26; BORGEN, (1995), 33–47. For early Christian examples, see BRUNT (1985), 113–124.

[33] CONZELMANN (1975), 171; BRUNT, 25–27; FISK, 62–63, 69.

2.4 Idol-Meat Observations in Light of Socio-Anthropological Studies

We have noted how Paul's discussion on idol meats focuses on social tensions. The problem at Corinth arises from a conflict of discord among the weak and strong and the conflict of unity with idolaters and demons. If a Greco-Roman view of the physical body is seen as a microcosm of the social body of the community, as socio-anthropological studies have suggested (cf. ch. 1:3.1.1; 3.3.1), then the idol-meat situation in Corinth might emphasise a social conflict based on this model.[34] From this vantage point, Paul would be claiming that if the strong cause the weak to stumble, they would be sinning against the weak and also against Christ (1 Cor. 8:12). Paul affirms, in fact, that the Christians in Corinth all partake in a solidarity with the body of Christ (10:16–17 cf. 12:13ff). They are all members of that one body; hence, for one member to harm another member is to disrupt the unity of that body. Elsewhere in the letter Paul writes that the Corinthians belong to Christ and are joined to him through the Spirit (1:13f; 6:13; 12:13).

The perspective I have just presented may shed light on Paul's use of boundary language. Paul stresses his anxiety over the thought of the Corinthians having fellowship (κοινωνία) with demons (10:20–21). Contextually, this potential union does not take place *merely* by means of idol meats (8:1ff; 10:25), or unbelievers (10:27f), or even attending idol precincts (8:10); it rather takes place by means of having communion with idolaters when they are committing idolatry.[35] In 1 Corinthians 6:12–20 Paul relates a similar situation wherein Corinthian congregation members were apparently committing fornication with temple prostitutes. Paul's anxiety over that situation, as Martin argues, was that a member of the body of Christ would be united with a member of the fallen *cosmos*. The unthinkable union of Christ and the *cosmos* rendered such an activity off-limits for Paul, and so he exhorts the Corinthian members to flee from fornication (6:18).[36] In 10:1–22 he warns the Corinthians to "flee from idolatry" (10:14). It seems likely that Paul would have thus considered fellowship with demons in 10:20–21 as another violation of the boundary between Christ and the *cosmos*. If the Corinthians were united with demons they would be blurring the boundary between the body of Christ and the realm of demons.

Although Paul uses forceful language to denounce such a union, he does not list an inventory of rules or principles to determine when a particular situation

---

[34] Cf. DOUGLAS (1973), 98; MEEKS (1983a), 97.

[35] Paul and the Corinthian congregation may have heard of stories such as the one in the *'Abodah Zarah* (55a) which claims that despite the belief that there is no such thing as other gods, a cripple may come out of an idol temple cured (cf. Sanh. 63b). Perhaps Paul felt he needed to explain such phenomena, and he would probably do so by attributing such things to demons (cf. WINTER, 1990:215–16, 223–24).

[36] D. MARTIN (1995), 176–78.

becomes idolatry. The only indication of this seems to be that the strong were not to participate in idol sacrifices at pagan altar tables.[37] In this sense Paul reflects more the attitude of the strong who tend to mitigate the boundaries *vis-à-vis* outsiders by defending their right to eat idol meats. The weak, on the other hand, seem to have well-defined boundaries: to them all forms of idol meat appeared to be prohibited.[38] Then again, temples and meals in Greco-Roman society functioned in diverse ways. Some meals were knowingly offered to a god while others were not; some meals were held in temples, others were not. The line between the "secular" and "sacred" was not always clear.[39] Regarding invitations to such meals, von Soden suggests, "Das Formular καλεῖν dient zu Tempelmählern ebenso wie zu solchen in privaten Häusern ... und an sich war das Essen in einem Raum, der ein Götzenbild enthielt, wenn dieses dabei igno-riert wurde, wohl nicht bedenklicher als etwa das Baden."[40] Hence, Paul's am-biguity in relation to outsiders seems to reflect that of the larger Corinthian culture: the boundary between religious and non-religious meals was blurred.

It is not that Paul wishes to side with the strong against the weak by not specifying clearer boundaries in reference to meals. His priority was to see people saved (9:19–22), and perhaps he realised that dinner invitations by non-Christians presented an ideal opportunity for him to preach the Gospel. As long as the strong did not offend the weak nor succumb to idolatry, he thinks they may accept such invitations (10:23 ff). On the other hand, Paul's soteriological objective also enabled him to empathise with the weak. He was free to lower his own status to a slave by performing the menial task of manual labour rather than accepting finances for his preaching (1 Cor. 9:12, 15–19). He apparently does this to gain the lower classes and those who might see financial support from preaching as a stumbling block.[41] In this regard, Paul is siding with the weak who, generally speaking, may have been from the lower classes.[42] Hence,

---

[37] Cf. BORGEN, 56; J. T. SANDERS (1997), 70.

[38] Cf. MEEKS (1983a), 98.

[39] Cf. P. OXY. 926; P. KÖLN; P. YALE 85; P. OSLO 157. On further sources and examples of the diversities of ancient Greco-Roman meals in relation to idols, see W. WILLIS, 17–62; GOOCH, 1–46; HORRELL (1996), 145–46; GARDNER 18–19; BARRETT (1964–65), 144–47; POGOLOFF (1992), 238–39.

[40] VON SODEN, 268–69.

[41] Cf. D. MARTIN (1990), 76–77, 121, 124, 132, 144.

[42] THEISSEN (1982:124–28) and MEEKS (69–70) have noted that invitations to dinner would normally be given to those of high status (cf. 1 Cor. 10:27). Meeks, however, writes that the strong in Corinth may have enjoyed high status in certain aspects (e.g., wealth, holding civic office, support by dependants and clients) while they shared affinity with the lower status in other aspects (e.g., origin, sex, occupation). On other criticisms against Theissen's view, see GOOCH, 148–50. Horrell has reservations regarding clear socio-eco-nomic statuses between the strong and weak, but he still maintains a generally high social standing for the strong on that basis that 1) the Corinthian letter reflects the perspective of the strong who also happen to be literate; 2) the strong are the ones who receive invitations to

he attempts to walk a fine line between the weak and strong, but he does so in a way that might have seemed unsatisfactory to some of his readers despite his rhetoric. In short, the boundary between idolatry and idol meats remained blurred to his audience.[43]

If the strong represented a desire to mitigate boundaries between the Christian community and the host society, it is appropriate to consider possible reasons for this. At least two may be noted here. First, some of the strong in Corinth were apparently socially affluent (cf. 1 Cor. 10:27).[44] It would be difficult to advance in society and maintain relationships with outsiders if the strong always turned down dinner invitations because they did not wish to offend the weak. Idol food pervaded weddings, birthday celebrations, funerals, and the like, as well as temples and private homes.[45] Second, the strong may have felt uneasy about the possibility of becoming social outcasts by avoiding such common meeting grounds. As Horrell affirms, the strong "may lose friends and position in the city if they refuse to attend celebrations and banquets to which they are personally invited. And they may have to do this, according to Paul, merely because a weak nobody, a slave even, is troubled by their conduct."[46]

When socio-anthropological dimensions are considered in relation to the situation in Corinth, they bring into sharp relief how acute the problem really was. These observations add to the reasons why Paul seems unclear in his thought in 1 Corinthians 8–10. It is not that there is a discontinuity regarding the unity of message in 1 Corinthians 8–10. The dangerous and complex situation in Corinth warranted Paul to discuss the controversial matter of idol meat while at the same time attempting not to offend either weak or strong. After Paul agrees with the perspective of the strong in chapter 8, he presents his main problem with their consumption of idol meats: they may offend the weak. In chapter 9 he uses himself as a model on how to avoid becoming offensive to others, and in chapter 10 he warns the strong against idolatry but affirms that there is nothing intrinsically wrong with eating idol meats.

---

dine; 3) socially prominent members of the congregation would stand more to lose and thus would tend to defend their right for social interactions (107–08).

[43] That Paul's message here essentially failed to be clearly communicated may be observed in the writings of the early church fathers who largely misunderstand and misinterpret Paul's discussion on idol meats (cf. BRUNT, 1985:120–21). On the other hand Paul's perspective can be seen as successful in a larger framework. J. T. Sanders notes that new religious movements are successful when they maintain cultural continuity yet partially deviate from it. This reflects a "medium level of tension" between continuity and deviance which helped Christianity survive beyond the Roman Empire era: "Paul and others like him found the winning formula, which we can now express in Rodney Stark's terms, *mutatis mutandis:* cultural continuity with the conventional faith of Jewish society, an attempt to accommodate as much as possible to Graeco-Roman culture, and a medium level of tension with the Gentile environment" (83 cf. 79–80).

[44] Cf. footnote 42 above.

[45] Cf. GOOCH, 45–46.

[46] HORRELL (1996), 148.

3. Outline of Paul's Argument in 1 Corinthians 10:1–13

As we noted in chapter one Margaret Mitchell argues that 1 Corinthians is a unified letter which, as a whole, may be characterised by deliberative rhetoric. The primary function of the letter for Paul was to warn against factionalism; that is, he wished to foster reconciliation among the various Christian groups at Corinth. I concur with Mitchell's outline for 1 Corinthians 8:1–11:1 (cf. 2.2 above).[47] It appears that 10:1–13 is connected with the larger context of idol meats (cf. 10:7), and to a lesser extent, the theme of unity and discord (cf. "all"/ "some" 10:1–10).[48] In 10:1–13 Paul seems to be using an inductive argument by means of examples (*paradeigmata*). He draws upon examples from Israelite history and derives his conclusion based on the examples. George Kennedy notes that in ancient rhetoric the conclusion drawn from *paradeigmata* is not often made explicit to the audience.[49] A similar case may be made regarding the first conclusion of Paul's argument in 1 Corinthians 10:1–12. The conclusion is implied, and it then becomes the first premise to a second, related argument. In the first argument Paul asserts the following:

All the Israelites partook of divine blessings in the wilderness (vv. 1–4).

Many Israelites were destroyed in the wilderness because God was displeased with them (vv. 5b, 7–10).

Therefore the Israelites' privileges did not prevent many from divine judgement when they displeased God (implied in v. 5).

Paul's second argument rests on the conclusion of his first, and it is more clearly directed at the Corinthian congregation:

The Israelites' privileges did not prevent many from divine judgement when they displeased God (implied in v. 5).

The things that happened to Israel in the wilderness are primarily given as negative examples for the Corinthians not to follow (vv. 6, 11).

Therefore, the Corinthians should beware, lest some of them, like Israel, commit vices in the wilderness and suffer divine judgement as a result (vv. 11–12).[50]

Lawrence Willis also notes how Paul's message in 10:1–14 follows a rhetorical structure which is exhortational and is found in Hellenistic Jewish and early Christian sermonic forms. This structure has three distinct repetitions: exempla,

---

[47] However, it can be argued that the placement of the foot-race in 9:24–27 has more in common with the wilderness trek in 10:1–13 than with the passage that precedes it. The former passage is transitional. On a structural level it appears to function as a corollary argument to Paul's exhortation for the strong which began in chapter 8. The content, however, anticipates his next section on the wilderness journey.

[48] My assumptions here will be defended in chs. 3–4.

[49] G. KENNEDY (1984), 16.

[50] 10:13 would seem to be anticlimactic to the strong language of 10:12; hence, its role in Paul's argument here is less significant. The verse will be dealt with in chapter 5 of this work.

conclusion, and exhortation. In 1 Corinthians 10:1–14 the forms appear in three cycles: exampla (10:1b–5; 7–10; 13a), conclusions (6, 11, 13b), and exhortations (7–10 "let us not," 12, 14).[51] A definitive affirmation of these rhetorical models is hard to determine. Willis's third cycle, for instance, seems questionable because 10:13a and 10:13b both appear to serve as a form of encouragement to the readers. Also, 10:14 has been normally linked more with what follows than what precedes it. Nevertheless if Paul is drawing on a kind of rhetoric characterised by exhortation or *paradeigmata*, he may be expressing in cogent terms a real concern for the spiritual dangers being encountered in the Corinthian congregation. His message here also seems deliberative in that it involves persuading the Corinthians to take some positive action by learning from a negative example. Paul seems to have strung together Israelite wilderness examples for the sake of reinforcing his argument. This shows us that what Paul is communicating to the Corinthians is important.

In this preliminary chapter on 1 Corinthians, I have attempted to establish the unity of Paul's thought in his idol meat discourse (1 Cor. 8:1–11:1). I have suggested how 10:1–13 fits into the larger context. Although problems on the disunity of the text have been raised, the literary integrity of 1 Corinthians 8:1–11:1 can be reasonably obtained. Moreover, recent socio-anthropological and rhetorical studies have tended to underscore this unity rather than disrupt it. I will therefore proceed on the basis that 10:1–13 is a literary unit which functions as a segment of Paul's larger argument in 8:1–11:1.[52] The central topic of 1 Corinthians 8:1–11:1 has to do with Paul's response to the Corinthian congregation's discord over meat sacrificed to idols.

---

[51] LAWRENCE WILLIS (1984), 298 cf. 288–89. Also see Collier who more recently reaffirmed Willis's structure on the same passage (COLLIER, 1994: 55–75).

[52] Some sections of the second half of the letter are characterised by the opening phrase "περὶ δέ" (7:1, 25; 8:1; 12:1; 16:1; 16:12; cf. HURD, 63ff). Thus, 8:1–11:1 is located in the second part of the letter which began with Paul's response to the Corinthian correspondence in 7:1.

Chapter 3

The Election of Israel through Initiation and Sustenance in the Exodus/Wilderness Episode

Now that we have established that 1 Corinthians 10:1–13 can be interpreted as a literary unit in the larger setting of 8:1–11:1, we will examine the first segment of the unit: 1 Corinthians 10:1–4. This segment forms a single long sentence in Greek and is marked off from what follows by the adversative ἀλλά in 10:5.[1] The unit presents Paul's description of Israel's exodus from Egypt at the Red Sea and the people's subsequent wilderness experiences of divine provision. In the passage Paul claims that all the Israelites were "baptised" into Moses in the cloud and in the sea, and that they all partook of spiritual food and drink. The source of this sustenance, he believes, came from Christ, the spiritual "rock." This segment of the passage is characterised by God's preservation of Israel in the wilderness. The text thus seems related to the concepts of election and perseverance, which are therefore important for interpreting the corollary apostasy of Israel in the verses which follow. We will examine the nature of Paul's interpretation of Israel's Red Sea experience as a baptism into Moses and his use of rhetoric to describe the wilderness provisions in an effort to determine what he means by terms such as "our fathers," "all," baptism in the "cloud," and the consumption of "spiritual" food. These observations are significant for Paul because he is attempting to communicate a message relevant for the Corinthian congregation's problem with idol meat. Perhaps this issue is in view when we consider the implications of Paul's appeal to the Israelites' consumption of spiritual food and drink. We will therefore ascertain the function of 10:1–4 in relation to its larger context.

1. Israel's Baptism in Moses as a Mark of Solidarity (1 Corinthians 10:1–2)

1.1 Paul's Introduction to the Pericope

Paul opens 1 Corinthians 10:1–13 with the introduction formula "for I do not wish you to be ignorant" (οὐ θέλω γὰρ ὑμᾶς ἀγνοεῖν). The word "for" (γάρ)

---

[1] Cf. FEE (1987), 449.

associates this section with the preceding passage (9:24–27).[2] This suggests that Paul intends to argue that members of the church at Corinth must exercise self-control on their way to incorruptible glory, or else they – like Paul's hypothetical situation in 9:27 – might be disqualified from their own race.

W. L. Willis suggests that οὐ θέλω ὑμᾶς ἀγνοεῖν was Paul's formula for introducing concepts which his listeners had not previously understood (cf. Rom. 1:13; 11:25; 1 Cor. 12:1; 2 Cor. 1:8; 1 Thes. 4:13).[3] Paul is still focusing on the same issue taken up at the beginning of chapter 8. As the context demonstrates, he is here providing examples from Israelite traditions to warn the Corinthian congregation members against committing idolatry and other vices. If the Acts account of Paul's initial visit to Corinth is reliable,[4] the first converts in the Corinthian congregation may have been Jews (Acts 18:1–17).[5] Luke may at least have thought that Paul sometimes included wilderness episodes in his messages when he preached in the synagogues (Acts 13:17–18 cf. 7:36 ff). If the representation in Acts has any basis in tradition about Paul's activity, then it is not impossible that the Jewish wilderness traditions would have been familiar to a number of his Corinthian hearers. Since Paul uses this tradition to address the Corinthian situation, we might ask in what sense this information about the wilderness functioned as deliberative rhetoric in the immediate context.

In the last chapter we noted that in 8:1–11:1 Paul is primarily addressing the strong members of the congregation, and that this group – as is evident by their intention to have fellowship with idolaters – seems to consist of Gentiles who were not formerly Jewish proselytes. Nevertheless it seems difficult to imagine that they would have never heard about the wilderness tradition once they be-

---

[2] FEE, 443.

[3] W. WILLIS (1985), 125–26.

[4] For arguments in favour of the reliability of the book of Acts, see HENGEL (1979); HEMER (1989); cf. further ftn.5 below.

[5] Acts describes Aquila, Priscilla and Apollos as Jews (18:1–2, 24, 27 cf. 1 Cor. 1:12). Crispus (and possibly Sosthenes – Acts 18:17 cf. 1 Cor. 1:1) is described as a synagogue ruler who was converted to Christianity (Acts 18:8 cf. 1 Cor. 1:14; cf. further HEMER, 187–89). Kee studies the evidence available for the status of the synagogue in the first part of the first century C. E. He claims that the Luke-Acts idea of Paul entering into synagogues to preach follows the patterns of synagogue practice developed after 70 C. E. (1990:1–24; esp. 18). Oster, however, contends that Kee's evidence is inaccurate and that there is no evidence supporting Luke's description of Jewish synagogues (1993:178–208). Moreover, evidence from literature and inscriptions from the Second Temple period suggests that many Jews resided in Corinth due to the Diaspora, and that the Jews met in synagogue there (Schürer, 1986:3.1:4–5, 64–66 cf. 141). His evidence demonstrates that the Jews at least met in houses for worship in virtually every city where they lived (cf. Strabo in Josephus, *Ant.* 14.7.2[111–115]; *Bell.* 7.3[43–45]; Philo, *In Flaccum* 7; *Legat. ad Gaium* 36). Acts 18:7 suggests that the synagogue in Corinth may have been situated in a house (οἰκία).

came Christians.[6] Paul may be extending a motif on the exodus/wilderness narrative which was already integrated into early Christian tradition.[7]

Bandstra suggests that Paul is making explicit an underlying theme of Jesus accomplishing an "exodus" in Jerusalem with a baptism of suffering and death (Luke 12:49 f cf. Mark 10:35–45). Hence, Paul believed that the Christians embark on a final exodus as the new Israel by being baptised.[8] Similarly, Friedrich Lang writes regarding Paul's introduction: "Das Neue ist hier die typologische Anwendung der Exoduserzählung auf die christliche Gemeinde ... deshalb bildet die Grundlegung des alten Gottesvolkes durch Gottes Wirken (Exodus und Wüstenzug) einen Typos, eine 'Voraus-Darstellung' für die Grundlegung des neuen, eschatologischen Gottesvolks durch das Christusgeschehen."[9] There is a close association in this passage between the old and new people of God, and (as we will examine in the following chapter) the experiences of Israel are advanced presentations for the Corinthians.

There is then reason to conclude that Paul is not appealing to previously unknown narratives about Israel in the wilderness; rather, he is attempting to relate these narratives to a predominantly Gentile situation. The strong may have known about Israel's escape from the Egyptians which occurred at the Red Sea. They may have known that many from Israel had been severely judged by God in the wilderness. But Paul is convinced that they did not realise this tra-

---

[6] Earlier in the letter, for instance, Paul linked Jesus to the Passover tradition in a way that assumes that the Corinthians already knew the exodus narrative (1 Cor. 5:6–8). Moreover, as John Gager demonstrates, Moses was not unknown in ancient Greco-Roman literature. See GAGER (1972); cf. BADKE (1988), 27–28.

[7] On the use of the new exodus motif in Paul, see SAHLIN (1953), 121–36; HOWARD (1969), 97–108; HANSEN (1945), 174–77. Other works on this theme in the NT include MAUSER (1963); NIXON (1963); FISHER (1977), 69–79; O. PIPER (1957), 3–22; WIEBE (1939); ALLISON (1993); WATTS (1997). For standard treatments in the OT, see VON RAD (1962), 1:280–89; FOHRER (1972), 60–86; RINGGREN (1966), 28–40; VRIEZEN (1963), 124–53.

[8] BANDSTRA (1971), 8. Bandstra, however, speaks of this baptism as a baptism into Christ's death. He seems to rely too heavily upon the Pauline theology of baptism as portrayed in other passages (cf. Rom. 6:1–4; Col. 2:11–13). Kreitzer argues instead that the place where Paul most often discusses baptism is in the Corinthian letters. Baptism is not even the central theme in Romans 6, the passage that is often assumed as the matrix of Paul's theology on baptism. There it functions as little more than an illustration: "the unity that exists between the believers *as the basis for the Christian's ethical lifestyle*" (1991:69). Hence, we think it is safe to assume that baptism into Christ's death is not at the forefront of Paul's thought in 1 Corinthians 10:1–13. In this passage, death is seen in reference to divine judgement rather than as a baptismal perspective on dying to oneself or to one's sins. Bandstra also stresses the wilderness narrative as the "new exodus" in 1 Corinthians 10:1–13. But perhaps it would be better to describe Paul's view in this passage as a new exodus/wilderness; in light of the entire passage, the emphasis is not so much on the Israelite departure from Egypt as it is on their behaviour in the wilderness.

[9] LANG (1986), 123. Cf. CONZELMANN (1975:165): "The material [1 Cor. 10] is assumed to be known: 'the' cloud, etc. The new element which Paul has to offer is the *interpretation* introduced by οὐ θέλω γὰρ ὑμᾶς ἀγνοεῖν."

dition referred to them and that they too could also be judged by God in a similar manner. Paul juxtaposes the experiences of the Israelites and the Corinthians within the framework of covenantal promises, solidarity, and initiation, as we will consider below.

1.2 The "Fathers" of the Corinthians

Paul's use of "our fathers" (οἱ πατέρες ἡμῶν) does not indicate that he is exclusively concerned with the Jewish members of the Corinthian congregation. Rather, Paul assumes that the Corinthian members – whether Jew or Gentile – are elect heirs of the covenantal promises given to the Israelites (Rom. 2:26–29; 4:1f; 9:8; 11:17–24; Gal. 3:6–9, 29; 4:28; 6:16; Phil. 3:3). Bandstra rightly claims, "Behind this manner of speaking is the conviction that the Christian church is the true eschatological Israel (cf. vs.[1 Cor. 10:]11), a truth which Paul also expresses or implies elsewhere in his epistles."[10] This makes the thrust of Paul's rhetoric even more cogent: what happened to Israel in the wilderness correlates to what could happen to the Corinthian members. Some scholars have noted that Paul may have adopted the phrase "our fathers" from previous Israelite wilderness traditions (cf. Num. 20:15; Neh. 9:9–34; Ps. 78:5; 106:6–7; Wisd. 18:6; 1QS1.25; 2 En. 53:4).[11] This view is no doubt correct. Paul uses a Hebrew expression which often referred to the Israelites, and now he includes Gentile Christians within the same category. What happens to the Israelites in the Jewish scriptures is unequivocally relevant for the Corinthians. Thus, we can already note that even though Paul refers back to Israel's experiences in the wilderness, he implies that the things which happened to them are ultimately related to the Corinthian situation.

1.3 The Solidarity of the Israelites' Experiences

In 10:1–4 Paul uses the pronominal adjective πάντες five times: 1) "all" the Israelites were under the cloud; 2) "all" the Israelites went through the sea; 3) "all" had themselves baptised into Moses; 4) "all" ate the same spiritual food; and 5) "all" ate the same spiritual drink. The repetitive "all" stands in contrast with the phrase "not with many of them" in verse 5 and with the references to "some" in verses 7–10, as we will discuss in the next chapter.

Apart from setting up a sharp contrast between "all" and "some," Paul may be using the repetitive "all" to stress the essential unity of the Israelite commu-

---

[10] BANDSTRA, 6; cf. SCHRAGE (1995), 388.
[11] GARDNER (1994), 116, 133; MARTELET (1956), 326–27.

nity. The Israelites certainly had a shared identity in the sense that they followed their leader Moses through the Red Sea to escape the Egyptians. In so doing, they were set apart as followers of Moses and his God. However, Paul is not stressing the idea that all the Israelites were unified in order to set up a contrast between the unity of Israel and the disunity in Corinth. Instead, Paul attempts to *compare* the Israelites with the Corinthians throughout this passage.

Moreover, it is not enough to affirm that Paul is commending the initial unity of Israel or implying that the Corinthians once had a harmonious relationship at the outset of their Christian journey. The stress on Israel's solidarity in this passage arises from a conviction concerning their common experiences as an elect people. They all experienced the exodus from Egypt, and they all partook of God's miraculous gifts and blessings in the wilderness. In Gardner's words, Paul is stressing that *all* the Israelites were "covenant community members."[12] His view appears correct because Paul uses the phrase "our fathers" (cf. 1.2 above), utilising the motif of a prophetic exodus, as we will discuss below. No doubt Paul, influenced by the wilderness traditions of his Hebrew upbringing, would have affirmed the importance of Israel's election in such traditions. Mauser rightly suggests that, "Within certain limitations it can be said that Israel's fundamental belief in her election as God's chosen people is rooted in the wilderness tradition."[13] This sets up a persuasive argument when later on Paul demonstrates that even these elect children of Israel turned away from God and suffered a fatal judgement. Although "all" were initiated and protected by God, "many" were destroyed in the wilderness.

As noted in the previous chapter, Paul is extending a discussion on failing to complete one's journey through a lack of self-control (9:24–27). In the footrace analogy, "all" entered the race, but only "one" receives the prize. We find a similar pattern in the exodus/wilderness: "all" set off for the journey, but "many" did not finish (cf. 10:5); more precisely, if Paul is specifically relying on the Numbers tradition as one of his sources, only two made it (Num. 13:22–24; cf. Josh. 14:6ff)! Hence, Paul is using the language of "all' to make a contrast which will become more evident in 10:5–10: all the Israelites participated in the journey, but not all finished it.

1.4 Correlation of Baptism into Moses with Baptism into the Body of Christ

After explaining that all the Israelites were under the cloud and passed through the sea during the exodus, Paul tells the Corinthians that all the Israelites were "baptised" into Moses in the cloud and sea (10:2). It is commonly asserted that

---

[12] GARDNER, 115.
[13] MAUSER (1963), 15.

Paul has created the phrase based on a prior conception of baptism into Christ. The construction of "into Moses" (εἰς τὸν Μωϋσῆν) in fact parallels "into Christ" (εἰς Χριστὸν) found in Galatians 3:27 and Romans 6:3. Paul is comparing two figures, Moses and Christ, but in what sense? At the heart of this question may rest a problem arising from a difference in viewpoints regarding baptism. The Corinthians, on the other hand, may have presupposed that baptism provides some sense of immunity. We will find that both positions have implications on how Paul and the Corinthian congregation perceived the conversion experience in relation to perseverance and apostasy; albeit, the full impact of this will not be discerned until we examine 1 Corinthians 10:11–12. I will argue that Paul's perspective is ultimately reminiscent of cultural anthropological rites of passages and early Jewish eschatological traditions.

1.4.1 Paul and the Antecedents toward His View on Baptism

Regarding Paul's perspective on baptism, some scholars have maintained that Paul was influenced by the Gnostic or mystery religions of his day. Perhaps the most influential of these is Schmithals who argues that Paul contends a heretical theology in Corinth in the form of Jewish Gnosticism. It is said that Paul held to some Gnostic elements. Based on the Gnostic idea of the spirit's escape from the body, Paul believed that through the symbolic act of baptism, one's spirit could escape the body of flesh because of the death of Christ (Rom. 6:3–4).[14] Schmithals' thesis, however, suffers from anachronisms. Clear Gnostic distinctives essentially begin as a second century phenomenon; Paul is writing to the Corinthians 50 to 100 years earlier than this.[15] Yamauchi argues that Gnosticism did not have a unified system of belief in the first century; hence, it is faulty to presuppose a Gnostic *system* as an explanation for New Testament thought.[16] As a whole, in comparing Gnosticism with the New Testament, Yamauchi is struck by the profound differences between the two, not the similarities.[17] Nevertheless, some proto-Gnostic ideas, such as superior knowledge, may have been influential in the first century, and Paul addresses issues related

---

[14] SCHMITHALS (1971), 248–49. In reference to baptism for the dead in 1 Corinthians 15:29, Schmithals claims that this is the only "account of the Gnostic baptismal praxis [that] has been handed down to us in the Corinthian epistles." He admits that baptism for the dead was popular among the mystery religions, but he believes that the Gnostic nonetheless practised it because he/she "must have thought of a magical effect through which the deceased, in spite of a lack of Gnosis, still experienced the liberation from the power of the demonic forces and was led homeward to the Pleroma" (258).

[15] So WEDDERBURN (1987), 148.

[16] YAMAUCHI (1973), 169–74. Yamauchi notes that Schmithals derives his arguments on Gnosticism from the Patristics, Jewish Gnosticism, and Mandaeanism – none of which can be proven as pre-Christian.

[17] YAMAUCHI, 179.

to knowledge and wisdom in 1 Corinthians (e.g., 1:18–2:16; 8:1–3). Is there some connection, then, between Gnostic or mystery influences and Paul?

Wedderburn questions the idea that baptism as a participation in Christ's death and resurrection originated in the Hellenistic churches where it was "understood on analogy of the initiation rites of the mysteries."[18] He argues that the Christians would not have had ideas from the mystery religions pervade the church unchallenged. What most likely happened was that Paul and the Jewish Christians unwittingly adopted language common to the mystery religions and that the Gentiles interpreted their faith in light of this language. However, once the Jewish Christians recognised what the Gentiles were doing, they repudiated these mystery associations.[19]

For Wedderburn, the parallels between Christian baptism and mystery initiations do not stem from the latter influencing the former. Instead, similarities may have arisen from similar presuppositions held by both groups. Both mystery and Christian initiation rites would fall under the category of "rites of passage" from a death event to a kind of transformation, and both "drew it from the general stock of ideas of their time, and indeed of most other times as well. This was an imagery that was current then in their environment as it has been and is in a multitude of other cultures."[20] Common initiation patterns between the mysteries and early Christianity might best be explained by a "rites of passage" matrix. If Wedderburn's suggestion is correct, this lends credibility to at least a subconscious separation rite (observed by the studies of Turner and van Gennep) in the mind of Paul. Wedderburn also suggests that: "The reversal of values with which Paul describes apostolic existence, and the transcending of distinctions or opposites, which he sees as marking the new creation and the new age (Gal. 3:28; 6:15), bears a surprising resemblance to some of the characteristics of 'liminal' or 'marginal' existence as described in anthropologists' descriptions of rites of passage."[21]

Wedderburn focuses on whether the mysteries influenced Paul and concludes that the answer is negative. Unlike the Gnostics who were prominent in the second century, we can suggest affirmatively that the mystery religions were widespread in the first century. They did seem to influence some of the

---

[18] WEDDERBURN, 3.

[19] WEDDERBURN, 162–63, 368–69, 396. Wedderburn uses 1 Corinthians 5:10 and 8:5 as two such examples. The mysteries had no standard theology resting on salvation in the ritual experience of participating in the death and resurrection of their deity, and their identifying in any suffering experience relates more to the deity that was bereaved of its loved one rather than the one who died (cf. 331; AUNE, *DPL*, 794–95).

[20] WEDDERBURN, 386–87. Alternatively, on language usage, Segal argues that there is no need to posit a relationship between mystery religions and Paul's vocabulary on baptismal conversion. Such language was available to both Hellenistic and Jewish mystic traditions, and Paul's conversion experience resembles Merkabah mysticism (1990:136 cf. 11, 34–38).

[21] WEDDERBURN, 386f.

members of the Corinthian congregation (as we will observe below regarding immortalisation), and Paul's correspondence implies that he is aware of this.[22] At the same time, Paul's own perspective is similar to a rites of passage, since a clear boundary of separation is implied by Israel's departure from Egypt through their "baptism" at the Red Sea (1 Cor. 10:2). With this pattern in mind, Israel's journey through the wilderness corresponds to their transition period, and their arrival in the promised land may be identified with their aggregation.

Early Jewish and Christian initiation patterns also seem to have influenced Paul. There is evidence from Tannaitic tradition that baptism was one of the means of initiation into early Judaism,[23] but more important for our purposes is whether baptism as an initiation ritual was practised by the Jews during the time of Paul, and if it influenced him. Although some scholars have argued that Jewish proselytising in this period lacks conclusive evidence,[24] Feldman responds that the Jewish attitude against idols would have been at least one incentive for attempting to convert the Gentiles, and the cumulative sources for Jewish missionary activities is considerable (e.g., Jud. 14:10; Sib. Or. 3.5–10; 2 Macc. 9:17; Letter of Aristeas 227; T. Joseph 4.4–5; Philo *De Vir.* 20.103–04 cf. Matt. 23:15).[25] If Feldman is correct, did such initiation include water baptism? McKnight makes a distinction between baptism as a lustration ritual and baptism as an unrepeatable initiation and argues that the former was practised in the first century C. E. while the latter cannot be proven until the third century. Nevertheless, he admits that "in light of needed rituals for women, it is more than likely (in my opinion) that baptism became a requirement for most of Judaism during the Second Temple Period."[26] He then suggests that Judaism

---

[22] Cf. e.g., RICHARD and CATHERINE KROEGER (1978), 332 ff. The Kroegers argue that some of the problems with women's hair/head/covering and use of prophetic gifts in the Corinthian congregation (chs. 11–14) may have stemmed from some of the Corinthian women's prior experiences as Maenads in the Dionysus religion.

[23] As the Israelites came into the covenant through circumcision, baptism, and sacrifice (which were said to occur during the exodus/wilderness episode), so the proselyte was to enter the covenant by the same means (cf. G. MOORE, 1966:1.331, 334). G. E. Moore, who refers to Rabbi Judah the Patriarch, writes that the Israelites were said to be circumcised before departing from Egypt (inferred by Josh. 5:2f), baptised in the desert (inferred by Exodus 19:10), and were sprinkled with the blood of the covenant in Exodus 24:3–8. After a proselyte was initiated, he became a full member of the religious community (MOORE, 1:332). Evidently, the Jews considered Gentiles as unclean (cf. Acts 10:28; Ezra 9–10; T. LEVI 14.6). Hence, the waters of baptism may have been used as a means to cleanse them of that impurity (cf. JEREMIAS, 1960:26–27; BEASELY-MURRAY, 1962:18–31).

[24] E.g., McKNIGHT (1991); GOODMAN (1994).

[25] FELDMAN (1993), 291–98; cf. DE RIDDER (1971), 102 ff, 120–27.

[26] McKNIGHT, 84 cf. 82 f. McKnight also admits the possibility that T. Pesah. 7.13 (c. 67 C. E.) mentions soldier proselytes who appear to be water-baptised on the Passover, but he explains this example as a purification ritual rather than proselyte baptism (83).

received its impetus from John the Baptist, Jesus, and earliest Christianity.[27] On the other hand, Oepke argues that Jewish opposition to Christianity, at least in the late first century, was too distinct to permit such a Christian ritual; hence, "Proselyte baptism must have preceded Christian baptism."[28] Again, it is always possible that baptism emerged more or less concurrently in both Jewish and Christian traditions. Although the issue cannot be finally decided here, one observation is almost certain: baptism is antecedent to Paul. We will suggest that Paul may be influenced by earlier baptism motifs which are often found, in varying degrees, within both traditions.

If we surmise that Jewish sources, though sometimes later than Christian sources, might reflect earlier traditions which are concurrent with, or ante-date, the Christian traditions, a few observation are worth noting.[29] Joachim Jeremias argues that the term "to baptise" (βαπτίζειν) and derivatives do not come from non-Jewish Hellenism but from Hellenistic Jews. He also notes that baptism in the middle voice "Is just as bad Greek as it is good Jewish-Greek," and cites an account of Judith washing herself (Jud. 12:7) in which the middle voice is used after "the Hebrew *tabhal*, Aramaic *t^e^bhal*, which in the Qal has the meaning 'to take the baptismal bath', 'to dip oneself'."[30]

Paul likely uses the middle voice in 1 Corinthians 10:2. Here the word ἐβαπτίσαντο follows the Textus Receptus, Codex B, and P-46, and is perhaps more original than ἐβαπτίσθησαν (supported by ℵ and A). In the passive, the word may be translated "they were baptised." The middle voice would allow for a rendering in the reflexive sense: "they baptised themselves." Since the middle voice is the more difficult reading, it is to be preferred over the passive sense. This reading appears to denote the Jewish practise of baptising oneself.[31] A less likely possibility is Gander's suggestion that βαπτίζω in this verse was substituted for the original Aramaic word, "to pass."[32] In either case, Paul's

---

[27] McKnight, 85.

[28] Oepke, *TDNT* 1:535.

[29] The early Christian use of "in the name" (εἰς τὸ ὄνομα) is also found in the Hebrew term לשם which was used in various rites. Paul's baptismal phrase εἰς τὸ ὄνομα, and similar phrases, may be related to an early Christian tradition which finds its matrix in the Hebrew term לשם (1 Cor. 1:13; 6:11; 10:2; Rom. 6:3; Gal. 3:27; cf. Acts 2:38). But again the problem arises in relation to the question of which tradition is older. On other possible Jewish influences, see Jeremias, 29–32; Moore (1966), 1:335.

[30] Jeremias, 29.

[31] Cf. Héring (1949), 78. Thus, Metzger is likely correct when he reasons that it is more probable that copyists replaced the middle with the passive than vice versa (1975:559). Zuntz, supporting the middle voice in 1 Corinthians 10:2, adds a number of examples of baptism in the middle voice including Mark 1:5; 7:4; Acts 8:12, as well as the aorist middle imperative βάπτισαι in Acts 22:16. He writes, "Such meaningful subtleties do not arise from corruption; but they are easily obliterated by more commonplace variants – as here by the passive" (1953:234).

[32] Gander claims that in an Aramaic first draft Paul used the word "pass" (*'mar*) instead of "baptise" (*'mad*) and wrote עמדו, but "Son secrétaire lut: *'madou*, et tourna, en grec:

perspective of baptism may be divorced from Jewish influence only with diffi-culty. Nevertheless, we must raise the question as to whether the early Christians literally baptised themselves. At least in Paul's experience at Corinth, apostles and leaders baptised the converts instead of the converts baptising themselves (1 Cor. 1:13–17). For Paul, then, the middle voice for βαπτίζω would not neces-sarily imply a self-performed baptism; in 10:2 he may be emphasising the Isra-elites' *choice* to identify with and follow Moses and his God.[33] This aspect would tend to underscore that Israel's initiation through the cloud and sea was an experience shared by all.

These considerations notwithstanding, Paul's model of baptism may have been derived ultimately from prophetic traditions found in the Hebrew scrip-tures, which were developed in later apocalyptic traditions. Sahlin suggests that the Old Testament is sufficient to find Paul's source for baptism (cf. Isa. 40:1ff), which is related to the eschatological baptism of John the Baptist.[34] John's baptism was a proclamation anticipating the coming judgement in the eschatological era (Mark 1:8; cf. Luke 12:49).[35] The Qumran community also seemed to hold a similar view regarding initiation, but they added an escha-tological dimension that can be summarised as entering into a new covenant (1QS 1:7ff, 3:6ff, 4:14–23; cf. 5.13).[36] Both John and Qumran also seemed to have believed in an eschatological purification involving the Spirit of God (Mark 1:8; John 1:33; 1QS 4:20–21).[37] The earliest Christians saw themselves as en-tering this eschatological era through baptism in water and the Spirit (cf. Acts 2). Holding to similar initiation assumptions, Paul seemed to understand an aspect of conversion in terms of entrance into a new covenant involving God's

---

ἐβαπτίσαντο ..., soit: «Ils se batisèrent». Voilà comment put s'introduire dans le texte la mention du baptême." (Gander, 1957:98). Gander's ingenious suggestion fails to be con-vincing because it leads to more remote speculations. An example of this can be seen when he hypothesises that Paul's secretary also changed Paul's wording before "Moses" to εἰς τὸν to allude to a baptism formula (101) even though there are no early manuscript witnesses to support his reading.

[33]   Since Paul often used the passive voice for baptism (1 Cor. 1:13; 12:13; Rom. 6:3; Gal. 3:27), he may have intended the middle voice to follow the passive in relation to baptism; both may be translated as an intransitive active: "underwent baptism" (cf. DAVIDSON, 1981:213; BARRETT, 1971:221). Perhaps "they had let themselves be baptised" is an alterna-tive way to render the word (cf. Acts 22:16; *BDF* 166).

[34]   SAHLIN (1953), 89–92.

[35]   Cf. BEASLEY-MURRAY (1962), 290f.

[36]   BLACK (1961), 91–94.

[37]   But the similarities between John the Baptist and Qumran should not be overtly stres-sed. PIERRE BENOIT (1990:6–8) notes that although both John and Qumran connect the Spirit with eschatological purification, John's teaching can be adequately explained on Old Testa-ment grounds (Ezek. 11:19; 36:25–27; Isa. 11:1–2; 32:15; 42:1). Benoit also notes, among other things, that it was not uncommon in first century Palestine for messianic groups to make their home in the desert and stress ablutions (e.g., the hermit Banos in Josephus *Vita* 11).

Spirit and an eschatological escape from the wrath of God (Gal. 1:1–4; 1 Thes. 1:9–10; Rom. 1:18ff; cf. 1 Cor. 11:23–26; 12:13; 2 Cor. 3; Acts 2:38–39).[38]

This eschatological nuance on baptism is significant for our study because Paul echoes themes associated with a prophetic exodus in relation to Israel's initiation in the cloud and sea (cf. Hos. 11:8–11; 12:9–13; 13:4–6, 14f; Amos 2:10–3:2; Mic. 4:1–8; 7:11–15; Hab. 3:1–7; Hag. 2:4f; Zech. 10:8–12; 12:8; 14:8f; Isaianic tradition below). Moreover, if Paul's view of baptism is influenced by both ritualistic and eschatological aspects, these influences might provide a broader focus on the nature of Paul's wilderness discourse in relation to his understanding of apostasy and perseverance. We have also noted that mystery/proto-Gnostic influences probably influenced some of the Corinthian congregation members, and to this issue we now turn.

1.4.2 Baptism from the Corinthian Congregation's Perspective

As noted earlier, the mystery religions may have influenced some of the members of the Corinthian community. Perhaps the key to understanding the problematic "baptism for the dead" in 1 Corinthians 15:29 underlies this inference. Some in Corinth may have been influenced by a mystery belief similar to that of the Orphic groups who ritually washed their dead.[39] As well, an immersion in water was thought to have regenerative powers in Greco-Roman religions, including Cybele sects.[40] If so, vicarious baptism, incited by a "magical" idea that water-regeneration secures one's future, may have influenced certain Corinthian members who originally came from a mystery religious background (cf. 1 Cor. 6:9–11; 12:2).[41] This interpretation would support the idea that a problem related to overconfidence is at stake in 10:1–4. Certainly, this would be the case in the larger context in which the strong were justifying their eating of meat sacrificed to idols (cf. ch. 2). Also, in 1 Corinthians 1:13–17, Paul

---

[38] This does not mean, however, that Paul's baptism was directly influenced by the Qumran sect. Early Christian baptism seemed to be an unrepeatable event (cf. Eph. 4:4–6; Heb. 6:1–4) while ablutions constituted a repeated ritual for Qumran (cf. BLACK, 97–98; BENOIT, 7–8).

[39] Cf. *Orphicorum fragmenta* (232) as stated in MESLIN, *ER*, 2:59. Baptism and immortality are also associated with the spring of Mnemosyne (Cretan funeral tablets), according to Meslin. For further references see OEPKE, *TDNT*, 1:542; WEDDERBURN (1987), 289.

[40] For references, see ELIADE (1964), 170–71. On the connection between water and regeneration with agriculture, Eliade writes, "Le rituel du bain sacré était pratiqué habituellement dans le culte des Grandes Déesses de la fécondité et de l'agriculture. Les forces taries de la divinité se réinégraient ainsi, assurant une bonne récolte (la magie de l'immersion provoquait la pluie) et la féconde multiplication des biens. Le 27 mars (*hilaria*) avait lieu le «bain» de la Mére phrygienne, Cybèle."

[41] In addition to the Corinthians' struggle with idolatry and sex, perhaps the "drunkenness" and "revelry" associated with certain mystery cults still influenced congregation members as well (1 Cor. 6:9–11 cf. 10:7; 11:21; 15:32–34).

deliberately seems to play down the importance of baptism.[42] His strategy here may reflect a reaction against those in Corinth who overemphasised its importance.

If this reading is correct, then the strong in Corinth thought that some type of immunity status accompanied their baptism.[43] This view was similar to a belief held in certain Greco-Roman religions whose adherents generally held to an attainment of immortal status through initiation.[44] Among Cybele circles, the Great Mother guaranteed future blessing to the votaries.[45] The Eleusinian mysteries also affirmed an immortality after initiation and ablution functioned as a preamble to this.[46] In the sect of Dionysus initiates were described as being possessed by the god through drinking wine, attaining a state of ecstasy (or drunkenness), being filled with Dionysus' spirit, and being called by his name. When the divinity entered the votary (*entheos*), he or she attained a sense of immortality.[47] Wedderburn notes that "the mysteries seem to have concentrated on assuring their initiates of the power of the god or goddess into whose rites they were entering. They were shown the deity's power both in this life and in the next."[48] It is possible that the Corinthian Gentiles viewed their Christianity with presuppositions shared with Greco-Roman traditions such as these.

On a social dimension another Corinthian misconception regarding baptism could have arisen from an earlier Christian tradition on baptism.[49] In Galatians 3:27–28, Paul stresses the egalitarian nature of Christian initiation.[50] The social freedom of neither "male nor female" might have been abused by the Corinthians. Mystery sects influenced by Cybele and Dionysus, which both appar-

---

[42] This is not to say that Paul did not consider baptism as important (cf. Rom. 6:3f), but since factions arose over the issue of which leader had baptised the Corinthians, Paul claims "οὐ γὰρ ἀπέστειλέν με Χριστὸς βαπτίζειν ἀλλὰ εὐαγγελίζεσθαι" (1 Cor. 1:17a).

[43] Cf. SCHLATTER (1974), 120–21; CONZELMANN (1975), 168.

[44] Cf. RICHARD and CATHERINE KROEGER (1984), 742–44.

[45] WEDDERBURN, 328. In later times, a baptism in the blood of a bull procured a new birth into an eternal state for Cybele worshippers (*renatus in aeternum* – *Corpus inscriptionum Latinarum* 6.510). In the early Christian era, however, the initiations were probably more diversified. MESLIN (2:59–60) notes that Pausanias (c. 150) affirms that a bath in the Trophonios sanctuary provided contemporary immortality to the initiate (*Desc. Gr.* 9.39:5). Hermetism (c. 200–400) was said to provide for initiates a transformation into a spiritual being who obtained *gnosis* or knowledge of the soul's origin (*Corpus Hermeticum* 1.4.4).

[46] Cf. MESLIN, 2:60; GUTHRIE (1950), 284 (cf. Isocrates *Panegyricus* 28–29; Plutarch *How to Study Poetry* 22F in D. AUNE, "Religions, Greco-Roman," *DPL*, 792–93).

[47] WILLOUGHBY (1960), 71–75; GUTHRIE, 148, 174–76, 180; WEDDERBURN, 322–23.

[48] WEDDERBURN, 331; cf. OROPEZA (1995), 133–40.

[49] Meeks suggests that the binary aspect of male/female in Galatians 3:28 is from an older baptismal *paradosis* which may have come from Paul. This was misconstrued by the pneumatics in Corinth (1974:180–82, 201–02).

[50] Galatians 3:28 transcends three barriers of human society: national (Jew/Gentiles), social (slave/free), and sexual (male/female). Cf. BOUCHER (1969), 56. The Jewish social religious system, on the other hand, may reflect four major categories: priest, Levites, common Israelites, and proselytes (cf. MOORE, 1:335).

ently were practised in the vicinity of Corinth during the first century,[51] included the expression of reversing sex roles and transvestism.[52] Such groups might have provided adherents, especially women, a sense of power, freedom, and ecstatic release from everyday routines.[53]

Perhaps some of the congregation members' prior involvement in religious groups which either reversed or equalised sex roles had led to a misconception about social roles with respect to early Christian initiation instruction (e.g., Gal. 3:27–28; cf. Col. 3:11). The apparent eradication of male and female categories in Christ may have led them to believe that the social roles of the sexes no longer applied. Likely, this is one reason why Paul stresses male and female distinction in 1 Corinthians 11:3–16.[54] It may also be the reason why, in a similar baptismal verse (1 Cor. 12:13), he excludes the phrase "neither male nor female," implying that in Paul's mind the congregation lacked a proper perception about gender roles.

Related to all this is Turner's notion that in liminal situations the neophytes find themselves as neither representing male nor female, or conversely, they are assigned the characteristics of both sexes. Turner relates this to "a kind of human *prima materia* – as undifferentiated raw material. It was perhaps from the rites of the Hellenic mystery religions that Plato derived his notion expressed in his *Symposium* that the first humans were androgynes."[55] In Galatians 3:27 Paul may be using androgynous language in common with the mysteries, but in 1 Corinthians he revises what he means by the phrase "neither male nor female" once he became aware that the Corinthians were abusing the "androgyne" idea due to their previous religious assumptions. Apparently, both Paul and the Corinthians held to some kind of equality between male and female related to the new status one receives as a Christian neophyte. Paul may have received his primary instruction on the androgynous implications through the Hebrew Scriptures (Gen. 1:26–27; 5:2 cf. 1 Cor. 11:7–8).[56] The Corinthians, on the other hand, may have based their androgynous perception on the mysteries. Paul must now begin to redefine and clarify boundaries, as he attempts to convince the Corinthians that they have misunderstood their new status as Christians.

---

[51] BRONEER (1971), 178–79; C.&R. KROEGER (1978), 332–35; GUTHRIE, 154; cf. Pausanius *Desc. Gr.* 2.7.5f; 6.7.5; Catallus *Poems* 63; Juvenal *Satires* 6.314–41; 474–541.

[52] GRAF (1996), 1547; FANTHAM, *et al* (1994), 90–91; DILLON, *ABD*, 2:202; L. MARTIN (1987), 95; MEEKS, (1974), 180, 184. Mourning rites included women cutting their hair and men growing theirs long (Plutarch, *Moralia* 267B). Also, devotees from the Cybele sect would castrate themselves in a state of ecstatic frenzy.

[53] E.g., LEFKOWITZ and FANT (1982), 250–51; MEEKS (1974), 169–70; C.&R. KROEGER (1978), 335; GUTHRIE, 148.

[54] So also C.&R. KROEGER (1978).

[55] TURNER (1967), 98.

[56] Cf. JERVIS (1993), 231–46; MEEKS (1974), 181, 185.

The upshot of this misperception was that some members in the Corinthian congregation had been overconfident and too secure in their present position – this due to their misunderstanding of baptismal-initiation teachings. The security in baptism may have caused the strong in Corinth to become ethically careless.[57] The boundary demarcating their previous from present existence was so complete that behaviour could hardly be thought of as undermining their transference. Although misconceptions arose from earlier Christian initiation instructions, the Corinthians' previous upbringing in the mystery religions was likely the presupposition for their misconceptions about immortalisation. As we will observe in the following sections, Paul's use of "baptism into Moses" underscores this view.

1.4.3 The Relationship Between the Persons of Moses and Christ

The analogy between Moses and Christ is virtually unmistakable in 10:2. It may be tempting to think that Paul *merely* uses Moses' name in reference to baptism as a means of extracting the analogous implication of the Corinthian congregation's baptism into Jesus Christ. But his decision to mention Moses seems to serve a purpose beyond this. Barrett posits a parallel between Moses and Christ based on the Jewish conception that the Messianic "latter redeemer" would be like the "former redeemer," who was Moses (cf. Deut. 18:18–19).[58] The Hebrew tradition often understood the Israelite redemption from Egypt as pointing to the eschatological messianic redemption (Isa. 11; 43:16–21; Mic. 7:11–15; cf. Hos. 2:14–18; 12:9). In the Isaianic tradition (ch. 11), the eschatological "branch" (11:1: נֵצֶר/ἄνθος) and "root" (11:10: שֹׁרֶשׁ/ῥίζης) of Jesse becomes a banner for the Gentiles, and they will find great rest in him. In that day, אֲדֹנָי will lead the remnant of his people through the wilderness a second time to escape the nations (11:10–16). Allison suggests that the probable cause of a Mosaic messiah arose from the conception that the Jewish eschatological redemption would be another exodus, which was inextricably related to Moses.[59]

In a similar way, certain Qumran texts predict that 40 years are to pass from the death of the Righteous Teacher until the destruction of all the followers of

---

[57] If one could generalise, then Schnakenburg might be correct when he writes that the mystery religions had "sacramental views divorced from ethics" (1964:94).

[58] BARRETT (1971), 221. For early Jewish sources on the messianic interpretation of Deuteronomy 18:15f and former/latter redeemer, see JEREMIAS, *TDNT* 4:857–60; E. E. ELLIS (1957b), 132. Like the messianic figure, Moses is called the "Chosen One" in Lives of the Prophets 2:14 (c. 1st century CE).

[59] ALLISON (1993), 90; cf. SAHLIN, 81–82. Allison suggests the expectation of a Mosaic messiah arose in the first century (88f). If Acts (3:17–26) and John's Gospel (1:15ff; 4:19ff; 6:14) reflect fairly well the attitudes of the people and times in which they intend to portray, this might suggest that the expectation was already known in the early first century.

the Man of Lies, which is to occur in the final eschatological war (CD 19:35–20:1, 20.13ff[8:21ff]; cf. 1QM). Mauser asserts concerning Qumran eschatology, "The forty years are certainly a prophetic number; as Israel had to live in the desert for forty years, so the community has to undergo the time of test for forty years, living a life of repentance in the wilderness by strict adherence to the law and thus preparing the way of the Lord."[60] In the document called the Words of Moses, the year 40 in relation to the wilderness is also stressed (1Q22 2.5f cf. 1.1). Mauser notes some other similarities between the texts of Qumran and Israel in relation to the wilderness: the subdivision of covenant members into thousands, hundreds, fifties, and tens (1QS 2.21ff cf. Exod. 18:25; Deut. 1:15); the assembling of members who live in camps (CD 7.6; 20.26[B] cf. Num. 2:1–5:4); and the regulations regarding living in camps (1QM 7.3–7; cf. Num. 5:1–4).[61]

The idea of an eschatological messiah as a kind of Moses figure who would lead followers into the desert seemed a prominent belief with the Qumran sect as well as other religious and political groups (cf. 1QS 8.13–16; 4Q175:1–13; Josephus *Ant.* 20.97–99; 188; *Bell.* 2.259–260; Matt. 24:26; Luke 3:15; John 1:19ff; Acts 21:38).[62] After examining various sources from the Second Temple period, Allison concludes that the eschatological expectation of another prophet like Moses "was not little known, or just the esoteric property of the Qumran coventile and Jewish-Christian churches. It was instead very much in the air in first-century Palestine and helped to instigate several short-lived revolutionary movements."[63] In Tannaitic literature, the messiah is expected to lead God's people into the wilderness just like Moses. The entire eschatological messianic era was depicted in the 40 years of the Israelite wilderness period (e.g. Tanhuma 'Ekeb 7b).[64]

Hence, for Paul, the relationship between Moses and Jesus might reflect his belief in the motif of a second redeemer who would lead God's people through a new exodus/wilderness experience. Other early Christian traditions also seemed to hold to this belief. Sahlin notes how Jesus appears to be the new Moses in Matthew through his extraordinary birth and childhood, his Sermon

---

[60] MAUSER, 60. Here the 40 years in the wilderness seems to reflect Deuteronomy 2:7 and 14 (cf. KNIBB, 1987:73–74). However, we should not overlook that the 40 years fits into the larger framework of Ezekiel's prophecy concerning 390 + 40 years (Ezek. 4:4–8; cf. CD 1:3–11). This prophetic calculation might indicate that the origin of the community began 390 years after the Babylonian exile (587 BCE). See SCOTT (1993), 654; KNIBB, 19–20.

[61] MAUSER, 60–61. On comparisons between Moses and the Teacher of Righteousness, see ALLISON (1993), 84–85ftn196.

[62] Cf. JEREMIAS, 4:861; RUSSELL, (1987), 126f.

[63] ALLISON, 83 cf. 73–82.

[64] I.e., "How long will the days of the Messiah last? R. Aqiba (c. 90–135) said: Forty years. As the Israelites spent 40 years in the wilderness, so he (the Messiah) will lead them forth and take them into the wilderness and cause them to eat bitter herbs and roots (Job 30:4)." Cf. JEREMIAS, 4:860–61.

of the Mount as the New Law, and the 10 miracles in Matthew 8–9 as the antithesis of the 10 plagues on Egypt.[65] One significant parallel between Christ and Moses is Christ's 40 day fast in the wilderness after his baptism, which is reminiscent of Moses' 40 day fast and his 40 years in the wilderness (Matt. 4:1–2; Exod. 34:28; Acts 7:29–30).[66] In the speech of Stephen, Luke has it that Moses was rejected by his own people, yet he became their deliverer-redeemer from Egypt (λυτρωτὴν – Acts 7:35; cf. Heb. 3:16), even though the Israelites later apostatised from God (Acts 7:20–43).[67] Here again the parallel between the life of Moses and Christ is evident.[68] It is very likely, then, that Paul and other early Christians would consider themselves to be a people who were living in an era which was characterised by the fulfilment of the "new exodus" under a messianic redeemer (cf. 10:6, 11).[69]

Paul, no doubt, considered the new era to be greater than the old (2 Cor. 5:17; cf. Isa. 43:16–19). He would regard the Corinthians as a new redeemed people of God who are inheriting the greater future fulfilments of the Israelites (10:6, 11 cf. Gal. 4:21–31; 6:16; Rom. 9–11; 15:4). Paul's reference to Moses is therefore created in order to suggest an Israelite experience similar to that of the Corinthians.[70] But more than this, he was convinced that the Corinthian Christians were experiencing the prophetic *fulfilment* of another exodus under a new redeemer, and he considers this redeemer to be greater than the former. The latter redeemer is the Christ, the Lord who was spiritually present with the Israelites on their journey.[71]

---

[65] SAHLIN, 82. However, Allison affirms that although the new Moses theme appears in Matthew, we should be cautious about claiming it as the most important theme (267–68).

[66] Cf. ALLISON (165–72), who, in addition, views the structure of Matthew 1–8 as a new exodus (194 ff cf. 298–300, 307 ff). The plot line of Matthew 1–5 and the exodus narrative are similar; both refer to: 1) the slaughter of infants (Exod. 1–2; Matt. 2:1–18); 2) return of the hero (Exod. 3–6; Matt. 2:23; 3:13 f); 3) a passage through water (Exod. 14; Matt. 3:16–17); 4) temptation in the wilderness (Exod. 15:22 ff; Matt. 4:1–11); and 5) a mountain of law-giving (Exod. 19 ff; Matt. 5:1 ff). See ALLISON (310; cf. 268) who is referring to GOULDER'S (1964) Mosiac allusions in Matthew.

[67] Cf. CHAVASSE (1951b), 289–90. CHAVASSE (1951a:245–46) also lists 10 similarities between Moses and the prophetic Servant of Yahweh in Isaiah and notes how the early Christian may have understood the Servant-Messiah as the second Moses (cf. Acts 3:22–26).

[68] It may be also interesting to note that Luke has Paul as possibly listening to Stephen's speech (cf. Acts 7:58).

[69] In 1 Corinthians 10:2–4, however, Paul also affirms that Christ is the rock. Hence, in Paul's mind, Moses should not be thought of as on the same level with Christ, for he identifies Christ with the κύριος of the Old Testament in 10:9. For Paul, then, Moses is more a "Typos Christi" (cf. KLAUCK, 1982:253) while Christ himself was God the "rock" (cf. ch. 5:3.2.1). See also HANSON (1945:174–75).

[70] Nevertheless, as Feuillet rightly affirms, Paul's originality does not preclude that he may have adapted or have been influenced by early Jewish literature. Feuillet sees these influences coming primarily from wisdom sources and "elles doivent provenir plus précisément du livre de la Sagesse" (1966:92 cf. 97). I will argue in chapter 4 that other sources were also prominent.

[71] Cf. SCHNACKENBURG (1964), 23; MARTELET (1956), 328.

1.4.4 Baptism in the Name of Jesus Christ and Moses

We have thus given a plausible explanation why Paul may have decided to mention Moses in this narrative, but why does he use his name as part of a baptismal formula? The phrase εἰς τὸν Μωϋσῆν not only parallels Gal. 3:27 but also the εἰς τὸ ὄνομα in 1 Corinthians 1:13, where Paul rhetorically asks the Corinthians if they were baptised in his own name. The latter construction is no doubt an allusion to baptism in the name of Jesus, a tradition which is used in Lukan narratives and placed in the mouth of Paul in Acts 19:3–5 (cf. Acts 2:38; 8:16; 10:48).[72] Hence, εἰς Χριστὸν in Galatians 3:27 appears to be an abbreviated form for εἰς τὸ ὄνομα τοῦ κυρίου Ἰησοῦ Χριστοῦ. The passage likely refers to an incorporation into the body of Christ at baptism which is depicted in terms of "putting on" (ἐνδύσασθαι) Christ as one puts on a garment (cf. 1 Cor. 12:13).[73] This understanding also appears to form the backdrop of 1 Corinthians 10:2. But we do not find a true parallel for baptism into Moses in the Hebrew scriptures or Jewish traditions of antiquity.[74] Moreover, unlike baptism into Christ, Paul does not seem to believe that the Israelites were somehow incorporated into a spiritual union with Moses or that the Israelites belonged to Moses. The question can therefore be raised concerning Paul's use of εἰς τὸν Μωϋσῆν. Should we settle for an arbitrary explanation? Why did he not simply mention Moses in this verse without using his name within a baptismal formula? I presently suggest a possible alternative.

Initiation "in the name" of something could mean to be initiated "with respect to" or "for the purpose of (achieving)," or "to the account of."[75] In Jewish tradition, non-Jewish slaves obtaining their freedom were immersed "in the name of a free man" and "in the name of freedom" (b. Yebamot 45b; cf. 47b).[76] The phrase also carries a sense of one's affixation to the referent with a sense of

---

[72] The construction of this phrase varies. Acts 2:38 uses ἐπὶ τῷ ὀνόματι; 10:48 uses ἐν τῷ ὀνόματι; 8:16 and 19:5 use the εἰς τὸ ὄνομα construction Paul uses in 1 Corinthians 1:13–14. In 1 Corinthians 5:4 and 6:11 Paul uses ἐν τῷ ὀνόματι rather than εἰς τὸ ὄνομα. Contrary to Fee, who believes that 6:11 refers to the authority of Christ (FEE, 247 cf. 206f), it seems connected with baptismal initiation because ἀλλὰ contrasts the previous unconverted lifestyle of the Corinthians (6:9–11a) with their current state in which they are cleansed, sanctified, and justified in the name of Christ and in the Spirit of God (6:11b). Elsewhere Paul uses the name of Christ and the Spirit to refer to conversion-initiation (1:13f; 12:13). These phrases might suggest that, like the Lukan narrative, Paul is not always consistent in distinguishing ἐν τῷ ὀνόματι from εἰς τὸ ὄνομα. In 1 Corinthians 5:4 Paul may be employing a "reverse initiation" or exit ritual (cf. ch. 1). Although Paul sometimes replaces εἰς with ἐν, in baptismal passages, he seems to stress the former word (cf. Gal. 3:27; Rom. 6:3; 1 Cor. 1:13). On the confusion between the two prepositions in Hellenistic Greek, see ZERWICK, *Gramm.*, 33ff.

[73] Cf. BETZ (1979), 186–91.

[74] Cf. W. WILLIS (1985), 129.

[75] Cf. HEITMÜLLER (1903), 105–09, 127; DUNN (1970), 117f; Str.B. 1:1054–55.

[76] Str.B. 1:1054–55.

obligation: the Samaritans circumcised "in the name of Mount Gerizim" (m. 'Aboda Zara 3.12f).[77] There seems to be a type of ownership or belonging in which the baptisand declares an allegiance to a new lord and trusting in the lord's deliverance and protection.[78] Schnackenburg writes, "a man [sic!] belongs to the one in whose name he is baptised as to his master."[79]

Conversion-initiation also may have taken a form in which both the baptiser and the baptisand participated "in the name of Jesus." Early Christian literature often emphasises the confession of Christ's lordship and perhaps a calling on the name of the Lord for deliverance from one's preconverted status at baptism (Rom. 10:9–13; 1 Cor. 1:2; cf. Acts 2:21, 38; 22:16; 8:26ff Codex E; 1 Pet. 3:21).[80] The baptiser may have invoked the name of Jesus and laid hands on the candidate, asking Jesus to somehow bless or protect the individual (cf. James 2:7). The idea of God's name being carried on his people in the sense of ownership was prevalent in the Jewish tradition (Num. 6:22–27; Deut. 28:10; 2 Sam. 6:2; 2 Chron. 7:14; Isa. 43:7; Jer. 15:16; 4 Ezra 4:25). We may assume that such a background influenced Paul's understanding of baptism in the name of Jesus.

Paul often uses the language of election and belonging/ownership with terms such as "called ones" (κλητοί) and "saints" (ἅγιοι) (Rom. 1:7; 1 Cor. 1:2), "known by God" (γνωσθέντες ὑπὸ θεοῦ) (Gal. 4:9; 1 Cor. 8:3), "beloved by God" (ἠγαπημένοι ὑπὸ θεοῦ) (1 Thes. 1:4), and adoption language (Gal. 3:26–4:6; Rom. 8:15–17). His use of terms denoting familial relationships also imply a sense of belonging (1 Thes. 2:5; 4:10; Gal. 4:4–6; 4:19; 1 Cor. 4:14f; 2 Cor. 6:13).[81] Paul seems concerned with this type of language in 1 Corinthians 10:1–13 because he opens the pericope with the phrase "our fathers." Meeks notes that such language reinforces a sense of *communitas* wherein the Christian community has turned from idols to serve God and set up boundaries that reinforce solidarity through one God, knowledge from the Spirit, and a Christology which is dramatised in baptism and recalled in the Lord's Supper.[82] In essence, Paul's formula for baptism implies a solidarity and a belonging to God and Christ. Accountability is therefore imbedded within the structure of Paul's view of baptism. In other words, Paul does not divorce his baptismal perspective

---

[77] Ibid.

[78] Cf. WEDDERBURN, 57–60. I. Abrahams notes that those Jews who were baptised "in the name of heaven" were baptised for the sake of God (Gerim 1.7): "It is a pure, unselfish act of submission to the true God" (1917:45).

[79] SCHNACKENBURG, 20.

[80] White suggests that "Jesus is the Christ" was the earliest church confession in Judean circles while "Jesus is Lord" was the early Gentile confession (1960:146). This is possible, but we do not know the exact words used in the earliest confessions.

[81] Cf. MEEKS (1983a), 85–88.

[82] MEEKS (1983a), 89–93.

from ethical obligation.[83] As we noted earlier, the same idea did not hold true for some of the Corinthian congregation members.

For many Gentile Christians, the baptiser's invocation of the appropriation of Christ upon the convert may have seemed quite similar to the magical presuppositions of the power of names used in Greco-Roman religions.[84] Aune states, "The fundamental significance of the magical use of the names of divinities, supernatural beings or great men of the past is the supposition that such names share the being and participate in the power of their bearers; to possess a name is to possess power over the one who bears the name."[85] For Paul, however, the emphasis of power may not have been grounded in the name of Jesus Christ itself but in the *person* of Jesus who bore the name. Charlesworth notes that in Jewish biblical and "apocryphal" writings, God's name is revered as holy and often ineffable – "the name was powerful because God was behind it" – while in the magical papyri, the divine name seems secretive and intrinsically efficacious (Exod. 3:13–15; 1 En. 69:14; Josephus *Ant.* 2.275–76; cf. Prayer Jacob 9, 15).[86] It is likely that Paul had adopted a similar approach to the concept of efficacy; the name of Jesus Christ was powerful to believers because of the person who represented that name. Hence, in Paul's view, "baptism in the name of Jesus" seemed to have little to do with the recital of magical formulas whereby the prescribed words, "I baptise you in the name of Jesus" had to be pronounced over the baptisand to authenticate the baptism.[87] Schnackenburg

---

[83] Cf. KREITZER (1991), 69.

[84] Cf. AUNE (1980:2.1545–1549) who borrows the idea from HEITMÜLLER, 221, 236, 253f. I am associating the term "magic" with the practice of a person who uses a proper technique or method – in this case, invoking the name of a powerful figure – as a means to accomplish his/her own end whether or not that person is seeking to conform to the will or teachings of that power or supernatural force.

[85] AUNE, 2:1546.

[86] Charlesworth, *Pseud.*, 2:717. AUNE (2:1548) notes that in the second century, the formula "in the name of Jesus Christ crucified under Pontius Pilate" entered baptismal liturgies "which originally functioned as magical rituals which expelled demons from baptismal candidates."

[87] There is no clear evidence that the phrases "I baptise you in the name of Jesus" or "I baptise you in the name of the Father, Son, and Holy Spirit" were pronounced by the earliest Christians while performing water baptisms. Evidence for such pronouncement traditions does not arise until about the second century (Trinitarian formula: Didache 7 [c. 100 C. E.]; "Jesus name" formula : Acts of Paul and Thecla [c. 150]). This observation supports the idea that at least some of the Christians in the second century emphasised the power of names more than their predecessors. In the latter source, Thecla requests from Paul the seal of Christ to protect her from temptation (*Acts of Paul and Thecla*, 25). When she is thrown into a stadium with wild beasts, she prays and sees a tank of water. She then casts herself into the water, saying, "In the name of Jesus Christ do I baptise myself on the last day." The beasts were not able to touch Thecla because a cloud of fire protected her, and some women who were present had special leaves whose odours put the beasts to sleep (*Acts of Paul and Thecla*, 34–35). Origen (c. 160–220) claimed that Jesus' name is so effective that even bad men can use it successfully (*Contra Celsus* 1.6). The sacred character of Jesus Christ's name

appears to be correct when he affirms that the name of Jesus does not effect conversion in a magical sense.[88]

On the other hand, the Corinthians – who seemed to hold to some Greco-Roman religious presuppositions (as argued above) – may have placed their emphasis on the intrinsic power of a name. There is evidence that non-Christians from the first century employed the name of Jesus when performing exorcisms (Acts 19:13–16; cf. Mark 9:38–40). Similarly, the name of Moses played a prominent role in both Jewish-Hellenistic and Greco-Roman magic/mystery traditions from about the first century.[89] Gager notes that many advocates of the magical arts, as well as Hellenistic Jews, believed that since Moses revealed God's name in the exodus narrative, he possessed a knowledge higher than that of other humans (Philo *Vit. Mos.* 1.155–57; Josephus, *Antiquities* 2.276; Sir. 45:1–5; cf. Exod. 3:1–4:31; Test. Mos. 1:14; 11:16–19).[90] Philo speaks of an initiation "under Moses the God-beloved into his greater mysteries," apparently borrowing ideas from the Eleusinian "mysteries" (*De Cherub.* 49).[91] The prominence of Moses' name among certain early Christians can be seen in the Egerton papyri (c. late second or third century) where Moses' name is considered sacred, abbreviated to μω (Papyrus 2, frag. 1.13, 15).[92]

The Greek Magical Papyri 5.108–18 reads: " I am Moses your prophet to whom you have transmitted your mysteries/celebrated by Israel; you have revealed the moist and the dry and all nourishment; hear me. I am the messenger of Pharaoh Ososronophris [the good Osiris];/this is your true name which has been transmitted to the prophets of Israel."[93] Hence, many believed that Moses' "very name guaranteed the efficacy of magical charms and provided protection

---

may also be seen in other second and third century sources (e.g., Egerton Papyrus 2 cf. HURTADO, 1997:1–22).

[88] SCHNACKENBURG, 4–5: "The name of Jesus and the Spirit of God do not stand on the same plane, as though the name effects in a magical way the new Christian life that the Spirit of God produces. The baptisand becomes the property of Jesus through calling on the name of Jesus, while the Spirit of God is bestowed as a gift on them (Rom. v. 5: τοῦ δοθέντος ἡμῖν) and at the same time effects holiness and justification."

[89] E.g., FELDMAN (285) notes that Justin (*Historiae Philippicae* 36, *Epitomia* 2.7) quotes Pompeius Trogus (early first century) who claimed that Moses inherited the knowledge of Joseph his father, who was a master in magical arts. Pliny also mentions a form of magic which was derived from Moses (*Natural History* 30.11, 18; cf. GAGER, 1972:138). For a list of various sources on Moses in Greco-Roman literature, see GAGER, 134–160.

[90] Jeremias claims that Hellenistic Judaism's conception of Moses as a kind of superhuman and genius was influenced by the "Hellenistic depictions of the θεῖος ἀνήρ" (*TDNTa* 4:855; cf. SEGAL 33–35). For Jewish legends of Moses' unusual childhood and adult life, consult RUSSELL, 99 ff; GINZBERG (1956), 288–302.

[91] COLSON and WHITAKER (1979), 2:483.

[92] HURTADO (1997), 2 and cf. BELL and SKEAT (1935), 4, 8 for source. HURTADO (19) also mentions that Justin claims that God disclosed his name to Moses as Jesus, the name of the angel in Exodus 23:20 (*Dia. Tryph.* 75:1–2). Moses is also considered a sorcerer by Celsus (Origen, *Contra Celsus* 5.42), but this work is polemical in nature.

[93] For source, see BETZ (1992), 103.

against the hostile forces of the cosmos."[94] Gager cites in one magical formula (GMP 2.114) a piece which is possibly rendered "in the house [land?] of Moses" (γης εισμουσεως).[95] If so, the word εἰς is in reference to Moses as it is in 1 Corinthians 10:2. Not all of these traditions were developed during Paul's era, but we have observed enough evidence to warrant a connection between Moses and magic in the first century.

Perhaps Paul understood that some Corinthian members had a magical/mystery understanding of their baptism εἰς Χριστὸν 'Ιησοῦν and an implicit view that Moses was a powerful magician. It is therefore possible that his use of the name of Moses as a baptismal invocation was prompted by this awareness. By the end of the entire pericope, Paul's intention for the Corinthians' view of magical names would be as follows: Our spiritual fathers who were initiated in the name of Moses – the chief miracle-worker in the Jewish tradition whose name both Jews and Gentiles invoke for spiritual protection – could not escape punishment when they sinned against God. So how is it that you Corinthians think that you can evade divine judgement just because you have been baptised in the name of Jesus?

Paul might be using Moses' name to argue persuasively *against* the idea of placing too much confidence in names associated with baptismal initiation – that the invocation of such names at baptism somehow makes the Corinthians exempt from apostasy and divine judgement in the Corinthian situation. Here Paul may be also echoing the earlier problem regarding initiation-allegiances to human persons at the expense of unity of fellowship (cf. 1 Cor. 1:13f).[96] The notion of magic may be important in this regard: it shows the significance of associating names with figures and the identification of oneself with those figures. Whether or not a magic tradition is in view, Paul's overall intention in this clause is to prompt the Corinthians to see how the Israelites' "baptism" parallels their own.

In the final analysis Paul may have understood the phrase "in the name of Jesus" not as a magical or semi-magical pronouncement as perhaps some of the

---

[94] GAGER (1972), 160. Moses was also regarded as the author of magical texts such as the *Maza*, the *Diadem*, the *Key of Moses*, the *Archangelical Book of Moses*, the *Secret Moon of Moses*, the *Eighth Book of Moses,* and the *Sword of Moses*. Most of the names of these magical books are found in the GMP (13.343–44, 1077 cf. GAGER, 146–55, 160).

[95] GAGER, 143ftn29. But GAGER notes it may be a scribal error for επι γη σεισμου.

[96] In 1 Corinthians 1:10–17 Paul's rhetorical "were you baptised in the name of Paul?" implies that he wants the Corinthians to say "no, we were baptised in the name of Christ." He is attempting to bring the Corinthians to realise the folly of their factions over which minister (Apollos, Peter, or Paul) had baptised them, and hence, which minister to whom they were in allegiance. (The party who are "of Christ" seem to be congregation members who claim they submit to no human leader.) Paul attempts to persuade the Corinthians that by being baptised in the name of Christ, the Corinthians have become members of the body of Christ (1:13: "Is Christ divided'?). Therefore, the Corinthian members should not be divided, for this is in effect, "parting out" the body of Christ.

Corinthians did; rather, he saw it in terms of conversion-initiation in which the baptisand confesses the name of the Lord Jesus Christ and is bound in union with his person. At baptism there is a strong sense of belonging to Christ and becoming a member in the elect and consolidated body of Christ. Baptism in the name of Jesus thus incorporates a convert into a community of members who are seen as the body of the name which that community represents. The stress on baptism rests not so much on immersion in water as it does on the confession of one's faith in Christ and the immersion in the Spirit, both occurring presumably at one's baptism (1 Cor. 6:11; 12:13; cf. Tit. 3:5; Acts 2:38f; 9:17–18).[97] Paul's language thus assumes that the Corinthian congregation's conversion was genuine (cf. ch. 5:2.2.1). The problem, at least from the analogy in 10:1–2, is that the strong were convinced that in some sense they were immune because of their election and initiation (which concepts we will examine further). In theological terms, they held to a form of final perseverance that Paul considered unacceptable.

2. Israel's Initiation in the Cloud and Sea

Paul claims that Israel's initiation occurs at the Red Sea. The Israelites were baptised in the cloud and sea (1 Corinthians 10:2). No doubt, Paul is alluding to the waters of baptism by mentioning the "sea," but his purpose for the "cloud" is less obvious. Fee suggests the possibility that the cloud refers to the Spirit, but he believes it is more likely that Paul's use of the cloud is in keeping with common wilderness language which normally combines the sea with the cloud. As such, "Paul himself did not 'mean' anything by it at all."[98] But νεφέλη appears twice in 10:1–2. Sequentially, "cloud" stands before the word "sea" in both verses,[99] and in the second instance, it is identified as the element of Israel's baptism along with the sea. This seems to suggest that it is not entirely void of meaning. I will argue that Fee's first suggestion is correct: Paul intended the cloud to represent the Spirit of God.[100] Our examination of this issue will be

---

[97] This also relieves the tension somewhat on how Paul's earlier declaration to the Corinthians that preaching the Gospel was more important than baptism itself (1 Cor. 1:14–17).

[98] FEE (1987), 446.

[99] Here Paul might be attempting to keep the order found in the exodus narrative. The Israelites experienced the cloud before they experienced the Red Sea (Exod. 13:21f; 14:19f). Ellicott is almost certainly wrong when he claims that it is inconsistent to affirm that the cloud represents the Holy Spirit since this would invert the doctrinal order ("born of water and Spirit") in John 3:5 (174). It is far from certain that Paul needed to retain the same word order as John or that John is even referring to water baptism.

[100] Cf. CONZELMANN, 166; ALLÓ (1956), 231; MARTALET, 336f; SCHRAGE (1995), 389. Hanson argues that the cloud represents another image of the preexistent Christ (1965:11–16). However, since Christ is identified as the rock (10:4), it is difficult to conceive of Paul implying that Christ was also the cloud: Christ is the goal, not the *element*, of baptism.

significant for ascertaining the nature of the Corinthians' conversion experience. If the cloud represents God's Spirit, what might be Paul's purpose for associating the Spirit with the cloud? How does this relate to the concepts of baptism and initiation? In order to address properly such questions, we will first examine some possible Jewish influences on Paul's interpretation of the cloud and sea.

2.1 Red Sea Traditions

We might be able to ascertain more accurately Paul's interpretation of 1 Corinthians 10 if we knew which Red Sea traditions may have influenced him. Bandstra, after Meredith Kline, thinks the cloud and sea signify elemental powers of ordeal: the cloud denotes fire (Exod. 13:21) and the sea denotes water. Bandstra suggests that in 1 Corinthians 10:2, βαπτίζω should be understood in its secondary sense of "judgement ordeal" (cf. Mark 10:38). The Israelites passed under the cloud of fire and through the sea (πάντες ὑπὸ τὴν νεφέλην ἦσαν καὶ πάντες διὰ τῆς θαλάσσης διῆλθον). This is how God brought the Israelites into an ordeal; an ordeal in which God found them acceptable as his servants.[101] The conception of an ordeal may in fact underlie certain traditions of the Red Sea that mention the Israelites being tested by fire and water as silver when it is purified (cf. Psa. 66:6–12; Isa. 43:1–3). Anthropological models affirm that ordeals are part of the ritual process. Van Gennep's transition stage may be so interpreted (cf. ch. 1.3.2).

Still, we should have some reservations about finding an ordeal in 10:1–2. Paul's use of the phrase "under the cloud" in 1 Corinthians 10:1 seems to reflect an idea of protection instead of judgement. If there is an ordeal implied by the context of 10:1–13, it seems more likely that Paul sees it taking place *in the wilderness* of 10:5–10. The desert is where the Israelites are tested (and most of them fail the test – cf. 10:5f), and the desert, not the Red Sea as such, is Paul's primary locus in the pericope. This leads to a further observation: Paul does not emphasise anywhere in 1 Corinthians 10:1–13 the virtues of Israel. If he did, this would seem to imply that the Corinthian congregation had some virtues as well, for Paul compares instead of contrasts the Israelite and Christian communities. It would seem rather odd for Paul to underscore rhetorically that the Israelites passed a test when he is trying to warn overconfident Corinthians about the dangers of *failing* one.

The exodus tradition emphasises the Red Sea as the place where Israel's deliverance and redemption from Egypt takes place (Exod. 14:13, 30; 15:2, 13, 16). Similarly, secondary reflections on the Red Sea narrative sometimes em-

---

[101] BANDSTRA (1971), 8–9; cf. KLINE (1968), 55ff.

phasise God's salvation of Israel and Egypt's punishment (Psa. 136:13–16; Wisd. 18:3–7, 13; 19:6ff, 19f; 3 Macc. 2:6–8; 6:4; cf. Hellenistic Synagogal Prayers 12:73f). Other traditions contrast the event at the Red Sea with Israel's rebellion and judgement in the wilderness and in the land of Canaan (e.g., Psa. 106:7–11, 13–21; Neh. 9:9–21; 4 Ezra 1:10–13 cf. 1 En. 89:16–40). One psalm describes the Israelites' belief in God's promises as a result of the Red Sea deliverance (106:12), but the writer then contrasts this thought with how, later on, the Israelites did not believe God's promises; hence, they were punished in the wilderness (106:24f). Another psalm tradition refers to the event in order to stress God's blessings and Israel's apostasies. Despite God's miracles in the exodus/wilderness episode, Israel rebelled against God, no longer believing God or trusting in his deliverance (Psa. 78:11–55). God therefore punishes them and puts them to death (78:31, 33–34 cf. v. 21). Both the Deuteronomic and Isaianic traditions emphasise God's power through the Red Sea event; the former uses this motif as an incentive for keeping God's commands (Deut. 11:1–8) while the latter points to a new eschatological fulfilment for God's redeemed people (Isa. 43:16f; 51:10–11; 31:5; cf. Mic. 7:15ff).[102]

From these traditions certain motifs emerge; they include God's salvation of Israel, God's demonstration of power through miracles, and Israel's apostasy despite God's deliverance. Although Paul does not appear to be citing any one source, he works out the same basic motifs in his allusion to the Red Sea in 10:2. Like the Israelites, God delivered the Corinthians from an oppression. The Egyptians oppressed Israel, but vices associated with the Corinthians' pre-converted background oppressed them (1 Cor. 6:9–10; 12:2). God's supernatural power was present for the Israelites, and the gifts of the Spirit were present for the Corinthians (1 Cor. 1:7–8; 12:7–11; 14 cf. 2:4–5; 4:19–20). Despite the redemption and miracles the Israelites experienced in the wilderness, many of them rebelled and were punished. Likewise, Paul warns the Corinthians that they too could suffer punishment as a result of rebellion (10:5–10).

2.2 Pillar of Cloud Traditions

The pillar of cloud first appears in the exodus narrative when Israel departs from Egypt at the Red Sea (Exod. 13:21–22; 14:19–24; cf. Deut. 4:37). In the Numbers tradition, during the 40 years in the wilderness, the Israelites would set up camp only when the cloud rested at a certain location. As soon as the cloud lifted, they would depart to a new destination (Num. 9:15–23; cf. Ps. 78:14). The cloud in the wilderness signified the Divine Presence for the Israelites – God was in the cloud and spoke through the cloud (Exod. 16:10–11;

---

[102] Cf. VON RAD (1962), 1:284.

19:9f; 24:15–18; 33:14; Num. 12:5–6; Deut. 1:32–33; 31:15f; Ps. 99:6–7).[103] In 1 Corinthians 10:1–2, Gardner regards the pillar cloud as essentially a sign of God's protection or covering. The cloud is depicted as overshadowing (σκιάζω) God's people as they went through the Red Sea (cf. Wisd. 19:7).[104] Indeed this is the function of the cloud in a number of wilderness narratives (Exod. 14:19–22; Josh. 24:7; Ps. 105:37–39; Isa. 4:4–6; 52:12). It is possible that Paul implies some sense of protection when he refers to the children of Israel moving "under the cloud" in 10:1.[105] But when this reference is combined with the baptism "in the cloud" in verse 2, something more than protection is probably in view.

In the Isaianic tradition the Red Sea/wilderness episode stands out as a major motif, and it forms the background for discussion regarding the "new exodus" which is characterised by the eschatological redemption from Babylon or another foreign power, the return from exile, and Zion's restoration (e.g., Isa. 4:2–6; 11:1–15; 26:20; 27:12–13; 31:5; 40:3–5; 43:2–17; 48:20–21).[106] The Divine Presence in the wilderness is associated with the Holy Spirit (Isa. 63:7–14; cf. 19:1; Psa. 106:32–33). J. Luzarraga identifies the "Spirit of glory" with the cloud of glory (Isa. 4:5), and he argues that the imagery of birds hovering over their nests in Isaiah 31:5 is reminiscent of the floating cloud of the exodus narrative. This characterises the Spirit hovering over creation (Gen. 1:2) and points to a new creation: "Este texto sugiere la liberación *Pascual* a la salida de Egipto, cuando Israel fue cubierto por las nubes de la gloria; comparándolo con 1 Cor 10,2 se puede descubrir también en él una alusión al Espíritu que revoloteaba en la primera creación."[107]

One wilderness tradition seems very significant for our discussion. Isaiah 63 speaks of God redeeming the Israelites in their distress as slaves, but they rebelled against and grieved God's Spirit; as a result, Yahweh fought against them (Isa. 63:9–10). The passage also mentions Yahweh who sets his Holy Spirit among the Israelites and divides and leads the Israelites through the waters of the Red Sea (Isa. 63:11–13). The Israelites were given rest by the Spirit of Yahweh, and so God guided his people (Isa. 63:14 cf. 52:12).[108] Perhaps the

---

[103] On the various cloud traditions and motifs in the exodus/wilderness event, see LUZARRAGA (1973), 101–92; DAVIDSON (1981), 211f. Source J is said to stress the cloud as a covering while E stresses an oracular pillar, but later Jewish interpretations collapse the two (SABOURIN, 1974:300–02).

[104] GARDNER (1994), 116, 119. Here SMIT (1997:43) understands the cloud as indicating a baptism under God's wing (cf. Neh. 9:12).

[105] Robertson and Plummer indicate that the accusative case in 10:1 (ὑπὸ τὴν νεφέλην) might imply motion: "They marched with the cloud above them" (199–200).

[106] Cf. ANDERSON (1962), 181–82, 187.

[107] LUZARRAGA, 234–35 cf. 114, 131, 236ff; but see also SABOURIN (1974), 311. Luzarraga also notes the association between the Spirit and "sangre y fuego y columnas de humo" of the eschatological Passover (cf. Isa. 4:4–6; Joel 3:3; Acts 2:19f).

[108] The LXX tradition brings out the guidance of the Spirit more clearly by omitting the notion of rest and stating that the Spirit came down from the Lord and guided the people; God

Isaianic tradition associated the Spirit with the cloud of Divine Presence because it also mentions the Spirit as a metaphor for water being poured forth in the desert (Isa. 32:15f; 35:6–10; 41:17–20; 43:16–21; 44:3–4; 49:8–10; 51:3; cf. 42:1; 61:1f; Psa. 126:4), and water comes from the clouds. The earliest Christians understood this imagery as anticipating the refreshing and renewal of God's people in the eschatological era by means of the outpouring or rainstorm of the Spirit (Acts 1:5; 2:3–4, 17, 33; 3:19 cf. Ezek. 47:1–12; Zech. 14:8; 1 En. 48:1; Odes of Sol. 6).[109] A rainstorm also appears to be implied as coming from the pillar cloud in the Red Sea narrative (Exod. 13:17–14:31; Psa. 77:16–20).[110] As the cloud was associated with the first exodus and the Mosiac covenant, so the Spirit is associated with an eschatological exodus and a renewed covenant (Isa. 59:21; cf. 2.4 below).[111]

The Isaianic tradition's identification of the cloud-presence with the Holy Spirit seems strengthened by several observations based on the other wilderness traditions. First, the Spirit given in Isaiah 63:11 may echo the prophetic/ecstatic gift of the Spirit distributed from the cloud-presence to the 70 elders in the wilderness at the Tent of Meeting (Num. 11:16–30; cf. Exod. 40:34–38; Ezek. 43:5). God places the Spirit upon Moses and distributes the Spirit among the 70 elders who begin to prophecy (Num. 11:16–17, 25f). Paul may have seen a parallel here with the distribution of spiritual gifts in the Corinthian congregation (1 Cor. 12:11ff). Second, different wilderness traditions refer to the idea of the Divine Presence or Spirit guiding the Israelites as does Isaiah 63:14 (cf. Num. 9:15f; Ps. 78:14; Neh. 9:12, 19–20). Third, we find that the Spirit is seen in terms of someone who is grieved or provoked at Israel's rebellion in the wilderness (Isa. 63:10), while God is grieved (MT – עצב) for the same reason in the wilderness episode of the *Maskil* of Asaph (Ps. 78:40 MT), and provoked (LXX – παροξύνειν) in other wilderness traditions (Num. 14:11, 22–23; Psa. 105[106]:29; 106[107]:11).[112] Fourth, in distinct wilderness accounts, we find

---

thus led his people to make a glorious name for himself (κατέβη πνεῦμα παρὰ Κυρίου, καὶ ὡδήγησεν αὐτούς. οὕτως ἤγαγες τὸν λαόν ...). It is difficult to finally determine which tradition would have influenced Paul more on this point. Virtually all of Paul's major citations from the Isaianic tradition do not seem to follow closely the LXX or the MT, and one follows both (1 Cor. 15:32 cf. Isa. 22:13; cf. Koch, 1986:35, 61–65, 107, 115, 203–4; Silva, DPL, 630–32). In any case, either reading of Isaiah 63:14 does not affect the implication that the Spirit represents the Divine Presence.

[109] It may be significant to acknowledge that the third stanza in Psalm 68 (vv. 7–10) mentions God (apparently through the pillar cloud) showering rain upon the Israelites during the wilderness episode. The Pauline writer associates this Psalm with the distribution of the gifts of the Spirit (Eph. 4:8–12 cf. Ps. 68:18).

[110] Cf. I. Abrahams (1917), 30.

[111] On the cloud motif in early eschatological Jewish and Christian sources, cf. Luzarraga, 193–212; Sabourin, 303–07.

[112] Once again, we do not know if Paul had the MT, LXX, both, or neither in mind. Psalm 105:33 LXX mentions another provocation (παρεπίκραναν) of the Holy Spirit by the wilderness generation.

the notion that both the Spirit (Isa. 63:14) and the Divine Presence give rest to the Israelites in the wilderness travels (Isa. 63:14; Exod. 33:14).[113]

Paul would seem influenced by these motifs because he often associates the Spirit with various aspects related to eschatology (Gal. 6:8; Rom. 8:11; 14:17; 2 Cor. 5:5).[114] Moreover, as we have already noted, it is likely that Paul considered the Corinthians as having participated in a "new exodus," and the Isaianic tradition might be his ground for doing so. Related to this, he often draws on the Isaianic tradition as a source (e.g., 1 Cor. 1:19 cf. Isa. 29:14; 1 Cor. 2:16 cf. Isa. 40:13; 1 Cor. 14:21 cf. Isa. 28:11–12; 1 Cor. 15:54 cf. Isa. 25:8).[115] The latter tradition, in turn, echoes the Song of Moses in Deuteronomy 32 on several occasions (e.g., Isa. 1:2 cf. Deut. 32:1; Isa. 30:17 cf. Deut. 32:30; Isa. 43:11–13 cf. Deut. 32:39), and the Song of Moses seems to be a primary source-tradition for Paul in 1 Corinthians 10:1–22.[116] Both the Isaiah and Song of Moses traditions are concerned with apostasy through idolatry; the latter sets it in the future, the former in the present. Paul employs the same theme of apostasy in the wilderness in 1 Corinthians 10:1–13 (cf. ch. 5:3.2.1). We find this theme in the Numbers tradition which also associates the Spirit with the cloud (cf. Num. 11:16f). As we will see in the next chapter, Paul alludes more than once to the Numbers tradition in 1 Corinthians 10:1–13, and he may have noticed this particular narrative due to the similarities between the prophetic distribution of God's Spirit in Numbers 11 and the prophetic problems at Corinth (cf. 1 Cor. 11–14).

We therefore have a plausible reason to suspect that the primary source of Paul's cloud reference derives from a tradition similar to that of the Isaianic and Numbers texts. In these traditions, the cloud-presence was linked with God's Spirit, and this presence was in the wilderness. As well, we will observe that the latter tradition is Paul's primary source in 10:5–10. These observations have ramifications for how we might interpret Paul's use of the term "cloud" in relation to baptism.

2.3 The Cloud as a Metaphor for Baptism in the Holy Spirit

We have noted above that Paul's motifs are similar to those in early Red Sea traditions. We have also observed that Paul echoes the Isaianic and Numbers

---

[113] If it could be demonstrated that Paul is using only the LXX tradition and not the MT tradition in 1 Corinthians in reference to Isaiah, this argument would be weakened. But this does not appear to be the case for reasons mentioned above. The author of Hebrews also mentions the Holy Spirit as saying "they shall not enter into my rest" in relation to Israel's rebellion in the wilderness (Heb. 3:7–11; cf. Psa. 95:7–11; see ch. 5:2.2.2 below).

[114] Cf. HAMILTON (1957).

[115] Cf. SILVA, 631. Also see WILK (1998) for examples primarily in Romans.

[116] Cf. KRAUSE (1988), 184f; HAYS (1989), 94.

traditions in 1 Corinthians. In the latter, the Spirit of God is given to the elders of Israel from the cloud-presence, and in the former, the cloud-presence is identified as the Spirit. Since Paul is aware of the Corinthian congregation's tendency toward "spiritual things," we might expect him to imply that the Israelites themselves had the Spirit in 1 Corinthians 10:1–4. This would make his argument more persuasive. Yet Paul is not arbitrary in his equating the cloud with the Spirit if he is following the Isaianic or Numbers tradition on this matter. Other Christian and Jewish traditions also affirm the connection between the exodus cloud and God's Spirit.[117] Another passage in 1 Corinthians might similarly reflect a connection between the Spirit and God's presence. The cloud of the Presence was depicted as filling the Israelite sanctuary at the dedication of the tabernacle and again at the dedication of Solomon's temple (Exod. 40:34–38; 1 Kings 8:10–13; cf. Rev. 15:6f). In a similar way, Paul proceeds on the assumption that the Corinthian Christians, whom he describes as a temple of God made without hands, were filled with the Spirit (1 Cor. 3:16–17).[118]

We now arrive at the probable conclusion regarding the association of the Spirit/cloud and Israel's baptism in 1 Corinthians 10:2. Through analogy with the Corinthians' experience, Paul may be affirming two elements into which the children of Israel were baptised: in the cloud (ἐν τῇ νεφέλῃ), which represents Spirit baptism, and in the sea (καὶ ἐν τῇ θαλάσσῃ), which represents water baptism. Contrary to scholars who claim that 12:13 primarily refers to water baptism,[119] the passage stresses a baptism in one Spirit (ἐν ἑνὶ πνεύματι ἡμεῖς πάντες εἰς ἓν σῶμα ἐβαπτίσθημεν). Here the Spirit is the element in which the Corinthians were baptised. Dunn rightly argues that ἐν does not have an instrumental force so as to be interpreted as a baptism "by the Spirit." Whenever the New Testament authors combine this preposition with βαπτίζειν it always indicates "the element in which the baptisand is immersed (or with which he is deluged) – except, of course, when it is part of a fuller phrase like ἐν τῇ ἐρήμῳ or ἐν τῷ ὀνόματι."[120] In this passage, the ἐν has the same force as it does ἐν τῇ νεφέλῃ and ἐν τῇ θαλάσσῃ in 10:2. The "baptism" (as well as the

---

[117] Davies notes that Jewish traditions associated the Shekinah with the presence of the Holy Spirit, for "both expressions were used as metonymies for God; the sins that drive away the Holy Spirit also drove away the Shekinah; the virtues that qualify one for the Holy Spirit also qualify for the Shekinah" (DAVIES, 1980:211; cf. MOORE, 1:435–37). For examples in the early Christian era, see HAYKIN (1986), 135–44; DANIELOU (1956), 91f; LUZARRAGA, 234, 237ff; John of Damascus (*Orthodox Faith* 4.9).

[118] See also LUZARRAGA, 209–10.

[119] E.g., BEASLEY-MURRAY (1962), 162–71.

[120] DUNN (1970), 128. Dunn also argues that the εἰς in 1 Corinthians 12:13 should not be understood as having the sense of "in," "for the sake of," or "with a view to," which renditions are sometimes used to support an instrumental interpretation. The preposition should be understood in terms of a "motion towards" or "into" a certain goal. In this case, the goal of being baptised in the Spirit is an incorporation into the Body of Christ or union with Christ.

Spirit "drink" – καὶ πάντες ἕν πνεῦμα ἐποτίσθημεν) may be a metaphor for being immersed or filled with the Spirit. The Spirit is never the agent for baptism, but like water, the Spirit serves as an element (cf. Mark 1:8; Matt. 3:11; Luke 3:16; John 1:26–33; Acts 1:5; 11:6).[121]

For Paul, the inception of Spirit is connected with conversion-initiation (Rom. 8:9; 10:9–13; 1 Cor. 6:11; 12:3; Gal. 3:2; 2 Thes. 2:13; Eph. 1:13–14; Tit. 3:5; cf. Phil. 1:19). Hence, in 1 Corinthians 10:2, Paul is implying that the Corinthians were baptised in (ἐν) the element of the Spirit in(to) (εἰς) the name of Jesus Christ; which for him in this context is an incorporation into the body of Christ (12:13). He equates the church with the body of Christ (1:13; 6:15, 17; 10:16–17;12:12–27).[122] The essential element in which one was initiated into this fellowship was the Spirit.[123] Paul is therefore arguing that all the Israelites had a divine encounter during their initiation through the Red Sea, and this experience was parallel to that of the Corinthians who were all baptised in the Spirit at their conversion and had become members of the body of Christ. The experiences of both groups were genuine. The irony in 1 Corinthians 10:1–13 is that even though the Israelites experienced God's presence, they still committed apostasy in the wilderness. This leads to certain ramifications regarding the election of God's people.

2.3.1 Excursus: The Body of Christ and Ethical Obligation

Since I have suggested that Paul's perspective of baptism involves a transfer of ownership in which a convert becomes a member of the body of Christ, it may be relevant to elaborate on how Paul views this body. In 1 Corinthians 12:13 the congregation's immersion in the element of the Spirit marked them as members in the body of Christ. To be a member of the body of Christ was to be a Christian, a member of the new elect people of God. Since the body of Christ represents the church, this conception might help us understand what Paul meant in certain contexts by the related phrase "ἐν Χριστῷ." The Pauline "in Christ-Christ in us" metaphor (1 Cor. 1:30; 2 Cor. 5:17; Rom. 6:11; 8:1; Gal. 2:20; Col. 1:27; Eph. 3:17) suggests that being "in Christ" means to be joined with him in some

---

[121] FEE (1987), 604–06.

[122] Does Paul consider the church as simply a human body rather than the body of Christ (cf. Yorke, 1991; 32, 119–23)? This seems difficult to reconcile with the implications of 1 Corinthians 1:13 which relates division in Corinth as dividing Christ, and that the bodies of church members are members of Christ (1 Cor. 6:15). See also "Ὑμεῖς δέ ἐστε σῶμα Χριστοῦ καὶ μέλη ἐκ μέρου" (1 Cor. 12:27); DAINES (1978), 71f. For a critique of Käsemann's view that the church is the post-resurrected body of Christ, see WEDDERBURN (1971), 71, 74–86. Best rightly argues that if we accept a material/realistic view of Christ's body as the church, then the "dead in Christ" (1 Thes. 4:16f) would seem to have no place in it (1955:113–114).

[123] Cf. DUNN, 129.

sense of solidarity/representation as part of the body of Christ.[124] The individual members are to work together for the benefit of all the members (1 Cor. 12). In 1 Corinthians, Paul rhetorically adjusts the congregation's misperception of advantage (e.g., slogans in 6:12ff; 10:23ff) by removing it from the individual frame of reference to the body of Christ.[125]

Paul presents various images of understanding Christian solidarity with Christ. For example, he construes the idea of solidarity in Abraham as the head of the family of faith whose posterity, Jesus Christ, receives God's promises and passes those promises to those whom he represents (Gal. 3:7–18).[126] In 1 Corinthians, however, Paul seems to compare Adam and Christ as two corporate representatives for humankind (1 Cor. 15:20–50; cf. Rom. 5:12–21).[127] Then again, in 1 Corinthians 3:16–17 he speaks of the congregation as collective members of the temple of God. He also speaks in the imagery of a marital union of two becoming one. It thus seems that the result of baptism in the Spirit joins in one Spirit the initiate with Christ (1 Cor. 6:15–17; cf. 2 Cor. 11:2; Rom 7:4; Eph. 5:25–32; Gen. 2:23–24).[128] Since Paul depicts the relationship between the church and Christ in more than one way, it may be that Paul's use of the body of Christ should not be oversimplified or finally reduced to a single point.[129]

Through the Corinthians' baptism in the name of Jesus there exists a strong sense of belonging/ownership (1:11ff; 10:2; cf. 1.4.4).[130] For Paul, to be a mem-

---

[124] Suggesting that baptism into Christ places one "in Christ," Best claims, "We enter by baptism εἰς Χριστόν and the resulting state is ἐν Χριστῷ ..." (1955:70).

[125] Cf. M. MITCHELL (1991), 233.

[126] Cf. WEDDERBURN (1971), 88.

[127] Greco-Roman literature has a similar notion of comparing the human body with the polis/community (e.g., Epictetus *Diss.* 2.10.4–5; Seneca *De Clem.* 1.51; Dio Chrysostom *Or.* 39.5; Livy, *Hist.* 2.32). For more references see M. MITCHELL, 160; Klauck 339. Differently, Philo speaks of the high priest offering sacrifice so that the nation might be welded into one family as if it were the same body (*Spec. Leg.* 3.131). The Adam-Christ idea, however, need not be equated with the Gnostic Anthropos myth of KÄSEMANN (1964:109f), as Wedderburn argues (1971:90–96; cf. Best, 85–87).

[128] White argues that in the Servant of Yahweh songs, the whole of the purified Israel is incorporated so that the elect's destiny is worked out through the Servant's experience. The Servant acts as the "inclusive representative" of the remnant people, for in him the children of Israel have been judged, died and revived again to a new life. Thus he concludes, "Such ideas, of the collective 'Servant of Yahweh,' the personal Representative of the remnant and the people, the corporate personality of the descendants of Adam, the representative Sacrifice that gathers into itself the penitence of the whole community (Isa. liii), are germane to the deepest Hebrew thinking, and there is no room for serious doubt that it is upon such theological foundation that Pauline 'mysticism' ultimately rests" (White 1960:223; cf. 222). If this is the basis of Paul's perspective, he does not directly expose such ideas in our passage. Nevertheless, Paul does allude to the Isaianic tradition, and he has some sense of corporate election in mind. Certain traditions affirm the messiah as God's elect one, and people who cling to the Lord of spirits are called elect ones (Isa. 42:1; 1 En. 40:4; 45:3–5; 61:8; cf. Luke 9:35).

[129] Cf. DUNN (1988), 2:724.

[130] Regarding "in Christ," Sanders writes, "What is important to note is that Paul did not consider *belonging* to Christ to be different from being *in* him" (1977:462).

ber of the body of Christ is to recognise a notion of accountability regardless of whether he had in mind the body imagery of Adamic/Servant solidarity, corporate/political, or marital union. If there is a collective sense of belonging to Christ, then obligation to both Christ and fellow members of the body of Christ naturally follows, and this appears to be the basis for Paul's ethics in Corinth (cf. 1 Cor. 3:23; 6:19–20; 7:22–23; 15:23; cf. 2 Cor. 5:14–15; Rom. 14:8–9).[131] Paul also affirms that the Spirit introduces an aspect of ethical purification in baptism (1 Cor. 6:11; cf. Eph. 5:25f; Tit. 3:5). Sahlin argues that "the Christian becomes 'holy' through baptism. He now belongs to the *true* people of God ... St Paul calls the Christians 'the saints' ... they belong to the body of Christ." Hence, Paul's assumption may be, "As you *have become* holy by your baptism, you must *lead a holy life.*"[132]

2.4 Baptism as a Boundary Marker for the Body of Christ

Since my reading of 10:2 implies an incorporation into the body of Christ, it may be significant to examine Paul's perspective of body language in relation to baptism. Here Paul defines boundaries in terms of body imagery. Douglas discerns the body in terms of boundaries related to cleanliness and uncleanliness. From the Levitical and Deuteronomic traditions she affirms that holiness means separateness, but she also maintains that one is to understand holiness in terms of wholeness or completeness: "In short the idea of holiness was given an external, physical expression in the wholeness of the body seen as a perfect container."[133] A deformed or mutilated body was deemed unacceptable to approach the God of Israel (cf. Lev. 21:16–20). Similarly, Paul believed that the wholeness of the body of Christ can be threatened through the vices and divisions at Corinth, and this plays a significant part in Paul's rhetoric in 10:1–11: "all" of God's people embarked on the wilderness journey, but "many" were destroyed (10:5).

Martin suggests that Paul's consigning the sexual offender to Satan in 1 Corinthians 5:1–5 reveals Paul's apocalyptic war between "sarx" and "pneuma." He argues that there is no clear boundary which separates the body of the fornicator from the church; the man's presence in the community indicates an "invasion of sarx" into the congregation. Hence, it is necessary for the "sarx" to be destroyed in both the offender and the church if the "pneuma" is to be saved in both.[134] Mere contact with the *cosmos*, however, does not threaten the body, for in the same message, Paul does not advocate complete separation from

---

[131] Cf. FURNISH (1990), 157.
[132] SAHLIN (1953), 92.
[133] DOUGLAS (1966), 51–52.
[134] D. MARTIN (1995), 174.

unregenerate sinners (1 Cor. 5:9–12). A disguised pollutant, according to Martin, is the real threat for Paul because it could penetrate the boundary between *cosmos* and the body of Christ.[135] If Martin's observations are correct, Paul considered expulsion necessary because the contamination and condemnation that could result are real threats to the wholeness of the body. One member can affect others. Likewise, through the Israelite exodus/wilderness episode, Paul is marking clear boundaries for the Corinthians regarding who is "in" and who is "out" in relation to the body of Christ.[136] He begins first with those who are "in." The opening verses indicate that "all" the Israelites were originally "in" (10:1–4), and by implication so were all the Corinthian members. In the proceeding verses (10:5–10), he begins to inidicate who is "out."

In 1 Corinthians 10 "in" and "out" language is already implied by the phrase "our fathers" in verse 1: elect language also implies non-elect.[137] For Paul, then, the cloud and sea in 10:1–2 function as boundary markers to separate elect Israel from non-elect Egypt. The divine presence was an identifying marker for Israel and distinguished them from other nations (Exod. 33:15–16); likewise, the Spirit identifies the people of God in the new era.[138] In the exodus event, the cloud of divine presence became a boundary indicator by providing light to Israel but darkness to Egypt. Moreover, the cloud and sea which "saved" Israel are the same elements which destroyed Egypt (Exod. 14).

In Jewish traditions of antiquity, the cloud is understood as an extraordinary sign, a separator between Israel and Egypt or other nations (Deut. 4:9–14, 32f; Neh. 9:9ff; Philo, *Quis Her.* 202–204; *Mos.* 1:178–79, 2:254).[139] According to Philo, the sea is both an instrument of salvation and an instrument of destruction (*Mos.* 2.254–55; cf. *Vit. Cont.* 85–86). Although the Egyptians may be implied as the "binary" of the Israelites in 10:1–2, we will discover that the identity of who is "out" in 10:5–11 centres on the Israelites in the desert. This thought is in keeping with the warning that if the Israelites' hearts turned back to their previous bondage in Egypt, they too would suffer the fate of their oppressors and their instruments of blessing would become instruments of cursing (cf. Deut. 28–32).

---

[135] D. MARTIN, 170.

[136] The "unleavened bread" (ch. 5:6f) and "one bread" (ch. 10:16f) in 1 Corinthians appear to suggest that both are related to the church as the body of Christ (cf. HOWARD, 1969:102).

[137] Barton notes how boundary-markers are essentially binary: "They divide or separate into categories: inner and outer, up and down, right and left (spatial); and presents and past/future, beginning and end, first and second/last (temporal). This binary structure is what makes boundary-markers so important for the communication of social *values*, for they can be made to represent the difference between the positive and the negative, right and wrong" (1986:227).

[138] Alló sees the Christians here as "le peuple élu" (1956:230).

[139] Cf. GARDNER (1994), 119. For a list of references in Jewish tradition sources regarding blessing and curse, see GARDNER, 134fnt117.

One of the rhetorical aims of Paul in 10:2 was to have the Corinthians comprehend that the cloud and sea were metaphors for baptism in the Spirit and water – the identifying marks of a truly converted initiate.[140] In his exhortation, the cloud and sea are the spatial boundaries between Israel and Egypt. Paul may be implying for the Corinthians that baptism functions as the boundary between the body of Christ and those who are in the present wicked world. This is certainly in keeping with Paul's cosmology which is divided into the categories of light and darkness (1 Thes. 5:4–5; Rom. 1:21; 2:19; Col. 1:13; 2 Cor. 6:14; cf. Eph. 4:17–18), sobriety and drunkenness (Rom. 13:11–14; 1 Thes. 5:6–7; cf. Eph. 5:18), the kingdom of Christ and the domain of Satan (2 Cor. 4:4; cf. Eph. 2:2; 5:5; 6:12), the age to come and the present age (Rom. 8:18–25; 1 Cor. 2:8; Gal. 1:4), and so forth. In his letter to the Corinthians, Paul is provoked by the ambiguous limits of the strong, and so he sets out to create clearer boundaries. He writes in terms of members and non-members (1 Cor. 1:1–2; 5:12–13; 6:1–11), saints and the perishing cosmos (1 Cor. 1:18–28; 2:12; 5:10; 7:31; 11:32), believers and unbelievers (1 Cor. 6:6; 7:12–15; 10:27; 14:23), clean/pure and unclean/polluted (1 Cor. 1:30; 6:11; 7:14, 34; 8:7; cf. 2 Cor. 7:1; 12:21), and so forth.[141]

Related to these binary conceptions is Neyrey's suggestion that in Paul's letters rituals denote the marking of boundaries. Entrance and exit rituals involve status transformation in the case of entrance rituals, or status reversal in the case of exit rituals (cf. ch. 1:3.3.2).[142] Neyrey affirms that the most noted entrance ritual for Paul is baptism and puts it well when he suggests, "In short, candidates for baptism leave one world, cross a boundary, and enter another world. The difference between the two worlds is itself expressed in terms of dualistic expressions that describe the irreconcilable differences between the before-and-after state of the entrance ritual of baptism."[143] Paul may have understood this entrance in terms of entering into a covenant. As the Israelites were delivered from Egypt through their "baptism" and received their covenant in the wilderness of Sinai, so the Corinthians entered an eschatological covenant through their baptism.[144] The allusion to baptism (10:2) precedes partici-

---

[140] Alló speaks of these opening verses of chapter 10 as a type of Christian regeneration (230).

[141] Cf. NEYREY (1990), 41–55.

[142] NEYREY, 79–80.

[143] NEYREY, 87–88.

[144] JEREMIAS (1969:88–94; 1960:32) argues that Paul may be adopting the Hillelite assumption that proselytes should be accepted into the Israelite covenant, as the elect Israelites were accepted into the Sinaitic covenant after their exodus through the Red Sea (cf. Exod. 24:8). From this belief may have arisen the notion that the Israelites in the wilderness were baptised through their deliverance from Egypt at the Red Sea. Jeremias asserts, "1 Cor. 10.1–2 shows us that this doctrine of the baptism of the desert generation, which is of fundamental importance for proselyte baptism, was already familiar to Paul [Acts 21:39–22:3], the pupil of the Hillelite Gamaliel I" (1960:32). However, other scholars have argued that such a view

pating in the Lord's Supper (10:3–4) because for Paul, only those who are identified as part of the elect community in Christ may partake in the new covenant established by Christ (1 Cor. 11:25 f).

Another observation worth noting is that the Isaianic and Deuteronomic traditions (both of which Paul alludes to in 10:1–4) describe the faithfulness of God in terms of God's renewing of the covenant to a new exodus/wilderness generation. The latter tradition describes this renewal in terms of the binary aspects of life/death and blessings/curses; these are attributed to the children of the wilderness generation depending on whether or not they are faithful toward God's covenant (Deut. 29:1 ff; 29:12 ff; cf. 7:7 ff; 28; 30–32). The former tradition predicts an everlasting covenant which is established by God's eschatological servant in a renewed wilderness setting (Isa. 42:6 ff; 49:6–11; 54:10; 55:3; 61:8; cf. 9:7). Similarly, in reference to initiation, the Qumran community saw themselves as entering a new covenant (1QS 1, 3, 4:14 ff; cf. 5.13). They apparently bound themselves with oaths including a public confession of sin, blessing from the priest, and a curse to those who were "of Belial and apostates of the 'new covenant'."[145]

It is likely, then, that Paul thinks of baptism in 10:2 as a ritual by which the initiate enters into an eschatological covenant community. This idea is reinforced by allusions to the eucharist in 10:3–4 which is considered part of the new covenant (11:23–25; 10:16–17). Hence, 10:1–13 may be seen in terms of a binary notion of entrance/exit ritual; the covenantal entrance phase occurs in 10:1–4, and Paul will work out the exit phase through the remainder of the pericope (10:5 ff).

2.5 Baptism as a Rite of Separation

Cultural anthropological studies on initiation may also add another insight to our text. Richard Hanson lists four common initiation patterns found in ancient Christian, Jewish, and Greco-Roman religions: 1) a death to one's former status or existence and a rebirth into a better existence; 2) a transformation process based on separation and incorporation into a new state; 3) a participation into the sacred history of the community; 4) the rite itself effects a transition; the act is more than symbolic. Hanson claims that these patterns account for why Paul

---

lacks clear evidence. The question of early Jewish proselytism aside, these scholars have argued that no Tannaitic passages directly connect proselyte baptism with the Red Sea experience rather than with ritual purification at Sinai (cf. MARTELET, 330–32; CONZELMANN, 165–66: DAVIDSON, 213–14). In any case, if Paul's view of baptism is derived from the Isaianic tradition, as I have argued, it seems a moot point to distinguish between the Red Sea and Sinai events – the two events should not be separated. The Isaianic tradition views the exodus/wilderness in multiple images including water, spirit, mountain, and desert.

[145] Cf. BLACK (1961), 94–95.

considers baptism as a negation (cf. 1 Cor. 6:9–11a), inauguration (cf. 1 Cor. 6:11b), and anticipation (cf. 1 Cor. 6:12–20).[146]

In varying degrees Hanson's initiation patterns appear in our text.[147] First, Paul relates how the Israelites departed from their former existence as slaves in Egypt to a new life in the land of Canaan. The Corinthians also departed from their former status of dependency on former vices (1 Cor. 6:9–11; 12:2). Second, Paul establishes that the cloud and sea separated Israel from their former existence as did the initiation for the Corinthians (cf. 2.4 above). Third, Paul conceives of the Corinthians as participating in a sacred history once possessed only by the Israelites (1 Cor. 10:6, 11; cf. Gal. 3:6f). Finally, Paul conveys to the Corinthians that the Israelites' baptism into Moses is a kind of initiation similar to their own conversion experience (cf. 1.4.4; 2.3 above). Thus, Hanson's model might suggest that 1 Corinthians 10:1–2 may be understood in relation to a separation rite.

In light of a rite of passage, Paul seems to regard baptism as a separation rite that ushers the baptisand into a state of liminality. The Israelites were separated from Egypt and lived a marginal existence in the wilderness. Since some of the Corinthian converts thought themselves immune through the act of initiation, they might have perceived themselves as already spiritually complete.[148] In the ritual process, they considered themselves to be in some state of aggregation (cf. ch. 4:8.4ff above). In the larger context of 1 Corinthians, however, Paul adds a new dimension to the congregation's thinking. Baptised members have not completed their process, and their initiation did not make them presently "immune." Rather, they are to live in a marginal existence until the completion of the eschaton (cf. 1 Cor. 4:8; 10:5–6, 11–12; 13:8–10; 15:12ff).[149]

Separation in the desert was a noted motif in early Jewish literature. For Philo, the wilderness keeps the Israelites away from the evils of the city and provides for them a training ground. For Josephus, the wilderness provides a retreat for various Messianic groups (cf. Matt. 24:26), and for Qumran, the new

---

[146] R. HANSON (1945), 174–77.

[147] R. HANSON's three stages are similar to that of Turner and van Gennep. Hanson's negation is virtually the same as Turner's separation stage, but in Hanson's model, the inauguration (which Turner calls "aggregation") occurs before the anticipation (which Turner calls "liminal") phase. If we were discussing the rite of baptism itself without any precedent or antecedent aspects, Hanson's model is quite attractive. However, by using the desert and journeying motifs (clear symbols of liminality; cf. ch. 1.3.2 above) *after* the baptism-initiation in 1 Corinthians 10:1–2, Paul delineates a pattern which is closer to Turner's model.

[148] Cf. CONZELMANN, 168; SCHLATTER (1974), 120; BARRETT, 220; WITHERINGTON (1995), 220.

[149] McVann argues that in baptism the early Christian converts "repudiate their precious allegiances and the *status quo*, and thus make themselves marginal … Jesus' own baptism … has the effect of radically transforming his status, rendering him marginal, an outsider. It therefore provides a model for Christian initiation" (1991:151–52; cf. WAETJEN, 1989:68–69).

covenantal people live in the wilderness to be separate from the apostate major-ity.[150] As a first century Jew, Paul almost certainly knew the motif of separation in the wilderness. Gardner rightly observes regarding 10:2 that baptism in the cloud and sea "was one of *separation* and group identification ... The compari-son between the old and new [group] is 'covenantal'. The Israelites were iden-tified as God's covenant community, separated by cloud and sea. For the new covenant people the word 'baptism' epitomised that process."[151] Thus, we see the initial stage of a liminal journey which shall be elaborated in fuller detail in chapter 4. Baptism marks the beginning of status change. Israel had broken away from their Egyptian oppressors through the Red Sea, and by implication, the Corinthians abandoned the oppression of their pre-Christian status through baptism. In both cases, the separation was real, and the salvation/deliverance experienced by all the members of the communities was genuine.

3. The Solidarity of Spiritual Consumption in the Wilderness (1 Corinthians 10:3–4)

Paul's account of Israel's consumption of spiritual food and drink in 1 Corinthians 10:3–4 echoes the incident at Massah and Meribah, where the children of Israel were eating manna in the desert and drinking the water which came from the rock (Exod. 16:1–17:7; cf. Num. 20:1–13). Paul probably intended the spiritual character of the food and drink in 10:3–4a to convey the same kind of spirituality attributed to the "spiritually following rock" (πνευματικῆς ἀκολουθούσης πέτρας) in 10:4b.[152] Perhaps the main difference between the sustenance and the rock is that the rock is the source of the sustenance.[153] The rock language

---

[150] For references, see MAUSER, 53–61.

[151] GARDNER, 120.

[152] Related to this assumption is the question of whether Paul intended that only the spiritual water derived its source from the spiritual rock, or if he intended that both the food and drink come from the spiritual rock. Davidson argues that since the spiritual origin of the drink is not so evident, Paul needed to address why it was. The spiritual nature of the manna was already self evident (cf. Deut. 8:3; Exod. 16:4); hence, Paul did not bother to insert a γὰρ clause before the βρῶμα (1981:245). Alternatively, since πνευματικός modifies both the food and drink, it appears that both the elements derived their πνευματικός from the rock. Also, since Paul is implying the consumption of the eucharist, the drink would not be quali-tatively different from the food. Paul may be employing an ellipsis at this point because "they were *eating and* drinking from the spiritually following rock" might have sounded redundant. BANDSTRA (1971:12–13) argues that the rock also provided food (honey and oil) which was associated with manna (Deut. 32:13 cf. Exod. 16:8; Num. 11:8). We should not make too much of this last point. Although the Deuteronomic verse might allude to the miraculous rock which provided water in the wilderness, the immediate context is set in the milieu of blessings depicted in the promised land (cf. 32:13a, 14c–15).

[153] The passage does not refer to Christ as the spiritual nourishment; he is rather the giver of the nourishment (cf. BORNKAMM, 1969:145).

was likely triggered by Paul's allusion to the rock at Massah and Meribah, which had become a symbol for rebellion in the wilderness in the presence of God's miraculous provision. Various interpretations of the rock have been set forth based on Jewish [154] or Philonic/Wisdom literature.[155] However, the rock in 10:4 most likely is derived directly from the Song of Moses which identifies God as "the Rock" in Deuteronomy 32:4, 15, 18, 30–31 (ch. 5:3.3.1).[156] Paul is stressing to the Corinthians that Christ was present with the Israelites in the wilderness just as he was present with them – the rock (ἡ πέτρα) "was" (ἦν) Christ.[157]

---

[154] E. ELLIS summarises in Jewish legends that there was a rock-shaped well the size of an oven or beehive which was created on the 6th day of creation and followed the Israelites in the wilderness. When the princes gathered around it and cried "Spring up, O well," water gushed forth from its openings. Sometimes the well provided drinks to people at their tents. It also provided healing and could swell up to crush Israel's enemies. It dried up after Miriam's death (her merit was why it was given), but it was restored for the Patriarchs' sake and did not rest until it reached the Sea of Tiberius where one might be able to still see its reflection in the depths (cf. E. ELLIS 1957a:53–56; 1957b:209–212; Str.-B., 3:406–408). Bandstra claims these traditions may be relatively late (c. 4th century), and the first century tradition from which it may have derived may not have mentioned it as a rock but as a stream of water (11–12; cf. W. WILLIS, 137). It is hardly conceivable that Paul thought Christ was somehow resident inside a literal rock (cf. 1 Cor. 10:9). While it is possible that Paul is repackaging a Jewish "following rock/stream" tradition, this explanation is insufficient to explain 10:4.

[155] Philo asserts that the flinty rock is the wisdom of God, which was the greatest of God's powers, and from which he provides the thirsty with drink. The thirsty are also filled with manna, which is the "primary genus of everything (τί ὅ πάντων ἐστὶ γένος), but the primal existence (γενικώτατόν) is God, and next to God is the word of God" (*Leg. All.* 2.86 cf. 2.84). The symbols of rock, water, and manna are associated with the word of God (cf. *Quaes. in Gn.* 2.62). When interpreting Deuteronomy 32:13, Philo affirms that oil and honey come from the rock, which is the divine wisdom of God and is called manna, the most ancient word of God (*Det.* 115–118). Wisdom is also associated with God in the Red Sea and wilderness narratives (Wisd. 10:15–11:4; Cf. FEUILLET, 105 f). If the Philonic wisdom/rock motif seems to be based on the Song of Moses (Deut. 32), both traditions may have influenced Paul. Alternatively, Paul and Philo may share common assumptions regarding the rock and divine wisdom. Paul refers to his sources in 10:1–13 as γραφή (10:11), and nowhere in 1 Corinthians does he appear to regard Philo's writings as fitting this category.

[156] Cf. HAYS (1989), 94; FEE, 449; McEWEN (1986), 7. The missing premises that Paul fails to write in his argument in 10:4b are his belief in a literal rock from which the water sprang and his belief in God as the metaphorical rock of Israel. As ambiguous as it may sound, Paul wants to communicate the symbol "rock" as both 1) the literal rock at Massah/Meribah and 2) the Lord God, the metaphorical rock whom Paul claims is the pre-existent Christ. It was Christ who followed the Israelites in their journey and customarily provided them with spiritual sustenance.

[157] Dunn's allegorical interpretation here does not appear to be correct: "the rock *represents* Christ" (1989:183; but see his alterations in 1998:279–80). The imperfect "was" contrasts Paul's use of the present tense "are" in "Hagar and Sarah *are* two covenants" (Gal. 4:24–25; cf. also present tense "is" in Jesus' parables) to demonstrate that rock was not merely a type of Christ, but in some sense it really was Christ (cf. ROBERTSON and PLUMMER, 201). Héring seems correct by affirming that the "rock" is the Messiah himself: "c'est-à-dire le Christ préexistant" (77). Moreover, if Moses is seen as a prefiguration of Christ in 10:2, it seems awkward that Paul would now say that the rock prefigures Christ. Moses can only be a precursor to Christ because he was *not* Christ – Christ was the rock.

Nevertheless, the hermeneutic focus of 1 Corinthians 10:1–13 is not christo-centric but, as Hays affirms, "ecclesiocentric: he [Paul] makes the biblical text pass through the filter of his experience of God's action of forming the church. The full meaning of God's eschatological redemptive purpose is now definitively enacted in the Christian community."[158] Paul depicts Israel as a collective com-munity held together and sustained by spiritual elements that came from Christ. In this sense, they were the body of Christ before the Corinthian congregation was.[159] The Corinthians, no doubt, would have understood the spiritual food as pointing to the Lord's supper (cf. Didache 10.3).[160] If this is the correct reading of 10:3–4, our purpose in this section will be to focus on the nature of the Lord's supper and the term πνευματικός in relation to the community's sustenance in order to determine its possible meaning for the Corinthians. What is Paul trying to convey to the Corinthians by mentioning Israel's consumption of spiritual food and drink in the wilderness? What Corinthian problem might he be attempting to counter? What might Paul be saying rhetorically? In what sense is he attempting to underscore his warning in 10:1–13? To these questions we now turn.

3.1 Antecedents to the Lord's Supper

If an issue related to the eucharist may be at stake in 10:3–4, we should attempt to ascertain if there were any problems with the Corinthian congregation's view of the Lord's supper. The problem in 11:17–34 might suggest that some of the members saw no connection between their gathering to partake of the eucharist and their ethical conduct. Paul portrays their meetings to be characterised by selfishness, drunkenness, and a lack of consideration for the "have nots." Since it appears that immunity was a problem related to their view of baptism (10:1–2), some sense of immunity may also be at stake in 10:3–4. We previously noted how a Dionysian-type of influence may well have left its mark on the Corin-thian community (1.4.2 above). It is possible that some of the Christian women in Corinth had carried over their former style of worshipping in a state of ec-static frenzy as Maenads. They were used to unbinding and tossing their hair when they felt at one with Dionysus; they may have resorted to similar phe-nomena when sensing the Spirit's presence (e.g., Juvenal, *Satires* 6.316–19; cf. 1 Cor. 11:2–16; 12:2; 14:23).[161] Regarding ecstatic states, Neyrey notes that

---

[158] HAYS, 102; cf. KREITZER (1993), 111.

[159] Jeske perhaps goes a little too far, however, by affirming that "the rock was Christ" refers to the corporate body of Christ, the church (1980:248). This would seem to indicate that the Israelites, and by implication the Corinthians, were the source of their own sustenance.

[160] So also KREITZER, 122–23; SCHLATTER, 120–21; KLAUCK, 255f; HÉRING, 79; LANG, 122.

[161] SCHATTENMANN, *NIDNTT*, 1:528–29; PAINTER (1982), 242–46; R.&C. KROEGER, 333–34; FERGUSON (1993), 247.

"where trance is not regarded as at all dangerous, but as a benign source of power and guidance for the community ... group boundaries [tend to be] unimportant, [and] social categories undefined."[162] The body often represents society, and the spirit the individual; hence, attitudes regarding the spirit often reflect cultural attitudes. A benign attitude toward spirit-possession reflects a low view of the body and society; an attitude which sees spirit-possession as dangerous may reflect a high regard for societal conformity.[163] Such presuppositions may have been operative in the Corinthian congregation (cf. ch. 1:3.1.2–3.3.2). The upshot of all this is that Dionysian groups are said to believe that Dionysus manifested himself through the wine they drank so that the drink mediated divine power and immortality confirmed by spiritual ecstasy.[164] It is likely that some of the Corinthian members, who may have come out of such a religious upbringing, associated immortality with the consumption of the eucharist and confirmed their "immortal" status through spiritual ecstasy (cf. 1 Cor. 11–14).

Given the former religious background of some of the Corinthian members, it is not unreasonable to assume that they took to an extreme some previous apostolic instruction on the Lord's Supper which may have suggested the notion of incorruptible life in the eschatological age. Dennis Smith observes that basic foods such as bread, water, and wine are often considered sacred in early Jewish literature (cf. Odes Sol. 6:8–18; Wisd. 16:20).[165] In Joseph and Aseneth, there is mention of the bread of life, the blessed cup of immortality, and the ointment of incorruptibility in which Joseph is said to partake in contrast to the food and drink of the heathen (JosAsen 8:5; cf. John 6:35, 48).[166] The idea of consuming the bread of life is associated with the election of God's people and with entering into eternal "rest" (JosAsen 8:11 cf. 5:7; 22:13; Psa. 94[95]:11; Heb. 3:7ff). Aseneth is fed a supernatural honeycomb representing manna (16:7–8 cf. Exod. 16:14, 31), and this, she is told by an angel, is her participation in the sacred bread, cup, and ointment (15:5; 16:1–15; 19:5).[167]

The Qumran community's sacred meal consisted of bread and/or wine (e.g., 1QSa 2:17–21; 1QS 6:4–6). Black argues that the meal of the Qumran community resembles the Messianic banquet in certain Jewish traditions (Isa. 25:6f; 1 En. 60:7f, 24; 62:14; 4 Ezra 6:49–52; 2 Bar. 29:3–6 cf. Matt. 8:11–12; Rev. 19:9). The Messianic banquet motif may have been associated with the Show-

---

[162] NEYREY (1990), 122; cf. (1988), 180–85; DOUGLAS (1970), 79.

[163] NEYREY (1988), 178–83.

[164] Cf. WILLOUGHBY (1960), 71–75.

[165] D. SMITH (1991), 66. We should note that in early Jewish feasts and sabbaths, thanksgiving was offered to God, and the meals included bread and wine (KLAUCK, 66–67; MARSHALL, 1993:570).

[166] Cf. CHESNUTT (1995), 128–36.

[167] See C. Burchard's comments in *Pseud.* 2:190, 211–13i, f2; 228–29f, o. In Greek mythology, ambrosia serves a similar function as a food for the gods (cf. D. SMITH, 1991:65).

bread or Bread of the Presence in the Holy Place. Black suggests that Ezekiel 44:3 ff speaks of the messianic Prince entering the temple and eating the Bread of the Presence, and this idea perhaps influenced the Qumran sect in their anticipation of a future Messianic banquet and a foreshadowing of the Zadokite priesthood that operates a completed Temple rite.[168]

It is not entirely clear how mythological texts were related to ritual, and so we are left with surmises as to what extent a messianic banquet motif may be attributed to the early Lord's Supper traditions.[169] We may cautiously affirm that like the Qumran community, Paul and the Christian community saw themselves as participating in a meal related to a new covenant as a new people with an eschatological destination, and this apparently was derived from the Lord's Supper tradition Paul claims to have received ἀπὸ τοῦ κυρίου (1 Cor. 11:23 cf. Mat. 26:26 ff; Mark 14:22 f; Luke 22:19 f).[170] With respect to meat sacrificed to idols, Paul mentions a cup of blessing in relation to the Lord's Supper which perhaps is reminiscent of a Jewish tradition similar to Joseph and Aseneth (1 Cor. 10:16–17). He also infers an obtaining of eschatological rest which is connected with the eating and drinking of spiritual food and drink (9:25 f; 10:1–10).

Sahlin posits a connection between the Jewish *Pesach* celebration and the Lord's Supper in Paul (cf. 1 Cor. 5:7) and suggests that the non-recurrent act of baptism signifies the beginning of the new exodus for Christians while the eucharist points both backward to a remembrance of Christ and forward to a final eschatological goal. "The Eucharist is the viaticum of the pilgrims of the New Exodus and the antitype of the manna and water from the rock in the first Exodus (cp. 1 Cor. 10:3f., 16f.)."[171] This view seems to reflect Paul's own perspective here. The Corinthian congregation was to participate in the eucharist until Christ returns (1 Cor. 11:26); thus, Paul views this celebration in an eschatological setting which marks the beginning of the final era.[172]

The eucharistic antecedents we have examined provide us with a plausible reconstruction of the problem in Corinth by revealing an underlying association between sacred meals and eschatological motifs.[173] The imperfect ἔπινον ("they used to drink") in 10:4 might suggest that the Israelites customarily drank from their spiritual source until they reached the promised land. This tense might imply Paul's assumption that the Corinthians were to continue participating in the Lord's Supper until Christ returns (cf. 11:26). The problem

---

[168] BLACK, 105 f.

[169] Cf. D. SMITH, 72–73. He addresses the same difficulty in ascertaining the relation between myth and ritual in Dionysian meals (70–71).

[170] Cf. MARSHALL (1993), 572.

[171] SAHLIN, 93–94.

[172] Cf. FEE, 557.

[173] Cf. SUGGIT (1987), 11–24.

with the congregation's perspective was eschatological. Perhaps the Corinthians misinterpreted their consumption of the eucharist as confirming immortal life in the culmination of the eschaton. In this sense, they perceived themselves as being immune from any spiritual harm in the present age. This situation resurfaces again in 10:6, 11. Davidson rightly affirms that the natural/earthly food, drink, and rock point beyond themselves to a supernatural/heavenly reality: Christ is "the true Rock and Provider of both bread and water as gifts of grace which are supernatural/salvific/sacramental and at the same time advance presentations of the NT Lord's Supper."[174]

3.2 Food and Drink as Sacramental

If Paul is alluding to the Lord's supper by mentioning Israel's spiritual food and drink, the passage would appear to be sacramental, pointing to the grace which was given to Israel and, by implication, to the Corinthian congregation.[175] Gardner has recently challenged this view by arguing that the spiritual food, when summarised with other Israelite and Christian traditions, "was a *gift* of God and needed to be properly *understood*; it may have indicated the Spirit as the specific source."[176] This leads him to affirm that the spiritual food and drink in the wilderness are not sacramental in nature; they refer instead to God's gifts to God's covenantal people. The Corinthian congregation may have understood this as indicating verbal-revelatory spiritual gifts such as wisdom, knowledge, and prophecy.[177]

Gardner rightly notes an underlying theme in Isaiah 40–66: the Spirit is poured forth like water in the desert. The water in the desert becomes a picture for the gifts or blessings of the Spirit poured out upon the elect (e.g., Isa. 43:18–21; 44:3; 48:20–21; cf. 51:3).[178] However, if the sacramental aspect of this passage is denied, Gardner has not provided a persuasive reason why Paul is not anticipating a subject which he discusses in the very next pericope (10:16–22) and refers to again in greater detail: the Lord's Supper (1 Cor. 11:17–34). This problem is especially relevant because 10:3–4 and 10:16 share a similar construc-

---

[174] DAVIDSON (1981), 247.

[175] We should note how the use of the word "sacrament" implies grace because it theologically tends toward a eucharist that is something more than a commemorative meal (and a baptism that is more than a symbolic act). Whether this view is the case in our passage depends primarily on how one interprets πνευματικός. My use of grace centres on the act of God's delivering and sustaining Israel in the exodus/wilderness rather than the meal itself. Unless otherwise indicated, I am using the word sacrament in a general sense to mean a rite or ceremony which was instituted or recognised by Christ; the most common ones being the eucharist and water baptism.

[176] GARDNER, 142.

[177] GARDNER, 141–43.

[178] GARDNER, 128.

tion.[179] In addition, if the eucharist is being stressed instead of spiritual gifts, this lends more force to the consequences of disobedience to God in relation to sustenance in both the Israelite and Corinthian situations. For the Israelites, even though God gave them manna and quail, the food that was intended to sustain them through the wilderness turns out to destroy some of them because of their disobedience (Num. 11:4–10, 18–20, 31–34). In Corinth, Paul suggests that some died because of their impiety in the context of partaking of the eucharist (1 Cor. 11:27–30).[180] It may also be worth noting that in 10:3–4 Paul uses the word πνευματικός, not χάρισμα. Although the two words are somewhat interchangeable for Paul, the former term, which emphasises the spiritual (cf. 1 Cor. 12:1; 14:1), seems more general than the latter, which emphasises spiritual gifts (cf. 1 Cor. 1:7; 12:4, 9, 28–31).[181] More is at stake than spiritual gifts. Bandstra is accurate in claiming that the food and drink are intended as gifts of God which somehow convey "the saving work of God in Christ."[182]

Scholars have often maintained that Paul is demolishing the notion of "super-sacramentalism" that creates a sense of false security. Nigel Watson suggests that Paul's mentioning of "spiritual food and drink" is probably borrowed from the Corinthians' own language who perhaps boasted, "'We '...' have partaken [of] spiritual food and drink; therefore we are secure'."[183] If so, Paul's response is primarily rhetorical. Mitchell, however, stressing the factional aspect in Corinth, argues that Paul is not attacking a magical-sacramental misconception on the congregation's part. The sacramental language conveys Israel's solidarity at the beginning of their journey before factions divided them.[184] But as we

---

[179] Davidson astutely compares the "all" eating the "same" manna in 10:3 with the "all" eating the "now" bread in 10:16 (224).

[180] Whether Paul looks at death in 1 Corinthians 11 as falling away from grace has been an issue of debate. Engberg-Pedersen associates the Lord's Supper in 1 Corinthians 11:17–34 with a loss of salvation (1991:120, 123–24). Fee suggests (565–66), on the other hand, that in 11:32, those who were "chastised by the Lord" (κρινόμενοι δὲ ὑπὸ [τοῦ] κυρίου παιδευόμεθα) with sickness and death are chastised so that they would not be "condemned with the world" (σὺν τῷ κόσμῳ κατακριθῶμεν). It is not certain, however, whether Paul had in mind both death and sickness as particular examples of this chastisement. Paul is not dealing with precisely the same eucharistic situation in 1 Corinthians 10 as he is in chapter 11. Although both judgements can lead to physical death, in chapter 11, the judgement is a current event caused by improper social behaviour in a Christian gathering, and the judgement *prevents* Christians from suffering eschatological judgement. In 10:1–22 the potential judgement is found in the milieu of an idolatrous social setting and has severe eschatological ramifications (10:6, 11f cf. 9:25). Fee correctly recognises this distinction between the two chapters because he affirms that the judgement in 10:1–12 is associated with the loss of salvation, not merely chastisement (442, 459).

[181] Cf. FEE, 576. The "gift" (χάρισμα) reflects the root χάρις, meaning "grace."

[182] BANDSTRA, 10.

[183] N. WATSON (1992), 98; cf. KÄSEMANN (1964), 114; BORNKAMM, 147. On slogans in 1 Corinthians, see HURD (1965), 67.

[184] M. MITCHELL, 139, 251–52. While it is true that the sacraments imply a sense of unity, the factions which later threaten the Israelites in this context are not dependent on the obe-

have already observed, "immunity" through baptism is not as weak as Mitchell claims, and the Corinthians held to certain "magic" presuppositions in common with their contemporary environment in the first century. There is no reason to exclude categorically a Corinthian sacramental misconception for the sake of emphasising unity and discord.

The sacramental interpretation, however, does not overshadow the importance that election and conversion-initiation play in this passage; it is intended to complement it. Paul is affirming through the Israelites' experience that the Corinthian congregation had genuinely received the blessing of salvation in baptism. This is evident to him because they are all members of the body of Christ and are filled with the Spirit. They are God's elect just as the Israelites in the exodus were God's elect. Another identifying marker of this election is the provision of spiritual nourishment or "grace" which is given to both Israelite and Corinthian communities. For the Israelites, manna and water are given to them; for the Corinthians, it was bread and wine. Although Gundry Volf recognises some sacramental dimensions in 10:1–4, she interprets these as "external signs" and overlooks the salvific and elective aspects of the passage. This is perhaps the main reason why she misinterprets those who fall in 10:5–12 as "ungenuine recipients of the promise [of entering the promised land]."[185]

3.3 The Function of Πνευματικός

3.3.1 Interpretations of Πνευματικός

The nature of Paul's use of the term πνευματικός in 1 Corinthians 10:3–4 has been open to various interpretations. Wedderburn lists four major competing views on how the word has been interpreted in this passage: 1) the food and drink were made of or permeated by πνεῦμα; 2) they were given by the Spirit; 3) they mediated the Spirit to the participants; 4) they pointed to higher or more spiritual things.[186] He argues that position 1 may be too literal because it suggests the idea that those who ate and drank, ate and drank the spirit. The weakness of position 2 is that in the immediate passage, Christ, not the Spirit, is the giver of spiritual gifts. (Yet Wedderburn admits that the connection between Christ and the Spirit is so close that this distinction cannot be pressed – cf. 1 Cor. 15:45.) Position 4 is anachronistic for Wedderburn because it is doubtful that such a sense of πνευματικὸν was given to the Greek adjective in the time of Paul.[187] Wedderburn

---

dience of Israel in 10:1–4 as opposed to their disobedience in 10:5–10. Their solidarity finds its matrix in their experiences as an elect community.

[185] GUNDRY VOLF (1990), 125–27.

[186] WEDDERBURN (1987), 241–242.

[187] WEDDERBURN does note that the adverb πνευματικῶς may have been used this way (cf. Rev. 11:8), but this point is arguable (cf. SCHWEIZER *TDNT*, 6:449).

seems to think that position 3, which supports a sacramental view, is the most attractive. Ultimately he suggests, however, that the meaning of "spiritual" in 10:3–4 is either uncertain or that a combination of the positions (such as 2 and 3) might capture the meaning.[188] Paul does seem to think that πνευματικός refers to something or someone that is a conveyer of the Spirit (1 Cor. 9:11; 12:1; 14:1; 15:44; cf. Rom. 1:11; 7:14; 15:27),[189] but if this meaning is behind 10:3–4, the Spirit would be associated with two distinct symbols: the baptism in the cloud (10:2) and the sustenance in the wilderness (10:3f). As we have noted, Paul directly associates the Spirit with baptism, but a connection between the eucharist and the Spirit is not as direct.[190] Still this may be the best of Wedderburn's options, but it does not exhaust Paul's meaning of this polyvalent term.

Scholars have also suggested that, in this passage, πνευματικός may be interpreted as "miraculous" or "supernatural."[191] The connection between food and drink in the wilderness and the eucharist seems to be that both share a supernatural quality. Paul sets in contrast the natural/carnal and supernatural/spiritual in this letter (1 Cor. 9:11; 15:44 cf. Rom. 15:27).[192] This may suggest, like certain Jewish traditions, that the manna was of divine origin, or "heaven sent," perhaps giving a foretaste of heavenly blessings.[193] On the other hand, Paul does not seem to deny that the water and rock at Massah and Meribah were natural elements; in the Israelite traditions, these were rather used by God in a miraculous way. The same may be said of the quail, which are also mentioned as a food sent by God (Exod. 16:12–35). We have noted how baptism and the eucharist are connected with a sense of immunity in the eschatological age.

If Paul is connecting the heavenly/supernatural realm with the eschatological age of "now and not yet" (cf. ch. 4§7 below) – which is not to deny the present corrupt or "earthly" age – the tension of the πνευματικός would rest in

---

[188] WEDDERBURN, 245–47. Barrett's view is similar to the fusion of positions 3 and 4 (1971:222).

[189] Cf. BARRETT, 222.

[190] This is not to deny that the Spirit may in fact operate through the eucharist. GROSHEIDE (1953:220–21) notes that "In Paul's letters all manifestations of the grace of God in this sinful world are spiritual (*pneumatic*) since they are manifestations of the Holy Spirit" (cf. Gal. 4:29). Also, in 1 Corinthians 12:13, D. SMITH (1981:326–37) considers the metaphor of drinking as alluding to the sharing of a bowl of wine with perhaps the Christian eucharist in view (cf. Eph. 5:18).

[191] Cf. ROBERTSON and PLUMMER, 200; HÉRING, 78.

[192] Käsemann argues that Paul holds this in common with the Corinthians whose Hellenistic thinking contrasted spiritual and natural worlds (1964:115f).

[193] Josephus claims that the manna was "divine" and provided sustenance for Israel so that it was substituted for the want of other foods (*Ant.* 3.26–32). Philonic literature speaks of manna as spiritual food and heavenly nourishment is associated with the divine word and wisdom (*Fug.* 137–39 cf. *Leg. All.* 3.169–70). This aspect of manna is also in other traditions which sometimes call it the "food of angels" or the "bread of heaven" (Psa. 77[78]:24–25; cf. Exod. 16:4; John 6:31ff). See E. ELLIS (1993), 170.

the overlap of the old and new ages. The natural elements point to the super-natural or heavenly, just as the "now" points to "not yet." But here we might have expected Paul to use ἐπουράνιος (instead of πνευματικός) which in this letter stresses the eschatological dimension with greater precision (cf. 1 Cor. 15:40, 48). If Paul intended the spiritual to denote the supernatural/miraculous, he did not make his intention very clear. This may suggest that a better expla-nation lies elsewhere.

3.3.2 Πνευματικός *as Rhetoric*

Paul may be using πνευματικός in this context as part of his rhetorical scheme to correct a Corinthian misperception. Since the Corinthians thought them-selves "spiritual" – whether through wisdom or the excessive use of spiritual gifts (1 Cor. 2:6ff; 1 Cor. 12:7ff), through tongue speaking or the ecstatic (14:1ff), through their low regard for the physical body (1 Cor. 15:12ff), or some other way – Paul uses the term in a broad sense to persuade the Corinthians that the spirituality they received from the Lord, the Israelites also received. If this is the case, then choosing between precise definitions for πνευματικός is not an issue. The elements of supernatural, eschatological, and Spirit-conveyance may all be implied because Paul is essentially saying that regardless of which ways the Corinthians thought themselves *pneumatics*, the Israelites were like-wise *pneumatics*. Since the direct medium for πνευματικός in this text is food and drink, it is quite likely that the Corinthians believed their eucharistic cel-ebration was a medium for *their* spirituality. Despite any eschatological or "magical" perspective of their meal, Paul is implying that the Corinthians can-not claim any final sense of immunity/immortality in the present age.

A rhetorical reading of 1 Corinthians 10:3–4 suggests that this passage is best understood in terms of its function in the larger wilderness framework. Paul is attempting to convince the Corinthians that as Israel and the Corinthians share a common spirituality (10:1–4), they might also share a common fate (10:5ff). This theme is enhanced by the role food and drink play in the early wilderness traditions. The motifs of testing, God's miracles and Israel's idola-try and apostasy are not only present in 1 Corinthians 10:1–13, but they are also found in these traditions (cf. ch. 4:1.2.1 below).

3.4 Meal Sharing in Corinth

Before we close this passage we should attempt to understand it within the larger framework of 10:1–22 in order to surmise what it might say in relation to idolatry. A precursor to the warning which Paul later elaborates in 1 Corinthians 10 may be implied in 10:3–4. First, Paul uses the phrase τὸ αὐτό in reference to both the eating and drinking of the Israelites.[194] They all partook of *the same* spiritual food and *the same* spiritual drink. That the Israelites shared the *same* identity is understood by their partaking in the *same* spiritual meal. On Paul's use of the word "same," Barrett asserts, "Paul's point is probably that *all* the Israelites, good and bad, those who would be saved and those who would be rejected, enjoyed the *same* privileges."[195] Thus, all Israel enjoyed the same amount of special graces (cf. Rom. 9:4–5), but their privileges did not exempt them from God's judgement. Héring correctly answers why τὸ αὐτό stands before the food and drink in this passage: "Sans doute, parce que le sacrament de l'eucharistie exige l'identité de la nourriture pour tous les participants, peut-être aussi pour souligner que la majorité des rejetés a reçu exactement les mêmes privilèges que la petite minorité des sauvés."[196]

Meeks observes that Paul's anathema curse is placed in a eucharistic setting (1 Cor. 16:22; cf. Didache 10:6) and suggests that the sacred meals are considered a region that is under taboo, bringing disaster upon violators (1 Cor. 11:30). Since the *communitas* experienced in baptism ought to be visible in the Lord's Supper, Paul is creating a strong boundary by contrasting the eucharist with idol meats (1 Cor. 10:16–22).[197] The eucharist would perhaps indicate a liminal ritual regularly performed by the Corinthians, who according to Paul, will remain in this state until the completion of the eschaton (1 Cor. 11:26). The unity of fellowship in their sacred meals reinforced a sense of *communitas*; the Corinthians were to live in a state of solidarity, perpetually set apart on the margins of society.[198] Paul's implication seems to be that there should be no social distinction between the Corinthian strong and weak in relation to the sharing of the spiritual meal.

The meal sharing among members also reinforced their identity as the body of Christ. If they violated this sacred meal, they were not discerning their identity as the body of Christ (1 Cor. 11:29). As baptised members of an eschatological community who experienced the manifestation of the Spirit, some of the Corinthian members may have believed themselves exempt from judgement. Perhaps they deemed themselves immune to the possibility of falling away from their conversion experience through misperceptions about baptism,

---

[194] Regarding the omission of the two cases of αὐτό in the P-46 text of 10:3–4, I concur with Zuntz that the evidence is too weak to support the omission (64–66). The two cases of the omission receive divided support from other witnesses, and the stronger P-46/B combination does not support either case.

[195] BARRETT, 221–22. The word "same" probably should not be taken in a sense that the Israelites share the same food that the Corinthians eat. Paul is concerned with relating in a rhetorical manner his "same" language with his "all" language, which in the text refer to the Israelites and their experiences.

[196] HÉRING, 79.

[197] MEEKS (1983a), 150–59.

[198] Cf. MEEKS, 161.

the eucharist, and πνευματικός.[199] If so, it is plausible that Paul directs his rhetorical argument at this situation by comparing the Israelites' partaking of spiritual food and drink in the wilderness with the Corinthians' partaking of the Lord's Supper and manifestations. No one was exempt from these experiences; they all partook of the same manifestations. In theological terms, this notion would underscore that Paul believed the Corinthians were genuine Christians who were being sustained by God's grace. The ramifications of this are made clear in 10:5–13.

Conclusion

In 1 Corinthians 10:1–4 we have examined the way in which Paul attempts to compare the Corinthian congregation with the children of Israel in their entirety in terms of the exodus/wilderness narrative. All the Israelites participated in the spiritual experiences of the exodus/wilderness trek as covenant community members, and likewise, all the Corinthian congregation experience spiritual benefits as God's eschatologically elect people. As all the Israelites were initiated in the cloud and Red Sea with Moses as their leader, all the Corinthian congregation were initiated in the Spirit and water into a union with Christ. As all the Israelites enjoyed the same privileges of eating and drinking supernatural food and drink in the wilderness, so all the Corinthian congregation enjoy the same privileges and grace related to the Lord's Supper. In both communities Christ is the divine source of the spiritual sustenance.

Behind Paul's wilderness rhetoric, there lies an assumption drawn from a resource of ideas held in common with many cultures: a liminal or marginal state that is implicit through Israel's example in wilderness. Parallel to Israel's initiation-separation from Egypt through the Red Sea which ushered them into the wilderness, the Corinthian congregation's initiation into Christ has separated them from their pre-converted origins into a new era. The Israelites' initiation separated them from Egypt and became a boundary marker for the embarkation of their journey in the wilderness; similarly, the Corinthians' baptism-initiation separated them from the hostile *cosmos* and became a kind of entrance ritual into a new solidarity set on the margins of society in an ambiguous state of liminality. This is in keeping with certain Jewish assumptions of Paul's day that the people of the eschatological messianic era partake in a "new exodus."

As the children of Israel customarily ate manna and drank water throughout their journeying, so the Corinthians relive their new status by partaking of the Lord's Supper until Christ returns. Beasley-Murray observes that "baptism,

---

[199] Käsemann asserts, "the sacrament [eucharist] does *not* provide insurance against apostasy or against the divine rejection" (1964:117).

like the Lords' Supper, sets the believer between the two poles of redemption – the death and resurrection of Jesus and the future coming of Jesus."[200] Thus, we have observed in 10:1–4 that all the Corinthian congregation members have experienced a genuine conversion-initiation and election. Moreover, their new status was continually being reinforced by spiritual nourishment coming from Christ. We will now observe how this section sets up Paul to declare a strong warning beginning in 10:5.

---

[200] BEASLEY-MURRAY, *DPL*, 65.

Chapter 4

The Divine Judgements on the Wilderness Generation: Eschatological Prefigurations for the Corinthians

In 1 Corinthians 10:1–4 we have argued that Paul is making a comparison between Israel's election and grace received by God in the exodus/wilderness episode and that of the congregation in Corinth. He underscored the solidarity of Israel's experience by referring to their initiation through the cloud and Red Sea. It was through this shared initiation that all were enabled to experience further benefits in the wilderness. In 10:5–10, however, Paul continues his argument by claiming that the Israelites' privileges did not prevent some from being judged by God when they fell in the wilderness. God was not pleased with the majority of them; he judged them in the wilderness. The Corinthian congregation were to learn from the example of Israel so that they do not covet things which displease God. Paul then lists four vices that were displeasing to God: idolatry, fornication, tempting Christ, and grumbling. He draws on Israelite traditions, even citing one tradition in the case of idolatry. Some of the Israelites participated in each of these vices and were thus destroyed by God in the wilderness.

Since Paul alludes to a number of sources in his discussion, we shall attempt to uncover which he may be using and why Paul seems to merge certain wilderness traditions. If certain events in the wilderness *should* be read together, this would underscore the implication that the vices listed in this section were being committed by some in the Corinthian congregation. Paul would not be selecting examples arbitrarily; he would be targeting problems and potential consequences associated with the Corinthian situation. Hence, it is important that we attempt to shed light on Paul's original intent for appealing to these various tradition histories. A thorough analysis of 10:5–11 is thus in order. Moreover, we noted in the previous chapter the idea of separation in the Israelite initiation. As Israel now embarks on the trek through the wilderness, our attention will be drawn to the question of liminality and its relation to Paul's eschatological perspective because in 10:6 and 11 he identifies the Corinthians as the eschatological successors of the Israelites. These issues might be significant for understanding his outlook on apostasy, divine judgement, purity, and the boundary markers. They might also point to some possible eschatological misperceptions held by some of the Corinthian members.

1. God's Rejection of Israel in the Wilderness (1 Corinthians 10:5)

Paul begins the next section of his pericope with a sharp contrast to what preceded it: God was not pleased with the majority of them (ἀλλ' οὐκ ἐν τοῖς πλείοσιν αὐτῶν εὐδόκησεν ὁ θεός). In 1 Corinthians 10:5, "but" (ἀλλὰ) is set in contrast to the miraculous benefits which were previously mentioned. On a rhetorical level, this is highlighted by Paul's negative words "not with the majority of them" which contrasts the positive "all" (πάντες) language in the previous four verses of the passage.[1] Hence, what Paul writes in 1 Corinthians 10:5 is important. If 10:1–4 emphasised the election, initiation, and provision of Israel in the wilderness, 10:5 stresses their rejection and judgement. As we will observe below, these aspects suggest that apostasy rather than perseverance is now in view.

1.1 "All," "Many," and "Some" Wilderness Rhetoric

We have argued that all the Israelites participated in the separation-initiation experience through the cloud and sea, identifying with Moses their leader, and all had participated in the spiritual sustenance which came from Christ. Despite all this, Paul affirms that God rejected most of them because they lusted after evil things (10:5–6). The "many" Israelites are further broken down into units of "some of them" (τινες αὐτῶν) in verses 7–10. The "some" language is important because it exposes a contrast to the "all" language in 10:1–4. We may see in this discourse an aspect of Paul's view of Israel's election. "All" had been chosen by God to experience his grace and to enter the promised land, but "many" did not make it due to their desiring evil things.[2] "Some" fell by idolatry, "some" fell by fornication, "some" fell by testing Christ, and "some" fell by murmuring. Only a remnant of the original people of God made it through the journey. In the "all" language of 10:1–4, the corporate ideas of election and mutual experience reflect Paul's intent. In the "some" language of

---

[1] Moule argues that the article τοῖς before πλείοσιν should make the phrase read "the majority" rather than "the many" (*Idiom*:108). But either translation captures the meaning clearly enough. Only Joshua and Caleb were said to have survived from the older generation (Num. 14:30; 26:65). Schrage suggests that Paul's language here is an understatement. He asks if Paul is rhetorically attempting to avoid bringing discouragement (1995:396). It is possible, however, that Paul is taking into consideration the younger generation who also survived (Num. 1:46; 26:51ff).

[2] In later Jewish tradition Israel is elect as opposed to the Gentiles. All Israel had a share in the world to come, but only some Gentiles. Contrast Rabbi Eliezar's "All the nations have no share in the world to come" (Tos. Sanh. 13.2 cf. Mekilta 1.238–39; Psa. 9:17) with Rabbi Joshua's "There are righteous men among the nations who have a share in the world to come" (BT, Sanh. 601; cf. Mekilta Bahodesh 2.236; Roetzel, 1972: 59–60).

10:7–10, Paul begins to move away from his original ideas to smaller collective units. The original sense of solidarity is being replaced by partitions now that divine judgement is in view.

1.2 Divine Judgement in the Wilderness

1.2.1 God's Rejection of the Majority

In 10:5, despite the graces Israel received in the wilderness, Paul claims that God was "not pleased" (οὐκ … εὐδόκησεν) with the majority of them. This statement does not merely refer to God's displeasure with them; it refers to God's rejection of many Israelites which resulted in judgement and the forfeiture of their election.[3] The Israelites became God's elect "son" through the solidarity of experiences they shared during the exodus (Exod. 4:22; Deut. 1:31 cf. 4:34; 32:8–10; Hos. 11:1).[4] Paul continues using this language of election in 10:5. When God is the subject of εὐδοκέω or εὐδοκία, Paul normally has the idea of election in mind (Gal. 1:15; 2 Thes. 1:11; Phil. 2:13 cf. Eph. 1:5, 9, 11), and this is probably borrowed from Jewish traditions (LXX Isa. 42:1; Psa. 67:16; 2 Macc. 14:35). When the word is combined with οὐκ, as in 10:5, the concept of God's displeasure implies God's rejection (cf. Heb. 10:38; Hab. 2:4 LXX).[5] Regarding the situation in 1 Corinthians, Paul might be setting up a contrast between God's pleasure in saving those who believe (1:21) and his displeasure and rejection of the majority of his elect people (10:5).[6]

The wilderness traditions of Israel often share a theme in common with 10:5 ff: God rejects the Israelites because they rejected God. We have noted that the ancient Israelite traditions combine the motifs of God's miraculous sustaining of Israel and Israel's provocation of God (ch. 3:2.1 f). In the Deuteronomic tradition, the manna brings a deeper meaning to the Israelites' dependency on

---

[3] W. Willis rightly argues that the displeasure does not merely refer to God's unhappiness but to the withdrawal of the election of the majority. "The evidence of this loss is then given (γὰρ), 'for' they were destroyed in the desert" (1985:143). SCHRAGE (1995:396) writes, "Der Erwählung folgte jedenfalls paradoxerweise die Verwerfung. Großer Segen schützte nicht vor großem Fall (vgl. auch Hebr. 3,16 f)." In the wilderness rebellion in Psalm 77[78] George Coats writes that Israel's rejection is a reversing of their election (1968:220, 251).

[4] Mauser observes that Israel had two distinct election traditions: election through the patriarchs and through the exodus event (1963:28). Although the election of the patriarchs is logically prior to the exodus, it does not nullify the election motif of the latter. He responds: " While in the election of Abraham the nation which is to issue from him is already represented, it is not until the events of exodus that Israel as a whole is declared to be the elect of Yahweh." Mauser also notes that בחר is a prominent word in both Deuteronomy and Deutero-Isaiah. Both of these traditions are influential as sources for Paul in 1 Corinthians 10 (cf. ch. 3 above).

[5] Cf. SCHRENK, *TDNT* 2:739–47; CONZELMANN (1975), 167; W. WILLIS (1985), 143.

[6] Cf. GARDNER (1994), 149.

God. They travel through a waterless desert infested with snakes and scorpions. Yahweh warns Israel not to forget their God after they have enjoyed the blessings of the land of Canaan (cf. Deut. 8:2–3, 10–16).[7] If they abandon God and follow other gods, God would destroy them as he did the nations for Israel's sake (Deut. 8:19–20). God's warning about the Israelites forsaking God due to their blessings seems to become the basis for the Song of Moses, which Paul alludes to in 1 Corinthians 10 verses 4, 13, 20, and 22 (Deut. 32:17, 21; cf. ch. 5:3.2.1 below).

In other early traditions, the testings at Massah and Meribah are interpreted as a symbol for apostasy and rebellion in the presence of God and his miraculous power. The Israelites are not to harden their hearts as they did at Massah and Meribah when they tested God and failed to enter into his rest (Psa. 95:7–11; cf. Psa. 80LXX[81]:5–7, 11–12).[8] Psalm 77[78] depicts the miraculous way God delivered the Israelites from the Egyptians and how he fed them with manna, birds, and water from rocks in the desert (LXX 77:13–30). Yet despite these wonders, they still did not believe God (77:22, 32). They grieved God, and when he slew them, they returned to their Rock (MT 78:35, 40).[9] Another psalm claims the Israelites rebelled against the Spirit of God at Meribah (ἀντιλογίας), and when they entered the land of Canaan, they mingled with the nations, worshipped idols, and sacrificed their children to demons (Psa. 105[106]:32–37). Philo describes the mighty work of God sending quail for the Israelites to eat in the wilderness. Instead of being filled with piety, however, the Israelites lusted greedily for more and perished (*Spec. Leg.* 4.126–31). In 1 Corinthians 10:5, the same basic theme as these early wilderness traditions seems to appear: God rejected Israel in the wilderness because they rejected God. This might suggest that Paul's view of the desert was similar to that of many ancient Jews.

1.2.2 Wilderness as a Place

Paul follows the biblical traditions which place God's rejection of the majority of Israelites "in the desert" (ἐν τῇ ἐρήμῳ). The term "desert" (מדבר) depicts various images in Israel's traditions.[10] The wilderness is often associated with a sense of unprotection, barrenness, banishment, and perishing (Deut. 1:19, 31; 8:15; 32:10; Psa. 107:40; Jer. 17:5–6; 1 Kings 19:3ff; Job. 6:18; 12:24). There Hagar and Ishmael wandered in the desert and almost died of thirst until Yahweh

---

[7] Cf. Von Rad (1962), 1:282.

[8] In the MT, Psalm 95 mentions Massah and Meribah, but the LXX replaces this with παραπικρασμῷ. It may also be worth noting that John 6 may represent a similar development of the wilderness tradition combining manna in the desert with disobedience (cf. Gardner, 132–33; R. Brown, 1966:1.282–94).

[9] "Rock" is replaced by "God" in the LXX. In the LXX, the manna is called ἄρτον οὐρανοῦ and ἄρτον ἀγγέλων (77:24–25).

[10] For the geographical-spatial connotations of term, see Talmon (1966), 40–42.

helped them (Gen. 21:14ff). The psalmist writes that the life of the Israelites wasted away in the wilderness until they cried out to God who then made rivers in the desert and sustained them (Psa. 107:4–9, 35–38).[11] Wild animals and demons were thought to reside in the desert (Isa. 13:21–22; 34:11–15; Job 24:5; Lam. 4:3; Zeph. 2:14f; Tob. 8:3; Lev. 16:10ff cf. 1 En. 10:4).[12] Likewise, early Christian traditions portray the wilderness as a place which endangers the body (e.g., Heb. 11:38) and as an abode where wild animals and demons live (Mark 1:12–14; Matt. 12:43; Luke 8:29; cf. Rev. 18:2).[13] Paul no doubt thought about the desert in similar terms of negativity because this was where he himself suffered physical hardship (2 Cor. 11:26).

Shemaryahu Talmon notes that the wilderness is sometimes viewed as taking on a positive connotation of purity with regard to the "nomadic ideal" epitomised by the Rechabites (Jer. 35). Still, he argues that the older Israelite traditions originally and essentially consider the desert as a place of punishment and an unavoidable transitory stage to obtain Israel's ideal place as an organised society in its own land. The desert as a transitional period in the epoch of Israel's exodus prepares it "for the ultimate transfer from social and spiritual chaos to an integrated social and spiritual order. The 'trek in the desert' motif represents on the historical and eschatological level what 'creatio ex nihilo,' the transfer from chaos to cosmos, signifies on the cosmic level" (Gen. 1:2; cf. Psa. 68:7–10; 74:13f).[14] In cultural anthropological terms, this depiction of the wilderness could be seen as the archetype of liminality.[15]

A motif of re-creation in the wilderness emerges in some of the prophetic literature. The wilderness functions not only as a place of abandonment and punishment (e.g., Ezek. 20), but also as an eschatological location where God blesses the barren lands with new life as he transforms the wilderness into a paradise. At times this motif suggests the rejuvenation of the human heart through the spirit of God.[16] The re-creation of the wilderness is particularly emphasised in the Isaianic tradition which often depicts it as a new exodus (e.g., Isa. 35; 41:18f; 44:3f; cf. Ezek. 36). As Otto Böcher suggests, the hope of

---

[11] The LXX (Psa. 106:5) claims that they fainted for hunger and thirst.

[12] In Canaanite myth, Mot, god of the underworld, was also said to have lived in the wilderness (TALMON, 52; cf. Jacob, 1963:250–9).

[13] Cf. KITTEL, *TDNT* 2:657f; Str.-B. 4:516; AUNE, *ISBE* 1:919.

[14] TALMON, 37 cf. 31–36; MAUSER, 37, 43–44. Similarly, Brueggemann states that the wilderness is a "space far away from ordered land. It is Israel's historical entry into the arena of chaos which, like the darkness before creation, is 'formless and void' ..." (1978: 29).

[15] Cf. McVANN (1993), 16–17; TURNER (1969), 95.

[16] TALMON, 54–55. The tradition of Hosea emphasises a return to the wilderness and restoration under the imagery of a betrothal to a wayward woman (Hos. 2:14ff; 13:4f; 14:4f cf. Jer. 2). Talmon claims that this conception serves as a "*rite de passage*," which is a re-enactment of the punishment of national slavery to freedom by a covenant relationship with God. This results in the re-establishment of Israel as a bride in the promised land (50).

eschatological salvation was linked to desert imagery (Isa. 40:3; Jer. 31:2 LXX; Ezek. 34:25; Hos. 2:16–25).[17]

In the Community Rule there is a synthesis of the ideas of retreat and eschatology in the concept of the wilderness.[18] Apparently, the Qumran community had retreated into the desert as a renewed covenant people who had separated themselves from wicked men of deceit who were outside the community (cf. 1QS 8:13–16; 4Q171 3:1). As in the exodus/wilderness generation, the period of the Qumran group's reclusion amounted to 40 years before the wicked would be destroyed and the meek would inherit the earth in a new era (4Q171 2–3; CD 19.33–20.1; 20:13–15[8:21ff]). The way was being prepared in the wilderness for God during the transitional period (1QS 8:13–14; 9:19–20).[19] In Talmon's words, the community's retreat into the wilderness is their "hiatus between the 'historical' exodus from the Jewish society of their day, and the 'eschatological' conquest of Jerusalem and the Land of Israel, which lies ahead of them."[20] For the Qumran community, then, the wilderness was seen in terms of a purification which would culminate in the conquest of the land of Jerusalem wherein the Zadokite priesthood would be established forever. Eschatological preparation in the desert was a means to that end.[21] Although Paul may hold to a similar eschatological view of the desert (cf. §8), he considers it a dangerous place of testing and judgement, as we will observe in our text.

1.2.3 Corporate and Eschatological Judgement in Jewish Tradition

Roetzel defines judgement in the prophetic and priestly literature as indicative of moral seriousness, demonstrating that God, who is the ultimate judge, counsellor, and king of Israel, has the right to condemn and destroy based on his sovereign authority over creation. God preserves his righteousness in destroying both other nations and those in Israel who break God's covenant (e.g., Judges 5:11).[22] Roetzel claims that these writers, along with those from the apocalyptic tradition, emphasised the notions of corporate judgement and eschatology (1 En. 1:9; 5:6–10; 4 Ezra 7:46–61; Psa. Sol. 18:3–7). While Roetzel acknowledges some differences between apocalyptic literature and Paul on issues related to judgement,[23] he affirms that Paul shares motifs in common with

---

[17] BÖCHER, *NIDNTT* 3:1005.

[18] Philonic literature similarly views the wilderness as a place of separation for training where the air is pure (*Vit. Cont.* 22–23). The desert functions as a means to keep Israel away from the wickedness of city life (*De Decal.* 1.2; 2.10–13). This aspect of the wilderness is carried over by the early ascetic Christians (cf. DE PLANHOL, *ER* 4:304–305).

[19] Cf. KNIBB (1987), 73–74, 250; BETZ (1967), 89–107.

[20] TALMON, 57.

[21] TALMON, 63; cf. MAUSER, 58–61.

[22] ROETZEL, 15–17.

[23] For instance, the Jews in Paul's day believed that God's condemnation comes upon the

these traditions, such as the belief that divine wrath is a function of God's righteousness upon corporate entities (Jub. 36:10; 1 En. 103:5–7; cf. Rom. 1:17–3:20), the outpouring of God's wrath on the last Day (1 En. 91:7–8; cf. Rom. 2:5f), and God's forbearance in relation to the wicked (2 Bar. 59:6; cf. Rom. 2:3–5).[24]

Two observations are worth noting regarding the nature of judgement as described by Roetzel for our text. First, as we examine 1 Corinthians 10:5–11, we will notice the influence of Jewish apocalyptic thought on Paul. Allusions to the eschaton were already implied by Paul's metaphor of winning an eschatological crown at the end of a race (9:24f), and this concept of completing a course/journey arises again in his narrative of the wilderness. This suggests that Paul's examples in the wilderness should be interpreted eschatologically so that the divine punishments are eschatological judgements (cf. 8.1f below).

Second, the judgements related to the traditions which Paul seems to echo in 10:5–10 are corporate in nature. God threatens to annihilate Israel completely and raise up a new Israel through Moses (Exod. 32:9–10). At the instigation of the ten spies, the entire community murmured against Moses and was sentenced to 40 years in the wilderness (Num. 14). In Korah's rebellion, his very household and possessions were swallowed by the earth (Num. 16:31–33). The corporate nature of judgement in the Corinthian situation may be seen with Paul's "all" and "some" language. Whereas 10:1–4 stressed the solidarity of experience, 10:5–10 focuses on the diversities of judgement. Paul stresses the corporate nature of judgement by emphasising the large number of Israelites who were killed (10:8), but the solidarity is now broken down under various groups of "some." On the one hand, Paul does not seem to infer that those who did not participate in the vices would necessarily suffer the same judgement as those who did. On the other hand, it seems that the individual participants of the vices were able to wield enough influence to gather a following. In the Corinthian correspondence, the tension between individual and corporate wrongdoing is discernible when Paul advises that the sexual offender be cast out of the congregation before he contaminates other members (1 Cor. 5:5–7).

1.2.4 Judgement in the Wilderness Traditions

We have observed the potential corporate and eschatological nature of 10:5–11. What specific points might our passage share in common with early Jewish traditions regarding the motif of wilderness as a place of judgement? The Damascus document speaks of males who were cut off in the wilderness due to the

---

Gentiles and apostate Jews. For Paul, however, judgement looms against those "outside" the church but it also impinges upon those "inside" (cf. 1 Cor. 5). Cf. Roetzel, 179.

[24] Roetzel, 66, 80–82. See also Synofzik (1977); N. Watson (1983), 209–221; Donfried (1976), 90–110.

Kadesh-Barnea episode where the Israelites murmured in their tents and did not pay attention to God's voice or the commands of their teacher (CD 3:6–10). They forsook the covenant to follow their own will; hence, God raised up a remnant and made an everlasting covenant with them (CD 3.11ff).[25] The Psalm tradition offers variant pictures of the exodus/wilderness motif, either stressing the goodness of God in his miraculous provisions for Israel (Psa. 66; 68; 105; 107; 114; 136), or affirming the rebellion and judgement of the Israelites who despised God's benevolence (Psa. 78; 95; 106). Paul adapts these same themes of grace/provision and rebellion/judgement in his narrative (1 Cor. 10:1–4 provision; 10:5–10 judgement).[26]

In the Deuteronomic tradition, the wilderness trek is understood in terms of election and utter dependency on Yahweh (e.g., Deut. 8:2–3). We observe the paraenetic nature of the tradition in its tendency to call the Israelites to remember their dependency on Yahweh, or else they might abandon God after they have experienced the goodness of the promised land (Deut. chs. 8; 31–32). The tradition recollects the rebellious behaviour of Israel in Massah, Taberah, and Kibroth-Hattaavah (Deut. 6:16; 9:22), but it stresses the rebellions at Kadesh-Barnea (1:26–46; 9:25f) and the golden calf incident (9:7–21). Paul seems to allude to at least the latter three in 1 Corinthians 10:5–10 (see *ad. loc.*). The Deuteronomic tradition, however, only recollects the events found in the Numbers and Exodus traditions.

The largest number of wilderness judgements appear in the Numbers tradition. The sin of grumbling in Taberah ("burning") is the first of a series of passages which focuses on the theme of divine punishment by death. In this particular case God consumes the murmurers by fire until Moses intercedes for them (Num. 11:1f). In the following episode at Kibroth Hattaavah ("grave of lust"), God sends a plague on the Israelites after they lusted for the food they once ate in Egypt (11:4–6, 31–35). After this episode Miriam and Aaron grumbled against Moses' authority, and God strikes Miriam with leprosy (Num. 12), but both she and Aaron escape death. In Kadesh, ten of the twelve spies gave a negative report concerning the land of Canaan, and because of this the Israelites begin to grumble. God threatens to destroy them all, but Moses intercedes for them. God then declares that those over 20 years of age would eventually die in the wilderness and their children would inherit the land. (God also kills the instigators by plague.) After this, the Israelites attempt to take over the promised land without Yahweh's intervention and are defeated in battle (Num. 13–14).

---

[25] Other traditions about Kadesh-Barnea emphasise Israel's rebellion and murmuring (Deut. 9:23; Psa. 105[106]:24f; Josephus *Ant.* 4:306–16).

[26] Similarly, the writer of Revelation apparently picks up these themes (Rev. 12 provision; Rev. 17–18 judgement).

In the subsequent narrative, a Sabbath violator is stoned to death (Num. 15:32–36); and this is followed by an account of Korah's rebellion against Moses. God consumes 250 men by fire while others are swallowed by the earth (Num. 16:1–35). Immediately after these judgements, the Israelites grumble against Moses, claiming that he had killed Yahweh's elect. God then sends another plague which kills 14,700 until Aaron offers up incense to atone for Israel's sin (Num. 16:41–50). At Meribah ("quarrelling") the Israelites grumble against Moses and Aaron because of thirst, and Moses disobeys God's direction to the extent that he is denied access to the promised land (20:1–13). After Aaron dies, the Israelites grumble because of the manna, and so Yahweh kills many of them by sending venomous snakes to bite them. Consequently, Moses places a bronze serpent on a pole which heals those who look upon it (Num. 21:4–9). Finally, when the Israelites commit fornication and idolatry with the women of Moab at Baal Peor, God commands Moses to kill the leaders, and Phineas stops a plague by thrusting a spear through a Simeonite leader (Num. 25). The plague kills 24,000.[27]

Several patterns emerge from these wilderness accounts in Numbers. First, judgement by death is almost always the inevitable consequence of the Israel's sins. The Exodus tradition stands in contrast to this. With the exception of the golden calf incident (Exod. 32), none of the Israelite rebellions – which often centre upon the notions of eating, drinking, and grumbling – result in punishment by death (Exod. 14:10–12; 15:22–27; 16:1–4, 19–20, 27–30; 17:1–4). Second, some type of intercession or atonement was necessary to put an end to the judgements. Moses intercedes in the Kadesh incident, and in the Korah rebellion Aaron atones through incense. At Baal Peor, Phineas atones for the sins of the people.[28] Third, the judgements often take on the binary notion of cursing and blessing which is frequently manifested by means of the same instrument – that which was once a blessing now becomes a curse or vice versa (see 8.5.2 below).[29] The miraculous provision of quail, for instance, results in death by a plague; the serpents' bite, which causes death, is healed by looking at a bronze serpent. Fourth, the leaders of the community were not exempt from punishment. The tribal spies, Korah, and Zimri the Simeonite are punished by death due to their respective rebellions. Finally, grumbling is the most pervasive vice which permeates these accounts.

---

[27] Apparently the Numbers tradition implies that a number of Simeonites were killed in this plague. At the beginning of the 40 years, their number totalled 59,300, by the end of it their number dwindled to only 22,200 (Num. 1:23 cf. 26:14).

[28] In Psalm 105[106] the psalmist observes this aspect by having Moses as the former intercessor and Phineas as the latter (105[106]:23, 30).

[29] The entire wilderness journey might be seen in this light if we accept Brueggemann's statement: "The wilderness is either the way to the land or the way to death" (39).

Paul evidently picks up on some of the themes underlined by his Jewish predecessors. As we will observe, the vices in 1 Corinthians 10:7–10 are related to incidents of apostasy through eating and drinking, and the vices result in judgement by death. Related to this are the notions of grace and judgement which seem to be played off against each other when the blessing motif of eating and drinking in 10:3–4 becomes a curse in 10:7–10. Paul may be contrasting two spheres of eating: the spiritual nourishment provided through the Lord's Supper and the spiritual contamination that could result from idol meats (cf. 1 Cor. 10:16–22). As well, it appears to be more than coincidental that Paul lists "grumbling" as one of the vices in 10:7–10. Like the Kadesh and the Korah incidents, the grumblings were sometimes instigated by the influential people in the community against Moses. Perhaps Paul is indirectly suggesting that some of the "strong" in Corinth are rebelling against his own authority. Paul may have noticed a Corinthian parallel in the Kadesh judgement: the "weak" children inherit the land instead of the "strong" adults.[30] He also echoes the same judgement, as we will examine below.

1.2.5 Κατεστρώθησαν

Paul's reference to the Israelites being scattered abroad in the wilderness (κατεστρώθησαν γὰρ ἐν τῇ ἐρήμῳ) follows closely Numbers 14:16 (LXX) where Moses intercedes on behalf of Israel at the Kadesh grumbling. He pleads that Yahweh would not destroy Israel or else the other nations will claim that God could not bring the Israelites into the promised land and therefore "overthrew them in the wilderness." The word καταστρώννυμι (commonly understood as to "slay" "overthrow" or "spread about") also follows closely the conception of judgement in Numbers 14:29, 32 even though the word itself does not appear in these verses. These verses relate how God would cause the bodies of the Israelites to fall in the wilderness. The word seldom appears in the Septuagint, but when it does, it normally carries a special kind of killing. In the Judith narrative, the Edomites and Moabites conspire with Holophernes of Assyria to overtake Israel by famine so that Israels corpses would be "strewn out" (κατεστροθήσονται) in their streets (Jud. 7:14 cf. v. 25; 14:4). In the Maccabees tradition, Antiochus slew (κατέστρωσε) great multitudes of Jews (2 Macc. 5:26A), and the Maccabeus brothers slew 11,000 foot-soldiers and 16,000 horseman on one occasion (2 Macc. 11:11), 25,000 soldiers on another (12:28), and 35,000 on yet another (15:27). Hence, the word normally stands in relation to a destroying of human life in large quantities. When God is the subject of the slaying, the word combines mass slaying with a judicial connotation (cf. Job 12:23).[31] A divine massacre or slaughter might capture the intended meaning.

---

[30] Cf. BRUEGGEMANN, 38–39.
[31] Cf. ELLICOTT (1887), 176.

Perhaps Paul employs the word because of its use in these traditions. The deaths he describes in 1 Corinthians 10:5–10 are in massive proportions. The huge numbers would relate to his statement that the majority of Israelites did not make it to the promised land. Rhetorically, the large numbers are intended to discourage the Corinthians from participating in the activities condemned in 10:5–10.[32]

We noted that Paul very likely views judgement in the wilderness eschatologically. This perspective has implications for the notion of the desert itself. Like the Qumran community, Paul seems to consider the desert as a penultimate destination whereby the elect of God must be prepared and purified before entering Canaan. He combines the aspects of conversion-initiation, transition-transformation, and the eschaton all in the imagery of the Israelite wilderness trek. It is evident that Paul believed in an initiation which freed a person from eschatological wrath (1 Cor. 6:9–11; Col. 3:3–4; 1 Thes. 1:10 cf. Luke 3:7, 16–17).[33] In terms of the Israelites' initiation imagery in the wilderness, a successful journey through the wilderness would then imply the inheritance of an eschatological reward. Failure to finish the journey would imply an eschatological loss.

Grosheide is almost certainly wrong when he argues that some of God's covenant people do not share in God's blessings and that Paul does not speak of a loss of regeneration in this passage.[34] His observation overlooks Paul's repetitive use of inclusive language in reference to "all" Israel partaking of the blessings of God (10:1–4), and some of these are clearly connected to redemptive metaphors implying grace, election, baptism and conversion-initiation. This makes Grosheide's following argument rather meaningless, namely that Paul is here only referring to the "outward manifestation" of blessings and life.[35] Likewise, Gundry Volf incorrectly claims that 10:5 refers to the rejection of those "not chosen" to enter the promised land. Instead of deriving an interpretation through the immediate context, she maintains this view because of her interpretation of unconditional election which she finds in Paul's letter to the Romans.[36] For Paul, conversion-initiation in 10:1–2 is not merely a symbolic gesture; it represents an actual transference of ownership into the person of Christ (cf. ch. 3 above). The whole person comes to Christ and is considered a member of the body of Christ, conjoined by Christ's Spirit. This work is both external and

---

[32] GODET (1887.2:59–60) comes close to Paul's intention here: "What a spectacle is that which is called up by the apostle before the eyes of the self-satisfied Corinthians: all those bodies, sated with miraculous food and drink, strewing the soil of the desert!"

[33] For divine judgement in reference to baptism, see MOULE (1956), 464–81.

[34] GROSHEIDE (1953), 222.

[35] Ibid.

[36] GUNDRY VOLF (1990), 126. I have already argued that the Corinthian letter should be interpreted in light of its *own* particular situation and not that of Romans (cf. ch. 1:1.3.3–1.4 above).

internal, related to the "all" who participate in it (e.g., 1 Cor. 12:13; Rom. 8:9–11).[37] Since the election is genuine in 10:1–4, it follows that the rejection is just as real in 10:5. Some of the children of Israel, who were delivered and initiated through the exodus event, were later destroyed in the wilderness when they lusted after the things of their pre-redemption. There is an implicit warning here in 10:5 to the Corinthian congregation. Although they were initiated in the Spirit and water baptism, some of them could incur divine rejection if they crave after things associated with their life prior to their conversion-initiation.

2. Types: That the Corinthians Would Not Lust After Evil Things (1 Corinthians 10:6)

If 1 Corinthians 10:5 introduces Paul's contrast between Israel's election and apostasy, in 10:6–11 he begins to formulate more clearly how these concepts pertain to the Corinthian congregation members. Verses 6 and 11 form an *inclusio*, apparently created by Paul to heighten the intensity of his warning: the things which happened to Israel in the wilderness are types for the Corinthians not to follow. We will notice that the vices Israel committed are very similar to the ones some of the Corinthian Christians were committing. All these vices may be associated with Paul's discourse on meat sacrificed to idols.

2.1 Chiasm and Ταῦτα Δὲ

Beginning in 10:6 Paul relates how the things that happened to the Israelites in the wilderness are set as examples for the Corinthians. In this verse, he appears to be stressing the importance of this similarity by implementing a chiasm which ends in 10:11. After beginning 10:6 with "now these things" (ταῦτα δὲ), Paul continues to persuade his readers by using "neither" (μηδὲ) followed by a second person plural imperative in verse 7. In verses 8–9 he uses two hortatory subjunctives ("let us not") followed by another second person plural imperative to complete an ABC–CBA pattern which forms a complete *inclusio* ending with the second "now these things" in verse 11:[38]

---

[37] W. Willis, affirming Grosheide on this point (cf. 142–43 ftn88), drives a wedge between personal salvation and the corporate people of God. This bifurcation is unhelpful given that Paul depicts election *and* initiation in a corporate sense in 10:1–5, and this has ramifications for the conversion-initiation language Paul uses in this passage. The question of apostasy and perseverance on an individual level will become more evident in 10:12–13.

[38] Cf. COLLIER (1994), 60–61.

A: 10.6 ταῦτα δὲ τύποι ἡμῶν ἐγενήθησαν
εἰς τὸ μὴ εἶναι ἡμᾶς ἐπιθυμητὰς κακῶν καθὼς κἀκεῖνοι ἐπεθύμησαν
  B: 10.7 μηδὲ εἰδωλολάτραι γίνεσθε
  καθώς τινες αὐτῶν
  ὥσπερ γέγραπται ᾿Εκάθισεν ὁ λαὸς φαγεῖν καὶ πεῖν καὶ ἀνέστησαν
  παίζειν
    C: 10.8 μηδὲ πορνεύωμεν
    καθώς τινες αὐτῶν ἐπόρνευσαν
    καὶ ἔπεσαν μιᾷ ἡμέρᾳ εἴκοσι τρεῖς χιλιάδες
    C: 10.9 μηδὲ ἐκπειράζωμεν τὸν Χριστόν
    καθώς τινες αὐτῶν ἐπείρασαν
    καὶ ὑπὸ τῶν ὄφεων ἀπώλλυντο
  B: 10.10 μηδὲ γογγύζετε
  καθάπερ τινὲς αὐτῶν ἐγόγγυσαν
  καὶ ἀπώλοντο ὑπὸ τοῦ ὀλοθρευτοῦ
A: 10.11 ταῦτα δὲ τυπικῶς συνέβαινεν ἐκείνοις
ἐγράφη δὲ πρὸς νουθεσίαν ἡμῶν
εἰς οὓς τὰ τέλη τῶν αἰώνων κατήντηκεν

A few observations about Paul's argument are in order. Paul opens and closes his examples with a note on how "these things" pertain to the Corinthians (10:6, 11). The examples are derived primarily from the mistakes of the Israelites in the wilderness; hence, these are negative examples for the Corinthians *not* to follow.[39] This is made evident by the negative purpose clause εἰς τὸ μὴ εἶναι ἡμᾶς ἐπιθυμητὰς, where Paul ventures to include himself in the exhortation with ἡμᾶς and the ἡμῶν which preceded it.[40] The opening (10:6) names the vice of lusting, but in contrast to the other vices, it is set apart as the only vice on the A level of the chiasm. It does not follow the structural pattern of the other vices listed on the B and C levels. This difference may have implications for the way coveting was intended to be interpreted (cf. 2.5 below). Another observation is that all the references to the wilderness were intended as allusions to Israel's tradition; the only clear exception is 10:7 which is directly cited from Exodus 32:6. Finally, each of the four vices in 10:7–10 are comprised of three components: 1) a negative exhortation for the Corinthians not to follow; 2) an indica-

---

[39] However, I do not wish to deny that 10:6 points back to the events in 10:1–5, which are primarily positive examples. But even in retrospect, the events in 10:1–5 finish on a negative note: the Israelites were rejected by God, and this appears to be what is emphasised in verse 6. Moreover, Paul did not relate the events in 10:1–4 as examples for the Corinthians to follow but as examples that they had *already* been following.

[40] FEE (1987:452) notes that Paul's "we" stems from using himself as an exemplary model in 9:24–27. This may be true of 10:6, but it is more difficult to ascertain Paul's first person plurals in 10:8–9. They do not seem to indicate that Paul felt himself more capable of falling in the areas of fornication and tempting Christ than in idolatry or grumbling. Apparently, their primary function is to serve as a production of Paul's chiasm. At any rate, 9:24–27 indicates that Paul did not consider himself exempt from falling short of his own eschatological aim.

tion that "some" in Israel committed the vice which the Corinthians are to avoid (καθώς τινες αὐτῶν); and 3) a description of divine judgement against those who committed the vice.[41]

The chiasm may not only have served as a symmetrical memory aid but also as a rhetorical enhancement for Paul's argument. The repetitive patterns would tend to emphasise the importance of the content with perhaps a special stress on the opening and closing sentences (10:6, 11). The examples in the wilderness are important in this pericope because they are examples for the Christians in Corinth.

2.2 Τύπος

The τύποι – τυπικῶς word group is found in 10:6 and 11. It functions to underscore a correspondence between the Corinthian congregation's activities and the events which Israel experienced in the wilderness.[42] We find similar wording in Romans 15:4 (ὅσα γὰρ προεγράφη εἰς τὴν ἡμετέραν διδασκαλίαν ἐγράφη), which is located in a similar context where eating food which offends weaker Christians is at stake (Rom. 14:1–15:4). Here Paul cites early Jewish tradition (Psa. 68:9 LXX) as an example for the Christians' instruction. This idea would be in conformity with the majority of references in Pauline literature that use the word τύπος (2 Thes. 3:9; 1 Tim. 4:12; Tit. 2:7). Some would thus suggest that Paul is merely interpreting τύπος as "example" or "warning" in 1 Corinthians 10:6.[43]

On the other hand, beginning with Paul's use of "our fathers" in 10:1, Goppelt argues for a definite connection between the Israelites as the first *Gottesvolk* and the Corinthians as the latter *Gottesvolk* for whom the "end of the ages has come" (10:11). He affirms that "τύπος bedeutet hier nicht wie sonst verschiedentlich bei Paulus vorbildliches Beispiel im allgemeinen Sinn; sondern heilsgeschichtliche Vorausdarstellung des Kommenden."[44] Goppelt recognises a redemptive history that begins with Israel and finds its fulfilment in the eschatological character of the Christ-event, and thus it has ramifications for the witnesses of Christ. Paul would see himself along with the Corinthians as the *actual* fulfilment of the historically elect people of God (1 Cor. 10:11; Rom. 4:23f; Gal. 4:4).[45] In similar

---

[41] Although verse 7 omits this third aspect, a judgement may be implied (see *ad loc.*).

[42] For the etymology of τύπος and its hermeneutical development see R. DAVIDSON (1981), 15–190.

[43] E.g., BARRETT (1971), 223, 226f; YOUNG (1994), 37–38. Young presents the "example" interpretation with hesitancy but affirms it may be correct if "our reading were not affected by typological assumptions."

[44] GOPPELT, (1969), 176.

[45] GOPPELT (1966), 33–34, 37; cf. E. ELLIS (1957b), 127; CARREZ (1971), 87–88; HAYS (1989), 121. Wolff affirms a Vorausdarstellung reading and writes that in this passage,

terms, Feuillet writes, "ici il est clair qu'il [Paul] entend prendre son point d'appui en des événements réels de l'histoire d'Israël, mais il les exploite comme des préfigurations de la religion du Christ."[46] In essence, this position asserts that it is not enough to affirm τύπος merely as an example in 1 Corinthians 10 when Paul is making the Corinthians the eschatological people of God who now partake in the election of the Israelites of old.[47]

Davidson is correct in affirming the events in 10:1ff as advance presentations, but he may be going too far by utilising Martelet's aspect of "devoir-être" ("must-needs-be") to argue that the pre-presentation or "type" *demands* a kind of inherent cause-effect fulfilment in the presentation or "anti-type".[48] More likely, Paul saw a correspondence of Israelite events to the Corinthian situation *post facto.*[49] The information Paul gives to the Corinthians was new information (10:1). Bandstra points out the two basic positions which we have already noted: 1) the "paraenetic" correlation which interprets this passage as a "pattern," "warning," or "example" (cf. 1 Thes. 1:7; Phl. 3:17), and 2) the "pre-representation" (*Vorausdarstellung*) model which interprets this passage as a hermeneutic type (cf. Rom 5:14). He suggests a view somewhere in between these poles, opting for a "hypothetical type" which indicates the possibility of fulfilment of disaster.[50]

Bandstra is correct in pointing out a middle option between the two poles. It may not be adequate to understand τύποι merely as "examples" or "warnings." Paul seems to believe there is some sense of a correspondence in history; the way God worked with Israel prefigures the way God works through the Corinthian congregation. On the other hand, Paul is not interpreting the type as someone/something proleptically pointing to its more significant fulfillment in an ultimate or inevitable sense. If so, the rock in 10:4 would not be the pre-existing Christ but a "Christ-type." As well, the judgements Israel experienced in the wilderness would find a greater fulfilment among the Corinthian Christians. Indeed, similar judgements *can* occur upon the Corinthians, but they do not necessarily need to. If "type" is only to be understood in a strictly hermeneutic or *Vorausdarstellung* sense in 1 Corinthians 10:1–13, there would be no need

---

"Wüstenzeit und Heilszeit entsprechen einander" (1982:43). Goppelt adds, "Alttestamentliches wie neutestamentiches Handeln Gottes auf das Heil hin ereignet sich für Paulus nicht zufällig, sondern *seinem Wesen nach in und durch Geschichte*" (37). The importance of church prefiguration should not be underestimated, yet we should note that what is foremost in the prefiguration of 10:6, 11 are ταῦτα – "these things" which happened to Israel in the wilderness, not Israel *per se.*

[46] FEUILLET (1966), 87.

[47] For examples of ancient Jewish prefigurations, see GOPPELT, *TDNT* 8:253–55.

[48] R. DAVIDSON, 223, 251ff, 266–69; cf. MARTELET (1956), 527–31.

[49] Cf. FEE, 444ftn10 cf. 458ftn39.

[50] BANDSTRA (1971), 15–16; cf. HÉRING (1949:80): "Les 'types' indiquent seulement la possibilité de pareilles catastrophes. Elles ne se réaliseront que si les chrétiens désobéissent et commettent certains péchés graves à la manière de leurs ancêtres spirituels."

for Paul to admonish the Corinthians about what is inevitable – they *must* fulfil the examples.[51] But Paul is primarily giving these examples as warnings to the Corinthians, hoping that the judgements will *not* take place in their community. Thus, if one wishes to affirm that Paul is employing a "type," one's definition should also take into consideration the freedom the Corinthians have in deciding to choose *not* to fulfil the "anti-type."

Michael Fishbane draws attention to various typologies in ancient Jewish literature, including: 1) cosmological correlations, 2) historical correlations, 3) spatial correlations, and 4) biographical correlations.[52] Space does not permit an overview of these typologies; we will focus on number 2 alone because of its relevance to our passage. In historical correlations, the exodus *traditum* was regularly being transformed into a variety of new exodus *traditios* (cf. Isa. 19:19–20; 43:16–21; Ezek. 20). For Fishbane, the historical type serves "as the means whereby the deeper dimensions perceived to be latent in historical events are rendered manifest and explicit to the cultural imagination."[53] Fishbane's examples help us recognise the diverse nature of early types.[54] It would seem that Paul's exodus/wilderness account falls under the category of historical correlations employing a Christian *traditio* from the exodus/wilderness *traditum*. Apparently, in Paul's day, there was enough flexibility in the way prefigurations were interpreted that he could create his own point of departure by combining types (10:1–4a), hypothetical types (10:5–11), and Christ as an actual figure who pervades the communities of both the "anti-type" and its fulfilment (10:4b cf. 9a). Hermeneutic typology, if it existed in Paul's day, seemed to be in its early developmental stage.[55]

In 10:1–13, then, we might wish to suggest that τύπος is to be understood primarily as "hypothetical prefigurations" for lack of a better term. Until a better word arises, we may leave the translation as "types" provided we understand that this does not impinge upon Paul's view that Christ is ontologically present in the blessing prefigurations, in the hypothetical warnings, and in the situation of the Corinthian congregation to which these τύποι point. Perhaps the most important aspect of τύποι for this study is that it affirms in no uncertain terms a close correlation between the Israelites in the wilderness and the Christians in Paul's era. As God rejected many of the Israelites in the wilderness, God could also reject many of the Corinthian Christians.

---

[51] On this point see A. T. Hanson (1965), 23–24, but note how Hanson opts for the "warning example" interpretation thus mitigating the facet of 1 Corinthians 10:6 which looks back to 10:1–4 where no warning is implied.

[52] Fishbane (1985), 353ff.

[53] Fishbane, 360 cf. 364–68.

[54] Cf. Young (1994), 39f.

[55] Cf. W. Willis, 160.

2.3 Midrash and Paul's Wilderness Account

We have noticed that the vices Paul mentions in 10:6–11 follow a particular pattern; hence, the question arises as to why these particular vices are mentioned. Is there a central motif or vice in the chiasm? Did Paul create this section or did he borrow it from an already extant homily or midrash which coincidentally strings together traditional elements relevant to the situation in 1 Corinthians 8–10? These questions are important if we are to assess the nature of these vices in their larger context.

Meeks argues that 1 Corinthians 10:1–13 was a Christian midrash composed prior to its present form in the Corinthian setting.[56] The central source behind Paul's passage is the quotation from Exodus 32:6 (1 Cor. 10:7). The phrase "sat down to eat and drink" suggests the spiritual food in 1 Corinthians 10:1–4, and the phrase "rose up to play" relates to the five vices which follow in 10:6–10. For Meeks, four of the vices (idolatry, fornication, testing Christ, and grumbling) are related to the Jewish definitions of παίζειν among the rabbis and the Septuagint, while the first vice ("lusting after evil things") is reflected by an understanding of the golden calf incident as found in Philo (*Mos.* 2.162 cf. *Spec. Leg.* 3.125f; *Ebr.* 95; *Fug.* 90).[57]

Gary Collier argues instead that Numbers 11, along with Exodus 32:6, is the main text of the passage. The former is the "midrashic basis" of the passage with "lusting after evil things" as the main theme (1 Cor. 10:6). The vices that follow illustrate this theme and are "midrashically derived by way of Exod. 32.6, not on the basis of παίζειν alone (Meeks), if at all, but primarily on the basis of the phrase, Ἐκάθισεν ὁ λαὸς φαγεῖν καὶ πεῖν."[58] Collier's insights uncover the importance of Numbers 11 for our passage, and they underscore the importance of the theme of eating and drinking in the text. Perhaps Paul intended ἐπιθυμία in verse 6 as a general reference for the vices which follow (cf. 2.5 below).

---

[56] MEEKS (1982), 65–66. The term "Midrash" ("to seek") is rather ambiguous. A "midrash" often can be used in a general sense to mean "interpretation," but when capitalised, it can refer to a type of Jewish literature consisting of various scriptural expositions with the emphasis lying in the creative exegetical application of the text rather than the original meaning. Jewish writers often list 7 rules for interpreting Midrash, but longer lists contain 32. For the shorter list, see Snodgrass, (1991), 421; for the longer list, see Strack (1963), 93–98. The precise nature of midrashic hermeneutics in Paul's day remains questionable since the rules are commonly derived from sources later than the first century C. E. (cf. SILVA, *DPL*, 637–38). Neusner defines three meanings for midrash: 1) a process of interpretation of a text (an hermeneutic); 2) a compilation of the results of the process (a book); 3) an exegetical composition on a unit of the process. He concludes that the word "Midrash" bears no meaning when it stands alone (1994:223–24). Meeks is using the term as a pre-Pauline "homily" or "literary unit" (1982:65ff).

[57] MEEKS (1982), 69–71.

[58] COLLIER (1994), 63.

That Paul is borrowing from a previous midrashic source or homily, how-ever, is not ultimately convincing. The Exodus and Numbers traditions defi-nitely appear in 1 Corinthians 10:5–10, but when they are placed under the entire rubric of 10:1–13, Paul is borrowing from several detectable sources including Deuteronomic and Isaianic traditions which permeate not only this text but the entire context of 1 Corinthians 8:1–11:1 (cf. chs. 3:2.2; 2.4; 5:3.2.1).[59] This observation casts doubt on pre-Pauline "midrashic" theories concerning this passage.

Paul is more likely weaving together the selected wilderness tradition ac-counts. As we have been arguing, the provisions and vices in the various tradi-tions all relate to the Corinthian situation (cf. the remainder of this chapter). Charles Perrot compiles examples from Targumic literature demonstrating that the various vices in 1 Corinthians 10:6–10 shared in common the notion of eating and punishment: "En effet, la tradition juive rappelait bien le danger des repas idolâtres (les trois premiers péchés: la convoitise, l'idolâtrie et la dé-bauche) et aussi lest déviations provoquées par la manducation de la manne (les deux derniers: la tentation et le murmure)."[60] Furthermore, we find a proleptic allusion to the Lord's Supper – Paul's very next topic (10:16–22) – intimated by the miraculous sustenance in 10:3–4. Additionally, the "all"/"some" language is an extension of Paul's race illustration in 1 Corinthians 9:24–27. The combi-nation of all these circumstances could hardly be coincidental had Paul simply adapted an interpretative tradition. That Paul placed all these innuendoes in an already existing "midrash" is also unconvincing.[61] Rather, the entire pericope of 1 Corinthians 10:1–13 is probably an original paraenesis of Paul in which he stringed together the Israelite traditions himself. The relevance of his message to the Corinthian situation makes his warning all the more serious. We will argue that the vices were not listed on an entirely random basis.

2.4 The Central Issues in Paul's Wilderness Narrative

Mitchell focuses on the notion of factionalism in her discussion of Israel's wilderness wanderings in 1 Corinthians 10:5–6. She connects the lusting after quail event in Numbers 11:4, 34 with Josephus who recounts the incident in

---

[59] Collier does mention Psalm 77[78] and 105[106] in reference to 1 Corinthians 10:1–4, but he believes the entire section (10:1–13) is a midrash on Numbers 11 (71–75). On Psalm 77[78] see 5.1.1 below. On Psalm 105[106] see the excursus below.

[60] PERROT (1983), 443; cf. 438–442.

[61] Fee rightly argues that if the text existed as a prior Midrash, it has been so thoroughly adapted by Paul as to make its prior existence almost irrelevant (442 fnt.5). He responds further: "Why, given its perfect fit in this context with no clear 'seams' and given Paul's own rabbinic background and acknowledged genius, could he not have composed such a Chris-tian 'midrash' *ad hoc*?" See OROPEZA (1998a) for further treatment.

terms of factionalism (στασιάζειν – *Ant.* 3.295). She also argues that Paul's allusions to Exodus 32 (1 Cor. 10:7), Numbers 25 (1 Cor. 10:8), and Numbers 16 (1 Cor. 10:10) are all connected with terms related to division and found in such sources as Josephus and Philo (*Ant.* 4.12–15, 32, 36, 59, 66, 140; *Ebr.* 99; *Post.* 182–85; *Mos.* 2.174, 283).[62] For Mitchell, Paul's wilderness rhetoric in 1 Corinthians 10:1–13 emphasises his warning against the Corinthian congregation's factional behaviour by using a "then and now" comparison of "divinely assisted beginnings and with later misfortunes." Like Israel of old, the Corinthians are in danger of not surviving due to factions over the same issues.[63]

As Mitchell's thesis demonstrates, factionalism is at the heart of the Corinthian letter, and we should not be surprised at its appearance in our text. Moreover, factionalism is implied by Paul's use of "some" in terms of various partitions of the "all" in 10:1–10. He also uses τινες in the context of various factions elsewhere in 1 Corinthians (4:18; 8:7; 15:12, 34 cf. 1:10–12, 26f). Mitchell's examples of discord might suggest the traditions picked up in Josephus and Philo lie at the centre of Paul's sources. But these traditions are not clearly alluded to in 1 Corinthians 10:1–13.[64] If the notion of factionalism is the central thought of this passage, it seems peculiar that this idea does not come from the Numbers and Exodus traditions, Paul's primary sources in 10:5–10. Mitchell also makes no reference to a faction related to the tempting Christ/bitten by snakes account in 10:9. It may be appropriate to conclude that a division among community members is implied in 1 Corinthians 10:1–13, and perhaps expressed in 10:10, but it does not seem to be what Paul is emphasising in relation to the entire passage.

Collier is perhaps correct in suggesting that "lusting after evil things" (10:6) is the *Leitmotiv*. The Numbers 11 tradition, from which this phrase is derived, demonstrates that this vice had special reference to "eating" in the wilderness. This motif makes good sense in the macro-context of eating meat sacrificed to idols (8:1–11:1). The next vice, which is the only formal scriptural citation in the passage, is related to the problem of idolatry (10:7).[65] For Paul, all the vices may be encapsulated under the general heading of "lusting after evil things."[66] In 10:6, "they lusted" (ἐπεθύμησαν) is not qualified by "some" as are the other vices in verses 10:7–10, perhaps implying a more general usage that covers all the wilderness rebellions. The chiastic structure of the argument reinforces this

---

[62] M. MITCHELL (1991), 139–40.

[63] M. MITCHELL, 252–53.

[64] Even the celebrated idea that Paul is borrowing from Philo in 1 Corinthians 10:4 is problematic (cf. ch. 3:3 ftn.153 above).

[65] COLLIER (65) observes that "they sat down" (Num. 11:4 LXX) and "rose up" (Num. 11:32 LXX) is similar to the wording found in 1 Corinthians 10:7.

[66] Cf. ALLÓ: "la seconde partie du verset [10:6b] est comme un sommaire des fautes qui vont être détaillées, 7–10" (1956:233).

hypothesis. The example of lusting is the only vice that does not follow the structural pattern of the other vices mentioned in 10:7–10; "lusting after evil things" with special reference to food seems to be the underlying theme about the nature of the vices in this account.[67] Paul then elaborates on specific examples of this and specific divine judgements which followed (10:7–10). These observations seem central to Paul's wilderness account in 10:5–10.

2.4.1 Excursus: Psalm 105[106] in Relation to Paul's Wilderness Narrative

Psalm 105 LXX [106] is significant because it combines all the vices in the wilderness that Paul mentions in the Corinthian account. After God saved and redeemed the children of Israel from the enemy at the Red Sea (Psa. 105:8–11, 21), they initially trusted God's promises, but through the wilderness hardships, they no longer believed (105:12f, 24). After a brief introduction of praise to Yahweh, the psalmist emphasises the apostasy of Israel in the wilderness. Like Paul's paraenesis, this psalmist tradition mentions eating and drinking in relation to the Israelite rebellion. They tempted God when they craved food in the wilderness (105:14–15), they participated in eating heathen sacrifices at Baal-Peor (105:28), and they provoked God and Moses by thirsting at the waters of Strife (105:32). The psalmist emphasises Israel's rebellions and God's judgements in ways similar to Paul's.

First, the Israelites emphatically lusted (or "lusted a lust") in the wilderness (ἐπεθύμησαν ἐπιθυμίαν ἐν τῇ ἐρήμῳ), and tempted God. This echoes the earlier Numbers tradition of craving fowl (Psa. 105:13–14; cf. Num. 11:4).[68] Paul also opens up his chiasm with this particular account, and like the psalmist, he uses ἐπεθύμησαν to describe the Israelites' vice which happens in the desert: ἐν τῇ ἐρήμῳ (1 Cor. 10:5–6).

Second, the psalmist recalls the golden calf incident in which the Israelites forgot the God who saved them and exchange the glory of God to worship the metal image of a bull that eats grass. But God did not destroy them; Moses stood in the gap for Israel (Psa. 105:19–23). Both Paul (1 Cor. 10:7) and this psalm tradition share in common the absence of any judgement mentioned in relation to this rebellion. The exodus tradition, on the other hand, records that 3,000 were slain by the Levites at the command of Moses, and God also struck the people with a plague (Exod. 32:28, 35).

Third, the Israelites despised the desirable land, disbelieved the promise of God, and grumbled in their tents, and so God swore that he would cast them

---

[67] Cf. KLAUCK: "Die Fehlhaltungen des Volkes haben es im alttestamentlichen Kontext mit Gelüsten nach Nahrung zu tun. Das Volk will irdische Speisen statt der Gaben, die Gott ihm schenkt" (1982:256).

[68] As a result of this rebellion, the Massoretic tradition includes that God then punished them with a plague (Psa.106:15 cf. Num. 11:33).

down in the desert and scatter their seed among the nations (Psa. 105:24–26). Here the psalmist seems to echo the Israelites murmuring in their tents in Deuteronomy 1:27.[69] The event recalls Numbers 14 where God swore that the older generation of Israelites would not enter the promised land. Paul may be relating this grumbling to 1 Corinthians 10:10.

Fourth, the Israelites are said to have joined themselves to Baal-Peor, eating sacrifices to lifeless gods and provoking Yahweh who then sends a plague on them, but Phineas stands in the gap to keep the plague in check (Psa. 105:28–31). This tradition reflects the fornication instigated by Balak the Moabite (Num. 25; Hos. 9:10b). Paul seems to be reflecting on the sin at Baal-Peor in 1 Corinthians 10:8.

Finally, the Israelites provoked God at the water of Meribah, causing Moses to speak rashly (105:32–33). The Israelites eventually prostituted and defiled themselves with the neighbouring nations and sacrificed their children to demons (καὶ ἔθυσαν τοὺς υἱοὺς αὐτῶν καὶ τὰς θυγατέρας αὐτῶν τοῖς δαιμονίοις [Heb. שֵׁדִים] Psa. 105[106]:37). Thus God handed them over to their enemies (105:34ff). The psalmist here reflects the strife at Meribah in Numbers 20. Their sacrificing to demons reflects the situation in 1 Corinthians 10:20–22. The idea of provoking or tempting God is repeated in the psalm several times (Psa. 105:7, 14, 28, 32–33, 43 cf. 16). This bears resemblance with Paul's exhortation not to tempt Christ in 1 Corinthians 10:9.[70]

Nevertheless, the genre of this psalm is confessional, not exhortational like Paul's narrative.[71] Also, the order of rebellions in Psalm 105 are in a different order than Paul's account. Moreover, the judgements that follow the rebellions in Psalm 105 do not find good corollaries in Paul's account. In 1 Corinthians 10:9, for instance, the Israelites' tempting of Christ is followed by their being bitten by snakes, which no doubt, alludes to Numbers 21. The psalmist, on the other hand, does not mention any aspect of this particular judgement from the Numbers tradition. While Paul may have derived some ideas from this psalm tradition, his wilderness account does not seem to depend on it.

---

[69] In the Massoretic tradition, both accounts have לֹא רָגַן, which locates the murmuring in the tents of Israel. Coats suggests that the psalm reflects deuteronomic influence (1968:230).

[70] We might be tempted to combine Psalm 104[105] with 105[106] to decipher the entire 1 Corinthians 10:1–10 pericope. In 104, God's miracles and spiritual provision are in focus (esp. 104:37–41), but in Psalm 105 the Israelites' rebellion is stressed. This pattern would be similar to the Corinthian account. Nevertheless, although both psalms are similar in that they portray somewhat of a chronological narrative of Israel's early traditions, if we combine the latter psalm with the former, the parting of the Red Sea disrupts the general flow since it is not mentioned until the latter (105:7f cf. v. 22) and this occurs *after* God's spiritual provision in the wilderness (104:37f).

[71] Cf. MEEKS, 66.

2.5 That We Should Not Lust After Evil Things

The Kibroth-Hattaavah ("graves of lust") incident appears to be the primary source behind Paul's reference to lusting after evil things (Num. 11 cf. Psa. 77[78]:26–31; 105[106]:14–15; Deut 9:22). The relationship of this passage to 1 Corinthians 10:5–6 is evident in the similarities in Greek (cf. 1.2.5): Ἐπι- θυμητὰς κακῶν καθὼς κἀκεῖνοι ἐπεθύμησαν in 10:6 is similar to ἐπεθύμη- σεν ἐπιθυμίαν in Numbers 11:4. But more specifically, the noun ἐπιθυμητής, which occurs only here in the New Testament, is found only in the LXX pas- sages of Numbers 11:34 and Proverbs 1:22.[72] Both Paul and the Numbers tra- dition set the vice of lusting toward the beginning of the rebellion in the wilder- ness. In Numbers 11 the people, having despised God's manna, greatly lusted for the foods of Egypt (Num. 11:4–9, 34).[73]

This account would be appealing to Paul for several reasons. Egypt repre- sented Israel's former state of bondage, and for the people to crave the food of Egypt in general – and meat (κρέα, Num. 11:4) in particular – coincided with the Corinthian situation of eating meat in the context of idols. As the foods of Egypt signified for the Israelites a turning back to the former things of their pre- redemption, so idolatry would be a thing associated with the Corinthians' pre- Christian status (cf. 1 Cor. 6:9–11; 12:2) and eating idol meat with idolaters could draw the Corinthians back to their former status. In the Numbers account, the mixed multitude (ὁ ἐπίμικτος ὁ ἐν αὐτοῖς) instigated the Israelites to lust after food (Num. 11:4). It is possible that this observation may have influenced Paul's judgements regarding the co-mingling of Christians with non-Christians in the Corinthian situation (cf. 10:16–22). Paul would also find in Numbers 11 the connection between God's Spirit and the cloud in the wilderness (cf. 1 Cor. 10:2).

By exhorting the Corinthians to avoid lusting after evil things, Paul primarily seems to have food in mind, but food as it was related to rebelling against God by craving things associated with their pre-converted status (cf. 10:5). Paul uses ἐπιθυμία in a negative sense of desiring (Rom. 7:7–8; 13:8–10).[74] The "evil things" refer to the desiring of things that incur God's displeasure. In both the Numbers and Corinthian contexts, lusting after evil things is associated

---

[72] Cf. FEE, 452 ftn 9. W. Willis seems incorrect to suggest that Paul may have drawn on the OT in a general way here (144). For references on how other Greek works use the term, see LIDDELL/SCOTT, 634.

[73] Coats affirms that the name *kibroth hattaavah* "might well suggest that the desire was the cause of punishment which resulted in death" (111).

[74] Cf. W. WILLIS, 144 f. For Paul, coveting is listed as a work of "the flesh" (Gal. 5:16–21, 24; Rom. 1:24 f). In certain early Jewish literature, coveting became the chief of all sins (cf. T. Jud. 16:1; BÜSCHEL, *TDNT*b, 3:169). It is interesting to observe that Paul also emphasises this vice in our passage.

with the pre-redemptive status, and the vices which follow in Paul's account may be specific examples of lusting after evil things. Hence, salvific activities in 10:1–4 are contrasted with the non-salvific activities in 10:5–11. In 10:7–10, four vices follow "lusting after evil things." We will now turn to these.

3. The Golden Calf and the Problem of Idol Meats (1 Corinthians 10:7)

3.1 The Golden Calf Incident and Idolatry

The only scriptural citation in 1 Corinthians 10:1–13 occurs in verse 7 where Paul warns the Corinthians not to become idolaters as did the Israelites, for it is written that the people sat down to eat and drink and rose up to play (ἐκάθισεν ὁ λαὸς φαγεῖν καὶ πεῖν καὶ ἀνέστησαν παίζειν). The citation comes from Exodus 32:6 (LXX) where Israel worships the golden calf.[75] When Moses received the covenant from God on Mount Sinai, the Israelites, under the leadership of Aaron, moulded a golden calf image out of the plunder they took from Egypt.[76] They proclaimed the image as the deity who had led them out of Egypt, and they celebrated a feast in its honour. When Moses descended from Sinai and saw the idolatry, he threw down the covenant (a sign of Israel's breaking of God's covenant – cf. Deut. 31:16–20; Jer. 11:10), destroyed the calf, and forced the Israelites to drink the residue.

The vice of idolatry is set apart from the other vices proceeding it in two ways: 1) It is the only vice in which Paul directly cites an older tradition, and 2) Paul makes no reference to any judgement occurring as a result of Israel committing the vice. The quotation may have been intended to stress idolatry over the other vices since this was the focus of his paraenesis in chapters 8–10. The golden calf incident would appeal to Paul's argument because it was the epitome of God's chosen people committing apostasy through idolatry (cf. Deut. 9:12–21; 1 Kings 12:26–14:11; Hos. 8:5; 10:5–6; Tob. 1:5).[77]

---

[75] The LXX, however, spells "to drink" as πεῖν.

[76] The bull was a prominent image in idol worship in the ancient world symbolising power and fecundity. The Egyptian god Amon-Re, the Canaanite Baal, and the Assyrian Asshur were all cast in images of a bull (OSWALT, 1988:12). One tradition has it that the golden calf was patterned after the bull image that formed part of the divine throne (Ezek. 1:10; cf. 1 Kings 7:25; 12:28, 32). The calf was thus a sign which pointed to the divine Presence (cf. FAUR, 1978:11). However, Ezekiel 20:8, 24 (cf. Bar. 1:20–22) might indicate the idea that the golden calf was originally an idol which came from Egypt. If this is the case, then the image itself was another indication of the Israelites coveting after an evil thing of their pre-deliverance. But the issue cannot be finally settled here. For a study of various interpretations related to the calf's identity, see HALPERIN (1988); SPENCER, *ABD*, 2:1068–69. On other possible Pauline allusions to the golden calf, see CALLAN (1990), 1–17.

[77] Cf. SPENCER (1992), 2:1065. One Jewish source asserts there was enough iniquity in

In this incident, however, Paul does not focus on the idolatry itself but on the cultic meal and celebration associated with the event. He wanted the Corinthians to see that the Israelites were "eating and drinking" in the presence of an idol. By way of contrast, the same Israelites ate and drank of miraculous sustenance and confirmed their covenant by eating a meal in the presence of God (Exod. 15:22–17:7; 24:11; cf. 1 Cor. 10:3–4). In the Corinthian situation it seems as though Paul already had in mind the contrast he expounds in 10:16–21: the Corinthians cannot be both partakers of the Lord's table and partakers at the table of demons associated with idols. Such participation could lead to idolatry (10:7, 14).

The "sitting" and "rising" of the people of God in the golden calf event also may have been significant for Paul. The concept of sitting was often associated with moral degradation by the later Jewish writers so that it became common for some rabbis to affirm that where one finds "sitting" one finds seduction.[78] The idea of sitting and rising also finds place in the rebellion at Kibroth-Hattaavah which Paul alludes to in 10:5–6 (cf. Num. 11:4, 32).[79] For the Jews, the notion of "playing" (פחצ/παίζειν) – though having a wide range of meanings – included cultic dancing (Judges 21:21; 1 Kings 18:26) and could denote erotic behaviour (cf. Gen. 26:8).[80] In the golden calf narrative, the "playing" may have borne both these connotations. The Exodus tradition records that when Moses descended from Sinai, he saw the Israelite dances (מחולה/χορός – Exod. 32:19) associated with the cultic meal,[81] and that the people were without restraint (פרע/διασκεδάζειν – 32:25). In Philo the incident included "blasphemous" dances, intoxication, and pleasant sins (*Mos.* 1:302; 2.162). If Paul understood that sensuality was involved in the playing, this would anticipate the πορνεία he mentions in 10:8.

Unlike the corollary vices, Paul mentions no judgement resulting from this incident. Perhaps for the sake of the chiasm Paul was developing, it would not have been advantageous to include another sentence describing Israel's judgement, especially when the judgement was rather complex. God declares that because the Israelites have transgressed, God would blot out (מחה) the Israelites and

---

the event to punish Israel until the dead are raised (Eliezar ben Jacob ARNa 9; cf. Meeks, 69). In 1 Corinthians 10:7 λαός designates God's chosen people (cf. Lenski, 1963:397). Paul may have not picked the best example of "some" of the people committing idolatry; the people as a corporate community do evil by moulding the idol out of their jewellery (Exod. 32:1–3; cf. 11, 21, 30). Nevertheless, the participation of "all" is later qualified as all those who had gold (Exod. 32:24). Also, the Levites stand with Moses and kill 3,000 Israelites at his command (32:26–29). Paul's stress on the language of "some" is not necessarily a contradiction of the incident.

[78] ExR 41 (98a) in Str.-B., 3:409f.

[79] Cf. Collier, 65.

[80] Cf. Bertram, *TDNT* 5:627, 629–30.

[81] In the LXX the word connotes the dancing of women (Exod. 15:20; Judges 11:34; 1 Kings 29:5).

make a great nation out of Moses. But Moses intercedes on Israel's behalf, and God relents (Exod. 32:7f, 32f; cf. Deut. 9:14–19). However, the Levites, in obedience to God and Moses, kill 3,000 idolaters (Exod. 32:26–29), and God sends a plague on the people (Exod. 32:34–35) killing an undisclosed number of Israelites. It may have been difficult for Paul to include a brief summary of these judgements, and he may have thought the 3,000 who died were not a large enough number to include in his description of the event (cf. 1.2.5 above).[82]

In the Hebrew scriptures, idolatry appears to be the dominating vice associated with apostasy, and the golden calf cultus epitomises this vice. Not only does it appear in the wilderness traditions (e.g., Psa. 105[106]:20; Deut. 9:14) but it also arises in the tradition-history of the divided monarchy when king Jeroboam sets up a golden calf image in Dan and Ephraim (1 Kings 12:25–33). This event leads the entire northern tribes into idolatry which finds its zenith during the reign of Ahab when Elijah complains to God that he alone of all Israel had not worshipped Baal (1 Kings 18–19). Jeroboam's wicked influence finally ends in Northern Israel's captivity. Sometimes the imagery of prostitution and adultery is associated with the idolatry of Israel as well (Num. 25; Ezek. 16; Hos. 1–2).

Forkman lists several kinds of activities which resulted in expulsion by means of the death penalty in the Hebrew scriptures. Serving other gods heads his list (Lev. 20:2–4; Deut. 13:6ff).[83] Expulsion portrayed in these traditions involve removing the object of defilement from the community of Israel. Defilement is especially potent in things associated with other gods or idolatry (Deut. 7:5, 25–26 cf. Jer. 2:22–23; Ezek. 20:30; Psa. 105[106]:37f). The cutting off of an individual meant that that person was no longer considered a member of the community of Israel; he or she was no longer considered to be a member of God's elect. As such, expulsion refers to a punishment that is meted out against those who commit apostasy. Such a person is denied the protection and blessings provided by the covenant of the community; instead, he or she is given over to covenantal curses, misfortune, or death.[84] In the Deuteronomic tradition, the individual idolater as well as an entire community who serve other gods must go under the חרם (Deut. 13:1–19 cf. Deut 7; 20:15–18; Exod. 22:19).

---

[82] In the minds of at least some of those who were familiar with the narrative, Paul's allusion to it would probably conjure up a remembrance of some kind of judgement associated with it.

[83] FORKMAN (1972), 17. FORKMAN (19–20, 36) observes that those who committed grievous sins such as these were "cut off" from the community (Lev. 20:5;1 Kings 14:10–14; 21:21; Ezek. 14:7f). The term "cut off" (כרה) normally has God either as the agent or the subject, and in principle, the term connotes putting an offender to death (cf. Exod. 31:14).

[84] Cf. FORKMAN, 25–34. Forkman notes that death is the normative rule for those who deviate from the covenant, but there are also degrees of expulsion in relation to impurity. Some forms can potentially lead to death if the cleansing procedures are ignored (cf. Num. 19:20).

D. P. Wright correctly observes that in Deuteronomy, "idolatry is apostasy for which the remedy is death."[85] In 1 Corinthians 10:7, Paul also depicts idolatry in the context of divine judgement/expulsion by death, but this becomes more evident in the proceeding verses (10:8–10 cf. v. 5).

3.2 Idolatry in the Corinthian Situation

The importance of Israelite traditions as the backdrop of Paul's argument against idolatry may be discerned in his appeal to the *shema* at the beginning of his exhortation on the issue of eating idol meats (1 Cor. 8:5–6). There was at least two distinctive perspectives on idolatry among the early Jews. The Isaianic tradition was prominent in depicting the impotence of idols as false gods who were lifeless products of human craftsmanship (Isa. 40:18–20; cf. 1 Chron. 16:25–26; Jer. 10:3–11), while another view connected the idea of demons and idols such as found in the Deuteronomic tradition (Deut. 32:17; Psa. 105 [106]:37; Bar. 4:7).[86] While Paul acknowledges the tradition of worthless idols in 1 Corinthians 8:1ff (cf. 12:2), his focus shifts in 1 Corinthians 10 to the Deuteronomic tradition of idols as demons (1 Cor. 10:20f). He thus seems to accept the tension of both traditions: while the idols are not gods but lifeless images, demons are a real power behind the idols.[87] In the context of 1 Corinthians 10:1–22, then, demons were associated with the vice of idolatry.[88]

In 10:1–22 the heart of the problem with eating idol meat is that Paul sees an irreconcilable contradiction with the Corinthians having fellowship both at the table of demons and at the Lord's table.[89] The real threat rested not so much in the idol meat itself, but in having fellowship with demons. As fornication with a prostitute constituted the joining of a member of the body of Christ with a member of the *cosmos* (1 Cor. 6:15–17), likewise, fellowship with idolaters constituted the unthinkable notion of adjoining Christ with demons and confused the boundary between Christians and non-Christians. One of the things

---

[85] D. WRIGHT (1987), 284.

[86] Cf. HORSLEY (1980–81), 38–39; Str.-B. 3.48–60. This does not mean, however, that the traditions affirming the connection between demons and idols had no conception that idols were lifeless products (Deut. 29:17; 32:17–21; Psa. 105[106]:28–37). Some of these traditions apparently hold to both perspectives, as did Paul.

[87] The term εἴδωλον can convey the idea of a phantom or apparition (Jos. *Bell.* 7.452; cf. BÜCHSEL, *TDNT* 2:376; WITHERINGTON, 1993:246).

[88] Other early Christian traditions also made a connection between demons and vices in special reference to idolatry (e.g., Rev. 9:20–21 cf. 2:14, 20–22). For early Jewish references to vices associated with demons, see G. BARTON, *ERE*, 4:599.

[89] Cf. PERROT, 443. Malan goes too far in classifying idolatry here as eating, drinking, and amusing oneself at an idol celebration (1981:153). Although Paul views idolatry occurring here in a cultic setting, fellowship with idolaters and demons is his ultimate concern. No doubt, the cultic setting is still a means to this end.

which made Israel a solidarity in the wilderness was their unity in the shared spiritual meal.[90] Thus, to have fellowship with demons via idols is to join a member of the body of Christ in participation or union with demons.[91]

Paul's warning against idolatry in 10:7 has special significance for the context of 1 Corinthians 8:1–11:1 where the problem of idol meats arises (cf. ch. 2 above). It may be helpful to observe that Paul used the term "idolaters" (εἰδωλολάτραι) in 1 Corinthians 10:7 (and 10:14) instead of the term "meat sacrificed to idols" (εἰδωλόθυτον) which he uses in 8:1–13. The former word is understood as a gross vice for Paul, the participation in which will exclude one from the kingdom of God (1 Cor. 5:10–11; 6:9–11; Gal. 5:20–21; Col. 3:5f; Eph. 5:5; cf. Rev. 21:8). The latter word appears nowhere else in Paul's letters except here in 1 Corinthians 8–10, and it rarely appears in Jewish literature (4 Mac. 5:2; Sib. Or. 2.95–96).[92] In the Sibylline Oracles, εἰδωλόθυτον is forbidden among a number of other practices which can defile a person who enters the contest of receiving a crown of life and immortality (2.39–55; 149–153 cf. 1 Cor. 9:24–27). In the Maccabees tradition the word is used in reference to the Jews being forced by Gentiles to eat meat offered to an idol in an effort to get them to reject their faith. Thus, the early Jewish accounts of εἰδωλόθυτον seemed to be concerned with the notion of apostasy as is the case with εἰδωλολάτραι.

While this study on the words does not intend to be exhaustive, it nevertheless underscores the argument that the problem concerning idol meats in 1 Corinthians 8 is not necessarily a separate issue from the idolatry which is mentioned in 10:1–13. Paul brings out primarily in chapter 8 how the strong in Corinth could cause the weak to apostatise through idol meats; in 10:1–13 Paul builds up an argument that the strong themselves could apostatise through idolatry.

4. Πορνεία Cultus (1 Corinthians 10:8)

4.1 Sexual Immorality

4.1.1 Πορνεία at Baal-Peor

The second vice warning in 10:7–10 is against sexual immorality (πορνεία). The situation Paul alludes to is the incident at Baal-Peor where the Moabites send their daughters to commit fornication with the Israelites and influence them to sacrifice to idols (Num. 25:1–18). There are several reasons why Paul

---

[90] Cf. BADKE (1988), 26.

[91] Κοινωνία generally means to share with someone in something (HAUCK, *TDNT* 3:804). In the context of 1 Corinthians 10:16–22, it may mean "to participate in" (Best, 1955:90).

[92] Cf. BÜCHSEL, 2:378–79.

seems to have this incident in view. First, the vice which stands out in this episode is fornication. In later Jewish and Christian traditions, the Baal-Peor incident demarcated cultic fornication that was inextricably linked with idolatry (Philo *Mos.* 1:295–303; Psa. 105 [106]:28–31; Wisd. 14:12; Rev. 2:14, 20). Second, in these traditions there is a connection between the aspects of fornication, idolatry, and eating and drinking.[93] The Israelites ate of the sacrifices of Moab and worshipped their idols (Num. 25:2). In the Baal Peor incident Paul could once again suggest the problems of eating and idolatry. Third, the account appears in the wilderness tradition of Numbers, Paul's main source in the pericope of 10:5–11 (cf. 2.3–5 above). Finally, the divine judgement that occurs as a result of the rebellion seems to be the same judgement described by Paul in 10:8b.

4.1.2 A Great Number of Deaths

Paul claims that 23,000 perished in one day (καὶ ἔπεσαν μιᾷ ἡμέρᾳ εἴκοσι τρεῖς χιλιάδες).[94] The Baal-Peor incident, however, records that 24,000 perished as a result of a plague sent by God (Num. 25:9), and there are no known variant readings in early Jewish tradition. Conzelmann suggests the discrepancy of Paul's 23,000 instead of 24,000 stems from either his bad recollection of the 23,000 Levites in Numbers 26:62, or the 3,000 killed in Exodus 32:38, or both.[95] Morris explains the discrepancy by asserting that "both are obviously round numbers, and in addition Paul may be making some allowance for those slain by the judges (Nu. 25:5)."[96] However, Morris does not escape this discrepancy by claiming the judges slew 1,000 Israelites; the passage clearly states that 24,000 died because of the *plague*.[97]

Godet argues that Paul would have known his own tradition claimed 23,000, as did all the other Jewish traditions which count the number at 24,000. Hence, Paul's discrepancy may be "a piece of Rabbinical refinement, similar to the: *forty stripes save one*" (2 Cor. 11:24) in which Paul does not wish to exaggerate.[98] But this explanation is hard to reconcile with Paul's wilderness rhetoric

---

[93] In ancient literature, fornication is often inseparable from a cultic matrix (Josephus *Ant.* 18:65–80; Rev. 2:14 cf. HAUCK/SCHULZ, *TDNT* 6:581–82, 586).

[94] In this context πίπτω means "to perish" or "be destroyed" (cf. Job. 14:10 LXX; Rev. 17:10; Philo *Aet.* 127–128). It carries a different nuance in 10:12 (see *ad loc*). A variant reading of 10:8 (including the secondhand correctors of ℵ and D) inserts the preposition εν between ἔπεσαν and μιᾷ. But the shorter reading, which has better manuscript evidence, is to be preferred. However, the insertion does not appear to change the text's meaning in any significant way.

[95] CONZELMANN (1975), 168; cf. SCHRAGE (1995), 400.

[96] MORRIS (1985), 141.

[97] Cf. ROBERTSON/PLUMMER (1911), 205.

[98] GODET, 2:62. On various Jewish sources of the numbering, see SCHRAGE, 400ftn97.

which tends to dramatise the genre of judgement. There seems to be no satisfying explanation why he would have rounded the number downward instead of upward.[99] It is possible that Paul is quoting by memory without verifying his source. This option aside, perhaps we can only surmise that he was using a source unknown to us,[100] or as Héring suggests, a very ancient copyist error lies behind this discrepancy.[101]

At any rate, the gist of Paul's argument is not effected so much by the exact number of those who died as in the affirmation that a very large number of Israelites did in fact die, emphasising the corporate influence of the vice and the notion of mass slaughter in the wilderness (cf. 10:5). Paul wishes to stress that God did not spare the Israelites who sinned, and by implication, neither will he spare the Corinthians.

4.2 The Corinthian Situation

In the ancient world, Corinth was famous for its prostitution in cultic settings. The Corinthian prostitutes, who were often known as the *hetairai*, partook of religious festivals in honour of Aphrodite (cf. Strabo, *Geogr.* 8.6.20[C378]; Athenaeus *Deipnos.* 571c–74e).[102] It would be easy to affirm that such a background underlies the problem Paul faces in Corinth; however, Conzelmann argues that the records about Corinthian sexual immorality originate centuries before the Common Era and thus may not be related to the first century church of Corinth.[103] Nevertheless, the prevalence of fornication in first century Greco-Roman society often seemed to create tension in the early Gentile churches, suggesting that πορνεία was wide-spread and sometimes may have been performed in a religious context (Acts 15:20, 29; Eph. 5:3f; Jude 4–7; Rev. 2:20f; cf. Jos. *Ant.* 18.65–80). Corinth would be no exception to this. Evidence of a cultic setting, however, should be examined within the Corinthian letter itself.

---

[99] Lenski argues that Paul would have used the conservative number in keeping with his context that only "some" of the Israelites participated in this sin (398). But this explanation still runs counter to Paul's rhetoric of dramatisation. More likely, if he knew about the 24,000, he would have used it.

[100] We may attempt to evade the difficulty by relating this incident to the promiscuity in the golden calf episode, assuming Conzelmann's conjecture of Exodus 32:6 that "they sit down to meal" indicates idolatry, and "rise up to play" suggests fornication (167 ftn33). Paul would thus be claiming that 23,000 died from the plague in Exodus 32:35. But this departure also suffers the set-back that no source locates the number of those who died in this plague at 23,000.

[101] In this case, the abbreviated letters τϱϛ (τέτταϱες) may have been mistaken for τϱεῖς (HÉRING, 82).

[102] For a brief study on ancient prostitution in relation to the biblical literature, see FORD (1993), 128–35.

[103] CONZELMANN, 12 ftn97.

In 1 Corinthians 6:12–20 (and 10:8), it seems that Paul understood πορνεία as referring to cultic prostitution.[104] This understanding is borne out by means of the prostitution and temple imagery in the passage. Paul also combines food and sex in 6:13. The Baal Peor incident would seem to parallel the fornication in 6:13; in both cases, the language compliments the idea of cultic fornication with strange women in a temple precinct. In 1 Corinthians 6, then, "prostitute" may be the best way to interpret πόρνη, perhaps suggesting a cultic setting for the situation and thus confirming a close conception with 10:8.[105]

At the heart of the Corinthian problem was the assumption that some of the strong in the Corinthian congregation seemed to believe that committing πορνεία was relatively harmless (cf. 1 Cor. 6:13).[106] Paul argues that such an activity does not build up the body of Christ, and it brings a member under the power of a prostitute (1 Cor. 6:12f). Some apparently did not understand that what happened to their personal body also affected the Spirit (6:16–17, 19–20). Paul therefore argues that fornication places the Corinthian Christian in the hands of someone other than the Spirit of God.[107] A sense of ownership may be the key to understanding this passage.

For Paul, committing fornication carries with it the idea of violating another person's possession (1 Cor. 7:4, 36–38; 1 Thes. 4:1–6; cf. Hos. 3:1–3; Isa. 54:5).[108] Paul sees the body of the Christian as belonging to Christ, and this body will be raised up by God at the completion of the eschaton (6:13–14, 19–20; 15:20f; cf. 2 Cor. 5:14–17).[109] The entire person is a member of the body of Christ through the Spirit, and this is seen in terms of the primordial marital maxim of two becoming one (1 Cor. 6:16–17; Gen. 2:24 cf. 2 Cor. 11:2–3; Rom.

---

[104] Nevertheless, Paul, who seems influenced by the Jewish traditions of his time, would understand the term πορνεία in a wider sense to also include incest (1 Cor. 5:1f), adultery and homosexuality (6:9–11 cf. Rom. 1:24, 26–29), and pre-marital sex in 1 Corinthians 7:1–2, 8–9 where he contrasts married and single statuses. All of these acts were denounced in Jewish traditions (Deut. 23:13–29; Lev. 18:22; 20:10ff; Prov. 5; 6:24–35; cf. Hauck/Schulz, 6:585–90).

[105] Cf. Wolff, 44. Kempthorne, however, argues that 1 Corinthians 6 continues on the topic of incest from chapter 5. He interprets πόρνη (1 Cor. 6:15–16) as an immoral woman and this term points back to the stepmother in 1 Corinthians 5:1 (1967:570–71, 574). But there is no clear evidence that πόρνη has a wider meaning than a "prostitute," as Kempthorne admits.

[106] D. Martin (1995:175–76) suggests that among the Greco-Roman elite, the body was often depreciated. The strong at Corinth were perhaps influenced by this perspective.

[107] Cf. Witherington (1995), 168–69.

[108] Cf. Rosner (1994), 136–37.

[109] On belonging to Christ in relation to ethics, see Furnish (1968), 176–81, 215f. For Paul both the spirit (πνεῦμα) and the body (σῶμα) are to be sanctified (1 Cor. 15:35ff; 2 Cor. 7:1; 1 Thes. 4:3f; cf. 1 Cor. 7:34), and the body of a Christian is the temple of the Spirit (6:19–20). In the Philonic account of Baal Peor, Phineas is grieved because the Israelites gave both their bodies to pleasure and their souls to transgressing the law and doing wicked works (*Mos.* 1.301).

7:4b; Eph. 5:21–23). Christ, as the "husband" of the believer, exercises authority over the believer's body. For Paul, to become one with a prostitute is to rob Christ of a member (ἄρας οὖν τὰ μέλη τοῦ Χριστοῦ ποιήσω πόρνης μέλη – 6:15b), breaking the union the Christian has with Christ through the Spirit. Robertson and Plummer rightly argue that the force of ἄρας in 6:15 is not merely "to take" (i.e., λαμβάνειν) but "to take away" (cf. 1 Cor. 5:2; Col. 2:14; cf. Eph. 4:31). They affirm that this passage speaks of "apostasy from the spiritual union with Christ."[110] Paul argues that fornication causes a man to sin against his own body, and consequently, the body of Christ (1 Cor. 6:15–18).[111] Thus, like idolatry, the Corinthians were to flee from fornication (6:18a; cf. 10:14).

Martin suggests that eating and sex in 1 Corinthians 6:12f are "boundary-transgressing activities." The prominent ideology of Greco-Roman society thought of these activities on the low end of the hierarchical perspective of the body. Paul, on the other hand, holds to a cosmological/ethical-dualism in which Christ is opposed to the hostile *cosmos*. Martin argues that Paul views fornication and prostitution as representatives of the *cosmos* while the Christian is perceived in terms of participating in the body of Christ. Copulation between the Christian and a prostitute violates the boundary set between Christ and the *cosmos*: "The man, by penetrating the prostitute, is himself penetrated by the sinful cosmos."[112] But Martin does not discuss the term ἄρας in this passage. It is not so much an issue of penetration as it is a transference of ownership by "taking one out" of fellowship with the body of Christ and attaching that person to a prostitute.[113] This interpretation stresses the idea of expulsion from the body of Christ. Nevertheless, the boundaries between Christ and the *cosmos* are definitely ambiguous in such a case, and this is a sociological concern Paul seems to have in the Corinthian situation. Fornication, like fellowship with idolaters, confuses the boundary between the body of Christ and the world.

4.3 Divine Judgement and Sexual Immorality

The early Jewish traditions often characterised sexual relationships with foreign women as leading to idolatry. It was thought that an Israelite would be tempted to start serving the foreign woman's gods (Deut. 7:3–6; 1 Kings. 11:1ff; cf. Wisd. 14:12). Israel's unfaithfulness to Yahweh was portrayed in the metaphorical imagery of an adulteress or prostitute who is unfaithful to her husband

---

[110] ROBERTSON/PLUMMER, 125.

[111] The Stoics similarly believed that the man who has sex with a *hetairae* sins against himself, and against the god within himself (HAUCK/SCHULZ, 6:583).

[112] D. MARTIN, 178 cf., 176–77.

[113] Cf. M. Mitchell who refers to political rhetoric to support a similar reading (1991:119).

(Hos. 1–3; Jer. 2:1–4:4; Ezek. 16). The author of the Testament of Reuben declares that the first of 7 spirits of error is the spirit of promiscuity (Test. Reub. 3.2–3). It separates a person from God, it leads to idolatry because it deceives the mind and perceptions, and it leads youths to "hell."[114] It also provides Beliar an opportunity to cause a person to stumble (4.6–8). The faithful Jews believed that sexual mingling with Gentiles defiles both the individual and the entire community of Israel; there is no forgiveness of sins for the persons who commit this act (Jub. 30:7–17; cf. Deut. 23:17–18). Borgen argues that Josephus' account of Numbers 25:1–16 reflects the apostates of his own era who wished to exercise freedom over the law of Moses and said "yes" to mingling with the idolatry of the Gentiles (Josephus *Ant.* 4.126–158).[115] The woman who commits fornication will be burned with fire (Jub. 20:4–5; cf. Gen. 38:24).

The upshot of these observations is that the Jews believed sexual misconduct and co-mingling with the Gentiles defiled the land of Israel. Martin rightly notes, "The condemnation of porneia in Jewish circles was a way of solidifying the boundary between the chosen people and everyone else with their idols and loose morals: porneia was something 'they' did."[116] To prevent contamination among the people of God, such activities were punishable by death (Deut. 22:20–24; Lev. 20:10f; 21:9; cf. Philo *Spec. Leg.* 1.54–57). In Paul's era the sexually immoral were said to suffer eternal punishment (Jub. 39:6; cf. Sib. Orac. 2.250–282; Rev. 21:8). In short, these traditions affirm that fornication leads to apostasy (cf. Sir. 18:30–19:3).[117]

Paul seems to hold to a similar view. Those who were outside the community of God were depicted as contaminating themselves with licentious practices (1 Thes. 4:5; Col. 3:5–10; cf. Eph. 4:17–24). Along with those who commit idolatry and other vices, those who committed sexually immoral acts would not inherit the kingdom of God (1 Cor. 5:10f; 6:9–11; 2 Cor. 12:20f; Rom. 1:18–32; Gal. 5:19–21; Col. 3:5, 8f; cf. Rev. 17:3; 21:8; 22:15).[118] The Corinthian congregation members were themselves once on the "outside" practising these vices, but they had been cleansed from such contamination by the name of Jesus and the washing of the Spirit which set the boundary between the Corinthians and corrupt outsiders (1 Cor. 6:11).[119] Since the incident at Baal Peor is placed in a cultic milieu, the Corinthian situation resembling this setting would seem to be very similar if not the same as the one Paul mentions in 6:12–20 and

---

[114] H. C. KEE translation, *Pseuda.* 1:783.

[115] BORGEN (1994), 33–38.

[116] D. MARTIN, 169.

[117] Cf. HAUCK/SCHULZ, 6:588.

[118] Cf. HAUCK/SCHULZ, 6:594. Note that Paul often mentions πορνεία alongside ἀκαθαρσία (2 Cor. 12:21; Gal. 5:19; Col. 3:5 cf. Eph. 5:3–5). Paul may have adopted this connection from Jewish writers. Uncleanliness as connoting sexual immorality seems to be prominent in the Second Temple period (1 En. 10:11; T. Jos. 4.6).

[119] Cf. D. MARTIN, 175.

10:8. Ποονεία would then take on a judgement of eschatological proportions (cf. 1 Cor. 6:9–11) akin with Jewish judgements on the fornicator as an apostate who was excluded from the community of God (cf. 1 Cor. 5:1–5). For the Corinthians who were involved in ποονεία, this indicates that the destruction of 23,000 at Baal Peor is an example of punishment with eschatological ramifications, as we will observe more fully in 10:11. Nevertheless, it has already become apparent that fornication and a form of idolatry which blurred the boundaries between the body of Christ and the *cosmos* were being committed by both the Israelites in the wilderness and by some in the Corinthian congregation. Hence, Paul is warning the Corinthians that some of them may suffer divine judgement and expulsion from the community if they continue to commit these vices.

5. The Provocation of Christ in the Wilderness (1 Cor. 10:9)

5.1 Tempting the Lord Past and Present

5.1.1 Paul's Sources

The concept of tempting appears twice in 1 Corinthians 10:9 (μηδὲ ἐκπειράζω-μεν τὸν Χριστόν, καθώς τινες αὐτῶν ἐπείρασαν).[120] Πειράζω appears in the Massah incident where the Israelites thirsted and questioned whether Yahweh was really with them (Exod. 17:1–7; cf. Num. 20:1ff; Deut. 33:8; Psa. 94[95]: 8f). Moses interrogatively urges them not to test Yahweh (Exod. 17:2). Ἐκπει-ράζω appears in Deuteronomy 6:16 where Israel was warned not to put Yahweh to the test as they did at Massah. Christ is said to have quoted this passage when tempted by Satan in the wilderness (Matt. 4:1ff; Luke 4:1ff). In the Deuteronomic tradition the passage lies in contextual proximity to the *shema* which Paul adopts at the beginning of his discussion on meat sacrificed to idols (Deut. 6:4f cf. 1 Cor. 8:5–6). Seesemann notes the intent of tempting God in light of Deuteronomy 6:16: "If we love God and keep his commandments we cannot test him or question his power by an attitude of doubt and unbelief."[121]

These observations might shed some light on Paul's idea of "testing Christ" in 10:9, but the Massah tradition does not seem to be Paul's focus. He writes that when the people tested God they were destroyed by serpents, and no such judgement occurred at Massah. The serpent incident takes place in Numbers

---

[120] On the Χριστόν reading, see the excursus below. The ἐκ- before πειράζω in 10:9a has a perfective function which may imply the idea of putting through a thorough test or a testing which is severe and prolonged (cf. ROBERTSON/PLUMMER, 205).

[121] SEESEMANN, *TDNT* 6:32. On other early "tempting the Lord" traditions, see VON RAD, 1:283 ftn6.

when the Israelites evaded the Edomites by walking along the path of the Red Sea (Num. 21:4–9). They began to speak against Moses and God along the route by detesting the provision of manna and desiring other kinds of food and drink. This provoked God, who then causes deadly serpents to bite them along the journey. After Israel repents, God tells Moses to make a bronze serpent and place it on a pole so that whenever the Israelites are bitten, they could look upon the serpent and live. However, no πειράζω variant is found in the account.[122]

Paul may have adopted ἐκπειράζω and πειράζω in 10:9 from Psalm 77[78]: 18, 41, 56.[123] The psalmist recollects the rebellion of Israel in the wilderness and how they provoked and tempted God by craving food in the wilderness (77:17–18), turning away from God and remembering not his deliverance from Egypt (77:40f), and breaking his covenant through graven images (77:56–58). In this tradition Coats describes God's rejection in terms of reversing Israel's election (e.g., 77:59–72).[124] Here the vice of tempting/provoking God is similar to the Corinthian motifs of eating, idolatry, apostasy and divine judgement. What may finally solidify the psalmist tradition as Paul's conceptual source is its mention that Israel tempted God by speaking against him (77:18–19: καὶ κατελάλησαν τοῦ Θεοῦ). This echoes the "speaking against God" found in the bronze serpent incident (Numbers 21:5 LXX: κατελάλει ὁ λαὸς πρὸς τὸν Θεὸν; cf. v. 21:7: κατελαλήσαμεν κατὰ τοῦ Κυρίου) and is not repeated again in any other wilderness tradition in the LXX narratives.

Although the Numbers tradition does not actually speak of "testing God" in the bronze serpent incident, Paul may have been prompted by the poetic parallelism of Psalm 77[78]:18–19 to equate "they tested God" (Psa. 77[78]:18) with "they spoke against God" (Psa. 77[78]:19). For the psalmist, speaking against God *is conceptually* the same thing as putting God to the test. Paul may have had a similar or the same conception in his assessment of Israel's vice and punishment in Numbers 21.[125] Both the Numbers and psalmist tradition share in common the vice of testing God in relation to eating, but the latter sets the

---

[122] The "ἐπείρασαν" conjugation in 1 Corinthians 10:9b appears in the Kadesh Barnea incident when God claims that Israel "tempted him ten times" in the wilderness (Num. 14:22), but this event is not related to the serpent incident.

[123] In other manuscripts, ἐπείρασαν in 10:9b (A B *Byz*) is replaced with ἐξεπείρασαν ([p 46] ℵ D). The textual evidence for both sides is almost even. The latter follows Psalm 77:18 (ἐξεπείρασαν), the former (ἐπείρασαν) 77:41 and 56. Both variants find support through the psalmist tradition. Robertson/Plummer favour ἐπείρασαν since ἐξεπείρασαν might be an assimilation to ἐκπειράζωμεν in 10:9a (206).

[124] Coats, 220 (cf. 1.2.1 above). Coats argues that the Psalm is intended as a polemic against the northern cult informing them that their election was forfeited by their fathers in the wilderness. Jerusalem and the Davidic posterity now enjoy the new election (251).

[125] Meeks may not be correct, then, when he argues that 10:9 is a "midrashic cross-reference to Deuteronomy 32:15, 'He [Jeshurun = Israel] scoffed at the Rock of his salvation'" (72). Likewise W. Willis seems incorrect in suggesting that Paul does not have any particular tradition in mind (1982:152).

vice in a wider context of apostasy through idolatry. In early Christian traditions, when humans tempt God, some form of apostasy is normally in view (Acts 5:9; Heb. 3:8f). This also seems to be the case in 1 Corinthians 10:9.

5.1.2 Israel's Destruction

The judgement Israel experiences in 10:9 is in keeping with punishment related to committing apostasy. Paul's language is sharp when he describes that Israel's calamity was a result of their testing Christ: they were being destroyed by serpents (καὶ ὑπὸ τῶν ὄφεων ἀπώλλυντο). He uses the imperfect tense of ἀπόλλυμι, indicating that this judgement may have had some sense of prolongation about it.[126] The incident took place as the Israelites travelled an apparently long route along the Red Sea (Num. 21:4). As was the case in God's judgement against the fornicators, a large number of Israelites were destroyed when they tested God (Num. 21:6). In essence, ἀπόλλυμι refers to moral ruin or eternal damnation.[127] Early Jewish traditions often used the word to describe a cutting off and cursing of the covenant people who rebelled against Yahweh or an eschatological ruin sometimes associated with the underworld (Lev. 20:3–6; Deut. 28:20; Prov. 15:10–11).[128] Early Christian traditions normally use the word for those who are eternally lost (Mark 8:35; Matt. 7:13; Luke 15:4, 8). Both Judas Iscariot and the man of lawlessness are called "sons of destruction" (ὁ υἱὸς τῆς ἀπωλείας – John 17:12; 2 Thes. 2:3).

Especially significant are traditions which associate ἀπόλλυμι with allusions to events in Israel's wilderness experiences. The Johannine text has Jesus contrasting ἀπόλλυμι with ζωή αἰώνιος using the bronze serpent in the wilderness as the background for his discussion (John 3:14–16). The epistle of Jude records that even though the Lord (Christ) saved the wilderness generation out of Egypt, he afterward destroyed (ἀπόλλυμι) those who did not believe (Jude 5).[129] In this letter, the author is speaking against apostate Christian teachers who deny their Master (Christ) and partake in the fellowship of the Christian love feasts but will suffer divine judgement (cf. vv. 4, 10, 12–13, 15).[130] The wilderness vices of Balaam (coveting) and "murmuring" are also mentioned (vv. 11, 16). A parallel passage to Jude in 2 Peter 2 interprets the apostates as eschatological false prophets who deny their Master and lead others astray. They walk in the lust of defilement (ἐπιθυμία μιασμοῦ – 2 Pet. 2:10), have gone astray,

---

[126] In some texts (C D Byz Lect), ἀπώλλυντο is replaced by απωλοντο, but the textual evidence favours the former reading ([p 46] ℵ [A] B).

[127] Cf. W. WILLIS, 106; CONZELMANN, 149; ROBERTSON/PLUMMER, 172.

[128] Cf. HAHN, NIDNTT 1:463.

[129] Here Bigg argues that κύριος refers to Christ, noting the similar language in 1 Corinthians 10:9 (1901:328).

[130] Cf. Bauckham (1983), 49–50.

following the way of Balaam (2:15–16), and bring upon themselves swift destruction (ἀπώλεια) (2:1 cf. 3:9; Jude 5). They are scoffers, though at one point they had been redeemed by Christ (2 Pet. 2:1; cf. Jude 4). The writer also affirms that as God spared not the angels who sinned, so will God not spare these prophets – they will suffer eternal damnation (2 Pet. 2:4–9, 12–13a, 17).[131] Φθείρω in 2 Peter 2:12 and Jude 10 is associated with eternal destruction and is used by Paul in 1 Corinthians 3:17b to refer to those who will be destroyed if they defile the temple of the Holy Spirit.[132]

Similar to other early Christian wilderness traditions, then, the Pauline writings – when using ἀπόλλυμι to refer to judgement on humans – attribute the word to those who are lost, fallen away, or eschatologically destroyed (1 Cor. 1:18; 15:18; 2 Cor. 2:15; 4:3; 2 Thes. 2:10; Rom. 14:15). Paul warns the strong not to cause the weak to be destroyed by their eating of idol meats (1 Cor. 8:8–13).[133] Oepke writes concerning Paul and John's use of the word: "In contrast to σῴζεσθαι or to ζωὴ αἰώιος, ἀπόλλυσθαι is definitive destruction, not merely in the sense of the extinction of physical existence, but rather of an eternal plunge into Hades and a hopeless destiny of death in the depiction of which such terms as ὀργή, θυμός, θλῖψις and στενοχωρία are used (Rom. 2:8f)."[134] This being the case, it would seem rather odd if all Paul had in mind in 1 Corinthians 10:9 is the physical death of the apostate Israelites. He implies more than this; he has an eschatological death in mind which is spelled out more clearly in 10:11–12.

In early Jewish and rabbinic traditions, serpents are often connected with some idea of the opening of their mouth by either their nature to bite or their presence in the notion of eating or coveting food.[135] Philo connects the pleasures of the belly with the bronze serpent incident in his interpretation of Numbers 21:5–6. These pleasures separate the soul from body not in the sense of death but in the destruction of the soul: "For in real truth there is nothing which so much bringeth death upon the soul as an immoderate indulgence in pleasures (*Leg. All.* 2.77)."[136] A serpent was also present during the primordial sin in Jewish tradition. The serpent was cursed to eat dust for tempting the primordial couple to eat the forbidden fruit which had special potency (Gen. 3). In later

---

[131] Cf. BAUCKHAM, 277–78. Bauckham affirms this apostasy is similar to those found in second century traditions (Hermas, Sim. 9.18:1–2; Irenaeus, *Adv. Haer.* 4.27:2–3).

[132] Cf. *BAGD*, 857.

[133] In 8:11 the word is emphatic by its position of standing first in the sentence.

[134] OEPKE, *TDNT*, 1:396.

[135] Cf. Str.-B., 3:411 for rabbinic sources. Coats associates the seraph/seraphim in Isaiah (6:1ff; 14:29; 30:6) with the bronze serpent (Num. 21:4b–9; 2 Kings 18:4 cf. Deut. 8:15) and suggests the possibility that the serpent was both part of the pre- and post-Davidic cults in Jerusalem (117–118). If so, the serpent may have been associated not only with eating but also with religious temple activities.

[136] Yonge translation of Philo (1993).

traditions the serpent became a symbol for Satan (e.g., Rev. 12:7), but there is no indication in 10:9 that Paul is warning the Corinthians against a judgement from Satan or demonic forces. The destruction by serpents serves to reinforce Paul's portrayal of the ghastly amount of human carnage that happens when the people of God commit acts of apostasy.

5.1.2.1 Excursus: Textual Criticism in 10:9a: "Christ" or "Lord"?

Text traditions vary on whether Paul's exhortation in 1 Corinthians 10:9 is for the Corinthians not to tempt "Christ" (p46 D E *Byz* 1739 Clement) or the "Lord" (א B C 33 Epiphanius).[137] Carroll Osburn argues that the former is older than the latter on the ground that there is no evidence prior to the fourth century for the κύριον tradition, which is predominantly Alexandrian. The Χριστόν tradition, on the other hand, dates back to the second century with the witness of p46.[138] It seems that κύριον, the easier reading, replaced the more difficult Χριστόν because it may have seemed awkward that Christ was with the Israelites in the desert.[139]

Others have noted that the second time the concept of tempting appears in verse 9 (τινες αὐτῶν ἐπείρασαν) it has no object; hence, "God" should be the implied object. The Corinthians should not tempt Christ the Lord as did the Israelites with God.[140] This interpretation fails to be convincing for at least two reasons. First, Paul has already affirmed that Christ was actually present with the Israelites as the "rock" (10:4), so it is not awkward for him to now claim that the Israelites tempted Christ. Second, the chiastic structure of Paul's argument at the B and C levels excludes an object when Paul warns the Corinthian Christians not to behave as the Israelites did (cf. 2.1). In the four warnings against idolatry, fornication, tempting Christ, and grumbling, the abrupt ending of "καθώς καθάπερ τινες αὐτῶν" has no object in every case. It would appear odd at this juncture for Paul to imply an object of dissimilarity between Israel and the Corinthians.

Bart Ehrman argues that 1 Corinthians 10:9 is an example of how the acts of God were predicated of Christ by the early church fathers. He suggests the "proto-orthodox" Christians of the second and third centuries altered 10:9 from

---

[137] A few texts (A,81) insert θεόν as the direct object, but the weight of textual evidence favours either Christ or Lord. The θεόν rendition may have been inserted to conform with the LXX tradition.

[138] OSBURN (1981), 201–212.

[139] Epiphanius (c. 315–403), Bishop of Salamis, claimed that Marcion (c. 160) changed the text to "Christ" instead of "Lord" (*Haer.* 42.12.3). Osburn, however, argues that there is no compelling reason for Marcion to alter the text, and it seems unlikely that a Marcionite text would have influenced Clement and the presbyter mentioned by Irenaeus who used the "Christ" text (203–05 cf. Zuntz, 232–33). Osburn suggests that Epiphanius, who lacked critical acumen, in his zeal against Marcion and other heretics, assumed that Marcion altered the text. Zuntz finds that the Marcion explanation apparently contradicts Marcion's objectives (126–127).

[140] Cf. PLUMPTRE (1878), 90.

"Lord" to "Christ" in their ongoing effort to combat adoptionistic and patri-passianistic heresies. Although he affirms that "Christ" is the sustainer in 1 Corinthians 10:4, it is "God" who brings judgement on Israel in 10:5: "the Israelites were destroyed after putting *God*, not 'Christ' to the test in 1 Corinthians 10:9."[141] But there are significant weaknesses in his position. First, he argues that the Alexandrian κύριος is the older witness, and this supports the idea that God, not Christ, is intended in the original reading. Yet in 1 Corinthians Paul almost categorically equates κύριος with Christ (1 Cor. 1:7–10; 9:1; 9:5; 12:3), whom he *distinguishes* from θέος (1:2–3; 7:17; 12:4–6).[142] Paul is most explicit about this in the idol-meat situation where he alludes to the *shema* and claims there is one God the Father and one Lord Jesus Christ (1 Cor. 8:5–6). Second, Paul implies that Christ is the Lord whom the Corinthians are provoking by their fellowship with demons (10:16–22). The testing of Christ in 10:9 appears to be the harbinger verse to 10:21–22. Third, Paul does not see any conflict in understanding Christ as "Lord" in terms of bringing judgement on the church (1 Cor. 4:4–5; 5:4–5; 11:32f). He can be both the sustainer in 10:4 and the executor of divine judgement in 10:9. Ellis rightly claims, "As in Jude 5, Christ in 1 Corinthians 10 [:4, 9] is the manifestation of Yahweh in his roles as redeemer and destroyer (cf. Exod. 12.23; Deut. 32.39; 1 Sam. 2.6; Isa. 45.6–7)."[143] The thrust of these observations demonstrates that Ehrman has not established his case adequately. Even if "Lord" were the original reading in 10:9 Paul would have "Christ" in mind, not "God."

Still the original reading in 10:9 is tipped in favour of "Christ" instead of "Lord." Osburn shows that in a fragment of book four of Origen's *Stromateis* written before 232 (preserved in codex 1739), Origen speculates on how his rivals would attempt to explain away Christ in the wilderness with Israel in 10:9. Apparently, he knew of no biblical alteration of this text in the third century Alexandrian region. Additionally, the bishops at the Synod of Antioch

---

[141] EHRMAN (1993), 90, cf. 87–89.

[142] There are at least 17 explicit references to Christ as Lord in 1 Corinthians and a higher number of implicit references. It seems that, whenever Paul himself was speaking, he intended "Lord" to refer to Christ. The only exceptions would be when he is citing someone else (e.g., 3:19–20). Yet in at least some of these exceptions, Paul still may have Christ in mind. In 1 Corinthians 1:31, for instance, Paul may be citing a variant of 1 Kings[1 Samuel] 2:8–10 (LXX) when he writes: "the one who boasts, let him boast in the Lord." Jeremiah 9:22–23 is a parallel source, but the source Paul is citing may have more in common with the Kings tradition. (Alternatively, he may have had both passages in mind – cf. MALAN, 1981: 141). The passage shares the words καυχάσθω ὁ καυχώμενος and κύριος in common with 1 Corinthians 1:31. The LXX passage also speaks of the θρόνον δόξης which may be the source behind Paul's mentioning of Christ as τόν κύριον τῆς δόξης in 1 Corinthians 2:8. If the Kings tradition is Paul's source for 1:31 and 2:8, then this underscores the assumption that he is reading Christ into his source and is perhaps thinking of Christ as Lord in 1 Corinthians 1:31 (cf. 1:29–30).

[143] E. ELLIS (1993), 173.

(268), using the Χριστόν reading of 10:9, condemned Paul of Samosata for denying the pre-existence of Christ, which might imply that neither they nor the monarchian knew of other variants of this passage in the third century.[144] Thus, the evidence favours "μηδὲ ἐκπειράζωμεν τὸν Χριστόν" in 10:9a.[145]

Contextually, the "Christ" rendition compliments Paul's wilderness rhetoric. We have argued that Christ was present with the Israelites in the wilderness episode (10:4).[146] It thus follows that the Israelites were able to tempt Christ in wilderness. Christ, who was Israel's provider in 10:4, is the same Christ who judged them in 10:9. The rendition of "Christ" instead of "Lord" in 10:9 serves to strengthen the analogy between Israel and the Corinthian church even more. Paul's implication is now becoming very evident: if Israel did not escape the judgement of Christ, neither should the Corinthians expect to escape it.

5.2 Testing Christ in Corinth

We noted earlier how Paul probably believes that testing God is interrelated with speaking against God. Did Paul think the Corinthians were partaking in such a practice with reference to Christ? The notion of speaking against Christ is found in 1 Corinthians 12:3 where Paul claims that no one who is speaking by the Spirit of God calls Jesus *anathema*. But there are not many clues that some people in the congregation were actually cursing Christ in an ecstatic state. It is

---

[144] OSBURN, 209–211.

[145] This interpretation, however, does not explain why Paul uses "God" instead of "Christ" in 10:5. Is Paul understanding "God" to mean "Christ" in this exceptional case? It would not be difficult for Paul to draw the inference that if the rock metaphorically refers to God in the Deuteronomic tradition, and Christ was the rock, then Christ was God. (A few witnesses in fact [e.g., 81] omit "God" in 10:5, making Christ the Rock in 10:4 as the subject who was displeased with the Israelites in 10:5. But the textual support is too weak to sustain the reading.) More probable is the solution that Paul may have believed God and Christ were both present in the wilderness. VON RAD (1962:1.284–85) observes that in Exodus 33, as a result of the golden calf rebellion, three divergent mediating traditions arise to lead Israel in the wilderness: 1) the angel of Yahweh; 2) the tabernacle of Moses; and 3) the פנים of Yahweh which has an "almost hypostatising independence." The last tradition appears in Deuteronomy 4:37 and Isaiah 63:9, but Von Rad affirms the first tradition has a wider basis (Exod. 14:19; 23:20f; 32:34; Num. 20:16). Paul may have identified the angel of Yahweh with Christ by observing how early traditions have Yahweh present in the cloud yet also present with the angel of Yahweh (מלך יהוה) (Exod. 3:2, 13–14; 14:19; 33:9–10; Gen. 19:23–24; Zech. 3:2; Philo *Mos.* 1.165f; Acts 7:30–38 cf. R. DAVIDSON, 242). Smit argues that the believers' unification with and separation from God, Christ, and the Spirit is an issue in this pericope (1997:43–44, 46). Alternatively, Paul may not have seen any tension created by having both God and Christ in his account of the wilderness epic.

[146] Cf. METZGER (1971), 560. It is also significant that in Psalm 78 MT (cf. 5.1.1 below) God is identified as the Rock (v. 35). It is possible that Paul's use of "Christ" in 10:9a (cf. 10:4) was instigated by this passage since he seems to have this psalm tradition in mind in 10:9b (see below).

almost inconceivable that a Christian would repeat such a thing or that the utterance would be confused with someone under the influence of the Spirit.[147] Ultimately, Paul seems to convey that not all ecstatic utterances come from the Spirit; some may in fact be demonic.[148] Yet there is no clear indication that Paul thought some in the congregation were speaking against Christ in this manner.

We have noted how coveting after food in the wilderness traditions is the incentive for the people of Israel "testing God." One aspect of the psalm tradition connected with testing God is the related notion of provoking God to jealousy with idols (παραζηλόω – LXX Psa. 77:58).[149] Such provoking may be significant because we find the same word (παραζηλόω) used by Paul in 10:22. After Paul tells the Corinthians they cannot have fellowship at the Lord's table and the table of idol-demons, he rhetorically asks, "Or do we provoke the Lord to jealousy? We are not stronger than he is, are we?" It is probably correct to affirm that Paul has this situation in mind in 10:9a when he exhorts the Corinthians not to test Christ.[150] 1 Corinthians 10:20–22 seems to be the immediate conceptual backdrop to 10:9a ("let us not tempt Christ"), and the conceptions found in Psalm 77[78] are behind 10:9b ("just as some of them tempted"), and Numbers 21 is behind 10:9c ("and were being destroyed by serpents").

The Corinthians, particular those of the strong group (10:22b), were testing and provoking Christ through their presumptuous attitude of eating idol meat and their abuse of liberty at the expense of loveless behaviour toward the weak.[151] As in the wilderness traditions, Paul may have connected food and idols with the notion of testing/provoking the Lord. These conceptions are interrelated in the macro-context of 1 Corinthians 8:1–11:1 and they also seem to be in 10:9. Roetzel argues that the loveless attitude of the strong in this situation links Paul's *anathema* in 16:22 with 8:3 (cf. 14:38; Matt. 25:12).[152] Paul is thus

---

[147] An *anathema* against Christ might be connected with the apostasy of Christians under persecution of their enemies (cf. Acts 26:11; Pliny to Traj. Ep. 10.96), but it would seem awkward for Paul to mention this connotation in the context of spiritual gifts. For an overview of various interpretations of this phrase, see FEE (1987), 578–82.

[148] Cf. FEE, 581. Perhaps in favour of this interpretation is the view that the *anathema* was declared in a mystery or non-Christian setting as implied by 12:2 (cf. STROBEL, 1989:185). On a similar note, ALLÓ (234) suggests that 10:9 implies tempting Christ through charismatic disorder.

[149] Παραζηλόω appears in the Song of Moses where an idolatrous setting is also in view (Deut. 32:21), and Paul echoes Deuteronomy 32:17 in 1 Corinthians 10:20. The only other LXX passage where the same word appears and has God as the subject is 3 Kings 14:22–23. The object of the provocation in this passage is also an idol.

[150] Cf. FEE, 457; R. DAVIDSON, 261–63.

[151] BARRETT (1971:107) observes that "puffed up" (φυσιοῦσθαι) is almost unique to the Corinthian situation (cf. 4:6, 18, 19; 5:2; 8:1; 13:4; 2 Cor. 12:20), appearing nowhere else in the NT except Colossians 2:18.

[152] ROETZEL (1972), 158f.

warning the Corinthians that if they continue to tempt Christ in such a manner, divine judgement would await them. Paul's language of tempting and destruction both suggest that a real and serious apostasy is an issue here.

6. Discord and the Grumbling Motif (1 Corinthians 10:10)

6.1 Sources behind the Grumbling Vice

In the final vice of Paul's wilderness episode, the apostle urges the Corinthian congregation not to grumble as did Israel, who were destroyed by the Destroyer (1 Cor. 10:10: μηδὲ γογγύζετε, καθάπερ τινὲς αὐτῶν ἐγόγγυσαν καὶ ἀπώλοντο ὑπὸ τοῦ ὀλοθρευτοῦ).[153] There is much ambiguity surrounding the wilderness tradition(s) Paul alludes to on this point mostly because the corollary judgement upon Israel cannot be found directly in the Exodus or Numbers wilderness traditions. Willis suggests that Paul is speaking only generally of the "Exodus experiences" without having a particular passage in mind.[154] The Israelites do grumble repetitively (Exod. 16:7f; 17:3; Num 11:1; 14:27–29; 16:11, 41; 17:5, 10).[155] Between Exodus and Numbers, only the latter tradition specifically relates grumbling with divine judgement; therefore, this is the tradition we will examine.[156]

---

[153] The second person plural imperative γογγύζετε (A B C 1739 *Byz Lect*) is preferred over the first person plural subjunctive γογγύζωμεν (א D 33). Apparently, the scribes of the latter witnesses did not recognise Paul's chiasm. Metzger suggests that scribes may have altered the γογγύζετε to γογγύζωμεν to keep the reading consistent with ἐκπειράζωμεν in 10:9 (560).

[154] W. WILLIS, 152; cf. CONZELMANN, 168; BARRETT, 226.

[155] In this study I am taking "murmuring" and "grumbling" as synonymous. Coats normally understands the word γογγύζω and its variants as "murmuring." The LXX consistently uses these variants for the Hebrew לון (COATS, 125 cf. 21).

[156] I have selected Exodus and Numbers because these appear to be Paul's primary sources in 10:5–10. Other traditions normally recollect and interpret the events in these traditions. The death of Nadab and Abihu (Lev. 10) and the death of Moses (Deut. 34) would be among the most significant exceptions to this. Two other traditions that recollect the Kadesh Barnea incident and are significant for this discussion are Deuteronomy (1:27) and Psalm 105[106]. GARDNER (151) proposes that the verb ἐξολεθρεύω appears in Psalm 105[106]23–25 and this is Paul's main source in 10:10. However, the more likely reading of ἐξολεθρεύω is in reference to God threatening to destroy the Israelites because of their worship of the golden calf (105[106]:19–23). The psalmist places the murmuring in Kadesh Barnea, which has its own distinctive judgement unrelated to ἐξολεθρεύω (105[106]:24–27). Deuteronomy 1:27 connects Israel's murmuring with ἐξολεθρεύω in Kadesh Barnea, but the destruction here is only in the imagination of the Israelites: they murmur that God hates them and so he plans to destroy them by delivering them to the Amorites. Although it is certainly possible that Paul has changed the destroying language from a verb to a noun in one of the above cases, evidence for the Korah rebellion as Paul's main source seems a bit stronger.

It does not seem wrong to affirm that the subject of grumbling and its conse-
quences is the most prominent theme of the entire wilderness rebellion in the
Numbers tradition. Paul could simply have the entire Numbers tradition in mind.
The weakness with this option, however, is that it creates a lopsided effect on
Paul's corollary judgement by the Destroyer. We would expect judgement by
the Destroyer to be a prominent means of judgement throughout Israel's rebellions, but it is not. Paul, of course, could somewhat arbitrarily consider the
Destroyer as the instrument of God's judgement against Israel throughout their
journey. This would be similar to Pseudo Philo 15:5f which apparently has an
angel bringing judgement on a continual basis. But as we have seen in 10:6–10,
Paul intends to convey particular incidents which can be traced to particular
sources. He also uses the aorist ἐγόγγυσαν in 10:10b which might also argue
against a prolonged incident (contrast the imperfect ἔπινον in 10:4) as does the
aorist ἀπώλοντο in 10:10c, which in contrast to the imperfect ἀπώλλυντο in
10:9, supports the idea of an immediate judgement.[157] Consequently, it would
be awkward both grammatically and contextually to argue that grumbling is the
only vice in 10:5–10 which does not echo a specific tradition.

Three of the grumbling incidents in Numbers are attached to an immediate
judgement: the Taberah murmuring (Num. 11:1–3), the Kadesh Barnea incident (Num. 13–14), and the Korah rebellion (Num. 16–17). In favour of the
Taberah incident as Paul's source is its general description of grumbling, and
that it is the first grumbling incident in the tradition. But there is no mention of
a judgement by the Destroyer unless we identify the Destroyer as Yahweh – it
is the fire of Yahweh which consumes a part of the camp. Also, the grumbling
at Taberah is not specifically mentioned in relation to eating or coveting,[158] and
there is no indication that a large number of people were killed. God's fire
strikes only the outskirts of the camp before the people cry out to Moses to
appease God's wrath. The prominent motifs in 1 Corinthians 10:5–10 of eat-
ing/coveting and judgement resulting in the death of large numbers are not
apparent.

In favour of the Kadesh Barnea incident is the corollary judgement by an
angel depicted in the later tradition of Pseudo Philo which records that God sent
an angel of wrath to burn with fire those who participated in the incident (Ps.
Philo 15:5f). Although the angel is not specified as the Destroyer, this passage
connects the ideas of the Kadesh incident with judgement by an angel. It is
possible that Paul linked this judgement with the older Numbers account of

---

[157] Paul uses the aorist tense to describe all the vices Israel commits in this narrative:
ἐπεθύμησαν (v. 6), ἐκάθισεν, ἀνέστησαν (v. 7), ἐπόρνευσαν (v. 8), ἐπείρασαν (v. 9), and
ἐγόγγυσαν (v. 10).

[158] It may implied in the MT, however, that when the people were grumbling about their
wilderness hardships, they had food in mind.

grumbling (Num. 14).[159] However, in other traditions, the Destroyer is normally understood as bringing a judgement by plague resulting in the death of large numbers, and this is probably Paul's conception of the term as well (Exod. 12:12–23; 1 Chron. 21:12–15 cf. 2 Sam. 24:15–17). This observation would tend to connect the Destroyer in Paul's narrative with the Kadesh judgement by plague. It would *not* seem to refer to the other Kadesh judgement in which God sentenced Israel to 40 years in the desert (cf. 1 Cor. 10:5).[160] At Kadesh, however, the murmurers did not die from the plague; only the 10 spies were struck down (Num. 14:37–38).[161] Hence, the death by plague mentioned at Kadesh Barnea does not fit well with Paul's description of large numbers dying in the desert and the normal Jewish conception of massive slaughter caused by the Destroyer.[162]

The final example combining grumbling and judgement is the Korah rebellion.[163] In the Wisdom account of the incident, a substantive participle is used of a messenger called the Destroyer (ὁ ὀλοθρεύων) who is connected with the judgement by plague in a recollection of the Korah rebellion (Wisd. 18:20–25). Perrot notes that Targumic literature also associated the destroying angel (מהבלע) with the grumbling of the Israelites immediately after Korah's death (Num. 16:41–50).[164] In Numbers, 14,700 die as a result of the plague (Num. 16:49), coinciding with Paul's understanding of καταστρώννυμι as indicating a divine massacre (cf. 1 Cor. 10:5; 1.2.5 above).[165] The notion of eating may be indi-

---

[159] Since Pseudo-Philo does not specifically mention grumbling, it seems less likely that Paul would only have this passage in mind in 10:10.

[160] Once again, the aorist ἀπώλοντο in 10:10c may support the immediate nature of the judgement at hand.

[161] There is a remote connection between eating and grumbling in this record. The spies bring back some fruit from the land and mention the food of Canaan in their report (Num. 13:26–27). Then they spoke discouraging words about the land and its inhabitants so that their report caused the Israelites to murmur (13:28–14:2). The connection between grumbling and eating in Numbers 16, however, is not as strained as this one (see below).

[162] Fee, however, sees the repetition of the 40 years judgement in 10:10 (cf. 10:5) as strengthening the argument in favour of Numbers 14 as Paul's source. The tradition accounts for the death of everyone over 20 except Joshua and Caleb, and so Paul is able to account for all the rest of those who had not previously been condemned in the wilderness (458). What may be problematic with this interpretation is that Paul has not repeated any of his other sources in the pericope, and 10:5 is not included as part of the chiasm of 10:6–11 wherein we would more likely expect such a repetition.

[163] Fee incorrectly claims that grumbling does not play a significant part in this incident (1987:457). If the rebellion of Korah does not centre on the enactment of grumbling against Moses and Aaron's authority, what does it centre on? Variants of the word "grumble" appear in the actual rebellion of Korah (Num. 16:11), the day after it occurred (16:41), and, perhaps more importantly, as an interpretation of the rebellion (Num. 17). The purpose of God making Aaron's staff bud was for a sign to establish his priestly authority and rid the Israelites of their constant grumbling against God's leaders (17:5, 10).

[164] Perrot, 440.

[165] If this is the case, why did Paul not record the large number of Israelites who died? In the Wisdom 18 account, the Destroyer does not give a specific number but claims that "a

rectly related to the incident because Dathan, one of the leaders of the rebellion, complains against Moses about the frustration of not being able to enter the land flowing with vineyards, milk and honey (Num. 16:11–14). This may have significance in relation to the perspective of the strong in Corinth who may think Paul was holding them back from the full benefits of a realised eschatology (cf. §8 below). Moreover, Coats observes that the persons who murmur in the wilderness traditions are consistently *all* the people of Israel (Exod. 16:2, 7–9; Num. 14:2, 27f, 35f). An exception to this is the Korah narrative in which only a group of families murmured.[166] Paul may have selected the Korah case in 10:10 since he is stressing the factions of "some" in 10:7–10 rather than the participation of "all" in 10:1–4.

Admittedly, 1 Corinthians 10:10 requires a little more conjecture than the previous verses, and this opens up various options for interpretation. It is always possible that Paul had the entire sphere of Numbers 13–17 in mind when he wrote 10:10 so that our choosing between the incidents in Numbers 13–14 and 16–17 becomes irrelevant. Yet the topics in Numbers 15 are not directly associated with either grumbling or judgement by a destroying angel; this weakens a suggestion that the surrounding accounts should be naturally linked together as one incident.[167] The Korah rebellion would seem to be the most consistent account for Paul's purposes in Corinth. The Korah traditions interpret the grumbling as resulting in a massive plague of death caused by the Destroyer, and this perspective would seem to fit well with Paul's argument.

6.2 The Grumbling Situation in Corinth and Corollary Judgement

At the heart of the Korah incident is the notion that influential members of the community came against God's established leaders because those leaders did not usher the people into the blessings of the promised land. Although the word "grumbling/murmuring" (γογγύζω) does not appear anywhere else in 1 Corinthians except in 10:10, some basic conceptions of the Korah incident pervade the letter. Some in Corinth struggled with issues of leadership (cf. 1:10–17), and Paul seems to associate envy and division with questions about leadership and authority (e.g., 1 Cor. 3:1–4, 21–23; 4:4f). In the situation regarding idol meats, Paul thinks it necessary to defend his leadership and uphold himself as

---

multitude" (πλήθους) were destroyed by the plague. This is the account which Paul apparently refers to in 10:10c. In the Numbers account, the deaths occur by means of three separate venues: some were swallowed by the earth (Num. 16:31 cf. Ps. Philo 16:3–7), 250 were consumed by fire (16:35), and 14,700 died of the plague (16:49).

[166] Coats, 26. The word כל often appears in these traditions.

[167] One could surmise that chapter 15 was a later insertion or that it functions as the centre of a chiasm, but these explanations provide no evidence that Paul would have read the Numbers tradition in such ways.

an example of self-restraint for the sake of others (cf. 9:1ff). All this may have particular relevance to the grumbling in 10:10. Maybe Paul, alluding to the Korah tradition, understood grumbling in the Corinthian situation as having special reference to their questioning of leadership authority. The concept of murmuring expressed itself through the vices of jealousies, envyings, and factions.[168] More specifically, Paul may be anticipating the grumbling of the strong who would complain about his solutions regarding idol meats.[169] Nothing in 10:10 suggests that the murmuring was specifically directed at God. As in the majority of wilderness traditions, it was directed at God's human representatives.[170] Hence, γογγύζω could be Paul's "catch-word" for these related issues. Mitchell affirms that factionalism and general discordant behaviour are related to grumbling in Corinth. In the only other passage where Paul uses γογγύζω (Phil. 2:14), factionalism is also an issue.[171]

The severe consequences related to the vice are seen in the corollary judgement.[172] Those who grumbled were destroyed by the Destroyer (10:10c). Paul's mention of the Destroyer seems deliberate. Since the Numbers tradition did not mention the Destroyer, he had to find or recollect another Korah tradition which mentions the Destroyer. The Destroyer was often understood as the personal name of an angel of destruction in Jewish tradition (Exod. 12:23; 1 Chron. 21:15; cf. Heb. 11:28).[173] Paul seemed to share this belief by using the definite article with ὀλοθρευτοῦ to identify this "special destroying angel."[174] The idea of a personal destructive angel of evil disposition can be seen in Jubilees which considers the spirit "Mastema" as the destroyer of the first-born in Egypt (Jub. 49:2). In other traditions, the Destroyer was the prince of the underworld (cf. Rev. 9:11ff).[175] The War Rule and Thanksgiving Hymns also mention destructive angels (1 QM 13:12; 1QH 3:35–36). Those who walk in the spirit of falsehood and practice vices such as greed, haughtiness, lust, and lewdness are to receive eternal damnation by the hand of the destroying angels (1QS 4.2–14; cf. 2.7–8; CD 2.6).[176] Such ideas of a destructive force may have influenced Paul.

---

[168] Noteworthy is the MT tradition which has the Korah rebels envying (קָנְאוּ) Moses in Psalm 106:16–18.

[169] Cf. PERROT (1983), 440; SCHRAGE (1995), 402.

[170] Cf. COATS, 27.

[171] M. MITCHELL, 140–41.

[172] COLLIER (62) suggests an intensity of judgements beginning with "forincation"/"fell," then "tempt Christ"/"were being destroyed," and then "grumble"/"were destroyed" in 10:8–10. If so, Paul's language here does not necessarily reflect Paul's sources. More Israelites died in the fornication at Baal Peor (Num. 25) than in the rebellion of Korah (Num. 16).

[173] See also Str.-B., 3:413–16.

[174] The phrase is found in BARRETT, 226.

[175] Cf. HAHN, 1:464–65. These traditions, however, use אבדון and ἀπολλύων, not ὀλοθρευτής or its variants as do Paul and the Wisdom writer he apparently alludes to.

[176] Interestingly, in the same Qumran context, the sons of truth who practice virtues will receive a crown of glory (cf. 1 Cor. 9:24–27).

Ultimately, whether Paul thought this messenger was Satan, another specific messenger, or a general reference to a destructive angel is difficult to determine.[177] Earlier in the same letter, Paul suggested Satan as the agent who would cause "the destruction of the flesh" (εἰς ὄλεθρον τῆς σαρκός) upon the man who committed fornication with his stepmother (1 Cor. 5:5; cf. 2 Cor. 12:7; 1 Tim. 1:20; 5:15).[178] Paul may have identified the Destroyer as Satan. On the other hand, he may be utilising the language of the Destroyer on a primarily rhetorical basis, emphasising what the Destroyer *does* rather than who or what it is. In LXX episodes, the Destroying angel is always associated with killing large numbers of people (Exod. 12:12–23; 1 Chron. 21:12–15; cf. Heb. 11:28). Thus, Paul's primary intention may be to convey that the Destroyer destroys large amounts of God's people. Such language would emphasise the severity of repercussions resulting from the practise of discord in Corinth. Perhaps Paul, like other orators of his era, perceived of factionalism as a disease which could spread throughout the entire body (cf. Juvenal *Sat.* 2.79 ff; Josephus *Bell.* 4.406–07).[179] If so, divine expulsion from the body of Christ would be the likely consequence for those members who persisted in such vices.

Paul's use of the verb ἀπόλλυμι in 10:10 also implied a severity in judgement. Earlier we noted that Paul uses this word to describe the Israelites' destruction by serpents in 10:9 (cf. 5.1.2 above) and that the word normally connotes an eschatological destruction associated with those who are excluded from the presence and kingdom of God (LXX Psa. 36:20; 67:2–3; 91:9; Isa. 41:11; Matt. 10:28; Luke 9:25; John 17:12).[180] Paul's thought may be similar to a Qumran text on this point; it too mentions Korah's judgement in the apparent context of a warning. Those who follow Korah's influence will suffer eschatological judgement (4Q423 fr. 5). The Community Rule also has it that those who murmur against the authority of the community would be expelled from the eschatological community of God forever (1QS 7:18; cf. 1QH 5:24 f).[181]

Although Paul uses "destroy" to denote physical death in the wilderness, the word is not entirely divorced from the eschatological death normally associated

---

[177] Str.-B. (4:412) note that several angels were named as personifications of destruction in Jewish tradition, and later traditions identified angels of destruction with Satan's angels, but "Ob der Apostel Paulus bei dem ὀλοθρευτής 1 Kor 10,10 speziell an den Gerichtsengel namens Maschchith oder allgemein an irgendeinen der vielen Engel des Verderbens gedacht hat, wird kaum zu entscheiden sein. Für das erster spricht der bestimmte Artikel vor ὀλοθρευτής, für das letztere, daß der Apostel auch 2 Kor 12,7 unter der Bezeichnung 'Satansengel' allgemein von Engle des Verderbens redet" (4:413).

[178] It is not true that Paul always called Satan "σατανᾶς." He seems to identify Satan as the god of this age (2 Cor. 4:4), Belial (2 Cor. 6:15), and the tempter (1 Thes. 3:5). These passages indicate that Paul believed Satan as an adversarial power opposed to the work of God.

[179] Cf. M. MITCHELL, 229 ftn238.

[180] For other references, see *BAGD* 95.

[181] Cf. M. NEWTON (1985), 44.

with it. Paul has employed extremely strong language in 10:5–10 in the geographic matrix of a hostile desert. Terms such as ἀπόλλυμι, καταστρώννυμι, and conceptions such as death by serpents, death in large numbers, and now death by the Destroyer were intended to graphically portray what happens to those who commit vices. Those who grumble in Corinth would suffer a severe judgement. This severity is consistent with the wilderness murmuring motif in the Hebrew scriptures, which portrays murmuring as a grave sin. Coats argues that this motif does not describe a mere complaint; it depicts open rebellion: "The act of murmuring poses a challenge to the object of the murmuring which, if unresolved, demands loss of office, due punishment, and perhaps death."[182]

The severe judgements on Israel spelled physical death in large numbers for that community and prevented the majority of them from entering the land God promised them. Moreover, these judgements happened to God's elect people in the wilderness, and Paul has consistently attempted to compare the similarities between the Israelite and Corinthian communities. In 10:11 he spells out more clearly what this all means in terms of the Corinthian situation.

7. The Wilderness Vices in Relation to Paul's Ethics

In retrospect we may notice that the vices Paul mentions in 1 Corinthians 10:5–10 all have relevance to the Corinthian situation and with eating and drinking (cf. 1 Cor. 8:1–11:1).[183] These observations suggest the probability of why Paul chose the particular wilderness examples he did: he wanted to emphasise examples related to the problem of idol meats. This prompts us to ask what the significance of vice language is for Paul's ethics.[184]

We have seen how our text links the wilderness experiences of the Israelites with the Christians in terms of initiation, divine sustenance (grace), and hypothetically, divine judgements. Rosner rightly argues that the Hebrew scriptures were crucial in the formation of Paul's ethics in 1 Corinthians (6:16; 9:10; 14:34).[185] Paul uses the scriptures (cf. ἐγράφη – 10:11) as an authoritative appeal which is intended to add persuasiveness to his argument (cf. 1 Cor. 4:6; 15:3).[186] In 1 Corinthians 10, then, the vices would be ethically "wrong" for

---

[182] COATS, 249. In later Jewish traditions Rengstorf suggests a softening against the severity of grumbling language (*TDNT* 1:731–33). The severity can still be seen, however, in the Qumran community (see above).

[183] Cf. SMIT (1997:49–51) and FEE (451–53) who arrive at a similar conclusion.

[184] I am understanding "ethics" here as describing Paul's ideas of daily living patterns of conduct on what is "right" and "wrong" (cf. FURNISH, 1968:209).

[185] ROSNER (1994), 177, 190–93.

[186] Cf. FURNISH, 77. Rosner also observes that "Paul cites Scripture most commonly when in the throes of controversy" (191).

Paul because they were wrong in the scriptures which he considered authoritative and which the Christians had inherited. The moral seriousness of these vices was evident by the dire consequences they had on Israel. If such vices incited divine rejection back then, they would do so now. Both the Israelites and Corinthians serve the same Lord; in fact, Christ was present with Israel back then just as he is present with the Corinthians now – a point which strengthens Paul's rhetoric here.

In addition, the language of belonging seems important for Paul because he emphasises that the Corinthians were baptised into Christ (10:2). The Corinthians belong to Christ, and since the members of the congregation are the body of Christ, there is a corresponding relationship between the individual and the πάντα (cf. 1 Cor. 12:26–27). The Corinthians should not give themselves over to vices and thereby defile the body of Christ.[187]

The vices were also wrong because they did not exemplify Paul as an imitator of Christ who had given up his ἐξουσία for the sake of others (1 Cor. 10:30– 11:1; cf. 9:18ff). In the discourse on idol meats, *imitatio Christi* would include giving up one's own freedom for the sake of loving and building up others (8:2 cf. 13:1ff; Rom. 13:8; 1 Thes. 3:12).

In 10:5–10 Paul employs the use of vice or virtue listing which was common in Jewish traditions (Hos. 4:1–2; Ezek. 18:5–17; Psa. 15; Wisd. 14:22–31; Test. Reub. 3.3–6; 1QS 4:2–6, 9–11; CD 4:17–19).[188] He included a number of vice lists in his own writings (Gal. 5:19–21; Rom. 1:29–31; 13:13; 2 Cor. 12:20–21; Col. 3:5, 8).[189]

Several observations are worth noting regarding Paul's vice lists. First, Paul uses the lists to identify specific vices in order to discourage Christians from such activities.[190] In essence, they became a channel for communicating Paul's boundary markers to his addressees. Second, Paul's lists often contain "social vices" reflecting an animosity toward sins that disrupted the community. These vices included malice, envy, strife, and so forth. Furnish writes, "Paul's vice

---

[187] See also FURNISH 162–181, 211–15.

[188] Vice lists also appear in certain Greco-Roman traditions. A list in Juvenal's Satires (Juvenal, Sat. 6.314–41) comes close to Paul's in 1 Corinthians 10 according to WITHERINGTON (1995:223). Greco-Roman lists, however, do not seem to be grounded in Jewish tradition, and since Paul is appealing to vices in the Israelite wilderness, he is undoubtedly utilising the latter tradition. For an extended overview of virtue and vice lists in Jewish and Christian traditions, see DUNN (1998), 662–65; ZAAS (1988), 622–29; McELENEY (1974), 203–19; SCHWEITZER (1979), 195–209; WIBBLING (1959); EASTON (1932), 1–12.

[189] Note also the amount of vice lists occurring in the disputed letters (Eph. 4:25–32; 5:3– 5; 1 Tim. 1:3–11; 4:1–3; 6:4–5; 2 Tim. 2:22–25; 3:1–9).

[190] One must refrain, however, from concluding that all of Paul's vice lists exhaust all the activities he considered contrary to Christian conduct. Furnish notes that in Galatians 5:19– 20, Paul includes the addendum "and such as these" (cf. Rom. 1:29) indicating there were more activities he considered as vices which he did not bother to mention. Hence, no complete ethical system should be extracted from Paul's lists (cf. FURNISH, 91).

lists, unlike those of the Hellenistic world in general which emphasized 'personal' vices, are particularly formed for the life of the community."[191] The lists reflect a similarity with the Jewish practice of listing sins that violate the Torah and which were set in the matrix of establishing order in the holy community (Exod. 20; Deut. 28–29; Lev. 18).[192] Third, the vices were sometimes contrasted with virtue lists (2 Cor. 6:6f; Gal. 5:22–23; Phil. 4:8; Col. 3:12f). The virtue lists would help identify how Christians were supposed to act in the present age. The vices were to reflect the behaviour of those who are not part of God's community but were the objects of his wrath (Gal. 5:21; 1 Cor. 6:10; Rom. 1:18ff).[193] Finally, the vice lists are not exhaustive so as to provide a complete catalogue of every conceivable sin Paul condemned. At the end of his lists in Galatians and Romans, he warns against those who do "things such as these" (καὶ τὰ ὅμοια τούτοις – Gal. 5:19a) and "things like these" (τὰ τοιαῦτα – Gal. 5:19b; Rom. 1:32).[194] The vices Paul lists are thus intended as samplings of sins he wishes the Christians to avoid. Moreover, he does not have a preconceived list that he inserts in the letters. No term appears in every list.[195]

It is significant, then, that the vice lists in the Corinthian letters are mostly situational. Paul is targeting specific vices that may already be harmful to the congregation.[196] The Corinthian lists help Paul establish boundary markers which identify the activities of those who should be considered "outside" of the Christian sphere. He writes that those who participate in the vices will not inherit the kingdom of God (1 Cor. 6:9–10). Yet Paul claims that *some* in the Corinthian church were also practising these vices (e.g., fornication: 5:1ff; 6:12ff; tempting Christ: 10:22; covetousness: 10:5–6). Gager rightly argues that the ἄδικοι refer to outsiders in 6:1–8, but then Paul says to the Corinthians in 6:9–11: "'You have been such as these!' (vs. 11a), with the clear implication that unless they change their ways, they, too will be numbered among the *adikoi*" and be excluded from the kingdom.[197] What is more, in 1 Corinthians he includes more vice lists than any of his other letters (1 Cor. 5:9–11; 6:9–10; 1 Cor.

---

[191] FURNISH, 84.

[192] Cf. MCELENEY, 217.

[193] For Philo, certain aspects of Jewish festivals and sacrifices are associated with vices and virtues (*Spec. Leg.* 1.172–74, 191–92, 213–15).

[194] FURNISH, 76f.

[195] Furnish observes that in 6 vice lists in the "Pauline homologoumena" 42 terms identify 39 distinct vices. Ἔρις (rivalry) and μέθη (drunkenness) appear 4 times; πορνεία (fornication), ἀσέλγεια (indecency), εἰδωλολατρία (idolatry), ζῆλος (jealousy), πλεονεξία (greed) appear 3 times; 8 terms appear twice, and 24 once (76 cf. WIBBLING, 86ff).

[196] Although Furnish argues that Paul's vice lists are mostly random, he acknowledges the vices in Corinth seem to be an exception to this (84).

[197] GAGER (1970), 334. GAGER (335) also notes how Paul uses the prospect of the kingdom to motivate ethical conduct among the Christians. After writing a list of vices to the Galatians Paul exhorts the Christian community: "I warn you now, as I warned you before, that those who do such things will not share in the kingdom of God" (Gal. 5:21b).

10:6–10; 13:4–7; cf. 1 Cor. 1:11f; 3:3; 4:6, 18–19; 5:1ff; 6:12ff; 8–10; 11:18–21).[198] Even in the chapter on love there rests an implicit vice list relevant to the Corinthian situation wherein Paul mentions jealousy and boasting (13:4 cf. 3:3, 21), rudeness and insisting on one's own way (13:5 cf. 6:7; 8:5ff), and rejoicing in wrongdoing (13:6 cf. 5:2).[199] Hence, Paul warns the Corinthians to "stop sinning" (μὴ ἁμαρτάνετε – 1 Cor. 15:34).[200] Gundry Volf is therefore mistaken when she uses the conventional language of the New Testament vice lists (she cites Luke 18:11) to interpret 1 Corinthians 6:9–11 as referring to non-believers.[201]

The situational nature of Paul's vices in 1 Corinthians appears again in the case of 10:7–10 (idolatry, fornication, tempting Christ, and grumbling). We have observed that the vices in this passage reflect the actual activities of some members in the congregation. Paul was not warning the Corinthians against the commencement of these activities – at least in a seminal form, some were *already* committing the vices.[202] Thus, he must use very strong language in the

---

[198] Also, in his second letter, Paul writes as though the Corinthians had already been participating in rivalries, fornication, and other vices related to his first letter (2 Cor. 12:20–13:2). Paul's lists to the Corinthians stress a social dimension and are closely linked with the problems of fornication, idolatry, drunkenness, envy, discord, and conceit (Cf. FURNISH, 84).

[199] Cf. THISELTON (1977–78), 522.

[200] On this verse Fee writes: "The present prohibition implies the cessation of action already going on; and apparently it is not the action of one or a few. The letter is replete with examples of sinning to which this could refer" (1987:774).

[201] GUNDRY VOLF (1990), 135. Her argument also presupposes that genuine believers cannot fall away (136ff). Although she rightly connects the ἄδικοι in 6:9–11 with 6:1, 6, this association does not exclude the assertion that some genuine Christians could fall away so as to become unrighteous. As we have observed in the main text, some of the Corinthians were committing the vices mentioned in 6:9–11 and elsewhere in the letter. Paul considers them to be *genuine* believers (cf. ch. 3 above), yet they were in danger of divine judgement and expulsion. ROSNER (1996:250–53) suggests that Paul's view of the kingdom of God in 6:9–11 may have come from Deuteronomy 1–6 and Exodus 18–19 which combine the notions of inheritance and covenant. If so, both the blessings and curses of the covenant would seem to apply to the same elect people depending on whether they were faithful or unfaithful to God. The unfaithful Israelite would suffer the same judgement as Israel's enemies (cf. Deut. 28–32). Evidently, Paul would hold to a similar view regarding the Corinthians. The entire community is considered elect, but only those who are faithful to God will inherit the kingdom; those who are unfaithful will not inherit it. They would suffer the same fate as the unbeliever.

[202] R. Davidson supports this point by interpreting the present imperative prohibition in 10:7 as "quit continuing to be idolaters" (1981:256). However, Paul's intention may have had more to do with creating a chiastic balance with the other imperative prohibition of grumbling in 10:10 (cf. 2.1 above). Were idolatry and grumbling more pervasive problems in the congregation than fornication and provoking Christ? It is interesting to note that they both appear on the B level of Paul's chiasm. It is possible that this implies some related significance between the two vices. For the Corinthian situation at hand, though, coveting and idolatry (vv. 6–7) seem to be the primary concern of Paul. They are the central vices related to the macro-theme of idol meats in chapters 8–10. On the other hand, if grumbling is understood by Paul as division/envy/rebelling against authority, then it is at the heart of the main theme of the letter itself (1 Cor. 1:10f).

pericope to discourage any further participation, or else God would reject those in Corinth who were practising these vices and they be marked off with those who are excluded from God's kingdom. In Paul's estimation, committing these vices was wrong just as it was wrong for the Israelite "fathers" before the Corinthians; just as the Israelites incurred divine judgements because of the vices, so some in Corinth were in danger of incurring a divine rejection that would identify them with non-community members who were not part of God's kingdom.

8. Eschatology and Boundaries in a Liminal State
(1 Corinthians 10:11)

In 1 Corinthians 10:11 we arrive at the conclusion of the subsection of 10:5–11 in Paul's larger argument (10:1–13). Here, as in 10:6, he once again stresses a comparison between the Israelites in the wilderness and the Corinthian congregation. But this passage is more significant for Paul's larger argument because he now adds an eschatological dimension in relation to the Corinthians' present state. The location of the Israelites' journey was in the wilderness, but the Corinthians' journey is "located" in the matrix of eschatological ages, and this for Paul is extremely important because it concludes his entire chiasm.

8.1 The Ends of the Ages Have Come upon the Corinthians

8.1.1 "These Things"

As ταῦτα δὲ opened Paul's chiasm in 10:6, a second ταῦτα δὲ closes it in 10:11.[203] Here Paul claims that "these things by way of type" (τυπικῶς)[204] were happening to the Israelites, but they were written for the Corinthians' warning (συνέβαινεν ἐκείνοις ἐγράφη δὲ πρὸς νουθεσίαν ἡμῶν). Since this passage concludes his chiasm, Paul intimates he has something crucial to say here. Once

---

[203] A variant reading has παντα δε ταυτα in 10:11a (א D 81) instead of ταῦτα δὲ (A B 33 1739). Metzger observes that the παντα differs in position in varying manuscripts suggesting it was probably a gloss (1971:560). But Collier suggests that it may be original (1994:62). The variant version increases the intensity of the pericope which builds to a climax in 10:11. The evidence for both witnesses is almost even, but Collier admits that the variant is only a possibility and the intensity still builds without παντα. One way Collier observes this intensity is by recognising that ἐγενήθησαν (the verb which opens the chiasm in 10:6a) is weaker than συνέβαινεν (the verb which closes the chiasm in 10:11a). The latter normally indicates events in the NT with dire consequences (see main text).

[204] The strong combination of א with B with the apparent p46 argues for τυπικῶς rather than the τυποι ([A] D Byz) which seems to be a later insertion to harmonise it with 10:6.

again, as in 10:6, he informs the Corinthian congregation that the things which happened to Israel in the wilderness are prefigurations for the Corinthians. In 10:11b he adds that the Corinthians stand at the climax of redemptive history.[205] Unlike 10:6, however, the "things" in 10:11 do not find their "type" in God's provisions for Israel (10:1–4); rather, the "things" hypothetically prefigure God's judgements on Israel in the wilderness (10:7–10). Paul intended the Corinthians to take warning from Israel's mistakes. This demonstrates once again that he is using deliberative rhetoric in an attempt to persuade the Corinthians against a certain action: they are not to copy Israel's apostasies in the wilderness.

As well, the idea of a sharp warning is implicit in some of the other terms Paul uses. First, Collier notes that συνέβαινεν "nearly always indicates an advent with (dire) consequences" (Mark 10:32; Luke 24:14; 1 Pet. 4:12).[206] The imperfect tense may add a dimension of continuity to the consequence. Robertson and Plummer highlight this aspect by translating 10:11a as follows: "Now these things by way of lesson happened one after another to them."[207] Second, Paul's use of ἐγράφη implies that he considered these as authoritative examples; he uses γράφω when referring to statements found in the Hebrew/LXX scripture traditions (cf. 1 Cor. 1:19; 2:9; 3:19; 9:9; etc.), which he considered to be the oracles of God (τὰ λόγια τοῦ θεοῦ) (Rom. 3:1–2 cf. 1:2).[208] Third, νουθεσία appears only once in the LXX and this is in the milieu of the Israelites in the wilderness who received "admonition" for a little while by having the bronze serpent as a sign of salvation (Wisd. 16:6).[209] It is possible that Paul may have had this passage in mind in 10:11 since he appears to use the Wisdom wilderness tradition in his previous sentence (1 Cor. 10:10c cf. Wisd. 18:22, 25).[210] In Paul's letters, the variants of this word denote a moral appeal leading to amendment (1 Cor. 4:14; Rom. 15:14; Col. 1:28; 3:16; 1 Thes. 5:12, 14; 2 Thes. 3:15; cf. Eph. 6:4).[211] Hence, the chiasm begins and ends with a sense of warning, stressing Paul's anxiety over the reality of divine judgement that could occur in the Corinthian situation.[212] The Israelite events were written to place a stern sense of caution in the minds of the readers.[213]

---

[205] R. Davidson writes that the "movement from OT events to NT realities involves an *historical progression* or *Steigerung* ("escalation") because the NT realities constitute the climatic, eschatological destination toward which the OT events point" (281).

[206] COLLIER, 62.

[207] ROBERTSON/PLUMMER, 207.

[208] On Paul's attitude toward scripture, see E. ELLIS (1957b), 20–37.

[209] Cf. BEHM, *TDNT* 4:1021.

[210] We should also note that the verb form νουθετέω appears in Wisdom (11:10; cf. 12:2, 26).

[211] ROSNER (1994), 193 ftn34.

[212] FEE (458) rightly exhibits the stress on warning by interpreting the second δέ as "slightly adversative" and contrasting what happened to them (Israel) with what was written πρὸς ... ἡμῶν: "for the purpose of (warning) us (objective genitive)."

[213] Cf. ROBERTSON/PLUMMER, 207.

8.1.2 Εἰς Οὓς τὰ Τέλη τῶν Αἰώνων Κατήντηκεν

In 10:11b Paul claims that he and the Corinthians exist at a time in which the "ends of the ages have come." In Jewish literature τέλος is often placed in eschatological contexts to refer to the "end" or "goal."[214] The word was used in certain traditions to convey a sense of salvation in the context of the return of Israel (Hos. 3:5; Isa. 2:2).[215] For Paul, the idea of τέλος as a "goal" in eschatological salvation is carried over from Jewish traditions, but with Christ as the object of faith (1 Cor. 1:8; 15:24). In light of Jewish traditions, the "ends of the ages" in 1 Corinthian 10:11 bears resemblance to the "end of days" phrases in ancient Jewish literature (Dan. 12:13; 4Q174 1:2, 15, 19; 1QSa 1:1; Test. Mos. 12:4; 4 Ezra 6:25; Sib. Or. 8.311),[216] or other eternity and eschatological expressions which have plural "ends" or "ages" (Heb. 9:26; 4 Ezra 11:44 cf. 14:10–12; Test. Levi 14:1).[217]

In 10:11b Conzelmann argues for either a singular or formal sense of "the end of a unity" having only one world-age from "the point of view of its limitation."[218] Another perspective has the plural "ends of the ages" indicating the termination of the present and past age, and the beginning of the new one. It would thus signify a meeting or overlap of two ages in unison with Paul's theology.[219] A third view interprets the phrase as the "aim[s] of the ages." The Israelite wilderness journeys would be one of those previous ages or epochs which finds its fulfilment in the present age of the eschatological era inaugurated through the Christ event (cf. 1 Thes. 5:1f; Acts 1:7; 1 QpHab 7:13).[220] This final reading is supported by the older apocalyptic traditions which divide their history into several eras. Daniel's images of beasts and Enoch's Apocalypse of Weeks provide two examples (Dan. 2:31ff; 7:3ff; 8:3ff; cf. 1 Enoch 91:12–17; 93:1–10). In addition, several periods seem depicted in the Qurman Commentary on Habakkuk (1QpHab 7:13), The Ages of Creation (4Q180), and

---

[214] Cf. DELLING, *TDNT*, 8:52–54.

[215] DELLING, 8:53.

[216] Cf. BARRETT, 227–28; DELLING, 8:54; Str.-B., 3.416f.

[217] Cf. SASSE, *TDNT* 1:203.

[218] CONZELMANN, 168. The perfect singular κατήντηκεν does not necessarily argue for the conceptual unity of the plural τὰ τέλη τῶν αἰώνων. Here Paul is more likely utilising the ancient grammarian principle of having the plural neuter subject adopt a singular verb (cf. *BDP*, 73–4).

[219] Cf. Soards: "upon whom the ends of the ages have *met* [emphasis mine]" (1986:149). Barrett, however, argues that this view "might not be an inaccurate account of Paul's eschatological beliefs, though he never (unless he does so here) expresses them in this way; it is scarcely admissible as a translation" because the "end" refers to a termination, not a beginning, and "arrive" is constructed with "upon whom," not with an implied "each other" (227). Hence, the "ends" come upon "us" (Paul and the Corinthians) not upon one another. J. Court adds that there is no indication in Greek use which clearly supports the idea of a "back-end" meeting a "front-end" (1982:62–63).

[220] Cf. DELLING, 8:54.

The Heavenly Prince Melchizedek (11QMel. 4–18).[221] In a similar way, Paul does not necessarily consider the "not yet" eschaton as one epoch; rather, he sees it fulfilled in several stages (1 Cor. 15:23 ff).[222] In 1 Corinthians, it is not unreasonable to think that Paul viewed the past the same way.

Two observations are important here in 10:11. First, whether a singular or plural conception is intended, τὰ τέλη τῶν αἰώνων for Paul finds its fullest meaning in an eschatological context.[223] Second, Paul is speaking from the vantage point of the beginning of a new era looking at the end of an old one which perhaps had multiple epochs. We will note the significance of these conclusions below.

8.2 Jewish Eschatological Influence on Paul

We have not answered thoroughly how Paul intended the conceptions of death and incompletion to be understood by the Corinthian believers in 10:5–11. In what sense might "death" hinder *them* from finishing their journey and what *was* their journey? Is there any indication envisioned that the Corinthians might actually turn away from finishing their trek? To formulate a plausible answer, we must step back to examine Paul's perspective of eschatology in light of the eschatological framework he establishes at the end of his chiasm in 10:11.

Many scholars have noted how Paul's thinking is similar to the Jewish apocalyptic traditions.[224] Apocalyptic literature of his era often perceived reality with

---

[221] Cf. J. Collins (1997), 54–57.

[222] See also Holleman (1996). In 1 Corinthians 15:24 Donfried observes Paul's indebtedness to the apocalyptic tradition as found in 1 Enoch 91–93 and the Sibylline Oracles 4:47–91 (1987:176).

[223] Καταντάω in Pauline literature can also point to an arrival, reception, or attaining in an eschatological setting (Phil. 3:11; Eph. 4:13). No doubt, the idea is similar here where a realised eschatological framework is in view (cf. Court, 63). M. Bogle suggests that τέλος could refer to a connotation of a "mystic rite" associated with the Mysteries (cf. 1 Cor. 2:7; 4:1; 15:51). He thus translates the phrase as "to whom the eternal mysteries have come down," or the more free translation: "Who are the heirs of the Mysteries of the ages" (1955–56:246–47). But this unusual interpretation emphasises a sacramental view, when Paul's view, as the choice of words and phrase shows, is clearly eschatological.

[224] E. g., Rowland (1982), 374–86; Collins (1984), 207–209; A. Brown (1995), xviii; Aune, *DPL*, 25–35. I am understanding the term *apocalypse* as a genre of literature which characterises segments of Jewish and Christian belief (c. 200 B.C.E. – 200 C. E.) in which a narrative and revelatory structure is said to have been mediated by a supernatural source to a human agent. The revelatory nature of this genre may be temporal in relation to eschatology and spatial in relation to cosmology (D. Russell, 1992:12 cf. J. Collins, 1979). However, I recognise that not all themes or motifs in apocalyptic literature are necessarily eschatological. Nevertheless, in this section, I will be focusing on apocalyptic eschatological themes. Some of these themes include a type of expectation often characterised by temporal and ethical dualism, insights into the secret plan of God which may be divided into historical

a dualistic approach toward cosmological categories.[225] The present age (often ruled by wicked spirits) was perceived as hostile and corrupt (4 Ezra 4:2ff; 7:31; 2 Bar. 44:9–12; 2 En. 66:6).[226] In the Community Rule and the War Rule, there is a distinction between the sons of light and the sons of darkness (1QS 3:17–4:11; 1QM 13:9–12), and between the people of God and the Kittim (1QM 1:6; 18:2–3). Apocalyptic traditions often predicted that at the end of the age, the Lord would punish wicked people and wicked spirits (2 Bar. 54:21; 1 En. 10:13ff; CD 7:9–8:3[19:9–13]). The tension between righteousness and wickedness permeated the reality of life in this world.

The dualistic nature of apocalyptic also appears on a temporal level, although it is perhaps not as explicit as it is in the later Tannaitic traditions.[227] In other words, certain apocalyptic writings make a contrast between two ages.[228] This seems to be attested in the Similitudes of Enoch (possibly c. 105–64 B.C.E.) where it is said that the "antecedent of time" shall proclaim peace in the name of the world which is to come (1 En. 71:15). 4 Ezra (c. 100 C.E. or earlier) affirms that the Most High has not made one age but two (4 Ezra 7:50). The present generation is characterised by corruption, ungodliness, and unbelief, and the coming era – which is heralded by the judgement day – is characterised by immortality and righteousness (7:51ff, 112–114 cf. Ps. Philo 3:10; 19:7–13; 2 En. 65:7–10).

In the Apocalypse of Abraham (c. 70–150 C.E.), the righteous of the coming age will destroy the heathen who ruled them in this age, which consists of 12 periods (Apoc. Abr. 31 cf. 29).[229] In the Syriac Apocalypse of Baruch (c. 100–120 C.E.) the future age is characterised by the passing away of that which is corruptible. The righteous will be raised from the dead, but there will be torment upon the wicked (2 Bar. 30:1–2; 44:9–15; cf. 15:7–8; 21:23; 40:3). Vestiges of

---

segments, an imminence of the reign of God and God's intervention in the cosmic order, and the introduction of a new royal mediator (cf. AUNE, 25–27).

[225] I am not saying, however, that these are the only important motifs in apocalyptic literature. Space does not permit an extensive apocalyptic study, which is currently in a state of flux. For a fuller treatment on apocalyptic themes from a fairly recent source, see COLLINS, 1–19. For earlier perspectives, see P. HANSON (1979), 1–31; KOCH (1972), 18–35; VIELHAUER, (1963–65), 2:581–607.

[226] Cf. RUSSELL (1964), 254ff, 267–68.

[227] Tannaitic literature often categorised eras in terms of "this age" (עוֹלָם הַזֶּה) and the "age to come" (עוֹלָם הַבָּא – Pirqe 'Aboth 2:7; 4:1, 21–22; 6:4, 7; M. Sanhedrin 10.1f; cf. Sasse, *TDNT*, 1:206; Str.-B. 1:829; LADD 1994:402; ROWLAND, 35).

[228] Rowland notes that there is indeed a dualism in apocalyptic eschatology which contrasts the weakness of present history with the future glory, but "only occasionally is this implicit dualism turned into an explicit doctrine of two ages" (28 cf. RUSSELL, 1992:104). HENGEL (1974:1.190) argues that the Jewish "present" and "coming" ages were not present in this form when the NT was written (cf. DALMAN, 1909:147–54). But this is no argument against a two (or more) age *conception* which appears during the Second Temple period (see main text).

[229] Cf. COLLINS (1984), 184.

this aspect of apocalyptic, however, seem to be much older (Dan. 12:2–3 cf. Tob. 13:2; 2 Macc. 7:9).[230] The imminence of the coming age is pronounced in the older traditions, but it also appears in the later ones (Dan. 8:17f; 12:11–13; 4 Ezra 4:44–52; 2 Bar. 85:10).[231]

In Jubilees (c. 161–140 B.C.E.), the coming age may be seen as already arriving in a preliminary stage (Jub. 1:23–29; 23:26–31).[232] In the Community Rule, the coming age has already arrived in an inceptual manner (1QS 3:17–4:21). In the Commentary on Habakkuk, there appears to be a delay in the final age (1QpHab. 7:2–14; 5:7–8). These traditions point to a transitional era even though the transition may not appear to be a smooth one.[233] In some traditions David's son was seen as a messianic king who would inaugurate or precede the new age (4 Ezra 7:26–44, 12:31–34; Test. Sim. 7:1–2; Psa. Sol. 17:21ff cf. 1 En. 91:1–17; 2 En. 32:2–33:1; Jub. 23:26–31).[234] The coming messianic age was sometimes seen as an intermediary era between the present and final ages (Dan. 2:44–45; 4 Ezra 7:26ff; 2 Bar. 29–30 cf. 1 En. 91:12–17).[235]

The messianic age was related to a kingdom motif that could be traced back to embryonic stages in the Hebrew scriptures. 1) In the Exodus tradition God had proclaimed that Israel would be a kingdom of priests and a holy nation (Exod. 19:5–6). 2) In other traditions God was viewed as ruling the kingdom of Israel in a theocratic system until the Israelites desired to establish a human king under Saul and then David (cf. 1 Sam. 8–10, 16).[236] 3) When Israel's moral corruption resulted in their defeat and captivity by the neighbouring nations, the prophetic writers proclaimed a final day of judgement. In the Day of Yahweh a new era of righteousness would be established. God would rule over his people, and the enemies of Israel would be routed (Amos 5:18–20; Joel 1–3; Zeph. 1–3; Zech. 14:4–9). 4) Some traditions proclaimed a new era in which a messianic deliverer would arise out of the line of David (2 Sam. 7:12ff; Isa. 7:14; 9:1f; 11:1f; Mic. 5:1–5) who was often identified as "David" (Amos. 9:11; Ezek. 34:23; 37:24; Jer. 23:5–6) or the "Branch" (Isa. 9:6; 11:1; Jer. 30:9; 33:15f; Zech. 3:8; 6:12).[237] 5) The coming messianic kingdom is also depicted as a new exodus and an inheriting of the promised land. This was often por-

---

[230] Cf. RUSSELL, 366–77.

[231] Cf. ROWLAND, 27f.

[232] Cf. RUSSELL, 269ftn4.

[233] Cf. COLLINS, 131f, 161; Cf. LINCOLN (1981), 177; RINGGREN (1963), 152–66; COLLINS (1997), 57, 62.

[234] Cf. RUSSELL, 91–97; SCHOEPS (1961), 93–98. In later Jewish literature there is a conception that the aeons consisted of 2000 years of chaos, 2000 years of Torah, and 2000 years of Messiah before the eternal rest (SCHOEPS, 98; cf. Sanh. 97a, Jer. Megilla 70d, Pesiq. Rabb. 4a–c).

[235] But on the diversity and complexities related to early Messianic sources, see CHARLESWORTH (1992), 3–35.

[236] Cf. SCHOEPS, 89ff.

[237] Cf. RUSSELL, 88–97.

trayed with the imagery of water in the desert, which was interpreted as an outpouring of God's spirit or the revitalisation of life (Isa. 11:10–16; 32:15; 44:3; Jer. 31:33–34; Ezek. 36:24–27; Joel 2:28–32; Zech. 12:10–13:1). The early Christian perspective does not appear to be an abandonment of this motif (cf. ch. 3.1.4.3 above). The wilderness episode came to be recognised as "the interval between the premessianic age and the consummation, between deliverance and final bliss."[238]

8.3 Paul in the Age of "Now" and "Not Yet"

We have viewed a sampling of Jewish sources which may have influenced Paul's perspective of eschatology, and we have discovered that these sources sometimes portray a temporal aspect which may be similar to Paul's language in 1 Corinthians 10:11. In order to gain more insight on Paul's meaning here, we will now examine his eschatological perspective in light of his Christian experience and writings.

8.3.1 Paul and the Apocalyptic Centre

J. Christiaan Beker argues that Paul's gospel has an apocalyptic centre which has been modified by the Christ-event. Apocalypticism is the symbolic expression of Paul's calling (Gal. 1:11–17 cf. Acts 9:2ff; 26:12–18) and the language of his symbolic universe as a Pharisaic Jew (Gal. 1:14; Phil. 3:5). Beker affirms this is the case because Paul believed the crucified Messiah revealed himself to him and confirmed the truth about the resurrected Christ, and resurrection language would be understandable to a Pharisee only in terms of apocalyptic categories.[239] Hence, Paul's eschatological perspective reflects an apocalyptic pattern of two ages, but he affixes the resurrection of Christ as a definitive sign of the impending kingdom. This event is tied into the future resurrection of the dead (1 Cor. 15:20–28; Rom. 1:2–4; 8:29; Col. 1:18).[240]

Beker seems right in affirming the centrality of Jewish apocalyptic influence in Paul's thought patterns.[241] Whether Paul has an apocalyptic centre in *all* his

---

[238] O. PIPER (1957), 17.

[239] J. C. BEKER (1980), xvii–xviii, xx cf. 16, 367 cf. SOARDS (1986), 149f. On Paul's Pharisaic background in relation to apocalyptic, see J. C. BEKER 137, 143–45. Segal argues that Paul's conversion was similar to the experience of Jewish Merkabah mysticism, which in first century Judea, was apocalyptic (1990:34).

[240] J. C. BEKER, 167, 177f.

[241] Although Beker seems a bit ambiguous about his definition of "apocalyptic," he understands apocalyptic literature as revolving around the three basic notions of historical dualism, cosmic expectation on a universal scale, and especially the imminence of the end of

letters seems less likely. The centre was probably adjusted to fit the situation of the audience whom he was attempting to reach.[242] Nevertheless Paul does perceive a contrast between a past/present and future age similar to certain Jewish apocalyptic writers. His view may have also been influenced by his own experience as well as by the earliest Christian communities who seemed to reflect a similar eschatological view (e.g., Mark 10:30; Luke 18:30). They affirmed Jesus' proclamation that the end of the ages had come and that the kingdom of God was now dawning through the activity of the Spirit in his ministry (Luke 3:16ff; 4:17f; 11:20; Matt. 12:28–29; 13 cf. Heb. 6:4–5).[243] The Pentecost sermon attributed to Peter proclaims the eschatological fulfilment of the last days outpouring of the Spirit made possible by the death and resurrection of Christ (Acts 2:17ff).

Cullmann rightly suggests that the Jewish tension between "this age" and the "age to come" finds its mid-point in the Christian redemptive history through the resurrection of Christ. The earliest Christians understood themselves to live at the beginning of the end of this history (cf. Acts 1:7;1 John 2:18; Heb. 1:1–2; 2 Pet. 3:1ff; Rev. 1:1–3, 19). The Christians live with the decisive battle having already taken place (e.g., D-Day) but its culmination as not yet fulfilled (e.g., V-Day).[244]

8.3.2 The Tension of "Now" and "Not Yet"

Paul held to a form of temporal dualism set in terms of the past and future age which seem to overlap in the present.[245] For him the kingdom of God was both a present "now" and future "not yet." The blessings of the kingdom could be experienced in this age (1 Cor. 4:20; 1 Thes. 2:12; Rom. 14:17), but the full benefits and inheritance was yet to come (1 Cor. 6:9–10; 15:24, 50; Gal. 5:21; 2 Thes. 1:5). The Christians are said to possess both the present and the future in Christ (1 Corinthians 3:22; cf. Rom. 8:38–39). The ungodly of this age, how-

---

the world (136). (But for qualifications, see 136–38.) We are concerned with supporting Beker's basic understanding of apocalyptic literature as influencing Paul's thought world.

[242] Cf. GAGER (1970), 237.

[243] Cf. DUNN (1975), 47–49. Dunn writes that Jesus distinguished his exorcisms from other Jewish exorcisms in that he operated his by the Spirit of God; hence, "Jesus saw his exorcisms ... as that binding of the powers of evil which was looked for at the end of the age. The final battle was already joined and Satan was already being routed (cf. Luke 10:18). These claims imply a *clear sense of the eschatological distinctiveness of his power*: Jesus' mighty acts were in his own eyes as epochal as the miracles of the Exodus and likewise heralded a new age" (48). On the expectation of a messianic figure who would drive out demons after the authority of David and Solomon, see AUNE, ISBE, 1:923.

[244] CULLMANN (1952), 81–83, 145–46.

[245] Yet it appears that Paul also believed the past and future ages were each composed of several epochs (cf. 8.1.2). Apparently, he saw no contradiction in using both apocalyptic perspectives.

ever, are subject to God's wrath and will perish with the age (Rom. 1:18ff;1 Cor. 1:18; cf. Col. 1:21; Eph. 2:3, 11–12). But the Christians are delivered from the present evil age (Gal. 1:4; Phil. 2:15 cf. 2 Tim. 4:10; Tit. 2:12) and from the coming wrath (1 Thes. 1:9–10; 5:9 cf. Rom. 5:9).[246]

The present age is controlled by the devil (2 Cor. 4:4 cf. Eph. 2:2) and is set in contrast to the future era where all sufferings shall cease and all creation will be renovated (Rom. 8:18–23 cf. Eph. 1:20–22).[247] He exhorts Christians not to conform to the manner of this age (ὁ αἰών οὗτος) which is influenced by human wisdom instead of the wisdom given to the renewed in spirit (1 Cor. 1:20; 2:6, 8; Rom. 12:2). He uses the phrase ὁ νῦν καιρός when speaking of the justification and election of God's people in the present time (Rom. 3:26; 11:5), and ὁ κόσμος οὗτος which denotes the moral corruption and/or transience of it (1 Cor. 3:19; 5:10; 7:31).[248]

Paul's eschatology in 1 Corinthians 10 appears to be similar to the perspective of Jewish apocalyptic writers who seem to have two ages which mingle or overlap in a transitional era and place the resurrection at the end of the messianic age (e.g., 2 Bar. 29–30; 39–40; 72–74).[249] The writer of 4 Ezra 7:26–44 marks a preliminary period of 400 years of political and salvific realisation before the end. Then the messiah dies and seven days of primeval silence follow (7:30). After this a general resurrection of the dead and day of judgement occur (7:32–38).

Schoeps noted that Tannaitic and later traditions fix the eschatological overlap of two ages at 40 years, after the number of years Israel spent in the wilderness (cf. Deut. 8:2).[250] Similarly, the Qumran community seemed to have retreated in the desert and there awaited 40 years to lapse (35 years of service plus 5 sabbatical years) from the time of the community congregation's preparations to the overthrow of the wicked (1 QS 1:15f; 11QPsa. 37 cf. CD 20:15; 1Q22 1:1; 2:5f).[251]

---

[246] Cf. FURNISH, 122–23.

[247] But this does not mean that Paul always thinks the things of cosmos are necessarily evil; his language is contingent on this point. In 1 Corinthians 7:29–31, the things pertaining to "this world" are not intrinsically evil; rather, they are transient and therefore unworthy of serious commitment on the part of the Corinthians (cf. WIMBUSH, 1987:33 cf. 42).

[248] Sasse (1:205) notes that ὁ αἰών οὗτος is substituted for ὁ καιρός οὗτος in early Christian sources (e.g., Mark 10:30). In general, αἰών reflects more a duration of time than καιρός in NT writings (cf. CULLMANN, 39, 45). Other Pauline literature affirms the mystery of Christ's presence in the Christian has been revealed in this age (Col. 1:26; Eph. 3:5).

[249] Cf. SCHOEPS, 98f; AUNE, 29. On comments and characteristics of the two ages in 4 Ezra, see STONE (1990), 92–93; STONE (1989), 44–83.

[250] R. Eliezer ben Hyrcanus: Bar. in Sanh. 99a; R. Aqiba: Midr. Teh. on Psa. 90:15; cf. Tanch. Eqeb 7b, Pes. Rabb. 4a: see SCHOEPS, 100f.

[251] According to COLLINS, the 40 years may be a period which is included in a larger framework related to eschatological calculations found in Ezekiel (4:1ff) and Daniel (9:24–27), and totalling 490 years (1997:55–56, 66).

Schoeps argues that Paul thought the interim period before Christ's return was very short and that Paul probably held a "short-term" messianic era of 40 years in common with certain Jewish traditions of his era. However, Schoeps seems to be going too far in suggesting that Paul thought the interim would literally last 40 years. Pauline writings do not indulge in setting dates for the end or in calculating eschatological predictions as do some apocalyptic writers (cf. 2 Thes. 2:1ff). Paul seemed to affirm the Jesus tradition that Christ's return would be unpredictable (1 Thes. 5:1–3 cf. Matt. 24:32–25:14). It has *not* been established that the Pauline passages used to support Christ's imminence indicate that Paul believed the *parousia* would definitely occur in his own lifetime (e.g., 1 Cor. 7:29–31; 15:51–52; Rom. 13:11–12; 1 Thes. 4:16–18).[252] Such passages must be set in tension with other ones in which Paul anticipates his death before Christ's return (Phil. 1:20–23; cf. 2 Cor. 1:9; 5:1–11; 2 Tim. 4:6–7). He maintains both Christ's imminence and his own death in the Philippian letter (Phil. 1:6, 1:20f; 3:20; 4:5). Paul may be simply borrowing from traditional and contemporary prophetic language which stressed the coming eschatological events were near (קָרוֹב) even though those events might point to the distant future (Joel 2:1, 15; Obad. 15; Ezek. 12:23–25; 4 Ezra 11:44; cf. Rev. 1:1–3). He would thus be convinced, as were some other Jews and Christians, that God does not work on the same time tables as do humans (cf. Psa. 90:4; 2 Pet. 3:8).[253] Therefore, it is not known whether Paul consistently believed he would live to see Christ's return. He probably did not know whether he would or not, and this is precisely *why* he could anticipate the *parousia* while at the same time maintaining the possibility of his death before then (Phil. 1:20; 3:20 cf. 1 Thes. 4:17–18).

In 1 Corinthians 10:1–11, apocalyptic influences seem to have coloured Paul's perspective of the wilderness epoch, and we have already noted how Paul was influenced by the Isaianic tradition which discloses a new exodus/ wilderness trek for God's people (cf. 8.2; ch. 3:2ff). Like the Israelites of the exodus, Paul views himself and the Corinthian congregation in a transitional "wilderness" state between the inception of the messianic age and the future completion of the messianic kingdom era which would be heralded by Christ's return (cf. 1 Cor. 15:23ff). It is not known, however, whether Paul personally

---

[252] In 1 Corinthian 7:29–31, for instance, the phrase "time is short" is set in the context of transient worldly things which become relative to the Christian in the new era. WITHERINGTON (1992:28) notes that the time has been shortened in a sense that ever since the Christ-event has taken place, "No one could say that there was necessarily a long time before God would bring his plan of history to a climax, since Jesus could return at any moment, like a thief in the night (see 1 Thes. 5:1–11)." Cf. MOISER (1983), 113; BORNKAMM (1969b), 206f. However, if Paul is the author of 2 Thessalonians, it would be more appropriate to say that Paul believed certain eschatological events must first take place before the *parousia* (2 Thes. 2:1–12).

[253] Cf. BLOMBERG, *DJG*, 246.

believed the present liminal period would last 40 years. What seems to be the backdrop of 10:11 is an eschatological interim which Paul thinks is reflected in the imagery of Israel's wilderness journey. This notion is associated with ideas about the transient present age inclusive of its hostile forces (cf. 1 Cor. 5:5 cf. 2 Cor. 4:4). Some other early Christian traditions also hold to an eschatological exodus. In the Apocalypse of John, for example, the woman (who represents God's people) gives birth to the messianic ruler (Rev. 12:1–5). She then escapes from the Leviathan dragon (who is often represented as Egypt or another oppressive power)[254] into the wilderness where she is miraculously fed for 1,260 days or 3 1/2 times. This time period apparently represents the transitional epoch from the coming of the messiah to the completion of the eschaton (Rev. 12:6ff cf. 11:2,5; Dan. 9:24–27).

8.3.3 Paul's Existential and Salvific Dualism

Don Howell observes the various tensions created by Paul's eschatological perspective in terms of the Christians' new standing with Christ and their old standing with Adam, which is set in a new age of unrealised fulfilments (cf. Rom. 5:12–20).[255] Some of these tensions of "now" and "not yet" are seen in the language of the flesh versus the spirit, the "firstfruits" of the Spirit, and salvation. First, the flesh wars against the spirit (Rom 7:5, 18, 25; 8:3–13; Gal. 5:13–19), and in this sense, it is seen as unregenerate and alienated from God, being "in cosmic solidarity with the old order." For Paul, those who are dominated by the "flesh" (σάρξ) will experience spiritual death (Rom. 8:6, 13; Gal. 6:8; Col. 2:13), and the σάρξ, along with sin and death, reigns in the present age (Rom. 5:21; 6:12f; 1 Cor. 15:56).[256] Second, the Spirit is viewed by Paul as a foretaste of the eschatological blessings in metaphors such as ἀπαρχή (Rom. 8:23) and ἀρραβών (2 Cor. 1:22; 5:5; cf. Eph. 1:14) which captivate an idea of an initiatory instalment that finds a greater completion in the future.[257] Third, Paul's metaphors for salvation are seen as eschatological realities which are "provisionally" realised (Rom. 1:17; 4:5–6; 5:10–11; 1 Cor. 1:21, 30; 2 Cor. 5:17–20 cf. Eph. 2:8; Tit. 2:11). Various examples of Paul's use of "once … but now" sets in contrast the believers' former status with their new salvific status in Christ (Rom. 6:21–22; 11:30; Gal. 4:8–9; Col. 3:7–8 cf. Eph 5:8).[258]

---

[254] Cf. Psa. 74[75]:13–14; Ezek. 29:3–5; Isa. 27:1, 12f; 51:9–11 cf. 30:7.

[255] HOWELL (1993), 16–24.

[256] HOWELL, 12–13.

[257] HOWELL, 22. To use these passages, however, as a guarantee of final perseverance does not suffice. The terms associated with the pledge or instalment of the Spirit (2 Cor. 1:22; 5:5; cf. Eph. 1:13–14) are related to baptism and conversion (cf. LAMPE, 1951; BARRETT, 1973:80–81). Paul writes to the same congregation (1 Cor. 10:1–4) that such aspects do *not* guarantee final perseverance, as the rest of the passage and this study demonstrate.

[258] HOWELL, 16; cf. FURNISH, 126–35.

Howell's perspective brings to light some of Paul's eschatological tensions, but he does not take this salvific tension into further areas related to judgement, perseverance, and apostasy. If the tension of "now" and "not yet" covers salvific aspects in Paul, then salvation in the present age is not fully realised but is both a present and future reality (Rom. 1:16;1 Cor. 1:18; Rom. 8:24; 13:11; 1 Cor. 3:15; 10:33; 1 Thes. 5:8 cf. Rom 5:9–10; 10:9).[259] Paul's notion of justification, then, is now and not yet (Rom. 5:1 cf. Gal. 5:5), as well as redemption (Rom. 3:24 cf. 8:23–24), resurrection (Col. 2:12; Rom. 6:5; 8:11), and other metaphors related to salvation such as adoption (Gal. 4:4 cf. Rom. 8:23) and marriage (Rom. 7:4f cf. 2 Cor. 11:2f).[260] Hence, Paul seems to have salvation as an on-going process in the present age. This perspective thus raises the question of perseverance and apostasy. What happens to those who do not complete the process?

In 1 Corinthians 10:11 the idea of Israel's incompletion takes on new importance in light of Paul's eschatology. Paul would tend to regard Israel's trek in the wilderness as prefiguring the eschatological venture of Christians in a transitional era. This in turn would create the dynamic tension emanating from the Corinthian situation on how the Christian ought to run his or her life in the present so as to attain the future life expressed in imagery of completing a race (1 Cor. 9:24–27) and completing a journey (1 Cor. 10:1–11). Mauser rightly affirms the function of Paul's wilderness theme when he writes, "'The end of the ages has come' (1 Cor. 10.11), but the new age itself has not yet arrived ... The wilderness is a parable of this condition. As Israel was delivered from Egypt and had to pass through the desert in order to reach the promised land, so the Christian is delivered by Christ from the bondage of the old age and is on the way to the new age which in faith is already present."[261] If faith is seen not only as a commitment to Christ but also as the ability to sustain the tension of the present status of "now" and "not yet," then Paul believed the Corinthian congregation must live out that tension in perseverance until the end of their natural lives.[262] A persistent failure to do so would result in the forfeiture of the future life. In such a case, the Corinthian member would thus perish with the corrupt and transient world and not attain that final future salvation in the age of incorruption. This could happen to the Corinthian *despite* his or her genuine initiation, election, membership in the body of Christ, and participation in the eucharist (cf. 10:1–4).

---

[259] Cf. ROETZEL, 102–04.

[260] Cf. DUNN, 309–10.

[261] MAUSER, 67–68.

[262] Cf. J. C. BEKER, 356. Along ethical lines, Ladd claims, "we must conclude that Paul uses the motivation of the final attainment of salvation in the Kingdom of God as a motivation to faithful and devoted Christian living" (566).

In essence, Paul maintains that those Corinthians who do not make it to the completion of their course because of their practising of vices will not attain the fully realised salvation expressed in the imagery of the Israelites' rest in the promised land (cf. Num. 14:23–24, 30–35; Deut. 1:35; 12:9–10; Josh. 1:13; Isa. 63:14). This view is supported by the fact that Paul considers the Corinthians as living in a new exodus/wilderness journey in 1 Corinthians 10. The rest to which the Corinthians may attain at the completion of their journey is the eschatological rest of the new exodus anticipated by earlier Jewish traditions (Isa. 40:3f; 43:16–21; Jer. 16:14–15; 31:2ff: Hos. 2:14ff; Psa. 95:8–11; cf. 2 Bar. 73:1) and implied as the goal of the hypothetical prefigurations drawn from the old exodus (cf. 1 Cor. 10:6, 11). For Israel, apostasy in the wilderness resulted in death (10:5–10).[263] For the Corinthians, Paul is implicitly warning against apostasy which results in eschatological death (cf. also Rom. 1:32; 7:13; 8:6, 11, 13).[264] The Corinthian members who commit vices are in danger of divine rejection and the forfeiture of their place in the eschatological kingdom (1 Cor. 10:5; 6:9–11).

8.4 The Eschatological Journey of the Corinthians

We have addressed the issue of the role death plays for the Corinthians in 10:5–11 and that Paul views the congregation members as living in an overlap of eschatological ages. We will now examine how some of the Corinthians may have viewed their own eschatological plight. Paul describes the future or "not yet" eschaton in terms of reward and judgement. At the beginning of the letter, he hopes that the Corinthians would be blameless at Christ's coming (1:7–8), and he concludes the letter with a declaration about the *parousia* in relation to judgement (16:21–22). Moreover, the Corinthians are exhorted to refrain from judging Paul and other leaders until Christ returns and reveals the inner motivations of the human heart (4:4–5). They themselves will judge angels at a future time (1 Cor. 6:3), and their own works will be judged on the day of the Lord (1 Cor. 3:13f). The members were to practise the Lord's Supper until Christ returns, and because of social problems related to the eucharist, they were being chastised in the present so that they would not be condemned with the world in the future (11:26, 32).[265] For Paul, the vice-doers of the present age were "outside" the Christian community and would be judged by God (1 Cor. 5:8–13).

---

[263] For Paul and his Jewish contemporaries, death comes from sin (Rom. 5:12–20; cf. Gen. 3:3, 19; 4 Ezra 8:53; 2 En. 30:16; Str.-B., 1.815–816; 3.155–57).

[264] In Roetzel's words, "Death is God's eschatological verdict for those who reject Christ" (86 cf. 85–90).

[265] In this case, the "chastisement" refers to some of the Corinthians getting sick or dying (11:29).

Satan resides in this "outside" world, and this was where the man who was committing fornication was to be banished so that his spirit might be saved in the last day (5:5, 13).

In 1 Corinthians 15 Paul refers to those who had misperceptions about the future resurrection of the body (1 Cor. 15:12, 35 ff). It is possible that because of their Hellenistic background, the body was not regarded as important, and hence, some in Corinth felt justified in claiming that the body does not partake in any future resurrection (cf. 1 Cor. 6:13–14). The thrust of Paul's argument over the issue of resurrection in 1 Corinthians 15 is related to the "not yet" eschaton (1 Cor. 15:12–28, 51ff). It seems that the Corinthians needed more information about the nature of the resurrection in reference to both the eschaton and the body. Their assumption may have been that if "Christ is risen, we are risen too."[266] Paul makes an effort to establish the order of eschatological events in relation to the resurrection, beginning with Christ's resurrection (1 Cor. 15:20–22) and then the future resurrection of those at Christ's second coming (15:23). Then Paul claims that the kingdom of God will be fully realised when all powers, including death, are placed in submission to Christ and turned over to God (15:24–28). Thus, if the Corinthians had misconceptions about the eschatological state of the body, these misunderstandings were probably not to the exclusion of others they had regarding the "not yet" future.

Paul does speak to the Corinthians as though they had "already" been perfected and had reigned as kings (1 Cor. 4:7–8).[267] Here, however, Paul is ironic. The Corinthians may have thought that the kingdom of God had fully arrived in relation to their spirituality and wisdom (cf. 1 Cor. 1:18–3:3). In contrast, Paul argues that the present kingdom of God does not rest in wisdom of words but in God's power (4:20), and the full realisation of the kingdom will not take place until every enemy of God is placed under Christ's feet (1 Cor. 15:24f).

Thiselton posits that the Corinthians espoused a realised eschatology closely connected to their over-enthusiastic spirituality (cf. chs. 12–14). He traces this thesis through all the major sections of 1 Corinthians.[268] The Corinthian congregation's enthusiasm spills over into their autonomy (1 Cor. 1:12ff), their

[266] MEARNS (1984), 26. Mearns adds that with "ὅταν δέ ... τότε" in 1 Corinthians 15:54 Paul was readjusting a Corinthian overrealised misperception by saying, "only at the time when ... [these events take place] then shall come to pass" the saying of death swallowed up in victory (27).

[267] The kingship issue raised in this passage may have as its background the Stoic belief that the person who possessed wisdom was considered a king (cf. MEEKS, 1990:316). But this interpretation, if it is correct, does not necessitate that 4:7–8 cannot also allude to the kingdom of God (cf. 4:20). I argue that wisdom and perfection are both connected with the Corinthian misperceptions about eschatology.

[268] THISELTON (1977–78), 512ff. Thiselton understands "enthusiasm" in the sense of an excessive use of gifts and workings of the Holy Spirit which cause a person to be considered "spiritual." Implicit in this explanation is an irrelevant attitude toward the things of the passing order such as food and body.

pride in self-spirituality (2:15–3:1; 5:2), their indifference toward the importance of food and body (6:13ff), their preoccupation with Christian liberty (10:23), and so forth.[269] Perhaps the Corinthians abused earlier Christian teachings, believing their excessive use of spiritual gifts confirmed their realised status. Apparently, the Corinthian members were deeply influenced by the early Christian tradition of the coming of the Spirit as a sign of the coming kingdom (cf. 8.3.1 above).[270] Since the Spirit belonged to the eschatological age, the abundance of spiritual manifestations the Corinthians experienced would have easily registered in their minds that the kingdom was now fully realised.

Thiselton seems correct that an overrealised eschatology rests at the heart of the Corinthian misperception.[271] In turn, this misperception may have been reinforced by the congregation's enthusiasm and participation in the sacraments (cf. ch. 3 above), and this all had repercussions on their ethics and their perception of the physical body. The congregation's misperception caused them to think they were spiritually mature, while Paul tells them just the opposite. Chapter 13 of 1 Corinthians is a prime example of how these issues interrelate. Here Paul intends that the central ethic upon which the Corinthians were to operate is love instead of spiritual gifts or vices. Love is a sign of maturity, and rhetorically, Paul is addressing the Corinthian congregation's *immaturity* by associating it with their enthusiasm (13:1f) and eschatology (13:7f), which are related to the problems of their spiritual gifts, such as wisdom of speech (13:1a) and knowledge (13:2, 8f). The vices Paul mentions in 13:4–6 allude to the Corinthian factions and to misperceptions about wisdom and knowledge discussed earlier in the letter (cf. §7 above).

If the correct inference from 13:1 is that some of the Corinthians were speaking with "tongues of angels" (13:1b cf. 14:2), this suggests both a strong sense of enthusiasm and a realised eschatological status among the strong.[272] If these

---

[269] Cf. Thiselton, 523.

[270] Cf. Wenham (1997), 138–39.

[271] Kuck (1992: 217 cf. 27–30, 218–22), however, maintains that Paul is not writing a polemic against overrealised eschatology in 1 Corinthians 1:10–4:21. He suggests that 4:8 is best understood in terms of the Corinthians' ethical (rather than eschatological) overconfidence. Paul is writing against their belief of having advanced to maturity on a faster track than he has without facing the sufferings he has faced (4:8–13). In Kuck's view the Corinthians deemed themselves as kingly because of their wisdom in speech, and "they may think that they are perfect already, but Paul says 'not yet' (οὔπω in 3:2)." But this division between immaturity/wisdom and eschatology may be hard to defend since these issues seem very much inter-related (see main text).

[272] Some of the *pneumatics* in Corinth may have believed that their tongue-speaking reinforced a high status of spirituality *within* the congregational setting. Ecstatic language was sometimes viewed in terms of angelic language (Test. Job 48; cf. Tertullian *On the Soul* 9). D. Martin notes that "for many [ancient] cultures glossolalic-like activity (that is, the practice of esoteric speech acts) was a valued status indicator, unproblematically linked with people in the society who had access to other forms of esoteric but valued knowledge" (1995:88).

members believed they spoke in heavenly languages, this may underscore that they believed themselves to participate already in a heavenly state. The Corinthians' low view of sexuality and marriage (7:1ff; 11:2ff) and the body (15:12ff) might also reflect that some in the congregation saw themselves as already perfected in a future eschatological status similar to the angels who neither marry nor die (cf. Luke 20:35–36).[273] In response to this, Paul sets up a contrast of incompletion by stating that the "now" (τότε) is set in contrast to the "then" (ἄρτι) perfection of the future (1 Cor. 13:8–12). The misperceptions about wisdom, knowledge, and body all seem related to the Corinthians' misperception of eschatological status incited by the exuberance of spiritual gifts.

In terms of the apocalyptic two ages, then, the Corinthian error rests on emphasising the "not yet" as if it were an "already" reality. Beker rightly claims that a D-Day which is celebrated as V-Day "loses sight of the reality of things because it ignores God's plan of cosmic redemption and is caught in an overheated spiritualistic illusion."[274] Thus, Paul's repeated emphasis on the "not yet" in the letter is intended to correct this.

The discussion in sections 8.1–4 above places us in a position to establish a plausible reading for 1 Corinthians 10:1–13. Paul is implying that the journey of Israel in the wilderness prefigures the Corinthians' "now" eschatological journey to the "not yet" future. They have experienced an eschatological "now" salvation through their conversion-initiation (10:1–2) but its culmination still lies in their future (cf. 9:24ff). Paul implies further that the notion of death in this passage prefigures an eschatological separation which is able to exclude some Corinthians from the "not yet" kingdom. This danger is imminent despite the fact that they "now" partake of the salvation experience of that kingdom (10:5–11 cf. 6:9–10; Gal. 5:19–21; 6:8; Rom. 8:13a). In short, Paul warns the Corinthian Christians that if they continue to practice vices, they will not finish their eschatological trek but will end up apostatising from the Christian community.

8.5 Purity and Contamination

8.5.1 Individual and Corporate Contamination

One observation emerging from our study of 10:5–11 is that a large numbers of Israelites were killed in the wilderness when they committed apostasy. This may be Paul's way of emphasising the corporate effects of vices, if tolerated in the Corinthian congregation. In the Hebrew scriptures, corporate judgement is seen in Achan's covetousness. As a result of his sin, the Israelites stoned both

---

[273] Cf. MEEKS (1974), 202; ARRINGTON (1978), 117; FEE, 630–31; cf. D. MACDONALD (1987).

[274] J. C. BEKER, 177.

him and his entire household (Josh. 7). Elsewhere, because of David's sin in numbering the Israelites, the entire community suffered a plague (2 Sam. 24:1–17). Such judgements may represent an idea of corporate solidarity whereby the guilt of the head of a social body implicates all those who are under that head.

Although Paul stressed the notion of solidarity with his "all" language (10:1–4), it is the "some" who never make it through the wilderness. Paul never mentions that the head of the community participated in any of the vices or was causing the guilt to come upon the Israelites. This may be significant because, in the case of the golden calf incident, he does not mention how it was Aaron who moulded the calf. Also, Paul does not allude to Moses and Aaron's own failure to enter the promised land (Num. 20:10–13). Since Paul at least indirectly seems to defend his apostolic authority in the Corinthian letter (9:1ff), he may have thought it counterproductive to attribute vices to the leaders.[275] Perhaps Paul is suggesting that only those Corinthians who in some sense participate in the various vices will be punished (10:5–10). Even though Paul is using corporate language, he does not appear to have a fully corporate, representational view in mind. Namely, the entire Corinthian community will not be judged because of some members who commit various vices.

It seems rather that Paul is thinking of corporate *influence*. He sees that contamination could occur as a result of the "some" who influence many to participate in the vices. But he goes beyond explicit influence to contamination, which by its very nature, should be excised. In the expulsion of the sexual offender (5:1–5), Paul uses the illustration of the effect of leaven upon a loaf of bread, which is a type of pollution. One of his reasons for ostracising the offender was to prevent him from polluting the entire body of Christ (1 Cor. 5:6–7).[276] For Martin, the body of Christ is not contaminated by its contact with the *cosmos*, but if that which is "outside" permeates the boundaries of the body, then expulsion of the invader becomes mandatory to keep the body healthy. Martin describes the offender in this situation as a "disguised presence" in the body of Christ that should be "out there" with the *cosmos*.[277]

The emphasis on purity and contamination in the Qumran community, for example, demonstrates how Jews in the Second Temple period could be concerned with such issues (1QS 5:13–20; 8:4–10; 9:3–6). Expulsion was carried out on those who were considered impure and immoral because they might pollute the community (1QS 7:4–5, 15–18; 8:21–24). The members of the Qumran

---

[275] This does not mean, however, that Paul thought himself beyond the capability of these vices. He often includes himself by using first person plurals in 10:1–13. He has also illustrated that he himself could fail to reach his eschatological goal (9:24–27).

[276] Cf. D. MARTIN (1995), 168–69.

[277] D. MARTIN, 170. Similarly, Douglas speaks of the danger of social pollutions as: 1) coming from outside a group; 2) transgressing the internal lines and norms in the group; 3) not distinguishing the margins of inside and outside; and 4) having internal contradictions (1966:122).

community apparently saw themselves as representing the Jewish temple, constituting the holy place and in the holy of holies, and having an expiatory role.[278] Since they seemed to have believed that the temple was defiled in Jerusalem (CD 5.6–7; 1 QpHab. 12.7–9), the presence of God had departed from there and now rested with the Qumran community. Hence, purity must thus be maintained in the community to guarantee the abiding presence of the divine (e.g., 1QS 8.5–10).[279] In a similar way Paul describes the Corinthian congregation members as the temple of the Holy Spirit and members of the body of Christ (1 Cor. 3:16–17; 6:19–20; 1 Cor. 12:13ff). Anyone who defiled the temple of the Spirit would be destroyed (1 Cor. 3:16–17 cf. 6:19–20).

For Paul, then, the large numbers of Israelites destroyed in the wilderness (10:5–10) serve as another indication that the Corinthian members, contaminated through their illegitimate contact with the *cosmos*, might in turn contaminate a larger segment of the congregation's community. Those who practise vices potentially threaten other members who will be influenced to practise them as well. Paul's thought is that offenders should either be expelled from the community (e.g., 5:5) or rejected and judged by God (e.g., 5:13; 10:12 cf. 11:29f).

8.5.2 Boundary Blurring and Exit Rituals

In the larger issue related to idol meats, Paul may have some anxiety over pollution entering into the body of Christ through the mingling or blurring of the boundary between legitimate and illegitimate fellowship in relation to eating. He illustrates this by showing the contrast between eating idol meat and partaking of the Lord's supper (10:16–22). Fellowship with both Christ and demon-idols was a categorical confusion of the worst sort because it joined a member of the body of Christ with the hostile powers of the *cosmos*. Neyrey rightly claims, "Just as in marriage there cannot be two husbands, so there cannot be two Lords of the covenant, Jesus and demons. Hence one cannot eat at both tables. The pure and the polluted are mutually exclusive realms."[280] Paul was thus creating a boundary between Christ and idolatry in order to maintain purity in the Corinthian community.

Although Paul was primarily concerned about the negative influence some members might have upon others in the idol meat situation, a larger corporate issue in chapter 10 may have also been at stake. Without a clear distinction between those who are "in" and those who are "out," the community could lose its identity as a genuine Christian congregation. In order to preserve the Corinthian community's identity in the present eschatological tension, Paul saw a need to

---

[278] Cf. M. NEWTON (1985), 46–47, 49.

[279] Cf. M. NEWTON, 42–43, 49f; cf. KNIBB (1987), 9, 129–34.

[280] NEYREY (1986), 144.

establish stronger boundaries in relation to the practising of vices (10:7–12).[281] He wished to maintain the cultural distinction of the Christian community within a larger Hellenistic context.[282] In terms of boundary language, the Israelites would be considered "insiders" in 10:1–4 because they all identified with Moses and his God through the cloud and sea and shared the experience of divine activity in the wilderness. In 10:5–11, however, the Israelites whom God rejected function as "outsiders." By committing idolatry and coveting the foods of Egypt, they would be identifying with their previous lord Pharaoh, who rejected Yahweh. In the Corinthian situation the non-Christian Gentiles are typified as following idols and practising other vices (1 Cor. 12:2; cf. 5:1). For Paul, they are οἱ ἔξω who belong to the *cosmos* (5:10–13) and will be judged by the Corinthian Christians in the future (6:2). In 10:1–13, however, Paul implies that some of the Corinthian Christians, not οἱ ἔξω, are in danger of judgement for practising vices. This implies that they were in danger of being expelled as "outsiders" from the body of Christ into the *cosmos* where other vice-doers await destruction.[283] Yet, unlike the fornicator whom the congregation was to expel, Paul emphasises divine rather than human judgement in 10:5–10.

Neyrey affirms that there are entrance and exit rituals which function as boundary markers, and these rituals involve status transformation in the case of entrance rituals, or status reversal in the case of exit rituals.[284] Excommunication is an exit ritual which occurs in the "now" (cf. 1 Cor. 5:1–5),[285] and the other ritual is divine judgement, which occurs as a "future" separation: "that is, a ritual whereby a boundary is maintained – and what does not belong is expelled" (cf. Matt. 13:24–30, 47–50).[286] Neyrey rightly includes 1 Corinthians

---

[281] Cf. MEEKS (1983a), 84ff. MEEKS (1979:8ff) uses the Corinthian congregation as his primary paradigm for suggesting his five different indicators of group boundaries in the Pauline churches: 1) language of separation (cf. 1 Cor. 5:12–13); 2) rules and rituals of purity (cf. 1 Cor. 10:25–28); 3) membership sanctions (1 Cor. 5:11); autonomous institutions (1 Cor. 6:1–8); and 5) sanctioned interaction with the larger society (1 Cor. 7:16).

[282] Cf. PERROT, 443.

[283] In Jewish tradition, "outside" in the Kidron Valley was where idolatrous impurities were discarded from the city and where the scapegoat was led after the sins of the community were pronounced over it (2 Chron. 29:5, 16; Lev. 16; cf. D. WRIGHT, 1987:18ff, 284–86). In latter traditions, those who died outside of Palestine were said to have no share in the life to come (MEKILTA, Bahodesh 2.236; cf. ROETZEL 60).

[284] NEYREY, (1990), 79–80. Similar to this in anthropological studies are the rites of banishment, separation, and de-sanctification (cf. VAN GENNEP, 1960:113–14).

[285] Perhaps Paul's use of "in the name of Jesus," when expelling the fornicator, functions as an exit ritual reversing the phrase which was commonly associated with early Christian baptisms (1 Cor. 5:4f). He would be handed over to the *cosmos* and Satan from whence he originally came (cf. M. NEWTON, 88). Havener suggests here that a curse is involved by invoking Jesus' name (1979:334–44; cf. HEITMÜLLER, 1903:74).

[286] NEYREY, 89–91.

10:2 as an entrance ritual and 10:6–13 as an indication of status degradation and an exit ritual of judgement.[287]

We are able to confirm that this viewpoint is supported by the Jewish sources Paul echoes. It is evident that divine judgement is seen as a reversal ritual in the Jewish wilderness traditions. Mauser observes that the Exodus and Numbers traditions normally combine two elements: danger and divine help. The wilderness threatens Israel's existence, but God's power is manifest there.[288] Sometimes both the danger and deliverance arise from the same source, depending on Israel's obedience or disobedience. We could suggest a mutual relationship between the danger/deliverance aspect of the wilderness motif and the cursing/blessing aspect of Israelite covenant (cf. Deut. 28–30).[289] These conceptions figure strongly in Paul's rhetoric if we understand that Paul emphasises deliverance and blessing in 1 Corinthians 10:1–4 while he later stresses danger and curse in 10:5, 7–10.

At the beginning of the exodus account, the plagues upon Egypt are indications of God's faithfulness to Israel. The Destroyer who kills the firstborn of Egypt passes over the homes of the Israelites (Exod. 12). At the Red Sea, the symbol of deliverance for the Israelites (water) became the instrument of death to the Egyptians (Exod. 14). However, once the "outside" threat of the Egyptians no longer existed, God turned the instruments of blessing and judgement on the "inside" – within the Israelite camp itself. In the Kibroth Hattaavah incident, the food God sends as a divine blessing to feed Israel in the wilderness becomes cholera (χολέραν Num. 11:20, 33) which destroys a number of them. The plagues that Yahweh once performed upon the Egyptians now strike Israel during the golden calf rebellion and the fornication at Baal Peor (Exod. 32:35; Num. 25:8, 18). The serpent, another symbol of Israel's deliverance over Egypt (i.e., the rod of Moses – Exod. 7:8f; 14:16f), now becomes an instrument of death for Israel along the route of the Red Sea (Num. 21:4f). The Destroyer, who once killed the Egyptian firstborn (Exod. 12:23), now strikes the murmurers in the Korah rebellion. We may also notice that it is fire that consumes the men of Korah, yet through the censor of Aaron, fire is the element which stops the plague (Wisd. 18:20–25 cf. Num. 16).[290]

Such reverse rituals support Neyrey's suggestion that 10:1–13 be viewed in terms of entrance and exit rituals. The imagery of entrance is seen in the concepts of initiation and election in 1 Corinthians 10:1–4, and the exit ritual of judgement and eschatological death associated with the apostasy describe 10:5–10. The binary aspects of blessing/cursing, danger/deliverance, and en-

---

[287] NEYREY, 90–91.

[288] MAUSER, 21.

[289] Note how Paul also places both cursing and blessing in an eschatological setting when he ends his first epistle to the Corinthians (1 Cor. 16:22). Cf. MILLARD (1970), 248.

[290] Similarly, in Numbers 11:1f, the fire that guided the Israelites (ch. 9) now burns them.

trance/exit serve to reinforce the idea that Paul is warning the Corinthians how elect covenant members who are "inside" the kingdom of God might find themselves "outside" of it. The divine judgement in 10:5–10 may be seen thus as a warning of the potential transformation of the status of some Corinthian members from insiders to outsiders. If they practised the things that the Gentile outsiders practised, they would also suffer the same fate as the outsiders.

8.6 Misperception in a Liminal Journey

As we previously argued, Paul described the current era as a transient "now" and "not yet," and similar to certain Jewish traditions, he depicts the eschatological era in terms of the Israelite wilderness trek (cf. 8.3). Turner's state of liminality or "betwixt and between," often spatially depicted by the symbol of "desert," might shed some new insight on the Corinthian situation (cf. ch. 1:3.2.2).[291] Leach affirms that the crossing of thresholds is important to biblical studies because inspired sacred persons "almost always experience their inspiration in a 'betwixt and between' locality, described as 'in the wilderness', which is neither fully in This World nor in The Other."[292]

Wedderburn argues that the similarities between Christian baptism and mystery initiations may share the common presupposition which is basic to numerous cultures. They share a common "rites of passage" enacting of a type of death to transformation.[293] He notes the parallel of Turner's liminality state with Paul's perception of the new age in Christ: "When we compare Paul's descriptions of the apostolic condition and the characteristics of the new creature, it is as if he had taken the imagery and the symbolism of the transitional state, and was saying that this limbo-like state between normal conditions was in fact the final state, or in the case of the apostles the state in which they must live out the rest of their earthly lives."[294] For Wedderburn, the future of the Christian's existence is to be fixed in a liminal mode, and "the theme of 'life in death' arises out of the symbolism of the Christian's transition from the old life to the new."[295]

Wedderburn, however, does not address liminality in reference to the baptism found in 1 Corinthians 10:1–13; rather, his points depict the state of Christian existence under Paul's ministry. We can suggest that behind Paul's apocalyptic language lies an assumption drawn from a resource of ideas held in common with many cultures – a liminal or marginal state that Paul (along with certain

---

[291] Turner himself does not hesitate to use the phrase "no longer" and "not yet" to describe this liminal status of ambiguity and paradox (e.g., 1967:96–97).

[292] LEACH (1983a), 15–16. Similarly, Van Gennep, suggested that transitional neutral zones "waver between two worlds" (18).

[293] WEDDERBURN (1987), 391 cf. 380–82.

[294] WEDDERBURN, 386–87.

[295] WEDDERBURN, 392.

Jewish and Christian traditions) considers as the transitional overlap of two ages.[296] Such liminality is marked by the "rite of passage" of baptism initiation that ushers a neophyte into a community and bears similarities to Turner's idea of marginal social groups who value egalitarianism, anti-structure, and preserve spontaneity.[297] They share certain characteristics with millenarian groups.[298] For Meeks, the description of Turner's *communitas* is paralleled by the characteristics of the *church* or *ekklesia*.[299]

If we consider the Corinthian congregation as an eschatological group analogous to Turner's idea of marginal groups, we may discover some fresh insight regarding the Corinthian situation. Paul may be communicating a message to the Corinthians in terms of liminality. Evidence warrants this possibility because religious liminal structures are almost universally embedded within various cultures, including ancient Jewish and Graeco-Roman societies.[300] If this is the case, the structures of cultural liminality would be comparable to Paul's "now" and "not yet" eschatology. The Corinthian members did share some common characteristics of Turner's *communitas*.[301] They were certainly spontaneous enthusiasts (chs. 12–14), and certain members seemed to reverse or equalise the roles of men and women (11:1–16; 14:31f; cf. Gal. 3:28).[302]

---

[296] This perspective seems to be characteristic of early Christian thinking. Ladd traces a "now" and "not yet" eschatology throughout the entire body of New Testament writings (1994:63–80, 203–10, 322–41, 363–73, 550–68).

[297] V.&E. TURNER, 250; Pentikäinen (1979), 156.

[298] Gager has also noted the similarities between millenarian movements and early Christianity. These traits include an imminent eschatology, an overthrow or reversal of the social order, a community life characterised by a release of emotional energy, a brief communal existence, and the central role of a charismatic leader (1975:21 cf. 2, 22f, 43ff). Like millenarian groups the Corinthian congregation seemed to have had extreme views regarding spirituality, eschatology, and the social order (cf. 1 Cor. 4:7ff; 11:2–16; 12–14). Nevertheless it may be best to refrain from drawing more specific parallels since it is questionable whether early Christianity could be classified as a millenarian movement. On criticisms of Gager's perspective, as well as others, see Holmberg (1990), 77–117. Holmberg concludes that millenarian models should not be misunderstood as delivering explanations; rather, "[what] ... we should expect from the comparative application of the church-sect typology is not verification but rather interesting new ideas and hypotheses for future work" (116f).

[299] MEEKS, (1983a), 157; cf. HARRIS (1991), 12–13, 21. For Turner, apart from a normative *communitas*, two other *communitas* are: 1) the spontaneous *communitas*, defying all construction; 2) the ideological *communitas* which formulates a *communitas* of the past as a utopian guideline for contemporary reform (1979:47; 1974:169–70; V.&E. TURNER, 252).

[300] It is difficult to determine, however, whether Paul is consciously using such a model on a purely structural level. In any case, the concept of liminality seems embedded in the wilderness traditions that Paul is consciously using (cf. ch. 1 above).

[301] I am not saying, however, that the Corinthians necessarily share all the characteristics of *communitas*. They do appear to be anti-structural regarding their boundaries, but they do not seem to be anti-ritualistic, as we have noted by the high regard for the baptism and the eucharist. Apparently, there was much diversity among apocalyptic groups in the first century (cf. COLLINS, 1984:141).

[302] Cf. TURNER (1967), 99.

With this perspective in mind, in 1 Corinthians 10:1–11 the Israelites may be regarded as "liminars" in Paul's narrative. Cohn describes Israel's wilderness journey in terms of the Turner/Van Gennep model; the separation stage occurs at the Red Sea, the transitional period takes place in the wilderness, and the reincorporation transpires at the crossing of the Jordan river into the new land.[303] Paul, however, uses the Israelites primarily as a paradigmatic example for the Corinthians not to follow. As Israel coveted the food of Egypt in the wilderness, so the Corinthians desired the things of the fallen world. Instead of holding to a social attitude of universalism and indifferentiation *internally*, among their members, they were opening this invitation to the influence of the larger society which practised vices and social inequality. In the situation regarding idol meats, the Corinthians were being anti-structural on the issue of vices, and structural regarding the internal social statuses of the strong and weak. Hence, Paul's narrative can be understood as a means whereby he, as a "guardian of structure" is reinforcing the external boundaries of the Corinthian congregation while at the same time encouraging internal egalitarianism (cf. 10:16–22; 12:13).[304] For Paul, unity among comrades is a sign of purity; homogeneity with the world is taboo.

Moreover, some of the members of the congregation appeared to be indifferent toward the things pertaining to the body. They had few rules regarding proper conduct in the areas of idol meats and human sexuality (chs. 5–10). Paul considers their behaviour as going too far and attempts to bring order and "structure" to their "anti-structural" assumption; at the same time, he seeks to instil a more anti-structural approach to the status distinctions between the strong/rich and weak/poor throughout his letter.

Paul's "now" and "not yet" and the cultural-anthropological "betwixt and between" may capture two facets of the same reality. For Cullmann, the "now" and "not yet" depict an overlap of the current evil age and the new age. For Turner, the "betwixt and between" primarily involves an overlap or transition of two states:[305] the neophyte has been separated from his or her previous state but has not completely arrived at the new. Paul could be viewed as merging the ideas of two eras and two states. The Corinthians are eschatological pilgrims in a liminal period between two eras, and they are also inheritors of eschatological life who have not yet reached their final state of perfection. As in a rites of passage ordeal, if the neophyte fails to pass the test in the liminal phase, he or

---

[303] COHN (1981), 13.

[304] Paul does not mention "no male nor female" in 12:13. It seems that Paul wanted to maintain some form of egalitarianism while at the same time denying it in reference to the roles of men and women.

[305] Turner identifies "state" as a culturally recognised stable or recurring condition, the change of which encompasses the notions of place, social position, status, office, and age (1969:94).

she could die in the process or be ostracised from the community.[306] In any case, the neophyte cannot receive the anticipated new identity unless the neophyte completes the transitional stage.[307] In liminal quests, then, arriving at the completion or the "aggregative stage" is necessary, and this aspect is the implicit goal in Paul's wilderness rhetoric. Half finished projects are not conducive to a final state of holiness and wholeness (cf. Deut. 20:6–7).[308]

For the Israelites, the aggregative stage was the promised land. There are those in Corinth who, however, collapsed the liminal and aggregative stages. They perceived that life in the "now" eschaton was already more or less completed, and the new status was already achieved. For Paul, the Corinthians are like the Israelites of old: they must complete their journey in the current phase in order to make it to the final eschaton, and they would not received the full realisation of their spiritual status until then.[309] The aggregative stage for Paul's Christianity would still remain in the "not yet" future.

Conclusion

The main theme of 1 Corinthians 10:5–10 centres on the concept of Israel coveting after food and committing idolatry, and this results in their apostasy and divine judgement *en masse*. In stark contrast to 1 Corinthians 10:1–4, 10:5–11 demonstrates that the Israelites' election, deliverance/salvation, and spiritual provisions in the exodus/wilderness (10:1–4) did not prevent the majority of them from being punished by God when they committed vices which displeased him. Paul stresses that the things which happened to Israel in the wilderness are hypothetical prefigurations for the Corinthian congregation. Namely, what happened to Israel could happen to the Corinthians because some of the Corinthians were already beginning to commit the same kinds of vices.

The Israelites coveted the food of Egypt and ate before the golden calf; likewise, some in the Corinthian congregation were participating in cultic meals in an idolatrous setting (cf. 1 Cor. 8:10; 10:14–22). Some Israelites fell into sexual play, and some of the Corinthians were participating in sexual immorality in a cultic context. The Israelites tested Christ, and so did the strong at Corinth by their presumptuous liberty and by not being considerate toward weaker Chris-

---

[306] Cf. Douglas (1966), 96; Olson (1992), 115.

[307] Similarly, Christian liminars who do not complete their religious pilgrimage cannot come to the ultimate meeting-place with the object of their devotion.

[308] Cf. Douglas, 51f. The comparison breaks down in relation to another aspect of aggregation: reincorporation into the old society's structural system. Paul did not want the Corinthians to be reincorporated into Greco-Roman society at the end of their journey; rather, Greco-Roman society was to be overruled by the kingdom of God (1 Cor. 15:24).

[309] Cf. McVann's connection between eternal life and the Van Gennep/Turner aggregation stage (1991:153–54).

tians. As the Israelites grumbled against the leadership of Moses and Aaron, some in Corinth were struggling against Paul. Paul was thus warning them to stop committing these vices. In relation to Paul's other vice lists, the practices of 10:5–10 identifies the activities of those whom God rejects. Those who persist in doing such things would not inherit God's kingdom.

Paul wishes to demonstrate through the imagery of the Israelite wilderness experience that the Corinthians are at present on an eschatological trek characterised by the tension of "now" and "not yet." This thought is evident in Paul's own Jewish tradition, and it resides deep in the structures of the religious psyche. In light of this common cultural pattern, the Corinthians' baptism into Christ had ushered them into a liminal state of "betwixt" and "between" their former lower status and a future higher one. The Corinthians, however, perceived themselves as already having attained the completed or aggregative state. But for Paul, the Corinthian congregation must until the culmination of the eschaton live in a perpetual state of liminality. The salvation experience itself is not fully realised until the end. The Christian life for Paul is set on the margins of society in an ambiguous state of life and death, and apostasy in the current disposition means eschatological death.

Chapter 5

A Warning against Apostasy and a Word of Perseverance

1. Introduction

In 1 Corinthians 10:12–13 we arrive at the conclusion of Paul's argument which he began in 10:1. I wish to examine the following points: 1) In 10:12 Paul articulates his main purpose for writing 10:1–13. Here Paul warns the Corinthians to beware, or else some of them – like Israel in the wilderness – will fall and suffer divine judgement. 2) The proper nuances of the binary terms "stand"/ "fall" must be determined in order to interpret what Paul means in relation to apostasy. 3) There are some implications related to Paul's use of the third person singular and this may shed fresh light on his view of election. After stressing "all" and "some" in the previous verses, Paul's rhetoric changes in 10:12. 4) The conclusions derived from 10:12 will assist us in our interpretation of Paul's discourse on meat sacrificed to idols. 5) In 10:13 Paul claims that God is faithful and will not permit temptation to go beyond the Corinthians' capability of enduring it. The purpose of this verse seems to affirm perseverance in Paul's message; hence, 10:13 must be taken into consideration to appreciate the overall thrust of the argument.

2. Apostasy: Falling Away (1 Corinthians 10:12)

2.1 The One Who Thinks He Stands, Let Him Beware, Lest He Fall

At the beginning of 1 Corinthians 10:12 ὥστε appears and may be translated as "therefore," "so then," or "for this reason."[1] Paul often uses the word in this letter with an imperative to denote an inferential conclusion to an argument (3:21; 4:5; 11:33; 14:39; 15:58). He also uses this construction when encouraging Christians to persevere (Phil. 2:12; 4:1). We may infer from Paul's use of the third person singular (ὥστε ὁ δοκῶν ἑστάναι βλεπέτω μὴ πέσῃ) that he is not singling out one particular person in the congregation. His indirect address may suggest his exhortational style of not wanting to sound too harsh to his

---

[1] Cf. *BAGD*, 899; MOULE, *Idiom*, 144.

readers.[2] The construction of this verse suggests a conclusive warning to Paul's argument in 10:1–11. In fact, the interpretation of 10:1–11 almost compels a particular interpretation for 10:12.

W. Willis argues that in the pericope of 10:1–13 Paul is not primarily concerned with correcting an overconfident view of sacramentalism; rather, he is concerned with the danger of "apostasy" and "loss of salvation" through idolatry. He affirms that the "point of the entire pericope is clearly and concisely stated in 10:12."[3] Willis may be correct by stressing apostasy over sacramentalism; however, the two subjects do not need to be set in opposition to one another. We have noted that Paul intended the language of baptism and eucharist as marks of a genuine participation in the elect community (cf. ch. 3 above). This would make the danger of apostasy all the more apparent. If one expands and paraphrases 10:12, Paul may be saying: "For this reason – the summation of what I have just written regarding the Israelites in the wilderness – the individual Christians in your congregation who think they stand securely in their faith because of their conversion-initiation and partaking of spiritual graces, beware! They too could apostatise by practising the same vices as the Israelites, and they would also suffer divine judgement so that they do not enter the future kingdom of our Lord."

2.2 Standing and Falling

2.2.1 The One Who "Seems" to Stand

Gundry Volf suggests that in 10:12 Paul addresses someone who may not be a genuine Christian: the person only "seems to stand" (ὁ δοκῶν ἑστάναι); hence, in reference to "fall" (πίπτειν), she thinks that "we should take it to refer not to losing salvation but to losing the appearance of salvation."[4] She also insists that 10:5 cannot mean the forfeiture of election because "Divine election stands (cf. Rom. 11:1, 2; 8:29, 30, 33)!"[5] Instead of taking the particular situation of the Corinthian congregation into account, Gundry Volf allows the presupposition of an irrevocable divine election of individuals, which she finds primarily in Paul's letter to the Romans, to govern her interpretation of 1 Corinthians 10:12. For her, Paul is saying in this verse: "Let the one who appears to be saved by virtue of being a partaker of the Lord's Supper beware that she does not behave like a non-Christian (in committing idolatry) and fall under judgement, thereby

---

[2] Cf. Roetzel (1972), 93–94. Nevertheless Paul does connect punishment to sin in relation to his judgement paraeneses (1 Cor. 3:16–17; 11:17–34; 1 Thes. 4:3–8; Gal. 6:7–10).

[3] W. Willis (1985), 155; cf. Gardner (1994), 155.

[4] Gundry Volf (1990), 127.

[5] Gundry Volf, 126.

disproving her Christian profession!"[6] She finds support for her interpretation of ὁ δοκῶν ἑστάναι by making a cross-reference to her previous interpretation of the fornicator who was a "so-called" (as opposed to genuine) Christian brother (1 Cor. 5:11 – ὀνομαζόμενος).[7]

There are at least two important considerations which make this interpretation untenable. First, Paul begins 10:1–13 with the metaphors of salvation through the concepts of election and baptism-initiation in the Spirit and water (10:1–4).[8] Elsewhere in 1 Corinthians those whom Paul addresses are considered to be saints, called, saved, cleansed, justified, sanctified, members of the body of Christ, and operating in the Spirit (e.g., 10:1, 6, 11 cf. 1:1–9, 18, 31; 4:15; 6:6, 11, 19f; 12:13).[9] Paul stresses the solidarity of "all" the Israelites who were called into these divine privileges indicating the *genuine* nature of these experiences. In Israel's tradition-history which Paul adopts, both Caleb (who made it through the journey) and Korah (who did not make it) participated in the "same" (τὸ αὐτὸ) exodus/wilderness experiences. Paul thus implies a *common* election that was experienced by *all*.[10] Moreover, Paul calls the Israelites "our fathers" and transfers the salvific language of this passage to the Corinthians whom he believes are Christians.[11] In his discourse on idol meats, Paul's lan-

---

[6] Gundry Volf, 127.

[7] Gundry Volf, 124–25. In 5:11 the middle/passive participle of ὀνομάζω is probably better rendered "is called" or "calls himself" (rather than "so-called," *contra* BAGD, 573–74) indicating that the Corinthians should not have fellowship with someone who is called a brother yet commits the vices Paul mentions in the context (1 Cor. 5:9f). The text has generated much discussion and little agreement. On the ambiguities in this passage, see Thiselton (1973), 204–28. My own view is this: 1) the offender is a believer whose conduct is denounced for following (or being worse than … [5:1]) conduct in the *cosmos*; 2) the offender is assigned to the *cosmos*, which is controlled by Satan; 3) as explained in previous chapters, his expulsion is from the body of Christ; if he does not repent, he will perish with the *cosmos* (cf. 5:6–7, 13); 4) the "destruction of the flesh" and "spirit saved", whether physical, ethical, etc., seems at least intended to bring him to repentance (cf. 1 Tim. 1:20; 2 Thes. 3:14f). If the offender were a non-Christian, it would be rather odd that a non-believer is expelled from the region of believers so that in the region of non-believers, he might become a believer!

[8] As noted in chapter 3, Gundry Volf acknowledges the sacramental language of this passage but does not properly address salvific aspects (125f).

[9] See also Fung (1980), 246–61. The objection that 11:19 opens up a case for ungenuine believers will not do. The verse does not address those who were in danger of participating in idolatry (1 Cor. 8:1–11:1); rather, it is related to the social problem in 11:17–34. Earlier, we argued that the judgement in the latter is different than the former (ch. 3.3.2). In relation to the social problems associated with the Lord's supper, the approved ones in 11:19 would be those who behave in a Christian manner and thus stand out from the ones who do not (cf. Barrett, 1971:262).

[10] M. Mitchell uses the paraphrase, "*all* Israel was unified at the beginning in *common* baptism, *common* experiences and *common* spiritual food and drink" (1991:252 cf. 88–90).

[11] *Contra* Gundry Volf who claims that those Israelites who did not make it to the promised land showed themselves as ungenuine recipients of the promise, and they function as "types" for the Corinthians. Her implication is that if any Corinthians fall away, they were not genuine Christians in the first place (126–127). But every indication in the text argues

guage assumes the strong are genuine believers: 1) they, along with Paul, find their life through the same God and Lord (8:5–6); 2) they are not to offend the weaker ἀδελφὸς who belongs to Christ (8:11f); 3) they became Christians directly through Paul's effort (9:1ff); 4) they participate in spiritual matters and the new era (9:11, 24ff); and 5) they are members of the body of Christ (10:16ff).

Second, Paul's binary usage of the words "stand" (ἵστημι) and "fall" (πίπτω) in 10:12 reinforce an interpretation that a genuine standing in grace and a real danger of falling into apostasy is at stake.[12] Paul uses the perfect tense of ἵστημι here as in Romans 11:20–22 where he gives another warning in the milieu of apostasy and high-mindedness (cf. 2.2.2 below). He also uses the word elsewhere in relation to apostasy and perseverance (Gal. 5:1ff; cf. 2 Thes. 2:15). Related to this usage is Paul's understanding of ἵστημι as denoting the idea of one's standing in faith and grace or in the message of the Gospel (1 Cor. 15:1f; 16:13; 2 Cor. 1:24; Rom. 5:2; 11:20; Phil. 4:1 cf. 1 Pet. 5:12).[13] Wolff writes regarding 10:12, "'Stehen' ist hier abgekürzt für 'Stehen im Glauben' ... Den Gegensatz dazu bezeichnet πίπτειν, die Abwendung von Gott und damit verbunden den Verlust des Heils."[14]

The idea of standing in faith might have as its basis the ancient Jewish concept of one establishing or standing on the word of the covenant (cf. Psa. 104:8–10 LXX).[15] In the Deuteronomic tradition, standing in the covenant is set in contrast with departing from it (Deut. 29:13–18). In a broad sense, then, Paul may have understood this nuance of "stand" as pointing to the new eschatological covenant of the Christians. Hence, the converse of standing in a new covenant would be to fall away from it.[16] The "stand" which Paul seems to intimate in 10:12 is reminiscent of the divine privileges found in 10:1–4 which some in Corinth understood in terms of eschatological security. Here ἑστάναι

---

against any non-genuine experiences in the wilderness, of which "all" were partakers. Moreover, Gundry Volf confuses the Israelites as the "types" when it was actually "the things" Israel experienced in the wilderness which are the "types" (10:6, 11 cf. ch. 4 above). The "things" as "types" in 10:6 included the retrospective salvific language in 10:1–4 and thus indicates that these experiences affected *both* Israel and the Corinthian congregation.

[12] Here Paul may be attempting to correct the high-minded attitude of the strong by showing the real danger attached with the situation at hand (Cf. BROER, 1989:317f; W. WILLIS, 156). On this point Godet rightly claims, "Paul allows indeed that the person addressed by him *is standing*, for he afterwards speaks of the danger he is in of falling" (2:68).

[13] In spite of divine assistance through grace, for Pauline thought, such standing required effort on the Christian's part (1 Cor. 16:13; Col. 4:12; Eph. 6:11–14).

[14] WOLFF (1982), 40; cf. LANG (1986), 126; ALLÓ (1956), 235; *Contra* CONZELMANN (1975), 168.

[15] Cf. GRUNDMANN, *TDNT*, 7:641ff, 649; GARDNER (1994), 152–53.

[16] GRUNDMANN (7:645–46) observes that the Qumran community held to the notion of the righteous as standing in the eschaton while the unrighteous loses his place (1QH 2:21ff; 11:13; 1QM 4:3f). Similar to the irony Paul portrays in the Corinthian situation, the Qumran group believed that God gives strength to the weak whereas "heroes and strong men" of the nations have no standing-place (1QM 14:6–7).

implies one's standing in a salvific relationship in Christ with the blessings of divine graces in the eschatological "now" and "not yet."

2.2.2 Apostasy: Falling from Grace into Eschatological Death

We therefore conclude that Paul's use of "fall" in 10:12 does not *merely* indicate a falling from fidelity or into a state of sin.[17] Such a "fall" would no doubt have a humiliating effect on the "secure-minded" strong, but Paul has more than sin or a secure status in mind. Some in Corinth had *already* begun to sin by committing the vices mentioned in 10:6–10 (cf. ch. 4.7 above). Moreover, we should avoid equating the precise nuance of πίπτω in 10:7 with that of πίπτω in 10:12. Although Paul describes the physical death of Israelites in terms of a "fall," he does not seem to suggest the same thing regarding the Corinthians' "fall."[18] They may in fact suffer divine judgement resulting in physical death, but Paul suggests more than this – he is thinking of an *eschatological* death.[19] The context implies that "death" for the Corinthians will prevent them from entering the "not yet" eschaton and kingdom of God. Similarly, Roetzel ascribes to Paul the view that the Corinthian congregation cannot take their salvation for granted. The imperative language of watching in 10:12 (cf. 3:10; 16:13) "has eschatological connotations. Πέσῃ in 10:12 means more than falling into sin or unbelief; it refers to the danger of falling out of grace (Gal. 5:4) or into eschatological ruin (Rom. 11:22)."[20]

Therefore, μὴ πέσῃ in 10:12 most likely suggests a falling from salvific grace,[21] the result of which leads to eschatological consequences of divine rejection. Paul would have no problem associating πίπτω with an apostasy of the high-minded which results in eschatological destruction, for such ideas were linked together in early Jewish wisdom literature (Sir. 1:30; 28:22–26; Psa. Sol. 3:9–12 cf. Prov. 16:18; 18:12). If there is a Jewish tradition behind his words, he is perhaps echoing the wisdom of Sirach. The grammatical construction of the subjunctive πίπτω with a negative particle in 10:12 is found several times in this tradition (Sir. 1:30; 2:7; 22:27–23:1), and Sirach also associates falling with forsaking the Lord. The author warns the readers to beware, lest they fall into an evil death and be destroyed by an unquenchable flame (28:22–26).

Paul himself associates the terms "stand"/"fall" and "beware" with apostasy in some of his other letters. If the Galatian Christians stand in the liberty of

---

[17] *Contra* GODET (1887), 2:68.

[18] Nor does the typology in 10:1–13 necessitate this equation. Regarding Paul's typology in this passage, Hays writes, "even the most antithetical typology must contain elements of likeness, and even the most positive typology must contain elements of contrast. Otherwise, the figure would not work at all" (1989:101).

[19] *Contra* MICHAELIS, *TDNT*, 164–65.

[20] ROETZEL (1972), 172.

[21] Cf. GARDNER, 153; W. WILLIS, 157; FEE (1987), 459; WOLFF, 40.

Christ, they could escape falling from grace which occurs by attempting to be justified through the law (Gal. 5:1–4).[22] Paul warns that those among them who are seeking to be justified by the law are "cut off" from Christ and "fallen from grace" (5:4: κατηργήθητε ἀπὸ Χριστοῦ, οἵτινες ἐν νόμῳ δικαιοῦσθε, τῆς χάριτος ἐξεπέσατε). In this letter, Paul is anxious that the Galatians will fall back into confining ritual and social practises; hence, he fears that the original gospel of liberty through the Spirit they received may have been in vain (3:4; 4:11; cf. 2:2; 2 Cor. 6:1; 1 Cor. 15:2).[23] Smiles takes seriously the danger of apostasy in Galatia when he compares the grace of God (2:21), which belongs to the *propositio* of Paul's argument in the letter (Gal. 2:16–21), with the falling from grace in 5:4.[24] It is not wrong to affirm that apostasy in Galatians is the reversal of justification and grace as found in the *propositio* of 2:16–21.

Particularly significant is that the Corinthian argument of Paul in 10:1–13 is perfectly consistent with what he does in other letters.[25] Similar to the Corinthian situation, the Galatian warning (βλέπετε μὴ – Gal. 5:15 cf. 1 Cor. 10:12) is set in the situation of falling from grace (Gal. 5:1, 4 cf. 1 Cor. 10:5, 12), being hindered from running a course (Gal. 5:7 cf. 1 Cor. 9:24ff), and being severed from Christ (Gal. 5:5; 4:30 cf. 1 Cor. 5:5; 10:4–10). Paul also mentions leaven as a negative influence on the believers in both letters (Gal. 5:9 cf. 1 Cor. 5:7) and a condemnation on those who practise vices such as discord, dissensions, and factions. Such works of the flesh prevent one from entering the kingdom of God (Gal. 5:19–21; 6:7–8 cf. 1 Cor. 5:8f; 6:9–10; 10:7–10; Rom. 8:12–13). In relation to apostasy, the essential difference between the two letters is that the Corinthian warning focuses on the danger of apostatising through the abuse of liberty. In Galatians the congregations were erring in the opposite extreme – they were entangled by the works of the law and needed more liberty in Christ (Gal. 3–5). For Paul, those who taught another Gospel that hindered one's liberty in Christ were accursed and their message was a perversion and desertion or turning away (μετατίθημι) from the true Gospel (Gal. 1:6–9 cf. 1 Cor. 16:22).

---

[22] GUNDRY VOLF (214–15) affirms that the present loss of salvation is at stake in Galatians 5:4; however, she claims that "From the perspective of God's faithfulness, Paul is certain that the Galatians will not finally turn away from the Gospel" (cf. Gal. 5:10). She suggests that the faithfulness of God in this situation can actually become manifest through Paul's warning (215). This is no doubt a case of special pleading and an introducing of theological concepts foreign to the text itself. Would the Galatians have then been able to genuinely apostatise if Paul had *not* given this warning? (On the faithfulness of God, see 3.2.1 below.) J. Barclay affirms that in passages such as Galatians 5:4, 21 and 6:6–10 eternal life or destruction are in some sense dependent on the work of those who believe. Faith involves commitment to obey the truth and walk in the spirit (1991:227, 236).

[23] Cf. DUNN (1993), 157. In Galatians, apostasy centred on Paul's response to teachings from Jewish-Christian missionaries (Gal. 1:6ff; 2:2, etc.; cf. DUNN, 9–11).

[24] SMILES (1998), 187–90 cf. 99–100.

[25] Very few scholars seem to properly address the comparisons between 1 Corinthians and Galatians 5–6. Osten-Sacken is a refreshing exception (1989:81–82).

Moreover, Paul and other early Christian writers often use the exhortation to "watch out" by combining βλέπω with a negative particle and an aorist subjunctive. This construction appears in warnings against deception, unbelief, and apostasy (Col. 2:8; Acts 13:40f; Luke 21:8; Heb. 3:12; 12:25). With reference to idol meats, Paul warns (βλέπετε) the strong in Corinth to avoid becoming a stumbling-block to the weak (1 Cor. 8:9, 13; cf. Rom 14:13). In 10:12, however, his warning does not centre on how the strong could negatively influence the weak; rather, he seems to be primarily warning the strong that they themselves could fall away through idolatry and related vices (cf. 10:14; 2.4 below).[26]

Romans 14:1–15:4 also has the binary aspects of standing and falling with language similar to 1 Corinthians 8:1–11:1. In Romans 14:4 these aspects are set in the context of Christians judging other Christians because of what they eat. Paul discourages judging another person's servant because the servant stands or falls to his or her own master. The metaphors here denote a master's approval ("stand") or rejection ("fall") of his servant.[27] Paul then applies the imagery to the Lord who approves of the Christian's eating (Rom. 14:4b). The "fall" in 1 Corinthians 10:12, however, does not simply refer to a generic divine disapproval. Paul is warning overconfident Christians of the reality of falling away. In Romans he is concerned with encouraging the readers that God accepts them regardless of what they eat or do not eat. The pericope in Romans seems to be a general paraenesis adapted from the more specific account in 1 Corinthians.[28] Both accounts are concerned nevertheless over the possible apostasy and destruction of weak Christians due to the liberty of strong ones (1 Cor. 8:9–13; Rom. 14:15, 20ff).

In Romans 9–11, Paul claims that the Jews have stumbled so that salvation might come to the Gentiles who stand by faith (Rom. 11:11–12, 20–22).[29] Paul explains that many Jews of his day have been cast away because they had not submitted to the righteousness found in Christ (cf. Rom. 11:15ff; 9:1–4; 10:1–4).[30] For Paul, such Jews did not share the present salvific experience of the

---

[26] Here Sandelin holds that Paul is addressing all believers (1995:269). Nevertheless, the strong are the ones who are over-confident in their liberty, and so they seem to be the ones whom Paul primarily targets in 10:12.

[27] Cf. DUNN (1988), 2.804.

[28] So KARRIS (1991), 65–84.

[29] The metaphor of stumbling likely points to Israel tripping over the stumbling-block in 9:32–33. W. Willis rightly observes that it "is clear from Rom 11:11, 12 that 'falling' means the loss of salvation, not just occasional slips" (157). Garlington argues that in Romans disobedience and sin are related to apostatising from God's covenant (1994:22–25, 89–94, 100, 145ff). His work, however, does not cover chapters 9–11.

[30] Paul's language of expulsion may allude to Jewish traditions on a deeper level (cf. Deut. 13:1ff; 29:9–20; 1QS 2.11–17). Expulsion refers to a punishment that is meted out to those who commit apostasy (Cf. FORKMAN 1972:25, 32–34). On Hebrew terms related to expulsion see FORKMAN, 16–34. One also finds a similar thought in 2 Baruch 13:9–10 where

Christians (ch. 10). Although Paul speaks of God having hardened the hearts of some of them (11:7, 25; cf. 9:18), they nevertheless are without excuse because they do not respond in faith to the message of righteousness (9:32–33; 10:17–21; 11:7ff). Yet God has not completely rejected his elect people; there will come a future day when all Israel will be saved (Rom. 11:26–29; cf. 11:12, 15).[31] With the metaphor of an olive tree Paul affirms that the falling away of many Israelites has opened the way for the Gentiles to be saved and grafted in with the elect people of God (Rom. 11:11ff). To the boasting Gentiles, he directs a warning that they too could be "cut off" (ἐκκόπτω) from the elect people; if God spared not the natural branches, neither would he spare the Gentiles (Rom. 11:17–24).[32] In both 1 Corinthians and Romans, then, we find Paul severely warning those who are presumptuous, whether Jews (Rom. 2:1–16) or Gentiles (Rom. 11:17ff; 1 Cor. 8:1–11:1).

Here we find the argument that many Jews who belonged to the elect people of God (Rom. 11:28) are "cut off" so that they do not participate in the salvation provided in Paul's era (i.e., the eschatological "now" and "not yet"). Longenecker suggests that Paul establishes this temporal perspective in Romans 1–8. In 9–11, he affirms that Israel has stumbled (προσκόπτειν) in the present time (9:32); thus, in the eschatological "now," they are excluded from the community of grace: "they are down, and therefore out. They have lost the race (cf. 9.30–31)."[33] Stuhlmacher affirms that the Israelites are in a condition of enmity which "characterizes sinners and the flesh as they stand over against God (in the

---

God did not spare his own sons, but God afflicted them as if they were his enemies (cf. Rom. 11:28). On Israel's responsibility in Romans 9–11 see BARRETT (1977), 99–121. On difficulties in Romans 9:19–23, see DUNN (1988), 2:559f; cf. OESTERREICHER (1961), 320; M. BARTH (1983), 13.

[31] Although the term "Israel" here is hotly debated, a number of recent studies (e. g., FITZMYER, 1993:623–24) argue for the implausibility that Israel here means a "spiritual Israel" made up of Christians or Jews and Gentiles. Rather, it refers to corporate Israel in an ethnic sense, as the context of Romans affirms.

[32] Gundry Volf admits that Paul's warning here allows for the possibility of the falling away of those who do not put their trust in God's grace (197, 200). She also affirms that even though God has temporarily "cut off" Israel because of its unbelief, God's election of Israel will stand sure in the future day when "all Israel shall be saved" (Rom. 11:26). But she argues further that although many Jews were hardened, God has not rejected them, and Paul "does not consider the hardened majority [of Jews to be] permanently excluded from salvation" (172, 195). This explanation does not clearly address the eternal destination of the temporarily-hardened majority of Jews. *Until* that future time (the eschatological "not yet") when "all Israel shall be saved," does Paul believe that Jews who reject Christ are eternally condemned? Open is the counter-claim that certain of God's elect (in this case, those who make up the temporarily-hardened Jewish majority) might be condemned because of their exclusion from salvation in Paul's day. If these Israelites were to die in the present state, they would appear to suffer eternal death as would Christians who follow their sinful nature (cf. Rom. 8:5–8, 13 and main text above). On the connection between Romans 8 and 9 in relation to the assurance of salvation, see SCHOEPS (1961), 236.

[33] LONGENECKER (1991), 257.

judgement) (cf. 5:10; 8:7)."[34] Nevertheless, the Israelites have stumbled (πταίειν) temporarily (11:11ff). In the eschatological "now," they are depicted as vessels of wrath (9:21–23) and cut-off branches (11:20ff), but they will be saved in the eschatological "not yet" (11:26ff).[35]

What is significant in relation to apostasy here is that Paul warns how the same thing could happen to the Christians; namely, they could fall away through unbelief so as to lose their salvation status in the present age (Rom. 11:22f).[36] Similar to Paul's language of election in 1 Corinthians 10:1–13, we find in Romans 11 that an entire Israelite community was elected (cf. "all" 1 Cor. 10:1–4), but individuals were severed from the community (cf. "many"/"some" 1 Cor. 10:5, 7–10) so that only a remnant of the original people remained (i.e., the implied converse of the "many" [Joshua, Caleb, and the children of the rebels] 1 Cor. 10:5; cf. 2.3 below). Moreover, in both passages Paul warns the Christians that they should not become overconfident; what happened to Israel could also happen to them (Rom. 11:22 cf. vv. 17–24; 15:4; 1 Cor. 10:12 cf. vv., 6, 11).

The language of falling away in 1 Corinthians 10:12 also reflects a later pattern in early Christian discourse where the meaning may be construed as conveying the idea of apostasy. Several examples of the wilderness apostasy motif that may be related to Paul's warning in 10:1–12 include passages from Hebrews, Jude/2 Peter, 1 & 2 Clement, Barnabas, and the Reliques of the Elders.

In the macro-context of Hebrews, McKnight rightly observes five basic warning pericopes (Heb. 2:1–4; 3:7–4:13; 5:11–6:12; 10:19–39; 12:1–29) and argues that the epistle teaches an inaugurated salvation for believers whose final salvation is in the future. They are presently able to lose faith and the privilege of inaugurated salvation.[37] In cultural anthropological terms, Johnsson recognises a *rites de passage* pattern in Hebrews involving baptism and persecution (separation – "then"), journeying and "proleptic participation" (transition – "now"), and seeing God and attaining his city (incorporation – "not yet").[38] The apostate in Hebrews would suffer eschatological retribution of a far greater magnitude than the punishments received by the rebels in Israel's traditions (2:2–3; 6:6–8; 10:26–31; 12:25).

---

[34] STUHLMACHER (1994), 173.

[35] Similarly, LONGENECKER, 257. This salvation comes apparently through a deliverer who removes their sins (11:26b–27). Still, in the eschatological "now," some of them could believe and be saved (cf. 11:23–24).

[36] In reference to Paul's warning that the Gentiles might be "cut off," Gundry Volf suggests that there might also exist the possibility that if Gentiles were "cut off," they could also be grafted in again at a later time just like the Jews (200–01). But this explanation would then seem to infer the possibility that some former Gentile Christians could also be excluded from salvation in the *eschatological "now."*

[37] MCKNIGHT (1992), 21–59. Against Grudem's view (1994:788–807 [revised in SCHREINER & WARE, 1995:1.133–82]), see SCHREINER (1998), 49–51.

[38] JOHNSSON (1978), 246.

Hebrews 3:7–4:13 is a prime example of how the wilderness narrative was used to warn against apostasy. It is similar to Paul's admonition. The writer warns the audience to beware (βλέπετε) lest they fall (ἵνα μὴ ... πέσῃ) into apostasy (ἀποστῆναι) through unbelief (Heb. 3:12; 4:11).[39] Using the same Israelite tradition as Paul in 1 Corinthians 10:5 (Kadesh in Num. 14), the Hebrews writer mentions the Israelites' carcasses which fell in the desert (ἔπεσεν ἐν τῇ ἐρήμῳ) (Heb. 3:17). If the Christians in the message to the Hebrews apostatised, they would fail to enter into God's day of eschatological rest just as the wilderness generation failed to enter into the promised land (Heb. 3:7–4:11). This warning extends to every one of the congregation members, who are to look out for each other (3:12–13; 4:1, 11; cf. 12:15). Holding firmly to one's confidence is the antithesis to apostasy.[40] The strong "if" of 3:14 (ἐάνπερ) stresses the conditional aspect of partaking in Christ.[41] In relation to the wilderness pericope, Lane writes, "A major theme in Hebrews is that Christians are the people of God who, like the generation in the desert, experience the tensions of an interim existence between redemption and rest, between promise and fulfilment."[42] God may exclude the apostate from God's promised rest (κατάπαυσις), which has both "now" and "not yet" aspects. Until the final rest "the believers are on probation."[43]

Another example comes from the epistle of Jude. In the first of three warning examples from the traditions of Israel, the author records that the Lord delivered the people of God from Egypt yet destroyed many of them in the wilderness because of their unbelief (Jude 5). The writer is denouncing apostate Christian teachers who have turned away from the gracious favour of God and deny their allegiance to their master, Christ (Jude 4).[44] They will suffer divine eschatolo-

---

[39] Mauser relates both 1 Corinthians 10 and Hebrews 3:7–4:13 as similar to the language of the wilderness generation described in Deuteronomy. All three accounts function as warning examples (1963:74). Interestingly, it is possible that the Hebrews writer may be using "some" to describe those who perish and those who survive (Heb. 3:16; 4:6; but see ELLINGWORTH, 1993:229f, 250).

[40] Cf. LANE (1991), 85–88; HOFIUS (1970), 133.

[41] Carson notes the perfect tense γεγόναμεν in Heb. 3:14 and posits the present result of past action: "we have become partakers ..." He emphasises the past to explain that partaking in Christ has perseverance "for its inevitable fruit" (1996:84–85). S. E. Porter, however, contends against Carson. The perfect tense is a timeless perfect in this case: "we are become partakers of Christ if we might hold firmly to our beginning confidence until the end" (1989:269f). Porter's view makes better sense in both the immediate context (cf. present tense with similar conditional language in Heb. 3:6) and macro-context in which genuine believers are in danger of apostasy (cf. McKNIGHT, 1992; and main text above). See also similar conditionality related to perseverance in Col. 1:22–23; Rom. 11:22.

[42] LANE, 89–90. CULLMANN (1952:44) notes that the language of the wilderness warning in Hebrews stresses the "now" aspect of the eschaton (Heb. 3:7, 13, 15).

[43] The phrase is taken from LAANSMA (1997), 314.

[44] NEYREY (1993:55–56; cf. 188–89) describes their apostasy as turning away (μετατίθημι) from God's favour into debauchery. The concept finds parallels in changing loyalties (Polybius

gical punishment (Jude 5 ff, 10, 12–15). Similar to 1 Corinthians 10:4, 9, there is enough text evidence to support that the Lord who delivers and destroys in Jude 5 is "Jesus" or "Christ" (p72, A, B, 33, 81, etc.).[45] These apostates practise vices related to the wilderness generation by running after the error of Balaam (covetousness v. 11) and murmuring (v. 16).[46] Bauckham recognises that Jude, Hebrews 3–4, and 1 Corinthians 10:7–11 are examples of how Christian traditions used the exodus/wilderness experiences to instruct an "eschatological people of God in the period of the new Exodus."[47]

The discourse in 2 Peter 2 parallels Jude and affirms that the apostates deny allegiance to their master, Christ (2 Pet. 2:1 cf. Jude 4). They are scoffers, followers of the vices of Balaam, and *were once redeemed* (τόν ἀγοράσαντα αὐτοὺς δεσπότην ἀρνούμενοι – 2 Pet. 2:1; cf. 1 Cor. 6:20; 7:23) but fell away through covetousness and false doctrines (2 Pet. 2:1–3, 15–16, 19–22; 3:2–4 cf. Jude 17–18). They had escaped (through Christ) the pollution of the world but became entangled in evil again so that their last state was worse than the first. The writer claims that it would have been better for them not to have known the way of righteousness than to have known it and then turn away (2 Pet. 2:20–21). Early wisdom literature is also used to speak of their apostasy in the imagery of a dog returning to its vomit and a washed pig returning back to its wallowing in the mire (2 Pet. 2:22 cf. Prov. 26:11).[48] They will suffer eternal damnation (2 Pet. 2:4–9, 12–13a, 17; cf. ch. 4.5.1.2 above).

The occasion of 1 Clement appears to be related to a sedition in the Corinthian congregation; it thus resembles Paul's correspondence to the same church. The Corinthians are exhorted to be obedient to the leadership; apostasy and destruction await the disobedient (1 Clem. 11 cf. 47). The Corinthian instigators are to entreat to obtain forgiveness and not harden their hearts as did the condemned sedition against Moses in the wilderness (1 Clem. 51). The author of 2 Clement makes a contrast between the now and not yet world in relation to a final state of rest. The Christians who do the will of Christ find rest, those who do not will not escape eternal punishment (2 Clem. 6:7; cf. 5:1–6:9).[49]

In the epistle of Barnabas, the readers are exhorted to take heed in the eschatological era and abstain from wickedness and practising vices. The Christian

---

5.111.8; 24.9.6), apostatising from ancestral traditions (2 Macc 7:24; Gal. 1:6), and party ideology (Diog. Laert. 7.37, 166). The turning away denotes a "failure of faithfulness and shame to one's party or family."

[45] C. Osborn argues that the original text read Ἰησοῦς and compares the passage with 1 Corinthians 10:9 and Hebrews 11:26 (1981:107–15).

[46] Balaam is also considered the instigator of the Israelites' fall into idolatry and fornication at Baal Peor (Num. 31:15–16 cf. 25:1ff).

[47] BAUCKHAM (1983), 50; cf. BIGG (1901), 327.

[48] Cf. D. WATSON (1988a), 122–23, 173f.

[49] Laansma compares the *Epistula Apostolorum* (c. 150) with 2 CLEMENT 5–6. For further examples of the "rest" motif in the post-apostolic era, see LAANSMA, 129–51.

life involves struggle in the present evil age. The believers are to be prepared for the impending age to come when everything associated with evil will be destroyed (*Barn.* 2:1; 4; 18–21). Careless Christians could lose their salvific life (2:10). A background and construction similar to 1 Corinthians 10:12 appears when the author of Barnabas reflects on the golden calf incident and affirms that Israel lost their covenant in the wilderness when they turned to idols. Although so many signs and wonders were done in Israel, God abandoned them. The writer then warns the Christians, "let us take heed" (προσέχωμεν), lest we be found as the Scripture "many are called but few chosen" (Barn. 4:6–14 cf. 2:10; 11:2; 19:2).

One final case comes from the second century church fragments known as the Reliques of the Elders (ch. 9)[50] and attributed to Irenaeus who writes about a certain elder who heard from the apostles and their scribes. This elder claimed that Christians were not to transgress after the manner of those in Paul's writings (in reference to Romans 11:17, 21 and 1 Corinthians 10:1–12), or else they would have no remission for sins and be excluded from the kingdom of God (*sed excludamur a regno eius*). Christians who practise vices akin to the people of the wilderness generation in Paul's narrative would be sent to eternal fire (*in ignem aeternum mitti tales*).

These examples from Paul and other early Christian writers strengthen our view that in 1 Corinthians 10:12 Paul implies through God's rejection of Israel in the previous verses that some in Corinth were in danger of apostasy. We find a strong sense of continuity not only between Paul and his Jewish predecessors, but also between Paul and later Christian writers of the first and second centuries. They all affirm that the motif of apostasy in the wilderness involved *genuine* people of God who could fall away and suffer God's condemnation. The judgement we find in the Christian sources – some, if not all, of which seem to echo 1 Corinthians 10:1–12 – affirm that *eternal* destruction awaits the apostate. This study has shown that Paul does not alter his perception of apostasy in a radically different way than the traditions he cites and echoes. He does, however, introduce eternal consequences as a result of defection, which would be more in keeping with the apocalyptic traditions of his day. The early Christian traditions we have noted pick up that aspect of apostasy without dropping the thought that eschatological condemnation could happen to genuine believers. There is no severe disjunction in this chain of events. Namely, it is extremely unlikely that Paul would argue or assume that individual Christians who fall away into eschatological ruin are not "real" Christians when the Jewish traditions he adopts on the one hand, and the early Christian traditions that adopt his writing on the other, *both* affirm the idea that genuine followers of God could (and sometimes do) fall into devine rejection and eternal destruction.

---

[50] For source in Latin, see LIGHTFOOT and HARMER (1984:556–57).

In 1 Corinthians, most of the Israelites who in 10:1–4 were the recipients of election, initiation, and divine grace fell in 10:5–11.[51] By implication, Paul is affirming that even though the Corinthians were the recipients of grace through their election as baptised Christians and through participation in spiritual blessings such as Lord's Supper, they too could fall away from grace (10:12). The term "stand" presupposes initiation, grace, and election (10:1–4); "fall" is indicative of the opposite (10:5–12). Hence, the fullest impact of the word "fall" in 10:12 means a fall from salvation expressed in the language of initiation, grace, and election into eschatological death.

2.3 Sub-Group and Individual Falling Away

In 10:1–4 we noted that the word "all" conveyed the corporate ideas of election and mutual experience, and the original social "whole" was reduced to smaller corporate units in the "some" language of 10:7–10. This language is particularised even further in 10:12 when Paul uses third person singulars. His language thus moves from community to individual. Mitchell claims that in 10:12 the Corinthians were so threatened by factions that the very survival of the community was at stake: "even if you think you yourselves stand, you will indeed fall if others do."[52] But this statement must be qualified. Paul does not place the emphasis on the "all" who are in danger of falling away but on the individuals and sub-groups committing vices *within* the all. The point of diminished numbers makes adequate sense in the wilderness traditions of antiquity. Paul has been stressing the warning that the Corinthian congregation is in danger of experiencing similar apostasies and judgements to those Israel experienced in the wilderness. In the Hebrew and Jewish tradition, however, "all" Israel did not fall – a remnant completed the entire journey. Paul no doubt recognised this;[53] he is warning that some of the Corinthians could fall away, and the total amount of apostates may come to many but not necessarily all (cf. 10:5).

Paul's differentiation between the "all" and the "some"/individual in this passage is likely a key to understanding his conception of election. All the Corinthians are elect through their participation in the body of Christ just as all the Israelites were God's elect people in the exodus/wilderness episode. The Corinthian congregation's conversion-initiation was genuine just as was Israel's initiation, and both were sustained in their status as God's people through

---

[51] For a similar perspective, see MAUSER, 73; J. BEKER (1993), 110 cf.196.

[52] M. MITCHELL, 254.

[53] Paul perhaps implies his awareness of this by his use of the "one" who receives the prize in 9:24–27.

spiritual provisions. Paul's notion of election here is collective. If subgroups and individuals within the elect body are judged and expelled from the body, this does not mean that the "all" have also apostatised or that the "some" who did apostatise never really participated in the "all." Individuals and subgroups within the community are not immune to falling away; nevertheless, those who made it through the wilderness journey demonstrate that God does preserve a remnant of his elect people. This notion is borne out again and again in Israel's tradition history (cf. Deut. 4:23–31; 1 Kings 19:18; Isa. 1:9f; T. Naph. 4:2–3; CD 3:12–14; Philo *Praem.* 152–72).[54] Hence, the forfeiture of divine election is not necessarily incompatible with the idea of an irrevocable election (cf. Rom. 11:28–29).

In 1 Corinthians 10:1–12 Paul may be supporting the irrevocable perseverance of the elect people of God *as a whole* ("all"), but he still believes that some members who were once part of that elect community can fall away so as to lose the salvific benefits of the elect community. One's identity as an elect individual may only find meaning if that individual belongs to the elect community. Similarly, Christian "individuality" is identified by its participation in the collective community identified as the body of Christ.[55] Paul's metaphorical use of believers being "in Christ" (or Christ in them) includes an aspect of having been joined to Christ in solidarity as one body (1 Cor. 1:30; 10:16–17; 12:27; 2 Cor. 5:17; Gal. 3:27–28; Rom. 6:11; 8:1; 12:5; Col. 1:27; Eph. 3:17; cf. Rom. 5:12ff).[56] For the Corinthian individuals and sub-groups in 10:1–12, removal from the body of Christ constituted a loss of elect membership privileges.[57]

This notion of individual identity as bound up in the collective community is in keeping with social perceptions in Paul's day. The ancient world of the New Testament did not share the modern Western perspective of individuality. Socio-

---

[54] For more examples, see HASEL (1974); CLEMENT (1980), 106–21; ROWLEY (1950), 70–94; ROBINSON (1964); Str.-B. 3:409. One of the most extreme examples of this idea is found in the exodus tradition. Even when God threatened to destroy all Israel in the golden calf incident, he promised to raise up a *remnant* through Moses (Exod. 32:9f). Differently, the forsaking of the "remnant" in Jerusalem (2 Kings 21:14) is not absolute when compared with the accounts of the poor who remained in Jerusalem during the exile and those who returned to the city after it (2 Kings 25:12, 22ff, 27ff; cf. Ezra).

[55] For a similar perspective, see D. MARTIN (1995), 176 cf. 21, 132.

[56] If early Christians understood Christ as the "elect one" (e.g., Luke 9:35; 23:35; 1 Pet. 2:4ff; John 1:34 [p5, א]; cf. Isa. 42:1ff; 1 En. 45:3ff; 48:10; etc.), it is not impossible to assume that Christian election was intricately connected with Christ's election. Klein (1990) argues for a corporate view of election and suggests that Christ is the elect one. The believers are thus elect because they are "in Christ"; they are corporately God's chosen people, the church, and the body of Christ (e.g., Eph. 1:4–11). On Paul's use of the phrase "in Christ," see DUNN (1998:396–401; cf. 548ff).

[57] Note the severity of Paul's excommunication of the sexual offender in 1 Corinthians 5. M. Mitchell rightly observes that the expulsion of the offender meant that he was not to be "included in the unity to which Paul calls the Corinthian church"; he was now considered an enemy belonging to the outside world (112; cf. ftn293: Dio Chrys. *Or.* 34.40).

anthropological studies demonstrate that self-identity is shared in relation to others, whether family, clan, social groups, or nations.[58] Paul's stress on individual and sub-group defections from the body of Christ is analogous to the solidarity of a Greco-Roman political body in which fellow companions are seen as limbs of one another: when one member quarrels with a companion and adjoins with an extraneous member, it is like cutting off one's own limb (Plutarch Mor. 479B cf. 1 Cor. 6:14–15, 20; 12:13).[59] Similar patterns of "cutting off" do not seem foreign to early Christian thinking. Paul himself may have been influenced by the Jesus tradition which claims that, rather than suffer eternal judgement, one should pluck out his/her right eye or cut off his/her hand if it offends him/her (cf. Matt. 5:29–30; Mark 9:43 ff).

For the Israelites, it was only *as* an Israelite that a person was elect; for Paul, Christians are elect in the body of Christ.[60] On a social level, the Pauline and early Jewish communities were in general agreement.[61] Moreover, both communities abide in a covenant relationship with God (cf. 1 Cor. 11:25; 2 Cor. 3:6; cf. Gal. 4:24), and (as we noted previously) Paul believes that the Christian community is eschatological; it is making a new exodus/wilderness journey. Breaking the covenant would result in a forfeiture of the benefits of election (cf. Deut. 28–31; Isa. 24:5; Ezek. 16; Hos. 6:7).[62] Paul holds to a similar view of forfeiture by claiming in essence that God rejects those who reject God (1 Cor. 10:5 f; cf. 4:8.5.2). The result of this for Israel was expulsion by death, and Paul implies for the Corinthians an expulsion by eschatological death.

2.3.1 Excursus: Election in Romans 8:28–39 in Light of Israel's Election and Apostasy

Our perspective of 1 Corinthians 10 and Romans 9–11 calls into question the assumption that unconditional election to final perseverance is a guarantee for the individual Christian (as supposed by some in Romans 8:28–39).[63] Since Paul in Romans 9–11 seems to consider both Israel and the Christians as corpo-

---

[58] Cf. MALINA's dyadic concept (1981:51–70). Neyrey writes, "The identity of people in Paul's world is not individualistic, but is found in terms of some other person. For example, people are know in terms of the town of their birth (Paul of Tarsus), one's family (sons of Zebedee), trade (Paul, the worker in leather) or some other identifying stereotype" (1990:192).

[59] Cf. M. MITCHELL, 119 f.

[60] Cf. JOCZ (1958), 138.

[61] Hays, arguing for an ecclesiocentric hermeneutic in Paul, observes that Paul's Gospel finds continuity with the Torah through an interpretative lens that reads the Hebrew scriptures "primarily as a *narrative* of divine election and promise" (1989:157 cf. 97).

[62] On "breaking the covenant" in Israel's tradition, see WEINFELD, *TDOT* 2:261–62; FORKMAN, 32 f, 70–73; THIEL (1970), 214–29.

[63] In support of this view of election in Romans 8:28 ff (and similar wording in 2 Thes. 2:13–14), see GUNDRY VOLF, 9–14, 56–69. On criticisms of her interpretation of Thessalonians, see MARSHALL (1990c), 259–76.

rately elect (cf. 2.2.2 above), this may help one interpret Paul's perspective of election when final perseverance is in view in the letter. As in 1 Corinthians 10, the language of election in Romans 11 is applied to both Jews (11:28 f cf. 9:11; 11:5) and Christians (11:7 cf. 9:24 ff; 10:20). This is not to say, however, that all the language of election in Romans 9–11 is completely void of individuality (cf. Rom. 9:13, 19),[64] but that individuality seems bound up in illustrations (e.g., Esau, Jacob, Pharoah), which are used as a means to argue conclusions about attaining righteousness by faith instead of works (9:30 ff) and the rejection and/or salvation of corporate groups or sub-groups such as ethnic Israel (e.g., 9:1–6; 10:18–21; 11:26 ff), the Israel of promise (e.g., 9:6–8), the remnant (11:1–7), and Gentile Christians (e.g., 9:30 cf. v. 24; 11:13–22).[65] The individual language in the text points rhetorically to a climax ultimately concerned with corporate Israel in chapter 11.[66]

Our perspective supports that when election with the goal of final perseverance is in view, Paul seems to be speaking of communities rather than individuals. Namely, the predestination and election of Christians in Romans 8:29–30 may rest on Paul's assumption that election to final perseverance refers to the election of a *community* rather than individuals as such.[67] Paul stresses the use of plural and collective terms such as "those," "many," and so forth to refer to the Christians in 8:28–39 (e.g., "τοῖς κατὰ πρόθεσιν κλητοῖς οὖσιν," "πολλοῖς ἀδελφοῖς," "οὓς ... τούτους," "ἡμῶν πάντων," "ἐκλεκτῶν θεοῦ," "ὑπερνικῶμεν διὰ τοῦ ἀγαπήσαντος ἡμᾶς"). Like the Christian community, Israel itself is called, elect, and beloved of God (Rom. 11:28–29; cf. 11:2),[68] yet

---

[64] J. PIPER (1983:163–86) and SCHREINER (1995:89–106) draw our attention to this fact.

[65] Likewise, while it is true that Paul is an individual (11:1), he uses himself to illustrate that he is a member of a corporate remnant of Israel and that God has not entirely rejected ethnic Israel. Romans 16:13 is an example of individual election in Romans, but it is not concerned with final perseverance.

[66] Here Cosgrove's "rhetorical suspense" is helpful though some would question his discussions on polyvalence (1996:271–287).

[67] Cf. WITHERINGTON: "To suggest that in Romans 8 Paul has a different concept of election from the group notion of election enunciated in Rom. 9–11, applied first to Israel after the flesh and then to those in Christ, is not convincing" (1994:232 f cf. 227 ff).

[68] Israel itself was also foreknown by God from the foundation of the world (cf. προγινώσκω 11:2; DUNN 1988:2.636). There is nothing intrinsic about προγινώσκω which necessitates that it refer to the elect individual instead of the elect community in Romans 8:29. Scholars have noted that the word conveys a Hebraic sense of "forelove" (e.g., MURRAY, 1967:1.317). The concept was used of both individuals (Jer. 1:5) and the collective Israelite community (cf. Exod. 2:25; Hos. 13:5; Amos 3:1–2). (Both senses may be implied in the case of Abraham because he is the father of the nation – Gen. 18:19.) Paul's collective use of προγινώσκω in Romans 11:2 might suggest that he primarily had a community in view as well in 8:29. This would also seem to make προώρισεν refer to the community in 8:29. In Romans 9–11, Paul is not primarily concerned with the predestination to final perseverance of *individuals* (or reprobation to final damnation of individuals). Apparently, the "vessels of wrath" in Romans 9:21–22 – which in the larger context seems to represent ethnic Israelites rather than generic individuals – can still repent in the eschatological "now" (11:23–24 cf.

many in Israel fell away so that in the present age, they do not participate in the salvific experience. Israel's corporate election is clearly in view when Paul claims that all Israel will be saved in the "not yet" future (Rom. 11:26). Nevertheless, in the "now" eschaton, Romans 11 (and 1 Corinthians 10) suggests that *individuals* and subgroups who are part of the elect community (whether Jews or Gentiles) may apostatise and be cut off from salvation (cf. Rom. 11:22).

If Paul is speaking about the assurance of election to final perseverance in Romans 8:28–39, then this promise – like Romans 11 and 1 Corinthians 10 – would seem to be affixed to a community rather than individuals *per se* (cf. 2.2 above).[69] First, as in 1 Corinthians 10, the Deuteronomic tradition is clearly evident in the background for Paul's argument in Romans, especially in chapters 9–11.[70] In this tradition, Paul seems to adopt a corporate view of election (cf. Deut. 7:6ff) while at the same time affirming that apostasy can happen to individuals and sub-groups (cf. Deut. 13:1ff; 29:18–20).

Second, the Christians in Rome who are called in accordance with God's purpose are identified as "the ones who love God" (τοῖς ἀγαπῶσιν τὸν θεόν – Rom. 8:28). Paul seems to adapt this phrase from the Deuteronomic tradition where Israel is identified as a community of those who love God *and keep his commandments* (Deut. 5:10; 7:9; cf. Sir. 2:15–16; T. Iss. 5:1–2; CD 19:1–2).[71] Paul probably does not intend to suggest that "the ones who love God" be understood as a *mere* designation or *terminus technicus* for Christians – the phrase takes on the additional implication that a responsibility rests among the people of God to demonstrate their love for God through obedience. God works for good with those who are obedient to God.[72]

9:22b; 2:4) and, by implication, they become "vessels of mercy" in 11:26. Paul's anguish (9:3; 10:1) seems misplaced if ethnic Israel (as the vessels of wrath) are destined to never repent. Conversely, his anguish is real because – even though he believes that Israel will be saved in the "not yet" – in the "now," many of them are not saved and could apparently suffer eternal death as long as they remain in that state. Nevertheless, Paul himself did not seem to entirely fathom his subject (cf. 11:33ff), and we may also wish to opt for a "mystery" at some point in this discussion. A list of studies on predestination can be found in the appendix.

[69] Gundry Volf argues that individuals make up a community and a community is made up of individuals. Hence, for Paul, "there can be no certainty for the group then without certainty for its individual members" (14). But this is too simplistic. Certainly, benefits of the community are experienced by the individuals, yet Romans 9–11 demonstrates that branches (members/sub-groups) which once genuinely belonged to the olive tree (community) were cut off so as to lose the benefits of the latter. Moreover, in 1 Corinthians 10:1–13, Paul holds the tension that God could preserve the people of God as a whole ("all") despite "some" individuals and subgroups who may fall away from the "all." This tension is in perfect keeping with Israel's ancient traditions.

[70] Cf. Scott (1993), 645–47, 659–65; *DPL*, 800–805.

[71] Cf. Dunn (1988), 1:481.

[72] On this interpretation of Romans 8:28, see Zerwick (*Greek*:1988), 477; E. P. Sanders (1977), 446. The former notes that the textual addition of ὁ θεός after συνεργεῖ supports the more emphatic reading: "God works with those who love God ...". The variant may actually be the older reading since it is supported by strong witnesses (p46, A, B, 81).

Third, in Romans it is evident that if a believer lives after the flesh or does not continue in Christ, he or she may become eternally separated from God (Rom. 8:12–13 cf. 11:22; 14:13, 15, 23). But in 8:28–39 Paul does not contemplate whether personal sin or unbelief could finally disrupt a Christian's salvific relationship with God.[73] Hence, the promise of any final perseverance in this passage does not necessarily apply to Christians who follow their sinful nature. In other words, Paul in 8:28–39 may indeed affirm that the collective community of God is foreknown, predestined and elect in the eternal plan of God and will persevere to final glorification.[74] This would be a great comfort to Paul's readers when he mentions the various trials that the Christians in Rome may face.[75] The readers, as individuals, could take comfort in the promises of this passage, but *only* as they are identified as members of the Christian community (cf. 2.2 above). The passage centres on the Christian community as elect, not the Christian individual. A person who is not part of this community has no claim to its promises.

Thus, Paul's use of terms related to predestination and election in Romans 8:28–39 give no necessary indication that genuinely elect individuals cannot finally apostatise. It seems that Paul believes that God can choose, foreknow, and predestine an elect people to final perseverance even though individual members can fall away (cf. Rom. 11). Some elect may fall away, perhaps even most, but never all.

Paul's thought here is consistent with many ancient Israelite traditions which portray the reality of individual and sub-group apostasies within the elect

---

[73] Cf. E. P. SANDERS, 446; GUNDRY VOLF, 13 ftn.29. Witherington writes that 8:35–39 assures the Christian that no external force can separate him or her from God, but what "Paul does not include in his listing in 8:35–39 is the individual himself or herself, who may indeed commit apostasy – hence all Paul's warnings and urgings about faithfulness and perseverance" (1994:232f). But if the pericope refers to the collective community rather than individuals as such, the most Paul could be saying is that the Christian church *as a whole* cannot sever itself from the love of God. Nevertheless, Witherington's point is well taken. Doubtless, Paul did not intend to include the Christians themselves as hostile enemies of their own communion with God by the phrase "another creature" or "any other creature" (Rom. 8:39 – κτίσις ἑτέρα may be textually closer to the original than the more emphatic τις κτίσις ἑτέρα because the τις does not appear in certain early witnesses [p46, D]). Paul is stressing *external* or objective hostile forces, be they natural or supernatural. He is neither focusing on the internal or subjective volition/nature of the Christians themselves, nor on temptation through vices. As elsewhere in Romans, he is not using "another/any other" (ἕτερος or τις ἕτερος) in some unqualified sense that transcends even the categories and parameters at hand (Rom. 13:9; cf. 1 Tim. 1:10). If we could paraphrase Paul, he probably implies this: "and if there is a different (external) opposing force out there which I have failed to mention, neither can it separate us (the ones who love God) from the love of God in Christ."

[74] Note also the parallel in 1 Peter 1:2 where it is said that God elected the Christian communities based on his foreknowledge. In Romans 8, God foreknows "those who love him" (8:28) – the collective elect (Rom. 8:31ff) – and they are predestined to be conformed to Christ's image (cf. Eph. 1:5).

[75] Cf. MARSHALL (1969), 93–94; E. P. SANDERS, 446–47.

community while at the same time maintaining the continuity of that community *as a whole*. In every episode of Israel's tradition history, a faithful remnant always survives after apostasy and judgement/expulsion occur (e.g., Deut. 4:23–31).[76] Paul habitually cites or echoes the Jewish traditions for authoritative support of his arguments, and for him, there is an analogy between Israel and Christians in relation to election (Rom. 11; 1 Cor. 10). It seems implausible that he would have divorced himself so completely from the presuppositions of his Jewish heritage that he now teaches that individuals which make up the elect body are each unconditionally preserved so as to never be able to completely fall away.

2.4 Apostasy and Idol Meats

Since Paul is warning the Corinthians against apostasy in 10:1–13, it would seem peculiar if his discussions concerning the perishing of weaker Christians (ch. 8) and his own potential failure to finish his course (9:24–27) do *not* also suggest the real possibility of falling away. This observation is especially poignant given that Paul begins and finishes his discussion on idol meats with the problem of the strong offending the weak (8:1–13; 10:23–11:1): why would Paul stress the seriousness of offending the weak if there is no real danger of apostasy through that venue? It seems far more consistent to affirm that in 1 Corinthians 8–10 Paul is describing various ways genuine members of the Body of Christ could fall away. This would tend to reinforce the unity of his message in the entire discourse on meat sacrificed to idols. In essence, Paul stresses three dangers in the situation, two potentially committed by the strong and one by the weak: 1) the error of the strong sinning against the weak by eating idol meat in their presence and thereby sinning against Christ (8:11–12); 2) the error of the weak who may be defiled and perish because they eat meat as if to an idol (8:7, 9–13); and 3) the sin of idolatry committed by the strong (10:14–22). In addition, Paul uses himself as an example of self-control and completing his apostolic mission with the implicit intention of deflating the overconfidence of the strong (9:23–27) – even an apostle can be rejected if he is not careful.[77] Therefore, in the situation at hand, there exists a threat of apostasy to real believers.

---

[76] Likewise Danell affirms that judgement on elect Israel is never total annihilation (1953:31). For more examples of this, see Meyer, *ABD*, 5:670 ff. The act or promise of restoration is normally given to a faithful remnant who are purified and restored through an act of repentance or who do not fall away along with Israel's apostates (Num. 14:23–24; Deut. 4:28–31; Judges 2–6; 1 Kings 19:14–18; Ezek. 20:35–38). The nation of Israel may suffer corporate judgement – such as a military mass slaughter (2 Chron. 28:6) or a generation which goes into captivity (Jer. 7:24–29) – but because of God's promises to Israel's forefathers, he does not forsake "all" Israel (Jer. 5:10, 18; 31:36–37; Mic. 7:18–20).

[77] Cf. ROETZEL, 171; *contra* GUNDRY VOLF (247) who, in this passage, attempts to separate

In a collective sense, Paul affirms that when the strong sin against the weak, they sin against Christ (8:12). Martin rightly argues that if the strong place a stumbling block before the weak, they are in essence placing a stumbling block before the body of Christ and hinder the Gospel itself (cf. 1 Cor. 9:12).[78] Moreover, Paul affirms that the stumbling of the weak can lead to ἀπόλλυμι, and Paul normally uses this word when he has eschatological ruin in mind (cf. 10:9–12). We therefore have good reason to suspect that the destruction of the weak in 1 Corinthians 8:7–13 is another way Paul is describing a potential apostasy. He warns that the liberty of the strong could destroy the salvation of the weak. In Paul's conclusion to his message on idol meats, he exhorts the strong to avoid hindering the salvation of anyone, whether Jews, Gentiles, or the church of God (10:32–33).

When we compare 2 Corinthians to these conclusions, the meaning of the warning exhortations found in the second letter become rather apparent (e.g., 2 Cor. 5:20–6:2; 11:3ff; 12:20–21).[79] Some Corinthian members were still in danger of falling away: they could receive the grace of God "in vain", they could be led astray by false apostles, and they could still be trapped by a number of vices. Some form of reconciliation did take place (2:5–11), but at least for some members in the congregation, Paul's warnings in his previous correspondence and visits had failed to bring about the repentance among the members which he had hoped. In 12:20–21 Paul's fear over those who had sinned "before" (προημαρτηκότων) suggests that some of the vices the members were committing in 1 Corinthians were still a problem in 2 Corinthians.[80] Paul was

---

Paul's apostolic calling from his salvation. Pfitzner correctly argues that "Paul cannot separate his apostolic commission from his own salvation. The two go hand in hand" (1967:85).

[78] D. Martin (1990), 145.

[79] I have refrained from including Paul's message against idolatry found in 2 Corinthians 6:14–7:1 because I am not convinced that this passage was written at a later time than 1 Corinthians. It may have been a separate unit that was later connected with the chs. 1–9 and 10–13. Some suggest that the text was originally the letter (or a portion of it) mentioned in 1 Corinthians 5:9. Questions have also been raised about Pauline authorship in this unit (on the debate see Fee, 1977:140–47). My view is that it seems difficult to explain the superficial treatment of idolatry in this section if it were written by Paul after he wrote 1 Corinthians. Fee (1977:143–61) attempts to argue that 1 Corinthians 8–10 is the earlier background to the 2 Corinthians text, but in the end he admits that "meat sacrificed to idols" does not appear in the latter.

[80] A comparison of the vice lists in the Corinthian letters, as well as Paul's mentioning of his prior visits (2 Cor. 13:1ff), supports this conclusion. Cf. Barrett (1973:332); R. Martin (1986:467f); *contra* Gundry Volf (217–25). It may be true that the members' self-examination (13:5ff) would help them to arrive at the conclusion that if Paul is a false apostle, then the message in which they believed is also false because they were converted through Paul's preaching; hence, they would be false believers. Nevertheless, Paul is using rhetoric here with the intention that their examination would lead them to vindicate both themselves and Paul's apostolic message. Paul seems to believe that they *are* genuine Christians, and yet he fears that some of them may have not repented over the vices they were committing *as* Christians.

still concerned about their practising fornication, conceit, disorder, and other vices. He writes that in a third visit he will have to step in and perhaps expel members from the congregation if they continue to oppose him and commit vices (13:1–2, 10; cf. 1 Cor. 5). As we have argued, these sins were being committed by converted members (cf. ch. 4.7 above).

Although we have observed apostasy in reference to 1 Corinthians 8–10 and selections from 2 Corinthians, Galatians, and Romans, it does not follow from this that Paul considered all vices, apostasies, and divine judgements to be the same. His letters involve separate sets of people and circumstances. The occasions are different. Even in the Corinthian situation, not all judgements were alike. While the dangers of apostasy related to idol meats and vices involve eschatological destruction, this does not appear to be the case everywhere else in the epistle. The ones who build (leaders such as Paul and Apollos) without the correct foundation of Christ appear to suffer eschatological loss of reward rather than eschatological death (1 Cor. 3:10–15).[81] But the individuals in the congregation who defile the temple of the Spirit (i.e., the Corinthian congregation members) will be punished with eternal ruin (3:16–17).[82] The members who were creating social problems at the Lord's supper (11:17–34) are punished with illness and physical death, not necessarily eschatological destruction. The incidents related to the vices in 1 Corinthians 5–6, however, depict a genuine danger of loss of eschatological salvation (e.g., 5:5; 6:10), and some of the Corinthians were committing the sexual immorality that Paul was condemning (5:1ff; 6:15ff; cf. chs. 3:2.4; 4:4.2; 4:7; 4:8.5 above).[83]

3. Perseverance: God Will Not Allow You to Be Tempted beyond Your Capabilities (1 Corinthians 10:13)

In the final verse of our pericope (1 Cor. 10:13), Paul assures the Corinthian congregation that every temptation has its limits. The Corinthians could overcome temptation because they serve a faithful God who will not permit them to be enticed above their ability to endure it. Here it seems that Paul is stressing perseverance rather than apostasy. We will therefore examine what he intends to accomplish by this apparent turn in his argument.

---

[81] A similar judgement may be portrayed in 1 Corinthians 4:1–5 and 2 Corinthians 5:9–10.

[82] Here Paul uses φθείρω, which involves a punishment associated with eternal destruction (cf. *BAGD*, 857; 2 Pet. 2:12; Jude 10).

[83] See also footnote 7 above.

3.1 Human Temptation

The difficult phrase "no temptation has seized hold of you except what is human"[84] (πειρασμὸς ὑμᾶς οὐκ εἴληφεν εἰ μὴ ἀνθρώπινος) in 1 Corinthians 10:13a is often interpreted as a statement of comfort.[85] Alternatively, it may be interpreted as a further warning. Paul is perhaps implying to the Corinthians that severer trials await them in the future, and so they should not think that they have proved exceptionally resistant to the trials they have already faced.[86] But if the greater temptation remains in the future,[87] this might seem to mitigate the significance and concern for the present temptation which the Corinthians faced. The source of the temptation in 10:13 seems revealed as a current problem in 10:14: "Therefore ... Flee idolatry!" The problem with idol meats is occurring in the eschatological present.

It would be a plausible step for Paul to comfort the Corinthians after a stern warning in 10:1–12. In this sense, 10:13 seems anticlimactic to 10:12. Some suggest that the strong are in view in 1 Corinthians 10:12 and the weak in 10:13.[88] If so, it would seem awkward that in 10:14 Paul reverts again to address the strong to flee from idolatry. More likely the strong are still primarily (but not necessarily exclusively) in view throughout these verses. In case they become overwhelmed by the fear of falling away, Paul gives them a word of assurance. The temptations are bearable because no matter how severe they are, they will not go beyond the human capability to endure them.[89] As Paul will claim in 2 Corinthians, the congregation should not lose heart, for the severe troubles they face are actually light and momentary when compared with the perspective of eternity (2 Cor. 4:17; cf. Rom. 8:17–18).

For Paul, the idea of succumbing to temptation is in reference to something *believers* face. It normally indicates a fall into sin or apostasy (1 Cor. 7:5; 1 Thes. 3:5; Gal. 6:1),[90] but successful perseverance is always possible. Paul's idea of temptation may have been adopted from the Israelite meaning for test-

---

[84] The force of λαμβάνω here seems to connote a seizing or taking hold of (cf. Wisd. 11:12; Luke 9:39).

[85] Cf. CONZELMANN (1975), 169; CALVIN (1960), 331.

[86] Cf. BARRETT (1971), 229. Godet uses the paraphrase: "If you should fall thus (ver. 13), you would be without excuse; for the temptations which have met you hitherto have not been of an irresistible nature, and as to those which may come on you in the future, God is always ready to sustain you and to save you in time from peril" (1887:2.69).

[87] A future temptation by means of eschatological persecution is often proposed. Basil applied this passage to the persecution of the early church (cf. ROBERTSON/PLUMMER, 1911:209).

[88] See discussion in HAHN (1981), 149–204.

[89] Cf. JEREMIAS, *TDNT*c, 1:366–67.

[90] Cf. KUHN (1992), 95–96; W. WILLIS, 157–58. In Paul's letters, πειρασμὸς appears only in 10:13 and Galatians 4:14. The verbal form is used in the passages cited in the main text and in 2 Corinthians 13:5 where the Corinthian members are to test their own selves to see if they are in the faith.

ing (נסה) in which covenant partners with God are tested to see whether they will keep their end of the agreement (cf. Exod. 16:4; Deut. 8:2; 13:4).[91] Paul may understand that one's failure through temptation resulted in unfaithfulness toward (or apostasy from) the covenant. But if so, he does not regard God as the direct agent of πειρασμός in 10:13; in fact, God is seen as the one who limits the power of temptation (cf. Sir. 33:1).

3.2 Bearing up under Temptation with the Help of a Faithful God

3.2.1 The Faithful God Provides a Way to Escape

Paul comforts the Corinthian congregation members by assuring them that they are able to endure temptation. He adds to this a second reason why they need not be anxious: God is faithful (πιστὸς δὲ ὁ θεός ὃς οὐκ ἐάσει ὑμᾶς πειρασθῆναι ὑπὲρ ὃ δύνασθε).[92] Earlier in the letter Paul also affirmed the faithfulness of God (1 Cor. 1:9). Although Paul wishes to encourage his readers that God's grace and divine assistance are always available to them, he did not intend πιστὸς δὲ ὁ θεός to be understood as some guarantee for final individual perseverance. Marshall rightly claims, "The faithfulness of God does not rule out the possibility of the faithlessness of men [sic!]."[93] It seems that Paul mentions election, assurance, and the faithful God in the opening of the letter because he has a rhetorical purpose in mind. The introduction (1:1–9) serves as an epistolary thanksgiving formula and prelude (προοίμιον). It also functions as an exordium with the intent of securing the goodwill of the recipients.[94] Hence, in the introduction, Paul first praises the Corinthians for their spiritual enthusiasm before he addresses the *excesses* of that enthusiasm.[95] In reference to the "faith-

---

[91]   Cf. SCHNEIDER/BROWN, *NIDNTT*, 3:799f.

[92]   In 10:13 δέ could be translated as "and," for it appears to support that the faithfulness of God is another reason in addition to the humanness of temptation for the Corinthians to take heart. COLLIER (1994:61) suggests a chiasm for 10:12–13 with "God is faithful" at the centre (A: 10:12a, 13e; B: 10:12b, 13d; C: 10:13a, 13c; D: 10:13b). But this structure is not convincing. Unlike 10:6–11, parallel words and tenses are not consistently found.

[93]   MARSHALL (1969), 107.

[94]   Cf. M. MITCHELL, 194–95, 197. Likewise, Philippians 1:6 is sometimes construed to support a guaranteed final perseverance. But it is found in an exordium involving thanksgiving and prayer and is insufficient in itself to support the claim (Phil. 1:3–11). Paul is not stating his theological assumptions about final perseverance; he is trying to build rapport with his audience. He intends to secure the goodwill of the readers and briefly mentions some central topics that will later be discussed (and direct mention of the believers' security in final perseverance does not appear to be one of them). In this case, he is encouraging and anticipating Christian maturity (cf. D. WATSON, 1988b:63f).

[95]   The introduction contains a number of themes which Paul addresses in the body of his letter. He mentions or implies baptism (1:2), wisdom of speech and knowledge (1:5), spiritual gifts and the eschaton (1:6–7), and eschatological assurance and fellowship (1:8–9). As we have noted, the Corinthians had misconceptions about all these issues.

ful God" (1:9), Paul mentions election and fellowship with Christ because the Corinthians had misperceptions about such things. As we have argued in his discussion on idol meats, these misperceptions are made manifest in the area of eschatological immunity and overconfidence whereby the strong were in danger of having fellowship with demons (10:1–22).

Paul's use of the phrase "God is faithful" (πιστὸς ὁ θεός) likely arises from Hebrew and Jewish traditions.[96] In Deuteronomy 7:9 the faithful God keeps his covenant with those who love him and destroys those who hate him. God's faithfulness to his covenant suggests that God will not tolerate his own elect if they violate the covenant, and this is vividly spelled out in the blessings and cursings of Deuteronomy 28–30. God is seen as faithful even when judging elect Israel. More precisely, in 1 Corinthians 10:1–13, Paul appears to adopt πιστὸς δὲ ὁ θεός straight from the wilderness traditions. The metaphor of God as the "Rock" implied the covenantal faithfulness of God in the Deuteronomic tradition. Both 1 Corinthians 10:1–13 and the Deuteronomic tradition are concerned with a new eschatological journey (cf. ch. 3:2.1).[97] It should also be noted that the Deuteronomic tradition has some of the most penetrating discussions on the subject of election among ancient Israelite traditions.[98]

It is not by coincidence that the Song of Moses (Deut. 32) – the song about Israel's apostasy – emphasises the faithfulness of God as the "rock" in the wilderness. Hays rightly argues that Christ as "the rock" in 1 Corinthians 10:4 comes from Deuteronomy 32. (The clearest echo of Deuteronomy 32 in 1 Corinthians 10 is the phrase in 10:20: ἀλλ' ὅτι ἃ θύουσιν, δαιμονίοις καὶ οὐ θεῷ, which follows Deut. 32:17 LXX.) He explains that Paul uses a text similar to the wording of the Hebrew rather than the Greek text in 10:4. The former identifies God as "the Rock" in Deuteronomy 32:4, 15, 18, 30–31. This is perhaps why Paul does not actually cite a Deuteronomic passage in the 10:1–13 pericope: "To explain to the Corinthians the difference between their Greek Bible and its Hebrew *Vorlage* would interrupt Paul's argument."[99]

I will mention several other reasons for entertaining the Song of Moses in Deuteronomy 32 as a backdrop to 1 Corinthians 10:1–22. First, both the Deuteronomic and 1 Corinthians 10 texts are concerned with God's elect offering sacrifices to idols/demons (cf. 32:16–17, 21, 37–39; cf. 1 Cor. 10:20f). The Song of Moses is concerned with defending the monotheistic nature of God who is provoked to jealousy by foreign gods who are really "no-gods" (Deut.

---

[96] Cf. Gardner, 153–54; *BAGD*, 664.

[97] Cf. Scott (1993), 650.

[98] So Patrick (1992), 2:436.

[99] Hays, 94; cf. Fee, 449; McEwen (1986), 7. In reference to the Isaianic texts, Paul does not seem to follow closely either the MT or LXX, and in at least one case, he follows both in 1 Corinthians (cf. ch. 3:2.1 footnotes). A similar case may be made for the Deuteronomic sources he uses. On the influence of the Song of Moses in reference to other Pauline texts, see Scott, 645–65.

32:16, 21; 31:29; Psa. 105[106]:37; 1 Cor. 10:22; cf. Psa. 95[96]:5; 113[115]:4–7; 134[135]:15–18; 1 Chron. 16:26). God is considered the one true God who declares, "I (am) he, and there is no god with me" (Deut. 32:39 cf. vv. 12, 31; 1 Cor. 8:1–6).[100] Regarding this phrase, van Ruiten notes that the Hebrew wording אני הוא in reference to God is found nowhere else in the Old Testament except in Deutero-Isaiah (Isa. 41:4; 43:10, 13; 46:4; 48:12). It later became a prooftext for the Jews, confirming there are not two gods.[101]

The monotheistic structure of the passage leads us to another observation. Both the Deuteronomic and Isaianic texts are as concerned with defending monotheism as is Paul in the context of 1 Corinthians 8–10. We observed that in 1 Corinthians 10:2, Paul seems to hold an Isaianic notion by associating the cloud in the wilderness with the Spirit of God. The Isaianic tradition echoes the Song of Moses on a number of occasions (cf. ch.3:2.1 above).[102] We may assume that Paul is borrowing from both Isaianic and Deuteronomic traditions in the immediate narrative because both texts are concerned with idolatry and its relation to a new generation of God's people in a wilderness milieu.

Second, a warning against apostasy in light of the spiritual provisions of God permeates both the Deuteronomic tradition and 1 Corinthians 10:1–13. The Song of Moses was written as a testimony against the Israelites when they entered into the land of Canaan and turned away from God (Deut. 31:16–22; cf. 8:10–20). God tells Moses that the Israelites will turn to foreign gods and forsake (עזב) him and break his covenant (Deut. 31:16, 20; cf. Lev. 26:15, 44; Judges 2:1; Jer. 11:10). Though the Israelites were the elect of God (Deut. 32:8–14), and Moses affirms that God will never forsake them (31:8), God claims that he *will* forsake them when they turn to idols (Deut. 31:16–17; 32:18–20; cf. Isa. 8:17; Mic. 3:4; 2 Chron. 12:5).[103]

Van Ruiten outlines the Song of Moses as follows: 32:1–6: Introduction and YHWH's loyalty versus Israel's disloyalty; 32:7–18: YHWH's mercy in connection with Israel's apostasy; 32:19–25: YHWH's reaction and judgement against Israel; 32:26–36: complaint against Israel's enemies; 32:37–42: results of recompense; and 32:43: a call to joy due to judgement.[104] Although Paul develops a different outline in 1 Corinthians 10:1–13, similar motifs appear: 1) God is faithful despite the unfaithfulness of God's people (10:13 cf. 7–10); 2) God gives gracious sustenance and gifts in the face of the people's apostasy

---

[100] Van Ruiten argues that the proclamation of God in Deuteronomy 32:39 is the climax of the entire passage, emphasising monotheism in the Song (1994:225).

[101] Ibid.

[102] Cf. KRAUSE (1988), 184f.

[103] On Israel's election in the Deuteronomic text, see VON RAD (1966), 196; THOMPSON (1974), 299.

[104] Van Ruiten, 224. CRAIGIE (1976:376–89) breaks down Deuteronomy 32:15–22 into two sections: 1) Israel's prosperity and apostasy (32:15–18); 2) the results of Israel's apostasy (32:19–22). Von Rad understands 32:15–18 as a description of Israel's backsliding (1966:196).

(10:1–10); and 3) God brings judgement on Israel (10:5, 7–10). Both the Song of Moses and Paul's rhetoric in 1 Corinthians 8–10 serve to remind God's people of the implications of breaking their covenant with God to serve idols.[105]

Third, the Israelites are said to lack wisdom and understanding in the Song of Moses, and God wishes they would be wise enough to enact in a positive way on account of the song (Deut. 32:28–29). Likewise in 1 Corinthians, Paul deals with a situation in which many of the members of the congregation in Corinth lack proper wisdom and discernment (e.g., 1 Cor. 2:6ff; 3:1ff; 4:8ff; 12–14), and though they claim to have knowledge in the area of things offered to idols, they seem to lack wisdom from Paul's perspective (8:1–3; 10:14–15).

Finally, Paul's idea of the rock as Christ does not conflict with the Deuteronomic idea that the rock is God. If Paul is equating the rock with some sense of Christ's pre-existence, he seems to affirm this idea in other letters (Gal. 4:4; Rom. 8:3–4; Phil. 2:6–11; Col. 1:15–20). Moreover, in 10:9, he associates Christ with the Lord from heaven (cf. Rom. 10:6–13; 14:9; Phil 2:9–11).

In the Song of Moses, the theme of God's faithfulness and the unfaithfulness of God's people in reference to idolatry would seem to attract Paul to the conception of Christ as the Rock-Deity of the Israelites in 1 Corinthians 10:4.[106] Peter Craigie suggests that the Israelite's conception of God as the rock (הַצּוּר) emphasises "the stability and permanence of the God Israel" (2 Sam. 23:3; Psa. 18:3, 31; 28:1; 61:2; 62:2; 71:3; 89:26; 95:1; Isa. 17:10; 30:29; Hab. 1:12).[107] The "rock" metaphor highlights the unchanging nature of the covenantal God in contrast with the fickle nature of God's covenant people.[108] God as the rock is associated with perfection, justice, and faithfulness (Deut. 32:4). After God provides Israel with honey and oil from the rock, and other delights, Israel the upright one (Jeshurun) grew fat and deserted the Rock their Saviour (Deut. 32:13–15, 18). Hence, they were "sold out" by the Rock (כִּי־צוּרָם מְכָרָם) in a kind of reverse redemption whereby the promise of putting their enemies to flight was now given to their enemies to put Israel to flight (Deut. 32:30; cf. Lev. 26:8). All this notwithstanding, the "rock" or gods of Israel's enemies cannot compare to the Rock of Israel; Yahweh will once again have compassion on his people and demonstrate that there is no god besides him (Deut. 32:31, 37–39; cf. Exod. 12:12). We can observe that the upshot in both 1 Corinthians 10 and

---

[105] We should also note that when Paul exhorts the Corinthian congregation to cast out the fornicator in 1 Corinthians 5:13, he quotes from Deuteronomy 17:7 (LXX) "ἐξάρατε τὸν πονηρὸν ἐξ ὑμῶν αὐτῶν"; the context of which speaks of purging the land by putting to death the person who worships others gods (cf. Deut. 19:19; 21:21; 22:21f; 24:7).

[106] The "rock" is also associated with the redemptive work of God (Deut. 32:15, 18; cf. Psa. 62:2; 78:35; 89:26; 95:1). Hence, beyond what has already been suggested, it is possible that Paul associated the "rock" with the redemptive work of Christ (cf. Kistemaker, 1993:325; Gardner, 161).

[107] Craigie, 378; cf. Driver (1902), 350–51.

[108] Ibid.

Deuteronomy 32 is similar: "Even though God gave them 'spiritual food,' they rejected him for their idols."[109]

Gundry Volf argues that Paul's mention of the faithfulness of God in 10:13 demonstrates a belief in the final perseverance of individual believers.[110] But this does not appear to be what Paul meant. For Paul and the traditions he echoes in 10:1–13, the motif of God's faithfulness is *not* a guarantee against apostasy – in fact, the phrase often appears in the very context of the defection of God's people. God is faithful despite his people's unfaithfulness. We conclude that in 10:13, then, Paul uses πιστὸς δὲ ὁ θεός to encourage the Corinthians that God is on their side and will faithfully help them when they are tempted (cf. Heb. 10:23). He is not affirming that since God is faithful, God will never allow any individual Christian to fall away. That idea is contrary to the sources Paul is using, and we have observed that Paul holds to a sense of covenantal election and apostasy which is similar to that of the ancient Jews.[111]

3.2.1.1 Excursus: The Faithful God, Ἀποστασία, and Encouragement in the Thessalonian Correspondence

In 2 Thessalonians, as in 1 Corinthians, the faithfulness of God stands in the context of eschatology and perseverance (2 Thes. 3:3).[112] If Paul is the author of this letter, this is the only text where he uses the term apostasy (ἡ ἀποστασία) (2 Thes. 2:3). The Septuagint often translates ἀποστασία or its variants from the Hebrew concepts of acting unfaithfully (מָעַל, בָּגַד) or rebelling/going astray (מֶרֶד, שָׁגָה, פָּשַׁע).[113] The Lukan narrative uses the word to describe the reaction of

---

[109] FEE, 449. This same motif of God's faithfulness in the wilderness despite Israel's unfaithfulness can be found in the Psalm traditions as well as Nehemiah (Psa. 78:8ff; Psa. 81; 95:1, 7–10; 106:6ff; 107; Neh. 9:7f, 17, 20f, 28 cf. vv. 31–32, 35). Like 1 Corinthians 10:1–13, Nehemiah's confession speaks of "our fathers" who experienced the parting of the Red Sea, the pillar cloud, and the miraculous provision of God. All this aside, Israel still apostatised in the wilderness.

[110] GUNDRY VOLF, 69–79.

[111] Cf. HAYS: "No reading of Scripture can be legitimate if it denies the faithfulness of Israel's God to his covenant promises. That criterion binds Paul's interpretive freedom to a relation of continuity with Israel's story" (191).

[112] On the literary integrity of the Thessalonian letters as Pauline, see WANAMAKER (1990), 27–63.

[113] E.g., Num. 14:9; Josh. 22:22f; 2 Chron. 29:19; Neh. 2:19; Isa. 30:1. Cf. RIGAUX (1956), 654; LIDDEL/SCOTT. Ἀφίστημι is sometimes translated for the same Hebrew words. It is also used for the notion "turning away" (e.g., שׁוּב, [שׁוּר]סוּר, מְשׁוּבָה, פָּנָה, הָפַךְ – Deut. 13:10, 13; Josh. 22:18; Jer. 3:14; Dan. 9:9; Cf. BAUDER, *NIDNTT*, 1:606–07). The word appears in the Parable of the Sower where it depicts the falling away of those who endure for a season before affliction and persecution offends them (Luke 8:13; cf. S. BROWN, 1969:12–15). It also appears in the Hebrews account of the wilderness rebellion (Heb. 3:12). In Pauline tradition, ἀφίσταμαι describes an eschatological falling away (1 Timothy 4:1). On other NT words and derivatives related to apostasy, see BAUDER, 1:608; N. BROWN (1963), 84–92. Campbell is only of minimal use (1957), 10–40. Some relevant terms are: ἀποστάσιον, ἀπόστασις, ἀρνέομαι, ἀδόκιμος, [παρα]πίπτω, σκανδαλίζω, ἀπιστέω, πλανάω. Other Hebrew words

the Jewish leaders who accuse Paul of teaching apostasy from Moses (Acts 21:21). Schlier notes that the related term διχοστασία connotes the idea of objective disunity which Paul denounces in his letters (Rom. 16:17; Gal. 5:20 cf. 1 Cor. 1:10; 3:3).[114]

In 2 Thessalonians, the author speaks of a great eschatological apostasy that will occur with the revelation of the man of lawlessness as its zenith (2 Thes. 2:3ff). Giblin suggest that the apostasy here is "a revolt against God that probably takes the form of disbelief and entails a separation of the wicked from the faithful, plus the manifestation of a personalized anti-God figure."[115] The followers of the lawless one are called the ἀπολλυμένοις, and they believe falsehood instead of the truth (2:9–11). The nature of this apostasy is not merely political or social; it is also religious and moral (2:3–4, 9–12).[116] Although it seems to be futuristic from Paul's vantage point, the "mystery of lawlessness" was already in some sense at work (2:7). The pericope may reflect the eschatological tradition of apostatising and being led astray by iniquity and false prophets (Jub. 23:14–21; 4 Ezra 5:1–13; Matt. 24:4ff; Mark 13:5ff; Luke 17:30–33; 21:8–18 cf. 1 Macc. 1:10ff).[117]

Early Christian sources affirm that the eschatological apostasy would include genuine Christians (cf. 1 Tim. 4:1f; 2 Pet. 2–3), but 2 Thessalonians does not directly address this issue. For the Thessalonian Christians, there is a present anticipation that they will not be led astray if they stand fast and keep the apostolic traditions (2 Thes. 2:13–3:5). The Thessalonians are assured that despite evil persons who have no faith, the faithful God will protect them from the evil one (2 Thes. 3:1–3).[118]

In 1 Thessalonians, the congregation is assured of their election and that God intends to save them from the eschatological wrath to come (1 Thes. 1:4, 10; 5:9; 5:24). This assurance is probably given because the congregation had been standing faithful in the midst of persecution (1 Thes. 1:6f; 2:13ff).[119] Unlike the Corinthians, whom Paul warns about turning from Christ to serve idols, the Thessalonian Christians are commended because they have turned from idols to serve God (1 Thes. 1:9)! There was nevertheless a real possibility that Satan

---

for apostasy include: "to forsake/abandon" (עזב, נטש); "to reject/despise" (מאס, בזה, נאץ); "to forget" (שׁכח); and "to exchange/change" (מור). Other concepts related to apostasy include רמה (defect/betray: 1 Chron. 12:17) and קשׁר (treason/rebellion: 1 Kings 11:14). But in the OT they stress turning away in a political rather than religious sense.

[114] SCHLIER, *TDNT*, 1:514.
[115] GIBLIN (1967), 245 cf. 81–88.
[116] Cf. BRUCE (1982), 166; HUGHES (1989), 58–59. The approximation of themes such as idolatry, deception, and lawlessness argue that "apostasy" (religious in connotation) rather than "departure" is perhaps the better translation.
[117] Cf. SCHLIER, 1:513.
[118] Cf. BRUCE, 200.
[119] Apparently in this case, persevering through trials increases the likelihood of Christian hope in the future eschaton (cf. DENTON, 1981:313–320).

could have tempted the congregation members to the point of apostasy, making Paul and his co-labourers' work among them all in vain (1 Thes. 3:5; cf. Gal. 4:11; 2 Cor. 6:1). Moreover, a brief paraenetic section on sexual immorality warns that those who reject/despise (ἀθετέω) the writer's exhortation reject/despise God and his spirit (1 Thes. 4:1–8).

The concept of encouragement plays a prominent role in the Thessalonian correspondence. Marshall is correct in affirming that such language would be important to a congregation which felt threatened by persecutions, afflictions, temptations, and anxiety about eschatological matters. Still he affirms that "we have not found any clear evidence in these epistles to support the view that the elect are a body of specific individuals chosen before the foundation of the world to be effectually called and to attain final salvation without any possibility of their falling away."[120]

3.2.2 The Way of Escaping Temptation

Paul assures the Corinthian congregation that "with the temptation, [God] will make the way to escape so that you are able to bear up under it" (ἀλλὰ ποιήσει σὺν τῷ πειρασμῷ καὶ τὴν ἔκβασιν τοῦ δύνασθαι ὑπενεγκεῖν). He is not claiming that God is the author of the temptation; rather, he affirms that when the Corinthians face temptation, God will provide a way to escape it. For Paul, temptation (πειρασμὸς) normally indicates the work of Satan (cf. 1 Cor. 7:5; 1 Thes. 3:5; cf. Gal. 6:1), yet in 10:13, Satan does not appear to be the direct agent. The temptation refers to the vices Paul mentioned in 10:7–10, and it also anticipates the idolatry in 10:14.[121] Hence, vices (especially idolatry) that lead to apostasy are the source of the temptation in 10:13.

Paul never specifies exactly what is "the way to escape" (τὴν ἔκβασιν).[122] Perhaps he intended the escape route to be connected with the next sentence to "flee idolatry" (10:14ff).[123] If so, this would suggest that escaping temptation is not a passive discipline, but the Corinthians must decide to flee temptation or avoid placing themselves in a tempting condition in the first place. Paul's use of ἔκβασις may also have a wider application than running away from idol temples. The Corinthians were to flee from every form of temptation (1 Cor. 6:18;

---

[120] MARSHALL (1990c), 276.

[121] Cf. KUHN (1992), 96, 108–09.

[122] On ἔκβασις, see *BAGD*, 237–38. Others understand ἔκβασις as the "end" (cf. Heb. 13:7), noting the difficulty of the idea that the Christian escapes the temptation and yet still endures it in the next phrase: τοῦ δύνασθαι ὑπενεγκεῖν (cf. CONZELMANN, 169). But since φεύγετε (10:14) is a present imperative: "keep on fleeing," this may imply a temptation which has a continual or repetitive nature. The deliverance would thus seem to suggest the same sense.

[123] Cf. FEE, 462.

cf. 1 Thes. 5:22; 2 Tim. 2:22).[124] Yet even this conception does not entirely capture Paul's meaning. Since God is the one who provides the way to escape, it is unlikely that the *only* thing the Corinthians had to do was make a self-determined effort to run away from temptation. Paul no doubt believed that the Corinthians would receive some form of unspecified divine assistance if they were resisting the temptation; he would affirm that God delivers the righteous out of temptation (2 Thes. 3:3; cf. 2 Tim. 3:11; 2 Pet. 2:9; Rev. 3:10). The result of this assistance is that the Corinthian Christians would be able to endure or "bear up under" the temptation (τοῦ δύνασθαι ὑπενεγκεῖν).[125] Nevertheless, in this pericope, divine assistance does not preclude the dangers of apostasy. Paul's word on escaping temptation was not intended to comfort the Corinthian members who would choose to continue in their vices or remain presumptuous. Barrett astutely writes, "The *way out* [of temptation] is for those who seek it, not for those who (like the Corinthians) are, where idolatry is concerned, looking for the way in."[126]

3.3 Warning and Encouragement in the Corinthian Situation

We therefore find Paul balancing the notions of apostasy and perseverance in 10:12–13. He warns the Corinthians not to fall away, but he refuses to end the discussion on an extremely negative note.[127] He encourages the members not to despair; God will make a way to escape temptation.[128] No one will fall away who is not careless and presumptuous, and God will never permit a person to fall away who really does not want to do so.[129] That God provides a way to escape, however, does not release the Corinthians from their moral responsibility. Paul did not write an intense warning in 10:1–12 just to assure the congregation in 10:13 that, ultimately, they have nothing to be concerned about. There would be no reason to warn them so severely if he believed they were all going to persevere to the end anyway. Moreover, there is no indication that he believed his very message would somehow instil effectual grace so as to guarantee their perseverance. *Despite* their election, the warning could either be ac-

---

[124] Perhaps behind the thought of fleeing, Paul is echoing Joseph's flight from Potiphar's wife in the milieu of adultery and fornication (Gen. 39:12–13).

[125] Cf. 2 Macc. 7:36; 2 Tim. 3:11; 1 Pet. 2:19; ROBERTSON/PLUMMER, 209. Τοῦ with the infinitive expresses purpose or result (cf. Rom. 1:24; Gal. 3:10; Luke 1:77, 79).

[126] BARRETT (1971), 229; cf. Plumtre (1878), 92.

[127] Cf. 1 Cor. 11:31–32 for another example of this.

[128] We should not assume that Paul never encourages the strong in this letter (cf. 1:1–9).

[129] Gundry Volf rightly affirms, "Fear and uncertainty is no substitute for over-confident carelessness. Instead Christians should trust in God while they attend to the task of not falling" (74).

cepted or rejected, obeyed or disobeyed with the real consequences of eternal life or death. Nigel Watson's comment is most instructive:[130]

> Wherever the gospel is misused to provide a basis for security, the message of judgement must be preached. Yet after the word of judgement there comes to expression once again, and often in direct sequence, the whole gospel, full assurance: God is faithful, he will bring it to pass. That can and must be said to him who has been shaken, after it has been said to him who is secure that everything can be lost ... Yet each of these words, the word of judgement as well as the word of assurance, is unconditionally valid *in its own situation.*

Conclusion

In this chapter we arrived at the conclusion of our pericope and have determined that Paul is warning the Corinthian congregation against a real danger of apostatising from the Christian faith (1 Cor. 10:12). The Christian who stands in a genuine relationship with Christ is the same one who is in danger of falling away in the eschatological "now." Paul had already illustrated the potential results of this apostasy when he discussed the divine judgements on the Israelites in the wilderness in 10:5–11. We have also found that similar language is used in discussions on apostasy in Galatians, Romans, and other early Christian sources. Moreover, in the context of Paul's discussion on idol meats (1 Cor. 8:1–11:1), he addresses a few other potential venues for apostasy: the strong sinning against Christ by offending the weak; the weak being destroyed by the liberty of the strong; and Paul's own potential failure to complete his course. Nevertheless, Paul encourages the congregation at the end of 10:1–13 by affirming a perseverance that does not diminish the dangers of apostasy or personal responsibility. For Paul, perseverance here implies divine assistance plus human endurance. He is conveying to the Corinthians that apostasy is a real danger, while perseverance is a real hope.

---

[130] N. WATSON (1983), 219f. (Emphasis mine.) In the context, Watson is summarising Joest's position and adds that such an understanding of Paul does not make the apostle's teaching chaotic and contradictory. Paul uses a word of justification or a word of judgement to address different hearers in different states of mind.

Chapter 6

Conclusion: Paul and Apostasy

1. Paul's View of Apostasy

For Paul in 1 Corinthians 10:1–13 I have argued that apostasy is a turning away from God for the things of the fallen eschatological "now," which is depicted as a transitional state between conversion-initiation and the final entering of the future kingdom of God. Apostasy occurs when a person who belongs to the elect people of God persists in vices associated with his or her pre-conversion. The result of apostasy in this state is something more than a physical death in the present age. It means being rejected by God and cut off from the grace of God and from God's elect people; the apostate is denied access to the salvific benefits of the "not yet" eschaton.

Problems related to idol meats may be implied by Paul when he mentions "evil things" in 1 Corinthians 10:6, but the neuter plural κακῶν has a wider application than this. Contextually, it is a reference to desiring things that incur God's displeasure, and for both the Israelites and Corinthians, these things are associated with their pre-redemptive status. As the "things of Egypt" represented Israel's former state of bondage, so the vices in this passage were associated with the Corinthians' pre-Christian state (cf. 1 Cor. 6:9–11; 12:2). By exhorting the Corinthians not to lust after evil things, Paul may have idol meats in mind, but idol meats as related to idolatry and rebelling against God by craving things associated with a pre-redemptive status.

On a rhetorical level, we have observed that Paul makes use of group, subgroup, and individual language in 10:1–13. The "all" of Israel did not apostatise, but "some" did – and that "some" were included in the "all" who were elected, delivered, and initiated through the exodus episode. Paul's language suggests that he wanted to make an impact on his readers: if some of the elect in Israel were rejected by God, the same thing could happen to some of the elect in Corinth despite their common fellowship "in one God (8:6; 12:6), one spirit (3:16; 6:11, 17; 12:4–11), one Lord Jesus Christ (1:10; 6:11; 8:6; 12:3, 5), and one body (6:16; 10:17; 12:12–27)."[1]

This understanding of the Corinthian situation favours an interpretation of the election of the people of God as a collective body, yet at the same time, it

---

[1] Quote from M. MITCHELL (1991), 90.

does not deny the possibility of the apostasy of individuals or sub-groups who belong to that body. It supports the perspective that Paul believes in a form of predestination and election of the collective people of God which does not preclude the possibility that some of those people may genuinely fall away. Our study suggests that if perseverance to final salvation is promised to the elect "all," Paul still believes that perseverance is conditional for the *individual* who belongs to the "all." Regardless of what we may think about his logic, Paul believes in the election of the people of God as a solidarity, but individuals within that unit can fall away so that those individuals no longer participate in the grace of God's elect. A rhetorical understanding of 10:1–13 reinforces this hypothesis. The "all" is not what finally apostatises, but the "some." In the Corinthian situation, Paul emphasises that the *individuals* should beware of falling away (1 Cor. 10:12 cf. 3:16–17; 5:1–5; 6:18f; 9:24–27; 16:22). This was no less true for the Christians in Corinth than it was for the Israelites in the wilderness.

Paul's emphasis on the falling away of individuals and sub-groups from the body of Christ resembles the solidarity language related to Greco-Roman political bodies. The members of such a group were viewed as limbs of one another, and the cutting off of a member was like cutting off one's own limb (e.g., Plutarch Mor. 479B). Paul, however, views the cutting off of apostates as a necessary function to preserve the purity of the body of Christ. In the Corinthian situation, he rhetorically corrects some of the members' appeal to advantage by removing it from the individual sphere of reference to the body of Christ. Every Corinthian congregation member belongs to the body of Christ; thus, each member should not seek his or her own benefit but the benefit of others (cf. 1 Cor. 10:33).

Paul's language is also relevant in relation to the recent socio-anthropological discussions of body boundaries and exit rituals. For Paul, the collective "all" in 10:1–13 suggests the Corinthian congregation as the body of Christ (1 Cor. 12:13). The physical body and its boundaries are a microcosm of the social body and its boundaries, and an invasion or penetration from the outside becomes threatening to the open regions of the body because such an opening could contaminate the body. Regarding idol meats, Paul is more concerned with maintaining the boundary between Christ and the fallen world of demons than with the mere eating of the idol meat. Idolatry is a real threat because it blurs the distinction between the body of Christ and the body of the *cosmos*. Paul thus warns that Christians cannot have fellowship with non-believers while they are in the process of committing idolatry (and hence, worshipping demons). When the Corinthians commit vices such as idolatry, they run the risk of expulsion from the social body, which is concomitant to being cut off from the elect community (cf. 1 Cor. 5:1–13). In 10:1–13 Paul implies that those who commit idolatry or other vices run the danger of being expelled from the body of Christ through divine judgement. This brings to light a reason *why* judgement occurs on an apostate. The apostate is a pollutant that must be expelled from the body in order to preserve the body from contamination and maintain the body's wholeness.

If Paul reflects the prominent ideas of the early Israelite sources, such as those found in the Deuteronomic tradition, it would seem that his understanding of apostasy is not identified with a single act of sin or disobedience; rather, it is an abandonment of one's covenantal relationship with God. Apostasy presupposes that the one who apostatises was once faithful to God's covenant but is no longer so. It points to the potential result of committing vices: rejection of God or God's covenant through one's actions or unbelief. Paul warns the Corinthians against turning away from God to serve idols. In the Corinthian situation apostasy arises primarily through the practising of destructive vices associated with the status of pre-conversion; in Romans 9–11 it seems to occur through unbelief, disobedience, and high-mindedness (Rom. 9:31–32; 10:16, 21; 11:22–23); in the Galatian congregations, it appears to centre on accepting a belief which contradicts the essence of the Gospel (Gal. 1:8–9; 5:4).

2. Final Conclusion

We have observed that in 1 Corinthians 10:1–13 Paul warns members in the Corinthian congregation that if they continue to participate in vices related to those which the Israelites practised, they would suffer divine rejection and judgement. Paul's method of persuading the Corinthians about this danger is by comparing Israel in the wilderness with the Corinthians, who are viewed as being in a state of eschatological overlap. The experiences of Israel in the wilderness are types pointing to the Corinthians' experiences, and the judgements are hypothetical prefigurations of what might happen to the Corinthians (10:6, 11a). Paul compares the two communities in relation to election, conversion-initiation, and divine graces. Israel's unified initiation through the cloud and sea under Moses prefigured the Corinthians' Spirit- and water baptism which made them members of the body of Christ (10:1–2). Israel's consumption of supernatural sustenance in the wilderness represented for the Corinthians their participation in the Lord's Supper and any other means whereby they might have deemed themselves as spiritual. Paul claims that Christ was the provider of these blessings for Israel; hence, Christ was spiritually present with the Israelites in the wilderness just like he was present with the Corinthians (10:3–4).

Despite these privileges, the majority of Israelites did not make it to the promised land; their bodies fell in the wilderness. God rejected them because they coveted the food of Egypt, committed idolatry and fornication, tempted Christ, and murmured against their leaders. Likewise Paul implies that the Corinthians may be rejected by God if they participate in idolatry, commit fornication, provoke Christ through their inconsiderate liberties, and continue in their factions and perhaps their opposition toward Paul (10:5–10). Many in Israel were destroyed in the wilderness; likewise, many in the Corinthian congregation could be destroyed in the present eschaton. For Paul, this period covers the overlap between the eschatological present and future ages. The eschatological "rest" for Paul is in the "not yet" kingdom of God (cf. 10:11b). Paul's eschatological framework is added to his argument, in part, because the Corinthians had an overrealised perspective of eschatology. In cultural-anthropological terms, they believed they had already achieved an aggregative status because of their initiation and separation from their pre-converted status. Paul attempts to bring them back to the realisation that they are still in a state of liminality. Paul warns them to watch out or else they will commit apostasy; namely, they will fall away from grace in this marginal state and fail to enter the "not yet" kingdom of God (10:12). After such a stern warning, he provides them some comfort by giving them assurance about persevering through temptation (10:13). This assurance, however, was not intended to contradict or mitigate his previous warning about the genuine possibility of their apostasy.

In reference to the larger framework (8:1–11:1), we have argued that the golden calf and Baal Peor incidents in 10:7–8 combine the notions of idolatry, fornication, and the eating of food in a cultic setting. The coveting in 10:6 is also associated with food and seems interrelated with all the vices Paul mentions. Paul intended the idolatry in 10:1–13 to be associated with his discourse on idol meats. Still he does not equate idolatry with idol meats even though this passage would have provided him with an expedient opportunity to do so. Paul does not condemn the eating of idol meats in a temple precinct *per se*; he condemns idolatry which may occur by participating in fellowship with idolaters and demons (cf. ch. 2). Nevertheless, he assumes that idolatry is likely to occur in a cultic setting, and for him, idolatry leads to apostasy (cf. 10:7–8).

If the strong in Corinth confuse the boundary between Christ and the *cosmos* by having fellowship with demons, they run the risk of contaminating the body of Christ. As such, they could be expelled from the body through divine judgement. Such a judgement may be considered an exit ritual in which the expelled persons have their status reversed from elect community members to non-elect members of the *cosmos*. The dangers of defection, however, are not always in reference to the strong. The liberties of the strong could result in the falling away of weaker members (ch. 8), and Paul affirms that even he himself is not immune to the possibility of apostasy (ch. 9:24 ff).

There are several closing remarks I wish to make concerning this study.

1. Intertextual analysis complements the conclusion that Paul is warning the Corinthians about a real danger of apostasy in 1 Corinthians 10:1–13. The wil-

derness examples from the traditions of Numbers, Exodus, Deuteronomy, Isaiah, Psalms, and Wisdom suggest that the Israelites were seen as an elect community, but individuals and sub-communities – who once participated as elect members of the community – could be expelled from it. Even in the Song of Moses, where Israel may fall away corporately, restoration is made possible to a remnant (Deut. 32). Paul holds to a similar sense of election in 10:1–13, illustrating the fall of "some" but not "all." Moreover, he claims that the Israelite experiences are hypothetical precursors to the Corinthian experiences and that both communities benefited from the spiritual nourishment bestowed to them by Christ. Paul also grounds his interpretation of the scriptures in an eschatological and ecclesiological matrix by implying that the Christian community is a restored covenant community who is making a new exodus/wilderness journey as described by early Jewish traditions.

2. Early Christian traditions also complement the conclusion that Paul is speaking of the apostasy of genuine believers in 10:1–13. First, Paul's use of terms such as "destroy," "fall," and "beware" in his other letters (where apostasy was also an issue) convey the same or similar meanings as in the Corinthian passage (e.g., Gal. 5; Rom. 11). Paul argues that individuals from among God's elect and the body of Christ are not exempt from defection. Second, other early Christian traditions, which describe the Israelites in the wilderness, and seem to be echoing Paul, portray a similar sense of apostasy which is then related to the Christian experience (e.g., Heb. 3–4; Jude/2 Peter; 1 Clem. 51; Barn. 4; Reliques 9). There is thus a strong case for supporting continuity of thought on apostasy in relation to Israel's traditions, Paul's writings, and some of the later Christian traditions of the first and second centuries.

3. Paul's rhetoric affirms that a paraenetic issue was at stake. Paul intends to convey a warning in order to compel the Corinthian members to a positive ethic. This was related to the overall theme of unity and discord in the letter. Paul's use of "all" in relation to Israel implies an elect solidarity for the Corinthian community. His use of "some" implies that certain members of the community could be judged and expelled despite their privileges in the "all." The graphic number of Israelites who were destroyed in the wilderness is intended to convince the Corinthians not to participate in similar vices. Paul warns them to watch out because no one is entirely immune to apostasy.

4. The socio-anthropological concepts of liminality, body boundaries, purity, and exit rituals underscore the conclusion of this study. Turner's liminal state of "betwixt" and "between" complements Paul's perspective of the Christian community in the eschatological "now" and "not yet." In both schemes, the idea of completion is necessary in order to achieve a new status. Paul implies that the

Corinthians have not achieved their final state. Paul's metaphor of the Corinthians as members of the body of Christ is analogous to the orators of his time who consider the human body as a microcosm of the larger social body. Community members who endanger others in the body are libel to be extricated from the body in order to maintain the body's wholeness. In such a case, the status of the member is reversed.

5. As stated in chapter 1 of this study, the phenomenon of defection is uncontested on historical and sociological grounds. The *interpretation* of that phenomenon is what is often disputed. Theologians from both Calvinist and Arminian persuasions have too often assumed that the authors of the New Testament all had the same opinion and wrote univocally on the subjects of apostasy and perseverance (as though perhaps these ancient writers were themselves systematic dogmaticians). This does not appear to be the case. Jewish and Gentile Christians did not always act and think alike (e.g., Gal. 2; Acts 21). The early congregations faced numerous variations of difficulties and temptations, and they had different attitudes and opinions related to these challenges. The authors were primarily involved in meeting the situational needs of these churches rather than creating a systematic and universally acceptable approach to apostasy and perseverance. As was the case in later church history, the New Testament Christians may have been unified on more central beliefs but diversified on less central ones. Paul offers the hope of restoration for apostate Israel (Rom. 11), and James offers it to Christians who have gone astray (James 5:19–20); the author of Hebrews, on the other hand, does not offer any hope of restoration for the apostate (Heb. 6:4–6). An honest and careful examination of both the unity and diversity of early Christian beliefs, I would argue, is perhaps the only true key to resolving the impasse between Calvinists and Arminians.

6. This work concludes that the undisputed Pauline letters, and 1 Corinthians 8–10 in particular, support the reality of apostasy as a falling away of genuine believers, and recent New Testament interpretative methods underscore that reality. I have intended to go beyond the common Calvin-Arminian theological debates by removing the question of apostasy from a systematic theological matrix in order to examine it in light of more recent interpretative methods. I selected one Pauline passage in relation to the macro-situation of the letter it appears in, and this was my starting point. I added the Hebrew scriptures and early Jewish sources which Paul seems to echo or which may have influenced him, and read the passage in light of some rhetorical and socio-anthropological methods. I have concluded that Paul's views on perseverance and election do not nullify his affirmation that genuine believers could fall from grace. For Paul, the tension between predestination/election/perseverance on the one hand, and apostasy/divine judgement on the other, is alleviated on a corporate level.

I hope that in future studies those who wish to contribute to the subject of apostasy and perseverance will take seriously the added dimension of recent interpretative methods.

Appendix

Selected Works Related to Apostasy and Perseverance

Consult the General Bibliography for complete data. Older works are often listed as reprints. For more sources see Chapter 1, the General Bibliography, dictionary entries listed below, and Peterson (1992). Some works overlap in subject areas.

1. Works Related to Apostasy and Perseverance in the Hebrew Scriptures

Coats (1968)
M. A. Ellis (1988) 16–26
Forkman (1972) 16–38
Franklyn (1986)
Gileadi (1988)
Holladay (1958)
B. Kelly (1996)
Marshall (1969) ch. 1

Noth (1981)
Patrick & Shogren (1992) 2:434–44
Snaith (1945) 131–42
Sundell (1983)
Thiel (1970) 214–229
Vranik (1993)
Waltke (1988) 123–39
Weinfeld TDOT 2:253–79

2. Works Related to Apostasy and Perseverance in Jewish Second Temple and Hellenistic Literature

J. Barclay (1995b) 114–21
Borgen (1994) 30–59
N. Brown (1963)
Eskola (1998) 27–94
Feldman (1993) 76–83
Forkman (1972) 39–86
Garlington (1991)
Haas (1989) 117–54

Harvey (1985) 79–96
Horbury (1985) 13–38
Kippenberg (1987) 1:353–54
McKnight (1991) 16–19
M. Newton (1995)
E. P. Sanders (1977)
Williamson (1970) 252–67

3. Works Related to Apostasy and Perseverance in Tannaitic Literature and Later Judaism

Charmé (1987) 17–33
Dov (1972) 3:201–16
Forkman (1972) 87–114
Harrington (1993)
Kaufman & Gottheil (1901) 2:12–18

E. P. Sanders (1977)
J. T. Sanders (1993) 58–67
Schereschewsky (1975) 377–79
Sjöberg (1938)
Zeitlin (1963) 84–86

4. Recent New Testament Works Related to Apostasy and Perseverance

Baker (1997) 326–330
J. Barclay (1995a) 89–120
Bauder NIDNTT 1:606–11
Borgen (1994) 30–59
S. Brown (1969)
Campbell (1957)
Cole (1964)
DeSilva (1996) 91–116
Didier (1955)
M. A. Ellis (1988)
Forkman (1972)
Garlington (1994)
Giblin (1967)
Gundry (1985) 1–38
Gundry Volf (1990)
Hofius (1973) 135–45

Hahn (1981) 149–204
Joest (1968)
McKnight (1992) 21–59
Marshall (1969); (1990b) 306–24
Monson (1980)
Prassel (1989)
Roetzel (1972)
Schlier TDNT 1:512–14
Schreiner (1998) 32–62
Segal (1990)
Smiles (1998)
Synofzik (1977)
Warren (1983)
Whisenand (1985)
Windisch (1908)

5. Works Related to Apostasy and Perseverance in Early and Medieval Christianity

Barnett (1997) 75–76
Beugnet (1909) 1:602–11
Bouché (1935) 1:640–52
Bowersock (1997)
Connelly (1967) 11:154–55
Croix (1954) 75–114
Doignon (1992) 111–14
Doskocil (1958)
Ermoni (1907) 1:98–104
Foakes-Jackson (1908) 1:623–25
Frend (1952); (1965); (1985)
Friedberg (1951) 1:238–39
Gaudemet (1949) 64–77

Guzzetti (1968) 1:75–76
Hyland (1928)
Jaroszewicz (1932)
Kippenberg (1987) 354–55
Moltmann (1986) 5:226–27
Nock (1933) 56–63
Petit (1909) 1:76–90
Saloom (1946) 7–46
Sato (1992) 619–33
Van Hove (1913) 1:624–26
Vodola (1986)
Wendebourg (1987) 295–320

6. Works Related to the Calvinism and Arminianism Controversy

Bangs (1971); (1963) 421–28
Berkouwer (1958)
Boettner (1932) 182–201
Browning (1860)
Curtiss (1894)
Davis (1991) 213–28
Harrison (1926); (1937)
Hegle (1961)
Hoekema (1989) 234–56
Hoenderdaal (1970) 49–92

Hunt (1971) 234–40
Jessop (1942)
Kendall (1983)
Mell (1851)
Moody (1991)
Muller (1991)
Murray (1955) 151–60
Nash (1871)
Oliphant (1878)
Peterson (1990) 119–125

Pinnock (1975); (1989)
Porter (1793)
Potter (1827)
Praamsma (1968) 22–38
Schreiner & Ware (1995)
Sell (1983)
Sellers (1987)
Shank (1961)

Starbuck (1908) 2:319–21
Steele (1899) 132–60
Tipson (1984) 301–330
Wakefield (1960) 253–58
W. White (1817)
Wilkin (1982)
Worman (1877) 3:973–75

7. Modern Systematic-Theological Works Related to Apostasy and Perseverance/ Election

Calvinist-Reformed
Berkhof (1953) 507–09 545–54
Hodge (1946) 3:104–13
Heppe (1950) 581–89
Dabney (1878) 687–713
Shedd (1894) 2:558

Arminian-Wesleyan
Wiley (1940–46) 249–51
Pope (1876) 3:100–47
Miley (1894) 2:268–70; 339–54
Beet (1906) 289–97
Rahlston (1874) 444–56

Anglican-Episcopal
H.C.G Moule (1894) 36–56

Baptist-Evangelical
Erickson (1985) 985–97
Moody (1981) 348–65
Strong (1907) 881–86

Charismatic/ Third Wave
Grudem (1994) 788–807
J. R. Williams (1990) 2:119–36

Dispensational
Chafer (1947) 3:267–355; 7:17–24
   285–86
Theissen (1949) 385–91

Eastern Orthodox
Karmires (1973) 75–82

Lutheran
Pieper (1950–57) 2:467–70 540–52;
   3:89–100

Neoorthodox
K. Barth (1957) 2.2
Brunner (1950) 1:346–53

Universalism
Schleiermacher (1926) 510–17

Pentecostal
E. S. Williams (1953) 1:207–78
Pearlman (1937) 267–76

Roman Catholic
Ott (1955) 242–46
Rahner (1992) 23:3–15; (1990) 97–106

8. Sociological and Miscellaneous Works Related to Apostasy and Perseverance

Barbour (1994)
Beckford (1981)
Berger (1987) 6–17
Bromley (1988)
Greeley (1971) 125–34

Hadaway (1992) 26–34
Hadaway & Roof (1988) 194–200
Nelson & Bromley (1988) 47–61
Hunsberger (1983) 121–38; (1980) 158–70

9. Studies on Assurance, Perseverance and/or Apostasy

Beeke (1991)
Bell (1985)
Borchert (1987)
Carson (1992) 1–29
Cook (1993) 147–53
Cureteu (1987)
Foxgrove (1980) 220–32

Goguel (1938) 105–44
Letham (1979)
Noll (1975) 161–77
Perkins (1988) 57–60
Stoeffler (1965) 128–39
Wolterstorff (1990) 396–417
Yates (1952)

10. Studies on Election

M. Barth (1983)
Berkouwer (1960)
Clements (1980) 106–21
Elwell (1993) 225–29
Hasel (1972)
Jewett (1985)
Jocz (1958)
Klein (1990)
Kraus (1995)
MacDonald (1989) 207–29
Marshall (1990c) 259–76

Meyer (1993) 5:669–71
Montagnini (1977) 57–97
Pannenberg (1977)
Patrick & Shogren (1992) 2:434–44
H. Robinson (1964)
Roetzel (1993), 211–33
Rowley (1950)
Schreiner 1995:89–106
Shank (1970)
Stendahl (1953) 63–80
Westblade (1995) 63–85

11. Studies on Predestination

W. Abraham (1989) 231–42
Boethius (1973)
Buis (1958)
Carson (1981)
Clark (1969)
Clines (1975) 110–26
Davidson (1946)
Dinkler (1967) 241–69
Eskola (1998)
Garrigou-Lagrange (1946)
Grider (1987) 56–64

Jacobs (1937)
P. Jewett (1985)
Lange (1996)
Marshall (1990a) 290–305
Merril (1975)
Moltmann (1961)
Mozley (1883)
Muller (1986)
Ockham (1983)
Röhser (1994)

Abbreviations Bibliography

ABD	*The Anchor Bible Dictionary*. David Noel Freedman, ed. Doubleday: New York/London/Toronto/Sydney/Auckland, 1992. 6 Volumes.
Apostolic Fathers	(see Lightfoot, J. B., and Harmer, J. R.).
BAGD	Bauer, Walter, Arndt, William F., Gingrich, F. Wilbur. *A Greek-English Lexicon of the New Testament and Other Early Christian Literature*. Second Edition. Revised and Augmented by F. W. Gingrich and Frederick W. Danker from Walter Bauer's 5th edition, 1958. Chicago: University of Chicago Press, 1979.
BDB	Brown, Francis, Driver, S. R., Briggs, Charles A. *The New Brown-Driver-Briggs-Gesenius Hebrew and English Lexicon with an appendix containing the Biblical Aramaic*. Peabody: Hendrickson, 1979.
BDF	Blass, F., Debrunner, A. *A Greek Grammar of the New Testament and Other Early Christian Literature*. A Translation and Revision of the 9th–10th German edition incorporating supplementary notes of A. Debrunner by Robert W. Funk. Chicago/London: The University of Chicago Press, 1961.
DDS	*The Dead Sea Scrolls in English*. Revised and Extended Fourth Version. Geza Vermes. London: Penguin Books, 1995.
DPL	*Dictionary of Paul and His Letters*. Gerald F. Hawthorne, Ralph P. Martin, Daniel G. Ried, eds. Downers Grove, IL/Leicester: InterVarsity Press, 1993.
DJG	*Dictionary of Jesus and the Gospels*. Joel B. Green, Scot McKight, I. Howard Marshall, eds. Downers Grove: InterVarsity Press, 1992.
DLGT	Muller, Richard A. *Dictionary of Latin and Greek Theological Terms: Drawn Principally from Protestant Scholastic Theology*. Grand Rapids: Baker Book House, 1985.
EDT	*Evangelical Dictionary of Theology*. Walter A. Elwell, ed. Grand Rapids: Baker Book House, 1984.
ER	*Encyclopedia of Religion*. Mircea Eliade, ed. Macmillan Library Reference USA. New York: Simon & Schuster, 1995. 16 Volumes.
ERE	*Encyclopaedia of Religion and Ethics*. James Hastings, ed. Edinburgh: T. & T. Clark, 1908–21. 12 Volumes.
GMP	*The Greek Magical Papyri*. (see Betz, Hans Dieter).
Fragments	(see Bell, H. Idris, and Skeat, T. C.).
Greek	Zerwick, Maximilian. *A Grammatical Analysis of the Greek New Testament* Unabridged, 3rd Revised Edition. Rome: Editrice Pontificio Istituto Biblico,1988.
Gram.	Zerwick, Maximilian. *Biblical Greek*. Reeditio photomechanica (1979). from 4th Latin edition. Rome: Scripta Pontficii Instituit Biblici, 1963.
Idiom	Moule, C. F. D. *An Idiom Book of New Testament Greek*. Second Edition. Cambridge: Cambridge University Press, 1959.
ISBE	*International Standard Bible Encyclopedia*. Revised Edition. Geoffrey W. Bromiley, ed. Grand Rapids: Eerdmans, 1979–88. 4 Volumes.

Liddell/   Liddell, Henry George, and Scott, Robert. *A Greek-English Lexicon*. 9th
Scott   edition. Oxford: Clarendon Press, 1940.

LCL   Loeb Classical Library.

NIDNTT   *New International Dictionary of New Testament Theology*. Expanded and Revised. Colin Brown, ed. Grand Rapids: Regency Reference Library/ Zondervan, 1975–1986. 4 Volumes.

ODC   *The Oxford Dictionary of the Christian Church*. Revised Second Edition. F. L. Cross and E. A. Livingstone, eds. Oxford: Oxford University Press, 1983.

Philo   (see Yonge).

Pseud.   *The Old Testament Pseudepigrapha*. James A. Charlesworth, ed. New York/ London/Toronto/Sydney/Auckland: Doubleday, 1983–85. 2 Volumes.

Schaff   Philip Schaff, ed. David S. Schaff, rev. *The Creeds of Christendom: With a History and Critical Notes*. 3 Volumes. Sixth edition. Reprint. Grand Rapids: Baker Book House, 1993. (See also [Ante-] [Post-] Nicene Fathers under respective ancient authors).

Str.B.   Strack, Hermann L. und Billerbeck, Paul. *Kommentar Zum Neuen Testament Aus Talmud Und Midrash*. München: C. H. Becksche Verlagsbuchhandlung, 1963–1965. 6 Volumes.

Syntax   Burton, Ernest De Witt. *Syntax of the Moods and Tenses in the New Testament*. Revised Edition. Grand Rapids: Kregel, 1976.

TDNT   *Theological Dictionary of the New Testament*. Gerhard Kittel, Gerhard Friendrich, eds. Translated and edited by Goeffrey Bromiley. Grand Rapids: Eerdmans, 1964–76. 10 Volumes.

TDOT   *Theological Dictionary of the Old Testament*. Johannes Botterweck, Helmer Ringgren, Heinz-Josef Fabry, eds. Revised edition translated by John T. Willis. Grand Rapids: Eerdmans, 1974–95. 7 Volumes.

Textual   (see Metzger, Bruce M.).
Commentary

Weimar   Weimar (H. Bohlau) Edition. *D. Martin Luthers Werke: Kritische Gesamtausgabe*. 1883. (see also Luther, Martin).

Works   Luther's Works. *Lectures on Titus, Philemon, and Hebrews*. Volume 29. Jaroslav Pelikan, ed. St. Louis: Concordia Publishing House, 1968. (see also Luther, Martin).

Yonge   *The Works of Philo: Complete and Unabridged*. New Updated Edition. Translated by C. D. Yonge. Introduction by David M. Scholer. Peabody, MA: Hendrickson Publishers, 1993. (see also Philo in General Bibliography).

Commentaries Bibliography

Alló, Le P. E.-B. *Saint Paul Première Épitre aux Corinthiens*. Études Bibliques. Paris: Librairie Lecoffre, J. Gabalda, 1956.

Bachmann, Philip. *Der erste Brief des Paulus an die Korinther*. Leipzig & Erlanger: Diechert, 1936.

Barrett, C. K. *The Second Epistle to the Corinthians*. Black's New Testament Commentaries. Peabody, MA: Hendrickson, 1973.

Barrett, C. K. *A Commentary on the First Epistle to the Corinthians*. Black's New Testament Commentaries. London: Adam & Charles Black, 1968. 2nd ed. 1971.

Bauckham, Richard J. *Jude, 2 Peter*. Word Biblical Commentary. Waco: Word Books, 1983.

Betz, Hans Dieter. *Galatians: A Commentary on Paul's Letter to the Churches in Galatia*. Hermeneia – A Critical and Historical Commentary on the Bible. Philadelphia: Fortress Press, 1979.

Bigg, Charles. *A Critical and Exegetical Commentary on the Epistles of St. Peter and St. Jude*. International Critical Commentary. Edinburgh: T. & T. Clark, 1901.

Brown, Raymond E. *The Gospel According to John: Introduction, Translation, and Notes*. The Anchor Bible. 2 Volumes. Garden City, NY: Doubleday, 1966–70.

Bruce, F. F. *1 and 2 Corinthians*. New Century Bible. London: Oliphants, 1971.

Bruce, F. F. *1 & 2 Thessalonians*. Word Biblical Commentary. Waco: Word Books, 1982.

Calvin, John. *The First Epistle of Paul the Apostle to the Corinthians*. Calvin's Commentaries. John W. Fraser, translator. David W. Torrance, T. F. Torrance, eds. Edinburgh: The Saint Andrew Press, 1960.

Conzelmann, Hans. *1 Corinthians*. Hermeneia – A Critical and Historical Commentary on the Bible. Philadelphia: Fortress Press, 1975.

Craigie, Peter C. *The Book of Deuteronomy*. New International Commentary of the Old Testament. London: Hodder & Stoughton, 1976.

Cranfield, C. E. B. *A Critical and Exegetical Commentary on the Epistle to the Romans*. International Critical Commentary. 2 Volumes. Edinburgh: T. & T. Clark, 1979.

Driver, S. R. *A Critical and Exegetical Commentary on Deuteronomy*. International Critical Commentary. Edinburgh: T. & T. Clark, 3rd ed., 1902.

Dunn, James D. G. *1 Corinthians*. New Testament Guides. Sheffield: Sheffield Academic Press, 1995.

Dunn, James D. G. *Romans 1–8*. Word Biblical Commentary. Dallas: Word Publishing, 1988.

Dunn, James D. G. *Romans 9–16*. Word Biblical Commentary. Dallas: Word Publishing, 1988.

Dunn, James D. G. *The Epistle to the Galatians*. Black's New Testament Commentaries. London: A & C Black, 1993.

Ellicott, Charles J. *St. Paul's First Epistle to the Corinthians: With a Critical and Grammatical Commentary*. London: Longmans, Green, and Co., 1887.

Ellingworth, Paul. *The Epistle to the Hebrews: A Commentary on the Greek Text.* New International Greek Testament Commentary. Grand Rapids/Carlisle: Eerdmans/The Paternoster Press, 1993.

Evans, Ernest. *The Epistles of Paul the Apostle to the Corinthians.* Oxford: The Claredon Press, 1930.

Fee, Gordon D. *The First Epistle to the Corinthians.* New International Commentary on the New Testament. Grand Rapids: Eerdmans, 1987.

Fitzmyer, Joseph A. *Romans: A New Translation with Introduction and Commentary.* The Anchor Bible. London: Geoffrey Chapman, 1993.

Frör, Hans. *You Wretched Corinthians!: The Correspondence Between the Church in Corinth and Paul.* London: SCM Press, 1995.

Godet, F. *Commentary on St. Paul's First Epistle to the Corinthians.* Edinburgh: T. & T. Clark, 1887. 2 Volumes.

Goudge, H. L. *The First Epistle to the Corinthians.* Westminster Commentaries. London: Methuen and Co., 1903.

Grosheide, F. W. *Commentary on the First Epistle to the Corinthians: The English Text with Introduction, Exposition and Notes.* New International Commentary on the New Testament. Grand Rapids: Eerdmans, 1953.

Hargreaves, John. *A Guide to 1 Corinthians.* Theological Education Fund. Study Guide. London: SPCK, 1978.

Héring, Jean. *La Premiére Épitre de Saint Paul Aux Corinthians.* Commentaire du Nouveau Testament 7. Paris: Delachaux & Niestlé, 1949.

Horsley, Richard A. *1 Corinthians.* Abingdon New Testament Commentaries. Nashville: Abingdon Press, 1998.

Kistemaker, Simon J. *Exposition of the First Epistle to the Corinthians.* New Testament Commentary. Grand Rapids: Baker Book House, 1993.

Knibb, Michael A. *The Qumran Community.* Cambridge: Cambridge University Press, 1987.

Lang, Friedrich. *Die Briefe an die Korinther.* Das Neue Testament Deutsch. Göttingen und Zürich: Vandenhoeck & Ruprecht, 1986.

Lenski, R. C. H. *The Interpretation of St. Paul's First and Second Epistles to the Corinthians.* Minneapolis: Augsburg Publishing House, 1963.

Lietzmann, Hans. *An die Korinther.* Handbuch zum Neuen Testament. Tübingen: J.C.B. Mohr (Paul Siebeck), 1969.

Marshall, I. Howard. *The Epistles of John.* New International Critical Commentary of the New Testament. Grand Rapids: Eerdmans, 1978.

Martin, Ralph P. *2 Corinthians.* Word Biblical Commentary. Waco, TX: Word Books, 1986.

Moffat, James. *The First Epistle of Paul to the Corinthians.* The Moffat New Testament Commentary. London: Hodder and Stoughton Limited, 1938.

Morris, Leon. *The First Epistle of Paul to the Corinthians.* Tyndale New Testament Commentaries. Leicester: Inter-Varsity Press/Grand Rapids: Eerdmans, 1958. 2nd ed., 1985.

Murray, John. *The Epistle to the Romans: The English Text with Introduction, Exposition and Notes.* London/Edinburgh: Marshal, Morgan & Scott, 1967.

Neyrey, Jerome H. *2 Peter, Jude: A New Translation with Introduction and Commentary.* The Anchor Bible. New York/London/Toronto/Sydney/Auckland: Doubleday, 1993.

Orr, William F., and Walther, James A. *1 Corinthians*. The Anchor Bible. Garden City, NY: Doubleday, 1976.

Quast, Kevin. *Reading the Corinthian Correspondence: An Introduction*. New York: Paulist Press, 1994.

Parry, John. *The First Epistle of Paul the Apostle to the Corinthians*. Cambridge: University Press, 1916.

Plumptre, E. H. *St. Paul's Epistles to the Corinthians*. New Testament Commentary for English Readers. London: Cassell and Company, Limited, Revised Reprint, 1878.

Rigaux, B. *Saint Paul Les Épistres Aux Thessaloniciens*. Paris: J. Gabalda et Cie, 1956.

Robertson, Archibald and Plummer, Alfred. *A Critical and Exegetical Commentary on the First Epistle of St. Paul to the Corinthians*. International Critical Commentary. Edinburgh: T. & T. Clark, 1911.

Ruef, J. S. *Paul's First Letter to Corinth*. The Pelican New Testament Commentaries. Harmondsworth, Middlesex: Penguin Book, 1971.

Schlatter, Adolf. *Die Korintherbriefe: Ausgelegt für Bibelleser*. Erläuterungen zum Neuen Testament 6. Stuttgart: Calwer, 1974.

Schrage, Wolfgang. *Der erste Brief an die Korinther: 1 Kor 6,12–11,16*. Evangelisch-Katholischer Kommentar zum Neuen Testament. Zürich: Benziger/Neuchirchen-Vluyn: Neukirchener, 1995.

Stone, Michael Edward. *Fourth Ezra: A Commentary on the Book of Ezra*. Hermeneia. Minneapolis: Augsburg Fortress, 1990.

Strobel, A. *Der Erste Brief and die Korinther*. Zürich: Theologischer, 1989.

Stuhlmacher, Peter. *Paul's Letter to the Romans: A Commentary*. Louisville: Westminster/John Knox, 1994.

Thompson, J. A. *Deuteronomy: An Introduction and Commentary*. Tyndale Old Testament Commentary. London: InterVarsity Press, 1974.

Thrall, M. *I and II Corinthans*. Cambridge Bible Commentary. Cambridge: Cambridge University Press, 1965.

Von Rad, Gerhard. *Deuteronomy: A Commentary*. London: SCM Press, 1966.

Wanamaker, Charles A. *The Epistles to the Thessalonians: A Commentary on the Greek Text*. New International Greek Testament Commentary. Grand Rapids/Exeter: Eerdmans/The Paternoster Press, 1990.

Watson, Nigel. *The First Epistle to the Corinthians*. Epworth Commentaries. London: Epworth Press, 1992.

Weiss, Johannes. *Der erste Korintherbrief*. Kritisch-exegetischer Kommentar über das Neue Testament. Göttingen: Vandenhoeck & Ruprecht, 1925.

Wenbland, Heinz-Dietrich. *Die Briefe an die Korinther*. Das Neue Testament Deutsch. Göttingen: Vandenhoeck & Ruprecht, 1965.

Whiteley, D. E. H. "Commentaries on 1 and 2 Corinthians." *Theology* 65 (1962), 188–91.

Witherington, Ben. *Conflict And Community In Corinth: A Socio-Rhetorical Commentary on 1 and 2 Corinthians*. Grand Rapids: Eerdmans/Carlisle: The Paternoster Press, 1995.

Wolff, Christian. *Der erst Brief des Paulus and die Korinther: Zweiter Teil: Auslegung der Kapitel 8–16*. Theologischer Handkommentar zum Neuen Testament. Berlin: Evangelische Verlagsanstalt, 1982.

General Bibliography

Aageson, James W. *Written Also for Our Sake: Paul and the Art of Biblical Interpretation.* Louisville: Westminster/John Knox Press, 1993.

Abraham, William J. "Predestination and Assurance." In *The Grace of God and the Will of Man: A Case for Arminianism*, Clark H. Pinnock, ed. Grand Rapids: Academie-Zondervan, 1989. 231–42.

Abraham, William J. "Soteriology in the Gospel of John," In *The Grace of God, The Will of Man: A Case for Arminianism*, Clark H. Pinnock, ed. Grand Rapids: Academie-Zondervan, 1989. 243–60.

Abrahams, I. *Studies in Pharisaism and the Gospels.* Cambridge: Cambridge University Press, 1917.

Adam, D. S. "Perseverance." In *Encyclopaedia of Religion and Ethics.* James Hastings, ed. Edinburgh: T. & T. Clark, 1908. 9:769–71.

Aldrich, Willard M. "Perseverance." *Bibliotheca Sacra* 115 (1958), 9–19.

Allison, Dale C. *The New Moses: A Matthean Typology.* Edinburgh: T. & T. Clark, 1993.

Ames, William. *The Marrow of Theology: William Ames (1576–1633).* Introduction by John Dykstra Eusden. Durham, NC: The Labyrinth Press, 1968.

Anderson, Bernhard W. "Exodus Typology in Second Isaiah." In *Israel's Prophetic Heritage: Essays in honor of James Muilenburg.* Bernhand W. Anderson and Walter Harrelson, eds. London: SCM Press, 1962. 177–95.

Aquinas (see Thomas Aquinas).

Aristotle, *The "Art" of Rhetoric.* Reprinted in Loeb Classic Library. Cambridge, MA: Harvard, 1926.

Arminius, Jacob. *The Works of James Arminius.* Reprinted by James and William Nichols, translators. Introduction by Carl Bangs. Grand Rapids: Eerdmans, 1968. 3 Volumes.

Arrington, French L. *Paul's Aeon Theology in 1 Corinthians.* Washington: University Press of America, 1978.

Augustine, Aurelius. *De Baptisimo, contra Donatistas.* Translation by J. R. King. Reprint. A Select Library of the Nicene and Post-Nicene Fathers of the Christian Church. Philip Schaff, ed. Grand Rapids: Eerdmans, 1983. 4:405–514.

Augustine, Aurelius. *De Correptione et Gratia Liber Unus.* Translation by Robert Ernest Wallis. Reprint. A Select Library of the Nicene and Post-Nicene Fathers of the Christian Church. Philip Schaff, ed. Grand Rapids: Eerdmans, 1971. 5:468–91.

Augustine, Aurelius. *De Dono Perseverantiae.* Translation and introduction by Mary Alphonsine Lesousky. Catholic University of America: Patristic Studies. Washington: Catholic University of America Press, 1956.

Augustine, Aurelius. *De Libero Arbitrio.* Translation and annotation by Dom Mark Pontifex. Ancient Christian Writers. New York/Ramsey, NJ: Newman Press, 1955.

Augustine, Aurelius. *De Praedestinatione Sanctorum.* Translation by Robert Ernest Wallis. Reprint. A Select Library of the Nicene and Post-Nicene Fathers of the Christian Church. Philip Schaff, ed. Grand Rapids: Eerdmans, 1971. 5:521–52.

Aune, David E. "Demonology." In *The International Standard Bible Encyclopedia.* Revised Edition. Geoffrey W. Bromiley, ed. Grand Rapids: Eerdmans, 1979. 1:919–23.

Aune, David E. "Apocalypticism." In *Dictionary of Paul and His Letters*. Gerald F. Hawthorne, Ralph P. Martin, Daniel G. Ried, eds. Downers Grove, IL/Leicester: InterVarsity Press, 1993. 25–35.

Aune, David E. "Magic in Early Christianity." In *Aufstieg Und Niedergang der Römischen Welt*. II.23. Wolfgand Haase, ed. Berlin/New York: Walter de Gruyter, 1980. 2:1507–1557.

Aycock, D. A. "The Fate of Lot's Wife: Structural Mediation in Biblical Mythology." In *Structuralist Interpretations of Biblical Myth*. Edmund Leach and D. Alan Aycock. Royal Anthropological Institute of Great Britain and Ireland. Cambridge: Cambridge University Press, 1983. 113–19.

Bacon, Nathaniel. *A Relation of the Fearful State of Francis Spira: After He Turned Apostate from the Protestant Church to Popery*. Philadelphia: David Hogan, 1798.

Badke, William B. "Baptised into Moses – Baptised into Christ: A Study in Doctrinal Development." *Evangelical Quarterly* 88 (1988), 23–29.

Bailey, Kenneth E. "The Structure of 1 Corinthians and Paul's Theological Method with Special Reference to 4:17." *Novum Testamentum* 25 (1983), 152–81.

Baird, William. "1 Corinthians 10:1–13." *Interpretation* 44 (1990), 286–90.

Baker, William R. "Endurance, Perseverance." In *Dictionary of the Later New Testament and Its Developments*. Ralph P. Martin and Peter H. Davids, eds. Downers Grove, IL/Leicester: InterVarsity Press, 1997. 326–330.

Bandstra, Andrew J. "Interpretation in 1 Corinthians 10:1–11." *Calvin Theological Journal* 6 (1971), 5–21.

Bangs, Carl. "Recent Studies in Arminianism." *Religion in Life* 32 (1963), 421–28.

Bangs, Carl. *Arminius: A Study in the Dutch Reformation*. Grand Rapids: Francis Asbury/ Zondervan, 1971.

Barbour, John D. *Versions of Deconversion: Autobiography and the Loss of Faith*. Charlottesville: University Press of Virginia, 1994.

Barclay, John M. G. "Deviance and Apostasy: Some applications of deviance theory to first-century Christianity." In *Modelling Early Christianity: Social-Scientific Studies of the New Testament in its Context*. Philip F. Esler, ed. London and New York: Routledge, 1995b. 114–27.

Barclay, John M. G. "Paul Among the Diaspora Jews: Anomaly or Apostate?" *Journal for the Study of the New Testament* 60 (1995a), 89–120.

Barclay, John M. G. *Obeying the Truth: Paul's Ethics in Galatians*. Minneapolis: Fortress Press, 1991.

Barclay, William. "Paul's Uncertainties." *Expository Times* 69 (1958), 324–27.

Barnett, Paul W. "Apostasy." In *Dictionary of the Later New Testament and Its Developments*. Ralph P. Martin and Peter H. Davids, eds. Downers Grove, IL/Leicester: InterVarsity Press, 1997. 73–76.

Barrett, C. K. "Things Sacrificed to Idols." *New Testament Studies* 11 (1964–65), 138–53.

Barrett, C. K. "Christianity at Corinth." *Bulletin of the John Rylands Library* 46 (1964), 269–97.

Barrett, C. K. "Romans 9:30–10:21: Fall and Responsibility of Israel." In *Die Israelfrage nach Röm 9–11*. L. de Lornenzi, ed. Monograph Series of Benedictina. Rome: St. Paul vor den Mauern, 1977. 3:109–21.

Barth, Karl. *Church Dogmatics*. Volume 2 Part 2. Goeffrey W. Bromiley and T. F. Torrance, eds. Edinbrugh: T. & T. Clark, 1957.

Barth, Markus. *The People of God*. Journal for the Society of New Testament Supplemental Series. Sheffield: JSOT Press, 1983.

Barton, George A. "Demons and Spirits (Hebrew)." In *Encyclopaedia of Religion and Ethics*. James Hastings, ed. Edinburgh: T. & T. Clark, 1908. 594–601.

Barton, Stephen C. "Paul's Sense of Place: An Anthropological Approach to Community Formation in Corinth." *New Testament Studies* 32 (1986), 225–46.

Bauder, Wolfgang. "Fall, Fall Away/ἀφίστεμι, πίπτω." In *NIDNTT* 1:606–11.

Bauer, Gerhard. "1 Korinther 9,24–27." In *Herr Tue meine Lippen auf*. G. Eichholz, ed. Wuppertal & Barmen: Müller, 1959. 2:158–165.

Bauer, Walter. *Orthodoxy and Heresy in Earliest Christianity*. Reprint. Fortress: Philadelphia, 1977.

Baugh. S. M. "The Meaning of Foreknowledge." In *The Grace of God, The Bondage of the Will: Volume 1 Biblical and Practical Perspectives on Calvinism*. Thomas R. Schreiner and Bruce A. Ware, eds. Grand Rapids: Baker Book House, 1995. 183–200.

Baumert, Norbert. "ΚΟΙΝΩΝΙΑ ΤΟΥ ΑΙΜΑΤΟΣ ΤΟΥ ΧΡΙΣΤΟΥ (1 Kor 10,14–22)." In *The Corinthian Correspondence*. R. Bieringer, ed. Leuven: Leuven University Press, 1996. 617–22.

Bavinck, Herman. *Our Reasonable Faith*. Reprint. Grand Rapids: Eerdmans, 1956.

Baxter, Richard. *Catholicke Theologie: Plain, Pure, Peaceable: For Pacification of the Dogmatic Word-Warriors*. London: Robert White for Nevill Simmons, 1675.

Beasley-Murray, George R. "Baptism." In *Dictionary of Paul and His Letters*. Gerald F. Hawthorne, Ralph P. Martin, Daniel G. Ried, eds. Downers Grove, IL/Leicester: InterVarsity Press, 1993. 60–66.

Beasley-Murray, George R. *Baptism in the New Testament*. New York/London: Macmillan & Co., 1962.

Beckford, James A. *Conversion and Apostasy: Antithesis or Complementary*. Durham: University of Durham, 1981.

Beeke, Joel R. *Assurance of Faith: Calvin, English Puritanism, and the Dutch Second Reformation*. New York: Peter Lang, 1991.

Beet, Joseph Agar. *A Manual of Theology*. London: Hodder & Stoughton, 1906. 289–97.

Begg, C. "The Golden Calf Episode According to Pseudo-Philo." In *Studies in the Book of Exodus: Redaction-Reception-Interpretation*. Marc Vervenne, ed. Bibliotheca ephemeridum theologicarum lovaniensium. Leuven: Peeters, 1996. 577–94.

Behm, Johannes. "νουθετέω, νουτεσία." In *TDNT* 4:1019–22.

Beker, J. Christiaan. *Paul the Apostle: The Triumph of God in Life and Thought*. Philadelphia: Fortress Press, 1980.

Beker, Jürgen. *Paul Apostle to the Gentiles*. Louisville: Westminster/John Knox, 1993.

Bell, Charles M. *Calvin and Scottish Theology: The Doctrine of Assurance*. Edinburgh: Handsell, 1985.

Bell, H. Idris, and Skeat, T. C., eds. *Fragments of an Unknown Gospel and Other Early Christian Papyri*. London: British Museum, 1935.

Belleville, Linda L. "Continuity of Discontinuity: A Fresh Look at 1 Corinthians in the Light of First-Century Epistolary Forms and Conventions." *Evangelical Quarterly* 59 (1987), 15–37.

Benoir, Pierre. "Qumran and the New Testament." In *Paul and the Dead Sea Scrolls*. Jerome Murphy-O'Connor and James H. Charlesworth, eds. New York: Crossroad, 1990. 1–30.

Beougher, Timothy K. "Conversion: The Teaching and Practice of the Puritan Pastor Richard Baxter with Regard to Becoming a 'True Christian.'" Ph.D. dissertation, Trinity Evangelical Divinity School, 1990.

Berger, Peter L. "Different Gospels: The Social Sources of Apostasy." The 1987 Erasmus Lecture. *This World* 17 (1987), 6–17.

Berkhof, Hendrikus. "The Christian Life: Perseverance and Renewal." In *Major Themes in the Reformed Tradition*. Grand Rapids: Eerdmans, 1992. 155–65.

Berkhof, Louis. *Systematic Theology*. Fourth Edition. Grand Rapids: Eerdmans, 1953.

Berkouwer, G. C. *Divine Election*. Studies in Dogmatics. Grand Rapids: Eerdmans, 1960.

Berkouwer, G. C. *Faith and Perseverance*. Studies in Dogmatics. Grand Rapids: Eerdmans, 1958.

Bertram, Georg. "παίζω, ἐμπαίζω, ἐμπαιγμονή, ἐμπαιγμός, ἐμπαίκτης." In *TDNT* 5:625–36.

Best, Ernest. *One Body In Christ: A Study in the Relationship of the Church to Christ in the Epistles of the Apostle Paul*. London: SPCK, 1955.

Betz, Hans Dieter, ed. *The Greek Magical Papyri in Translation: Including the Demotic Spells*. Volume 1: Texts. Chicago & London: University of Chicago Press, 1992.

Betz, Hans Dieter. "The Eschatological Interpretation of the Sinai-Tradition in Qumran." *Revue de Qumran* 21 (1967), 89–107.

Beugnet, A. "Apostasie." In *Dictionnaire de Théologie Catholique*. A. Vacant & E. Mangenot, eds. Paris: Letouzey et Ané, 1909. 1:1602–11.

Bevan, E. R. *Holy Images: An Inquiry into Idolatry and Image Worship in Ancient Paganism and Christianity*. New York: AMS, 1979.

Bicknell, E. J. *A Theological Introduction to the Thirty-Nine Articles of the Church of England*. London/New York/Toronto: Longmans, Green, and Co., 1925. 2nd ed.

Bjerkelund, Carl J. "«Vergeblich» als Missionsergebnis bei Paulus." In *God's Christ and His People: Studies in Honour of Nils Alstrup Dahl*. Jacob Jervell and Wayne A. Meeks, eds. Oslo/Bergen/Trömso: Universitetsforglaget, 1977. 175–91.

Black, Matthew. *The Scrolls and Christian Origins: Studies in the Jewish Background of the New Testament*. London/Edinburgh/Paris/Melbourne/Johannesburg/Toronto/New York: Thomas Nelson, 1961.

Blomberg, Craig. "Form Criticism." In *Dictionary of Jesus and the Gospels*. Joel B. Green, Scot McKight, I. Howard Marshall, eds. Downers Grove: InterVarsity Press, 1992. 243–50.

Blue, B. B. "Food Offered to Idols and Jewish Food Laws." In *Dictionary of Paul and His Letters*. Gerald F. Hawthorne, Ralph P. Martin, Daniel G. Ried, eds. Downers Grove, IL/Leicester: InterVarsity Press, 1993. 306–10.

Böcher, Otto. "ἔρημος." In *NIDNTT*. 3:1004–1008.

Bochert, Gerald L. *Assurance and Warning*. Nashville: Broadman, 1987.

Boethius, Anicius Manlius Torquatus Severinus. *The Consolation of Philosophy*. Revised Edition. Translation by S. J. Tester. Loeb Classical Library. London: Heinemann, 1973.

Boettner, Loraine. "The Perseverance of the Saints." In *The Reformed Doctrine of Predestination*. Loraine Boettner. Grand Rapids: Eerdmans, 1932.

Bogle, M. M. "τὰ τέλη τῶν αἰώνων: 1 Corinthians x.11 A Suggestion." *Expository Times* 67 (1955–56), 246–47.

Bonnington, Mark. "The Antioch Episode in Historical and Cultural Context" Ph.D. Thesis, Nottingham University, 1994.

Borchert, Gerald L. *Assurance and Warning*. Nashville: Broadman, 1987.

Borgen, Peter. "'Yes,' 'No,' 'How Far?': The Participation of Jews and Christians in Pagan Cults." In *Paul in his Hellenistic Context*. Troels Engberg-Pedersen, ed. Edinburgh: T. & T. Clark, 1994. 30–59.

Borgen, Peter. "Catalogues of Vices, the Apostolic Decree, and the Jerusalem Meeting." In *Early Christianity and Hellenistic Judaism*. Peder Borgan. Edinburgh: T. & T. Clark, 1996. 233–51.

Bornkamm, Günther. "Das Anathema in der urchristlichen Abendmahlsliturgie." *Theologische Literaturzeitung* 75 (1950), 227–30.

Bornkamm, Günther. *Early Christian Experience*. The New Testament Library. London: SCM, 1969.

Bouché, J. "Apostasie." In *Dictionnaire de droit canonique, contenant tous les termes du droit canonique, avec un sommaire de l'histoire et des institutions et de l'âetat actuel de la discipline*. R. Naz, ed. Paris: Letouzey et Ané. 1935–65. 1:640–52.

Boucher, Madeleine. "Some Unexpected Parallels to 1 Cor. 11, 11–12 and Gal. 3,28: The New Testament on the Role of Women." *CBQ* 31 (1969), 50–58.

Boudinhon, A. "Excommunication." In *The Catholic Encyclopedia: An International Work of Reference on the Constitution, Doctrine, Discipline, and History of the Catholic Church*. Charles G. Herbermann, Edward A. Pace, C. B. Pallen, Thomas J. Shahan, John J. Wynne, eds. New York: The Encyclopedia Press, 1913. 5:678–91.

Bouttier, Michel. "1 Co 8–10 considéré du point de vue de son unité.". In *Freedom and Love: The Guide for Christian Life (1 Co 8–10. Rm 14–15)*. L. de Lorenzi, ed. Monograph Series of Benedictina. Rome: St. Paul vor den Mauern, 1981. 6.205–61.

Bowersock, G. W. *Julian the Apostate*. Cambridge, MA: Harvard University Press, 1997.

Bratcher, Dennis A. "The Concepts of Conditionality and Apostasy in Relation to the Covenant." Th. M. Thesis, Westminster Theological Seminary (Philadelphia), 1986.

Broer, Ingo. "Darum: Wer da meint zu stehen, der sehe zu, daß er nicht falle: 1 Kor 10,12 im Kontext von 1 Kor 10,1–13." In *Neues Testament Und Ethik: Für Rudolph Schnackenburg*. Helmut Merklein, ed. Freiburg: Herder, 1989. 299–325.

Bromley, David G. ed. *Falling From the Faith: Causes and Consequences of Religious Apostasy*. Sage Focus. Newbury Park/Beverly Hills/London/New Delhi: Sage, 1988.

Broneer, Oscar. "Paul and the Pagan Cults at Isthmia." *Harvard Theological Review* 64 (1971), 169–88.

Brown, Alexandra R. *The Cross and Human Transformation: Paul's Apocalyptic Word in 1 Corinthians*. Minneapolis: Fortress, 1995.

Brown, Basil S. "The Great Apostasy in the Teaching of Jesus." *Australian Biblical Review* 10 (1962), 14–20.

Brown, Colin, Hahn, Hans-Cristoph, Merkel, Friedmann, and Packer, J. I. "Destroy, Perish, Ruin." In *NIDNTT* 1:462–71.

Brown, Harold O. J. *Heresies: The Image of Christ in the Mirror of Heresy and Orthodoxy from the Apostles to the Present*. Grand Rapids: Baker Book House, 1984.

Brown, Lawrence Duane. "The New Testament Doctrine of Apostasy." Th.D. Dissertation, Bob Jones University, 1966.

Brown, Nobel B. "The Concept of Apostasy in Jewish and Christian Apocalyptic." Ph.D. Dissertation, Southern Baptist Theological Seminary, 1963.

Brown, Raymond E. *An Introduction to the New Testament*. The Anchor Bible Reference Library. New York/London/Toronto/Sydney/Auckland: Doubleday, 1997.

Brown, Schuyler. *Apostasy and Perseverance in the Theology of Luke*. Analecta Biblica: Investigationes Scientificae in Res Biblicas. Rome: Pontifical Biblical Institute, 1969.

Browning, W. H. *An Examination of the Doctrine of the Unconditional Final Perseverance of the Saints as Taught by Calvinists*. Thomas V. Summers, eds. Nashville: Southern Methodist Publishing House, 1860.

Brueggemann, Walter. *The Land: Place as Gift, Promise, and Challenge in Biblical Faith.* London: SPCK, 1978.

Brunner, Emil. *The Doctrine of God.* Dogmatics Volume 1. Philadelphia: The Westminster Press, 1950. 346–52.

Brunt, John C. "Love, Freedom, and Moral Responsibility: The Contribution of 1 Cor. 8–10 to an Understanding of Paul's Ethical Thinking." *Society of Biblical Literature* 1981 Seminar Papers 20. Kent Harold Richards, ed. Chico, CA: Scholars Press, 1981. 19–33.

Brunt, John C. "Rejected, Ignored, or Misunderstood: The Fate of Paul's Approach to the Problem of Food Offered to Idols in Early Christianity." *New Testament Studies* 31 (1985), 113–124.

Büchsel, Friedrich. "εἴδωλον, εἰδωλόθυτον, εἰδωλεῖον, κατείδωλος, εἰδωλολάτρης, εἰδωλολάτρία." In *TDNT* a 2:375–81.

Büchsel, Friedrich. "θυμός, ἐπιθυμία, ἐπιθυμέω, ἐπιθυμητής, ἐπιθυμέομαι, ἐνθύμησις." In *TDNT* b, 3:167–72.

Buis, Harry. *Historical Protestantism and Predestination.* Philadelphia: Presbyterian and Reformed Publishing Co., 1958.

Bultmann, Rudolf. *Theology of the New Testament.* New York: Schribner, 1951. 2 volumes.

Bünker, Michael. *Briefformular und rhetorische Disposition im 1. Korintherbrief.* Göttinger theologische Arbeiten. Göttingen: Vanderhoeck & Ruprecht, 1983.

Byrne, Brenden. "Eschatologies of Resurrection and Destruction: The Ethical Significance of Paul's Dispute with the Corinthians." *Downside Review* 104 (1986), 288–99.

Cadbury, H. J. "The Macellum of Corinth." *Journal of Biblical Literature* 53 (1934), 134–41.

Callan, Terrance. "Paul and the Golden Calf." Paper presented in Proceedings: 10th Eastern Great Lakes and Midwest Biblical Society. Pittsburg, April 20, 1990. 1–17.

Calvin, John. *Concerning the Eternal Predestination of God.* Introduction by J. K. S. Reid. London: James Clarke, 1961.

Calvin, John. *Institutes of the Christian Religion.* 2 Volumes. John T. McNeill, ed. Translation by Ford Lewis Battles. The Library of Christian Classics. Philadelphia: Westminster, 1960.

Cambier, Jules-Marie. "La chair et l'esprit en 1 Cor. V.5." *New Testament Studies* 15 (1968–69), 221–32.

Cambier, Jules-Marie. "La liberté chrétienne est et personnelle et communautaire (Rm 14,1 – 15,13)." In *Freedom and Love: The Guide for Christian Life (1 Co 8–10. Rm 14–15).* L. de Lorenzi, ed. Monograph Series of Benedictina. Rome: St. Paul vor den Mauern, 1981. 6.53–126.

Campbell, A. Glenn. "The Problem of Apostasy in Greek New Testament." Th.D. Dissertation, Dallas Theological Seminary, 1957.

Caneday, Ardel B. "The Doctrine of Perseverance of the Saints from the Life and Epistles of Paul." Th.M. Thesis, Grace Theological Seminary, 1978.

Carlson, Richard P. "The Role of Baptism in Paul's Thought." *Interpretation* 47 (July, 1993), 255–66.

Carrasco, David. "Those Who Go on a Sacred Journey: The Shapes and Diversity of Pilgrimages." *Concilium* (1996/4), 13–24.

Carrez, Maurice. "Le Méthode de G. Von Rad Appliquée a Quelques Textes Pauliniens: Petit Essai de Vérification." *Revue Des Sciences Philosophiques Et Theologiques* 55 (1971), 81–95.

Carson, D. A. "Reflections on Christian Assurance." *Westminster Theological Journal* 54 (1992), 1–29.

Carson, D. A. *Divine Sovereignty and Human Responsibility: Biblical Perspectives in Tension*. Atlanta: John Knox Press, 1981.

Carson, D. A. *Exegetical Fallacies*. Second Edition. Carlisle, Cumbria/Grand Rapids: Paternoster/Baker Book House, 1996.

Chafer, Lewis Sperry. *Systematic Theology*. 8 Volumes. Dallas: Dallas Seminary Press, 1947–48.

Charlesworth, James H. "From Messianology to Christology: Problems and Prospects." In *The Messiah: Developments in Earliest Judaism and Christianity*. The First Princeton Symposium on Judaism and Christian Origins. James H. Charlesworth, ed. Minneapolis: Fortress Press, 1992.

Charmé, Stuart L. "Heretics, Infidels, and Apostates: Menace, Problem or Symptom?" *Judaism* 36 (1987), 17–33.

Chavasse, Claude. "Jesus: Christ *and* Moses – I." *Theology* 54 (Jan.-Dec., 1951a), 244–50.

Chavasse, Claude. "Jesus: Christ *and* Moses – II." *Theology* 54 (Jan.-Dec., 1951b), 289–96.

Chestnutt, Randall D. *From Death to Life: Conversion in Joseph and Asenath*. Journal for the Study of the Pseudepigrapha Supplement Series. Sheffield: Sheffield Academic Press, 1995.

Ciocchi, David M. "Understanding Our Ability To Endure Temptation: A Theological Watershed." *Journal of the Evangelical Theological Society* 35 (Dec. 1992), 463–479.

Clark, Gordon H. *Biblical Predestination*. Nutley, NJ: Presbyterian and Reformed Publishing Co., 1969.

Classen, C. Joachim. "Paulus und die antike Rhetorik." *Zeitschrift für die Neue Testamentliche Wissenschaft* 82 (1991), 1–31.

Clements, Ronald E. "'A Remnant Chosen by Grace' (Romans 11:5): The Old Testament Background and Origin of the Remnant Concept." In *Pauline Studies: Essays presented to Professor F. F. Bruce on his 70th Birthday*. Donald A. Hagner and Murray J. Harris, eds. Exeter, Devon: The Paternoster Press/Grand Rapids: Eerdmans, 1980. 106–21.

Clines, David J. A. "Predestination in the Old Testament." In *Grace Unlimited*. Clark Pinnock, ed. Minneapolis: Bethany, 1975. 110–26.

Coats, George W. *Rebellion In the Wilderness: The Murmuring Motif in the Wilderness Traditions of the Old Testament*. Nashville/New York: Abingdon Press, 1968.

Cohn, Robert L. *The Shape of Sacred Space: Four Biblical Studies*. American Academy of Religion – Studies in Religion. Chico, CA: Scholars Press, 1981.

Cole, Victor Grady. "Apostasy and Perseverance in the Pauline Epistles as Conditioned by the Recipients." Th.M. Thesis, Southwestern Baptist Theological Seminary, 1964.

Collier, Gary D. "'That We Might Not Crave Evil: The Structure and Argument of 1 Corinthians 10:1–13." *Journal for the Study of the New Testament* 55 (1994), 55–75.

Collins, John J. ed. *Apocalypse: The Morphology of a Genre*. Semeia 14. Chico, CA: Scholars Press, 1979.

Collins, John J. *Apocalypticism in the Dead Sea Scrolls*. The Literature of the Dead Sea Scrolls. London and New York: Routledge, 1997.

Collins, John J. *The Apocalyptic Imagination: An Introduction to the Jewish Matrix of Christianity*. New York: Crossroad, 1984.

Connelly, J. J. "Perseverance, Final." In *New Catholic Encyclopedia*. William J. McDonald, ed. San Francisco/Toronto/London/Sydney: McGraw-Hill, 1967. 11:154–55.

Constantelos, Demetrios J. *Understanding the Greek Orthodox Church: Its Faith, History, and Practice*. New York: Seabury, 1982.

Cook, Robert R. "Apostasy: Some Logical Reflections." *Evangelical Quarterly* 65 (1993), 147–53.

Cope, Lamar. "First Corinthians 8–10: Continuity or Contradiction?" *Anglican Theological Review: Supplementary Series 11*. Christ and His Communities: Essays in Honour of Reginald H. Fuller (Mar. 1990), 114–123.

Cosgrove, Charles H. "Rhetorical Suspense in Romans 9–11: A Study in Polyvalence and Hermeneutical Election." *Journal of Biblical Literature* 115 (1996), 271–87.

Cottle, Ronald E. "All Were Baptized." *Journal of the Evangelical Theological Society* 17 (1974), 75–80.

Countryman, L. William. *Dirt, Greed, and Sex: Sexual Ethics in the New Testament and their Implications for Today*. London: SCM Press, 1988.

Court, John M. "Paul and the Apocalyptic Pattern." In *Paul and Paulinism: Essays in Honour of C. K. Barrett*. M. D. Hooker and S. G. Wilson, eds. London: SPCK, 1982. 57–66.

Couser, Charles B. "The Theological Task of 1 Corinthians." In *Pauline Theology: Volume II: 1 & 2 Corinthians*. David M. Hay, ed. Minnesota: Fortress Press, 1993. 90–102.

Craig, William Lane. "'Lest Anyone Should Fall': A Middle Knowledge Perspective on Perseverance and Apostolic Warnings." *International Journal for Philosophy of Religion* 29 (1991), 65–74.

Cranfield, Loren. "Encountering Heresy: Insight from the Pastoral Epistles." *Southwestern Journal of Theology* 22 (1980), 23–40.

Croix, G. E. M. De Ste. "Aspects of the 'Great Persecution'." *Harvard Theological Review* 47 (1954), 75–114.

Cullmann, Oscar. *Christ and Time*. London: SCM Press, 1952.

Cureteu, Octavian. "Apostasy: A Biblical, Theological, and Pastoral Approach." M.A. Thesis, Loma Linda University, 1987.

Curtiss, George L. *Arminianism in History: Or, the Revolt from Predestination*. Cincinnati: Cranston & Curts, 1894.

Daines, Brian. "Paul's Use of the Analogy of the Body of Christ – With Special Reference to 1 Corinthians 12." *Evangelical Quarterly* 50 (1978), 71–78.

Dalman, Gustaf. *The Words of Jesus: Considered in the Light of Post-Biblical Jewish Writings and the Aramaic Language*. Edinburgh: T. & T. Clark, 1909.

Damer, T. Edward. *Attacking Faulty Reasoning*. Second Edition. Belmont, CA: Wadsworth, 1987.

Danell, G. A. "The Idea of God's People in the Bible." In *The Root of the Vine: Essays in Biblical Theology*. Anton Fridrichsen and other members of Uppsala University. London: Dacre, 1953. 23–36.

Danélou, Jean. *The Bible and the Liturgy*. London: Darton, Longman & Todd, 1956.

Davidson, Francis. *Pauline Predestination*. The Tyndale New Testament Lecture. London: Tyndale Press, 1946.

Davidson, Richard M. *Typology In Scripture: A Study of Hermeneutical τύπος Structures*. Andrews University Seminary Doctoral Dissertation Series 2. Berrien Springs, MI: Andrews University Press, 1981.

Davies, W. D. *Paul and Rabbinic Judaism: Some Rabbinic Elements in Pauline Theology*. Fourth Edition. Philadelphia: Fortress, 1980.

Davis, John Jefferson. "The Perseverance of the Saints: A History of the Doctrine." *Journal of the Evangelical Theological Society* 34 (1991), 213–228.

Dawes, Gregory W. "The Danger of Idolatry: First Corinthians 8:7–13." *Catholic Biblical Quarterly* 58 (1996), 82–98.

De Boer, Martinus C. *The Defeat of Death: Apocalyptic Eschatology in 1 Corinthians 15 and Romans 5*. Journal for the Study of the New Testament Supplement Series. Sheffield: JSOT Press, 1988.

De Letter, P. "Faith, Loss of." In *New Catholic Encyclopedia*. William J. McDonald, ed. San Francisco/Toronto/London/Sydney: McGraw-Hill, 1967. 5:804–05.

De Planhol, Xavier. "Deserts." In *The Encyclopedia of Religion*. Mircea Eliade, ed. Macmillan Library Reference USA. New York: Simon & Schuster, 1995. 4:304–307.

De Ridder, Richard R. *The Dispersion of the People of God: The Covenant Basis of Matthew 28:18–20 Against the Background of Jewish, Pre-Christian Proselytising and Diaspora, and the Apostleship of Jesus Christ*. Vrije Universiteit Te Amsterdam. J. H. Kok N. V. Kampen, 1971.

Delling, Gerhard. "τέλος, τελέω, ἐπιτελέω, συντελέω, συντέλεια, παντελής, τέλειος, τελειότης, τελειόω, τελείωσις, τελειωτής." In *TDNT* 8:49–87.

Denton, D. R. "Hope and Perseverance." *Scottish Theological Journal* 34 (1981), 313–320.

Derrett, J. Duncan M. "Judgement and 1 Corinthians 6." *New Testament Studies* 37 (1991), 22–36.

DeSilva, David A. "Exchanging Favor for Wrath: Apostasy in Hebrews and Patron-Client Relationships." *Journal of Biblical Literature* 115 (1996), 91–116.

Didier, G. *Désintéressement du Chrétien: La Rétribution dans la Morale de Saint Paul*. Paris: Aubier, 1955.

Dillon, John. "Dionysus." In *The Anchor Bible Dictionary*. David Noel Freedman, ed. New York/London/Toronto/Sydney/Auckland, 1992. 2:201–02.

Dinkler, Erich. "Apostasy." In *The Interpreter's Dictionary of the Bible*. G. A. Buttrick, ed. New York: Abingdon Press, 1962. 1.170.

Dinkler, Erich. "Prädestination bei Paulus: Exegetische Bemerkungen zum Römerbrief." In *Signum Crucis: Aufsätze zum Neuen Testament und zur christlichen Archäologie*. Erich Dinkler. Tübingen: J. C. B. Mohr (Paul Siebeck), 1967. 241–269.

Doddrige, Philip. *The Works of the Reverend Philip Doddridge*. 5 Volumes. Memoir by Job Orton. Leeds: Edward Baines, 1802–04.

Doignon, Jean. "La défection en nombre des disciples de Jésus (*Jean* 6,66) et l'apostasie de la foi chez Hilaire de Poitiers." In *«Humanitas» Classica E «Sapientia» Cristiana: Scritti offerti a Roberto Iacoangeli*. Sergio Felici, ed. Biblioteca di Scienze Religiose. Roma: Las, 1992. 111–14.

Donfried, Karl Paul. "The Kingdom of God in Paul." In *The Kingdom of God in 20th-Century Interpretation*. Wendell Willis, ed. Peabody: Hendrickson, 1987. 175–90.

Donfried, Karl Paul. "Justification and Last Judgment in Paul." *Zeitschrift für die Neue Testamenliche Wissenschaft* 67 (1976), 90–110.

Doskocil, Walter. *Der Bann in der Urkirche: Eine rechtsgeschichtliche Untersuchung*. München: K. Zink, 1958.

Doughty, Darrell J. "The Presence and Future of Salvation in Corinth." *Zeitschrift für die Neutestamentliche Wissenschaft* 66 (1975), 61–90.

Douglas, Mary. *Cultural Bias.* Occasional Paper 34. London: Royal Anthropological Institute of Great Britain & Ireland, 1978.

Douglas, Mary. *Natural Symbols: Explorations in Cosmology.* London: Barrie & Rockliff/The Cresset Press, 1970.

Douglas, Mary. *Purity and Danger: An Analysis of Concepts of Pollution and Taboo.* London: Routledge & Kegan Paul, 1966.

Dov, Noy. "Apostasy." In *Encyclopaedia Judaica.* Cecil Roth and Geoffrey Wigoder, eds. Jerusalem: Keter Publishing House Jerusalem Ltd., 1972. 3:201–16.

Dreyfus, François. "Le passé et le présent d'Israël (Rom., 9, 1–5; 11, 1–24)." In *Die Israelfrage nach Röm 9–11.* L. de Lorenzi, ed. Monograph Series of Benedictina. Rome: St. Paul vor den Mauern, 1977. 3:131–51.

Driver, S. R. "Notes on Three Passages in St Paul's Epistles," *The Expositor,* 3rd Series 9 (1889), 15–23.

Duff, Nancy J. "The Significance of Pauline Apocalyptic for Theological Ethics." In *Apocalyptic and the New Testament: Essays in Honor of J. Louis Martyn.* Joel Marcus and Marion L. Soards, eds. Journal for the Study of the New Testament Supplement Series. Sheffield: Sheffield Academic Press, 1989. 279–96.

Dunham, Duane A. "An Exegetical Study of 2 Peter 2:18–22." *Bibliotheca Sacra* 140 (1983), 40–54.

Dunn, James D. G. *Baptism in the Holy Spirit: A Re-examination of the New Testament Teaching on the Gift of the Spirit in relation to Pentecostalism today.* Studies in Biblical Theology. London: SCM Press, 1970.

Dunn, James D. G. *Christology in the Making: An Inquiry into the Origins of the Doctrine of the Incarnation.* Second Edition. London: SCM Press, 1989.

Dunn, James D. G. *Jesus and the Spirit: A Study of the Religious and Charismatic Experience of Jesus and the First Christians as Reflected in the New Testament.* New Testament Library. London: SCM, 1975.

Dunn, James D. G. *The Parting of the Ways between Christianity and Judaism.* London: SCM, 1991.

Dunn, James D. G. *The Theology of Paul the Apostle.* Cambridge, U.K./Grand Rapids: Eerdmans, 1998.

Dunn, James D. G. *Unity and Diversity in the New Testament: An Inquiry into the Character of the Earliest Christianity.* Second Edition. London: SCM Press/Valley Forge: Trinity Press International, 1990.

Easton, Burton S. "New Testament Ethical Lists." *Journal of Biblical Literature* 51 (1932), 1–12.

Eaton, Michael A. *A Theology of Encouragement.* Carlisle: Paternoster Press, 1995.

Edwards, Jonathan. "Concerning the Perseverance of the Saints." Chapter VII in *Remarks on Important Theological Controversies (Miscellaneous Remarks).* In *The Works of Jonathan Edwards.* Reprint. Memoir by Sereno E. Dwight. Revised and corrected by Edward Hickman. Carlisle, PN/Edinburgh: The Banner of Truth Trust, 1974. 2:596–603.

Edwards, Jonathan. *A Careful and Strict Inquiry into Prevailing Notions of the Freedom of the Will.* In *The Works of Jonathan Edwards.* Reprint. Memoir by Sereno E. Dwight. Revised and corrected by Edward Hickman. Carlisle, PN/Edinburgh: The Banner of Truth Trust, 1974. 1:1–93.

Ehrman, Bart D. *The Orthodox Corruption of Scripture: The Effect of Early Christological Controversies on the Text of the New Testament.* New York/Oxford: Oxford University Press, 1993.

Eliade, Mircea. *Traité D'Histoire Des Religions*. Revised Edition. Paris: Payot, 1964.

Ellis, E. Earle. "A Note on First Corinthians 10,4." *Journal of Biblical Literature* 76 (1957a), 53–56.

Ellis, E. Earle. "χριστός in 1 Corinthians 10.4, 9." In *From John To Jesus: Essays on Jesus and New Testament Christology in Honour of Marinus de Jorge*. Martinus C. De Boer, ed. Journal for the Study of the New Testament Supplement Series 84 (1993), 169–173.

Ellis, E. Earle. "'Wisdom' and 'Knowledge' in 1 Corinthians." In *Prophecy and Hermeneutic in Early Christianity: New Testament Essays*. E. Earle Ellis. Wissenschaftliche Untersuchungen zum Neuen Testament. Tübingen: J. C. B. Mohr (Paul Siebeck), 1978.

Ellis, E. Earle. *Paul's Use of the Old Testament*. Edinburgh/London: Oliver and Boyd, 1957b.

Ellis, Mark A. "Apostasy and Perseverance in the Pastoral Epistles." Th.M. Thesis, Dallas Theological Seminary, 1988.

Elwell, Walter A. "Election and Predestination." In *Dictionary of Paul and His Letters*. Gerald F. Hawthorne, Ralph P. Martin, Daniel G. Ried, eds. Downers Grove, IL/ Leicester: InterVarsity Press, 1993. 225–29.

Engberg-Pedersen, Troels. "Proclaiming the Lord's Death: 1 Corinthians 11:17–34 and the Forms of Paul's Theological Argument." In *Pauline Theology: Volume 2 – 1 & 2 Corinthians*. David H. May, ed. Minneapolis: Fortress Press, 1991. 103–32.

Epp, Jay Eldon, and MacRae, George W. eds. *The New Testament and Its Modern Interpreters*. The Bible and Its Modern Interpreters. Atlanta: Scholars Press, 1989.

Eriksson, Anders. *Traditions as Rhetorical Proof: Pauline Argumentation in 1 Corinthians*. Coniectanea biblica, New Testament. Stockholm: Almqvist & Wiksell, 1998.

Ermoni, V. "Abjuration." In *Dictionnaire D'Archéologie Chrétienne Et De Liturgie*. Frenand Cabrol, ed. Paris: Letouzey et Ané, 1907. 1:98–104.

Eskola, Timo. *Theodicy and Predestination in Pauline Soteriology*. Wissenschaftliche Untersuchungen zum Neuen Testament. Tübingen: J. C. B. Mohr (Paul Siebeck), 1998.

Eusebius. *Historia Ecclesiastica*. Translation by Arthur Cushman McGiffert. Reprint. A Select Library of the Nicene and Post-Nicene Fathers of the Christian Church. Philip Schaff and Henry Wace, eds. Grand Rapids: Eerdmans, 1982. 1:1–403.

Evans-Pritchard, E. E. "Social Anthropology: Past and Present." In *Essays in Social Anthropology*. London: Faber and Faber, 1962. 13–28.

Fantham, Elaine, Foley, Helene, Kampen, Natalie, Pomeroy, Sarah, Shapiro, H. A. *Women in the Classical World: Image and Text*. Oxford: Oxford University Press, 1994.

Faur, José. "The Biblical Idea of Idolatry." *Jewish Quarterly Review* 79 (1978), 1–15.

Fee, Gordon D. "Εἰδωλόθυτα Once Again: An Interpretation of 1 Corinthians 8–10." *Biblica* 61 (1980), 172–97.

Fee, Gordon D. "Toward a Theology of 1 Corinthians." In *Pauline Theology: Volume II: 1 & 2 Corinthians*. David M. Hay, ed. Minnesota: Fortress Press, 1993. 37–58.

Fee, Gordon D. "II Corinthians VI.14-VII.1 and Food Offered to Idols." *New Testament Studies* 23 (1977), 140–161.

Feldman, Louis H. *Jew and Gentile in the Ancient World: Attitudes and Interactions from Alexander to Justinian*. Princeton: Princeton University Press, 1993.

Ferguson, Everett. *Backgrounds of Early Christianity*. Grand Rapids: Eerdmans, 1993.

Feuillet, André. *Le Christ Sagesse De Dieu: d'après les épitres Pauliniennes*. Études Bibliques. Paris: Libraire Lecoffre, J. Gabalda et Cie Éditeurs, 1966.

Filson, Floyd V. *St. Paul's Conception of Recompense*. Untersuchungen zum Neuen Testament. Leipzig: J. C. Hinrichs, 1931.

Finney, Charles. *Finney's Lectures on Systematic Theology*. Reprinted and Edited by J. H. Fairchild. Grand Rapids: Eerdmans, 1957.

Fiorenza, Elisabeth Schüssler. "Rhetorical Situation and Historical Reconstruction in 1 Corinthians." *New Testament Studies* 33 (1987), 386–403.

Fishbane, Michael. *Biblical Interpretation In Ancient Israel*. Oxford: Clarendon Press, 1985.

Fisher, Fred L. "The New and Greater Exodus: The Exodus Pattern in the New Testament." *Southwestern Journal of Theology* 20 (1977), 69–79.

Fisk, Bruce B. "Eating Meat Offered to Idols: Corinthian Behavior and Pauline Response in 1 Corinthians 8–10." *Trinity Journal* 10 (1989) 49–70.

Fitzmyer, Joseph A. *According to Paul: Studies in the Theology of the Apostle*. New York: Paulist Press, 1993.

Foakes-Jackson, F. J. "Apostasy." In *Encyclopaedia of Religion and Ethics*. James Hastings, ed. Edinburgh: T. & T. Clark, 1908. 1:623–25.

Fohrer, Georg. *History of Israelite Religion*. Nashville: Abingdon Press, 1972.

Ford, J. Massynbaerde. "Bookshelf on Prostitution." *Biblical Theology Bulletin* 23 (1993), 128–35.

Forkman, Göran. *The Limits of the Religious Community: Expulsion from the Religious Community within the Qumran Sect, within Rabbinic Judaism, and within Primitive Christianity*. Coniectanea Biblica – New Testament Series 5. Lund: CWK Gleerup, 1972.

Foxgrove, David. "Temporary Faith and Certainty of Salvation." *Calvin Theological Journal* 15 (1980), 220–32.

Franklyn, Paul N. "Prophetic Cursing of Apostasy: The Text, Forms, and Traditions of Hosea 13." Ph.D. Dissertation, Vanderbilt University, 1986.

Frend, W. H. C. *Martyrdom and Persecution in the Early Church: A Study of a Conflict from the Maccabees to Donatists*. Oxford: Oxford University Press, 1965.

Frend, W. H. C. *Saints and Sinners in the Early Church: Differing and Conflicting Traditions in the First Six Centuries*. London: Darton, Longman & Todd, 1985.

Frend, W. H. C. *The Donatist Church: A Movement of Protest in Roman North Africa*. Oxford: Clarendon Press, 1952.

Friederg, E. "Apostasy." In *The New Schaff-Herzog Encyclopedia of Religious Knowledge*. Samuel Macauley Jackson, ed. Grand Rapids: Baker Book House, 1951. 1:238–39.

Fung, Ronald Y. -K. "Body of Christ." In *Dictionary of Paul and His Letters*. Gerald F. Hawthorne, Ralph P. Martin, Daniel G. Ried, eds. Downers Grove, IL/Leicester: InterVarsity Press, 1993. 76–82.

Fung, Ronald Y. -K. "Justification by Faith in 1 & 2 Corinthians." In *Pauline Studies: Essays presented to Professor F. F. Bruce on his 70th Birthday*. Donald A. Hagner and Murray J. Harris, eds. Exeter, Devon: The Paternoster Press/Grand Rapids: Eerdmans, 1980. 246–61.

Furnish, Victor Paul. "Belonging to Christ: A Paradigm for Ethics in First Corinthians." *Interpretation* 44 (1990), 145–157.

Furnish, Victor Paul. "Elect Sojourners in Christ: An Approach to the Theology of 1 Peter." *Perkins Journal* 28 (1975), 1–11.

Furnish, Victor Paul. *Theology and Ethics in Paul*. Nashville/New York: Abingdon Press, 1968.

Gager, John G. "Functional Diversity in Paul's Use of End-Time Language." *Journal of Biblical Literature* 89 (1970), 325–337.

Gager, John G. *Kingdom and Community: The Social World of Early Christianity.* Prentice-Hall Studies In Religion Series. Englewood Cliffs, NJ: Prentice-Hall, 1975.

Gager, John G. *Moses in Greco-Roman Paganism.* Society of Biblical Literature Monograph Series 16. Nashville/New York: Abingdon Press, 1972.

Gander, G. "1 Cor. 10:2 parle-t-il du baptême?" *Revue D'histoire et de philosophie religieuses* 37 (1957), 97–102.

Gardner, Paul Douglas. *The Gifts of God and the Authentication of a Christian: An Exegetical Study of 1 Corinthians 8–11:1.* Lanham, MD/New York/London: University Press of America, 1994.

Garlington, Don B. *Faith, Obedience and Perseverance: Aspects of Paul's Letter to the Romans.* Wissenschaftliche Untersuchungen zum Neuen Testament. Tübingen: J. C.B. Mohr (Paul Siebeck), 1994.

Garlington, Don B. *'The Obedience of Faith': A Pauline Phrase in Historical Context.* Wissenschaftliche Untersuchungen zum Neuen Testament. Tübingen: J.C.B. Mohr (Paul Siebeck), 1991.

Garrigou-Lagrange, Reginald. *Predestination.* St. Louis: B. Herder, 1946.

Gaston, Lloyd. "Israel's Misstep in the Eyes of Paul." In *The Romans Debate.* Revised and Expanded Edition. Karl P. Donfried, ed. Peabody, MA: Hendrickson, 1991. 309–26.

Gaudemet, J. "Notes sur les formes anciennes de l'Excommunication." *Recherches de science religieuse* 23 (1949), 64–77.

Gavin, Jos. B. "The York House Conference, 1626: A Watershed in the Arminian-Calvinist-Puritan Debate over Predestination." In *Trinification of the World: A Festschrift in Honor of Frederick E. Crowe.* Thomas A. Dunne and Jean-Marc Laporte, eds. Toronto: Regis College Press, 1978. 280–311.

Geeley, Andrew M. "A Social Science Model for the Consideration of Religious Apostasy." In *Perspectives of a Political Ecclesiology.* J. B. Metz, ed. New York: Herder & Herder, 1971. 125–134.

Gennep, Arnold van. *The Rites of Passage.* London: Routledge & Kegan Paul, 1960.

Giblin, C. H. *The Threat to Faith: An Exegetical and Theological Re-Examination of 2 Thessalonians 2.* Analecta Biblica. Rome: Pontifical Biblical Institute, 1967.

Gileadi, Avraham, ed. *Israel's Apostasy and Restoration: Essays in Honor of Roland K. Harrison.* Grand Rapids: Baker Book House,1988.

Gill, David W. J. "In Search Of The Social Élite In The Corinthian Church." *Tyndale Bulletin* 44 (1993), 323–337.

Gill, David W. J. "The Meat-Market at Corinth (1 Corinthians 10:25)." *Tyndale Bulletin* 43 (1992), 389–93.

Ginzberg, Louis. *Legends of the Bible.* Philadelphia: The Jewish Publication Society of America, 1956.

Girardeau, John L. "Calvinism and Evangelical Arminianism Compared as to Election." *Methodist Quarterly Review* 37 (1893), 29–45.

Gitay, Yehoshua. "Rhetorical Criticism." In *To Each Its Own Meaning: An Introduction to Biblical Criticisms and their Application*, Steven L. McKenzie and Stephen R. Haynes, eds. Louisville, KT: Westminster/John Knox Press, 1993. 135–49.

Goguel, Maurice. "Le caractere, à la fois actuel et futur, du salut dans la théologie paulinienne." In *The Background of the New Testament and its Eschatology: In Honour of Charles Harold Dodd.* W. D. Davies and D. Daube, eds. Cambridge: Cambridge University Press, 1956. 322–41.

Goguel, Maurice. "Les fondements de l'assurance du salut chez l'apôtre Paul." *Revue d'histotoire et de philosophie religieuses* 17 (1938), 105–44.

Gooch, Peter D. *Dangerous Food: 1 Corinthians 8–10 in Its Context.* Studies in Christianity and Judaism. Ontario: Wilfrid Laurier University Press, 1993.

Goodman, Martin. *Mission and Conversion: Proselytizing in the Religious History of the Roman Empire.* Oxford: Clarendon Press, 1994.

Goodwin, John. *Redemption Redeemed.* London: John Macock for Lodowick Lloyd and Henry Cripps, 1651.

Goodwin, John. *Triumuiri.* London: Henry Eversden, 1658.

Goppelt, Leonard. "Paulus und die Heilsgeschichte: Schlussfolgerungen aus Röm. IV und I. Kor. X. 1–13." *New Testament Studies* 13 (1966), 31–42.

Goppelt, Leonard. "τύπος, ἀντίτυπος, τυπικός, ὑποτύπωσις." In *TDNT* 8:246–59.

Goppelt, Leonard. *Typos: Die Typologische Deutung des Alten Testaments im Neuen. Anhang Apokalyptik und Typologie bei Paulus.* Second Edition. Darmstadt: Wissenschaftliche Buchgesellschaft,1969.

Gorman, Frank H. "Ritual Studies and Biblical Studies: Assessment of the Past; Prospects for the Future." In *Transformations, Passages, and Processes: Ritual Approaches to Biblical Texts.* Mark McVann, ed. *Semeia* 67 (1995), 13–36.

Goulder, M. D. *Type and History in Acts.* London: SPCK, 1964.

Graf, Fritz. "Transvestitism, ritual." In *The Oxford Classical Dictionary.* 3rd ed. Simon Hornblower, Antony Spawforth, eds. Oxford/New York: Oxford University Press, 1996.

Greeley, Andrew M. "A Social Science Model for the Consideration of Religious Apostasy." In *Perspectives of a Political Ecclesiology.* J. B. Metz, ed. New York: Herder & Herder, 1971. 125–34.

Grider, J. Kenneth. "Predestination as Temporal Only." *Wesleyan Theological Journal* 22/2 (1987), 56–64.

Grossi, Vittorino. "Heresy – Heretic." In *Encyclopedia of the Early Church.* Angelo Di Berardino, ed. New York: Oxford University Press, 1992. 1:376–77.

Grudem, Wayne. *Systematic Theology: an Introduction to Biblical Doctrine.* Leicester: InterVarsity Press/Grand Rapids: Zondervan, 1994.

Grundmann, Walter. "στήκω, ἵστημι." In *TDNT* 7:636–53.

Gundry Volf, Judith. "Apostasy, Falling Away, Perseverance." In *Dictionary of Paul and His Letters.* Gerald F. Hawthorne, Ralph P. Martin, Daniel G. Ried, eds. Downers Grove, IL/Leicester: InterVarsity Press, 1993. 39–45.

Gundry Volf, Judith. *Paul and Perseverance: Staying In and Falling Away.* Wissenschaftliche Untersuchungen zum Neuen Testament. Tübingen: J. C. B. Mohr (Paul Siebeck), 1990. Reprinted in Louisville: Westminster/John Knox Press, 1990.

Gundry, Robert. "Grace, Works, and Staying Saved in Paul." *Biblica* 66 (1985), 1–38.

Guthrie, W. K. C. *The Greeks and Their Gods.* Boston: Beacon Press, 1950.

Guzzetti, G. B. "Apostasy." In *Sacramentum Mundi: An Encyclopedia of Theology.* Adolf Darlap, gen. ed., Karl Rahner, ed. London: Burns and Oates, 1968. 1:75–76.

Haarbeck, Hermann. "δόκιμος." In *NIDNTT* 3:808–11.

Haas, Cees. "Job's Perseverance in the Testament of Job." *In Studies in the Testament of Job.* M. A. Knibb and P. W. van der Horst, eds. Cambridge: Cambridge University Press, 1989. 117–54.

Hadaway, C. Kirk, and Roof, Wade Clark. "Apostasy in American Churches: Evidence from National Survey Data." In *Falling From the Faith: Causes and Consequences of Religious Apostasy*. David G. Bromley, ed. Sage Focus. Newbury Park/Beverly Hills/London/New Delhi: Sage, 1988. 29–46.

Hadaway, C. Kirk. "Five Types of Apostates." *Urban Mission* 9 (Jan. 1992), 26–34.

Hägglund, Bengt. *History of Theology*. St. Louis: Concordia Publishing House, 1968.

Hahn, Ferdinand. "Teilhabe am Heil und Gefahr des Abfalls: Eine Auslegung von 1 Ko 10,1–22." In *Freedom and Love: The Guide for Christian Life (1 Co 8–10. Rm 14–15)*. L. de Lorenzi, ed. Monograph Series of Benedictina. Rome: St. Paul vor den Mauern, 1981. 6.149–204.

Hahn, Ferdinand. "Zum Stand der Erforschung des urchristlichen Herrenmahls." *Evangelische Theologie* 35 (1975), 553–63.

Hahn, Hans-Cristoph. "ἀπώλεια." In *NIDNTT* 1:462–65.

Halperin, David J. *Faces of the Chariot: Early Jewish Responses to Ezekiel's Vision*. Texte und Studien zum Antiken Judentem. Tübingen: J. C.B. Mohr (Paul Siebeck), 1988.

Hamilton, Neill Q. *The Holy Spirit and Eschatology in Paul*. Scottish Journal of Theology Occasional Papers 6. London/Edinburgh: Oliver & Boyd, 1957.

Hansen, F. Allan. *Meaning in Culture*. International Library of Anthropology. London/Boston: Routledge & Kegan Paul, 1975.

Hanson, Anthony Tyrrell. *Jesus in the Old Testament*. London: SPCK, 1965.

Hanson, K. C. "Transformed on the Mountain: Ritual Analysis and the Gospel of Matthew." In *Transformations, Passages, and Processes: Ritual Approaches to Biblical Texts*. Mark McVann, ed. *Semeia* 67 (1995), 147–70.

Hanson, Paul D. *The Dawn of Apocalyptic: The Historical and Sociological Roots of Jewish Apocalyptic Eschatology*. Philadelphia: Fortress Press, 1979.

Hanson, Richard. "Moses in the Typology of St. Paul." *Theology* 48 (1945), 174–77.

Harrington, Hannah K. *The Impurity System of Qumran and the Rabbis: Biblical Foundations*. Society of Biblical Literature Dissertation Series. Atlanta: Scholars Press, 1993.

Harris, Gerald. "The Beginnings of Church Discipline: 1 Corinthians 5." *New Testament Studies* 37 (1991), 1–21.

Harrison, A. W. *Arminianism*. Duckworth's Theology Series. London: Gerald Duckworth & Company, 1937.

Harrison, A. W. *The Beginnings of Arminianism to the Synod of Dort*. London: University of London Press, 1926.

Hartman, Lars. "Baptism." In *The Anchor Bible Dictionary*. David Noel Freedman, ed. New York/London/Toronto/Sydney/Auckland, 1992. 1:583–94.

Harvey, A. E. "Forty Strokes Save One: Social Aspects of Judaizing and Apostasy." In *Alternative Approaches to New Testament Study*. A. E. Harvey, ed. London: SPCK, 1985. 79–96.

Hasel, Gerhard F. *The Remnant: the History and Theology of the Remnant Idea from Genesis to Isaiah*. Berrien Springs, MI: Andrews University Press, 1972.

Hauck, Friedrich, and Schulz, Siegfried. "πόρνη, πόρνος, πορνεία, πορνεύω, ἐκπορνεύω." In *TDNT* 6:579–95.

Havener, Ivan. "A Curse for Salvation – 1 Corinthians 5:1–5." In *Sin, Salvation, and the Spirit: Commemorating the Fiftieth Year of the Liturgical Press*. Daniel Durken, ed. Collegeville, MN: The Liturgical Press, 1979. 334–44.

Haykin, Michael A. G. "'In the Cloud and in the Sea': Basil of Caesarea and the Exegesis of 1 Cor 10:2." *Vigiliae Christianae* 40 (1986), 135–144.

Hays, Richard B. *Echoes Of Scripture In the Letters Of Paul*. New Haven & London: Yale University Press, 1989.

Hebblewaite, Margaret, and Donovan, Kevin. *The Theology of Penance*. Theology To-day. Butler, WS: Clergy Book Service, 1979.

Hegle, Maurice Edward. "A Comparative Study of the Wesleyan-Arminian and Calvin-istic Doctrines of the Perseverance of the Saints as Set Forth by Selected Representa-tives." B.D. Thesis, Western Evangelical Seminary, 1961.

Heitmüller, W. *Im Namen Jesu: Eine Sprach und Religionsgeschichtliche Untersuchung zum Neuen Testament, Speziel zur Altchristliche Taufe*. Göttingen: Vandenhoeck & Ruprecht, 1903.

Helm, Paul. "Persevering Perseverence [sic!]." *International Journal for Philosophy of Religion* 33 (1993), 103–109.

Hemer, Colin J. *The Book of Acts in the Setting of Hellenistic History*. Wissenschaftliche Untersuchungen zum Neuen Testament. Tübingen: J. C. B. Mohr (Paul Siebeck), 1989.

Hendel, Ronald S. "Sacrifice as a Cultural System: The Ritual Symbolism of Exodus 24, 3–8." *Zeitschrift für die alttestamenliche Wissenschaft* 101 (1989), 366–90.

Hengel, Martin. *Acts and the History of Earliest Christianity*. London: SCM Press, 1979.

Hengel, Martin. *Judaism and Hellenism: Studies in their Encounter in Palestine during the Early Hellensitic Period*. London: SCM, 1974. 2 Volumes.

Heppe, Heinrich. *Reformed Dogmatics*. Foreword by Karl Barth; Revised and Edited by Ernst Bizer, London: George Allen and Unwin, 1950.

Heyd, Michael. "The Reaction To Enthusiasm in the 17th Century: From Antistructure to Structure." *Religion* 15 (1985), 279–289.

Hill, C. E. "Paul's Understanding of Christ's Kingdom in 1 Corinthians 15:20–28." *Novum Testamentum* 30 (1988), 297–320.

Hinz, Christoph. "'Bewahrung und Verkehrung der Freiheit in Christo': Versuch einer Transformation von I. Kor 10,23-II,1 (8,1–10,22)." In *Gnosis und Neues Testament: Studien aus Religionswissenschaft und Theologie*. Karl-Wolfgang Tröger, ed. Berlin: Gütersloher Verlagshaus/Gerd Mohn, 1973. 405–422.

Hodge, Charles. *Systematic Theology*. 3 Volume Reprint. Grand Rapids: Eermans, 1946.

Hoekema, Anthony A. "The Perseverance of True Believers." In *Saved by Grace*. Anthony Hoekema. Exeter: Paternoster/Grand Rapids: Eerdmans, 1989. 234–56.

Hoenderdaal, G. J. "Remonstrantie en Contraremonstrantie." *Nederlands Archief Kerk-geschiedenis* 51/1 (1970), 49–92.

Hofius, Otfried. "Die Unabänderlichkeit des göttlichen Heilsratschlusses: Erwägungen zur Herkunft eines neutestamentlichen Theologumenon." *Zeitschrift für die neutesta-mentliche Wissenschaft* 64 (1973), 135–145.

Hofius, Otfried. *Katapausis: Die Vorstellung vom endzeitlichen Ruheort im Hebräer-brief*. Wissenschaftliche Untersuchungen zum Neuen Testament. Tübingen: J. C. B. Mohr (Paul Siebeck), 1970.

Holladay, William L. *The Root Sûbh in the Old Testament: With Particular Reference to its Usages in Covenantal Contexts*. Leiden: E. J. Brill, 1958.

Holleman, Joost. *Resurrection and Parousia: A Traditio-Historical Study of Paul's Es-chatology in 1 Corinthians 15*. Novum Testamentum Supplement Series. Leiden/New York/Cologne: E. J. Brill, 1996.

Holmberg, Bengt. *Sociology and the New Testament: An Appraisal*. Minneapolis: For-tress Press, 1990.

Horbury, William. "Extirpation and Excommunication." *Vetus Testamentum* 35 (1985), 13–38.

Horrell, David G. "Theological Principle of Christological Praxis? Pauline Ethics in 1 Corinthians 8.1–11.1." *Journal for the Study of the New Testament* 67 (1997), 83–114.

Horrell, David G. *The Social Ethos of the Corinthian Correspondence: Interests and Ideology from 1 Corinthians to 1 Clement.* Studies of the New Testament and its World. Edinburgh: T. & T. Clark, 1996.

Horsley, Richard A. "Consciousness and Freedom among the Corinthians: 1 Corinthians 8–10." *Catholic Biblical Quarterly* 40 (1978), 574–589.

Horsley, Richard A. "Gnosis in Corinth: 1 Corinthians 8.1–6." *New Testament Studies* 27 (1980–81), 32–51.

Horsley, Richard A. "Pneumatikos vs. Psychikos: Distinctions of Spiritual Status Among the Corinthians." *Harvard Theological Review* 69 (1976), 269–88.

Howard, J. K. "'Christ Our Passover Lamb': A Study of the Passover-Exodus Theme in 1 Corinthians." *Evangelical Quarterly* 41 (1969), 97–108.

Howell, Don N. "Pauline Eschatological Dualism and Its Resulting Tensions." *Trinity Journal* 14NS (1993), 3–24.

Hübner, Hans. *Gottes Ich und Israel: Zum Schriftgebrauch des Paulus in Römer 9–11.* Göttingen: Vanderhoek & Ruprecht, 1984.

Hughes, Frank Witt. *Early Christian Rhetoric and 2 Thessalonians.* Journal for the Society of New Testament Supplement Series. Sheffield: JSOT Press, 1989.

Hughes, Philip E. "Hebrews 6:4–6 and the Peril of Apostasy." *Westminster Theological Journal* 35 (1973), 137–55.

Hunsberger, Bruce. "A Reexamination of the Antecedents of Apostasy." *Review of Religious Research* 21 (1980), 158–70.

Hunsberger, Bruce. "Apostasy: A Social Learning Perspective." *Review of Religious Research* 25 (1983), 21–38.

Hunt, W. Boyd. "The Perseverance of the Saints." In *Basic Christian Doctrines.* Reprint. Carl F. H. Henry, ed. Grand Rapids: Baker Book House, 1971. 234–40.

Hurd, John C. *The Origin of 1 Corinthians.* London: SPCK/New York: Seaburg, 1965.

Hurtado, Larry W. "The *Nomina Sacra* and Christian Origins." Unpublished Paper, University of Edinburgh: 1997. 1–22.

Hurtado, Larry W. *One God, One Lord: Early Christian Devotion and Ancient Jewish Monotheism.* London: SCM, 1988.

Hyland, Francis Edward. *Excommunication: Its Nature, Historical Development and Effects.* Washington: Catholic University of America, 1928.

Isenberg, Sheldon R. "Millenarism in Greco-Roman Palestine." *Religion* 4 (1974), 26–46.

Isenberg, Sheldon R. "Some Uses and Limitations of Social Scientific Methodology in the Study of Early Christianity." In *Society of Biblical Literature 1980 Seminar Papers.* Paul J. Achtemeier, ed. Chico: Scholars Press, 1980. 29–49.

Jacob, E. "L'Héritage cananéen dans le livre du prophète Osée." *RHPR* 3 (1963), 250–9.

Jacobs, Paul. *Prädestination und Verantwortlichkeit bei Calvin.* Neukirchen: Neukirchner Verlag, 1937.

Jaroszewicz, Joannes. *De dono perseverantiae finalis secundum doctrinam sancti Thomae Aquinatis.* Diss. Theol. Friburg. Helvetiorum. Kielciis: Typis Officinae S. Josephi, Karczówka, 1932.

Jeremias, Joachim. "Chaismus in den Paulusbriefen." *Zeitschrift für die Neue Testamentliche Wissenschaft* 49 (1958), 145–56.

Jeremias, Joachim. "ἄνθρωπος, ἄνθρώπινος." *TDNT*c 1:364–67.

Jeremias, Joachim. "λίθος, λίθινος." *TDNT*b 4:268–80.

Jeremias, Joachim. "Μωϋσῆς." In *TDNT*a 4:848–73.

Jeremias, Joachim. "Paulus Als Hillelit." In *Neotestamentica Et Semitica: Studies in Honour of Matthew Black.* E. Earle Ellis and Max Wilcox, eds. Edinburgh: T. & T. Clark, 1969. 88–94.

Jeremias, Joachim. *Infant Baptism in the First Four Centuries.* The Library of History and Doctrine. London: SCM Press, 1960.

Jervis, L. Ann. "'But I Want You to Know': Paul's Midrashic Intertextual Response to the Corinthian Worshipers (1 Cor 11:2–16). *Journal of Biblical Literature* 112 (1993), 231–46.

Jeske, Richard L. "The Rock was Christ: The Ecclesiology of 1 Corinthians 10." In *Kirche: Festschrift Günther Bornkamm*, D. Luhrmann & G. Strecker, eds. Tübingen: Mohr (Paul Siebeck), 1980. 245–55.

Jessup, Harry E. *Foundations of Doctrine.* Chicago: Chicago Evangelistic Institute, 1938.

Jessup, Harry E. *That Burning Question of Final Perseverance.* Winons Lake, IN: Light and Life Press, 1942.

Jewett, Paul K. *Election and Predestination.* Grand Rapids: Eerdmans, 1985.

Jocz, Jakób. *A Theology of Election: Israel and the Church.* London: SPCK, 1958.

Joest, W. *Gesetz und Freiheit: Das Problem des Tertius Usus Legis bei Luther und die neutestamentliche Parainese.* Göttingen: Vandenhoeck & Ruprecht, 1968.

John of Damascus. *Saint John of Damascus Writings.* Translated by Frederic H. Chase, Jr. The Fathers of the Church: A New Translation. Washington: The Catholic University of America Press, 1958.

Johnson, Elizabeth. *The Function of Apocalyptic and Wisdom Traditions in Romans 9–11.* Society of Biblical Literature Dissertation Series. Atlanta: Scholars Press, 1989.

Johnsson, William G. "The Pilgrimage Motif in the Book of Hebrews." *Journal of Biblical Literature* 97 (1978), 239–51.

Karmiris, John. *A Synopsis of the Dogmatic Theology of the Orthodox Catholic Church.* Scranton, PN: Christian Orthodox Edition, 1973.

Karris, Robert J. "Romans 14:1–15:13 and the Occasion of Romans." In *The Romans Debate.* Revised and Expanded Edition. Karl P. Donfried, ed. Peabody, MA: Hendrickson, 1991. 65–84.

Käsemann, Ernst. "The Pauline Doctrine of the Lord's Supper." In *Essays on New Testament Themes.* Studies in Biblical Theology 41. London: SCM, 1964. 108–135.

Käsemann, Ernst. *The Wandering People of God: An Investigation of the Letter to the Hebrews.* Minneapolis: Augsburg, 1984.

Kaufmann, Kuhler, and Gottheil, Richard. "Apostasy and Apostates from Judaism." In *The Jewish Encyclopedia.* Isidore Singer, ed. New York: KTAV Publishing House, 1901. 2:12–18.

Kee, Howard C. "The Transformation of the Synagogue After 70 C. E.: Its Import for Early Christianity. *New Testament Studies* 36 (1990), 1–24.

Kelly, J. N. D. *Early Christian Doctrines.* Revised Edition. San Francisco: Harper & Row, 1978.

Kelly, Brian E. *Retribution and Eschatology in Chronicles.* Journal for the Study of the Old Testament Supplement Series. Sheffield: Sheffield Academic Press, 1996.

Kempthorne, R. "Incest and the Body of Christ: A Study of 1 Corinthians VI. 12–20." *New Testament Studies* 14 (1967), 568–74.

Kendall, R. T. *Once Saved, Always Saved.* Chicago: Moody Press, 1983.

Kennedy, Charles A. "1 Cor. 8 as a Mishnaic List." In *Religious Writings and Religious Systems: Systemic Analysis of Holy books in Christianity, Islam, Buddhism, Greco-*

Roman Religious, Ancient Israel, and Judaism. Jacob Neusner, Ernest S. Frerichs, A. J. Levine, eds. Atlanta: Scholars Press, 1989. 2:17–24.

Kennedy, Charles A. "The Cult of the Dead in Corinth." In *Love and Death in the Ancient Near East: Essays in Honor of Marvin H. Pope.* John H. Marks, Robert M. Good, eds. Guilford, CT: Four Quarters Publishing Company, 1987. 227–36.

Kennedy, George A. *New Testament Interpretation through Rhetorical Criticism.* Studies in Religion. Chapel Hill/London: University of North Carolina Press, 1984.

Kim, D. "Perseverance in Hebrews." *Skrif en Kerk* 18 (1997), 280–90.

Kippenberg, H. G. "Apostasy." In *The Encyclopedia of Religion.* Mircea Eliade, ed. New York: Macmillan Publishing/London: Collier Macmillan Publishers, 1987. 1:353–56.

Kittel, Gerhard. "ἔρημος, ἐρημία, ἐρημόω, ἐρήμωσις." In *TDNT* 2:657–60.

Klauck, Hans-Josef. *Herrenmahl Und Hellenistischer Kult: Eine religionsgeschichtliche Untersuchung zum ersten Korintherbrief.* Münster: Aschendorff, 1982.

Klein, William W. *The New Chosen People: A Corporate View of Election.* Grand Rapids: Zondervan, 1990.

Kline, Meredith. *By Oath Consigned: A Reinterpretation of the Covenant Signs of Circumcision and Baptism.* Grand Rapids: Eerdmans, 1968.

Koch, Dietrich-Alex. *Die Schrift als Zeuge des Evangeliums: Untersuchungen zur Verwendung und zum Verständnis der Schrift bei Paulus.* Tübingen: J.C.B. Mohr (Paul Siebeck), 1986.

Koch, Klaus. *The Rediscovery of Apocalyptic: A Polemical Work on a Neglected Area of Biblical Studies and Its Damaging Effects on Theology and Philosophy.* London: SCM, 1972.

Kraus, Wolfgang. *Das Volk Gottes: Zur Grundlegung der Ekklesiologie bei Paulus.* Wissenschaftliche Untersuchungen zum Neuen Testament. Tübingen: J. C. B. Mohr (Paul Siebeck), 1995.

Krause, Alfred E. "Historical Selectivity: Prophetic Prerogative or Typological Imperative?" In *Israel's Apostasy and Restoration: Essays in Honor of Roland K. Harrison.* Avraham Gileadi, ed. Grand Rapids:Baker Book House,1988. 175–212.

Kreitzer, Larry. "Baptism In the Pauline Epistles: With Special Reference to the Corinthian Letters." *Biblical Quarterly* 34 (1991), 67–78.

Kroeger, Richard and Catherine. "An Inquiry into Evidence of Maenadism in the Corinthian Congregation." In *Society of Biblical Literature 1978 Seminar Papers.* Paul J. Achtemeier, ed. Missoula, MT: Scholars Press, 1978. 331–38.

Kroeger, Richard and Catherine. "Mystery Religions." In *Evangelical Dictionary of Theology.* Walter A. Elwell, ed. Grand Rapids: Baker Book House, 1984. 742–44.

Kuck, David W. *Judgement and Community Conflict: Paul's Use of Apocalyptic Judgment Language in 1 Corinthians 3:5–4:5.* Supplements To Novum Testamentum. Leiden/New York/København/Köln: E. J. Brill, 1992.

Kuhn, Georg Karl. "New Light on Temptation, Sin, and Flesh in the New Testament." In *The Scrolls and the New Testament.* Christian Origins Library. Revised Edition. Krister Stendahl, ed. with James H. Charlesworth. New York: Crossroad, 1992. 94–113.

Laansma, Jon. '*I Will Give You Rest' The Rest Motif in the New Testament with Special Reference to Mt 11 an Heb 3–4.* Wissenschaftliche Untersuchungen zum Neuen Testament. Tübingen: J. C. B. Mohr (Paul Siebeck), 1997.

Ladd, George Eldon. *A Theology of the New Testament.* Revised Edition. Donald A. Hagner, ed. Cambridge: The Lutterworth Press, 1994.

Lamgor, Uri. "Long Time and Short Time: Ritual and Non-Ritual Liminality In An East-African Age System." *Religion* 15 (1985), 219–34.

Lampe, G. W. H. "Church Discipline and the Epistles to the Corinthians." In *Christian History and Interpretation: Studies Presented to John Knox.* W. R. Farmer, C.F.D. Moule, Richard R. Niebuhr, eds. Cambridge: Cambridge University Press, 1967. 337–361.

Lampe, G. W. H. *"The Seal of the Spirit: A Study of Baptism and Confirmation in the New Testament and the Fathers."* London: Longmans, Green and Company, 1951.

Lampe, Peter. "Das korinthische Herrenmahl im Schnittpunkt hellenistisch-römischer Mahlpraxis und paulinischer Theologia Crucis (1 Kor 11,17–34)." *Zeitschrift für die neutestamentliche Wissenschaft* 82 (1991), 183–213.

Lane, William L. *Hebrews 1–8.* Word Biblical Commentary, Dallas: Word Books, 1991.

Lange, Armin. *Weisheit und Prädestination in den Textfunden von Qumran.* Studies on the Text of the Desert of Judah. Leiden: E. J. Brill, 1996.

Larsson, Edvin. *Christus als Vorbild: Eine Untersuchung zu den paulinischen Tauf- und Eikontexten.* Acta seminarii neotestamentici upsaliensis. Uppsala: Almquist & Wiksell, 1962.

Latourette, Kenneth Scott. *A History of Christianity.* 2 Volumes. Revised Edition. San Francisco: Harper & Row, 1975.

Laurence, Richard. *An Attempt to Illustrate those Articles of the Church of England which the Calvinist Improperly Consider as Calvinistical.* Oxford: Oxford University Press, 1805.

Leach, Edmund. "Anthropological Approaches to the Study of the Bible during the Twentieth Century." In Edmund Leach and D. Alan Aycock. *Structuralist Interpretations of Biblical Myth.* Royal Anthropological Institute of Great Britain and Ireland. Cambridge: Cambridge University Press, 1983a. 7–32.

Leach, Edmund. "Why Did Moses Have a Sister?" In Edmund Leach and D. Alan Aycock. *Structuralist Interpretations of Biblical Myth.* Royal Antropological Institute of Great Britain and Ireland. Cambridge: Cambridge University Press, 1983b. 33–66.

Leach, Edmund. *Culture and Communication: The Logic by which Symbols are Connected.* Themes in the Social Sciences. Cambridge: Cambridge University Press, 1976.

Lee, Max J. "Perseverance and Apostasy in Jewish Literature" Unpublished Paper. Fuller Theological Seminary, 1995. 1–25.

Lefkowitz, Mary R., and Fant, Maureen B. *Women's Life In Greece and Rome.* London: Gerald Duckworth & Co. 1982.

Letham, Robert "Saving Faith and Assurance in Reformed Theology: Zwingli to the Synod of Dort." 2 Volumes. Ph.D. Thesis, Aberdeen University, 1979.

Lightfoot, J. B., and Harmer, J. R. *The Apostolic Fathers.* Revised Greek Texts with Introduction and English Translations. Grand Rapids: Baker Book House, 1984.

Lincoln, Andrew T. *Paradise Now and Not Yet: Studies in the Role of the Heavenly Dimension in Paul's Thought with Special Reference to His Eschatology.* Society For New Testament Studies Monograph Series. Cambridge/London/New York/New Rochelle/Melbourne/Sydney: Cambridge University Press, 1991.

Lindemann, Andreas. "Paulus und die Korinthische Eschatologie: Zur These von einer 'Entwicklung' im Paulinischen Denken." *New Testament Studies* 37 (1991), 373–399.

Lodge, John G. *Romans 9–11: A Reader-Response Analysis.* International Studies in Formative Christianity and Judaism. Atlanta: Scholars Press, 1996.

Loh, I-Jin. "A Study of an Early Christian Hymn in II Tim. 2:11–13." Th.D. Dissertation, Princeton Theological Seminary, 1968.

Longnecker, Bruce W. "Different Answers to Different Issues: Israel, the Gentiles and

Salvation History in Romans 9–11." *Journal for the Study of the New Testament* 36 (1989), 95–123.

Longnecker, Bruce W. *Eschatology and the Covenant: A Comparison of 4 Ezra and Romans 1–11*. Journal for the Study of the New Testament Supplement Series 57. Sheffield: JSOT/Sheffield Academic Press, 1991.

Lübking, Hans-Martin. *Paulus und Israel im Römerbrief: Eine Untersuchung zu Römer 9–11*. Europäische Hochschulschriften – Theologie. Franfurt am Main/Bern/New York: Peter Lang, 1986.

Lüdemann, Gerd. *Heretics: The Other Side of Christianity*. London: SCM, 1996.

Luther, Martin. *The Babylonian Captivity*. Revised and Reprinted in *Three Treatises*. Austin, TX: Augsburg Fortress, 1970a.

Luther, Martin. *The Freedom of a Christian*. Revised and Reprinted in *Three Treatises*. Austin, TX: Augsburg Fortress, rev. ed. 1970b.

Luzarraga, J. *Las tradiciones de la nube en la biblia y en el judaismo primitivo*. Analecta Biblica. Rome: Biblical Institute Press, 1973.

MacDonald, Dennis. *There is No Male and Female*. Philadelphia: Fortress, 1987.

MacDonald, Margaret Y. *The Pauline Churches: A Socio-Historical Study of Institutionalization in the Pauline and Deutero-Pauline Writings*. Society For New Testament Studies Monograph Series. Cambridge: Cambridge University Press, 1990.

MacDonald, William G. "The Biblical Doctrine of Election." In *The Grace of God, the Will of Man: A Case for Arminianism*. Clark Pinnock, ed. Grand Rapids: Zondervan, 1989. 207–29.

MacPherson, P. "τὰ τέλη τῶν αἰώνων: 1 Corinthians x.11," *Expository Times* 55 (1943/44), 222.

Maier, Johann. *Jüdische Auseinandersetzung mit dem Christentum in der Antike*. Erträge der Forschung. Darmstadt: Wissenschaftliche Buchgesellschaft, 1982.

Malan, F. S. "The Use of the Old Testament in Corinthians." *Neotestamentica* 14 (1981), 134–70.

Malherbe, Abraham J. "Determinism and Free Will in Paul: The Argument of 1 Corinthians 8 and 9." In *Paul in His Hellenistic Context*. Troels Engberg-Pedersen, ed. Minneapolis: Fortress Press, 1995. 231–255.

Malina, Bruce J. *Christian Origins and Cultural Anthropological Interpretation*. Atlanta: John Knox Press, 1986.

Malina, Bruce J. *The New Testament World: Insights from Cultural Anthropology*. Atlanta: John Knox Press, 1981.

Maly, Karl. *Mündige Gemeinde: Untersuchungen zur pastoralen Führung des Apostels Paulus im 1. Korintherbrief*. Stuttgarter biblische Monographien. Stuttgart: Verlag Katholisches Bibelwerk, 1967.

Mann, Thomas W. "The Pillar of Cloud in the Read Sea Narrative." *Journal of Biblical Literature* 90 (1971), 15–30.

Marsh, H. G. *The Origin and Significance of the New Testament Baptism*. Publications of the University of Manchester. Theological Series. Manchester: Manchester University Press, 1941.

Marshall, I. Howard. "Lord's Supper." In *Dictionary of Paul and His Letters*. Gerald F. Hawthorne, Ralph P. Martin, Daniel G. Ried, eds. Downers Grove, IL/Leicester: InterVarsity Press, 1993. 569–75.

Marshall, I. Howard. "Predestination in the New Testament." In *Jesus the Saviour: Studies In New Testament Theology*. I. H. Marshall. London: SCPK, 1990a. 290–305.

Marshall, I. Howard. "The Problem of Apostasy in New Testament Theology." In *Jesus the Saviour: Studies In New Testament Theology*. I. H. Marshall. London: SCPK, 1990b. 306–24.

Marshall, I. Howard. "Election and Calling to Salvation in 1 and 2 Thessalonians." In *The Thessalonian Correspondence*. Raymond F. Collins, ed. Bibliotheca Ephemeridum Theologicarum Lovaniensium. Leuven: Leuven University Press/Uitgeverij Peeters, 1990c .259–76.

Marshall, I. Howard. *Kept By The Power Of God: A Study of Perseverance and Falling Away*. Library of Ecumenical Studies. London: Epworth, 1969.

Martelet, Gustave. "Sacraments, Figures et Exhortation en 1 Cor. X, 1–11." *Recherches de Science religieuse* 44 (1956), 323–59.

Martin, Dale B. *Slavery as Salvation: The Metaphor of Slavery in Pauline Christianity*. New Haven/London: Yale University Press, 1990.

Martin, Dale B. *The Corinthian Body*. New Haven/London: Yale University Press, 1995.

Martin, Luther H. *Hellenistic Religions: An Introduction*. Oxford: Oxford University Press, 1987.

Mauser, Ulrich. *Christ in the Wilderness: The Wilderness Theme in the Second Gospel and its Basis in the Biblical Tradition*. Studies in Biblical Theology. London: SCM Press, 1963.

McClelland, J. C. "The Reformed Doctrine of Predestination According to Peter Martyr." *Scottish Journal of Theology* 8 (1955), 255–71.

McEleney, Neil J. "The Vice Lists of the Pastoral Epistles." *Catholic Biblical Quarterly* 36 (1974), 203–19.

McEllingott, C. J. *The Crown of Life: A Study of Perseverance*. St. Louis: B. Herder, 1963.

McEwen, A. "Paul's Use of the Old Testament in 1 Corinthians 10:1–4." *Vox Reformata* 47 (1986), 3–10.

McKnight, Scot. "The Warning Passages of Hebrews: A Formal Analysis and Theological Conclusions." *Trinity Journal* 13 (1992), 21–59.

McKnight, Scot. *A Light Among the Gentiles: Jewish Missionary Activity in the Second Temple Period*. Minneapolis: Fortress Press, 1991.

McVann, Mark, ed. *Transformations, Passages, and Processes: Ritual Approaches to Biblical Texts. Semeia* 67 (1995).

McVann, Mark. "Baptism, Miracles, and Boundary Jumping in Mark." *Biblical Theology Bulletin* 21 (Winter, 1991), 151–57.

McVann, Mark. "One of the Prophets: Matthew's Testing Narrative as a Rite of Passage." *Biblical Theology Bulletin* 23 (Spring, 1993), 14–20.

Mearns, Christopher L. "Early Eschatological Development in Paul: The Evidence of 1 Corinthians." *Journal for the Study of the New Testament* 22 (1984), 19–35.

Meeks, Wayne A. "And Rose Up to Play: Midrash and Paraenesis in 1 Corinthians 10:1–22," *JSNT* 16 (1982), 64–78.

Meeks, Wayne A. "Since Then You Would Need To Go Out Of The World: Group Boundaries in Pauline Christianity." In *Critical History and Biblical Faith: New Testament Perspectives*. College Theology Society Annual Publication Series. Thomas J. Ryan, ed. Lanham, MD: University Press of America, 1979. 4–29.

Meeks, Wayne A. "Social Functions of Apocalyptic Language in Pauline Christianity." In *Apocalypticism in the Mediterranean World and the Near East*. Preceedings of the International Colloquium on Apocalypticism Uppsala, August 12–17, 1979. David Hellholm, ed. Tübingen: J.C.B Mohr (Paul Siebeck), 1983b. 687–705.

Meeks, Wayne A. "The Circle of Reference in Pauline Morality." In *Greeks, Romans, and Christians: Essays in Honour of Abraham J. Malherbe*. David L. Balch, Everett Ferguson, and Wayne Meeks, eds. Minneapolis: Fortress Press, 1990. 305–17.

Meeks, Wayne A. "The Image of the Androgyne: Some Uses of a Symbol in Earliest Christianity." *History of Religions* 13 (Feb. 1974), 165–208.

Meeks, Wayne A. *The First Urban Christians: The Social World of the Apostle Paul*. New Haven/London: Yale University Press, 1983a.

Meggit, Justin J. "Meat Consumption and Social Conflict in Corinth." *Journal of Theological Studies* 45 (1994), 137–41.

Meissner, Stefan. *Die Heimholung des Ketzers: Studien zur jüdischen Auseinandersetzung mit Paulus*. Wissenschaftliche Untersuchungen zum Neuen Testament. Tübingen: J. C. B. Mohr (Paul Siebeck), 1996.

Mell, Patrick Hues. *Predestination and the Saints' Perseverance, Stated and Defended*. Charleston: Southern Baptist Publication Society, 1851.

Merklein, Helmut. "Die Einheitlichkeit des ersten Korintherbriefes." *Zeitschrift für die Neutestamentliche Wissenschaft* 75 (1984), 153–83.

Merrill, E. H. *Qumran and Predestination*. Leiden: E. J. Brill, 1975.

Meslin, Michel. "Baptism." In *The Encyclopedia of Religion*. Mircea Eliade, ed. New York: Macmillan Library Reference USA/Simon & Schuster Macmillan, 1995. 2:59–63.

Metzger, Bruce M. *A Textual Commentary on the Greek New Testament*. A Companion Volume to the United Bible Societies' Greek New Testament. Third Edition. Stuttgart: United Bible Societies, 1971.

Meyer, Lester V. "Remnant," In *The Anchor Bible Dictionary*. David Noel Freedman, ed. New York/London/Toronto/Sydney/Auckland, 1992. 5:669–71.

Michaelis, Wilhelm. "πίπτω, πτῶμα, πτῶσις, ἐκπίπτω, καταπίπτω, παραπίπτω, παράπτωμα, περιπίπτω." In *TDNT* 6:161–73.

Michel, Otto. *Paulus und Seine Bibel*. Darmstadt: Wissenschaftliche Buchgesellschaft, 1972.

Miley, John. *Systematic Theology*. 2 Volumes. New York: Hunt & Eaton, 1894.

Millard, A. R. "Covenant and Communion in First Corinthians." In *Apostolic History and the Gospel: Biblical and Historical Essays presented to F. F. Bruce on his 60th Birthday*. W. Ward Gasque and Ralph P. Martin, eds. Exeter: The Paternoster Press, 1970. 242–48.

Mitchell, Alan C. "1 Corinthians 6:1–11: Group Boundaries and the Courts of Corinth" Ph.D. Dissertation, Yale University, 1986.

Mitchell, Margaret M. *Paul and the Rhetoric of Reconciliation: An Exegetical Investigation of the Language and Composition of 1 Corinthians*. Hermeneutische Untersuchungen Zur Theologie. Tübingen: J. C. B. Mohr (Paul Siebeck), 1991. Reprinted by Louiesville: Westminster/John Knox Press, 1991.

Moberly, R. Walter L. "Towards An Interpretation of the Shema." Unpublished paper, University of Durham, 1996. 1–17.

Moiser, Jeremy. "A Reassessment of Paul's View of Marriage with Reference to 1 Cor. 7." *Journal for the Study of the New Testament* 18 (1983), 103–22.

Moltmann, Jürgen. "Perseveranz." In *Religion in Geschichte und Gegenwart*. Kurt Galling, ed. Tübingen: J.C.B. Mohr (Paul Siebeck), 3rd ed., 1986. 5:226–27.

Moltmann, Jürgen. *Prädestination und Perseveranz: Geschichte und Bedeutung der reformierten Lehre 'de perseverantia sanctorum'*. Neukirchen: Neukirchner Verlag, 1961.

Monson, Robert. "The Dangers of Apostasy in Jude 8–10." M.Div. Thesis, Talbot Theological Seminary, 1980.

Montagnini, Felice. "Elezione e libertà, grazia e predestinazione a proposito di Rom. 9, 6–29. In *Die Israelfrage nach Röm 9–11*. L. de Lornenzi, ed. Monograph Series of Benedictina. Rome: St. Paul vor den Mauern, 1977. 3:57–97.

Moody, Dale. "Salvation and Apostasy." In *The Word of Truth: A Summary of Christian Doctrine Based on Biblical Revelation*. Dale Moody. Grand Rapids: Eerdmans, 1981. 348–65.

Moody, Dale. *Apostasy: A Study in the Epistle to the Hebrews and in Baptist History*. Greenville, SC: Smyth & Helwys, 1991.

Moore, G. E. *Judaism In the First Centuries of the Christian Era: The Age of the Tannaim*. Cambridge: Harvard University Press, 1966.

Moule, C. F. D. "The Judgement Theme in the Sacraments." In *The Background of the New Testament and its Eschatology: In Honour of Charles Harold Dodd*. W. D. Davies and D. Daube, eds. Cambridge: Cambridge University Press, 1956. 464–81.

Moule, H. C. G. *Outlines of Christian Doctrine*. Revised. London: Hodder and Stoughton, 1894.

Mozley, J. B. *Augustinian Doctrine of Predestination*. London: John Murray, 1883.

Muller, Richard A. "Grace, Election, and Contingent Choice: Arminius' Gambit and the Reformed Response." In *The Grace of God, The Bondage of the Will: Volume 2: Historical and Theological Perspectives on Calvinism*. Thomas R. Schreiner and Bruce A. Ware, eds. Grand Rapids: Baker Book House, 1995. 251–78.

Muller, Richard A. *Christ and the Decree: Christology and Predestination in Reformed Theology from Calvin to Perkins*. Grand Rapids: Baker Book House, 1986.

Muller, Richard A. *God, Creation, and Providence in the Thought of Jacob Arminius: Sources and Directions of Scholastic Protestantism in the Era of Early Orthodoxy*. Grand Rapids: Baker Book House, 1991.

Murphy-O'Connor, Jerome. "Freedom or the Ghetto (1 Cor., VIII, 1–13. X, 23 - XI, 1)?" *Revue Biblique* 85 (1978), 543–74.

Murphy-O'Connor, Jerome. "Food and Spiritual Gifts in 1 Cor. 8:8." *Catholic Biblical Quarterly* 41 (1979), 292–298.

Murphy-O'Connor, Jerome. "The Corinth that Saint Paul Saw." *Biblical Archaeologist* (1984), 147–59.

Murray, John. "Perseverance." In *Redemption Accomplished and Applied*. John Murray. Grand Rapids: Eerdmans, 1955. 151–60.

Nash, Albert. *Perseverance and Apostasy: Being an Argument in Proof of the Arminian Doctrine*. New York: N. Tibbals & Son, 1871.

Neale, D. "Was Jesus a Mesith?: Public Response to Jesus and His Ministry." *Tyndale Bulletin* 44 (May 1993), 89–101.

Nebe, Gottfried. *'Hoffnung' bei Paulus: Elpis und ihre Synonyme im Zusammenhang der Eschatologie*. Studien zur Umwelt des Neuen Testaments. Göttingen: Vandenhoeck & Ruprecht, 1983.

Nelson, Lynn D. and Bromley, David G. "Another Look at Conversion and Defection in Conservative Churches." In *Falling From the Faith: Causes and Consequences of Religious Apostasy*. David G. Bromley, ed. Sage Focus. Newbury Park/Beverly Hills/London/New Delhi: Sage, 1988. 47–61.

Neusner, Jacob. *Introduction to Rabbinic Literature*. The Anchor Bible Reference Library. New York/London/Toronto/Sydney/Auckland: Doubleday, 1994.

Newton, Derek. "Food Offered to Idols in 1 Corinthians 8–10: A Study of Conflicting Viewpoints in the Setting of Religious Pluralism in Corinth." Ph.D. Thesis, University of Sheffield, 1996.

Newton, Michael. *The Concept of Purity at Qumran and in the Letters of Paul.* Society for New Testament Studies Monograph Series. Cambridge: Cambridge University Press, 1985.

Neyrey, Jerome H. "Body Language in 1 Corinthians: The Use of Anthropological Models for Understanding Paul and His Opponents. In *Social-Scientific Criticism of the New Testament and Its Social World.* John H. Elliott, ed. *Semeia* 35 (1986), 129–70.

Neyrey, Jerome H. *An Ideology of Revolt: John's Christology in Social-Science Perspective.* Philadelphia: Fortress Press, 1988.

Neyrey, Jerome H. *Paul, In Other Words: A Cultural Reading Of His Letters.* Louisville: Westminster/John Knox, 1990.

Nicole, Roger. "Perseverance of the Saints." In *Encyclopedia of the Reformed Faith.* Donald K McKim, ed. Louisville: Westminster/John Knox Press/Edinburgh: Saint Andrew Press, 1992. 275–76.

Nixon, R. E. *The Exodus in the New Testament.* The Tyndale New Testament Lecture, 1962. London: Tyndale Press, 1963.

Noack, Bent. *Satanás und Sotería: Untersuchung zur neutestamentliche Dämonologie.* Copenhagen: Gads, 1948.

Nock, Arthur Darby. *Conversion: The Old and New in Religion from Alexander the Great to Augustine of Hippo.* Oxford: Oxford University Press, 1933.

Noll, Mark A. "John Wesley and the Doctrine of Assurance." *Bibliotheca Sacra* 132 (1975), 161–77.

Noth, Martin. *The Deuteronomistic History.* Reprint. Sheffield: Journal for the Study of the Old Testament, 1981.

Nuttall, Geoffrey Fillingham. *Richard Baxter and Philip Doddridge: A Study in a Tradition.* Friends of Dr. William's Library. Fifth Lecture. Oxford: Oxford University Press, 1951.

Occam (see William of Ockham).

Oepke, Albrecht. "ἀπόλλυμι, ἀπώλεια, Ἀπολλύων." In *TDNT* 1:394–397.

Oesterreicher, John M. "Israel's Misstep and her Rise: The Dialectic of God's Design in Romans 9–11." In *Studiorum Paulinorum Congressus Internationalis Catholicus 1961.* Cesario D'Amato, ed. Volume 1. Analecta Biblica. Romae: E Pontificio Instituto Biblico, 1963. 317–327.

Oliphant, James H. *The Doctrine of the Final Perseverance of the Saints.* Indianapolis: Baker and Radolph, 1878.

Olson, Carl. *The Theology and Philosophy of Eliade: A Search for the Centre.* London: Macmillan Academic and Professional, 1992.

Oropeza, B. J. "Laying to Rest the Midrash: Paul's Message on Meat Sacrificed to Idols in Light of the Deuteronomic Tradition." *Biblica* 79 (1998a), 57–68.

Oropeza, B. J. "Situational Immorality: Paul's 'Vice Lists' at Corinth." *Expository Times* 110 (1998b), 9–10.

Oropeza, B. J. *A Time To Laugh: The Holy Laughter Phenomenon Examined.* Peabody, MA: Hendrickson Publishers, 1995.

Oropeza, B. J. *99 Reasons Why No One Knows When Christ Will Return.* Downers Grove, IL: InterVarsity Press, 1994.

Osborne, Grant R. "Exegetical Notes on Calvinist Texts." In *Grace Unlimited.* Clark Pinnock, ed. Minneapolis: Bethany, 1975. 167–89.

Osburn, Carroll D. "The Text of 1 Corinthians 10:9." In *New Testament Textual Criticism: Its Significance for Exegesis: Essays in Honour of Bruce M. Metzger*. Eldon Jay Epp and Gordon D. Fee, eds. Oxford at the Clarendon Press, 1981. 201–212.

Osburn, Carroll D. "The Text of Jude 5." *Biblica* 62 (1981), 107–15.

Osten-Sacken, Peter von der. *Die Heiligkeit der Tora: Studien zum Gesetz bei Paulus.* München: Chr. Kaiser, 1989.

Oster, Richard E. "Supposed Anachronism in Luke-Acts' Use of συναγωγή: A Rejoinder to H. C. Kee." *New Testament Studies* 39 (1993), 178–208.

Oswalt, John N. "Golden Calves and the 'Bull of Jacob': The Impact on Israel of Its Religious Environment." In *Israel's Apostasy and Restoration: Essays in Honor of Roland K. Harrison*. Avraham Gileadi, ed. Grand Rapids:Baker Book House,1988. 9–18.

Ott, Ludwig. *Fundamentals of Catholic Dogma*. James Canan Bastible, ed. St. Louis: Herder, 1955.

Owen, John. *The Doctrine of the Saints' Perseverance Explained and Confirmed*. Reprinted in *The Works of John Owen*. Volume 11. Carlisle, PA: The Banner of Truth Trust, 1980.

Painter, John. "Paul and Πνευματικοί at Corinth." In *Paul and Paulinism: Essays in Honour of C. K. Barrett*. M. D. Hooker and S. G. Wilson, eds. London: SPCK, 1982. 237–50.

Pannenberg, Wolfhart. *Human Nature, Election, and History*. Philadelphia: Westminster Press, 1977.

Patrick, Dale and Shogren, Gary S. "Election." In *The Anchor Bible Dictionary*. David Noel Freedman, ed. New York/London/Toronto/Sydney/Auckland, 1992. 2:434–44.

Paulsen, Henning. "Schisma und Häresie: Untersuchungen zu 1 Kor 11,18.19." *Zeitschrift für Theologie und Kirche* 79 (1982), 180–211.

Pearlman, Myer. *Knowing the Doctrines of the Bible*. Revised Edition. Springfield, MO: Gospel Publishing House, 1981.

Pearson, Berger A. *The Pneumatikos – Psychikos Terminology in 1 Corinthians: A Study in the Theology of the Corinthian Opponents of Paul and Its Relation to Gnosticism.* Society of Biblical Literature Dissertation Series. Missoula, MT: Society of Biblical Literature, 1973.

Pentikäinen, Juha. "The Symbolism of Liminality." In *Religious Symbols and Their Functions*. Haralds Biezais, ed. Scripta Instituti Donneriani Aboensis. Stockholm: Almqvist & Wiksell International, 1979. 154–65.

Perkins, Robert L. "Two Notes on Apostasy." *Perspectives in Religious Studies* 15 (1988), 57–60.

Perkins, William. *William Perkins (1558–1602), English Puritanist – His Pioneer Works on Casuistry: 'A Discourse of Conscience' and 'The Whole Treatise of Cases of Conscience.'* Edited with Introduction by Thomas F. Merrill. Nieuwkoop: B. De Graaf, 1966.

Perrot, Charles. "Les examples du désert (1 Co. 10.6–11)." *New Testament Studies* 29 (1983), 437–52.

Peterson, Brian K. *Eloquence and the Proclamation of the Gospel in Corinth*. Society of Biblical Literature Dissertation Series. Atlanta: Scholars Press, 1998.

Peterson, Robert A. "Perseverance and Apostasy: A Bibliographic Essay." *Presbyterion* 16 (1990), 119–125.

Peterson, Robert A. "Apostasy." *Presbyterion* 19 (1993), 17–31.

Peterson, Robert A. "Preservation, Perseverance, Assurance, and Apostasy: A Bibliography." Paper from Covenant Theological Seminary, 1992.

Peterson, Robert A. "The Perseverance of the Saints: A Theological Exegesis of Four Key New Testament Passages." *Presbyterion* 17 (1991), 95–112.

Petit, L. "Abjuration pour entrer dans l'Église orthodoxe, grecque et russe." In *Dictionnaire de Théologie Catholique*. A. Vacant & E. Mangenot, eds. Paris: Letouzey et Ané, 1909. 1:76–90.

Pfitzner, Victor C. *Paul and the Agon Motif*. Leiden: Novum Testamentum Supplement,1967.

Pfürtner, Stephanus. *Luther and Aquinas – A Conversation: Our Salvation, Its Certainty and Peril*. London: Darton, Longman & Todd, 1964.

Philo. Colson, F. H. and Whitaker, G. H., translators. Loeb Classical Library. London: William Heinemann LTD/Cambridge, Mass: Harvard University Press, 1959–68. 10 Volumes.

Philo. *The Works of Philo: New Updated Edition*. Complete and Unabridged in One Volume. C. D. Yonge, tr.. Foreword, David M. Scholer. Peabody: Hendrickson, 1993.

Pieper, Francis. *Christian Dogmatics*. 4 Volumes. Saints Louis: Concordia, 1950–57.

Pinnock, Clark H. ed. *Grace Unlimited*. Minneapolis: Bethany, 1975.

Pinnock, Clark H. ed. *The Grace of God, the Will of Man: A Case for Arminianism*. Grand Rapids: Zondervan, 1989.

Piper, John. *The Justification of God: An Exegetical and Theological Study of Romans 9:1–23*. Grand Rapids: Baker Book House, 1983.

Piper, Otto. "Unchanging Promises: Exodus in the New Testament." *Interpretation* 11 (1957), 3–22.

Plag, Christoph. *Israels Wege zum Heil: Eine Untersuchung zu Römer 9–11*. Arbeiten zur Theologie. Stuttgart: Calwer, 1969.

Plantinga, Alvin. *God, Freedom and Evil*. London: Allen and Unwin, 1975.

Pogoloff, Stephen M. *Logos and Sophia: The Rhetorical Situation of 1 Corinthians*. Atlanta: Scholars Press, 1992.

Pope, William Burt. *A Compendium of Christian Theology*. 3 Volumes. New York: Phillips & Hunt, 1881.

Porter, Samuel. *A Discourse of the Decrees of God, and the Perseverance of the Saints, and Sinless Perfection*. Pittsburgh: Samuel Porter, 1793.

Porter, Stanley E. *Verbal Aspect in the Greek of the New Testament with Reference to Tense and Mood*. Studies in Biblical Greek. New York: Peter Lang, 1989.

Potter, Ray. *A Vindication of the Doctrine of the Final Perseverance of the Saints*. Pawtucket, RI: n.p., 1827.

Praamsma, Louis. "The Background of the Arminian Controversy (1586–1618)." In *Crisis in the Reformed Churches: Essays in Commemoration of the Great Synod of Dort, 1618–19*. Peter Y. De Jong, ed. Grand Rapids: Reformed Fellowship, Inc., 1968. 22–38.

Prassel, Richard C. "Atonement in Paul's Theology as a Key to His Understanding of Perseverance." Th.M. Thesis, Southern Baptist Theological Seminary, 1989.

Pratt, Dwight M. "Apostasy." In *International Standard Bible Encyclopedia*. Revised Edition. Geoffrey Bromiley, ed. Grand Rapids: Eerdmans, 1979. 1.192.

Prestige, George L. *Fathers and Heretics: Six Studies in Dogmatic Faith with Prologue and Epilogue*. Reprint. London: SPCK, 1977.

Preston, James J. "Expulsion." In *The Encyclopedia of Religion*. Mircea Eliade, ed. New York: Macmillan Publishing/London: Collier Macmillan Publishers, 1987. 5:233–36.

Prichard, Robert W. "Nineteenth Century Episcopal Attitudes on Predestination and Election." *Historical Magazine of the Protestant Episcopal Church* 51 (1982), 23–51.

Probst, Hermann. *Paul und der Brief: Die Rhetorik des antiken Briefes als Form der paulinischen Korintherkorrespondenz (1 Kor 8–10)*. Wissenschaftliche Untersuchungen zum Neuen Testament. Tübingen: J. C. B. Mohr (Paul Siebeck), 1991.

Quasten, Johannes. *Patrology*. 4 Volumes. Reprint. Angelo Di Berardino, ed. 4th Volume. Westminster, MD: Christian Classics, Inc. 1983–86.

Rahlston, Thomas N. *Elements of Divinity*. Nashville: A. H. Redford, 1974.

Rahner, Karl. *Foundations of Christian Faith: An Introduction to the Idea of Christianity*. New York: Crossroad, 1978.

Rahner, Karl. *Theological Investigations*. Volume 23: Final Writings. New York: Crossroad, 1992.

Räisänen, Heikki. *Paul and the Law*. Wissenschaftliche Untersuchungen zum Neuen Testament. Tübingen: J. C. B. Mohr (Paul Siebeck), 1983.

Ramsaran, Rollin A. *Liberating Words: Paul's Use of Rhetorical Maxims in 1 Corinthians 1–10*. Valley Forge: Trinity Press International, 1996.

Ready, Charles. *The Possibility of Apostasy*. Clifton, TX: Nichol Publishing Company, 1951.

Rengstorf, K. H. "γογγύζω, διαγογγύζω, γογγυσμός, γογγυστής." *TDNT* 1:728–37.

Rese, Martin. "Die Rettung der Juden Nach Römer 11." In *L'Apôtre Paul: Personnalité, Style et Conception du Ministére*. Bibliotheca Ephemeridum Theologicarum Lovaniensium. A. Vonhoye, ed. Leuven: Leuven University Press, 1986.

Rese, Martin. "Israel und Kirche in Römer 9." *New Testament Studies* 34 (1988), 208–17.

Resenfeld, Harald. "The Meaning of the Verb ἀρνέσθαι." *Coniectanea Neotestamentica* 11 (1947), 207–19.

Rice, George E. "Apostasy as a Motif and Its Effect on the Structure of Hebrews." *Andrews University Seminary Studies* 23 (1985), 29–35.

Rich, Gregory P. "Jonathan Edward's View of the Freedom Requisite for Moral Agency." In *Religions and Philosophy in the United States of America*. Arbeiten zur Amerikanistik. Peter Freese, ed. Essen: Die Blaue Eule, 1987. 2:641–55.

Ringgren, Helmer. *Israelite Religion*. Philadelphia: Fortress Press, 1966.

Ringgren, Helmer. *The Faith of Qumran*. Philadelphia: Fortress Press, 1963.

Robbins, Vernon K. *The Tapestry of Early Christian Discourse: Rhetoric, Society and Ideology*. London/New York: Routledge, 1996b.

Robbins, Vernon K. *Exploring the Texture of Texts: A Guide to Socio-Rhetorical Interpretation*. Valley Forge: Trinity Press International, 1996a.

Robinson, H. W. *Corporate Personality in Ancient Israel*. Philadelphia: Fortress Press, 1964.

Roetzel, Calvin J. "The Grammar of Election in Four Pauline Letters." In *Pauline Theology: Volume II: 1&2 Corinthians*. David M. Hay, ed. Minnesota: Fortress Press, 1993. 211–233.

Roetzel, Calvin J. *Judgement in the Community: A Study of the Relationship Between Eschatology and Ecclesiology in Paul*. Leiden: E. J. Brill, 1972.

Rogerson, J. W. "The Hebrew Conception of Corporate Personality: A Reexamination." *Journal of Theological Studies* 21 (1970), 1–16.

Rohrbaugh, Richard L. "'Social Location of Thought,' As a Heuristic Construct in New Testament Study." *Journal for the Study of the New Testament* 30 (1987), 103–119.

Röhser, G. *Prädestination und Verstockung: Untersuchungen zur frühjüdischen, paulinischen und johanneischen Theologie*. Tübingen: Francke, 1994.

Rosner, Brian S. "The Origin and Meaning of 1 Corinthians 6,9–11 in Context." *Biblische Zeitschrift* 40 (1996), 250–53.

Rosner, Brian S. *Paul, Scripture and Ethics: A Study of 1 Corinthinas 5–7.* Arbeiten Zur Geschichte Des Antiken Judentums Und Des Urchristentums. Leiden/New York/Köln: E. J. Brill, 1994.

Rosscup, James E. "The Overcomer of the Apocalypse." *Grace Theological Journal* 3 (1982), 261–86.

Rowland, Christopher. *The Open Heaven: A Study of Apocalyptic in Judaism and Early Christianity.* London: SPCK, 1982.

Rowley, H. H. *The Biblical Doctrine of Election.* London: Lutterworth Press, 1950.

Ruegg, Uli. "Paul et la Rhetorique Ancienne." *Bulletin du Centre Protestant d'Etudes* 35 (1983), 5–35.

Russell, D. S. *Divine Disclosure: An Introduction To Jewish Apocalyptic.* Minneapolis: Fortress Press, 1992.

Russell, D. S. *The Method and Message of Jewish Apocalyptic: 200 BC – AD 100.* The Old Testament Library. London: SCM Press, 1964.

Russell, D. S. *The Old Testament Pseudepigrapha: Patriarchs & Prophets in Early Judaism.* London: SCM Press, 1987.

Sabourin, Leopold. "The Biblical Cloud: Terminology and Traditions." *Biblical Theology Bulletin* 4 (1974), 290–311.

Sahlin, Harald. "Der neue Heilsexodus bei Paulus." *Judaica* 7 (1951), 121–136. "The New Exodus of Salvation according to St. Paul." In *The Root of the Vine: Essays in Biblical Theology.* Anton Fridrichsen and other members of Uppsala University. London: Dacre, 1953. 81–95.

Saloom, Ernest. "The Doctrine of Final Perseverance of the Saints." Th.D. Disseration, Southwestern Baptist Theological Seminary, 1946.

Sandelin, Karl-Gustav. "'Do not Be Idolaters!' (1 Cor 10:7)." In *Texts and Contexts: Biblical Texts in Their Textual and Situational Contexts, Essays in Honor of Lars Hartman.* David Hellholm and T. Fornberg, eds. Oslo: Scandinavian University Press, 1995. 257–73.

Sanders, E. P. *Paul and Palestinian Judaism: A Comparison of Patterns of Religion.* London: SCM Press, 1977.

Sanders, E. P. *Paul, the Law, and the Jewish People.* Philadelphia: Fortress, 1983.

Sanders, Jack T. "Paul Between Jews and Gentiles in Corinth." *Journal for the Study of the New Testament* 65 (1997), 67–83.

Sanders, Jack T. *Schismatics, Sectarians, Dissidents, Deviants: The First One Hundred Years of Jewish-Christian Relations.* London: SCM, 1993.

Sasse, Hermann. "αἰών, αἰώνιος." In *TDNT* 1:197–209.

Sato, Yoshiaki. "Martyrdom and Apostasy." In *Eusebius, Christianity, and Judaism.* Attridge, Harold W. and Hata, Gohei, eds. Detroit: Wayne State University Press, 1992. 619–34.

Schattenmann, Johannes. "μαίνομαι." In *NIDNTT* 1:528–29.

Schereschewsky, Ben-Zion. "Apostate." In *The Principles of Jewish Law.* Encyclopedia Judaica. Menachem Elon, ed. Jersusalem: Keter Publishing House Jerusalem LTD, 1975. 377–79.

Schleiermacher, Friedrich. *The Christian Faith.* Second Edition. H. R. Mackintosh and J. S. Stewart, eds. Edinburgh: T. & T. Clark, 1928.

Schlier, Heinrich. "ἀφίστεμι, ἀποστασία, διχοστασία." In *TDNT* 1:512–14.

Schmithals, Walter. *Gnosticism in Corinth: An Investigation of the Letters to the Corinthians.* Nashville/New York: Abingdom Press, 3rd ed. 1971.

Schnackenburg, Rudolf. *Baptism in the Thought of St. Paul.* Oxford: Basil Blackwell, 1964.

Schneider, B. "The Corporate Meaning and Background of 1 Cor 15,45b – O ESCHATOS ADAM EIS PNEUMA ZOIOPOIOUN." *Catholic Biblical Quarterly* 29 (1967), 450–67.

Schneider, Walter, and Brown, Colin. "πειρασμός." In *NIDNTT* 3:798–808.

Schoeps, H. J. *Paul: The Theology of the Apostle in the Light of Jewish Religious History.* London: Lutterworth Press, 1961.

Schrage, Wolfgang. *The Ethics of the New Testament.* Philadelphia: Fortress Press, 1988.

Schreiner, Thomas R. "Does Romans 9 Teach Individual Election unto Salvation?" In *The Grace of God, The Bondage of the Will: Volume 1 Biblical and practical Perspectives on Calvinism.* Thomas R. Schreiner and Bruce A. Ware, eds. Grand Rapids: Baker Book House, 1995. 89–106.

Schreiner, Thomas R. "Perseverance and Assurance: A Survey and a Proposal." *Southern Baptist Journal of Theology* 2 (1998), 32–62.

Schreiner, Thomas R., and Ware, Bruce A. eds. *The Grace of God, The Bondage of the Will: Volume 1 Biblical and practical Perspectives on Calvinism.* eds. Grand Rapids: Baker Book House, 1995.

Schreiner, Thomas R., and Ware, Bruce A. eds. *The Grace of God, The Bondage of the Will: Volume 2: Historical and Theological Perspectives on Calvinism.* Thomas R. Schreiner and Bruce A. Ware, eds. Grand Rapids: Baker Book House, 1995.

Schrenk, Gottlieb. "εὐδοκέω, εὐδοκία." In *TDNT* 2:738–51.

Schürer, Emil. *A History of the Jewish People In the Age of Jesus Christ (175 B. C. – A. D. 135).* Revised Edition. Geza Vermes, Fergus Millar, Martin Goodman, eds. Edinburgh: T. & T. Clark, 1986. Volume 3.1.

Schweitzer, Eduard. "Traditional Ethical Pattern in the Pauline and Post-Pauling Letters and their Development (Lists of Vices and House-Tables)." In *Text and Interpretation: Studies in the New Testament Presented to Matthew Black.* Ernest Best and R. McL. Wilson, eds. Cambridge: Cambridge University Press, 1979. 195–209.

Scott, James M. "Paul's Use of Deuteronomic Tradition." *Journal of Biblical Literature* 112 (1993), 645–665.

Scott, James M. "Restoration of Israel." In *Dictionary of Paul and His Letters.* Gerald F. Hawthorne, Ralph P. Martin, Daniel G. Ried, eds. Downers Grove, IL/Leicester: InterVarsity Press, 1993. 800–805.

Seeseman, Heinrich. "πεῖρα, πειράω, πειράζω, πειρασμός, ἀπείραστος, ἐκπειράζω." In *TDNT* 6:23–36.

Segal, Alan F. *Paul the Convert: The Apostolate and Apostasy of Saul the Pharisee.* New Haven and London: Yale University Press, 1990.

Sell, Alan P. F. *The Great Debate: Calvinism, Arminianism and Salvation.* Grand Rapids: Baker Book House, 1983.

Sellers, C. Norman. An Analysis and Evaluation of the Writings of Robert Shank in the Light of the New Testament Doctrines of Election and Perseverance." Th.D. Dissertation, Grace Theological Seminary, 1977.

Sellers, C. Norman. *Election and Perseverance.* College Studies Series. Miami Springs: Schoettle Publishing Co., 1987.

Sellin, Gerhard. *Der Streit um die Auferstehung der Toten: Eine religionsgeschichtliche und exegetische Untersuchung von 1 Korinther 15.* Forschungen zur Religion und Literatur des Alten und Neuen Testaments. Göttingen: Vanderhoeck & Ruprecht, 1986.

Shank, Robert. *Elect in the Son.* Springfield: Westcott, 1970.

Shank, Robert. *Life in the Son.* Second Edition. Springfield: Westcott, 1961.

Shedd, William G. T. Dogmatic Theology. 3 Volumes. Grand Rapids: Zondervan, 1969.

Silva, Moisés. "Old Testament in Paul." In *Dictionary of Paul and His Letters.* Gerald F. Hawthorne, Ralph P. Martin, Daniel G. Ried, eds. Downers Grove, IL/Leicester: InterVarsity Press, 1993. 630–42.

Simon, Marcel. "From Greek Hairesis to Christian Heresy." In *Early Christian Literature and the Classical Intellectual Tradition: In Honorem Robert M. Grant.* William R. Schoedel and Robert L. Wilkin, eds. Paris: Éditions Beauchesne, 1979. 101–116.

Sinnema, Donald W. "The Issue of Reprobation at the Synod of Dort (1618–19) in the Light of the History of This Doctrine." Ph.D. Thesis, University of St. Michael's College, 1985.

Sjöberg, Erik. *Gott und die Sünder im Palästinischen Judentum.* Stuttgart: Kohlhammer, 1938.

Smiles, Vincent M. *The Gospel and the Law in Galatia: Paul's Response to Jewish-Christian Separation and the Threat of Galatian Apostasy.* Collegeville, MN: Liturgical Press, 1998.

Smit, J. "'Do Not Be Idolaters': Paul's Rhetoric in First Corinthians 10:1–22." *Novum Testamentum* 39 (1997), 40–53.

Smit, J. "1 Cor 8,1–6: A Rhetorical Partitio: A Contribution to the Coherence of 1 Cor 8,1–11,1." In *The Corinthian Correspondence.* R. Bieringer, ed. Leuven: Leuven University Press, 1996. 577–91.

Smith, Dennis E. "Meals and Morality in Paul and his World." Society of Biblical Literature Seminar Papers. Kent Harold Richard, ed. (1981), 319–339.

Smith, Dennis E. "The Messianic Banquet Reconsidered." In *The Future of Early Christianity: Essays in Honor of Helmut Koester.* Birger A. Pearson, ed. Minneapolis: Fortress, 1991. 64–73.

Smith, John Clarke. "Calvin: Unbelief in the Elect." *Evangelical Quarterly* 54 (1982), 14–24.

Smith, Mark S. *The Pilgrimage Pattern in Exodus.* Journal for the Society of the Old Testament Supplement Series. Sheffield: Sheffield Academic Press, 1997.

Snaith, Norman H. *The Distinctive Ideas of the Old Testament.* London: Epworth, 1945.

Snodgrass, Klyne. "The Use of the Old Testament in the New." In *New Testament Criticism and Interpretation.* David Alan Black and David S. Dockery, eds. Grand Rapids: Zondervan/Academie and Professional Books, 1991. 409–434.

Soards, Marion L. "Paul: Apostle and Apocalyptic Visionary." *Biblical Theology Bulletin* 16 (1986), 148–150.

Songer, Harold S. "Problems Arising from the Worship of Idols: 1 Corinthians 8:1–11:1." *Review and Expositor* 80 (1983), 363–75.

Spencer, John R. "Golden Calf." In *The Anchor Bible Dictionary.* David Noel Freedman, ed. New York/London/Toronto/Sydney/Auckland, 1992. 2:1065–69.

Stambaugh, John E. and Balch, David L. *The New Testament in Its Social Environment.* Library of Early Christianity. Philadelphia: The Westminster Press, 1986.

Starbuck, Edwin D. "Backsliding." In *Encyclopaedia of Religion and Ethics.* James Hastings, ed. Edinburgh: T. & T. Clark, 1908. 2:319–21.

Steele, Daniel. *A Substitute for Holiness.* Chicago: The Christian Witness Company, 1899.

Stegemann, Wolfgang. "Paul and the Sexual Mentality of His World." *Biblical Theological Bulletin* 23 (1993), 161–66.

Stendahl, Krister. "The Called and the Chosen: An Essay on Election." In *The Root of the Vine: Essays in Biblical Theology*. Anton Fridrichsen and other members of Uppsala University. London: Dacre, 1953. 63–80.

Stoeffler, F. Ernest. "The Wesleyan Concept of Religious Certainty – Its Pre-History and Significance." *London Quarterly & Holborn Review* (1965), 128–39.

Stone, Michael Edward. *Features of the Eschatology of IV Ezra*. Harvard Semitic Studies. Atlanta: Scholars Press, 1989.

Strack, H. L. *Introduction to the Talmud and Midrash*. Cleveland: World, 1963.

Strong, Augustus H. *Systematic Theology*. Westwood, NJ: Revell, 1907.

Stuhlmacher, Peter. "Erwägungen zum Problem von Gegenwart und Zukunft in der paulinischen Eschatologie." *Zeitschrift für Theologie und Kirche* 64 (1967), 423–450.

Suggit, J. N. "The Eucharist as Eschatological Proclamation, according to St. Paul." *Neotestamentica* 21 (1987), 11–24.

Sundell, Dennis D. "A Study of the Seven Penitential Psalms as Related to David's Apostasy." M. Div. Thesis, Concordia Theological Seminary (Ft. Wayne), 1983.

Swartley, Willard M. *Israel's Scripture Traditions and the Synoptic Gospels: Story Shaping Story*. Peabody, MA: Hendrickson, 1994.

Sweet, J. P. M. "Maintaining the Testimony of Jesus: The Suffering of Christians in the Revelation of John." In *Suffering and Martyrdom in the New Testament: Studies presented to G. M. Styler by the Cambridge New Testament Seminar*. William Horbury and Brian McNeil, eds. Cambridge, UK: Cambridge University Press, 1981. 101–117.

Synofzik, Ernst. *Die Gerichts- und Vergeltungsaussagen bei Paulus: Eine traditionsgeschichtliche Untersuchung*. Göttinger Theologische Arbeiten. Göttingen: Vandenhoeck & Ruprecht, 1977.

Talmon, Shemaryahu. "The 'Desert Motif' in the Bible and in Qumran Literature." In *Biblical Motifs: Origins and Transformations*. Alexander Altmann, ed. Philip W. Lown Institute of Advanced Judaic Studies – Studies and Texts 3. Cambridge, MA: Harvard University Press, 1966. 31–63.

Tambasco, Anthony J. *In the Days of Paul: The Social World and Teaching of the Apostle*. New York: Paulist Press, 1991.

Tanca, R. "La defezione dei discepoli di Gesù (Io. 6,66) nella tradizione patristica." *Studi e materiali di storia delle religioni* 8 (1984), 139–46.

Thackeray, Henry St. John. *The Relation of St. Paul to Contemporary Jewish Thought*. London/New York: Macmillan and Co., 1900.

Theissen, Gerd. *Psychological Aspects of Pauline Theology*. Philadelphia: Fortress Press, 1987.

Theissen, Gerd. *The Social Setting Of Pauline Christianity*. Minneapolis: Fortress Press/ T. & T. Clark: Edinburgh, 1982.

Thiel, W. "Zum Bundbrechen im AT." *Vetus Testamentum* 20 (1970), 214–229.

Thiessen, Henry Clarence. *Introductory Lectures in Systematic Theology*. Grand Rapdis: Eerdmans, 1949.

Thiselton, Anthony J. "Realized Eschatology at Corinth." *New Testament Studies* 24 (1977–78), 510–526.

Thiselton, Anthony J. "The Meaning of ΣΑΡΞ in 1 Corinthians 5:5: A Fresh Approach in the Light of Logical and Semanitc Factors." *Scottish Journal of Theology* 26 (1973), 204–228.

Thomas Aquinas. *Summa Contra Gentiles.* 4 Volumes. Translation, introduction and notes by A. C. Pegis, J. F. Anderson, V. J. Bourke, and C. J. O'Neil. Nortre Dame: University of Nortre Dame Press, 1975.

Thomas Aquinas. *Summa Theologica.* 2 Volumes. Translation by the Fathers of the English Dominican Province. Revised by Daniel J. Sullivan. Great Western Books of the World. Chicago/London/Toronto: Encyclopaedia Britannica, 1952.

Thomson, Ian H. *Chiasmus in the Pauline Letters.* Sheffield: Sheffield Academic Press, 1996.

Tipson, Baird. "A Dark Side of Seventeenth-Century English Protestantism: The Sin Against the Holy Spirit." *Harvard Theological Review* 77 (1984), 301–30.

Tomson, Peter J. *Paul and the Jewish Law: Halakha in the Letters of the Apostle to the Gentiles.* Compendia Rerum Iudaicarum ad Novum Testamentum (Section III): Jewish Traditions in Early Christian Literature. Assen/Maastricht: Van Gorcum/Minneapolis: Fortress Press, 1990.

Toussaint, Stanley D. "The Eschatology of the Warning Passages in the Book of Hebrews." *Grace Theological Journal* 3 (1982), 67–80.

Turner, Edith. "Pilgrimage: An Overview." In *The Encyclopedia of Religion.* Mircea Eliade, ed. New York: Macmillan Publishing/London: Collier Macmillan Publishers, 1987. 11:327–30.

Turner, Victor and Turner, Edith. *Image and Pilgrimage in Christian Culture: Anthropological Perspectives.* Oxford: Basil Blackwell, 1978.

Turner, Victor. "Liminality, Kabbalah, and the Media," *Religion* 15 (1985), 205–18.

Turner, Victor. "The Center Out There: Pilgrim's Goal." *History of Religions* 12 (1973), 191–230.

Turner, Victor. *Dramas, Fields, and Metaphors: Symbolic Action in Human Society.* Ithaca/London: Cornell University Press, 1974.

Turner, Victor. *Process, Performance and Pilgrimage: A Study in Comparative Symbology.* Ranchi Anthropology Series 1. New Delhi: Concept Publishing, 1979.

Turner, Victor. *The Drums of Affliction: A Study of Religious Processes among the Ndembu of Zambia.* Oxford: Clarendon Press/The International African Institute, 1968.

Turner, Victor. *The Forest of Symbols: Aspects of Ndembu Ritual.* Ithaca/New York: Cornell University Press, 1967.

Turner, Victor. *The Ritual Process: Structure and Anti-Structure.* Symbol, Myth, and Ritual Series. Ithaca, NY: Cornell Paperbacks. Cornell University Press, 1969.

Van Hove, A. "Apostasy." In *The Catholic Encyclopedia: An International Work of Reference on the Constitution, Doctrine, Discipline, and History of the Catholic Church* , Charles G. Herbermann, Edward A. Pace, C. B. Pallen, Thomas J. Shahan, John J. Wynne, eds. New York: The Encyclopedia Press, 1913. 1:624–626.

Van Ruiten, J. T. A. G. M. "The Use of Deuteronomy 32:39 in Monotheistic Controversies in Rabbinic Literature." In *Studies in Deuteronomy: In Honour of C. J. Labuschagne on the occasion of his 65th birthday.* F. García Martínez, A. Hilhorst, J. T. A. G. M. Van Ruiten, A. S. Van Der Woude, eds. Supplements to Vetus Testamentum 53. Leider/New York/Köln: E. J. Brill, 1994. 223–241.

Vielhauer, Philipp. "Introduction [to Apocalypses and Related Subjects]." In *New Testament Apocrypha.* E. Hennecke, W. Schneemelcher, eds. Philadelphia: Westminster, 1963–65. 2:581–607.

Vodola, Elisabeth. *Excommunication in the Middle Ages.* Berkeley: University of California Press, 1986.

Von Rad, Gerhard. *Old Testament Theology: The Theology of Israel's Historical Traditions*. Edinburgh/London: Oliver & Boyd, 1962. Volume 1.

Von Soden, Hans. "Sakrament Und Ethik Bei Paulus: Zur Frage der Literarischen und Theologischen Einheitlichkeit von 1 Kor. 8–10." In *Urchristentum und Geschichte*. Hans Von Campenhausen, ed. Tübingen: J. C. B. Mohr (Paul Siebeck), 1951. 239–75.

Von Wahlde, Urban C. "Community in Conflict: The History and Social Context of the Johannine Community." *Interpretation* 49 no. 4 (1995), 379–89.

Vranik, Barbara. "The Roots of Apostasy in the Northern Kingdom." M. A. Thesis, Trinity Evangelical Divinity School, 1993.

Vriezen, Theodorus C. *The Religion of Ancient Israel*. Philadelphia: Westminster Press, 1963.

Waetjen, Herman C. *A Reordering of Power: A Socio-Political Reading of Mark's Gospel*. Minneapolis: Fortress, 1989.

Wakefield, Gordon. "Arminianism in the Seventeenth and Eighteenth Centuries." *London Quarterly and Holborn Review* 185 (1960), 253–58.

Walter, Nikolaus. "Christusglaube und Heidnische Religiosität in Paulinischen Gemeinden." *New Testament Studies* 25 (1978–79), 422–42.

Walter, Nikolaus. "Zur Interpretation von Römer 9–11." *Zeitschrift für Theologie und Kirche* 81 (1984), 172–95.

Waltke, Bruce K. "The Phenomenon of Conditionality within Unconditional Covenants." In *Israel's Apostasy and Restoration: Essays in Honor of Roland K. Harrison*. Avraham Gileadi, ed. Grand Rapids: Baker Book House,1988. 123–39.

Ware, Timothy. *The Orthodox Church*. Revised. Harmondsworth, Middlesex: Penguins Books, 1972.

Warren, William Leon. "Apostasy in the Book of Revelation." Ph.D. Thesis, Southern Baptist Theological Seminary, 1983.

Watkins, Oscar Daniel. *A History of Penance: Being a Study of Authorities*. Reprint. New York: B. Franklin, 1961

Watson, Duane F. "1 Corinthians 10:23–11:1 in the Light of Greco-Roman Rhetoric: The Role of Rhetorical Questions." *Journal of Biblical Literature* 108 (1989), 301–318.

Watson, Duane F. *Invention, Arrangement, and Style: Rhetorical Criticism of Jude and 2 Peter*. Society of Biblical Literature Dissertation Series. Atlanta: Scholars Press, 1988a.

Watson, Duane F. "Rhetorical Criticism." In *Dictionary of Jesus and the Gospels*, Joel B. Green, Scot McKnight, I. Howard Marshall, eds. Downers Grove, IL/Leicester: InterVarsity Press, 1992. 698–701.

Watson, Duane F. "A Rhetorical Analysis of Philippians and Its Implications for the Unity Question." *Novum Testamentum* 30 (1988b), 57–88.

Watson, Duane F. "Rhetorical Criticism of the Pauline Epistles since 1975." *Currents in Research: Biblical Studies* 3 (1995), 219–248.

Watson, Francis. "The Two Roman Congregations: Romans 14:1–15:13." In *The Romans Debate*. Revised and Expanded Edition. Karl P. Donfried, ed. Peabody, MA: Hendrickson, 1991. 203–215.

Watson, Nigel M. "Justified by Faith: Judged by Works – An Antimony?" *New Testament Studies* 29 (1983), 209–221.

Watson, Thomas. *A Body of Divinity*. London: Reprint. London: The Banner of Truth Trust, 1965.

Watts, Rikki E. *Isaiah's New Exodus and Mark*. Wissenschaftliche Untersuchungen zum Neuen Testament. Tübingen: J. C. B. Mohr (Paul Siebeck), 1997.

Wedderburn, A. J. M. "The Body of Christ And Related Concepts In 1 Corinthians." *Scottish Journal of Theology* 24 (1971), 74–97.

Wedderburn, A. J. M. *Baptism and Resurrection: Studies in Pauline Theology against its Greco-Roman Background.* Wissenschaftliche Untersuchungen zum Neuen Testament. Tübingen: J. C. B. Mohr (Paul Siebeck), 1987.

Weinfeld, M. "בְּרִית‎ bᵉrîth." In *TDOT* 2:253–79.

Welborn, L. L. *Politics and Rhetoric in the Corinthian Epistles.* Macon: Mercer University Press, 1997.

Wendebourg, Dorothea. "Das Martyrium in der Alten Kirchen als ethisches Problem." *Zeitschrift für Kirchengeschichte* 98 (1987), 295–320.

Wenham, David. "Whatever Went Wrong in Corinth?" *Expository Times* 108 (Feb. 1997), 137–141.

Wenham, David. "A Note on Matthew 24:10–12." *Tyndale Bulletin* 31 (1980), 155–162.

Wesley, John. *The Letters of the Reverend John Wesley, A. M.: Sometime Fellow of Lincoln College, Oxford.* John Telford, ed. Reprinted Standard Edition. London: The Epworth Press, J. Alfred Sharp. 1931. 3:295–331.

Wesley, John. *The Works of John Wesley.* 14 Volumes. T. Jackson, ed. Reprint. Grand Rapids: Zondervan, 1958–59.

Westblade, Donald J. "Divine Election in the Pauline Literature." In *The Grace of God, The Bondage of the Will: Volume 1 Biblical and practical Perspectives on Calvinism.* Thomas R. Schreiner and Bruce A. Ware, eds. Grand Rapids: Baker Book House, 1995. 63–87.

Whisenand, Gary D. "Perseverance in II Peter." Th.M. Thesis, Talbot Theological Seminary, 1985.

White, R. E. O. "Perseverance." In *Evangelical Dictionary of Theology.* Walter Elwell, ed. Grand Rapids: Baker Book House, 1984. 844–45.

White, R. E. O. *The Biblical Doctrine of Initiation.* London: Hodder & Stoughton, 1960.

White, William. *Comparative Views of the Controversy between the Calvinists and the Arminians.* 2 Volumes. Philadelphia: M. Thomas, 1817.

Whitefield, George. *Whitefield's Journals.* Reprint. London: The Banner of Truth Trust, 1960.

Whitlock, Luder G. "Apostasy." In *Evangelical Dictionary of Theology,* Walter Elwell, ed. Grand Rapids: Baker Book House, 1984. 70.

Wibbling, Siegfried. *Die Tugend und Lasterkataloge im Neuen Testament.* Berlin: A. Töpelmann, 1959.

Wiebe, Willi. "Die Wüstenzeit als Typus der messianischen Heilszeit." Ph.D. Thesis, Göttingen University, 1939.

Wiley, H. Orton. *Christian Theology.* 3 Volumes. Kansas City, MO: Beacon Hill Press, 1940–49.

Wilk, Florian. *Die Bedeutung des Jesajabuches für Paulus.* Forschungen zur Religion und Literatur des Alten und Neuen Testaments. Göttingen: Vandenhoeck & Ruprecht, 1998.

Wilkin, Robert Nicholas. "An Exegetical Evaluation of the Reformed Doctrine of the Perseverance of the Saints." Th.M. Thesis, Dallas Theological Seminary, 1982.

William of Ockham. *Predestination, God's Foreknowledge, and Future Contigents.* Marylin McCord Adams and Norman Kretzman, translators with introduction and appendices. Indianapolis: Hackett, 1983.

Williams, Ernest. *Systematic Theology.* 3 Volumes. Springfield: Gospel Publishing House, 1953.

Williams, J. Rodman. *Renewal Theology.* 3 Volumes. Grand Rapids: Zondervan, 1988–92.

Williamson, Ronald. *Philo and the Epistle to the Hebrews*. Arbeiten zur Literatur und Geschichte des hellenistischen Judentums. E. J. Brill: Leiden, 1970.

Willis, Lawrence. "The Form of the Sermon in Hellenistic Judaism and Early Christianity." *Harvard Theological Review* 77 (1984), 277–99.

Willis, Wendell Lee. *Idol Meat In Corinth: The Pauline Argument in 1 Corinthians 8 and 10*. Society Of Biblical Literature Dissertation Series. Chico, CA: Scholars Press, 1985.

Willoughby, Harold R. *Pagan Regeneration: A Study of Mystery Initiations in the Graeco-Roman World*. Chicago: University of Chicago Press, 1960.

Wilson, Robert R. "This World – and the World to Come: Apocalyptic Religion and the Counterculture." *Encounter* 38 (1977), 117–24.

Wimbush, Vincent L. *Paul the Worldly Ascetic: Response to the World and Self-Understanding according to 1 Corinthians 7*. Macon, GA: Mercer University Press, 1987.

Windisch, Hans. *Taufe und Sünde im ältesten Christentum bis auf Origenes*. Tübingen: Mohr, 1908.

Winter, Bruce W. "Theological and Ethical Responses to Religious Pluralism – 1 Corinthians 8–10." *Tyndale Bulletin* 41.2 (1990), 209–226.

Wire, Antoinette Clark. *The Corinthian Women Prophets: A Reconstruction through Paul's Rhetoric*. Minneapolis: Augsburg Fortress, 1990.

Witherington, Ben. "Not So Idle Thoughts About *Eidolothuton*." *Tyndale Bulletin* 44.2 (1993). 237–54.

Witherington, Ben. *Jesus, Paul and the End of the World: A Comparative Study in New Testament Eschatology*. Exeter: The Paternoster Press, 1992.

Witherington, Ben. *Paul's Narrative Thought World: The Tapestry of Tragedy and Triumph*. Louisville: Westminster/John Knox Press, 1994.

Wolterstorff, Nicholas. "The Assurance of Faith." *Faith and Philosophy* 7 (1990), 396–417.

Worman, J. H. "Perseverance." In *Cyclopaedia of Biblical, Theological, and Ecclesiastical Literature*. John McLintock & James Strong, eds. New York: Harper & Brothers, 1874. 3:973–75

Wright, David P. *The Disposal of Impurity: Elimination Rites in the Bible and in Hittite and Mesopotamian Literature*. Society of Biblical Literature Dissertation Series. Atlanta: Scholars Press, 1987.

Wright, N. T. "One God, One Lord, One People: Incarnational Christology for Church in a Pagan Environment." *Ex Auditu* 7 (1991), 45–58.

Wright, N. T. *The Climax of the Covenant: Christ and the Law in Pauline Theology*. Edinburgh: T. & T. Clark, 1991.

Wuellner, Wilhelm H. "Der vorchristliche Paulus und die Rhetorik." In *Tempelkult und Tempelzerstörung (70 n. Chr): Festschrift für Clemens Thoma zum 60. Geburstag*. S. Lauer und H. Ernst, eds. Bern: Peter Lang, 1995. 133–65.

Wuellner, Wilhelm H. "Paul as Pastor: The Function of Rhetorical Questions in First Corinthians." In *L'Apôtre Paul: Personnalité, Style et Conception du Ministère*. A. Vanhoye, ed. Leuven: Leuven University Press, 1986. 49–77.

Yamauchi, Edwin. *Pre-Christian Gnosticism: A Survey of the Proposed Evidence*. London: Tyndale Press, 1973.

Yarbro Collins, Adela. "The Function of Excommunication in Paul." *Harvard Theological Review* 73 (1980), 251–63.

Yates, A. S. *The Doctrine of Assurance: With Special Reference to John Wesley*. London: Epworth, 1952.

Yeo, Khiok-Khng. *Rhetorical Interaction in 1 Corinthians 8 and 10: A Formal Analysis with Preliminary Suggestions for a Chinese, Cross-Cultural Hermeneutic*. Biblical Interpretation Series. Leiden/New York/Köln: E. J. Brill, 1995.

Yorke, Gosnell L.O.R. *The Church as the Body of Christ in Pauline Corpus: A Re-examination*. Lanham, MD/New York/London: University Press of America, 1991.

Young, Frances. "Typology." In *Crossing the Boundaries: Essays in Biblical Interpretation in Honour of Michael D. Goulder*. Stanley E. Porter, Paul Joyce, and David E. Orton, eds. Biblical Interpretation Series 8. Leiden/New York/Köln: E. J. Brill, 1994. 29–48.

Zaas, Peter S. "Catalogues and Context: 1 Corinthians 5 and 6." *New Testament Studies* 34 (1988), 622–629.

Zeitlin, S. "Mumar and Meshumad." *Jewish Quarterly Review* (July, 1963) 84–86.

Zuntz, G. *The Text of the Epistles: A Disquisition upon the Corpus Paulinum*. London/ Oxford: Oxford University Press, 1953.

Zwemer, Samuel M. *The Law of Apostasy in Islam*. London/New York: Marshall Brothers, 1924.

References

Old Testament (with Apocrypha)

Pseudepigrapha

Qumran Literature

Philo and Josephus

Tannaitic, Mishnaic, and Related Literature

New Testament

References

Early Christian Literature

10.2–4   5

Tertullian

On Repentance
7   5

On the Soul
9   181

De Praescriptione Haereticorum
3   6
40   6

Thomas Aquinas

Summa Theologica
Ia IIae Q. 109 Art. 10 11
Ia IIae Q. 114 Art. 9   11
IIa IIae Q. 12 Art. 1–2 11
IIa IIae Q. 12 Art. 3f 11

Classical, Hellenistic, and other Ancient Writings & Inscriptions

Aristotle

Rhetoric
3.1.1358a   35

Athenaeus

Deipnosophistae
571c–74e   145

Catallus

Poems
63   81

Corpus Hermeticum
1.4.4   80

Corpus Inscriptionum Latinarum
6.510   80

Dio Chrysostom

Orationes
34.40   205
39.5   98

Diogenes Laertius

7.166   202
7.37   202

Epictetus

Dissertationes
2.10:4–5   98

Greek Magical Papyri
2.114   89
5.108–18   88
13.343–44   89
13.1077   89

Isocrates

Panegyricus
28–29   80

Juvenal

Satires
2.79ff   162
6.314–41   81
6.474–541   81
6.316–19   106
6.314–41   164

Livy

History
2.32   98

Orphicorum Fragmenta
232   79

P. Oxy.
926   65

P. Köln
57   65

P. Yale
85   65

P. Oslo
157   65

Pausanius

Description of Greece
2.7.5f   81
9.39:5   80

Pliny (the elder)

Natural History
30.11   88

Pliny (the younger)

Epistles
10.96   7

Plutarch

How to Study Poetry
22F   80

Moralia
267B   81
479B   206, 224

Polybius
5.111   201
24.9.6   202

Seneca

De Clementia
1.51   98

Strabo

Geography
8.6.20   145

Authors

Subjects

Wissenschaftliche Untersuchungen zum Neuen Testament

Alphabetical Index of the First and Second Series

Ådna, Jostein: Jesu Stellung zum Tempel. 2000. *Volume II/119.*

Anderson, Paul N.: The Christology of the Fourth Gospel. 1996. *Volume II/78.*

Appold, Mark L.: The Oneness Motif in the Fourth Gospel. 1976. *Volume II/1.*

Arnold, Clinton E.: The Colossian Syncretism. 1995. *Volume II/77.*

Avemarie, Friedrich und *Hermann Lichtenberger* (Ed.): Bund und Tora. 1996. *Volume 92.*

Bachmann, Michael: Sünder oder Übertreter. 1992. *Volume 59.*

Baker, William R.: Personal Speech-Ethics in the Epistle of James. 1995. *Volume II/68.*

Balla, Peter: Challenges to New Testament Theology. 1997. *Volume II/95.*

Bammel, Ernst: Judaica. Volume I 1986. *Volume 37* – Volume II 1997. *Volume 91.*

Bash, Anthony: Ambassadors for Christ. 1997. *Volume II/92.*

Bauernfeind, Otto: Kommentar und Studien zur Apostelgeschichte. 1980. *Volume 22.*

Bayer, Hans Friedrich: Jesus' Predictions of Vindication and Resurrection. 1986. *Volume II/20.*

Bell, Richard H.: Provoked to Jealousy. 1994. *Volume II/63.*

– No One Seeks for God. 1998. *Volume 106.*

Bergman, Jan: see *Kieffer, René*

Bergmeier, Roland: Das Gesetz im Römerbrief und andere Studien zum Neuen Testament. 2000. *Volume 121.*

Betz, Otto: Jesus, der Messias Israels. 1987. *Volume 42.*

– Jesus, der Herr der Kirche. 1990. *Volume 52.*

Beyschlag, Karlmann: Simon Magus und die christliche Gnosis. 1974. *Volume 16.*

Bittner, Wolfgang J.: Jesu Zeichen im Johannesevangelium. 1987. *Volume II/26.*

Bjerkelund, Carl J.: Tauta Egeneto. 1987. *Volume 40.*

Blackburn, Barry Lee: Theios Aner and the Markan Miracle Traditions. 1991. *Volume II/40.*

Bock, Darrell L.: Blasphemy and Exaltation in Judaism and the Final Examination of Jesus. 1998. *Volume II/106.*

Bockmuehl, Markus N.A.: Revelation and Mystery in Ancient Judaism and Pauline Christianity. 1990. *Volume II/36.*

Böhlig, Alexander: Gnosis und Synkretismus. Teil 1 1989. *Volume 47* –Teil 2 1989. *Volume 48.*

Böhm, Martina: Samarien und die Samaritai bei Lukas. 1999. *Volume II/111.*

Böttrich, Christfried: Weltweisheit – Menschheitsethik – Urkult. 1992. *Volume II/50.*

Bolyki, János: Jesu Tischgemeinschaften. 1997. *Volume II/96.*

Büchli, Jörg: Der Poimandres – ein paganisiertes Evangelium. 1987. *Volume II/27.*

Bühner, Jan A.: Der Gesandte und sein Weg im 4. Evangelium. 1977. *Volume II/2.*

Burchard, Christoph: Untersuchungen zu Joseph und Aseneth. 1965. *Volume 8.*

– Studien zur Theologie, Sprache und Umwelt des Neuen Testaments. Ed. by D. Sänger. 1998. *Volume 107.*

Byrskog, Samuel: Story as History – History as Story. 2000. *Volume 123.*

Cancik, Hubert (Ed.): Markus-Philologie. 1984. *Volume 33.*

Capes, David B.: Old Testament Yaweh Texts in Paul's Christology. 1992. *Volume II/47.*

Caragounis, Chrys C.: The Son of Man. 1986. *Volume 38.*

– see *Fridrichsen, Anton.*

Carleton Paget, James: The Epistle of Barnabas. 1994. *Volume II/64.*

Ciampa, Roy E.: The Presence and Function of Scripture in Galatians 1 and 2. 1998. *Volume II/102.*

Crump, David: Jesus the Intercessor. 1992. *Volume II/49.*

Deines, Roland: Jüdische Steingefäße und pharisäische Frömmigkeit. 1993. *Volume II/52.*

– Die Pharisäer. 1997. *Volume 101.*

Dietzfelbinger, Christian: Der Abschied des Kommenden. 1997. *Volume 95.*

Dobbeler, Axel von: Glaube als Teilhabe. 1987. *Volume II/22.*

Du Toit, David S.: Theios Anthropos. 1997. *Volume II/91*

Dunn, James D.G. (Ed.): Jews and Christians. 1992. *Volume 66.*

– Paul and the Mosaic Law. 1996. *Volume 89.*

Ebertz, Michael N.: Das Charisma des Gekreuzigten. 1987. *Volume 45.*

Eckstein, Hans-Joachim: Der Begriff Syneidesis bei Paulus. 1983. *Volume II/10.*

– Verheißung und Gesetz. 1996. *Volume 86.*

Ego, Beate: Im Himmel wie auf Erden. 1989. *Volume II/34*

Ego, Beate und *Lange, Armin* sowie *Pilhofer, Peter (Ed.):* Gemeinde ohne Tempel – Community without Temple. 1999. *Volume 118.*

Eisen, Ute E.: see *Paulsen, Henning.*

Ellis, E. Earle: Prophecy and Hermeneutic in Early Christianity. 1978. *Volume 18.*

– The Old Testament in Early Christianity. 1991. *Volume 54.*

Ennulat, Andreas: Die ‚Minor Agreements‘. 1994. *Volume II/62.*

Ensor, Peter W.: Jesus and His ‚Works‘. 1996. *Volume II/85.*

Eskola, Timo: Theodicy and Predestination in Pauline Soteriology. 1998. *Volume II/100.*

Feldmeier, Reinhard: Die Krisis des Gottessohnes. 1987. *Volume II/21.*

– Die Christen als Fremde. 1992. *Volume 64.*

Feldmeier, Reinhard und *Ulrich Heckel* (Ed.): Die Heiden. 1994. *Volume 70.*

Fletcher-Louis, Crispin H.T.: Luke-Acts: Angels, Christology and Soteriology. 1997. *Volume II/94.*

Förster, Niclas: Marcus Magus. 1999. *Volume 114.*

Forbes, Christopher Brian: Prophecy and Inspired Speech in Early Christianity and its Hellenistic Environment. 1995. *Volume II/75.*

Fornberg, Tord: see *Fridrichsen, Anton.*

Fossum, Jarl E.: The Name of God and the Angel of the Lord. 1985. *Volume 36.*

Frenschkowski, Marco: Offenbarung und Epiphanie. Volume 1 1995. *Volume II/79*

– Volume 2 1997. *Volume II/80.*

Frey, Jörg: Eugen Drewermann und die biblische Exegese. 1995. *Volume II/71.*

– Die johanneische Eschatologie. Band I. 1997. *Volume 96.* – Band II. 1998. *Volume 110.* – Band III. 2000. *Volume 117.*

Freyne, Sean: Galilee and Gospel. 2000. *Volume 125.*

Fridrichsen, Anton: Exegetical Writings. Ed. von C.C. Caragounis und T. Fornberg. 1994. *Volume 76.*

Garlington, Don B.: ‚The Obedience of Faith‘. 1991. *Volume II/38.*

– Faith, Obedience, and Perseverance. 1994. *Volume 79.*

Garnet, Paul: Salvation and Atonement in the Qumran Scrolls. 1977. *Volume II/3.*

Gese, Michael: Das Vermächtnis des Apostels. 1997. *Volume II/99.*

Gräbe, Petrus J.: The Power of God in Paul's Letters. 2000. *Volume II/123.*

Gräßer, Erich: Der Alte Bund im Neuen. 1985. *Volume 35.*

Green, Joel B.: The Death of Jesus. 1988. *Volume II/33.*

Gundry Volf, Judith M.: Paul and Perseverance. 1990. *Volume II/37.*

Hafemann, Scott J.: Suffering and the Spirit. 1986. *Volume II/19.*

– Paul, Moses, and the History of Israel. 1995. *Volume 81.*

Hamid-Khani, Saeed: Relevation and Concealment of Christ. 2000. *Volume II/120.*

Hannah, Darrel D.: Michael and Christ. 1999. *Volume II/109.*

Hartman, Lars: Text-Centered New Testament Studies. Ed. by D. Hellholm. 1997. *Volume 102.*

Heckel, Theo K.: Der Innere Mensch. 1993. *Volume II/53.*

– Vom Evangelium des Markus zum viergestaltigen Evangelium. 1999. *Volume 120.*

Heckel, Ulrich: Kraft in Schwachheit. 1993. *Volume II/56.*

– see *Feldmeier, Reinhard.*

– see *Hengel, Martin.*

Heiligenthal, Roman: Werke als Zeichen. 1983. *Volume II/9.*

Hellholm, D.: see *Hartman, Lars.*

Hemer, Colin J.: The Book of Acts in the Setting of Hellenistic History. 1989. *Volume 49.*

Hengel, Martin: Judentum und Hellenismus. 1969, ³1988. *Volume 10.*

To My Parents
Mr. and Mrs. Wayne Arnold

Wissenschaftliche Untersuchungen
zum Neuen Testament · 2. Reihe

Herausgegeben von
Martin Hengel und Otfried Hofius

77

The
Colossian Syncretism

The Interface Between Christianity
and Folk Belief at Colossae

by

Clinton E. Arnold

J. C. B. Mohr (Paul Siebeck) Tübingen

BS
2715.2
.A75
1995

Die Deutsche Bibliothek – CIP-Einheitsaufnahme

Arnold, Clinton E.:
The Colossian syncretism : the interface between Christianity
and folk belief at Colossae / by Clinton E. Arnold. – Tübingen : Mohr, 1995
  (Wissenschaftliche Untersuchungen zum Neuen Testament : Reihe 2 ;
  77)
  ISBN 3-16-146435-4
NE: Wissenschaftliche Untersuchungen zum Neuen Testament / 02

The book was printed and bound by Druck Partner Rübelmann in Hemsbach on acid-
free paper from Papierfabrik Niefern. Printed in Germany.

ISSN 0340-9570

Acknowledgments

The beginnings of this work reach back to my doctoral study at the University of Aberdeen (Scotland). Although my dissertation focused primarily on the letter to the Ephesians, the seeds of the present study were planted and took root there. Accordingly, I would like to express my appreciation to Professor I. Howard Marshall for his earlier guidance.

Much of the research for this book was carried out in Tübingen during 1991. I am grateful to Biola University for granting me the study leave and also to the Association of Theological Schools (ATS) for a research grant which made the trip to Germany possible. Our time was made particularly enjoyable by the hospitality of some very dear friends: Wilfried and Judith Sturm, Lienhard and Renate Pflaum, and Jürgen and Franziska Schwarz.

I owe a special debt of gratitude to Professor Peter Stuhlmacher for faithfully serving as my "mentor" under the provisions of the ATS grant. I appreciate the many opportunities to discuss the chapters with him and for his numerous insightful comments. I also want to extend my thanks to Professor Robert McL. Wilson (St. Andrews) for reading much of the manuscript and for the opportunity to discuss it with him in his home. I have also benefitted significantly from the remarks of a great number of scholars who commented on portions of this study given as papers in the regional and annual meetings of the Society of Biblical Literature, the Evangelical Theological Society, and seminars in Aberdeen and Tübingen.

I would like to thank Professor Martin Hengel for reading a portion of this manuscript at an early stage and providing helpful feedback. I am grateful that he has now included this work in the WUNT monograph series.

It has been wonderful to serve at Talbot School of Theology with a group of colleagues that are encouraging and supportive friends. I want to express my appreciation to three, in particular, who contributed to me in a variety of ways toward the completion of this project: Dr. Michael J. Wilkins (my Department Chair), Dr. Dennis Dirks (my Dean), and Dr. W. Bingham Hunter (my former Dean). I also want to thank Heather Johnson for her very careful proofreading of this manuscript.

I am exceedingly grateful to my family—my wife, Barbara, and our sons Jeffrey, Dustin, and Brandon—for participating with me in this project through the years. They packed up and moved to Germany for the sake of this project and shared with me in all of the emotional ups and downs of research and writing.

Finally, I dedicate this work to my parents, Mr. and Mrs. Wayne Arnold. I am grateful to my father for imparting to me a sense of vision and perseverance for taking on big projects and seeing them to the end. My mother has always been very supportive of my endeavors, putting up with long periods of separation, and yet providing significant help along the way. Thanks to both of you!

March, 1995   Clinton E. Arnold
La Mirada, California

Table of Contents

Abbreviations

References to classical sources and the associated literature are abbreviated according to N. G. L. Hammond and H. H. Scullard, eds., *The Oxford Classical Dictionary* (2d ed.; Oxford: Clarendon, 1970) and supplemented by H. G. Liddell and R. Scott, eds., *A Greek-English Lexicon* (rev. ed., with Supplement; Oxford: Clarendon, 1978) and the "Notes for Contributors and Abbreviations," in *American Journal of Archaeology* 90 (1986) 381-94. For biblical sources and the associated literature, abbreviations are as listed in the *Journal of Biblical Literature* 107 (1988) 579-96, with the following additions:

ARWAW, PC   Abhandlungen der Rheinisch-Westfälischen Akademie der Wissenschaft, Papyrologica Coloniensia

Bauer[6]   *Griechisch-deutsches Wörterbuch zu den Schriften des Neuen Testaments und der frühchristlichen Literatur.* 6., völlig neu bearbeitete Auflage. Hrsg. K. Aland & B. Aland. Berlin/New York: Walter de Gruyter, 1988.

BCH   *Bulletin de correspondance hellénique*

Conflict   *Conflict at Colossae.* Eds. F. O. Francis & W. A. Meeks. SBLSBS 4. Missoula: Scholar's Press, 1973.

DPL   *Dictionary of Paul and His Letters.* Eds. G. F. Hawthorne, R. P. Martin, and D. G. Reid. Downer's Grove: InterVarsity Press, 1993.

Encycl. Rel.   *The Encyclopedia of Religion.* Ed. M. Eliade. 16 Vols. New York: Macmillan, 1987.

GGR   *Geschichte der Griechischen Religion.* Zweiter Band: Die Hellenistische und Römische Zeit. Handbuch der Altertumswissenschaft 5,2. Zweite Auflage. München: C. H. Beck'sche Verlagsbuchhandlung, 1961.

GMPT   *The Greek Magical Papyri in Translation.* Vol. 1: Texts. Ed. H. D. Betz. Chicago: University of Chicago Press, 1986.

HJP²   Emil Schürer. *The History of the Jewish People in the Age of Jesus Christ.* Revised and edited by Geza Vermes, Fergus Millar, and Martin Goodman. Vol. 3, Part 1. Edinburgh: T. & T. Clark, 1986.

IGRR   *Inscriptiones Graecae ad Res Romanas Pertinentes.*

I.Strat.   *Die Inschriften von Stratonikeia.* Ed. M. Cetin Sahin. 2 Parts. IGSK 21 & 22. Bonn: Rudolf Habelt, 1981 & 1982.

JhhÖArchInst   *Jahreshefte des Österreichischen Archäologischen Instituts in Wien*

JSP   *Journal for the Study of the Pseudepigrapha*

KP   *Der Kleine Pauly.* Lexikon der Antike in fünf Bänden. Hrsg. K. Ziegler & W. Sontheimer. München: Alfred Druckenmüller (Artemis) Verlag, 1979.

MAMA   *Monumenta Asiae Minoris Antiqua.* Ed. W. M. Calder, et al. 8 Vols. London: Longman's, Green & Co., 1928-62.

SEG   *Supplementum Epigraphicum Graecum*

Introduction

The problem of identifying the precise nature of the teaching and practices of the opponents reflected in Colossians is notorious. There have been intervals in the history of the interpretation of the letter when a consensus appeared to be emerging only to find it fall apart in the next decade based on fresh studies of the letter.

Syncretism is a word that has long been used to characterize the beliefs and practices of the opponents in Colossians. There is clearly some mixture of religious ideas behind this self-styled "philosophy." The difficulty has been in discerning the nature and extent of the syncretism.[1]

For years it appeared that a Gnostic interpretation of the Colossian "philosophy" would prevail. This view was expressed in a variety of ways ranging from pure Gnosticism (E. Lohmeyer), to a Jewish Gnosticism (J. B. Lightfoot; G. Bornkamm; H. Conzelmann; H. -M. Schenke; F. F. Bruce), to a Gnosticism more closely resembling mystery cult beliefs and practice (Dibelius; Lohse). This interpretation has fallen into disfavor, however, based on studies pointing to the later development of the Gnostic religion of redemption and to substantive differences in thought when compared to the teaching of the Colossian opponents. This has led other interpreters to dismiss the "Gnostic" part of the interpretation and stress the correlation with pagan mystery cults (J. Gnilka).

More recently a consensus seemed to be surfacing that rooted the deviant teaching at Colossae in Jewish mysticism. This brand of mysticism, it was argued, involved a visionary ascent to heaven for which the adept prepared by rigorous ascetic practices. The initial catalyst for this view was provided through two essays by F. O. Francis. The argument was taken up and developed by C. Rowland, A. T. Lincoln, P. T. O'Brien, R.

---

[1] The use of the term "syncretism" here and in the title of the book is not intended to prejudge the teaching of the opponents as bad, heretical, or unorthodox (thus, the previous references to "the Colossian heresy," or "die kolossische Irrlehre"). The designation is descriptive insofar as the competing teaching represents a blending of a variety of religious traditions. Of course, as we will see in the course of this investigation, the author of the letter has significant problems with the particular set of beliefs that combine to form the Colossian "philosophy."

Yates, and most recently, T. J. Sappington.[2] This would probably come close to the majority view at present, but many aspects of this view are receiving just criticism.

The idea that the Colossian "philosophy" is best explained by some stream of contemporary philosophical thought has found few supporters. E. Schweizer, an exception, contends that the various strands of evidence about the Colossian teaching point away from Judaism to a world view that he finds dominant in neo-Pythagoreanism. Quite recently, R. DeMaris has argued that the opposing teaching at Colossae is actually best interpreted as an expression of Middle Platonism.[3] He has argued effectively that the sources on which Schweizer depends upon as articulations of neo-Pythagoreanism are quite eclectic and are not clear representations of neo-Pythagorean thought. He points rather to the importance of Plutarch and other writers in the Middle Platonic tradition as providing the most appropriate context for interpreting the various strands of evidence in the letter about the Colossian "philosophy."

Two other scholarly treatments are worthy of special mention because of their stress on local religious traditions. In his 1968 Harvard dissertation, A. T. Kraabel argued that the Colossian teaching has much in common with Anatolian Judaism and what M. P. Nilsson has called "the Lydian-Phrygian mentality" in which the Jews of the region participated.[4] Kraabel was the first to uncover many of the local religious traditions that seemed to have much in common with the teaching and practice of the Colossian opponents. His treatment of angelic veneration in the area as well as his discussion of the local Judaism seemed to advance the discussion significantly. Unfortunately, his analysis has seldom factored into the discussion on Colossians, probably in part because his study was never published. Three years later, unaware of Kraabel's work, J. Lähnemann published a major monograph on Colossians in which he characterized the Colossian "philosophy" as a product of Anatolian syncretism.[5] He claimed that the competing teaching was a form of Christianity with roots in local Phrygian religions (especially the cults of Cybele and Men), an Iranian

---

[2] T. J. Sappington, *Revelation and Redemption at Colossae* (JSNTSS 53; Sheffield: JSOT Press, 1991).

[3] R. DeMaris, *The Colossian Controversy* (JSNTSS 96; Sheffield: JSOT Press, 1994).

[4] A. T. Kraabel, "Judaism in Asia Minor under the Roman Empire with a Preliminary Study of the Jewish Community at Sardis, Lydia" (Unpublished Doctoral Dissertation; Harvard, 1968) 139-54, esp. 141.

[5] J. Lähnemann, *Der Kolosserbrief. Komposition, Situation und Argumentation* (SNT 3; Gütersloh: Mohn, 1971).

myth of the elements, and hellenized Judaism. Although his analysis of Phrygian Judaism is weak and his appeal to Iranian myth is dubious, his characterization of "the philosophy" as a syncretism involving both pagan and Jewish elements and his emphasis on the distinctively Phrygian features is helpful. Surprisingly, since the publication of these two works no serious studies correlating the local Phrygian religious traditions and Anatolian Judaism to the Colossian "philosophy" have been undertaken.

Of course, quite a variety of other views has been suggested from time to time to take into account the disparate evidence of the letter in reconstructing the teaching of the opponents. It is not our purpose here to provide a history of the research on Colossians; such an endeavor would fill pages. The reader can be brought up to date by the review of the literature in another recent monograph on Colossians.[6] The intent of this study is to point to some needed revisions in the method of research, to undertake a fresh investigation of the problem, and to suggest a new framework for interpreting the teaching of the opponents. Of course this needs to be carried out in dialogue with the data and conclusions of past research. Thus, the various views of the Colossian "philosophy" will be discussed at the appropriate intervals throughout this volume.

1. Revising the Method

Following the lead of Kraabel and Lähnemann, one of the distinctive methodological traits of this work will be to stress the utilization of local primary evidence whenever possible for the illumination of terms and concepts characteristic of "the philosophy." Thus, inscriptions and archaeological evidence from Phrygia, Lydia, Caria, and Asia Minor as a whole will be investigated and employed when appropriate. Although there is a limited amount of relevant local evidence, compounded all the more by the fact that the site of Colossae remains unexcavated, there is more local evidence that is relevant to this study than most biblical scholars realize. We will attempt to bring this material to light and consider its significance for understanding the views of the opponents. Especially significant in this regard are the many "angel" inscriptions discovered in Asia Minor, the ἐμβατεύω inscriptions from Claros and Notion, inscrip-

---

6 DeMaris, *Controversy*, 18-40 (= Chapter 2: "History of Scholarship on the Colossian Philosophy").

tional and literary evidence pertaining to the Judaism of Asia Minor, and the inscriptional and literary evidence illuminating our understanding of local pagan cults (such as the cults of Apollo, Men, *Theos Hypsistos,* Cybele and Attis, et al.).

One of the greatest difficulties for any interpreter attempting to reconstruct the Colossian "philosophy" is discerning the difference between a "catchword" used by the opponents and the author's polemic (or his own positive theological affirmations). There has been an almost universal recognition in the history of the interpretation of Colossians that the letter writer has quoted words and slogans in use by the advocates of "the philosophy" as part of his polemic. Scholars have also discerned that the author has taken over some of the opponents' terms and turned these against them by infusing the words with a different meaning. It is more likely that this takes place, however, in the polemical sections of the letter (2:4-8, 16-23) than in other portions of the letter, particularly in the hymn of 1:15-20 and the core theological section of 2:9-15. As I will argue later, this makes it less likely that a term such as πλήρωμα, often previously understood to reflect a Gnostic background to the opponents, was a catchword of "the philosophy."

A final methodological consideration is the criterion of determining what religious/cultural background best explains the pre-Christian religious background of the Colossians and the purveyors of the "philosophy." Any reconstruction of the teaching and practices of "the philosophy" should be consistent with what we might reasonably expect to surface in this area of Asia Minor. Thus, it is important for us to keep in mind that Colossae was not an important cultural center such as Alexandria, Athens, or Rome. In fact, Colossae was a rather insignificant city in Roman times, eclipsed by its neighbor Laodicea. Most of the people of Colossae would have made their living by raising sheep, by farming crops, or by wool-dying. This is certainly not a new criterion, but one that we need to apply more rigorously in an attempt to gain a more accurate appraisal of the situation.

Those arguing for some form of Gnosticism have claimed an advantage here by contending that Gnosticism was a world view that permeated the entire Mediterranean world in the Roman period. This assumption is now seriously questioned in terms of the date of the rise of Gnosticism and in terms of the extent of its sphere of influence.

The current Jewish mystical view also claims this advantage. It is certainly beyond dispute that Jewish communities existed in the Lycus Valley, and it is quite possible that the Colossian church had its beginnings among

Jews and godfearers who looked on Christ as Messiah and Son of God. It is also clear that there are references in Colossians to distinctively Jewish practices that were an integral part of the Colossian "philosophy." But is there any evidence of some form of communal mysticism in the Judaism of Asia Minor? Qumran is a long way from Phrygia both in distance and in belief and practice.

The recent proposal that the Colossian opponents were a group of Middle Platonists advocating their ideas to the community at Colossae[7] weakens when faced with this criterion. Is it really plausible that this kind of school philosophy would reach the rural sections of Asia Minor and have the kind of appeal and impact that is presupposed in Colossians?

The thesis of this monograph is that the beliefs and practices of the opponents at Colossae best cohere around the category of what might loosely be called folk religion. In affirming this, I am not intending to establish a commitment to one particular anthropological model of folk belief. Rather, I am suggesting that the best explanation for the Colossian "philosophy" lies in the quite general classification of folk religion. This forces us to think more deeply about what is most likely from the standpoint of the belief structures of common people in Phrygia. As one of the best windows into folk belief, current scholarship has been pointing us in the direction of the so-called magical texts. These clearly represent a dimension of belief held by common people, but reflecting a mixture of religious ideas.

2. The Importance of Reconstructing the Situation

One does not need to grasp the precise contours and details of the teaching and practices of the Colossian "philosophy" to interpret and appreciate much of the theology of the letter. The image of Christ as the exalted Lord of heaven and earth, the presence of salvation for those who believe, and the ethical responsibilities for Christians is equally apprehensible whether one sees the opponents as Gnostics or Jewish mystics.

It is important for us to recognize, however, that Colossians is more than a creedal statement or a kind of theological treatise. It is a genuine letter written at a particular point in time to a specific group of people who were faced with the threat of a teaching that was deemed dangerous

---

[7] DeMaris, *Controversy,* 131-33.

and deceptive by the author. The letter points to a group of factional teachers who were advocating a certain set of theological beliefs and practices to this Christian community. The primary motivation for the composition of the letter was to oppose this teaching. Without investigating the content of this teaching, we have little idea how this letter corresponds to the reality of the historical situation in the church. Furthermore, we are left in the dark as to how we might interpret many words and lines from the letter that need to be understood in light of the deviant teaching as a whole; for example: θρησκεία τῶν ἀγγέλων, ἃ ἑόρακεν ἐμβατεύων, στοιχεῖα τοῦ κόσμου, philosophy, wisdom, honor, humility, severe treatment of the body, freely-chosen worship, do not handle! do not taste! do not touch! festivals, New Moons, Sabbaths, eating, drinking, and others. Recent Pauline scholarship has rightly emphasized the occasional nature of the letters. As documents of history, they give to us the obligation of interpreting them historically.

Perhaps an even more important reason for attempting a reconstruction of the Colossian controversy is to help us understand why certain developments took place in Paul's thought and why certain features of his theology were emphasized over others. Understanding the setting will help us to grasp the manner of his contextualization of the gospel, that is, the contingent application of his theology to the situation.

3. The Issue of Authorship

When compared with the seven chief letters written by Paul, Colossians exhibits significant theological developments. The issue has long been debated whether the apostle himself was capable of these theological innovations: Does the theology represent the development of his thought (or more mildly, the fresh application of his thought to a new situation) or a later formulation that is inconsistent with what Paul would have said? Without minimizing the uniqueness of the theology of this letter, I have come down on the side of consistency with Pauline thought. It is imperative that one not undervalue the role of the unique and threatening situation facing the Colossian church in catalyzing a fresh application and development of Pauline thought.

It is well known that the author cites hymnic material (esp. 1:15-20), makes ample use of traditional language and imagery, and quotes and alludes to the unique teaching of the syncretistic "philosophy." When one

takes into consideration the Apostle Paul's ability for varied manners of expression, the arguments against the authenticity of the letter based on stylistic matters and *hapax legomena* are somewhat blunted.[8] This is not to deny that there are some significant differences in style between this letter and the earlier Paulines. The matter is more of a judgment call as to whether Paul was capable of such a style of writing or whether we need to hypothesize another hand behind the letter.[9]

Throughout this volume I will therefore refer to Paul as the author of the letter (in line with a fairly strong stream of scholarship).[10] In doing so, there is nothing in my argument throughout the book that presupposes Paul as the author or depends on this conclusion.

---

[8] In spite of the monographs by W. Bujard (*Stilanalytische Untersuchungen zum Kolosserbrief* [SUNT 11; Göttingen: Vandenhoeck & Ruprecht, 1973]) and M. Kiley (*Colossians as Pseudepigraphy* [Sheffield: JSOT Press, 1986], the question of whether Paul was (in)capable of the style of writing and argumentation in Colossians is far from decided. With J. Zmijewski, *Der Stil der paulinische "Narrenrede,"* (BBB 52; Köln/Bonn: Verlag Peter Hanstein, 1978) 37-39, I would fault Bujard's study for relying too much on statistical comparisons, minimizing the dynamic possibilities and individuality of style, and neglecting the theological issues at stake in the letter to the Colossians. See my critique of Kiley's work in *EQ* 60 (1988) 69-71.

[9] Of course, it is also possible that the style of Colossians reflects the proclivities of a particular amanuensis. See now the study by E. R. Richards, *The Secretary in the Letters of Paul* (WUNT 2/42; Tübingen: J.C.B. Mohr [Paul Siebeck] 1991). Richards aptly notes, "If no attempt is made to determine the secretarial role, then anything apparently 'non-Pauline' could be the secretary's. And if the secretary's, then ultimately it must be Paul's: he permitted it to remain in his letter."

[10] See the various writings of the following scholars who also conclude that Paul is the author: R. P. Martin, N. T. Wright, P. T. O'Brien; J. -N. Aletti ("très probablement de Paul"); P. Benoit; G. Fee; M. D. Hooker; F. F. Bruce; M. Barth; N. Kehl; C. F. D. Moule; J. L. Houlden; W. G. Kümmel; F. W. Beare; W. L. Knox; E. Percy; M. Dibelius; et al.

Part I: The "Worship of Angels"

The phrase "worship of angels" (θρησκεία τῶν ἀγγέλων) in Colossians 2:18 provides one of our most specific clues about the nature of the competing teaching at Colossae. The expression has properly been at the center of the debate, although it has been variously interpreted.

For many years the prevailing interpretation has been that the phrase represents part of the author's polemic against a Gnostic-oriented cult of angels. In this view, the angels were identified with the *stoicheia* and regarded as the objects of veneration. The angels were then seen either as helpful mediators or as evil beings who could hinder the ascent of the soul on the day of death.[1] Along similar lines, J. B. Lightfoot emphasized an angelolatry, of a *Jewish*-Gnostic type with strong affinities to Essenism, in which the angels (also called *archai, exousiai, thronoi*, etc.) function as intermediaries between God and humanity.[2]

A variety of other opinions has also been expressed. Prior to Lightfoot, J. Eadie argued that the phrase reflected Essene-type Jewish ideas about angels and spirits influenced by local Phrygian beliefs (not Gnosticism).[3] He suggested that these Colossian Christians venerated angels as mediators and protectors. He claims, in fact, that the object of the teaching was "to

---

[1] Martin Dibelius, "The Isis Initiation in Apuleius and Related Initiatory Rites," in *Conflict*, 84, 89; Dibelius-Greeven, *Kolosser*, 27-29, 35; G. Bornkamm, "The Heresy of Colossians," in *Conflict*, 130; Hans-Martin Schenke, "Der Widerstreit gnostischer und kirchlicher Christologie im Spiegel des Kolosserbriefes," *ZTK* 61 (1964) 391-99. He speaks of the phrase as the key point for identifying the heresy as actual Gnosis. For him the phrase refers to a Gnostic cult of the archons, with the archons understood as the rulers of the planetary spheres who demand worship. See also H.-F. Weiss, "Gnostische Motive und antignostische Polemik im Kolosser- und im Epheserbrief," in *Gnosis und Neues Testament* (Gütersloh: Gerd Mohn, 1973) 312-14; Lohse, *Colossians,* 118 and Martin, *Colossians* (NCB), 14-15; Gnilka, *Kolosserbrief,* 149-50 (although Gnilka sees a significant Jewish contribution to "the philosophy."); Pokorný, *Colossians,* 119; et al.

[2] Lightfoot, *Colossians,* 29-30. He sees the Colossian aberration as consisting of a doctrine of intermediate agencies who were involved in creation and now in the government of the world. The Colossians errorists worshipped these beings as their link to God. Lightfoot, however, did not equate the angels with the *stoicheia.* See also, Moule, *Colossians,* 31-32.

[3] Eadie, *Colossians, 179-82.*

secure spiritual protection, by communing with the world of spirits."[4] E. Schweizer argued that it refers to the practice of offering worship to souls (identified as angels) as they ascend to heaven.[5] R. DeMaris has recently contended that the passage refers to a devotion to demons or heroes. Some have even seen the phrase as pointing to a rendering of honor to the angels who assisted in the giving of the law and now watch over its observance.[6]

The majority of interpreters in the past decade (especially in Great Britain and North America) have accepted Fred O. Francis' conclusion that angels were not the object of the veneration, but God himself was the unexpressed object of worship by the angels before his heavenly throne.[7] This explanation then characterizes "the philosophy" as a Jewish mysticism in which the earthly congregation sought to participate in the heavenly angelic liturgy, i.e. by worshiping *with* the angels. Accordingly, Francis argued that the genitive expression τῶν ἀγγέλων should be understood as the subject of the action of worship (θρησκεία). This interpretation, as I will argue below, falls short both on grammatical grounds and in terms of its inability to account for all the facets of "the philosophy" as revealed in Colossians.

In an insightful but neglected article written shortly after the turn of the century, A. L. Williams suggested that the phrase points to an angelolatry (a worship of the angels = objective genitive), but a type of angelic veneration that had its roots in the fringes of Judaism.[8] Specifically, he contends that "there is almost no evidence for the worship of them [angels]

---

[4] Eadie, *Colossians,* xxxiii.

[5] Schweizer, *Colossians,* 131-33, 160.

[6] E. Percy, *Die Probleme der Kolosser- und Epheserbriefe* (Lund: Gleerup, 1964) 168; S. Lyonnet, "Paul's Adversaries in Colossae," in *Conflict,* 149-50.

[7] Fred O Francis, "Humility and Angelic Worship in Col 2:18," in *Conflict,* 177. He has been followed in this interpretation by: T. J. Sappington, *Revelation and Redemption at Colossae* (JSNTSS 53; Sheffield: JSOT Press, 1991) 158-64; J. Sumney, "Those Who 'Pass Judgment': The Identity of the Opponents in Colossians," *Bib* 74 (1993) 377-78; W. Carr, *Angels and Principalities* (SNTSMS 42; Cambridge: University Press, 1981) 69-72; "Two Notes on Colossians," *JTS* 24 (1973) 499, 500; O'Brien, *Colossians,* 143; R. Yates, "'The Worship of Angels' (Col. 2:18)," *ET* (1987) 12-15; C. Rowland, "Apocalyptic Visions and the Exaltation of Christ in the Letter to the Colossians," *JSNT* 19 (1983) 73-83; C. A. Evans, "The Colossian Mystics," *Biblica* 63 (1982) 188-205; A. T. Lincoln, *Paradise Now and Not Yet* (SNTSMS 43; Cambridge: University Press, 1981) 111-12; L. Hurtado, *One God, One Lord* (Philadelphia: Fortress, 1988) 32-33. Hurtado comments, "I am not aware of a refutation of Francis, and in view of his work citation of Col. 2:18 as evidence of a first-century Jewish cult of angels must be considered a misinterpretation of the passage."

[8] A. Lukyn Williams, "The Cult of the Angels at Colossae," *JTS* 10 (1909) 413-38.

being recognized in early times by thoughtful Jews, save indeed in connexion with exorcism and magic."[9] He argues that local religious influences would have reinforced this attitude toward angels and, consequently, was adopted by some of the Colossian Christians. For Williams, the essence of the problem at Colossae stems from Jewish influences, albeit a syncretistic Judaism—with an affinity of type to Essenism (as Eadie and Lightfoot suggested)—but also betraying Phrygian, Persian, and Syrian characteristics, especially of a magical character.

Although there are some significant weaknesses in Williams' presentation when seen as a whole,[10] I am convinced that the heart of his thesis is correct. The "worship of angels" in Colossians 2:18 refers essentially to a magical invocation of angels, especially for apotropaic purposes. In the following pages, I will attempt to substantiate and develop this claim by building on the foundation already laid by Williams. Surprisingly, Williams reached this conclusion without ever referring to the magical papyri, the amulets, and the lead curse tablets. This material, especially that of a Jewish character, significantly strengthens his central idea. Perhaps most importantly, no previous work has sought to collect all the information about local (Phrygian and Carian) attitudes about "angels." A surprising amount of material is forthcoming from the inscriptions of Asia Minor that illuminates local beliefs about angelic mediation.

This section will serve not only to interpret the phrase "worship of angels," but will help to set "the philosophy" into the milieu of a magical understanding of spirituality and human existence, namely, the domain of folk belief. In the process of describing how the ancients would call on angels, divine mediators, and supernatural assistants, many other facets of the teaching of the opponents at Colossae will be exposed.

---

[9] Williams, "Cult," 432.

[10] For example: (1) he speaks of a "cult" of angels, but he does not clarify what he means by a cultic context of veneration and ends up with an idea that sounds more like a private invocation of angels; (2) the foregoing observation also points to an inadequate analysis of the meaning of the term θρησκεία; (3) he does not compare and discuss his understanding of the use of the term "angels" in Col. 2:18 with the occurrences of στοιχεῖα in Col. 2:8, 20 nor with the ἀρχαὶ καὶ ἐξουσίαι in Col. 1:16; 2:10, 15.

CHAPTER 1

The Veneration of Angels in Magic

Before we begin looking at the role of angels in magic, it is imperative to define our understanding of magic and to describe its significance for understanding folk religion among Jews and pagans of Asia Minor. It will also be important for establishing the proper context of certain pagan, Jewish, and Christian amulets discovered in Asia Minor.

1. Defining Magic

A generation ago, "magic" was defined in rather objective terms, viz. a technique for manipulating supernatural beings while guaranteeing the results one intends. The term "magic" sometimes also functioned as a value judgment when it was set against "religion" as a base or perverse way of approaching a deity. Thus Martin Nilsson could refer to magic as "the decay of the old religion" or as an inferior way of believing *(der niedere Glaube)*.[1] Similarly, Sam Eitrem, a Norwegian scholar who published a number of magical texts, went so far as to refer to the magical papyri as "interesting relics of degenerate religions and of the human mind gone astray."[2]

In more recent times, assisted by the disciplines of anthropology and sociology, many interpreters have become wary of seeing "magic" as an objective category that describes a set of beliefs and practices. They are pointing rather to the sociological function of the labels "magic," "sorcery," "witchcraft," and similar terms. They suggest that "magic" is a

---

[1] See his *Greek Popular Religion* (New York: Columbia University Press, 1940) 115, and *GGR*, 2.520, where the expression, "der niedere Glaube," is used as a section head for his discussion of magic (pp. 520-80). For his distinction between "religion" and "superstition," he was sternly criticized by E. R. Goodenough in a review of *Greek Popular Religion* appearing in *JBL* 60 (1941) 345-48.

[2] As cited in D. E. Aune, "Magic in Early Christianity," *ANRW* II.23.2 (1980) 1511, note 7.

negative value judgment placed by one person (or group) upon another. "Magic" therefore becomes a vehicle of accusation, for indicting the beliefs and practices of others as less than honorable or even illegal. In the process of emphasizing the sociological function of the term, many scholars have evacuated it of any objective meaning at all.[3]

In an important article titled "Magic In Early Christianity" David Aune has provided a more balanced approach to the issue. He provides a definition of magic that is appropriately sensitive to the sociological function of the term, but also recognizes that there is some objective content to the concept of magic. His two-fold definition is as follows:

> 1. Magic is defined as that form of religious deviance whereby individual or social goals are sought by means alternate to those normally sanctioned by the dominant religious institution.
> 2. Goals sought within the context of religious deviance are magical when attained through the management of supernatural powers in such a way that results are virtually guaranteed.[4]

The first part of the definition recognizes the nature of "witchcraft accusations" in the social context of antiquity. In narrative and polemical texts, the description of a person or group as practicing "magic" must be interpreted with a sensitivity to the social relationships between the people represented. The charge may be hollow since the accusers may be using the term as a slanderous device to mark the others as practicing something deviant to their own preferred form of ritual or piety. The actual content of the alleged deviance needs to be more closely examined.

On the other hand, some in antiquity were happy to wear the label of

---

[3] See, for example, J. G. Gager, *Curse Tablets and Binding Spells from the Ancient World* (Oxford: University Press, 1992) 24-25, who claims to avoid using the word "magic" in his corpus of texts, because "magic, as a definable and consistent category of human experience, simply does not exist." Is it not inconsistent with his introductory remark that Gager has no difficulty referring to the creators of the *defixiones* and practitioners of the rituals contained in the texts he discusses as *magoi*? (pp. v, 5, 10, 16, 20, 24, 31, 78, 112, 118, 204, 205, 265). In a similar fashion, Alan Segal, "Hellenistic Magic: Some Questions of Definition," *The Other Judaisms of Late Antiquity,* Brown Judaic Studies 127 (Atlanta: Scholar's Press, 1987) 79-108, contends, "no definition of magic can be universally applicable because 'magic' cannot and should not be construed as a properly scientific term. Its meaning changes as the context in which it is used changes" (p. 81). Such definitions fail to deal with the self-understanding of various *magoi* in the Mediterranean world.

[4] Aune, "Magic in Early Christianity," 1515. See my *Ephesians: Power and Magic* (SNTSMS 63; Cambridge: University Press, 1989) 19.

"magician" (μάγος,[5] or γόης[6]) and regarded what they did as a special-ized art which they could practice even within the context of the sanc-tioned cult, but often privately as well. These people were shamans, and they claimed to possess special insight into supernatural powers and could use their knowledge to accomplish a variety of purposes.[7]

"Magic" was typically judged by its effectiveness in obtaining the in-tended results. This is well illustrated by a spell reportedly originating from the prophet/magician Pachrates perhaps the same person described by Lucian (Lucian, *Philops.* 34):

> Pachrates, the prophet of Heliopolis, revealed it [the spell] to the emperor Hadrian, revealing the power of his own divine magic (μαγείας). For it attracted in one hour; it made someone sick in 2 hours; it destroyed in 7 hours, sent the emperor himself dreams as he thoroughly tested the whole truth of the magic (μαγείας) within his power. And marveling at the prophet, he ordered double fees to be given to him (*PGM* IV.2445-55).

This paragraph functions to underline the effectivness of a love spell of attraction that immediately follows it in the papyrus. It can be described as magic, partly because it works—even within a specified period of time!

The second part of Aune's definition is also correct by stressing "the management of supernatural powers." R. MacMullen has described magic as an "art" that "brings about the intervention of superhuman powers in the material world."[8] Aune has also emphasized that the implementation of the art brings "guaranteed results." Those who use magic attempt to co-erce these powers through a variety of means to obtain what they want.[9] The assurance of success is well illustrated by the text above. The notion of magic as managing or manipulating supernatural powers will become increasingly apparent in the various texts we discuss in PART I.

---

[5] *PGM* IV.243, 2081, 2289.

[6] For a history of this term in Greek literature, see W. Burkert, "ΓΟΗΣ. Zum Griechischen 'Schamanismus,'" *Rheinisches Museum für Philologie* NS 105 (1962) 36-55.

[7] See Burkert's discussion on the γόης as a shaman in Hellenistic and Roman religon; Burkert, "ΓΟΗΣ," 36-55.

[8] R. MacMullen, *Paganism in the Roman Empire* (New Haven: Yale University Press, 1981) 70.

[9] M. P. Nilsson, "Letter to Professor Arthur D. Nock on some Fundamental Concepts in the Science of Religion. May 15, 1947," in *Opuscula Selecta* (Lund: Gleerup, 1960) 3.369-71. Nilsson attempts to distance himself from J. G. Frazer in this article, but stresses that there is a difference between magic and religion. The fundamental difference for him is that "magic tries to attain its purpose by coercion" (p. 370).

In their recent book, *Ancient Christian Magic,* Marvin Meyer and Richard Smith subtitle the volume, *Coptic Texts of Ritual Power.*[10] They prefer the subtitle as a description of the contents of the volume because it is a less value-laden description than "magic" or even "religion." Yet they recognize that these texts need some kind of designation that sets them apart from other kinds of cultic practices. They contend that the descriptive label "ritual power" best represents the nature of these texts. As texts of ritual power, "they direct the user to engage in activities that are marked off from normal activity by framing behavior through rules, repetitions, and other formalities."[11] As Aune, they stress that these texts are "overt in their manipulation of power and force" but they stop short of describing them as guaranteeing results.[12]

Although the designation "texts of ritual power" is an accurate descriptive label of the kinds of materials we find in papyri, it does not go far enough in describing the full extent of beliefs and practices of what has traditionally been labeled "magic." In spite of the increasing unpopularity of the term "magic," I will retain this designation for the purposes of this study and use it in the two-fold sense that Aune has set forth.

I would go beyond Aune, however, in establishing a number of more objective factors that characterize magic as it was practiced in the Greco-Roman world particularly as exhibited in the primary documents—the papyri, amulets, and the lead curse tablets. I summarize what I regard as some of these more objective features of magic below:

1. There is an identifiable form to the charms and spells. Most of the so-called magical texts can be observed to have two or three of the following elements: (a) a rite to perform, (b) an invocation (including a list of the appropriate names to call upon), and (c) a statement of command (versus request), usually given in the aorist imperative (in Greek texts).
2. As we have already seen above, magic was perceived to guarantee results; it was effective (ἐνέργεια). If one followed all the details of the instructions for the prescribed rite and invocation, one would experience success.
3. Magical documents have an array of terminology given specialized significance. Perhaps the most common is the term for conjuration that appears in the vast majority of the documents: ὁρκίζω or ἐξορκίζω. For example, in one Jewish exorcistic recipe (*PGM* IV.3007-86), the phrase, "I conjure you" (ὁρκίζω σε) appears fourteen times.

---

[10] Marvin Meyer and Richard Smith, eds., *Ancient Christian Magic. Coptic Texts of Ritual Power* (San Francisco: Harper Collins, 1994).

[11] Meyer and Smith, *Ancient Christian Magic,* 4.

[12] Meyer and Smith, *Ancient Christian Magic,* 5.

4. The documents invariably include a series of names (often unknown to the modern interpreter) or characters. Scholars often refer to these as "Ephesia Grammata."[13] The document may also include a figure or drawing, thought to be laden with power.

These characteristics are not necessarily present in all of the magical texts all at the same time. An amulet for instance, may consist of nothing more than a drawing, a series of magical names and/or characters, and an invocation with a demand.

These objective characteristics were all a part of the magician's "technique" (τέχνη)[14] or "art" (*ars*)[15] that distinguished them from priests and other religious officials. In saying this, however, one cannot distance the magician too far from the organized cult. As Aune has rightly observed, magic often functioned as a substructure to the organized cults.[16] The "holy man" who practiced the magic could very well have been a priest of the cult.

2. Magic as a Key to Understanding Popular Belief— Even Within Judaism

An increasing number of scholars are recognizing the value of the magical papyri as a key for unlocking our understanding of the beliefs of common folk in the Greco-Roman world.[17] Georg Luck is correct in noting that, "the world of the ancients was full of magical powers, acting in all directions, and many people must have felt constantly threatened."[18] The belief in magic was an essential part of the spiritual atmosphere of antiquity, especially from the beginning of the Roman Imperial period to the time of Neoplatonism.[19] This is well-documented in the second volume

---

[13] See Karl Wessely, "Ephesia Grammata aus Papyrusrollen, Inschriften, Gemmen, etc.," *Zwölfter jahresbericht über das k. k. Franz-Josef-Gymnasium in Wien* (Wien: Franz-Joseph-Gymnasium, 1886) 1-38.

[14] Note the following use of the term τέχνη in Jewish magic: "And God granted him [Solomon] knowledge of the art used against demons (τὴν κατὰ τῶν δαιμόνων τέχνην) for the benefit and healing of men" (Josephus, *Ant.* 8.2.5 §45).

[15] See Pliny, *HN* 30.1.1 and 30.2.10.

[16] Aune, "Magic in Early Christianity," 1520.

[17] See my previous comments in *Ephesians*, 19-20.

[18] Georg Luck, *Arcana Mundi* (Baltimore and London: Johns Hopkins University Press, 1985) 19.

[19] Nilsson, *GGR*, 2.529. A. D. Nock, "Astrology and Cultural History," *Arthur*

of Martin Nilsson's classic work, *Geschichte der Griechischen Religion.*[20] A. D. Nock went so far as to emphasize the *necessity* of using the magical texts to interpret the religion of the common people. He writes, "we may and must make use of magical papyri in our attempt to reconstruct the religious attitude of the mass of mankind in the Roman world."[21]

The value of the magical texts for interpreting the beliefs of common folk in the Greco-Roman world extends beyond paganism to Judaism. E. R. Goodenough argued this point most strongly in the second volume of his massive *Jewish Symbols in the Greco-Roman Period.*[22] Although the work has been criticized on many fronts, he nevertheless convincingly demonstrates—with a significant amount of material evidence—that magic had penetrated deeply into the Judaism of the diaspora. He argued that the magical material "increasingly seems to represent popular Judaism."[23]

Jewish scholar Ephraim Urbach reached a similar conclusion. He first clarifies the official position of the rabbis: "On commenting on the verse, 'There is none else beside Him' (Deuteronomy 1 v 35) R. Hanina commented: 'Even in respect of sorceries' *(T.B. loc. cit.).* Rashi gives the explanation with precision: 'They are impotent before His decree, for there is no power besides Him.'"[24] Urbach follows this up with what he regards to be the more common view: "But this was not the accepted view among the broad masses of the people, and hence the prolonged debates and discussions on these questions. Magical practices and sorcery were widespread in the ancient world in the areas where the Sages lived, that is,

---

Darby Nock: Essays on Religion and the Ancient World (ed. Z. Stewart; Oxford: Clarendon, 1972) 1.502, concurs: "Astrology, magic, and the expression of devotion to the Emperor were the universal phenomena of paganism in Roman times."

[20] See especially his chapters dealing with astrology ("Die Astrologie und die Sonnenreligion," 486-520), superstition ("Die niedere Glaube," 520-43), and belief in the underworld ("Der Toten- und Unterweltsglaube," 543-58).

[21] A. D. Nock, "Studies in the Graeco-Roman Beliefs of the Empire," *Arthur Darby Nock: Essays on Religion and the Ancient World* (ed. Z. Stewart; Oxford: Clarendon, 1972) 1.34.

[22] See Erwin R. Goodenough, *Jewish Symbols in the Greco-Roman Period,* Volume 2: The Archaeological Evidence from the Diaspora (Bollingen Series 37; New York: Bollingen Foundation, 1953).

[23] Goodenough, *Symbols,* 2.170. Similarly, he later notes, "The [magical] charms actually give us an extensive body of literary evidence regarding the Judaism of the Greco-Roman world—evidence that comes as early from what we might call the religious 'lower classes' of Judaism ..." (p. 207).

[24] Ephraim E. Urbach, *The Sages. Their Concepts and Beliefs* (Jerusalem: Magnes Press, 1975) 98.

throughout the Orient."[25] He sees this tendency widespread not only among the common people of the land, "but also among the scholars in Eretz-Israel and even more so in Babylon."[26] James Charlesworth has acknowledged his indebtedness to Urbach for influencing his thinking on this subject.[27]

In the recent revision of Emil Schürer's *History of the Jewish People,* P. S. Alexander emphatically stresses the value of the magical texts for opening up to us the religion of the common people. He writes:

> To fail to consider magic would be to neglect an area of immense importance in the study of early Judaism. Incantations and books of magic ... open up areas of popular religion which are often inadequately represented in the official literary texts, and which are in consequence frequently ignored by historians. As an indicator of the spiritual atmosphere in which large sections of the populace lived—rich and poor, educated and ignorant—their importance can hardly be overestimated. Magic flourished among the Jews despite strong and persistent condemnation by the religious authority.[28]

These comments regarding the importance of using the magical texts for understanding popular belief not only give us a warrant, but a mandate, to explore their relevance for interpreting the teaching of "the philosophy" at Colossae.

3. Addressing the Issue of Date

An oft-heard criticism directed toward those who use the magical papyri for illuminating first-century A.D. documents is that the papyri are too late. It is true that that most of the papyri date into the third and fourth centuries A.D. But does this fact automatically render them worthless for the enterprise of interpreting earlier documents? An initial response can be given on the basis of the parallels with the phenomenon of early Christianity. We do not date the beginning of the Jesus movement to the early

---

[25] Urbach, *Sages,* 98.

[26] Urbach, *Sages,* 101. With regard to the widespread nature of Jewish magic, he observes, "In actuality, even the Sages of the Talmud and Midrash—despite their fundamental recognition that there is none besides God and that consequently witchcraft does not exist—could not ignore the facts, to wit, that broad masses of the people believed in and made use of these practices" (p. 101).

[27] James H. Charlesworth, "Prayer of Jacob," in *OTP* 2.716, note 3.

[28] P. S. Alexander, "Incantations and Books of Magic," in *HJP²*, 342.

second century merely because most of the papyrus fragments of the gospels date to the third and fourth centuries A.D. We know on the basis of other historical grounds that the Jesus movement got its start early in the first century. Similarly, with magic, if one wants to argue for its lateness, it needs to be done on a basis other than the actual date of the papyrus texts. It happens, however, that we know from other historical sources that the magic we have represented in the papyri was not only practiced in the first century, but also for many centuries previously. In contradistinction to Christianity and Gnosis, magic was not a movement, but a way of approaching the divine that historians regard as reaching back before recorded history.

In Asia Minor we know that the local populations practiced magic in the Hittite period. Numerous tablets with conjuration rituals have been discovered.[29] Similarly, for the Greco-Roman period, more than 1500 lead curse tablets *(defixiones)* have been discovered, not only in Asia Minor, but throughout the Mediterranean world. Tablets using the Greek language are attested as early as the fifth century B.C. and appear until the sixth century A.D.[30] Among these defixiones, Audollent's corpus includes thirteen that were found in Caria, and range in date from B.C. 300 to 100.[31] He also includes some from the territory of Phrygia.[32] These tablets represent the same kind of magic that is seen in the recipes of the magical papyri.[33]

Similarly, magical amulets were in use throughout the Mediterranean world from the earliest times. Evidence of their use is traceable to the time of Homer and Pindar.[34] Numerous magical amulets have been found

---

[29] For a discussion of these texts and the practice of magic in Asia Minor in the Hittite period, see Albrecht Goetze, *Kulturgeschichte des Alten Orients: Kleinasien* (Handbuch der Altertumswissenschaft 3.1.3.3.1; 2d ed.; München: Beck, 1957) 151-61.

[30] See David R. Jordan, "A Survey of the Greek Defixiones Not Included in the Special Corpora," *GRBS* 26 (1985) 151-54. Professor Jordan is currently in the process of preparing a corpus of the Greek defixiones. A representative corpus of *defixiones* translated into English has now been published by J. G. Gager, *Curse Tablets and Binding Spells from the Ancient World* (New York: Oxford University Press, 1992). For a good introduction and discussion of the *defixiones*, see Karl Preisendanz, "Fluchtafel (Defixio)," *RAC* 8.1-24. See also Nilsson, *GGR*, 2.524.

[31] Augustus Audollent, *Defixionum Tabellae* (Paris: Alberti Fontemoing, 1894) 5-19.

[32] Audollent, *Defixionum*, 20ff.

[33] R. Wünsch, *Antike Fluchtafeln* (Kleine Texte für Vorlesungen und Übungen 20; 2d ed.; Bonn: A. Marcus and E. Weber, 1912) 3-4, remarks, "the curse tablets stand on precisely the same level as the Greek magical papyri of the third and fourth centuries."

[34] See R. Kotansky, "Incantations and Prayers for Salvation on Inscribed Greek Amulets," in *Magika Hiera. Ancient Greek Magic and Religion* (eds. C. A. Faraone and

that date to the first century A.D. or prior. The names, incantations, and words of command inscribed on them correspond closely to the recipes given for their creation recorded in the *Papyri Graecae Magicae.*

In the mid-first century, Pliny complained that "the fraudulent art has held sway throughout the world for many ages" (Pliny, *NH* 30.1.1). He also speaks of "the greatness of its influence" in his day (30.1.1) noting that "magic rose to such a height that even today it has sway over a great part of mankind" (30.1.2; cf. also 30.4.13). His testimony is now well illustrated by the material evidence we have available.

The curse tablets as well as the magical amulets reinforce the claim of many historians who assert that the magical papyri represent a tradition much earlier than the date of the actual papyri on which they appear. Georg Luck, for instance, contends, "Although their [the magical papyri] date is relatively late (third or fourth century A.D.), they reflect much older ideas, and the doctrines and techniques they embody were probably developed in the late Hellenistic period. Many are considered to be copies of copies."[35]

Because of the antiquity of the content of the papyri, scholars of classical antiquity make use of them for illuminating much earlier literary documents. To cite one example, A. S. Gow uses the *PGM* for explaining the magic that is present in Theocritus's Idyll II (θεοκρίτου φαρμακεύτρια), written sometime between 300 and 260 B.C.[36] He remarks, "their [the magical papyri's] numerous points of agreement with T. [Theocritus] and with the Latin poets from Virgil onward show that much of the material which they systematise is far older than themselves, and some of it must be of immemorial antiquity."[37] He suggests that the traditions can be dated to as early as the third century B.C.

Nevertheless, one must exercise caution in using the papyri because of some later intrusions. The name "Jesus," for example, does appear in a few recipes in the papyri.[38] This may mean that the recipe or formula postdates the beginning of Christianity, although it is entirely possible that only the name was added to an ancient formula because a magician heard

---

D. Obbink; New York: Oxford University Press, 1991) 107-110.

[35] Luck, *Arcana Mundi,* 16. With respect to Jewish magic, compare the same contention of Alexander, "Incantations," 344. See also, Meyer and Smith, *Ancient Christian Magic,* 7.

[36] A. S. F. Gow, *Theocritus* (2 vols.; Cambridge: University Press, 1965).

[37] Gow, *Theocritus,* 2.35-36.

[38] See, for example, *PGM* IV.3019-20: "I conjure you by the god of the Hebrews, Jesus." For a discussion, see W. L. Knox, "Jewish Liturgical Exorcism," *HTR* 31 (1938) 193-94.

that it was a name laden with power. One needs certainly to be discerning of possible Gnostic influences on the papyri. But even here most of the influence has been one way, that is, with magical ideas and formulas contributing to Gnosis. With Georg Luck, we may safely conclude the following about the magical papyri:

> What emerges from the evidence is the permanence and universality of magic in the ancient world. Although some testimonies may be relatively late, the doctrines and practices they reveal are often much older. Certain formulas and recipes were handed down for generations, perhaps with minor changes, and though they are found on tablets and papyri dating from the early Christian era, they probably had been practiced for centuries. Moreover, it is clear that the same type of magic was practiced throughout the Roman Empire.[39]

4. The Veneration of "Angels" in Magic

One of the distinctive traits of magic was the high regard for "angels" and other supernatural beings that were invoked by the practitioner. It should initially be pointed out that "angels" known from Judaism figure prominently in the magical papyri.[40] In Preisendanz' collection, "Michael" is mentioned 20 times, "Gabriel" seven times, and a great number of angel names are mentioned once or twice.[41] The term ἄγγελος itself occurs more than 70 times. In the numerous lead curse tablets (defixiones) found throughout the Mediterranean world, "angels" and "archangels" are called upon with corresponding frequency.

In the magical texts these angels are invoked for a multiplicity of reasons: They fulfill an apotropaic function by providing protection to the conjurer from harmful spirits; they are the agents for revelatory magic, viz. dream oracles and light divination; they fulfill aphrodisiacs and love potions; they are powerful assistants, πάρεδροι, that can help the suppliant in any way he/she requests. They are commonly viewed as the assistants to

---

[39] Luck, *Arcana Mundi*, 20.

[40] For a discussion of the nature and function of "angels" in magic, see the section entitled "Die Erzengel und Engel" in Theodor Hopfner, *Griechisch-Ägyptischer Offenbarungszauber* (Studien zur Palaeographie und Papyruskunde 21; Amsterdam: Adolf M. Hakkert, 1974 [originally published in Leipzig: Haessel, 1921]) §§135-162.

[41] Cf. M. P. Nilsson, "Die Religion in den griechischen Zauberpapyri," *Kungl. Humanistiska Vetenskapssamfundet I Lund. Årsberattelse* 1947-48 (Lund: Gleerup, 1948) 65-66.

the gods and can bring aid as a representative of the god. They are also associated with stars and planets and are therefore viewed as active in influencing one's fate, and, conversely, as susceptible to magical manipulation.[42]

a. The Invocation of Angels for Protection

The following texts illustrate the apotropaic function of angels in the context of magic. The need for protection from evil spirits and curses was felt quite acutely by people in the Mediterranean world. Regarding curses, Pliny said, "There is no one who does not fear to be spellbound by curse tablets" (*Nat. His.* 28.4.19). One of the most common means of seeking protections was through the use of an amulet. In fact, the normal word in the magical papyri for an amulet is φυλακτήριον, which is formed from the verb φυλάσσειν, "to protect."

The examples discussed here are drawn from both the magical papyri and the *defixiones*. The first text calls on the angels of Helios:

> I call upon you (ἐπικαλοῦμαι), lord Helios, and your holy angels (ἁγίους ἀγγέλους) on this day, in this very hour: Preserve me, NN, for I am THENOR, and you are holy angels (ἅγιοι ἄγγελοι), guardians (φύλακες) of the ARDIMALECHA and [nine lines of *voces magicae* follow], I beg you (δέομαι), lord Helios, hear me NN and grant me power over the spirit of this man who died a violent death (βιοθανάτου πνεύματος), from whose tent I hold [this], so that I may keep him with me, [NN] as helper and avenger for whatever business I crave from him (*PGM* IV.1932-54).

The formulaic invocation is then followed by a prayer to recite to Helios and a rite to perform. The recipe is to be used to protect the suppliant from an evil spirit, specifically a *Biaiothanatos* spirit, viz. one who had suffered a violent or premature death and could not enter the underworld and now roamed the earth as a tormenting spirit.[43] The recipe assumes that the spirit can not only be thwarted but may be harnessed and used as a personal assistant.

The apotropaic function of angels is also clearly seen in *PGM* XXXVI. 168-78, where specific angels are even prescribed:

> For reinforcement by words, write this on a papyrus: 'I am Chphyris, give me success! Michael, Raphael, Rubel, Nariel, Katiel, Rumbuthiel, Azariel, Joel, Juel,

---

[42] Hopfner, *Offenbarungszauber,* 1.§162.
[43] See J. H. Waszink, "Biothanati," *RAC* 2.391-92.

Ezriel, Suriel, Nariel, Metmuriel, Azael, Aziel, Saumiel, Rubuthiel, Rabieel, Rab-
chlu, Enaezrael, ἄγγελοι, protect me (φυλάξατέ με) from every bad thing that
comes upon me (translation mine).'

As in the previous text where the angels are called φύλακες, in this text
their function is to protect (φυλάσσω). This text also demonstrates a
strong Jewish influence through the Hebrew-sounding names for angels.[44]
The matter of importance for the magician is that these "angels" have a
reputation as powerful beings that can be invoked for assistance.

In the third example, the Egyptian "Headless One" is the object of the
invocation (*PGM* V.96-72). Although he is ascribed the most exalting
ephithets (lord, king, master, the one who created heaven and earth), he is
also spoken of as the assistant of Osiris: "a good angel of god" (εὐάγγελος
τοῦ θεοῦ; line 143) and the "angel (ἄγγελος) of Pharaoh Osoronnophris"
(lines 113-14), i.e. the angel of the ruling benefactor Osiris.[45] The apotropaic function of the charm comes out clearly as seen in the following
lines:

Lines 119-20: "... listen to me and turn away this daimon (τὸ δαιμόνιον)."
Lines 125-26: "Holy Headless One, deliver him, NN, from the demon (δαίμονος)
    which restrains him."
Lines 164-71: "Subject to me all daimons (τὰ δαιμόνια πάντα), so that every dai-
    mon, whether heavenly or aerial or earthly or subterranean or terrestrial or aquatic,
    might be obedient to me ..."

This text is also interesting because of the incorporation of many Jewish
elements into an otherwise Egyptian text. E. R. Goodenough, in contrast,
accounts for the Jewish elements by suggesting that this Egyptian charm
was adapted by a Jew for Jewish use.[46] Since the primary deities are still
Egyptian (Osiris and the Headless One), it is best to regard it as an essentially Egyptian charm with the infusion of a few Jewish ideas (such as a

---

[44] Goodenough, *Symbols,* 2.195, actually regarded this as a Jewish charm.

[45] The Greek text of line 114 reads: ἐγώ εἰμι ἄγγελος τοῦ Φαπρω 'Οσορονννωφρις.
'Οννωφρις was an epithet of Osiris, transliterated from Coptic (see the Coptic expression
in *PGM* IV.128), and equivalent to the Greek ὄμφις = εὐεργέτης; see Hopfner, *Offenbarungszauber,* 1.§157. Preisendanz, *PGM,* 1.185, translated the expression: "Ich bin
der Engel des Wohltäters" ("I am the angel of the benefactor"), but he earlier translates σὺ
εἶ 'Οσορονννωφρις (line 101), "du bist der Gute Osiris" ("you are the good Osiris").
Robert Ritner, *GMPT,* 337, suggests, "Osiris the beautiful being." Similarly, Φαπρω is a
Greek transliteration of a Coptic term meaning "pharaoh" or "king"; see Hopfner, *Offenbarungszauber,* 1.§157.

[46] Goodenough, *Symbols,* 2.197.

Moses tradition; lines 109-11). Now, in addition to φυλάσσω, we see a repertoire of other terms for averting/thwarting evil spirits: ἀποστρέφω, ἀπαλλάσσω, and ὑποτάσσω.

Other texts speak of "angels" more in the sense of astral spirits who hold the keys of cruel fate. The stars were thought of as "gods" and "angels" who threaten humanity (*PGM* IV.571). Helios is often invoked against these "angels":

> You are the holy and powerful name considered sacred by the angels (τῶν ἀγγέλων); protect me (διαφύλαξόν με), so-and-so, from every excess of power and every violent act ... you who created gods, archangels (ἀρχαγγέλους), and decans. The ten thousands of angels (ἀγγέλους) stood by [you] and exalted the heaven ... (*PGM* IV.1190-1205).

Here the suppliant seeks protection from more than just foul fate. These angels seek to exercise their harmful influence in the affairs of daily life. Similarly, *PGM* I.214-16 seeks Helios's protection from these evil angels: "[Wherefore, come] to me, you who are lord over all angels (ἀγγέλων); shield (ὑπεράσπισόν μου) me against all excess of magical power of aerial daimon [and] fate."

The most common function of the magical amulets was for protection, as Campbell Bonner demonstrates in his superb analysis of Greek and Egyptian amulets.[47] Consequently, one of the most common inscriptions is a one-word request for protection: φύλασσε, διαφύλασσε, φύλαξον, or διαφύλαξον. Another typical command is the word "flee" (φεῦγε), which is directed to the evil spirits bringing harm or ill health. The names of helpful gods, spirits, and *paredroi* were often inscribed on amulets. They would have been invoked in the chant or invocation (ἐπῳδαί) that went along with the use of the amulet. These practices also characterized Jewish magic (see below), but in that context the names of angels were most commonly invoked.

b. The Invocation of Angels in Revelatory Magic and Dream Divination

Angels not only appear in apotropaic magic, but also in the context of revelatory magic. A common theme in the magical texts, revelatory magic

---

[47] Campbell Bonner, *Studies in Magical Amulets Chiefly Graeco-Egyptian* (Ann Arbor: Univ. of Michigan Press, 1950) 45-50.

often involved performing a rite and saying a chant (ἐπῳδή/ἐπαοιδή) as the means of summoning a deity to make an appearance and impart information.

The oracular god Apollo is frequently called upon in the magical texts. In one text a number of "angels"—including those known to Judaism—are called upon together with Apollo for revelation:

> O lord Apollo, come with Paian.
> Give answer to my questions, lord. O master ...
> Whene'er my priestly lips voice secret words:
> First angel (ἄγγελε) of the god, great Zeus. *Iao*
> And you, *Michael,* who rule heaven's realm,
> I call (καλῶ), and you, archangel (πρωτάγγελε) *Gabriel*
> Down from Olympos, *Abrasax,* delighting
> In dawns, come gracious who view sunset from
> The dawn, *Adonai.* Father of the world
> ... (other names invoked) ...
> I adjure (ὁρκίζω) these holy and divine names that
> They send me the divine spirit and that it
> Fulfill what I have in my heart and soul
> Hear blessed one, I call you who rule heav'n
> And earth and Chaos and Hades where dwell ...
> Send me this demon (δαίμονα) at my sacred chants ...
> (*PGM* I.296-327; italics mine)[48]

The invocation is prefaced by a recipe for constructing an amulet to serve as a protective charm for the rite ("daimons [avoid] the characters' magical powers"; l. 274). The suppliant faced danger from "the heavenly gods and chthonic daimons" that would be summoned; he needed protection in order to perform the rite fearlessly. Morton Smith regards this charm as having been written "by a completely assimilated Jew."[49] It is perhaps better, in this instance, to follow the (uncharacteristic) caution of Goodenough, who allows the possibility that this is a Jewish charm recast by a pagan, but finds it more probable that it is pagan since Apollo is addressed first and the Jewish personages are all declared secondary to

---

[48] For a similar invocation, but invoking Helios together with some Jewish angel names (including the term ἄγγελος), see *PGM* III.198-229 (= Hymn 5; see Preisendanz, *PGM* 2.241-42).

[49] Morton Smith, "A Note on Some Jewish Assimilationists: The Angels (P. Berlin 5025b, P. Louvre 2391)," *Journal of the Ancient Near Eastern Society* 16-17 (1984-85) 209. He believes there is a tinge of monotheism still present when he says that the author of this text "invoked these Jewish angels as powerful, albeit subordinate, members of the imaginary supernatural society."

Zeus.[50] If the text was a pagan creation, it well illustrates how Jewish angelology penetrated pagan magic.[51]

Another revelatory text identifies "angels" with stars. In *PGM* VII.795-845, the angel "Zizaubio" is invoked to come and reveal whatever the conjurer wishes to know. Zizaubio is called a "holy angel" (ἅγιε ἄγγελε) who is subordinate to the sun, probably the sun god Ra or Helios. The angel comes from the constellation Pleiades and makes his appearance as a fiery star. The text assumes that there are many other angels that are under his authority who also can aid in accomplishing the revelation. The preparatory rite for the dream oracle involves taking a branch of laurel (a plant sacred to Apollo) and inscribing on each leaf a sign of the Zodiac. Although in this particular text the word στοιχεῖα never appears, we will find ample reason for making the further identification of ἄγγελοι with στοιχεῖα in other texts as I will describe in Chapter 6.

A similar astral emphasis appears in the so-called "Eighth Book of Moses,[52]" but here the content of the revelation is more closely linked to acquiring a knowledge of astral fate. The basic purpose of this spell, which appears in each version of the Eighth Book of Moses, is "divination and correction of fate."[53] The invocation is addressed to a superior deity (perhaps Serapis), but the magician expects to see the appearance of an angel: "An angel (ἄγγελος) will come in, and you say to the angel, 'Greetings, lord'" (*PGM* XIII.603-609). Once the angel appears, the suppliant not only has the opportunity to inquire about his/her fate, but if it is bad, to have it changed. The conjurer says, "'Both initiate me by these rites I am performing and present me [to the god], and let the fate determined by my birth be revealed to me.' And if he [the angel] says anything bad, say, 'Wash off from me the evils of fate'" (ἀπάλειψόν μου τὰ τῆς εἱμαρμένης κακά; ll. 613-14). At the end of the invocation, the magician

---

50 Goodenough, *Symbols,* 2.194.

51 The text also illustrates the translation of the Tetragrammaton into Greek ('Ιάω). Iao here functions as a name of power on much the same level as Michael, Gabriel, and the rest.

52 The presence of the name of Moses does not force us to regard this charm as essentially Jewish. Moses had great fame as a magician among the Gentiles who passed on Moses magical legends and circulated magical texts under his name. See Morton Smith in *GMPT,* 172, note 2, and John Gager, *Moses in Greco-Roman Paganism* (SBLMS 16; Nashville: Abingdon, 1972), Chapter 4: "Moses and Magic," 134-61.

53 Morton Smith, "The Eighth Book of Moses and How it Grew (*P. Leid.* J 395)," *Atti del XVII Congresso Internazionale di Papirologia* (Napoli: Centro Internazionale per lo Studio Dei Papiri Ercolanesi, 1984) 2.685-86. This purpose is set in contrast to the revelation of the name of God, which is not found in our passage.

assures the deity that he serves his angel (δουλεύω ὑπὸ τὸν σὸν [κόσμον τῷ σῷ] ἀγγέλῳ; l. 617; cf. also l. 74).

"Lamp divination" represents still another form of revelatory magic involving angels. The form of this kind of divination is quite similar to what we have just discussed. It includes the preparation of an amulet for protection, purity prohibitions, the performance of a rite, and the actual invocation. The difference is the inclusion of a lamp in the performance of the rite and invocation. A vision of the god and the angels, usually described by the word ὁράω, also plays a significant part, as is evident in *PGM* IV.1104-14: "After saying the light-bringing spell, open your eyes and you will see (ὄψῃ) the light of the lamp becoming like a vault. Then while closing your eyes say ... , and after opening your eyes you will see (ὄψῃ) all things wide-open and the greatest brightenss within, but the lamp shining nowhere. Then you will see (ὄψῃ) the god ... while being carried in the hands of 2 angels (ἀγγέλων) with 12 rays around them."

c. The Invocation of Angels for Other Purposes

Some of the magical texts give recipes for ensuring prosperity and success in any kind of endeavor. The angels of various deities could be called upon to perform the request, as in *PGM* IV.3165-67: "Give me all favor, all success, for the angel (ἄγγελος) bringing good, who stands beside [the goddess] Tyche, is with you. Accordingly, give profit [and] success to this house." The request is actually addressed to 18 different names, presumably representing 18 angels, written on an amulet and recited. Similarly, after reciting nine names (including the Jewish names Iao, Sabaoth, Adonai, Eloai, and Abrasax), *PGM* XXXVI.35-68 summarizes the demand for power: "supreme angels (κύριοι ἄγγελοι), give to me ... victory, favor, reputation, [and] advantage over all men and over all women ..."[54]

Aphrodisiacs are among the most common spells in the magical texts. Again, angels are often invoked as the functionaries of this magic. The angels of Judaism are present in *PGM* XXXVI. 295-311, in which the suppliant is directed to invoke "the angels of God who overturned the five cities" (including Sodom and Gomorrah). The recipe then instructs, "so also serve me, in regards to her, and do not allow her to go to bed or to

---

[54] Because of the inclusion of the Jewish names, Goodenough, *Symbols,* 2.196, regards this as another example of Judaism taking over a pagan charm.

find sleep until she comes and fulfills the mystery rite of Aphrodite." A number of magical names are then given, which include the Jewish terms Sabaoth, Michael, Zouriel, Gabriel, Istrael (probably a corruption of "Israel"), and Abraam.

The syncretistic mixing of Jewish and pagan divine names is evident in another love magic text (*P. Colon.* Inv. T. 1.1-83).[55] Whereas in the previous text the term "angels" summarized the names invoked, in this text the word "demons" is used: "I adjure all ghosts (δέμονας) in this place to come to the assistance of this ghost (δέμονι). Raise yourself up for me from the repose that keeps you and go out into every district and every quarter and every house and every shop, and drive, spellbind Matrona ... that she may not ... be able to go with any other man than Theodorus" (ll. 14-23). The deities invoked in this text—Pluto, Kore, Persophoneia, Ereschigal, Anubis, Hecate, Artemis—belong to the underworld with its terrors, perhaps explaining why the term δέμων is used (versus the more neutral δαίμων). The conjuration also seeks the assistance of the untimely dead. The magical words, however, demonstrate a strong Jewish influence: line 3: Iaō; Adōnelēe, Baruch, Adōnai; line 34: Baruch, Adōnai; line 35: Abrasax.

Finally, numerous examples could be cited of angels invoked to bring a curse upon another person. This is primarily the domain of the curse tablets *(defixiones)*.[56] The use of these lead tablets is well attested in the first century A.D. as illustrated by Tacitus. He tells us of Germanicus's suspicion that Cnaeus Calpurnius Piso had poisoned him, which resulted in the search of Piso's home (A.D. 16): "Examination of the floor and walls of his bedroom revealed the remains of human bodies, spells, curses, and lead tablets inscribed with the name of Germanicus (*et nomen Germanici plumbeis tabulis insculptum*), charred and bloody ashes, and other malignant objects which are supposed to consign souls to the powers of the tomb" (Tacitus, *Annals* 2.67).[57]

---

[55] The text is published with critical notes by Dierk Wortmann, "Neue Magische Texte," *Bonner Jahrbücher* 168 (1968) 60-80. The English translation of the text here depends on D. R. Jordan, "A Love Charm with Verses," *ZPE* 72 (1988) 245-49.

[56] See Audollent, *Defixionum,* 466-69. See especially the following texts: §§156.39; 157.18-19; 162.22; 163.34; 164.29; 168b.7; 187.54. See also: 155a.44-45; 155b.20.

[57] For additional references to the lead desecration texts in literary sources, see Gager, *Curse Tablets,* 243-64 (= Chapter 8: Testimonies). See also Audollent, *Defixionum,* CXVII-CXXV. They draw attention to their use by the Greeks as early as the time of Homer and Plato.

Typical of this type is a well-known *defixio* discovered in Rome in which "angels" are invoked to bring loss and destruction to a charioteer:

> I invoke (ἐξορκίζω) you holy angels (ἅγιοι ἄγγελοι) and holy names, join forces with this restraining spell and bind, tie up, block, strike, overthrow, harm, destroy, kill, and shatter Eucherios the charioteer and all his horses tomorrow in the arena of Rome. Let the starting gates not [open] properly. Let him not compete quickly. Let him not pass. Let him not squeeze over. Let him not win ... let him be bound, let him be broken up, and let him drag behind by your power. Both in the early races and in the later ones. Now, now! Quickly, Quickly![58]

This desecration text is one of a group of tablets discovered in Rome known as the Sethian tablets—so named after the deity Typhon/Seth whose image is inscribed on most of the texts. Many of these tablets use the term ἄγγελοι and/or ἀρχάγγελοι, demonic assistants to Typhon/Seth who perform the harmful curse.[59] The phrase, "I conjure you holy angels" (ὑμᾶς ὁρκίζω ἁγίους ἀγγέλους [sic]) appears repeatedly.

In an Attic curse tablet, underworld spirits are invoked with the expression ἀγγέλης καταχθονίοις [sic] together with a number of other deities such as Hermes, Hekate, Pluto, Kore, Persephone, and the Moira (Audollent, *Defixionum,* §§74.1 and 75.2-3). The Jewish angel Michael together with "Iaō," El, and the Egyptian goddess Nephthō (Nebtha t) are invoked on a late second-century A.D. tablet found in Puteoli, near Rome.[60] Many other examples of the term ἄγγελοι being used in the *defixiones* could be cited. In his survey of curse tablets not included in special corpora, D. R. Jordan cites a few examples of angels invoked to perform the curse.[61]

The magical papyri contain many recipes on how to construct such curse tablets. "Angels" are invoked in the same formulaic manner. On some occasions, ἄγγελοι can referred to absolutely without any explicit

---

[58] Audollent, *Defixionum,* §187; text given and discussed on pp. 243-47. Translation by Gager, *Curse Tablets,* 73-74 (= no. 15). See also the translation and discussion in Segal, "Hellenistic Magic," 358.

[59] See Audollent, *Defixionum,* §§155a.44-45; 155b.20; 156.39; 157.18-19; 162.22; 163.34; 164.29; 168b.7; 187.54.

[60] Gager, *Curse Tablets,* 216 (no. 118); Audollent, *Defixionum,* §208; Wünsch, *Fluchtafeln,* 7-9.

[61] Jordan, "Defixiones," 151-97. See §164, Nysa-Skythopolis, Beth-Shean (the κύριοι ἄγγελοι are invoked to bind the parts of three women); §167, Berytus (the ἅγιοι ἄγγελοι are invoked against 34 intended victims); §169, Claudiopolis (an adjuration to κύριοι Θεοὶ ἄγγελοι).

connection to a known deity, as in *PGM* XXXVI. 246-255: "Supreme angels (κύριοι ἄγγελοι), just as this frog drips with blood and dries up, so also will the body of him, NN whom NN bore, because I conjure you (ὀρκίζω), who are in command of fire MASKELLI MASKELLO." In this instance, the "angels" are merely perceived as powerful beings that can be manipulated to fulfil the request. The conjuration needs to be written on a lead tablet and used in an elaborate frog ritual.

In other instances, the "angels" are connected to a known deity. *PGM* III.1-164 describes an involved cat-drowning ritual as part of a recipe for a *defixio* to gain victory in chariot races. The ritual is associated with the "cat-faced god," probably to be identified with the Egyptian deity Sekhmet-Bastet, known in the Egyptian magical texts. This god is referred to as a spirit, angel, and a demon as seen below:

> Lines 3-8: "Come hither to me ... you the cat-faced god (θεός) ... and accomplish the NN deed ... because I am calling upon you, O sacred spirit (πνε[ῦμ]α)."
>
> Lines 49-53: "I conjure you (ὀρκίζω), the daimon (δαίμονα) that has been aroused in this place, and you, the daimon (δ[αί]μονα) of the cat that has been endowed with spirit (πνευματωτοῦ); come ... and perform for me the NN deed."
>
> Lines 71-76: "I conjure you (ὀρκίζω), the powerful and mighty angel (ἄγγελον) of this animal in this place ... rouse yourself for me against my enemies, NN, and perform NN deed."
>
> Lines 90-: "I conjure you (ὀρκίζω), Maskelli Maskellō, (formula). Perform for me this, the NN deed, by virtue of your visage, cat-faced spirit (ἄγγελος)."

At the end of the recipe, the Jewish influence is clearly seen in the syncretistic invocation of the Jewish god and archangels: "I conjure (ἐνεύχομαι) you by the god Iaō, by the god Abaōth, by the god Adōnai, by the god Michaēl, by the god Souriēl, by the god Gabriēl, by the god Raphaēl, by the god Abrasax [followed by a string of magical names] (ll. 147-50)." It appears that the pagan writer only borrowed the names from Judaism and not the formula since Iao and Adonai are set parallel as two distinct gods and placed on the same level as the archangels.

d. *Paredroi*: The Mighty Assistants Who Perform Anything

The magical papyri and the *defixiones* know a special category of divine assistant termed a *paredros* (πάρεδρος). These *paredroi* are special divine assistants subordinate to the gods, but they are also spirits who can serve

people through being compelled by the magical arts.[62] By definition, the *paredroi* appear to be quite similar to angels, and, indeed they were perceived by the practitioners of magic to be roughly identical. In the Sethian tablets they are indistinguishable, e.g. "I conjure you (ὁρκίζο [sic]) holy angels and archangels and holy Eulamonas and holy assistants (παρέδρους) and holy Symphonia and holy characters" (Audollent, *Defixionum,* §155b.20-23; see also §163.22; 16b.72-73). Here the angels and paredroi are regarded as the demonic servants of Typhon-Seth.[63]

The *paredroi* fulfill a similar function in the magical papyri. A good example is a recipe for love magic in which Selene, here identified with Aphrodite, is adjured to send an *aggelos* or a *paredros* to draw a woman for whom the conjurer longs (*PGM* VII.862-918). In every subsequent reference to the divine assistant, the conjuration uses the word *aggelos*. The recipe assumes that there is a different angel/paredros for every hour of the night and proceeds to recite each by name, e.g. "send forth your angel (ἄγγελος) who is appointed over the 1st hour: Menebain, and the one over the 2nd hour: Neboun, and the one over the 3rd hour: Lēmnei, and the one ..." (ll. 897-99).

It appears that *aggelos* and *paredros* are used interchangeably in the context of magic. Perhaps the only distinction would be that the term *paredros* carries a slightly stronger emphasis on the action of assisting. This may be seen in a line out of the previous recipe where the participial form of the term appears: "Mistress, send forth your angel (ἄγγελον) from among those who assist (παρεδρεύοντων) you ..." (ll. 891-92). For the magician who endeavors to make use of the divine power of each of these supernatural beings, they truly provide the assistance one needs to accomplish the task at hand.

5. Summary

(1) There is a clear veneration of "angels" that takes place in the context of magic. First, the angels are called upon in the place of the deity: such expressions as ἐπικάλουμαί σε, καλῶ σε, δέομαί σε, (ἐξ)ὁρκίζω σε, and ἐνεύχομαί σε are common in the appeal to angels. Secondly, the angels are spoken to directly and are given commands or directions by the human suppliants, e.g. protect me, preserve me, hear me, give me, come

---

62 Karl Preisendanz, "Paredros," *PW* 18/2.1428-29.

63 See the comments of Audollent, *Defixionum,* 211, note on line 20.

to me, serve me, fulfill for me, and perform for me. Thirdly, the angels take on many of the attributes and functions of deity: an angel may be called a κύριος or a θεός and may be the recipient of human service (δουλεύω).

(2) The term ἄγγελος itself functions as a summary expression for the intermediaries and assistants of the gods. In many of the texts, the term ἄγγελος is used interchangeably with πνεῦμα, δαίμων, δαιμόνιον, δέμων, and sometimes even θεός.

(3) In the pagan magical texts, angels are frequently associated with the stars, especially in terms of their power over fate. As we will see in Chapter 6, this fact suggests an association of the angels with the στοιχεῖα τοῦ κόσμου. "Angels" are also commonly associated with the underworld and the underworld deities.

(4) The pagan magical texts we have surveyed show a few connections with other characteristics of the Colossian "philosophy": (a) we have noticed the importance of vision in revelatory magic (cf. ἑόρακεν in Col 2:18); (b) magical rites often had stringent purity regulations that consisted of many prohibitions; (c) "knowledge" is important for magic— knowing the right names to call upon, having the appropriate protective amulet, knowing the proper invocation, etc.

(5) These magical texts are not as concerned with ultimate salvation, of obtaining life after death; their primary concern focuses on improving life here and now. Apotropaic magic, in particular, is concerned to thwart the influence of evil forces for the present. In this way, magic distinguishes itself from Gnosis, which is chiefly concerned about the dangers of the heavenly ascent after death.

(6) The texts also are a good illustration of the religious syncretism of the time. Jewish angels, as well as the names and titles of Yahweh, are mixed up with pagan intermediaries and all referred to as "angels." The personalities of the deities and the spirits are lost in favor of a pragmatic concern about which ones have power and which ones will help.

CHAPTER 2

The Veneration of Angels in Judaism

Angels become very significant in the Jewish literature from the second century B.C. through the New Testament era.[1] This interest in angels continues in the literature of Judaism evidenced in the Talmudim and Midrashim, but especially in the later Hekhalot texts and the various pieces of evidence documenting the practice of Jewish magic.

Much of the interest in angels was taken up with speculation about the heavenly sanctuary and the throne of God. The ascent to heaven motif was becoming a popular theme. Speculation about the activities of angels in the heavens and the origin of evil angels and demons was a significant concern in the apocalyptic literature. The Qumran documents as well as the apocalyptic literature also demonstrate a curiosity about the part the angels play in God's war against evil, especially at the end of time.

What continues to remain as a question is the accuracy of saying that there was a strand of Judaism involved in "worshiping" angels. As we will see at the end of this section, this accusation was directed against the Jews in the first few centuries of our era. It is clear that the Qumran community, especially as seen in the Sabbath liturgies, viewed themselves as participating with the angels in the worship of God. But, in what sense can we say the Jews "worshipped" angels?

This charge is especially validated in the context of magic and mysticism. Just as divine intermediaries were invoked in pagan magic, a similar practice occured with Jews invoking angels.

---

[1] For a comprehensive overview of the development of Jewish belief in angels, see M. Mach, *Entwicklungsstadien des jüdischen Engelglaubens in vorrabbinischer Zeit* (TSAJ 34; Tübingen: J.C.B. Mohr [Paul Siebeck], 1992). See also M. J. Davidson, *Angels at Qumran* (JSPSS 11; Sheffield: JSOT Press, 1992). Davidson's study focuses on a comparison of the angelology of *1 Enoch* with the writings of Qumran.

1. Calling on Angels: The Literature of Judaism

R. Judan said … 'If trouble comes on a man he must not cry either to Michael or to Gabriel but he must cry to Me, and I answer him at once. That is what is written: Every one that calleth on the name of the Lord shall be delivered' (T. Jerus. *Berachoth* ix.1, p. 13a).[2]

Peter Schäfer regards the polemic of this passage as pointing to concrete instances in popular Judaism of people turning to angels instead of directly to God.[3] He contends that this is one of a series of texts in the Rabbinic writings that attest to actual cults of angels within Judaism.[4]

Whether or not we agree with Schäfer that there were angel cults, it does appear that individuals within Judaism had moved beyond participating with the angels in the worship of God to making the angels themselves an object of veneration. Many Jews were increasingly inclined to appeal to angels rather than to God for deliverance and for the provision of their needs. Angels were becoming mediators in a manner like the *angeloi* and *paredroi* in pagan religion and magic. Against this, we find polemic in the Rabbinic texts and traces of the tendency in the apocryphal and pseudepigraphal literature.

Why would Jews invoke angels rather than God for protection and help? Perhaps one of the chief reasons stems from their increasing consciousness (in the time leading up to the NT era) that angels were active in the struggle against Satan and his forces. We see this particularly in the book of Daniel, the forerunner to the apocalyptic literature. The book unveils the heavenly struggle between Michael, "the great prince who protects your people" (Dan 12:1), and the opposing angelic princes of Persia and Greece (Dan 10:13, 20). Gabriel, the angel who reveals these heavenly insights to Daniel (Dan 8:16), says that he has come in response to Daniel's prayer and humility: "Do not be afraid, Daniel. Since the first day that you set your mind to gain understanding and to humble yourself before your God, your words were heard, and I have come in response to them" (Dan 10:12). Nowhere does the book say that Daniel directed his prayers to Michael or Gabriel; Daniel's humility was before God and his prayers were directly to God. Nevertheless, it is now only a small step for

---

[2] As cited in A. Lukyn Williams, "The Cult of the Angels at Colossae," *JTS* 10 (1909) 429-30.

[3] Peter Schäfer, *Rivalität zwischen Engeln und Menschen* (Studia Judaica 8; Berlin: Walter de Gruyter, 1975) 70.

[4] Schäfer, *Rivalität*, 67-74.

succeeding generations to direct their prayers to Michael and the other angels rather than directly to God. The idea of invoking mediators would also have been reinforced by the influence of Hellenism on the Jews of Palestine and, especially, the diaspora.

We can see this next step taking place in some of the Pseudepigraphal literature. The protective angel becomes an increasing object of veneration, as seen in the Testament of Dan: "And now fear the Lord, my children, be on guard against Satan and his spirits. Draw near to God *and to the angel* who intercedes for you, because he is the mediator between God and men for the peace of Israel. He shall stand in opposition to the kingdom of the enemy" (*Testament of Dan* 6:1-2; italics mine).

Learning the names of the angels was also perceived as important so that the appropriate one could be invoked when there was need in order to provide deliverance. To his revealing angel, Levi said, "I beg you, Lord, teach me your name, so that I may call on you in the day of tribulation" (*Testament of Levi* 5:5). The Testament of Solomon, as we will see below, becomes the prime example of calling on angels to thwart evil, especially the evil inflicted by demons and rebellious angels.

This may have been one of the reasons that an initiate into the Essene sect had to take an oath of admission that bound him "to guard carefully the books of their sect and the names of the angels" (Josephus, *J.W.* 2.8.7 §139). This interpretation is strengthened by the immediately preceding context in Josephus, which reveals that the Essenes diligently studied ancient books that gave them special insight into the qualities of roots and the properties of stones (*J.W.* 2.8.6 §136). As Lightfoot observed a century ago, "this expression ... points clearly to the study of occult sciences, and recalls the alliance with the practice of magical arts."[5] Although there is no direct confirmation of the Qumran community's magical/medical use of stones and herbs, the group was interested in healing. Furthermore, the discovery of fragments of the books of Jubilees and 1 Enoch at Qumran illustrates their combined interest in angels and healing.[6] There are even a few instances of exorcistic healing in the traditions of Qumran. In the Prayer of Nabonidus, Nabonidus explains

---

[5] Lightfoot, "Colossian Heresy," in *Conflict*, 23. However, he described these magical practices as "a distinguishing feature of Gnosticism." One wonders if he had the benefit of our revised understanding of Gnosticism and our advanced knowledge of Hellenistic magic whether he would refrain from this identification.

[6] See Todd S. Beall, *Josephus' Description of the Essenes Illustrated by the Dead Sea Scrolls* (SNTSMS 58; Cambridge: University Press, 1988) 72.

that, "I was afflicted [with an evil ulcer] for seven years ... and an exorcist pardoned my sins. He was a Jew from among the [children of the exile of Judah]" (4QPrNab 1-3). The Genesis Apocryphon also relates a story regarding the exorcism of Pharaoh at the hand of Abraham after the ruler of Egypt had experienced two years of torment by an evil spirit while he possessed Sarah: "So I prayed [for him] ... and I laid my hands on his [head]; and the scourge departed from him and the evil [spirit] was expelled [from him], and he lived" (1QapGen 20:19-20). Émile Puech has recently identified two exorcism rituals in the Psalms scroll of Qumran cave 11 (11QPsApᵃ 4:4-5:3; 5:4-14).[7] B. Nitzan has argued that two hymns from cave 4 were written in an incantation form and were recited as protection against evil spirits (4Q510, 511).[8]

The apotropaic use of herbs is well illustrated in the book of Jubilees. The book explains that Noah was taught by the angels of God how to heal demonic afflictions and illnesses by the the use of herbs. Noah then wrote these recipes down in a book that he passed on to his oldest son, Shem, with the result that "the evil spirits were restrained from following the sons of Noah" (*Jubilees* 10:10-14).

The book of 1 Enoch may lend help in clarifying one of the reasons why "guarding the names of the angels" would have been important to the Essene sectarians and how they may have used these names.[9] 1 Enoch 69 gives an extended list of the names and specific evil activities of the chiefs of the fallen angels (69:1-13). One of the fallen angels had revealed the names to Michael. The same angel also revealed a secret "oath" that causes the angels to respond (69:13, 21, 26). Michael, in turn, revealed these names to the people of God because they are the key to thwarting the evil influence of these fallen beings (69:15). Specifically,

> He [Beqa, a fallen angel] spoke to Michael to disclose to him his secret name so that he would memorize this secret name of his, so that he would call it up in an oath in order that they [the fallen angels] shall tremble before it and the oath. He (then) re-

---

[7] E. Puech, "*11QPsApᵃ*: Un Rituel de'Exorcismes. Essai de Reconstruction," *RevQ* 55 (1990) 377-408; idem, "Les Deux Derniers Psaumes Davidiques du Rituel d'Exorcisme, 11QPsApᵃ IV 4-V 14," in *The Dead Sea Scrolls. Forty Years of Research* (STDJ 10; eds. D. Dimant & U. Rappaport; Leiden: Brill, 1992) 64-89.

[8] B. Nitzan, "Hymns from Qumran—4Q510-4Q511," in *The Dead Sea Scrolls. Forty Years of Research* (STDJ 10; eds. D. Dimant & U. Rappaport; Leiden: Brill, 1992) 53-63.

[9] It must be noted, however, that the Book of Parables (*1 Enoch* 37-71) was not found among the many fragments of 1 Enoch discovered at Qumran.

vealed these to the children of the people, (and) all the hidden things and this power of this oath, for it is power and strength itself. The Evil One placed this oath in Michael's hand (*1 Enoch* 69:14-15).[10]

Interestingly, the names are also related to the stars (69:21):[11] "and by the same oath the stars complete their courses of travel; if they call (or, if he calls) their names, he causes them to respond." This is significant in light of the function of the *stoicheia* in the Colossian teaching (see Chapter 6). The teaching of this passage comes very close to what is represented in the Jewish magical tradition. Here we have secret names (the names of the fallen angels) and a formula (the oath) which guarantees success ("this oath has become dominant over them"; *1 Enoch* 69:26). All of this takes place still within a monotheistic context. The mediation of angels, however, has eclipsed the direct personal involvement of God himself in the affairs of his people, and indeed, in the workings of much of creation.

On the other hand, within the same literature there is a stream of tradition that runs counter to the use of magic. In *1 Enoch* 7:1 and 8:3 it is the fallen angels who teach people about magical medicine, "the cutting of roots," plants, incantations, and astrology. It is quite possible that these comments go beyond an indictment of pagan practice to forms of magic practiced within Judaism which were considered evil and off limits.

Such a judgment may be partially confirmed by Pseudo-Philo (1 c. A.D.), a Jewish document that serves as an excellent witness to the beliefs of the Palestinian synagogues just before A.D. 70.[12] Chapter 34 describes a certain magician from Midian called Aod who successfully lured Israel into serving the gods of the Midianites ostensibly during the time of Gideon (cf. Judges 6). In agreement with 1 Enoch 7-8, the writer of Pseudo-Philo explains that magic was revealed by the evil angels before their condemnation. Aod could perform amazing deeds (such as making the sun appear in the middle of the night) because he was actually given supernatural assistance by fallen angels. Pseudo-Philo explains that, "he went away and worked with his magic tricks and gave orders to the angels who were in charge of magicians, for he had been sacrificing to them for a long time" (34:2). His magic successfully fulfilled his intent "and the people of Israel were deceived and began to serve the gods of the

---

[10] Translation by E. Isaac, "1 (Ethiopic Apocalypse of) Enoch," in *OTP* 1.48.

[11] For a survey of Jewish texts in which angels are identified with stars, see "Exkurs 1 - Die Engel und die Sterne," in Mach, *Entwicklungsstadien,* 173-84.

[12] See the introductory comments by D. J. Harrington, in "Pseudo-Philo," *OTP* 2.297-302.

Midianites" (34:5). This story about Aod is unique to Pseudo-Philo and causes one to ask his motive for including it in his work. Perhaps the most plausible explanation is that it represents an indirect polemic against certain Jewish circles who had been deceived in the same way that Israel was deceived in the time of Gideon. Some Jews were sacrificing to angels and invoking them ("giving them orders") to carry out certain supernatural feats. The author of Pseudo-Philo regards this as tantamount to serving pagan gods, which he connects with being led astray by evil angels.

Finally, as noted earlier, Peter Schäfer has gathered evidence out of the Rabbinic literature that he thinks reveals clear traces of angel cults within Judaism.[13] Schäfer contends, "References to such a practice are found admittedly only indirectly, however, these polemical references are enough to posit the actual existence of an angel cult within Rabbinic Judaism."[14] He gathers his evidence into four categories: (1) prohibitions against images, (2) prohibitions against offerings, (3) prohibitions against invocations, and (4) prohibitions against veneration. He believes such a phenomenon may have come about through an overemphasis on "the otherness" and distance of God, which may have led some to believe that there was now no longer the necessity or even the possibility of turning directly to God[15]; instead, they turned to angelic mediators.

One could add to the testimony adduced by Schäfer the polemic of Rabbi Maimonides against the use of the Mezuzah as an amulet. He chastises those who write the names of angels or figures (probably pictorial representations of angels) on the scroll as fools who will have no share in the future world (*Yad: Teefillin*, v, 4).[16] This appears to be nothing more than the magical invocation of angels for protection and well-being.

The concrete instances presupposed by the Rabbinic polemic may also have taken place simply as part of an encroaching magical understanding of God and his angels on the part of certain Jews, as we have been point-

---

[13] Schäfer, *Rivalität*, 67-74. See his book for the references. Erwin R. Goodenough, *Jewish Symbols in the Greco-Roman Period*, Volume 2: The Archaeological Evidence from the Diaspora (Bollingen Series 37; New York: Bollingen Foundation, 1953) 146, reaches the same conclusion: "The rabbis consistently opposed any type of angel worship, and their prohibitions are usually naïvely quoted to prove that Jews did not practice it ... their very protest also bears witness to its practice."

[14] Schäfer, *Rivalität*, 67 (translation mine).

[15] Schäfer, *Rivalität*, 74.

[16] See Goodenough, *Symbols*, 2.209-11.

ing to above and will demonstrate below. Goodenough explains it in terms of a Jewish adaptation to hellenistic polytheism.[17]

In an insightful monograph titled *The Commerce of the Sacred,* Jack N. Lightstone has suggested that the fear of demons and the invocation of angels for apotropaic purposes was a distinctive feature of Diaspora Judaism.[18] He says, "In the Graeco-Roman Diaspora ... belief in demons seems everywhere, and in all periods."[19] He observes that the Diaspora Jews relied on certain priests who in reality functioned as shamanistic holy men to mediate the angelic powers of heaven for protection and other highly specific ends.[20] He illustrates his thesis with Jewish incantation texts from the *Papyri Graecae Magicae,* a collection of Coptic magical texts, and the *Sepher Ha-Razim.* At the minimum, he clearly demonstrates shamanistic tendencies in the Judaism of the Diaspora.[21]

Both Goodenough and Lightstone have pointed us in the proper direction for understanding the kind of angelic veneration we find in the Judaism of Asia Minor and in the situation of the church at Colossae. We will now illustrate this tendency among Jews to invoke angels for protection and aid.

2. Calling on Angels: Amulets and Incantations

Widespread use of magical amulets is well attested in the Judaism of the Greco-Roman period. Amulets were worn for their protective power (apotropaic function) against demons, illness, enemies, and accidents. Jewish amulets were often engraved with cult objects (such as the menorah) and usually bore the names of angels, patriarchs, and/or magical signs and symbols. Sometimes pagan names, figures, and symbols appeared on amulets that were otherwise Jewish. Amulets were made out of a variety of objects, but most often precious stones.

---

[17] Goodenough, *Symbols,* 2.146.

[18] Jack N. Lightstone, *The Commerce of the Sacred* (Brown Judaic Studies 59; Chico, CA.: Scholar's Press, 1984).

[19] Lightstone, *Commerce,* 50; see also pp. 11-12.

[20] Lightstone, *Commerce,* 23-24.

[21] I do not agree with his thesis that the fear of demons and shamanistic mediation of heavenly powers was strictly a unique feature of the Diaspora and was alien to those who had direct access to the temple and its system of purification.

Literary evidence for the use of magical amulets is forthcoming from 2 Macc 13:32-45 in the account of Judas Maccabeus's campaign against the troops of Gorgias, the governor of Idumea. Judas won the battle, but a number of his men were killed in the fighting. When his men returned to retrieve the bodies of the dead soldiers, "under the tunic of every one of the dead they found sacred tokens of the idols of Jamnia, which the law forbids the Jews to wear" (13:40).[22] Goodenough aptly observes, "the passage tells us directly that in Palestine itself in the hellenistic period, even Jews who were so loyal to Judaism that they fought in the army of Judas Maccabeus had begun to syncretize, at least in the realm of magic and amulets."[23] He regards this passage as a polemic against a widespread Jewish custom of wearing amulets. Commenting on this passage, Bonner notes, "there were probably a good many Jews who wore images of heathen gods as amulets."[24]

The invocation of angels was common on Jewish amulets and was a fundamental feature of Jewish magic as a whole.[25] The following section will illustrate the role of angels in Jewish magic.

a. The Book of Tobit—An Angel Reveals Magical Rites and Binds a Demon

One needs only to look to the second-century B.C. book of Tobit to find angelic intervention against the demonic forces. Although this book does not represent the characters as calling directly on angels, it teaches that angels are involved in the human situation in an intimate way. In the story, the angel Raphael appears to Tobias in the form of an ordinary man and accompanies him on a journey from Ninevah to Ecbatana (Media). During the trip, Raphael instructs Tobias to take the liver, heart, and gall out of a huge fish that he caught. These organs were used in two separate magical rites that Raphael directs Tobias to perform. In the first, Tobias burns the heart and liver of the fish in the bedchamber of the woman to

---

[22] For a discussion of this passage, see Ephraim E. Urbach, *The Sages. Their Concepts and Beliefs* (Jerusalem: Magnes Press, 1975) 23, and Goodenough, *Symbols*, 2.216.

[23] Goodenough, *Symbols*, 2.216.

[24] Campbell Bonner, *Studies in Magical Amulets Chiefly Graeco-Egyptian* (Ann Arbor: Univ. of Michigan Press, 1950) 28.

[25] This was also noticed by Goodenough, *Symbols*, 2.145, and well illustrated throughout volume 2.

whom he was betrothed. This young lady, Sarah, had been possessed by the evil demon Asmodeus, who expressed his intense jealousy for her by murdering the seven successive men she married before they were able to physically consummate the marriage. By burning the organs with the incense, Tobias causes the evil demon to flee to the remotest part of Egypt where the angel Raphael bound him. Tobias is then able to safely marry the girl. In the second magical rite, Raphael instructs Tobias to apply the gall of the fish to the eyes of his recently blinded father, Tobit. In this instance, the author of the book does not trace the etiology of the blindness to a demon, but nevertheless the rite revealed by the angel was a success.

The book of Tobit, valuable for the picture it gives of Jewish culture and religious life in the first two centuries B.C., further confirms and illustrates how angels were becoming an increasing focus of attention in popular Jewish piety. Although every instance of prayer in the book of Tobit is directed toward God, we will see in the following examples from Jewish magic that this was not always the case.

b. Magical Papyri—Invocation of Angels

As we have already seen, the magical papyri provide numerous examples of people calling on "angels" to carry out their directives. When we return to the same corpus of texts to find examples of Jewish incantations, we face the difficulty of determining precisely what is Jewish in origin. There is such extensive two-way borrowing, i.e. pagans from Jews and vice-versa, that to determine which text is distinctively Jewish and which is not is rather subjective, and to some extent unnecessary. Perhaps the only difference between the Jews who practiced magic and their pagan counterparts has to do with the quantity of Jewish themes used in the conjuration; the techniques, magical words, and aims were largely the same. M. Simon, however, contends that there are three qualitative features that distinguish Jewish magic: (1) a great respect for Hebrew phrases that seemed to some Jews to have magical power; (2) a sense of the efficacious power of the divine name; and (3) an overwhelming regard for angels and demons.[26] Nevertheless, because of the reciprocal borrowing, many of the

---

[26] Marcel Simon, *Verus Israel. Etude sur les Relations entre Chrétiens et Juifs dans l'Empire Romain (132-425)* (Paris: Editions E. DeBoccard, 1964) 399-404. In this description of Jewish magic, he has been followed by Goodenough, *Symbols*, 2.161 and J. Charlesworth, "Prayer of Jacob," in *OTP* 2.716. See my previous discussion of this issue in *Ephesians: Power and Magic* (SNTSMS 63; Cambridge: University Press, 1989), 31.

texts we discussed in the previous chapter have relevance to our understanding of Jewish magic. In this section we will focus on a few texts that
are widely agreed to be Jewish in origin.

Our first example is an aphrodisiac recipe that instructs the user to call
on the angels of God who destroyed Sodom and Gomorrah to fulfill the
spell of attraction (*PGM* XXXVI.295-311). The text, which is widely
agreed to be Jewish,[27] involves performing a simple rite using sulfur and
then pronouncing the formula:

> The heavens of heavens opened, and the angels of God descended and overturned the
> five cities … you are the sulfur which God rained down on the middle of Sodom and
> Gomorrah … you are the sulfur which served God—so also serve me, NN, in re-
> gards to her, NN, and do not allow her to go to bed or to find sleep until she comes
> and fulfills the mystery rite of Aphrodite (ll. 298-306).

As the conjurer throws lumps of sulfur into a fire (as part of the rite), he
is to call on specific angels to perform the deed: "I conjure you (ὀρκίζω)
… by the great Michael, Zouriel, Gabriel" (ll. 307-10). In addition to the
angel names are a list of other names that include magical words (e.g. se-
sengenbarpharanges) and other Jewish names: Iaō, Sabaōth, Istraēl, and
Abraam. The reference to "the mystery of Aphrodite" probably has reference to sexual union and betrays the religious syncretism of this document.

In a very brief text of only eight lines, Jewish angels are invoked to
bring a dream revelation (*PGM* VII.1009-16). Following the performance
of a rite, the suppliant is required to say the following spell:

> I call upon (ἐπικάλουμαι)[you], Sabaoth, Michael, Raphael and you, [powerful ar-
> chang]el Gabriel, do not [simply] pass by me [as you bring visions], but let one of
> you enter and reveal [to me] concerning the NN matter, AIAI ACHĒNĒ IAŌ (ll.1012-
> 15).

In this text, as in the previous, angels are directly called upon. Sabaoth, if
this is a reference to Yahweh, is not regarded as the supreme God in this
instance, but is placed on the same level as the archangels. The final instruction is for the conjurer to write the spell on leaves of laurel and sleep
by them. This instruction reflects the syncretism of the recipe insofar as
laurel (δάφνη) was a plant sacred to the oracular god Apollo.[28]

---

[27] Goodenough, *Symbols*, 2.197; P. S. Alexander, "Incantations and Books of
Magic," in *HJP²*, 359.

[28] See *PGM* II.81: "Laurel (δάφνη), Apollo's holy plant of presage."

In the same papyrus, Michael is summoned together with Helios to bring favor and victory to the one who uses the formula (*PGM* VII.1017-26). The text is fragmentary, but it should be reconstructed to include the names of at least two additional angels. The spell is as follows:

> "[Hail, Helios!] Hail, Helios!, [Gabriel! Hail, Raphael! Hail,] Michael! Hail, whole [universe! Give me] the [authority] and power of SABAŌTH, the [strength of IAŌ,] and the success of ABLANATHANALBA, and [the might of] AKRAMMACHAMEREI. Grant that I [gain] the victory, as I have summoned you" (then write the 59-[letter] IAEŌ formula). "Grant [victory] because I know the names of the Good Daimon ('Αγαθοῦ Δαίμονος) ... accomplish this for me." Speak to [no one].

In this text, the names of the angels are freely mixed with the sun god. This does not conflict with the assessment that this is basically a Jewish in-cantation, since, as Goodenough has correctly observed, the mention of Helios here causes us to recall the figures of Helios in the ornamentation of the Jewish synagogues.[29] The syncretism of this spell, however, is fur-ther heightened by reference to "Agathos Daimon," a god common in the magical texts.

In a text that moves still further away from orthodox Judaism, the conjurer asks for an appearance of an "archangel" who is later identified with the sun-god Helios (*PGM* XIII.255-59). Morton Smith regards the spell as "unmistakably Jewish."[30] Although arguable, he is probably cor-rect because of the strong Jewish motifs. The conjurer appears to appeal to the power of Yahweh to solicit the appearance of the archangel: "I am he upon the two cherubim" (l. 255; cf. 1 Sam 4:4; 2 Sam 6:2).

Mention must also be made of one other Jewish magical text that does not directly invoke angels but in which angels play a significant role. The text is included in the second volume of Charlesworth's, *Old Testament Pseudepigrapha*, commonly referred to as "The Prayer of Jacob" (= *PGM* XXIIb.1-26).[31] Charlesworth contends that the text could be dated as early as the first century A.D. Much could be said about this 26-line text which Preisendanz regarded as a recipe for an amulet[32] and Charlesworth sees as a serious prayer. The fact that it ends with a formula—"say the prayer of Jacob seven times to the North and East" (l. 26)—gives it more the flavor of a magical text, although many other magical motifs are missing and it

---

[29] Goodenough, *Symbols*, 2.199-200. Alexander, "Incantations," 359, also regards this as a Jewish text.

[30] Morton Smith in *GMPT*, 179, note 64.

[31] See J. H. Charlesworth, "Prayer of Jacob," in *OTP* 2.713-19.

[32] Preisendanz, *PGM*, 2.148.

is directed to Yahweh. What is significant for us is the prominence given to angels: Yahweh is described primarily in terms of his relationship to the "powers" and "angels":

l. 2 = "[Fathe]r of (the) powe[rs (δυνάμεων) of the co]sm[os]"
l. 3 = "Creator of the angels and archang[e]l[s]"
l. 3 = "C[r]eator of the re[deeming] nam[es];"
l. 4 = "O Father of powe[r]s altogether,"
l. 5 = "[O Father] [to whom the] ch[erubim are sub]j[e]c[t]e[d];
l. 7 = "(You) the God o[f the p]owers,"
l. 7 = "the G[od of ang]els a[nd a]r[cha]ngels,"
l. 14 = "you who [si]t [u]pon th[e ...] ... Abri͞el, Lou͞el

Although the prayer is specifically addressed to the Father, the extraordinary emphasis on angelic powers could imply that they are intended as the functionaries for fulfilling the request. The specific request of the prayer is for wisdom and empowerment (πλήρωσόν με σοφίας, δυνάμωσ[ό]ν με), but the purpose for the power and the kind of wisdom intended are not explicitly stated. Both requests could have an intent similar to other magical texts for favor and success. The request to "fill my heart with good things," however, leans us in a more positive direction.

Finally, I will cite a Jewish-influenced Coptic magical text that illustrates the invocation of angels for protection from the demonic realm:

> May there hearken unto me
> All angels and archangels ...
> Help me, ye holy angels,
> May all my enemies flee before me
> ... (23 angelic names are invoked) ...
> That you come to me and stand beside me,
> And drive from before my face
> All impure spirits ...[33]

The text significantly post-dates the NT (fifth century A.D.), although it could very well contain some ancient traditions predating Christianity[34];

---

[33] Goodenough, *Symbols*, 2.175-76; Marvin Meyer and Richard Smith, eds., *Ancient Christian Magic. Coptic Texts of Ritual Power* (San Francisco: Harper Collins, 1994) 133-46 (= no. 71). For the text, see A. M. Kropp, *Ausgewählte koptische Zaubertexte* (Brussels: Foundation Reine Elisabeth, 1931) 2.176-99. Goodenough is insistent that incantations of this sort be sharply distinguished from Gnosticism (esp. pp. 174, 189). The magician is concerned only with manipulating the spirit world, whereas the Gnostics were concerned with organizing and systematizing the spirit realm.

[34] Goodenough, *Symbols*, 2.190, notes: "This is primitive raw material, and as here

however, we need to exercise significantly more caution in using it to illustrate the NT. More important for our purposes, at this point, is the observation that the text as a whole contains some definite Christian interpolations. It is still another example of Christians taking over Jewish magical tradition—precisely what may have happened in the mid-first century at Colossae!

c. Inscriptions—Invocation of Angels

There are three Jewish inscriptions that are particularly significant for illustrating the invocation of angels. This tendency may be illustrated by a pair of funerary inscriptions found on Rhenea, an island owned by Delos and used as a burial place for its inhabitants (CIJ 1.725 = SIG³.1181).[35] The two gravestones date to the first or second century B.C., have almost identical inscriptions, and are probably Jewish.[36] The inscriptions call for divine vengeance on the murderers of two girls, Heraclea and Marthina. The texts initially call upon Yahweh (ἐπικαλοῦμαι καὶ ἀξιῶ τὸν θεὸν τὸν ὕψιστον), but describe him as "the Lord of the Spirits" (τὸν κύριον τῶν πνευμάτων). Ultimately, they invoke God *and his angels* (κύριε ὁ πάντα ἐφορῶν καὶ οἱ ἄγγελοι θεοῦ) to avenge the innocent blood. There is no cultic worship of angels reflected in this text.[37] The angels are looked upon as functionaries of the most high God who could exact the justice so deeply desired by the grieving family.

---

presented it is overwhelmingly Jewish in its names and in its Old Testament phrases."

[35] For the texts, translations, and a full discussion, see Deissmann, *Light from the Ancient East* (4th ed.; New York: Harper and Brothers, 1927) 413-24 (= Appendix I: Jewish Prayers for Vengeance Found at Rheneia). See also J. G. Gager, *Curse Tablets and Binding Spells from the Ancient World* (Oxford: University Press, 1992) 185-87 (= no. 87). For additional discussion of the inscription, see M. Simon, "Remarques sur l'Angélolâtrie Juive au Début de l'Ére Chrétienne," *CRAIBL* (1971) 123; M. Hengel, "Die Synagogeninschrift von Stobi," *ZNW* 57 (1966) 156, note 32; A. T. Kraabel, "The Diaspora Synagogue: Archaeological and Epigraphic Evidence Since Sukenik," *ANRW* II.19.1 (1979) 493; *HJP²*, 3.1.70.

[36] Although A. T. Kraabel, "New Evidence of the Samaritan Diaspora Has Been Found on Delos," *BA* 147 (March 1984) 44-46, has suggested that the building on Delos traditionally described as a Jewish synagogue may have been Samaritan. He bases his argument for a Samaritan presence at Delos on two inscriptions that contain the term Ἀργαριζείν, which he interprets as the Greek equivalent of *Har Garizim*, Hebrew for Mount Gerizim.

[37] So also, Deissmann, *Light*, 418, who notes, "The invocation of the ἄγγελοι θεοῦ (line 10) does not warrant us in assuming a special cult of the angels."

One other example of this kind of appeal to angels for protection is represented in a Jewish magical tablet found in Patras (Achaia) (*CIJ* 717). The precise date of the inscription is uncertain. The apotropaic character of the tablet is clearly seen by the following lines:

l. 17   [O angels], protect (διαφυλάξατε) the household and lives of
        John and Georgia [...

l. 23   ēlailail Sabaōth Elo[e]ei[n ...

l. 27   Arīel, [Ga]brīel [...]īel [...
        Arīel, Michaēl, Raphaēl, [...]droēl, Thelchīe[l
        Sisīe[l], O[urīel, Raph]aēl, Danīel, [...
        Ourīel [...] Bore[e]l, Iaō Sabaō[th]
        Charīel [...

l. 47   [O] power of these angels and characters
        give victory and favor to John and Georgia and
        this household while they live.[38]

This text well illustrates how popular Judaism was calling directly upon the angels for protection, favor, and success in daily living. Additional inscriptions demonstrating this tendency in Asia Minor will be discussed in the next chapter.

d. Amulets—Invocation of Angels

Numerous examples of amulets using angel names could be cited. I have provided a few examples of local Jewish amulets in the following section. For a full discussion of this topic, one should consult the superb collection and discussion of Jewish amulets (with many pictures and illustrations) in the second volume of E. R. Goodenough's *Jewish Symbols of the Greco-Roman Period*. C. Bonner published a few amulets in which the angels of Judaism are invoked (esp. Michael and Gabriel).[39] More recently, E. Zwierlein-Diehl has published a second-century amulet from Egypt that

---

[38] The lines that I have cited are also the only lines given by J. B. Frey, *CIJ*, 517 (no. 717). Translation is mine.

[39] Bonner, *Amulets*, §§309, 310, 311, 338, et al.

includes the angel names Michael and Ouriel.[40] Another second-century amulet also invokes Michael as well as Iaō.[41]

I will give one example of a Greek amulet to illustrate the Jewish practice of invoking angels for protection. This particular amulet was discovered in Syria and appears to be distinctively Jewish, not showing any definite signs of Christian influence. It is a rectangular gold leaf with a Greek inscription that dates to the end of the Roman empire (perhaps the 4th century A.D.).[42] The inscription reads:

> I call upon (ἐπικάλουμαι) Iao, Michael, Gabriel, Ouriel, Arbathiao, Arbathiao, Adonai, Ablanathanalba, Sabaoth, Sesengenbarpharanges, Akrammachamari, Semesilamps, Laalam, Chorbeth, Thaubarrabau, Thobarimmauo, Eloai, α ε η ι ο υ ω ... [this is followed by three lines containing magical "characters" or symbols] ... Lords, archangels, gods, and ye divine characters, drive away every evil and every convulsion and every stomach ailment from the child whom NN has borne, beginning today and from the present hour, forever ...[43]

Here, as we have seen before, Yahweh receives no prominence of place. "Iao," "Sabaoth," and "Adonai" are strung together with all the other names thought to be laden with power. Although this is not consistent with official Judaism, it is consistent with many examples of Jewish magic.

e. Summary

The angels of Judaism played a significant part in Jewish magic. In some cases, God was directly called upon with the assumption that he could dispatch his angels for the benefit of the person(s) as he would see fit (e.g. Prayer of Jacob). In many other cases, however, Jews took the next larger step. Rather than focusing their attention on God, they called directly upon the angels to do their bidding.

It is quite difficult to reconstruct the social context of each of the amulets and inscriptions, but it would appear that most of these were created for individual rather than group use. These individual practices, however,

---

[40] E. Zwierlein-Diehl, *Magische Amulette und ander Gemmen des Instituts für Altertumskunde der Universität zu Köln* (ARWAW, PC 20; Opladen: Westdeutscher Verlag, 1992) 71-73 (= no. 13).

[41] Zwierlein-Diehl, *Magische Amulette*, 65-68 (= no. 9).

[42] Paul Perdrizet, "Amulette Grecque Trouvée en Syrie," *Revue des Études Grecques* 41 (1928) 73-82. For a discussion of the amulet, see Goodenough, *Symbols*, 2.204.

[43] Translation by Goodenough, *Symbols*, 2.204.

cannot be seen in total isolation from the local cults. It is quite conceivable that the attitude toward the angels in private devotion would have had an influence on the worship of the local synagogues.[44] This is precisely one of the points Goodenough was attempting to make in his massive *Jewish Symbols of the Greco-Roman World*. He contends, and I think rightly, that individuals practiced syncretism before the group did. He applies this conclusion not only to their local worship, but also to the kind of decorations exhibited in the synagogues. He concludes his second volume by arguing that "the amulets have suggested that a much more genuine syncretism may be reflected in the symbols of the synagogues than we have dared or shall dare to say."[45]

3. Testament of Solomon—Thwarting the Demons

Angels and demons are the primary focus of the *Testament of Solomon*. The document is the epitome of the magical invocation of angels in the context of popular Judaism. The book collects and builds upon a widespread Jewish and early Christian tradition that Solomon's vast wisdom extended to managing the demonic realm through calling on the help of angels. The self-attested purpose of the book is as follows: "at my death I wrote this testament to the sons of Israel and I gave (it) to them so that (they) might know the powers of the demons and their forms, as well as the names of the angels by which they are thwarted" (*TSol* 15:14).

The book represents an amalgam of magical recipes for thwarting the influence and harmful activities of the cruel demons. The good angels from the throne of God play the key role in most of the recipes. Any given demon can only be thwarted by knowing the right angel to call upon.

The loose putative framework for the work is Solomon's narration of how he learned to manipulate demons to accomplish the construction of the temple. Into this overall structure are incorporated traditions about the names of demons and detailed descriptions of the nature of their evil activities. This is generally followed by an apotropaic formula which in-

---

[44] Lightstone, *Commerce*, 13, goes so far as to speak of the synagogue liturgy in the Diaspora as a "communal incantation."

[45] Goodenough, *Symbols*, 2.290.

volves invoking an angel. The following examples illustrate the role of the
angels in thwarting (καταργέω) the demons:

> (1) The demon Asmodeus (from the constellation of the Great Bear) who at-
> tacks newlyweds and virgins: "Then I [Solomon] adjured (ὤρκισα) him by the name
> of the Lord Sabaoth, 'Asmodeus, fear God, and tell me by which angel you are
> thwarted.' The demon said, 'Raphael, the one who stands before God; but also a
> liver and a gall of a fish smoking on coals of charcoal drives me away'" (*TSol* 5:9).
> In this instance, the demon is not thwarted only by calling on an angel, but also by
> performing a rite using a fish. This tradition closely resembles what we have already
> observed in the book of Tobit.
>
> (2) The demon Lix Tetrax who spreads disunity and makes whirlwinds:
> "Finally, I asked him, 'By what name are you thwarted?' He responded, 'the name
> of the archangel Azael.' Then I placed my seal on the demon and commanded him to
> pick up stones ... ; compelled, the demon complied with his orders" (*TSol* 8:7-8).
> This "seal" (σφραγίς) represents an amulet that was allegedly given to Solomon by
> God through the archangel Michael (*TSol* 1:6). The magical ring also gave him
> power over demons. The text does not specify the contents of the inscription on the
> precious stone, but presumably it bore the names of angels. This tradition perpetuated
> the creation of numerous Solomonic magical amulets.[46]
>
> (3) The second planetary angel: "The second said [to Solomon], 'I am Strife. I
> cause strife by making available clubs, pellets, and swords, my implements of war.
> But I have an angel who thwarts me, Baruchiel'" (*TSol* 8:6).
>
> (4) The so-called Winged Dragon who attacks women: "After I glorified God I
> asked the dragon-shaped demon, saying, 'Tell me by what angel you are thwarted.'
> He replied, 'By the great angel who is seated in the second heaven, who is called in
> Hebrew Bazazath.' When I, Solomon, heard these things and invoked
> (ἐπικαλεσάμενος) his angel, I condemned him to cut marble for construction of the
> Temple of God" (*TSol* 14:7-8).
>
> (5) The 29th of the thirty-six στοιχεῖα τοῦ κόσμου: "I am called Rhyx
> Anoster. I unleash hysteria and cause pains in the blatter. If anyone mashes up the
> seeds of laurel into pure oil and massages (the body with it), saying, 'I adjure
> (ὀρκίζω) you by Marmaraoth,' I retreat immediately" (*TSol* 18:33).

As one can observe from these few examples from the Testament of
Solomon, the invocation of the appropriate angel is presented as essential
to alleviating demonic affliction. For its readers, the value of the work lay
in the book's insight into the names of the demons and their specific areas
of evil activity, but most importantly, in the names of angels who appear
to have power over individual demons. In these recipes, the Jewish (or
Christian) reader is not instructed to pray directly to Yahweh for deliver-

---

[46] For many examples, see Goodenough, *Symbols*, 2.227-35.

ance. The focus has now been shifted to the angelic intermediaries. One is expected to call upon angels.

The primary value of the Testament is the invaluable insight that it provides into common folk belief. C. C. McCown, the editor of the critical edition of the text, comments, "It is as a leaf from the common man's thinking that the *Testament* has its chief value."[47] The recipes and formulas contained in the Testament correspond in large measure to what we have already seen in the magical papyri and amulets (and see below). Taken together, this mass of magical material gives us a rare glimpse into the widespread belief in demonic powers in antiquity and some of the mechanisms used to deal with this kind of evil. The Testament is a prime example of Jewish apotropaic magic that was widely used in the Roman world.

The date of the final form of the Testament is impossible to fix with any certainty. As D. Duling has noted, "Whether one follows McCown's early third-century dating or Preisendanz's earlier one [first or second century A.D.], there is general agreement that much of the testament reflects first-century Judaism in Palestine."[48]

There is no doubt that the Testament, even if compiled by a Christian author, incorporates mainly Jewish traditions about demons and angels. And herein lies its value for interpreting the New Testament. Duling rightly notes, "It is perhaps in this area of demonology (and angelology) that the Testament offers information which could be exploited for New Testament interpretation."[49] Similarly, P. Alexander affirmed that the Testament "clearly contains much Jewish material, and can surely be used to throw light on early Jewish demonology."[50]

The difficulty in using the Testament for the interpretation of the NT is the problem of discerning Christian additions to originally Jewish material. In most places, Christian additions are readily identifiable (e.g. the Arabian demon Ephippas is said to be thwarted "by the one who is going

---

[47] Chester C. McCown, *The Testament of Solomon* (Untersuchungen zum Neuen Testament 9; Leipzig: J. C. Heinrichs, 1922) 1.

[48] D. C. Duling, "Testament of Solomon," in *OTP* 1.942.

[49] D. C. Duling, "The Testament of Solomon: Retrospect and Prospect," *JSP* 2 (1988) 102.

[50] Alexander, "Incantations," 374. See also McCown, *Testament*, 3, who contends that the Testament represents pre-Talmudic Palestinian demonology. J. H. Charlesworth, "Jewish Interest in Astrology During the Hellenistic and Roman Period," *ANRW* II.20.2 (1987) 935, agrees with McCown and concludes, "in its present form [the Testament] probably dates from the third century and is Christian; but it seems to contain Jewish traditions that are traceable back to the first century."

to be born from a virgin and be crucified by the Jews" [*TSol* 22:20]). It is
somewhat more awkward to make a decision regarding certain concepts
that appear in the NT that may also have been present in the Jewish environment but are not otherwise attested (e.g. the discussion about Beelzeboul as the prince of demons [*TSol* 3:1-5; cf. Mark 3:22 and pars.]). In
general, however, since the NT was not concerned to take up speculation
about demonic beings, it is probably safer to conclude that the NT reflects
the common Jewish terminology for demons (as one encounters in the
Testament of Solomon) rather than seeing the NT as the protogenitor of
neologisms for demons (e.g. Beelzeboul, στοιχεῖα, κοσμοκράτορες, etc.

The fact that the Testament of Solomon came into Christian use (some
entertain the possibility that it was actually compiled by a Christian) also
has great significance for our investigation. Not only does the Testament
reflect a common magical piety among certain Jewish circles, it also
serves as an illustration of the adoption of these ideas and practices by
early Christianity.[51] The entry of magical practices into the Christian
church, therefore, did not necessarily come through paganism; they just as
easily could have entered through Judaism.

It is impossible to determine the precise social background of the Testament. Given the foregoing discussion, it is also imperative that we speak
in the plural, i.e. of social locations, both Jewish and early Christian.
McCown conjectured that the Testament might be traced to the Ophites or
some other similar but unknown sect.[52] McCown's suggestion leaves the
door open to the possibility that the Testament may have had a cultic as
well as a private use.

The Testament quite possibly has additional significance for our understanding of the Judaism of Asia Minor since it may have stemmed from
western Asia Minor. C. C. McCown had, in fact, argued for an Asia Minor provenance of the document,[53] although this suggestion has not re-

---

[51] The Solomonic magical tradition was also known to the writers of some of the Nag
Hammadi documents; see S. Giversen, "Solomon und die Dämonen," *Essays on the Nag
Hammadi Texts in Honor of Alexander Böhlig* (NHS 3; ed. M. Krause; Leiden: Brill,
1972) 16-21.

[52] McCown, *Testament*, 14, 70. Duling, "Retrospect," 98-101, briefly discusses the
issue, but does not speculate on the Testament's proximity to any known sect. Rather, he
rightly concludes that the Testament does not correspond to the testament genre. He suggests that the author of the work made use of the word "testament" with reference to his
work as a device for enhancing the reputation of his collection of Solomonic magical legends in the face of the illegality of magic in the empire.

[53] McCown, *Testament*, 110.

ceived much support in recent years.[54] Although there are some good reasons to commend an Asia Minor provenance,[55] the identification will never be certain given the paucity of evidence at hand. As we saw in the first section of the paper, the Solomonic magical tradition (which included the invocation of angels) was firmly established in the Judaism of Asia Minor.

4. Sepher Ha-Razim

The *Sepher Ha-Razim* (סֵפֶר הָרָזִים: "Book of Mysteries") provides us with still another glimpse of the popular Judaism that venerated angels. The text of this document has only recently been restored to an approximation of the original form by the efforts of Mordecai Margalioth.[56] He based his reconstruction on a series of Hebrew Genizah fragments. Peter Schäfer, however, has doubted that the fragements originally constituted one book, particularly in the form constructed by Margalioth.[57] Schäfer also distinguishes *Sepher Ha-Razim* from the Hekhaloth literature.[58] It is therefore more accurate to see *Sepher Ha-Razim* as a collection of Jewish incantation texts.

---

[54] Most recently, Duling, "Retrospect," 97, however, has argued for (Syria-) Palestine; so also K. Preisendanz, "Salomo," in *PWSup* 8.690. Alexander, "Incantations," 374, suggests Egpyt.

[55] (1) The Solomonic magical tradition is epigraphically attested for Asia Minor. (2) One of the only two geographical terms in the document is Lydia (southwest Asia Minor; see 8:4). The other is Olympus (northeastern Greece; see 8:4). While it is explainable why the writer of the document would have mentioned Olympus, famous as the reputed home of the gods in Greek mythology and religion, it is difficulty to see why the writer would have mentioned the territory of Lydia unless the writer lived there or near there and was familiar with some local traditions. (3) The document explicitly names "Lix Tetrax" (7:5), two of the six *Ephesia Grammata* purportedly written on the cultic statue of the Ephesian Artemis. (4) *T. Sol.* also reports a demon telling Solomon, "I shall harm when I order (you to be bound) with the bonds of Artemis" (8:11), which is best understood as the Ephesian Artemis, a patronness of magic.

[56] Mordecai Margalioth, *Sepher Ha-Razim* (Jerusalem: Yediot Achronot, 1966) (in Hebrew). Michael Morgan has provided an English translation of the work in his *Sepher Ha-Razim: The Book of Mysteries* (SBLTT 25, Pseudepigrapha Series 11; Chico: Scholar's Press, 1983).

[57] P. Schäfer, "Tradition and Redaction in Hekhaloth Literature," in *Hekhalot-Studien*, (TSAJ 19; Tübingen: J.C.B. Mohr [Paul Siebeck], 1988) 15.

[58] Schäfer, "Hekhalot Literature," 15.

The general contents of the book had been previously known through extracts scattered in *Sepher Razi'el*. Although the book probably dates to the fourth century, scholars agree that it represents a compilation of much earlier material.[59] The high quality of its Hebrew has led some to postulate a Palestinian provenance,[60] although one cannot be certain.

Although the work consists only of about 800 lines, nearly 700 angel names are mentioned. These occur in an overall framework giving a description of the seven heavens and their subdivisions. The names of the angels populating each of the six heavens and a description of their activities are given. Interwoven within these descriptions are numerous magical formulas. I. Gruenwald accurately notes that the book "displays a highly developed angelology, and the invocation of these angels comes in the place of the magical formula (*Zauberwörter*) in the magical papyri."[61] Morgan believes that the magical formulas and spells were placed within the cosmological frawework to make them appear as legitimate, i.e. legal, Jewish practices.[62] In the description of the seventh heaven, wherein is the throne of God, a semblance of monotheism is retained. God is praised as the "king of kings" and "lord of hosts": "by all the angels he is revered" (7.20) and "[he is] exalted among the angels of heaven" (7.23). Although angels are the object of invocation and veneration until the description of the seventh heaven, at this point Yahweh becomes the focus of praise and adoration.

In our earlier description of the veneration of angels in magic (see the previous chapter), we saw that angels were invoked for protection from evil (apotropaic magic), to make an appearance for interrogation (revelatory magic), as well as to fulfill aphrodisiacs, to bring prosperity or success, or to perform a curse against someone. *All of these functions are also illustrated in the Jewish* Sepher Ha-Razim. In fact, the *Sepher Ha-Razim* is best illustrated by the magical formula contained in the *Papyri Graecae Magicae*. The magical rites that are prescribed, the characters and

---

[59] Morgan, *Sepher Ha-Razim*, 9, comments, "It is crucial to recognize that what fascinates us most about this text, the magic, is part of a folk tradition which dates from an earlier time... In dating SHR we are not dating the antiquity of the praxeis themselves." Alexander, "Incantations," 349, places the *terminus a quo* for the compilation at c. A.D. 350. Charlesworth, "Jewish Interest in Astrology," 936, dates the document from around the third century, but argues that it probably contains earlier Jewish traditions. See also Chen Merchavya, "Razim, Sefer Ha-," *Encyclopaedia Judaica* 13 (1971) 1595.

[60] Alexander, "Incantations," 349. He also leaves open the possibility of Egypt.

[61] I. Gruenwald, *Apocalyptic and Merkavah Mysticism* (AGJU 14; Leiden: Brill, 1980) 231.

[62] Morgan, *Sepher Ha-Razim*, 9.

symbols, and the purity regulations are all paralleled in the magical papyri. *Sepher Ha-Razim* also illustrates the syncretistic nature of Jewish
magic by the presence of formulas in which pagan deities are invoked: a
prayer to Helios (4.61-63), Aphrodite is invoked as the evening star
(1.126), Hermes is invoked under his title, "the ram-bearer" (1.178), and
the moon (perhaps Selene) is invoked twice (2.50-54 and 2.166-71).[63]

A few typical examples will help to illustrate the prominent role of angels in the *Sepher Ha-Razim* (the angel names are given in transliteration
without vowels):

(1) Apotropaic Magic: "Upon the eighth step [in the second heaven] stand
these: 'BRH, BRQY'L, 'DWNY'L, ᶜZRY'L, BRKY'L, ᶜMY'L, QDSY'L,
MRGY'L, PRW'L, PNY'L, MRBNY'L, MRNYS'L, SMY'L, ᶜMNY'L, MTN'L,
HWD HWD ... They rule the spirits that wander in the earth, and in a place where
their name is invoked an evil spirit cannot appear. If you wish to drive off an evil
spirit so it will not come to a woman when she is in childbirth and so it will not kill
her child, before the woman's pregnancy write (the names of) these angels on a
golden *lamella* and place it in a silver tubular case and let her wear it, and at the time
of childbirth take four silver *lamellae* and write upon them (the names of) the angels
and place them in the four sides of the house and no (evil) spirit will come in"
(2.118-29).

(2) Revelatory Magic: "These are the names of the angels who serve BNHL in
the third encampment [in the first heaven]: ... [the names of thirty-six angels are now
given] ... These angels tell everyone who, in purity, gains power over them, what
will happen on the earth in each and every year, whether for plenty or for famine,
whether rains will be abundant or sparse ... and whether death or suffering will befall
mankind" (1.84-94). The fact that thirty-six angels are named who have knowledge
about future events on earth makes it quite possible that these are the angelic guardians of each 10° of the heavenly sphere; in Greek literature they would be known as
the "decans" or the στοιχεῖα (see *TSol.* 18).[64] It is also significant to note that successful interrogation of the angels depends on having attained ritual purity. This is
reiterated at the end of the charm: "And do, (as in) every operation, act in purity, and
you will succeed" (1.108).

(3) For love magic: "If you wish to put the love of a man into the heart of a
woman, or to arrange for a poor man to wed a rich woman, take two copper *lamellae*
and write upon them, on both sides, the names of these angels, and the name of the
man and the name of the woman and say thus: 'I ask of you, angels who rule the
fates of the children of Adam and Eve, that you do my will and bring in conjunction

---

[63] See the discussion of this in Alexander, "Incantations," 347. See also P. Schäfer,
"Jewish Magic Literature in Late Antiquity and Early Middle Ages," *JJS* 41 (1990) 82.

[64] On the astral decans, see Wilhelm Gundel, *Dekane und Dekansternbilder. Ein Beitrag zur Geschichte der Sternbilder der Kulturvölker* (2d ed.; Darmstadt: Wissenschaftliche Buchgesellschaft, 1969) esp. 27-28, 69-70.

the planet of N son of N into conjunction with (the planet of) the woman N daughter of N. Let him find favor and affection in her eyes and do not let her belong to any man except him'" (2.31-35). Reflected in this spell is again the belief in astrological destiny. However, there is no resignation to fate. By following the appropriate formula and calling upon the right angels, fate can be altered and one's personal desires can be realized.

(4) For the creation of a defixio: "If you wish to give your enemy trouble in sleeping, take the head of a black dog that never saw light during its days and take a *lamella* from a strip of (lead) pipe from an aqueduct, and write upon it (the names of) these angels [the 16 angels on the fourth step of the second heaven] and say thus: 'I hand over to you, angels of disquiet who stand upon the fourth step, the life and the soul and the spirit of N son of N so that you may tie him in chains of iron and bind him to a bronze yoke ... let him weep and cry like a woman at childbirth, and do not permit any (other) man to release him (from this spell)'" (2.62-67).

The veneration of angels, as we find in the *Sepher Ha-Razim,* may bring us a long way toward interpreting the polemical expression, "veneration of angels," in Colossians. People are not encouraged to bring their supplications and requests to God in *Sepher Ha-Razim* but to angels. The emphasis on ritual purity and humility in the book also finds parallels in the competing teaching at Colossae. Even the *stoicheia* may be present in the thirty-six angels who have dominance over astrological fate.

J. N. Lightstone may also be correct in seeing *Sepher Ha-Razim* as a piece of evidence demonstrating the presence of certain Jewish holy men functioning as shamans in the Diaspora.[65] The visionary ascent to heaven, according to Lightstone, "grounds the authority of the theurgist and provides the measure of the extent of that authority."[66] This shaman is therefore in no danger of being overcome by demons and is in a position to help others deal with the influence of these hostile forces.

Sepher Ha-Razim serves as an excellent piece of evidence for the practice of magic and astrology in "official" Judaism. P. Alexander notes that, "there is good evidence to suggest that such material circulated at the very heart of Rabbinic society."[67] If this is the case, as I. Gruenwald would also affirm, how much more involved in these kinds of practices were the common Jews of the diaspora. Gruenwald remarks, "We may well assume that the common people were less conscientious in restricting their use of magic."[68] Accordingly, Gruenwald considers the *Sepher Ha-Razim* and similar books more reliable than the rabbinic writings for transmitting to

---

65 Lightstone, *Commerce,* 31.
66 Lightstone, *Commerce,* 43.
67 Alexander, "Incantations," 349.
68 Gruenwald, *Apocalyptic,* 228, 230.

us the nature and scope of occult practices among the common people. M. Margalioth regards it as an apt illustration of why the Church Fathers attacked the Jews for praying not to God but to angels and for practicing magic.[69]

5. The Hekhalot Literature

Thanks to the editing and publishing efforts of Peter Schäfer and his colleagues, the Jewish Hekhalot literature has now become accessible.[70] This material helps us to better understand one important stream of early Jewish mysticism.

Since the Second World War, biblical scholars have relied heavily on the works of Gershom Sholem for insight into the earliest forms of Jewish mysticism known as *Merkabah Mysticism*, visionary ascent to heaven with a focus on the divine throne-chariot (Ezekiel 1).[71] Scholem suggested that this mysticism arose as early as the second century (possibly even earlier) and was deeply influenced by Gnostic speculation about the ascent of the soul through the planetary spheres controlled by hostile angelic powers.[72] I. Gruenwald has successfully challenged Scholem's conclusion that Merkabah mysticism, even in its most developed form, was Gnostic.[73] In particular, he pointed to the absence of anti-cosmic dualism in Merkabah mysticism as well as to the presupposition that the mystic always returns from his heavenly ascent and visionary experiences to his body on earth.[74]

---

[69] Margalioth, *Sepher Ha-Razim*, 14 (cited in Gruenwald, *Apocalyptic*, 230).

[70] P. Schäfer, ed. *Synopse zur Hekhlot-Literatur* (TSAJ 2; Tübingen: J.C.B. Mohr [Paul Siebeck], 1981).

[71] G. Scholem, *Major Trends in Jewish Mysticism* (London: Thames and Hudson, 1955); idem, *Jewish Gnosticism, Merkabah Mysticism, and Talmudic Tradition* (New York: Jewish Theological Seminary of America, 1960).

[72] Scholem, *Major Trends*, 39-78 (= Chapter 2: "Merkabah Mysticism and Jewish Gnosticism").

[73] I. Gruenwald, "The Problem of Anti-Gnostic Polemic in Rabbinic Literature," in *Studies in Gnosticism and Hellenistic Religions* (EPRO 91, FS. G. Quispel; Leiden: Brill, 1981) 176-77. See also A. F. Segal, "Heavenly Ascent in Hellenistic Judaism, Early Christianity and Their Environment," *ANRW* II.23.2 (1980) 1368, who argues that the merkabah texts should be seen as offshoots of apocalyptic literature rather than Gnosticism.

[74] Gruenwald, "Anti-Gnostic Polemic," 176-77; idem, *Apocalyptic*, 110-11; idem, "Knowledge and Vision," *IOS* 3 (1973) 91.

The lack of a redemptive quality in these writings further distinguishes them from Gnosis.[75]

The recent work of Peter Schäfer has resulted in further modifications to Scholem's view and greater insight into the nature of the Hekhalot literature.[76] Whereas Scholem contended that the ascent of the Merkabah mystic through the seven palaces (*hekhalot*) to the throne-chariot was the major theme of the Hekhalot literature, Schäfer argues that descriptions of the ascent itself are actually peripheral to the main concerns of the Hekhalot literature. He suggests that there were two aims reflectected in the literature: (1) to participate in the heavenly liturgy and thereby to confirm that the earthly congregation stands in direct contact with God, and (2) to make a comprehensive knowledge of Torah available through magical adjuration (versus intense study). What we have in the Hekhalot materials then is a unique combination of magic and mysticism into a theurgic ritual.

Schäfer stresses the strongly magical character of the literature. He notes, "we are concerned here with eminently magical texts which deal with forceful adjurations."[77] As in much of the Jewish magical materials we have already assessed, the objects of invocation and adjuration are the angels. In some of the rituals, the intent is actually to bring the angel down to earth to fulfill the requests of the person. Schäfer describes this as, in effect, "a reverse heavenly journey: instead of the mystic ascending to heaven, the angel descends to carry out the mystic's wishes."[78]

Visionary experience, according to Schäfer, is a minor part of the heavenly journey of the mystic. He says, "The first surprising result of an examination of the texts is that the ascent accounts say almost nothing at all about what the mystic actually sees when he finally arrives at the goal of his wishes."[79] The emphasis is rather on the mystic's participation in he heavenly liturgy rather than on a culminating vision.

Schäfer also places a much later date on the form of Jewish mysticism reflected in the Hekhalot literature than did Scholem. Schäfer contends that the material is not a product of Rabbinic Judaism but rather a post-

---

[75] Gruenwald, *Apocalyptic*, 110.

[76] See especially P. Schäfer, "The Aim and Purpose of Early Jewish Mysticism," *Hekhalot-Studien* (TSAJ 19; Tübingen: J.C.B. Mohr [Paul Siebeck], 1988) 277-95.

[77] Schäfer, "Early Jewish Mysticism," 282.

[78] Schäfer, "Early Jewish Mysticism," 282. See also idem, "Jewish Magic Literature," 76, where Schäfer notes, "One of the major characteristics of Hekhalot literature is the conjuring of angels to execute the will of man."

[79] Schäfer, "Early Jewish Mysticism," 285.

Rabbinic phenomenon.[80] This makes the material essentially irrelevant for NT interpretation. The Hekhalot literature instead gives us a fascinating picture of how a post-Rabbinic circle of Jews drew on some much earlier traditions—the magical invocation of angels and mystical participation in heavenly liturgy (as reflected in the Qumran *Songs of the Sabbath Sacrifice*—and developed their own unique form of theurgic ritual. This interpretation thus precludes an understanding of the Colossian "philosophy" as an early form of Jewish Gnosticism or Merkabah mysticism.[81]

We could examine still more examples of Jewish magic to demonstrate the tendency to call on angels for help and revelation. Documents such as *Harba de Moshe (The Sword of Moses)*[82] and additional Jewish amulets[83] would further corroborate our thesis. J. Neusner has also documented well the extent to which Babylonian Jews in the Talmudic era feared demons, invoked angels, and practiced magic.[84] What is clear in what we examined is a long-lasting tendency withing Judaism to invoke angels for protection and help and a strong impulse to assimilate local pagan beliefs in the realm of magic and folk belief.

6. Accusations of Jewish Angel Worship

The Jews frequently faced accusations from both pagans and Christians that they worshipped angels. One of the clearest pagan statements to this effect can be found in Origen, *Contra Celsum* 1.27: "Let us see how Celsus, who professes to know everything, misrepresents the Jews when he says that 'they worship (σέβειν) angels and are addicted to sorcery (γοητεία) of which Moses was their teacher." Celsus is quoted again later in the same book: "The first thing about the Jews which may well cause amazement is that although they worship the heaven and the angels in it (ἀγγέλους σέβουσι)" (5.6; cf. also 6.30).[85] It is true that Origen dis-

---

[80] Schäfer, "Early Jewish Mysticism," 285.

[81] See, for example, Bruce, *Colossians*, 21-26.

[82] The document is discussed in Alexander, "Incantations," 350-52.

[83] See especially J. Naveh & S. Shaked, *Amulets and Magic Bowls: Aramaic Incantations of Late Antiquity* (Jerusalem/Leiden: Brill, 1985). For a good description of this material, see Schäfer, "Jewish Magic Literature," 82-85.

[84] See J. Neusner, *The Wonder-Working Lawyers of Talmudic Babylonia* (Studies in Judaism; Lanham, MD.: University Press of America, 1987) 184-222.

[85] Both translations taken from H. Chadwick, *Origen: Contra Celsum* (Cambridge:

missed the accusations as they were framed by Celsus, but he did so on the basis of how Jews ought to have approached God as based on OT revelation, not by appealing to known Jewish practices.[86] As Williams rightly observed, "It is clear that although Origen knew of this accusation against the Jews the whole tone of his remarks suggest that he did not believe it, save perhaps in connexion with sorcery (cf. 5.9)."[87] This confirms the direction to which the evidence we have looked at thus far points.

The *Kerygma Petrou* as recorded by Origen (*Comm. Joh.* 13.17) and Clement (*Strom.* 6.5.41) also calls attention to the Jewish "worship of angels." The key indictment, as recorded by Clement, reads as follows: "They also who think that they alone know God, do not know him, worshiping angels and archangels the months and the moon (λατρεύοντες ἀγγέλοις καὶ ἀρχαγγέλοις, μηνὶ καὶ σελήνῃ)."[88] In the Syriac recension of the *Apology of Aristides*, the accusation is made against the Jews that, "In the methods of their actions their service is to angels and not to God, in that they observe sabbaths and new moons and the passover and the great fast, and the fast, and circumcision, and cleanness of meats."[89] Jerome even goes so far as to speak of "victims offered not to God but to the angels and to the impure spirits" in Judaism (Jerome, *Epist.* 121.10).[90]

It is true that all these statements were made by unsympathetic outsiders. Therefore, we must exercise caution in basing too much on their evaluation since they may represent generalization and caricaturization.[91]

University Press, 1979) 26. For Greek text, see M. Borret, *Origène, Contre Celse* (SC 132; Paris: Editions du Cerf, 1969) 24.

[86] L. Hurtado, *One God, One Lord: Early Christian Devotion and Ancient Jewish Monotheism* (Philadelphia: Fortress, 1988) 33, does not take this consideration into account in his dismissal of the veracity of Celsus's statement. Furthermore, given Celsus's effort to portray the Jews as inconsistent, it is possible that he capitalized on the variety of practices he witnessed in Judaism, i.e. he tried to make a point based on some groups who venerate angels knowing full well that this was not representative of all of Judaism.

[87] Williams, "Cult," 428.

[88] *Clemens Alexandrinus, Band II: Stromata Buch I-VI* (GCS; eds. O. Stählin & L. Früchtel; Berlin: Akademie, 1985) 452. The citation in Origen's commentary only varies slightly: λατρεύοντες ἀγγέλοις καὶ μηνὶ καὶ σελήνῃ; C. Blanc, *Origène—Commentaire sur Saint Jean* (SC 222; Paris: Editions du Cerf, 1975) 86. W. Lueken, *Michael* (Göttingen: Vandenhoeck & Ruprecht) 5, regarded this statement as a direct witness for angel veneration (Engelverehrung) among the Jews.

[89] Translation by Williams, "Cult," 426. See also Lueken, *Michael*, 5.

[90] Migne, *PL* 22 (1854) 1032: "omnis Judaicarum observationum cultura destructa est, et quascumque offerunt victimas, non Deo offerunt, sed Angelis refugis et spiritibus immundis."

[91] As Hurtado, *One God*, 33-34, and Simon, "L'Angélolâtrie Juive," 126-32, observe.

However, we must ask why these writers would choose to characterize the Jews as worshiping/serving angels? The consistent testimony on this one point would lead us to believe that angels do have a prominent place in the religous life of at least some Jewish circles. These writers were probably familiar with Jewish circles that gave undue attention to angels (from their perspective) such that they felt justified in describing this practice as "worship" or "service." One cannot dismiss this testimony as having no basis in historical reality.

7. Summary

(1) It is now clear that there were certain circles within Judaism that venerated angels, namely, those which engaged in the practice of magic. Rather than calling upon (ἐπικάλουμαι) Yahweh for deliverance from their plight (cf. Joel 3:5 and Acts 2:21: "And everyone who calls on (ἐπικαλέσηται) the name of the Lord will be saved"), they called upon (ἐπικάλουμαι) angels and neglected turning to their God. The widespread fear of malevolent powers led many to practice apotropaic magic.

(2) In form, Jewish magic appears quite similar to pagan magic. The main difference is that the Jewish angels are usually substituted for pagan deities and intermediaries. Like their pagan counterparts, Jews used magical techniques for more than just protection from evil spirits. They sought revelation from angels about the future. They also invoked angels for help with all matters of day-to-day life, from having success in undertakings to finding a lover and cursing an enemy. The relationship of Yahweh with his people was displaced for a manipulative relationship with his angels.

(3) Michael surfaces as perhaps the most prominent of the angels in Jewish magical texts (including the Jewish angel inscriptions from Asia Minor in the next chapter), but he is only called upon for help, not worshipped in a cultic sense. He is called upon as a warrior against evils, a protector of the people of God. Because they called upon Michael and other angels, some groups of Jews and, subsequently, some groups of early Christians could be accused of "worshiping" Michael, or worshiping angels in general. But this is worship and veneration in a qualitatively different manner from the early Christian worship of Christ. Michael and the angels protect in matters of temporal importance—they fight against evil spirits, protect graves, avert natural disasters; Christ was worshipped for providing help not only in temporal matters but primarily for pro-

viding deliverance in an eternal perspective. There is no evidence of cultic activity in which Michael (or the other angels) was adored, sung to, sacrificed to, praised, and worshipped jointly with God.[92]

(4) It is very difficult to reach behind the texts we have examined and reconstruct their social setting in Judaism. It is clear, particularly with material evidence such as amulets, that angels were invoked privately. Other evidence (such as the *Testament of Solomon*, the *Sepher Ha-Razim*, among others) would leave open the possibility of corporate involvement in these practices.

(5) In spite of the fantastic concentration on angels in this material, one can still say that in most instances monotheism is retained. God has become more remote, but he is still supreme—above all the angels—and thus worthy of praise and blessing (cf. *Sepher Ha-Razim*). The angels are seen as more accessible and easily moved to action if one has sufficient knowledge, viz. their names and the appropriate rites and formulas.

(6) These Jewish texts reveal many other points of contact with the teaching of the opponents at Colossae (which we will develop later): (a) there are often purity regulations with stringent prohibitions (e.g. "do not touch …; "do not eat … ," etc.); (b) "knowledge" is important for success; (c) concern about the evil powers is a strong motivation for using the magic; (d) the Jews often engaged in revelatory magic (cf. the importance of vision in 2:18); (e) "humility" is mentioned in the *Sepher Ha-Razim* as a prerequisite for the effectiveness of the spell; (f) "wisdom," in the magical Solomonic tradition, is highly valued, viz. Solomon knew how to manage the angels and to control the demons.

---

[92] This confirms, in part, the conclusion reached by Hurtado, *One God*, 28-35, who attempts to refute the idea that some Jews, either in a Palestinian or a Diaspora setting, were involved in the worship of angels. Hurtado goes much too far, however, in denying any form of Jewish angel worship. In his recent critique of Hurtado's work, Paul Rainbow, "Jewish Monotheism as the Matrix for New Testament Christology: A Review Article," *NovT* 33 (1991) 83, also rejects Hurtado's conclusion and correctly notes that, "surely such worship of angels as there might have been was a declension from a socially shared ideal."

The Local Veneration of Angels

Local evidence for the veneration of angels will have the greatest significance for us as we attempt to discern the practices of "the philosophy" at Colossae. What makes this evidence particularly enticing is that there is so much of it. A relatively high number of inscriptions mentioning angels have been discovered in Asia Minor. Surprisingly, this material is not often used by biblical scholars in their discussion of the passage.

The prevalence of angel inscriptions has led scholars to speak of a distinctively Carian/Lydian/Phrygian piety (which gives a prominent place to angels) and to postulate the existence of "cults of angels" in Asia Minor during the Roman imperial period. Some have seen these cults as essentially pagan and have regarded the angels as mediator figures either (1) in the context of a tendency toward the worship of one "high god" in Asia Minor[1] or (2) by connecting the angels with the underworld (in the tradition of Hermes and Hekate) and regarding them as helpful or protective divine beings or agents.[2] Other scholars, however, have regarded the angel cults as Jewish and find corroborating evidence for their existence in rabbinic polemic and Christian sources.[3]

---

[1] See, for example, Nilsson, *GGR*, 1.577. See also A. R. R. Sheppard, "Pagan Cults of Angels in Roman Asia Minor," *Talanta* 12-13 (1980-81) 77-101. Sheppard, however, argues that certain features of the religious language of the angel inscriptions are best explained as borrowings from the religious language of Judaism. He thinks "angel" designates "a particular type of supernatural being" rather than a messenger of the gods.

[2] See, for example, F. Sokolowski, "Sur le Culte d'Angelos dans le Paganisme Grec et Romain," *HTR* 53 (1960) 225-29, who thinks many of the occurrences of ἄγγελος in the inscriptions refer to Hekate. See also, M. Dibelius, *Die Geisterwelt im Glauben des Paulus* (Göttingen: Vandenhoeck & Ruprecht, 1909) 209-21, and F. Andres, "Angelos," *RE* Supp. 3 (1918) 101-14.

[3] See especially M. Simon, "Remarques sur l'Angélolâtrie Juive au Début de l'Ere Chrétienne," *CRAIBL* (1971) 120-34. More recently, see M. Hengel, "Der Alte und der neue 'Schürer'," *JSS* 35 (1990) 37-38.

There is no doubt about the later Christian veneration of angels in Asia Minor, particularly the archangel Michael.[4] What is crucial for us to discern is the relationship of these inscriptions and the later veneration accorded to angels by Christians to the phrase "worship of angels" in Colossians 2:18.

Many of the inscriptions have been notoriously difficult to interpret. Some of the most foundational issues have failed to gain a consensus, viz. is a given inscription pagan, Jewish, or Christian? What is the identity and function of the "angel" in the text? Does the text betray assimilation and syncretism, and, if so, in what direction?

In this chapter I have collected these local inscriptions and make an attempt to interpret the nature and function of the angelic (mediator?) figure referred to in each. I have focused exclusively on inscriptions that use the word ἄγγελος, ἀγγελικός, or name one or more of the angel figures known to Judaism.[5] As part of the conclusion I will try to articulate a more precise understanding of what are commonly referred to as "angel cults" in Asia Minor. The ultimate aim, however, is to explain the relevance of these inscriptions not only for an understanding of θρησκεία τῶν ἀγγέλων, but for providing additional insights into the nature of the Colossian "philosophy."

1. "Angels" in the Context of Magic: Pagan, Jewish, and Christian

The angel inscriptions most easily explained are those that can clearly be identified as connected to the practice of magic. In most of these inscriptions, angels are invoked for their help or protection by individuals or groups within Asia Minor. These texts are often neglected in the discussion and interpretation of other "angel" texts, yet they may very well provide a significant key for helping to interpret other more enigmatic angel inscriptions.

---

[4] On the development of the worship of the archangel Michael in the Lycus Valley, see W. M. Ramsay, *The Church in the Roman Empire Before A.D. 170* (New York: Putnam's, 1893) 465-80 (= Chapter 19: "The Miracle at Khonai").

[5] The investigation does not extend to inscriptions that mention Hekate or Hermes unless they are explicitly identified as an ἄγγελος.

a. The Pergamum Magical Apparatus

In 1905, Richard Wünsch published the remarkable discovery of a "magical apparatus" discovered at Pergamum in the 1890s by the Athens Institute.[6] The apparatus consisted of a triangular-shaped bronze table, a bronze disk, a bronze spike, two bronze rings, two bronze plates, and three black burnished stones. All of the components of the apparatus are inscribed with magical names and signs. The materials were clearly used for performing magical arts. It is not clear whether it was used in a cultic context or by a private magician. Wünsch dates the apparatus to A.D. 200-250.

The underworld goddess Hekate, famed for her connection with witchcraft and sorcery, figures most prominently in the magical instruments. She is depicted on the three corners of the triangular table and the epithets πασικράτεια ("universal queen"; cf. *PGM* IV.2774) and πασιμέδουσα ("ruler over all"; *PGM* IV.2775) are used of her in an inscription in the center of the table. The inscription also makes reference to Persephone and Artemis Leukophryene (a epiklese of the local Artemis at Magnesia am Maeander).

The three polished black stones display Jewish influence. Each of the stones bears the same inscription. Of special significance for our inquiry is the fact that the names of the Jewish angels Michael, Gabriel, Ragouēl, and Raphaēl appear on the fifth line of the common inscription. Most of the 14 lines of the inscription consist of magical names.

1   ιαεωβαφρενεμουνοθιλαρικριφιαευ
      εαιφιρκιραλιθοννομενερφαβωεαι
      καρτανοαιαξ
      ναζαερχαοζαυφραυκαξ

5   Μιχαηλ Γαβριηλ Ῥαγουηλ[7] Ῥαφαηλ
      ψανχονιαια αβρια φριξακτειρα Σθεννω
      πιμιαξαερομενδεινα ορεοτερουξαρα
      πληξιπαν πυρινου Μερχουρι μνα
      ρονο αμωσιαια Αβερραβερρα

10   διρορθε αμεινον

---

[6] Richard Wünsch, *Antikes Zaubergerät aus Pergamon* (Jahrbuch des Kaiserlich Deutschen Archäologischen Instituts, Ergänzungsheft 6; Berlin: Georg Reimer, 1905). A brief description of the find was first published in *AM* 24 (1899) 199f.

[7] Two of the inscriptions read Ῥαγουσηλ.

δενδρα κυμινδραχητα
χρημιλλον δενδρουφι
νηνεμον

Wünsch also finds Jewish influence in the palindrome of lines 1 & 2, which he contends begins and ends with the secret and powerful name of Yahweh (here spelled Ἰαεω; cf. *PGM* 4.396, 3069).[8] It is not surprising to find these four angels named in the context of magic; they appear frequently in the papyrus texts (e.g. *PGM* 4.1814-15, 2356).

Two pagan deities are also named in the inscription: Stheno and Mercury. Hesiod refers to Stheno ("the strong one") as one of the two immortal sisters of Gorgo (or, Medusa) (Hes. *Theog.* 270, 77). Stheno is here characterized by the epithet φριξάκτειρα, "the one who brings shivers." The writer of the text transliterate the Latin name of the god Mercury instead of using the name of his Greek counterpart, Hermes. This is not unusual in the magical texts. "Mercury πυρίνος" is possibly a way of referring to him as a fiery spirit.[9]

Because of the predominant pagan motifs and minimal Jewish themes, it is certain that the apparatus as a whole was used by pagans. It is most likely that the stones functioned as amulets and may have been used for protection by the magician as he performed his rituals and incantations.[10] Comparable to the high regard for Jewish angels in the magical papyri, the Pergameme magicians had no problem incorporating these powerful, albeit Jewish, angels into their formulas for protective amulets. It is possible that they drew on local Jewish magical traditions, which invoked angels for apotropaic purposes, as the following amulet illustrates.

b. Local Amulets

(1) *Cyzicus*. The names of Jewish angels appear in a bronze disk found at Cyzicus (c. 140km north of Pergamum).[11] The disk measures 4.3 X 4.6

---

[8] Wünsch, *Zaubergerät*, 36.

[9] Wünsch, *Zaubergerät*, 28, translates, "Feuergeist."

[10] Wünsch, *Zaubergerät*, 16. Surprisingly, these amulets go unnoticed by Goodenough.

[11] A. Sorlin Dorigny, "Phylactère Alexandrin," *Revue des Études Grecques* 4 (1891) 287-96; see also P. S. Alexander, "Incantations and Books of Magic," in *HJP²*, 377; E. R. Goodenough, *Jewish Symbols in the Greco-Roman Period*, Volume 2: The Archaeological Evidence from the Diaspora (Bollingen Series 37; New York: Bollingen Foundation, 1953) 229-30 (Fig. 1052); and Wünsch, *Zaubergerät*, 37.

cm. in diameter and was found in the Roman cemetery in Boulgar-keui. Dorigny dates the amulet to the second half of the third century A.D.[12] The text provides still more evidence for the angels of Judaism being invoked in the magical practices of Asia Minor.

Μιχαήλ, Γαβριήλ, Οὐριήλ, Ῥαφαήλ διαφύλαξον τὸν φοροῦντα.
Ἅγιος, Ἅγιος, Ἅγιος
ΠΙΠΙ ΡΠΣΣ
Ἄγγελος Ἀρααφ, φεῦγε μεμισμένη· Σολομών σε διώκι.

Michael, Gabriel, Ouriel, Raphael
Protect the one who wears this.
Holy, holy, holy.
ΠΙΠΙ RPSSS.
Angel, Araaph,
Flee, O hated one:
Solomon pursues you.

With the exception that Ouriel has been favored over Ragouel, these are the same four angels named in the Pergamum text. The same four angels named here are also listed in book 2 of the *Sibylline Oracles* (probably written in Asia Minor). There the angels are commissioned by God to lead the souls of people to judgment (2.215). The *trisagion* of Isa 6:3 appears after the invocation of the angels. ΠΙΠΙ is probably a pseudo-transcription in Greek of the Hebrew name יהוה.[13] The talisman calls for the help of good angels in the tradition of Solomonic magic (see *Testament of Solomon* 18). In the center of the amulet there is the figure of a horseman led by an angel spearing a woman and a snake. Dorigny takes this as a symbol of Horus fighting Typhon.[14] The explicit reference to Solomon, however, points one toward interpreting the horseman as Solomon, a motif common among amulets.[15] This amulet points to the awareness and use of the Solomonic magical tradition in Asia Minor.

The term ἄγγελος is also used in a negative sense to refer to "the hated one," the evil emissary, "Araaph." Dorigny described Araaph as an evil

---

[12] Dorigny, "Phylactère Alexandrin," 296.

[13] Dorigny, "Phylactére," 291. Wünsch, *Zaubergerät*, 38, regards this as possible but not certain.

[14] Dorigny, "Phylactére," 287-88.

[15] On the cavalier Solomon represented on amulets, see Goodenough, *Symbols*, 2.227-35 and Campbell Bonner, *Studies in Magical Amulets Chiefly Graeco-Egyptian* (Ann Arbor: Univ. of Michigan Press, 1950) 208-21.

female demon, possibly responsible for causing bloody noses.[16] It is preferable to take Ἀραάφ as an alternative spelling of Ἄραψ of *TSol* 11.4.[17]
The demon is there called "lion shaped" (Λεοντοφόρον) and is said to
watch over those who are sick and to render them unable to recover. This
explanation also finds support in the image of a lion on the obverse side of
the amulet, where a figure of a lion appears below the images of Helios
and Selene and next to the Horus eye.

The pagan motifs—Helios, Selene and the Horus eye—included in an
otherwise Jewish amulet point to a Jewish borrowing from paganism, a
syncretism consistent with the milieu of magic.

(2) *Smyrna.* T. Homolle published a similar amulet found at Koula,
near Smyrna.[18] The diameter of the amulet is 4.8 cm.

Σφραγὶς τοῦ ζῶντος θεοῦ
φύλαξον τὸν φοροῦντα.
Ἅγιος, Ἅγιος, Ἅγιος Κύριος.
Σαβαώθ πλίρις ὁ οὐρανὸς καὶ ἡ γῖ τῖς δόξις.
Φεύγε μισιμένι,
Ἀραὰφ ὁ ἄγγελος, σε διό[κι] κὲ
Σολομὸν ἀπὸ τοῦ φοροῦντ(ος).

Seal of the living God.
Protect the one who wears this.
Holy, Holy, Holy is the Lord.
Sabaoth, heaven and earth are full of your glory.
Flee, hated one, O angel Araaph; Solomon chases you from the one wearing this.

This protective amulet, devoid of any pagan motifs, is clearly Jewish.[19]
The dependence on Isaiah 6:3 is clear. Here again, ἄγγελος is used to refer to the evil demon Araaph. In contrast to the previous amulet, angels
are not called upon to ward off harm. Rather, trust is placed strictly in the
effectiveness of the amulet, regarded as the seal of the power God (cf.

---

[16] Dorigny, "Phylactère," 294-95, reaches this conclusion based on the meaning of the
Semitic root רעף. He notes, "En arabe, la signification est plus précise: *Araaf* est le pluriel
régulier du mot-racine *Rahafa* (ré, aïn, élif, fé), qui désigne le sang coulant goutte à goutte
du nez."

[17] D. C. Duling, "Testament of Solomon," in *OTP* 1.973, translates it "Arab," i.e. the
descent of the demon. In note e, however, he leaves open the possibility that it may be a
name.

[18] T. Homolle, "Nouvelles et Correspondance: Ionie," *BCH* 17 (1893) 638.

[19] See Alexander, "Incantations," 377.

Test. Sol. 1.6, 7, 8; 2:5). The tradition of Solomonic magic is once again attested for Asia Minor.

(3) *Thera.* Not far off the coast of Asia Minor on the island of Thera, some 40+ gravestone inscriptions using the term ἄγγελος were discovered.[20] There has been much debate as to whether these inscriptions are pagan,[21] Jewish,[22] or Christian[23] in origin. M. P. Nilsson said it remains an open question,[24] and J. Schniewind simply described the texts as "syncretistic."[25]

Most of the texts simply have the term ἄγγελος followed by a name in the genitive case (e.g. 934 = ἄγγελος 'Αγαθόποδος; 935 = ἄγγελος Βοϊθίονος). Using another inscription found outside Thera to explain the rest (*IG*, XII.3.1238: καὶ ἐπὶ γέμι τὸ θηκίον τοῦτο, ἐνορκίζω ὑμᾶς τὸν ὧδε ἐφεστῶτα ἄνγελον μή τίς ποτε τολμῇ ἐνθάδε τινὰ καταθέσθε), J. H. Moulton argues that the Christians in Thera had taken over the pagan belief that the souls of the dead remain in or near their tombs.[26] The most likely explanation, however, is that an angel is invoked for the protection of the grave from robbers or tomb spoilers. Curses on grave spoilers were very common on the graves of pagans, Christians, and Jews alike, particularly in Asia Minor.[27] If this is the case, then there is a functional similarity to the Jewish tomb inscriptions found at Acmonia.

---

[20] *IG* XII.3.455, 933-73, 1056, 1057.

[21] Dibelius, *Geisterwelt*, 215, who denies any Christian influence on these inscriptions, observes: "Doch sind die Inschriften heidnisch, so gehören sie in eine Linie mit den hier besprochenen Zeugnissen und reden von ἄγγελοι als offenbar unterirdischen Schutzgeistern oder als den Seelen der Verstorbenen."

[22] *HJP²*, 3.1.71, interprets the inscriptions as either Jewish or Christian in origin.

[23] L. Robert, "Reliefs Votifs et Cultes d'Anatolie," *Opera Minora Selecta* (Amsterdam: Hakkert, 1969 [originally published in 1958]) 1.421, note 71; J. Michl, "Engel I (heidnisch)" *RAC* 5.55-56, describes them as syncretistic and reflecting a Jewish-Christian influence. See also A. Deissmann, *Light from the Ancient East* (4th ed.; New York: Harper and Brothers, 1927) 280, note 1.

[24] Nilsson, *GGR*, 2.540, note 7.

[25] J. Schniewind, *Euangelion. Ursprung und erste Gestalt des Begriffs Euangelium* (Darmstadt: Wissenschaftliche Buchgesellschaft, 1931) 2.234. W. Grundmann, "ἄγγελος," *TDNT* 1.75, follows Schniewind.

[26] J. H. Moulton, "It is His Angel," *JTS* 3 (1902) 519-20.

[27] See J. H. M. Strubbe, "'Cursed Be He That Moves My Bones,'" in *Magika Hiera. Ancient Greek Magic and Religion* (eds. C. A. Faraone & D. Obbink; New York/Oxford: Oxford University Press, 1991) 33-59. Strubbe's study focuses exclusively on the pagan grave imprecations found in Asia Minor.

(4) *Vicinity of Smyrna.* In the late 1800s, Henry J. Van Lennep reported seeing many signet stones from the regions south of Smyrna (*CIJ* 743).[28] They all bore the same Greek inscription (θωβαρραβο υλακασακις αβρασασε ωαωη ναλη εχεχε), and one of them had a clear representation of the Jewish menorah. That the amulets invoke angels may be inferred from the fact that the first word, θωβαρραβο, appears in a list of angel names invoked on another apotropaic magical amulet found in Syria.[29]

(5) *Ephesus.* A magical amulet discovered in Ephesus and published by J. Keil is quite Jewish in character.[30] On one side is a Greek inscription (printed below) and the reverse side is inscribed with Hebrew letters, viz. the "At-Basch" form of writing, which plays a significant role in the Kabbalistic literature. In fact, the final eleven syllables of the Greek inscription represent a transliteration of the Hebrew At-Basch (viz. דק גר בש את etc.). The amulet invokes the Jewish God with a series of epithets:

Οὐρανοειδῆ, {θ}σκοτοειδῆ, θαλασσοειδῆ καὶ παντόμορφε, αἰώνιε, μυριαγωγέ, χιλιαγωγέ, ἀκατάλημπτε, ὦ μυριάδες ἀνγέλων παρεστήκασιν, [ἀ]ίζων Ἀδωναῖε, ὁ ὢν γὰρ εἶ. Ετ βος γαρ δακ ας ο{ο}φ ζ[α] ας ταν ιαν χαλ.

O heaven-like one, darkness-like one, sea-like one, you who have the form of the all, eternal one, leader of 10,000's, leader of 1000's, incomprehensible one, beside whom stand myriads of angels, forever-living Adonai, for you are the one who is. ET BOS GAR DAK AS OOPH ZA AS TAN IAN CHAL.

Some of the epithets are attested in *PGM* IV.3007-86, esp. 3065 ff., a charm that is widely regarded as essentially Jewish in character.[31] In this amulet, God is described as the one who is served by tens of thousands of

28 Henry J. van Lennep, *Travels in Little-Known Parts of Asia Minor* (2 vols.; London: John Murray, 1870) 1.19-20.

29 See P. Perdrizet, "Amulette Grecque Trouvée en Syrie," *Revue des Études Grecque* 41 (1928) 73-82. The Syrian inscription reads: [επικ]αλουμαι Ιαω Μιχα[η]λ Γαβριηλ Ου[ρ]ι]ηλ Αρβαθιαω αβραθια ... Χω|ρβηθ Θαυβαρραβαυ Θω|[β]αριμμαυω Ελωαι ... (p. 72). In the Smyrna amulets, the word ωαωη may have been an attempt to transliterate the sound "Yahweh" into Greek characters. The expression αβρασασε may be a variant of the term "Abrasax," a solar symbol of Yahweh (see Goodenough, *Symbols*, 2.221, 250-51).

30 J. Keil, "Ein rätselhaftes Amulett," *JhhÖArchInst,* Hauptblatt 32 (1940) cols. 79-84. The amulet was actually purchased in Smyrna in 1912 and was only reported to have come from Ephesus. G. H. R. Horsley, "The Inscriptions of Ephesos and the New Testament," *NovT* 34 (1992) 125, is therefore correct in observing that an Ephesian provenance is not certain.

31 See W. L. Knox, "Jewish Liturgical Exorcism," *HTR* 31 (1938) 191-203; Deissmann, *Light*, 256-64; Goodenough, *Symbols*, 2.191.

angels. This fact is important for the bearer of the amulet because it implies that God can easily dispatch angelic assistance to the one who invokes him. The amulet not only further confirms Jewish involvement in magical practices in the region, but also demonstrates they could invoke their God in a magical sense.

c. Local Defixiones

(1) *Claudiopolis, Bithynia.* In Claudiopolis (Bithynia), a lead curse tablet was discovered invoking κύριοι θεοὶ ἄνγελοι to spellbind 42 men and women.[32] The defixio measures 35 cm. wide by 15 cm. in height and dates to the third or fourth century A.D. It consists of five columns of script with the first 2 1/2 columns listing the names of the people to be cursed. The deities/angels are instructed to prevent these people from spying on a certain Capetolinus and to prevent them from saying anything against him.

The powerful names invoked include Iaō (common in pagan magic), the cosmic deity Abrasax,[33] three deities connected with the underworld (Ortho [= Artemis], Baubo [= Hekate], and Ereschigal), and long strings of magical names (e.g. σανκιστη δωδεκακιστη ἀκρουροβόρε κοδηρε ιω ιω ιω αρβεθε). Apart from the occurrences of 'Ιαω and ἄγγελος, the pagan defixio shows no other signs of possible Jewish influence.

The use of ἄγγελος here does not necessarily betray Jewish influence. It may be a pagan application of the term to the underworld deities that has precedence in other magical documents.

(2) *Maeander Valley (north of Colossae).* One other curse tablet dates to the second century A.D. and was found in the upper Maeander Valley.[34] On one side, "demons" (δαίμονες) are invoked to fulfill a curse

---

[32] J. G. Gager, *Curse Tablets and Binding Spells from the Ancient World* (Oxford: University Press, 1992) 137 (= no. 47); J. M. R. Cormack, "A *Tabella Defixionis* in the Museum of the University of Reading, England," *HTR* 44 (1951) 25-34. See also David R. Jordan, "A Survey of the Greek Defixiones Not Included in the Special Corpora," *GRBS* 26 (1985) 194-95.

[33] Abrasax is the god of the heavens who appears many times in magical documents. He was believed to contain in himself the seven planets (thus the seven letters of his name) and the 365 days of the year (based on the numeric value of his name: 1 + 2 + 100 + 1 + 60 +1 + 200). See R. Merkelbach & M. Totti, *Abrasax* (ARWAW, PC 20; Opladen: Westdeutscher Verlag, 1990) 1.ix; K. Preisendanz, "Abrasax," *KP* 1.17-18.

[34] See Jordan, "Defixiones," 194 (§ 168).

against six people. On the reverse side, the same curse is repeated, but instead of the summary term "demons," Hekate, Hermes, and other underworld gods are invoked. This is significant for our investigation because both Hekate and Hermes can also be referred to as "angels" in their roles as messengers of the underworld (see below).

d. Summary

In all of these texts angels are best described as powerful supernatural beings who are accessible to people as functionaries of magic, whether guarding a grave, protecting someone from evil spirits, or performing a curse. Although some of these texts are predominantly Jewish and others are predominantly pagan, the point of commonality is the utilitarian posture toward the angels. The angels are not worshipped, but they are invoked and commanded. The context of each text is also highly individual and not cultic.

2. Pagan "Angel" Texts

The following texts are distinguished from those above by the lack of an explicit magical character, viz. there is no invocation of deity or superhuman messengers to fulfill a certain task, they are not written on magical materials, and there is no use of magical names or formulas. These text are also loosely interpreted as "pagan" because of their predominantly non-Jewish character.

a. The ἄγγελος and ἀγγελικός Inscriptions in Stratonicea (Caria)

Well known is a series of dedicatory inscriptions found in Caria near the city of Stratonicea (approximately 40 miles SW of Aphrodisias and 40 miles S of Tralles), which dates to the second century A.D.[35] Each inscription makes use of the term ἄγγελος or ἀγγελικός:

---

[35] The most recent publication and discussion of these texts is by Sheppard, "Pagan Cults," 77-101.

1. Διὶ Ὑψίστῳ καὶ Ἀγαθῷ Ἀγγέλῳ Κλαύδιος Ἀχιλλεὺς καὶ Γαλατία ὑπέρ σωτηρίας μετὰ τῶν ἰδίων πάντων χαριστήριον.³⁶
2. Διὶ Ὑψίστῳ καὶ Θείῳ Ἀγγέλῳ Νέ[ω]ν καὶ Εὐφροσύνη ὑπέρ τῶν ἰδίων.³⁷
3. Θείῳ Ἀγγελικῷ εὐχαριστοῦμεν ὑπέρ σωτηρίας.³⁸
4. Θείῳ Ἀγγελικῷ εὐχαριστοῦμεν. ³⁹

1. To Zeus Most High and the good angel, Claudius Achilles and Galatia, with all their household, made a thank offering for deliverance.
2. To Zeus Most High and the divine angel, Neon and Euphrosune [give thanks] on behalf of their household.
3. We give thanks to the angelic divinity for deliverance.
4. We give thanks to the angelic divinity.

The root issue for us is the problem of determining whether ἀγαθῷ ἀγγέλῳ / θείῳ ἀγγέλῳ / θείῳ ἀγγελικῷ refer to a second independent deity next to the high god, another deity with mediatorial functions (e.g. Hekate or Hermes), or a mediator figure serving the high god. To answer this, one needs first to interpret the meaning of θείῳ, which in turn affects the way one interprets ἄγγελος: Should θείῳ be regarded as masculine (θεῖος) and thereby interpreted as an adjective, "divine," (Nilsson; Schniewind), or should it be regarded as a neuter noun (τὸ Θεῖον) and thus as an independent deity, viz. a god called "Θεῖον," = "The Divinity" (Robert; Sokolowski)?⁴⁰ If θείῳ is a masculine adjective, we would translate no. 2 "divine angel" and nos. 3 & 4 "the divine angelic being" or "the angelic divinity." If θείῳ is a neuter noun, no. 2 would be interpreted as "Theion, the angel/messenger" or "Theion Angelos" and nos. 3 & 4 as "the angelic Theion" or "Theion Angelicon."

---

³⁶ *I. Strat.* 1118; P. LeBas and W. Waddington, *Voyage archéologique en Grèce et en Asie Mineure*, vol. III.v (Inscriptions - Asie Mineure) (Bibliotheque des Monuments Figures Grecs et Romains 1; Paris: Firmin-Didot et Cie, 1870) 515. See also Robert, "Reliefs Votifs," 420; Sokolowski, "Sur le Culte," 226 (no. 4); Sheppard, "Pagan Cults," 78 (no. 1).

³⁷ *I. Strat.* 1117; A. Hauvette-Besnault & M. Dubois, "Inscriptions de Carie," *BCH* 5 (1881) 182 (no. 3). See also Robert, "Reliefs votifs," 414; Sokolowski, "Sur le Culte," 226 (no. 1); Sheppard, "Pagan Cults," 78 (no. 2).

³⁸ *I. Strat.* 1119. A. Laumonier, "Inscriptions de Carie," *BCH* 53 (1954) 337-39 (no. 22). See also Robert, "Reliefs Votifs," 414; Sokolowski, "Sur le Culte," 226 (no. 2); Sheppard, "Pagan Cults," 78 (no. 3).

³⁹ *I. Strat.* 1120. L. Robert, "Rapport Sommaire sur un Second Voyage en Carie," *Revue Archéologique* 6 (1935) 154-155. See also Robert, "Reliefs Votifs," 414; Sokolowski, "Sur le Culte," 226 (no. 3); Sheppard, "Pagan Cults," 78 (no. 4).

⁴⁰ Cf. Herodotus 1.32; 3.108.

Two of the "angel" inscriptions (nos. 1 & 2) are coupled with "the most high god." This does not necessarily imply that these are Jewish inscriptions or even that they are Jewish-influenced inscriptions. Recent research has demonstrated (contra F. Cumont) that Zeus Hypsistos/Theos Hypsistos was a title used for the popular pagan belief in Asia Minor (especially in Lydia and Phrygia) in the "Highest God."[41] Without any other signs of Jewish provenance or influence, it is probably best to interpret these texts as pagan.

Taking θείῳ as a masculine adjective, M. P. Nilsson contends that the inscriptions should be understood exclusively within the context of the cult of the "high god" (Zeus Hypsistos/Theos Hypsistos) in Asia Minor and the tendency toward monotheism. The expressions Θεῖος, Θεῖος ἄγγελος, and Θεῖος ἀγγελικός therefore must refer to a mediator figure who intercedes between the high god and humanity.[42] Nilsson refers to this figure as a second god, but interprets it as an inferior, subordinate god fulfilling a mediatorial function. This mediator could be referred to simply as "the divine one,"[43] or as "divine angel," "good angel," or "angelic divinity"— expressions well-suited to express the figure's mediatorial role.

L. Robert, taking θείῳ as neuter, concludes that the good angel (Θεῖον) is a separate deity distinct from Zeus Most High.[44] However, he sees "Theion" as an intermediate divinity (or emanation) subordinate to the most high god. Thus, the texts give further evidence of the tendency toward monotheism in Asia Minor. His conclusion, therefore, does not differ markedly from Nilsson's.

A. Sheppard also takes Θείῳ as neuter but contends that it refers to a nameless divine being, not one of the traditional gods or goddesses.[45] He sees the use of the ἄγγελος/ἀγγελικός terminology as stemming from Jewish influence on this pagan cult. Specifically, he suggests the influence of philonic traditions that he supposes circulated among the Jews of Asia Minor. He points particularly to the story of Balaam and the angel where Balaam refers to the angel as τὸ θεῖον (*De Vit. Mos.* 1.281). Apart from

---

[41] A. T. Kraabel, "Ὕψιστος and the Synagogue at Sardis," *GRBS* 10 (1969) 81-93. Now see P. Trebilco, *Jewish Communities in Asia Minor* (SNTSMS 69; Cambridge: University Press, 1991) Chap. 6: 'Theos Hypsistos' and Sabazios, 127-44, esp. 131-33.

[42] Similarly, see Georg Petzl, "Vier Inschriften aus Lydien," *Studien zur Religion und Kultur Kleinasiens* (EPRO 66; FS. F. K. Dörner; eds. S. Sahin, E. Schwertheim & J. Wagner; Leiden: Brill, 1978) 2.516-39. So also Trebilco, *Communities*, 132.

[43] Another dedication from Stratonicea omits any reference to "angel/angelic": Διεὶ ὑψίστῳ καὶ Θείῳ ἀγαθῷ Σόκρατης (= Laumonier, no. 21; Sheppard, no. 5).

[44] Robert, "Reliefs Votifs," 421.

[45] Sheppard, "Pagan Cults," 79-80.

no clear evidence affirming the knowledge and use of philonic traditions in the Judaism of Asia Minor (which Sheppard concedes), it is even more speculative to assert that Stratonicean pagans would have been familiar with one specific philonic tradition. Also, one must observe that this identification of τὸ θεῖον with an angel is an isolated instance in Philo, not a common motif in his angelology. In fact, Sheppard himself observes that θεῖον is a regular substitute for θεός in Philo (*Quod. Det.* 55; *Fug. et Inv.* 99). If this is the case, would it not be less likely for the Stratonicean pagans to apply θεῖον to a mediator figure?

F. Sokolowski also takes θείῳ as neuter and sees two gods in view, the well-known Zeus Hypsistos and the relatively unknown "Theion" or "Theion Angelos." He contends, however, that the second god should be identified with Hekate. The dedications were therefore offered to the two great deities of the region, Zeus and Hekate.

I am convinced that Sokolowski was essentially correct in his view. (1) He rightly observes that the underworld deity Hekate bore the epithet ἀγγέλη or even the masculine form ἄγγελος.[46] (2) He is also correct in pointing to the prominence of both Zeus and Hekate at Stratonicea; their cultic images adorned the council chamber, and they were reputed to "perform good deeds of divine power," for which the people render their thanks.[47] The main sanctuary of Hekate was, in fact, located in nearby Lagina.[48] (3) One could add to Sokolowski's evidence the fact that Hekate was venerated in Stratonicea as Σώτειρα ("deliverer"),[49] which corresponds well with the thanksgiving for σωτηρία in inscription nos. 1 & 3 (perhaps implied but not made explicit in nos. 2 & 4). (4) In a similar θείῳ inscription to those found at Stratonicea, Θεῖον/θεῖος is given the epithet ἐπιφανής: Θεῷ ὑψίστῳ καὶ μεγ[ά]λῳ Θείῳ ἐπιφανεῖ Δημὼ θυγάτηρ Τυράννου θεὰν Λαρμηνὴν ἀνέστησεν ἔτους σνζ' ("Demo, daughter of Tyrannus, set up [a statue of] the goddess Larmene, in the year 256, to the Most High God and to the great and manifest divinity").[50] The adjectives ἐπιφανής and ἐπιφανεστάτη were very common epithets

---

[46] For references, see Sokolowski, "Sur le Culte," 227-29.

[47] Specifically, the city of Stratonicea on one occasion attributed its deliverance to the help of Zeus Panamaros and Hekate (*CIG* 2715 a, b). See Nilsson, *GGR*, 2.227, note 2, and R. Lane Fox, *Pagans and Christians* (New York: Alfred A. Knopf, 1989) 135.

[48] A. Kehl, "Hekate," *RAC* 14. 312; Herta Sauer, "Hekate," *KP* 2.982.

[49] See Kehl, "Hekate," col. 316, and T. Kraus, *Hekate. Studien zu Wesen und Bild der Göttin in Kleinasien und Griechenland* (Heidelberger Kunstgeschichliche Abhandlungen 5; Heidelberg: Carl Winter, 1960) 43-44, for references. See also *CIG* 3827 (Cotiaeum, just north of Acmonia in Phrygia).

[50] Robert, "Reliefs Votifs," 411; Sheppard, "Pagan Cults," 99 (no. 12).

for Hekate.[51] (5) In the city of Panamara, just south of Stratonicea, Hekate was referred to as the second in a pair of deities named in an inscription: [Διὶ] Ὑψίστῳ καὶ Ἑκάτῃ Σω[τείρᾳ].[52] (6) In the popular magical practices, as Sokolowski notes, Hekate was also associated with Hermes as a messenger of the underworld. In such a context, both could be called "angels": καταγράφω καὶ κατατίθω ἀγγέλοις καταχθονίοις, Ἑρμῇ καταχθονίῳ καὶ Ἑκάτῃ καταχθονίᾳ.[53]

The major difficulty with his view is the lack of evidence for the use of Θεῖον as a way of referring to Hekate.[54] This does not render his view impossible, however, and the prominence of Hekate in Stratonicea prompts us to retain his view as a viable possibility.

If the terms refer to a second unnamed deity (Robert; Nilsson; Sheppard), then this being is understood by people in western Asia Minor as a messenger of Zeus, viz. a mediator between Zeus and his worshippers in Asia Minor. Nilsson discusses the Stratonicean inscriptions as part of his larger treatment of the widespread religious inclination toward monotheism during the Roman period.[55] In popular belief, an increasing number of people were beginning to speak of one god as the master of the universe. Consequently, the other gods were often subordinated to a supreme god and could be referred to as "angels," viz. messengers or assistants to the powerful god. It is also illustrated in the tendency to identify the gods with one another, as Apuleius did with Isis (*Metamorph.* 11.5).

If our interpretation is correct and the terms refer to Hekate, then the figure should still be seen as a mediator—not so much between Zeus and humanity, but as a messenger of the underworld, an accessible goddess who can be called on for protection. The ἄγγελος terminology was used because of her mediatorial functions. In this explanation, Hekate is not necessarily seen as an equal to Zeus. He is more remote, and she is more accessible.

Unfortunately, we have little additional information to help us determine precisely how this mediatorial role was understood in Stratonicea. The inscriptions demonstrate that it was appropriate to render praise to this "angel" (εὐχαριστοῦμεν). On two occasions the angel is praised for

---

[51] See Kraus, *Hekate*, 43-44, for references.

[52] G. Deschamps & G. Cousin, "Inscriptions du Temple de Zeus Panamaros," *BCH* 12 (1888) 271, note 5.

[53] Sokolowski, "Sur le Culte," 228. The text is from A. Audollent, *Defixionum Tabellae* (Paris: Alberti Fontemoing, 1904) 102 (nos. 74, 75).

[54] So Nilsson, *GGR*, 2.577, note 1.

[55] Nilsson, *GGR*, 2.569-78.

providing deliverance (ὑπὲρ σωτηρίας).[56] It is likely that the people of the region looked to this deity for protection from various forms of evil (including natural calamities), a common function for Hekate. By setting up these monuments, some people express thanksgiving for her help in a time of trouble. In this respect, their practice is not far from the kind of angelic invocation we discussed in the previous section of this paper under the category of "'angels' in the context of magic."

b. Lydia: "Holy and Just"

Similar to the Stratonicean inscriptions is another ἄγγελος inscription discovered at Temrek, near Borlu (Lydia), about 30 miles north of Philadelphia. The inscription dates to the second or third century and measures 56 x 53 x 8 cm.

... ιιων καὶ Λουκία ... καὶ 'Αγγέλῳ 'Οσίῳ Δικαίῳ εὐχαριστοῦντες ἀνέστησαν διὰ προφητοῦ 'Αλεξάνδρου Σαϊττηνοῦ.[57]

[s.o.] and Lucia ..., [to a certain god(dess)] and to the holy and just angel, with thanksgiving have set up [this monument] with the help of Alexander of Saittae.

The part of the text missing before καὶ 'Αγγέλῳ assumes the presence of another honored deity, perhaps Ζεὺς Ὕψιστος as in the Stratonicean inscriptions. The term ἄγγελος here does not include the name (or, epithet) θεῖος, but it does include the epithets ὅσιος and δίκαιος. It is not necessary here to explain these epithets as reflecting Jewish influence since they are also well-attested in pagan literature and inscriptions.[58] We are left with the same possibilities for interpreting ἄγγελος here as in the Stratonicean texts.

---

56 It is doubtful that σωτηρία should here be interpreted as life after death. The inscriptions point to something already accomplished for which thanks could be rendered.

57 Robert, "Reliefs Votifs," 419. See also, Sheppard, "Pagan Cults," 90-92; Sokolowski, "Sur le Culte," 226 (no. 5).

58 See *LSJ*, s.v.

c. Men Text from Lydia

A monument set up to the Anatolian moon-god Men in Lydia makes clear reference to angelic intermediaries who functioned on behalf of the deity. Lane dates the monument to A.D. 164-65.

Μέγας Μεὶς 'Αξιοττηνὸς Τάρσι βασιλεύων. 'Επεὶ ἐπεστάθη σκῆπτρον εἴ τις ἐκ τοῦ βαλανείου τι κλέψι, κλαπέντος οὖν εἱματίου ὁ θεὸς ἐνεμέσησε τὸν κλέπτην καὶ ἐπόησε μετὰ χρόνον τὸ εἱμάτιον ἐνενκῖν ἐπὶ τὸν θεὸν καὶ ἐξωμολογήσατα. 'Ο θεὸς οὖν ἐκέλευσε δι' ἀνγέλου πραθῆναι τὸ εἱμάτιν καὶ στηλλογραφῆσαι τὰς δυνάμεις. "Ετους σμθ'.59

Great is Men Axiottenos, King in Tarsi! When the sceptre had been set up in case anyone stole anything from the bath-house, since a cloak was stolen, the god took vengeance on the thief and made him bring the cloak to the god after a time, and he made confession. So the god gave orders through an angel that the cloak should be sold and his powers written up on a stele. In the year 249 (= AD 164/65).60

This text provides unequivocal evidence for the use of ἄγγελος in a pagan context in Asia Minor. The angel functions as the messenger of the god. Sheppard, however, argues that the appearance of ἄγγελος reflects borrowing from Judaism. He suggests that some pagans could have thought that Jews worshipped a supreme 'One' god of the moon, and have applied some of the language used by the Jews to their own cult.61 While such a borrowing is not impossible, it is certainly not necessary to posit this influence, particularly on a text that shows no other signs of Jewish influence.

Men was viewed in some contexts as the supreme deity (cf. Zeus Hypsistos) illustrated by the inscription from Saittae, Lydia: Εἷς θεὸς ἐν οὐρανοῖς, μέγας Μὴν οὐράνιος, μεγάλη δύναμις τοῦ ἀθανάτου θεοῦ.62 Like Zeus, Men could be served by supernatural assistants and intermediaries.

It is here noteworthy that Men himself took vengeance on the thief, not an angel. The angel functions strictly as a messenger of the god. In this

---

59 E. Lane, *Corpus Monumentorum Religionis Dei Menis* (EPRO 19, Part 1; Leiden: Brill, 1971) 45-46 (no. 69); Sheppard, "Pagan Cults," 92 (no. 10).

60 Translation by Sheppard, "Pagan Cults," 92-93.

61 Sheppard, "Pagan Cults," 93.

62 J. Keil & A. Premerstein, *Bericht über eine zweite Reise in Lydien* (DenkschrWien, philosophisch-historische Klasse Band 54.2; Vienna: Alfred Hölder, 1911) 2.107, no. 210, as cited in A. D. Nock, "Studies in the Graeco-Roman Beliefs of the Empire," *Essays on Religion and the Ancient World* (ed. Z. Stewart; Oxford: Clarendon, 1972) 38.

way the text differs from the magical texts we have examined as well as
the Stratonicean texts where angels were involved in protecting and delivering.

d. Didyma Text

An inscription from Didyma, perhaps dating to the first century A.D., refers to a feminine deity named "Angel." The text extolls the benefactions
of a father and son who served as comptrollers. Among their benefactions
was the construction of an enclosure to "Angel."

ταμίαι πατὴρ καὶ υἱὸς ᾽Αντίγονος ᾽Απολλωνίου καὶ ᾽Αντίγονος ᾽Αντιγόνου
παρήδρευσαν τῷ θεῷ δι᾽ ὅλου τοῦ ἐνιαυτοῦ εὐσεβῶς, τοῖς δὲ ἀνθρώποις
εὐαρέστως, ποιήσαντες παραπράσεις πάντων διηνεκῶς· οἰκοδόμησαν δὲ καὶ
τὸν περίβολον τῆς ᾽Αγγέλου ἐκ τῶν ἰδίων καὶ ἀνέθηκαν τῷ ᾽Απόλλωνι βωμόν·
λιπόντος δὲ ὕδατος τῷ τόπῳ ἤντλησαν τὰ καινὰ ... φρέατα.[63]

Treasurers, father and son, Antigonus, son of Apollonius, and Antigonus, son of
Antigonus, attended the god reverently throughout the year. To people who were
well-pleasing [to the god] they regularly made sales of items below the market value.
And they also constructed the enclosure of Angelos at their own expense and set up
an altar to Apollo. Because of the lack of water in the place, they dug new wells.

What appears as unique in this inscription is the use of the feminine article
with the noun ἄγγελος. This probably indicates that ἄγγελος should be
understood as an epithet of one of the known female deities of the region,
e.g. Hekate, Artemis, Cybele, or Demeter, rather than indicating an entirely new deity and cult—the cult of the goddess Angelos—which would
otherwise be unattested.

A number of scholars have identified this "angel" with Hekate.[64] Hekate
bore the epithet ἄγγελος in other texts, as did Artemis with whom she
was closely associated. Some also find support in the testimony of the
Syracusan Sophron, a writer of mimes, who told a story about a certain
Angelos, a daughter of Zeus and Hera, who became an underworld

---

[63] Theodor Wiegand, ed., *Didyma. Zweiter Teil: Die Inschriften* (Berlin: Gebr. Mann,
1958) 243 (no. 406). For recent discussion of the text, see Joseph Fontenrose, *Didyma.
Apollo's Oracle, Cult, and Companions* (Berkeley: University of California Press, 1988)
159. See also Sokolowski, "Sur le Culte," 227-28.

[64] Wiegand, *Didyma*, 243; Sokolowski, "Sur le Culte," 227; Kehl, "Hekate," 321.

spirit.[65] J. Fontenrose has raised the only dissenting voice in identifying Hekate with the "Angelos" of our text. He says, "It seems to me that the two Antigonoi would have identified Angelos as Artemis or Hekate if she were the deity for whom they made the enclosure."[66] But this is merely to argue from silence. It is therefore most likely that the inscription is referring to Hekate as Angelos rather than to some unknown Angelos.

On the basis of this inscription, all that we can determine about Hekate-Angelos is that she had a cultic center in Didyma. The functions of her cult in Lagina (near Stratonicea) would perhaps serve as the best analogy to her cult in Didyma. The reference to Hekate as Angelos may also bring us closer to her popular function as a goddess of the underworld who was frequently called upon as a functionary of magic (cf. the Pergamum magical apparatus, above).

e. Oenoanda (Lycia)

This inscription was discovered and copied in 1966 when an archaeologist was lowered by a rope from the top of a remaining portion of the old city wall of Oenoanda. The text records an oracle given by the Clarian Apollo to the city of Oenoanda in the late second or early third century. It represents an alternative viewpoint of Oenoandans to the Epicureanism that flourished in the second and third centuries. The words from Apollo were written in hexameter verse and contain a refence to "angels":

αὐτοφυής, ἀδίδακτος, ἀμήτωρ, ἀστυφέλικτος,
οὔνομα μὴ χωρῶν, πολυώνυμος, ἐν πυρὶ ναίων.
τοῦτο θεός, μεικρὰ δὲ θεοῦ μερὶς ἄγγελοι ἡμεῖς.
τοῦτο πευθομένοισι θεοῦ πέρι ὅστις ὑπάρχει,
Αἰ[θ]έ[ρ]α πανδερκ[ῆ θε]ὸν ἔννεπεν, εἰς ὃν ὁρῶντας
εὔχεσθ' ἠῴους πρὸς ἀντολίην ἐσορῶ[ν]τα[ς].[67]

Self-born, untaught, motherless, unshakeable,
Giving place to no name, many-named, dwelling in fire,
Such is God: we are a portion of God, his angels.
This, then, to the questioners about God's nature

---

[65] The Scholiast on Theocritus, II, 12 (as cited in Sokolowski, "Sur le Culte," 227-28).

[66] Fontenrose, *Didyma*, 159.

[67] L. Robert, "Un Oracle Gravé à Oinoanda," *CRAIBL* (1971) 597-619, esp. p. 602. See also A. S. Hall, "The Klarian Oracle at Oenoanda," *ZPE* 32 (1978) 263-67.

The god replied, calling him all-seeing Ether: to him, then, look
And pray at dawn, looking out to the east.[68]

The text as a whole, particularly the first three lines, has much in common
with the theological ideas of Platonism in the second and third century.[69]
While there are many intriguing aspects of the text that we could endeavor
to interpret, the portion that concerns us most is the third line: "we are a
portion of God, his angels." It is not necessary for us to assume that
Apollo is the god in view in this text. The various epithets point to a supreme god. In fact, a second altar under our text was dedicated to "the
Most High God."

The text would therefore seem to provide further evidence of the tendency toward a belief in one god who is served by intermediaries, often
termed ἄγγελοι in Asia Minor. This would support the conclusion
reached by R. Lane Fox, "The mention of 'angels' raises no problem in a
pagan context. Angels occur freely in pagan cults of abstract divinities of
Asia Minor."[70] However, as Nilsson observes, it is particularly conspicu-
ous that Apollo would include himself as a portion and indeed an ἄγγελος
of the great god.[71]

This text differs from most of the epigraphical "angel" texts that we
have already examined. There is not only a greater sophistication to the
expression of theology; it also has a strongly Platonic tone. In fact, with
regard to the use of "angel" in this passage, Lane Fox has observed that
"the tone of this text suggests that it had derived the word from school
theology."[72] In this respect he sees the text reflecting the Platonic idea of a
supreme abstract notion of divinity with intermediaries serving between
the gods and people. Nevertheless, as an authentic oracle of the Clarian
Apollo, it gives us valuable insight into the local view of a high god
served by intermediaries termed ἄγγελοι.

---

[68] Translation by Lane Fox, *Pagans and Christians*, 169.

[69] Lane Fox, *Pagans and Christians*, 170.

[70] Lane Fox, *Pagans and Christians*, 170.

[71] Nilsson, *GGR*, 2.478. Nilsson's comment was based upon the quotation of the first
three lines of the oracle in Lactantius, *Div. Inst.* 1.7, which he rightly regarded as authentic testimony of the oracle prior to the epigraphic discovery in Oenoanda.

[72] Lane Fox, *Pagans and Christians*, 170.

f. Summary

With the possible exception of the Didyma text, each of these inscriptions point to the local belief in a supreme deity (whether Theos Hypsistos, Zeus, or Men). This deity is served by intermediaries who bridge the gap between the high god and humanity. It is appropriate to render thanks to these intermediaries when they provide help, and one may even erect a holy place for the angel (Didyma).

It is possible in some of these instances to identify the intermediary as the underworld goddess Hekate (Stratonicea, Temrek, and Didyma). In popular belief she was known as an apotropaic deity.

3. Jewish "Angel" Texts

We have already discussed a few texts in Chapter 2 of a Jewish character that illustrate the invocation of angels for protection. Angel names such as Michael, Gabriel, Raphael, and others, as well as the terms ἄγγελος and ἅγιος, figured prominently in these texts. Here we will discuss a few inscriptions of a similar type.

a. Eumenia

A grave inscription in Eumenia, about 60 km north of Colossae, warns against disturbing the burial place. It is inscribed on a white marble bomos with a pediment; it measures 67.5 cm. X 29 cm. (shaft), 38.5 cm. (base):

> εἴ τις δὲ ἕτερον θήσει, ἔστε αὐτῷ πρὸς τὸν θεὸν καὶ τὸν ἄγγελον τὸν Ρουβῆδος.[73]

> If anyone inters another [here], he will have to reckon with God and the angel of Roubes.

---

[73] L. Robert, "Épitaphes d'Eumeneia de Phrygie," *Hellenica. Recueil d'Épigraphie de Numismatique et d'Antiquites Grecques*, vols. 11-12 (Paris: Adrien-Maisonneuve, 1960) 429-30. The most recent publication of the text appears in A. R. R. Sheppard, "Jews, Christians and Heretics in Acmonia and Eumenia," *Anatolian Studies* 29 (1979) 175-76. See the discussion in Lane Fox, *Pagans and Christians*, 294-95, who regards "Roubes" as a Christian (although possibly a converted Jew).

Roubes (or, Reuben) had been a greatly respected person in Eumenia. Lycidas, the man who provided for this *heroon* and the inscription, now places it under the protection of the guardian angel of Roubes, a righteous person now dead.[74] It is possible that the spirit of the deceased was believed to still inhabit or frequent the tomb (as in pagan belief) and therefore protect the grave. This is less likely, however, in a Jewish or Christian context.

It is not completely certain whether the inscription is Jewish or Christian, but even if it is Christian,[75] it demonstrates that the Jewish idea of calling upon angels for protection also penetrated early Christianity. The threat to the potential intruder—ἔστε αὐτῷ πρὸς τὸν θεόν—is a variation of a stock formula on Eumenian burial tombs,[76] although only this one also invokes an angel. This formula was also common among the pagan burial inscriptions in Asia Minor (e.g. ἔστι αὐτῷ πρὸς Ἥλλιων κὲ Σελήνην ["he will have to reckon with Helios and Selene]).[77]

b. Kalecik, Galatia: "Theos Hypsistos and His Angels"

A recently published text honors "Theos Hypsistos and his holy angels" on a monument discovered in Kalecik, NE of Ankara. The text was inscribed on a column of red marble measuring 46 cm high with a diameter of 28 cm, which Mitchell tentatively dates to the third century.

Τῷ μεγάλῳ Θεῷ Ὑψίστῳ καὶ Ἐπουρανίῳ καὶ τοῖς ἁγίοις αὐτοῦ ἀγγέλοις καὶ τῇ προσκυνητῇ αὐτοῦ προσευχῇ τὰ ὧδε ἔργα γείνεται ...[78]

The works here set forth are for the Great and Most High God of Heaven and for his holy angels and for his venerable house of prayer ...[79]

---

[74] Thus Sheppard, "Jews," 176.

[75] This is the opinion of Robert, "Épitaphes," 432.

[76] See Trebilco, *Communities*, 79.

[77] See Strubbe, "'Cursed Be He,'" 34-35. See also E. Rohde, *Psyche* (New York: Harcourt, Brace & Co., 1925) 552-54.

[78] Sheppard, "Pagan Cults," 94 (no. 11). See also, S. Mitchell, *Regional Epigraphic Catalogues of Asia Minor II. The Ankara District. The Inscriptions of North Galatia* (British Institute of Archaeology at Ankara Monograph 4; Oxford: British Archaeological Reports International Series 135, 1982) 177-78, no. 209b; Trebilco, *Judaism*, 137.

[79] Translation by Sheppard, "Pagan Cults," 94.

Trebilco has recently argued that this text can be included among the Jewish inscriptions using Theos Hypsistos with a high degree of certainty.[80] He bases his conclusion on the following observations: (1) it is customary to find the article with Theos Hypsistos in the LXX and in some Jewish inscriptions, but not in pagan epigraphic dedications; (2) προσευχή is characteristically used in the inscriptions to refer to a Jewish house of prayer[81]; (3) there is an absence of pagan or polytheistic elements; and, (4) the expression ἅγιοι ἄγγελοι is found in Jewish sources but not in pagan texts.[82]

The text appears to be a thanksgiving text (χαριστήριον), but it breaks off at the point where "the works" would have been enumerated. One may surmise that God has somehow delivered the dedicants from some great evil through the agency of his holy angels. If this is the case, then in form and intent it differs little from the Stratonicean inscriptions.

Hengel takes the inscription as "a plain reference to a Jewish angel cult, as attested in Christian sources, rabbinic polemic, and also in the Hekhalot and magical texts."[83] One could wish for Hengel—and the many others who use this expression[84]—to be more precise in what they mean by "angel cult." If they mean that angels figure prominently in the belief system of this Jewish circle and that these Jews invoke angels for protection while maintaining their devotion to "one God," then yes. If, however, he means that groups of Jews gathered regularly to adore, pray to, and worship angels, either in place of or alongside of the one God, then no.

This text is best explained by the larger Jewish tendency to invoke angels for protection from various forms of evil or to exact vengeance. We have no way of knowing, however, if these people rendering their thanks had originally prayed directly to God or invoked his divine angels directly

---

[80] Trebilco, *Communities*, 137. *HJP²*, 3.1.35 also regards this text as "probably Jewish."

[81] Hengel, "Schürer," 37, regards the προσκυνητὴ προσευχή as a decisive factor in identifying this text as Jewish since προσευχή applied to a building for divine worship occurs almost exclusively in Jewish sources. So also, Mitchell, *Catalogues*, 178. Sheppard, "Pagan Cults," 96, likewise sees προσευχή as marking "the inscription as either Jewish or connected in some way with Judaism." However, he still erroneously (in my opinion) interprets the text as pagan, although conceding a high degree of borrowing from the religious terminology of the local Jews.

[82] "Holy angels," however, does appear in the Jewish-influenced magical texts. See R. Wünsch, *Defixionum Tabellae* (= *IG* III.3 [1897]) nos. 16.52, 72; 17.39; 18.19; et al. (as cited in K. Preisendanz, "Paredros," *RE* 18.2 [1949] col. 1432).

[83] Hengel, "Schürer," 37-38.

[84] See, for example, Robert, "Un Oracle," 614, note 2; M. Simon, *Verus Israel* (Paris: Editions E. De Boccard, 1964) 429-30.

to respond to their need. The latter possibility is not out of the questions in light of the Jewish magical tradition in Asia Minor.

In an inscription from Catania, Sicily, which dates to the third century A.D. (CIJ 1.719), personified δυνάμεις—in the sense of angels—are invoked for the protection of a grave.[85] The two Jewish inscriptions we discussed in the previous chapter (CIJ 725 and 717) also represent appeals directly to angels for vengeance and for protection respectively. None of these texts can be adduced, however, to support the notion of angel cults.

Both the inscription from Eumenia and the one from Kalecik may very well betray a tendency toward a magical approach to divinity.[86] As we saw in the first section of the paper, the invocation of angels for protection and aid was common in the Jewish, pagan and Christian magic of western Asia Minor.

4. Christian "Angel" Texts

The following texts have been identified as Christian (although not without dispute in some cases).

a. Miletus Angel Inscription (*CIG* 2895)

Continuing to reflect the tendency to invoke angels for protection in Asia Minor is a curious inscription discovered in the theater at Miletus in which angels are invoked for the protection of the city (*CIG* 2895).[87] The inscription is difficult to date, no earlier than the third century A.D. and perhaps as late as the fifth.[88] It is commonly referred to as the "planetary inscription" because of the presence of planetary symbols.

---

[85] See M. Hengel, "Die Synagogeninschrift von Stobi," *ZNW* 57 (1956) 156, note 32.

[86] Hengel, "Die Synagogeninschrift," 156, speaks of a "magical-syncretistic tendency."

[87] A good discussion of the text together with a photograph appears in Deissmann, *Light*, 453-60 (= Appendix XI: "The So-Called 'Planetary Inscription' in the Theatre at Miletus a Late Christian Protective Charm").

[88] See D. F. McCabe and M. A. Plunkett, *Miletos Inscriptions* (Princeton Epigraphic Project; Princeton, 1984) no. 631, bibliog. on p. 174, as cited by Horsley, "Inscriptions of Ephesos," 123, note 83. Informed by T. Wiegand's analysis of the style of the characters, Deissmann was one of the first to break with the consensus that regarded the inscription as pre-Christian and as either pagan or Jewish-pagan.

At the very top of the stone panel is one line of text consisting of 37 vowels (with perhaps 14 others broken away):

ιεουαηωιαωαιεουαηωιωαεηουιαωιηεουενον ...

Below this, the rock face is divided into five and one-half (originally seven) well-defined sectors (a column of text with a circle inscribed around it). Above each sector is a monogram, or symbol, of one of the seven planetary angels.[89] Within each sector, at the top, is an inscription with the seven vowels of the Greek alphabet arranged in exact alphabetic permutation (αεηιουω, εηιουωα, ηιουωαε, ιουωαεη, ουωαεηι, υωαεηιο, ωαεηιου). Following the vowels in each compartment is the inscription, "Holy One, protect the city of the Milesians and all those inhabiting it ("Αγιε, φύλαξον τὴν πόλιν Μιλησίων καὶ πάντας τοὺς κατοικοῦντας)." Situated below these sectors across the bottom of the entire panel is the summarizing invocation: "Archangels ('Αρχάγγελοι) protect the city of the Milesians and all those inhabiting it."

Deissmann has correctly observed that the series of vowels within each oval have their parallel in a magical text, *PGM* 10.36-50. In the magical text, the names of seven angels from Judaism are given as the counterparts to the series of vowels: Michael, Raphael, Gabriel, Souriel, Zaziel, Badakiel, and Suliel.[90]

It is probable, *pace* Deissmann, that the ἀρχάγγελοι of this text are thought of in connection with astrological powers. This is the way ἀρχάγγελος is commonly used in the magical papyri;[91] see, for example, *PGM* IV.1205; XIII. 257, 337, 454-55. Although most interpreters regard the inscription as Christian, there are no distinctively Christian terms or concepts in the text apart from the references to ἅγιος and ἀρχάγγελος, which could just as easily be Jewish or Jewish-influence on a pagan text. Most importantly, the text provides an additional example illustrating a local tendency to invoke angels in a magical sense that spanned quite a

---

[89] Theodor Hopfner, *Griechisch-Ägyptischer Offenbarungszauber* (Studien zur Palaeographie und Papyruskunde 21; Amsterdam: Adolf M. Hakkert, 1974 [originally published in Leipzig: Haessel, 1921]) §151 (p. 75). See also Gager, *Curse Tablets*, 11.

[90] Hopfner, *Offenbarungszauber*, §§151-52 (pp. 75-76) on the basis of his study of the planetary signs and the rows of vowels (thought to correspond to angels), concludes that the following angels were intended to be connected with the seven days of the week (also corresponding to the planets): Raphael, Gabriel, Samael, Michael, Sadakiel, Anael, and Caphriel. On the connection of planets and angels, see Michl, "Engel I (heidnisch)" *RAC* 5.57.

[91] See Hopfner, *Offenbarungszauber*, §154 (p. 77).

number of years throughout the Greco-Roman and into the late-Christian period.

b. A Magical Inscription From Pisidian Antioch

D. M. Robinson, former director of the excavations at Pisidian Antioch, has published a Christian magical inscription he discovered there that contains an invocation of angels.[92] The inscription was on a piece of silver foil rolled up inside a bronze tube. Robinson dated the inscription to the third century on the basis of the cursive script and identified it as "at least partly Christian."[93]

πρὸς πνεῦμα θαθωαθφρο. ἀναχώρησον ἀποβὰς εἰς τοὔπὶ δεξιᾷ "Αγιοι τοῦ θ(εο)ῦ καὶ τὸ ἔμα (= αἷμα) τὸ Χ(ριστο)ῦ καὶ τοῖ[ς] ἀνγέλοις ἄτης καὶ ἰκλησία.

To the evil spirit Thoathphro: Depart, going off to the right! (I call on you) O holy ones of God and the blood of Christ and the angels *ates*(?) and the church.

This text represents an invocation of angels against a demon that is causing some problem, the nature of which is not indicated. The angels are invoked twice, first as "holy ones of God" (ἄγιοι τοῦ θεοῦ) and second, by the term ἄνγελοι. The spelling is not unusual for magical texts. Robinson could not read line 12 (ἄτης καὶ) with certainty. He suggested also the possibilites "Απις or "Ατης. Both of these are possible given the kind of syncretism taking place in the realm of magical practices.

c. Council of Laodicea

The invocation of angels continued to be a practice of some of the churches in western Asia Minor through the fourth century A.D. Angels were invoked by Christians for protection from various forms of evil. One of the clearest illustrations of this utilitarian posture toward the angels can be seen in two decrees of an ecclesiastical council held at Laodicea c. A.D. 350:

---

[92] D. M. Robinson, "A Magical Inscription From Pisidian Antioch," *Hesperia* 22 (1953) 172-74.

[93] Robinson, "Magical Inscription," 172.

35. Christians shall not forsake the church of God and turn to the worship of angels (ἀγγέλους ὀνομάζειν), thus introducing a cultus of the angels. This is forbidden. Whoever, therefore, shows an inclination to this hidden idolatry, let him be anathema, because he has forsaken our Lord Jesus Christ, the Son of God, and gone over to idolatry.

36. Neither the higher nor the lower clergy may be magicians, conjurors, mathematicians, or astrologers, nor shall they make so-called amulets, which are chains for their own souls. And those who wear these amulets shall be shut out from the church.[94]

The 35th decree presupposes that some people in the churches were secretly involving themselves in a magical invocation of angels. It is of interest that the framers of this decree interpreted the activity as idolatry and tantamount to abandoning Christ. The reference to the cults of angels probably corresponds to the rise of churches dedicated to the archangel Michael in Phrygia (see below).[95] This became an attraction to numerous Christian pilgrims in the Byzantine era.[96] There are a number of inscriptions attesting the worship of Michael in Asia Minor, such as the following:

ὁ μέγας 'Αρχ(άγγελος) Μη(χαήλ). Κ(ύρι)ε Βοήθη τὸν δοῦλον[...][97]
O great archangel Michael! Lord, help the servant!

Κύριος φυλάξι τοὺς ἐργαζομένους ἐν τῷ οἴκῳ τοῦ 'Αρχαγγέλου Μιχαήλ.[98]
Lord, protect those working in the house of the archangel Michael.

The 36th decree of the Laodicean Council demonstrates the ongoing problem in the early church of Christians involving themselves in magical practices. This is true also of the "mathematicians" (μαθηματικοί), who are to be understood as astrologers who cast horoscopes.[99] The practice of

---

[94] Text and translation from C. J. Hefele, *A History of the Councils of the Church,* Vol II: A.D. 326-429 (Edinburgh: T. & T. Clark, 1896). For more discussion, see Lightfoot, *Colossians,* 69; Hopfner, *Offenbarungszauber,* § 146 (pp. 70-71).

[95] Hefele, *History of the Councils,* 317.

[96] N. Merisch, "Chonai," in *Phrygien und Pisidien* (eds. K. Belke & N. Merisch; Tabuli Imperii Byzantini 7, Österreichische Akademie der Wissenschaften, Philosophisch-Historische Klasse Denkschriften 211; Wien: Verlag der Österreischischen Akademie der Wissenschaften, 1990) 222-25.

[97] *MAMA* 1.434. The inscription is on a marble slab with a Latin cross.

[98] *MAMA* 4.307. The inscription was found in Dionysopolis, about 30 miles NE of Colossae.

[99] Hefele, *History of the Councils,* 318.

magic can be traced to the very beginning of the church in Asia Minor in Paul's ministry at Ephesus (Acts 19) and, I would contend, observable also at Colossae. The decrees illustrate that Christians not only invoked angels, but constructed amulets, and presumably, because of the summary character of the statement, were involved in all forms of magical practices. The fact that the 36th decree prohibits church leaders from functioning as magicians hints at the extent of the problem at that time.

The history of the church at Colossae, not far from Laodicea, points to a special place the Christians there accorded one angelic mediator, the archangel Michael. Michael was believed to have saved the population of Colossae from inundation by the Lycus river by making a new opening in the bank that diverted the waters from the city. This is the legend behind the origin of the great church of Michael the Archistratēgos at Colossae.[100] There was also a miraculous spring, made effective by Michael, located between Colossae and Hierapolis at Chaeretopa. Allegedly, the spring healed all who called upon the Father, Son, and Spirit in the name of the archangel. M. Simon suggests that Michael may very well have replaced here some pagan deity of the hot springs.[101] He goes on to suggest that "the substitution was in all likelihood pre-Christian, and had been engineered by those syncretizing Jews whose influence can be glimpsed through the polemical arguments of the epistle to the Colossians."[102]

The Laodicean Council apparently had little affect on curbing the invocation of angels. Writing in the first half of the fifth century, Theodoret notes in his commentary on Col 2:18: "[This disease] long remained in Phrygia and Pisidia. For this reason also a synod convened in Laodicea of Phrygia forbad by a decree the offering prayer to angels [noted above]; and even to the present time oratories of the holy Michael may be seen among them and their neighbours."[103] The tendency for Christians to call on angels for help and deliverance continued for many years and is well attested in the literature.[104]

---

[100] For more details, see Sir William M. Ramsay, *The Cities and Bishoprics of Phrygia* (Oxford: Clarendon, 1895) 214-16. See also L. Robert, *Villes d'Asie Mineure* (Paris: de Boccard, 1962) 105; Lightfoot, *Colossians*, 70-71.

[101] M. Simon, *Verus Israel* (Oxford: Oxford University Press, 1968) 368.

[102] Simon, *Verus Israel*, 368.

[103] Translation from Lightfoot, *Colossians*, 68, note 2. See also Hopfner, *Offenbarungszauber*, § 146 (p. 71).

[104] See J. Michl, "Engel IV (christlich)" *RAC* 5.199-200.

5. Conclusions

We are now in a position to affirm a fairly common function for the "angels" in the inscriptions of Asia Minor: They were perceived as accessible supernatural beings who came to the aid of people in need. They delivered people from all kinds of difficulties, and they protected the tombs of the deceased. This much was true in pagan, Jewish, and Christian contexts. In the context of magic, good angels would protect people from other angels of a baser character (e.g. Araaph).

In many of the pagan texts (Stratonicea, Temrek, and Didyma), I have interpreted "angel" as referring to Hekate. These inscriptions were found in areas where Hekate worship is widely attested. In popular belief, Hekate was famed as a goddess of the underworld. Although she is not seen as a rival to Theos Hypsistos in Stratonicea, she could be regarded as "universal queen" (πασικράτεια) and "ruler over all" (πασιμέδουσα) in her own right. Most importantly, she was perceived as an accessible deity and one to invoke for protection, deliverance, or help. As such, she could be referred to as ἄγγελος. This function is consonant with her prominent role in the magical papyri as a divine assistant (πάρεδρος), or a functionary of magic. This is also consistent with her prominence in the Pergamum magical apparatus and in the defixio found in the upper Maeander valley.

In the Jewish and Christian texts, the angels are best interpreted as the supernatural servants and emissaries of Yahweh. There is no indication that the angels had taken on divine status even though they were *directly* invoked on occasion for help.

May we now speak confidently of "angel cults" in Asia Minor? I would respond by saying 'yes' with regard to pagan cults of angels, but 'no' to Jewish or Christian cults of angels. In the many texts where ἄγγελος is used as an epithet of Hekate, there is a cultic dimension in the response of people to this goddess: she is regarded as a deity (Θεῖον); she is rendered praise alongside Theos Hypsistos; people render thanksgiving to her for providing deliverance/salvation; beneficiaries of her favor set up monuments in her honor; she has a cultic image, which, in fact, adorned the council chamber in Stratonicea. Her devotees could even erect a holy place—a temple precinct (περίβολος)—for her. On the other hand, in those texts where angels are regarded simply as mediators of a supreme deity (e.g. the Men text from Lydia; the Oenoanda inscription), it would be inappropriate to speak of "angel cults." Therefore, in the paganism of Asia Minor, an "angel cult" is coextensive with a cult of Hekate.

The evidence of the Jewish inscriptions (including those in the category of magical) does not point to an organized cult in which angels were worshipped in the same way as Yahweh—with ascriptions of praise and glory, with singing and worship, with sacrifices, etc. Our texts point to a specific kind of angel veneration, viz. calling on angels, invoking them, praying to them. The purpose of these invocations was largely apotropaic: people called on the angels as divine mediators to protect them or their property from various forms of evil, including evil angels who could bring harm, grave robbers, etc. They also may have called on angels to help them with the affairs of daily life (success in business, healing, bringing vengeance on enemies, etc.). While much of the evidence we have examined would have been used privately, some may have been used in a corporate context. In the inscriptions, there is no evidence for calling on angels in a mystical sense for visionary revelation. The silence of the extant inscriptions, however, does not imply this was not happening.

In short, the local inscriptional evidence demonstrates that "angel" was an important term in the religious life of the people of Asia Minor. People in the area commonly called upon ἄγγελοι—regardless of primary religious orientation—for protection and help.

CHAPTER 4

The Veneration of Angels at Colossae

The vast amount of material covered in the first three chapters to interpret the concise expression "worship of angels" (θρησκεία τῶν ἀγγέλων) performs a broader function than merely illustrating the one phrase; this material provides the primary basis for interpreting the whole teaching of the Colossian "philosophy." This material, often given the label "magic," gives us insight into the realm of folk religion in Asia Minor. It is precisely this realm of folk belief, illustrated by various magical texts, that helps us reconstruct a composite picture of the Colossian "philosophy." This assertion will, of course, need further demonstration in our discussion of the other elements of "the philosophy."

1. The Use of Θρησκεία

It will now be important for us to determine the meaning of θρησκεία in the context of Col 2:18 as well as to interpret the relationship of the term to its accompanying genitive, τῶν ἀγγέλων.[1]

a. Subjective Genitive: Worshiping *With* the Angels?

The angels have almost universally been regarded as the object of the veneration throughout the history of the interpretation of the passage.[2] In re-

---

[1] C. Rowland, "Apocalyptic Visions and the Exaltation of Christ in the Letter to the Colossians," *JSNT* 19 (1983) 75, suggests that the genitive τῶν ἀγγέλων should be taken with both θρησκεία and ταπεινοφροσύνη. He therefore thinks that Paul is referring to the activities of the angels in heaven, their humility and worship. But this interpretation misses the significance of the governing participial expression θέλων ἐν, normally translated "taking pleasure in" (BAGD, 355) or "insisting on" (RSV). The reference is to something that the advocates of "the philosophy" were practicing *and were prescribing* to the community.

cent years this has been challenged by the influential 1962 study of Fred O. Francis.[3] He argued that τῶν ἀγγέλων should be taken as a subjective genitive and interpreted as, "the worship which the angels perform."[4] He then set this phrase into the larger framework of angelic liturgies in Judaism, especially as seen in the Qumran literature, the Ascension of Isaiah, Testament of Job, Apocalypse of Abraham, 3 Enoch, and the Arabic Testament of Isaac. The rival teaching at Qumran, Francis argued, was calling for a visionary heavenly ascent followed by a participation in the angelic liturgy.

Francis found precedent for the use of θρησκεία with a subjective genitive in 4 Macc 5.7 and Josephus (*Ant.* 12.5.4 §253). In both instances, θρησκεία is modified by the accompanying genitive Ἰουδαίων and should be understood as "the religion" or "the worship" of the Jews. Francis also pointed out a few examples of θρησκεία where the accompanying genitive must be interpreted as objective, as for example in Josephus (*Ant.* 12.6.2 §271. In that passage the term θρησκεία occurs in a genitive relation to θεοῦ, which could only be taken as an objective genitive. Francis, therefore, argued that since a genitive following θρησκεία could be either in a subject or objective relationship to the noun, each instance needs to be interpreted according to the demands of the context. He insisted that his evidence "precludes a purely lexical determination of θρησκεία τῶν ἀγγέλων in Col 2:17 (sic)."[5]

There is reason, however, to disagree with his conclusion. A survey of the usage of θρησκεία fails to turn up one example of a divine being, or a typical object of worship (e.g. an "idol"), related to θρησκεία in the genitive case that should be taken as a subjective genitive.[6] This observation

---

[2] See Eadie, *Colossians,* 180, for a concise discussion of a few interpreters prior to 1900 who interpreted the phrase as the worship that the angels perform (i.e. as θρησκεία ἀγγελική).

[3] Fred O Francis, "Humility and Angelic Worship in Col 2:18," in *Conflict,* 163-95.

[4] Francis, "Angel Worship," 177.

[5] Francis, "Angelic Worship," 180. I have found three additional occurrences of the subjective genitive with θρησκεία in Josephus: (1) *Ant.* 16.4.3 §115, θρησκεία τοῦ παντὸς ἔθνους ("the worship of every Gentile"); (2) *J.W.* 2.10.4 §198 is the phrase, θρησκείας τῶν ἀνδρῶν ("the worship of men"). See also Chariton, *De Chaerea et Callirhoe* 7.6.6 (2nd century A.D. Greek romance writer from Aphrodisias in Caria) where the expression θρησκεία τῶν βαρβάρων ("the worship of barbarians") occurs.

[6] My survey of the usage of θρησκεία was facilitated greatly by the use of the Thesaurus Linguae Graecae database of Greek literature.

upholds the statement in BAGD that, "the Being who is worshipped is given in the obj. gen."[7]

b. Objective Genitive: Invoking Angels

The noun θρησκεία is not very common in the Greco-Roman secular writers.[8] In Jewish writings it only appears four times in the LXX and five times in Philo. The term is very common in Josephus, however, occurring a total of 91 times. It should also be pointed out that no occurrences of the word are reported in Denis's Greek concordance of the Pseudepigrapha.[9] From this survey of the usage, numerous examples can be cited of a divine object given in the genitive case:

> "Worship of god" (θρησκεία τοῦ θεοῦ)[10]
> "Worship of the gods" (θρησκεία θεῶν)[11]
> "Worship of idols" (εἰδώλων θρησκεία)[12]
> "The Worship of Apollo" ([τὴ]ν θρησκεί[αν τ]οῦ Ἀπό[λλωνος τοῦ Πυθίου])[13]
> "The Worship of Sarapis" (θρησκεία τοῦ Σαράπιδος)[14]

In light of this evidence, it appears highly probable that the writer of Colossians would have intended the genitive expression τῶν ἀγγέλων as the

---

[7] BAGD, 363. So also Bauer[6], col. 738: "das Wesen, dem die Verehrung gilt, wird im gen. obi. hinzugefügt."

[8] It never appears in a host of writers and occurs only once in Dio Chrysostom (but a textual difficulty renders this occurrence tenuous), Strabo, Dionysius of Halicarnassus, Chariton, Lucian, and Xenophon of Ephesus, twice in Plutarch, Soranus, and Galen, five times in Sextus Empiricus. The term does appear eighteen times in Iamblichus.

[9] See Albert-Marie Denis, ed., *Concordance Grecque des Pseudépigraphes d'Ancien Testament* (Louvain: Université Catholique de Louvain, 1987) s.v.

[10] Josephus, *Ant.* 1.13.1 §222. Cf. also 4.4.1 §61; 4.8.44 §306; 7.14.2 §341; 8.8.4 §225; 8.10.2 §251; 8.15.2 §395; 9.5.1 §96; 9.6.6 §133; 9.7.5 §157; 9.13.3 §273; 10.4.1 §53; 12.6.2 §271; 13.6.3 §200; 17.9.3 §214. See also Xenophon Ephesius, *Ephesiaca*, 1.5.1; Herodianus, *De Prosodia Catholica* 4.8.7 (τήν τε τοῦ θεοῦ θρησκείαν καὶ τὴν τοῦ ἥρωος); 5.7.2.

[11] Philo, *Spec. Leg.* 1.315 (this is the only occasion in which a genitive is joined to θρησκεία in Philo). See also Iambl., *De Vita Pythagorica* 4.19; 6.32; 28.137; *Protrepticus* 111.27; 112.9; *Myst.* 3.31; Porphyry, *De Philosophia ex Oraculis* 148.2; Simpl., *in Cael.* 7.370; *BGU* 13.2215,3. For two additional papyrus examples of θρησκεία θεῶν, see F. Preisigke, *Wörterbuch der griechischen Papyruskunden* (Göttingen: Hubert & Co, 1925) 1.373.

[12] Wisdom 14:27.

[13] This line occurs in the famous Delphi inscription, *SIG[3]* § 801d, line 4 (p. 494).

[14] Ael. *NA* 10.28 (cited in Bauer[6]).

object of the noun θρησκεία; if he did not, his readers would surely have misunderstood him. Furthermore, I can find no example in extant Greek literature of θρησκεία used with some expression of accompaniment, i.e. worshiping with someone. Francis's intepretation is therefore quite doubtful.[15]

An additional difficulty with Francis's view can be seen in Col 2:23 where ἐν ἐθελοθρησκίᾳ (as well as ταπεινοφροσύνῃ and ἀφειδίᾳ σώματος) is used to describe the activity of the people involved in the practice of "the philosophy." The fact that this freely-chosen worship is here performed by people (not angels) and also is viewed in a negative sense reinforces our impression that the worship of 2:18 is also performed by people and should be seen in a negative light.[16] The objection stands, in spite of the recent attempts to rescue the view by arguing that humans still participate in the worship even if θρησκεία τῶν ἀγγέλων refers to worship that angels perform.[17]

Having established that the angels are the objects of "worship," we must now endeavor to determine the precise significance of θρησκεία within the context of Col 2:18 and the Colossian "philosophy" as a whole. The term is commonly used, especially in Josephus, for the cultic activity of worshiping God.[18] It can also be used with regard to the cultic veneration of the pagan gods (see above).

The term can also denote the simple act of worship and one's own response to deity apart from the cult. This usage has not been adequately described in Bauer's lexicon,[19] and some have missed the non-cultic use of the term.[20] One can see this use of the term even in Jas 1:27. This usage of

---

[15] Likewise, the evidence suggests just the opposite of the conclusion reached by Rowland, "Apocalyptic Visions," 76: "When taken in isolation from its surrounding context, there is every reason to suppose that *tōn angelōn* should be taken as a subjective genitive."

[16] See R. DeMaris, *The Colossian Controversy* (JSNTSS 96; Sheffield: JSOT Press, 1994) 77; Lohse, *Colossians,* 119, note 36; Schweizer, *Colossians,* 159.

[17] See A. T. Lincoln, *Paradise Now and Not Yet* (SNTSMS 43; Cambridge: University Press, 1981) 223, note 9, and Rowland, "Apocalyptic Visions," 77.

[18] Thus, rightly, BAGD, 363, "the worship of God, religion, esp. as it expresses itself in religious service or cult." So also Bauer[6], col. 738: "d. Gottesverehrung, bes. auch soweit sie sich äußert als d. Gottesdienst, d. Kultus."

[19] This observation holds true both for the English translation of the fourth edition (BAGD) and the new 6th edition.

[20] Even prior to Bauer, Lightfoot, *Colossians,* 196, overstressed the cultic use: "The word referes properly to the external rites of religion, and so gets to signify an over-scrupulous devotion to external forms." This negative understanding of the word also misses its positive usage, which is common in Josephus.

the term is well illustrated in Josephus's account of Abraham's offering of Isaac where H. St. J. Thackeray actually uses the word "piety" to translate the occurrences of θρησκεία: Josephus records that God desired "to make trial of [Abraham's] piety towards himself" (τῆς περὶ αὐτὸν θρησκείας) (*Ant.* 1.13.1 §223) and that by offering Isaac, "thus would he manifest his piety towards himself" (τὴν περὶ αὐτὸν θρησκείαν) (*Ant.* 1.13.1 §224); because of Abraham's willingness to sacrifice his dear son to God, the Lord "knew the ardour and depth of his piety" (θρησκεία; *Ant.* 1.13.3 §234).

The idea of "veneration" may also be prominent in the use of the term, again, detached from cultic ritual. In Josephus, Laban accuses Jacob of "making off with the sacred objects of my family which my forefathers venerated (τιμηθέντα) and I have deemed worthy of the same worship (θρησκείας) as they" (*Ant.* 1.19.9 §316).

Finally, and very significant for our investigation, is the use of θρησκεία to signify *conjuration* or *invocation*. In Strabo's only use of the term, he connects it with the magical arts (μαντική and γοητεία; *Geog.* 10.3.23). In a context where he is describing the enthusiasm of certain devotees of the gods, he notes, "juggling and magic are closely related to religious frenzies, worship, and divination" (τῶν δ' ἐνθουσιασμῶν καὶ θρησκείας καὶ μαντικῆς τὸ ἀγυρτικὸν καὶ γοητεία ἐγγύς). In this context, "invocation" or "conjuration" would be more appropriate translations than the more general "worship." A similar use of the verbal form appears in Origen's *Contra Celsum*. This passage is highly significant for our purposes because it is the same paragraph in which Celsus accuses the Jews of worshiping heaven and the angels in it (Origen, *Contra Celsum*, 5.6; see the discussion of this passage in the previous chapter). Celsus continues his invective against the Jews by saying:

> They behave as though it were possible that the whole could be be God but its parts not divine, or that one might quite rightly worship (θρησκεύειν) beings which are alleged to draw near to people blinded in darkness somewhere as a result of black magic (ἐκ γοητείας), or who have dreams of obscure phantoms (δι' ἀμυδρῶν φασμάτων).[21]

In disputing this characterization of the Jews, Origen does not repeat Celsus's use of θρησκεύειν, but uses his own preferred term προσκυνεῖν. The

---

[21] Translations taken from H. Chadwick, *Origen: Contra Celsum* (Cambridge: University Press, 1979) 26. For Greek text, see M. Borret, *Origène, Contre Celse* (SC 132; Paris: Editions du Cerf, 1969) 26.

passage gives clear evidence, however, of the continued use of θρησκεύειν in connection with magical practices.

The term θρησκεία thus has a wide range of usage extending from cultic activity to personal piety to private veneration and even involvement with magical practices. Thus, no fixed lexical determination of the meaning can be established. One needs to determine the more precise meaning of the term by seeing it in relationship to its genitive qualifier (τῶν ἀγγέλων) in the context of what can be discerned about the nature of the teaching of "the philosophy" in general.

At the minimum we can say that the errorists were making "angels" the object of their veneration. The phrase does not tell us whether this was happening in a cultic context or in terms of private devotion. The larger context of "the philosophy," as we shall see below, points to some cultic overtones, but could also include private activities. If we are correct in approaching the nature of the false teaching partially from the standpoint of pagan and Jewish magic, it is likely that the phrase represents the Colossian author's critique of "the philosophy's" practice, as opposed to representing a phrase quoted by the errorists, since the term θρησκεία does not appear in the magical texts.[22] "The veneration of angels" is probably a polemical phrase created by the author to describe what the faction was doing and perhaps even rhetorically conceived to reduce the reader's estimation of the practice of the opponents.

2. Jewish Mysticism or Gnosticism?

Before we give an exposition of what the phrase does mean in the context of "the philosophy," it will be necessary to give a brief indication of what it does not mean. In particular, we need to examine the increasingly popular view that the phrase has something to do with "worshiping *with* the angels" around the heavenly throne in the context of Jewish mysticism as well as the formerly popular view that the phrase is evidence of a Gnostic background to "the philosophy."

---

[22] At least the phrase does not appear in the index to the *PGM* (Karl Preisendanz, *Papyri Graecae Magicae. Die Griechischen Zauberpapyri*, Vol. 3 [Leipzig: Teubner, 1942]) nor in the index to Audollent's corpus of defixiones.

a. Participation in Angelic Liturgy

Liturgical documents from Qumran (esp. 4QShirShabb [=4Q400-407];
4QSerek Sirot; 11QSirSab; 1QSb; but also portions of 1QH; 1QS; and CD)
have given us a unique insight into a group of pious Jews, separated from
the Jerusalem temple, who sought to worship God in a meaningful way.
Angels, and speculation about the angels, abound in these documents. They
contain a more extensive range of angel terminology than any of the other
Qumran writings.

The Songs of the Sabbath Sacrifice (4QShirShabb) are especially significant in this regard.[23] The thirteen compositions give an account of the
angelic worship performed on the Sabbath in the heavenly sanctuary.
Carol Newsom notes that, "the highly descriptive content and the carefully
crafted rhetoric direct the worshipper who hears the songs recited toward
a particular kind of religious experience, a sense of being in the heavenly
sanctuary and in the presence of the angelic priests and worshippers."[24]
She says that "the effect of this style is to direct attention to the angels who
praise rather than to the God who is praised."[25] It is likely that these Palestinian Jews perceived heaven to be closer, and thus more conducive to
liturgical communion with the angels, on Sabbaths and holidays than during the ordinary weekday liturgy.[26] Thus, according to Newsom, the
Songs of the Sabbath were not intended as vehicles for the incubation of
visions or of mystical ascent by individuals, but as a vehicle for communion with the angels that would have had as a byproduct the increased possibility of ecstatic experience among some of the worshippers.[27] The
communal mysticism of the angelic liturgies thus enabled the Qumran
community, separated from the impure worship of the Jerusalem temple,
to participate in the sacrificial cult of the heavenly temple itself. It would
have also helped to assure the Qumran worshippers in their belief that
they were the legitimate and holy priesthood.[28]

Although he did not know these texts, F. O. Francis pointed in this direction as the solution to the problem of θρησκεία τῶν ἀγγέλων in Colos-

---

[23] See Carol Newsom, *Songs of the Sabbath Sacrifice: A Critical Edition* (Harvard
Semitic Studies 27; Atlanta: Scholars Press, 1985). See also the discussion in also M. J.
Davidson, *Angels at Qumran* (JSPSS 11; Sheffield: JSOT Press, 1992) 235-54 (= Chap-
ter 12).

[24] Newsom, *Songs,* 17.

[25] Newsom, *Songs,* 16.

[26] Newsom, *Songs,* 20-21.

[27] Newsom, *Songs,* 17-18.

[28] Davidson, *Angels at Qumran,* 237.

sians 2:18 on the basis of other related texts.[29] The followers of Francis
have found these recently published documents as confirmation of a
"Jewish mysticism" view of the competing teaching at Colossae.[30] The
strength of this approach is that it can be used to explain "the philosophy's" emphasis on keeping special days, particularly the Sabbath (Col
2:16). It can explain the food and drink prohibitions (2:16), which might
also be described as "humility" (2:18), by appealing to the food and drink
laws of Qumran as a preparation for the act of worship. The new liturgical texts may also help this interpretation (if one sees the genitive as subjective, "worshiping with the angels") by illustrating how the angels may
be seen as taking on too prominent of a role in the minds of the human
worshippers, i.e. although they were not the objects of worship, they received too much attention.

Nevertheless, the Jewish mystical interpretation still does not give an
adequate understanding of how the angels could be regarded as the objects
of worship. In my opinion, Francis's interpretation of θρησκεία τῶν
ἀγγέλων as "worshiping with the angels" is untenable. We have already
seen that it is quite unlikely that a first-century author would have used
"angels" in a genitive relationship to θρησκεία as the subjects of the act of
worshiping. There are also many other weaknesses to this view, mainly
stemming from its inability to explain some of the key elements of "the
philosophy" and important aspects of the polemic of the letter. Namely:
(1) this view does not take into account the emphasis on evil angelic
powers in Colossians, especially the fact that Col 2:15 gives us the fullest
description of the devastating defeat of the powers by Christ's work on the
cross; (2) the view does not give adequate credence to the connection of
the term ἐμβατεύω (2:18) with the local mystery rites; (3) it does not help
us to understand in what sense the false teaching had "a reputation of
wisdom" (σοφία; 2:23); (4) the emphasis on moral and ritual purity at
Qumran appears inconsistent with the vices listed in 3:5-11, especially the
emphasis on sexual sin; (5) the view does not explain how the στοιχεῖα

---

[29] Francis, "Humility," 177.

[30] Some had already made use of the two fragments of angelic liturgies published in
1960 by John Strugnell ("The Angelic Liturgy at Qumran—4QSerek Sirot Olat Hassabat,"
in *Congress Volume: Oxford, 1959* [VTSup 7; Leiden: Brill, 1960] 318-45) to give further support to Francis's conclusions prior to the publication of Newsom's edition of the
Sabbath Songs. See, for example, Roy Yates, "The 'Worship of Angels' (Col. 2:18),"
ET 97 (1985) 14-15, and Rowland, "Apocalyptic Visions," 77. T. J. Sappington, *Revelation and Redemption at Colossae* (JSNTSS 53; Sheffield: JSOT Press, 1991) 20, mentions the Sabbath Liturgies but does not use them for nearly as much profit as he could to
support his thesis.

τοῦ κόσμου should be factored into the competing teaching (Francis himself completely neglected treating this concern)[31]; (6) certain features of the polemic in Colossians appear inappropriate to the Jewish mystical interpretation, e.g. how could Paul speak of Jewish-Christian advocacy of participation in angelic liturgy as "vain deceit" (2:8)?; (7) how can we be sure that the kind of mystical worship that we find at Qumran made its way to the west coast of Asia Minor, especially among a large number of Jews who likely had no prior contact with the Dead Sea community (one must remember that many came directly from Persia); (8) finally, this view neglects the importance of the Gentile presence and influence within the churches of Asia Minor.

This leads us to conclude that we need to look beyond the borders of Jewish mysticism, as defined by Francis and his followers, for a more precise understanding of the "worship of angels" (θρησκεία τῶν ἀγγέλων) within the Colossian context. We do not need to leave Judaism, however, to find a more relevant understanding of the idea.

b. Gnostic Veneration of Angels

Petr Pokorný recently has revived the hypothesis that the Colossian "philosophy" is best explained on the basis of Gnostic models.[32] Although admitting that Gnosticism is not unequivocally attested until the second century, Pokorný contends that its roots existed a few decades prior to the first documented evidence and that we see a form of Gnosticism reflected in "the philosophy" at Colossae.

Pokorný argues that the veneration of angels by the opponents at Colossae represented a concern with the archons who could ultimately prevent a unification with the highest deity. He thus regards the angels as evil, coextensive with the *archai kai exousiai* and the *stoicheia*. He claims that Gnostics learned how to disguise themselves from the archons by participating in their cult and thus averting their wrath.

Pokorný follows in large measure the presentation of Hans-Martin Schenke, who also affirmed the identity of the angels in 2:18 with the evil

---

[31] Sappington, *Revelation and Redemption,* 164-70, has partly rectified this weakness of the view in his discussion of στοιχεῖα τοῦ κόσμου. He erroneously (in my opinion) reduces the significance of the expression to secondary evidence for discerning the error at Colossae and contends that it refers to basic principles of religion.

[32] Pokorný, *Colossians,* 117-21.

principalities and powers and the *stoicheia.*[33] Schenke argued that Gnostics, in spite of their redemption, regarded themselves as still under the rule of archons and facing a dangerous road after death in their journey through the kingdom of the archons to the kingdom of light.[34] Consequently they needed to make special preparation for this journey by acceding during life to the demands of the archons for worship. This present worship would enable these Gnostics, on the day of their death, to successfully pierce through the various planetary spheres and arrive safely to the kingdom of light.

Schenke and Pokorný have provided further precision and elucidation of earlier gnostic interpretations of "the worship of angels" as one element of the gnostic-oriented teaching. G. Bornkamm, for instance, merely pointed to θρησκεία τῶν ἀγγέλων as the author's "characterization of the στοιχεῖα-cult."[35] Similarly, M. Dibelius provided no more explanation of the phrase than his assertions that the term "angels" is another way of referring to *stoicheia* and that the advocates of "the philosophy" were involved in the cultic worship of *stoicheia*/angels.[36]

There are numerous difficulties with the gnostic view, not least of which is the question of the appropriateness of illustrating first-century tendencies and practices on the basis of later well-developed gnostic systems. I have argued in a different context that priority should be given to exploring traditions that were *known* to exist in the first century before appealing to the later developments,[37] especially if the catalyst for the development of the anticosmic dualism and the demiurge concept in Gnosis postdates the composition of Colossians.[38] Both Schenke and Pokorný, for

---

[33] H.-M. Schenke, "Der Widerstreit gnostischer und kirchlicher Christologie im Spiegel des Kolosserbriefes," *ZTK* 61 (1964) 393-96.

[34] Schenke, "Widerstreit," 396.

[35] G. Bornkamm, "The Heresy of Colossians," in *Conflict,* 130. Bornkamm saw the phrase as pointing to the Jewish origin of the heresy since many documents in second-temple Judaism coordinate angels with *stoicheia* and constellations. He wrongly assumes, however, that the Judaizing movement sprang from gnosticizing Judaism.

[36] M. Dibelius, "The Isis Initiation in Apuleius and Related Initiatory Rites," in *Conflict,* 83-84, 89; Dibelius-Greeven, *Kolosser,* 27-29.

[37] See my *Ephesians: Power and Magic* (SNTSMS 63; Cambridge: University Press, 1989) 7-13.

[38] See I. Culianu, "The Angels of the Nations and the Origins of Gnostic Dualism," *Studies in Gnosticism and Hellenistic Religions* (EPRO 91; FS. G. Quispel; Leiden: Brill, 1981) 78-80; A. F. Segal, *Two Powers in Heaven* (SJLA 25; Leiden: Brill, 1977) 265; E. Yamauchi, "Jewish Gnosticism? The Prologue of John, Mandaean Parallels, and the Trimorphic Protennoia," *Studies in Gnosticism and Hellenistic Religions* (EPRO 91; FS. G. Quispel; Leiden: Brill, 1981) 491.

instance, illustrate the meaning of "worship of angels" in Colossians on the basis of a passage in *The Hypostasis of the Archons* (= *NHC* II,4) 92:29-32, where an archon demands that Norea (the daughter of Eve) render service to them. This document, however, represents a well-developed Gnosticism of the third century and actually begins by quoting what "the great apostle" said in Colossians and Ephesians![39]

Among the other major difficulties with the gnostic view is that the Colossian letter gives no indication that the advocates of "the philosophy" were concerned about the dangers of the ascent of the soul on the day of death, while this was a major emphasis in all gnostic systems. It is true that the opponents had a deep concern about hostile spirit powers, but this concern is capable of another explanation. By identifying the angels with the hostile *stoicheia* and the evil principalities and powers, the gnostic view fails to consider that the angels may be viewed by the opponents as good and helpful beings. It is easier to explain "worship of angels" in Col 2:18 by the supposition that the faction was venerating good angels who were assisting and helping them than by arguing that they were worshiping hostile archons as a means of averting their wrath.

The gnostic interpretation thus rightly points to angels as the object of veneration (versus participating in an angelic liturgy), characterizes the *stoicheia* and the principalities and powers as evil, and points to the diminution of Christ's status in relation to other spirit beings. This view, however, relies too heavily on a well-developed system of a later time that, even in its incipient form, is not appropriate for explaining the Colossian "philosophy." We would prefer to give priority to the streams of tradition that were known to exist—mystery traditions, magic, astrology, local religions, and Judaism—than to explain "the philosophy" on the basis of Gnosis.

---

[39] Pokorný, *Colossians,* 119, also suggests that "veneration of angels" may be explained by the gnostic teaching that the aeons are spiritual reflections of the highest deity with the implication that the worship of these beings is appropriate as long as the gnostic recognizes the light behind the mask of the material world. Pokorný concedes that these gnostic conceptions come from a later time and are not present in all gnostic layers of tradition. He contends, however, that because there is gnostic speculation about the archons present in all gnostic groups, it is appropriate to retroject this speculation back into the first century. It is precisely at this point where I disagree with Pokorný.

3. Invoking Angels at Colossae

The cumulative evidence of the foregoing chapters leads us to conclude that "the philosophy" at Colossae included an element of "invoking angels" probably for protection, help, and assistance. This accords well with the role of angels in popular religion, the role of angels in the inscriptions of Asia Minor, and the "Christ alone" emphasis in the letter to the Colossians.

As we have seen, the term θρησκεία has a broad usage ranging in meaning from cultic activity to personal piety to involvement in the magical arts. The precise meaning of the term, therefore, must be contextually determined. It is probable that the entire expression, θρησκεία τῶν ἀγγέλων, was chosen by the author as descriptive of the opponents' activity, but also as a rhetorically powerful way of shocking the readers into viewing their own practice less favorably. As a descriptive term, it could be interpreted as *"veneration of angels,"* and thereby function as an appropriate description of calling on angels in magical invocations. As rhetorically conceived, the expression would help the readers to see that the focus of their attention was neither on God or Christ, but on angelic beings.

The evidence we have gathered here does not point to an organized cult in which angels were worshipped in the same way as Yahweh—with ascriptions of praise and glory, with singing and praying, with sacrifices, etc. Nor does the evidence point in the direction of an actual cult modeled on the Hellenistic mystery religions.[40] Our texts point to a specific kind of angel veneration, viz. calling on angels, invoking them, praying to them. The purpose of these invocations was largely apotropaic: People called on the angels as intermediaries of God to protect them from the evil powers— the στοιχεῖα τοῦ κόσμου, the ἀρχαὶ καὶ ἐξουσίαι, the θρόνοι and κυριότητες, and every other invisible power that could bring harm. They probably also called on angels for revelation that would have taken place in a visionary manner. They also may have called on angels to help them with the affairs of daily life (success in business, healing, bringing vengeance on enemies, etc.). While much of the evidence we have examined would have been used privately, there is also a large amount that could have been used in a corporate context.

---

[40] *Contra* Gnilka, *Kolosserbrief,* 168. Dibelius, "Isis Initiation," 82, 90, argued that there was a "cult of the elements" present at Colossae.

The magical material—both pagan and Jewish—has many other parallels with the Colossian teaching that remain to be developed. In a summary fashion, we can here note the main motifs: concern over evil powers and perhaps astral powers, in particular knowledge, wisdom, vision, humility, and ritual prohibitions.

The local evidence from Colossae and the regions around serves to confirm that "angels" played a very significant role in the religious life of the people. People in the area commonly called upon angels for protection and help. Later tradition shows that this was perceived as a problem in the churches of the Lycus valley.

It is possible that the advocates of "the philosophy" thought of Christ in terms similar to the way pagans thought of Hekate or Hermes (as an "angel") in relation to Zeus, or the way Jews thought of Michael in relation to Yahweh. The alleged pagan tendency in Asia Minor toward the worship of one high god served by angelic mediators would be consonant with this conception of Jesus on par with Hekate and/or Michael.

It appears that the practice of invoking angels at Colossae does not have as much to do with matters of ultimate spiritual significance as it does with the issues of day-to-day life. As with the veneration of angels in the Judaism of magic and incantations, the Colossian practice involved a diminution of one's relationship to Yahweh (and now Christ) in favor of a manipulative relationship with his angels. In spite of the focus on angels, monotheism is probably retained. The angels are "called upon" and invoked, but they are not worshipped in a cultic fashion. The greater implication is with Christology where it appears that Christ is either neglected in favor of calling upon angels, or that he is regarded on the same level as the angels and is invoked in the same fashion as in the incantation texts.

The author of Colossians judged the advocates of "the philosophy" as having gone too far in addressing angels. The Pauline tradition leaves little room for directly seeking angelic assistance. The emphasis is rather on seeking to appropriate the benefits of union with the exalted Christ as the means for overcoming evil.

Part II: Reconstructing the Colossian "Philosophy"

Our conclusion that "worship of angels" in Colossians 2:18 represents the practice of invoking angels for protection, help, and deliverance takes us a long way toward identifying the matrix of beliefs in the Colossian syncretism. There still remain a number of other important clues for discerning the nature of the factional teaching.

The connection of "the philosophy" to local mystery cult beliefs hinges partly on interpreting the phrase ἃ ἑόρακεν ἐμβατεύων, also appearing in Col 2:18. There has been a longstanding dispute over whether the term ἐμβατεύω was a technical term of the local mysteries. The nature of the local Phrygian/Lydian/Carian religious traditions needs to be further explored, however, for other possible similarities to the deviant teaching at Colossae. This investigation will need to include an examination of the alleged presence of highly syncretistic Jewish cults in Asia Minor—the cults of Sabazios and Theos Hypsistos. Further inquiry also needs to be undertaken regarding any evidence that can help us understand the magical substructure of the local cults. Our research will be aided here by the increasing amount of information available about the worship of Hekate.

The expression στοιχεῖα τοῦ κόσμου (Col 2:8, 20) provides still another important window on the teaching of "the philosophy." Among the issues that surface with regard to this expression is the foundational question of whether it refers to angelic powers, basic principles of religion, or the four elements.

Finally, the many additional "catchwords" and allusions to the practices and beliefs of the opponents need to be taken into account and correlated with the conclusions reached on these previous issues of interpretation. A composite portrait of the Colossian "philosophy" will be drawn as the final chapter of PART II. An attempt will then be made to locate the place of "the philosophy" in the context of local beliefs and as part of a broader trajectory in early Christianity.

Chapter 5

The Term Ἐμβατεύω, Mystery Initiation, and the Local Cults

The phrase ἃ ἑόρακεν ἐμβατεύων in Colossians 2:18 has proven to be the single most perplexing exegetical problem of the letter. The difficulty of interpreting the phrase can be traced very early in a few textual variants that record attempts at clarifying the meaning.[1] Some scholars, including Lightfoot, even resorted to textual emendation to explain the ambiguous phrase.[2]

Most scholars since Lightfoot accept the text as it stands but debate the most appropriate meaning of ἐμβατεύω for this context. Some opt for the meaning "investigate" and suggest that the term points either to careful investigation into visions seen in ecstatic experience[3] or to careful philosophical investigation leading to important insights regarded as authoritative for "the philosophy."[4] Others contend that the term should be taken as "entering into possession of [something]" and understand the heavenly realm as the unexpressed object. F. O. Francis then explains that, "the Colossians sought to enter heaven in order to possess themselves of salvation, a portion in the Lord."[5] Francis's explanation has proven compelling to those who see the background of the Colossian "philosophy" in Jewish mystical ascent to heaven and worship with the angels.[6]

---

[1] Two variant textual traditions add a negative between ἃ and ἑόρακεν: (1) The majority text together with א², C, D², Ψ, 075, 0150, the Vulgate, and a few other witnesses add μή; (2) the uncials F and G add οὐκ.

[2] Lightfoot, *Colossians,* 196-97, emends the text to: ἃ ἑώρα (or, αἰώρᾳ?) κενεμβατεύων, "to indulge in vain speculations."

[3] H. Preisker, "ἐμβατεύω," *TDNT* 2.535-36. Lexical precedent for this meaning can be found in 2 Macc 2:30 and Philo, *De plant.* 80.

[4] R. E. DeMaris, *The Colossian Controversy* (JSNTSS 96; Sheffield: JSOT Press, 1994) 64-66.

[5] F. O. Francis, "The Background of EMBATEUEIN (Col 2:18) in Legal Papyri and Oracle Inscriptions," in *Conflict,* 199.

[6] See most recently, Thomas J. Sappington, *Revelation and Redemption at Colossae* (JSNTSS 53; Sheffield: JSOT Press, 1991) 156-58. See also O'Brien, *Colossians,* 143; R. Yates, "'The Worship of Angels' (Col. 2:18)" *ET* (1987) 14; C. Rowland,

There is another interpretation, however, that proves more compelling. Shortly after the turn of the century, Theodore Macridy, working on behalf of the Turkish Imperial Museum at Notion (Roman Colophon), published a series of inscriptions from the then recently discovered Apollo temple at Claros, 30 km north of Ephesus.[7] A short time later, Sir William Ramsay and Martin Dibelius, although working independently, both came to realize the relevance of the inscriptions for the interpretation of Col 2.18. They noted that the term ἐμβατεύω occurred three times in a technical sense, signifying the second stage of the initiation into the mystery of the local Apollo cult.[8] They concluded that, in a pattern of ritual similar to that at Eleusis, there was a lower and higher stage in the mystery initiation at Claros. The lower stage was the initiation proper (μύησις), and the higher stage was called "entering" (ἐμβατεύω; termed the "Epoptika" at Eleusis). They concurred that the Colossian "philosophy" could now be described as having some connection with a local pagan mystery cult. They argued that the term would have been readily intelligible to the readers of the epistle as a technical term for mystery initiation in one of the local cults—"what he had seen when he reached the climax of his initiation." It thus appeared that an influential member of the Christian community at Colossae, still swayed by his past experience in mystery initiation, was introducing these ideas into the

---

"Apocalyptic Visions and the Exaltation of Christ in the Letter to the Colossians," *JSNT* 19 (1983) 76; C. A. Evans, "The Colossian Mystics," *Biblica* 63 (1982) 198; A. T. Lincoln, *Paradise Now and Not Yet* (SNTSMS 43; Cambridge: University Press, 1981) 112-13. W. Carr, "Two Notes on Colossians," *JTS* 24 (1973) 496-99, argues that the more precise meaning is, "to tread upon a sacred place," which he finds attested in Aeschylus, *Pers.* 449; Sophocles, *OC* 679 and *OT* 825; Euripides *Rhes.* 225 and *El.* 595.

[7] The inscriptions were published by Theodore Macridy in two stages: (1) "Altertümer von Notion," *JhhÖArchInst* 8 (1905) 155-173, and (2) "Antiquités de Notion II," *JhhÖArchInst* 15 (1912) 36-67.

[8] Sir William M. Ramsay, *The Teaching of Paul in Terms of the Present Day* (2d ed.; London: Hodder & Stoughton, 1914) 283-305 (= Chapter 46: "The Relation of St. Paul to the Greek Mysteries"; the chapter is a revision and enlargement of "The Mysteries in their Relation to St. Paul," *Contemporary Review* 104 [1913] 201. Ramsay's initial publication on the relevance of the inscriptions for Col 2:18 was "Ancient Mysteries and their Relation to St. Paul," *Athenaeum* (Jan. 25, 1913) 106-107); idem, "Sketches in the Religious Antiquities of Asia Minor," *The Annual of the British School at Athens* 18 (1911-12) 44-51. Martin Dibelius, "The Isis Initiation in Apuleius and Related Initiatory Rites," in *Conflict,* 87 (this is a translation of "Die Isisweihe bei Apuleius und verwandte Initiations-Riten," *Sitzungsberichte der Heidelberger Akademie der Wissenschaften, Philosophisch-historische Klasse* 4 [1917], later reprinted in *Botschaft und Geschichte* [eds. G. Bornkamm & H. Kraft; Tübingen: J.C.B. Mohr [Paul Siebeck], 1956] 2.30-79.

church. This interpretation of ἐμβατεύω has attracted a sizeable following of scholars.[9]

Dibelius and Ramsay differed in their interpretations of the extent to which the local mysteries should be viewed as part of the Colossian "philosophy." In looking at the other indications of the nature of the competing teaching in Colossians, Dibelius's myopic approach totally closed the door on seeing any Jewish elements in the heresy—a conclusion which has made his position the object of substantial criticism.[10] Ramsay, on the other hand, stressed the syncretistic background of the movement threatening the Colossian church. In fact, he suggested that concepts from the mystery cults were combined "with Jewish thought in a popular superstitious form," alluding to a possible connection with Jewish magic (Acts 19:13).[11] Unfortunately, Ramsay's study has gone largely unnoticed and the general position that the Colossian heresy had something to do with the local mystery religions has been attacked mainly on the basis of the refusal of Dibelius (and so also Lohse) to see any direct Jewish contribution to "the philosophy." This has been corrected, in part, by J. Lähnemann, but still stands in need of further refinement.

I am convinced of the essential appropriateness of interpreting ἐμβατεύω as a technical term of the local mysteries and as a catchword of the teaching of the opponents. In the following pages, I will endeavor to provide additional support to this contention (against the critics of Dibelius) and to clarify the relationship of the teaching of the opponents to lo-

---

[9] (Beginning with the most recent) Pokorný, *Colossians,* 115-17, 146-47; (although he roots the heresy not in the mystery religions but in Gnosis, which drew many of its terms and concepts from the mysteries); Randal A. Argall, "The Source of Religious Error in Colossae," *CTJ* 22 (1987) 14-15; Horacio B. Lona, *Die Eschatologie im Kolosser- und Epheserbrief* (FzB 48; Würzburg: Echter, 1984) 210-11; Martin, *Colossians* (NCB), 94-95; Gnilka, *Kolosserbrief,* 150-51; Johannes Lähnemann, *Der Kolosserbrief. Komposition, Situation und Argumentation* (SNT 3; Gütersloh: Mohn, 1971) 86, 138; J. L. Houlden, *Paul's Letters From Prison* (Pelican New Testament Commentaries; Harmondsworth: Penguin, 1970) 198; Lohse, *Colossians,* 120; A. T. Kraabel, "Judaism in Asia Minor under the Roman Empire with a Preliminary Study of the Jewish Community at Sardis, Lydia" (Unpublished Doctoral Dissertation; Harvard, 1968) 147; C. Maurer, "Die Begründung der Herrschaft Christi über die Mächte nach Kol. 1,15-20," *Wort und Dienst* N.S. 4 (1955) 80-81; Beare, *Colossians,* 202-204; Lohmeyer, *Kolosser,* 176-77; Dibelius-Greeven, *Kolosser,* 35; G. Bornkamm, "The Heresy of Colossians," in *Conflict,* 140, note 13 (Bornkamm still leaves open the possibility that the term has the more general meaning, "investigate."); Scott, *Colossians,* 55; S. Eitrem, "'EMBATEYΩ. Note sur Col. 2, 18," *ST* 2 (1948) 90-94; idem, "Apollonische Weihe," in *Orakel und Mysterien am Ausgang der Antike* (Albae Vigiliae 5; Zürich: Rhein-Verlag, 1947) 73.

[10] So also E. Lohse, who interprets the heresy as having no Jewish elements.

[11] Ramsay, *Teaching of Paul,* 299, note 1, and "The Mysteries," 206.

cal mystery rites and to the understanding of mystery initiation which we find in the context of magic. This chapter will also serve to describe some of the local religions from which adherents to "the philosophy" may have derived some of the beliefs and practices.

In describing mystery rites, it will be important for us to keep in mind that mystery initiation should properly be seen as "a special form of worship offered in the larger context of relgious practice."[12] In saying this, we distance ourselves from a past generation of scholarship (viz. the History-of-Religions School) who spoke of "mystery religions" as typifying a certain group of cults. It is important also to recognize the further advance made in recent scholarship in denying that there is a common pattern of belief—a mystery religion theology—of cults offering mystery initiation rites in Greco-Roman antiquity. There were a variety of different cults in this period that had their own unique histories, informing myths, rituals, symbols, and practices. There were often points of convergence as well as outright borrowing and assimilation, but each cult needs to be interpreted on its own.

1. Pagan Cults at Colossae

Our knowledge of the pagan cults at Colossae is somewhat limited by the paucity of references to Colossae in literature and by the fact that the site of the ancient city has never been excavated.[13] Numismatic evidence, however, has given us at least a partial picture of some of the deities worshipped in the city. Our knowledge of the local cults is also enhanced by a comparatively better understanding of the cults that were active in nearby Laodicea and Hierapolis.

The coins point to the presence of the worship of the following deities at Colossae: the Ephesian Artemis, the Laodicean Zeus, Artemis (the huntress), Asclepios and Hygieia, Leto, Demeter, Helios, Selene, Men,

---

[12] W. Burkert, *Ancient Mystery Cults* (Cambridge, Mass.: Harvard University Press, 1987) 10.

[13] On Colossae in general, see my entry, "Colossae," in *ABD* 1.1089. See also N. Merisch, "Kolossai," in *Phrygien und Pisidien* (eds. K. Belke & N. Merisch; Tabuli Imperii Byzantini 7, Österreichische Akademie der Wissenschaften, Philosophisch-Historische Klasse Denkschriften 211; Wien: Verlag der Österreichischen Akademie der Wissenschaften, 1990) 309-11.

Dionysus, Athena, Nike, Tyche, Zeus,[14] Boule, Isis, Sarapis, and the flood god of the Lycus.[15] Undoubtedly, many other deities were worshipped there, probably including the Magna Mater (Cybele) and Attis. We have no idea how many of these deities had temples in the city. Our knowledge of the religions of Colossae would be greatly assisted by the excavation of the site.[16] Most of the same deities were worshipped in nearby Laodicea and Hierapolis, and indeed, throughout Asia Minor.

Those who have argued that the teaching of the opponents reflects Jewish mysticism have discounted the need for an awareness of the local cults. If, on the basis of the term ἐμβατεύω and other indicators of the nature of the competing teaching, we see a connection with mystery rites as represented in the local religions, then an investigation into the nature of these religions becomes quite important. At the minimum it is necessitated by the likelihood that there were many Gentile converts in the Colossian church who, prior to conversion (or prior to their attachment to the synagogue), had been participants in these cults.

Lightfoot, in spite of the fact that he saw the teaching of the opponents as a form of Jewish Gnosticism, pointed to the local popular worship of the Phrygian Cybele, Sabazios, and the Ephesian Artemis as producing a climate favorable to the growth of the kind of teaching we see developed in "the philosophy."[17] Dibelius sought to explain the nature of the false teaching mainly on the basis of parallels to the Isis initiation in Apuleius, a description he used as evidence to generalize about the character of Hellenistic mysteries as a whole. His essay was extremely helpful (and influential) but limited by its failure to take into account more specific traits

---

[14] On the worship of Zeus throughout Phrygia, see T. Drew-Bear and C. Naour, "Divinités de Phrygie," *ANRW* II.18.3 (1990) 1907-2044.

[15] Based on the coins published by Hans von Aulock, *Münzen und Städte Phrygiens,* Part 2 (Istanbuler Mitteilungen, Beiheft 27; Tübingen: Ernst Wasmuth, 1987) 24-27, 83-93 (nos. 443-595). See also Barclay V. Head, ed., *Catalogue of the Greek Coins of Phrygia in the British Museum* (London: British Museum, 1906) 154-57; Also, F. Imhoof-Blumer, *Kleinasiatische Münzen* (Sonderschriften des Österreichischen Archäologischen Institutes in Wien; Wien: Alfred Hölder, 1902) 260-61. Most of the coins that can be dated with any certainty are from the second century A.D.

[16] One group has made repeated attempts to gain permission to begin excavation, but has consistently been turned down. See W. Harold Mare, "Archaeological Prospects at Colossae," *Near East Archaeological Society Bulletin* 7 (1976) 39-59. Prof. Daria de Barnardi Ferrero, director of the Italian mission currently excavating Hierapolis, informed me (by letter) that she is not aware of any group with plans to excavate the site. At the present time, it does not appear that the Turkish government is granting permission for the excavation of any new sites.

[17] J. B. Lightfoot, "The Colossian Heresy," in *Conflict,* 26.

about the local religions and especially in terms of its failure to consider the influence of Asia Minor Judaism. Johannes Lähnemann advanced the discussion significantly beyond Dibelius by emphasizing the importance of placing the Colossian heresy into its local religious context, especially into the sphere of the Cybele cult and the local Phrygian cult of the moon-God Men.[18] He also suggested that Hellenized Judaism had a significant part to play in the formation of the teaching of the opponents at Colossae. Ralph Martin has reiterated many aspects of the argument of Lähnemann, including the importance of recognizing the role of the local Phrygian religions as background to the controversy, especially the cults of Cybele and Men.[19]

In line with these interpreters, I am convinced that a knowledge of the beliefs and practices of these local cults is crucial to a proper understanding of the Colossian "philosophy." This is not to argue for a direct influence by saying, for instance, that the opponents were actually priests of the Cybele cult. Rather, I am emphasizing that Gentiles were coming into the church from a background of worship and devotion in these cults and may very well have brought some of their ideas and practices with them.

I would like to advance the discussion even further by four other streams of tradition that should be considered for sharpening our perspective on the Colossian "philosophy": (1) the cult of Apollo (surprisingly neglected by Dibelius and his followers), (2) the association of Artemis, Hekate, Selene, and Cybele as underworld goddesses with a close connection to magical practices, (3) "magical" mysteries, e.g. the so-called "Mithras Liturgy"; and finally, (4) the role of local "syncretistic" Judaism as a possible co-bearer of these ideas to the Christian congregation at Colossae.

2. Ἐμβατεύω As a Technical Term of the Local Mysteries

There are four inscriptions associated with the Apollo temple at Claros that use the term ἐμβατεύω. Three of these inscriptions were found at the actual site at Claros, and the fourth was discovered in Pergamum. The

---

[18] Lähnemann, *Kolosserbrief,* 85-87. He also sees an Iranian (Persian) root implicit in the cosmology of the opponents and a philosophical root similar to what is displayed in Dio Chrysostom.

[19] Martin, *Colossians* (NCB), 4-5.

first three were published by Theodore Macridy in 1905 and 1912; the fourth was published in 1922 by Charles Picard. As far as I am aware, no one has published a translation of these inscriptions. It would therefore be appropriate here to print the full text of each inscription and to provide a translation. By this means we shall have the full context of each occurrence of ἐμβατεύω for our comparison to the text of Colossians 2:18.

1. A Delegation from Amisus (Pontus) [20]

This inscription from the Apollo temple at Claros was first published in 1894. Its reference to the 63rd *prytanis* of Apollo enables us to date it to A.D. 132.[21]

> Ἀγαθῇ τύχῃ. Ἀμισοῦ ἐλευθέρας καὶ αὐτονόμου καὶ ὁμοσπόνδου Ῥωμαίοις. Ἐπὶ πρυτάνεως Ἀπόλλωνος τὸ ἕξ̄γ̄, ἱερατεύοντος Μ(άρκου) Ο(ὐ)λ(πίου) Ἀρτεμιδώρου, θεσπιωδοῦντο[ς] Ἀσκληπίδου τοῦ Δημοφίλο[υ] τῶν ἀπ' Ἄρδυος Ἡρακλειδῶν Πατρο[ξ]ενίδου, προφητεύοντος Ἑρμίου Ἀττάλου, γραμματέων Ἀττάλου β̄ καὶ Ἑρμογένους Δαδέου. Θεοπρόποι ἦλθο[ν] Κρίσπος Τρύφωνος καὶ Π(όπλιος) Πούπιος Καλλικλῆς, οἵτινες μυηθέντες ἐνεβάτευσαν. Ἔτους ρ̄ξ̄γ̄ τῆς ἐλευθερίας.

> Good Luck! [The embassy] from Amisus [that is] free and independent and bound by treaty to the Romans. During the 63rd *prytanis* of Apollo, in the priesthood of Marcus Ulpius Artemidorus and while Asclepiadus, son of Demophilus (he belonged to the Heraclidae [having descended] from Ardys Patrogenis) was the versifier of the oracles, while Hermius Attalus was the prophet [and] while Attalus II and Hermogenes Dadaeus were recorders. *Theopropoi* came [to inquire of the oracle], namely Crispus Tryphonus and Poplius Poupius Kallikes. These men were initiated and then *they entered*. The 163rd year of freedom.

This was the first ἐμβατεύω inscription from Claros to be published. Even in the initial publication, the term was interpreted as referring to mystery initiation. J. Chamonard and E. Legrand, who published the inscription, argued that ἐμβατεύω does not point merely to the mantic consultation, "but to a session for initiation."[22]

In 1898, B. Haussoullier disputed their interpretation of ἐμβατεύω and suggested that it meant that the embassy from Amisus had simply entered into the oracle grotto. In spite of the presence of the term μυηθέντες, he

---

[20] Macridy, "Altertümer," 170 [= § V.4] (1905); *OGIS* 530 (pp. 192-97); *IGRR* 4.1586 (p. 521).

[21] On dating the inscription, see B. Haussoullier, "L'Oracle d'Apollon a Claros," *Revue de Philologie* 22 (1898) 263-64; Macridy, "Altertümer," 171.

[22] J. Chamonard and E. Legrand, "Inscriptions de Notion," *BCH* 18 (1894) 221.

did not think that the evidence was sufficient to affirm the presence of mystery rites in the ceremonies leading up to the consultation of the oracle.[23]

Before writing his 1917 essay "The Isis Initiation in Apuleius," Martin Dibelius followed Haussoullier in regarding ἐμβατεύω as the entry into the oracle grotto simply for the purpose of consultation. He published this conclusion in the first edition of his Handbuch zum Neuen Testament commentary on Colossians. It was not until the other inscriptions from Claros were assembled and published by T. Macridy (see below) that Dibelius changed his position and argued that ἐμβατεύω was employed here as a technical expression for the second higher stage of initiation.

2. An Envoy from Lappa (Crete) [24]

The inscription was engraved on a column of the Apollo temple. As with all of the embassy inscriptions at the Apollo temple, this one dates to the second century A.D. The inscription provides a clear example of the use of ἐμβατεύω in connection with mystery rites.

Κρητῶ[ν Λ]αππα[ίω]ν. ἐπὶ πρυτάνε[ως Κλα]ρίου Ἀπόλλων[ος τὸ] ρ΄, θεσπι-
ωδοῦ[ν]τος Τιβ[ερίου] Κλ(αυδίου) Ἄρδυος τῶν ἀπὸ Ἄρδ[υος] Ἡρακλειδῶν
Πατρογενίδου, ἐπὶ ἱερέως Πο(πλίου) Αἰλ(ίου) [Φιλί]ππου θεοπρόπος
Ἀνδρικὸς Ἀλεξάνδρου παραλ[αβ]ὼν τὰ μυστήρι[α] ἐνεβάτευσεν. Ὑμνωδοί·
Φά(βιος) Ἀντιγένης, Ἐπίγονος β΄, Ἀλέξανδρος β΄, Σεραπίων Κλωδίου
Ζωσίμου, Ῥάντος Ἀσκληπιάδου, ὑμνοδιδάσκαλος κ(αὶ) κιθαριστὴς Μ(ᾶρκος)
Πεδουκαῖος Ἀλέξανδρος.

[This memorial was erected by the delegation] from [the city of] Lappa, Crete. During the 100th *prytanis* of the Clarian Apollo, while Tiberius Claudius Ardys was the versifier of the oracles (he belonged to the Heraclidae [having descended] from Ardys Patrogenis), during the priesthood of Poplius Aelius Phillipus. Andricos, son of Alexander, was the *theopropos*. *He received the mysteries and then he entered.* The choral singers were: Phabius Antigenes, Epigonus II, Alexander II, Serapion (son of Clodius Zosimus), and Rhantus (son of Asklepiades). The hymn teacher and *cithara* player was Marcus Pedoucaius Alexander.

---

23 Haussoullier, "L'Oracle," 268-70. See the critique of Haussoullier in Charles Picard, *Éphèse et Claros: Recherches sur les Sanctuaires et les Cultes de L'Ionie du Nord* (Bibliothèque des Écoles Françaises d'Athenes et de Rome 123; Paris: Anciennes Maisons Thorin et Fontemoing, 1922) 304.

24 Macridy, "Antiquités," 46 [= Série I.1] (1912).

3. An Embassy from Hadrianeia Neocaesareia (Pontus) [25]

The third inscription containing ἐμβατεύω is much like the first but with the addition of the technical term χράομαι for consulting the oracle.

Ἀδ[ριανῶ]ν [Νεο]καισαρέων τῆς μητροπό[λε]ως τοῦ Πόντου. Ἐ[π]ὶ πρυτάνεως καὶ προφήτου Κ[λ(αυδίου)] ['Ρο]ύφο(υ), ἱερατεύοντος Ο(ὐ)λ(πίου) Ἀρτεμιδώρου, θεσπιωδοῦντος Ἀσκληπίδο[υ,] γραμματέων Κλ(αυδίων) Κριτολάου καὶ Βάσσου β̄. Θεοπρόποι Ἀντώνιος Νεικήτης ἰατρὸς καὶ Φλαβουλήιος Βᾶσσο[ς] μυηθέντες καὶ ἐνβατεύσαντες ἐχρήσαντο ἄρχοντος Νεοκαισαρείας Ἀντωνίου Βλάνδου, τοῦ ξ̄θ̄ ἔ[τ]ο[υς] τῆς ἐπαρχείας.

[This memorial was erected by the embassy from] Hadrianeia Neocaesareia, the metropolis of Pontus. They came when Claudius Rufus was both *prytanis* and prophet during the priesthood of Ulpius Artemidorus, and while Asclepiades was the versifier of the oracles, and while Claudius Critolaos and Bassus II were recorders. The *theopropoi* were: Antonius Neiketes, the physician, and Flabulaeus Bassus. After *they were initiated and they entered*, they consulted the oracle about the ruler of Neocaesareia, Antonius Blandus, during the 69th year of his reign.

4. An Embassy from Laodicea [26]

This inscription was originally discovered in 1818 and published shortly thereafter.

['Επὶ - - - - · θεοπρόποι ἦλθον Κ]λα[ύ]δ̣ιος[- - - - - - - - - - Κ]λ[α]ύδιος[- - - - - - - - - - - - -] καὶ Κλαύδιος[- - - - - - - - - - - [οἵτινες μυ]ηθέντες καὶ ἐμβα[τεύσαντες ἐχρήσαντο καὶ ἀπέδωκαντ]ὸν ὑπογεγραμμένον [τοῦ Κλαρίου Ἀπόλλωνος ἀκέρ]αιον χρησμόν [ὅ]ν χρησμὸν ἔδοξεν τῆι βουλῆι καὶ τῶι δήμωι τῆς μητροπόλεως τῆς Ἀσίας καὶ δίς νεωκόρου πρώτης Περγαμηνων πόλεως, ἐν στήλαις ἀνα[γ]ραψάντας ἐπί τε τῆς ἀγορᾶς καὶ τῶν ἱερῶν ἀναστῆσαι.

[On (date?). *Theopropoi* came.. They included C]laudius - - - - - - - - - - - - - Claudius - - - - - - - - - - - - and Claudius. *They were initiated and then they entered.* Following this they consulted the oracle and received a pure response, copied [by the recorder], from the Clarian Apollo. The oracular response seemed good to the council and the people of the metropolis of Asia, twice Neocorate, the preeminent city of the Pergamenes. [This memorial was] written on steles and raised up in the agora and the temples.

---

[25] Macridy, "Altertümer," 165 [= § II.2] (1905).

[26] *CIG* II.3538; Charles Picard, "Un Oracle d'Apollon Clarios a Pergame," *BCH* 46 (1922) 190-97 (full bibliography on p. 190).

Although this inscription is in a particularly bad state of preservation, its similarity to inscription no. 3 (for lines 5 and 6) enables us to have a high level of confidence in the reconstruction.

Many other inscriptions associated with the Apollo temple were discovered at Claros. Macridy published a total of 47 (14 in 1905 and 33 in 1912). The vast majority of these record the visits of various delegations. In addition to the four ἐμβατεύω inscriptions, four others commemorate the initiation of the delegate(s) into the mysteries of the god with the usual technical language of mystery initiation. Rather than print the full text of these four inscriptions (which are of a similar form to the four given above), I will cite the crucial lines that refer to mystery initiation in each inscription. For convenience of comparison, I will also repeat the relevant lines from the four ἐμβατυεύω inscriptions given above:

(1) θεοπρόποι ... μυηθέντες ἐνεβάτευσαν.
(2) θεοπρόπος ... παραλ[αβ]ὼν τὰ μυστήρι[α] ἐνεβάτευσεν.
(3) θεοπρόποι ... μυηθέντες καὶ ἐνβατεύσαντες ἐχρήσαντο.
(4) [θεοπρόποι ... μυ]ηθέντες καὶ ἐμβα[τεύσαντες ἐχρήσαντο].
(5) θεοπρόπος ... [ἐπε]τέλεσε καὶ μυστήρια.[27]
(6) θεοπρόπος ... [ἐπε]τέλεσε καὶ μυστήρια.[28]
(7) θεοπρόπος ... [ἐπ]ετέλεσε καὶ μυστήρια.[29]
(8) θεοπρόπος ... οἵ καὶ ἐμυήθησαν τῷ θεῷ ... συνμυηθέντος καὶ αὐτοῦ.[30]

These inscriptions now demonstrate beyond doubt that mystery initiation rites were celebrated at the temple of Apollo at Claros. Unfortunately, our understanding of these rites is not helped by looking to inscriptions associated with the cult of Apollo at Didyma. Whereas the inscriptions mention the fact that mystery rites were performed, J. Fontenrose laments, "the fact is that we have no more than the terms 'mysteries' and *teletai;* we have no information at all on their meaning."[31]

The main question that remains is how to interpret the term ἐμβατεύω. Could it still possibly be understood simply in the sense of simply

---

[27] An envoy from Dionysopolis (Moesia Inferior). Macridy, "Antiquités," 50 (= no. 15).

[28] An envoy from Odessus (Moesia Inferior). Macridy, "Antiquités," 51 (= no. 16).

[29] An envoy from Stobi (Macedonia). Macridy, "Antiquités," 52 (= no. 20 [Picard, *Éphèse,* 303, erroneously notes this as no. 27]).

[30] Unpublished inscription (= inv. no. 94); found on a column south of the propylaeum. Lines 7-13 cited in Picard, *Éphèse,* 303-304.

[31] J. Fontenrose, *Didyma. Apollo's Oracle, Cult, and Companions* (Berkeley: University of California Press, 1988) 130.

"entering" the oracle grotto for consultation (as Haussoullier suggested). Or does it refer to entering the *adyton*, the innermost sanctuary of the temple, after performing the μύησις (and thereby the term acquires a technical significance for the second higher stage of initiation)?

After carefully studying these inscriptions, W. M. Ramsay, M. Dibelius, and C. Picard argued that ἐμβατεύω refers to the mystery initiation rite, specifically to the second stage of ritual initiation. They observed that the term μυηθῆναι (nos. 1, 3, 4) appears to be equivalent to the phrase παραλαμβάνειν τὰ μυστήρια (No. 2) because both of these expressions are used to characterize an action that is performed just prior to the action expressed by ἐνεβάτευσαν. For them, this opened the possibility that there was a two-stage act of initiation following the general pattern found at Eleusis expressed by the terms μύησις and ἐποπτεία (μυεῖν καὶ ἐποπτεύειν)[32] but in Asia Minor by the terms μύησις and ἐμβατεύσις (μυεῖν and ἐμβατεύειν).[33] The phrase ἐπιτελεῖν τὰ μυστήρια (nos. 5, 6, 7) could then best be explained as functioning as a summary expression to refer to the two-stage initiation as a whole (since none of the other three expressions are used when this phrase appears).[34]

Ramsay suggested there was a literal, ritual "entry" into an *adyton* included in the meaning of ἐμβατεύω, but he emphasized this "entry" as part of the second stage of the initiation.[35] He illustrated the two-stage ritual by drawing an analogy to the mystery celebration held in the sanctuary of Men at Kara Kuyu, outside Pisidian Antioch, which he had just excavated under the sponsorship of the Asia Minor Exploration Fund.[36] He explained that the μύστης performed the first stage of the rite on the west side of the initiation hall. The second stage took place on the east side of the sanctuary. For the latter part, the initiate would be brought to the center of the hall where he/she would then enter the most holy place (presumably the *adyton,* although Ramsay does not refer to it as such).

---

[32] See, for example, Plato, *Epistulae* 7 [333E]: μυεῖν καὶ ἐποπτεύειν. See LSJ, s.v. "ἐποπτεία."

[33] Ramsay coined the noun ἐμβατεύσις based on the verbal form. The noun form is not yet attested in Anatolian inscriptions.

[34] Dibelius, "Isis Initiation," 86-87; Ramsay, "Sketches," 44-51; Picard, *Éphèse,* 304-305.

[35] Ramsay, "The Mysteries," 201, notes, "The initiated person, at the conclusion of his initiation, 'makes entrance,' or 'sets foot on—.' In the ritual the action was performed in some apparent fashion, and this performance of the action was the prelude to another stage of the ritual."

[36] Ramsay, "Sketches," 37-56. This remains the only temple of Men that has been excavated.

Ramsay then explains, "When the *mystēs* 'set foot on' the entrance way, the act constituted the *embateuein;* and he emerged from the entrance way into the presence of the god on his throne. The mortal, fresh from the initiation, had thus entered on a new life, which he now was to live in the divine company."[37] As Ramsay reiterates in a different context, the use of the term ἐμβατεύω highlights the ultimate meaning of the rite to the initiate—union with the deity, "new life":

> The term ... evidently indicates the climax or final act in the mystic ceremonial; [after] "being initiated" or "receiving the mystic things and words" [indicated by μυηθέντες and παραλαβὼν τὰ μυστήρια], they performed the act called ἐμβατεύειν, symbolizing that they had entered on a new life, and intended to continue therein.[38]

Ramsay was followed in his explanation of ἐμβατεύω by Charles Picard, Directeur de l'École Française d'Athènes, in his massive work *Éphèse et Claros*. Surprisingly, Picard shows no knowledge of Dibelius's work on the same topic (Dibelius published in 1917, Picard in 1922). Picard also affirmed that a literal action—entry into the ἱερόν—symbolized a deeper, spiritual meaning for ἐμβατεύω. He therefore interpreted ἐμβατεύω as placing the foot on the divine threshold, viz. "an act which symbolised the new life of the initiate" ("acte qui symbolisait la vie nouvell de l'initié").[39]

Similarly, Dibelius contended that, "ἐμβατεύειν is to be connected with the 'entering' of the inner shrine (in the temple)."[40] Dibelius was careful, however, to distinguish this from the oracle grotto. I am not sure why it was important to him to maintain this distinction unless he wanted to avoid devaluing ἐμβατεύειν to simply "entering to consult the oracle" versus "entering the holy place" as the ritual part of the second stage of initiation.

---

[37] Ramsay, "The Mysteries," 202; idem, *Teaching of Paul*, 291-96. See also his "Religious Antiquities," 46-51, for a full discussion of the second stage of initiation.

[38] Ramsay, "Sketches," 48. He provides a popular presentation of the two-stage initiation rite that Pisidian Antioch and Claros had in common in an encyclopedia entry: "Phrygians," *Encyclopaedia of Religion and Ethics* (ed. J. Hastings; New York: Charles Scribner's Sons) 9.902-903.

[39] Picard, *Éphèse*, 308.

[40] Dibelius, "Isis Initiation," 87. On p. 114 (note 79) Dibelius notes: Ramsay (*Athenaeum* 1 [1913] 107) offers an explanation which I do not understand: "Perhaps, then, ἐμβατεύειν implies 'to put foot on the threshold,' i.e. enter of [sic] the new life of the initiated." Dibelius's confusion would have been clarified had he referred to Ramsay's article on "Sketches in the Religious Antiquities of Asia Minor," which I cited above. Ramsay, however, never indicates whether he would accept a literal "entering" into the ἱερόν as the ritual basis for the metaphorical understanding.

Louis Robert, the scholar who directed the systematic excavation of the Apollo Temple at Claros from 1950 to 1960, also sees the technical significance of ἐμβατεύω as stemming from a ritual act of "entering" into the holy place:

> The consultants had been "initiated" and they had performed the act which is called *embateuein,* that is to say, "to enter" ... It refers to entering into the *adyton* [the most holy room of the temple]. Certain consultants were the object of the performance of special ceremonies and secrets, of mysteries according to the usage of the time.[41]

H. W. Parke, in his recent monograph on the oracles of Apollo in Asia Minor, explains ἐμβατεύω as entering the holy place, but explains this as the same place where the oracles were given. He notes, "the 'entrance' was presumably the formal approach to the hall of consultation by means of the basement passages."[42] Drawing on the extensive archaeological work undertaken at Claros, Parke describes the labyrinth under the temple.[43] He says that a series of underground passages led to a subterranean chamber of inquiry, the *adyton.* It was here, on a "holy night," that the temple officials would lead individual inquirers or official embassies to consult the oracle. The prophet would then go to the farthest part of the *adyton* to seek inspiration from Apollo and return with his message from the god. Parke gives a vivid description of the process:

> The ceremony itself in its reformed style[44] must have been very impressive. Meeting in the temple in the dark and escorted by *mystagogoi* in batches down the steps and along the passages to the lamp-lit room, where they presented their enquiries and waited while the prophet went beyond them into the chamber containing the spring. His voice may have been heard indistinctly from within, and was taken up by the

---

[41] Louis Robert, "Les fouilles de Claros," in *Opera Minora Selecta* (Amsterdam: Adolf M. Hakkert, 1989) 6.548-49 (originally published in 1954).

[42] H. W. Parke, *The Oracles of Apollo in Asia Minor* (London: Croom Helm, 1985) 146. For a concise description of the structure, see E. Akurgal, *Ancient Civilizations and Ruins of Turkey* (Istanbul: Mobil Oil Türk, 1969) 136-39.

[43] Parke, *Apollo,* 219-24, provides a full reconstruction of how he believes the oracle of Apollo at Claros functioned.

[44] In trying to reconcile Tacitus's description of the procedure of the events at Claros (*Annals* 2.54) with the account by Iamblichus (*de Mysteriis* 3.11), Parke proposes that the Clarian oracle underwent something of a revival during the reign of Hadrian. See Parke, *Apollo,* 219-24. This is certainly not to deny the popularity of the oracle during the Hellenistic era. Parke speculates that it may have faced somewhat of a decline during the first century A.D., but our lack of information about the oracle during the first century may imply nothing more than the fact that we have an inadequate amount of source material.

thespiodos, who chanted the response in verse ... After the enquirers had emerged they must have been supplied with a copy of the *thespiodos's* poem, which had been taken down in shorthand by the secretaries.[45]

He contends that this whole procedure was described as a "mystery."[46] To be more precise, however, it is important to distinguish the delegations who came to consult the oracle from those who consulted the oracle *and* undertook the mystery initiation rites. The inscriptions make clear this distinction.

Parke's work brings us up to date on the impact of the excavation work on the Apollo temple for its bearing on the προσκυνήματα (embassy) inscriptions. Unfortunately, a precise explanation of the full meaning of ἐμβατεύω in the context of the mystery rites celebrated in the temple was not part of his purpose.[47] Therefore, he does not enter the debate on the possibility that ἐμβατεύω has here become a technical expression for the second stage of mystery initiation. The idea that it was the functional equivalent of ἐποπτεία is still a viable possibility given Parke's exposition of the entire process of consulting the oracle. The weaknesses of Parke's work for our purposes is his failure to correlate the distinctively "mystery" traits of the Apollo cult at Claros with other mystery religions (Phrygian, Eleusinian, and otherwise). This will become an important task for us in the following sections.

F. O. Francis, arguing against Dibelius, contended that, "'entering' at Claros had no particular technical meaning to distinguish it from other verbs of 'entering' in the contemporary oracle literature."[48] He sees the mystery initiation as something separate and preparatory to "entering" that only had reference to consulting the oracle. His analysis, however, draws too sharp a distinction between mystery initiation and consultation of the oracle.[49] Furthermore, it minimizes the importance and significance

---

[45] Parke, *Apollo,* 223.

[46] Parke, *Apollo,* 222.

[47] T. L. Robinson, "Oracles and Their Society: Social Realities as Reflected in the Oracles of Claros and Didyma," *Semeia* 56 (1992) 63, likewise affirms that mystery rites were sometimes carried out by the inquirers, but he does not attempt to interpret the ἐμβατεύω inscriptions. His study underlines the extent to which the Clarian oracle, in contrast to the Didymaean, sought to extend its influence to cities throughout Asia Minor and beyond. Three-quarters of the inscriptions found at the Apollo temple at Claros reveal that delegations from various Anatolian cities sought the services of Claros, especially during times of crisis, such as plagues and famines.

[48] Francis, "EMBATEUEIN," 202-203.

[49] Francis, "EMBATEUEIN," 201, 206 (note 17), points to the fact that there were a variety of verbs used in Plutarch and Pausanius for "entering" (esp. "descending" to a

of mystery initiation for those who performed this rite. There is no doubt that ἐμβατεύω had a broad range of usage, but to deny the technical significance that it appears to have had at Claros is to go too far. The weakness of this part of Francis's interpretation of the term may be partially belied by the fact that some interpreters, who otherwise follow Francis's overall reconstruction of the Colossian "philosophy," concede that ἐμβατεύω may have had the technical significance we have been describing.[50]

It is therefore with good reasons that the standard lexicons include the technical meaning as one of the accepted usages of the term.[51] While this technical use of ἐμβατεύω is not currently attested in other parts of Asia Minor, it is still quite possible that it was used to refer to the higher stage of initiation in other Phrygian mystery rites. Nevertheless, this technical usage would have been known in the Lycus valley since five of the Clarian

---

subterranean grotto) to consult an oracle. He uses this argument as further proof that ἐμβατεύω had no technical mystery significance at Claros. There are two difficulties with this observation: (1) the texts that he cites only have to do with consultation and nothing to do with mystery initiation; at Claros, both parts were important. (2) He assumes there was no descent at Claros into an underground chamber; therefore, he contends that ἐμβατεύειν is especially appropriate because it conveys the notion of entry without descent. The archaeological work at Claros, as we have noted above in our discussion of H. W. Parke, demonstrates that the chamber for consultation was indeed subterranean.

[50] W. Carr, *Angels and Principalities* (SNTSMS 42; Cambridge: University Press, 1981) 68-69; idem, "Two Notes on Colossians," 498, where he says, "The inscriptions ... represent a specific, technical sense of the word ἐμβατεύειν." See also, Lincoln, *Paradise,* 112-13. H. Preisker, "ἐμβατεύω," *TDNT* 2.535, also contends that the inscriptions demonstrate that ἐμβατεύω was used in a technical sense for mystery initiation, although he thinks the meaning "investigate" is more appropriate to the context of Colossians.

[51] Thus, LSJ, s.v. "'to be initated' into the mysteries"; Bauer[6], s.v., "Drei kleinas. Inschr. [II n], die sich auf den Apollon von Klaros beziehen, erweisen ἐμβατεύω als t.t. der Mysteriensprache. Dann etwa *der* (das Heiligtum) *betritt, welches er* (in der Ekstase) *geschaut hat.*" BAGD, s.v., "Three inscr. of Asia Minor [II AD], which refer to the Apollo of Klaros ... show that ἐ[μβατεύω] was a t. t. of the mystery religions." MM, s.v., "More significant however than any of the above citations for the meaning of the verb in its only occurrence in the NT (Col 2:18) is its use in the mystery religions to denote the climax of initiation, when the mystes 'sets foot on' the entrance to the new life which he is now to share with the God." J. P. Louw and E. A. Nida, *Greek-English Lexicon of the New Testament Based on Semantic Domains* (2d ed.; New York: United Bible Societies, 1989) 533, classify the term under the domain of "Religious Activities" and the subdomain of "Religious Practice." They conclude that, "ἐμβατεύω in Col 2.18 is a technical term derived from the mystery religions" and then suggest the translation, "by what he saw when he was initiated."

inscriptions record the coming of embassies from Laodicea ad Lycum (only eleven miles distant from Colossae).[52]

Ramsay finds the concept of "entering" new life expressed in a common coin type, characteristic almost exclusively of Asia Minor, including Laodicea ad Lycum. Although the term ἐμβατεύω is not engraved on the coins, they depict the concept of "'entering' new life" by portraying a hero stepping onto a ship looking back as if he were calling others to follow. The hero, representing the leader of a foreign emigration, encourages his countrymen to join him in embarking on a new life in a different land.[53] Ramsay concludes,

> The idea common to all these coins is the new city life, symbolized by the hero founder stepping on to the land of the colony, or on to the ship that is to bear him to that land across the sea. The entrance on a new life, the settlement in a new home—that is ἐμβατεῦσαι ... This thought of stepping into a new life, therefore, was familiar in Asia Minor, and it would be in accord with the philosophic thought which underlay the Mysteries that a similar idea should find some symbolic expression in them.[54]

Ramsay's suggestion is plausible. The weaknesses of his view are, however, (1) that there is no explicit evidence linking the motif of life in the new world as illustrated by the coins with the idea of new life as found in the mysteries, and (2) it may be overly dependent on the erroneous emphasis of the History-of-Religions School on the concept of rising from death with the deity as the basis for new life. In support of Ramsay, one must recognize that the concept of gaining deliverance and salvation was central to mystery initiation in general. Insofar as the appeasement of the gods and hostile spirits sets one on a new course, yes, the person will experience a new life along with the other initiates. At the minimum it is surprising that this aspect of Ramsay's treatment of ἐμβατεύω in the context of the mysteries has dropped out of contemporary discussion.

---

[52] See Macridy, "Altertümer," 164 (§ II.1), 166-67 (§§ III.1, 2), 168-69 (§ V.3); Macridy, "Antiquités," 49 (no. 12).

[53] See, for example, Imhoof-Blumer, *Kleinasiatische Münzen*, 290 (photograph in Tafel XI, 15). This particular coin comes from Stectorium, Phrygia (50 miles NE of Colossae, near Eumeneia) depicting the hero Mygdon (see Homer, *Iliad* 3.184ff.) stepping onto a ship with his right foot while looking behind him. He is wearing a helmet and armor. In his right hand he holds a torch high into the air and in his left hand he carries a shield and spear. According to Homer, Mygdon called his fellows to join him so they could travel to Phrygia and gain dominion over the land. Imhoof-Blumer notes that this is a coin type common to other cities in Phrygia.

[54] Ramsay, "Sketches," 47-48.

It would be a mistake to minimize the Apollo initiation as a rather unimportant ritual prerequisite to getting to what was really important—consulting the oracle. Mystery rites typically involved intense religious feeling and aimed at some form of salvation through a closeness to the divine.[55]

Thus, if the advocates of "the philosophy" had experienced one or more forms of mystery initiation in the local cults, they had undergone a powerful experience that was life-changing. We cannot underestimate the difficulty they would have faced in reinterpreting their past experience after becoming Christians. Certainly it would have been tempting, and natural, for them to assimilate their past experience and knowledge with the Christianity they had now received.

3. The Determinative Influence of the Inscriptions on Interpreting Col 2:18

If one can accept the technical significance of ἐμβατεύω in the Clarian inscriptions, it still remains to show that this is the most appropriate meaning for the use of the term in Col 2:18. The term, although rare, has a wide range of well-attested meanings: (1) to enter; to step on/into; to visit; to frequent or haunt; to enter into discussion about something; (2) to come into possession of something; to enter into an inheritance; (3) to enter into study; to research; to investigate; (4) to undergo the second, higher stage of a mystery initiation rite. Each of these attested meanings has had one or more interpreters who have argued its relevance for interpreting Col 2:18. It is not our purpose here to review all of the proposed interpretations, but rather to demonstrate that the fourth meaning best fits the Colossian context syntactically and in terms of its appropriateness to explaining the Colossian "philosophy."

It can initially be said in favor of our view that the Claros inscriptions illustrate both a local and a religious use of the term. We can be certain that people living in the Lycus Valley would have been familiar with this usage because of the contact between Laodicea and the Clarian Apollo temple. The inscriptions are also sufficiently close chronologically to the composition of Colossians. Although they postdate the writing of the letter

---

[55] Burkert, *Ancient Mystery Cults*, 12-13; see also his Chapter 4: "The Extraordinary Experience" (pp. 89-114).

(the earliest inscription was probably engraved in A.D. 132), it is very likely that the same terminology was being used 70 years earlier for the two-stage initiation rite. Further inscriptional evidence from Phrygian mystery rites might very well demonstrate that this language was a local way of referring to initiation in other cults, as Ramsay suggests in his observation about the coins (see above).

Perhaps the greatest challenge is in demonstrating the syntactical appropriateness of our interpretation of ἐμβατεύω to the context of Col 2:16-18. Since the author of Colossians has given such brief snippets of information about the false teaching, this is an enormous challenge for anyone who approaches this section of the letter. The basic structure of the passage can be graphically depicted as follows:

> Μὴ οὖν τις ὑμᾶς κρινέτω
>   ἐν βρώσει καὶ ἐν πόσει ἢ ἐν μέρει ἑορτῆς ἢ νεομηνίας ἢ σαββάτων·
>   <u>ἅ</u> ἐστιν σκιὰ τῶν μελλόντων,
>   τὸ δὲ σῶμα τοῦ Χριστοῦ.
>
> μηδεὶς ὑμᾶς καταβραβευέτω
>   θέλων ἐν
>   ταπεινοφροσύνῃ καὶ
>   θρησκείᾳ τῶν ἀγγέλων,
>   <u>ἅ</u> ἑόρακεν <u>ἐμβατεύων</u>,
>   εἰκῇ <u>φυσιούμενος</u> ὑπὸ τοῦ νοὸς τῆς σαρκὸς αὐτοῦ,
>   καὶ <u>οὐ κρατῶν</u> τὴν κεφαλήν,

The overall structure of this passage is clear. Both of the main clauses serve warning against the danger of the teaching of the opponents who are arrogantly foisting their variant beliefs and practices onto the Colossian Christians. The one major issue that surfaces is the question of the precise syntactical relationship between the relative clause ἅ ἑόρακεν and its immediately preceding and following contexts, viz. (1) Does the phrase serve as the direct object of the participle ἐμβατεύων, or (2) does it refer back to "humility" and "worship of angels" as the object of vision during a time of "entering" or "being initiated."

The latter view has a strong syntactical reason to commend itself to us. Most notably, some intepreters have observed that the two clauses have a parallel structure, viz. they both use the neuter relative pronoun ἅ (underlined above) to sum up a list, the first with five members and the second with two. We find a similar use of ἅ (with reference to the preceding Μὴ ἅψῃ μηδὲ γεύσῃ μηδὲ θίγῃς) in Col 2:22 and δι' ἅ (with reference to the preceding list of five vices) in Col 3:6. In his 1917 essay,

Dibelius held the first view, but later changed his opinion in favor of the second view because of "the formal parallelism to 2:16."[56] Dibelius then translated the clause, "Let no one purposefully condemn you, relying on 'humility' and angel veneration, as he has seen them in his initiation."[57] This interpretation of the relative clause has also been the preferred explanation by those who see the opponents as Jewish visionaries. They explain that the heavenly realm is the unexpressed but implied object of entering. The visionary sees angels worshiping before the heavenly throne.[58]

There are stronger reasons, however, for taking ἃ ἑόρακεν as the object of ἐμβατεύων, which I will enumerate. (1) If the entire phrase, ἃ ἑόρακεν ἐμβατεύων, is a quotation from the teaching of the opponents, the relative pronoun may not conform to the syntactical patterns of the rest of the book. In other words, the relative pronoun would need to be interpreted as a distinct syntactical unit with ἐμβατεύων. (2) Col 2:17, 22 and 3:6, which use the neuter plural of the relative pronoun to sum up a list, are not exactly parallel to Col 2:18. In all three passages the pronoun is used to refer back to the list so that a judgment can be made about the elements in the list: ἅ ἐστιν σκιὰ τῶν μελλόντων ("which are a shadow of things to come"); ἅ ἐστιν πάντα εἰς φθορὰν τῇ ἀποχρήσει ("these are all destined to perish with use"; 2:22); δι᾽ ἃ ἔρχεται ἡ ὀργὴ τοῦ θεοῦ ("because of these, the wrath of God is coming"; 3:6). Furthermore, in 2:18 there is no parallel use of the copulative ἐστιν following ἅ to introduce judgment. No judgment is made in 2:18; rather, the author uses the relative pronoun as the direct object of the participle ἐμβατεύων. (3) It is therefore likely that ἅ refers to objects of visionary experience that are not explicit in the context (although visions of angels would certainly be a part of the experience). In the letters attributed to Paul, there are plenty of examples of the neuter plural of the relative pronoun used to refer to something not explicitly stated in the context. See, for example, 1 Cor 10:20 (ἃ θύουσιν); 1 Cor 4:6 (ἃ γέγραπται); 2 Cor 5:10 (ἃ ἔπραξεν).[59] (4) The alternative interpretation is stretched beyond credibility when it makes "humility" an object of heavenly vision. Whereas it makes sense to contend that angels are the objects of vision, it is not intelligible to hold

---

[56] Compare Dibelius, "Isis Initiation," 87-88, to Dibelius-Greeven, *Kolosser,* 35-36 (this is the third edition of the commentary).

[57] Dibelius-Greeven, *Kolosser,* 34.

[58] See most recently, Sappington, *Revelation,* 157-58. This has also been the explanation of Francis, "Humility," 130; Lincoln, *Paradise,* 112; Evans, "Mystics," 197-98; Rowland, "Apocalyptic Visions," 74-76.

[59] See also 1 Cor 2:9 (an OT quotation), 4:6; Phil 4:9; et al.

that the abstract idea of "humility" is also an object of the visionary experience. Francis tries to escape this difficulty by arguing that ταπεινοφρο-σύνη should be understood as "instruction in humility for the purpose of obtaining visions," i.e. angelic instruction is the object of the vision.[60] Such an explanation grossly over-interprets ταπεινοφροσύνη. Further, this explanation is inconsistent with the emphasis throughout his article on participation in the angelic liturgy as the object of vision. This particular difficulty has been softened, however, by the contention of C. Rowland and T. Sappington that the visionaries saw angels performing worship and exhibiting humility.[61]

The best explanation, however, is to interpret the relative pronoun with demonstrative force and to take it as the object of entering, viz. "entering the things he had seen." The *adyton* would still be the primary object of entry, but the language also takes into account the whole visionary experience of the mystery initiate as he/she entered the most holy chamber of the temple. The priest would have led the adept through ecstatic visionary experiences—perhaps including descent to the underworld and ascent to heaven—ultimately culminating in a vision of the god/goddess. The neuter relative pronoun sums up the totality of the visionary experience as part of the second stage of mystery initiation.

The participle ἐμβατεύων is thus parallel with θέλων and dependent on the verb καταβραβευέτω. The first participle should then be interpreted as modal ("by insisting on ...") and the second as causal. I would suggest the following translation and paraphrase of 2:18:

> Let no one condemn you
>> by insisting on
>>> ascetic practices and
>>> invoking angels
>> because he "entered the things he had seen"
>> [i.e. he based his knowledge/authority on visionary experiences he received during the final stage of his mystery initiation].

The meaning of the verse could also be simply put, "Let no one condemn you ... because he has been initiated [and you have not]." It appears that the experience of initiation, with the incredible visions that went along

---

[60] Fred O Francis, "Humility and Angelic Worship in Col 2:18," in *Conflict,* 180. Evans, "Mystics," 195-98, and Lincoln, *Paradise,* 111-12, do not appear to have sensed this difficulty as they both contend that "humility" refers to cultic practice.

[61] Rowland, "Apocalyptic Visions," 75; Sappington, *Revelation,* 160.

with it, served as the basis for the arrogant belittling of the Colossian congregation by the opposing faction.

Visionary experience held an important place in mystery initiation.[62] Receiving a vision from a deity was one of the reasons for seeking initiation. Pausanias reports that the underworld gods (θεοὶ καταχθόνιοι) near the Maeander river in western Asia Minor would send visions (ἀποστέλλουσιν αὐτοῖς ὀνειράτων ὄψεις) to all whom they wished to enter their *adyta* (Paus. 32.13). The initiation itself was full of visionay experience. H. D. Betz observes that the word "I saw" (ὁράω) occurs frequently in underworld myths.[63] This is further illustrated by the fact that vision held an important place in magic as evidenced by the numerous occurrences of ὁράω in the magical papyri. The papyri contain many recipes for conjuring a "god" with the goal of having an appearance and eliciting the spirit power to fulfill a request or provide protection from other evil spiritual beings.[64]

The process of initiation and vision is well summarized by two texts contained in Preisendanz's collection of magical papyri which may contain pieces of authentic liturgies from mystery cults. The first text, *PGM* LXX.4-25 (= *P.Mich.* III, 154), is regarded by H. D. Betz as containing liturgical remnants from the mystery cult of the Idaean Dactyls.[65] The text follows the pattern that we have described above: a two-stage initiation with a visionary experience as part of the second stage. The relevant section reads as follows:

τετέ[λ]εσμαι καὶ εἰς μέγαρον κατέ[βη]ν Δακτύλων καὶ [τ]ὰ ἄλλα εἶδον κάτω,
παρθένος, κύων, καὶ τὰ λοιπὰ πά[ν]τα.

I have been initiated, and I went down into the [underground] chamber of the Dactyls, and I saw the other things down below, virgin, bitch, and all the rest.

It is clear that the vision (εἶδον) is part of the experience of being in the underground chamber. Two objects of the vision are explicitly named, "the virgin," perhaps an epithet of the goddess, and "the dog," a reference

---

63 H. D. Betz, "Fragments from a Catabasis Ritual in a Greek Magical Papyrus," *HistRel* 19 (1980) 293. He cites evidence from Plato's myth of Er, *Rep.* 10.614bff.; Lucian, *Necyom.* 2.10, and *Philops.* 22.
64 See, for example, *PGM* IV. 2479 ff.; VII. 335ff.; XII. 145ff.; 154ff.
65 Betz, "Catabasis Ritual," 287, 294-95. The papyrus dates to the third or fourth century; cf. Preisendanz, *PGM,* 2.202.

either to Hekate or to a chthonic demon.[66] An injunction of secrecy may have prevented the person from speaking of everything he saw, apart from the use of these codewords. The vision is described in the ambiguous neuter construction, τὰ ἄλλα. It is not surprising, then, to find the author of Colossians quoting ἃ ἑόρακεν ἐμβατεύων as a formula from a local mystery that summarizes the visionary experience of the one initiated.

A comparison of the pattern of the stages in mystery initiation (ἐπιτελεῖν τὰ μυστήρια) may appear as follows:

Eleusis:	(1) μύεσθαι	(2) ἐποπτύειν — with visionary experience
Claros:	(1) μύεσθαι	(2) ἐμβατεύειν — with visionary experience
Idaean Dactyls:	(1) τέλεσθαι	(2) καταβαίνεσθαι — εἴδειν

The Idaean Dactyls text is also significant for our inquiry because it may have originated in Asia Minor.[67] This is likely insofar as the text represents a liturgical fragment from the mysteries of the Idaean Dactyls.[68] According to Strabo (*Geog.* 10.3.22), the name originally applied to the settlers of the lower slopes (*dactyli* [Latin] = "fingers" or "toes") of mount Ida in Phrygia (near Troas). He claims that Sophocles (in a work now lost) stated that there were originally five male Dactyls who were the first to discover and work with iron. Strabo further remarks that all ancient writers "have assumed that they were wizards (γόητας) and attendants of the Mother of the gods [Cybele], and that they lived in Phrygia about Ida." Here they are represented as divine beings in their own right with a cultic mystery initiation for their adherents. This connection with Asia Minor is further enhanced through the appearance of two of the six *Ephesia Grammata*, ἄσκει κατάσκει, in a magical formula in line eleven.[69] In ad-

---

[66] Hekate had a close connection with the image of the dog. The Chaldean Oracles also refer to chthonic demons as "dogs" (frs. 90, 91, 135, 156), but assume Hekate as their mistress. See Sarah I. Johnston, *Hekate Soteira. A Study of Hekate's Roles in the Chaldean Oracles and Related Literature* (American Classical Studies 21; Atlanta: Scholar's Press, 1990) 87, 134-42.

[67] See my previous discussion of this text in *Ephesians: Power and Magic* (SNTSMS 63; Cambridge: University Press, 1989) 57-58.

[68] On the Idaean Dactyls, see Bengt Hemberg, "Die Idaiischen Daktylen," *Eranos. Acta philologica suecana a Vilelmo Lundström condita* 50 (1952) 41-59.

[69] See my discussion of the *Ephesia Grammata* in, *Ephesians*, 15-16. See also R. Kotansky, "Incantations and Prayers for Salvation on Inscribed Greek Amulets," in *Magika*

dition, the goddess of the underworld, Hekate-Ereschigal (line 4), was widely worshipped in Asia Minor.

Visionary experience as part of mystery initiation may also be illustrated by the so-called Mithras Liturgy (*PGM* IV.475-829; see below for a full discussion of this text). The term ὁράω appears repeatedly throughout this text to introduce what the initiate sees in the mystery rites. At the high point of the initiation rite ("the immortal birth"; l. 501; the "rebirth" [μεταγεννάω], l. 509), the initiate experiences a visionary ascent to heaven:

> You will see (ὄψη) yourself being lifted up and ascending to the height, so that you seem to be in midair ... you will see (ὄψη) all immortal things. For in that day and hour you will see (ὄψη) the divine order of the skies: the presiding gods rising into heaven, and others setting. Now the course of the visible gods (ὁρωμένων θεῶν) will appear through the disk of god ... And you will see (ὄψη) the gods staring intently at you and rushing at you ... Then you will see (ὄψη) the gods looking graciously upon you and no longer rushing at you, but rather going about in their own order of affairs. So when you see (ἴδης) that the world above is clear and circling, and that none of the gods or angels is threatening you, expect to hear a great crash of thunder, so as to shock you ... and [after you have said the second prayer] you will see (ὄψη) many five-pronged stars coming froth from the disk and filling all the air. Then say again: 'Silence! Silence!' And when the disk is open, you will see (ὄψη) the fireless circle, and the fiery doors shut tight (*PGM* IV.539-85)

One can readily observe the importance of vision in this brief text. Here entry into the *adyton* is never mentioned, but is probably assumed as the climax of the ritual. The stress is on the spiritual significance of the entry—the μύστης ascends to heaven and gains an incredible visionary experience. A large part of this vision is seeing the hostile gods, angels, planets, and stars. However, because of the adept's ἀπαθανατισμός and knowledge of a magical formula, these beings change from a posture of hostility to favor. The initiation provides protection from these malignant forces.

When the adept is ultimately given a revelation of Helios-Mithras, he/she decides to worship (προσκυνῆσαι) him. In this text, Helios is not regarded as the supreme god, but as an intermediary or messenger of the supreme god who remains unnamed. The adept then asks Helios to take with him the horoscope of that day and hour, for a revelation of the supreme god, and for protection (φύλαξόν με) from the seven fates of

Hiera: Ancient Greek Magic and Religion (eds. C. A. Faraone & D. Obbink; New York/Oxford: Oxford University Press, 1991) 110-12, 126-27.

heaven (αἱ ζ' Τύχαι τοῦ οὐρανοῦ), who are subsequently revealed (*PGM* IV.639-65).

In this portion of the Mithras Liturgy, we have observed four motifs that appear to be prominent in the Colossian "philosophy": (1) fear of supernatural hostile powers, viz. the stars and heavenly bodies; (2) worship of an intermediary; (3) a prayer to the intermediary for protection from the hostile powers; (4) initiation into a mystery rite for "new life"—but especially a new life which provides protection from the fates and hostile planetary powers; and, (5) vision as part of the experience of the climax of mystery initiation.

As W. Burkert has noted, "one of the main characteristics of mysteries is the *makarismos*, the praise of the blessed status of those who have 'seen' the mysteries."[70] This blessed status involves the appeasement of hostile forces leading to the possibility of a safer and happier existence in this world.

4. The Clarian Apollo and the Teaching of "the Philosophy"

Surprisingly in past intepretation, those who have argued that ἐμβατεύω is a technical term from the mysteries on the basis of the Claros inscriptions have not looked to the Apollo oracle/cult for additional information about the Colossian "philosophy." This is understandable, in part, because of the paucity of information we have about the nature and significance of this local mystery initiation. Likewise, these interpreters have probably correctly worked from the assumption that ἐμβατεύω reflects the language of Phrygian mysteries in general. More information, however, is now available which may illuminate a few aspects of the Apollo cult which bear a similarity to the teaching of the opponents at Colossae.

Of course, we have already seen that it is the four inscriptions from the Apollo temple at Claros that inform us of the technical use of ἐμβατεύω for the climax of mystery initiation. These inscriptions say little, however, about the meaning of this initiation to the μύσται.

The god Apollo was often seen as a "messenger" (ἄγγελος) of Zeus rather than as the supreme deity. The church father Lactantius preseves an oracle from Apollo at Claros in which Apollo characterizes himself as a

---

[70] Burkert, *Ancient Mystery Cults*, 93.

"messenger" of god: μικρὰ δὲ θεοῦ μερὶς ἄγγελοι ἡμεῖς ("and we, his messengers, are a slight portion of god"; Lactantius, *Div. Inst.* 1.7). M. P. Nilsson says that the authenticity of this oracle is generally acknowledged.[71]

There is direct evidence linking the Apollo at Claros with magical practices.[72] One line of evidence recorded by Tacitus, dated to A.D. 49, involves an accusation brought against Lollia Paulina who tried unsuccessfully to attract the emperor Claudius into marrying her. She was charged with consulting astrologers, magicians, and an image of the Clarian Apollo (Tacitus, *Annals,* 12.22).[73] The Apollo of Claros is also specifically invoked in a magical text (*PGM* II.139).[74] There is ample evidence in the magical papyri linking Apollo with the invocation of angels, viz. Apollo is invoked along with other "angels" or "divine messengers" (*PGM* I. 296-327; discussed in Chapter 1). Finally, Philostratus points to a tradition that the magician Apollonius of Tyana shared the same kind of mantic wisdom with the Apollo oracle at Claros.[75] This is not to say that the cult of Apollo was "magical," but that there was a magical substructure to the cult (whether official or unofficial). In popular belief and practice, the cult may have been approached in a distinctively magical sense. Furthermore, as in other cults, the mysteries of Apollo had a reciprocal relationship with the practices and beliefs of magic—magicians were commonly said to have established mysteries and certainly drew material from them.[76]

---

[71] Nilsson, *GGR,* 2.478.

[72] See S. Eitrem, "Apollon in der Magie," in *Orakel und Mysterien am Ausgang der Antike* (Albae Vigiliae 5; Zürich: Rhein-Verlag, 1947) 47-52.

[73] Parke, *Oracles,* 145, comments, "[the passage] implies that Lollia possessed an image dedicated to the Clarian Apollo—probably a miniature copy of his cult statue — and by the use of magicians was alleged to have tried to extract from it a divination about Claudius."

[74] The context also includes one of the *Ephesia Grammata* (δαμναμενευς; line 164), magical terms associated with the Ephesian Artemis. Karl Wessely recognized the connection of the Clarian Apollo with magic long ago when he noticed that the phrase δάφνη μαντοσύνης ἱερὸν φυτὸν Ἀπόλλωνος ("the divining laurel is a sacred plant of Apollo") occurs in magical texts (e.g. *PGM* II. 81), see Richard Wünsch, *Antikes Zaubergerät aus Pergamon* (Jahrbuch des Kaiserlich Deutschen Archäologischen Instituts, Ergänzungsheft 6; Berlin: Georg Reimer, 1905) 45.

[75] Philostratus, *Vita Apoll.* 4.1: "Thus from the oracle at Colophon it was announced that he [Apollonius] shared its peculiar wisdom (σοφίας) and was absolutely wise (ἀτεχνῶς σοφόν)."

[76] See M. Smith, *Clement of Alexandria and a Secret Gospel of Mark* (Cambridge, Mass.: Harvard University Press, 1973) 220.

There is one small strand of evidence showing some connection between Judaism and the Clarian oracle. Macrobius (*Sat.* 1.18, 19-21) reports that the oracle once issued a reply concerning the god Ἰάω
(probably here to be understood as Yahweh). This is taken as a possible
indication of Jewish influence in Colophon in the new edition of
Schürer.[77] At this time, however, we have no explicit evidence about influence working the other way, viz. the influence of the Clarian Apollo on
local Judaism.

There is an interesting inscription discovered in the Apollo temple at
Hierapolis that demonstrates the significant influence of the Clarian
Apollo in the Lycus valley.[78] The inscription (second century A.D.[79])
gives the response of the Clarian Apollo to an embassy from Hierapolis
who came to seek a remedy for the difficulties they were facing. The inscription is probably to be associated with the epidemic that struck portions of the empire after the Parthian campaign of Lucius Verus in A.D.
162-166.[80] The disease had apparently been brought by the returning soldiers.[81] At the same time, western Asia Minor was facing a famine due to
crop failure.[82] In addition to Hierapolis, Caesarea Troceta, Pergamum,
and Callipolis also consulted the Clarian Apollo about the plague. It is
rather astonishing that Hierapolis appealed to Apollo at Claros for help
rather than seeking an oracular response from their own local Apollo
(known as Apollo Kareios) especially in light of the famous Plutonium at
the city. Parke suggests that this may have happened because the Clarian
Apollo had acquired a special reputation for averting plagues.[83]

Significant for our purposes is the fact that the epidemic and famine
are not only attributed to the wrath of the Earth Goddess, but to evil powers—heavenly and earthly—who need to be appeased. Because of the im-

---

[77] *HJP²*, 22. See also G. Kittel, "Das kleinasiatische Judentum in der hellenistisch-
römischen Zeit," *TLZ* 1/2 (1944) 16.

[78] G. Pugliese Carratelli, "ΧΡΗΣΜΟΙ Di Apollo Kareios e Apollo Klarios a Hierapolis
in Frigia," *Annuario della Scuola Archaeologica di Atene e delle Missioni Italiane in Oriente* 61-62 (1963-64) 351-70. For an English translation and additional discussion of the
text, see Parke, *Oracles,* 153-55.

[79] This is probably to be associated with the pestilence that gripped the area in A.D.
166, during the reign of Marcus Aurelius; cf. Carratelli, "ΧΡΗΣΜΟΙ," 362.

[80] Robinson, "Oracles and Their Society," 71.

[81] D. Magie, *Roman Rule in Asia Minor* (Princeton: University Press, 1950) 1.663.

[82] Magie, *Roman Rule,* 1.663.

[83] Parke, *Oracles,* 155.

portance of this inscription for illuminating popular belief near Colossae, I will provide the full translation of the text:[84]

> [The first lines of the inscription are lost] But you are not alone in being injured by the destructive miseries of a deadly plague, but many are the cities and peoples which are grieved at the wrathful displeasures of the gods. The painful anger of the deities I bid you avoid by libations and feasts (εἰλαπίναις) and fully accomplished sacrifices.
>
> Firstly then to Earth the mother of all bring a cow from the herd into her hall of four measures, and sacrifice it with sweet-smelling incense and then ravage it with fire, and when the flame has consumed it all, then sprinkle around with libations and a mixture of honey and soil all together.
>
> Secondly sacrifice an unfeasted offering to the Aither and to the gods of the heavens (ἐπουρανίοις θεοῖς), all sweet-smelling with incense.
>
> To Demeter, as your custom is, and to the gods of the underworld (ἐνερτερίοις θεοῖσιν), perform rites (ἱερὰ ποιήσασθε) with victims free from pollution, and to the heroes in the ground pour drink-offerings in accordance with the precepts, and continually be mindful of Apollo Kareios (Καρείου Ἀπόλλωνος). For you are descended from me in family and from Mopsus, the city's patron.
>
> Also around all your city gates consecrate precincts for a holy statue of the Clarian Phoebus (Κλαρίου Φοίβου) equipped with his bow, which destroys diseases, as though shooting with his arrow from afar at the unfertile plague.
>
> Moreover when after you have wrought appeasement and the evil powers (Κῆρες) have departed, I instruct your boys with maidenly musicians to come together to Colophon accompanied by libations and hecatombs in willing spirit. For indeed often I have saved you, but I have not received a share of fat to gladden my heart. Yet it is right not even to be forgetful of men who have done you benefit. If you perform what it is seemly for godfearing men to accomplish, never will you be in painful confusions, but with more wealth and better safety … [the remainder of the text is missing]

As one can observe from this text, the appeasement of the gods takes place through performing a series of sacrifices and libations, providing offerings, holding feasts, and also by erecting a statue of Apollo wielding his bow as the averter of evil.[85] The gods in heaven, on earth, and under the earth are represented as pouring out their wrath on the people of Hierapolis. Once they are appeased, and Apollo thwarts the plague, the people of Hierapolis are instucted to send an embassy to Colophon (Claros) to provide a thank-offering to Apollo.

We do not know if the delegation from Hierapolis went through the two-stage ritual initiation ceremony at Claros. Their situation would have provided a powerful incentive for them to seek this. Walter Burkert has

---

[84] Translation by Parke, *Oracles,* 153-54.

[85] The cities of Trocetta and Callipolis were also instructed to set up this statue.

suggested that the central idea of mystery initiation had to do with appeasing the active powers of destruction that are a threat to daily life in the present.[86] These powers, whether they are gods or the disembodied spirits of ancestors, would be made to feel cheerful and happy as they joined in the celebration. Perhaps this perspective may help us to discern why some delegations consulting the Clarian oracle experienced mystery initiation and some did not.

The inscription provides vivid evidence of local belief in the reality of evil powers (or, gods) who can bring destruction and harm. The people turned to another god to deliver them from the suffering that was devastating them.[87] The Clarian Apollo is commemorated as having had the answer for averting the destruction wrought by these powers. Even the observance of "festivals" had a part in the solution (cf. Col 2:16). There is no indication, however, that the Colossian opponents advocated the performance of sacrifices and libations which play a significant role in this text.

5. The Isis Initiation in Apuleius

Given the paucity of literary witnesses to the essence of the mystery rites, the eleventh book of Apuleius's *Metamorphoses* takes on considerable importance. In this text, Apuleius describes the heart of the rite of initiation into the mystery of Isis at Cenchrae, the eastern port of Corinth. Although Apuleius writes in Latin, we can be certain that the spoken parts of the rite at Cenchrae were performed in Greek. It is likely that the *Metamorphoses* were written about A.D. 170 and were probably based largely on Apuleius's own experience including his own initiation into the mystery of Isis earlier in his life.[88] It is rather doubtful that the form or meaning of

---

[86] Burkert, *Ancient Mystery Cults*, 24.

[87] We can only speculate about Jewish involvement in this appeal to Apollo. Based on a number of Jewish burial epitaphs from Hierapolis (*CIJ* II.775, 776, 777) and the information in Josephus about the considerable number of Jews settled by Antiochus the Great in Phrygia (Josephus, *Ant.* 12.3.4 §§147-53; see *HJP²*, 27-28), we can be certain that there was a strong Jewish population in Hierapolis. If the Jews here were as involved in civic life as in other cities within Asia Minor, this situation may have produced a crisis of conscience for them. On the other hand, if the Jews were strongly assimilated, they may have condoned such an action by recourse to explaining these gods as "angels."

[88] J. Gwyn Griffiths, *The Isis-Book (Metamorphoses, Book XI)* (EPRO 39; Leiden: Brill, 1975) 10, 15.

the mystery initiation would have changed in any substantive way from the first to the second centuries.[89]

The chief character of the story is an unfortunate young man named Lucius who has been transformed into an ass through an inappropriate use of the magical arts. Much of the book is taken up with a humorous description of the many dreadful situations Lucius encounters as a result of his transformation. The climax of the book occurs with Lucius being rescued from his asinine captivity by the goddess Isis and his initiation into her mystery rite.

At a point when Lucius is deeply discouraged over his condition, Isis reveals herself to him while he is by the sea. She is described in the text with many glorious epithets, including "the mistress of the elements" (see Chapter 6).

Lucius is then instructed by the goddess to perform a number of purification rites and observe a set of carefully delineated prohibitions as preparation for initiation into the mystery of Isis. As the time for his initiation approaches, Lucius goes to the sacred temple in a procession of devotees. He is then dressed in a linen garment and is taken by the priest into the temple where he is led to the very heart of the holy shrine and is consecrated into the mystery of Isis. Apuleius describes the sacred act of initiation:

> Listen then, but believe, for my account is true. I approached (*accessi*) the boundary of death and treading on Proserpine's threshold, I was carried through all the elements (*per omnia vectus elementa*) after which I returned (*remeavi*). At dead of night I saw the sun flashing with bright effulgence. I approached close to the gods above and the gods below and worshipped them face to face (Apuleius, *Metamorphoses* 11.23; = 284-85).

Martin Dibelius aptly summarized the content of this section as an entry into the realm of the dead, a vision of the underworld gods, a joyous return connected with a journey through all the elements, and an epiphany of light with a vision of the gods above.[90]

---

[89] A. J. M. Wedderburn, *Baptism and Resurrection: Studies in Pauline Theology Against Its Graeco-Roman Background* (WUNT 44; Tübingen: J.C.B. Mohr [Paul Siebeck], 1987) 162, has recently noted, "[there is no] adequate reason for saying that the beliefs of their devotees then were greatly different from those a century later, so that it is not illegitimate to read back whatever we may infer from, for instance, Apuleius's account of Lucius's initiation into the mysteries of Isis."

[90] Dibelius, "Isis Initiation," 64. Dibelius spends much effort in attempting to argue through form-critical analysis that this passage was a σύνθημα, i.e. a formulaic password of the cult that enabled mutual recognition of initiates when they were in a foreign envi-

Dibelius made substantive use of the eleventh book of the *Metamorphoses* for illustrating the nature of mystery initiation, which for him served as background for understanding the initiation rite alluded to in Col 2:18. Others have followed his lead in using this material not only for shedding light on ἐμβατεύω, but also on other aspects of the teaching of the opponents.[91] I am convinced that Dibelius is essentially justified in using this text as an example of one mystery rite which may serve, in many respects, as typical of mystery initiation in the first century A.D. Of course, one must respect the distinctive traits of each mystery cult and avoid repeating the past generalizations regarding a unified theology among the mysteries.[92] In light of progress in Gnostic studies over the past decade, Dibelius's further conclusion that pagan cults had already been strongly influenced by Gnosticism[93] must clearly be rejected.[94]

It would be helpful at this point to list the major similarities between the Isis initiation in Apuleius and the teaching of "the philosophy" at Colossae:

(1) *"Entering"* (cf. Col 2:18): In the description of his initation, Lucius was said to have "aproached *(accessi)* the boundary of death" and, after being carried through all the elements, he returned *(remeavi)* (11.22). The term *accedere* ("to enter") approximates very closely to the use of the term ἐμβατεύω in the Claros inscriptions. It introduces the long-awaited culmination of the mystery rite.[95] Dibelius argues that this term (or, more precisely, its Greek equivalent) was used in a technical sense.[96] He notes, "The initiation itself is an 'entering,' sanctioned by the goddess, into the sanctuary, its secrets, and its celebrations."[97] He suggests that the mystagogue led the initiate into an underground room where the descent to the underworld and the ascent through the elements were enacted with special

---

ronment (pp. 65-74). Griffiths, *Isis-Book,* 295, has adequately refuted this conclusion and contends that the passage is indeed descriptive of the initiate's movements and what he has seen, albeit in a heightened symbolic sense.

[91] See, most recently, Argall, "Religious Error," 14-20. See also, Lohse, *Colossians, ad. loc.;* et al.

[92] Dibelius, "Isis Initiation," 61, exercised some sensitivity to this point, as illustrated by his criticism of R. Reitzenstein: "because this scholar's interest is fixed on the continuous lines of connection, the individual structure does not always emerge into clarity."

[93] Dibelius, "Isis Initiation," 91-96, esp. 91.

[94] See my previous discussion of this issue with regard to the background of Ephesians (*Ephesians,* 7-13). See also Wedderburn, *Baptism and Resurrection,* 139.

[95] Griffiths, *Isis-Book,* 297.

[96] He also points to three other terms for entering: *pervadere* (11.21), *deducere* (11.23), and *aditus* (11.28). See Dibelius, "Isis Initiation," 75.

[97] Dibelius, "Isis Initiation," 75.

effects. The ecstatic mood and the visual effects, according to Dibelius, heightened the fantasy of the initiate and began to blur the distinction between reality and unreality.[98] J. G. Griffiths upholds many of the details of Dibelius's earlier interpretation. He contends that the ceremonies probably took place in an underground chamber—which the initiate would have "entered"—since crypts were a regular feature of temples of Isis and Serapis.[99] Likewise, he does not explain the experience of the initiate as a dream or trance, but as "the reality of revelation" induced by the sacred drama.[100]

(2) *Vision* (cf. Col 2:18): As I have just described above, the visionary experience of entering the holiest chamber was the high point of the initiation rite. The μύστης saw the underworld and elements as he passed through the heavenly spheres. Lucius says, "At dead of night I saw *(vidi)* the sun." Then he approached close enough to the gods to see them and worship them face to face.

(3) *Stoicheia* (cf. Col 2:8, 20): The vision of passing through the *elementa* and the role of the *elementa* elsewhere in the eleventh book of the *Metamorphoses* provides background to the concept of the *stoicheia* in Colossians (see Chapter 6).

(4) *Fasting and Prohibitions* (cf. Col 2:16, 18, 21, 23): As with other mystery rites, ritual purity was prerequisite to initiation in the Isis cult. This is expressed in 11:23: "One command, however, he announced clearly for all present to hear, that for the ten following days I should curb my desire for food, abstaining from all animal flesh and from wine. After I had kept these rules with reverent restraint, now came the day of the divine pledge [his initiation]." The regulations were not easy: "for I [Lucius] had taken care to ascertain how arduous was the service of the faith, how extremely hard were the rules of chastity and abstinence" (11.19; see also 11.21). Lucius faced a similar set of restrictions in his preparation for later performing the rites of Osiris: "and straightway [I] submitted to the rigour of a vegetarian diet; indeed I added, with a voluntary discipline" (11:30; see also 11.28).

---

[98] Dibelius, "Isis Initiation," 77.

[99] Griffiths, *Isis Book,* 298.

[100] Griffiths, *Isis Book,* 299. He explains the drama by suggesting that the experience of the realm of the dead was imparted through representations on the walls of the rooms. He sees the Egyptian New Kingdom tombs, which provide a sequence of scenes divided between several rooms and passages, as background to what may have been on the walls of the crypt in Cenchrae (where Apuleius himself was probably initiatated).

(5) *Freely Chosen Worship* (cf. Col 2:23): Although the Greek word ἐθελοθρησκία certainly does not appear, the concept of "freely chosen worship"—in line with other mystery rites as voluntary cults—is present. Lucius refers to his initiation as "the day of my constant desire" (11.22). Similarly, the priest of Isis tells Lucius, "The day is at hand for which you have longed with constant prayers, the day when you shall enter ... into the most sacred mysteries of the holy rites" (11.22). Plutarch's account of the Isis and Osiris mysteries further illustrates the nature of the rigid requirements (see Plutarch, *De Is. et Os.* 4.352c-d; 7.353b).

(6) *Tradition* (cf. Col 2:8): As with other mystery cult rituals, the Isis rite is passed on to the initiate in terms of secret and venerable tradition. Lucius receives the tradition of the Isis rite and performs it accordingly: "For the gates of hell and the guarantee of life were alike in the power of the goddess and the very rite of dedication (*traditionem*) itself was performed in the manner of a voluntary death and of a life obtained by grace" (Apul. *Met.* 11.21 = 283, 5).[101]

(7) *Fear of the Powers* (cf. Col 1:16; 2:8, 10, 15, 20): One of the most significant motives for initiation was to gain immunity from and authority over the hostile powers. This assumes a widespread fear of the evil heavenly, terrestrial, and underworld powers. Dibelius thus appropriately summarizes the overall significance of the rite:

> Insofar as Lucius traverses this way [to the underworld and through the heavens] unharmed, he proves himself charmed against chthonic, earthly, and heavenly powers. The deification at the end of the ceremony imparts confirmation and duration to this superiority ... Thus the initiate becomes a participant in the cosmic rule of his goddess ... This freedom from the rule of the cosmic powers means freedom also from the coercion of fate ... One sees what significance is here attributed to the Isis mystery: the rule of the cosmic powers and the blind Fortuna represented by them is replaced by the rule of the gracious *Fortuna videns* [Fortune who sees], whom all those powers obey, Isis.[102]

J. G. Griffiths agrees with Dibelius in affirming that the primary meaning of the union with Isis is that now "the initiate shares adoringly in her cosmic sovereignty."[103] This union also ultimately leads to a eternal happiness with the promise of immortality.[104]

---

[101] Griffiths, *Isis-Book,* 280.
[102] Dibelius, "Isis Initiation," 81-82.
[103] Griffiths, *Isis-Book,* 307.
[104] Griffiths, *Isis-Book,* 307. *Pace* Nilsson, *GGR,* 2.636.

This account of the Isis initiation is also important for our study of Colossians because we know, based on numismatic evidence, that Isis was worshipped at Colossae.[105] The famous "Invocation of Isis" (*P.Oxy.* 1380) demonstrates the exceptional popularity of Isis outside of Egypt. More than 55 locales outside of Egypt are named as places where Isis was worshipped. Interestingly for our purposes, this document twice associates her with Hekate, the goddess of witchcraft and sorcery, in terms of how she was identified and worshipped in Asia Minor:

> line 90: "In Asia [she is] worshipped at the three ways"
> line 113: "In Caria [she is known as] Hecate"

Her power over the realm of evil spirits is lauded in line 164: "the ... spirits become thy subjects" (δ[α]ίμονες ὑπήκοοι σοὶ [γ]ίνο[ν]ται). This further heightens the importance of our investigation of the Hekate tradition in Asia Minor (see below).

6. The "Mithras Liturgy"—A Magical Mystery Rite

Any boundary between mystery and magic was exceedingly thin at times. In line with our definition of magic as a substructure to official religion is the notion that magic had a place in the mystery cults. Hans Dieter Betz has recently noted, "Information about and relics from the Greek mystery-cults definitely suggest that magic was a constituent element in the rituals of the mysteries."[106] Conversely, the *PGM* contain much of the terminology and ideas of the mystery cults.[107]

In 1903, Albrecht Dieterich published a study in which he claimed to have identified in the Great Paris Magical Papyrus (*PGM* IV.475-829) an actual liturgy of the mysteries of the Mithras cult.[108] The text contained

---

[105] See Françoise Dunand, *Le Culte d'Isis dans le Bassin Oriental de la Méditerranée*, vol. 3: Le Culte d'Isis en Asie Mineure Clergé et Rituel des Santuaires Isiaques (EPRO 26; Leiden: Brill, 1973) 46.

[106] Hans Dieter Betz, "Magic and Mystery in the Greek Magical Papyri," *Hellenismus und Urchristentum,* Gesammelte Aufsätze I (Tübingen: J.C.B. Mohr [Paul Siebeck], 1990) 220.

[107] Betz, "Magic and Mystery," 219-20.

[108] See Albrecht Dieterich, *Eine Mithrasliturgie* (3d ed. by Otto Weinrich; Darmstadt: Wissenschaftliche Buchgesellschaft, 1966). The text has been translated by Marvin W. Meyer in three venues: (1) in *The "Mithras Liturgy,"* (SBLTT 10, Greco-Roman Religion

much of the terminology of the mysteries (e.g. παραδοτὰ μυστήρια, μύσται, ἀπαθανατισμός) and many of the central ideas of the Greek mystery cults (e.g. union with the deity, immortality, the ascent of the soul through the elements; re-birth). Dieterich's claim was disputed by Franz Cumont, not for his analysis of its connection with mystery rites, but over his contention that it belonged to the Mithras cult.[109] Recent scholarship upholds Cumont's criticism insisting that the text is not an authentic liturgy from the Mithras cult.[110] It is possible, however, that in the general context of Hellenistic syncretism, the so-called "Mithras Liturgy" represents one expression of Egyptian Mithraism.[111] As W. Burkert has observed, it is more important to see the text as describing "a private trip in a quest for oracular revelations, not a communal mystery rite."[112] For our purposes it is not important to insist on the text's identification with Mithraism as much as to reaffirm its character as a document of religious mystery with significant magical overtones.

The Egyptian provenance does not remove it so far from the sphere of Asia Minor religions so as to render it irrelevant to our concerns. It must be remembered that the magical tradition encompassed by the *PGM* transcends the borders of Egypt and represents in large measure what was typical of magic and popular religion in the Roman period. Furthermore, the presence of Egyptian deities at Colossae (illustrated by the numismatic evidence) demonstrates that the local populace had imbibed Egyptian re-

---

Series 2; Missoula: Scholar's Press, 1976), (2) in *GMPT,* 48-54, and now in (3) *The Ancient Mysteries: A Sourcebook* (San Francisco: Harper & Row, 1987) 211-21. Dieterich regarded lines 475-723 as the actual liturgy and lines 723-834 as instructions for the magical use of the liturgy. There is an extensive discussion of the text in R. Reitzenstein, *Hellenistic Mystery-Religions* (Pittsburgh Theological Monograph Series 15; Pittsburgh: Pickwick, 1978) 200-36.

[109] F. Cumont, *Textes et Monuments Figurés Relatifs aux Mystères de Mithra* (Brussels: H. Lamertin, 1896, 1899) 2.55ff., 1.41.

[110] Burkert, *Ancient Mystery Cults,* 68-69. Gary Lease, "Mithraism and Christianity: Borrowings and Transformations," *ANRW* II.23.2 (1980) 1308, notes, "this rejection is widely held today." See also Alan F. Segal, "Heavenly Ascent in Hellenistic Judaism, Early Christianity and their Environment," *ANRW* II.23.2 (1980) 1382, note 193, who concludes, "though Dieterich's evidence that the document represents a religious mystery is sound, important aspects of his argument for its mithraic origin must be dismissed." *Pace* Betz, "Magic and Mystery," 224-25.

[111] Maarten J. Vermaseren, "La Sotériologie dans les Papyri Graecae Magicae," *La Soteriologia Dei Culti Orientali Nell' Impero Romano* (EPRO 92, eds. U. Bianchi & M. J. Vermaseren; Leiden: Brill, 1982) 25.

[112] Burkert, *Ancient Mystery Cults,* 68. He further notes, "On the whole, the overlap between mysteries and magical papyri is not extensive enough to extract 'mystery liturgies' from the latter" (p. 69).

ligion to some degree. This was no doubt stimulated by consistent commerce and communication with Egypt carried through the port city of Ephesus.

The papyrus itself dates to the fourth century (possibly in the time of Diocletian), but it is widely recognized to preserve much earlier traditions. Dieterich conjectures that the liturgy may have been created as early as A.D. 100.[113] He links it with this period because of the rapid expanse of Mithraism from the East after A.D. 100. An even earlier date is conceivable if the text is not linked directly to Mithraism. One needs to allow some time to pass to account for its annexation to a book of magical recipes, although I am convinced that this could have happened in less than a generation after its creation.

The text prescribes the proper rites and invocations for a prospective initiate to become immortal (ἀθανασία, ll. 477-78). The process involves a visionary ascent to heaven and a mystery rite in which an ointment is created and applied. The result is the initiate's immortality (ἀπαθανατισμός; ll. 647-48, 741, 747, 771). This is imparted through union with the deity: when Mithras appears to the initiate, he or she responds by saying, "dwell with me in my soul" (μένε σὺν ἐμὲ ἐν τῇ ψυχῇ μου [l. 710]).[114] The experience is described throughout as a re-birth (ἡ ἀθάνατος γένεσις, [sic] l. 501; μεταγεννάω, ll. 508-509, 647; [ἐγὼ] θνητὸς γεννηθεὶς ... βεβελτιωμένος ὑπὸ κράτους μεγαλοδυνάμου, ll. 517-19)

Günther Bornkamm was the first to call attention to the relevance of this text for interpreting the teaching of the opponents at Colossae.[115] After pointing out some of the parallels of thought between the liturgy and the Colossian "philosophy," he concludes that, "The Colossians also seem to have celebrated a mystery of rebirth."[116] Many of the parallels he draws are convincing, as I will show below. Bornkamm goes too far, however, in assuming that the "Mithras Liturgy" represents Gnosticism. It is better to see it as representing a syncretistic mystery religion with many magical elements. It should be said, however, that texts of this kind fed into the developing Gnosis. Below I would like to highlight a few charac-

---

[113] Dieterich, *Mithrasliturgie*, 46.

[114] On this topic, see Dieterich, *Mithrasliturgie*, 95-97.

[115] Bornkamm, "Heresy," 127-28. He is followed with some modifications by H. Hegermann, *Die Vorstellung vom Schöpfungsmittler im hellenistischen Judentum und Urchristentum* (TU 82; Berlin: Akademie, 1961) 161-62.

[116] Bornkamm, "Heresy," 128.

teristics of the "Mithras Liturgy" that bear similarity to the competing teaching at Colossae.

(1) The liturgy was received as "tradition" (cf. Col 2:8). The author of the text describes what he is writing down as παραδοτὰ μυστήρια (1. 476).

(2) The initiation provides deliverance from dreaded fate and the threat of hostile supernatural powers (cf. Col 1:16; 2:8, 10, 15, 20). The liturgy actually begins by imploring Providence and Tyche[117] to show favor (1. 475). Magical names are given to the devotee to invoke for protection from "the pressing and bitter and inexorable necessity" (ἀνάγκη, ll. 605-606). When the adept ascends to heaven, he will see "the divine order of the skies: the presiding gods rising into heaven, and others setting" (ll. 544-47). These astral deities are dangerous to the mere mortal, and when they see the person they stare intently and rush at him (ll. 556-57). But the initiate is protected by his immortalization and an apotropaic formula that he then utters (ll. 558-60). Thus protected, the adept will "see the gods looking graciously upon you and no longer rushing at you" (ll. 565-67). These hostile gods are also termed ἄγγελοι (1. 571) or "stars" (ἀστέρες, 1. 574, 580). The text never uses the term στοιχεῖα for these hostile gods, but the term is used elsewhere in *PGM* in this sense.

(3) The four elements are assumed to prevent the immortalization (cf. Col 2.8, 20). Without using the term στοιχεῖα, the text also speaks of the human body as composed of spirit, fire, water, and earth (πνεῦμα, πῦρ, ὕδωρ, οὐσία γεώδης). These are then invoked as gods and told to give the initiate over to his immortal birth (ματαπαραδῶναι με τῇ ἀθανάτῳ γενέσει, 1. 501).[118] This is followed by the initiate "gazing on the im- mortal, beginning with the immortal spirit" (ll. 505-506), that he might "be born again in thought" (ἵνα νοήματι μεταγεννηθῶ, ll. 509-10), and that "the sacred spirit may breathe in me" (1. 510). Finally, he is granted a vision of the immortal Aion (1. 520). Bornkamm describes the revelation and function of Aion in this text in terms of a cosmic macroanthropos, a world-deity whose gigantic body is composed of the elements of the uni- verse.[119] In this fashion he imputes Gnostic ideas into the Mithras Liturgy and through it into the Colossian "philosophy." His characterization of Aion, however, does not hold for the Mithras Liturgy. Although Aion is

---

[117] Dieterich, *Mithrasliturgie*, 2, reads the text as Τύχη, whereas Preisendanz, *PGM*, 1.87, takes it as Ψυχή.

[118] Dieterich, *Mithrasliturgie*, 55, correctly points to the fact that this personalized un- derstanding of the elements is attested in Persian religion in ancient times.

[119] Bornkamm, "Heresy," 127.

described as the master of the four elements, he is not depicted here as a "body" with the elements as the constituent parts. The emphasis of the passage is on the immortality of Aion and the transformation of the mortal μύστης into an immortal being by contact with the divine. The four elements are represented as under his control: Aion is "master of the water ... founder of the earth ... ruler of the wind ... [and the] bright lightener" (δέσποτα ὕδατος, κατάρχα γῆς, δυνάστα πνεύματος, λαμπροφεγγῆ, ll. 713-15). It is important not to read this text in terms of developed Gnosticism. One must allow it to stand on its own terms as a mystery initiation text.

(4) Vision of the gods, angels, and astral powers was very important (cf. Col 2:18). The term ὁράω actually appears 21 times in this text (see above).

(5) An angel is said to have revealed these mystery traditions (cf. Col. 2:8, 18). Helios Mithras ordered his archangel (ἀρχάγγελος, l. 483) to reveal the instructions for the rite and invocations.

(6) The text includes instructions for procuring a fellow initiate (cf. θέλω in Col 2:18): "If you wish to use a fellow initiate ... (ἐὰν δὲ θέλῃς καὶ συνμύστῃ, l. 732). "The philosophy" at Colossae also sought to gain adherents. It is possible that the appearance of θέλω in Col 2:18, a passage containing another catchword from mystery cult usage, may have been influenced by such a formulation as we have here. If this is the case, we might translate 2:18a as follows: "Let no one condemn you who wishes for you to participate as a συνμύστη ..." The further context of instructions for acquiring a συνμύστη could also help to explain Paul's condemnation of the errorists as extremely arrogant. The liturgy calls for them to function as a judge over the participant: "And if you also wish to show him, then judge whether he is completely worthy as a man" (ll. 738-40).

(7) Dietary and purity regulations are imposed on the fellow initiate (Col 2:16, 21): "let him remain pure with you for [seven] days, and abstain from meat and the bath" (ll. 734-36; so also ll. 783-84: " ... having kept yourself pure for three days in advance").

(8) Performance of the mystery rite during the new moon was essential (cf. νεομηνία in Col 2:16): "Begin to prepare [the scarab] on the new moon in the lion, according to the god's [reckoning] (ἐν λέοντι κατὰ θεὸν νουμηνίᾳ, ll. 786-87; so also l. 780).

Not only the direct polemic, but also much of the positive teaching in Colossians could be understood as a response to this kind of teaching infiltrating the church. In contrast to Dibelius and Lohse, however, who saw the mystery cults as explaining all of the characteristics of the Colossian

"philosophy," it will be necessary to give just weight to some of the Jewish factors as well, e.g. especially "sabbaths" (see below).

7. The Goddess of Witchcraft and Magic: Hekate

In light of the prominent role of supernatural powers in the letter to the Colossians, it is especially important for us to consider the evidence illustrating the worship of Hekate in Asia Minor. As we saw above, Hekate was often identified with Isis in Asia Minor. The testimonies about this underworld goddess gives us a unique glimpse into the spiritual atmosphere of Asia Minor, especially regarding the fear of demons and evil spirits.

Hekate is a uniquely Asia Minor goddess. Her veneration was concentrated primarily in the territories of Caria and Phrygia, at least according to the distribution of material evidence (statues, coins, and inscriptions) that has been discovered as well as some literary testimony.[120] Her main cult center was in Lagina (about 70 miles SW of Colossae, near Stratonicea). She was probably also worshipped and feared at Colossae since every surrounding city attests to her worship, viz. Hierapolis, Laodicea, Apamea, Aphrodisias, Acmonia, Stratonicea, Alabanda, and Tralles. The veneration of Hekate was also quite popular during the mid-first century A.D. In fact, the whole tradition for Hekate in Caria and Phrygia belongs mainly to the Hellenistic and Roman Imperial era.[121] From Asia Minor, her worship spread to many other cities and villages in the Mediterranean world, including Athens and Rome.

Hekate is never mentioned in Homer or the Homeric fragments. The earliest literary testimony about Hekate associates her with the Asia Minor "Great Mother" (Hesiod *Theog.* 409-52).[122] In origin, she was probably a localized expression of the mother goddess (perhaps ultimately stemming from the Hittite goddess Kubaba). This explains, in part, her close association with Cybele and the Ephesian Artemis. From the 5th century B.C. on there are numerous references to Hekate in literature and epigraphical

---

[120] Theodor Kraus, *Hekate. Studien zu Wesen und Bild der Göttin in Kleinasien und Griechenland* (Heidelberger Kunstgeschichtliche Abhandlungen 5; Heidelberg: Carl Winter, 1960) 51-52 and Anhang I: "Hekate-Zeugnisse aus Karien und Phrygien," 166-68.

[121] Kraus, *Hekate,* 54.

[122] See Alois Kehl, "Hekate," *RAC* 14.315.

sources. According to these sources, Hekate was revered as the goddess of demons and evil spirits.[123]

Hekate uniquely belongs to popular folk belief.[124] Alois Kehl remarks, "in the common belief of Greco-Roman civilization, Hekate appeared above all as the ruler of darkness, of terror, of the dead, of demons, and of magic."[125] From an early stage she is compared with Persephone (bride of Hades) and characterized as mistress of the underworld (Orpheus, *Hymn* 1.7). She possesses the keys to the door of Hades as a symbol of her power.[126] Because she controlled the passageway to the underworld, she could enable people to communicate with the dead. Her custodianship of Hades also enabled her to control the apparitions or souls who ascended to do the magician's bidding.[127]

She was also recognized as ruler over the souls of the dead in folk belief.[128] She could use her power over these disembodied spirits to order them to do her evil bidding. She was responsible for sending frightful apparitions and night terrors to people, for bringing various kinds of sickness, and for causing insanity. As goddess of the underworld, Hekate is often invoked because of her ability to command an army of spirits. These were generally believed to be ἀλάστορες ("avenging spirits"), both ἄωροι (the spirits of those who had died before the completion of their 'destined' years) and βιαιοθάνατοι (the spirits of those who had died violent deaths).

"The Goddess of the Crossroads" was a well-known epithet for Hekate.[129] In popular belief, the intersection of roads was commonly believed to be dangerous and haunted by evil spirits. Her statue—usually a three-sided figure *(triformis)*[130]—was erected at crossroads throughout Asia Minor where she was believed to function as an averter of evil. Meals were brought to the Hekate image at a certain time each month to

---

[123] Joseph Heckenback, "Hekate," *PW* 7.2770. See Johnston, *Hekate Soteira*, Chapters 3 ("The Mistress of the Moon") and 9 ("The Chaldean Daemon-dogs").

[124] Heckenbach, "Hekate," 2776, notes, "Hekate is therefore a greatly feared image of Greek folk belief."

[125] Kehl, "Hekate," 315 (translation mine).

[126] Kraus, *Hekate,* 50-51; Kehl, "Hekate," 320; Heckenbach, "Hekate," 2773.

[127] See Johnston, *Hekate Soteira,* 146.

[128] Kehl, "Hekate," 320; Heckenbach, "Hekate," 2774; E. Rohde, *Psyche* (New York: Harcourt, Brace & Co., 1925) 593-95.

[129] E.g. *PGM* IV.1432: "O mistress Hekate ... O Lady of the Crossroads."

[130] For this image on amulets, see Campbell Bonner, *Studies in Magical Amulets Chiefly Graeco-Egyptian* (Ann Arbor: University of Michigan Press, 1950) 263-64 (nos. 63-66).

appease her and to avert (ἀποτρόπαιος) evil (see Plutarch, *Quaest. Rom.* 111). J. Heckenbach supposes that her origin may have been nothing other than a goddess to protect the way.[131]

Hekate was also believed to have cosmic power. Her authority extended over earth, sea, and heaven. Some texts point to her connection with the lunar element, and she becomes associated with the moon-goddess Selene. A few ancient writers even emphasize her role as a cosmic soul.[132]

Her sway over the underworld, demons, and disembodied souls led to her vastly popular function as the goddess of witchcraft and magic.[133] She is called on numerous times in the magical papyri and in the defixiones.[134] She gave magic its effective power because she controlled the spirits who would perform the deeds.[135] Hekate would dispatch the demons to carry out the magician's wishes. Perhaps one of the most significant pieces of local evidence for her prominence in magic is the magical apparatus found at Pergamum. An image of Hekate holding keys (to the underworld) is inscribed in the three corners of the triangular bronze magical table.[136]

In this function she is closely associated with the Ephesian Artemis, who is also worshipped as a goddess of the underworld.[137] In fact, a common linkage of Hekate, Artemis, and the moon goddess Selene becomes traditional in the magical papyri.[138] Persephone, Cybele[139], and the Babylonian underworld deity Ereschigal are also often associated with the other three. These goddesses of witchraft and sorcery were thought to

---

131 Heckenbach, "Hekate," 2775.

132 See the recent book by Sarah Johnston, *Hekate Soteira*, that documents and illustrates this theme in the ancient literature.

133 M. P. Nilsson, *Greek Popular Religion* (New York: Columbia University Press, 1940) 80, 90-91, 111; Heckenbach, "Hekate," 2772-73; Kehl, "Hekate," 320-21; C. Downing, "Hekate," in *The Encyclopedia of Religion* (ed. M. Eliade; New York: Macmillan, 1987) 6.252.

134 See, for example, *PGM* III.47; IV.1432, 1443, 1462, 2119, 2610, 2632, 2692, 2714, 2727, 2730, 2745, 2751, 2815, 2880, 2957. For an indication of how often she is invoked in defixiones, see A. Audollent, *Defixionum Tabellae* (Paris: Alberti Fontemoing, 1904) 461-70 (= Index IV: Nomina et Cognomina Deorum Daemonumque Invodatorum).

135 Kehl, "Hekate," p. 320.

136 Wünsch, *Zaubergerät,* 11-13. See also Heckenbach, "Hekate," 2773.

137 See Arnold, *Ephesians,* Chapter 2, Section: "Artemis and Magic." See futher, Heckenbach, "Hekate," 2770-71; Kraus, *Hekate,* 34-36.

138 Theodor Hopfner, "Hekate-Selene-Artemis und Verwandte in den griechischen Zauberpapyri und auf den Fluchtafeln," *Pisciculi. F. J. Dölger zum 60. Geburtstage* (Münster: Aschendorff, 1939) 125-45. Hopfner sees the equation of these deities beginning in the syncretism of the fifth century B.C. (126).

139 Cybele herself was said to have been surrounded by a company of wizards known as the Idaean Dactyls (see the discussion above on *PGM* LXX).

possess power and authority over underworld demons, terrestrial spirits, and even the astral spirits believed to control one's fate. Through a series of spells and formulae the initiate could avert the tyranny of the "powers." This is well illustrated by a number of "hymns" in the magical papyri dedicated to Hekate-Selene-Artemis.[140]

These deities themselves were referred to as ἄγγελοι. In fact, ἄγγελος was a well-known epithet of the Asia Minor goddesses Artemis and Hekate.[141] An Attic curse tablet explicitly invokes Hekate and other pagan deities as ἄγγελοι καταχθόνιοι.[142] It is difficult to know why this epiklesis was given to these deities. J. Schniewind thinks it may have to do with the euphemistic quality of the name for underworld deities.[143] We have already pointed to the *"Angelos-Angelikos"* inscriptions of Carian Stratonicea, which may very well refer to Hekate (see Chapter 3). Another Asia Minor inscription, a defixio from Claudiopolis (Bithynia), also makes the association: "Ortho (Artemis), Baubo (Hekate), ... Ereschigal, ... sovereign gods and angels (κύριοι θεοὶ ἄνγελοι), bind with your spell all those herein written."[144]

One could also be initiated into the mystery rite of Hekate. One inscription briefly mentions an ἐπιμελέτης τῶν μυστηρίων connected with her cult in Lagina.[145] Unfortunately, none of our evidence gives us any specific information about the rites. Because of her reputation as an apotropaic goddess, one may conjecture that someone would be initiated into the mysteries of Hekate to gain immunity from harmful spirits. There is

---

[140] See Preisendanz, *PGM* (Stuttgart edition) 250-60, for hymns 18 (= PGM IV. 2786-2870), 19 (= PGM IV. 2574-2610 and 2643-74), 20 (= PGM IV. 2522-67), and 21 (= PGM IV. 2714-83). For further discussion, see Hopfner, "Hekate-Selene-Artemis," 125-45, who devotes special attention to the variety of epithets ascribed to these deities.

[141] For the texts, see Julius Schniewind, *Euangelion. Ursprung und erste Gestalt des Begriffs Euangelium* (Darmstadt: Wissenschaftliche Buchgesellschaft, 1931) 2.225-35. See also Sokolowski, "Sur le Culte," 226-29 and Dibelius, *Geisterwelt,* 212-13. This has been brought out in recent literature by David Aune, "The Apocalypse of John and Graeco-Roman Revelatory Magic," *NTS* 33 (1987) 489.

[142] Audollent, *Defixionum,* 103 (= 75a.1-9): Καταγράφω καὶ κατατίθω ἀνγέλοις καταχθονίοις Ἑρμῇ καταχθονίῳ καὶ Ἑκάτῃ καταχθονίᾳ Πλούτωνι καὶ Κόρη καὶ Περσιφόνη καὶ Μοίραις καταχθονίαις καὶ πάντοις τοῖς θεοῖς. In a similar way, so also 74.1-5. See Aune, "Apocalypse," 489.

[143] Schniewind, *Euangelion,* 228.

[144] J. M. R. Cormack, "A *Tabella Defixionis* in the Museum of the University of Reading, England," *HTR* 44 (1951) 25-34.

[145] For this and other references to mystery rites, see Heckenbach, "Hekate," 2779-81.

some evidence that people may have performed her rites in an effort to seek healing, especially from epilepsy and insanity.[146]

There is some evidence pointing to the influence of Hekate veneration in Judaism. E. R. Goodenough regards *PGM* XXXVI.187-210 as essentially Jewish.[147] P. Alexander corroborates Goodenough's conclusion by speaking of this text as one of his more convincing examples.[148] The recipe, to be inscribed on ostraca, calls on Hekate to perform love magic, but she is invoked by the god of the Jews:

> Hecate, you, Hecate, triple-formed ... I adjure you by the great name of ABLA-NATHANALBA and by the power of AGRAMARI ... because I am holding in my right hand the two serpents and the victory of IAŌ SABAŌTH (καὶ τὴν νίκην τοῦ Ἰαω Σαβαώθ) ... [Write] 8 characters like this: "Grant me, indeed the favor of all, ADŌNAI (᾿Αδωναί)" [one of the 8 symbols is a rectangular drawing with the term IAŌ in the middle].

Goodenough notes the close association of "Iao" and Hekate: "The chief value of the charm is that it shows how completely Hecate and Iao could be associated. The combination could have been made by a pagan or a Jew, but the way in which 'Iao' and 'Adonai' dominate suggests to me that the author was more probably a Jew."[149]

In another example, Solomon is depicted as a magician performing hydromancy on one side of a Jewish amulet (*CIJ* 394). On the reverse side an image of Hekate is inscribed (tri-formed) next to a five-branched menorah and various other symbols.[150] Another amulet bears an image of Hekate with the inscription, "Iao, Sabaoth, protect."[151] C. Bonner's collection of amulets includes one with an image of the triple Hekate with the inscription: Ιαω σαβαωθ αδωναι χω.[152] Goodenough cites many other amulets in which Hekate appears with the name(s) of the Jewish god and

---

[146] This was particularly true of her cult on the island of Aegina in the Saronic Gulf (Lucian, *Navig.* 15; Pausanius, 2.30.2); for further references, see Heckenbach, "Hekate," 2781.

[147] E. R. Goodenough, *Jewish Symbols in the Greco-Roman Period*, Volume 2: The Archaeological Evidence from the Diaspora (Bollingen Series 37; New York: Bollingen Foundation, 1953) 196.

[148] P. S. Alexander, "Incantations and Books of Magic," in *HJP*[2], 359.

[149] Goodenough, *Symbols*, 2.196.

[150] For discussion of this amulet, see Goodenough, *Symbols*, 2.233.

[151] Goodenough, *Symbols*, 2.237.

[152] Bonner, *Amulets*, 264 (no. 65). This amulet is also discussed in Goodenough, *Symbols*, 2.237.

various Jewish symbols. He concludes that Hekate was highly valued for Jewish magic and freely invoked for her operative power.[153]

Hekate's popularity in Jewish magic opens up the possibility that Jewish Christians may have introduced her veneration into the early church. If it was not a problem for certain Jews to maintain their fidelity to Yahweh while invoking the ἄγγελος Hekate for protection, then some Jewish Christians may not have had a scruples about calling on Hekate while worshiping Christ as Lord. In later Christian tradition, however, she was described as a satanic lieutenant in charge of a demonic horde: ἄρχουσα τῶν πονηρῶν δαιμόνων (Eusebius, *Praep. Ev.* 4.22).

In conclusion, having established in PART I the relevance of magic/folk belief to interpreting the features of the competing teaching in general and the "invocation of angels" in particular, Hekate becomes an extremely important local tradition to take into consideration. Because they feared terrestrial spirits and evil powers, people invoked Hekate—as an *angelos*—for protection. This practice even crept into Judaism.

8. Other Relevant Phrygian Cults

There are a few other local cults that should be considered for their possible contribution to an understanding of the teaching of the opponents at Colossae. In particular, one must consider the cult of the "Great Mother," Cybele. Also informative, however, are the cults of Men, Theos Hypsistos, and Sabazios.

I will make a few general comments about the characteristics of these cults and their relevance to understanding the Colossian "philosophy" here. Additional, more specific, comments will also be made when I describe the "catchwords" of the teaching of the Colossian "philosophy" in Chapter 7.

a. Cybele and Attis

A number of interpreters have looked to the cult of Cybele for providing at least some of the backdrop to the Colossian "philosophy."[154] Johannes

---

[153] Goodenough, *Symbols*, 2.237.

[154] This was particularly common among older interpreters. See, for example, Eadie,

Lähnemann has given the most attention to the cult among recent inter-preters.[155]

In exclusive dependence on F. Cumont's description of the cult, Läh-nemann calls attention to the following characteristics of the worship of Cybele as possible background to the Colossian teaching: the regular festi-vals (cf. Col 2:16), the voluntary nature of the cult (cf. ἐθελοθρησκία in Col 2:23), the bodily mutilations (ἀφειδία σώματος in Col 2:23 and the reference to 'spiritual' circumcision Col 2:11), the celebration of mystery rites (cf. Col 2:18), and the rigorous asceticism (cf. Col 2:16, 20-23). Lähnemann does not see this as a direct set of influences on the church, but looks to Hellenistic Judaism, which had assimilated some of these pa-gan beliefs and practices, as the carrier of these ideas.[156] Thus he roots the Colossian "philosophy" in the larger religious environment of what he terms "the Asia Minor syncretism" (*der kleinasiatische Synkretismus*).

One of the most striking aspects of the cult is the ecstatic worship.[157] The spring festival began with the singing of hymns accompanied by the rhythm of tambourines. The worshipers would join together in wild dancing, singing, and shrieking, with their arms and hands raised above their heads. According to the informing myth, Attis himself had danced in a feverish dance as he was driven insane by the goddess Cybele. Many terra cotta figurines depicting the dancing and frenzied Attis have been published by M. J. Vermaseren.[158] As part of the enthusiastic worship, the Galli—the priests of the cult—would flagellate their chests and upper arms with a leather scourge (*flagellum*) until they bled on the *dies sangui-nis* (the day of blood).[159] Those desirous of becoming Galli culminated their commitment to the goddess by castrating themselves in the frenzied worship in imitation of Attis's self-emasculation.[160]

Colossians, xii-xiii; Abbott, *Colossians,* xlix; et al.

[155] Lähnemann, *Kolosserbrief,* 85-86. He was followed in some of the details by Martin, *Colossians* (NCB), 4.

[156] Lähnemann, *Kolosserbrief,* 97.

[157] For a description of the ecstatic rites and references to the primary sources that at-test to them, see M. J. Vermaseren, *The Legend of Attis in Greek and Roman Art* (EPRO 9; Leiden: Brill, 1966) 42-44; idem, *Cybele and Attis. The Myth and the Cult* (London: Thames and Hudson, 1977) 24-32, 113-24; H. Graillot, *Le Culte de Cybéle* (Paris, 1912) 255 and *passim*. See also Rohde, *Psyche,* 257, who finds many points of similarity to the Thracian worship of Dionysus.

[158] See Vermaseren, *Legend,* plates XXVI-XXXVII.

[159] Vermaseren, *Cybele and Attis,* 115. See also Burkert, *Ancient Mystery Cults,* 35-36.

[160] Vermaseren, *Legend,* 43; idem, *Cybele and Attis,* 115; T. Hopfner, "Mysterien," *PW* 16/2.1331.

All of this celebration was preceded by a week of fasting, abstinence, and various forms of purification. Vermaseren discusses an inscription from the temple of Cybele at Maeonia, Lydia (about 70 miles NW of Colossae), dated to 147-146 B.C., that describes a series of ritual prohibitions.[161] These prohibitions included sexual contact, but there were also provisions for ritual purification (ἀγνεύειν).

Many scholars have characterized the ecstatic worship associated with cult of Cybele and Attis as illustrative of the so-called "Lydian-Phrygian spirit." I am persuaded that Lähnemann is correct in pointing to the Cybele cult as significant for gaining a better understanding of Phrygian religion, and thereby as providing important background to the syncretistic "philosophy" influencing the church at Colossae. There is certainly no question about the importance of the Magna Mater to religion in Asia Minor and, although we have no direct inscriptional or numismatic proof, she was undoubtedly worshipped at Colossae.[162] Vermaseren has noted, "in the Roman epoch there was no citadel, village or hamlet in Phrygia that did not remain true to the worship of Cybele."[163] Although it is difficult to discern what manner of influence this local form of worship may have had on Phrygian Judaism, there is no doubt that Gentile Christians converted from a background of devotion to Cybele and Attis would have had difficulty completely forsaking their prior forms of worship.

b. Men

F. A. Henle was the first to point to aspects of the worship of Men (Μήν, or Μείς) in Asia Minor for interpreting the Colossian problem.[164] J. Lähnemann has taken up the important parts of his study.[165] As we noted earlier, the worship of the moon-god Men at Colossae is confirmed by nu-

---

[161] Vermaseren, *Cybele and Attis*, 30. Editio princeps: F. Sokolowski, *Lois sacrées de l'Asie Mineure* (Paris: Editions de Boccard, 1955) 50, no. 18.

[162] See the recent collection of epigraphic evidence for Asia Minor by M. J. Vermaseren in *Corpus Cultus Cybelae Attidisque*, I. Asia Minor (EPRO 50; Leiden: Brill, 1987). For a brief discussion about Cybele worship at Hierapolis, see S. E. Johnson, "Laodicea and its Neighbors," *BA* 13 (1950) 6.

[163] Vermaseren, *Cybele and Attis*, 27.

[164] F. A. Henle, "Der Men- und Mithrakult in Phrgyien: Skizzen zur Vorgeschichte der kolossischen Irrlehre," *TQ* 70 (1888) 590-614 (as cited in Lähnemann, *Kolosserbrief*, 86-87).

[165] Lähnemann, *Kolosserbrief*, 86-87.

mismatic evidence.[166] F. Cumont has gone so far as to say that "no god enjoyed greater popularity in the country districts [of Asia Minor]."[167]

Lähnemann and Henle point in particular to the relevance of this cult for the interpretation of νεομηνία (Col 2:16) and as background for the opponents' understanding of πλήρωμα. Men was regarded as an androgynous being who could produce offspring by himself. This concept, they argue, could have been the basis for the emanation concept implied by πλήρωμα in the teaching of the Colossian opponents.

While I disagree with the latter suggestion (which is unduly speculative), it is possible that the festivals in Colossae associated with the new moon could have had some connection with the cult of Men (see my discussion in Chapter 7).

The concentration of material evidence for the worship of Men is located particularly in two areas of Asia Minor: the Maeonian region of Lydia and in Antioch of Pisidia.[168] E. N. Lane notes that the nature of the cult differs considerably from place to place, taking on concepts that characterize a particular area.[169] The Maeonian evidence is thus especially relevant for giving us insight into the Lydian-Phrygian worship of this deity.

One peculiar concept from the Maeonian region involves the local fear of offending the god, even unwittingly.[170] Those who were in some form of bondage because they had displeased him found it necessary to purchase their freedom with a price (λύτρον).[171]

Mystery rites for Men are attested in one inscription found in the Cayster Valley (near Ephesus and Claros).[172] As we observed above, Sir William Ramsay excavated a temple of Men near Pisidian Antioch where

---

[166] See also A. Lesky, "Men," *PW* 15/1.691. He also notes, "the numismatic references to the Men cult in Phrygia are numerous."

[167] F. Cumont, *Oriental Religions in Roman Paganism* (New York: Dover, 1911) 61. Similarly, E. Lane, *Corpus Monumentorum Religionis Dei Menis* (EPRO 19; Leiden: Brill, 1976) 1.31, comments, "From these inscriptions, I think that it is clear what an important role Men and the divinities associated with him played in the life of the common people of this area [Lydia]."

[168] E. N. Lane, "Men: A Neglected Cult of Roman Asia Minor," *ANRW* II.18.3 (1990) 2163-64."

[169] Lane, "Men," 2164.

[170] Lane, "Men," 2164; see *CMRDM*, I, nos. 61 and 66.

[171] Lane, "Men," 2164; see *CMRDM*, I, nos. 57, 61, and 90.

[172] *CMRDM*, I, no. 75. See Nilsson, *GGR*, 2.657; Lesky, "Men," 696.

mystery initiation rites were celebrated. It is also significant that purity rites had an important place in the cult.[173]

Men was a god people could call on for protection. Villagers invoked him to ward off evil from their farms and property.[174] People also placed graves under his protection.[175] In accordance with this function he was given the title, "the Underworld Men" (*Men Katachthonios*). This evidence thus furthers our contention that there was a keen fear of evil powers in Phrygia and Lydia and that people called on gods, goddesses, and various intermediaries for help and deliverance.

9. Syncretistic Judaism in Phrygia

One of the possibilities we must entertain is that the mystery terminology in "the philosophy" (esp. ἐμβατεύω, but perhaps also ἐθελοθρησκία, τιμή, ταπεινοφροσύνη, ἑορτή, and νεομηνία) was mediated *through Judaism* rather than directly through pagan religion. This relates to the overarching issue of syncretism within the Judaism of Asia Minor: To what extent did at least some segments of Anatolian Judaism assimilate the religious symbolism, terminology, and beliefs of their pagan neighbors.

It needs to be repeated at this point that the term ἐμβατεύω does not appear in any extant literary or epigraphical Jewish texts used in a religious sense. This does not obviate the possibility that it may have been used this way, which later inscriptional finds could confirm. Nevertheless, an equally important question is whether one can find evidence of the existence of Jewish mystery cults in Asia Minor.

Celebrated Yale scholar Erwin R. Goodenough argued strenuously that Jews throughout the Diaspora had developed mystery cults based upon and borrowing from the pagan mystery cults. He claimed to find a concrete example in Philo's account of the Theraputae (see Philo, *De Vita Contemplativa*), but also argues that Philo himself assimilated many pagan mystery cult beliefs.[176] He attempted to marshal additional support for his thesis in the material evidence of Diaspora Judaism, which he published in his

---

[173] See Nilsson, *GGR,* 2.657, note 9, for the inscriptions.

[174] Cumont, *Oriental Religions,* 61.

[175] *CMRDM,* I, nos. 70-71 (from Lydia). See also Nilsson, *GGR,* 2.657; Cumont, *Oriental Religions,* 61.

[176] See especially his work, *By Light, Light: The Mystic Gospel of Hellenistic Judaism* (New Haven: Yale, 1935). See also *Symbols,* 2.146-47.

stately twelve-volume series, *Jewish Symbols in the Greco-Roman Period.*[177] His overall thesis has largely been discounted, however, by the course of subsequent scholarship.[178] Although Philo often uses the language of the mysteries, he does so more to present his own ancestral faith in language that would have been comprehensible to pagans. There is little evidence that Philo either consciously or unconsciously assimilated pagan mystery-cult beliefs.[179] Further, it is quite unlikely that the Theraputae in Philo represent a Jewish mystery sect.[180]

The Judaism of the inscriptions has proven much more debatable. On certain points, Goodenough's thesis of Jewish syncretism has been defended by subsequent scholarship, most notably with regard to (1) *astrological beliefs and practices,* and (2) *magic.* J. H. Charlesworth has recently argued that the two Jewish astrological documents preserved in Cave 4 at Qumran and documents such as the *Treatise of Shem* (which he dates to the first century B.C.) suggest that synagogal mosaics that include depictions of the zodiac demonstrate that the Jews of those locations had assimilated astrological beliefs. Charlesworth concludes, "These early Jewish astrological documents ... tend to swing the debate in Goodenough's direction."[181] There also appears to have been a significant amount of Jewish assimilation of pagan terms, concepts, and beliefs in the practice of magic. Of course the borrowing went both ways. It is impor-

---

[177] Erwin R. Goodenough, *Jewish Symbols in the Greco-Roman Period* (12 vols.; Bollingen Series 37; New York: Pantheon, 1953-1965).

[178] See the summary of research by G. Lease, "Jewish Mystery Cults Since Goodenough," *ANRW* II.20.2 (1987) 858-80, who concludes, "we must also acknowledge that the existence of a peculiarly Jewish mystery cult, conceptualized and patterned after the Hellenistic mystery cults, is without evidence and unsupportable." The most thorough—and devastating—critique of Goodenough's *Symbols* was published by A. D. Nock in a series of articles in *Gnomon.* The reviews have been reprinted by Z. Stewart, ed., in *Essays on Religion and the Ancient World* (Oxford: Clarendon, 1972), with the titles "Religious Symbols and Symbolism I, II, III," 877-94, 895-907, 908-18. M. Smith has also written a valuable review titled "Goodenough's *Jewish Symbols* in Retrospect," *JBL* 86 (1967) 53-68. On pp. 66-67, Smith gives a list of all the published reviews of Goodenough's *Symbols.*

[179] See especially H. A. Wolfson, *Philo: Foundations of Religious Philosophy in Judaism, Christianity, and Islam* (Cambridge, Mass.: Harvard University Press, 1947 [4th ed., 1968]) 1.27-55; Lease, "Jewish Mystery Cults," 870, 873; D. Sänger, *Antikes Judentum und die Mysterien* (WUNT 2/5; Tübingen: J.C.B. Mohr [Paul Siebeck], 1980) 216.

[180] Lease, "Jewish Mystery Cults," 870; Sänger, *Antikes Judentum,* 49, 216.

[181] J. H. Charlesworth, "Jewish Interest in Astrology During the Hellenistic and Roman Period," *ANRW* II.20.2 (1987) 926-50, esp. 945-46.

tant to recognize, however, that there was a real syncretism in the sphere of magical practices.[182]

The case for more extensive assimilation of pagan beliefs in a cultic context has rested largely on inscriptions attesting the worship of the deities *Theos Hypsistos* ("the highest god") and *Sabazios*. We have already interpreted three *Hypsistos* inscriptions in connection with our discussion of angel figures in Asia Minor (see Chapter 3). One of these was clearly Jewish, but in the other two we found no evidence of Jewish influence. The two inscriptions from Stratonicea express thanksgiving to Zeus Hypsistos and an angelic being (Ἀγαθὸς Ἄγγελος/Θεῖον Ἄγγελος) that we interpreted as referring to Hekate. These inscriptions are representative of a much larger group of *Hypsistos* inscriptions from Phrygia and Lydia.[183]

F. Cumont argued that the pagan use of *Hypsistos* was stimulated by the Jewish worship of Yahweh as *Hypsistos* in Asia Minor.[184] He further suggested that a few pagan *thiasoi* (cult associations) had arisen independently of the synagogues devoted to the worship of the Most High and assimilated many Jewish religious concepts into a syncretistic fusion of pagan and Jewish ideas.[185] Cumont's view has been accepted, in part, by M. P. Nilsson[186] and M. Hengel.[187]

In the mid 1930s, A. D. Nock argued against assuming Jewish influence in the majority of the *Hypsistos* inscriptions while at the same time noting that some of the texts do betray "the impact of Jewish or Judaizing culture."[188] Others, most notably A. T. Kraabel and P. Trebilco, have disputed this view and have argued vigorously against the supposition of this kind of syncretism in the Judaism of Asia Minor.[189] They have effectively

---

[182] See Nock, "Religious Symbols. I," 889-91.

[183] See F. Cumont, "Ὕψιστος," *PW* 9.444-50. For additional inscriptions, now see Drew-Bear and Naour, "Divinités de Phrygie," 2032-43.

[184] Cumont, *Oriental Religions,* 62-66; idem, "Les Mystères de Sabazius et le Judaïsme," *CRAIBL* (1906) 63-79, esp. 64-65, 73.

[185] Cumont, *Oriental Religions,* 162.

[186] Nilsson, *GGR,* 2.636-40.

[187] M. Hengel, *Judaism and Hellenism* (Philadelphia: Fortress, 1981) 1.263; 2.177, note 60.

[188] A. D. Nock, C. Roberts, and T. C. Skeat, "The Guild of Zeus Hypsistos," *HTR* 29 (1936) 61-69 (= *Essays on Religion in the Ancient World* [Oxford: Clarendon, 1972] 422-27). See also Drew-Bear and Naour, "Divinités de Phrygie," 2033-35; G. H. R. Horsley, *New Documents Illustrating Early Christianity. A Review of the Greek Inscriptions and Payri Published in 1976* (Macquarie University: The Ancient History Documentary Research Centre, 1981) 26.

[189] See P. Trebilco, *Jewish Communities in Asia Minor* (SNTSMS 69; Cambridge: University Press, 1991) esp. Chapter 6: "Theos Hypsistos and Sabazios — Syncretism in

argued: (1) that ὕψιστος was used of pagan deities throughout the Roman world and that the term, therefore, does not necessarily reflect Jewish LXX usage; (2) that the term ἄγγελος was used by pagans, again without necessarily reflecting Jewish influence; (3) that ὕψιστος would have been a natural way to refer to the all-powerful deity in the tendency toward monotheism in the pagan religious beliefs of Asia Minor; and, (4) that it is best to discern other corroborating Jewish motifs on an inscription before concluding it is Jewish or Jewish-influenced strictly on the basis of the presence of the term *Hypsistos* (and perhaps also the presence of the term ἄγγελος).

The debate on the fact or extent of Jewish influence on the cult of *Theos Hypsistos* in Asia Minor is not yet over. Kraabel and Trebilco have struck out too far in denying the possibility of Jewish influence on some pagan *thiasoi* who worshiped *Theos Hypsistos.* One cannot be dogmatic on this issue, especially when there are clearly established tendencies for pagans to borrow from Jews in the sphere of magic.

Unfortunately, we know very little about the actual cultic worship of *Theos Hypsistos* in Asia Minor. We do not know, for instance, whether a mystery initiation rite was established in the cult or what kind of rituals and practice went along with the worship of this deity. It is important, however, to point out that the dedicants to *Theos Hypsistos* did not conceive of him as an abstract deity; they were predominantly concerned about the affairs of daily life—their cattle and their crops.[190]

F. Cumont and others have also argued that the Asia Minor cult of Sabazios (Σαβάζιος) represents the identification of the Jewish "Lord of Hosts" (LXX = κύριος Σαβαώθ) with a local Phrygian-Thracian deity (Sabazios) also identified with the Phrygian Jupiter and Dionysus.[191] In-

---

Judaism in Asia Minor," 127-44; A. T. Kraabel, "Hypsistos and the Synagogue at Sardis," *GRBS* 10 (1969) 81-93; idem, "The Roman Diaspora: Six Questionable Assumptions," *JJS* 33 (1982) 445-64, esp. 450-51; idem, "The Diaspora Synagogue: Archaeological and Epigraphic Evidence Since Sukenik," *ANRW* II.19.1 (1979) 477-510, esp. 491-93; idem, "Paganism and Judaism: The Sardis Evidence," in *Paganisme, Judaïsme, Christianisme. Influences et Affrontements dans le Monde Antique, Mélanges offerts à Marcel Simon,* (eds. A. Benoit, M. Philonenko, & C. Vogel; Paris: Éditions E. de Boccard, 1978) 13-33.

[190] Drew-Bear and Naour, "Divinités de Phrygie," 2034-35. They point, for example, to a Phrygian inscription (from Nacoleia) where the dedicant was concerned about the deliverance of his cattle; *MAMA* 5 (no. 212): Γάϊος Μανου ὑπὲρ βοῶν σωτηρίας τῶν ἰδί[ων π]άντων [Ὑψ]ίστῳ εὐχήν.

[191] Cumont, *Oriental Religions,* 64; idem, "Les Mystères de Sabazius," 63-79. So also Reitzenstein, *Mystery-Religions,* 123-25.

scriptional attestation for this cult is quite rare in Asia Minor and problematic—facts that should temper anyone's conclusions regarding the precise nature of this cult.

Recent scholarship has once again questioned the validity of Cumont's conclusion. Much of the debate has centered around the interpretation of a passage from Valerius Maximus that appeared to give evidence that there were Jews in Rome who worshipped Jupiter Sabazios around 139 B.C. (Valerius Maximus, *Epitome,* 1.3.3).[192] A recent study of the passage by E. N. Lane has demonstrated that it is better to take the passage as indicating two distinct groups: Jews and also worshippers of Sabazios.[193] Cumont also drew attention to a third-century A.D. tomb in Rome of a certain Vincentius who was a priest of Sabazios. One panel on the tomb depicts a winged figure called *angelus bonus.* Because Cumont assumed that angel terminology was not used in paganism, he found this to be a further example of Jewish influence on the cult, most probably representing the archangel Michael who would guide the soul of the just to the other world.[194] We have already demonstrated in Chapter 3, however, that pagans in Asia Minor (and, therefore, elsewhere) did use the term ἄγγελος.[195] Still other evidence points away from the conclusion that Sabazios represents a Jewish-pagan mixed cult.[196]

Sabazios was, nevertheless, a popular deity in Phrygia. Similar to Men, with whom he was sometimes identified, Sabazios was worshipped as the protector of the people of the Phrygian countryside.[197]

It now appears that there is a very slim basis for espousing the existence of any form of Jewish mystery cult in Asia Minor, especially by appealing to the worship of Theos Hypsistos and Sabazios. These appear to be pagan cults that, in some instances, use terminology in common with Judaism. Furthermore, the evidence from Philo does not corroborate the notion of a Jewish mystery cult. It is therefore unlikely that the advocates of the Colossian "philosophy" drew any of their mystery cult terms, concepts, or beliefs from an alleged Jewish mystery cult. On the other hand, because of the prominence of the cults of Theos Hypsistos and Sabazios in

---

[192] The text is cited and discussed in Hengel, *Judaism and Hellenism,* 1.263.

[193] E. N. Lane, "Sabazius and the Jews in Valerius Maximus: A Re-examination," *JRS* 69 (1979) 35-38. See also Trebilco, *Jewish Communities,* 140-41.

[194] Cumont, "Les Mystère de Sabazius," 72-74; idem, *Oriental Religions,* 64-65.

[195] Trebilco, *Jewish Communities,* 141, also rejects Cumont's claim that the representation of a banquet and the inscription "eat, drink, relax, and come to me," reflect the Jewish belief in a messianic banquet.

[196] See Trebilco, *Jewish Communities,* 140-42.

[197] See W. Fauth, "Sabazios," *KP* 4.1479.

Phrygia, it is not impossible that Gentile Christians espousing the Colossian "philosophy" may have been drawing on what they have learned in these cults.

On the issue of Jewish syncretism, I would contend that P. Trebilco has overstated his case when he concludes, "No evidence has arisen from this study to suggest that Judaism in Asia Minor was syncretistic or had been compromised by paganism. This is a very important finding."[198] This overlooks the evidence coming from Jewish astrological and magical beliefs, where there are clear instances of Jewish assimilation of pagan names, terms, concepts, and practices.[199] Thus, this form of Judaism becomes highly significant for our study.

10. Conclusion

(1) Our investigation of the term ἐμβατεύω has reaffirmed the earlier conclusions of W. M. Ramsay and M. Dibelius that (a) a technical usage of the term for the second stage of mystery initiation is clearly attested in the inscriptions from the Apollo temple at Claros, and (b) this technical usage of the term is the appropriate meaning for its use in Col. 2:18. The preceding clause, "the things he has seen" (ἃ ἑώρακεν), should be seen as the object of the participle ἐμβατεύων. The combination should thus be translated, "entering the things he had seen." This would be a technical way of summarizing the initiate's entry into the holy chamber of the temple, where the priest would have led the person through a whole series of ecstatic visionary experiences (perhaps including ascent to heaven and/or

---

[198] Trebilco, *Jewish Communities,* 142.

[199] I would offer the same criticism of some of the comments made by A. T. Kraabel. In his essay, "The Roman Diaspora: Six Questionable Assumptions," *JJS* 33 (1982) 450-51, the first assumption he questions is that "the Jewish Diaspora was *syncretistic*" [italics his]. In his development of the point, he only discusses the alleged syncretism reflected in the cults of Sabazios and Theos Hypsistos. At the minimum, he needs to clarify his definition of syncretism as well as to discuss the apparent syncretism in Jewish magic. He had no difficulty using the term to describe the phenomena he observed in Anatolian Judaism in his 1968 dissertation (A. T. Kraabel, "Judaism in Asia Minor Under the Roman Empire with a Preliminary Study of the Jewish Community at Sardis, Lydia" [Unpublished Doctoral Dissertation; Harvard: March, 1968] 145-46). There he indicts Anatolian Judaism as already participating in the "typical Lydian-Phrygian piety" and appears to agree with M. Simon, who suggests that in certain syncretistic Jewish groups, Judaism's basic monotheism was placed in serious danger by speculation regarding angels.

descent to the underworld). The initiation thus served as the basis of the knowledge and authority for the opponents to judge the Colossians—those in the faction had been initiated, seen the visions, and learned from them. This mystery rite may have signified the beginning of a new and victorious life experience for the initiate in relationship to the hostile powers—the chains of fate had been broken and a new power for warding off hostile spirits had been received.

(2) The quotation of this phrase from the teaching of "the philosophy" indicates that the competing teaching had some connection to mystery initiation. There is too little information in the context to know precisely what this connection may have been. At the minimum it seems to indicate that the advocates of "the philosophy" had gone through ritual initiation and were extolling the benefits of this ecstatic visionary experience. Can we imply more than this? Is it possible that the faction was going so far as to encourage Christians to pursue initiation into one of the Phrygian cults for additional protection from the powers? Were they in the process of establishing an actual Christian mystery initiation rite? The meager evidence may not be sufficient to satisfy our curiosity.

(3) The combination of Christianity with Phrygian mystery cult practice represents a rather bold syncretism. Rather than renouncing their past cultic involvements and beliefs (cf. 1 Thess 1:9: "you turned to God from the idols"), the advocates of "the philosophy" appeared to have embraced certain pagan beliefs and rituals—indeed even mystery initiation—as valuable for their Christian experience. For them, this was not a private matter. The opponents were attempting to foist their beliefs on the rest of the Colossian congregation. They apparently showed great disdain for those who did not follow their practices.

(4) Perhaps the most significant reason the opponents have retained and advocate certain pagan rituals and practices is their fear of evil spiritual powers. The apotropaic function that many of the local deities played heightens this prospect (e.g. the role played by the Clarian Apollo in averting a plague caused by evil powers). This would also fit well with the conclusions we reached about why the Colossians were invoking angels (Part I). Ritual initiation was one more means by which they could avert the hostile activity of astral, terrestrial, and underworld powers. Just as the initiate in the Mithras Liturgy could ascend to heaven and gain a vision of the evil powers changing from a mode of hostility to a mode of favor, others could gain this kind of protection from the foul spirits.

(5) The Hekate traditions of Asia Minor prove very relevant to our investigation by furthering the conclusions we reached in PART I. The fear

of evil spirits prompted many people in Phrygia, Caria, and Lydia to call on Hekate for help and protection. She was invoked as an *angelos*. There is even some evidence of Jewish involvement in this practice.

(6) The local cults, the "Mithras Liturgy," and the Isis initiation rite as reported by Apuleius not only provide background for understanding the meaning of initiation and the role it may have played in the Colossian "philosophy," they also may provide some important insight into other facets of the competing teaching. The evidence is informative on the following points: (a) the initiation liturgies could be referred to as "tradition"; (b) the four elements and the stars (also referred to as elements) are viewed as hostile, personal powers; (c) there were often dietary and purity regulations—ascetic practices—imposed on initiates; these could be phrased in prohibitory commands; (d) angelic beings and mediator figures are prominent in most of these traditions; in some cases they were worshipped or called upon for protection as in the "Mithras Liturgy"; (e) the local cults celebrated a variety of festivals; (f) the cult of Men Tyrannos specifically celebrated a new moon festival; (g) the bodily mutilations associated with the Cybele cult could contribute to our understanding of ἀφειδία σώματος in Col 2:23; and, (h) many of the mystery cults were viewed as voluntary associations, which may help to explain ἐθελοθρησκία in Col 2:23.

Chapter 6

Hostile Powers: The Problem of the *Stoicheia*

1. The Prominence of the Powers in Colossians

Many interpreters have rightly pointed to the hostile angelic powers as central to a proper interpretation of the letter. Hans-Martin Schenke, for example, has observed that the primary objective of the author was to set down for the readers the relationship of Christ to the powers. The author was not elaborating on this topic out of pure theological reflection, but was compelled to address it because of a concrete situation in which the readers faced a "false, heretical definition of the relationship of Christ to the powers."[1] Most would agree with Schenke up to this point but many would part ways with him over the precise role the powers play in the teaching of "the philosophy."

Do these references to the powers point to a Gnostic interpretation of the problem at Colossae? Was there possibly a pagan *stoicheia* cult that was influencing the church? Should these angelic powers be understood in the more positive sense of angels surrounding the throne (or divine chariot) of God?

Angelic powers hold a prominent place in Colossians. They are referred to as many as twelve times in the first two chapters of the letter with six different terms employed. The first supernatural power we encounter is the evil "authority of darkness" (ἐξουσία τοῦ σκότους) from whose grip believers have been rescued (1:13). The Christ-hymn (1:16) introduces us to four other categories of angelic powers when the author expands the expression "the invisible beings" (τὰ ἀόρατα). For him these are "thrones" (θρόνοι), "lordships" (κυριότητες), and the "principalities and authorities" (ἀρχαὶ καὶ ἐξουσίαι). He then refers to the "principalities and authorities" two more times in the second chapter of Colossians (2:10, 15). In 2:18, the writer specifically uses the word

---

[1] Hans-Martin Schenke, "Der Widerstreit gnostischer und kirchlicher Christologie im Spiegel des Kolosserbriefes," *ZTK* 61 (1964) 391.

"angel" (ἄγγελος). Finally, he speaks of τὰ στοιχεῖα τοῦ κόσμου in 2:8 and 20—an expression that is disputed, but which we understand to be a reference to hostile angelic powers. This extraordinary concentration of references to angelic powers in the span of just 52 verses points to the importance of investigating their meaning both for the writer and for the readers of the letter. This chapter will concentrate on interpreting the meaning of *stoicheia*. The final chapter will provide an exposition of Paul's response to the situation involving the powers at Colossae.

2. The Issue

The role of the *stoicheia* has often been accorded a significant place in descriptions of the competing teaching at Colossae. Martin Dibelius made the term the most important foundation in putting together the varied strands of evidence regarding "the philosophy." He argued for the presence in Colossae of a "cult of the elements" that Christians joined as a means of double insurance against the liabilities of the cosmic tyrants of fate.[2] Similarly, Günther Bornkamm observed that, "the first and most important part of the Colossian heresy is, according to 2:8, 20, its teaching about the cosmic elements."[3] Both of these interpreters have argued for a personal interpretation, taking the *stoicheia* to refer to cosmic spirit powers. This viewpoint has proven compelling to most interpreters.[4] Still nu-

---

[2] Martin Dibelius, "The Isis Initiation in Apuleius and Related Initiatory Rites," in *Conflict*, 82, 90.

[3] Günther Bornkamm, "The Heresy of Colossians," in *Conflict*, 123, 130-31.

[4] See, for example, the following interpreters (beginning with the most recent): D. G. Reid, "Elements/Elemental Spirits of the World," in *DPL*, 232; Martin, *Colossians* (Interpretation), 84-86; idem, *Colossians* (NCB) 10-14, 79; Lindemann, *Kolosserbrief*, 40; O'Brien, *Colossians*, 132; A. T. Lincoln, *Paradise Now and Not Yet* (SNTSMS 43; Cambridge: University Press, 1981) 114; Gnilka, *Kolosserbrief*, 127; J. J. Gunther, *St. Paul's Opponents and Their Background*, (NovTSup 35; Leiden: Brill, 1973) 177-79; H.-F. Weiß, "Gnostische Motive und antignostische Polemik im Kolosser- und im Epheserbrief," in *Gnosis und Neues Testament* (ed. K. -W. Tröger; Gütersloh: Gerd Mohn, 1973) 312-13; O. Böcher, *Christus Exorcista. Dämonismus und Taufe im Neuen Testament* (BZANT 16; Stuttgart, 1972) 20-32, 171; J. Lähnemann, *Der Kolosserbrief. Komposition, Situation und Argumentation* (SNT 3; Gütersloh: Mohn, 1971) 79-80; Lohse, *Colossians*, 99; J. Y. Lee, "Interpreting the Demonic Powers in Pauline Thought," *NovT* 12 (1970) 61-62; H. J. Gabathuler, *Jesus Christus: Haupt der Kirche—Haupt der Welt*, ATANT 45 (Zürich: Zwingli, 1965) 168; Conzelmann, *Kolosser*, 190 (although he emphasizes that the *stoicheia* are the members of the body of the macroanthropos); H.

merous differences exist among these interpreters regarding whether the *stoicheia* refer to spirits governing the physical elements ("elemental spirits"), spirits over the sun, moon, planets, and stars ("astral spirits"), a gnostic interpretation that sees the spirits as the heavenly powers comprising the "fullness" (πλήρωμα), or simply evil angels and demons.

More recently, however, many interpreters who have emphasized a Jewish mystical interpretation of the problem at Colossae—describing the teaching as a mystical ascent to heaven to worship with the angels around the throne of God—have devalued the importance of the term *stoicheia* for understanding the teaching. In his influential study on the background of the Colossian conflict, F. O. Francis completely neglects treating the role of the *stoicheia* — a glaring weakness of his study (if for no other reason than to attempt to demonstrate that the term *stoicheia* is exegetically insignificant).[5] Christopher Rowland, who follows in substance the interpretation of Francis, never refers to the role of the *stoicheia* in his treatment of the teaching at Colossae.[6] Similarly, Thomas Sappington treats the *stoicheia* passages as "only secondary evidence for discerning the error at Colossae" and argues for a "principial" interpretation of the expression, i.e. the religious ABC's of this world reflecting a spiritual infancy.[7]

Schlier, *Principalities and Powers in the New Testament* (London: Burns & Oates, 1961) 23-24; A. Lumpe, "Elementum," *RAC* 4.1089-1092; C. Maurer, "Die Begründung der Herrschaft Christi über die Mächte nach Kol. 1,15-20," *Wort und Dienst* N.S. 4 (1955) 81; G. H. C. MacGregor, "Principalities and Powers: The Cosmic Background of Saint Paul's Thought," *NTS* 1 (1954) 21-22; B. Noack, *Satanás und Sotería. Untersuchungen zur Neutestamentlichen Dämonologie* (Kobenhavn, 1948) 124; Scott, *Colossians,* 42-43; K. L. Schmidt, "Die Natur- und Geistkräfte bei Paulus," *Eranos Jahrbuch* 14 (1946) 136; L. E. Scheu, *Die "Weltelemente" beim Apostel Paulus (Gal. 4,3.9 und Kol. 2,8.20)* (Universitas Catholica Americae 37; Washington: Catholic University of America, 1933) 102-21; W. M. Ramsay, "The Mysteries in Their Relation to St. Paul," *Contemporary Review* 104 (1913) 208; Dibelius-Greeven, *Kolosser,* 27-29; F. Pfister, "Die στοιχεῖα τοῦ κόσμου in den Briefen des Apostels Paulus," *Philologus* 69 (1910) 411-27 (Pfister comments that the Pauline use of the term is best explained by the use of the term in the magical papyri; see p. 420); M. Dibelius, *Die Geisterwelt im Glauben des Paulus* (Göttingen: Vandenhoeck & Ruprecht, 1909) 78-85, 227-30; A. Deissmann, "Elements," *Encyclopaedia Biblica* (London: Adam & Charles Black, 1901) 2.1901; H. Diels, *Elementum* (Leipzig: Teubner, 1899) 50-55; O. Everling, *Die paulinische Angelologie und Dämonologie* (Göttingen: Vandenhoeck & Ruprecht, 1888) 66-76; et al.

[5] Fred O. Francis, "Humility and Angelic Worship in Col 2:18," in *Conflict,* 163-95.

[6] Christopher Rowland, "Apocalyptic Visions and the Exaltation of Christ in the Letter to the Colossians," *JSNT* 19 (1983) 73-83.

[7] Thomas J. Sappington, *Revelation and Redemption at Colossae* (JSNTS 53; Sheffield: Sheffield Academic Press, 1991) 164-70. Most interpreters who follow Francis's

Others also have understood στοιχεῖα τοῦ κόσμου in a non-personal sense. Some see in it a reference to the basic principles common to all religion,[8] the domain of Jewish ritual and worship,[9] the domain of flesh, sin, and death,[10] intermediaries such as the Jewish law or pagan deities that stand between God and humanity,[11] or even the actual physical elements[12] that may represent the foundational cosmological principles and, thus, the intellectual basis for the Colossian "philosophy."[13]

The term *stoicheia* appears only four times in the Pauline corpus, twice in Galatians and twice in Colossians (Gal. 4:3, 9; Col. 2:8, 20). Three issues need to be settled in order to arrive at an accurate appraisal of the meaning of the expression in Colossians: (1) What is the relevant background to the term in Colossians given its broad and diverse usage in the literature of antiquity? Related to this is the question of whether there is any evidence for the use of the term to denote spirit beings prior to the second century A.D. (2) What is the meaning of the term in Gal 4:3, 9, and is that usage determinative for its usage in Colossians? (3) Was the expression an integral part of the teaching and thus the theology of the

---

overall approach to the Colossian problem as reflecting Jewish mystical ascent to heaven also devalue the importance of the στοιχεῖα and adopt a "principial" interpretation. See, for example, Wesley Carr, *Angels and Principalities* (SNTSMS 42; Cambridge: University Press, 1981) 75.

[8] G. Delling, "στοιχεῖον," *TDNT* 7.685; W. Wink, *Naming the Powers* (Philadelphia: Fortress, 1984) 72; Moule, *Colossians,* 92. See also Lightfoot, *Colossians,* 180.

[9] Eadie, *Colossians,* 134-35.

[10] A. J. Bandstra, *The Law and the Elements of the World* (Kampen: J. H. Kok N. V., 1964) 68-69; Josef Blinzler, "Lexikalisches zu dem Terminus τὰ στοιχεῖα τοῦ κόσμου," *Studiorum Paulinorum Congressus Internationalis Catholicus* II (Rome: Pontifical Biblical Institute, 1963) 442.

[11] Pokorný, *Colossians,* 113-14, 152.

[12] E. Schweizer, "Die 'Elemente der Welt' Gal 4, 3.9; Kol 2, 8.20," *Verborum Veritas,* (FS. G. Stählin; Wuppertal: Brockhaus, 1970) 245-59, and now, more recently in his article, "Slaves of the Elements and Worshipers of Angels: Gal 4:3, 9 and Col 2:8, 18, 20," *JBL* 107 (1988) 455-68, sees the Colossian "philosophy" as influenced by neopythagorean ideas and interprets the στοιχεῖα as referring to the four Empedoclean elements (earth, air, fire, and water). N. Kehl, *Der Christushymnus im Kolosserbrief,* (SBS 1; Stuttgart, 1967) 70-74, 138ff., finds the physical elements playing a role in a teaching about the knowledge of God based on the works of creation, however, the heathen have substituted the worship of God for the worship of the creation (cf. Rom. 1:23). See also D. Rusam, "Neue Belege zu den στοιχεῖα τοῦ κόσμου," *ZNW* 83 (1992) 119-25.

[13] R. DeMaris, *The Colossian Controversy* (JSNTSS 96; Sheffield: JSOT Press, 1994) 83; idem, "Element, Elemental Spirit," in *ABD* 2.445.

opponents at Colossae, or does it reflect Paul's own thought as applied to the situation?

3. The Religions-Historical Background

Josef Blinzler has provided an excellent summary of the usage of *stoicheia*.[14] He suggests the following nine categories to describe the semantic range of the term:

1. Letters, characters
2. The alphabet, ABC's
3. The foundation or principles of a science or institution
4. The rudiments or initial basis for something
5. The physical elements (usually earth, air, fire, and water)
6. Fundamentals
7. The planets and stars
8. Spirits of the physical elements, star-spirits
9. Demons, spirits

It is certainly not necessary to rehearse the evidence that Blinzler (and others) has already set forth to illustrate these various uses of the term. It is my contention that the contexts of Col 2:8 and 20 (as well as Gal 4:3, 9) point toward categories 8 and 9—a personal interpretation of *stoicheia* as spirits/angels—as the most likely meaning of the term. I would also contend that there is ample evidence to demonstrate that *stoicheia* was used in this sense in the religious vocabulary of both Jews and pagans in the mid-first century. In the following section, I will endeavor to provide a deeper and more illuminating discussion of *stoicheia* as spirit beings than is found in Blinzler. In the exegesis of Colossians 2:8 and 20, I will demonstrate why this background is the most relevant given the nature of the teaching of the opponents and the meaning of the Pauline polemic.

---

[14] Blinzler, "Lexikalisches," 429-43. See his bibliography for additional studies. See also Lumpe, "Elementum," 1073-1100.

a. Babylonian, Persian, and Greek Antecedents

The Babylonians worshipped the four elements—earth, air, fire, and water—as divine cosmic powers long before the first century, as F. Cumont explains:

> The domain of the divine god did not end at the zone of the moon, which is nearest to us. The Chaldeans also worshipped, as beneficent or formidable powers, the Earth, whether fruitful or barren, the Ocean and the Waters, that fertilise or devastate, the Winds which blow from the four points of the horizon, and Fire which warms and devours. They confounded with the stars under the generic name of Elements (στοιχεῖα) these primordial forces, ...[15]

In Babylon, the sun, moon, planets, and stars were also connected with special gods.[16] These astral deities had no special cult, but came to be connected with the mystery religions—especially Mithraism, which had more astral elements than the others.

The Persian worship of the four physical elements as well as the sun and the moon is attested by Herodotus and Strabo (Herodotus 1.31; Strabo 15.3.13).[17] The Arabic tradition of Al-Biruni reports that the Persians worshiped the sun, moon, planets, and the elements before Zoroaster (the eighth or ninth century B.C. or earlier).[18] Still other Persian sources refer to the worship of the four elements as deities.[19] This influence can be seen in Dio Chrysostom (from Prusa, Bithynia, Asia Minor) when he refers to the four elements as the four immortal and divine horses of Zeus, a concept that he explicitly adapted from the teaching of the magi (Dio Chrysostom 36.39-54).[20] This kind of divinization of the elements, however, was even present in Greek thought. Empedocles (5th c. B.C.), for instance, equated Zeus with fire, Hera with air, Hades with earth, and Nestis with water (see also Xenocrates, fragment 15.23).[21]

---

[15] Franz Cumont, *Astrology and Religion among the Greeks and Romans* (New York & London: G. P. Putnam's, 1912) 34; see pp. 1-35 for an extended discussion of the Chaldean background.

[16] Günter Haufe, "Hellenistische Volksfrömmigkeit," *Umwelt des Urchristentums,* I: Darstellung des neutestamentlichen Zeitalters (Berlin: Evangelische Verlagsanstalt, 1971) 83. See also Nilsson, *GGR,* 2.497, and Lumpe, "Elementum," 1081-82.

[17] See Lumpe, "Elementum," 1081, who also cites the reports of Theodoret, *Historia Ecclesiastica* 5.39.5, and *Epistulae* 82.

[18] Lumpe, "Elementum," 1081.

[19] Lumpe, "Elementum," 1081-82.

[20] See Schweizer, "Die 'Elemente der Welt,'" 248 and Lähnemann, *Kolosserbrief,* 92-94.

[21] Empedocles, Fragment 6 (as summarized in Lumpe, "Elementum," 1081). Although

The cult of Mithras has often been seen as important background to understanding the use of *stoicheia* in Asia Minor.[22] Central to Mithraism is the belief in seven planetary gods parallel to which are seven grades of initiation into the cult. Initiates hoped that, on the day of their death, their souls would successfully traverse the seven planetary spheres and arrive at the sphere of the fixed stars, their true home.[23] F. Cumont argued that Asia Minor was actually the place where Mithraism as a religion developed. He notes that communities of Magi, who brought with them their Persian Mazdaism, settled throughout Asia Minor including Galatia, Phrygia, and Lydia.[24] As Rome extended her conquests into Asia Minor in the first century B.C., the West began to have contact with the developing Mithraic religion.[25]

Cumont's views were subsequently adopted by scholars of the History of Religions School, where they held sway for many years. More recent scholarship, however, has largely dismantled many key features of Cumont's interpretation.[26] The Asia Minor origin and development of the cult has been called into question for, among other reasons, the fact that only four Mithraic monuments have been discovered there with the earliest dating to A.D. 150.[27] A pre-Christian date for the origin of Mithraic religion remains an issue. The earliest evidence of the presence of Mithraism in the west is the testimony of a passage in Dio Cassius (63.1-7) describing the visit of Tiridates, king of Armenia, to Nero in A.D. 66 where he makes known his worship of Mithras. In addition, the earliest

---

Schweizer, "Slaves of the Elements," 456-57, cites part of this fragment, he neglects mentioning this divinization of the elements.

[22] Note for instance Scheu, *"Weltelemente,"* 44-46, 112-116.

[23] For a concise description of Mithraic beliefs, see R. Merkelbach, "Mithras, Mithraism," in *ABD* 4.878. See also idem, *Mithras* (Königstein/Ts.: Verlag Anton Hain, 1984).

[24] F. Cumont, *Oriental Religions in Roman Paganism* (New York: Dover, 1956) 139, 143.

[25] For a concise presentation of his view, Cumont, *Oriental Religions,* 138-49. For a more extensive presentation, see his *The Mysteries of Mithra* (New York: Dover, 1956), and *Textes et monuments figurés relatifs aux mystères de Mithra* (2 vols.; Brussels: H. Lamertin, 1896-99).

[26] E. Yamauchi, *Persia and the Bible* (Grand Rapids: Eerdmans, 1990) notes, "Cumont's interpretations have been analyzed and rejected on all major points." See also R. Beck, "Mithraism Since Franz Cumont," *ANRW* II.17.4 (1984) 2002-2115, and D. Ulansey, "Mithraic Studies: A Paradigm Shift?" *Recherches de Science Religieuse* 13 (1987) 104-10.

[27] Yamauchi, *Persia,* 508.

Mithraic inscription in the West dates to the early second century A.D.[28]
E. Yamauchi thus observes, "Most scholars conclude that Mithraism,
which developed at the earliest late in the first century A.D., could not
have influenced nascent Christianity.[29] For our purposes, this evidence
makes it unlikely that the concepts of Mithraism informed popular usage
of *stoicheia* in Asia Minor in the mid-first century A.D.

Nevertheless, Persian influence on the religious and cosmological
thought in Asia Minor is still demonstrable, as we have already seen with
Dio Chrysostom. With this in mind, we may point to one other line of
evidence attesting the personal interpretation of *stoicheia* in the East. On
the basis of four passages from a Syriac work titled, *Περὶ Εἱμαρμένης*
(*Concerning Fate*) or *The Book of the Laws of the Countries,* ascribed to
Bardaisan of Edessa (A.D. 154-222) by patristic writers, W. Hatch demonstrated that *stoicheia* was commonly used in Mesopotamia in the second
and third centuries A.D. for "personal cosmic powers."[30] If the term was
in common currency in this sense in the second century, it is not unreasonable to suppose that the beginning of this usage took place in the first
century or prior.

Numerous texts from Greek literature could be cited that illustrate the
use of *stoicheia* for divinized heavenly bodies or the spirits that stand behind the sun, moon, planets, and stars: See, for example, Pseudo-
Callisthenes 1.12 and 1.1.3; the Hermetic fragment Κόρη Κόσμου of Hermes Trismegistus (in Stobaeus 1.49.44); Diogenes Laertius 6.102 ("an Ar-
cadian hat on his head with the twelve signs of the zodiac inwrought in
it")[31]; Vettius Valens 7.5 ("I conjure you by Helios and Selene, and by the
courses of the five stars, … and by the four *stoicheia*")[32]; Simplicius, *in
Cael.* 1.3 (θεοὶ στοιχειοκράτορες); *Corp. Herm.* 13.20 and 1.17; Pseudo-
Manetho, *Astrol.* 4; Eust. *ad Homeri,* 11.17.[33] H. Diels points out that the
noun στοιχείωσις was used in Tatian (second century A.D.) for the mate-

---

[28] Yamauchi, *Persia,* 510.

[29] Yamauchi, *Persia,* 518.

[30] W. H. P. Hatch, "Τὰ Στοιχεῖα in Paul and Bardaisan," *JTS* 28 (1927) 181-82.
This study is cited approvingly in MM, 591. One of the passages is as follows: "But I
[i.e. Bardaisan] say that God and the Angels and the Powers and the Governors and the
Elements and men and animals have this power; but to all these orders of which I have
spoken power is not given in everything" (Hatch, Τὰ Στοιχεῖα, 182).

[31] "Πῖλος Ἀρκαδικὸς ἐπὶ τῆς κεφαλῆς ἔχων ἐνυφασμένα τὰ δώδεκα στοιχεῖα."

[32] "Ὁρκίζω σε Ἥλιον καὶ Σελήνην καὶ τῶν πέντε ἀστέρων τοὺς δρόμους
φύσιν τε καὶ πρόνοιαν καὶ τὰ τέσσαρα στοιχεῖα μὴ ταχέως τινὶ μεταδοῦναι κτλ."

[33] These and other texts are cited and discussed in Lohse, *Colossians,* 96-99, Lumpe,
"Elementum," 1082-84, and Pfister, "Die στοιχεῖα," 411-27.

rialization of the astrological star spirits.[34] While it is true that all of these texts date to the second century and later, it is unimaginable that some of these astrological traditions incorporating the use of *stoicheia* for star spirits would not date to the first century A.D. or prior.

b. The Milieu of Magic and Astrology

If we continue to follow the lead of the previous chapters and explore the religious milieu of magic and astrology for insight into the meaning of *stoicheia* , we find a substantial amount of material that makes use of the term. The four elements—earth, air, fire, and water—are explicitly named as the *stoicheia* in one passage in Preisendanz's collection of magical papyri. The second-century A.D. *PGM* XVIIb.15 addresses the god Hermes as the one who rules over the elements (στοιχεῖα): fire, air, water, and earth (see also *PGM* LXII.15).

That the four elements are often identified as deities is made clear in the so-called "Mithras Liturgy" (*PGM* IV.475-829). The mortal initiate invokes the immortal "Beginning" (Γένεσις and Ἀρχή) to begin the process of his apotheosis. He then invokes "spirit," "fire," "water," "earth," and ultimately the "perfect body" (σῶμα τέλειον). R. Reitzenstein correctly notes that the initiate invokes these "not as the elements that are in him but as their divine prototypes, actual deities."[35]

The term *stoicheia* is used most commonly in the magical texts in connection with stars and/or the spirit entities (or gods) they represent. In the Great Paris Magical Papyrus, the constellation of the Bear (Arktos) is given the epithet στοιχεῖον: "Bear, greatest goddess, ruling heaven, reigning over the pole of the stars, highest, beautiful-shining goddess, incorruptible element (στοιχεῖον ἄφθαρτον) ... you who stand on the pole, you whom the lord god appointed to turn the holy pole with a strong hand ..." (*PGM* IV.1301-07). The invocation is part of a "Bear charm that accomplishes anything" (line 1275). Elsewhere in the Paris Papyrus, the στοιχεῖα are explicitly connected with spirits: "Hail, revolution of untiring service by heavenly bodies (στοιχείων) ... Hail, all spirits of the aerial images (ἀερίων εἰδώλων πνεύματα)" (*PGM* IV.1126-35).

Also in the Paris Papyrus, Helios is hymned as the one "from whom, indeed, all elements (στοιχεῖα) have been arranged to suit your laws

---

[34] See Diels, *Elementum*, 54-55.

[35] Richard Reitzenstein, *Hellenistic Mystery Religions* (PTMS 15; Pittsburgh: Pickwick, 1978) 280.

which nourish all the world with its four yearly turning points" (*PGM* IV.440-41; see also IV.1961). Toward the end of the text, Horus (equated with Helios) is invoked as the name "which is in number equivalent to those of the Moirai (fate):

αχαιφω θωθω φιαχα αιη ηια ιαη ηια θωθω φιαχα
(lines 455-56; see also IV.1986).

This series of thirty-six characters forms a palindrome that one can say forwards and backwards. Wilhelm Gundel has suggested that these thirty-six letters represent the astral decans that rule over every ten degrees of the heavens.[36] Given one of the common usages of στοιχεῖα as letters of the alphabet, it is easy to see how the term could be applied to these magical letters as representing the decans. Here they are thought of as subject to Helios, who is called upon to make effective a recipe for love magic.

The concept of "decans" is in the oldest astrological handbooks. It is known in Greek inscriptions of the third century B.C. and was also used of astral gods in Rome during the first century B.C. (see Manilius 4.298, 372).[37] It is of special significance for our interpretation of Colossians to note that the decans could also be referred to as "angels." Gundel observes, "the Egyptian designations 'star attendants' and 'envoys of Isis-Hathor' correspond to the Hellenistic characterizations 'Archangels,' 'Angels,' 'Archdemons,' and 'Mighty Demons,' ἀρχάγγελοι, ἄγγελοι, ἀρχιδαίμονες and κραταιοὶ δαίμονες."[38] There are a few texts that make the connection explicit, for example: χαίρουσι ἀρχάγγελοι δεκανῶν, ἀγγέλων (*PGM* XIII.328-29 [from the so-called "Eighth Book of Moses"]);[39] Helios is ὁ κτίσας δεκανοὺς κ[ρα]ταιοὺς καὶ ἀρχαγγέλους (*PGM* I.208); similarly, ὁ κτίσας θεοὺς καὶ ἀρχαγγέλους καὶ δεκανούς (*PGM* IV.1202-04).[40] J. G. Gager thus comments: "angels and archangels were thought to command and control not only spirits and demons

---

36 Wilhelm Gundel, *Dekane und Dekansternbilder. Ein Beitrag zur Geschichte der Sternbilder der Kulturvölker* (2d ed.; Darmstadt: Wissenschaftliche Buchgesellschaft, 1969) 27; see also pp. 68-70.

37 Gundel, *Dekane*, 28.

38 Gundel, *Dekane*, 27-28.

39 Gundel, *Dekane*, 28, note 1. The text is also discussed in A. Dieterich, *Abrasax. Studien zur Religionsgeschichte des spätern Altertums* (Leipzig: Teubner, 1891) 192, note 20.

40 See the discussion in Reitzenstein, *Mystery Religions,* 457. He contends that there is an ancient pre-Christian base to the text that was later influenced by Jewish magical literature.

generally, but the thirty-six decans specifically—that is, the thirty-six equally divided portions, also known as world rulers, of the heavenly sphere or zodiac according to Egyptian astrological tradition."[41]

We saw above (in *PGM* IV.440-41) that the "decans" or στοιχεῖα were associated with Helios/Horus in a love potion. Often, however, the decans were invoked for protection from other powers. The conjurer needed to know the names of the decans and make use of them in the prescribed way in order to affect the will of the gods and thereby secure personal protection.[42]

The decans/angels were also objects of fear because they held the keys of fate (εἱμαρμένη). It was possible to thwart these bearers of awful fate by seeking the aid of a powerful deity through magical means:

> I call upon you, Lord. Hear me, holy god who rest among the the holy ones ... eternal ruler of the celestial orb, standing in the seven-part region, [four lines of *voces magicae* follow] ... who possess the powerful name which has been consecrated by all angels. Hear me, you who have established the mighty Decans and archangels, and beside whom stand untold myriads of angels ... [Wherefore, come] to me, you who are lord over all angels (ὁ κυριεύων πάντων ἀγγέλων); shield me against all excess of magical power of aerial daimon [and] fate (ἐξουσίας δαίμονος ἀε[ρί]ου [καὶ εἱ]μαρμένης). Aye, lord, because I call upon your secret name, [four lines of *voces magicae* follow], rescue me in an hour of need (*PGM* I.195-222).

Similarly, Sarapis is invoked as the supreme god in another magical text to protect the suppliant from his foul astrological fate:

> I call on you, lord, holy, much hymned, greatly honored, ruler of the cosmos (κοσμοκράτωρ), Sarapis consider my birth and turn me not away, me, NN whom NN [bore], who knows your true name and valid name, [six lines of *voces magicae* follow], ... Protect me from all my own astrological destiny (ἀστρικῆς); destroy my foul fate (εἱμαρμένην); apportion good things for me in my horoscope; increase my life; and [may I enjoy] many good things, for I am your slave and petitioner and have hymned your valid and holy name, lord, glorious one, ruler of the cosmos (κοσμοκράτωρ) ... Sarapis (*PGM* XIII.618-40).

This formula is immediately followed by a rite in which magical names are to be spoken out loud to the four directions and thirty-six characters, presumably referring to the decans, are to be pronounced to the earth, moon, water, and sky (lines 640-46).

---

[41] J. G. Gager, *Curse Tablets and Binding Spells from the Ancient World* (Oxford: University Press, 1992) 57, note 41.

[42] Gundel, *Dekane*, 226.

Finally, I will call attention to one last text, part of "The Eighth Book of Moses" (*PGM* XIII.646-734), where the fear of astrological fate is vividly portrayed and the ability of a supreme deity to conquer it is affirmed. The text begins by giving the details of an elaborate initiation rite into the mystery of a god "who is greater than all." The rite involves using the names of the 365 gods set over the days and saying the names of the gods of the hours.[43] The supplicant is also required to carve an image of Apollo, who will provide help when the initiation is performed. During the performance of the initiation rite, the god will appear, during which time the initiate is to heed the following set of instructions:

> Now when the god comes in do not stare at his face, but look at his feet while beseeching him, and giving thanks that he did not treat you contemptuously, ... You, then, ask "master, what is fated (εἵμαρται) for me?" And he will tell you even about your star (ἄστρου), and what kind of daimon (δαίμων) you have, and your horoscope (ὡροσκόπος) and where you may live and where you will die. And if you hear something bad, do not cry out or weep, but ask that he may wash it off or circumvent it, for this god can do everything (δύναται γὰρ πάντα ὁ θεὸς οὗτος) (*PGM* XIII.708-14).

"Fate" is clearly in the hands of capricious deities who may be seen by their astral images in the heavens. By the use of magic, the horrors of fate can be averted. Nilsson comments, "The belief in *Heimarmene*, against which the old gods were able to do nothing, threw people in antiquity into the arms of magical practices, mystical redemption teachings, and Christianity."[44]

This description of the function of "decans" and the astral powers of fate in magic in some ways resembles Martin Dibelius's hypothesized "cult of the elements" at Colossae. He emphasized the apotropaic function of the cult, especially with respect to the powers of fate, "the cosmic tyrants of existence."[45] I think Dibelius was essentially correct about the fundamental nature of the problem addressed by "the philosophy," but his description of "the philosophy" itself was flawed by its reductionistic and speculative character. His hypothesis of a pagan cult of the "elements" at Colossae was severely weakened by the fact that no parallel cult of the "elements" exists in any other location. It would have proved more productive to see "the philosophy's" mechanism for dealing with the fear of the elements within

---

[43] A similar conception appears in the *Apocryphon of John* 19 (*NHLE*, 115): "this is the number of the angels: together they are 365."

[44] Nilsson, *GGR*, 2.507. See also his discussion on p. 506.

[45] Dibelius, "Isis Initiation," 81-82, 100-101.

the structure of one of the local cults (especially the mystery cults) or within the framework of the more individualistic practice of magic. Dibelius does not take into account the magic texts that were discussed above. By describing "the philosophy" in these broader terms, it becomes easier to account for the distinctively Jewish aspects of the competing teaching at Colossae. His failure to take the Jewish components seriously (also a problem with Lohse's work), has justly earned his reconstruction a great deal of criticism, but has enabled many of his critics to dismiss too easily some of the major components of his thesis that are substantially correct.

One of the passages in Preisendanz's collection of texts includes the genitive qualifier τοῦ κόσμου. The phrase στοιχεῖα τοῦ κόσμου appears in *PGM* XXXIX.18-21 as a designation for the zodiac: "I adjure you by the twelve elements of heaven (στοιχεῖα τοῦ οὐρανοῦ) and the twenty-four elements of the world (στοιχεῖα τοῦ κόσμου), that you attract Herakles whom Taaipis bore, to me, to Allous, whom Alexandria bore, immediately, immediately; quickly, quickly." On the papyrus, the conjuration appears immediately under a crude drawing of the god Bes, presumably the deity invoked. This manner of calling on the στοιχεῖα closely resembles the kind of magical invocation of angels we described in Part I of this volume.

In much of the past interpretation of *stoicheia* in Colossians and Galatians, the testimony of the magical papyri has been too quickly and simply dismissed by the fact that each of the papyrus texts postdates the first century. History-of-Religions specialists, however, are unanimous in their opinion that most of the traditions incorporated into the magical papyri are much earlier, including the astrological terms and concepts. H. G. Gundel sees the "Individual Astrology" mirrored in the concepts of the magical papyri as stemming from as early as the third-century B.C.[46]

The concept of thirty-six astral decans penetrated Judaism at an early stage as we can see in the third fragment of *Artapanus*. He recounts that when Moses ascended to prominence in Egypt, "he divided the state into thirty-six nomes and appointed for each of the names the god to be worshiped" (*Artapanus* 27:4).[47]

---

[46] Hans Georg Gundel, *Weltbild und Astrologie in den griechischen Zauberpapyri* (Münchener Beiträge zur Papyrusforschung und Antiken Rechtsgeschichte 53; München: Beck, 1968) 65.

[47] M. Mach, *Entwicklungsstadien des jüdischen Engelglaubens in vorrabbinischer Zeit* (TSAJ 34; Tübingen: J.C.B. Mohr [Paul Siebeck], 1992) 177-78, argues strongly in favor of this astrological explanation of this passage.

The term *stoicheia* is again applied to the thirty-six decans in the Testament of Solomon. It occurs twice in the introduction to chapter 18, an astrological document thought to have had an earlier independent existence, the archetype of which probably dates to the first-century B.C.[48] The text is as follows:

> Then I commanded another demon (δαίμονα) to appear before me. There came to me thirty-six heavenly bodies (τὰ τριάκοντα ἕξ στοιχεῖα), their heads like formless dogs. But there were among them (those who were) in the form of humans, or of bulls, or of dragons, with faces like the birds, or the beasts, or the sphinx. When I, Solomon, saw these beings, I asked them, saying, 'Well, who are you?' All at once, with one voice, they said, 'We are thirty-six heavenly bodies (στοιχεῖα), the world rulers (κοσμοκράτορες) of the darkness of this age. But you, King, are not able to harm us or to lock us up; but since God gave you authority over all the spirits of the air, the earth, and (the regions) beneath the earth, we have also taken our place before you like the other spirits. Then I, Solomon, summoned the first spirit (πνεῦμα) and said to him, 'Who are you?' He replied, 'I am the first decan (δεκανός) of the zodiac (ζωδιακός) (and) I am called Ruax. I cause heads of men to suffer pain and I cause their temples to throb. Should I hear only, 'Michael, imprison Ruax,' I retreat immediately (*Testament of Solomon* 18:1-5).

The text then recounts Solomon summoning each of the spirits and asking them to reveal their names. All thirty-six spirits, in turn, appear before Solomon, state their names, the kind of trouble they cause people, and how they can be thwarted (18:3-40). After the thirty-sixth has revealed himself to Solomon, the sage says: "When I, Solomon, heard these things, I glorified the God of heaven and earth and I ordered them to bear water. Then I prayed to God that the thirty-six demons (δαίμονας) who continually plague humanity go to the Temple of God" (18:41-42). Now knowing how to control each of the decans, Solomon would then coerce them to do the work of constructing the temple.

The means by which each of these demons/*stoicheia* could be thwarted was, in this case, not by Solomon's magical ring, but by invoking an angel. Thus, for each decan, a "good" angel is named who can protect the suppliant from the evil attack of the decan.

Chapter 18 is generally regarded as being free from Christian interpolations. Chester C. McCown, however, did assert that the term *stoicheia* as applied to the thirty-six decans stemmed from the language of the NT, viz.

---

[48] Gundel, *Dekane*, 45, 56-57. Gundel thinks that a Greek-speaking Jewish author took over an originally Hebrew text and transformed ('degenerated') many of the Egyptian names for the decans into evil demons. See also D. C. Duling, "Testament of Solomon," *OTP*, 1.977, note 18a.

Gal. 4 and Col. 2.[49] This to me seems unlikely for the following reasons: (1) There are no other signs of Christian interpolation in this passage. The only possible exception is the reference to κοσμοκράτορες τοῦ σκότους in 18:2 (cf. Eph 6:12); but there are no other terms or phrases that betray a dependence on the NT. Neither is there, for instance, any reference to the power of Christ over the decans or any other marker of Christian redaction. (2) It is less likely that Paul coined the use of this term as a designation for astral powers than that he appropriated the term from already existing Jewish tradition like the traditions behind the *Testament* as a means of referring to demonic forces.[50] In general, Paul was not concerned with speculations regarding the realm of angels and demons; he was concerned to provide perspective on this realm for the benefit of his Christian readers. The word was probably formed on the analogy of the LXX παντοκράτωρ in Jewish circles where there was much speculation about demonology and angelology. (3) McCown fails to give a motivation to the author of the Testament for adopting a term from a Pauline context in which there is no explicit link between the *stoicheia* and the decans. In fact, Paul never uses the word δεκανός, nor does he engage in any speculation about how astral demons cause headaches and the like. (4) Most scholars would now contend that the demonology of the *Testament* belongs to the earliest form of the text and is therefore one of the most useful parts of the *Testament* for illuminating the NT.[51] In summary, it is probable that the author of the Testament borrows the summary term *stoicheia* from already existing Jewish tradition and/or magical-astrological tradition that very well may have been a part of the religious *koine* language of the first century.

The term also appears at two other places in the Testament to refer to demonic astral powers. In 8:2 the seven planets are called the στοιχεῖα κοσμοκράτορες τοῦ σκότους:

> Again, I glorified God, who gave me this authority, and I commanded another demon to appear before me. There came seven spirits bound up together hand and foot, fair of form and graceful. When I, Solomon, saw them, I was amazed and asked them, 'Who are you?' They replied, 'We are heavenly bodies, rulers of this world darkness (στοιχεῖα κοσμοκράτορες τοῦ σκότους).' The first said, 'I am Deception ... The seventh said, 'I am The Worst. Our stars in heaven look small, but we are named like gods. We change our position together and we live together, some-

---

[49] Chester C. McCown, *The Testament of Solomon* (Untersuchungen zum Neuen Testament 9; Leipzig: J. C. Heinrichs, 1922) 68.

[50] *Contra* W. Michaelis, "κοσμοκράτωρ," *TDNT* 3.914.

[51] See Duling, "Testament of Solomon," in *OTP* 1.952-53, 955.

times in Lydia, sometimes in Olympus, sometimes on the great mountain (*Testament of Solomon* 8:1-4).

This text not only provides further illustration of the demonic use of *stoicheia,* it also suggests that the tradition has a connection to western Asia Minor. First, in 8:3 "Lydia" is mentioned as one of the places where these gods live together when they change their position. Lydia is a territory in the southwestern part of Asia Minor, the border of which lies only 30 miles from Colossae. Secondly, 8:11 mentions (the Ephesian) Artemis in the context of Solomon's interrogation of the seven planetary powers: "Similarly, the seventh said, 'I am The Worst, and you, King, I shall harm when I order (you to be bound) with the bonds of Artemis ('Αρτέμιδος δεσμοῖς)." These passages give indirect evidence of the presence of such magical/astrological traditions in western Asia Minor. McCown regarded the reference to Lydia, one of the two geographical terms in the document, as pointing to an Asia Minor provenance for the Testament.[52] One other use of the term can be found in 15:5 where the demon Enepsigos, probably to be identified with Hekate,[53] is described as a "heavenly body" (στοιχεῖον). She is said to be thwarted by the angel Rathanael (15:6).

Finally, we have already noted in Chapter 2 that the concept of decans appears in the *Sepher Ha-Razim* (1.84-94). In that work, thirty-six angels are named who have the ability to provide information about future events. These angels can be interrogated but must be approached with ritual purity.

In summary, one may safely conclude that in the context of magic and astrology, even in Jewish and early Christian circles, the term *stoicheia* was indeed used of personalized spiritual forces that have significant influence over the affairs of day-to-day existence. They are not only involved in the unfolding of fate, but may be the functionaries of a magical charm or bring such evils as sickness (e.g. fevers, chills, croup, kidney pain, and heart disease), jealousies, and squabbles. Furthermore, these traditions (including the demonic use of *stoicheia*) reach into the first century A.D. and even earlier.

---

[52] McCown, *Testament,* 110.

[53] She is referred to as a "goddess" (15.3), she is said to "hover near the moon" (15.4), and she possesses three forms (15.4, 5).

c. Mystery Cult Usage: The Isis Initiation in Apuleius

The term *elementa* (= στοιχεῖα) appears three times in Apuleius's eleventh book of the *Metamorphoses:* in Isis's first revelation to Lucius, in the description of the mystery initiation rite, and in the initiate's song of praise to the goddess.

Prior to his initiation, Isis reveals herself in a vision to Lucius as "the mistress of the elements":

> Lo, I am with you, Lucius, moved by your prayers, I who am the mother of the universe, the mistress of all the elements (*elementorum omnium domina*), the first offspring of time, the highest of deities, the queen of the dead, the foremost of heavenly beings, the single form that fuses all gods and goddesses; I who order by my will the starry heights of heaven (Apuleius, *Metamorphoses* 11.5; = 269).[54]

In this passage, *elementa* is not explicitly defined, but in light of the immediately following references to "deities," "heavenly beings," "gods and goddesses," and "the starry heights of heaven," it is probable that Apuleius is thinking of divine beings, perhaps astral deities—all of which are thought of as subordinate to Isis.

The term appears again in the important passage describing the consecration:

> I approached the boundary of death and treading on Proserpine's threshold, I was carried through all the elements (*per omnia vectus elementa*) after which I returned. At dead of night I saw the sun flashing with bright effulgence. I approached close to the gods above and the gods below and worshipped them face to face (Apuleius, *Metamorphoses* 11.23; = 284-85).

In this passage, Lucius's visionary ascent to heaven is the context for his passing through all the "elements." Some kind of astral significance for the "elements" is clear in this text. A. Lumpe suggests that the initiate is led by images of the elemental deities, representing the actual gods. The initiate thus experiences a ritual enactment of heavenly ascent with the help of the protective power of the goddess Isis.[55] It is also possible that this text speaks of a purely visionary experience without ritual enactment. Either way, the *elementa* should be understood as divine intermediaries.

---

[54] Text from J. Gwyn Griffiths, *The Isis-Book (Metamorphoses, Book XI)* (EPRO 39; Leiden: Brill, 1975).

[55] Lumpe, "Elementum," 1082.

Three days after his inititiation, Lucius eats a sacred meal and celebrates the consummation of his mystery initiation. He offers a prayer of
thanks to Isis, in which he praises Isis for her power over the *elementa:*

> ... and when thou has stilled the storms of life thou dost stretch out thy saving hand,
> with which thou unravelest even those threads of fate which are inextricably woven
> together; thou dost pacify the gales of Fortune and keep in check the baleful move-
> ments of the stars. Thee do the gods above honour, and thou art worshipped by those
> below; thou dost revolve the sphere of heaven, and illumine the sun, thou dost guide
> the earth, and trample Hell (*Tartarum*) under thy feet. For thee the constellations
> move, for thee the seasons return; the divine beings rejoice for thee, and the elements
> (*elementa*) are thy slaves (Apuleius, *Metamorphoses* 11.25; = 286-87).

In both the description of the initiation and the prayer of thanks to Isis,
elementa are viewed as hostile astral powers over which Isis wields control. Another Isis aretology expresses similar praise to Isis's control of the
stars: "I showed the paths of the stars" and "the stars do not move on their
own course unless they receive commands from me."[56]
    J. Gwyn Griffiths interprets Lucius's initiatory experience of being
"carried through all the elements" as a symbolic movement through the
cosmic regions. He sees the Mithraic concept of the soul's journey through
the separate spheres of the planets as in view. He suggests that these regions were visually depicted before the initiate on the surrounding walls
of the crypt.[57] While Griffiths is correct both in denying that the reference of *elementa* is to the four Empedoclean elements and in asserting an
astral signficance to the term, his spatial interpretation is less likely. R. E.
Witt is probably correct in his assertion that the *elementa* are spirit powers.[58] While the initiation passage in Apuleius could be interpreted in a
spatial sense, this view is rendered unlikely when the uses of *elementa* in
the vision passage and the prayer of thanksgiving passage are also considered. When Lucius praises Isis because "thou dost keep in check the baleful movements of the stars ... the divine beings rejoice for thee, and the
elements are thy slaves," a personalized interpretation becomes more
likely than a spatial.[59] If there is any spatial sense implied by *remeavi* ("I

---

[56] Dieter Müller, *Ägypten und die griechischen Isis-Aretalogien* (Abh. Leipzig, 53, 1;
Berlin, 1961) M 13 (as cited in Griffiths, *The Isis-Book,* 323).

[57] Griffiths, *The Isis-Book,* 301. He clearly dismisses the possibility of interpreting
the *elementa* here as the four Empedoclean elements of air, earth, fire, and water.

[58] R. E. Witt, *Isis in the Greco-Roman World* (Ithaca, N.Y.: Cornell University Press,
1971) 263.

[59] So also Dibelius, "Isis Initiation," 78.

was carried through [all the elements]"), then the emphasis falls on the astral deities who control each of the planetary spheres. However, there is nothing else in the context to support a spatial interpretation, and the more simple idea of "astral spirits/gods" surfaces as the most probable.

Dibelius rightly characterizes the effect of this initiation as a new-found freedom from the rule of the cosmic powers. He notes, "Insofar as Lucius traverses this way unharmed, he proves himself charmed against chthonic, earthly, and heavenly powers."[60]

Mysteries such as this that offered protection from the cosmic powers of fate proved to be a significant attraction to people during this time. Because of the fear of these powers, people were initiated to gain a means of protection and to avert the harmful influences of these forces.

d. Judaism

In addition to the Testament of Solomon and the Sepher Ha-Razim, which represent the demonology and angelology of Jewish folk belief, there are a variety of other Jewish documents that further illustrate the personal interpretation of *stoicheia*. The single most unambiguous text in support of our understanding of *stoichiea* is found in the longer recension of Slavonic Enoch (2 Enoch) 16:7: "Thus she [the sun] goes, day and night, in accordance with the heavenly winds, and *spirits and elements and flying angels*, with 6 wings to each angel." Wilhelm Bousset conjectured that the Greek text standing behind the italicized portion would have been πνεύματα, στοιχεῖα, ἄγγελοι. He also argued that the Greek original predates Paul and the text should therefore be interpreted as decisive for our understanding of Pauline usage in Colossians and Galatians.[61]

Blinzler disagreed with Bousset's conclusions, objecting that (1) we cannot be sure that *stoicheia* was the Greek word underlying the Old Slavonic term translated "elements," and (2) the date of 2 Enoch is in question (he points to the fact that Kirsopp Lake dated it to the seventh century A.D.); the date of the reading is further complicated by the absence of this portion of text from recension B (= recension A in *OTP*).[62] It is true that we have no way of knowing with certainty what the Greek *Vorlage* of 2 Enoch would have contained. However, there is still a strong possibility

---

[60] Dibelius, "Isis Initiation," 81.

[61] W. Bousset and H. Gressmann, *Die Religion des Judentums im späthellenistischen Zeitalter* (3d ed.; HBNT 21; Tübingen: J.C.B. Mohr [Paul Siebeck], 1926) 323.

[62] Blinzler, "Lexikalisches," 438.

that the Greek original did indeed read *stoicheia* and not δυνάμεις, the term Blinzler thinks stands behind the text. He argued that the Greek term *stoicheia* did not come to be used in a personal sense (as spirits or angels) until the Byzantine era. Thus, the translator could have used the Old Slavonic equivalent of "elements" to translate an assortment of Greek words denoting spirit powers. It seems unlikely to me, however, that the translator would have exercised this much liberty in his translation, especially when one considers that the Slavonic term for elements (*stikhii* or *stoukhii*) appears elsewhere in 2 Enoch in reference to stars and the physical elements (2 Enoch 12:1; 15:1; 23:1; 27:3). In these cases, the Greek original would surely have contained *stoicheia*. It is more likely that the translator would have been consistent in his rendering of *stoicheia* throughout the document, including 16:7.

The dating of the document is indeed a difficult problem. Recent scholarship, however, is leaning toward an early date (as early as the first century A.D.) for the original document[63]—thus partly confirming R. H. Charles's conclusion[64]—because of the apparent antiquity of the traditions contained in the recensions we currently have at hand.[65] C. Böttrich suggests that the primitive form of the text stood in the shadow of the more popular 1 Enoch prior to A.D. 70 and afterward became widely used in the esoteric circles of Jewish mysticism.[66]

2 Enoch conceives of the angels, both good and evil, as governing every aspect of creation. The angels are subject to a higher group of archangels who watch for evil activity and restore order and harmony to the cosmic order:

> And I saw there 7 groups of angels ... And these groups carry out and carefully study the movements of the stars, and the revolution of the sun and the phases of the moon, and the well-being of the cosmos. And when they see any evil activity, they put the commandments and instructions in order, and the sweet choral singing and

---

[63] C. Böttrich, *Weltweisheit, Menschheitsethik, Urkult: Studien zum slavischen Henochbuch* (WUNT 2/50; Tübingen: J.C.B. Mohr [Paul Siebeck], 1992) 54, summarizes the consensus of scholarship: "Grundlegende Bedeutung hat der Konsens der meisten Forscher, daß ganz allgemein von einem jüdischen Grundstock, Archetyp, Kern (oder auch immer) des slHen gesprochen werden kann, der zeitlich dem 1. Jh. zuzuordnen ist."

[64] R. H. Charles and W. R. Morfill, *The Books of the Secrets of Henoch* (Oxford: Clarendon, 1896) xxvi.

[65] See F. I. Andersen, "2 (Slavonic Apocalypse of) Enoch," in *OTP*, 1.92-97. Anderson sees the divergence in the two recensions as the result of transmission in Slavonic.

[66] Böttrich, *Weltweisheit*, 143. He argues that the text originated in Alexandria in the first century A.D. and subsequently made its way to Palestine and Asia Minor (see also pp. 213-15).

every kind of glorious praise. These are the archangels who are over the angels; and they harmonize all existence, heavenly and earthly; and angels who are over seasons and years, and angels who are over rivers and the ocean, and angels who are over the fruits of the earth and over every kind of grass, and who give every kind of food to every kind of living thing; and angels who regard all human souls, and all their deeds, and their lives before the face of the Lord (2 Enoch 19:4; cf. also 4:1-2).

If 2 Enoch reflects strands of Jewish tradition before or around the time of Paul, it attests to the currency of *stoicheia* as angelic beings in first-century Judaism—potentially illuminating Paul's use of the term in Colossians and Galatians.

In 1 Enoch, portions of which were known at Qumran, the term "elements" does not appear in the same simple equation with "spirits" and "angels," but the book does imply an identification of the angels with the stars in the heavens.[67] In *1 Enoch* 43:3 the number of the stars of heaven, which God calls by name, are as many as the angels. The document also contains clear teaching that the four physical elements and the stars are governed by angels. Various manifestations of the four elements are described in 1 Enoch 60:11-25 with the function of their angelic governors mentioned in a few instances. For example, it is noted that "the frost-wind is its own guardian (lit. "angel") and the hail-wind is a kind of messenger (lit. "angel") (60:17). According to 1 Enoch 75:1-3, the angel Uriel was appointed by God over all the luminaries, and under his authority are the angels appointed over all of the stars (see also 80:1, 6). Whereas the book maintains monotheism by conceiving of the stars as angels or by viewing the angels as governors over the planets and elements,[68] it charges the Gentiles of erring and taking the stars themselves to be gods (80:7).[69]

The book of Jubilees, also known at Qumran, conceives of spirits/angels as governors set over the physical elements and other aspects of creation:

> For on the first day he [God] created the heavens, which are above, and the earth, and the waters and all of the spirits which minister before him:
>> the angels of the presence
>> and the angels of sanctification
>> and the angels of the spirit of fire

---

[67] See the discussion in Mach, *Entwicklungsstadien*, 178-79.

[68] Although in the book of dream visions, it is the stars themselves that descend from heaven to earth (*1 Enoch* 86:1-6; 88:1-3).

[69] This statement clearly implies the opposition of the author of this portion of *1 Enoch* to astrology. See M. J. Davidson, *Angels at Qumran* (JSPSS 11; Sheffield: JSOT Press, 1992) 86.

and the angels of the spirit of the clouds and darkness and snow and hail and
frost,
and the angels of resoundings and thunder and lightning,
and the angels of the spirits of cold and heat and winter and springtime and har-
vest and summer,
and all the spirits of his creatures which are in heaven and on earth (Jub. 2:2).

In Jubilees 2:8, God's creation of the heavenly bodies on the fourth day is
mentioned: "And on the fourth day he made the sun and the moon and the
stars." A Greek fragment of *Jub.* 2:8 adds to this list the στοιχεῖα: καὶ
τὰς τῶν ἄστρων θέσεις καὶ τὰ στοιχεῖα.[70] Here the στοιχεῖα are not
explicitly called angels, but the larger context (esp. 2:2) conceives of the
elements as governed by angels.

Without using the term *stoicheia* to refer to the angels, still many other
Jewish texts could be cited that attest to a widespread Jewish belief in the
identification of the angels with the stars. The evidence is summarized
well by M. Mach in an excursus, "The Angels and the Stars."[71]

The high regard of the Qumran community for the sun and the stars is
well known. A few fragments even attest to the practice of astrology
within the community (e.g. 4Q Cryptic, or 4Q 186). Of course, with most
of the documents written in Hebrew, one would not expect to find the
Greek word *stoicheia* attested. Nevertheless, no Hebrew parallel to the
term *stoicheia* appears in the Qumran literature.[72] The movements of the
sun (they followed a solar calendar), moon, and stars, however, formed
the basis of their "appointed times" of worship (see 1QS 9.26-10.8). At
the same time, the Qumran community reflects a deep interest in angelology. In these ways the beliefs at Qumran have a remarkable affinity with
the contents of 1 Enoch and Jubilees and may explain the use of these
books by the Dead Sea group.

The term *stoicheia* appears in the LXX only three times. It occurs in 4
Macc. 12:13 with reference to the physical components of the human body
and in Wisdom 19:18 to refer to the four basic elements. The one remaining occurrence, found in the Wisdom of Solomon, is significant for

---

[70] See the text as printed in Albert-Marie Denis, ed., *Concordance Grecque des
Pseudépigraphes d'Ancien Testament* (Louvain: Université Catholique de Louvain, 1987)
902.

[71] Mach, *Entwicklungsstadien,* 173-84. Among the texts he discusses that point to this
identification are: *1 Enoch* 18:13-16; *Jub* 8:3; *TAbr* (recension A)16:6-12; *Ezekiel the
Tragedian* 79-80; *Pseudo-Phocylides* 71-75, 101-104; *TSol* 18.

[72] Herbert Braun, *Qumran und das Neue Testament* (Tübingen: J.C.B. Mohr [Paul
Siebeck], 1966) 2.229.

our investigation because of its use in connection with the stars. In this passage, Solomon claims to have extensive knowledge of various facets of creation, imparted to him by God through personified wisdom:

> For it is he [God] who gave me unerring knowledge of what exists, to know the structure of the world and the activity of the elements (ἐνέργειαν στοιχείων); the beginning and end and middle of times, the alternations of the solstices and the changes of the seasons, the cycles of the year and the constellations of the stars ... the powers of spirits ... the varieties of plants and the virtues of roots; I learned both what is secret and what is manifest, for wisdom, the fashioner of all things, taught me (Wisdom 7.15-22).

Here the term *stoicheia* is used as a collective term to refer either to the heavenly bodies or earth, air, fire, and water, whose movements result in seasons and the days of the year. The Gentiles are later condemned in Wisdom for venerating these elements as gods: "but they [the Gentiles] supposed that either fire or wind or swift air, or the circle of the stars, or turbulent water, or the luminaries of heaven were the gods that rule the world" (13.2). The burden of the author is to reaffirm strict monotheism to the readers, so that they may "know how much better than these [the divinized elements] is their Lord, for the author of beauty created them" (13.3).

The text is silent about the relationship of the angels to the physical elements and the stars, although chapter 18 implies that demons are involved in pagan worship. The writer notes that the Egyptians (representing idolaters) were "appalled by specters (ἰνδάλματα)" (17.3) and "dismal phantoms (φάσματα) with gloomy faces appeared" to them (17.4; cf. 18.17) when they trusted in their gods and magical arts.

A brief mention must be made of Philo, one of our chief witnesses to Hellenistic Judaism. He only reports the worship of the physical elements as deities, while he himself regards them as lifeless matter:

> [Some people] revere the elements (στοιχεῖα), earth, water, air, fire, which have received different names from different peoples ... Hephaestus ... Hera ... Poseidon ... Demeter ..., but the elements (στοιχεῖα) themselves are lifeless matter incapable of movement of itself (*Vit. Cont.* 3-4; cf. also *Spec. Leg.* 2.255).[73]

A. Lumpe sees this text as illustrating the tendency for people in Hellenistic times to use the word στοιχεῖον (*elementum*) as a direct designation

---

[73] As cited in Schweizer, "Slaves of the Elements," 460.

for the deity or spirit associated with the element.[74] Plato, of course, spoke of the deity of the stars, even referring to them as "visible gods" (Plato *Tim.* 40a, 40c, 40d, 41a). Philo himself regards the angels as inhabiting one of the elements, viz. air. For Philo, the Jewish angels are the same phenomena that the philosophers call *daimona,* disembodied souls that fly and hover in the air (*Somn.* 1.141; *Gig.* 6.16).

Unfortunately, we have little literary evidence to demonstrate how Jews in Asia Minor understood the term *stoicheia* in the first century A.D. The only extensive documents we have that come from Asia Minor are the substratum of the *Sibylline Oracles* (Books 1 & 2) and possibly the Jewish base of the *Testament of Solomon,* but the provenance of this book is disputed. We have already seen, however, that the Testament does give much positive evidence regarding our identification of the *stoicheia* with angels. As far as I am aware, the term *stoicheia* appears in none of the Jewish inscriptions collected thus far in Asia Minor.

One historical phenomenon, however, may lend insight into how certain sectors of Asia Minor Judaism may have understood *stoicheia.* Josephus informs us that as many as 2000 Jewish families in Lydia and Phrygia—perhaps as many as 10,000 people—came there directly from Mesopotamia and Babylon (*Ant.* 12.3.4 §§148-53), having been relocated by Antiochus III (c. 210-200 B.C.).[75] Given the Persian worship of the physical elements, the stars, and the heavenly bodies as deities, as well as the Babylonian astrological concept of thirty-six astral decans, it would not be surprising if some of these relocated Jews had adopted these concepts while in Mesopotamia and brought them to Asia Minor. As we have already seen, there is widespread evidence that Jews had begun to identify the stars as angels, and in this way had preserved their monotheism.

M. P. Nilsson notes that direct Persian influence on Asia Minor was much greater than is commonly supposed. He points to the great popularity of the Persian goddess Anahita, temples to Anahita and other Persian deities in Pontus and Lydia (Hierokaisareia and Hypaipa), the presence of Magi in Cappadocia, and the establishment of the religion of Mithras.[76] In

---

[74] Lumpe, "Elementum," 1081. Bauer[6], s.v. "στοιχεῖον," includes this text to support the usage of the term as "elemental spirit" (*Elementargeister*).

[75] See P. Trebilco, *Jewish Communities in Asia Minor* (SNTSMS 69; Cambridge: University Press, 1991) 5-6; *HJP*[2], 17. For further discussion, see also A. T. Kraabel, "Judaism in Asia Minor under the Roman Empire with a Preliminary Study of the Jewish Community at Sardis, Lydia" (Unpublished Doctoral Dissertation; Harvard, March 1968) 148; J. B. Lightfoot, "The Colossian Heresy," in *Conflict,* 50, note 45.

[76] Nilsson, *GGR,* 2.42. However, it needs to be said that more recent scholarship has demonstrated that F. Cumont greatly exaggerated the presence of Mithraism in Asia Minor

Lydia, Anahita was assimilated to Cybele and the Ephesian Artemis and was referred to as Mater Anahita or Artemis Anahita.[77] Perhaps most significant for our inquiry is the fact that Babylonian astral worship had penetrated Asia Minor.

It is therefore conceivable that the Persian concept of the elements may have gained a foothold in Judaism quite early and was then transported directly to Asia Minor and elsewhere. Of course, Anatolian Jews may have picked up these concepts from their pagan neighbors in Asia Minor. The term *stoicheia* may thus have been in use not only in the paganism of Asia Minor (especially in certain cults, astral religion, and magical practices), but also even in the Judaism of Asia Minor.

e. Summary

(1) The cavalier dismissal of the personal interpretation of *stoicheia* in Galatians and Colossians strictly on the basis of the late date of the evidence is wrong. The magical papyri and the *Testament of Solomon* are widely recognized to contain traditions that date to the first century A.D. and earlier. Similarly, the initiation rite of Isis reflected in Apuleius also represents a tradition that was probably unchanged since the first century. While the testimony of *Slavonic Enoch* cannot be known with certainty to date back to the first century, the testimony of the Wisdom of Solomon is certainly pre-Christian. In Wisdom, the term *stoicheia* is used with reference to the stars, and the author later points out that these are worshiped by the Gentiles, thus implying their divinity and thereby confirming a Jewish use of *stoicheia* for astral deities predating the NT. There is no doubt, however, that the four physical elements (as well as the sun, moon, planets, and stars) were personified and deified in the pre-Christian era by many segments of society—in spite of the fact that the precise term *stoicheia* may not have been employed on each occasion to refer to the elements. The fact that the *concept* of personified "elements" was present prior to the NT era should reduce the reluctance on the part of some to allow this interpretation to stand as a viable possibility. Once the possibility of this interpretation is admitted, it still remains to establish it as exegetically viable and to describe more precisely how Paul understood the term.

---

and wrongly assumed that it was a viable and popular religion in the early first century. For a summary of recent studies, see Yamauchi, *Persia,* 502-18.

[77] See F. R. Walton, "Anahita," in *OCD,* 58; Nilsson, *GGR,* 2.672-73.

(2) Perhaps the lowest common denominator in all of the traditions reviewed (magical, mystery, Jewish apocalyptic, and wisdom) is the linking of the term *stoicheia* with the stars. In the magical and mystery traditions, the *stoicheia* are commonly viewed as hostile, but are capable of being manipulated (in magic) or overcome (by mystery initiation). In the Jewish apocalyptic tradition, the stars are either identified with angels or are seen as governed by angels, both good and evil, yet ultimately subject to the one true God.

(3) Magic and the mysteries provided a way to escape the tyrants of fate and the terrors brought by the often corrupt guardians of cosmic order. Knowing the right names and performing the appropriate rites could alter a dreadful fate. On a more utilitarian vein, the "decans" could even be invoked and manipulated to perform something as individual and self-centered as love magic.

(4) Jews could turn to Yahweh and exercise faith in him alone to deliver them from the evils of the world. But not always. The *Testament of Solomon* gives evidence of another facet of Judaism. The hostile decans/*stoicheia* could be thwarted by invoking angels. This does not necessarily take place in a cultic context, but by personal knowledge of the appropriate angel names and formulas that will effectively compel the hostile forces to respond as commanded. This Jewish magic thus addresses a fundamental problem faced by all in the Hellenistic world: how to survive in a world filled with hostile supernatural forces.

4. The *Stoicheia* in Galatians 4

Before we can turn to Colossians it will be necessary to treat the chronologically prior letter of Paul to the Galatians, where the term *stoicheia* appears twice. The text of Galatians takes on additional significance for interpreting the term in Colossians since it too was addressed to believers in the hinterlands of Asia Minor. I have written an article-length treatment of this topic elsewhere and will merely summarize here the main points of that research.[78]

Having demonstrated that the semantic range of *stoicheia* for first-century usage—for Paul as well as for his Gentile readers—includes the

---

[78] See "Returning to the Domain of the Powers: *Stoicheia* as Evil Spirits in Gal 4:3, 9," *NovT* (forthcoming).

meanings "spirits," "angels," and "demons," it remains for us to determine whether this meaning best explains Galatians 4:3, 9. I am convinced that the contexts of both occurrences lend clear support to this interpretation.

When Paul says in Gal 4:3 that "when we were children, we were enslaved under the τὰ στοιχεῖα τοῦ κόσμου," he is describing the plight of both Jews and Gentiles prior to the coming of Christ. He has already established that Jews have been kept in custody by the law (Gal 3:23). He has also suggested that life "under the law" was tantamount to life "under sin" (Gal 3:22). Determinative for interpreting these concepts is Paul's two-age framework, in which he sees Christ as inaugurating the age to come "in the fullness of time" (Gal 4:4) and delivering his people from the present evil age (Gal 1:4). Elaborating on the plight of life under the old aeon, he clarifies in Gal 4:3 that both Jews and Gentiles have been enslaved to powers that belong to this present evil age. The genitive qualifier τοῦ κόσμου puts the *stoicheia* firmly into his two-age understanding. The reference to the *stoicheia* most likely stems from Paul's apocalyptic world view, which envisions the present evil age as dominated by hostile principalities and powers.

Paul continues his negative evaluation of the *stoicheia* in Gal 4:9 by describing them as "weak and beggarly" (τὰ ἀσθενῆ καὶ πτωχὰ στοιχεῖα). Here he is appealing to the Gentile Christians of Galatia not to turn to the law observances espoused by the Judaizing opponents (especially the rite of circumcision and the observance of food laws as well as festivals and sacred days). To orient one's life around the law in this fashion, according to Paul, is tantamount to returning to the domain of the demonic powers.

For Paul, these are the same demonic powers that enslaved the Galatian Christians in their pagan past when they worshipped false gods (see 4:8). Paul unmasks them by asserting that they were not really gods at all, but rather the weak and beggarly *stoicheia* that are now attempting to reassert their control by other means.

Paul has thus employed an expression from a reservoir of terminology commonly used in first-century Judaism to refer to the demonic powers of the present evil age. Because of the widespread use of the term in pagan magic, astrology, and mystery cults, it is likely that Paul's Gentile readers (some of whom may have been unfamiliar with the Jewish apocalyptic tradition) would have understood the term to refer to some kind of spirit powers. The context of the two uses of *stoicheia* in Galatians, however, would have helped all to understand that Paul regards them as evil spirit powers belonging to the present evil age.

5. The *Stoicheia* Inspired "The Philosophy" at Colossae (Colossians 2.8)

Having examined the relevant history of religions background to *stoicheia* and summarized its usage in Paul's letter to the Galatians, we are now better able to approach the two occasions of its use in Colossians. The first appearance occurs in the context of Paul's initial direct polemic against the opposing teaching at Colossae. The development of thought may be graphically depicted in the following syntactical arrangement:

βλέπετε μή τις ὑμᾶς ἔσται ὁ συλαγωγῶν
    <u>διὰ</u> τῆς φιλοσοφίας
    καὶ κενῆς ἀπάτης

    <u>κατὰ</u> τὴν παράδοσιν τῶν ἀνθρώπων,
    <u>κατὰ</u> τὰ στοιχεῖα τοῦ κόσμου
    καὶ οὐ <u>κατὰ</u> Χριστόν·

The passage is marked by the stern warning βλέπετε μή followed by five prepositional phrases, two coordinated with διά (the second assumed) and three coordinated with κατά. It is perhaps best to understand ἡ φιλοσοφία as the self-description of the teaching of the opponents (as I will discuss later). The κενῆς ἀπάτης would then be an adjectival adjunct conveying Paul's polemical characterization of "the philosophy."

With the warning βλέπετε μή (2:8), the author of Colossians begins in earnest his polemic against the new teaching threatening the church.[79] He warns against someone (τις) taking them captive (συλαγωγέω) through "the philosophy" (τῆς φιλοσοφίας), which Paul characterizes as "empty deception."

The use of the indefinite pronoun (τις) does not mean that there was no identifiable person(s) in view propagating this teaching among the Colossians.[80] On the contrary, Lightfoot correctly pointed out that the pronoun "is frequently used by St Paul, when speaking of opponents whom he knows well enough but does not care to name" (see Gal 1:7: εἰ μή <u>τινές</u>

---

[79] On βλέπετε as a serious warning with the sense of "beware!", see BAGD, 143 (6). Paul used this expression to warn of dangerous teachers; see Phil 3:2.

[80] *Contra* M. D. Hooker, "Were There False Teachers in Colossae," in *Christ and Spirit in the New Testament* (FS. C. F. D. Moule; Cambridge: University Press, 1973) 326, suggests that the term should be understood here as "anyone" in the sense of "in case anyone might teach these things."

εἰσιν οἱ ταράσσοντες ὑμᾶς).[81] Neither does the fact that the pronoun appears in the singular necessarily mean that there was only one opposing teacher. The τις may be used to refer to any individual from the opposing faction.

Paul's deep concern over the well-being of the church is expressed by his choice of the rare term συλαγωγέω, a hapax legomenon in the NT and in the LXX.[82] The dictionaries cite only two late occurrences of the term (third and fifth centuries A.D.), where in one instance the term was used in the sense of stealing property (to rob)[83] and, in the other instance, of taking a captive.[84] As Lightfoot has pointed out, additional light on the meaning of the term comes from the better attested cognate words σκευαγωγέω (to pack up and carry away goods), δουλαγωγέω (lead into slavery, make a slave), and especially λαφυραγωγέω (carry off as booty, plunder [λάφυρα = spoils taken in war]).[85] The neuter noun σῦλον (pl. = τὰ σῦλα), upon which συλαγωγέω is formed, was used to refer to booty or plunder that was seized or even for the right of seizure or reprisal (most commonly with reference to the cargo of a ship).[86] Thus, to "take as plunder" or "take as a captive" surface as possible meanings for συλαγωγέω. Because of the serious threat of the opposing teaching (characterized as "empty deception") and Paul's earlier emphasis on their deliverance (ἐρρύσατο ἡμᾶς) and redemption (ἀπολύτρωσις), the concept of "captivity" or "slavery" is most appropriate to this context. As such, the Colossians were in danger of being re-enslaved to a teaching instigated by the στοιχεῖα τοῦ κοσμοῦ. The thought is thus quite similar to Gal 4:3, 9 in that the Galatians also faced the danger of returning to the dominion of the *stoicheia*. The Galatians, however, would be victimized by the powers through embracing the Torah and the nomistic observances advocated by the Judaizing opposition.

The syntax appears awkward here with Paul using ἔσται ὁ συλαγωγῶν instead of the simpler ὃς συλαγωγήσει. The articular participle here

---

81 Lightfoot, *Colossians,* 178.

82 There does not appear to be any attested occurrence of the word prior to its use in this passage.

83 See Aristaenetus (fifth century A.D.), *Epistolographi* 2.22: ἐγχειροῦσα συλαγωγῆσαι τὸν ἡμέτερον οἶκον ("attempting to rob our house"). The Greek text is cited in MM, 596.

84 See Heliodorus (the third century A.D. novelist) 10.35: οὗτός ἐστιν ὁ τὴν ἐμὴν θυγατέρα συλαγωγήσας ([A priest said of his daughter's alleged kidnapper] "this is the one who took my daughter captive"). See MM, 596; LSJ, 1671; BAGD, 776.

85 Lightfoot, *Colossians,* 178.

86 LSJ, 1671.

"gives a directness and individuality to the reference"[87] and thus points to a person or group of people who are a danger. He thereby cautions his readers against the threat of a teaching inconsistent with the community's standing in Christ.

Paul then clearly states the specific danger he sees threatening the church: it is "the philosophy (ἡ φιλοσοφία)." In the two διά phrases, "the philosophy" serves as the means by which the Colossians may be led astray. Rather than directly connecting φιλοσοφία with the adjectives κενή and ἀπάτη (thus, "vain and deceptive philosophy"), immediately after φιλοσοφία Paul inserts a καί that functions epexegetically to introduce his own evaluation of "the philosophy." This enables him to refer to *the* philosophy—the probable designation of the opponents for their teaching—and then to deliver his extremely harsh opinion about it.

The presence of the Greek article before the noun implies that there is an identifiable "philosophy" on the horizon that could undermine the stability of the church in Colossae. The fact that he designates the competing teaching as a φιλοσοφία does not make it necessary to narrow the focus of our inquiry to known Greek philosophies, such as Platonism, Epicureanism, or Stoicism. The word itself was used much more broadly. It was even used to denote magical practices and mystery traditions (see Chapter 7), a meaning thoroughly consistent with the results of our investigation thus far.

This "philosophy" is denounced by Paul as "empty deception" (κενή ἀπάτη) in Col 2:8. The combination of these two terms, although rare in Jewish literature,[88] does occur in Jewish condemnation of pagan religion. In an oracle predicting the rise of a pious group within Judaism, the Sibyl describes their piety in terms of not being led astray by idols: "For to them alone did the great God give wise counsel and faith and excellent understanding in their breasts. They do not honor with empty deceits (ἀπάτῃσι κεναῖς) works of men, either gold or bronze, or silver or ivory, or wooden, stone, or clay idols of dead gods ... such as mortals honor with empty-minded (κενεόφρονι) counsel" (*Sib. Or.* 3.584-90). Similarly, *T. Naph.* 3.1 warns of letting your souls be deceived by empty phrases (ἐν λόγοις κενοῖς ἀπατᾶν τὰς ψυχάς) such as the Gentiles who have wandered into a devotion to idols. Significantly, the term ἀπάτη also appears in a condemnation of magical practices in *Sib. Or.* 3.226: the text praises the righteous because they do not get involved with "seers, nor

---

[87] Lightfoot, *Colossians,* 178.
[88] The combination never appears in the LXX.

sorcerers, nor soothsayers, nor the deceits of foolish words of ventrilo-quists (οὐ μύθων μωρῶν ἀπάτας ἐγγαστεριμύθων). Neither do they prac-tice the astrological predictions of the Chaldeans nor astronomy. For all these things are erroneous ..." (For a similar connection of ἀπάτη with magic, see Josephus, *Vit.* 40).

The author of Colossians then uses three κατά phrases to indicate the source[89] of the deceitful teaching. He regards "the philosophy" as based upon (1) the tradition of men and (2) the στοιχεῖα τοῦ κόσμου, (3) not on Christ. It is my contention that he regards "the tradition of men" as the intermediate source and the στοιχεῖα τοῦ κόσμου as the ultimate source in this context.

As with the term "philosophy," the notion of sacred "tradition" (παράδοσις) was foundational to magic, where recipes were transmitted from magician to magician. "Tradition," especially in an oral sense, was also important in the context of the mystery religions for the transmission of the sacred rites (see Chapter 7).

When he says that "the philosophy" stemmed from the στοιχεῖα τοῦ κόσμου, we again face the same issues that surfaced in treating Galatians: (1) should we understand *stoicheia* in a personal or non-personal sense, and (2) was the term used by the opposition as a characteristic part of their teaching, or does it only represent Pauline polemic? Resolving these two issues is prerequisite to determining precisely how *stoicheia* should be understood in Colossians 2:8 and 20.

Contextual perspective on the first question is forthcoming when we observe the third member of the trio of κατά phrases: "not according to Christ." By inserting the negative particle οὐ before the preposition, the author establishes a direct contrast with the immediately preceding phrase.[90] That he is thinking primarily of the immediately preceding phrase is clarified by the fact that only the final two phrases are linked by καί. This results in a contrast between two personal sources (the *stoicheia* and Christ), which are in turn set parallel to an impersonal source (the tradition of men). Paul is therefore saying that on the human level the source of "the philosophy" is in tradition, but on the supernatural/personal

---

[89] Technically, the author is using κατά to introduce "the norm which governs some-thing" (see BAGD, 407 [II.5.a]) and can be translated, "according to" or "in accordance with."

[90] Lohse, *Colossians,* 99, speaks of a "sharply formulated antithesis," which he sees as leading to a personal interpretation. See also Dibelius-Greeven, *Kolosser,* 27; Lähne-mann, *Kolosserbrief,* 114.

level it has its source in evil spiritual powers (the *stoicheia*) and not Christ.

Once again Paul appears to be citing the self-understanding of his opponents and then commenting on it. In this instance, he refers to their own positive evaluation of their teaching as venerable "tradition" (παράδοσις), but then he negatively characterizes it as inspired by demonic forces (στοιχεῖα), certainly not inspired by Christ. As tradition "of men" (τῶν ἀνθρώπων)[91] it was created by people and transmitted by people, but Paul's point here is that it was created and maintained by people influenced by demonic spirits—the powers of the present evil age.

We have already demonstrated that there is lexical justification for a personal interpretation of *stoicheia* as "angels" or "spirits." There is a rich history of use of the term in the mystery religions, magic, astrology, and certain strands of Judaism. With that being the case, and given our tentative conclusion that "the philosophy" has some connection with these, it is quite possible that the term *stoicheia* figured in the competing teaching. Although it is difficult to know with any certainty the precise sense in which the opposing teachers may have described the role of the *stoicheia*, I think there are at least two possibilities: (1) the entire phrase κατὰ τὰ στοιχεῖα τοῦ κόσμου could be seen as a reflection of the self-understanding of "the philosophy" as a veneration of the divinized elements (the four [or five] physical elements and the heavenly bodies as spirits or angels,[92] or (2) the term *stoicheia* (without the genitive qualifier τοῦ κόσμου) was simply part of the vocabulary of the adherents of "the philosophy" for various kinds of spirits: astral decans, spirits regulating the physical elements (and thus responsible for the harmony of the earth, including disasters such as plagues and earthquakes), and various kinds of spirit powers and divine intermediaries. This latter view is more likely. Paul may have employed the term *stoicheia* not only because of the Colossians' familiarity with the word as a designation of spirit powers, but also because the leaders of "the philosophy" seemed especially concerned about the role the *stoicheia* and other spirit powers played in the affairs of day-to-day life. The Colossian opponents did not understand their "philosophy" as imparted to them through the agency of harmful spirits, but as a tradition that was effective for averting the evil influence of these hostile forces.

---

[91] Mark reports Jesus as upbraiding the Pharisees for holding to the "traditions of men" (τὴν ταράδοσιν τῶν ἀνθρώπων) rather than to the command of God (Mk 7:8).

[92] This is essentially the view of M. Dibelius. See Dibelius-Greeven, *Kolosser*, 27-29, 36, 38.

Paul's polemic would have startled his readers as they realized that he was actually denouncing their "philosophy" as inspired by the same malicious powers from which they were seeking protection! Paul, of course, is not adopting their doctrine regarding the *stoicheia*, only the same terminology. This was made possible by the fact that Judaism and Hellenism shared much of the same terminology for angelic powers. Paul bases his polemic on Jewish (esp. apocalyptic) tradition, which associates the term *stoicheia* with angels and regards pagan religion and practices as the work of demons. The genitive expression τοῦ κόσμου was Paul's own addition, as it was in Galatians, to make it clear that these powers belong to the present evil age—they are not good angels, they are demonic spirits!

Colossians 2:8, therefore, warns the Colossian congregation against a "philosophy" that was really an empty deception, inspired by evil cosmic forces, and not inspired by Christ. The final phrase of the verse—οὐ κατὰ Χριστόν—underlines the author's concern that the competing teaching strikes directly at the root of Christology. For the Colossian Christians, "the philosophy" stands diametrically opposed to their faith in Christ.

6. Immunity to the *Stoicheia:* Union with Christ (Colossians 2.20)

In the next passage where Paul speaks of the *stoicheia,* he tells the Colossians the secret of deflecting the harmful influence of the powers. The answer is to be found in Christ alone.

He declares that they have died with Christ from the powers of evil (ἀπεθάνετε σὺν Χριστῷ ἀπὸ τῶν στοιχείων τοῦ κόσμου).[93] The idea of "dying to the powers" is a natural extension of Paul's thought on the implications of being united with Christ (see esp. Rom 6:3-11). In Col 2:12 Paul affirms that believers have been buried with Christ (συνταφέντες αὐτῷ) and now here, again using the preposition σύν, he reaffirms their identification with the death of Christ, but draws its implications with regard to the powers.

Throughout Romans and Galatians, Paul makes many comments about the implications of corporate identification with the death of Christ. In

---

[93] The "declaration" is actually part of a conditional sentence prefaced by the particle εἰ. The εἰ, however, does not express doubt, but affirms the reality of the initial statement and, therefore, should be translated "since [this is true]." With O'Brien, *Colossians,* 148, and most other commentators.

Galatians 2:19 he affirms that believers have died "to the law" (cf. also Rom 7:6). That is, through their identification with the death of Jesus, believers are not only free from a Torah-centered (nomistic) life-style, they are also freed from the jurisdiction of the Mosaic law.[94] They are called to a Christ-centered existence (Gal 2:20). In Romans 6:2, 7 and 10, Paul describes death with Christ for believers as a death "to sin"; believers have passed from an epoch ruled by the power of sin leading to death into an epoch of life in union with Jesus Christ.[95] And finally, Paul declares that believers have died to the world (the κόσμος) which for him at this juncture represents the present evil age (Gal 6:14).

Thus having established that all who are in Christ have died to the law, to sin, and to the world, Paul now interprets death with Christ as also including death to another category of powers associated with the present evil age: The Colossians have died to the influence of evil angelic powers.[96] This implication of identification with the death of Jesus flows out of Paul's colorful statements regarding Christ's victory over the hostile powers (ἀρχαὶ καὶ ἐξουσίαι [= στοιχεῖα]) through his death on the cross five verses earlier (Col 2:15). This death to the powers is already alluded to in Col 1:13 when Paul describes their conversion as God rescuing them "from the authority of darkness" and transferring them into the kingdom of his beloved son. In order to emphasize their decisive separation from the compelling influence of the powers of darkness, Paul uses the preposition ἀπό following ἀπεθάνετε, varying from his normal use of the dative following the verb "die."

This concept bears striking similarity to what we have already seen to be present in Galatians 4: Jewish believers were at one time enslaved to the *stoicheia* by virtue of the fact that life under Torah was life in the old aeon—an age dominated by Satan and his forces (Gal 4:3). But Christ has brought redemption (ἐξαγοράζω; Gal 4:5) for those "under law." Therefore, there is no reason for the Galatians to embrace Torah. To do so is tantamount to regressing to life in the old aeon where the evil *stoicheia* hold sway and where believers were formerly held in bondage by evil spirits through their idolatrous practices (Gal 4:8-10).

The most natural explanation for his emphasis on this aspect of the meaning of Christ's death is due to the fact that the powers, viz. the

---

94 See Longenecker, *Galatians*, 91.

95 See further, Dunn, *Romans 1-8*, 307-308.

96 Pokorný, *Colossians*, 152, also stresses the two-age distinction to explain the present passage. He notes, "the one baptized is part of the new age in which the powers of this world no longer have any power."

stoicheia, figure prominently in the teaching of the opponents and in the fears of his readers. It is doubtful that, as some commentators have surmised, the teachers of "the philosophy" were asserting that the *stoicheia* were controlling the heavenly realm and thus blocking a person's access to the presence of God either in the context of gaining a visionary experience of the divine throne[97] or on the day of death when the soul would ascend.[98] It is more likely that "the philosophy" was indeed teaching that the *stoicheia* controlled the heavenly realm, but the concern was much more directed toward their hostile influence on matters of daily life—causing sickness, effecting a curse, bringing poor crops, plagues, earthquakes, and "natural" disasters. By calling on good angels (Col 2:18), the advocates of "the philosophy" contended, the work of these evil spirits could be averted.

Now that Paul has declared their freedom from the powers, he asks the Colossians why they are submitting to regulations (τί ... δογμα-τίζεσθε;). He has in mind the regulations imposed by "the philosophy" (see Chapter 7), an example of which he quotes in the following verse: "Do not handle! Do not taste! Do not touch!" (2:21). He carefully links these regulations to the *stoicheia*, which, as we have just seen, are viewed by the author as the ultimate source of the errant teaching. Perhaps one of the greatest difficulties faced by the Colossians who were tempted to follow this teaching would have been to accept Paul's interpretation of it as demonically inspired.

Paul compares their penchant toward observing the regulations of "the philosophy" with their pre-Christian life experience. He asks, "why are you submitting to regulations as though you are living in the world (ὡς ζῶντες ἐν κόσμῳ)?" He here uses κόσμος in the theological sense of a pattern of life determined by the present evil age (cf. Gal 1:4). The use of κόσμος in this clause reinforces our impression that the τοῦ κόσμου that qualifies *stoicheia* in Col 2:8, 20 is Paul's own negative evaluation that these hostile angels are integrally linked to the present evil age. By contrast, Paul calls the Colossians to set their focus on the "things above" (τὰ ἄνω; Col 3:1, 2; cf. Phil 3:20)—the age to come—where Christ is, to whom they belong. By accepting the teaching of the opponents, the Colossians would be reverting into a slavery that they once experienced in their pagan past (see Gal 4:3, 8-10), when they lived under the dominion of the present evil age.[99]

---

[97] Lincoln, *Paradise*, 115.

[98] Schweizer, *Colossians*, 166.

[99] So also Lohse, *Colossians*, 123.

The pattern of teaching he commends to the Colossians is then: The powers of evil have no authority over you who are in Christ because you have participated in his death; therefore, do not submit to their regulations. With his emphasis on "with Christ" (Col 2:20), Christ as the "head" who supplies the body (Col 2:19), and Christ as the "substance" in contrast to the observances of the false teachers, which are only a "shadow" (Col 2:17), Paul strongly emphasizes Christ's claim on their lives. As E. Lohse has rightly said, "anything else that might put forward a claim to lordship has lost its authority."[100]

What Paul says here in 2:20-23 is merely a restatement of the same idea stated just a few verses earlier. In 2:15 he asserts the nullification of the influence of the powers through Christ's triumph over them on the cross; this is immediately followed by an injunction to desist from following various kinds of regulations others are imposing (2:16), which really are a part of the present age (2:17). The action Paul calls them to is only possible because of their participation in Christ's death and resurrection (2:12; cf. 2:10). Recognition of this pattern in Colossians gives contextual reinforcement to our understanding of *stoicheia* as evil powers.

Against these demonically inspired dictates, the author presents a message of freedom. He urges the readers to reconsider the meaning of their conversion.[101] Identification with the death of Christ necessarily implies immunity from demonic tyranny. The author does not imply that this immunity comes automatically; it must be appropriated by the believer, therefore the exhortation in vv. 20ff. If the Colossian Christians are immunized against the "powers," there is now no reason for them to be tempted to follow the regulations of "the philosophy," which, ironically, Paul claims were inspired by the "powers" themselves.

7. Summary and Conclusions

(1) The *stoicheia* are to be understood as evil spiritual "powers" equivalent to the ἀρχαὶ καὶ ἐξουσίαι (1:16; 2:10, 15).

(2) For the adherents of "the philosophy" the *stoicheia* were hostile powers to be feared. Although these spirits were frequently associated with the stars and cosmic fate, they were also perceived as operating in a

---

[100] Lohse, *Colossians,* 122.
[101] Expressed by the rite of baptism; see Col 2:12.

direct and immediate way in the day-to-day affairs of life. To avert the harmful influence of these forces, the opposing faction engaged in rites of a quasi-magical nature—including the invocation of angels for protection. There is no evidence to support the claim that there was a pagan *stoicheia* cult that influenced the church. Neither is there evidence to support the Gnostic interpretation, which sees the *stoichiea* as the heavenly powers comprising the *pleroma*.

(3) For Paul the *stoicheia* were an integral part of the present evil age. They function as masters and overlords of unredeemed humanity working through various means—including the Jewish law and pagan religions—to hold their subjects in bondage. The rules and regulations imposed by these "powers," ostensibly through sacred and venerable religious tradition, are therefore entirely unnecessary and actually represent a reversion to a form of slavery to the "powers" themselves. A reaffirmation of the community's freedom from this demonic tyranny is expressed by the author, who stresses the complete identification of believers with Christ. The identification includes death to the former lords, the στοιχεῖα τοῦ κόσμου, who would still seek to impose their control.

Chapter 7

"Wisdom," "Philosophy," and Ascetic Behavior

The previous three chapters have demonstrated that "the philosophy" at Colossae reflected aspects of local popular religion. In particular, we have identified a "magical" dimension (seen in the practice of invoking divine intermediaries for aid and protection), a connection with local mystery initiation ritual, and a concern about hostile spirits—especially those governing the physical elements and the heavenly bodies. We have yet to tie these seemingly disparate pieces of the overall picture together and suggest a coherent reconstruction of the competing teaching. Before we can do this, however, there are additional lexical items in the letter that provide us with clues regarding the nature of the teaching. An additional issue that needs to be addressed further is whether "the philosophy" has primarily Jewish or pagan roots and the extent to which these overlap or "syncretize."

1. The Jewish Contribution

There is more than a modicum of Jewish influence on the teaching of "the philosophy." We have already pointed to the significant contribution of the Jewish magical tradition, especially the Solomonic magical tradition, to the beliefs and practices of the variant teaching. We have also noted the slight possibility that there was a Jewish connection through a form of Judaism that was influenced by the structure of the mystery cults (esp. the worship of Sabazios).

The polemical section of 2:16-23 demonstrates many other points where "the philosophy" is indebted to Jewish traditions. One of the most obvious is the mention of "sabbaths" (Col 2:16) as one of the ritual observances. It is likely also that the "festivals" and "new moon" celebrations reflect, at least in part, Jewish traditions. This conclusion may be confirmed partly by the fact that the author gathers together the entire list of observances in Col 2:17 with the relative pronoun ἅ and refers to them as

merely a "shadow" (σκιά) of what is to come (cf. Heb 10:1). Although many scholars have pointed to circumcision as one of the regulations of the opponents based upon the author's mention of spiritual circumcision in Col 2:11, it is doubtful that this was one of their practices. First, the mention of circumcision does not occur as part of the author's polemic against the dangerous teaching, but as part of his positive teaching about the implications of being "in Christ." Second, based on the precedent of Galatians, one would expect Paul (or a Pauline disciple) to argue far more passionately and condemningly if the opponents were insisting on circumcision. Third, the whole nature of the teaching of the opponents at Colossae is significantly different than what Paul frequently encountered in his opposition by Judaizers. Thus, although circumcision may not have been part of the practice of "the philosophy," sabbath observance and various other Jewish calendrical observances did indeed have an integral role.

As far as external evidence about the nature of the Judaism at Colossae, there is very little information. Because the site has never been excavated, we have no material evidence of the Judaism there. It is very likely, however, that there was a strong Jewish presence in the city and perhaps also a synagogue. Based upon the amount of Temple tax confiscated by the proconsul Flacus in Laodicea in 62 B.C. (see Cic. *Flac.* 28.68), some have estimated that as many as 7,500 Jewish freemen were in the Lycus Valley region (consisting of Colossae, Laodicea, and Hierapolis).[1] Although the precise figure is impossible to detemine, there was nevertheless a sizable Jewish population in Colossae and its neighboring cities. A much larger Jewish population is attested for Apamea, less than 50 miles NE of Colossae. A few Jewish inscription have also been found there.[2] A Jewish synagogue and a number of Jewish inscriptions have been discovered in nearby Aphrodisias, 30 miles W of Colossae. The synagogue postdates the NT, but points to the likelihood of a Jewish presence in the city during the first century.

Many of the Phrygian Jews came directly from Mesopotamia, never having lived in Jerusalem or Judaea. Josephus reports that Antiochus III transferred two-thousand Jewish families—perhaps representing as many as 10,000 people—to the territories of Lydia and Phrygia in the second

---

[1] The determination of the number of men depends on whether the twenty pounds of gold seized from the Jews of Laodicea by the Roman governor L. Valerius Flaccus was the Temple tax for one year and also whether Cicero exaggerated the amount in his defense speech. See further, P. Trebilco, *Jewish Communities in Asia Minor* (SNTSMS 69; Cambridge: University Press, 1991) 12-16.

[2] See Trebilco, *Jewish Communities,* 85-103.

century B.C. (Josephus, *Ap.* 1.176-82; *Ant* 12.3.4 §§147-53). These people were resettled to secure Antiochus's hold on the land.[3] Scholars have often speculated regarding the extent to which these Mesopotamian Jews had assimilated Eastern religions and culture.[4] The paucity of evidence makes it difficult to assess the amount of syncretism. A recognition that there very well may have been some degree of religious assimilation, at least among some of the relocated Jews, must remain a viable possibility.

A document preserved by Josephus demonstrates that Sabbath observance was important to the Jews of Laodicea as it was for Jews in Asia Minor as a whole (Josephus, *Ant.* 14.10.20 §§241-42).[5] Although there is no evidence about Jewish observance of festivals or food laws in the Lycus Valley, there is evidence that the observance of food laws was a significant part of Jewish practice in Sardis.[6]

A huge issue that remains unresolved is whether and to what extent the Judaism of Asia Minor represents a syncretism, viz. a mixing of the Judaism with the local pagan cults. Much of the discussion of the issue has revolved around the worship of the gods "Theos Hypsistos" and Sabazios in Asia Minor. Although we may not be able to reach a firm conclusion regarding whether these cults are in some sense Jewish, we have already assembled adequate evidence to illustrate the syncretism that was occurring in the context of magic, astrology, and folk belief.

There is not enough evidence to suggest that all the elements of "the philosophy" came together in the synagogue before they were adapted and advocated in the church at Colossae. It is possible, however, to see that many did in fact come together under the rubric of syncretistic Judaism in Asia Minor.

We will now undertake a brief examination of some additional characteristics of the competing teaching at Colossae reflected in the polemic of 2:16-23. Given our hypothesis that many of these elements came together in the context of what we may call "folk Judaism" of Asia Minor, we will be especially sensitive to illustrating this particular dimension of Judaism

---

[3] For further discussion, see M. Stern, "The Jewish Diaspora," *The Jewish People in the First Century* (CRINT I/1; Philadelphia: Fortress, 1974) 143.

[4] Beare, *Colossians*, 139, goes so far as to say that the ancestors of these first-century Phrygian Jews "had been in touch with Iranian religion for centuries and could hardly have maintained their Judaism unimpaired ... Such a group would be particularly amenable to the prevailing syncretism of Hellenistic times."

[5] Trebilco, *Jewish Communities,* 17-18.

[6] Trebilco, *Jewish Communities,* 18.

as well as the relevant aspects of popular religion in Phrygia and Asia Minor as a whole.

2. The Structure of 2:16-23

Following the initial warning about "the philosophy" in 2:4, 8, the section 2:16-23 comprises the heart of the polemic against the variant teachers. The rhetoric is not directed toward the teachers themselves, but to the Colossian believers who were apparently tempted to let themselves accede to the demands these new teachers were imposing.

The section is simply structured around three very stern warnings—two imperatives and one rhetorical question:

1.   2:16   Μὴ οὖν τις ὑμᾶς κρινέτω
2.   2:18   μηδεὶς ὑμᾶς καταβραβευέτω
3.   2:23   τί ... δογματίζεσθε;

The first subsection warns the Colossians not to allow anyone to judge them with regard to dietary regulations (ἐν βρόσει καὶ ἐν πόσει) or calendrical observances (ἐν μέρει ἑορτῆς ἢ νεομηνίας ἢ σαββάτων). Referring to both lists with the relative pronoun ἅ, Paul then critiques these regulations as "a shadow of what is to come" (σκιὰ τῶν μελλόντων) and claims "the substance" (τὸ σῶμα) belongs to Christ.

The second subsection begins similarly with a third-person imperatival injunction not to allow anyone to serve as judge over them. This is followed by a series of four coordinated participles, the first of which is used to introduce two of the practices of the errorists that the Colossians should avoid. The second participial clause is a quotation from the opponents giving their self-attested basis for judging the Colossians—they have had incredible visionary experience in mystery cult initiation. The third and fourth participles offer two reasons why the Colossians should not follow the dictates of the deviant teachers. The entire subsection could be diagrammed as follows:

Imperatival Warning:
μηδεὶς ὑμᾶς καταβραβευέτω
   The Practices They Advocate:
   θέλων ἐν
      ταπεινοφροσύνῃ καὶ
      θρησκείᾳ τῶν ἀγγέλων,
   Their Basis for Judging—Initiation
   ἃ ἑόρακεν ἐμβατεύων,
   Paul's Critique:
   εἰκῇ φυσιούμενος ὑπὸ τοῦ νοὸς τῆς σαρκὸς αὐτοῦ,
   καὶ οὐ κρατῶν τὴν κεφαλήν,

In contrast to the first and final subsections, the relative pronoun ἃ is not
followed by ἐστιν and does not gather the preceding list (here
ταπεινοφροσύνη and θρησκείᾳ τῶν ἀγγέλων) as a means to introduce the
critique. Here the pronoun ἃ should be understood as an accusative and
the unit ἃ ἑόρακεν serving as the object of the participle ἐμβατεύων.[7]

The final subsection (see the diagram below) begins with a first-class
condition the apodosis of which is a rhetorical question that once again
warns the Colossians about submitting themselves to the rules of the variant teaching. Specifically, Paul asks, "why are you submitting yourselves
to regulations" (τί δογματίζεσθε;). This is immediately followed, by
asyndeton, with an expression that most interpreters have regarded as a
slogan of the teachers: Μὴ ἅψῃ μηδὲ γεύσῃ μηδὲ θίγῃς ("Do not handle!
Do not taste! Do not touch!). As in the first subsection, Paul sums these
regulations up with the neuter relative pronoun ἃ and provides his critique: ἅ ἐστιν πάντα εἰς φθορὰν τῇ ἀποχρήσει ("these are all destined to
perish with use"). This is then followed by a parenthetic prepositional
phrase that reaches back to τί δογματίζεσθε; as a critique of the source
of the δόγματα—they are κατὰ τὰ ἐντάλματα καὶ διδασκαλίας τῶν
ἀνθρώπων ("according to the commandments and teachings of men"). Paul
then refers to all the regulations of the opponents (those implied in the
quotation in v. 21 and all the regulations represented by v. 22b) with the
qualitative relative pronoun ἅτινα and provides additional critique in v.
23.

Colossians 2:23 has been notoriously difficult to interpret. Here we are
confronted with a sentence that is peculiarly complex syntactically. B.
Hollenbach, however, has made a convincing proposal that helps to clear

---

[7] See the more extensive comments on the syntax of ἃ ἑόρακεν ἐμβατεύων in Chapter 5.

up the confusion and which I follow here in the main.[8] He takes the main clause to be: ἅτινά ἐστιν ... πρὸς πλησμονὴν τῆς σαρκός ("Which things lead to the fulfillment of the flesh").[9] He understands μέν as marking out a subordinate concessive clause governed by the participle ἔχοντα, which stands in the middle of the main clause[10]: λόγον μὲν ἔχοντα σοφίας ἐν ἐθελοθρησκίᾳ καὶ ταπεινοφροσύνῃ καὶ ἀφειδίᾳ σώματος ("having a reputation for wisdom in the areas of self-chosen worship, humility, and severe treatment of the body"). The expression οὐκ ἐν τιμῇ τινι ("without any honor whatsoever") is understood to be subordinate to the concessive clause. Given this construction, I would contend that the four nouns of the subordinate clause—σοφία, ἐθελοθρησκία, ταπεινοφροσύνη, and ἀφειδία σώματος—as well as the noun τιμή in the final subordinate clause are catchwords of the opponents. Paul's critique comes in summing them all up (with ἅτινα, which looks backward to "the commandments and teachings" and forward to these specific practices) and describing them as nothing more than a "gratification of the flesh" (πλησμονὴν τῆς σαρκός). The entire third subsection could be diagrammatically represented as follows (with indentation designating subordination):

Conditional Sentence With a Rhetorical Question
Εἰ ἀπεθάνετε σὺν Χριστῷ ἀπὸ τῶν στοιχείων τοῦ κόσμου,
τί ὡς ζῶντες ἐν κόσμῳ δογματίζεσθε;
    Quotation: "Μὴ ἅψῃ μηδὲ γεύσῃ μηδὲ θίγῃς,"
        Critique: ἅ ἐστιν πάντα εἰς φθορὰν τῇ ἀποχρήσει,
    Parenthesis: Referring Back To τί ... δογματίζεσθε;
    (κατὰ τὰ ἐντάλματα καὶ διδασκαλίας τῶν ἀνθρώπων,)
        Critique of the Regulations
        ἅτινά ἐστιν -
                λόγον μὲν ἔχοντα σοφίας
                ἐν ἐθελοθρησκίᾳ καὶ
                ταπεινοφροσύνῃ [καὶ]
                ἀφειδίᾳ σώματος,
                οὐκ ἐν τιμῇ τινι
        - πρὸς πλησμονὴν τῆς σαρκός.

---

[8] B. Hollenbach, "Col. II.23: Which Things Lead to the Fulfilment of the Flesh," *NTS* 25 (1978-79) 254-61. His solution has been followed by O'Brien, *Colossians,* 152-53; Pokorný, *Colossians,* 155.

[9] This meaning for ἐστιν πρός can also be seen in John 11:4: Αὕτη ἡ ἀσθένεια οὐκ ἔστιν πρὸς θάνατον (cf. also 1 Cor 14:26). See Hollenbach, "Colossians II.23," 259.

[10] Hollenbach, "Colossians II.23," 257-58, finds precedent for this use of μέν in Rom 7:25; 8:10; and 2 Cor 12:1.

3. "Wisdom"

That some form of "wisdom" tradition played a part in the teaching of "the philosophy" is explicitly stated in the polemic of Col 2:23 where Paul says that the doctrine of the opponents "has a reputation[11] for wisdom" (λόγον μὲν ἔχοντα σοφίας). Given the characteristics of the teaching that we have already observed, it is highly unlikely that the opponents were claiming to propagate Jewish "wisdom" in the traditional sense (i.e. Proverbs, Ecclesiastes, Wisdom of Solomon, or Wisdom of Jesus ben Sirach). Neither is it likely that the reference is to wisdom in a Greek philosophical sense. It probably relates to wisdom of an esoteric nature that the adherents to "the philosophy" claimed to possess. There was already precedent for this in Greek literature where the term γόης was connected to σοφιστής.[12]

Jewish involvement in such practices and beliefs could have been justified by the local Jews on the basis of an already established tradition purportedly stemming from Solomon, which boasted in this patriarch as adept at magic and manipulating the evil spirits.[13] In contrast to understanding "wisdom" in line with the sapiential literature, the opponents may have understood "wisdom" in this *magical* sense. This view of wisdom is well

---

[11] On this meaning of the expression λόγον ἔχειν, see Lightfoot, *Colossians,* 205.

[12] For the references, see W. Burkert, "ΓΟΗΣ. Zum Griechischen 'Schamanismus,'" *Rheinisches Museum für Philologie* NS 105 (1962) 55.

[13] P. S. Alexander, "Incantations and Books of Magic," in *HJP²*, 3.375-79 (= "Appendix: Solomon and Magic"); K. Preisendanz, "Salomo," in *PW* Supplementband 8.660-704; E. Lohse, "Σολομών," *TDNT* 7.462-63; R. Kraft, "The Multiform Jewish Heritage of Early Christianity," in *Christianity, Judaism and Other Greco-Roman Cults* (FS. M. Smith; SJLA 12; Leiden: Brill, 1975) 3.196-97; M. P. Nilsson, "Die Religion in den griechischen Zauberpapyri," *Kungl. Humanistiska Vetenskapssamfundet I Lund. Arsberattelse 1947-48* (Lund: Gleerup, 1948) 64-65; H. G. Gundel, *Weltbild und Astrologie in den griechischen Zauberpapyri* (Münchener Beiträge zur Papyrusforschung und Antiken Rechtsgeschichte 53; München: Beck, 1968) 75-76; G. Luck, *Arcana Mundi* (Baltimore: Johns Hopkins University Press, 1985) 27; D. Aune, "Magic in Early Christianity," *ANRW* II.23.2 (Berlin: Walter de Gruyter, 1980) 1526. See also K. Berger, "Die königlichen Messiastraditionen des Neuen Testaments," *NTS* 20 (1973) 1-44, esp. 3-9, sees the Solomonic tradition as strong enough to argue that "son of David" (= Solomon) designates the Messiah as an exorcist and miracle worker. Berger is thus attempting to refute those who contend that Jewish messianic expectation was not tied to miracle working. See his article for the numerous references demonstrating the Solomonic magical tradition. Moses, however, is regarded as the greatest author of magical books by the magical papyri (*PGM* V.109; VII.619; XIII.1, 21, 343, 383, 725, 971, 1057, 1078); see further, J. G. Gager, *Moses in Greco-Roman Paganism* (SBLMS 16; Nashville: Scholar's Press, 1972) 134-61 (= Chapter 4, "Moses and Magic").

attested in the Judaism of the Hellenistic period. There were many Solomonic traditions portraying his expertise in manipulating the spirit world and bringing the hostile "powers" under control.[14]

The tradition has its roots in 1 Kings 3:5-12 and 4:29-34, where Solomon requests wisdom from the Lord and God promises to make him the wisest of all people. The Wisdom of Solomon interprets this as, among other things, a knowledge of astral powers, the realm of spirits, and magic: "For it is he [God] who gave me unerring knowledge of what exists, to know the structure of the world and the activity of the elements (ἐνέργεια στοιχείων) ... the constellations of the stars ... *the powers of spirits* (πνευμάτων βίας) ... and the virtues of roots (δυνάμεις ῥιζῶν)" (Wis 7:17-20 [italics mine]). There is an allusion to Solomon's power over demons in *Pseudo-Philo* 60:3: When David plays his lyre to drive away the demon from Saul, he sings, "after a time one born from my loins will rule over you." The Solomonic magical tradition appears in the Great Paris Magical papyrus[15] as well as many other magical papyri and amulets.[16]

The tradition of Solomon's great "wisdom" in dealing with evil spirits is perhaps best illustrated by Josephus (*Ant.* 8.2.5 §§ 41-49):

> Now so great was the prudence and wisdom (σοφίαν) which God granted Solomon that he surpassed the ancients, and even the Egyptians, who are said to excel all men in understanding, were not only, when compared with him, a little inferior but proved to fall far short of the king in sagacity ... There was no form of nature with which he was not acquainted or which he passed over without examining, but he studied them all philosophically (ἀλλ' ἐν πάσαις ἐφιλοσόφησε) and revealed the most complete knowledge of their several properties. And God granted him knowledge of the art used against demons (τὴν κατὰ τῶν δαιμόνων τέχνην) for the bene-

---

[14] See M. Hengel, *Judaism and Hellenism* (London: SCM, 1974) 1.130; cf. also 2.88, notes 175-77. Hengel asserts, "According to Josephus (*Ant.* 8.2.5 §§41-49), Solomon 'philosophized' [cf. Col. 2:8, φιλοσοφία] about the whole of nature, though according to the thinking of the Hellenistic period this all-embracing wisdom could only be understood in a *magical* [emphasis his] sense. In this way, Solomon took his place alongside Moses in the Hellenistic-Roman world as one of the great wise teachers of secret knowledge long before the first Greek philosophers, comparable with the 'magicians' Zoroaster and Ostanes or the Egyptian Hermes-Thoth. This explains his significance for ancient magic which, according to the witness of Wisdom and Josephus, goes back into the pre-Christian period. The number of astrological, alchemistic, iatromantic and other tractates ascribed to him, quite apart from amulets and magical gems, is almost incalculable."

[15] See *PGM* IV.850-929. The charm is introduced as Solomonic magic (Σολομῶνος κατάπτωσις [line 850]; ἡ Σολομῶνος πραγματεία [line 853]) and has a parallel in *T. Sol.* 1:3 in lines 899ff (see note by W. C. Grese in *GMPT*, 1.55 [note 121]).

[16] See Alexander, "Incantations," 376-77 and Preisendanz, "Salomo," 662-84.

fit and healing of men. He also composed incantations (ἐπῳδάς) by which illnesses are relieved, and left behind forms of exorcisms (τρόπους ἐξορκώσεων) with which those possessed by demons drive them out, never to return. And this kind of cure is of very great power among us to this day, for I have seen a certain Eleazar, a countryman of mine, in the presence of Vespasian, his sons, tribunes and a number of other soldiers, free men possessed by demons, and this was the manner of the cure ... And when this was done, the understanding and wisdom (σύνεσις καὶ σοφία) of Solomon were clearly revealed ..."[17]

It is quite possible that Solomonic magical traditions were even in use among the Essenes at Qumran (cf. Josephus, *J.W.* 2.8.6 §136).[18]

This Solomonic magical wisdom is epitomized in the *Testament of Solomon,* where σοφία can be defined in terms of the ability to command and manipulate demons.[19] In the superscription at the head of the various versions of the *Testament of Solomon,* the king is given the epithet σοφός or σοφώτατος.[20] Thus, Solomon is represented as saying, "When I saw the Prince of Demons approaching, I glorified God and said, 'Blessed are you, Lord God Almighty, who has granted to your servant Solomon wisdom (σοφίαν), the attendant of your thrones, and who has placed in subjection all the power of the demons (πᾶσαν τὴν τῶν δαιμόνων δύναμιν)'" (*T. Sol.* 3:5). Even the King of Arabia, according to a letter cited in the *Testament,* had heard of Solomon's wisdom: "King of Arabia, Adarkes, to King Solomon, greetings. I have heard about the wisdom (σοφίαν) which has been granted to you and that, being a man from the Lord, there has been given to you understanding (σύνεσις) about all the spirits of the air, the earth, and beneath the earth" (*T. Sol.* 22:1; cf. also 22:3).

As we have already noted in connection with Chapter 2, the *Testament of Solomon* likely represents Jewish magical tradition that was taken over by Christians as early as the late first century or early second century

---

[17] LCL translation by H. S. J. Thackeray and R. Marcus (cited in D. C. Duling, "The Testament of Solomon," in *OTP* 1.946-47).

[18] T. S. Beall, *Josephus' Description of the Essenes Illustrated by the Dead Sea Scrolls* (SNTSMS 58; Cambridge: University Press, 1988) 154, note 175. Beall comments, "Thus, although Eleazar is not named by Josephus as an Essene, perhaps among the writings studied by the Essenes were those containing such 'medicinal roots' and other remedies prescribed by Solomon." R. Marcus, in the LCL translation, puts it more confidently: "[the Essenes] possessed books of medicine attributed to Solomon" (in H. S. J. Thackeray, et al., *Josephus* [LCL; London: Heinemann, 1966] 5.595).

[19] C. C. McCown, *The Testament of Solomon* (Untersuchungen zum Neuen Testament 9; Leipzig: J. C. Heinrichs, 1922) 48, comments: "In the *Test* he is already the wise man and magician *par excellence,* the favorite of God, endowed by him with divine σοφία, which includes insight into the crafty wiles of his demonic captives."

[20] Preisendanz, "Salomo," 662.

A.D. The mere fact that this tradition was taken over and used by early Christians—perhaps even in Asia Minor—gives further credibility to our contention that it may have happened in Colossae. If our hypothesis is then correct that σοφία signifies the Solomonic magical-wisdom tradition in the context of "the philosophy," the Colossian teaching would then be the first example of Christians adapting this tradition for their own purposes. Representing "the philosophy" as based on "wisdom" may also have been an attempt by the opponents to present their teaching as deeply rooted in authoritative Jewish tradition and thereby consistent with the faith of the Colossian Christians.

J. B. Lightfoot came close to the same identification of the reputed "wisdom" of the Colossian "philosophy" with the Solomonic magical tradition when he associated it with the magical arts practiced by the Essenes (as described by Josephus [see *J.W.* 2.8.6 §136]).[21] He even called attention to Josephus description of Solomon's magic as "wisdom." Uninformed by the later Dead Sea Scroll finds, Lightfoot erred, however, in describing Essenism as "Gnostic Judaism."

4. "The Philosophy" and "Tradition"

The fact that the opponents at Colossae described their teaching as "philosophy" has long been recognized on the basis of Col 2:8. There the author tells the readers to beware that no one take them captive "through the philosophy" (τῆς φιλοσοφίας). The choice of this term, as opposed to a more general term such as διδασκαλία (such as he uses later in 2:22), as well as the presence of the article, point toward the likelihood that the opponents referred to their hybrid form of Christianity in this euphemistic and honorable manner.[22]

By the time of the Roman Imperial period, the term was used quite broadly to refer not only to the various Greek philosophies, but also to the Jewish religion (Philo, *Leg.* 156, 245; 4 Macc 5:11) and even by Josephus to describe the three major sects of Judaism (φιλοσοφίαι τρεῖς; *Ant.*

---

[21] J. B. Lightfoot, "The Colossian Heresy," in *Conflict,* 23, 47-49 (note 39).

[22] So also, Lightfoot, *Colossians,* 179, who contends, "The term was doubtless used by the false teachers themselves to describe their system." See also, G. Bornkamm, "The Heresy of Colossians," in *Conflict,* 126; Dibelius-Greeven, *Kolosser,* 27; O'Brien, *Colossians,* xxxix, 109.

18.1.2 §11; *J.W.* 2.8.2 §119). The term also came into use to describe popular religion and the mysteries.[23]

Of special significance for our purposes is to observe that even esoteric knowledge expressed through magical practices was termed "philosophy." G. Bornkamm goes so far as to say that, "For syncretistic thought it has long since ceased to designate rational learning, but has become equivalent to revealed doctrine and magic."[24] Without accepting his *religions-geschichtliche* assumptions, we can still agree that the term was used widely for magic.

In his anthology of excerpts from much earlier works, Stobaeus (1.407) relates how a prophet imbued with esoteric knowledge works "in order that philosophy and magic (φιλοσοφία μὲν καὶ μαγεία) might nourish the soul."[25] R. Reitzenstein has correctly observed that in the magical papyri σοφιστής [= philosopher] "denotes one who possesses secret knowledge and secret power, the magician."[26] In Judaism, the term "philosopher" could even be used to refer to magicians. One of the epithets used for Solomon because of his knowledge of magic and the demonic realm was φιλόσοφος.[27] In the previous section we saw in Josephus's description of the Solomonic magical tradition that Solomon allegedly studied nature "philosophically" (ἀλλ' ἐν πάσαις ἐφιλοσόφησε), which appears closely connected to his knowledge of the art of casting out demons. This concept of "philosophy" is also well illustrated by the Greek translations of the Hebrew הַחַרְתֻּמִּים הָאַשָּׁפִים in Dan 1:20, the magicians and sorcerer-priests at the court of the king of Babylon[28]:

LXX = ὑπὲρ τοὺς σοφιστὰς καὶ <u>τοὺς φιλοσόφους</u>
Theod. = παρὰ πάντας τοὺς ἐπαοιδοὺς καὶ <u>τοὺς μάγους</u>

---

[23] See Theon of Smyrna (A.D. 115-40), *Expositio rerum mathematicarum* 14: "One might say that philosophy (φιλοσοφία) is the rite of genuine initiation and the handing on of those mysteries which are genuine mysteries" (cited in Lohse, *Colossians,* 95).

[24] Bornkamm, "Heresy," 126. See also Nilsson, *GGR,* 2.712-13, who speaks of "occultism" taking on a philosophical garment beginning in Hellenistic times (especially as exemplified by Bolus of Mendes).

[25] As cited in Lohse, *Colossians,* 95.

[26] Richard Reitzenstein, *Hellenistic Mystery Religions* (PTMS 15; Pittsburgh: Pickwick, 1978) 297. See also Bornkamm, "Heresy," 139, note 12.

[27] For references, see Preisendanz, "Salomo," 662.

[28] See further, O. Michel, "φιλοσοφία," *TDNT* 9.179-80 and Gnilka, *Kolosserbrief,* 122.

It is therefore quite conceivable that the Colossian faction, emphasizing the acquisition of an esoteric knowledge based on magical and mystery traditions, could have referred to its teaching as "philosophy."

Few scholars have attempted to portray the Colossian "philosophy" as representing teaching from one of the contemporary philosophical schools. E. Schweizer, who has suggested that the Colossian teaching represented Neopythagoreanism, had essentially been the lone exception.[29] His overall reconstruction of the competing teaching has attracted few followers.

In a recent monograph titled, *The Colossian Controversy*, R. DeMaris has also now attempted to make a case for an actual school philosophy as the catalyst stimulating the Colossian controversy.[30] He sets forth the thesis that the opponents were a group of Middle Platonists who had joined the Christian community at Colossae and were propagating their beliefs. He characterizes their teaching as "essentially syncretistic" and thus finds in it certain features of Jewish belief (along the lines of Philo). The opponents, however, were not Jews (or Jewish Christians) according to DeMaris, but were pagans who had entered the community to aid their philosophical pursuits (127).

In many ways, DeMaris stands on the shoulders of Schweizer. He provides an excellent analysis of Schweizer's view, rejecting Schweizer's conclusion that the Colossian "philosophy" was Neopythagorean, but retaining some of Schweizer's sources and re-classifying them as actually Middle Platonic (esp. Diogenes Laertius's, *Hypomnemata*). He rightly criticizes Schweizer for not taking more seriously the Jewish elements of the Colossian teaching and for too readily accepting claims of ancient sources to represent Pythagoreanism when in reality they are Platonic or eclectic (88, 92).

DeMaris sees the term *stoicheia* as a crux and suggests that how one interprets the term is decisive for the understanding of "the philosophy" (40). He concludes that the term "points unequivocally to a philosophical background" (55) and sees the *stoicheia* referring to the four elements, which are metaphorically understood in philosophical circles to refer to the "guiding principles in the world" (55). I would agree that the term is crucial for helping to understand the Colossian teaching and that the term was understood the way he describes in certain philosophical communities. He is wrong, however, in some of his assumptions about the use of the term. First, it is incorrect now to assume that there is no evidence for the use of the term to denote personal beings in the first century A.D. or prior (see Chapter 6). Second, although he claims that there is no evidence for the identification of the *stoicheia* with angels, he overlooks 2 Enoch 16:7 and is unfamiliar with the pagan and Jewish tradition about astral decans.

---

[29] Schweizer, *Colossians,* 125-34 (= "Excursus: The Colossian Philosophy [2:8]); idem, "Slaves of the Elements and Worshipers of Angels: Gal 4:3, 9 and Col 2:8, 18, 20," *JBL* 107 (1988) 455-68.

[30] R. DeMaris, *The Colossian Controversy* (JSNTSS 96; Sheffield: JSOT Press, 1994).

He interprets the "worship of angels" (2:18) as a devotion to demons or heroes (62, 71), suggesting that the opponents took over the Jewish designation ("angels"), but that Jews would have strongly rejected this practice. He understands these beings in the Middle Platonic sense of mediators between gods and humans (104-105). DeMaris even points to some of the angel inscriptions from Asia Minor, but concedes that they show no sign of Middle Platonic influence (107). In general, I would agree with his understanding of the angels as divine mediators, but would not want to root this in Middle Platonism. Had DeMaris looked more carefully into the angel inscriptions of Asia Minor, he would have found that the mediatorial function of the angels was carried out in a context of invocations by people for protection and aid. As we suggested earlier, the magical texts and the realm of folk religion therefore provides a better social location for understanding this phrase than philosophical speculation.

DeMaris rejects the interpretation of ἐμβατεύω as a technical term of mystery initiation in Col 2:18. Rather, he follows Nock and Preisker in taking it in the sense of "investigating." He thereby interprets the phrase as referring to a close mental scrutiny that produces or deciphers a revelatory vision of some kind (66). Ultimately, he makes the *stoicheia*, the guiding principles (the Platonic forms?), the object of scrutiny (118). This conclusion does injustice to the passage, which never indicates that the *stoicheia* become the object of study or visionary experience. DeMaris never addresses the implications of his decision to see ἅ as gathering together the preceding phrases and commenting on them (63). In what sense does the philosopher see "humility" and "the worship of angels"? DeMaris seems unaware of the difficulties of the syntax of this verse, and his conclusions tend to muddle the problem even more.

Most of DeMaris's analysis is limited to the passage he has identified as the polemical core of Colossians, 2:9-15. His myopic approach thus fails to take into account much of the positive teaching of the letter that may, at least, give some insight into the problem by noticing the suggested antidote. I think he misses the prominent role given to the teaching about principalities and powers in the letter—beginning with the hymn and extending through Col 2. He likewise fails to grapple with some of the unique theological accents of the letter, especially the cosmic Christology and realized eschatology, for what these themes can contribute to an understanding of the problem. At the minimum he needs to ask why the Colossian congregation needs to receive this form of teaching if they are tempted to take up Middle Platonic ideas.

One of the greatest weaknesses of his study is his need to demonstrate the presence of Middle Platonic circles in Asia Minor. He assumes the widespread popularity of Middle Platonism, but can point to no examples of its influence in western Anatolia. His thesis could be slightly more convincing if the letter were written to a church in Alexandria or Athens, but a small community in a rural area? In discussing Neopythagoreanism, he concedes that a "preoccupation with religion, magic, and the occult typified the age" (102). I remain convinced that this is the most fruitful avenue to pursue. The kind of philosophical purity and noble pursuit of knowledge as extolled in Timaeus Locrus and other Middle Platonic authors is too removed from the lives of the common people we find in the churches of the Lycus Valley.

Paul also characterizes this "philosophy" as "tradition" (παράδοσις; Col 2:8) passed on by the hands of men. Although it is possible to see the term παράδοσις as part of Paul's critique of the opponents teaching,[31] it is more likely that the opponents presented their teaching as valuable because, in fact, it was based on ancient and venerable παράδοσις.[32]

The term παράδοσις was very important both in the context of magic and the mysteries. The idea of a "tradition" passed down from magician to magician was foundational to the magical papyri.[33] In fact, all magical literature is or pretends to be tradition. Recipes, spells, and conjurations have been collected and written down from purportedly old and valuable παράδοσις (*PGM* I. 54; IV. 476).[34] As we observed in Chapter 5, the so-called Mithras Liturgy is described as παραδοτὰ μυστήρια (*PGM* IV.476).[35] Similarly, a pagan magical text betraying the obvious influence of the Moses magical tradition speaks of passing on tradition (*PGM* V.109-10)[36]: "I am Moses your prophet to whom you transmitted your mysteries (παρέδωκας τὰ μυστήρια) celebrated by Israel." Here the (probably Egyptian) author conceives of the people of Israel as worshiping their God in the form of a mystery cult. The ultimate aim of this charm, however, was for the person to gain power over all kinds of demonic spirits.

In the cults that practiced mystery rites there were often no written liturgies or sacred documents. Ritual enactment of the informing myth—the "sacred tale (ἱερὸς λόγος)"—was central to the practice of the cult. The symbolic dramatic scene itself became an important part of the "tradition" together with any vow or cultic formula (σύνθημα). The term *tradition* (= παράδοσις) is used by Apuleius to refer to the heart of the rite Lucius received, performed, and experienced during his initiation into the mystery of Isis: "For the gates of hell and the guarantee of life were alike in the power of the goddess and the very rite of dedication (*traditionem*) itself

---

[31] So Schweizer, *Colossians,* 136-37.

[32] So also Dibelius-Greeven, *Kolosser,* 27; Bornkamm, "Heresy," 126.

[33] See H. D. Betz, "The Formation of Authoritative Tradition in the Greek Magical Papyri," in *Jewish and Christian Self Definition* (London: SCM, 1982) 3.161-70. For references to the importance of "tradition" in the mysteries, see Lohse, *Colossians,* 95-96, n. 25.

[34] Betz, "Authoritative Tradition," 164.

[35] For comment on this text, as well as on the role of παράδοσις/παραδιδόναι generally in the mystery cults, see Albrecht Dieterich, *Eine Mithrasliturgie* (3d ed. by Otto Weinrich; Darmstadt: Wissenschaftliche Buchgesellschaft, 1966) 53-54, esp. note 4.

[36] See the discussion of this text in Chapter 1 (section: "The Invocation of Angels for Protection").

was performed in the manner of a voluntary death and of a life obtained by grace" (Apul. *Met.* 11.21 = 283, 5).[37]

E. Lohse has collected and presented some of the most important texts illustrating the role of "tradition" (παράδοσις/*traditio*) in the mysteries.[38] One line in Cicero's *Tusculanae Disputationes* reads, "Recall, as you have been initiatied, the lore imparted to you in the mysteries (*quae tradantur mysteriis*) (Cic. *Tusc.* 1.13).[39] An inscription from Attica calls attention to a person who "entered into the tradition of the mysteries (εἰσαγαγὼν τὴν τῶν μυστηρίων παράδοσιν)."[40] Many other texts could be cited to illustrate how the transmission of tradition was fundamental to the practice of ritual initiation in the mysteries.[41]

The conclusion reached by Lohse regarding the role of παράδοσις in the teaching of the "philosophy" is still supported by the evidence:

> Obviously the proponents of that "philosophy" which had been introduced into the Asia Minor communities spared no effort to clothe their teaching with the aura of wisdom transmitted from of old. They did this by appealing to the "tradition" (παράδοσις) which would guarantee the unimpaired transmission of the divine revelation.[42]

The author of Colossians rejects their claim, however, and contends that it was a tradition *of men*. The genitive attribute τῶν ἀνθρώπων was probably added by Paul to devalue the opponents' claim that their tradition was based ultimately on divine revelation.[43] Paul takes it one step further, however, by suggesting that their "philosophy" was actually *demonically* inspired (κατὰ τὰ στοιχεῖα τοῦ κόσμου).

Although it is possible that the main perpetrator of the Colossian "philosophy" may have been a Gentile who was thinking in terms of the

---

[37] See J. G. Griffiths, *The Isis-Book (Metamorphoses, Book XI)* (EPRO 39; Leiden: Brill, 1975) 280.

[38] Lohse, *Colossians,* 95-96 (see esp. note 25).

[39] Translation from Lohse, *Colossians,* 96, note 25. See also Gnilka, *Kolosser,* 123.

[40] W. Dittenberger, *SIG³,* 704 E 12 (also cited in Lohse, *Colossians,* 95, note 25).

[41] See Plut., *De Is. et Os.* 2 (= *Moralia* 351E-F); *Demetr.* 26.1; Diod. Sic., 5.48.4; Athenaeus, *Deipnosphistae* 2.40d. See also the references in Griffiths, *Isis-Book,* 280, and M. Dibelius, "The Isis Initiation in Apuleius and Related Initiatory Rites," in *Conflict,* 102, note 3.

[42] Lohse, *Colossians,* 96.

[43] In this way it echoes Mk 7:8, where Jesus is represented as upbraiding the Pharisees and lawyers for their scrupulous observance of food laws to the point where they "have let go of the commands of God and are holding on to the traditions of men (τὴν παράδοσιν τῶν ἀνθρώπων)."

tradition he had received prior to his conversion (thus, mystery initiation), it is also certainly conceivable that the primary teacher was Jewish and was drawing on Jewish magical and mystical traditions. As we observed above, the Solomonic magical tradition may have been a significant source for the opponents. Once again, we can refer to Lightfoot for support, who, more than a century ago, pointed in this direction when he explained παράδοσις in Col 2:8 by appealing to the secret books of the Essenes that contained the names of the angels (Josephus, *J.W.* 2.8.7 §142).[44] Books with the names of angels that could be invoked for protection and aid—such as early forms of the tradition behind the *Testament of Solomon* and the *Sepher Ha-Razim*—may have been used by the Colossian opponents and extolled as "philosophy," which they had received as valuable "tradition."

In contrast to this Paul calls the Colossians back to the Lord Jesus Christ whom they had "received" (παρελάβετε) as embodied tradition (Col 2:6). Their emphasis on angelic mediators in the context of "the philosophy" was apparently threatening to overshadow their relationship to Christ. In fact, Paul accuses the disseminators of the variant teaching of "not holding tight to the head" (i.e. Jesus Christ; Col 2:19).

5. Dietary Regulations and Taboos

There are many indications in Paul's polemic that the teachers of "the philosophy" were imposing strict dietary regulations on their followers. This is evident in the admonition of Col 2:16 not to let anyone judge them regarding "food" (βρῶσις) and "drink" (πόσις). It comes out most strongly in the final section of the polemic (2:20-23), where they are again warned not to submit to regulations. Paul then quotes what appears to be one of the slogans of the opponents: "Do not handle! Do not taste! Do not touch!" (Μὴ ἅψῃ μηδὲ γεύσῃ μηδὲ θίγῃς) (2:21). In addition, Paul twice uses the word ταπεινοφροσύνη ("humility") to describe their practice (2:18, 23) and finally employs the rare expression ἀφειδία σώματος (2:23) to characterize the harshness with which they were treating their bodies. The sum total of this terminology seems to go beyond the cultic and ritual practices typical of Judaism.[45]

---

44 Lightfoot, *Colossians,* 180.
45 So also DeMaris, *Controversy,* 58.

The terms for eating and drinking (ἐν βρώσει καὶ ἐν πόσει; 2:16) were common words for the everyday practice of taking nourishment.[46] In religious usage, they could be found in many traditions. What is significant in Col 2:16 is that the dietary practices of some in the Colossian congregation were coming under scrutiny and judgment by the advocates of "the philosophy," presumably because they were not maintaining the specific food laws deemed crucial by the teachers.

The term ταπεινοφροσύνη ("humility") is used in Col. 2:8, 23 to characterize a facet of the false teaching and is likely connected with the practice of fasting.[47] Since elsewhere in this letter (3:12) as well as in Paul's letters (Phil 2:3; cf. also Eph 4:2) the term carries a positive significance and here it is used with negative connotations, it is likely quoted in these two verses as a technical term of "the philosophy." This observation is strengthened by the fact that the term appears in a series of three items that the opponents were "insisting on."

Fasting was practiced widely in the ancient world and for a variety of purposes. Jewish mystics fasted to ready themselves for visionary heavenly ascent.[48] In the local pagan cults, fasting was preliminary to receiving the oracular statements from Apollo at Didyma or Claros.[49] Initiation into the mysteries of Isis was preceded by a ten-day period of purification that included fasting (Apul. *Met.* 11.23 [=284-85]).[50] Fasting was also an important preparation for receiving a dream from the deity or performing spells effectively.

Of special significance for our inquiry is the well attested fact that fasting also had apotropaic significance—for driving off evil demons.[51] J. Behm observes,

---

[46] See *BAGD,* 148. The combination of the two are used by Paul in Rom 14:17 to describe Jewish religious scruples. The terms are also frequently used in pagan litrerature as well as the magical papyri.

[47] See, for example, Hermas, *Vis.* 3.10.6; *Sim.* 3.10.6, where ταπεινοφροσύνη is used of fasting. For discussion, see Francis, "Humility and Angelic Worship in Col 2:18," in *Conflict,* 167-71. This particular use of ταπεινοφροσύνη appears to be a distinctively Jewish description for fasting (normally indicated by νηστεία). The term ταπεινοφροσύνη came to be used perhaps as a way of expressing a contrite heart and a submissive spirit before God as evidenced through the practice of fasting.

[48] Francis, "Humility," 168; Thomas J. Sappington, *Revelation and Redemption at Colossae* (JSNTS 53; Sheffield: Sheffield Academic Press, 1991) 151, 162.

[49] See R. L. Fox, *Pagans and Christians* (New York: Knopf, 1986) 386.

[50] See Griffiths, *Isis-Book,* 290-91.

[51] See P. Gerlitz, "Fasten als Reinigungsritus," *ZRGG* 20 (1968) 212-22. He goes so far as to say, "Originally all fasting practices of religious history can be traced back to an apotropaic-cathartic reason and they were magically based." Still the most thorough study

The original and most powerful motive for fasting in antiquity is to be found in fear of demons who gained power over men through eating. Fasting was also an effective means of preparing for intercourse with the deity and for the reception of ecstatic or magical powers.[52]

This is true in both pagan and Jewish magical traditions. In this connection, Behm notes, "In magic fasting is often a pre-condition of success in the magical arts. The texts always demand sobriety, if not extended fasting to strengthen the magical force."[53] In Judaism, the apotropaic function of fasting is well-illustrated in the *Apocalypse of Elijah* 1:20-21: "But a pure fast is what I created, with a pure heart and pure hands. It releases sin. It heals diseases. It casts out demons."[54] Some segments of early Christianity also believed that evil spirits enter human bodies to enjoy food and drink (as well as other pleasures) through the person they possess. Thus, in Pseudo Clement, *Homily* 9.10, fasting is prescribed to cause demons to flee: "Hence, in order to the putting of demons to flight, the most useful help is abstinence, and fasting, and suffering of affliction."[55]

The referent of ταπεινοφροσύνη in Col 2:18 & 23 should not be limited, however, strictly to the practice of fasting. As Lohse notes, the term "describes the eagerness and docility with which a person fulfills the cultic ordinances."[56] Thus, it may be closely related to the slogan of prohibitions in v. 21. As we will see below, calendrical observances may also be in the purview of this word.

Nearly all interpreters have correctly regarded verse 21—"Do not handle! Do not taste! Do not touch! (Μὴ ἅψῃ μηδὲ γεύσῃ μηδὲ θίγῃς)"— as either a direct quotation from "the philosophy" or the author's stereotyping of their taboo-oriented regulations. Although this particular slogan

---

of this motive for fasting is found in P. R. Arbesmann, *Das Fasten bei den Griechen und Römern* (Religionsgeschichtliche Versuche und Vorarbeiten 21; Giessen: Töpelmann, 1929) esp. ch. 2, §6, "Das apotropäische Fasten," 21-63.

[52] J. Behm, "νῆστις," *TDNT* 4.926. See his article for the references. See also O'Brien, *Colossians,* 138-39, and Lohse, *Colossians,* 115, who cite Behm approvingly.

[53] Behm, "νῆστις," *TDNT* 4.927. See his article for the relevant texts.

[54] This appears in a portion of the book that probably reflects the original Jewish homily and not Christian redaction. See O. S. Wintermute, "Apocalypse of Elijah," in *OTP* 1.721-22. See also Behm, "νῆστις," *TDNT* 4.929.

[55] See Gerlitz, "Fasten," 212-13. He notes a similar conception in Porphyry, *De Philosophia ex Oraculis Haurienda* 149.

[56] Lohse, *Colossians,* 118. Sappington, *Revelation and Redemption,* 151 contends that Francis's research suggested that the term was used more broadly than fasting to include a whole range of bodily disciplines. He claims that Lohse (and others) misunderstood Francis's view when he criticized him for limiting the meaning to fasting.

is without a precise parallel, there are numerous parallels to the individual prohibitions in many traditions. The saying as a whole gives strong evidence that "the philosophy" had a collection of taboos. This was a common phenomenon in many of the popular religions of the time. Although most interpreters take the saying as referring to dietary regulations, there is no reason to limit the application to matters of food and drink. It may extend to sexual regulations and other types of taboos.

The careful observance of taboos was a precondition for the successful fulfillment of a magical recipe. In an invocation rite to summon the god Apollo in *PGM* I.262-347, the suppliant is called to "refrain from all unclean things and from all eating of fish and from all sexual intercourse" so that he or she could "bring the god into the greatest desire toward you" (*PGM* I.289-92). As we have already observed (in Chapter 5), the so-called Mithras Liturgy calls for the initiate to maintain certain dietary and purity regulations, including abstaining from meat for seven days (*PGM* IV.734-36, 783-84). Ritual prohibitions similar to these abound in the magical papyri. So also in Jewish magic, the practitioner needed to respect numerous taboos in order to ensure success. In the *Sepher Ha-Razim,* a recipe to conjure an appearance of Helios for the purpose of fulfilling the adept's request includes the following prohibitions: "guard yourself, take care, and keep pure for seven days from all (impure) food, from all (impure) drink, and from every unclean thing. Then on the seventh day ... invoke seven times the names of the angels that lead him during the day" (*Sepher Ha-Razim,* 4.25-30; cf. also 4:43-45).

Finally, dietary regulations and various kinds of taboos were an integral part of the rites in many local religions. The regulations were especially important in preparation for mystery initiation rites and ritual union with deities. As we have noted (in Chapter 5 and above), there was a ten-day period of ritual restraints in preparation for the Isis mysteries.[57] Similarly, Livy reports that a ten-day period of abstinence was required prior to initiation into the Dionysiac mysteries in Rome (Livy, 39.9). The Eleusinian rites also required periods of fasting as well as times of abstinence from wine and various kinds of meat.[58] The first statement of the *synthema,* or password, for the Eleusis initiates referred to the practice: "I

---

[57] Also, Plut., *De Is. et Os.* 4 (= *Moralia* 352c) and 6 (= *Moralia* 353b), describes the dietary regulations and taboos that the priests observed.

[58] Griffiths, *Isis-Book,* 291. See esp. Arbesmann, *Das Fasten,* 75-83.

fasted, I drank the *kykeon*, ..."[59] The rites of Attis and Cybele also had their periods of abstinence from food and sexual intercourse.[60]

The final expression that may point to dietary regulations and taboos in the context of "the philosophy" is the phrase "harsh treatment of the body" (ἀφειδία σώματος) in Col 2:23. We have already indicated above the structural probability that this expression was a self-description of the opponents.[61] The phrase probably refers to an "unsparing treatement" of the physical body.[62] It is quite doubtful that the Colossian opponents were engaging in rites that would have included flagellation and self-mutilation such as we find characteristic of the worship of Attis. These harsh practices were carried out in accordance with the informing Phrygian myth about Attis, who was driven mad by Cybele, flagellated himself, and ultimately performed an act of self-emasculation that led to his death. Because no such myth would inform the Colossian "philosophy," ἀφειδία σώματος should not be compared to the Attis rites. Rather, the phrase provides a fitting overall description of the ritual and ascetic observances practiced by the adherents of "the philosophy." The rites practiced by the adherents of the opposing teaching, however, could have taken on "enthusiastic" character insofar as they may be related to more common patterns of approach to deity characteristic of many local religions.

6. Observances: Festivals, New Moons, and Sabbaths

The first subsection of polemic (Col 2:16-17) contains a stern warning for the Colossians not to permit the errorists to judge them not only with respect to dietary regulations, but also regarding calendrical observances—

---

[59] Arnobius, *Adv. Nat.* 5.26: ἐνήστευσα, ἔπιον τὸν κυκεῶνα.

[60] Arbesmann, *Das Fasten,* 83-86; M. J. Vermaseren, *Cybele and Attis* (London: Thames and Hudson, 1977) 115; idem, *The Legend of Attis in Greek and Roman Art* (EPRO 9; Leiden: Brill, 1966) 44; H. Graillot, *Le Culte de Cybele* (Bibliotheque des Ecoles Francaises d'Athenes et de Rome 107; Paris: Fontemoing, 1912) 119. Less certain is the role fasting and food taboos played in the cult of Mithras. This is primarily due to the late date of the texts describing the ritual prohibitions. See Arbesmann, *Das Fasten,* 87-89.

[61] So also Lohse, *Colossians,* 126.

[62] Although the noun ἀφειδία never appears in the LXX, the adverb (ἀφειδῶς) appears four times. In Prov 21:26 it is said that "the righteous give *without sparing*" (similarly, see the use of the adjective in *Aristeas* 85:4). It is also used of the relentless slaughter (no one was spared) engaged in by Jason and his soldiers (2 Macc 5:6, 12).

"in the matter of a festival, a new moon, or Sabbaths" (ἐν μέρει ἑορτῆς ἢ νεομηνίας ἢ σαββάτων). There is no doubt that this collocation of terms come from Jewish practice since they appear together in the OT (see Hos 2:11; Ezek 45:17; 1 Chron 23:31; 2 Chr 2:4; 31:3; cf. also *Jub.* 1:14).

The major issue facing us, here, however is what the meaning of these festivals and observances was in the teaching of "the philosophy." Assuredly, they did not have the same significance they had in the OT. E. Lohse argued that "the philosophy" made use of "terms which stemmed from Jewish tradition, but which had been transformed in the crucible of syncretism to be subject to the service of 'the elements of the universe.'"[63] Similarly, J. Gnilka suggests discontinuity with the OT meaning and a close connection to the Colossians' fear of hostile powers: "They were not interested in the events of the OT salvation-history as the content of the festivals, neither were they interested in the Sabbath as a sign of the election of the people of God, but times and seasons as an expression of order ruled by cosmic powers who had control over the birth, death, sicknesses, and destiny of humanity."[64] These writers are certainly correct to remind us of the syncretistic nature of "the philosophy" and the deep concern at Colossae about the impact of hostile angelic powers. It is crucial, therefore, to interpret the calendrical obervances (as well as the taboos and dietary regulations) in light of the composite picture of the competing teaching.

Since "sabbaths" were not a part of the observances in local pagan religions or magical practices, it is likely that the teachers of "the philosophy" adapted sabbath observance from Jewish tradition. Sabbath observance was important to the Jews of Asia Minor.[65] It is possible that the Colossian teachers depended directly on the OT, but more likely that they drew on Jewish mystical traditions regarding the Sabbath. In the communal mysticism reflected in the Qumran *Sabbath Shirot,* heaven was perceived as closer on the Sabbath. This enabled the liturgical communion with the angels that is at the heart of the *Shirot* (the 4QShirShab and the 4Q400 texts).[66] Although it is doubtful that the communal and liturgical mysticism of Qumran is what the advocates of "the philosophy" were teaching, this kind of view of the Sabbath and holy days may have influenced the teachers.

---

[63] Lohse, *Colossians,* 116.

[64] Gnilka, *Kolosserbrief,* 146.

[65] See Trebilco, *Jewish Communities,* 17-18, 198-99 (here for the references).

[66] C. Newsom, *Songs of the Sabbath Sacrifice: A Critical Edition* (Harvard Semitic Studies 27; Atlanta: Scholar's Press, 1985) 20-21, 59.

Certainly the popularity of Asia Minor deities associated with the moon could have influenced the interpretation of "new moon" observances in the Colossian philosophy. The cult of the popular Phrygian moon-god Men (Μήν) surfaces as a viable condidate.[67] I have already pointed to the fact that numismatic evidence confirms that Men was worshipped at Colossae (see Chapter 5). Although we know little about the nature of the ritual observances that were a part of this cult, we do know from inscriptional evidence that Men was worshipped as a heavenly deity (Μὴν Οὐράνιος) as well as an underworld deity (Μὴν Καταχθόνιος).[68] Without any doubt, the various phases of the moon would have had significance to the devotees of this god. Another moon deity worshipped at Colossae was the goddess Selene (Σελήνη). She was closely associated with Artemis and Hekate. The three of these deities were very popular in magical practices and were believed to protect their worshippers from hostile spirits populating the heavens, the earth, and the underworld.[69] One text claims that "Selene, when she goes through the underworld, breaks whatever [spell] she finds" (*PGM* VII.455-56). In the *Testament of Solomon,* Selene appears as the evil demon Enepsigos (*T. Sol.* 15:1-7). Solomon discovers, however, that he can thwart this three-formed goddess by calling upon the angel Rathanael.

The observance of the new moon was significant for the performance of certain mystery initiation rites. Lucian describes how Menippus prepared for his initiation by following a set of ritual prohibitions and being ritually cleansed beginning on a new moon.[70] The "new moon" (νεομηνία) was also a crucial time for the performance of certain magical rites (*PGM* IV.787, 2389; XIII.30, 387). Concern about the phases of the moon was also true in Jewish magic evidenced in the traditions contained in *Sepher Ha-Razim.*[71] New moon festivals, however, do not hold a significant place in the observances of the Qumran community, presumably due to the emphasis on a solar calendar. This observation is significant for

---

[67] J. Lähnemann, *Der Kolosserbrief. Komposition, Situation und Argumentation* (SNT 3; Gütersloh: Mohn, 1971) 86-87, suggests the Men cult as the background to the interpretation of "new moon" observances in Col 2:16.

[68] For references, see W. Fauth, "Men," in *KP* 3.1195.

[69] See Theodor Hopfner, "Hekate-Selene-Artemis und Verwandte in den griechischen Zauberpapyri und auf den Fluchtafeln," in *Pisciculi. F. J. Dölger zum 60. Geburtstage* (Münster: Aschendorff, 1939) 125-45.

[70] Lucian, *Menippus* 4.72-109: "So the man took me in charge, and first of all, for twenty-nine days, beginning with the new moon (τῇ σελήνῃ ἀρξάμενος), he took me down to the Euphrates in the early morning, toward sunrise, and bathed me."

[71] See *Sepher Ha-Razim* 2.163-70, 48-51.

further demonstrating that there were some significant differences between Qumran Essenism and the Colossian "philosophy." Finally, it is significant to observe that "months" and the "moon" were observed in some sense in the Jewish "worship of angels" according to the *Kerygma Petrou.*[72] This text is important for reaffirming the connection between invoking angels (see Chapter 2) and calendrical observances in the context of Judaism.

The observance of various holy festivals (ἑορταί) was integral to the practice of Judaism, and there is some evidence confirming that Jews in Asia Minor continued to observe their special days.[73] A Jewish inscription from Hierapolis mentions Passover and Pentecost (*CIJ* 777).[74] If we can trust the historical reliability of Eusebius's assertion that Justin's *Dialogue With Trypho* (c. A.D. 160) was set in Ephesus, there would be further evidence concerning Jewish concern to observe the Sabbaths and feasts in Asia Minor.[75] It is important here to note that in the apocalyptic tradition the calendar (including the weekly sabbaths) is closely connected to the sun, planets, and stars as well as the angels that are over these heavenly bodies (see *Jub.* 2:9; *1 Enoch* 79:1-6; *2 Enoch* 19:3).

Festivals were also popular and important to pagan religion as a whole. Monthy festivals were characteristic of a number of the Phrygian cults.[76] The term ἑορτή itself, broadly used for any kind of religious festival[77], provides little help in sharpening our perspective on the Colossian "philosophy." Because it appears in a string of terms probably taken from the OT, it may point to the celebration of Jewish holy days. But, as we have noted, these may have undergone a fundamental reinterpretation along magical, mystical, and local religious lines.

---

[72] See Origen, *Comm. Joh.* 13.17 and Clement, *Strom.* 6.5.39. This passage is also quoted approvingly by Schweizer, *Colossians,* 155, as providing some insight into how the advocates of "the philosophy" may have understood these observances.

[73] See Trebilco, *Jewish Communities,* 18-19, 29-31, 190 note 70; *HJP²*, 144.

[74] Trebilco, *Jewish Communities,* 199, note 70, notes inscriptional evidence alluding to the observance of Jewish festivals at Aphrodisias.

[75] Trypho encourages Justin to "first be circumcised, then observe what ordinances have been enacted with respect to the Sabbath, and the feasts, and the new moons of God; and, in a word, do all things which have been written in the law (Justin, *Dialogue With Trypho* 8.4). See further, Trebilco, *Jewish Communities,* 29-30.

[76] E.g. the monthly festivals of Hekate; see T. Kraus, *Hekate: Studien zu Wesen und Bild der Göttin in Kleinasien und Griechenland* (Heidelberger Kunstgeschichtliche Abhandlungen 5; Heidelberg: Carl Winter, 1960) 50-51.

[77] See BAGD, 280; LSJ, 601.

There is one figure who may help us better understand how a Christian teacher may have combined magical, astrological, Jewish, and local pagan cult traditions into a new teaching. At the end of the first century, during the time of Trajan (A.D. 98-117), a Christian leader named Elchasai combined aspects of Jewish nomism (circumcision and law observance) with astrological beliefs and practices. The resultant syncretistic teaching emphasized the hostility of the stars (viewed as angels) and the need to regulate one's life according to the calendar (especially the Sabbath and the courses of the moon). Hippolytus quotes this aspect of the teaching of Elchasai:

> There exist wicked stars of impiety. This declaration has been now made by us, O ye pious ones and disciples: beware of the power of the days of the sovereignty of these stars, and engage not in the commencement of any undertaking during the ruling days of these. And baptize not man or woman during the days of the power of these stars, when the moon, (emerging) from among them, courses the sky, and travels along with them. Beware of the very day up to that on which the moon passes out from these stars, and enter on every beginning of your works. But, moreover, honour the day of the Sabbath, since that day is one of those during which prevails (the power) of these stars. Take care, however, not to commence your works the third day from a Sabbath, since when three years of the reign of the emperor Trajan are again completed from the time that he subjected the Parthians to his own sway, —when, I say, three years have been completed, war rages between the impious angels of the northern constellations; and on this account all kingdoms of impiety are in a state of confusion (Hippol. *Haer.* 9.11).[78]

Colossae was certainly not afflicted by the teaching of Elchasai, but "the philosophy" bore many similarities. At the minimum, the example of Elchasai points to emerging forms of localized syncretistic Christianity at an early stage. The Elchasaite teaching also demonstrates how a magical/astrological interpretation of sabbaths could surface in early Christianity.

---

[78] Translation by J. H. MacMahon in *The Ante-Nicene Fathers,* Vol. 5 (Grand Rapids: Eerdmans, n.d. [rpt. 1990]). It is better to affirm an affinity of type rather than a genealogical relationship between the Colossian "philosophy" and the teaching of Elchasai; *contra* Lähnemann, *Kolosserbrief,* 99. Similarly, A.J.M. Wedderburn, "The Theology of Colossians," in *The Theology of the Later Pauline Letters* (Cambridge: University Press, 1993) 6-7, has pointed to the teaching of Elchasai as providing "an instructive parallel." Neither do we need to conclude that the gigantic angelic figure that gives Elchasai the book of his teachings is derived from the so-called Iranian Aeon-myth (*contra* Bornkamm, "Heresy," 132-33); this angelic figure has more in common with Jewish mystical traditions such as that preserved in the *Shi'ur Qomah* (see M. S. Cohen, *The Shi'ur Qomah: Texts and Recensions* [TSAJ 9; Tübingen: J.C.B. Mohr [Paul Siebeck], 1985]).

7. "Freely Chosen Worship"

The fourth of the five expressions used by the opponents is ἐθελοθρησκία. This rare term denotes a *"voluntary* worship" formed with the prefix ἐθελο-.[79] E. Lohse is therefore correct in asserting that these teachers "proudly boasted that they had freely chosen the cult in which they participated."[80] This concept is thoroughly consistent with the character of local mystery cults as voluntary societies (θίασοι). The voluntary nature of the mysteries is clearly expressed by W. Burkert:

> [The mysteries were] cults which were not prescribed or restricted by family, clan, or class, but which could be chosen at will, still promising some personal security through integration into a festival and through the corresponding personal closeness to some great divinity. Mysteries were initiation rituals of a voluntary, personal, and secret character that aimed at a change of mind through experience of the sacred.[81]

Paul quotes the term here, as he does with ταπεινοφροσύνη, as a means of demonstrating that their claims are not valid. As O'Brien has said, "The apostle regards this worship as freely chosen but wrong."[82]

8. "Honor"

The final distinction which the advocates of "the philosophy" claim characterizes their spirituality is "honor" (τιμή; Col 2:23). In the context of "the philosophy" it probably indicates divine honor that they believe God confers upon them through visionary appearance, his election, bestowal of divine power, and possibly mystical union with him.

The term τιμή was used in this sense by some of the local Phrygian religions and in the mystery cults in general. For example, in the Phrygian cult of the goddess Hekate, the initiate is said to be conferred with honor

---

[79] A similarly formed term ἐθελοδουλεία was used in the sense of "voluntary subjection"; see LSJ, 479.

[80] Lohse, *Colossians,* 126. Similarly, see Bornkamm, "Heresy," 134; Pokorný, *Colossians,* 156 ("the reference is more likely to an additional act of devotion in the sense of a voluntary cult").

[81] W. Burkert, *Ancient Mystery Cults* (Cambridge, Mass.: Harvard University Press, 1987) 11. See also Nilsson, *GGR,* 2.345.

[82] O'Brien, *Colossians,* 153.

by the goddess. R. Reitzenstein has brought together the texts from which I will summarize the relevant lines below:[83]

1. <u>τιμηθέντα</u> ὑπὸ Σωτείρης Ἑκάτης κατιέρωσαν
   (They dedicated someone honored by Hekate Soteira)

2. Τρόφιμον καὶ ... Ἄμμιον ἔτι ζῶσαν ἀπειέρωσαν <u>τιμηθέντας</u> ὑπὸ Σωτείρης Ἑκάτης
   (They consecrated Trophimus and Ammius while they were still living after they were honored by Hekate Soteira)

3. ἀθάνατος Ἐπιτύνχανος <u>τιμηθ(ε)ὶς</u> ὑπὸ Ἑκάτης
   (Epitunchanos is immortal having been honored by Hekate)

In these three inscriptions, Hekate apparently honored the initiate by revealing herself to the person at the climax of the rites. In the case of the third inscription, it appears to have resulted in his immortality.

In a similar way, Lucius is accorded divine honor (*dignatio*) by the goddess Isis through her appearance to him in a dream and her invitation to be initiated into her mystery rites (Apul. *Met.*, 11.21-22). "Honor" (τιμή,*dignatio*) was thus often used with technical significance in local religions for privilege someone experienced of being chosen by a deity and going through a mystery initiation rite.[84]

These texts, therefore, serve to strengthen our impression that the Colossian "philosophy" has combined aspects of local religious traditions—particularly from the mystery cults as first indicated by ἐμβατεύω—into their beliefs and practice.

By his insertion of the negative οὐκ, Paul makes it clear that anyone (τις) who claims such honor is badly mistaken. The practices of "the philosophy" bring divine honor to no one! This is certainly part of the "empty deceit" (κενή ἀπάτη) he speaks of in 2:8.

9. Polemical Comments

The section 2:16-23 represents the heart of the polemic against the Colossian "philosophy." Having made an attempt to discern the nature of the

---

[83] For the references, see Reitzenstein, *Mystery-Religions,* 320-21.

[84] See Bornkamm, "Heresy," 134; J. Schneider, "τιμή," *TDNT* 8.177; Gnilka, *Kolosserbrief,* 161; Lohse, *Colossians,* 127.

opposing teaching in the polemical comments, we will now examine some of the reasons for Paul's antipathy toward "the philosophy" as reflected in his rhetoric[85].

a. The Teaching Belongs to "The World"

One of the most important points that Paul tries to make is that "the philosophy" is deeply rooted in the patterns and beliefs of the present evil age. He does this by twice using the term "world" (κόσμος), describing the teaching as a "shadow" (σκία), connecting its concerns with the part of creation that is passing away, emphasizing its human origins, and by twice connecting it with the term "flesh" (σάρξ).

Paul devalues the dietary regulations and calendrical observances in 2:17 by labeling them as merely a "shadow" (σκιά) of what is to come. He contrasts σκιά with σῶμα—the reality—which he describes as Christ. In spite of this criticism, it appears on the surface that Paul sees at least something of value in these practices to ascribe to them the semi-positive function of "shadow."[86] J. Gnilka disputes this, however, by pointing out that "shadow" often had very negative connotations for Greek speakers — unstable, shifting, weak, and empty.[87] He finds this use of σκιά present in the OT (e.g. 1 Chron 29:15: "Our days on earth are like a shadow, without hope") as well as in Hellenistic Judaism. In Philo, *Flaccus,* 165 the shadow (σκιά) is something that is exposed as falsehood (τὸ ψεῦδος). The main point of Paul's comments is that these practices are currently without value because of "the things which are coming" (τὰ μέλλοντα). This expectation has been fulfilled in the Lord Jesus Christ. The σκιά/σῶμα contrast is thus best explained as a reference to the turning of the ages with the coming of Christ.[88] In light of the present possibility of union with Christ, ritual observances, dietary regulations, and taboos motivated by

---

[85] A full analysis of the nature of the rhetoric of this section is beyond the scope of the present work. Such a study is needed, however. W. Bujard, *Stilanalytische Untersuchungen zum Kolosserbrief als Beitrag zur Methodik von Sprachvergleichen* (SUNT 11; Göttingen: Vandenhoeck & Ruprecht, 1973), has made an important initial contribution. Bujard's study is limited to a quantification of certain kinds of grammatical forms and structures and a comparison with the *Hauptbriefe.* One wonders whether his study suffers from an underlying *Tendenz* of disproving the possibility of the Pauline authorship of Colossians.

[86] So Lohmeyer, *Kolosser,* 122.

[87] Gnilka, *Kolosserbrief,* 147.

[88] Lohse, *Colossians,* 116-17; Gnilka, *Kolosserbrief,* 147.

fear of the hostile principalities and powers are wrong.[89] Christ has defeated the powers (Col 2:15), thus extending the possibility of living without a constrant dread of their influence, and he has introduced a new form of worship and service based upon a vital union directly with him, thus eliminating the need for mediator figures and assorted ritualistic observances and practices.

In the critique of the practices in the second subsection, Paul attributes to the advocates of "the philosophy" an exceeding arrogance, which he discerns as ultimately motivated by their own evil inclinations. He says that such a teacher is "puffed up without cause by the mind of his flesh" (εἰκῇ φυσιούμενος ὑπὸ τοῦ νοὸς[90] τῆς σαρκὸς αὐτοῦ; 2:18). "The mind of the flesh" is similar to Paul's statement in Rom 8:6-7 that τὸ φρόνημα τῆς σαρκὸς is hostile to God and is headed toward death. The mindset (νοῦς/φρόνημα) is the result of maintaining an attitude that is characteristic of the flesh (Rom 8:5). It refers to a pattern of thinking and living that is controlled by the evil inclination, the old self.[91]

Furthering his critique, in 2:20 Paul uses the term κόσμος twice in relation to the teaching of "the philosophy." He first affirms that the Colossians have died with Christ from the compelling influence of the hostile spiritual powers that belong to this world (see below). He then asks the Colossians the rhetorical question, "why are you submitting to regulations?" but emphatically inserts the clause, "as though you are still living in the world" (ὡς ζῶντες ἐν κόσμῳ). The contrast comes in 3:1-4, where Paul reminds them of their heavenly existence and calls them to seek the things above where Christ is seated at the right hand of God. Paul regards submission to the practices and teaching of the variant teachers at Colossae as a return to the structures of the present evil age (cf. Gal 4:9).

Two lines later, after quoting a slogan from "the philosophy" highlighting its ritual prohibitions, Paul claims that the food and other objects referred to by the prohibitions are destined to perish when they are used (ἅ ἐστιν πάντα εἰς φθορὰν τῇ ἀποχρήσει; 2:22). The point seems to be that the objects the variant teachers are prohibiting are of little consequence for true spirituality. God has given food to be consumed. Thus, it

---

[89] O'Brien, *Colossians,* 139, aptly comments, "So Paul is not condemning the use of sacred days or seasons as such; it is the wrong motive involved when the observance of these days is bound up with the recognition of elemental spirits."

[90] The entire clause is Paul's criticism of "the philosophy" and does not reflect a polemic against the role of *nous* in the teaching of the opponents; *contra* Pokorný, *Colossians,* 148.

[91] See O'Brien, *Colossians,* 146.

is perfectly appropriate for all foods to be consumed while recognizing them as God's gracious provision (cf. Mark 7:19). To create a series of taboos is to introduce a false legalism that actually contravenes God's intents.[92]

Following this remark, Paul makes the parenthetical comment that the regulations (δόγματα) of "the philosophy" have a human origin rather than a divine. He claims that the legal observances are "according to the commandments and teachings *of men*" (κατὰ τὰ ἐντάλματα καὶ διδασκαλίας τῶν ἀνθρώπων; 2:22). Here he makes use of the language of Isa 29:13 in which a woe is pronounced upon the people of God for only honoring him with their lips and worshiping him by their own rules. In Mark's gospel, Jesus quotes this passage in his criticism of the Pharisees, concluding that they "have let go of the commands of God and are holding on to the traditions of men" (Mark 7:6-8; Matt 15:7-9). The obvious point in Isa 29:13, Mark, and here is that the people of God need to be sensitive to what God desires from them in worship and service, that it is possible to have a facade of religiosity that actually repulses the one they are ostensibly trying to serve.

The final polemical comment Paul makes is that all the varied practices of "the philosophy" merely lead to a gratification of the flesh (πρὸς πλησμονὴν[93] τῆς σαρκός; 2:23). Quite apart from leading to a deeper union with Christ, these practices are considered by Paul as utterly rooted in the sensual dimensions of this present age.

b. The Teaching Devalues Christ

In all three subsections, Paul argues against the practices and/or beliefs of "the philosophy" based upon Christology. In the first subsection (2:17), he makes the point that "the reality"—in contrast to "the shadow"—is Christ. The implication is that those who decide to follow the variant teaching are detaching themselves from Christ.

In the second subsection—where Paul has revealed that the opponents invoke angels, have visionary experiences similar to what they experienced in pagan mystery initiation, and engage in ritual fasting and observe cultic prohibitions—he accuses the purveyors of this teaching of not being connected to Christ, literally, of "not holding tight to the head" (2:19).

---

[92] See Lohse, *Colossians,* 124; O'Brien, *Colossians,* 150.

[93] The word only appears here in the NT, probably with the meaning "satiety" or "gratification" (cf. LXX Ezek 39:19; Hos 13:6).

Rather than being inspired by Christ, they are following the tendencies of the evil inclination.

Finally, in the third subsection, Paul begins with the Christological point. He reminds the Colossians that by virtue of their union with Christ, they have effectively died to the influence of the world and the demonic powers within it (Col 2:20). This provides the basis for his urging that they not submit to the regulations that the opponents are trying to impose upon them.

It is highly doubtful that the advocates of "the philosophy" perceived themselves as detached from Christ or as teaching something that would lead others away from a genuine union with Christ. This is precisely, however, the implication that Paul draws for their teaching. Although the apostle does not argue here with the same obvious passion that he does toward the Galatians, he still sees the teaching as dreadfully dangerous because it demeans the role of Christ for believers and lessens the vitality of their union with him.

c. The Teaching is Demonic

Not only does the teaching demean the person of Christ, but Paul also contends that the tenets of "the philosophy" are demonic. He said this explicitly in Col 2:8 (κατὰ τὰ στοιχεῖα τοῦ κόσμου) and now implies it in Col 2:20. The reason he begins by asserting that they have died "from the elemental spirits of the world" (ἀπὸ τῶν στοιχείων τοῦ κόσμου) must be because these hostile spirits have some close connection to the imposition of regulations on the Colossians, as expressed in the apodosis clause. The natural conclusion is that Paul is viewing the variant teachers as led along by evil spirits and thus promoting teaching that is contrary to the Pauline gospel. There is a second reason that Paul reaffirms the identity of the Colossian believers with Christ over against the realm of evil spirit powers. This is due to the continued fear of that realm by the Colossians. The teachers of "the philosophy" were in fact prescribing these practices in response to the prevailing fear of astral spirits, capricious terrestrial spirits, and the awful spirits of the underworld. Paul here reaffirms that the Colossian Christians need not fear this realm nor do they need to adopt a supplemental system of beliefs and practices to deal with this realm.

d. The Teachers are Improper Judges

The beginning of each subsection urges the Colossians not to allow the advocates of "the philosophy" to function as their judges in matters of belief and practice. The key exhortations are as follows:

1. (2.16) Μὴ οὖν τις ὑμᾶς κρινέτω
2. (2.18) μηδεὶς ὑμᾶς καταβραβευέτω
3. (2.20) τί ὡς ζῶντες ἐν κόσμῳ δογματίζεσθε;

In the first, the idea of judgment is explicit and is directed toward the variant teachers' demands regarding dietary regulations and calendar observances. The teachers had put together a specific course of spiritual disciplines, and it appears that those who did not commit themselves to following their regulations (δόγματα) would face sarcastic criticism.[94]

Paul gives a similar warning in the second clause, but uses the rare and colorful word καταβραβεύω. The term was used in the context of the games and reflected the decision of the judge (βραβεύς) against someone.[95] Thus, an athlete who did not receive a favorable decision by the judge could be disqualified or deprived of the prize. For Paul, the opponents had no right to set themselves up as judges over the Colossians. Their flesh-oriented mindset was symptomized by an exceeding arrogance. Most damning is Paul's perception that they are not closely connected to Christ (2:19). Therefore, the Colossian believers should resist the insistence of these teachers to invoke angels and engage in ascetic practices, in spite of their visionary claims.

The concept of judgment is less explicit, but nevertheless present, in the final clause—"why are you submitting to [their] regulations?"[96] (τί ... δογματίζεσθε). The rhetorical question makes it clear that the teachers of "the philosophy" had effectively gained at least a limited following among the Colossians and that others were perhaps inclined to subscribe to the new teaching. Based on the two clauses we just discussed, it appears that one of the reasons people were taking up the regulations of "the philosophy" had to do with the harsh criticism they would receive from these influential teachers if they chose not to adhere to the rigorous practices.

---

[94] So also, Lohse, *Colossians,* 114.
[95] See LSJ, 885, 327.
[96] On this meaning for δογματίζω with the passive voice, see BAGD, 201.

Paul, however, declares these teachers unfit for leadership. The Colossians need to desist from these practices, cling to Christ, and ignore their damning criticisms.

10. Conclusion

(1) A careful examination of the characteristics of "the philosophy" based upon the polemic of Colossians 2 demonstrates a remarkable syncretism. There are features that appear to be clearly Jewish (such as Sabbath observances), some that are distinctively pagan (mystery initiation), others that are best explained as folk belief/magic (invoking angels), and many that could be explained from the perspective of a number of traditions.

(2) Traditions from Judaism are taken over by the purveyors of "the philosophy" and significantly adapted for their own purposes as well as combined with other traditions and beliefs from local cults, magic, and astrology. Some of the combinations and adaptations probably occured in the context of syncretism in some streams of Judaism in Asia Minor prior to the rise of "the philosophy" at Colossae. This is particularly true in the Jewish magical tradition in Phrygia and Asia Minor. This "folk Judaism" appears to have made a major contribution to the Colossian "philosophy."

(3) Many of the specific features of "the philosophy" are derived from this "folk Judaism": (a) the *wisdom* that the opponents valued and taught is best explained by the Solomonic magical tradition, in which wisdom is defined in terms of the ability to command and manipulate demons; (b) the term *philosophy* itself, the self-description of the opponents' teaching, can be explained as esoteric knowledge based on magic and mystery traditions, especially a knowledge of supernatural power and how to deal with spirits; (c) *Sabbath observance* is distinctively Jewish and is consistent with what we know of the conscientiousness of Anatolian Jews as recorded in Josephus; it may have been given a magical/astrological interpretation by the opponents; (d) likewise, *festivals and new moon celebrations* fit with the practices of local Jews; (e) *humility* is best understood in the Jewish sense of fasting and ascetic practice; in the context of "the philosophy," it may very well have been practiced for apotropaic reasons.

(4) Other features of "the philosophy" might be better explained as coming from a Gentile context of popular religion, particularly the local cults and magic: (a) *honor* is best explained by its use in the Phrygian

mystery cults, particularly the cult of the goddess Hekate, in which the initiate is said to be honored by the appearance of a deity at the climax of the initiatory rites; (b) *freely chosen worship* is consistent with the voluntary nature of the mystery cults; (c) although we mentioned *new moon celebrations* under Judaism, "the philosophy" may have reinterpreted the Jewish festival more in line with local traditions associated with the powerful moon god, Men; (d) likewise, the *festivals* may have been brought into conformity with local religious norms; and, (e) *dietary regulations* were an integral part of preparation for mystery initiation and for performing certain actions of ritual power that could provide protection from hostile powers.

(5) Because we are in the domain of folk religion, there is significant overlap in the practices of these people from different backgrounds. Therefore, in spite of the fact that the primary impetus for the Colossian "philosophy" may have been "folk Judaism," this Judaism had already assimilated certain beliefs and practices from the surrounding environment and, now, the teachers of "the philosophy" were combining a still greater variety of practices. The *traditions*, we can be sure, were varied, but probably had as their core a set of mechanisms for dealing with the threat of hostile powers.

(6) The content of Paul's polemical remarks clearly shows that he considered the teaching of "the philosophy" dangerous, especially because it demeaned the person of Christ and became a substitute for a vital relationship with the exalted Lord. Paul also saw the teaching as deeply rooted in the present evil age. As such it was a product of the minds of clever people who who were still controlled by their evil inclinations. Furthermore, "the philosophy" also had a demonic component and was regarded by Paul as ultimately inspired by evil spirits performing their work of deceiving people (cf. 2:8). The champions of "the philosophy" appear to have gained a foothold in the Colossian church. In the process of advocating their system of practices, they would bring harsh criticism on those who refused to follow their teachings. Paul urged the Colossian Christians to refuse their teachings and to ignore the scolding blasts they would receive at the hands of these teachers.

(7) We have suggested that all of these seemingly disparate practices cohere under the general framework of magic and folk religion. It is now necessary to pull all of these together and to attempt a reconstruction of the broad outlines of "the philosophy," which we will undertake in the next chapter.

Chapter 8

Toward a Reconstruction of "The Philosophy"

Where does this evidence lead us? We must now attempt a tentative reconstruction of the nature of the conflict at Colossae. In suggesting an overall framework for the Colossian "philosophy," it will be important to keep in mind E. R. Goodenough's comments in the inaugural volume of his *Jewish Symbols:* "Such a book, like all historical reconstructions, should properly be written in the subjunctive mood: what I say may be the case."[1]

Portraying the situation at Colossae with precision and clarity is really an impossible task for any interpreter. One feels that it is comparable to filling in the gaps of a 5,000 piece mosaic while possessing only 150 tiles and not knowing exactly where many should be placed! This is now an opportune time, however, to attempt a fresh portrait. Additional pieces of the mosaic have been discovered (e.g. new inscriptional evidence), we now have a better understanding of some of the pieces we already have (e.g. a new appreciation of the magical texts as giving us a glimpse of folk religion), and we have found that some of the pieces never belonged in our portrait to begin with (e.g. developed Gnosticism).

1. A Portrait of "The Philosophy"

It is sufficiently clear in the language of the letter that there is only one opposing front and that it has surfaced from within the church. Most likely a faction has developed in the church that is spreading unhealthy teaching and treating those who do not take up their practices with disdain and scorn. There may be one influential teacher—a shaman-like figure— behind the "philosophy," but this is not necessarily the case since the indefinite singular τις could be used for any representative of the group.

---

[1] E. R. Goodenough, *Jewish Symbols in the Greco-Roman Period. I: The Archaeological Evidence From Palestine* (New York: Pantheon, 1953) 31. Many scholars, however, are convinced that Goodenough failed to heed his own warning!

Paul never castigates them as outsiders or as proclaiming a different gospel; their greatest offence is that they are not adequately in contact with the risen Christ and that they reflect too much of the present evil age in their attitudes, teaching, and practice.

The issue of angelic beings is a matter of major consequence in the letter. The hymn makes it clear that Christ is not an angelic being—he is, in fact, the creator of all invisible entities and is therefore supreme by virtue of his temporal superiority and their subservient role as his creatures. The introduction to the hymn points to the hostility of the powers by associating them with darkness and describing the followers of Christ as being rescued from their realm. The danger of their realm and their dominance over the present age is revealed in Col 2:15 where the death and resurrection of Christ is explained in terms of its consequence for the demonic powers. Paul assumes the continuing influence of these powers when he calls the Colossians to consider themselves as dead to the control of these forces by virtue of their identification with the death of Jesus (2:20) and their present connection with him as Lord of these malignant forces (2:10).

Why is there such an emphasis on the realm of angelic figures, particularly those of a hostile bent? Part of the answer is forthcoming from Paul's description of the Colossian "philosophy" as an empty and deceitful teaching that is in accordance with the *stoicheia* of this evil age (2:8). As we concluded earlier, it appears that one of the ways that Paul sees the demonic agencies as still at work is through inspiring people to develop and propagate destructive teachings.

Part I of our investigation revealed that there is more to this theme than a charge of "demonic teaching" by a teacher in authority who sees his base of power and influence threatened. The descriptive phrase "worship of angels" suggests that the adherents of "the philosophy" themselves had a high regard for angelic beings and gave them a prominent place in their teaching. The veneration of angelic mediator figures was a widespread practice in the Mediterranean world of the first century both in Judaism and in pagan practice and seems to be particularly well attested for western Asia Minor. People called on angels for a variety of reasons, but especially for protection and assistance.

They needed supernatural aid because they faced supernatural threats and dangers in daily life: They lived in a world filled with evil spirits and capricious gods and goddesses. Astral spirits, decans, and the *stoicheia* often inflicted them with a foul fate. Enemies would curse them by invoking numerous *daimonia* and spirits of the dead through incantations and by

depositing *defixiones* in wells or graves. All kinds of evil spirits roamed freely and, at will or in fulfillment of a curse, caused fevers, headaches, seizures, and all kinds of sicknesses, induced terror through horrible dreams at night, brought harm and misfortune to people on journeys, and generally were the source of many forms of evil. Without being appeased by performing the proper rites, observing the right taboos, and making the acceptable offerings, the underworld deities and terrestrial spirits would manifest their displeasure by striking a region with a plague, a flood, or an earthquake. Even death itself did not provide a respite from the horrors of evil spirits: one might be forced to join their ranks through an untimely death and become a *biaoithanatos* spirit; even the underworld itself was ruled by deities who were not worthy of trust. Thus, in the Mediterranean world of the first century, an atmosphere of fear and anxiety prevailed about the activities of treacherous spirits. At the same time there was a keen sensitivity to do what was necessary—and what worked!—for protection.

All was not hopeless. There were mechanisms for dealing with this world of treacherous spirits. The phenomena that we call "magic" were the most common way of obtaining protection. Apotropaic magic was useful for warding off evil spirits. One could create a magical amulet to wear for protection. Various kinds of magical rituals could be performed to provide a defense against the attacks of evil powers. *Foundational to protective magic was the practice of invoking angels.* We have provided a detailed demonstration of this practice throughout Part I. Calling on angels for protection from evil spirits was something that was widely practiced and crossed all religious boundaries. Perhaps most significant for our purposes is how amply attested the practice was in the Jewish and pagan epigraphic evidence for western Asia Minor.

Protective magic not only involved calling on divine beings; other procedures such as the performance of ritual, the observance of taboos, and honoring deities through their festivals were often associated with it. Some magical rituals even had the appearance of a mystery initiation ritual (e.g. the so-called "Mithras Liturgy") that resulted in the adept's immortalization *(apothanatismos)* and deliverance from bitter fate and the awful workings of malignant powers.

By using magic one could avert a horrible fate, find healing from a spirit-induced sickness, cancel the effects of a curse, and summon a helper who could bring aid and protection.

As a substructure to the official religions, the practice of magic did not supplant the role of the local pagan cults, or in a Jewish context, the syna-

gogue. In other words, one did not decline using a magical amulet because one had been initiated into the cult of the Ephesian Artemis or was a member of the synagogue. Magic was practiced in varying degrees alongside the official, or recognized, religions.

The local cults did provide a second mechanism for dealing with the hostile powers. By experiencing ritual initiation in one of the cults that offered mysteries, a person could gain a certain immunity to the adverse spirits and deities. *This provides the most plausible context for the role of ritual initiation—suggested by the presence of the term ἐμβατεύω—in the Colossian "philosophy."*

Walter Burkert has recently suggested that "magic" is one of the main roots of the mysteries in the sense that the sacrifices, festivals, purifications, offerings, and initiations are performed to assuage the anger and envy of spirits who can wreak evil and destruction.[2] The mysteries do indeed evince a concern about the avoidance of danger in the present life. By offering a closeness to the divine through the extraordinary experience of initiatory encounter with a god or goddess, the mysteries extend a form of salvation that constitutes a deliverance from the greatest dangers of life.

We could certainly wish for more elaboration and specific information about the role of ritual initiation in the context of "the philosophy" from the author of Colossians. All we have is the almost cryptic indication that one or more of the proponents of "the philosophy" had experienced the highest stage of initiation and that they were appealing to their visionary experience in their advocacy of their beliefs and practice. There are three possible directions to which this evidence may point: (1) the leaders of the faction had experienced ritual initiation in one or more of the Phrygian cults. Although they were now followers of Christ, they viewed their past visionary experience as giving them authentic and helpful insight into the supernatural realm. They now appealed to this as a partial basis for their claim of wisdom and understanding in these matters. (2) The leaders of the faction had not only experienced ritual initiation in one of the local cults, but they were now "baptizing" this religious form and establishing an actual Christian mystery initiation rite. (3) The final possibility is that they were continuing in the spirit of polytheism and advocating ritual initiation into one of the Phrygian mysteries in addition to their new commitment as followers of Jesus Christ.

---

2 Walter Burkert, *Ancient Mystery Cults* (Cambridge, Mass.: Harvard University Press, 1987) 24. I cannot agree, however, with his claim that the mysteries had little concern with the afterlife in their emphasis on a happy and cheerful life for the present.

There is simply not enough information in Colossians to reach a certain conclusion. Of the three alternatives, the first appears to me as most plausible. The act of ritual initiation (ἐμβατεύων) is the context for visionary experience (ἃ ἑόρακεν), which appears to serve as the basis of the authority for the leaders of the Colossian faction. They are claiming a unique spiritual insight and therefore have the right to dictate to the Colossian congregation as a whole what is necessary and important for them to practice.

This would then suggest that the primary leaders of the Colossian "philosophy" were Gentile since it is doubtful that Jews in the Colossian congregation had been initiated into a local mystery cult. It is clear that the leaders of the group were not only drawing on their visionary experience in ritual initiation, but also on other religious beliefs and forms from their local cults. Their observance of festivals and new moons as well as the strict dietary regulations and taboos may have been taken over and adapted from the local religions.

"The philosophy" was certainly not just a Gentile movement in the churches of the Lycus valley. There are unmistakable Jewish contributions to this new teaching and, undoubtedly, Jewish Christians were involved in the faction itself. As we have noted earlier, the presence of "sabbaths" points to a kind of syncretism that is unique—sabbath day observances were not taken over and adapted in local pagan religions or magical practices. This aspect of "the philosophy," therefore appears to be a direct Jewish contribution. We know from Josephus that Sabbath observance was important to the Jews of Asia Minor. In the Colossian "philosophy," the Sabbath-day custom appears within a broader complex of observances that include new moon ceremonies and various other "festivals." It is difficult to discern the meaning attached to the Sabbath in the context of "the philosophy." We have already dismissed the specific suggestion that it reflects a kind of Sabbath-day communal, liturgical mysticism similar to what was practiced at Qumran. Nevertheless, in light of the composite picture we have already drawn of the Colossian teaching, it very well may be the case that the faction had a concept of the Sabbath that was similar to what we find in the *Sabbath Shirot* at Qumran. Specifically, they may have conceived of heaven as nearer on the Sabbath, the angels are more accessible, and their efforts at calling upon the angels for help and protection as meeting with greater success. There is also a sense in which the Sabbath would have been viewed as an important day to observe and that failure to observe it could displease God and thereby render one more susceptible to harm and influence by evil powers.

Local Judaism also appears to have made a significant contribution from its magical traditions and practices. In particular, the Solomonic magical tradition—viewed as "wisdom"—is an important part of "the philosophy." This tradition illustrates how Jews called on angels for protection and deliverance. Jews appealed to Solomon as the source of their knowledge of the proper angel names. The presence of this tradition in Asia Minor has significant epigraphical corroboration. Surprisingly, no one has ever taken this Jewish magical tradition into account in describing the kinds of Jewish influences on the churches of the Lycus Valley.

Certainly the whole complex of Jewish food and purity laws may be reflected in the teaching of "the philosophy." It is important to realize that they were probably refined into a system of taboos that needed to be observed in order to avoid offending not only God, but especially his angels, and thus lessening one's ability to call upon them and their effectiveness at providing help and protection.

The nature of the teaching of the opponents at Colossae is significantly different from the opposing teaching reflected in the polemic of Galatians. The law is a major issue in Galatians, whereas in Colossians, the term νόμος is never mentioned, nor are other terms associated with a law controversy, e.g. covenant, Moses, Abraham, etc. By implication, justification/righteousness terminology is not present in Colossians because the issue of covenant status with respect to the law is not part of the debate. Although some writers have contended that the opponents advocated circumcision, I think it is quite doubtful that they were insisting on the performance of this rite. The only reference to circumcision is in 2:11 where the author speaks positively about a spiritual circumcision. There is no direct polemic against the practice of circumcision anywhere in the letter. This is consistent with the nature of the controversy at Colossae as essentially Christological rather than a law controversy.

Thus, the Colossian faction was headed by one or more charismatic teachers who claimed special divine insight and were foisting their beliefs and practices onto the others.[3] At this stage they appear to have remained

---

[3] M. D. Hooker, "Were There False Teachers in Colossae," *Christ and Spirit in the New Testament* (FS. C. F. D. Moule; Cambridge: University Press, 1973) 315-31, questions the validity of any reconstruction such as what we have just laid out, questioning the supposition that there is any group of teachers advocating a particular doctrine. She points in particular to "the extraordinary calm" that characterizes how Paul writes, suggesting that Paul would have attacked any opposing teaching openly and explicitly. She argues that Paul writes the letter out of a general pastoral concern for the younger Christians at Colossae who are "under pressure to conform to the beliefs and practices of their pagan and Jewish neighbours" (329). Although I commend many of the observations made by

within the sphere of the Colossian church and had not broken away and formed a separate *thiasos*. The Apostle Paul judged their esoteric traditions and practices as extremely dangerous to the form of Apostolic Christianity he had passed on to them through Epaphras.

2. The Context of the Syncretism: Phrygian Folk Belief

Anthropologists have long recognized the persistence of local religious forms and beliefs even after a group converts to a newer religion. Syncretism is often regarded as a distinguishing feature of folk belief.

Robert Redfield has demonstrated, for instance, how Mayan religious beliefs and modes of practice have persevered in the peasant villages of the Yucatan for many years after that area's official conversion to Spanish Catholicism.[4] He cites numerous examples of the "naturalization" of Catholic practice by local reinterpretations of the rituals, symbols, and

---

Hooker in her study, I take exception to her overall thesis for two reasons: (1) Paul is not calm. There is a clear polemical tone to his remarks illustrated by his indictment of "the philosophy" as empty deception and demonic. (2) Hooker drastically undervalues the indications in Colossians that Paul is polemicizing against a specific group of opponents. Above all, Paul refers to the faction as *"the philosophy"*! Hooker neglects treating many of the key components of the teaching and practice of the faction, esp. ἐμβατεύω, the worship of angels, the set of taboos ("do not handle, do not taste, do not touch!"), etc. With Gnilka, *Kolosserbrief*, 163-64, n. 4, I would regard this view as "a gross oversimplification which does not take seriously the specific statements of our letter and does not reflect on the connection between the belief in the powers and the ritual prohibitions (the taboos)." On the other hand, Hooker has done an admirable job of describing many of the world view issues the Colossians would have been struggling with. In posing the question of why Paul wrote the letter, she asks, "Or was it because, living in a world which took the existence of such spiritual powers for granted, and wrested from their pagan beliefs and superstitions by Christian preachers, the Colossians would naturally have qualms about these beings, and wonder whether they still had power to influence their destiny?" (323). She aptly notes later, "what Paul has to say about ἀρχαί and ἐξουσίαι seems to suggest that the Colossians are still worried about the power of these spiritual beings, and need encouragement to be confident in Christ's power over them" (327).

[4] See R. Redfield, "A Selection from *The Folk Culture of Yucatan*," in *Anthropology of Folk Religion* (ed. C. Leslie; New York: Vintage, 1960) 337-88 (reprinted from *The Folk Culture of Yucatan* [Chicago: University of Chicago Press, 1941]). See also his *The Primitive World and Its Transformations* (Ithaca: Cornell University Press, 1953) 26-83. Redfield attempts to support the thesis that adherence to local beliefs and rituals after conversion to another religion is proportional to the distance of a village from a major city. This aspect of his thesis is doubtful. It fails to take into account the diversity of religious belief and expression in an urban context.

meanings through Mayan interpretive lenses. The prayers of a village shaman, for example, were directed to pagan deities as well as to Catholic saints. "Catholic" is not kept distinct from "Mayan," but rather the two traditions are integrated into a single web of religious belief. Conversion has only been partial; a new syncretistic religious form has emerged.

A similar situation emerged in Anatolia during the age of Hellenism. The worship of Greek deities spread across Ionia, Caria, Lydia, Phrygia, and the other territories of Asia Minor. The old gods and goddesses, however, were by no means displaced; their worship continued, albeit in a modified form. This phenomenon is readily observable in the context of the worship of the Ephesian Artemis. The Ephesian deity was originally a local fertility deity/mother goddess who was renamed Artemis by Greek settlers. Although now identified with the Greek goddess, the cult retained an oriental and orgiastic character. Even her cultic image was unaffected by the new identification—one can readily see the stark contrast between the richly ornamented Ephesian Artemis in a rigid, standing position and the elegant beauty of the the Greek Artemis depicted in many positions wearing smooth flowing robes. As I have documented elsewhere, there was also a strong magical substructure to the Artemis cult in Ephesus.[5] This popular veneration of the goddess likely issued in novel or unofficial interpretations of the ornamentation of her cult statue (e.g. her so-called breasts interpreted as planetary symbols). Her name is invoked in many magical papyri and curse tablets; her image is sometimes inscribed on the *defixiones* and amulets.

There is thus a tendency for local religious traditions to persist and there is also an additional factor to folk religion, which we have referred to throughout this book as "magic." In the first century of our era, Plutarch spoke of it as *deisidaimonia,* "fear of the gods" or "demon terror."[6] He held a much more positive view of the gods than much of the populace and argued that the gods were virtuous and kind, there was no cause for dread with them. His essay, titled *Deisidaimonia,* provides much insight into first-century folk belief.[7] According to Plutarch, such people were terrified by the gods and worried about potential attacks by evil spirits (προσβολαὶ δαίμονος). They experienced awful dreams and saw fright-

---

[5] *Ephesians: Power and Magic* (SNTSMS 63; Cambridge: University Press, 1989) 24.

[6] He was not the first to speak of this. Theophrastus wrote on this theme in Δεισιδαιμονίας ("Superstitiousness") *Characters,* XVI (in LCL, 79-83). For additional references and discussion, see K. Preisendanz, "Aberglaube," *KP* 1.8-12.

[7] See his essay, Περὶ Δεισιδαιμονίας ("Superstition") in Plutarch, *Moralia* 164E-171F (in LCL, 454-95).

ening and horrible apparitions (τεράστια φάσματα). These people also had a great fear of life after death, imagining that they would descend to the abysmal underworld where they would be greeted by hideous spectres, judges, and torturers and there face countless numbers of woes. This dread prompted people to wear protective amulets and to use magical charms and spells (γοητεῖαι καὶ μαγεῖαι), to seek the assistance of magicians and conjurers (γόητaι, μάντεις, ἀγύρται, περιμάκτριαι), to severely abuse their bodies as they confessed their errors, to offer sacrifices and perform purifications, and to pray with quivering voices. Plutarch says that these people "cast away all hope."

As a philosopher and one of the "enlightened" of his day, Plutarch saw the universe as an ordered and harmonious organism. His elevation of reason prevented him from finding a supernatural cause for every problem. His writings clearly reveal that the beliefs of the educated elite on spiritual matters were quite distinguishable from common piety. In other words, his Middle Platonism was distinct from folk belief.

This is an important point to establish as we consider the context of the church at Colossae. It is not appropriate for us to look to the philosophical schools and academies for an explanation of the Colossian "philosophy." The most plausible context for interpreting the teaching of the opponents at Colossae is in the domain of folk belief and *deisidaimonia*.[8]

Many scholars have recognized a certain commonality in the religious practices and beliefs of the Phrygian people that crosses their official religious affiliations. This is often referred to as the "Phrygian spirit." The following themes, which we have discussed throughout PARTS I and II, characterize this local folk belief and provide the context for the rise of the Colossian "philosophy":

• *A Tendency Toward Henotheism.* There was a distinct trend in Asia Minor in the Roman Imperial period to ascribe supremacy to one deity.[9] This is attested in part by many inscriptions to an anonymous *Theos Hypsistos* ("the most high god") in western Anatolia. In some cases the descriptive title may be a reference to Zeus, but some local deities were also worshipped as supreme in the universe (e.g. Men Tyrannos).

• *An Emphasis on Divine Intermediaries.* The trend toward a belief in one supreme deity did not imply a belief that all other gods and goddesses

---

[8] This conclusion has also been affirmed by R. Oster, "Christianity in Asia Minor," *ABD* 1.945-46.

[9] For a further discussion of this trend, see P. Trebilco, *Jewish Communities in Asia Minor* (SNTSMS 69; Cambridge: University Press, 1991) 128-29, 132-33; L. Robert, "Reliefs votifs et cultes d'Anatolie," *Anatolia* 3 (1958) 118-19; Nilsson, *GGR,* 2.569-77.

were now dead or impotent; rather, the highest god was envisioned as transcendent and served by many intermediate deities. This partly explains the existence of many *angelos* inscriptions in Asia Minor. These intermediaries were more directly involved in the day-to-day affairs of humanity than the supreme deity.

• *A Strong Belief In Dangerous Spirits and Powers—Deisidaimonia.* Not all gods, goddesses, spirits, and *daimones* were benevolent. They were to be feared. The curse tablets discovered in Asia Minor demonstrate the belief that various supernatual beings could be called upon to effect a curse. There were also spirits that posed a threat associated with wildlife, agriculture, crossroads and many other parts of daily life. Astral spirits, the zodiac, the planetary deities, and the constellations (*Arktos, Pleiades,* etc.) held sway over fate and were perceived as influencing the affairs of day-to-day life. The underworld was often perceived as a place of danger to which Hekate held the keys. One also needed to be wary of the spirits of deceased ancestors and the untimely dead who haunted and could wreak terror. Of course even the the gods and goddesses generally perceived to be charitable could be offended by improper or inadequate worship. As they did in Hierapolis, they could bring a severe plague or inflict other kinds of disasters. The common people of Asia Minor were thus gripped by *deisidaimonia;* these capricious and wicked powers brought sufficient reason for concern.

• *An Appeal to Intermediaries for Protection and Deliverance.* People in Asia Minor tended to call on intermediaries for help. The *angelos* inscriptions from the area well illustrate this trend. Angels were perceived as accessible supernatural beings that would come to the aid of people in need.

• *A Prominent Role for "Magic."* Acts of ritual power, wearing amulets, invoking supernatural beings, and a variety of other so-called magical practices were practiced in Phrygia. This is what we would expect from a people who lived in the dread of the hostile supernatural realm. Magic provided a mechanism for controlling these forces and a means of protection from their evil intent. The practice of magic among both pagans and Jews is well attested for Asia Minor.

• *Ecstatic Forms of Worship.* One final aspect of the Lydian-Phrygian spirit is the element of ecstasy in devotion that lead to the abuse of the body. This is best illustrated by the rites practiced in the worship of Cybele and Attis that involved, among other things, self-mutilations and flagellation. Of course, fasting and other forms of self-denial were a part of the preparation for mystery initiation in many of the local cults.

This local folk belief—the "Lydian-Phrygian spirit"—provides the best framework for understanding and interpreting the Colossian "philosophy." It provides a more natural explanation of the Colossian syncretism as stemming from local religious impulses that continued to wield a powerful draw on people converted to Christianity from the local Jewish communities and pagan cults.[10]

3. Christian Syncretism and Magic

The kind of syncretism we find at Colossae was not unique to that city or region. Paul had already written to a group of churches in central Asia warning them against the practice of εἰδωλολατρία and φαρμακεία ("idolatry and magic"), which he classified as deeds of the flesh (Gal 5:20). The burning of the magical books at Ephesus during Paul's stay in that city demonstrates the temptation that believers faced to continue practicing magic even after conversion to Christianity (Acts 19:18-19). Luke emphasizes that these were people "who had believed" (πολλοί τε τῶν πεπιστευκότων) that confessed their continued participation in the occultic arts (οἱ πράξαντες τὰ περίεργα) and brought their books out and publicly burned them. One cannot help but wonder how many did not participate in this act of renunciation! If many in Ephesus had continued their involvement in magic, it would not be surprising to find Christians elsewhere in Asia Minor doing the same.

I have argued elsewhere that the letter to the Ephesians addressed this issue in a general way.[11] Specifically, I suggested that the letter assumes a prior involvement of many of the readers in magical practices and a continuing fear of evil spirits and hostile powers. The letter thus provides apostolic perspective on the relationship of Christ to the powers in an effort to help the believers forsake their amulets and other magical practices, move away from a magical world view and approach toward their Christianity, and have assurance in their relationship to the risen Christ who has been exalted far above all powers.

---

[10] The distinctive characteristics of Lydian-Phrygian piety have been suggested as the most relevant background for interpreting the second-century Montanist movement. Most scholars now deny any direct link between Montanism and Phrygian local religion. See the discussion by R. Oster, "Christianity in Asia Minor," *ABD* 1.946.

[11] See my *Ephesians: Power and Magic* (SNTSMS 63 Cambridge: University Press, 1989).

2 Timothy, which has a likely connection to western Asia Minor, also reveals the continuing tendency toward a Christian syncretism involving magic. The opponents are compared to Jannes and Jambres (2 Tim 3:8)—the Egyptian magicians who opposed Moses in Jewish tradition.[12] The readers are subsequently warned about "magicians" (γόητες) who would continue to exert a deceiving influence on the churches (2 Tim 3:13).

D. Aune has described the presence of a strong anti-magic polemic in another document associated with Asia Minor, the Apocalypse.[13] The practice of magic is represented as something of which people should repent (Rev 9:21). Those who engage in the magic arts will not have a place in the heavenly city (Rev 22:15), and the judgment of God will come upon them severely (Rev 18:23; 21:8: "their place will be in the fiery lake of burning sulphur").

One piece of anti-magic polemic can even be detected in Ignatius's letter to the Ephesian Christians. He declares that with the coming of Christ "all magic and every kind of spell (πᾶσα μαγεία καὶ πᾶς δεσμός) were dissolved" (Ign., *Eph.* 19:3). Throughout the first few centuries of the church, there was a steady stream of anti-magic polemic from many Christian writers. Thus, a person of the stature of Irenaeus could declare, "Nor does she [the church] perform anything by means of angelic invocations, or by incantations, or by any other wicked curious art; but, directing her prayers to the Lord ..." (Irenaeus, *Adv. Haer.* 2.32.5). His very insistence that the true church does not do these things implies that there are some Christians who do practice them.

In spite of all the anti-magic polemic, the tendency for Christians to combine their apostolic faith with magical practices and local beliefs did not stop. The polemic itself bears testimony to this. There is much additional literary, inscriptional, and papyrus evidence, however, attesting the development of various forms of early Christian magic.

The *Testament of Solomon* bears testimony to a stream of Christianity that practiced the very kind of occultic arts that were condemned by other Christians.[14] Although the Testament is a compilation of Jewish magical

---

[12] This tradition is known in the *Testament of Solomon,* where the two magicians are represented as calling on an evil demon named Abezethibou to oppose Moses with supernatural signs and wonders (*TSol* 25:1-4). For a good overview of the Jannes and Jambres tradition in Judaism, see A. Pietersma, "Jannes and Jambres," *ABD* 3.638-40.

[13] D. Aune, "The Apocalypse of John and Graeco-Roman Revelatory Magic," *NTS* 33 (1987) 481-501; idem, *Prophecy in Early Christianity and the Ancient Mediterranean World* (Grand Rapids: Eerdmans, 1983) 44-45.

[14] See the prior discussion of the *Testament of Solomon* in Chapter 2.

traditions, it may have been put together by a Greek-speaking Christian author. At the minimum, the document was edited, used, and preserved by a group of Christians. It thus provides an important insight into a deviant form of early Christian belief and practice.

The few references to Christ in the Testament reveal that Christ is perceived as little more than an angel who can be invoked to subdue certain demons.[15] Certainly this was precisely the danger the Colossian believers faced in terms of Christology—demoting Christ to the role of a mediator on par with the angels. C. C. McCown, the editor of the standard edition of the Testament, expresses well the difficulty facing those who were newly converted not to combine the Apostolic faith with magic: "it was impossible all at once to replace the old sensuous paganism with a spiritual and ethical monotheism. During the long struggle Christianity was fearfully debased and weakened. How much of the old was carried over into the new religion the *Testament of Solomon* helps one partly to realize."[16] Although he overstates just how representative the Testament was of early Christianity—especially when he says that the document "stands as a representative of the great majority of the Christians of the time"[17]—the Testament nevertheless does provide surprising testimony about the nature and extent of syncretism in at least some early Christian groups.

The second volume of K. Preisendanz's corpus of magical papyri contains 35 papyrus documents that he classified as "Christian."[18] Most of these range in date from the fourth to the sixth centuries A.D. They are classified as "Christian" because of the predominance of Christian names and motifs, but "magical" because they are formulaic texts of ritual power. In addition some of the ostraca in Preisendanz's corpus could accurately be described as Christian.[19]

The recent publication of *Ancient Christian Magic* by M. Meyer and R. Smith has helped to draw more attention to this strand of early Christian belief and practice.[20] In the second chapter of the book, twenty-four of the thirty-five Christian papyri from Preisendanz's collection of Greek texts

---

[15] C. C. McCown, *The Testament of Solomon* (Untersuchungen zum Neuen Testament 9; Leipzig: J. C. Heinrichs, 1922) 50.

[16] McCown, *Testament,* 3.

[17] McCown, *Testament,* 3.

[18] K. Preisendanz, *Papyri Graecae Magicae. Die Griechischen Zauberpapyri,* 2nd rev. ed. by A. Heinrichs (Stuttgart: Teubner, 1973-74) 2.208-32 (originally published in 1931 [= pp. 189-208]. The revised edition includes four additional texts).

[19] Nos. O3 and O4. Both of these are amulets.

[20] M. Meyer and R. Smith, eds., *Ancient Christian Magic. Coptic Texts of Ritual Power* (San Francisco: Harper, 1994).

are translated into English.[21] The volume also included translations of eight more recently discovered papyri. The main purpose of the book, however, was to make available for the first time in English translation a representative selection of 135 Coptic texts. In addition to the many Christian texts included in these two corpora, a great many others could be added. There are many more Greek, Coptic, and Syriac texts published in a wide variety of journals, publications of insriptions, and archaeological bulletins.

These Christian "magical" texts demonstrate that Christianity could take "the form of a folk religion with a syncretistic interest in making use of ritual power for all sorts of practical purposes."[22] Although the texts in these two corpora come from Egypt, there is no reason to doubt that the same kind of syncretism was taking place in Asia Minor and elsewhere.

What is significant for our investigation is the correlation of these later developments with the nature of the problem we have discerned at Colossae. Many of the features of the variant teaching at Colossae are similar in type to the kind of syncretistic folk Christianity that we see reflected in these magical texts. I will highlight a few of these characteristics below:

• *A Tremendous Fear of Demons and Evil Spirits.* The numerous protective amulets reveal the terror people felt with respect to the threats and attacks of evil spirits. People felt the need to acquire additional protection from demons through mechanisms that they were familiar with from the surrounding religious environment. Thus, among other means, they wore amulets inscribed with pleas for protection. For example, the writer of one text pleads, "protect me from every evil spirit, and subject to me every spirit of impure, destroying demons—on the earth, of the water and of the land—and every phantom."[23]

• *A Tendency to Invoke Angels for Protection.* A prominent feature in the Christian magical texts is the practice of invoking angels for protection or fulfilling the requests of the petitioner. Angels are often directly called upon:

---

[21] Those they do not translate are: P2a; P5c, d; P6a, b, c, d; P11; P19; P20; P22. They also provide a translation of one of the two Christian ostraca (O3).

[22] Meyer and Smith, *Ancient Christian Magic,* 7.

[23] *PGM* P13a (Preisendanz, p. 222); Meyer & Smith, 46-47 (= no. 22).

- "O angels, archangels ... seize them [the headless demons] and release me ...!"[24]
- "O angels, archangels ... seize him [the headless demon] when he comes and release me ...!"[25]
- "Holy god, Gabriel, Michael, do what is sufficient for me, Mesa."[26]
- "Lord Gabriel, lord Gabriel, lord Gabriel, heal the patient."[27]
- "Protect, shelter her, Yao Sabbaoth ... archangel Michael, Gabriel, helper."[28]
- "I invoke you, 7 archangels, who are Michael, Gabriel, Uriel, Rakuel, Suriel, Asuel, Salaphuel ..."[29]

The number of examples of angel invocation could be multiplied many times over. This practice is also clearly seen throughout the *Testament of Solomon,* especially chapter 18. Local evidence of Christians invoking angels for protection can be seen in the planetary inscription found at Miletus (*CIG* 2895) and the legend behind the origin of the church of Michael the chief warrior at Colossae (both discussed in Chapter 3). Furthermore, the Laodicean ecclesiastical council expressly forbade the invoking of angels, the practice of magic, and the wearing of amulets (see the discussion in Chapter 3). Irenaeus claimed that the pure church does nothing of this sort: "Nor does she perform anything by means of angelic invocations, or by incantations, or by any other wicked curious art" (Irenaeus, *Adv. Haer.* 2.32.5). He is clearly aware of this continuing practice in some Christian communities and, in the spirit of the Laodicean council, believes that Christians should have no part in it.

• *The Diminution of Christ.* The resurrected Christ was viewed as something less than the almighty and pre-eminent Lord who wields a position of authority over all the hostile powers by early Christians who took up magical practices. Jesus is often seen as something of a mediator figure at roughly the same level as the angelic beings. His name is viewed as a name of power that could be added to a list of other beings whose names are known as powerful. The name of Jesus could even be invoked alongside of angels and pagan deities: "Hor, Hor, Phor, Eloei, Adonai, Iao, Sabaoth, Michael, Jesus Christ. Help us and this household. Amen."[30]

---

[24] *PGM* P15a (Preisendanz, p. 224); Meyer & Smith, 47 (= no. 23).

[25] *PGM* P15b (Preisendanz, p. 224); Meyer & Smith, 48 (= no. 24).

[26] Meyer & Smith, 52 (= no. 29). This text also demonstrates that some Christians went so far as to call on angels to effect a curse against another person! This recipe calls for the angels to "strike Philadelphe and her children."

[27] Meyer & Smith, 85 (= no. 43), lines 50-52 (Coptic text).

[28] Meyer & Smith, 64 (= no. 64), lines 33-35 (Coptic text).

[29] Meyer & Smith, 125-27 (= no. 66), lines 1-4, verso (Coptic text).

[30] *PGM* P6a (Preisendanz, p. 214). See also Meyer & Smith, 37 (no. 11), where Jesus is invoked next to the Egyptian "white wolf," a figure with connections to the Egyp-

• *The Solomonic Magical Tradition.* The Solomonic magical tradition came to hold a significant place in Christian magical practices. Again, the very fact that the *Testament of Solomon* was preserved and used by Christians attests to this fact. Many examples could also be given in the Greek and Coptic magical spells of references to Solomon and this tradition.[31] As we have attempted to demonstrate, it appears that the Solomonic magical tradition penetrated Christianity at Colossae prior to the writing of the letter to the Colossians.

These are the very kinds of practices and beliefs that many of the church fathers have warned of and polemicized against in their writings.[32]

4. Conclusion

The Colossian "philsophy" thus represents a combination of Phrygian folk belief, local folk Judaism, and Christianity. The local folk belief has some distinctive Phrygian qualities, but it also has much in common with what we could also describe as magic or ritual power. The Judaism of the area had already been influenced by these local beliefs and practices. Conversely, the magical substructure of Anatolian Judaism had already made its own contributions to pagan belief and practice. With the proclamation of the Pauline gospel in Colossae and the creation of a Christian community out of converted Jews and pagans, a controversy arose in the church a few years later over the practices and beliefs of an emerging faction within the church. This "philosophy," in the strongly held opinion of the Apostle Paul, compromised too much with the surrounding religious envi-

---

tian god Horus and the Greek god Apollo.

[31] See, for example, *PGM* P10 (Preisendanz, p. 218-19); Meyer & Smith, 44-45 (= no. 20). Meyer & Smith rightly note, "The person adjures the spirits by means of the power of god, the angels, the seven spheres of heaven, and the Christian liturgy. This means of adjuration is somewhat reminiscent of the Testament of Solomon." See also *PGM* P17 (Preisendanz, p. 226-27); Meyer & Smith, 45-46 (= no. 21). This incantation refers to itself as an "exorcism of Solomon against *every* unclean spirit" and speaks of myriads of angels who are available to help. Solomon himself is invoked in some of the formulas; see, for example, *PGM* P3 (Preisendanz, p. 210-11); Meyer & Smith, 49-50 (= no. 26). For a discussion of the Solomonic magical themes used in Christian amulets, see C. Bonner, *Studies in Magical Amulets Chiefly Graeco-Egyptian* (Ann Arbor: University of Michigan Press, 1950) 210-11. The most common feature of these amulets is the image of a rider on a horse (Solomon) spearing an evil spirit. See also the discussion in Goodenough, *Symbols,* 2.231.

[32] For references, see J. Michl, "Engel IV (christlich)," *RAC* 5.199-200.

ronment. Paul saw this syncretistic compromise as dangerous to the health of the church because it diminished the person of Christ and the present role he has in the church.

Part III: The Contextualized Theology of Colossians

Rather than undertake a complete description of the theology of Colossians, the final chapter will focus on how Pauline theology was adapted and developed with specific application to the setting at Colossae. The missiological term "contextualization" best captures the focal point of this chapter. Our intent will be to determine the nature of the contextualization of Pauline theology to the Colossian situation. This will involve not only discerning what aspects of theology are emphasized as a counter to the teaching of the opponents, but also to see how Paul has addressed some of the fundamental issues of world view. In other words, we will also seek to describe how Paul attempts to modify and refine their assumptions, understanding of life, and perception of reality. As we have already demonstrated, one of the key issues for Phrygian Christians was their fear of the realm of spirits and powers. The position of Christ in relationship to this supernatural realm as well as the nature and implications of their solidarity with Christ will emerge as key points of discussion.

CHAPTER 9

The Theological Response to the Situation

The conflict at Colossae was not over how to acquire knowledge of the divine or even how to attain a deeper experience of the fullness of God; the issue was of a more practical concern. The Christians in the Lycus Valley continued to fear astral powers, chthonic spirits, and underworld powers that raised problems for them in day-to-day life. Their folk religion roots provided a belief structure that some of them considered compatible with Christianity: One must call on intermediary spirits and angels for protection.

For the author of Colossians, this belief with its associated practices represented a misunderstanding of the identity of Christ and his present role in the church. The believers of Colossae thus faced a challenge to the concept of the Lordship of Christ they had received in apostolic tradition from the hands of Epaphras. "The philosophy" was demeaning the role of Christ in relationship to his creation and serving an implicit indictment against the sufficiency of Christ for the Colossian Christians: The power and authority of Christ, and their access to his power and authority, was not adequate for protection from the hostile "powers" in daily life.

The theological response to the Colossian Christians in opposition to the influence of "the philosophy" has a two-fold emphasis: (1) Paul attempts to purify their Christology by emphasizing the so-called "cosmic" role of Christ through clarifying his relationship to divine intermediaries; and, (2) Paul stresses a "realized eschatology" to emphasize their status as people who are united with Christ in his kingdom and who share in his power and authority over the demonic realm.

1. Poetic Praise to Christ's Supremacy Over the Powers (1:15-20)

The author of Colossians confronts this challenge at the outset of the letter with an eloquent affirmation of the cosmic supremacy of Christ. The im-

plication of the "Christ-hymn" is that believers have no need to fear the "powers" since they have been rescued from their domain and now live in connection to their powerful and loving Lord. As a corollary, the readers have no need for "the philosophy," with all of its rigorous ascetic demands, in view of their relationship to the omnipotent Lord.

Colossians 1:15-20 could accurately be described as a magnificent declaration of Christ as Lord. Although the title κύριος itself does not appear in the hymn, each line of the passage extols Christ in terms of supremacy and lordship. Building on this foundation, the author employs κύριος thirteen times elsewhere in the letter. He further elaborates on Christ's lordship by depicting him as "head" and describing him in exalted terms.

The hymn depicts Christ as παντοκράτωρ over creation. The passage poignantly affirms and beautifully praises the supremacy of Christ in relation to all of creation, earthly and heavenly. Most important, for the Colossian Christians, Christ is extolled as superior to all the evil spiritual "powers."[1] This is very important to the readers since they are represented as having been rescued from the dominion of the "powers" and brought under the reign of Christ (1:13). Paul's prayer for them now is that they would conduct their lives in a worthy manner before the Lord (1:10). By acceding to the demands of "the philosophy," the Colossians were living outside the boundaries of what Paul considered worthy of their exalted Lord.

a. The Nature and Structure of the Passage

The language and style of vv. 15-20 has led most interpreters since E. Norden to regard the passage as hymnic.[2] Voluminous material has been written about this passage mainly with the attempt to discern the content

---

[1] See also G. Münderlein, "Die Erwählung durch das Pleroma," *NTS* 8 (1962) 265, who suggests that the "Kernmotiv" of the entire hymn is: "Christ is Lord of all the powers of heaven and earth." Similarly, P. Müller, *Anfänge der Paulusschule* (ATANT 74; Zürich: Theologischer Verlag, 1978) 79, notes: "The hymn celebrates the installation of Christ as Lord (*die Herrscherstellung*) of Christ over all the principalities and powers." Pokorný, *Colossians,* 74, thus also comments: "Behind this hymn is the view of Christian worship as proclamation of the Lordship of Christ in the face of all powers that influence humanity and seek to determine its destiny."

[2] E. Norden, *Agnostos Theos. Untersuchungen zur Formengeschichte religiöser Rede,* (4th ed.; Stuttgart: Teubner, 1956 [= reprint of 1913 edition]) was the first to use form-critical tools to uncover what he considered to be old traditional material.

and provenance of the original hymn as the basis for detecting the letter writer's redaction of it.[3]

With regard to the history of religions background to the text, a consensus has been achieved in rejecting E. Käsemann's suggestion that the unredacted form of the passage was a pre-Christian Gnostic hymn, viz. a tribute to "the supra-historical and metaphysical drama of the Gnostic Redeemer."[4] It appears that a further consensus has been reached in rooting the essential framework of the passage in OT and Wisdom tradition (especially as seen in Proverbs, Wisdom, Sirach, and Philo). The hymn's portrayal of Jesus in terms reminiscent of divine Wisdom is quite appropriate to the polemical situation of the letter. The hymn is a perfect counter to the magical "wisdom" Christology of the opponents in which Jesus is seen on par with angels.

---

[3] Helpful summaries of the research on the exegesis of 1:15-20 are contained in H. J. Gabathuler, *Jesus Christus. Haupt der Kirche—Haupt der Welt* (ATANT 45; Zürich: Zwingli, 1965) 11-124, and in P. Benoit, "L'hymne christologique de Col 1, 15-20. Jugement critique sur l'état des recherches," *Christianity, Judaism and Other Greco-Roman Cults* (FS. M. Smith, SJLA 12; Leiden: Brill, 1975) 1.226-63. Gabathuler summarizes the work of eighteen scholars beginning with Schleiermacher and ending with Conzelmann (1962). Benoit summarizes treatments from Schliermacher to Pöhlmann (1973). L. Helyer, "Recent Research on Col 1:15-20 (1980-1990)," *GTJ* 12 (1992) 51-67, has provided a helpful critique of studies appearing in the 1980s.

[4] E. Käsemann, "A Primitive Christian Baptismal Liturgy," *Essays on New Testament Themes* (SBT 41; London: SCM, 1964) 155. Pokorný, *Colossians,* 66, however, has argued that in spite of the fact that it is not a Gnostic hymn and that the best framework for interpreting it is Hellenistic-Jewish wisdom speculation and *logos* teaching, the piece still reflects Gnostic influence. J. Fossum, "Colossians 1.15-18a in the Light of Jewish Mysticism and Gnosticism," *NTS* 35 (1989) 183-201, has returned much further in the direction of Käsemann. On the one hand, Fossum argues that (1) the second part of the hymn cannot speak of anyone other than Christ, and (2) there is no evidence for the existence of a Gnostic *Urmensch-Erlöser* until the time of Mani. On the other, he contends that the hymn is better interpreted in terms of a Gnostic heavenly-man (Anthropos) Christology rather than a Wisdom Christology. I am still of the opinion that the OT and Wisdom tradition provides the best framework for interpreting the text. Furthermore, Fossum's view flounders on the following points: (1) he is not able to explain the meaning of the πλήρωμα taking up residence in Christ (1:19); in Gnosis the πλήρωμα is generally understood as the totality of the aeons; (2) although Christ is here presented as the creator (the demiurge), the text emphasizes that he created the invisible powers; this is inconsistent with the Gnostic conception of the powers as emanations; (3) there is nothing in Gnosis about the heavenly man maintaining (συνέστηκεν) the universe; and, (4) if the hymn presents an Anthropos-Christology, it is somewhat surprising that the term ἄνθρωπος and the term δόξα (Fossum sees σῶμα coming from Gnostic dependence on the Jewish speculation concerning the body of the Glory) never appear.

The hymn reflects more than Wisdom Christology. The passage is perhaps best described as a Christian composition depending upon a variety of traditions including the OT (esp. Gen 1 and Isa 40-55), Wisdom, Hellenistic-Jewish traditions similar to what we see in Philo, common Hellenistic imagery, Christian liturgical traditions, and Pauline ideas (esp. his theology of the cross and eschatology).

It is certainly possible—indeed, it has been the majority opinion among interpreters—that the passage was a pre-Pauline Christian hymn that circulated perhaps in Asia Minor and has been taken up and edited by the author of the letter. This conclusion has not gone uncontested. A wide array of scholars, especially those who see Paul as the author of the letter, have suggested that it was the apostle himself, writing in an elevated style, who composed the passage.[5]

More recently, a few interpreters have emphasized the importance of a synchronic approach to the passage by concentrating on the final form of the hymn and attempting to discern its function in the context of the letter as a whole.[6] Since the early history of the hymn is not our concern in this context, our comments will be centered on the final form of the hymn and how the author has intended his readers to understand it, especially in light of the situation at Colossae.

All interpreters have noticed the parallelism in the basic structure of the passage:[7]

---

[5] Most recently, N. T. Wright, "Poetry and Theology in Colossians 1.15-20," *NTS* 36 (1990) 444-68 (now reprinted with some alterations in *The Climax of the Covenant* [Minneapolis: Fortress, 1991] 99-119), suggests that the passage is a carefully constructed piece of poetry composed by the Apostle Paul himself. S. E. Porter, *Καταλλάσσω in Ancient Greek Literature with Reference to the Pauline Writings* (Estudios de Filología Neotestamentaria 5; Cordoba: Ediciones El Almendro, 1994) 163-90, intimates that Paul himself is responsible for the creative use of language in this passage. See also S. Baugh, "The Poetic Form of Col 1:15-20," *WTJ* 47 (1985) 227-44; J. F. Balchin, "Colossians 1:15-20: An Early Christian Hymn? The Arguments from Style," *Vox Evangelica* 15 (1985) 65-94; L. R. Helyer, "Colossians 1:15-20: Pre-Pauline or Pauline?" *JETS* 26 (1983) 167-79; N. Kehl, *Der Christushymnus im Kolosserbrief* (SBM 1; Stuttgart: Katholisches Bibelwerk, 1967) 162-64 argues that the hymn is thoroughly Pauline and reflects his theology regarding the conversion of the Gentiles; C. Maurer, "Die Begründung der Herrschaft Christi über die Mächte nach Kolosser 1, 15-20," *Wort und Dienst* NF 4 (1955) 71-93, esp. 85, sees it as "hymnic," but as a Pauline composition; W. G. Kümmel, *Introduction to the New Testament* (London: SCM, 1982) 343; Dibelius-Greeven, *Kolosser,* 10-12; O'Brien, *Colossians,* 40-42; et al.

[6] See especially, S. E. Fowl, *The Story of Christ in the Ethics of Paul* (JSNTSS 36; Sheffield: JSOT Press, 1990) 31-45, esp. p. 45. See also Wright, "Poetry," 445, and Aletti, *Colossiens,* 89.

[7] This layout is given by Wright, "Poetry," 446.

ὅς ἐστιν (15a)
   ὅτι ἐν αὐτῷ (16a)
   δι' αὐτοῦ καὶ εἰς αὐτόν (16f)

καὶ αὐτός (17a)
καὶ αὐτός (18a)

ὅς ἐστιν (18c)
   ὅτι ἐν αὐτῷ (19)
   δι' αὐτοῦ ... εἰς αὐτόν (20)

This has led most interpreters to describe the passage as being composed of two strophes (vv. 15-16; 18b-20) with a transitional link or refrain (17-18a)[8] connecting the two strophes 'by summarizing the preceding strophe and introducing the following.[9] Disagreement arises over the inner conherence of each of the strophes. This has led most interpreters to speculate about the precise content of the original hymn and what the letter writer has deleted and inserted.[10] N. T. Wright, however, has recently challenged the long-standing assumption that a letter writer would redact a hymn. He quips, "Nothing would be more calculated to puzzle a congregation that tampering with a hymn they are in the act of singing."[11] Wright therefore contends that the passage is a poetic piece composed by the author of the letter. He and others have explored the possibility that the writer structured the passage chiastically.[12]

---

[8] Some would prefer to refer to this unit as a strophe.

[9] See, for instance, Pokorný, *Colossians*, 58-58, and P. Beasley-Murray, "Colossians 1:15-20: An Early Christian Hymn Celebrating the Lordship of Christ," *Pauline Studies* (FS. F. F. Bruce; Exeter: Paternoster, 1980) 169-70. For a helpful list of all the proposed solutions (including those who see 3, 4, or 5 strophes present), see Aletti, *Colossiens*, 90.

[10] The prime candidates for insertion are: (1) most of v. 16—"in heaven and upon earth, the visible and the invisible, whether thrones, dominions, principalities, or authorities"; (2) v. 18b—τῆς ἐκκλησίας; (3) v. 18c—"that in everything he might be pre-eminent"; (4) v. 20b—"making peace through the blood of his cross"; (5) v. 20c—"whether things upon the earth or things in heaven." See Gnilka, *Kolosserbrief*, 52-54, and C. Bürger, *Schöpfung und Versöhnung. Studien zum liturgischen Gut im Kolosser- und Epheserbrief* (WMANT 46; Neukirchen: Neukirchner, 1975) 9-11, 15-16, for a more complete list of supposed insertions and the corresponding proponents of such a reconstruction.

[11] Wright, "Poetry," 445.

[12] Baugh, "Poetic Form," 235-44, has argued that vv. 15-20 can be structured chiastically according to an ABCB'A' arrangement. In his analysis the A and A' sections correspond with what most interpreters have described as the first and final strophe (15-16 and 18b-20). The B and B' sections are 17a and 18a. The C section is 17b—καὶ τὰ πάντα ἐν

Whether or not the passage was a quoted hymnic piece or a poetic composition by the author, our goal here will chiefly be to interpret the passage in light of the larger context of the letter. We will therefore follow a synchronic approach and only comment on possible redaction where it makes a difference in how we interpret a given line or phrase. Although the passage does achieve a high degree of artistry, it is also clear that the demands of the content had priority over maintaining an artistic structure. The hymn celebrates Christ as Lord of creation (first strophe) and as Lord of reconciliation (second strophe).

b. The Powers are Not Supreme: Christ is Lord of Creation

The angelic "powers" are given the greatest prominence in the hymn as part of the creation over which Christ is Lord (v. 16). They are specifically enumerated in v. 16—θρόνοι, κυριότητες, ἀρχαί, ἐξουσίαι— and referred to in a variety of other ways throughout the hymn: as part of the creation (κτίσις [v. 15b]), "all things in heaven" (τὰ πάντα ἐν τοῖς οὐρανοῖς [v. 16a, c; 17a, b; 20a]), "the invisible" (τὰ ἀόρατα [v. 16b]), and "the things in heaven" (τὰ ἐν τοῖς οὐρανοῖς [v. 20c]). The structural emphasis on the "powers" as an elaboration of the invisible realm underlines our impression of the nature of the root problem facing the Colossian Christians—they continue to fear the realm of evil supernatural

---

αὐτῷ συνέστηκεν—which he contends should be seen as the focus of the poem. The image of Christ as maintaining the universe, however, is certainly not the central thought that Paul develops later in the letter. It is only one of a series of thoughts celebrating Christ as Lord. Wright, "Poetry," 446, has taken a similar approach but argues that the two καὶ αὐτός ἐστιν statements in 17a and 18a introduce the central members of the chiasmus: A = 15-16; B = 17; B' = 18a; A' = 18c-20. The center of the chiasmus would then be three lines larger that what Baugh proposed:

B   1. καὶ αὐτός ἐστιν πρὸ πάντων

     2. καὶ τὰ πάντα ἐν αὐτῷ συνέστηκεν

B' 1. καὶ αὐτός ἐστιν ἡ κεφαλὴ

     2. τοῦ σώματος τῆς ἐκκλησίας

Although his proposal has the merit of preserving the integrity of τῆς ἐκκλησίας as an original part of the passage and having a balanced syllable count (B = 19; B' = 18), it suffers the weakness of severe formal dissimilarity when one compares the second line of B and B'. The first is a complete clause and the second is only a genitive adjunct that depends on ἡ κεφαλή. Thus, B1 and B2 are two separate clauses that convey two distinct but overlapping ideas—temporal priority and maintenance of the universe. B'1 and B'2 comprise only one clause—Christ is the head of his body, the church. Wright does not address this difficulty nor does he discuss the resultant meaning of the central chiasm. Why the shift from the cosmic focus to an ecclesiological focus?

forces that bring harm.[13] Hence, the writer of our letter leads them in acclaiming Christ as Lord of the powers. We will now seek to determine the accuracy of this observation by examining the specific contents of the hymn in greater detail.

Many intepreters regard the specific delineation of the "powers" in v. 16 as an insertion by the author of the epistle into the original hymn to provide a concrete reference to the Colossian situation.[14] Those who see Paul as the author of the hymn also see an explicit reference to the Colossian situation in the terms for the "powers."[15] The author of Colossians extols Christ's supremacy and lordship *vis à vis* the "powers" as the basis and authority for his subsequent polemic against the Colossian heresy, which he perceives to be connected with the "powers."[16] I would suggest that this connection is three-fold: (1) the Colossians fear the powers and the influence they have on fate, "natural" disasters, health, and other issues of day-to-day life; (2) the Colossian "philosophy" claims to have an answer for averting the harmful workings of the hostile powers, and (3) the author of the letter actually discerns the teaching of the "philosophy" to be inspired by the powers.

Among the four terms the author uses for the "powers," the second pair—ἀρχαί and ἐξουσίαι—are the most common in the NT linked together elsewhere in Pauline writings (1 Cor 15:24; Eph 1:21; 3:10; 6:12). They also appear in tandem at two other points in this letter (Col 2:10, 15). Paul uses ἀρχαὶ elsewhere only in Rom 8:38, where it is linked with δυνάμεις and ἄγγελοι. The term ἐξουσία, detached from ἀρχή, is used with reference to the realm of Satan in Eph 2:2 and in the introduction to

---

[13] See also Schweizer, *Colossians,* 61.

[14] See, for example, A.J.M. Wedderburn, "The Theology of Colossians," in *The Theology of the Later Pauline Letters* (Cambridge: University Press, 1993) 15-16; E. Schweizer, "Die Kirche als Leib Christi in den paulinischen Antilegomena," *Neotestamentica: Deutsche und englische Aufsätze (1951-1963)* (Zurich: Zwingli, 1963) 297; idem, *Colossians,* 57; Kehl, *Christushymnus,* 46; R. Deichgräber, *Gotteshymnus und Christushymnus in der frühen Christenheit* (SUNT 5; Göttingen, 1967) 146; Beasley-Murray, "Colossians 1:15-20," 172-73; J. M. Robinson, "A Formal Analysis of Colossians 1:15-20," *JBL* 76 (1957) 270-87; F. F. Bruce, "The 'Christ-Hymn' of Colossians 1:15-20," *BibSac* 141 (1984) 103; Martin, *Colossians* (NCB), 56; Gnilka, *Kolosserbrief,* 57, 65; Gabathuler, *Jesus Christus,* 168; et al.

[15] E.g. O'Brien, *Colossians,* 46, remarks, "Probably with special reference to the Colossian heresy Paul now emphasizes that even the cosmic powers and principalities, which apparently received some prominence in that heresy, were created in Christ ... No doubt it is the hostile rather than the friendly powers Paul has particularly in view." See also Dibelius-Greeven, *Kolosser,* 10-11.

[16] Dibelius-Greeven, *Kolosser,* 11.

the hymn (Col 1:13). It should also be mentioned that 1 Peter, perhaps relying on a traditional formulation, speaks of Christ having subjected "angels and authorities and powers" (ἄγγελοι, ἐξουσίαι, δυνάμεις) in describing the heavenly exaltation of Christ in terms reminiscent of Psalm 110.

The use of the terms in these contexts is best explained by the Jewish usage of the terms to denote angelic powers (see *1 Enoch* 61:10; *2 Enoch* 20:1; *Test. Levi* 3:8; *TSol* 20:15; 3:6: "I am Beelzebul, the ruler [ἀρχή in ms. W] of the demons"; see also LXX Dan 7:27: καὶ πᾶσαι αἱ ἐξουσίαι [Theod. = ἀρχαί] αὐτῷ ὑποταγήσονται καὶ πειθαρχήσουσιν αὐτῷ).[17] In addition to these texts that have commonly figured into the discussion are three important yet overlooked passages that further illustrate the use of ἀρχαί and ἐξουσίαι as angelic powers. (1) The term ἀρχαί appears in a Greek fragment of *1 Enoch* 6:7-8 to designate ten angels who serve as chiefs of groups of ten (καὶ ταῦτα τὰ ὀνόματα τῶν ἀρχόντων αὐτῶν Σεμιαζὰ οὗτος ἦν ἄρχων αὐτῶν 'Αραθὰκ Κιμβρὰ ... οὗτοί εἰσιν ἀρχαὶ αὐτῶν οἱ ἐπὶ δέκα). It is noteworthy that in this passage the terms ἄρχοντες and ἀρχαί seem to be used interchangeably. (2) In *3 Baruch* 12:3, Baruch sees a group of angels carrying baskets filled with flowers. Michael reveals to him that "these are the angels over the principalities (οὗτοι εἰσιν ἄγγελοι ἐπὶ τῶν ἐξουσίων)." (3) The *Testament of Abraham* 13:10 (shorter recension), probably a first-century document,[18] lists not only ἀρχαί and ἐξουσίαι but also θρόνοι in a list of angelic powers:

> And Death said to Abraham, "I tell you, in all the creation which God created, there is not to be found one (like you. For he searched among the angels and archangels, and principalities and powers, as well as thrones [ἐν τοῖς ἀγγέλοις καὶ ἀρχαγγέλοις καὶ ἀρχαῖς καὶ ἐξουσίαις θρόνοις]; and upon all the earth,

---

[17] See my previous discussion of these terms in *Ephesians: Power and Magic* (SNTSMS 63; Cambridge: University Press, 1989) 52-53. See also my article, "Principalities and Powers," in *ABD* 5.467.

[18] The majority of scholars date the text to the first century B.C. or first century A.D. See J. R. Mueller, "Abraham, Testament Of," in *ABD* 1.44. F. Schmidt, "The Two Recensions of the Testament of Abraham: In Which Way Did the Transformation Take Place?" in *Studies on the Testament of Abraham* (SBLSCS 6; ed. G. W. E. Nickelsburg; Missoula: Scholar's Press, 1976) 80, argues that the Testament of Abraham was very likely written in the second half of the first century A.D. He suggests that the earliest form of the text was composed in a Semitic language and subsequently translated into Greek, thus forming the shorter recension. He contends that manuscript E and the Slavonic version are currently the best witnesses of this state of the tradition.

including four-footed animals and wild beasts of the earth and everything that is in the water, as far as heaven, and he did not find one like you).[19]

Although the terms ἀρχαί and ἐξουσίαι appear to be a firm part of Jewish vocabulary for angelic beings, they are not commonly used in Hellenism for gods, spirits, or mediator beings.[20]

As a classification of angelic "powers," the term θρόνοι occurs only here in the NT.[21] It is known in Jewish apocalyptic literature as a title for a class of angelic "powers" (*2 Enoch* 20:1). In the *Test. of Levi* 3:8 it is listed next to ἐξουσίαι, and also, as we saw above, in the *Testament of Abraham* 13:10 it appears in conjunction with ἄγγελοι, ἀρχαί, and ἐξουσίαι. The term also is used to designate the realm of angelic/demonic beings over which Solomon reigned in *TSol* 3:5: "the attendant of your thrones (τῶν σῶν θρόνων πάρεδρον)." The term does occur in a few magical texts to denote angelic "powers." *PGM* CI. 40[22] reads, "And again I conjure you by the one who is in charge of the air. And again I conjure you by the seven thrones (θρόνων) ... (7 magical names given) ... and by the relentless god (magical names)." A. Audollent cites two texts which use the term σύνθρονοι to denote spirit "powers."[23]

The term κυριότητες only occurs elsewhere in Paul at Eph 1:21.[24] This category of angel "powers," however, is also known from Jewish apocalyptic (*1 Enoch* 61:10; *2 Enoch* 20:1; *Cave of Treas.* 1:3)[25] and Jewish

---

[19] The translation is by E. P. Sanders, "Testament of Abraham," in *OTP*, 1.901. The most recent and best critical edition of the text is by F. Schmidt, *Le Testament grec d'Abraham, Introduction, édition critique des deux recensions grecques, traduction* (TSAJ 11; Tübingen: J.C.B. Mohr [Paul Siebeck], 1986) 78-79. The portion of the text that is enclosed in parentheses is found only in manuscript E; a similar list is in manuscript D. Schmidt contends, however, that manuscript E provides the best Greek text for the shorter recension, a point that Sanders acknowledges.

[20] However, in *PGM* I.215 ἐξουσία appears in an apotropaic formula to describe magical power that is exerted by an aerial demon: "Wherefore, come to me, you who are lord over all angels; shield me against all excess of magical power of aerial daimon and fate (πρὸς πᾶσαν ὑπεροχὴν ἐξουσίας δαίμονος ἀε[ρί]ου [καὶ εἱ]μαρμένης)." For a similar use, see *PGM* IV.1193

[21] See the discussion in O. Schmitz, "θρόνος," *TDNT* 3.166-67.

[22] This text was published subsequent to the appearance of K. Preisendanz's corpus. The *editio princeps* is by D. Wortmann, "Neue magische Texte," *Bonner Jahrbücher* 168 (1968) 88, 100.

[23] A. Audollent, *Defixionum Tabellae* (Paris: Alberti Fontemoing, 1894) 35:37; 240:1ff (both cited in Wortmann, "Neue magische Texte," 100).

[24] See my previous discussion of this term in *Ephesians*, 54.

[25] W. Foerster, "κυριότης," *TDNT* 3.1096-97. The term also appears in Jude 8 and 2 Pet 2:10, but it is not used there as a class of angelic beings.

magic (*TSol* 8:6 [ms. D: καὶ οἱ θρόνοι καὶ αἱ κυριότητες]).[26] Dibelius sees a line of continuity in the use of this term with Paul's reference to the "many lords" (κύριοι πολλοί) in 1 Cor 8:5 as "so-called gods" (λεγόμενοι θεοί).[27]

This list of angelic "powers" should be viewed as an expansion of the preceding ἀόρατα.[28] Furthermore, these beings are evil and hostile to the purposes of God.[29] This judgment is supported by the larger context of the letter. The hymn is introduced with a background of dramatic conflict with the powers: God *rescued* us from the authority of darkness (Col 1:13). This conflict reaches a high point in 2:15 where God's victory over the powers through Christ is eloquently exclaimed. Given also the fact that the influence of the powers is an issue for the readers and that the writer of the letter connects "the philosophy" to the powers, it is not surprising that the powers receive special attention in the hymn. It is also important to recognize that the ἀρχαί and ἐξουσίαι are consistently portrayed as evil beings in Paul.

The powers are not portrayed here as demi-gods blocking the heavenly ascent, nor are they depicted as mediators of divine knowledge, nor should they be seen as emanations from a high god or even as impersonal forces. The author of this letter conceives of the powers as angelic beings in league with the authority of darkness (1:13), foes of God and his son Jesus Christ. They oppose God's purposes in the church and are now instigating conflict in the Colossian community through "the philosophy."

In a variety of ways Christ is extolled as supreme and as Lord over these "powers":

---

[26] For the text, see C. C. McCown, *The Testament of Solomon* (Untersuchungen zum Neuen Testament 9; Leipzig: J. C. Heinrichs, 1922) 97.

[27] M. Dibelius, *Die Geisterwelt im Glauben des Paulus* (Göttingen: Vandenhoeck & Ruprecht, 1909) 128; cf. also Dibelius-Greeven, *Kolosser,* 13; O. Everling, *Die paulinische Angelologie und Dämonologie* (Göttingen: Vandenhoeck & Ruprecht, 1888) 88-89.

[28] E. Bammel, "Versuch zu Kol 1, 15-20," *ZNW* 52 (1961) 88-95. (followed by Houlden, *Letters From Prison,* 163), has argued on the basis of a complex chiastic structure that the "invisible" world consists of κυριότητες and ἀρχαί and is situated in the heavens, and correspondingly, the "visible" world consists of θρόνοι and ἐξουσίαι and is situated on the earth. This arrangement should be rejected, however, since it splits the one phrase that Paul normally keeps together, viz. the ἀρχαὶ καὶ ἐξουσίαι; see further, Wedderburn, "Theology," 15; W. Carr, *Angels and Principalities* (SNTSMS 42; Cambridge: University Press, 1983) 48; cf. also Deichgräber, *Gotteshymnus,* 147.

[29] *Contra* Pokorný, *Colossians,* 78 ("they are essentially neutral entities"); Carr, *Angels and Principalities,* 48-52; W. Wink, *Naming the Powers* (Philadelphia: Fortress, 1984) 64-67.

(1) "He is the image of the invisible God." As a probable reference to Christ as personified Wisdom,[30] this phrase identifies Christ's relationship to God implying his pre-existence. Lohse aptly portrays the contextual significance of this phrase by saying, "As the 'image' of the invisible God, he does not belong to what was created, but stands with the creator who, in Christ, is acting upon the world and with the world. He is absolutely superior to the cosmos, i.e. the whole creation on earth and in heaven."[31] There are no other images to which one should give devotion. Because in his pre-existence Christ participated in the creation of the universe, he is therefore "the one and only legitimate image of God."[32] J. Jervell rightly sees the spiritual milieu of the area, specifically "the power of the spirit realm," as motivating the inclusion of this Christological title in the hymn, and thus the inclusion of the hymn in Colossians.[33] He contends that as "the image of the invisible God," Christ is κοσμοκράτωρ, and "that in Christ God is presently working so that he establishes himself in Christ as more powerful than the powers of evil (die Mächte)."[34]

(2) "The firstborn of all creation." Again, the sovereignty of Christ is manifestly present in this phrase.[35] Rather than indicating that Christ is the first of all beings to be created the expression denotes a sovereignty of rank. This is a common usage of πρωτότοκος in the LXX (e.g. Psalm 89:27: "I will make him the 'firstborn,' the highest of the kings of the earth"). The title belongs to Christ not only as the Son of David, but as the Wisdom of God, "the Sovereign who is installed by God through resurrection as Lord over not only the Church but the whole universe."[36] As v. 16 will immediately clarify, "creation" includes the angelic "powers" that figure prominently in the Colossian situation.

---

[30] "Wisdom" was with the Lord at the time of the creation of the world (Prov. 8:22), and the personified divine wisdom can be described as the "image" (εἰκών) in Wisd. 7:26; cf. E. J. Schnabel, *Law and Wisdom from Ben Sira to Paul* (WUNT 2/16; Tübingen: J.C.B. Mohr [Paul Siebeck], 1985) 258; J. G. Gibbs, *Creation and Redemption* (NovTSup 26; Leiden: Brill, 1971) 102-103; Wedderburn, "Theology," 18; Kehl, *Christushymnus,* 61-67; O'Brien, *Colossians,* 43; et pl.

[31] Lohse, *Colossians,* 48.

[32] Kehl, *Christushymnus,* 158.

[33] J. Jervell, *Imago Dei. Gen 1, 26f im Spätjudentum, in der Gnosis und in den paulinischen Briefen* (FRLANT 76; Göttingen: Vandenhoeck & Ruprecht, 1960) 219-20.

[34] Jervell, *Imago Dei,* 220.

[35] Wedderburn, "Theology," 25.

[36] Gibbs, *Creation,* 104.

(3) Christ was the creator of all things,[37] including the "powers."[38] All things were created "by/through him" and not apart from him.[39] This is expressed in two different ways by the parallel clauses at the beginning and end of v. 16: ἐν αὐτῷ ἐκτίσθη τὰ πάντα // τὰ πάντα δι' αὐτοῦ ... ἔκτισται. The role of Christ as creator is well attested in early Christian tradition (see Heb. 1:2; John 1:3). Thus, Christ should in no sense be mistaken as in any way equal to the "powers," he is their creator!

(4) Christ is the goal ("for him;" εἰς αὐτόν) of all creation. This affirmation exceeds anything predicated for divine wisdom and now conceives of Christ in an eschatological sense. He is the one who will restore creation to what it was originally intended to be. The close affinity of Christ to God can be seen when comparing this declaration to 1 Cor 8:6 where the same thing is said of the one God.

(5) Christ is the pre-eminent one. The transitional verse (v. 17) reaffirms the pre-existence of Christ by describing him as "before all things" (πρὸ πάντων). It has much in common with John 8:58: "before Abraham was, I am." P. Beasley-Murray has aptly commented that the phrase is not merely an assertion of temporal priority, but "supremacy is above all involved."[40] As the one who is before all things, Christ is "Lord over the universe."[41]

(6) "All things hold together in him." This statement complements what has been said about the role of Christ in creation. Christ not only brought all things into being but he also maintains (συνέστηκεν) all things (cf. Heb 1:3).[42] The "powers" therefore were not only created by Christ, but their present existence depends entirely on him. As Lightfoot says, Christ is the

---

[37] This conception is also rooted in Wisdom speculation; see Wedderburn, "Theology," 27-28; Lohse, *Colossians,* 50.

[38] The expression τὰ πάντα refers to the whole of creation, but the angelic powers belong to this. See Pokorný, *Colossians,* 77.

[39] Lohse, *Colossians,* 50, correctly interprets ἐν αὐτῷ as instrumental. *Contra* those who argue for the local sense of ἐν αὐτῷ: see Bruce, *Colossians,* 61-62; E. Percy, *Die Probleme der Kolosser- und Epheserbriefe* (Skrifter Utgivna av Kungl. Humanistiska Vetenskapssamfundet i Lund XXXIX; Lund: Gleerup, 1964) 69-70; O'Brien, *Colossians,* 45; Schweizer, *Colossians,* 69, also takes it in a local sense, but he sees the Stoic concept of the "macroanthropos" behind it.

[40] Beasley-Murray, "Christian Hymn," 173.

[41] Lohse, *Colossians,* 52.

[42] There is close conceptual similarity here to the role of God's *logos* in Sirach 43:26 ("by his word all things hold together [σύγκειται]"). In Philo, the *logos* is described as the bond of the universe that maintains the creation (see esp. *De Fug.* 112; *Quis Rer. Div. Her.* 23 and 311).

one who makes creation "a cosmos instead of a chaos."[43] Not only does Christ keep the world from falling apart as a result of earthquakes, floods, plagues, and cosmic disturbances, he maintains a check on the baleful and multifarious workings of the hostile powers. Again, what is expressed here is "Christ's lordship over the world."[44]

The first strophe of the hymn thus extols Christ as Lord of creation. He is not portrayed here in his role as the incarnate earthly Jesus, but as the pre-existent mediator of creation.[45] He is supreme by virtue of his unique relationship to God that extends prior to the creation of the world. He is also shown to be supreme in his role as creator and maintainer of the created order. He is not just a mediator figure, however, because he is the goal of creation—a distinguishing characteristic of the one God.

The hymn has many points of commonality with poetic ascriptions of praise to Yahweh in the LXX, such as 1 Chron 29:10-13. In this passage, God's lordship over "all things" in heaven and on earth is stressed (v. 11: σὺ πάντων τῶν ἐν τῷ οὐρανῷ καὶ ἐπὶ τῆς γῆς δεσπόζεις). In his exalted role as ruler over all (v. 12: σὺ πάντων ἄρχεις), not only are all earthly kings and tribes frightened by him (v. 11: ταράσσεται πᾶς βασιλεὺς καὶ ἔθνος), but every heavenly principality is ruled by God (v. 12: κύριε ὁ ἄρχων πάσης ἀρχῆς). God is truly παντοκράτωρ (v. 12).[46]

In its present form, the Colossian hymn stresses the fact that the various ranks of the "powers" are part of this created order and therefore are subject to the Lordship of Christ. Christ is not just one deity among many,[47] nor is he some kind of angelic mediator figure. "Paul has modified Jewish monotheism so as to place Jesus Christ within the description, almost the definition, of the one God."[48] Christ is therefore Lord over all in the same way that Yahweh is Lord over all.

The hymn provides encouragement to the Colossians by declaring that the hostile powers are not ultimate; they do not reign supreme over the daily lives and future destiny of people. The hymn also provides a basis for the author's polemic against "the philosophy" (2:4-23), which is seen

---

[43] Lightfoot, *Colossians,* 156.

[44] Schweizer, *Colossians,* 71.

[45] See Schweizer, *Colossians,* 64.

[46] Neh 9 (= 2 Ezra 19) speaks of all the heavenly armies (v. 6: σοὶ προσκυνοῦσιν αἱ στρατιαὶ τῶν οὐρανῶν) worshiping God among its many affirmations of his Lordship (v. 6: σὺ εἶ αὐτὸς κύριος μόνος). See also Esth 4:17b-d.

[47] Wright, "Poetry," 454.

[48] Wright, "Poetry," 460.

by Paul as an attempt to deal with the problem of the powers, but with means inspired by the powers themselves.

Verse 18a marks the transition to the second stanza of the hymn by the movement from affirming Christ's lordship over all of creation to Christ's lordship with respect to the church. The relationship is expressed through the organic metaphor of head/body: "and he is the head of the body, the church." Many interpreters have argued that τῆς ἐκκλησίας is a secondary insertion by the letter's author into a metaphor that originally had a cosmic interpretation: σῶμα is regarded as a circumlocution for κόσμος and Christ is consequently understood as the "head" of his cosmic body, the "macroanthropos."[49] This interpretation, which depends heavily on Hellenistic or Gnostic concepts, faces some severe difficulties. I have argued in a different context that the metaphor is drawn from current physiological understandings of the head in relationship to the body as exhibited in the medical writers, some philosophers, and Philo.[50] In this view, the head functions not only as the ruling part of the body, but also as the supply center of the body since it is the source of sensation, movement, and will. As head of the church, Christ provides leadership and direction for his people while at the same time is the source of the church's life energy for its growth to maturity. I do have a few additional comments to make, however, at this juncture.

First, it is quite clear that the author of the epistle did not view Christ as head of a cosmic body in this hymn; otherwise he would not have explicitly identified the body as the church. He makes the same explicit identification a few lines later (v. 24) blatantly restricting the sense in which he intends his readers to take σῶμα. Furthermore, it is irrelevant for our purposes to discern whether or not σῶμα was used in the sense of a "macroanthropos" in the original hymn. We are concerned strictly with how the hymn would have been understood by the Christians at Colossae.

Secondly, Paul himself shows no sign of knowing the "macroanthropos" myth in the accepted epistles, there is no explicit Helle-

---

[49] E.g. Pokorný, *Colossians,* 82; Schweizer, *Colossians,* 58-59; idem, "σῶμα," *TDNT* 7.1054-55; *idem,* "Body," *ABD* 1.771; idem, "Die Kirche," 293-316; C. Colpe, "Zur Leib-Christi-Vorstellung im Epheserbrief," in *Judentum, Urchristentum, Kirche* (ed. W. Eltester; BZNW 26; Berlin: de Gruyter, 1964) 172-87, esp. 179-82; H. Hegermann, *Die Vorstellung vom Schöpfungsmittler im hellenistischen Judentum und Urchristentum* (TU 82; Berlin: Akademie, 1961) 138-57; et al.

[50] "Jesus Christ: 'Head' of the Church," in *Jesus of Nazareth: Lord and Christ. Essays on the Historical Jesus and New Testament Christology* (eds. M.M.B. Turner and J. B. Green; Grand Rapids: Eerdmans, 1994) 346-66.

nistic text affirming a head-body correlation as it is expressed in Col. 1:18, and interpreters have been too quick to cite texts from Philo as examples of the "macroanthropos" myth allegedly behind the Col. hymn. In fact, Philo never ascribes a cosmic function to κεφαλή when he elaborates on the world soul.[51]

This fresh concept of Christ as the head of his body, the church, is especially appropriate to the situation facing the believers at Colossae. The "body" concept maintains the emphasis on the unity of the fellow members within the church (as in 1 Cor. and Rom.), but the "head-body" analogy stresses the unity of the church with Christ. This is then further developed in the body of the letter when Paul calls on the Colossians to depend on Christ alone for leadership and for power and strengthening (Col 2:19). The Colossians therefore have no need for any additional help, namely that which "the philosophy" offers, in realizing their salvation and for coping with the onslaught of the "powers."

c. The Powers No Longer Enslave: Christ is Lord of Reconciliation

The second stanza of the hymn praises Christ as the Lord of reconciliation. Whereas the first strophe characterized Christ's relationship to creation and especially the angelic "powers," the second strophe describes Christ's relationship to the church by describing the three most important events in obtaining redemption: death on the cross, the resurrection, and the declaration of divine sonship. The scope of the redemption—here termed "reconciliation"—is expressed in universal terms.

The issue of the demonic powers is not lost in the second half of the hymn. Whereas the first strophe emphasized Christ's superiority to the powers, the second strophe not only reiterates Christ's pre-eminence as Lord, but also establishes the basis for the church's freedom from and superiority to the powers—those who are united with Christ are the redeemed people of God. Furthermore, the hymn does take up Christ's relationship to the "powers" (τὰ ἐν τοῖς οὐρανοῖς) again at the conclusion by referring to them as objects of "reconciliation."

The first line of the second stanza continues to develop the theme of pre-eminence from the first stanza and v. 17. Christ is praised as the ἀρχή ("the beginning"). In this respect he resembles the figure of Wisdom in Prov 8:22. G. Delling notes that ἀρχή denotes primacy, whether in a tem-

---

[51] See my "Jesus Christ: 'Head' of the Church," 348-49.

poral sense or with reference to dominion and power.[52] Both senses are present in this context. He is the beginning of a new humanity because he is the "firstborn from the dead" (v. 18). He holds the leading position of power and authority because he is "firstborn of all creation" (v. 15) and by virtue of the fact that he is πρὸ πάντων (v. 17). The idea of rulership also dominates in Rev 3:14 where Christ is named as "the ruler of God's creation" (ἡ ἀρχὴ τῆς κτίσεως τοῦ θεοῦ). When Christ as the beginning is correlated with the statement that he is the goal of creation (v. 16), we have here a concept similar to the declaration in the Apocalypse that Christ is the beginning and end, the Alpha and Omega (Rev 1:8; 21:6; 22:13). Pokorný thus rightly concludes, "'the beginning' is a description of authority and lordship."[53] Therefore, as the "beginning," Christ is Lord both over creation (which includes the powers) and the church.

As "firstborn from the dead," the power of Christ over one of his greatest enemies—death—is extolled. Although death is personified as an enemy in 1 Cor 15:26 and Rom 8:38, it is altogether a different class of enemy than what is conveyed with the terms ἀρχαί, ἐξουσίαι, θρόνοι, and κυριότητες. These hostile angelic forces, however, were also defeated by Jesus' death on the cross (Col 2:15), which has made possible the reconciliation and peace spoken of in the final lines of the hymn.

Contrasted with his exalted status as "the beginning" of all things is his assumed position as "the beginning" with respect to the new creation. Based on his victory over death by his resurrection, Christ, "the firstborn from the dead," is praised as having become "pre-eminent (πρωτεύων) in all things" (v. 18). The first and most prominent place in the church belongs to Christ alone[54]; he is the "head" of his body. Because he is "the beginning" and "before all things" (1:17), he holds first position over all things. The term πρωτεύων was used by the civic leaders of Ephesus in claiming the pre-eminence of their city in all of Asia (Josephus, *Ant.* 14.10.11 §224). The pre-eminence of Christ is here emphasized "to the evident depreciation of the cosmic rulers ... evidently because a similar position had been ascribed to them in the heretical doctrine."[55] Christ alone should hold the most prominent place in the hearts and lives of the Christians at Colossae.

---

[52] G. Delling, "ἀρχή," *TDNT* 1.481-84.

[53] Pokorný, *Colossians,* 83.

[54] For additional references illustrating the common use of πρωτεύω to signify rank, see W. Michaelis, "πρωτεύω," *TDNT* 6.881-82.

[55] R. Leivestad, *Christ the Conqueror* (London: SPCK, 1954) 97.

The pre-eminence of Christ is no vacuous claim. Christ possesses "all the fullness" (πᾶν τὸ πλήρωμα). All the fullness of God's power, essence, and glory dwells in Christ. Conversely, Christ is not a divine intermediary or an emanation of God. He is the presence of God himself.

Although the term πλήρωμα appears in Paul's earlier letters (see, for example, Rom 11:12, 25; 13:10; 15:29; 1 Cor 10:26; Gal 4:4), this is the first time that it appears with a technical theological significance. The passive sense of the term (a filled receptacle vs. a filling substance or entity) best fits the present context and is further supported by Paul's previous non-technical usage in which the term always bears a passive sense.

The interpretation of the term is informed by the accompanying phrases ἐν αὐτῷ εὐδόκησεν and κατοικῆσαι. The roots of the first phrase go deep into the OT and LXX where the term is used frequently of God's divine pleasure. The two terms are sometimes even found in the same context in the LXX referring to God's choice of a place to dwell.[56] Thus, the Psalmist speaks of Zion as "the mountain on which it pleased God to dwell" (τὸ ὄρος, ὃ εὐδόκησεν ὁ θεὸς κατοικεῖν ἐν αὐτῷ) (Ps 67:17 LXX; cf. also Ps 131:13-14; Isa 8:18; 49:20). Similarly, the temple was God's dwelling place: "O Lord of all ... thou was pleased (ηὐδόκησας) that there be a temple for thy habitation among us" (2 Macc 14:35). The subject of εὐδόκησεν is best understood in Col 1:19 as πᾶν τὸ πλήρωμα[57] rather than implying θεός.[58] The change of subject was signalled by the beginning ἐν αὐτῷ of 1:19, which continues the reference to Christ. This interpretation is also suggested by the parallel phrase in 2:9 where πᾶν τὸ πλήρωμα is indisputably the subject of κατοικεῖ. Some have objected to this view since πλήρωμα appears to be impersonal. As we will see below, however, the term πλήρωμα appears to be used in Colossians as a circumlocution for the Spirit.

Consonant with this image, the hymn takes up the term πλήρωμα as a means of denoting something similar to the OT notion of the *shekina*.[59] As G. Münderlein and others have suggested, the term therefore refers to the essence, power, glory, and full presence of God, who inhabits the place he has chosen as a dwelling.[60] Although the noun never appears in the LXX

---

[56] For references, see Lohse, *Colossians*, 58.

[57] Porter, Καταλλάσσω, 173-74; Pokorný, *Colossians*, 85; O'Brien, *Colossians*, 51; Lohse, *Colossians*, 56-57; Münderlein, "Erwählung," 266; et al.

[58] This is the view of G. Delling, "πλήρωμα," *TDNT* 6.303; Lightfoot, *Colossians*, 158; et al.

[59] See my previous discussion of this term in *Ephesians*, 82-85.

[60] Münderlein, "Die Erwählung," 264-76; Kehl, *Christushymnus*, 124; Gibbs, *Crea-*

in this sense, the verb (πληρόω) and the adjective (πλήρης) are used repeatedly of the presence of God "filling" the place of his habitation. Thus the prophet can exclaim: "I looked and saw the glory of the Lord filling the temple" (Ezek 44:4; see also 43:5; Isa 6:1; Hag 2:7). In this sense, the term may also serve as a circumlocution for the Holy Spirit.[61]

The hymn writer (Paul or otherwise) has thus found the term πλήρωμα helpful in communicating the sovereignty of Christ. The emphasis of the expression on the fullness of divine power is particularly acute, as F. Mußner notes: "by virtue of God's activity in raising Jesus, the firstborn from the dead comes into possession of the complete divine life-giving power and thereby Christ becomes Lord of all according to the divine purpose."[62] This expression has particular relevance to the situation confronting the Colossian congregation. O'Brien correctly observes, "The Colossian Christians need not fear those supernatural powers under whose control men were supposed to live, whether divine emanations, agencies or the like. God in all his divine essence and power had taken up residence in Christ."[63]

Πλήρωμα, therefore, does not appear to have been a catchword of the opponents for the following reasons[64]: (1) it was not used in the polemical sections of the letter (2:5, 8, 16-23); (2) it appears first as a positive Christological affirmation in the hymn (1:19); (3) the only other occurrence appears to be a reaffirmation of the hymnic statement for the purpose of developing the ecclesiological implications of all the fullness dwelling in Christ vis-a-vis the church is in Christ (2:9-10); (4) although we have already demonstrated that the roots to the author's understanding of fullness in the LXX, it must also be stated that the use of the term in Colossians is unrelated to the technical significance it is given in Gnostic

---

tion and Redemption, 99-100, 108.

[61] See esp. A. J. Bandstra, "Pleroma as Pneuma in Colossians," *Ad Interim* (FS. R. Schippers; Kampen: Kok, 1975) 96-102. He finds linguistic support for this interpretation in the unamended text of 2 *Apoc. Bar.* 21:4: "the one who fixed the firmament by his *fullness* and fastened the height of heaven by the *spirit.*" He also oberves that the Holy Spirit is brought into close association with fullness in 1QH 16:2-3. Münderlein, "Erwählung," 272, concludes that the term is "a striking paraphrase of the Holy Spirit." See also Pokorný, *Colossians,* 85.

[62] F. Mußner, *Christus, das All und die Kirche* (TTS 5; Trier: Paulinus, 1955) 57.

[63] O'Brien, *Colossians,* 53.

[64] So also Pokorný, *Colossians,* 121 ("That fullness was one of the opponents' concepts of God cannot be demonstrated.") See also Bürger, *Schöpfung und Versöhnung,* 112ff.; Percy, *Probleme,* 77.

literature.[65] "Fullness" is thus an appropriate expression for the sole-sufficiency and adequacy of Christ derived from the LXX.

The final line of the hymn reveals the ultimate aim of the outworking of the divine power through the Lord Jesus Christ—"all things," both earthly and heavenly, will be "reconciled" (ἀποκαταλάσσω) to Christ (v. 20). He promises to bring universal and cosmic peace.

As a backdrop to this optimistic picture of the future, E. Schweizer and many other interpreters have suggested that there was a widespread feeling of fear throughout the Mediterranean region about the instability of the world. There was conflict among the physical elements and heavenly bodies (which were regarded as animated by angelic beings) that was leading to a degeneration and break up of the world.[66] Schweizer is essentially correct in his portrayal of the common fear of the instability of the world, but he does not go far enough in describing the prominent role of the mediatorial divine powers and angels as the agents of destruction and harm. As we saw earlier in Chapter 5, nearby Hierapolis faced a deadly plague because of the wrathful displeasures of the gods. It was only through appeasing the evil powers that the plague could be averted. On the individual level, the fear of the harmful and destructive machinations of personal supernatural powers was just as critical. Consequently, people were initiated into the cults of benevolent deities for protection, they wore apotropaic amulets, and they participated in rituals, and invoked spirits,

---

[65] P. D. Overfield, "Pleroma: A Study in Content and Context," *NTS* 25 (1978-79) 384-96; P. Benoit, "The 'plèroma' in the Epistles to the Colossians and the Ephesians," *SEÅ* 49 (1984) 136-58. J. M. Dillon, *"Pleroma* and Noetic Cosmos: A Comparative Study," in *Neoplatonism and Gnosticism* (Studies in Neoplatonism: Ancient and Modern 6; Albany: State University of New York, 1992) 108, concludes regarding the use of the term in the Nag Hammadi Corpus, "We may accept, then, that the term *Pleroma* is derived from the language of the New Testament, even as is the term *aion* in the plural, and the mythological details are distinctive of Gnosticism, but the concept which it represents is, I would maintain, an implantation from the Platonist tradition into Gnosticism."

[66] See Schweizer, *Colossians,* 80-81. Philo, *Spec. Leg.* 2.190-92, speaks of nature at strife in herself, but presents God as the one who is the peacemaker and peacekeeper (εἰρηνοποιός καὶ εἰρηνοφύλαξ) destroying the factious hostilities in the various parts of the All (ἐν τοῖς μέρεσι τοῦ παντός). L. Hartmann, "Universal Reconciliation (Col 1,20)" *SNTU* 10 (1985) 109-21, regards the idea of reconciliation at the end of the hymn as similar to the Philonic way of thinking of the Logos—both Philo and the author of Colossians share the same basic perspective on the universe. According to Hartmann, the author of Colossians believes that the Christ event has changed the actual situation of the planets (which are viewed as living creatures) insofar as, "if anyone is afraid of them or of their ability to influence his destiny, he would know that the real power and the deepest divine principle of the world is the one he is ruled by, Christ's" (120).

gods, and angels for protection.[67] For the common folk of Asia Minor in the Roman period, the *kosmos* was not a smooth-working piece of machinery where they could enjoy a peaceful existence; there was every sort of invisible power that could overturn momentary tranquility and replace it with catastrophe.

The hymn extols Christ as the peacemaker (εἰρηνοποιήσας). He will create worldwide, indeed even cosmic, peace in spite of many powerful adversaries. As Pokorný has noted, this pronouncement has much in common with the promise of universal peace found in the Servant Songs of Isaiah, especially Isa 52:6-10.[68] Although the people of God had experienced slavery and oppression at the hands of the Egyptians and the Assyrians, they entertained the lively hope of peace when Yahweh would "lay bare his holy arm in the sight of all the nations" and bring salvation to his people (Isa 52:10). His act of redemption would lead to times of rejoicing and celebration. Worldwide peace would ensue as people would rightly proclaim, "your God reigns!" (Isa 52:7).

In language reminiscent of Isaiah, the Colossian hymn thus declares a time of universal peace that would come with the redemption (Isa 52:3, 9) and salvation (Isa 52:7, 10) of God. This is consonant with the role of the Messiah as "prince of peace" (שַׂר שָׁלוֹם)—"the guarantor and guardian of peace in the coming Messianic kingdom."[69] Because there is not yet peace in heaven and on earth from the vantage point of the Colossians, the passage has a distinctively futuristic eschatological flavor. It holds out the promise of universal peace. On the other hand, Paul clearly indicates that the Messianic peace is something the Colossians could currently experience. Thus, he begins the letter with his typical greeting, "grace *and peace* to you from God our Father" (Col 1:2). He also urges the Colossians to let the Messianic peace reign in their hearts (Col 3:15). Within the Pauline eschatological framework of the "now and not yet," the Messianic peace is presented as something both present and future. It is present through union with the Messiah and experienced in the forgiveness of sin and in protection from the hostile influence of the powers. It is future because the Messiah has not yet created worldwide and heavenly peace.

---

[67] Similarly, Wolter, *Kolosser, 87,* remarks, "The people of that time found the possibility of protection from the ongoing threats to their own existence and thereby the possibility of overcoming their own tremendous fears (*Weltangst*) above all in the various forms of magic, the mysteries, asceticism, and the cultic veneration of the world-governing powers."

[68] Pokorný, *Colossians,* 89.

[69] W. Foerster, "εἰρήνη," *TDNT* 2.405-406.

The peace is achieved "through the blood of the cross."[70] Here then the Pauline theology of the cross is employed, but it is shown not only to have implications for the sin of humanity, but also for cosmic peace.

In contrast to Isaiah and the other Pauline letters, the hymn links peace to a *universal* "reconciliation" (ἀποκαταλάσσω). The neuter τὰ πάντα clearly places the scope of reconciliation beyond redeemed humanity as is made clear by the explanatory statement of v. 20c, which stresses comprehensiveness: εἴτε τὰ ἐπὶ τῆς γῆς εἴτε τὰ ἐν τοῖς οὐρανοῖς. This would include the invisible powers of v. 16c.[71]

The subsequent reference to ἀποκαταλλάσσω in Col 1:22 has much in common with the earlier Pauline understanding of reconciliation, which he brings to expression with the terms καταλλάσσω (Rom. 5:10; 1 Cor. 7:11; 2 Cor. 5:18, 20) and καταλλαγή (2 Cor 5:18, 19; Rom. 11:15). Humanity is presented as at enmity with God, and he effects[72] a reconciliation through the death of Christ, which restores the relationship. Rom 5:1-11 also links the term peace with reconciliation (see Rom 5:1 and 10a).

What stand out as unique developments in Paul's concept of reconciliation is the use of the prefixed verb ἀποκαταλλάσσω and the universal extent of the reconciliation. The verb occurs only in Colossians and Ephesians (Col. 1:20, 22; Eph 2:16) in the entire NT.[73] In fact, this is the first time this prefixed form appears in all of Greek literature. Therefore, it is most likely that the author of the hymn has taken over the Pauline καταλλάσσω and intensified it by the addition of ἀπό, thus making it an emphatic use of the simple form.[74] This emphatic form would be consistent, then, with the expanded scope of reconciliation and consequent condition of universal peace.

---

[70] Many interpreters regard this phrase as the author's redactional addition to the hymn.

[71] Porter, *Καταλλάσσω*, 182.

[72] God is the implied subject of ἀποκαταλλάσσω in both Col 1:20 and 22. So also Lohse, *Colossians*, 64.

[73] For a full discussion of this term, see Chapter 8 ("'Αποκαταλλάσσω in Colossians 1:20, 22, and Ephesians 2:16") in Porter, *Καταλλάσσω*, 163-90.

[74] Porter, *Καταλλάσσω*, 184. Kehl's suggestion (in *Christushymnus*, 159-60) that the ἀποκαταλλαγή of Col 1:20 is the making amends for the Gentiles' ἀλλαγή in Rom 1:23 is a good example of a "root fallacy." While ἀλλάσσω and (ἀπο)καταλλάσσω do have the same etymology, the two terms have distinct semantic ranges in the Greek of the Hellenistic and Roman eras. This does not invalidate, however, Kehl's astute suggestion that Col 1:12-20 has a similar conceptual background to Rom 1:23 and its context.

The universal extent of reconciliation in 1:20 is clearly unique in scope, and its distinctiveness is brought into bolder relief when it is realized that the terminology played no role in Greek and Hellenistic pagan religion either with respect to the relation between humanity and the deity or with reference to the cosmos as a whole.[75] When the author of Colossians repeats ἀποκαταλλάσσω in the following section (vv. 21-23), however, he restricts the scope to humanity. The author never again repeats the term and explicitly elaborates on how this "reconciliation" is to be understood between the "powers" and God or between the "powers" and humanity.

The most natural way of explaining the meaning of this universal reconciliation is by interpreting it in light of the following qualifying participial clause—εἰρηνοποιήσας διὰ τοῦ αἵματος τοῦ σταυροῦ αὐτοῦ. Reconciliation would then be understood in Col 1:20 as referring primarily to the condition of peace in heaven and on earth. The universal scope of the reconciliation is thus an eschatological promise yet to be fulfilled from the standpoint of the author. It is the time of final redemption when even the enemies of God will proclaim, "Your God reigns!" As we have already seen, however, it is part of the present experience of the Colossian Christians in that they experience the peace of God because they are in Christ, no longer estranged from God, and set free from the tyranny of the powers.

W. Wink has recently argued that the reconciliation here indicates that the hostile powers will be redeemed.[76] The strength of his position lies in the fact that in all of the other occurrences of reconciliation terminology in Paul, the term is used of enemies brought into relationship with God or with each other.

It is certainly true that this passage is unique in extending reconciliation to "things/beings in heaven," but it is nowhere explicitly stated that the heavenly beings are redeemed. There are seven pertinent observations demonstrating that the hostile heavenly beings are not brought into a relationship with God in the same way as redeemed humanity: (1) It is con-

---

[75] See F. Büchsel, "καταλλάσσω," *TDNT* 1.254.

[76] W. Wink, *Engaging the Powers* (Minneapolis: Fortress, 1992) 73-85 (= a section titled, "The Powers Will Be Redeemed," in Chapter 4). See also *Naming the Powers*, 54-55. Pokorný, *Colossians*, 88, comes close to this when he asserts that this passage "denotes the restoration of the original function of the cosmic powers." W. Michaelis, *Versöhnung des Alls* (Bern: Siloah, 1950) 24-25 (cited in Gnilka, *Kolosserbrief*, 76), argued that this passage together with Eph. 1:10 and others indicate that since God's eternal plan and purpose was reconciliation, then nothing in his creation would finally or ultimately be lost, including the demonic "powers."

spicuous that the writer of the letter nowhere speaks of the powers in anything other than negative terms. (2) The hymn is introduced by praising Christ's rescue of his people from the dominion of darkness. (3) Reconciliation terminology is immediately applied to believers in the typical Pauline sense in 1:21-23 to describe the removal of alienation from God on the basis of the purification of the redeemed people. Conversely, the hostile powers are not mentioned in 1:21-23, nor is reconciliation terminology applied to them elsewhere in the letter. (4) The most telling point against Wink's position is Paul's dramatic and emphatic portrayal of the powers as defeated at the cross (Col 2:15). The language he uses leaves no room for a reconciliation as friends. (5) The notion of the redemption of the hostile powers is also difficult to maintain in light of the Jewish apocalyptic framework that informs Paul's thought. This world view looked forward to a time of final battle (see 1QM!) in which there would be a losing side. God would intervene and triumph over his enemies. (6) Even if one sees the author of the hymn depending upon the Philonic conception of God as universal peacemaker as expressed in *Spec. Leg.* 2.292, the means that God takes for achieving cosmic peace is through the destruction (ἀναιρέω) of factions in heaven and on earth. (7) Finally, Wink maintains this position in large measure because he contends that Paul has already moved a considerable distance toward demythologizing the powers.[77] As "the necessary social structures of human life,"[78] he argues that they are indeed capable of redemption and can thus fulfill a good and worthwhile purpose. I have argued more extensively elsewhere that this kind of reading of Paul's language for the powers is an inappropriate imposition of a Western post-Enlightenment world view onto the first-century writer of Colossians.[79]

The elaboration on the "powers" in 2:8, 10, 15, and 20 should thus be viewed as determinative for our understanding of the "reconciliation" of the powers. Through the work of Christ on the cross, God has denuded these malignant forces of their power and authority, he has publicly exposed them for what they really are, and, in short, he has led them away as vanquished foes in a victor's parade (2:15; see the discussion of this verse in the next section). Christ can now be proclaimed as sovereign, that is, as the "head" of the "powers." As vanquished foes who nevertheless

---

[77] Wink, *Naming,* 61-63.

[78] Wink, *Engaging,* 66.

[79] See my *Ephesians,* 48-51, 129-34; see also "'Principalities and Powers' in Recent Interpretation," *Catalyst* 17.2 (February 1991) 4-5, and *Powers of Darkness* (Downer's Grove, Ill.: InterVarsity Press, 1992) 198-201.

still seek to lead the saints astray (2:8), they have not entered a relationship of friendship with God. On the contrary, peace comes to the church and to the cosmos because they have been defeated and their power has been broken. Consequently, a number of interpreters have appropriately described the reconciliation of the "powers" in terms of "pacification"[80] or "subjection" (Unterordnung).[81]

The emphasis of Col 1:20 is on the future condition of peace and harmony in the cosmos as a result of the work of the peacemaker—the Lord Jesus Christ. Peace comes because the enemies have been dealt with and they will no longer be actors on the stage. "The new world will be a world of peace and reconciliation and Christ will be it's Lord."[82]

This declaration is quite relevant to the Colossians who are tempted to find the means of appeasing the hostile powers. The purveyors of "the philosophy" are offering a new means of appeasing the powers—through a unique mixture of their Christianity, Jewish and local Phrygian ascetic practices, mystery initiation concepts, visionary experience, and through invoking helpful angels.

The author of Colossians thus assures the readers that Christ is supreme and that there would be a time of universal peace. Christ's death is the basis for this restoration of harmony throughout heaven and earth.

d. Summary

In an eloquent and rhetorically powerful manner, the author lays the groundwork for his polemic against "the philosophy" in 2:4-23. He employs (or, composes) a moving piece of poetry especially relevant to his case. The passage magnificently recounts the unsurpassed supremacy of

---

[80] Aletti, *Colossiens,* 112-13; T. J. Sappington, *Revelation and Redemption at Colossae* (JSNTSS 53; Sheffield: JSOT Press, 1991) 175 ("a peace imposed on them by a superior force"); O'Brien, *Colossians,* 56; F. F. Bruce, "Christ as Conqueror and Reconciler," *BibSac* 141 (1984) 293. R. P. Martin, *Reconciliation* (Atlanta: John Knox, 1981) 126, although he sees Paul altering the original sense of the term as it was known in the hymn.

[81] Dibelius-Greeven, *Kolosser,* 19; Percy, *Probleme,* 105 ("unterworfen"); Gabathuler, *Jesus Christus ,* 143 ("Unterwerfung").

[82] Gnilka, *Kolosserbrief,* 75. Because of the contextual emphasis on the identity of the reconciler and the fact of a future condition of peace, Gnilka actually sees the question of whether the powers will be subjected or redeemed as inappropriate. Similarly, F. Mussner, *Christus,* 71, argues that one should not ask who or what is to be reconciled, but who is the mediator of reconciliation.

Christ over creation, most notably the hostile angelic powers. The powers are thus not ultimate. Christ is prior to the powers, he is in fact their creator, and is thus pre-eminent. The hymn also reminds the readers that Christ has inaugurated a new humanity through the cross and his resurrection. The author builds on the Pauline view of the body of Christ by naming Christ as the "head" of the new humanity known as his "body." This designation is particularly appropriate to the situation facing the Colossian readers, who need to be reassured of the complete adequacy of Christ for acquiring strength and guidance. Much to the reassurance of the readers, Christ is not unaware of the threat posed by these angelic "powers" nor is he unable to provide ultimate protection and security. The hymn also hold out the eschatological promise that God will bring about harmony throughout heaven and earth because of the cross of Christ, both for the redemption of estranged mankind and for the pacification of the hostile angelic agitators.

The author instructs the readers that they have actually been rescued from a dominion controlled by the "powers" of darkness. This teaching may have provoked a fearful awe in the emotions of the readers who may not have realized how deeply and thoroughly their fate and daily existence was at the hands of the evil "powers." The Colossian Christians no longer have any need to fear; rather they have every reason for thanksgiving, for they have been relocated into the kingdom of their loving and powerful Lord. Within this dominion, they have access to an abundant supply of divine power to protect them from the continuing and compelling influence of the evil "powers" and to strengthen them to resist the encroaching influence of the burgeoning "philosophy."

This section therefore provides a perfect basis for the author's polemic against "the philosophy." It answers the root question filling the minds of some of the Colossians, viz. do we need extra protection from the hostile "powers" in addition to our faith in and union with Christ?

2. Christ as *The* Mystery

Paul continues to extol the person of Christ as central to the divine plan of salvation by describing him as "the mystery" (τὸ μυστήριον). Three times in the section leading up to the polemic (1:24-2:5) Paul makes reference to the mystery (1:26, 27; 2:2).

He explicitly identifies Christ as "the mystery of God" in 2:2 by the use of Χριστοῦ as a genitive of apposition: "the mystery of God *which is* Christ."[83] The same construction reappears in 4:3 where Paul describes the content of his preaching as, "the mystery, which is Christ" (τὸ μυστήριον τοῦ Χριστοῦ).

As we have already seen in Chapter 5, the advocates of "the philosophy" continued to embrace certain aspects of mystery cult belief and practice, which they were combining with their Christianity. This may have taken on more of a magical form in terms of rituals of power for the purpose of gaining additional means of dealing with hostile powers and spirits. We do not know precisely how they were promulgating this influence among the Colossians: by advocating a ritual initiation into one of the Phrygian mysteries, by establishing a Christian initiation ritual modeled after the local rites, or merely by teaching what they had learned in their own previous visionary experience in pagan ritual initiation. What we do know is that, by taking up one of these approaches, they did not make a clean break with their idolatrous past. They mixed their Christian faith with Phrygian religion and/or magic in a fashion that Paul deemed unacceptable.

It is clear that Paul himself has not taken over mystery cult theology in his portrayal of Christ as the divine mystery. Current scholarship has shown conclusively that Paul's concept of mystery is deeply rooted in Judaism. M. Bockmuehl has asserted that K. Prümm's entry in the *Dictionnaire de la Bible, Supplément,* marks the "clear death-knell of the theory of pagan derivation."[84] Paul's concept of mystery should be interpreted on the basis of the use of "mystery" (רָז) in the book of Daniel where it is used to describe the hiddenness or secrecy of the redemptive plan of God. A similar usage appears in the Qumran materials and in some of the apocalyptic documents.[85]

---

[83] This phrase is beset with an array of textual alternatives. With the UBS[4] and the Nestle-Aland[27], it is best to see the readings of $\mathfrak{P}^{46}$, B, et al. as preserving the original form of the text. The variations represent attempts at smoothing out the text. See the discussions in Pokorný, *Colossians,* 107, and O'Brien, *Colossians,* 94.

[84] M. N. A. Bockmuehl, *Revelation and Mystery in Ancient Judaism and Pauline Christianity* (WUNT 2/36; Tübingen: J.C.B. Mohr [Paul Siebeck], 1990) 223, referring to K. Prümm, "Mystères," in *DBSup* 6.1-225, esp. 173-225.

[85] See Bockmuehl, *Revelation and Mystery,* 221-30; R. E. Brown, *The Semitic Background of the Term "Mystery" in the NT* (Philadelphia: Fortress, 1968) 1-30, 56-66; G. Bornkamm, "μυστήριον," *TDNT* 4.824; C. C. Caragounis, *The Ephesian Mysterion,* (ConB 8; Lund: Gleerup, 1977) 143-46; et al.

Given the nature of the situation at Colossae and the background of the Gentile readers, it is surprising that Paul does not avoid using the term altogether. Many of the believers at Colossae would have been Gentiles, presumably having a background in the cults of the local deities (whether they came to Christ through the intermediate step of the synagogue or not). Furthermore, the opponents themselves advocated some form of mystery cult theology and practice and may very well have been using the term "mystery"!

The fact that Paul does use the term—four times at that!—actually betrays a powerful rhetorical strategy. He points to Christ as *the* mystery! Christ is the divine reality. He is the central figure to the one God's plan of redemption. Christ is here conceived not only in terms of his divine being, but in his essential role in procuring salvation. As Bockmuehl has said with regard to Colossians: "Paul seems to condense his teaching about mysteries into a 'grander,' more universal conception of 'the mystery of Christ,' in which Christology and soteriology are one."[86] In light of Christ as *the* mystery, Paul implies that one should turn away from other so-called mysteries and their teaching. The Colossians should therefore not be led astray by what Paul calls the "empty deceit" (2:18) of "the philosophy," which depends upon teaching from the local mysteries.

The one aspect of this grand mystery that Paul appears to stress above all else is *the presence of the indwelling Christ in believers* (1:27).[87] He essentially makes it the content of the mystery: ὅ [τὸ μυστήριον] ἐστιν Χριστὸς ἐν ὑμῖν. The statement has much in common with what he has said before in Rom 8:10 (Χριστὸς ἐν ὑμῖν)—a passage that characterizes

---

[86] Bockmuehl, *Revelation and Mystery,* 228.

[87] Some interpreters, however, have argued that the ἐν ὑμῖν should be interpreted as "among you," that is, in the sense of the Gospel's proclamation among the Gentiles; so, Wolter, *Kolosser,* 105; Bockmuehl, *Revelation and Mystery,* 182; Pokorný, *Colossians,* 103; Lohse, *Colossians,* 76; et al. It is preferable, on contextual grounds, to see the phrase as referring to the pneumatic indwelling of Christ; thus, Wright, *Colossians,* 92; O'Brien, *Colossians,* 87; Caragounis, *Mysterion,* 30; Dibelius-Greeven, *Kolosser,* 25; Bornkamm, "μυστήριον," *TDNT* 4.820; Lightfoot, *Colossians,* 169; et al. The idea of "Messiah proclaimed among the Gentiles" is certainly presupposed, but this is not exactly what Paul is emphasizing here. He wants to convey the concept that the resurrected Christ *indwells* every person (see the double emphasis on individuals within the community in 1:28: πάντα ἄνθρωπον). The empowering presence of Christ in each person is what makes it possible for the Apostle to look forward to presenting every person "complete" (τέλειον) in Christ. The concluding ἐν Χριστῷ serves as merely another way of stressing the solidarity of believers with Christ. It is precisely this solidarity of Christ with believers that Paul is stressing here because it serves his theological purpose of building up the Colossian believers for the purpose of resisting "the philosophy."

the basis of Christian existence.[88] In that context the indwelling of Christ is made coextensive with possession of the Spirit (Rom 8:9, 11) and serves as the basis of future hope (8:11) as well as an empowering presence to overcome evil practices (8:13).[89] Although Colossians does not speak explicitly of the work of the Holy Spirit, the empowering presence of the Spirit does come to expression through the "fullness/filling" terminology (2:10; see discussion below). "Christ in you" thus conveys the concept of a present union with Christ through faith. This solidarity of believers with Christ becomes the basis for all that Paul says in the theological section of 2:9-15. There he expresses the concept with the phrases "in Christ" and "with Christ."

Although there is a distinct accent on the present revelation and knowability of the mystery, this does not diminish the future expectation of revelation. Thus Paul describes the presence of the indwelling Christ as the basis for their anticipation of a future union with Christ at his coming in glory (ἡ ἐλπὶς τῆς δόξης; 1:27; cf. 3:4).[90] In the previous verse, Paul used the aorist tense of φανερόω to express the present manifestation of this mystery, but he later uses the future tense of the same verb to maintain the vitality of a future hope centered on the return of the Lord Jesus Christ (3:4). He also states that the presence of the indwelling Christ is the source of the believers' hope of future glory (1:27; cf. 3:4). In addition, Paul looks forward to the day when he will be able to present every person he has worked with complete in Christ (1:28). This presupposes the return of Christ and a time of judgment. Thus, temporal categories have not completely given way to spatial. Even in this context of strong emphasis on the realized pole of eschatology, hope still has a temporal dimension.[91]

---

[88] Dibelius-Greeven, *Kolosser,* 25.

[89] See also 2 Cor 13:3, 5; Gal 2:20; 4:19; Eph 3:17.

[90] So also Sappington, *Revelation and Redemption,* 186. The tension between the temporal and spatial categories regarding glory can be observed in Paul's previous letters. In Rom 8:17, believers are said to await the experience of glory in the future whereas in 2 Cor 3:18 they experience a taste of that glory in the present age. They are being "transformed ... from glory to glory just as from the Lord, the Spirit." The Spirit (or, the exalted Lord) thus currently carries on a ministry in the saints that is characterized as ἐν δόξῃ (vv. 9, 11). This transformational experience under the new covenant is described by Paul as their "hope" (v. 12)—a hope experienced in the present through the glorious ministry of the Lord, but simultaneously providing a reassurance of future glory (thus, the εἰς δόξαν in 3:13). See further, R. Kittel, "δόξα," *TDNT* 2.251; V. P. Furnish, *Theology and Ethics in Paul* (Nashville: Abingdon, 1968) 126-27.

[91] Contra G. Bornkamm, "Die Hoffnung im Kolosserbrief. Zugleich ein Beitrag zur Frage der Echtheit des Briefes," in *Studien zum Neuen Testament und zur Patristik* (FS.

For the Colossians, Christ—"the mystery of God"—is not only the source of power and hope, but the wellspring of "all the treasures of wisdom and knowledge" (2:2-3). Paul here draws upon Wisdom tradition and transfers the functions of wisdom to Christ (see Prov 2:3-6).[92] Since wisdom and knowledge are "stored up" (ἀπόκρυφοι) in Christ, Christ is therefore the place where they are to be found.[93] The Colossians should invest their energy in seeking for wisdom and knowledge in the proper place (cf. 3:1, 2). Paul wants them to grasp Christ (cf. 2:19), not the tenets of "the philosophy."

The Colossian Christians, therefore, do not need to perform ritual initiation of any kind for added protection from the powers. Neither do they need πάρεδροι or angelic beings that would come to assist them and protect them after their performance of this kind of ritual (cf. *PGM* I.128-32). They have been given the ultimate mystery—Christ himself who indwells their lives. He is supreme above all the powers and is the source of all knowledge and wisdom.

3. "You Have Been Filled": The Structure and Function of 2:9-15

The hymn extols Christ as the one in whom all the fullness (πᾶν τὸ πλήρωμα) dwells (1:19). Paul reaffirms this immediately after he begins his polemic against the opposing teaching. After indicting the teaching as in accordance with demonic spirits and not in accordance with Christ (2:8), he declares that "in Christ all the fullness of the divine nature (πᾶν τὸ πλήρωμα τῆς θεότητος) dwells in bodily form" (2:9). He immediately makes this Christological statement ecclesiologically relevant. Paul declares that they share in this fullness by virtue of their identification with Christ. He exclaims: "and you have been filled in him (καὶ ἐστὲ ἐν αὐτῷ πεπληρωμένοι; 2:10a).

E. Klostermann, TU 77; Berlin: Akademie, 1961) 56-64. He contends that the meaning of hope has been recast through Gnostic influence so that it now possesses a strictly spatial sense indicating cosmic spheres of power. Hope has thus become an object (*res sperata*) that already lies in heaven prepared for believers.

[92] See Schnabel, *Law and Wisdom,* 259, and M. Hengel, *The Son of God* (Philadelphia: Fortress, 1976) 72.

[93] O'Brien, *Colossians,* 95, and Lohse, *Colossians,* 83.

Paul then develops this thought through verse 15, after which he again takes up his explicit polemic about the factional teaching. This section serves as the specific theological basis for denying the demands of the teachers in the opposing faction. The passage develops many of the Christological themes of the hymn by elaborating on their ecclesiological implications in light of the situation at Colossae. The overall structure of the passage can thus be depicted as follows:

• Christological Statement:
ἐν αὐτῷ κατοικεῖ πᾶν τὸ πλήρωμα τῆς θεότητος σωματικῶς (2:9)

• Ecclesiological Relevance:
ἐστὲ ἐν αὐτῷ πεπληρωμένοι
ὅς ἐστιν ἡ κεφαλὴ πάσης ἀρχῆς καὶ ἐξουσίας (2:10)
   1. ἐν ᾧ καὶ περιετμήθητε περιτομῇ ἀχειροποιήτῳ (2:11a)
   2. ἐν ᾧ καὶ συνηγέρθητε (2:12b)
   3. συνεζωοποίησεν ὑμᾶς σὺν αὐτῷ (2:13b)
      a. χαρισάμενος ἡμῖν πάντα τὰ παραπτώματα (2:13c)
      b. ἐξαλείψας τὸ καθ' ἡμῶν χειρόγραφον (2:14a)
      c. ἀπεκδυσάμενος τὰς ἀρχὰς καὶ τὰς ἐξουσίας (2:15a)

Paul's burden in this section is to demonstrate that the believers at Colossae share in the divine fullness, dwelling in Christ by virtue of their corporate solidarity with him. Thus ἐν αὐτῷ, ἐν ᾧ, and σὺν αὐτῷ are prominent throughout the section.

The relative clause ὅς ἐστιν ἡ κεφαλὴ πάσης ἀρχῆς καὶ ἐξουσίας (2:10b) immediately highlights one implication of Christ possessing all the divine fullness that is especially significant for the Colossians given their concerns about the realm of spirits. Paul here clearly affirms that Christ has authority over the realm of spirits and angels. In v. 15, Paul gives a reason for Christ's authority over this realm by explaining that God has decisively defeated the hostile powers and authorities through the work of Christ on the cross. *The relationship of Christ to the principalities and powers—the ἀρχαὶ καὶ ἐξουσίαι—thus functions as an inclusio for the central theological passage of the book.*

The basis upon which believers share in Christ's fullness is developed in the three sentences employing aorist verbs coupled with an affirmation of incorporation: (1) ἐν ᾧ καὶ περιετμήθητε, (2) ἐν ᾧ καὶ συνηγέρθητε, and (3) συνεζωοποίησεν ὑμᾶς σὺν αὐτῷ. There appears to be a progression of thought in this section—death, resurrection, new life—with no *parallelismus membrorum* or chiastic structure evident.

The final verb is developed by a series of three aorist participles that explain the basis for new life in Christ. The first two are interrelated—forgiveness of transgressions and the wiping out of the *cheirographon*. The third forms the climax of the section by describing the defeat of the powers on the cross. There is also a shift of persons from "you" to "we" in this section, which some have argued points to the inclusion of a hymnic fragment or traditional piece here.[94] I would concur, however, with some more recent studies of the passage that see vv. 13c-15 as composed by the author of the letter.[95]

The series of uncommon words and expressions in this section may partly be explained by the subject matter. In expounding on the theme of Christ's triumph over the powers—which receives more of an emphasis here than anywhere else in the Pauline corpus—the author has employed some colorful imagery: the stripping (ἀπεκδυσάμενος), the public exposure (ἐδειγμάτισεν), and the triumphal procession (θριαμβεύσας). The image of the triumphal procession, however, was used by Paul in 2 Cor 2:14 and the image of stripping he has used twice elsewhere in this letter (2:11 and 3:10). Only the image of public exposure is unique to this section.

The affirmation of God's forgiveness expressed with χαρίζομαι is also Pauline (see 1 Cor 2:12) as well as the term παράπτωμα (Rom 4:25; 5:15-20; 11:11-12; 2 Cor 5:19). The image that is particularly unique is the portrayal of forgiveness as the taking away of the *cheirographon* with its stipulations. All three of the terms in v. 14a (ἐκλείπω, χειρόγραφον, and δόγμα) are *hapax legomena* in Paul. It appears that the author has creatively appropriated an expression from the *koine* of commerce and finance to more powerfully convey the concept of God's forgiveness. This image thus further elucidates God's blessing of χαρισάμενος ἡμῖν πάντα τὰ παραπτώματα (2:13c). It seems to be called forth at least in part by the exigencies of the situation at Colossae in which the opposing teachers appear to have a ministry of judgment and condemnation toward those who do not measure up to their standards.

---

[94] See especially Deichgräber, *Gotteshymnus,* 168-69, and E. Lohse, "Ein hymnisches Bekenntnis in Kolosser 2, 13c-15," *Mélanges Bibliques en hommage au R. P. Béda Rigaux* (Gembloux: Duculot, 1970) 427-35.

[95] See, for example, Sappington, *Revelation and Redemption,* 206-207, who has recently cast doubt about the hypothesis that a pre-Pauline composition is embedded in the text. With Schweizer (*Colossians,* 136) he views vv. 13c-15 as composed by the author of the letter, who has employed a considerable amount of traditional imagery.

There is also a significant implication of our understanding of the structure of this passage for interpreting a key theological term in Colossians: the "fullness" (πλήρωμα). Because the term factors so significantly into the positive expression of the author's theology, it is doubtful that he has taken the term over from the teaching of the opponents. Our suspicions are first raised in this regard by recognizing that the hymn itself extols Christ as the one in whom "all the fullness" (πᾶν τὸ πλήρωμα) was pleased to dwell (1:19). Now Paul reiterates this truth and emphasizes how the church participates in the divine fullness present in Christ. Once again, Paul highlights this truth because of the needs of the present situation in Colossae. The opposing sphere of hostile principalities and powers is an issue for them (demonstrated structurally by the *inclusio* referencing the ἀρχαὶ καὶ ἐξουσίαι). Emphasizing their share in the divine fullness—expressed by their sharing in Christ's authority over the realm of hostile powers (2:10b) made possible by their participation in his death, resurrection, and new life—is perfectly suited to believers who are struggling with a fear of the powers and facing the temptation to succumb to an unacceptable teaching that offers a different approach for dealing with the issue of the powers.[96]

4. The Defeat of the Powers by Christ (2:15)

To allay the Colossians' fears of the threats and influence of the evil angelic powers, Paul declares that God has triumphed over them in Christ. In fact, this passage represents the most elaborate description of Christ's defeat of the powers in all the letters attributed to Paul. The declaration appears as the climax of the central theological passage in Colossians (2:9-15). The author uses three colorful images to portray the nature of Christ's conquering moment—a work that God himself has accomplished through Christ.[97]

---

[96] Pokorný, *Colossians,* 123, reaches the similar conclusion that the section 2:11-15 is "what the foundation is upon which one is able to build hope in the face of the threat of the supra-individual powers."

[97] It is best to understand God as the subject throughout this verse as well as in 13c and 14. Consequently, one should take ἐν αὐτῷ at the end of v. 15 as a reference to Christ, viz. "in him." This interpretation is consistent with our understanding of the structure of the passage, which does not see Paul incorporating a traditional piece here that could account for a potential shift in subject. God is the subject of συνεζωοποίησεν and remains the subject throughout the end of v. 15. To see a shift in subject from God to

a. Disarming the Powers

Paul first declares that God has "disarmed" (ἀπεκδυσάμενος) the "powers." Christ's death and resurrection have deprived the evil forces of any effective power against Christ himself or against those who are incorporated into him and appropriate his power.

The participle ἀπεκδυσάμενος appears in the middle voice and should be interpreted as having an active sense in this context—"to strip."[98] Some interpreters attempt to maintain the middle sense—"having stripped off from himself." There have been two major variations of this view. (1) Many of the Latin Fathers and some modern interpreters find "the flesh" (or the physical body) as the implied object, an apparent allusion to 2:11—ἐν τῇ ἀπεκδύσει τοῦ σώματος τῆς σαρκός.[99] In a variation of this interpretation, E. Käsemann sees the object as "body," viz. "the Adamic body tyrannized over by the demonic rulers of this aeon."[100] These explanations possess the insurmountable weakness that "flesh" and "body" are not in view in the immediate context. Finally, W. Carr has suggested that the participle should be interpreted absolutely, i.e. Christ undressed himself.[101] This view reads too much into the metaphor of triumph (θριαμβεύω) since it assumes that Christ will immediately don a victor's garment. None of these appropriately take into account the accusative expression τὰς ἀρχὰς καὶ τὰς ἐξουσίας which is most naturally understood as the object of the action of the participle. (2) Lightfoot and some of the

---

Christ (as, for example, Lightfoot, *Colossians*, 189-91, and Moule, *Colossians*, 100-102) is unwarranted in the context. Furthermore, because of the repeated use of ἐν αὐτῷ in the previous verses (vv. 6-12) in reference to Christ, there is no reason to see ἐν αὐτῷ refer to something different here (such as the cross). So also, Pokorný, *Colossians*, 140; Schweizer, *Colossians*, 151; Lohse, *Colossians*, 112; O'Brien, *Colossians*, 127; Gnilka, *Kolosserbrief,* 143.

[98] Sappington, *Revelation and Redemption*, 212; Pokorný, *Colossians*, 140-41; Gnilka, *Kolosser*, 142; Lohse, *Colossians*, 112; O'Brien, *Colossians*, 127-28; Schweizer, *Colossians*, 151; Dibelius-Greeven, *Kolosser*, 32; Scott, *Colossians*, 48; Eadie, *Colossians*, 167. On the use of the middle voice with an active sense, see BDF, par.316 (1).

[99] D. G. Reid, "Triumph," in *DPL,* 949; R. Yates, "Colossians 2.15: Christ Triumphant," *NTS* 37 (1991) 590; J. A. T. Robinson, *The Body* (SBT 5; London: SCM, 1952) 41; G. H. C. MacGregor, "Principalities and Powers: The Cosmic Background of Paul's Thought," *NTS* 1 (1954-55) 23; J. Y. Lee, "Interpreting the Demonic Powers in Pauline Thought," *NovT* 12 (1970) 64.

[100] Käsemann, "Baptismal Liturgy," 162. Martin, *Colossians* (Interpretation), 107-108.

[101] Carr, *Angels and Principalities,* 61. See my further criticism of his view in "The 'Exorcism' of Ephesians 6.12 in Recent Research," *JSNT* 30 (1987) 71-87.

Greek Fathers saw the "powers" as the object while maintaining Christ as the subject: the evil powers had clung "like a Nessus robe" about his humanity.[102] Thus Lightfoot sees Jesus as stripping himself of the hostile principalities and authorities which surrounded him and opposed him like a dirty garment throughout his earthly ministry. Lightfoot finds the image of the filthy garment, implied by the "stripping off," as stemming from the episode of Joshua the high priest standing before the angel of the Lord (Zech 3:1ff.). The Lord commands his angels to take away the filthy garments from Joshua. As with the previous set of interpretations, this view faces the difficulty of needing to assume a change in subject from God to Christ. As we have already noted above, this is quite unlikely. Furthermore, demonic spirits are never depicted as garments or filthy rags anywhere in the OT or the NT. The filthy garments that Joshua wore represented sinfulness.

The best intepretation of the participle here is to understand it as active in significance with God as the subject and the evil principalities and powers as the objects. This is more suitable to the following image of the triumphal procession, which implies not only the defeat but the disarming of the enemies.[103] This accords well with the use of the same participle in 3:9 (ἀπεκδυσάμενοι τὸν παλαιὸν ἄνθρωπον), which is also best explained as an active: "strip off the old self."

Since this is the first traceable use of ἀπεκδύομαι in the Greek language, we have no opportunity to investigate the contemporary usage to determine more precisely the nature of the image that Paul is using. Based on the usage of the participle in 3:9, the related noun ἀπέκδυσις in 2:11, and the meaning of the cognate verbal form ἀποδύομαι ("take off"), it appears that the simple ideas of "strip off," "take off," and "remove" are adequate for grasping Paul's meaning here.

Although Paul gives no explicit indication of the sense in which the powers have been stripped, the implication is that they have been stripped of their power toward Christ and his body. It is clear, however, that Paul does not conceive of the "powers" as having been taken off the scene or removed from the day-to-day affairs of life. Neither does Paul see them as having been totally divested of their power. The overall content of the letter leads us to conclude that the evil powers are powerless toward the Colossian Christians insofar as they recognize and appropriate their authority in Christ. The Colossian Christians have the possibility of living

---

102 Lightfoot, *Colossians*, 188.
103 Pokorný, *Colossians*, 141.

in a manner that would be pleasing to God and of resisting the influence
and demands of wayward teachers—even given the reality of supernatural
demonic opposition. The fairly common translation "disarm"[104] is thus
appropriate given this theological understanding.[105]

The fact that the Colossians fear the powers and are tempted to take up
the beliefs and practices of the opposing faction imply that they are not
automatically immune to the influence of the hostile powers. From Paul's
perspective, the Colossians need to grow in their awareness of their position in Christ—they have been filled—and then begin to appropriate this
fullness by resisting the opposing teaching and by living a life worthy of
Christ. For a group of people who fear the realm of hostile spirits, this
teaching would have also proved especially comforting.

b. Exposing the Powers

Paul continues[106] his portrayal of God's victory over the powers in Christ
by affirming that he publicly "exposed" (ἐδειγμάτισεν) them. The term
δειγματίζω is actually quite rare in the Greek language. It does appear,
however, one other time in the NT where it is used of Joseph's plan not to
"expose" Mary's pregnancy and thus bring public disgrace upon her (Matt
1:19). The notion of an exposure leading to disgrace may also be illustrated in a Cyprian law mentioned by Dio Chrysostom according to which
an adulteress had to cut her hair and was subjected to contempt by the
community (Dio Chrys. 47[64] 3).[107] Lohse cites a relevant use of the
term in Jewish tradition where it appears in connection with the exposure
of a demonic power, Sammael: "For Beliar harbored great wrath against
Isaiah on account of the vision of the exposure ([δει]γματισμοῦ) with
which he had exposed ([ἐ]δειγμάτισεν) Sammael" (*Asc. Is.* 3:13).[108] Finally, we note one further use of the word in the *Acts of Peter* where it is

---

[104] Suggested by BAGD, s.v., and incorporated, for example, into the NIV and
NASB translations.

[105] The caveat is essential to avoid a triumphalism that Paul did not intend. Commentators such as Eadie, *Colossians,* 166, go too far when they say that God "stript them of
all power and authority" without providing any note of explanation.

[106] Some manuscripts (𝔓46, B) include καί before ἐδειγμάτισεν. This is the preferred reading because of the strength of the testimony of these witnesses and because of
the balance this creates with the structure of the preceeding section: ἐξαλείψας ... καὶ
αὐτὸ ἦρκεν.

[107] Cited in BAGD, 142.

[108] Text and translation from Lohse, *Colossians,* 112, note 139. See also MM, 138.

used in connection with Peter's "exposure" of Simon Magus in Rome (*Acts of Peter* 32[3]).[109]

The idea of an exposure that leads to a public disgrace is well attested for δειγματίζω and fits the context quite well in this passage. The notion of a "public" exposure is emphasized by Paul's use of ἐν παρρησίᾳ following the verb. This expression was commonly used to convey the simple idea of "in public" in contrast to the thought of doing something "in secret" (see, for example, John 7:4).

The cross and resurrection of Christ continue to be in view here as the event in which the powers not only were disarmed but were also publicly exposed. In what sense were they exposed? Their claim to be plenipotentiaries was shown to be worthless. Their efforts to kill Christ once and for all and thereby to skew the redemptive plan of God (1 Cor. 2:6-8) was exposed as futile in light of God's wisdom and power in raising Jesus from the dead. Their authority to compel service and worship from humanity was likewise shown to be baseless. Christ has publicly exposed the weakness and inability of the "powers" to effectively hinder the plans of God. Paul therefore had adequate reason for referring to the *stoicheia* as "weak" and "miserable" when he wrote to the Galatians (Gal 4:9).

c. Leading the Powers in a Triumphal Procession

Paul now builds on the idea of a public exposure of the powers by appropriating the vivid image of a Roman triumph. When a general led his army to victory in a battle, the returning army would celebrate their conquest with a "triumphal procession" (θριαμβεύω). The successful general would lead a tumultuous procession marching through the streets followed by his army singing hymns of victory and jubilantly reveling in their conquest. The defeated king with all of his surviving warriors together with the spoils of war would also be paraded along as a spectacle for all to see.[110]

---

[109] For additional discussion of the usage of the word, see H. Schlier, "δειγματίζω," *TDNT* 2.31-32, and BAGD, s.v., MM, 137-38; and G. W. H. Lampe, *A Patristic Greek Lexicon* (Oxford: University Press, 1961) 334.

[110] See especially L. Williamson, "Led in Triumph. Paul's Use of Thriambeuo," *Int* 22 (1968) 317-32; S. J. Hafemann, *Suffering and the Spirit* (WUNT II/19; Tübingen: J.C.B. Mohr [Paul Siebeck], 1986) 18-39; C. Breytenbach, "Paul's Proclamation and God's 'Thriambos' (Notes on 2 Corinthians 2:14-16b)," *Neotestamentica* 24 (1990) 257-71. The majority of interpreters would see the author as adapting the image of the Roman triumphal procession to God's victory over the powers in Christ.

This use of this use of θριαμβεύω is well illustrated in Plutarch (*Aemilius Paulus,* 32-34). Included in the triumphal parade depicted in this passage was the disheartened king Perseus along with all of his arms, riches, children, and attendants. Plutarch narrates, "he [Perseus], too, was followed by a company of friends and intimates whose faces were heavy with grief." The primary focus, however, was on the victorious Aemilius: "The whole army also carried sprays of laurel, following the chariot of their general by companies and divisions, and singing, some of them divers songs intermingled with jesting, as the ancient custom was, and others paeans of victory and hymns in praise of the achievements of Aemilius, who was gazed upon and admired by all, and envied by no one that was good." Dionysus of Halicarnassus (8.67.9-10) also portrays the glory accorded to the victorious general in the θρίαμβος—a procession that included the defeated army as prisoners: "He accordingly drove into the city with the spoils, the prisoners (τοὺς αἰχμαλώτους), and the army that had fought under him, he himself riding in a chariot drawn by horses with golden bridles and being arrayed in the royal robes, as is the custom in the greater triumphs (θριάμβους)."

In a similar way, God has put the hostile principalities and powers on public display as defeated enemies through Christ's death and resurrection. God has thus paraded the "powers" in a triumphal procession (θριαμβεύσας) celebrating the victory over them in Christ. The "powers" are led in the celebration as the vanquished enemies.

R. Yates has recently challenged this common interpretation of Christ's triumph over the powers.[111] He contends that the ἀρχαὶ καὶ ἐξουσίαι are

---

[111] R. Yates, "Colossians 2:15: Christ Triumphant," *NTS* 37 (1991) 573-91. In a different way, R. B. Egan, "Lexical Evidence on Two Pauline Passages," *NovT* 19 (1977) 34-62, has challenged this interpretation. He has taken up the novel suggestion of G. G. Findlay that the background to Paul's use of the image was not the Roman triumph but rather the festal processions held in honor of Dionysus. Thus, the frame of reference is the inspiring deity leading his exultant worshipers in a festal or choral procession, not the Roman conqueror leading his wretched captives. In applying this image to Col 2:15, it is thus necessary for Egan to describe the ἀρχαὶ καὶ ἐξουσίαι as "intimates of Christ" rather than as enemies. This does severe injustice to the immediate context, which includes the thought of public humiliation as well as the notion of stripping them of power (see also below). Hafemann, *Suffering,* 36-39, has provided an effective refutation of other aspects of Egan's thesis. P. Marshall, "A Metaphor of Social Shame: ΘΡΙΑΜΒΕΥΕΙΝ in 2 Cor 2:14," *NovT* 25 (1983) 302-17, has provided additional support for rooting the background of the usage of the term in the context of a Roman triumphal procession. Specifically, he shows how Seneca used the Latin equivalent in a metaphorical way (*On Benefits* 2.11.1) and thereby provides an example of a metaphorical application of the image in the first century. He is not able, however, to adduce any exam-

not evil powers, but rather the good angels from the throne of God who are now adoring Christ in the celebration of his splendor.[112] He further argues that in adopting the image of the Roman triumphal procession, "the emphasis was not upon the procession of captives, nor even the trophies of victory, but rather on the triumphator as the bearer of good fortune."[113] Yates is quite correct in affirming that the emphasis of the triumphal procession was upon the victorious general, but he is certainly wrong to downplay the significance of the procession of defeated captives and the spoils of war.[114] Yates is even self contradictory on this point when he admits to their presence in the procession: "Not only were the spoils of war carried along ..., but also pictures of battle scenes and towns captured, and boards inscribed with the names of subjugated peoples. The chained prisoners walked right in front of the triumphal chariot ..."[115] I would contend, along with most commentators, that the presence of the defeated enemies in the procession helps magnify the glory of the victorious general and, ultimately, the god who granted the victory. Thus Lohse aptly comments, "As their devastating defeat is shown to the whole world, the infinite superiority of Christ is demonstrated."[116] Furthermore, as I have discussed above and elsewhere,[117] the phrase ἀρχαὶ καὶ ἐξουσίαι is consistently employed by Paul to refer to hostile angelic powers. Just as the captives in a Roman triumph were, in reality, being led to their death,[118] so the doom of the principalities and powers is sure based on the prior triumph of God in Christ. These are the entities he will do away with at the end (εἶτα τὸ τέλος ... ὅταν καταργήσῃ πᾶσαν ἀρχὴν καὶ πᾶσαν ἐξουσίαν καὶ δύναμιν; 1 Cor 15:24). Given the demonic character of these principalities and powers, it is therefore best to view them as the defeated foes that are paraded in the triumphal procession.

---

ples of θριαμβεύειν used in a metaphorical sense.

[112] In this he follows Carr, *Angels and Principalities,* 47-85. See my extensive critique of Carr's view in "The 'Exorcism' of Ephesians 6.12," 71-87. Egan, "Lexical Evidence," 39-40, 55-56, sees the ἀρχαὶ καὶ ἐξουσίαι as "intimates or attributes of Christ."

[113] Yates, "Christ Triumphant," 579.

[114] One needs merely to scan the many passages cited in the studies by Hafemann and Breytenbach to see that the defeated enemies play a significant and indispensable role in the triumphal procession.

[115] Yates, "Christ Triumphant," 579.

[116] Lohse, *Colossians,* 112.

[117] See my *Ephesians,* 52-56, and "The 'Exorcism' of Ephesians 6.12," 78-83.

[118] Hafemann, *Suffering,* 25. One of Hafemann's major contributions to our understanding of the Roman triumphal procession is the observation that the prisoners of war were being led to their execution.

Paul employs the image of the triumphal procession on one other occasion. In 2 Cor 2:14 he exclaims, "But thanks be to God, who always leads us in triumphal procession (θριαμβεύοντι) in Christ and through us spreads everywhere the fragrance of the knowledge of him." In this context, it is not God's supernatural enemies—the principalities and powers—that are in view, but Paul himself and his missionary companions. They are the defeated enemies that God leads along in his triumphal procession. This interpretation is required because the accusative following θριαμβεύειν invariably refers to the conquered foes.[119] S. Hafemann has suggested that Paul here portrays himself as one of the defeated foes now being led by God as a slave to death (through his suffering).[120] Paul, however, has been reconciled to God and can thereby celebrate God's own victorious work in his own life. He serves God as a "slave of Christ" and as an apostle which, above all, involves spreading the knowledge of Christ as a fragrance everywhere. C. Breytenbach has recently illustrated the presence of incense bearers in the procession who spread the aroma of cinnamon and incense all along the route of the parade.[121] He finds this aspect of the procession as a metaphor for Paul's apostolic activity in that, "wherever Paul preaches the gospel, the smell of cinnamon and incense is spread."[122] The triumphal procession, therefore, here represents God's celebration over his prior enemy, the persecutor of the church, now reconciled and serving as an apostle and slave of Christ. The ongoing triumphal procession is not only a celebration of God's victory, but a spreading of the aroma of Christ through the proclamation of the gospel. In Colossians, however, the emphasis is on the inimical powers who are led along as humiliated and defeated enemies of God.

The image of triumph over the powers also comes to expression in Ephesians, although in different terms. In Eph 4:8, the author cites Ps 68:18 (= Ps 67:19 LXX) to depict the triumphal procession of Christ ascending on high with a train of captives. It is best to interpret the clause,

---

[119] Hafemann, *Suffering*, 18-36, has convincingly shown that there is no lexical evidence to demonstrate that the direct object of the verb θριαμβεύειν could refer to Paul sharing as a co-victor in the procession or that the verb could have a causative sense, e.g. "God causes us to triumph in Christ." See also Breytenbach, "Paul's Proclamation," 265, who concludes, "it is clear that the function can only be in the role of one of those being conquered."

[120] Hafemann, *Suffering*, 34-35.

[121] See Breytenbach, "Paul's Proclamation," 265-69.

[122] See Breytenbach, "Paul's Proclamation," 269.

"he led captives in his train" (ἠχμαλώτευσεν αἰχμαλωσίαν) as a reference to the evil ἀρχαὶ καὶ ἐξουσίαι.[123]

In a rather splendid way, then, Paul declares to the Colossians that Christ's death and resurrection was not only effective for procuring the forgiveness of sins, but also in defeating the hostile forces of evil—the principalities and powers bent on thwarting God's redemptive purposes. There is a close connection between the forgiveness Christ has achieved for his people and the defeat of the powers. Sappington has suggested that it is precisely through the blessing of forgiveness, which includes the wiping out of the χειρόγραφον, that the evil principalities and powers are disarmed.[124] He supports this through appealing not only to the development of thought in 2:13-15, but also by correlating this passage to 1:12-14. There, he contends, it is divine forgiveness that rescues believers from the sphere of authority of the spiritual powers and transfers them into the kingdom of God's beloved son.[125] In 2:13-15 he argues that the author's reference to the disarming of the powers (2:15a) gathers up the thoughts of the two previous affirmations—the forgiveness of trespasses and the wiping out of the χειρόγραφον—and applies them directly to the principalities and powers.[126]

Sappington has provided a valuable insight into the connection between divine forgiveness and the defeat of the powers, but as we will see below he has overstated the case. In Paul's thought, the goal of the hostile powers had indeed been to thwart God's redemptive activity in Christ. By instigating the death of Christ on the cross, the powers thought they would put an end to God's merciful saving purposes (1 Cor 2:6-8). Christ's atoning death—procuring forgiveness of sins—and his exaltation uncovered the foolishness of their plans and highlighted the wisdom of God. As Scott observes, "They imagined that they had won a victory over God, but in the death of Christ he had vanquished them."[127] Forgiveness is thus a very important part of the meaning of Christ's defeat of the powers on the cross. God has been able to complete his redemptive purposes. Furthermore, the condemning power of the powers of evil has been blunted by the removal of any basis for condemnation.

---

[123] Pokorný, *Colossians,* 141. For a more detailed discussion of this passage, see my *Ephesians,* 56-58.

[124] Sappington, *Revelation and Redemption,* 211-13, 221-23.

[125] Sappington, *Revelation and Redemption,* 212.

[126] Sappington, *Revelation and Redemption,* 212.

[127] Scott, *Colossians,* 49.

Sappington's view, however, is too restrictive in limiting the interpretation of Christ's defeat of the powers to his work in achieving divine forgiveness: (1) A greater stress needs to be placed on the resurrection and the exaltation of Christ (3:1) as the basis for demonstrating his victory over death as well as his victory over all the power of the enemy spirits. The Colossian hymn highlights the resurrection by asserting that Christ is the firstborn from the dead (1:19) thus implying the defeat of the power of death (cf. also 1 Cor 15:55). In 2:12, Paul stresses that the Colossian believers have experienced co-resurrection with Christ that forms the basis for their new life with him (2:13). (2) Although it is true that one of the chief weapons of the spiritual forces is to incite feelings of guilt through their accusations, these pernicious powers use other means to enslave.[128] They are tempting the Colossians, for instance, to worship divine intermediaries. (3) When Paul says that the Colossians have died with Christ from the elementary spirits of this world (Col 2:20), he is affirming that they have died to the compelling influence of these hostile powers which are part of the present evil age—however they may manifest their influence. Here Paul is thinking primarily of the ascetic regulations that the opposing faction is attempting to foist onto the Colossian Christians. (4) The structure of 2:13-15 does not support Sappington's thesis that the "disarming" is an elucidation of the previous context. As we have demonstrated above in our analysis of the structure, there is a series of three co-ordinated participles that are dependent on συνεζωοποίησεν. Thus, there may be an interrelatedness of thought, but the third is not the amplification of the other two. (5) Finally, it is too restrictive to say that divine forgiveness alone is what rescues believers from the kingdom of Satan (see below in my treatment of Col 1:12-14).

The powers are defeated, but they are still very much active. Thus, Paul tells the Colossians to beware (βλέπετε μή) of a *stoicheia*-inspired teaching that was infiltrating the church (2:8). The main point of this passage appears to be that Christ did indeed "disarm" the powers on the cross, but not in an absolute sense. People need to be incorporated into Christ (thus, ἐν αὐτῷ in 2:10, ἐν ᾧ in 2:11 and 12, and σὺν αὐτῷ in 2:13), realize their participation in his divine fullness (2:10), and appropriate these resources for resisting the variety of ways the principalities and powers manifest their influence.[129]

---

[128] In Paul's thought, the powers continue to work in a variety of ways to thwart the divine plan: they tempt (1 Thess 3:5), deceive (2 Cor 11:3, 14), and do all they can to hinder the mission of the church (2 Cor 4:4; 1 Thess 2:18).

[129] Similarly, G. Bornkamm notes: "So the 'rulers' and 'powers' are still there, but for

The death and resurrection of Christ should inspire faith and give cause for celebration (3:16) to the Colossian Christians. The work of God in Christ utterly destroys any reason for doing obeisance to angels, or for entertaining fears about the evil spiritual realm. Scott recognized this implication for the situation of the Colossians over 60 years ago:

> His [the Colossian's] safety was to be found in the conciliation of the friendly powers by means of offerings, sacred rites, spells, and talismans, so that they would protect him against the opposing demons ... But he [Paul] insists always that this protection is offered by Christ and that all else is useless ... We have a power on our side which can overcome everything that is against us.[130]

5. Redemption: Deliverance from the Powers

With sensitivity to the Colossians' fear of the powers and his own concern that they may be led astray by the powers through the teaching of "the philosophy," Paul begins his letter by declaring that they have been rescued from the domain of the powers. This gives the Colossians more than sufficient reason to express joyous thanksgiving to God (1:12), to deny the promptings and demands of the deceitful teachers (2:4, 8, 16, 18, 20), and to appropriate the virtues of the Christian way of life (3:5-17).

a. Deliverance from the Domain of the Powers (1:12-14)

Their plight of captivity is over. Paul announces that God has rescued his people from bondage in the domain of Satan (1:12). He has also told this community that he regularly prays that they would conduct their lives in a way that would be pleasing to the Lord. This manner of life includes giving thanks for the work of God on their behalf in providing redemption.[131] Specifically, he encourages them to offer thanks to God for their

---

believers they no longer bear any weapons and thereby they glorify the victory of Christ" ("Baptism and New Life in Paul," *Early Christian Experience,* 80, as cited in Lohse, *Colossians,* 113, note 144).

[130] Scott, *Colossians,* 50.

[131] It is best to interpret the four participles καρποφοροῦντες, αὐξανόμενοι, δυναμούμενοι, and εὐχαριστοῦντες adverbially and dependent on περιπατῆσαι ἀξίως τοῦ κυρίου εἰς πᾶσαν ἀρεσκείαν. So also Sappington, *Revelation and Redemption,* 196-97.

divine inheritance, for their deliverance from the domain of the powers, and for their incorporation into the kingdom of Christ.

Some interpreters, however, do not see the transfer of dominion statements (1:13) as an integral and concluding part of the prayer-report section (1:9-14). They claim that the author of the letter has incorporated a traditional piece of a liturgical character (possibly from a baptismal context) that serves to commence a new section providing an introduction to the Christ hymn.[132] More recent commentators have rightly rejected this view and argue that the passage reflects the letter writer's own composition but with the use of traditional language.[133]

Paul's declaration that these believers have been rescued from "the authority of darkness" (1:13) highlights Christian freedom from the domain of the principalities and powers as a key theme in this letter. The phrase ἐξουσία τοῦ σκότους denotes the sphere over which the powers of darkness rule.[134] The expression occurs elsewhere in the NT only in Luke (Luke 22:53) as uttered by Christ indicating the motivating force behind his arrest. The closest parallel to the thought here is recorded by Luke in Acts 26:18 of Paul's Damascus christophany whereby he received his commission: "to open their eyes, that they may turn from darkness to light and from the power of Satan (ἐξουσία τοῦ Σατανᾶ)." Satan is thereby pictured as the arch-enemy possessing an "authority." In Colossians the emphasis is more on the domain and all that it entails rather than on the actual figurehead of Satan himself.

Comparable to God's deliverance (ῥύομαι) of his people from their bondage in Egypt (LXX Exodus 6:6; 14:30; Judg. 6:9, 13), Paul stresses that God has rescued believers from their bondage in the domain of darkness. Exodus terminology is found throughout this passage and justifies the conclusion that Paul is here portraying conversion as a second exodus experience.[135]

---

[132] Most notably, Käsemann, "Baptismal Liturgy," 149-68, argued that 1:12-14 was an early Christian baptismal liturgy that the author has adapted and incorporated into the letter. Some contend that the citation begins with εὐχαριστοῦντες (1:12), others that it begins with ὃς ἐρρύσατο (1:13).

[133] For a good critique of Käsemann's view, see Sappington, *Revelation and Redemption,* 193-97.

[134] Thus, Dibelius-Greeven, *Kolosser,* 9, comments, "ἐξουσία does not here designate an individual spirit being as in 1:16, 2:10, 15, but the sphere of their power (*Machtsphäre*)."

[135] See, for example, G. Shogren, "Presently Entering the Kingdom of Christ: The Background and Purpose of Col 1:12-14," *JETS* 31 (1988) 176-77.

The believing community has not only been rescued from this evil domain, but they have been incorporated into a new dominion. The next line clarifies that they have actually experienced a transfer (μεθίστημι) from one kingdom to another (1:13). The terminology may have reminded the readers of the time when Antiochus transferred several thousand Jews to Asia Minor in the second century B.C. (Josephus, *Ant.* 12.3.4 §149). Believers have been transferred to the kingdom of Christ, i.e. "the son of his love." The use of the aorist tense (versus the future tense) indicates that this action has already been accomplished for the community. They currently share in the benefits and blessings of the future kingdom. Paul clarifies the precise sense in which he understands the presence of the kingdom in the rest of the letter. It is closely tied in with helping these beleagured believers deal with the supernatural opposition they face in their struggle with the principalities and powers (see the next section below).

"Darkness" and "light" are the metaphors used by the author to describe the nature of the two opposing kingdoms. Although darkness and light imagery was commonplace among the varied religious traditions in the Mediterranean world in the first century,[136] especially relevant here are the abundant occurrences of this metaphor in the Qumran texts, most notably 1QM to describe the forces of God aligned against the forces of Belial (e.g. 1 QM 1:1, 5, 11; 4:2; 13:4-5, 10-11).[137]

Paul also enjoins the Colossians to give thanks to God because he authorized them "to share in the inheritance of the saints in the light" (1:12). This particular affirmation has much in common with 1QS 11:7-8: "[God] has caused them to inherit the lot (וינחילם בגורל)of the Holy Ones (קדושים). He has joined their assembly to the Sons of Heaven (בני שמים)." As Col 3:24 makes clear, however, Paul maintains the hope of a future inheritance while stressing the present participation in the inheritance.[138] Because the expression "holy ones" (קדושים = ἅγιοι) normally refers to angels in the Qumran literature, most scholars who see a strong influence of the language of Qumran on Col 1:12-14 contend that ἅγιοι thus refers

---

[136] In late Judaism, darkness and light imagery could be used to depict conversion to the God of Israel (e.g. *Joseph and Asenath* 8:9; 15:12). See H. Conzelmann, "φῶς," *TDNT* 9.333-43 for a description of its use in characterizing Gnostic dualism and pp. 310-32 for its use in various other pagan religious traditions.

[137] See Lohse, *Colossians,* 35-37, for further references from Qumran.

[138] A. T. Lincoln, *Paradise Now and Not Yet* (SNTSMS 43; Cambridge: University Press, 1981) 119. See also P. L. Hammer, "Inheritance (NT)," *ABD* 415-16.

to angels.[139] This evidence is not strong enough, however, to overturn the likelihood that Paul is using ἅγιοι here in precisely the same way he used it in his greeting (1:2), the introductory thanksgiving (1:4), as well as later in the letter (1:26; 3:12)—as a reference to the people of God.[140]

As Lohse has suggested, it is doubtful that the author of Colossians was directly influenced by the language of Qumran.[141] It is possible, however, that Paul was familiar with some of the ideas of Essenism from his pre-conversion life. Some of the concepts may also have been picked up by the Palestinian and diaspora synagogues and may thereby reflect a common pool of contemporary Jewish usage.

G. Shogren contends that Paul reflects in Col 1:12-14 the language and imagery of the exodus found throughout the LXX, but especially the book of Isaiah.[142] He intimates that Paul may even have had Isa 63:15-19 in mind as he wrote Col 1:12-14. The Isaianic passage is a prayer for deliverance (ῥῦσαι ἡμᾶς) and contains many of the themes of our passage: God is referred to as "our Father" (which is not typical of Qumran language) and redeemer, the people of God are his inheritance, they face enemies, and the rule of God is sought. Although this particular passage does not use light/darkness imagery, the metaphor is, however, prominent throughout Isaiah (see, for example, Isa 9:2; 42:6-7, 16; 49:6-9; 50:10-11; 60:1-3, 19-20).

The imagery of Isaiah is also particularly well suited for adaptation to the situation facing the Colossian believers because of the anti-syncretism polemic. Isaiah 2, for instance, speaks of the people of Israel compromising their faith by taking up the practices of their neighbors:

> They are full of superstitions from the East
> They practice divination like the Philistines
>   and clasp hands with pagans ...
> Their land is full of idols;
> they bow down to the work of their hands,
>   to what their fingers have made (Isa 2:6, 8).

---

[139] So Lohse, *Colossians,* 36; Pokorný, *Colossians,* 52; Gnilka, *Kolosserbrief,* 47; Martin, *Colossians* (Interpretation), 97; Sappington, *Revelation and Redemption,* 199-200; and O. Hofius, "Gemeinschaft mit den Engeln im Gottesdienst der Kirche. Eine traditionsgeschichtliche Skizze," *ZTK* 89 (1992) 187-88.

[140] So O'Brien, *Colossians,* 26; Schweizer, *Colossians,* 47; Wright, *Colossians,* 61.

[141] See Lohse, *Colossians,* 38, note 48.

[142] Shogren, "Presently Entering," 176-77 (see esp. note 14 for references). The article is based on his unpublished 1986 Aberdeen University Ph.D. Thesis: "The Kingdom of God in Paul."

The prophet implores the people, "Come, O house of Jacob, let us walk in the light of the Lord" (Isa 2:5). Just as Isaiah speaks of the arrogance of the wayward (see Isa 2:11, 17), Paul upbraids the arrogance of the factional teachers at Colossae (Col 2:18) who appear to be advocating a syncretistic compromise in place of the apostolic faith. The main difference here is that Paul argues that a new exodus of a spiritual nature has taken place. The people of God have been rescued from the ultimate enemy, the dominion of Satan and his evil powers. They have a present experience of the blessings of the future realm that enables them to deal with the ongoing hostility of the supernatural principalities and powers.

I would therefore contend that Paul is directly dependent on terms, ideas, and imagery from the book of Isaiah as he writes Col 1:12-14 as well as other portions of Colossians. However, I would not deny an indirect dependence on Essene (Qumran) and apocalyptic concepts—especially in his concern to give perspective on the realm of the domain of Satan. Paul appears to be comfortable in drawing on the terminology of contemporary Judaism (especially the apocalyptic literature) to refer to the evil forces of the present age. In a similar way, he drew on this imagery to contrast the two kingdoms when he wrote to the Corinthians, and exclaimed: "what fellowship has light with darkness? What accord has Christ with Belial?" (2 Cor 6:14).[143] This passage also shares with Col 1:12 the term μερίς ("share") which, in both passages, indicates membership in a community.

"Redemption" (ἀπολύτρωσις) has thus been enacted for believers. They have been freed from the bonds of a hostile dominion.[144] But this is only half the story. They have also entered the kingdom of Christ, here described as God's beloved son.

b. Forgiveness of Sins (1:14; 2:13c-14)

Another crucial aspect of this redemption is the forgiveness of sins committed while under the sway of the authority of darkness (1:14). Thus

---

[143] This, of course, depends on seeing Paul as the author (editor?) of the passage. On 2 Cor 6:14-7:1 as an original part of the letter, integral to Paul's argument, and reflecting (or at least consistent with) his thought; see R. P. Martin, *2 Corinthians* (WBC 40; Waco: Word, 1986) 195, and the works he cites. Martin himself thinks that Paul borrowed a writing of Essene origin and placed his own finishing touches on it.

[144] An expectation of this kind of redemption appears in the *Testament of Zebulon* 9:8: "He shall redeem (λυτρώσεται) all the captivity of the sons of men from Beliar."

Paul juxtaposes redemption with the forgiveness of sins: ἐν ᾧ ἔχομεν τὴν ἀπολύτρωσιν, τὴν ἄφεσιν τῶν ἁμαρτιῶν. The blessings of redemption are thus conceived as consisting of two aspects: liberation from bondage in the dominion of Satan (with the consequent incorporation into the kingdom of Christ) and forgiveness of sins. Christ is "our redemption" (1 Cor. 1:30) by virtue of his work on the cross where he not only paid the ransom for sin but also destroyed the power of the influence of the evil dominion (Col. 2:14-15).[145] This "redemption" is expressed as having already been realized in Colossians, a concept articulated by Paul (1 Cor. 1:30).

Paul reiterates the assurance that sins have been forgiven in 2:13c as he develops the implications of sharing new life with Christ. The forgiveness terminology shifts from ἄφεσις[146] to χαρίζομαι and instead of "sins" (ἁμαρτίαι) he now speaks of "transgressions" (παραπτώματα).

The next clause develops the notion of forgiveness even further by metaphorically representing forgiveness as the cancellation of a χειρόγραφον (2:14). Paul elaborates on the image by characterizing the *cheirographon* as having stipulations that stood against the community; he then portrays God as taking the damning document away and nailing it to the cross of Christ.

The term *cheirographon* was commonly used in the first and second centuries, especially in the papyri, to refer to a note of indebtedness.[147] This usage is even well attested in Jewish literature (see, for example, Tobit 5:3; 9:2, 5; *Test. Job* 11:11: "'Let us find how we might be able to repay you,' Without delay, I would bring before them the note (τὸ χειρόγραφον) and read it granting cancellation." Some interpreters have argued that there is a more specific Jewish background that Paul is appealing to. They contend that Paul has in mind the usage represented in *Apocalypse of Zephanaiah* 7 where the *cheirographon* refers to a heavenly scroll with a record of each individual's sins and the decrees of judgment that will follow.[148] As others have argued, because the term was used quite

---

[145] Some see a change of metaphors in Col. 1:14 from the victor who rescues the captive by force of arms (v. 13) to the philanthropist who releases him by the payment of a ransom; e.g. L. Morris, *The Apostolic Preaching of the Cross* (Grand Rapids: Eerdmans, 1965) 46-47.

[146] The term only appears here and in Eph 1:7 in the literature attributed to Paul.

[147] See references in BAGD, 880; MM, 687; A. Deissmann, *Light From the Ancient East* (4th ed.; New York: Harper & Brothers, 1922) 332-34, and idem, *Bible Studies* (Edinburgh: T. & T. Clark, 1901) 247. See also R. Yates, "Colossians 2,14: Metaphor of Forgiveness," *Bib* 90 (1990) 248-59.

[148] This view has most recently been advocated by Sappington, *Revelation and Re-*

frequently in the language of business and finance for a loan agreement, it is more likely that the author of Colossians creatively adopted this term and metaphorically applied it to conveying his understanding of the concept of the forgiveness of sins.[149] Yates has interpreted it as "a bond or certificate of indebtedness to which all men have subscribed because of their sin."[150]

Because Paul later expresses his concern that the Colossians would allow themselves to become subject to the regulations that the advocates of "the philosophy" were championing (τί ... δογματίζεσθε; 2:20), the presence of the term δόγματα in 2:14 may very well be an indication that Paul's comments have in mind the situation facing his readers.[151] That the opposing teachers were attempting to motivate compliance with their ascetic requirements through the inducement of guilt is clear from Paul's polemic. He encourages them not to permit anyone to judge them regarding dietary regulations or calendrical observances (2:16). He repeats his warning in 2:18 by urging the Colossians not to allow anyone to serve as their judge (as at an athletic contest) and disqualify them from the contest by their insistence on observing ascetic practices and invoking angels.

Because all of the transgressions of the Colossian Christians have been forgiven by the work of Christ on the cross, they do not need to live with a load of guilt nor do they need to give in to the demands of the factional teachers.

6. Participating in Christ's Fullness

Christ has not only delivered his people from the domain of darkness, but he has brought them into his kingdom and bestowed on them his salvation. Colossians emphasizes this as a present experience. There is a strong accent on the reception and actualization of this present salvation. This is

---

demption, 214-20. It was originally argued by O. A. Blanchette, "Does the Cheirographon of Col. 2,14 Represent Christ Himself," *CBQ* 23 (1961) 306-12, and then taken up by A. J. Bandstra, *The Law and the Elements of the Universe* (Kampen: Kok, 1964) 158-66. E. Lohse, "χειρόγραφον," *TDNT* 9.435-36, thinks that the term was employed to convey what he regarded as a common Jewish concept of God keeping an account of the debts of humanity against which there are divine penalties.

[149] See, for example, O'Brien, *Colossians*, 125.

[150] Yates, "Metaphor of Forgiveness," 256.

[151] So also Pokorný, *Colossians*, 139, who notes: "by 'legal demands' the author means the teachings and ascetic regulations of the opponents."

motivated by Paul's perception of the need of this community to have fresh perspective on their security and protection in Christ as well as the means available to them for dealing with the hostile supernatural powers. Paul is thus dealing with the root issue (their fear of the powers) as the means for diminishing the attraction of the teaching of "the philosophy."

a. Possessing the *Pleroma* (2:9-10)

Immediately following his very incisive invective against "the philosophy" in 2:8, Paul's begins his series of theological affirmations with the rather remarkable statement that the Colossian believers currently experience the divine fullness. He immediately ties this to the position of authority Christ has over the demonic powers in which believers share.

The first statement in the series is a reiteration of a declaration about Christ from the hymn (1:19), namely, that "all the fullness dwells in Christ." Here Paul makes explicit that he is referring to the fullness that properly belongs to God, the divine essence, through the use of the term θεότης which he links to πλήρωμα as an epexegetical genitive. In a stark juxtaposition, he then makes the assertion that the fullness dwells in Christ in his bodily existence (σωματικῶς).[152]

What Paul has said about Christ he immediately applies to the church by declaring, "in him you are filled" (ἐστὲ ἐν αὐτῷ πεπληρωμένοι). The "in him" (ἐν αὐτῷ) marks a major motif of the entire theological section of 2:9-15.[153] Paul is hereby attempting to help these believers understand the full significance of being in Christ, especially as it relates to their concern about supernatural powers and their temptation to follow the solution offered by "the philosophy." His solution is for them to gain a fuller appreciation for their resources in Christ and to grasp hold of their leader and supplier (2:19) and to concentrate on the things above where Christ is at the right hand of God (3:1).

---

[152] Lightfoot, *Colossians,* 182; O'Brien, *Colossians,* 112-13. Wedderburn, "Theology," 36-37, observes that the change of tense from the aorist (κατοικῆσαι) in 1:19 to the present (κατοικεῖ) in 2:9 presumably refers to the existence of the risen Christ as still a corporeal one.

[153] Note the use of the following phrases in the theological section: ἐν αὐτῷ (2:10); ἐν ᾧ (2:11, 12); the σύν-compounds: συνταφέντες (2:12), συνηγέρθητε (2:12), and συνεζωοποίησεν (2:13); σὺν αὐτῷ (2:13).

The fullness of God—his power and his grace—are bestowed on believers by virtue of their incorporation into Christ.[154] As Lightfoot has said, God's πλήρωμα is "transfused" into them.[155] The perfect periphrastic construction (ἐστὲ ... πεπληρωμένοι) emphasizes their share in the divine fullness as part of their present experience.

b. Sharing in Christ's Authority over the Powers (2:10)

Sharing in the divine fullness has implications for the relationship of believers to the powers. Paul immediately affirms that Christ is the "head" (κεφαλή) of every "principality and authority" (ἀρχὴ καὶ ἐξουσία). The emphasis in his use of "head" here falls on the certainty of Christ's control of the "powers"—not one angelic power stands outside of his sovereignty.[156] The metaphorical use of the term is in line with the OT and Hellenistic Jewish concept of "head" as "authority over," "superior," "ruler."[157] It is also similar to the Philonic idea of the ἡγεμονικός—the "governing part" or "leader"—which he uses in association with κεφαλή (e.g., *Op. Mund.* 119; *Fug.* 110, 182; *Somn.* 2.207; *Vit. Mos.* 2.30, 82; *Spec. Leg.* 3.184).

This proposition builds upon the theme of the pre-eminence of Christ in relationship to the powers that was an emphatic part of the Christ hymn. Not only is Christ superior to the powers as their creator and as the one who will be the agent for their final subjugation, he currently wields a position of dominance and authority over these beings.

What is now significant for the Colossians is the realization that because they are "in him," they share in his authority over the powers. The realization of this fact would take them a long way in overcoming their fear of the powers of darkness, which to them take the form of terrestrial

---

154 On the meaning of πλήρωμα, see my previous discussion of the use of the term in 1:19.

155 Lightfoot, *Colossians,* 182.

156 The term σῶμα does not appear here in connection with κεφαλή. It is thus improper to view the "powers" as the cosmic σῶμα with Christ as the complementing κεφαλή (contra Dibelius-Greeven, *Kolosser,* 29; Lohmeyer, *Kolosser,* 107; H. Koester, *Introduction to the New Testament* (Philadelphia: Fortress, 1982) 2.264). With the exception of 2:17, the term σῶμα functions strictly as a part of the author's ecclesiology (1:18, 24). For further discussion, see my, "Jesus Christ: 'Head' of the Church," 347-50, 364-65.

157 See J. A. Fitzmyer, "Another Look at ΚΕΦΑΛΗ in 1 Corinthians 11.3," *NTS* 35 (1989) 503-11.

spirits, stellar powers, spirits of nature and wildlife, and a host of other threatening beings. It would also help the community turn their backs to the demonically inspired "philosophy," which ostensibly offered a new solution to the daily plight of these people.

This statement then functions as the lead argument for a whole section stressing the sufficiency and adequacy of Christ for believers. They do not need to invoke angels or engage in the practices of "the philosophy."

c. The Basis: Participation in the Death and Resurrection of Christ (2:11-13)

The heart of Paul's theological argument lies in verses 12 and 13.[158] He declares that the Colossian believers currently possess a new life based on their participation with Christ in his death *and resurrection.* Not only does this reassure the Colossians that their sins are forgiven, that they are indeed reconciled to the Father and have fellowship with him, and that they will have life after death, it forms the basis for their participation in Christ's death to the influence of the powers, his exaltation and victory over the powers, and the present authority he wields over them.

The twice-repeated ἐν ᾧ καὶ ("in him also") of vv. 11-12, placed in an emphatic position in the sentences, signals that Paul is leading the Colossians into a deeper understanding of the significance and implications of what it means to be incorporated into Christ. He here reminds them of the faith they confessed particularly through the rite of baptism (2:12), the incorporation rite of the new age (2:11).

In an unusual twist, he introduces his remarks on baptism by first speaking of it metaphorically as circumcision.[159] He declares that the Colossians have been circumcised not in the physical sense of the removal of a small amount of skin, but in the removal of their solidarity with the first Adam, "the body of sin" (Rom 6:6), humanity under the rule of sin and death. His interpretation of circumcision as the "removal of the body of flesh" refers to the same reality that Paul speaks of in Rom 6:6 when he announces that "the old self has been crucified" and in Gal 5:24 in the pronouncement that "those who belong to Christ have crucified the

---

[158] Pokorný, *Colossians,* 126, suggests that verses 12 and 13 contain the argument of the entire epistle.

[159] Wolter, *Kolosser,* 128; Pokorný, *Colossians,* 124, speaks of baptism as "true circumcision"; Gnilka, *Kolosser,* 131. This is the only time that baptism is related to circumcision in the letters attributed to Paul.

flesh."[160] Paul here emphasizes that this spiritual circumcision was performed by Christ.[161] The following participial clause (συνταφέντες αὐτῷ ἐν τῷ βαπτισμῷ) explains this circumcision as having taken place through identification with Christ in his death and represented through the rite of baptism.

Many scholars have speculated that the unusual reference to circumcision here suggests that the rite was advocated by the opponents.[162] Although this may be true, doubt is cast on this conclusion by the fact that the reference to circumcision appears in a series of positive theological statements and is never mentioned in any part of the letter's polemic. The interpretation Paul gives to the spiritual circumcision also lays a good foundation for his subsequent and colorful emphasis on the forgiveness of sin (Col 2:14), for his call to refuse the flesh-oriented practices of "the philosophy" (Col 2:23), and for his injunction in the paraenetic section of the letter to get rid of (ἀπεκδυσάμενοι; cf. ἀπέκδυσις in 2:11) the practices of the old self (Col 3:9). Paul has here drawn on and adapted the OT tradition of the "circumcision of the heart" (see Deut 10:16; Lev 26:41; Jer 4:4; Ezek 44:7, 9).[163]

Paul now calls these believers to remember the meaning of their baptism as an identification with the death/burial of Jesus (Col 2:12). With some rhetorical flair, he employs his first of three σύν compounds—συνταφέντες, συνηγέρθητε and συνεζωοποίησεν (2:12-13)—to highlight the solidarity of this community with Christ.[164] The concept of dying with Christ is an integral part of Paul's theology, especially as it is expressed in Rom 6:3-11. The fact that this death with Christ has implications for sin is

---

[160] The interpretation of G. Schille (*Frühchristiliche Hymnen* [Berlin: Evangelische Verlagsanstalt, 1965] 35)—that the author has created a word play with the ἀπέκδυσις of 2:11 and the ἀπεκδυσάμενοι of 2:15 so his readers would think of Christ's removal of his flesh as a kind of cosmic circumcision in which he takes off the powers—is unconvincing.

[161] The genitive in the expression τοῦ Χριστοῦ is best understood as subjective.

[162] For example, Gnilka, *Kolosser,* 133; Lohse, *Colossians,* 101-102; et al. Building one speculation upon another, these and other interpreters contend that the meaning of circumcision as advocated by "the philosophy" was similar to the initiation rite of the mystery cults.

[163] 1QS 5:5 speaks of a circumcision of the foreskin of evil inclination and stiffness of neck. As Meyer has observed, this and other texts demonstrate that the idea of a figurative view of circumcision was known in Palestinian Judaism; see R. Meyer, "περιτέμνω," *TDNT* 6.79. Thus, Gnilka, *Kolosser,* 133, concludes, "this is the nearest background for v. 11."

[164] As Lohse, *Colossians,* 104, has observed, the phrase σὺν Χριστῷ is used in different contexts in Paul to describe the closest possible union with Christ.

made clear in the previous verse, and the victory over death is implied in the newness of life expressed in the following verse (cf. Rom 6:2, 4).

Paul now declares in explicit and emphatic terms what was only latent in his manner of previous theological expression—"in him also you were raised" (ἐν ᾧ καὶ συνηγέρθητε). Just how latent this concept of co-resurrection is in Romans 6 has been a matter of pointed debate. A number of interpreters have argued for a present, partial eschatological ful-fillment of two key expressions in Romans 6: "we will be united with him in the likeness of his resurrection" (ἀλλὰ καὶ τῆς ἀναστάσεως ἐσόμεθα; Rom 6:5) and "we believe that we will also live with him" (συζήσομεν αὐτῷ; Rom 6:8).[165] The prevailing interpretation, however, has been that in Romans 6 Paul is, in part, polemicizing against a Hellenistic church tra-dition that espouses an over-realized eschatology (similar to what we find in the theology of the opponents at Corinth, but perhaps not as realized as the enthusiasts in view in 2 Tim 2:18 [τὴν ἀνάστασιν ἤδη γεγονέναι]). Over against this Hellenistic view, Paul maintains an eschatological re-serve, consistent with his apocalyptic eschatological framework of thought. He thus stops short of saying, "you were raised with Christ."[166] J. C. Beker notes:

---

[165] Most recently, J. Fitzmyer, *Romans* (AB 33; New York: Doubleday, 1993) 435, has asserted: "Because the context describes the present experience of the Christian, the fut. *esometha* has to be understood as gnomic, expressing a logical sequel to the first part of the verse, for baptism identifies a person not only with Christ's act of dying, but also with rising. Though future, it describes a share in the risen life of Christ that the justified Christian already enjoys, as a result of the Christ-event. See also C. E. B. Cranfield, *Ro-mans,* (ICC; Edinburgh: T. & T. Clark, 1975) 1.307-308, 312-13; G. R. Beasley-Murray, *Baptism in the New Testament* (London: Macmillan, 1962) 138-39; S. Kim, *The Origin of Paul's Gospel* (WUNT 2/4; Tübingen: J.C.B. Mohr [Paul Siebeck], 1981) 302; Lincoln, *Paradise,* 122-23, comments concerning believers as now "alive to God" (Rom 6:13) that, "unless Paul thought of believers as already having been identified with Christ in his resurrection, this would simply be make-believe." R. Bultmann, *Theology of the New Testament* (New York: Scribner's, 1951) 1.140, remarks, "In Rom. 6:2ff., it is true, Paul makes an effort to bring freedom from sin into relation with the latter by teach-ing the readers to understand the future resurrection guaranteed by baptism as an already present resurrection which realizes itself in ethical conduct." Bultmann, however, wrongly attributes this Pauline explanation of participation in the death and resurrection of Christ to the Hellenistic church, which he alleges interpreted the rite on the analogy of mystery cult initiation rites (esp. the dying and rising of Attis, Adonis, or Osiris).

[166] See, for example, L. Hartmann, "Baptism," *ABD* 1.589; Koester, *Introduction,* 2.266; Schweizer, *Colossians,* 144-45; R. C. Tannehill, *Dying and Rising With Christ,* (BZNW 32; Berlin: Töpelmann, 1967) 10-11; J. Becker, *Auferstehung der Toten im Ur-christentum* (Stuttgart: KBW Verlag, 1976) 55; Lohse, *Colossians,* 103. Schille, *Früh-christliche Hymnen,* 31-37, goes so far as to suggest that an early Christian redeemer

When in Colossians and Ephesians baptism signifies that Christians have not only been buried with Christ but have also been raised with Christ in the heavenly places (Col 2:12; 3:1; Eph 2:4-6), the apocalyptic future collapses into the Christ-event. In this context the church becomes identified with Christ, becoming a heavenly entity and threatening to displace the apocalyptic future. Whereas Rom 6:1-11 limits our present identification with Christ to our participation in his death, Colossians and Ephesians extend it to our participation in his resurrection as well.[167]

While not denying the foundational importance of the eschatological future to Paul's theology, there are a number of significant difficulties with this view. A. T. Lincoln, V. Branick, and others have clearly shown that the seeds of realized eschatology are already present in Paul.[168] This can be seen in Paul's statement about "walking in newness of life" (Rom 6:4), his theme of inner transformation and renewal (e.g. 2 Cor 4:16), and his understanding of present existence "in Christ" based on participation in the new eschatological age (e.g. 2 Cor 5:17), as well as many other themes.[169] Lincoln summarizes well the scope of Paul's thought well on this issue when he states, "there are two poles to Paul's thinking about resurrection life. That life has been entered on by the believer in union with Christ yet its consummation still lies in the future."[170]

In his outstanding study of the themes of baptism and resurrection in Paul, A. J. M. Wedderburn has delivered a decisive blow to the history-of-religions interpretation of union with Christ as having derived from a

---

hymn with a connection to baptism lies behind Col 2:9-15. F. Zeilinger, *Der Erstgeborene der Schöpfung* (Wien: Herder, 1974) 54, also argues that a baptismal hymn has been incorporated here, but extends only through verses 11-15. J. D. G. Dunn preserves the eschatological reservation of 6:5 and 8, but he does stress that Rom 6:4 clearly implies a sharing in some degree in Christ's risen life; J. D. G. Dunn, *Romans 1-8*, (WBC 38a; Dallas: Word, 1988) 330.

167 J. C. Beker, *Paul the Apostle* (Edinburgh: T. & T. Clark, 1980) 163. Although some interpreters find the author of Colossians dependent upon an earlier tradition of realized eschatology that Paul opposed in Romans 6 (see above), others see the innovation as stemming from the author of Colossians himself (as Beker seems to); see G. Sellin, "'Die Auferstehung ist schon geschehen.' Zur Spiritualisierung Apokolyptisch Terminologie im Neuen Testament," *NovT* 25 (1983) 231 ("Before and during Paul's ministry there are no modifications of the resurrection statements of the Christological kerygma under the influence of hellenistic-mystery theology.").

168 Lincoln, *Paradise*, 122-23; V. P. Branick, "Apocalyptic Paul?" *CBQ* 47 (1985) 664-75; et al.

169 See Branick, "Apocalyptic Paul?" 670-75.

170 Lincoln, *Paradise*, 122; idem, *Ephesians* (WBC 42; Dallas: Word, 1990) 105-106.

common mystery religion theology of Paul's day.[171] He has argued convincingly that Paul is not setting out to correct an alleged Hellenistic view of over-realized eschatology in Romans 6.[172] In fact, for Wedderburn, the notion of rising with Christ did not originate in the so-called Hellenistic church. Among many other reasons, Wedderburn points out that initiates into the mysteries did not see their relationship to the deity as "dying" and "rising"; they put their hope on the power of the deity with whom they were now related through initiation.[173] Consequently, he concludes that it is possible that the future tenses of Rom 6:5, 8 "are as much logical as temporal, or, putting it another (perhaps better) way, they refer to a state of affairs that already obtains in some measure, however much it still looks to the future for its full consummation (as in 5:19?)."[174] When he turns to Col 2:12, Wedderburn then argues that the declaration of co-resurrection with Christ does not go back to a tradition already in existence and opposed by Paul in Romans 6, nor does it reflect a mystery religion or Gnostic influence on the writer of Colossians; rather, the author has here given expression to the meaning of baptism in terms borrowed from Romans 6.[175] For Wedderburn, this is a logical and natural development of the themes in Romans 6 that came into expression because of the nature of the situation facing the church at Colossae.

It is vitally important to observe that the author of Colossians has not lost sight of future fulfillment. As much as he uses spatial categories and emphasizes a realized eschatology, the future hope is preserved. The expectation of a future return of Christ shines brightly in Col 3:4 (see also 1:22, 28), and, at the same time, the anticipation of future judgment is brought out in Col 3:6 and 24.

The concept of co-resurrection is central to the theology of Colossians. Paul builds on it later in Col 3:1 and it is the foundation for his third σύν-statement: "he made you alive with him" (συνεζωοποίησεν ὑμᾶς σὺν αὐτῷ; 2:13). The verb συζωοποιέω appears elsewhere only in the closely related Eph 2:5. In both passages the expression refers to the new life that

---

[171] A. J. M. Wedderburn, *Baptism and Resurrection* (WUNT 44; Tübingen: J. C. B. Mohr [Paul Siebeck], 1987). Walter Burkert, *Ancient Mystery Cults* (Cambridge, Mass.: Harvard University Press, 1987) 101, comments that "there is hardly any evidence for baptism in pagan mysteries." He also stresses that although there is a dimension of death in all of the mystery initiations, "the concept of rebirth or resurrection of either gods or *mystai* is anything but explicit" (p. 75).

[172] Wedderburn, *Baptism,* 46. So also Sellin, "Die Auferstehung," 232.

[173] Wedderburn, *Baptism,* 356-57.

[174] Wedderburn, *Baptism,* 44.

[175] Wedderburn, *Baptism,* 73-74.

believers come to possess because of their participation in the death and resurrection of Christ.

What then was the situation that prompted this specific development in Paul's thought? Wedderburn rightly suggests that the writer had to emphasize the sufficiency and adequacy of the salvation brought by Christ over against the claims of the opponents.[176] Although the advocates of "the philosophy" had in all likelihood been baptized, they either misunderstood its significance or undervalued it; at any rate, they gave much greater prominence to their special knowledge derived from mystery initiation and their insight into the angelic realm.[177] Paul is therefore striving here to help the Colossians see the full implications of their incorporation into Christ so they will have the security and strength to refuse the demands placed upon them by the teachers of this faction.

The motive for this unique accent on realized eschatology goes deeper than this. As we have observed repeatedly, one of the continuing concerns for the Christians at Colossae was their relationship to the hostile powers. The readers' fear of the demonic realm necessitated the author's reaffirmation of the truth that Christ alone is sufficient to protect them from the "powers." Others have pointed this motive out as well. Pokorný, for instance, claims that the author shifted the emphasis to salvation as present so that he could "emphasize the sufficiency of salvation in Jesus Christ and to free the recipients from the fear that the superhuman powers might one day block the way to salvation for them."[178] Pokorný is right to a certain extent, but errs by still maintaining a Gnostic framework for interpreting the powers and stressing their threat only on the day of death. G. Sellin comes closer to the intent when he remarks: "Against the Colossian "philosophy" with its attention to the cosmic powers (the veneration of the elemental spirits), the author emphasizes that the destruction of the cosmic powers has already occured through the enthronement of Christ. Christians have a share in this overcoming of the powers: they are freed from these powers in baptism."[179] The concern of the Colossians, and for Paul, was the influence of the powers on daily life in the here and now. The

---

[176] Wedderburn, *Baptism*, 83.

[177] Similarly, see Pokorný, *Colossians*, 123.

[178] Pokorný, *Colossians*, 126. See also Schweizer, *Colossians*, 145.

[179] Sellin, "Die Auferstehung," 232. Sellin errs, however, by arguing that the powers have been *completely* defeated; there will be no future subjection of the powers as we find in Paul (1 Cor 15:20-28). He furthermore finds no future eschatology in Paul, which we have already shown to be false. As we have demonstrated in our discussion of Col 1:20, Colossians does indeed envisage a future subjugation of the powers that will result in a universal cosmic peace.

concept of co-resurrection affirms their participation with Christ in his exaltation and defeat of the powers (cf. Col 2:15).[180]

The Colossians had already exercised faith on the efficacy of God's power (ἐνεργείας τοῦ θεοῦ; 2:12)—a power sufficient to raise Christ from the dead—when they were initially incorporated into Christ. The author now implicitly encourages the same kind of faith in the power of God/Christ over the "powers" so the readers do not submit themselves to various practices because of their fear of the power of the *stoicheia* and the "principalities and powers." As A. T. Lincoln, comment, "all depends then on their appropriation by faith of God's saving actions in history in Christ, and it is this very thing which their baptism proclaimed (cf. 2:12)."[181]

As a side note it it worth observing that the rite of baptism came to have a much closer assocation with the victorious relationship of the believer to demonic powers in the subsequent history of the church. In the second through the fourth centuries A.D., baptism was laden with apotropaic significance in the church. This is a natural development from the understanding of baptism as presented in Colossians where incorporation into Christ is interpreted as solidarity with one who has defeated the demonic powers and has been exalted to a position of present authority over their realm.[182]

---

[180] I have argued in a different context that there was a similar concern behind the composition of Ephesians that prompted a continuing emphasis on realized eschatology. See my *Ephesians*, 147-50.

[181] Lincoln, *Paradise*, 122.

[182] See H. A. Kelly, *The Devil at Baptism* (Ithaca: Cornell University Press, 1985). O. Böcher, *Christus Exorcista. Dämonismus und Taufe im Neuen Testament* (BWANT 16; Stuttgart: Kohlhammer, 1972) 170-75, argues that the NT emphasizes baptism as a participation in the victory of Christ over the demonic realm. The NT, and above all Paul, did not understand baptism in a magical-sacramental sense, but as a transfer of dominions into the sphere of the Holy Spirit (175). Böcher finds the later church, however, transforming the Pauline understanding of baptism into a magical misunderstanding such that the waters of baptism drove out the demons and caused the entry of the Holy Spirit (175-80). M. Smith, *Clement of Alexandria and a Secret Gospel of Mark* (Cambridge, Mass.: Harvard University Press, 1973) 220-22, argues that the *Pauline* understanding of baptism was magical. This explanation reads too much into the evidence, as Böcher has shown.

d. The Power of the New Dominion (1:11)

One indication of the power available to believers in their present experience of union with Christ is given in 1:11. Paul here reports that he prays that they would conduct their lives in a manner worthy of the Lord Jesus Christ, pleasing him in every respect (Col 1:10). He indicates that they have extraordinary means[183] available for living in a Christ-pleasing manner: "with all power being strengthened according to the might of his glory for all endurance and patience" (1:11).

Paul stacks up four different power-denoting terms here to persuade them that they do indeed have access to incredible divine resources for living according to the standards the Lord has called them to: δύναμις, δυναμόω, κράτος, and δόξα. The accumulation of power terminology has parallels in Jewish documents, especially the Qumran texts (e.g. 1QH 4:32 בכח גברו; see also 1QH 7:9ff.; 18:8ff.; 1QS 11:19ff.).[184] The rhetorical impact is heightened by (1) the presence of πάσῃ to modify δυνάμει— "with all power," (2) the redundancy of δύναμις with δυναμόω, and (3) the further conceptual redundancy of the κατά phrase with κράτος as the object. These expressions combine to produce an extraordinary emphasis on the divine power ("being empowered with power by power!").

Rather than rooting the source of the power explicitly in θεός, Paul speaks of it as found in "his glory" (ἡ δόξα αὐτοῦ). The glory of God is often linked with his power in the OT[185] and the two terms can be used interchangably by Paul.[186] Paul has probably chosen to speak of God's glory here for the sake of emphasizing him as the source of power—the

---

[183] The author may have intended his readers to understand the participle in an imperatival sense, "be strengthened"! J. C. O'Neill, "The Source of the Christology in Colossians," *NTS* 26 (1979) 90-91, translates it as an imperative. Lohse, *Colossians*, 32, who takes the following participle, εὐχαριστοῦντες, with an imperative meaning, viz. "Give thanks." He points to the frequent use of the participle in this way in Jewish texts and occasionally in Paul (e.g. Rom. 12:9); for further examples of the participle appearing with an imperatival meaning, see D. Daube, "Participle and Imperative in I Peter," in E. G. Selwyn, *The First Epistle of St. Peter* (London: Macmillan, 1947) 467-88.

[184] For additional discussion, see R. E. Murphy, "GBR and GBWRH in the Qumran Writings," in *Lex Tua Veritas* (FS. H. Junker; Trier: Paulinus, 1961) 137-43. For OT (LXX) references, see W. Grundmann, "δύναμαι," *TDNT* 2.290-94; idem, *Der Begriff der Kraft in der Neutestamentlichen Gedankenwelt* (BWANT 8; Stuttgart: Kohlhammer, 1932) 109-10. The use of δυναμόω with δύναμις, however, is unparalleled in the LXX.

[185] See, for example, Ps 61:2 (LXX = 62:3): τοῦ ἰδεῖν τὴν δύναμίν σου καὶ τὴν δόξαν σου; Isa 2:10, 19, 21: ἀπὸ τῆς δόξης τῆς ἰσχύος αὐτοῦ.

[186] On the one hand, Paul can attribute the resurrection of Christ to the δύναμις of God (1 Cor 6:14), while on the other hand it can be regarded as a manifestation of the δόξα of God (Rom 6:4).

divine king in the splendor of his majesty. The angels assuredly have access to the glory of God, but believers can *directly* receive God's divine
power from his throne of glory at the present time. This does not replace
or diminish, however, the hope of being with Christ in his future glory
(see 1:27 and 3:4).

In contrast to the teaching and methods of "the philosophy," this prayer
teaches that (1) there is more than *adequate* power available for the needs
of the Christian life in a proper knowledge of God, (2) this power is
available to believers, (3) this power is mediated *through a relationship*—
it is associated with increasing in the knowledge of God (1:10), and (4)
prayer, which Paul models here, is the means for acquiring God's power.
Negatively put, one does not need to invoke the aid of angelic intermediaries, engage in ascetic behavior to curry favor with God or angels, or use
any ritual means for obtaining divine power.[187]

Paul sees the divine power as a foundational presupposition for Christian conduct, which he expresses as "walking worthy of the Lord" and
"pleasing him in every respect" (v. 10). Specifically, he writes that the divine power is essential to "endurance" (ὑπομονή) and "patience"
(μακροθυμία). Endurance and patience are necessary for persevering until
the final consummation.[188] However, Paul is probably thinking here of the
immediate conflict facing the church at Colossae in the form of the syncretistic "philosophy" (which he sees as demonic [2:8]) and the pressures
perceived by the congregation as coming from the realm of the evil powers.[189] He is thus asking God to impart his awesome power to these people
so they could hold out "against the pressure of evil forces in the Lycus
Valley that would lead them astray as well as make them dispirited."[190]

Paul presents himself as a model of this dependence upon the awesome
power of God in Col 1:29 (cf. Eph 3:7[191]). There he attributes his hard
work on behalf of the gospel not to his own strength and abilities, but to
"his [Christ's] strength, which works powerfully in me, in power" (κατὰ
τὴν ἐνέργειαν αὐτοῦ τὴν ἐνεργουμένην ἐν ἐμοὶ ἐν δυνάμει). Once again
Paul employs a Semitic manner of expression by piling up terms for
power as a means of bringing into bold relief the empowering presence of

---

[187] See my discussion of the closely related text, Eph 1:19, in *Ephesians,* 72-75.

[188] Schweizer, *Colossians,* 44.

[189] There is nothing in the larger context that would suggest that Paul is preparing the
congregation for persecution, as Gnilka, *Kolosserbrief,* 43, suggests.

[190] O'Brien, *Colossians,* 24. For a similar conclusion, see Lohse, *Colossians,* 30;
Martin, *Colossians* (NCB), 53.

[191] See my discussion of this text in *Ephesians,* 161-62.

Christ in his life. He uses the terms ἐνέργεια and ἐνεργέω to stress the operation of the divine power in his life.

e. Concentrating on the Heavenly Dimension (3:1-4)

The transitional section of 3:1-4 reaffirms and develops aspects of the theology presented in 2:9-15. The passage provides a fitting bridge to the ethical paraenesis of 3:5ff. and yet continues to show the author's concern to provide a stimulus for the community to deny the opposing teaching.

With two imperatives, Paul calls on the Colossians to "seek (ζητεῖτε) the things which are above" and to "set your minds on (φρονεῖτε) the things which are above." The first injunction has much in common with Matt 6:33 where the disciples are enjoined to seek (ζητεῖτε) the kingdom of God and his righteousness above all else. As H. Greeven has noted, the use of the word here and in so many of the contexts in which it is used has to do with the orientation of a person's will as part of the process of seeking after something.[192] The will also comes into view with the second imperative, φρονεῖτε. With this term, the thought life of the person comes more sharply into view. Paul was fond of this term as a means of helping to redirect the thought-life of the people in his communities. Perhaps most notable in this respect are his many admonitions to "think the same thing" (e.g., Rom 12:16; 15:5; 2 Cor 13:11; Phil 2:2; 4:2) and his call to the Philippian congregation to "let this mind be in you (φρονεῖτε τοῦτο) which was also in Christ Jesus" (Phil 2:5). The combination of these two terms with the repeated τὰ ἄνω represents his attempt to redirect the direction of their strivings.

Paul wants the Colossians to focus on the heavenly dimension, which he expresses by his repeated use of τὰ ἄνω. "Above" contrasts not with "below," but with the earth (3:2). In Pauline thought, the dust of the earth contrasts with heaven with the dust/earth being the place of origin of the first man Adam (1 Cor 15:47). As such it is temporal and inferior to a heavenly origin which is eternal and coextensive with the kingdom of God (1 Cor 15:50). The spatial category τὰ ἄνω only appears twice (in varied form) in the other Pauline letters, but both texts have much in common with these two occurences. In Gal 4:26, Paul speaks of "the Jerusalem above" (ἡ ἄνω Ἰερουσαλήμ) that is free which, in his view, corresponds to the new covenant. In Phil 3:14, Paul relates how he zealously seeks "the

---

[192] H. Greeven, "ζητέω," *TDNT* 2.893.

upward call of God" (ἡ ἄνω κλῆσις τοῦ θεοῦ). He later correlates this upward call to citizenship in heaven (Phil 3:20) and contrasts it to the unhealthy focus of the opponents whose mind is set on earthly things (οἱ τὰ ἐπίγεια φρονοῦντες; Phil 3:19). Furthermore, as background to this usage, Lincoln has demonstrated that in Judaism, the two-age eschatological framework could be completely paralleled by the concept of lower and upper worlds.[193] One does not, therefore, need to posit a dependence on Hellenistic spatial categories by the author of Colossians. In spite of the fact that the precise phrase τὰ ἄνω never appears in the accepted Paulines, this mode of thinking was already characteristic of Paul.

In the context of this letter, Paul is encouraging the Colossian believers to earnestly pursue everything that is associated with the heavenly dimension. This has both an objective and an ethical aspect. Above all, they are to pursue a deeper knowledge of Christ himself which Paul is attempting to facilitate through what he has already written in this letter. As a corollary, they are called to pursue a set of ethical imperatives that Paul views as essential to a life worthy of Christ (1:10; 2:6; 3:5ff.). Clearly, he sees the beliefs and practices of the opponents as inconsistent with a heavenly orientation. He places them in the category of τὰ ἐπὶ τῆς γῆς by associating them with the "world" (2:20), the "flesh" (2:23), and demonic powers (2:8, 20).

The heavenly dimension is where Christ is seated at the right hand of God (3:1b). The writer uses the language of Ps 110:1 (possibly in dependence on a traditional formulation)—a passage widely interpreted by the early Christians as a Messianic promise that God's anointed one would be exalted to a position of prominence after he defeated his enemies.[194] Although he does not explicitly cite the portion of the Psalm that speaks of the defeat of the enemies, the familiarity of this passage to the Christian readers would have prompted a recollection of the rest of the text. Early Christians typically identified the enemies of the Psalm with the hostile demonic powers that Christ subjugated by his death and exaltation. This allusion to Ps 110:1 is especially appropriate following the dramatic depiction in 2:15 of Christ's defeat of the principalities and powers on the cross. Lohse aptly comments, "Christ has been exalted above the powers and is enthroned at God's right hand. Whoever belongs to him is thereby freed for new life."[195] Paul therefore calls the Colossians to dwell on the

---

[193] See Lincoln, *Paradise,* 124, for references.

[194] See Mk 12:36 (// Matt 22:43-44; Lk 20:42-43); 14:62 (// Matt 26:64; Lk 22:69); Acts 2:34; 1 Cor 15:25; Rom 8:34; Eph 1:20; Heb 1:3, 13; 8:1; 10:12-13; 12:2.

[195] Lohse, *Colossians,* 133, note 8.

fact that they are united to a sovereign lord who has defeated his super-natural enemies—the same enemies which they have faced—and now sits enthroned in a position of authority at God's right hand.

The heavenly dimension is also a place of security. Paul exclaims that "your live is hidden (κέκρυπται) with Christ in God" (3:3). There has been much speculation about the background and meaning of the author's use of the term "hidden."[196] The best explanation is that the writer is here using language from Isaiah and the Psalms that expresses the security of the people of God as they trust in him when they face their enemies. It is said regarding the Servant of the Lord in Isa 49:2 that, "in the shadow of his hand he hid (ἔκρυψεν) me; he made me into a polished arrow and con-cealed (ἐσκέπασεν) me in his quiver." In Ps 27:5-6 (26:5-6 LXX), the Psalmist extols the protective intervention of the Lord: "For in the day of trouble he will keep me safe in his dwelling; he will hide (ἔκρυψεν) me in the shelter of his tabernacle and set me high upon a rock. Then my head will be exalted above the enemies who surround me." In a similar fashion, Ps 31:19-20 (30:19-21 LXX) declares: "How great is your goodness, which you have stored up (ἔκρυψας) for those who fear you, which you bestow in the sight of men on those who take refuge in you. In the shelter of your presence you hide them (κατακρύψεις αὐτοὺς ἐν ἀποκρύφῳ τοῦ προσώπου σου) ..." The enemies the Psalmist faced were idolaters; thus, he exclaims, "I hate those who cling to worthless idols; I trust in the Lord" (Ps 31:6 [30:7 LXX]). They also speak with "accusing tongues" (31:20 [30:21 LXX]) and "with pride and contempt they speak arrogantly against the righteous" (31:18; [30:19 LXX]). It is interesting to observe how Paul condemns the arrogance and judgmental attitudes the purveyors of "the philosophy" had toward the Colossian believers. Although he never calls them idolaters, his expression "worship of angels" (Col 2:18) and characterization of "the philosophy" as vain deceit (2:8) come close to this. It is therefore quite possible that Paul writes to the Colossians in the spirit of these Psalms and using some of the language contained in them.

Although Paul may have emphasized hiddenness to bring out the secu-rity of these believers, this concept is consistent with his overarching Jewish eschatological framework that also understands hiddenness as a historical concept. Here he speaks of the anticipated second stage of the awaiting revelation at Christ's parousia (3:4), whereas in Col 1:26-27 he could refer to the mystery hidden for ages that has already been revealed

---

[196] See the commentaries for a survey of the views.

in the first coming of Christ.[197] Although there is an extraordinary emphasis on spatial categories in this passage, the eschatological temporality is not lost. In traditional language, Paul refers to the second coming of Christ in 3:4.[198] The anticipation of the future *parousia* thereby serves as a partial basis for the ethical admonitions which follow.

Hence, in Col 3:1-4, Paul reaffirms to the Colossian believers that they have access to the heavenly dimension based on their death and resurrection with Christ. As Lincoln observes, "since resurrection life is heavenly life, by being united with Christ in his resurrection believers participate in the life of the realm above."[199] Here there is security, freedom of fear, and power for dealing with the influences of the hostile powers.

7. Conclusions

The letter to the Colossians was prompted by the threat of an opposing teaching that the Apostle deemed dangerous to the health of the church and demeaning to the person of Christ. This syncretistic "philosophy" was an enticement to the Colossians because it presented them with additional means for averting the harmful influence of chthonic spirits, astral powers, and every variety of evil spirit. With an ironic twist, Paul denigrates "the philosophy" by rooting it in the present evil age and explicitly linking it to the deceptive influence of the powers.

To counter the potential influence of "the philosophy," Paul directly polemicizes against certain features of the teaching and practice. He goes beyond this, however, by dealing with the root issue for the Colossians: the relationship of Christ and his people to the powers.

With an elegant piece of poetic praise, Paul declares the supremacy of Christ. He magnifies Christ as Lord by portraying him as superior to everything in heaven and on earth, including the hostile powers. He further develops the theme of cosmic Christology by giving eloquent testimony to Christ's defeat of the powers by the cross/resurrection event and announcing that Christ is the "head" over every power and authority. The

---

[197] Lincoln, *Paradise,* 129.

[198] Lincoln, *Paradise,* 123, rightly observes that this verse "demonstrates clearly" that Christ's return in glory still awaits.

[199] Lincoln, *Paradise,* 124.

"cosmic" emphasis of the Christology maintains a primary focus on Christ in relationship to the powers.

Paul also gives expression to the theme of redemption not only to express forgiveness of sin and reconciliation to God, but especially to highlight the change of dominions that takes place for believers. They are no longer under the authority of the ruler of darkness; they have been brought into the kingdom of Christ. He emphasizes the identification of believers with the death of Christ, which enables them to resist the influence of the hostile powers.

More than in any of his previous letters, Paul stresses the solidarity of the believer with the resurrected Christ. He explicitly refers to a present experience of resurrection with Christ and emphasizes the reality of new life. This strongly realized eschatology serves his purpose of helping the Colossian believers to see that they do not need additional protection from the powers. They have solidarity with one who has defeated the powers on the cross. They have access to all the fullness of God and thereby share in Christ's authority over principalities and powers. Christ alone is therefore sufficient for them. They are called to concentrate on him and hold on tight to him.

Contrary to what many scholars have said, the future hope has not been displaced by a spatial orientation. Paul speaks of hope in both a present and future sense. Christ will return in all of his glory. He has yet to perform his work of creating a cosmic peace. The Colossians can therefore take comfort in the fact that the principalities and powers are not ultimate. Christ is in control of history and will bring it to a consummation—a future marked by the absence of hostilities when peace will prevail in heaven and on earth.

Conclusions

The Christians at Colossae lived in an environment of religious pluralism. They coexisted with people who worshiped Anatolian, Persian, Greek, Roman, and Egyptian deities and with Jews who were devoted to the worship of one god and the observance of Torah. The manner of devotion and religious expression was quite varied among the different groups.

In spite of the rich diversity of beliefs and approaches to the divine in Asia Minor, there were some threads of commonality. The environment was characterized by a significant level of religious syncretism. There was a fair amount of borrowing from cult to cult. There was also a strong tendency for the newer religions to assimilate features of the older local religions.

Some of the beliefs and practices held in common can be attributed to the strength of the local Phrygian religious traditions. What many scholars have called the "Lydian-Phrygian spirit" permeated many of the cults, and to some degree, even Judaism. This local tradition included a tendency toward the worship of one high god served by many intermediary beings, ecstatic forms of worship that sometimes led to the abuse of the body, a strong belief in dangerous spirits and powers, and the practice of invoking divine intermediaries for deliverance, protection, and assistance.

These local beliefs overlap significantly with what we know about the practice of "magic" in western Asia Minor. Scholars have long recognized that the magical texts provide us with a unique glimpse into folk religion. In this popular substructure to the official doctrine and practice of the cults we find the highest degree of syncretism. Deities and intermediaries were seen primarily in terms of their power. The tremendous fear of spirits (often referred to as *deisidaimonia*) prompted people to call on helpful spirits or angels and engage in rituals of power. Various forms of ritual initiation could help to charm one against the powers and provide the much-sought-after protection. Fasting and other forms of ascetic practices often accompanied the rituals and incantations. It is in this area where we see the highest degree of syncretism among the Jews of western Asia Minor.

The early Christian movement in the Lycus Valley did not prove to be immune to this powerful set of local beliefs. As Colossian Gentiles and

Jews became Christians, accepting the Pauline gospel which they heard from Epaphras, they would have found it difficulty to shed many parts of their world view and religious practices in favor of this new tradition they embraced. Indeed, many did not and continued to struggle—especially with fear over the impact and potential impact the hostile powers could have on their day-to-day lives. They faced a great temptation to resort to the mechanisms for dealing with these supernatural adversaries that they had depended on for their entire lives.

It is within this context that a new teaching emerged within the Christian community at Colossae. Referring to itself as "the philosophy," the leaders of this faction had adapted the Pauline gospel to aspects of Phrygian-Lydian beliefs and practices as well as to the local Judaism. They advocated the invocation of angels for protection from the hostile powers. They appear to have overemphasized the transcendence of God and underemphasized the exalted position of Christ, functionally viewing him as a mediator, perhaps on the same level as the angels. As a means of countering this teaching and giving the Colossians perspective on the relationship of Christ to the powers, Paul gives eloquent expression to a *cosmic Christology*. Jesus existed before the powers, he in fact created them, he defeated the hostile powers on the cross, and he will intervene in the future and bring about a universal peace in heaven as well as on earth.

The advocates of the new teaching, in line with Lydian-Phrygian practice, emphasized a rigorous asceticism with a variety of taboos, ritual observances, and dietary regulations. These practices were motivated at least in part by a desire to gain ritual power over the harmful and malignant forces. In contrast to this, Paul rejects these mechanisms for ritual power in favor of a better understanding of their objective relationship to the exalted Lord and appropriating the divine power and resources that they have in him. In doing this, Paul places an extraordinary emphasis on *realized eschatology*. He goes beyond what he has said in his previous letters in emphasizing the presence of salvation. He stresses their co-resurrection with Christ, access to the heavenly realm (where Christ is), and the fact that they have been filled with the same fullness with which Christ had been filled. Paul has not displaced the future hope of believers, but has here placed a tremendous emphasis upon the solidarity of believers with Christ.

Contrary to a spirit of religious tolerance, Paul polemicizes strongly against the teaching of this opposing group within the church. He goes so far as to label their teaching "empty deception" and as inspired by the evil spirits of this present age.

Unfortunately, we only have one perspective on the controversy and have no access to the other side of the story. His opponents would certainly not have agreed with his analysis of the situation and would have been offended by his harsh language. Paul's letter may very well have intensified the debate within the church. It was Paul's hope, however, that the Christians of the Lycus Valley would no longer give the faction a hearing.

The kind of problem that surfaced in the Colossian church was not unique and represents a traceable trend in early Christianity toward a syncretism with folk religious beliefs and practices. The storm center of controversy in the years ahead would focus on a different form of Christian syncretism—the rise of Gnosticism. This had not yet surfaced at the time Colossians was written, yet some forms of Gnosticism would adopt aspects of the teaching and practice of this form of folk religion.

Bibliography

Commentaries

ABBOTT, T. K. *The Epistles to the Ephesians and to the Colossians.* ICC. Edinburgh: T. & T. Clark, 1897.

ALETTI, Jean-Noël. *Saint Paul Épitre aux Colossiens.* Études Bibliques, Nouvelle Série 20. Paris: Gabalda, 1993.

BEARE, F. W. *The Epistle to the Colossians.* IB 11. Nashville: Abingdon, 1955.

BRUCE, F. F. *The Epistles to the Colossians, to Philemon, and to the Ephesians.* NICNT. Grand Rapids: Eerdmans, 1984.

CAIRD, G. B. *Paul's Letters From Prison.* New Clarendon Bible. Oxford: University Press, 1976.

CONZELMANN, Hans. *Der Brief an die Epheser.* NTD 8. Göttingen: Vandenhoeck & Ruprecht, 1965, 56-91.

—. *Der Brief an die Kolosser.* NTD 8. Göttingen: Vandenhoeck & Ruprecht, 1965

DIBELIUS, Martin and GREEVEN, Heinrich. *An die Kolosser, Epheser, an Philemon.* HNT 12. 3rd ed. Tübingen: Mohr, 1953.

EADIE, John. *A Commentary on the Greek Text of the Epistle of Paul to the Colossians.* Grand Rapids: Baker, 1979 (originally, Edinburgh: T. & T. Clark, 1884).

ERNST, J. *Die Briefe an die Philipper, an Philemon, an die Kolosser, an die Epheser.* RNT. Regensburg: Pustet, 1974.

GNILKA, Joachim. *Der Epheserbrief.* HTKNT X 2. Freiburg: Herder, 1971.

—. *Der Kolosserbrief.* HTKNT X 1. Freiburg: Herder, 1980.

HOULDEN, J. L. *Paul's Letters from Prison.* Pelican New Testament Commentary. Baltimore, Md.: Penguin, 1970.

LIGHTFOOT, J. B. *St. Paul's Epistles to the Colossians and to Philemon.* London: Macmillan, 1875.

LINDEMANN, Andreas. *Der Kolosserbrief.* ZBK. Zürich: Zwingli, 1983.

LOHMEYER, Ernst. *Die Briefe an die Philipper, an die Kolosser und an Philemon.* MeyerK. 13th Ed. Göttingen: Vandenhoeck & Ruprecht, 1964.

LOHSE, Eduard. *Colossians and Philemon.* Tr. W. R. Poehlmann & R. J. Karris. Hermeneia. Philadelphia: Fortress, 1971.

MARTIN, Ralph P. *Colossians and Philemon.* NCB. London: Oliphants, 1981.

—. *Colossians: The Church's Lord and the Christian's Liberty.* Exeter: Paternoster, 1972.

MELLICK, Richard R. *Philippians, Colossians, Philemon.* New American Commentary. Nashville: Broadman, 1991.

MOULE, C. F. D. *The Epistles of Paul the Apostle to the Colossians and to Philemon.* CGTC. Cambridge: University Press, 1962.

O'BRIEN, Peter T. *Colossians, Philemon.* WBC 44. Waco: Word, 1982.

PATZIA, Arthur G. *Ephesians, Colossians, Philemon.* NIBC 10. Peabody, Mass.: Hendrickson, 1990.

POKORNÝ, Petr. *Colossians. A Commentary.* Peabody, Mass.: Hendrickson, 1991.

SCHLATTER, A. "Die Briefe an die Galater, Epheser, Kolosser und Philemon." *Erläuterungen zum Neuen Testament* 7. Stuttgart: Calwer, 1963, 152-352.

SCHWEIZER, Eduard. *The Letter to the Colossians.* Tr. A. Chester. Minneapolis: Augsburg, 1982.

SCOTT, E. F. *The Epistles of Paul to the Colossians, to Philemon, and to the Ephesians.* MNTC. London: Hodder & Stoughton, 1930.

STRACK, H. L. & BILLERBECK, P. *Kommentar zum Neuen Testament aus Talmud und Midrasch.* Vol. 3. München: Beck, 1926.

WILSON, R. McL. *The Epistle to the Colossians.* ICC. Edinburgh: T. & T. Clark (in process).

WOLTER, Michael. *Der Brief an die Kolosser. Der Brief an Philemon.* ÖTKNT 12. Würzburg: Echter Verlag, 1993.

Books and Articles

AKURGAL, Ekrem. *Ancient Civilizations and Ruins of Turkey*. Istanbul: Mobil Oil Türk, 1969.

ALETTI, J. N. *Colossiens, 1, 15-20. Genre et exégese du texte Fonction de la thématique sapientielle*. AnBib 91. Rome: Biblical Institute, 1981.

ALEXANDER, P. S. "Incantations and Books of Magic." In *The History of the Jewish People in the Age of Jesus Christ*. Revised and edited by Geza Vermes, Fergus Millar, and Martin Goodman. Vol. 3, Part 1. Edinburgh: T. & T. Clark, 1986, 342-79.

ANDRES, F. "Angelos." *PW* Supp. 3.101-14

ARBESMANN, P. R. *Das Fasten bei den Griechen und Römern*. Religionsgeschichtliche Versuche und Vorarbeiten 21. Giessen: Töpelmann, 1929 (rpt. 1966).

ARGALL, Randal A. "The Source of Religious Error in Colossae." *CTJ* 22 (1987) 6-20.

ARNOLD, Clinton E. *Ephesians: Power and Magic. The Concept of Power in Ephesians in Light of its Historical Setting*. Society for New Testament Studies Monograph 63. Cambridge: University Press, 1989 (reprinted under the same title: Grand Rapids: Baker, 1992).

—. "Returning to the Domain of the Powers: *Stoicheia* as Evil Spirits in Gal 4:3, 9." *NovT* (forthcoming).

—. "Principalities and Powers." *ABD* 5.467.

—. "Colossae." *ABD* 1.1089

—. "'Principalities and Powers' in Recent Interpretation." *Catalyst* 17.2 (February, 1991) 4-5.

—. "Jesus Christ: 'Head' of the Church." In *Jesus of Nazareth: Lord and Christ. Essays on the Historical Jesus and New Testament Christology*. Eds. M. M. B. Turner and J. B. Green. Grand Rapids: Eerdmans, 1994, 346-66.

AUDOLLENT, Augustus. *Defixionum Tabellae*. Paris: Alberti Fontemoing, 1894.

AULOCK, Hans von. *Münzen und Städte Phrygiens*. Istanbuler Mitteilungen Beiheft 27. Tübingen: Ernst Wasmuth, 1987.

AUNE, David E. *Prophecy in Early Christianity and the Ancient Mediterranean World*. Grand Rapids: Eerdmans, 1983.

—. "Magic in Early Christianity." *ANRW* II.23.2. Berlin: Walter de Gruyter, 1980, 1507-57.

—. "Magic." *ISBE* 3.213-19.

—. "The Apocalypse of John and Graeco-Roman Revelatory Magic." *NTS* 33 (1987) 481-501.

BALCHIN, J. F. "Colossians 1:15-20: An Early Christian Hymn? The Arguments from Style." *Vox Evangelica* 15 (1985) 65-94.

BAMMEL, E. "Versuch zu Kol 1, 15-20." *ZNW* 52 (1961) 88-95.

BANDSTRA, Andrew J. *The Law and the Elements of the World. An Exegetical Study in Aspects of Paul's Teaching*. Kampen: J. H. Kok N. V., 1964.

—. "Did the Colossian Errorists Need a Mediator?" *New Dimensions in New Testament Study*. Eds. R. N. Longenecker & M. C. Tenney. Grand Rapids: Zondervan, 1974, 329-43.

—. "Plēroma as Pneuma in Colossians." *Ad Interim. Opstellen over Eschatologie, Apocalyptiek en Ethiek*. FS. R. Schippers. Kampen: Kok, 1975, 96-102.

BARBOUR, R. S. "Salvation and Cosmology: The Setting of the Epistle to the Colossians." *SJT* 20 (1967) 257-71.

BAUGH, S. "The Poetic Form of Col 1:15-20." *WTJ* 47 (1985) 227-44.

BEALL, Todd S. *Josephus' Description of the Essenes Illustrated by the Dead Sea Scrolls*. SNTSMS 58. Cambridge: University Press, 1988.

BEASLEY-MURRAY, G. R. "The Second Chapter of Colossians." *RevExp* 70 (1973) 469-79.

—. *Baptism in the New Testament*. London: Macmillan, 1962.

BEASLEY-MURRAY, P. "Colossians 1:15-20: An Early Christian Hymn Celebrating the Lordship of Christ." *Pauline Studies*. FS. F. F. Bruce. Exeter: Paternoster, 1980, 169-83.

BECK, Roger. "Mithraism Since Franz Cumont." *ANRW* II.17.4 (1984) 2002-2115.

BECKER, J. *Auferstehung der Toten im Urchristentum*. Stuttgart: KBW Verlag, 1976.

BEKER, J. Christiaan. *Paul the Apostle*. Edinburgh: T. & T. Clark, 1980.

BENOIT, Pierre. "L'hymne christologique de Col i, 15-20. Jugement critique sur l'état des recherches." *Christianity, Judaism and Other Greco-Roman Cults* I. FS. M. Smith. SJLA 12. Leiden: Brill, 1975, 226-63.

—. "Pauline Angelology and Demonology. Reflexions on the Designations of the Heavenly Powers and on the Origin of Angelic Evil According to Paul." *Religious Studies Bulletin* 3 (1983) 1-18.

—. "The 'plèroma' in the Epistles to the Colossians and the Ephesians." *SEÅ* 49 (1984) 136-58.

BERGER, Klaus. "Die königlichen Messiastraditionen des neuen Testaments." *NTS* 20 (1974) 1-44.

BETZ, Hans Dieter, Ed. *The Greek Magical Papyri in Translation*. Vol. 1: Text. Chicago: Univ. of Chicago Press, 1986.

BETZ, Hans Dieter. "Fragments from a Catabasis Ritual in a Greek Magical Papyrus." *HistRel* 19 (1980) 287-95.

—. "The Formation of Authoritative Tradition in the Greek Magical Papyri." *Jewish and Christian Self-Definition III*. Eds. B. F. Meyer & E. P. Sanders. London: SCM, 1982, 161-70.

—. "The Delphic Maxim 'Know Yourself' in the Greek Magical Papyri." *HistRel* 21 (1981) 156-71.

—. "Magic and Mystery in the Greek Magical Papyri." In *Hellenismus und Urchristentum*. Gesammelte Aufsätze I. Tübingen: Mohr, 1990, 209-29.

—. "Magic and Mystery in the Greek Magical Papyri." In *Magika Hiera. Ancient Greek Magic and Religion*. Eds. C. A. Faraone and D. Obbink. New York: Oxford University Press, 1991, 244-59.

BIETENHARD, Hans. *Die himmlische Welt im Urchristentum und Spätjudentum*. WUNT 2. Tübingen: Mohr, 1951.

BLACK, Matthew. *The Book of Enoch or 1 Enoch*. Studia in Veteris Testamenti Pseudepigrapha 7. Leiden: Brill, 1985.

BLANCHETTE, O. A. "Does the Cheirographon of Col. 2,14 Represent Christ Himself?" *CBQ* 23 (1961) 306-12.

BLAU, Ludwig. *Das altjüdische Zauberwesen*. Berlin: Verlag von Luis Lamm, 1914.

BLINZLER, Josef. "Lexikalisches zu dem Terminus τὰ στοιχεῖα τοῦ κόσμου." *Studiorum Paulinorum Congressus Internationalis Catholicus* II. Rome: Pontifical Biblical Institute, 1963, 429-43.

BÖCHER, O. *Das Neue Testament und die dämonischen Mächte*. SBS 58. Stuttgart: Katholisches Bibelwerk, 1972.

—. *Christus Exorcista. Dämonismus und Taufe im Neuen Testament*. BWANT 16. Stuttgart: Kohlhammmer, 1972.

—. *Dämonenfurcht und Dämonenabwehr. Ein Beitrag zur Vorgeschichte der christlichen Taufe*. BWANT 10. Stuttgart: Kohlhammer, 1970.

BOCKMUEHL, Markus N. A. *Revelation and Mystery in Ancient Judaism and Pauline Christianity*. WUNT 2.36. Tübingen: Mohr, 1990.

BONNER, Campbell. *Studies in Magical Amulets Chiefly Graeco-Egyptian*. Ann Arbor: Univ. of Michigan Press, 1950.

BORNKAMM, Günther. "The Heresy of Colossians." *Conflict at Colossae*. Eds. F. O. Francis & W. A. Meeks. SBLSBS 4. Missoula: Scholar's Press, 1973, 123-45 (originally published in 1948).

—. "Die Hoffnung im Kolosserbrief. Zugleich ein Beitrag zur Frage der Echtheit des Briefes." *Studien zum Neuen Testament und zur Patristik*. FS. E. Klostermann. TU 77. Berlin: Akademie, 1961, 56-64.

—. "μυστήριον." *TDNT* 4.802-27

BÖTTRICH, C. *Weltweisheit, Menschheitsethik, Urkult. Studien zum slavonsichen Henochbuch*. WUNT 2/50. Tübingen: Mohr, 1992.

BOUSSET, Wilhelm. *Kyrios Christos*. Tr. J. E. Steely. Nashville: Abingdon, 1970.

BOUSSET, Wilhelm & GRESSMANN, Hugo. *Die Religion des Judentums im Späthellenistischen Zeitalter*. HzNT 21. 3rd ed. Tübingen: Mohr, 1966.

BRANICK, V. P. "Apocalyptic Paul?" *CBQ* 47 (1985) 664-75.

BRAUN, Herbert. *Qumran und das Neue Testament*. 2 Vols. Tübingen, 1966.

BREYTENBACH, Cilliers. "Paul's Proclamation and God's 'Thriambos.'" *Neotestamentica* 24 (1990) 257-71.

BROWN, Raymond E. *The Semitic Background of the Term 'Mystery' in the NT*. Facet Books, Biblical Series. Philadelphia: Fortress Press, 1968.

BRUCE, F. F. "The 'Christ-Hymn' of Colossians 1:15-20." *BibSac* 141 (1984) 99-111.

—. "The Colossian Heresy." *BibSac* 141 (1984) 195-208.

—. "Christ as Conqueror and Reconciler." *BibSac* 141 (1984) 291-302.

—. "Jews and Christians in the Lycus Valley." *BibSac* 141 (1984) 3-15.

BUJARD, Walter. *Stilanalytische Untersuchungen zum Kolosserbrief*. SUNT 11. Göttingen: Vandenhoeck & Ruprecht, 1973.

BULTMANN, Rudolf. *Theology of the New Testament*. 2 Vols. Tr. K. Grobel. New York: Charles Scribner's Sons, 1951, 1955.

BUNDRICK, David R. "*TA STOICHEIA TOU KOSMOU* (GAL 4:3)." *JETS* 34 (1991) 353-64.

BÜRGER, Christoph. *Schöpfung und Versöhnung. Studien zum liturgischen Gut im Kolosser- und Epheserbrief.* WMANT 46. Neukirchen: Neukirchener, 1975.

BURKERT, Walter. *Ancient Mystery Cults.* Cambridge, Mass.: Harvard University Press, 1987.

—. "ΓΟΗΣ. Zum Griechischen 'Schamanismus.'" *Rheinisches Museum für Philologie* NS 105 (1962) 36-55.

BURNEY, C. F. "Christ as the ARXH of Creation." *JTS* 27 (1926) 160-77.

CAIRD, G. B. *Principalities and Powers.* Oxford: Clarendon, 1956.

CANNON, George E. *The Use of Traditional Material in Colossians.* Macon: Mercer Univ. Press, 1983.

CARAGOUNIS, Chrys C. *The Ephesian Mysterion.* Meaning and Content. ConB 8. Lund: Gleerup, 1977.

CARR, Wesley. *Angels and Principalities. The Background, Meaning and Development of the Pauline Phrase hai archai kai hai exousiai.* SNTSMS 42. Cambridge: University Press, 1983.

—. "Two Notes on Colossians." *JTS* 24 (1973) 492-500.

CARRATELLI, G. Pugliese. "ΧΡΗΣΜΟΙ di Apollo Kareios e Apollo Klarios a Hierapolis in Frigia." *Annuario della Scuola Archeologica di Atene e delle Missioni Italiane in Oriente* 61-62 (1963-64) 351-70.

CERFAUX, Lucien. "Influence des Mystères sur le Judaïsme Alexandrin avant Philo." *Recueil Lucien Cerfaux. Études d'Exégèse et d'Histoire Religieuse de Monseigneur Cerfaux.* BETL 6-7. Gembloux: Éditions J. Duculot, 1954, 1.65-112.

CHADWICK, H. *Origen: Contra Celsum.* Cambridge: University Press, 1979.

CHAMONARD, J. and LEGRAND, A. "Inscriptions de Notion." *BCH* 18 (1894) 216-21.

CHARLES, R. H. *The Apocrypha and Pseudepigrapha of the Old Testament.* 2 Vols. Oxford: Clarendon, 1913.

CHARLES, R. H. and MORFILL W. R. *The Books of the Secrets of Henoch.* Oxford: Clarendon, 1896.

CHARLESWORTH, James H, Ed. *The Old Testament Pseudepigrapha.* 2 Vols. New York: Doubleday & Co., 1983.

—. *The Pseudepigrapha and Modern Research.* Society of Biblical Literature Septuagint and Cognate Studies 7. Missoula: Scholar's Press, 1976.

—. "Jewish Astrology in the Talmud, Pseudepigrapha, the Dead Sea Scrolls, and Early Palestinian Synagogues." *HTR* 70 (1977) 183-200.

—. *The Old Testament Pseudepigrapha and the New Testament. Prolegomena for the Study of Christian Origins.* SNTSMS 54. Cambridge: Univ. Press, 1985.

COHEN, M. S. *The Shi'ur Qomah: Texts and Recensions.* TSAJ 9. Tübingen: Mohr, 1985.

COLPE, C. *Die religionsgeschichtliche Schule. Darstellung der Kritik ihres Bildes vom gnostischen Erlösermythus.* FRLANT 78. Göttingen: Vandenhoeck & Ruprecht, 1961.

—. "Zur Leib-Christi Vorstellung im Epheserbrief." In *Judentum, Urchristentum, Kirche*. Ed. W. Eltester. BZNW 26. Berlin: de Gruyter, 1964, 172-87.

CORMACK, J. M. R. "A *Tabella Defixionis* in the Museum of the University of Reading, England." *HTR* 44 (1951) 25-34.

CULIANU, I. P. "The Angels of the Nations and the Origins of Gnostic Dualism." *Studies in Gnosticism and Hellenistic Religions*. FS. G. Quispel. Eds. R. van den Broek and M. J. Vermaseren. EPRO 91. Leiden: Brill, 1981, 78-91.

CUMONT, Franz. *Astrology and Religion Among the Greeks and Romans*. New York & London: G. P. Putnam's, 1912.

—. *The Oriental Religions in Roman Paganism*. New York/London: Dover, 1956.

—. "Les Mystères de Sabazius et le Judaïsme." *CRAIBL* (1906) 63-79.

—. *The Mysteries of Mithra*. New York: Dover, 1956.

—. *Textes et monuments figurés relatifs aux mystères de Mithra*. 2 Vols. Brussels: H. Lamertin, 1896, 1899.

—. "Ὕψιστος." *PW* 9.444-50

DANIEL, Robert and MALTOMINI, Franco. *Supplementum Magicum*. 2 Vols. Abhandlungen der Rheinisch-Westfälischen Akademie der Wissenschaften. Sonderreihe, Papyrological Coloniensia 16.1, 16.2. Opladen: Westdeutscher Verlag, 1990, 1992.

DAUBE, David. "Participle and Imperative in I Peter." In E. G. Selwyn. *The First Epistle of St. Peter*. Oxford: Univ. Press, 1947, 467-88.

DAVIDSON, M. J. *Angels at Qumran. A Comparative Study of 1 Enoch 1-36, 72-108 and Sectarian Writings from Qumran*. JSPSS 11. Sheffield: JSOT Press, 1992.

DEICHGRÄBER, R. *Gotteshymnus und Christushymnus in der frühen Christenheit. Untersuchungen zur Form, Sprache und Stil der frühchristlichen Hymnen*. SUNT 5. Göttingen: Vandenhoeck & Ruprecht, 1967.

DEISSMANN, Adolf. "Ephesia Grammata." *Abhandlung zur Semitischen Religionskunde und Sprachwissenschaft*. Eds. W. Frankenberg & F. Kuchler. BZAW 33. Gießen: Töpelmann, 1918, 121-24.

—. *Light from the Ancient East*. Tr. R. M. Strachan. New York: Doran, 1927.

—. *Bible Studies*. Edinburgh: T. & T. Clark, 1901.

—. "Elements." In *Encyclopaedia Biblica*. London: Adam & Charles Black, 1901, 2.1258-62.

DELLING, Gerhard. "στοιχεῖον." *TDNT* 7.670-87.

—. "ἀρχή." *TDNT* 1.481-84.

—. "ἄρχων." *TDNT* 1.488-89.

—. "πληρόω, πλήρωμα." *TDNT* 6.286-305.

DEMARIS, Richard E. *The Colossian Controversy. Wisdom in Dispute at Colossae*. JSNTSS 96. Sheffield: JSOT Press, 1994.

DENIS, Albert-Marie, Ed. *Concordance Grecque des Pseudépigraphes d'Ancien Testament*. Louvain: Université Catholique de Louvain, 1987.

DESCHAMPS, G. & COUSIN, G. "Inscriptions du Temple de Zeus Panamaros," *BCH* 12 (1888) 249-73.

DIBELIUS, Martin. "The Isis Initiation in Apuleius and Related Initiatory Rites." *Conflict at Colossae*. Eds. F. O. Francis & W. A. Meeks. SBLSBS 4. Missoula: Scholar's Press, 1973, 61-121 (originally published in 1917).

—. *Die Geisterwelt im Glauben des Paulus*. Göttingen: Vandenhoeck & Ruprecht, 1909.

DIELS, Hermann. *Elementum. Eine Vorarbeit zum Griechischen und Lateinischen Thesaurus*. Leipzig: Teubner, 1899.

DIETERICH, A. *Abraxas. Studien zur Religionsgeschichte des spätern Altertums*. Leipzig: Teubner, 1891.

—. *Eine Mithrasliturgie*. 3d Ed. Darmstadt: Wissenschaftliche Buchgesellschaft, 1966 (first edition, 1903; third edition: Leipzig and Berlin, 1923).

DILLON, J. M. "*Pleroma* and Noetic Cosmos: A Comparative Study." In *Neoplatonism and Gnosticism*. Ed. R. T. Wallis. Studies in Neoplatonism: Ancient and Modern 6. Albany: State University of New York, 1992, 99-110.

DITTENBERGER, Wilhelm. *Orientis Graeci Inscriptiones Selectae*. Supplementum Sylloges Inscriptionum Graecarum. Volumen Alterum. Hildesheim/Zürich/New York: Georg Olms, 1986. (Originally by Leipzig: Herzel, 1905.)

DORIGNY, A. Sorlin. "Phylactére Alexandrin." *Revue des Études Grecques* 4 (1891) 287-96.

DREW-BEAR, Thomas, and NAOUR, Christian. "Divinitès de Phrygie." *ANRW* II.18.3 (1990) 1907-2044.

DULING, Dennis. "Solomon, Exorcism, and the Son of David." *HTR* 68 (1975) 235-52.

—. "The Eleazar Miracle and Solomon's Magical Wisdom in Flavius Josephus's *Antiquitates Judaicae* 8.42-49." *HTR* 78 (1985) 1-25.

—. "The Testament of Solomon: Retrospect and Prospect." *JSP* 2 (1988) 87-112.

DUNAND, Françoise. *Le Culte d'Isis dans le Bassin Oriental de la Méditerranée*. Vol. 3. EPRO 26. Leiden: Brill, 1973.

EGAN, R. B. "Lexical Evidence on Two Pauline Passages." *NovT* 19 (1977) 34-62.

EITREM, S. E. *Some Notes on the Demonology of the New Testament*. Symbolae Osloenes Fasc. Supplement 12. Oslo: A. W. Brogger, 1950.

—. "'EMBATEϓΩ. Note sur Col. 2, 18," *ST* 2 (1948) 90-94

—. *Orakel und Mysterien am Ausgang der Antike*. Albae Vigiliae 5. Zürich: Rhein-Verlag, 1947.

EVERLING, Otto. *Die paulinische Angelologie und Dämonologie*. Göttingen: Vandenhoeck & Ruprecht, 1888.

EVANS, Craig A. "The Colossian Mystics." *Bib* 63 (1982) 188-205.

FAUTH, Wolfgang. "Apollon." *KP* 1.442-48.

—. "Men." *KP* 3.1194-96.

—. "Selene." *KP* 5.82-83.

FITZMYER, J. A. "Another Look at ΚΕΦΑΛΗ in 1 Corinthians 11.3." *NTS* 35 (1989) 503-11.

FOERSTER, W. "Die Irrlehrer des Kolosserbriefes." In *Studia Biblica et Semitica*. FS. T. C. Vriezen. Wageningen, 1966, 71-80.

—. "κυριότης." *TDNT* 3.1096-97.

FONTENROSE, Joseph. *Didyma. Apollo's Oracle, Cult, and Companions*. Berkeley/Los Angeles: University of California Press. 1988.

FOSSUM, Jarl. "Colossians 1.15-18 in the Light of Jewish Mysticism and Gnosticism." *NTS* 35 (1989) 183-201.

FOWL, S. E. *The Story of Christ in the Ethics of Paul*. JSNTSS 36. Sheffield: JSOT Press, 1990.

FOX, R. Lane. *Pagans and Christians*. New York: Alfred A. Knopf, 1986.

FRANCIS, Fred O. "Humility and Angelic Worship in Col 2:18." *Conflict at Colossae*. Eds. F. O. Francis & W. A. Meeks. SBLSBS 4. Missoula: Scholar's Press, 1973, 163-95.

—. "The Background of EMBATEUEIN (Col 2:18) in Legal Papyri and Oracle Inscriptions." *Conflict at Colossae*. Eds. F. O. Francis & W. A. Meeks. SBLSBS 4. Missoula: Scholar's Press, 1973, 197-207.

FREY, J. -B. "L'Angélologie Juive au temps de Jésus-Christ." *RSPT* 5 (1911) 75-110.

FURNISH, Victor P. *Theology and Ethics in Paul*. Nashville: Abingdon, 1968.

GABATHULER, Hans J. *Jesus Christus. Haupt der Kirche—Haupt der Welt. Der Christushymnus Colosser 1, 15-20 in der theologischen Forschung der letzten 130 Jahre*. ATANT 45. Zürich: Zwingli, 1965.

GAGER, J. G. *Moses in Greco-Roman Paganism*. SBLMS 16. Nashville: Abingdon, 1972.

—. *Curse Tablets and Binding Spells from the Ancient World*. New York: Oxford University Press, 1992.

GERLITZ, Peter. "Fasten als Reinigungsritus." *ZRGG* 20 (1968) 212-22.

GIBBS, John G. *Creation and Redemption. A Study in Pauline Theology*. SupNovT 26. Leiden: Brill, 1971.

GIVERSEN, S. "Solomon und die Dämonen." *Essays on the Nag Hammadi Texts in Honor of Alexander Böhlig*. Ed. M. Krause. NHS 3. Leiden: Brill, 1972, 16-21.

GOETZE, Albrecht. *Kulturgeschichte des Alten Orients: Kleinasien*. 2d Ed. Handbuch der Altertumswissenschaft 3.1.3.3.1. München: C. H. Beck'sche, 1957.

GOODENOUGH, Erwin R. *Jewish Symbols in the Greco-Roman Period. I: The Archaeological Evidence From Palestine*. New York: Pantheon, 1953.

—. *Jewish Symbols in the Greco-Roman Period. II: The Archaeological Evidence from the Diaspora*. New York: Pantheon, 1953.

—. *Jewish Symbols in the Greco-Roman Period. Volume 10.2: Symbolism in The Dura Synagogue*. Bollingen Series 37. New York: Bollingen Foundation, 1964.

—. *By Light, Light: The Mystic Gospel of Hellenistic Judaism*. New Haven: Yale, 1935.

—. Rev. of M. P. Nilsson, *Greek Popular Religion* in *JBL* 60 (1941) 345-48.

GOW, A. S. F. *Theocritus*. 2 Vols. Cambridge: University Press, 1965.

GRAILLOT, H. *Le Culte de Cybele. Mere des Dieux, a Rome et dans l'Empire romain*. Bibliotheque des Ecoles Francaises d'Athenes et de Rome 107. Paris: Fontemoing, 1912.

GRIFFITHS, J. Gwyn. *The Isis-Book (Metamorphoses, Book XI)*. EPRO 39. Leiden: Brill, 1975.

GRUENWALD, Ithamar. "The Problem of Anti-Gnostic Polemic in Rabbinic Literature." *Studies in Gnosticism and Hellenistic Religions*. FS. G. Quispel. Eds. R. van den Broek and M. J. Vermaseren. EPRO 91. Leiden: Brill, 1981.

—. "Jewish Apocalyptic Literature." *ANRW* II.19.1 (1979) 89-118.

—. *Apocalyptic and Merkavah Mysticism*. AGJU 14. Leiden: Brill, 1980.

—. "Knowledge and Vision." *IOS* 3 (1973) 63-107.

GRUNDMANN, Walter. *Der Begriff der Kraft in der Neutestamentlichen Gedankenwelt*. BWANT 8. Stuttgart: Kohlhammer, 1932.

—. "δύναμαι ." *TDNT* 2.292-99.

—. "ἄγγελος." *TDNT* 1.74-76.

GUNDEL, Hans Georg. *Weltbild und Astrologie in den griechischen Zauberpapyri*. Münchener Beiträge zur Papyrusforschung und Antiken Rechtsgeschichte 53. München: Beck, 1968.

—. "Imagines Zodiaci. Zu neueren Funden und Forschungen." *Hommages à Maarten J. Vermaseren* I. Eds. M. B. De Boer & T. A. Edridge. EPRO 68. Leiden: Brill, 1978, 438-54.

GUNDEL, Wilhelm. *Dekane und Dekansternbilder. Ein Beitrag zur Geschichte der Sternbilder der Kulturvölker*. 2nd Edition. Darmstadt: Wissenschaftliche Buchgesellschaft, 1969. (1st Edition: 1936, Studien der Bibliothek Warburg, XIX)

GUNTHER, John J. *St. Paul's Opponents and their Background. A Study of Apocalyptic and Jewish Sectarian Teachings*. NovTSup 35. Leiden: Brill, 1973.

HAFEMANN, Scott. *Suffering and the Spirit. An Exegetical Study of II Cor 2:14-3:3 Within the Context of the Corinthian Correspondence*. WUNT II/19. Tübingen: J.C.B. Mohr [Paul Siebeck], 1986.

HALL, A. S. "The Klarian Oracle at Oenoanda." *ZPE* 32 (1978) 263-67.

HARTMANN, Lars. "Universal Reconciliation (Col 1,20)." *SNTU* 10 (1985) 109-21.

HATCH, W. H. P. "Τὰ Στοιχεῖα In Paul and Bardaisan." *JTS* 28 (1927) 181-82.

HAUFE, Günter. "Hellenistische Volksfrömmigkeit." In *Umwelt des Urchristentums I: Darstellung des neutestamentlichen Zeitalters*. Eds. J. Leipoldt & W. Grundmann. Berlin: Evangelische Verlagsanstalt, 1971, 68-100.

HAUSSOULLIER, B. "L'Oracle d'Apollon a Claros." *Revue de Philologie* 22 (1898) 257-73.

HAUVETTE-BESNAULT, A. & DUBOIS, M. "Inscriptions de Carie." *BCH* 5 (1881) 179-94.

HAYMAN, Peter. "Was God a Magician? Sefer Yesira and Jewish Magic." *JJS* 40 (1989) 225-37.

HEAD, Barclay V. *Catalogue of the Greek Coins of Phrygia in the British Museum*. London: British Museum, 1906.

HECKENBACH, Josephus. "Hekate." *PW* 7.2769-82.

HEFELE, Charles J. *A History of the Councils of the Church*. Vol. II: A.D. 326 - A.D. 429. Edinburgh: T. & T. Clark, 1896.

HEGERMANN, Harald. *Die Vorstellung vom Schöpfungsmittler im hellenistischen Judentum und Urchristentum.* TU 82. Berlin: Akademie, 1961.

HELYER, Larry. "Recent Research on Col 1:15-20 (1980-1990." *GTJ* 12 (1992) 51-67.

—. "Colossians 1:15-20: Pre-Pauline or Pauline?" *JETS* 26 (1983) 167-79.

HEMBERG, Bengt. "Die Idaiischen Daktylen." *Eranos. Acta philologica suecana a Vilelmo Lundström condita* 50 (1952) 41-59.

HEMER, Colin. *The Letters to the Seven Churches of Asia in their Local Setting.* JSNTSS 11. Sheffield: JSOT Press, 1986.

HENGEL, Martin. *Judaism and Hellenism. Studies in their Encounter in Palestine during the Early Hellenistic Period.* 2 Vols. Tr. J. Bowden. London: SCM, 1974.

—. *The Son of God.* Philadelphia: Fortress, 1976.

—. "Die Synagogeninschrift von Stobi." *ZNW* 57 (1966) 145-83.

—. "Christology and New Testament Chronology: A Problem in the History of Earliest Christianity." *Between Jesus and Paul.* Philadelphia: Fortress, 1983, 30-47, 156-65.

—. "Der Alte und der neue 'Schürer.'" *JSS* 35 (1990) 19-72.

HENLE, F. A. "Der Men- und Mithrakult in Phrgyien: Skizzen zur Vorgeschichte der kolossischen Irrlehre."*TQ* 70 (1888) 590-614.

HOFIUS, O. "Gemeinschaft mit den Engeln im Gottesdienst der Kirche. Eine traditions-geschichtliche Skizze." *ZTK* 89 (1992) 172-96.

HOLLANDER, H. W. and DE JONGE, M. *The Testaments of the Twelve Patriarchs.* Studia in Veteris Testamenti Pseudepigrapha 8. Leiden: Brill, 1985.

HOLLENBACH, B. "Col. ii.23: Which Things Lead to the Fulfilment of the Flesh." *NTS* 25 (1978-79) 254-61.

HOMOLLE, T. "Nouvelles et Correspondance: Ionie." *BCH* 17 (1893) 638.

HOOKER, Morna D. "Were there False Teachers in Colossae?" *Christ and Spirit in the New Testament.* FS. C. F. D. Moule. Eds. B. Lindars & S. Smalley. Cambridge: Univ. Press, 1973, 315-31.

HOPFNER, Theodor. "Hekate-Selene-Artemis und Verwandte in den griechischen Zauberpapyri und auf den Fluchtafeln." In *Pisciculi. F. J. Dölger zum 60. Geburtstage.* Münster: Aschendorff, 1939, 125-45.

—. *Griechisch-Agyptischer Offenbarungszauber.* Studien zur Palaeographie und Papyruskunde 21. Amsterdam: Adolf M. Hakkert, I = 1974, II = 1983 (originally published in Leipzig: Haessel, I = 1921, II = 1924).

—. "Mysterien." *PW* 16/2.1315-50.

HORSLEY, G. H. R. *New Documents Illustrating Early Christianity. A Review of the Greek Inscriptions and Papyri Published in 1976.* North Ryde, NSW, Australia: Macquarie University, 1981.

—. "The Inscriptions of Ephesos and the New Testament." *NovT* 34 (1992) 105-68.

HURTADO, L. W. *One God, One Lord: Early Christian Devotion and Ancient Jewish Monotheism.* Philadelphia: Fortress, 1988.

IMHOOF-BLUMER, F. *Kleinasiatische Münzen.* Sonderschriften des Österreichischen Archäologischen Institutes in Wien. 3 Vols. Wien: Alfred Hölder, 1902.

JAMES, M. R. "The Testament of Solomon." *JTS* 24 (1922) 468.

JERVELL, Jacob. *Imago Dei. Gen 1, 26f im Spätjudentum, in der Gnosis und in den paulinischen Briefen.* FRLANT 76. Göttingen: Vandenhoeck & Ruprecht, 1960.

JOHNSON, Sherman E. "Laodicea and Its Neighbors." *BA* 13 (1950) 1-18.

—. "Asia Minor and Early Christianity." *Christianity, Judaism and Other Greco-Roman Cults II.* FS. M. Smith. SJLA 12. Leiden: Brill, 1975, 77-145.

—. "Unsolved Questions About Early Christianity in Anatolia." *Studies in New Testament and Early Christian Literature.* FS. A. P. Wikgren. Ed. D. E. Aune. NovTSup 33. Leiden: Brill, 1972, 181-93.

—. "The Present State of Sabazios Research." *ANRW* II.17.3 (1984) 1583-1613.

JOHNSTON, Sarah Iles. *Hekate Soteira. A Study of Hekate's Roles in the Chaldean Oracles and Related Literature.* American Philological Association. American Classical Studies 21. Atlanta: Scholar's Press, 1990.

JORDAN, D. R. "A Survey of Greek Defixiones Not Included in the Special Corpora." *GRBS* 26 (1985) 151-97.

—. "A Love Charm With Verses." *ZPE* 72 (1988) 245-59.

KÄSEMANN, Ernst. "A Primitive Christian Baptismal Liturgy." *Essays on New Testament Themes.* Tr. W. J. Montague. SBT 41. London: SCM, 1964, 149-68.

—. "Kolosserbrief." *RGG* (1959) 3.1727-28.

KEHL, Alois. "Hekate." *RAC* 14.310-38.

KEHL, Nicholas. *Der Christushymnus im Kolosserbrief. Eine motivgeschichtliche Untersuchung zu Kol 1, 12-20.* SBM 1. Stuttgart: Katholisches Bibelwerk, 1967.

KEIL, Josef. "Ein rätselhaftes Amulett." *JhhÖArchInst* 32 (1940) 79-84.

KEIL, J. & PREMERSTEIN, A. *Bericht über eine zweite Reise in Lydien,* DenkschrWien, philosophisch-historische Klasse Band 54.2. Vienna: Alfred Hölder, 1911.

KELLY, H. A. *The Devil at Baptism.* Ithaca: Cornell University Press, 1985.

KILEY, Mark. *Colossians as Pseudepigraphy.* Sheffield: JSOT Press, 1986.

KIM, Seyoon. *The Origin of Paul's Gospel.* WUNT 2/4. Tübingen: Mohr, 1981.

KITTEL, Gerhard. "Das kleinasiatische Judentum in der hellenistisch-römischen Zeit." *TLZ* 1/2 (1944) 9-20.

KNOX, Wilfred L. *St. Paul and the Church of the Gentiles.* Cambridge: University Press, 1961.

—. "Jewish Liturgical Exorcism." *HTR* 31 (1938) 191-203.

KOESTER, Helmut. *Introduction to the New Testament.* 2 Vols. (1= History, Culture, and Religion of the Hellenistic Age; 2= History and Literature of Early Christianity) Philadelphia: Fortress, 1982.

KOTANSKY, Roy. "Incantations and Prayers for Salvation on Inscribed Greek Amulets." In *Magika Hiera. Ancient Greek Magic and Religion.* Eds. C. A. Faraone and D. Obbink. New York: Oxford University Press, 1991, 107-37.

KRAABEL, A. T. "Judaism in Asia Minor under the Roman Empire with a Preliminary Study of the Jewish Community at Sardis, Lydia." Unpublished Doctoral Dissertation: Harvard, March 1968.

—. "The Roman Diaspora: Six Questionable Assumptions." *JJS* 33 (1982) 445-64.

—. "The Diaspora Synagogue: Archaeological and Epigraphic Evidence Since Sukenik." *ANRW* II.19.1. (1979) 477-510.

—. "Ὕψιστος and the Synagogue at Sardis." *GRBS* 10 (1969) 81-93.

—. "Paganism and Judaism: The Sardis Evidence." *Paganisme, Judaïsme, Christianisme. Influences et affrontements dans le Monde Antique.* Mélanges offerts à Marcel Simon. Eds. A. Benoit, M. Philonenko, and C. Vogel. Paris: Éditions E. de Boccard, 1978, 13-33.

—. "New Evidence of the Samaritan Diaspora Has Been Found on Delos." *BA* 147 (March 1984) 44-46

KRAFT, Robert. "The Multiform Jewish Heritage of Early Christianity." *Christianity, Judaism and Other Greco-Roman Cults III.* FS. M. Smith. SJLA 12. Leiden: Brill, 1975, 174-205.

KRAUS, Theodor. *Hekate. Studien zu Wesen und Bild der Göttin in Kleinasien und Griechenland.* Heidelberger Kunstgeschichtliche Abhandlungen 5. Heidelberg: Carl Winter, 1960.

KÜMMEL, Werner G. *Introduction to the New Testament.* Tr. H. C. Kee. London: SCM, 1982.

LÄHNEMANN, Johannes. *Der Kolosserbrief. Komposition, Situation und Argumentation.* SNT 3. Gütersloh: Mohn, 1971.

LANE, Eugene. *Corpus Monumentorum Religionis Dei Menis.* EPRO 19, Part 3. Leiden: Brill, 1976.

—. "Men: A Neglected Cult of Roman Asia Minor." *ANRW* II.18.3 (1990) 2161-74.

—. "Sabazius and the Jews in Valerius Maximus: A Re-Examination." *JRS* 69 (1979) 35-38.

LAUMONIER, Alfred. "Inscriptions de Carie." *BCH* 53 (1954) 291-380.

LEASE, Gary. "Mithraism and Christianity: Borrowings and Transformations." *ANRW* II.23.2 (1980) 1306-32.

—. "Jewish Mystery Cults Since Goodenough." *ANRW* II.20.2 (1987) 858-80.

LE BAS, P. & WADDINGTON, W. *Voyage archéologique en Grèce et en Asie Mineure.* Vol. III.v (Inscriptions - Asie Mineure). Bibliotheque des Monuments Figures Grecs et Romains 1. Paris: Firmin-Didot et Cie, 1870.

LEE, J. Y. "Interpreting the Demonic Powers in Pauline Thought." *NovT* 12 (1970) 54-69.

LEIVESTAD, Ragnar. *Christ the Conqueror. Ideas of Conflict and Victory in the New Testament.* London: SPCK, 1954.

LESKY, A. "Men," *PW* 15/1.689-97.

LIGHTFOOT, J. B. "The Colossian Heresy." *Conflict at Colossae.* Eds. F. O. Francis & W. A. Meeks. SBLSBS 4. Missoula: Scholar's Press, 1973, 13-59.

LIGHTSTONE, Jack. *Commerce of the Sacred. Mediation of the Divine among Jews in the Graeco-Roman Diaspora.* Brown Judaic Studies 59. Chico, Calif.: Scholars Press, 1984.

LINCOLN, Andrew T. *Paradise Now and Not Yet. Studies in the Role of the Heavenly Dimension in Paul's Thought with Special Reference to His Eschatology.* SNTSMS 43. Cambridge: University Press, 1981.

LINDEMANN, Andreas. "Die Gemeinde von 'Kolossä.' Erwägungen zum 'Sitz im Leben' eines pseudopaulinischen Briefes." *Wort und Dienst* 16 (1981) 111-34.

LOHSE, Eduard. "Ein hymnisches Bekenntnis in Kolosser 2, 13c-15." *Mélanges Bibliques en hommage au R. P. Béda Rigaux.* Eds. A. Descamps & A. Halleux. Gembloux: Duculot, 1970, 427-35.

—. "Pauline Theology in the Letter to the Colossians." *NTS* 15 (1968-69) 211-20.

—. "Christusherrschaft und Kirche im Kolosserbrief." *NTS* 11 (1964-65) 203-16.

—. "Σολομών." *TDNT* 7.462-63

LONA, Horacio E. *Die Eschatologie im Kolosser- und Epheserbrief.* FzB 48. Würzburg: Echter, 1984.

LUCK, Georg. *Arcana Mundi. Magic and the Occult in the Greek and Roman Worlds.* Baltimore: Johns Hopkins University Press, 1985.

LUEKEN, W. *Michael. Eine Darstellung und Vergleichung der jüdischen und der morgenländisch-christlichen Tradition vom Erzengel Michael.* Göttingen: Vandenhoeck & Ruprecht, 1898.

LUMPE, A. "Elementum." *RAC* 4.1073-1100.

LYONNET, Stanislaus. "Paul's Adversaries in Colossae." *Conflict at Colossae.* Eds. F. O. Francis & W. A. Meeks. SBLSBS 4. Missoula: Scholar's Press, 1973, 147-61.

—. "L'Épitre aux Colossiens (Col 2,18) et let Mystères D'Apollon Clarien." *Biblica* 43 (1962) 417-35.

MacGREGOR, G. H. C. "Principalities and Powers: the Cosmic Background of Paul's Thought." *NTS* 1 (1954-55) 17-28.

MacMULLEN, Ramsay. *Paganism in the Roman Empire.* New Haven: Yale Univ. Press, 1974.

MACH, Michael. *Entwicklungsstadien des jüdischen Engelglaubens in vorrabbinischer Zeit.* TSAJ 34. Tübingen: Mohr, 1992.

MACRIDY, Theodore. "Altertümer von Notion." *JhhÖArchInst* 8 (1905) 155-73.

—. "Antiquités de Notion II." *JhhÖArchInst* 15 (1912) 36-67.

MACRIDY, Theodore and PICARD, Charles. "Fouilles du Hiéron d'Apollon Clarios a Colophon." *BCH* 39 (1915) 33-52.

MAGIE, D. *Roman Rule in Asia Minor.* 2 Vols. Princeton: University Press, 1950.

MARE, W. Harold. "Archaeological Prospects at Colossae." *Near East Archaeological Society Bulletin* 7 (1976) 39-59.

MARGALIOTH, M. *Sepher Ha-Razim.* Jerusalem: Yediot Achronot, 1966.

MARSHALL, P. "A Metaphor of Shame: ΘΡΙΑΜΒΕΥΕΙΝ in 2 Cor 2:14." *NovT* 25 (1983) 302-17.

MARTIN, Luther H. *Hellenistic Religions.* Oxford: Oxford University Press, 1987.

MARTIN, Ralph P. *Reconciliation. A Study of Paul's Theology.* Atlanta: John Knox, 1981.

MARTIN, Roland. "Le Didymeion." In *La Civilisation Grecque de l'Antiquite a nos Jours.* Eds. C. Delvoye & G. Roux. Bruxelles: La Renaissance du Livre, 1967, 1.297-303.

MAURER, C. "Die Begründung der Herrschaft Christi über die Mächte nach Kol. 1, 15-20," *Wort und Dienst* N.S. 4 (1955) 79-93.

McCABE, D. F. and PLUNKETT, M. A. *Miletos Inscriptions*. Princeton Epigraphic Project. Princeton, 1984.

McCOWN, Chester Carlton. *The Testament of Solomon*. Untersuchungen zum Neuen Testament 9. Leipzig: J. C. Heinrichs, 1922.

MEEKS, Wayne A. *The First Urban Christians*. New Haven: Yale Univerisity Press, 1983.

MERISCH, N. "Chonai." In *Phrygien und Pisidien*. Eds. K. Belke & N. Merisch. Tabuli Imperii Byzantini 7, Österreichische Akademie der Wissenschaften, Philosophisch-Historische Klasse Denkschriften 211. Wien: Verlag der Österreichischen Akademie der Wissenschaften, 1990, 222-25.

MERKELBACH, Reinhold. "Mithras, Mithraism." *ABD* 4.877-78.

—. *Mithras*. Königstein/Ts.: Verlag Anton Hain, 1984.

MERKELBACH, Reinhold AND TOTTI, Maria. *Abrasax. Ausgewählte Papyri Religiösen und Magischen Inhalts*. 3 Vols. Abhandlungen der Rheinisch-Westfälischen Akademie der Wissenschaften. Sonderreihe, Papyrological Coloniensia 17.1, 17.2, 17.3 Opladen: Westdeutscher Verlag, 1990, 1991, 1992.

MEYER, Marvin W. *The "Mithras Liturgy."* SBL Texts and Translations 10, Graeco-Roman Religion Series 2. Missoula: Scholar's Press, 1976.

—. *The Ancient Mysteries: A Sourcebook*. San Francisco: Harper & Row, 1987.

MEYER, Marvin & SMITH, Richard. *Ancient Christian Magic. Coptic Texts of Ritual Power*. San Francisco: Harper, 1994.

MICHAELIS, W. *Versöhnung des Alls. Die frohe Botschaft von der Gnade Gottes*. Bern: Siloah, 1950.

—. "πρωτεύω." *TDNT* 6.881-82.

—. "κοσμοκράτωρ." *TDNT* 3.913-15.

MICHEL, O. "φιλοσοφία." *TDNT* 9.172-88

MICHL, J. "Engel." *RAC* 5.53-258.

MITCHELL, S. *Regional Epigraphic Catalogues of Asia Minor II. The Ankara District. The Inscriptions of North Galatia*. British Institute of Archaeology at Ankara Monograph 4. Oxford: British Archaeological Reports International Series 135, 1982.

MORGAN, Michael. *Sepher Ha-Razim. The Book of the Mysteries*. SBL Texts and Translations 25, Pseudepigrapha Series 11. Chico: Scholars Press, 1983.

MORRIS, Leon. *The Apostolic Preaching of the Cross*. Grand Rapids: Eerdmans, 1965.

MOULTON, J. H. "It is His Angel." *JTS* 3 (1902) 514-27.

MUELLER, J. R. "Abraham, Testament Of." *ABD* 1.44.

MÜLLER, Peter. *Anfänge der Paulusschule. Dargestellt am zweiten Thessalonicherbrief und am Kolosserbrief*. Zürich: Theologischer Verlag, 1988.

MÜNDERLEIN, Gerhard. "Die Erwählung durch das Pleroma." *NTS* 8 (1962) 264-76.

MURPHY, R. E. "GBR and GBWRH in the Qumran Writings." In *Lex Tua Veritas*. FS. H. Junker. Trier: Paulinus, 1961, 137-43.

MUSSNER, F. *Christus, das All und die Kirche. Studien zur Theologie des Epheserbriefes*. TTS 5. Trier: Paulinus, 1955.

NAVEH, Joseph & SHAKED, Shaul. *Amulets and Magic Bowls: Aramaic Incantations of Late Antiquity.* Jerusalem/Leiden: Brill, 1985.

NEUGEBAUER, Fritz. "Das Paulinische 'In Christo.'" *NTS* 4 (1957-58) 124-38.

NEUSNER, Jacob. *The Wonder-Working Lawyers of Talmudic Babylonia. The Theory and Practice of Judaism in its Formative Age.* Studies in Judaism. Lanham, MD.: University Press of America, 1987.

NEWSOM, Carol. *Songs of the Sabbath Sacrifice: A Critical Edition.* Harvard Semitic Studies 27. Atlanta: Scholars Press, 1985.

NILSSON, Martin P. *Geschichte der Griechischen Religion.* Zweiter Band: Die Hellenistische und Römische Zeit. Handbuch der Altertumswissenschaft 5, 2. Zweite Auflage. München: C. H. Beck'sche Verlagsbuchhandlung: 1961.

—. "Die Religion in den griechischen Zauberpapyri." *Kungl. Humanistiska Vetenskapssamfundet I Lund. Arsberattelse 1947-48.* Lund: Gleerup, 1948, 59-93. (= *Opuscula Selecta* 3. Lund: Gleerup, 1960, 129-66.)

—. *Greek Popular Religion.* New York: Columbia Univ. Press, 1940 (reprinted under the title, *Greek Folk Religion,* Harper Torch Books [New York: Harper & Bros, 1961).

—. "Letter to Professor Arthur D. Nock on some Fundamental Concepts in the Science of Religion. May 15, 1947." In *Opuscula Selecta.* Lund: Gleerup, 1960, 3.345-82 (= *HTR* 42 [1949] 71-107).

NITZAN, Bilha. "Hymns from Qumran—4Q510-4Q511." In *The Dead Sea Scrolls. Forty Years of Research.* STDJ 10. Eds. D. Dimant & U. Rappaport. Leiden: Brill, 1992, 53-63.

NOACK, Bent. *Satanâs und Soterîa. Untersuchungen zur neutestamentlichen Dämonologie.* Kobehhavn: G. E. C. Gads, 1948.

NOCK, A. D. "Greek Magical Papyri." *Arthur Darby Nock: Essays on Religion and the Ancient World I.* Ed. Z. Stewart. Oxford: Clarendon, 1972, 176-94 (= *Journal of Egyptian Archaeology* 15 [1929], 219-35).

—. "Studies in the Graeco-Roman Beliefs of the Empire." *Arthur Darby Nock: Essays on Religion and the Ancient World I.* Ed. Z. Stewart. Oxford: Clarendon, 1972, 32-48 (= *JHS* 48 [1928], 84-101).

—. "Astrology and Cultural History." *Arthur Darby Nock: Essays on Religion and the Ancient World I.* Ed. Z. Stewart. Oxford: Clarendon, 1972, 359-68.

—. "Vocabulary of the New Testament." *JBL* 52 (1933) 131-39.

—. *Early Gentile Christianity and its Hellenistic Background.* New York: Harper and Row, 1964.

—. *Conversion. The Old and the New in Religion from Alexander the Great to Augustine of Hippo.* London: Oxford University Press, 1933.

—. "Eunuchs in Ancient Religion." *Arthur Darby Nock: Essays on Religion and the Ancient World I.* Ed. Z. Stewart. Oxford: Clarendon, 1972, 7-15. (= *ARW* 23 [1925], 25-33).

—. "Religious Symbols and Symbolism I" [Review of E. R. Goodenough]. *Arthur Darby Nock: Essays on Religion and the Ancient World II.* Ed. Z. Stewart. Oxford: Clarendon, 1972, 877-94. (= *Gnomon* 27 [1955], 558-72).

—. "Religious Symbols and Symbolism II" [Review of E. R. Goodenough]. *Arthur Darby Nock: Essays on Religion and the Ancient World II.* Ed. Z. Stewart. Oxford: Clarendon, 1972, 895-907. (= *Gnomon* 29 [1957], 524-33).

—. "Religious Symbols and Symbolism III" [Review of E. R. Goodenough]. *Arthur Darby Nock: Essays on Religion and the Ancient World II*. Ed. Z. Stewart. Oxford: Clarendon, 1972, 908-18. (= *Gnomon* 32 [1960], 728-36).

NOCK, A. D., ROBERTS, C., and SKEAT, T. C. "The Guild of Zeus Hypsistos." *HTR* 29 (1936) 61-69 (= *Essays on Religion in the Ancient World*. Ed Z. Stewart. Oxford: Clarendon, 1972, 422-27)

NORDEN, E. *Agnostos Theos. Untersuchungen zur Formengeschichte religiöser Rede*. 4th ed. Stuttgart: B. G. Teubner, 1956 [= reprint of 1913 edition].

O'NEILL, J. C. "The Source of Christology in Colossians." *NTS* 26 (1979) 87-100.

OSTER, Richard E. "Christianity in Asia Minor." In *ABD* 1.938-54.

OVERFIELD, P. D. "Pleroma: A Study in Content and Context." *NTS* 25 (1978-79) 384-96.

PARKE, H. W. *The Oracles of Apollo in Asia Minor*. London: Croom Helm, 1985.

PERCY, Ernst. *Die Probleme der Kolosser- und Epheserbriefe. Skrifter Utgivna av Kungl. Humanistiska Vetenskapssamfundet i Lund XXXIX*. Lund: Gleerup, 1964 (reprint of 1946 edition).

PERDRIZET, Paul. "Amulette Grecque Trouvée en Syrie." *Revue des Études Grecque* 41 (1928) 73-82.

PETZL, Georg. "Vier Inschriften aus Lydien." *Studien zur Religion und Kultur Kleinasiens II*. FS. F. K. Dörner. Eds. S. Sahin, E. Schwertheim & J. Wagner. EPRO 66. Leiden: Brill, 1978, 745-61.

PFISTER, Friedrich. "Die στοιχεῖα τοῦ κόσμου in den Briefen des Apostels Paulus." *Philologus* 69 (1910) 411-27.

PICARD, Charles. *Éphèse et Claros. Recherches sur les Sanctuaires et les Cultes de L'Ionie du Nord*. Biobliothèque des Écoles Françaises d'Athenes et de Rome 123. Paris: Anciennes Maisons Thorin et Fontemoing, 1922.

—. "Un Oracle d'Apollon Clarios a Pergame." *BCH* 46 (1922) 190-97.

PORTER, Stanley E. *Καταλλάσσω in Ancient Greek Literature, with Reference to the Pauline Writings*. Estudios de Filología Neotestamentaria 5. Cordoba: Ediciones El Almendro, 1994.

PREISENDANZ, Karl. *Papyri Graecae Magicae. Die Griechischen Zauberpapyri*. Leipzig/Berlin: Verlag und Druck von B. G. Teubner, I: 1928; II: 1931; III: 1942. (2nd rev. ed. by A. Heinrichs, Stuttgart, 1973-74)

PREISENDANZ, Karl. "Die griechischen Zauberpapyri." *APF* 8 (1927) 104-67.

—. "Ephesia Grammata." *RAC* 5.515-20.

—. "Die griechischen und lateinischen Zaubertafeln." *APF* 11 (1935) 153-64.

—. "Fluchtafel (Defixio)." *RAC* 8. 1-29.

—. "Salomo." *PWSup* 8. 660-704.

—. "Paredros." *PW* 18.2.428-54.

—. "Aberglaube." *KP* 1.8-12.

PREISIGKE, F. *Wörterbuch der griechischen Papyruskunden mit Einfluss der griechischen Inschriften Ausschriften Ostraca Mumien Schilder usw. aus Ägypten*. 4 Vols. Göttingen: Hubert & Co, 1925-31.

PREISKER, H. "ἐμβατεύω," *TDNT* 2.535-36

PRÜMM, Karl. "Mystères." *DBSup* 6.1-225.

PUECH,Émile. "*11QPsAp^a*: Un Rituel de 'Exorcismes. Essai de Reconstruction." *RevQ* 55 (1990) 377-408.

—. "Les Deux Derniers Psaumes Davidiques du Rituel d'Exorcisme, 11QPsAp^a IV 4-V 14." In *The Dead Sea Scrolls. Forty Years of Research.* STDJ 10. Eds. D. Dimant & U. Rappaport. Leiden: Brill, 1992, 64-89.

RAINBOW, Paul A. "Jewish Monotheism as the Matrix for New Testament Christology." *NovT* 33 (1991) 78-91.

RAMSAY, W. M. *The Cities and Bishoprics of Phrygia.* 2 Vols. Oxford: University Press, 1= 1895, 2= 1897.

—. "Sketches in the Religious Antiquities of Asia Minor." *The Annual of the British School at Athens* 18 (1911-12) 37-79.

—. "The Mysteries in their Relation to St. Paul." *Contemporary Review* 104 (1913) 198-209.

—. *The Teaching of Paul in Terms of the Present Day.* London: Hodder & Stoughton, 1914.

—. "Phrygians." In *Encyclopaedia of Religion and Ethics.* Ed. J. Hastings. New York: Charles Scribner's Sons, 1925, 9.900-11.

—. *The Church in the Roman Empire Before A.D. 170.* New York: Putnam's, 1893.

—. "Ancient Mysteries and their Relation to St. Paul," *Athenaeum* (Jan. 25, 1913) 106-107.

REDFIELD, R. "A Selection from *The Folk Culture of Yucatan.*" In *Anthropology of Folk Religion.* Ed. C. Leslie. New York: Vintage, 1960, 337-88 (reprinted from *The Folk Culture of Yucatan.* Chicago: University of Chicago Press, 1941).

—. *The Primitive World and Its Transformations.* Ithaca: Cornell University Press, 1953.

REID, D. G. "Triumph." *DPL*, 946-54.

—. "Elements/Elemental Spirits of the World." *DPL*, 229-33.

—. "Principalities and Powers." *DPL*, 746-52.

REITZENSTEIN, Richard. *Hellenistic Mystery Religions. Their Basic Ideas and Significance.* Pittsburgh Theological Monograph Series 15. Pittsburgh: Pickwick Press, 1978.

RICHARDS, E. R. *The Secretary in the Letters of Paul.* WUNT 2/42. Tübingen: J.C.B. Mohr [Paul Siebeck], 1991

ROBERT, Louis. "Reliefs Votifs et Cultes d'Anatolie. I. Dédicace à Héraclès et aux Nymphes. II. Inscriptions de Lydie. *Opera Minora Selecta.* Vol. 1. Amsterdam: Adolf M. Hakkert, 1969, 402-35. (= *Anatolia* 3 [1958] 103-36).

—. "Les fouilles de Claros. Conférence donnée à l'Université d'Ankara à la fin de quatre campagnes de fouilles." *Opera Minora Selecta.* Vol. 6. Amsterdam: Adolf M. Hakkert, 1989. (= originally published in 1954).

—. "XXVII. Reliefs Votifs: 1. Relief à Hiérapolis." *Documents D'Asie Mineure.* Bibliotheque des Écoles Françaises d'Athès et de Rome 239. Paris: De Boccard, 1987, 355-59 (= *BCH* 107 [1983] 511-15).

—. "Rapport Sommaire sur un Second Voyage en Carie," *Revue Archéologique* 6 (1935) 152-63.

—. "Un Oracle Gravé à Oenoanda." *CRAIBL* (1971) 597-619.

—. "L'Oracle de Claros." *La Civilisation Grecque de l'Antiquité a nos Jours.* Vol. 1. Eds. C. Delvoye and G. Roux. Brussells: La Renaissance du Livre, 1967, 305-12.

—. *Villes d'Asie Mineure. Etudes de géographie ancienne.* 2d Ed. Paris: De Boccard, 1962.

—. "Épitaphes d'Eumeneia de Phrygie." *Hellenica. Recueil d'Épigraphie de Numismatique et d'Antiquites Grecques.* Vols. 11-12. Paris: Adrien-Maisonneuve, 1960, 414-39.

ROBINSON, D. M. "A Magical Inscription From Pisidian Antioch." *Hesperia* 22 (1953) 172-74.

ROBINSON, J. A. T. *The Body.* SBT 5. London: SCM, 1952.

ROBINSON, James M. "A Formal Analysis of Colossians 1:15-20." *JBL* 76 (1957) 270-87.

ROBINSON, Thomas L. "Oracles and Their Society: Social Realities as Reflected in the Oracles of Claros and Didyma." *Semeia* 56 (1992) 59-77.

RODD, C. S. "Salvation Proclaimed: XI. Colossians 2:8-15," *ET* 94 (1982) 36-41.

ROHDE, Erwin. *Psyche. The cult of Souls and Belief in Immorality Among the Greeks.* 8th Ed. Tr. W. B. Hillis. New York: Harcourt, Brace & Co., 1925.

ROWLAND, Christopher. *The Open Heaven. A Study of Apocalyptic in Judaism and Early Christianity.* London: SPCK, 1982.

—. "Apocalyptic Visions and the Exaltation of Christ in the Letter to the Colossians." *JSNT* 19 (1983) 73-83.

RUSAM, Dietrich. "Neue Belege zu den στοιχεῖα τοῦ κόσμου (Gal 4,3.9; Kol 2,8.20). *ZNW* 83 (1992) 119-25.

SÄNGER, D. *Antikes Judentum und die Mysterien.* WUNT 2/5. Tübingen: Mohr, 1980.

SCHÄFER, Peter. *Rivalität zwischen Engeln und Menschen.* Studia Judaica 8. Berlin: Walter de Gruyter, 1975.

—. "Tradition and Redaction in Hekhalot Literature." *Hekhalot-Studien.* TSAJ 19. Tübingen: Mohr, 1988, 8-16.

—. "The Aim and Purpose of Early Jewish Mysticism." *Hekhalot-Studien.* TSAJ 19. Tübingen: Mohr, 1988, 277-95.

—. "Jewish Magic and Literature in Late Antiquity and Early Middle Ages." *JJS* 41 (1990) 75-91.

SCHÄFER, Peter, Ed. *Synopse zur Hekhlot-Literatur.* TSAJ 2. Tübingen: J.C.B. Mohr [Paul Siebeck], 1981.

SCHENK, Wolfgang. "Christus, das Geheimnis der Welt, als dogmatisches und ethisches Grundprinzip des Kolosserbriefes." *EvT* 43 (1983) 138-55.

—. "Der Kolosserbrief in der neueren Forschung (1945-1985)." *ANRW* II.25.4 (1987) 3327-64.

SCHENKE, Hans-Martin. "Der Widerstreit gnostischer und kirchlicher Christologie im Spiegel des Kolosserbriefes." *ZTK* 61 (1964) 391-403.

SCHEU, Lawrence E. *Die "Weltelemente" beim Apostel Paulus (Gal. 4, 3.9 und Kol. 2,8.20)*. Universitas Catholica Americae 37. Washington: The Catholic University of America, 1933.

SCHILLE, G. *Frühchristliche Hymnen*. Berlin: Evangelische Verlagsanstalt, 1965.

SCHLIER, Heinrich. *Principalities and Powers in the New Testament*. QD 3. Freiburg: Herder, 1961.

SCHMIDT, F. *Le Testament gred c'Abraham, Introduction, édition critique des deus recensions grecques, traduction*. TSAJ 11. Tübingen: J. C. B. Mohr [Paul Siebeck], 1986.

—. "The Two Recensions of the Testament of Abraham: In Which Way Did the Transformation Take Place?" In *Studies on the Testament of Abraham*. SBLSCS 6. Ed. G. W. E. Nickelsburg. Missoula: Scholar's Press, 1976.

SCHMIDT, Karl L. "Die Natur- und Geistkräfte bei Paulus." *Eranos Jahrbuch* 14 (1946) 87-143.

SCHMITZ, O. "θρόνος." *TDNT* 3.166-67.

SCHNABEL, Eckhard J. *Law and Wisdom from Ben Sira to Paul*. WUNT 2.16. Tübingen: Mohr, 1985.

SCHNIEWIND, Julius. *Euangelion. Ursprung und erste Gestalt des Begriffs Euangelium*. Vol. 2. Darmstadt: Wissenschaftliche Buchgesellschaft, 1931.

SCHOLEM, Gershom. *Major Trends in Jewish Mysticism*. London: Thames and Hudson, 1955.

—. *Jewish Gnosticism, Merkabah Mysticism, and Talmudic Tradition*. New York: Jewish Theological Seminary of America, 1960.

SCHÜRER, Emil. *The History of the Jewish People in the Age of Jesus Christ*. Revised and edited by Geza Vermes, Fergus Millar, and Martin Goodman. Vol. 3, Part 1. Edinburgh: T. & T. Clark, 1986.

SCHWEIZER, Eduard. "Die 'Elemente der Welt' Gal 4, 3.9; Kol 2, 8.20." *Verborum Veritas*. FS. G. Stählin. Eds. O. Böcher and K. Haacker. Wuppertal: Brockhaus, 1970, 245-59.

—. "Die Kirche als Leib Christi in den paulinischen Antilegomena." In *Neotestamentica. Deutsche und Englische Aufsätze, 1951-1963*. Zürich & Stuttgart: Zwingli, 1963, 293-316.

—. "Slaves of the Elements and Worshipers of Angels: Gal 4:3, 9 and Col 2:8, 18, 20." *JBL* 107 (1988) 455-68.

—. "σῶμα." *TDNT* 7.1024-94.

—. "Body." *ABD* 1.767-72.

SEGAL, Alan F. *Two Powers in Heaven. Early Rabbinic Reports about Christianity and Gnosticism*. SJLA 25. Leiden: Brill, 1977.

—. "Hellenistic Magic: Some Questions of Definition." *The Other Judaisms of Late Antiquity*. Brown Judaic Studies 127. Atlanta: Scholar's Press, 1987, 79-108. (orig. in *Studies in Gnosticism and Hellenistic Religions*. FS. G. Quispel. Eds. R. van den Broek and M. J. Vermaseren. EPRO 91. Leiden: Brill, 1981, 349-75.)

—. "Heavenly Ascent in Hellenistic Judaism, Early Christianity and Their Environment." *ANRW* II.23.2 (1980) 1333-94.

SELLIN, G. "'Die Auferstehung ist schon geschehen.' Zur Spiritualisierung Apokolyptisch Terminologie im Neuen Testament." *NovT* 25 (1983) 220-37.

SHEPPARD, A. R. R. "Jews, Christians and Heretics in Acmonia and Eumeneia," *Anatolian Studies* 29 (1979) 169-80.

—. "Pagan Cults of Angels in Roman Asia Minor." *Talanta* 12-13 (1980-81) 77-101

SHOGREN, Gary. "Presently Entering the Kingdom of Christ: The Background and Purpose of Col 1:12-14." *JETS* 31 (1988) 173-80.

SIMON, Marcel. *Verus Israel. A Study of the Relations Between Christians and Jews in the Roman Empire (135-425)*. Oxford: Oxford University Press, 1986 (originally appeared as: *Verus Israel. Etude sur les Relations entre Chrétiens et Juifs dans l'Empire Romain [132-425]*. Paris: Editions E. DeBoccard, 1964).

—. *Le Christianisme Antique et Son Contexte Religieux*. WUNT 23. Tübingen: J.C.B. Mohr [Paul Siebeck], 1981.

—. "Remarques sur l'Angélolâtrie Juive au Début de l'Ère Chrétienne." *CRAIBL* (1971) 120-34 (= *Le Christianisme Antique*, 450-64).

SMITH, Morton. *Clement of Alexandria and a Secret Gospel of Mark*. Cambridge, Mass.: Harvard Univ. Press, 1973.

—. "A Note on Some Jewish Assimilationists: The Angels (P. Berlin 5025b, P. Louvre 2391)." *Journal of the Ancient Near Eastern Society* 16-17 (1984-85) 207-12.

—. "Goodenough's *Jewish Symbols* in Retrospect." *JBL* 86 (1967) 53-68.

—. "The Eighth Book of Moses and How it Grew (*PLEID*. J 395)." *Atti del XVII Congresso Internazionale di Papirologia*. Vol. 2. Napoli: Centro Internazionale per lo Studio Dei Papiri Ercolanesi, 1984, 683-93.

SOKOLOWSKI, F. "Sur le Culte d'Angelos dans le Paganisme Grec et Romain." *HTR* 53 (1960) 225-29.

—. *Lois sacrées de l'Asie Mineure*. Paris: Editions de Boccard, 1955.

STERN, M. "The Jewish Diaspora." In *The Jewish People in the First Century*. CRINT I/1. Philadelphia: Fortress, 1974.

STRUBBE, J. H. M. "Cursed Be He That Moves My Bones." In *Magika Hiera. Ancient Greek Magic and Religion*. Eds. C. A. Faraone and D. Obbink. New York: Oxford University Press, 1991, 33-59.

STRUGNELL, J. "The Angelic Liturgy at Qumran, 4QSerek Sirot 'Olat Hassabat," In *Congress Volume: Oxford, 1959*. VTSup 7. Leiden: Brill, 1960, 318-45.

STUHLMACHER, Peter. "Christliche Verantwortung bei Paulus und seinen Schülern." *EvT* 28 (1968) 165-86.

—. *Gerechtigkeit Gottes bei Paulus*. FRLANT 87. Göttingen: Vandenhoeck & Ruprecht, 1965.

SUMNEY, J. "Those Who 'Pass Judgment': The Identity of the Opponents in Colossians." *Biblica* 74 (1993) 366-88.

TANNEHILL, Robert C. *Dying and Rising with Christ. A Study in Pauline Theology*. BZNW 32. Berlin: Töpelmann, 1967.

TREBILCO, Paul. *Jewish Communities in Asia Minor*. SNTSMS 69. Cambridge: University Press, 1991.

ULANSEY, David. *The Origins of the Mithraic Mysteries. Cosmology and Salvation in the Ancient World*. New York: Oxford University Press, 1989.

—. "Mithraic Studies: A Paradigm Shift?" *Recherches de Science Religieuse* 13 (1987) 104-10.

URBACH, Ephraim E. *The Sages. Their Concepts and Beliefs.* 2 Vols. Trans. I. Abrahams. Jerusalem: Magnes Press, the Hebrew University, 1975.

van LENNEP, Henry J. *Travels in Little-Known Parts of Asia Minor.* 2 Vols. London: John Murray, 1870.

VERMASEREN, Maarten J. *Corpus Cultus Cybelae Attidisque (CCCA).* I. Asia Minor. EPRO 50. Leiden: Brill, 1987.

—. "La Sotériologie dans les Papyri Graecae Magicae." *La Soteriologia Dei Culti Orientali Nell' Impero Romano.* Eds. U. Bianchi & M. J. Vermaseren. EPRO 92. Leiden: Brill, 1982, 17-30.

—. *The Legend of Attis in Greek and Roman Art.* EPRO 9. Leiden: Brill, 1966.

—. *Cybele and Attis. The Myth and the Cult.* London: Thames and Hudson, 1977.

VIELHAUER, Philipp. "Gesetzesdienst und Stoicheiadienst im Galaterbrief." *Rechtfertigung. Festschrift für Ernst Käsemann zum 70. Geburtstag.* Eds. J. Friedrich, W. Pöhlmann, & P. Stuhlmacher. Tübingen: Mohr; Göttingen: Vandenhoeck & Ruprecht, 1976, 543-55.

WASZINK, J. H. "Biothanati." *RAC* 2.391-92.

WEDDERBURN, A. J. M. *Baptism and Resurrection: Studies in Pauline Theology Against Its Graeco-Roman Background.* WUNT 44. Tübingen: Mohr, 1987.

—. "The Theology of Colossians." In *The Theology of the Later Pauline Letters.* Cambridge: University Press, 1993, 1-71.

WEISS, H.-F. "Gnostische Motive und antignostische Polemik im Kolosser- und Epheserbrief." *Gnosis und Neues Testament.* Ed. K. W. Tröger. Gütersloh: Gerd Mohn, 1973, 311-24.

WESSELY, Karl. "Ephesia Grammata aus Papyrusrollen, Inschriften, Gemmen, etc." *Zwölfter jahresbericht über das k. k. Franz-Josef-Gymnasium in Wien.* Wien: Franz-Joseph-Gymnasium, 1886.

WIEGAND, Theodor, Ed. *Didyma. Zweiter Teil: Die Inschriften.* Berlin: Gebr. Mann, 1958.

WILLIAMS, A. L. "The Cult of the Angels at Colossae." *JTS* 10 (1909) 413-38.

WILLIAMSON, Lamar. "Led in Triumph. Paul's Use of Thriambeuo." *Int* 22 (1968) 317-32.

WILSON, R. McL. "Gnosis and the Mysteries." *Studies in Gnosticism and Hellenistic Religions.* FS. G. Quispel. Eds. R. van den Broek and M. J. Vermaseren. EPRO 91. Leiden: Brill, 1981, 451-57.

—. "Nag Hammadi and the New Testament." *NTS* 28 (1982) 289-302.

—. *The Gnostic Problem.* London: Mowbray, 1958.

—. *Gnosis and the New Testament.* Philadelphia: Fortress, 1968.

WINK, Walter. *Naming the Powers. The Language of Power in the New Testament.* Philadelphia: Fortress, 1984.

—. *Engaging the Powers. Discernment and Resistance in a World of Domination.* Minneapolis: Fortress, 1992.

WITT, R. E. *Isis in the Greco-Roman World.* Ithaca, N.Y.: Cornell University Press, 1971.

WOLFSON, Harry A. *Philo. Foundations of Religious Philosophy in Judaism, Christianity, and Islam.* 2 Vols. 4th Rev. Ed. Cambridge, Mass.: Harvard University Press, 1968.

WORTMANN, Dierk. "Neue Magische Texte," *Bonner Jahrbücher* 168 (1968) 56-111.

WRIGHT, N. T. "Poetry and Theology in Colossians 1.15-20." *NTS* 36 (1990) 444-68 [= reprinted with minor revisions in *The Climax of the Covenant. Christ and the Law in Pauline Theology.* Minneapolis: Fortress, 1992, 99-119.

WÜNSCH, Richard. *Antikes Zaubergerät aus Pergamon.* Jahrbuch des Kaiserlich Deutschen Archäologischen Instituts. Ergänzungsheft VI. Berlin: Georg Reimer, 1905.

—. *Antike Fluchtafeln.* 2d Ed. Kleine Texte für Vorlesungen und Übungen 20. Bonn: A. Marcus and E. Weber, 1912.

YAMAUCHI, E. M. *Persia and the Bible.* Grand Rapids: Baker, 1990.

—. "Jewish Gnosticism? The Prologue of John, Mandaean Parallels, and the Trimorphic Protennoia." *Studies in Gnosticism and Hellenistic Religions.* FS. G. Quispel. Eds. R. van den Broek and M. J. Vermaseren. EPRO 91. Leiden: Brill, 1981, 467-97.

—. "Magic in the Biblical World." *TB* 34 (1983) 169-200.

—. "Pre-Christian Gnosticism, the New Testament and Nag Hammadi in Recent Debate." *Themelios* 10 (1984) 22-27.

—. *Pre-Christian Gnosticism.* 2nd Edition. Grand Rapids: Baker, 1983.

—. "Sectarian Parallels: Qumran and Colosse." *BibSac* 121 (1964) 141-52.

YATES, R. "Colossians 2.15: Christ Triumphant." *NTS* 37 (1991) 573-91.

—. "'The Worship of Angels' (Col. 2:18)." *ET* 97 (1985) 12-15.

—. "Christ and the Powers of Evil in Colossians." *Studia Biblica 1978: III.* JSNTSS 3. Sheffield: JSOT Press, 1980, 461-68.

—. "Colossians 2,14: Metaphor of Forgiveness." *Biblica* 90 (1990) 248-59.

—. "A Reappraisal of Colossians." *ITQ* 58 (1992) 95-117.

ZEILINGER, F. *Der Erstgeborene der Schöpfung. Untersuchungen zur Formalstruktur und Theologie des Kolosserbriefes.* Wien: Herder, 1974.

ZWIERLEIN-DIEHL, Erika, Ed. *Magische Amulette und andere Gemmen des Instituts für Altertumskunde der Universität zu Köln.* Abhandlungen der Rheinisch-Westfälischen Akademie der Wissenschaften. Sonderreihe, Papyrological Coloniensia 20. Opladen: Westdeutscher Verlag, 1992.

ZMIEJEWSKI, J. *Der Stil der paulinische "Narrenrede."* BBB 52. Köln-Bonn: Hanstein, 1978.

Index of Authors

Index of References

Isaiah

2:5	291
2:6	290
2:8	290
2:10	303
2:11	290
2:17	290
2:19	303
2:21	303
6:1	263
6:3	65, 66
8:18	262
9:2	290
29:13	223
40-55	249
42:6-7	290
42:16	290
49:2	307
49:6-9	290
49:20	262
50:10-11	290
52:3	265
52:9	265
52:6-10	265
52:7	265
52:10	265
60:1-3	290
63:15-19	290
60:19-20	290

Jeremiah

4:4	297

Ezekiel

1	55
39:19	223
43:5	263
44:4	263
44:7	297
44:9	297

45:17	215

Daniel

1:20	205
7:27	253
8:16	33
10:12	33
10:13	33
10:20	33
12:1	33

Hosea

2:11	215
13:6	223

Joel

3:5	59

Haggai

2:7	263

Zechariah

3:1ff.	279

Old Testament Apocrypha

2 Maccabees

2:30	103
5:6	214
5:12	214
13:32-45	39
13:40	39
14:35	262

4 Maccabees

5:7	91
5:11	204
12:13	179

Index of Subjects

Wissenschaftliche Untersuchungen zum Neuen Testament

Alphabetical Index
of the First and Second Series

Hafemann, Scott J.: Suffering and the Spirit. 1986. *Volume II/19.*
– Paul, Moses, and the History of Israel. 1995. *Volume 81.*
Heckel, Theo K.: Der Innere Mensch. 1993. *Volume II/53.*
Heckel, Ulrich: Kraft in Schwachheit. 1993. *Volume II/56.*
– see *Feldmeier.*
– see *Hengel.*
Heiligenthal, Roman: Werke als Zeichen. 1983. *Volume II/9.*
Hemer, Colin J.: The Book of Acts in the Setting of Hellenistic History. 1989. *Volume 49.*
Hengel, Martin: Judentum und Hellenismus. 1969, ³1988. *Volume 10.*
– Die johanneische Frage. 1993. *Volume 67.*
Hengel, Martin und *Ulrich Heckel* (Ed.): Paulus und das antike Judentum. 1991. *Volume 58.*
Hengel, Martin und *Hermut Löhr:* Schriftauslegung. 1994. *Volume 73.*
Hengel, Martin und *Anna Maria Schwemer* (Ed.): Königsherrschaft Gottes und himmlischer Kult. 1991. *Volume 55.*
– Die Septuaginta. 1994. *Volume 72.*
Herrenbrück, Fritz: Jesus und die Zöllner. 1990. *Volume II/41.*
Hofius, Otfried: Katapausis. 1970. *Volume 11.*
– Der Vorhang vor dem Thron Gottes. 1972. *Volume 14.*
– Der Christushymnus Philipper 2,6–11. 1976, ²1991. *Volume 17.*
– Paulusstudien. 1989. ²1994. *Volume 51.*
Holtz, Traugott: Geschichte und Theologie des Urchristentums. Hrsg. von Eckart Reinmuth und Christian Wolff. 1991. *Volume 57.*
Hommel, Hildebrecht: Sebasmata. Volume 1. 1983. *Volume 31.* – Volume 2. 1984. *Volume 32.*
Kähler, Christoph: Jesu Gleichnisse als Poesie und Therapie. 1995. *Volume 78.*
Kamlah, Ehrhard: Die Form der katalogischen Paränese im Neuen Testament. 1964. *Volume 7.*
Kim, Seyoon: The Origin of Paul's Gospel. 1981, ²1984. *Volume II/4.*
– »The ›Son of Man‹« as the Son of God. 1983. *Volume 30.*
Kleinknecht, Karl Th.: Der leidende Gerechtfertigte. 1984, ²1988. *Volume II/13.*
Klinghardt, Matthias: Gesetz und Volk Gottes. 1988. *Volume II/32.*
Köhler, Wolf-Dietrich: Rezeption des Matthäusevangeliums in der Zeit vor Irenäus. 1987. *Volume II/24.*
Korn, Manfred: Die Geschichte Jesu in veränderter Zeit. 1993. *Volume II/51.*
Koskenniemi, Erkki: Apollonios von Tyana in der neutestamentlichen Exegese. 1994. *Volume II/61.*
Kraus, Wolfgang: Das Volk Gottes. 1995. *Volume 85.*
Kuhn, Karl G.: Achtzehngebet und Vaterunser und der Reim. 1950. *Volume 1.*
Lampe, Peter: Die stadtrömischen Christen in den ersten beiden Jahrhunderten. 1987, ²1989. *Volume II/18.*
Lieu, Samuel N. C.: Manichaeism in the Later Roman Empire and Medieval China. 1992. *Volume 63.*
Löhr, Hermut: see *Hengel.*
Löhr, Winrich A.: Basilides und seine Schule. 1995. *Volume 83.*
Maier, Gerhard: Mensch und freier Wille. 1971. *Volume 12.*
– Die Johannesoffenbarung und die Kirche. 1981. *Volume 25.*
Markschies, Christoph: Valentinus Gnosticus? 1992. *Volume 65.*
Marshall, Peter: Enmity in Corinth: Social Conventions in Paul's Relations with the Conrinthians. 1987. *Volume II/23.*
Meade, David G.: Pseudonymity and Canon. 1986. *Volume 39.*
Meadors, Edward P.: Jesus the Messianic Herald of Salvation. 1995. *Volume II/72.*
Mell, Ulrich: Die »anderen« Winzer. 1994. *Volume 77.*
Mengel, Berthold: Studien zum Philipperbrief. 1982. *Volume II/8.*
Merkel, Helmut: Die Wiedersprüche zwischen den Evangelien. 1971. *Volume 13.*
Merklein, Helmut: Studien zu Jesus und Paulus. 1987. *Volume 43.*
Metzler, Karin: Der griechische Begriff des Verzeihens. 1991. *Volume II/44.*
Metzner, Rainer: Die Rezeption des Matthäusevangeliums im 1. Petrusbrief. 1995. *Volume II/74.*
Niebuhr, Karl-Wilhelm: Gesetze und Paränese. 1987. *Volume II/28.*
– Heidenapostel aus Israel. 1992. *Volume 63.*

Nissen, Andreas: Gott und der Nächste im antiken Judentum. 1974. *Volume 15.*

Noormann, Rolf: Irenäus als Paulusinterpret. 1994. *Volume II/66.*

Okure, Teresa: The Johannine Approach to Mission. 1988. *Volume II/31.*

Philonenko, Marc (Ed.): Le Trône de Dieu. 1993. *Volume 69.*

Pilhofer, Peter: Presbyteron Kreitton. 1990. *Volume II/39.*

Pöhlmann, Wolfgang: Der Verlorene Sohn und das Haus. 1993. *Volume 68.*

Probst, Hermann: Paulus und der Brief. 1991. *Volume II/45.*

Räisänen, Heikki: Paul and the Law. 1983, ²1987. *Volume 29.*

Rehkopf, Friedrich: Die lukanische Sonderquelle. 1959. *Volume 5.*

Rein, Matthias: Die Heilung des Blindgeborenen. 1995. *Volume II/73.*

Reinmuth, Eckart: Pseudo-Philo und Lukas. 1994. *Volume 74.*

– see *Holtz.*

Reiser, Marius: Syntax und Stil des Markusevangeliums. 1984. *Volume II/11.*

Richards, E. Randolph: The Secretary in the Letters of Paul. 1991. *Volume II/42.*

Riesner, Rainer: Jesus als Lehrer. 1981. ³1988. *Volume II/7.*

– Die Frühzeit des Apostels Paulus. 1994. *Volume 71.*

Rissi, Mathias: Die Theologie des Hebräerbriefs. 1987. *Volume 41.*

Röhser, Günter: Metaphorik und Personifikation der Sünde. 1987. *Volume II/25.*

Rose, Christian: Die Wolke der Zeugen. 1994. *Volume II/60.*

Rüger, Hans Peter: Die Weisheitsschrift aus der Kairoer Geniza. 1991. *Volume 53.*

Salzmann, Jorg Christian: Lehren und Ermahnen. 1994. *Volume II/59.*

Sänger, Dieter: Antikes Judentum und die Mysterien. 1980. *Volume II/5.*

– Die Verkündigung des Gekreuzigten und Israel. 1994. *Volume 75.*

Sandnes, Karl Olav: Paul – One of the Prophets? 1991. *Volume II/43.*

Sato, Migaku: Q und Prophetie. 1988. *Volume II/29.*

Schaper, Joachim: Eschatology in the Greek Psalter. 1995. *Volume II/76.*

Schimanowski, Gottfried: Weisheit und Messias. 1985. *Volume II/17.*

Schlichting, Günter: Ein jüdisches Leben Jesu. 1982. *Volume 24.*

Schnabel, Eckhard J.: Law and Wisdom from Ben Sira to Paul. 1985. *Volume II/16.*

Schutter, William I..: Hermeneutic and Composition in I Peter. 1989. *Volume II/30.*

Schwartz, Daniel R.: Studies in the Jewish Background of Christianity. 1992. *Volume 60.*

Schwemer, A. M.: see *Hengel.*

Scott, James M.: Adoption as Sons of God. 1992. *Volume II/48.*

– Paul and the Nations. 1995. *Volume 84.*

Siegert, Folker: Drei hellenistisch-jüdische Predigten. Teil 1 1980. *Volume 20.* – Teil 2 1992. *Volume 61.*

– Nag-Hammadi-Register. 1982. *Volume 26.*

– Argumentation bei Paulus. 1985. *Volume 34.*

– Philon von Alexandrien. 1988. *Volume 46.*

Simon, Marcel: Le christianisme antique et son contexte religieux I/II. 1981. *Volume 23.*

Snodgrass, Klyne: The Parable of the Wicked Tenants. 1983. *Volume 27.*

Söding, Thomas: see *Thüsing.*

Sommer Urs: Die Passionsgeschichte des Markusevangeliums. 1993. *Volume II/58.*

Spangenberg, Volker: Herrlichkeit des Neuen Bundes. 1993. *Volume II/55.*

Speyer, Wolfgang: Frühes Christentum im antiken Strahlungsfeld. 1989. *Volume 50.*

Stadelmann, Helge: Ben Sira als Schriftgelehrter. 1980. *Volume II/6.*

Strobel, August: Die Stunde der Wahrheit. 1980. *Volume 21.*

Stuckenbruck, Loren: Angel Veneration and Christology. 1995. *Volume II/70.*

Stuhlmacher, Peter (Ed.): Das Evangelium und die Evangelien. 1983. *Volume 28.*

Sung, Chong-Hyon: Vergebung der Sünden. 1993. *Volume II/57.*

Tajra, Harry W.: The Trial of St. Paul. 1989. *Volume II/35.*

– The Martyrdom of St. Paul. 1994. *Volume II/67.*

Theissen, Gerd: Studien zur Soziologie des Urchristentums. 1979, ³1989. *Volume 19.*

Thornton, Claus-Jürgen: Der Zeuge des Zeugen. 1991. *Volume 56.*

Thüsing, Wilhelm: Studien zur neutestamentlichen Theologie. Hrsg. von Thomas Söding. 1995. *Volume 82.*

Twelftree, Graham: Jesus the Exorcist. 1993. *Volume II/54.*

Visotzky, Burton L.: Fathers of the World. 1995. *Volume 80.*

Wagener, Ulrike: Die Ordnung des ›Hauses Gottes‹. 1994. *Volume II/65.*

Wedderburn, A. J. M.: Baptism and Resurrection. 1987. *Volume 44.*

Wegner, Uwe: Der Hauptmann von Kafarnaum. 1985. *Volume II/14.*

Welck, Christian: Erzählte ›Zeichen‹. 1994. *Volume II/69.*

Wilson, Walter T.: Love without Pretense. 1991. *Volume II/46.*

Wolff, Christian: see *Holtz.*

Zimmermann, Alfred: Die urchristlichen Lehrer. 1984, ²1988. *Volume II/12.*

For a complete catalogue please write to the publisher
J. C. B. Mohr (Paul Siebeck), P. O. Box 20 40, D-72010 Tübingen

Wissenschaftliche Untersuchungen zum Neuen Testament

Williams, Catrin H.: I am He. 2000. *Volume II/113.*

Wilson, Walter T.: Love without Pretense. 1991. *Volume II/46.*

Zimmermann, Alfred E.: Die urchristlichen Lehrer. 1984, ²1988. *Volume II/12.*

Zimmermann, Johannes: Messianische Texte aus Qumran. 1998. *Volume II/104.*

Zimmermann, Ruben: Geschlechtermetaphorik und Geschlechterverhältnis. 2000. *Volume II/122.*

For a complete catalogue please write to the publisher
Mohr Siebeck · Postfach 2030 · D–72010 Tübingen.
Up-to-date information on the internet at http://www.mohr.de

– see *Burchard, Christoph*

Salzmann, Jorg Christian: Lehren und Ermahnen. 1994. *Volume II/59.*

Sandnes, Karl Olav: Paul – One of the Prophets? 1991. *Volume II/43.*

Sato, Migaku: Q und Prophetie. 1988. *Volume II/29.*

Schaper, Joachim: Eschatology in the Greek Psalter. 1995. *Volume II/76.*

Schimanowski, Gottfried: Weisheit und Messias. 1985. *Volume II/17.*

Schlichting, Günter: Ein jüdisches Leben Jesu. 1982. *Volume 24.*

Schnabel, Eckhard J.: Law and Wisdom from Ben Sira to Paul. 1985. *Volume II/16.*

Schutter, William L.: Hermeneutic and Composition in I Peter. 1989. *Volume II/30.*

Schwartz, Daniel R.: Studies in the Jewish Background of Christianity. 1992. *Volume 60.*

Schwemer, Anna Maria: see *Hengel, Martin*

Scott, James M.: Adoption as Sons of God. 1992. *Volume II/48.*

– Paul and the Nations. 1995. *Volume 84.*

Siegert, Folker: Drei hellenistisch-jüdische Predigten. Teil I 1980. *Volume 20* – Teil II 1992. *Volume 61.*

– Nag-Hammadi-Register. 1982. *Volume 26.*

– Argumentation bei Paulus. 1985. *Volume 34.*

– Philon von Alexandrien. 1988. *Volume 46.*

Simon, Marcel: Le christianisme antique et son contexte religieux I/II. 1981. *Volume 23.*

Snodgrass, Klyne: The Parable of the Wicked Tenants. 1983. *Volume 27.*

Söding, Thomas: Das Wort vom Kreuz. 1997. *Volume 93.*

– see *Thüsing, Wilhelm.*

Sommer, Urs: Die Passionsgeschichte des Markusevangeliums. 1993. *Volume II/58.*

Souček, Josef B.: see *Pokorný, Petr.*

Spangenberg, Volker: Herrlichkeit des Neuen Bundes. 1993. *Volume II/55.*

Spanje, T.E. van: Inconsistency in Paul?. 1999. *Volume II/110.*

Speyer, Wolfgang: Frühes Christentum im antiken Strahlungsfeld. Band I: 1989. *Volume 50.* – Band II: 1999. *Volume 116.*

Stadelmann, Helge: Ben Sira als Schriftgelehrter. 1980. *Volume II/6.*

Stenschke, Christoph W.: Luke's Portrait of Gentiles Prior to Their Coming to Faith. *Volume II/108.*

Stettler, Hanna: Die Christologie der Pastoralbriefe. 1998. *Volume II/105.*

Strobel, August: Die Stunde der Wahrheit. 1980. *Volume 21.*

Stroumsa, Guy G.: Barbarian Philosophy. 1999. *Volume 112.*

Stuckenbruck, Loren T.: Angel Veneration and Christology. 1995. *Volume II/70.*

Stuhlmacher, Peter (Ed.): Das Evangelium und die Evangelien. 1983. *Volume 28.*

Sung, Chong-Hyon: Vergebung der Sünden. 1993. *Volume II/57.*

Tajra, Harry W.: The Trial of St. Paul. 1989. *Volume II/35.*

– The Martyrdom of St.Paul. 1994. *Volume II/67.*

Theißen, Gerd: Studien zur Soziologie des Urchristentums. 1979, ³1989. *Volume 19.*

Theobald, Michael: see *Mußner, Franz.*

Thornton, Claus-Jürgen: Der Zeuge des Zeugen. 1991. *Volume 56.*

Thüsing, Wilhelm: Studien zur neutestamentlichen Theologie. Ed. von Thomas Söding. 1995. *Volume 82.*

Thurén, Lauri: Derhetorizing Paul. 2000. *Volume 124.*

Treloar, Geoffrey R.: Lightfoot the Historian. 1998. *Volume II/103.*

Tsuji, Manabu: Glaube zwischen Vollkommenheit und Verweltlichung. 1997. *Volume II/93*

Twelftree, Graham H.: Jesus the Exorcist. 1993. *Volume II/54.*

Visotzky, Burton L.: Fathers of the World. 1995. *Volume 80.*

Wagener, Ulrike: Die Ordnung des „Hauses Gottes". 1994. *Volume II/65.*

Walter, Nikolaus: Praeparatio Evangelica. Ed. by Wolfgang Kraus und Florian Wilk. 1997. *Volume 98.*

Wander, Bernd: Gottesfürchtige und Sympathisanten. 1998. *Volume 104.*

Watts, Rikki: Isaiah's New Exodus and Mark. 1997. *Volume II/88.*

Wedderburn, A.J.M.: Baptism and Resurrection. 1987. *Volume 44.*

Wegner, Uwe: Der Hauptmann von Kafarnaum. 1985. *Volume II/14.*

Welck, Christian: Erzählte ‚Zeichen'. 1994. *Volume II/69.*

Wilk, Florian: see *Walter, Nikolaus.*

Marshall, Peter: Enmity in Corinth: Social Conventions in Paul's Relations with the Corinthians. 1987. *Volume II/23.*

McDonough, Sean M.: YHWH at Patmos: Rev. 1:4 in its Hellenistic and Early Jewish Setting. 1999. *Volume II/107.*

Meade, David G.: Pseudonymity and Canon. 1986. *Volume 39.*

Meadors, Edward P.: Jesus the Messianic Herald of Salvation. 1995. *Volume II/72.*

Meißner, Stefan: Die Heimholung des Ketzers. 1996. *Volume II/87.*

Mell, Ulrich: Die „anderen" Winzer. 1994. *Volume 77.*

Mengel, Berthold: Studien zum Philipperbrief. 1982. *Volume II/8.*

Merkel, Helmut: Die Widersprüche zwischen den Evangelien. 1971. *Volume 13.*

Merklein, Helmut: Studien zu Jesus und Paulus. Volume 1 1987. *Volume 43.* – Volume 2 1998. *Volume 105.*

Metzler, Karin: Der griechische Begriff des Verzeihens. 1991. *Volume II/44.*

Metzner, Rainer: Die Rezeption des Matthäusevangeliums im 1. Petrusbrief. 1995. *Volume II/74.*

– Das Verständnis der Sünde im Johannesevangelium. 2000. *Volume 122.*

Mittmann-Richert, Ulrike: Magnifikat und Benediktus. *1996. Volume II/90.*

Mußner, Franz: Jesus von Nazareth im Umfeld Israels und der Urkirche. Ed. by M. Theobald. 1998. *Volume 111.*

Niebuhr, Karl-Wilhelm: Gesetz und Paränese. 1987. *Volume II/28.*

– Heidenapostel aus Israel. 1992. *Volume 62.*

Nielsen, Anders E.: Until it is Fulfilled. 2000. *Volume II/126.*

Nissen, Andreas: Gott und der Nächste im antiken Judentum. 1974. *Volume 15.*

Noack, Christian: Gottesbewußtsein. 2000. *Volume II/116.*

Noormann, Rolf: Irenäus als Paulusinterpret. 1994. *Volume II/66.*

Obermann, Andreas: Die christologische Erfüllung der Schrift im Johannesevangelium. 1996. *Volume II/83.*

Okure, Teresa: The Johannine Approach to Mission. 1988. *Volume II/31.*

Oropeza, B. J.: Paul and Apostasy. 2000. *Volume II/115.*

Ostmeyer, Karl-Heinrich: Taufe und Typos. 2000. *Volume II/118.*

Paulsen, Henning: Studien zur Literatur und Geschichte des frühen Christentums. Ed. von Ute E. Eisen. 1997. *Volume 99.*

Park, Eung Chun: The Mission Discourse in Matthew's Interpretation. 1995. *Volume II/81.*

Park, Joseph S.: Conceptions of Afterlife in Jewish Insriptions. 2000. *Volume II/121.*

Pate, C. Marvin: The Reverse of the Curse. 2000. *Volume II/114.*

Philonenko, Marc (Ed.): Le Trône de Dieu. 1993. *Volume 69.*

Pilhofer, Peter: Presbyteron Kreitton. 1990. *Volume II/39.*

– Philippi. Volume 1 1995. *Volume 87.*

– see Ego, Beate.

Pöhlmann, Wolfgang: Der Verlorene Sohn und das Haus. 1993. *Volume 68.*

Pokorný, Petr und *Josef B. Souček:* Bibelauslegung als Theologie. 1997. *Volume 100.*

Porter, Stanley E.: The Paul of Acts. 1999. *Volume 115.*

Prieur, Alexander: Die Verkündigung der Gottesherrschaft. 1996. *Volume II/89.*

Probst, Hermann: Paulus und der Brief. 1991. *Volume II/45.*

Räisänen, Heikki: Paul and the Law. 1983, [2]1987. *Volume 29.*

Rehkopf, Friedrich: Die lukanische Sonderquelle. 1959. *Volume 5.*

Rein, Matthias: Die Heilung des Blindgeborenen (Joh 9). 1995. *Volume II/73.*

Reinmuth, Eckart: Pseudo-Philo und Lukas. 1994. *Volume 74.*

Reiser, Marius: Syntax und Stil des Markusevangeliums. 1984. *Volume II/11.*

Richards, E. Randolph: The Secretary in the Letters of Paul. 1991. *Volume II/42.*

Riesner, Rainer: Jesus als Lehrer. 1981, [3]1988. *Volume II/7.*

– Die Frühzeit des Apostels Paulus. 1994. *Volume 71.*

Rissi, Mathias: Die Theologie des Hebräerbriefs. 1987. *Volume 41.*

Röhser, Günter: Metaphorik und Personifikation der Sünde. 1987. *Volume II/25.*

Rose, Christian: Die Wolke der Zeugen. 1994. *Volume II/60.*

Rüger, Hans Peter: Die Weisheitsschrift aus der Kairoer Geniza. 1991. *Volume 53.*

Sänger, Dieter: Antikes Judentum und die Mysterien. 1980. *Volume II/5.*

– Die Verkündigung des Gekreuzigten und Israel. 1994. *Volume 75.*

– Die johanneische Frage. 1993. *Volume 67.*
– Judaica et Hellenistica. Band 1. 1996. *Volume 90.* – Band 2. 1999. *Volume 109.*
Hengel, Martin and *Ulrich Heckel* (Ed.): Paulus und das antike Judentum. 1991. *Volume 58.*
Hengel, Martin und *Hermut Löhr* (Ed.): Schriftauslegung im antiken Judentum und im Urchristentum. 1994. *Volume 73.*
Hengel, Martin and *Anna Maria Schwemer:* Paulus zwischen Damaskus und Antiochien. 1998. *Volume 108.*
Hengel, Martin and *Anna Maria Schwemer* (Ed.): Königsherrschaft Gottes und himmlischer Kult. 1991. *Volume 55.*
– Die Septuaginta. 1994. *Volume 72.*
Herrenbrück, Fritz: Jesus und die Zöllner. 1990. *Volume II/41.*
Herzer, Jens: Paulus oder Petrus? 1998. *Volume 103.*
Hoegen-Rohls, Christina: Der nachösterliche Johannes. 1996. *Volume II/84.*
Hofius, Otfried: Katapausis. 1970. *Volume 11.*
– Der Vorhang vor dem Thron Gottes. 1972. *Volume 14.*
– Der Christushymnus Philipper 2,6–11. 1976, ²1991. *Volume 17.*
– Paulusstudien. 1989, ²1994. *Volume 51.*
Hofius, Otfried und *Hans-Christian Kammler:* Johannesstudien. 1996. *Volume 88.*
Holtz, Traugott: Geschichte und Theologie des Urchristentums. 1991. *Volume 57.*
Hommel, Hildebrecht: Sebasmata. Band 1 1983. *Volume 31* – Band 2 1984. *Volume 32.*
Hvalvik, Reidar: The Struggle for Scripture and Covenant. 1996. *Volume II/82.*
Joubert, Stephan: Paul as Benefactor. 2000. *Volume II/124.*
Kähler, Christoph: Jesu Gleichnisse als Poesie und Therapie. 1995. *Volume 78.*
Kamlah, Ehrhard: Die Form der katalogischen Paränese im Neuen Testament. 1964. *Volume 7.*
Kammler, Hans-Christian: Christologie und Eschatologie. 2000. *Volume 126.*
– see *Hofius, Otfried.*
Kelhoffer, James A.: Miracle and Mission. 1999. *Volume II/112.*
Kieffer, René and *Jan Bergman (Ed.):* La Main de Dieu / Die Hand Gottes. 1997. *Volume 94.*
Kim, Seyoon: The Origin of Paul's Gospel. 1981, ²1984. *Volume II/4.*

– „The ‚Son of Man'" as the Son of God. 1983. *Volume 30.*
Kleinknecht, Karl Th.: Der leidende Gerechtfertigte. 1984, ²1988. *Volume II/13.*
Klinghardt, Matthias: Gesetz und Volk Gottes. 1988. *Volume II/32.*
Köhler, Wolf-Dietrich: Rezeption des Matthäusevangeliums in der Zeit vor Irenäus. 1987. *Volume II/24.*
Korn, Manfred: Die Geschichte Jesu in veränderter Zeit. 1993. *Volume II/51.*
Koskenniemi, Erkki: Apollonios von Tyana in der neutestamentlichen Exegese. 1994. *Volume II/61.*
Kraus, Wolfgang: Das Volk Gottes. 1996. *Volume 85.*
– see *Walter, Nikolaus.*
Kuhn, Karl G.: Achtzehngebet und Vaterunser und der Reim. 1950. *Volume 1.*
Laansma, Jon: I Will Give You Rest. 1997. *Volume II/98.*
Labahn, Michael: Offenbarung in Zeichen und Wort. 2000. *Volume II/117.*
Lange, Armin: see *Ego, Beate.*
Lampe, Peter: Die stadtrömischen Christen in den ersten beiden Jahrhunderten. 1987, ²1989. *Volume II/18.*
Landmesser, Christof: Wahrheit als Grundbegriff neutestamentlicher Wissenschaft. 1999. *Volume 113.*
Lau, Andrew: Manifest in Flesh. 1996. *Volume II/86.*
Lichtenberger, Hermann: see *Avemarie, Friedrich.*
Lieu, Samuel N.C.: Manichaeism in the Later Roman Empire and Medieval China. ²1992. *Volume 63.*
Loader, William R.G.: Jesus' Attitude Towards the Law. 1997. *Volume II/97.*
Löhr, Gebhard: Verherrlichung Gottes durch Philosophie. 1997. *Volume 97.*
Löhr, Hermut: see *Hengel, Martin.*
Löhr, Winrich Alfried: Basilides und seine Schule. 1995. *Volume 83.*
Luomanen, Petri: Entering the Kingdom of Heaven. 1998. *Volume II/101.*
Maier, Gerhard: Mensch und freier Wille. 1971. *Volume 12.*
– Die Johannesoffenbarung und die Kirche. 1981. *Volume 25.*
Markschies, Christoph: Valentinus Gnosticus? 1992. *Volume 65.*